online resource centre
www.oxfordtextbooks.co.uk/orc/smith

Smith and Hogan's Text, Cases, and Materials on C
by several free online resources to further your understanding

Visit **www.oxfordtextbooks.co.uk/orc/smithandhogan/** to find the following features:

- Detailed post-publication **legal updates**.

- **Web links** to selected further reading and resources.

- A key to all **abbreviations** used in the text.

- The full **bibliography** to Smith and Hogan's Criminal Law.

New to This Edition

This edition has been comprehensively updated to take account of recent legislation and the major decisions of the appellate courts. These include:

- *Hughes* in the Supreme Court on doubly strict liability in causing death by driving unlawfully (Ch 7)
- *Gnango* in the Supreme Court on the law of 'joint enterprise' (Ch 8)
- *Coley, Harris, and McGhee*; and *Oye* on insanity and automatism (Ch 10)
- The further amendment to the law of self-defence by the Crime and Courts Act 2013 affecting householders who use force on trespassers (Ch 11)
- *S&H* on the correct interpretation of the offences under the Serious Crime Act 2007 (Ch 12)
- The partial defences of loss of control and diminished responsibility under the Coroners and Justice Act 2009 (Ch 16)
- *M(J)* on unlawful act manslaughter (Ch 17)
- *Assange, CPS v F* and *McNally* on deception in sexual offences (Ch 20)
- *Foster* on the Theft Act 1968 (Ch 21)
- Numerous cases under the Fraud Act 2006 including *UAE v Allen*; *Gilbert*; and *Augunas* (Ch 25)
- *Unsworth v DPP* on criminal damage (Ch 28)

About the Authors

David Ormerod QC is currently a Law Commissioner. He is seconded from Queen Mary, University of London, where he is Professor of Criminal Justice. David is the author of numerous journal articles and books and is: Editor of the *Criminal Law Review*; Editor-in-Chief of *Blackstone's Criminal Practice*; and Consultant Editor of *Halsbury's Laws of England on Criminal Procedure* (2010). He lectures regularly to the profession and for the Judicial College on a range of topics.

He is a Door Tenant in the chambers of Max Hill QC, 18 Red Lion Chambers, and is a Bencher of Middle Temple, and an honorary life member of the Criminal Bar Association.

Other titles from David Ormerod:
Fraud: Criminal Law and Procedure (2008) with Clare Montgomery QC;
Smith's Law of Theft (9th edn 2007)with David Williams QC; and
Smith & Hogan's Criminal Law (13th edn 2011, 14th edn forthcoming 2015).

Karl Laird is currently Lecturer in Law at Exeter College, Oxford and a Senior Retained Lecturer at Pembroke College, Oxford. In addition to teaching at the University of Oxford, Karl has also taught at the University of Bristol. He studied law at Queen Mary, University of London and at Oxford. Karl has published in the *Criminal Law Review* and the *Modern Law Review*.

SMITH and HOGAN'S

Text, Cases, and Materials on

CRIMINAL LAW

Eleventh edition

David Ormerod QC

Law Commissioner for England and Wales,
Professor of Criminal Justice, Queen Mary, University of London,
Bencher of Middle Temple,
Door Tenant at 18 Red Lion Chambers

Karl Laird

Lecturer in Law, Exeter College, Oxford

OXFORD
UNIVERSITY PRESS

OXFORD

UNIVERSITY PRESS

Great Clarendon Street, Oxford, OX2 6DP,
United Kingdom

Oxford University Press is a department of the University of Oxford.
It furthers the University's objective of excellence in research, scholarship,
and education by publishing worldwide. Oxford is a registered trade mark of
Oxford University Press in the UK and in certain other countries

© Oxford University Press 2014

The moral rights of the authors have been asserted

Eighth edition 2003
Ninth edition 2005
Tenth edition 2009

Impression: 1

Public sector information reproduced under Open Government Licence v1.0
(http://www.nationalarchives.gov.uk/doc/open-government-licence/open-government-licence.htm)

Crown Copyright material reproduced with the permission of the
Controller, HMSO (under the terms of the Click Use licence)

Published in the United States of America by Oxford University Press
198 Madison Avenue, New York, NY 10016, United States of America

British Library Cataloguing in Publication Data

Data available

Library of Congress Control Number: 2014930918

ISBN 978-0-19-969488-4

Printed in Great Britain by
Bell & Bain Ltd, Glasgow

*In memory of Gianni Sonvico, whose dedication to the
criminal law remains a source of inspiration.
1990–2013*

Outline Contents

Detailed Contents

Preface

In the preface to the first edition of their *Cases and Materials* book, Professors John Smith and Brian Hogan stated that their aim in producing a casebook was to facilitate the teaching of criminal law by the case method. In the forty years since that first edition was published not only has the law changed significantly, so too has legal pedagogy. This eleventh edition of *Smith and Hogan's Text, Cases, and Materials* is one that has undergone significant development in order to reflect these changes.

What should first strike the reader is that the title has now been modified to 'Text, Cases, and Materials'. This reflects a significant change that has been made to the fabric of the book. We have continued the Smith and Hogan tradition of including substantial extracts from cases and academic commentary in order to allow students the opportunity to develop their skills in analysing the key sources from which they must gain an understanding of the law. We have, however, juxtaposed these extracts with expanded sections of text explaining what the law is. Our aim in including more explanation and less primary material has not been to gloss over the complexities inherent in the criminal law, but rather to assist the student's understanding of them. We hope that we have been able to present the material in an even more accessible fashion thus ensuring the book's continued appeal to a broad readership. As with previous editions, questions are interspersed throughout the chapters and their aim is not only to ensure students understand the law but also to focus attention on some of the more difficult facets of it. The questions vary in their complexity, in order to reflect the broad readership that the book is aimed at.

The book remains doctrinal in nature, but we have sought to ensure that the text informs the reader of areas where there are conceptual controversies and theoretical debate. In keeping with the aim of the book, we have sought to present this material in a comprehensible fashion.

Another significant change to the book is that both its content and structure have been modified to reflect modern undergraduate criminal law courses. For example, we have amalgamated a number of chapters that examined separately various offences found in the Theft Act 1968 into a single chapter and removed some of the discussion of those more peripheral matters that are not found in the typical undergraduate course. We have also separated out the chapters dealing with offences against the person and consent. Chapters dealing with subjects which undergraduates find more complex have been rewritten and are given more extensive treatment (as with Ch 8 on participation). We hope that these improvements make the structure of the book more intuitive and aid clarity

What has not, of course, changed from previous editions is that the book retains its comprehensive and up-to-date coverage. The last edition of the book was published in 2009 and in addition to ensuring that the text incorporated the most recent authorities, developments since then have necessitated the rewriting of a number of chapters. There is now a new chapter (Ch 16) detailing the reforms to the partial defences to murder implemented by the Coroners and Justice Act 2009. This chapter examines the recent cases interpreting the 2009 Act and references the latest academic commentary. There has been a deluge of appeal cases concerning 'joint enterprise' and a significant proportion of the chapter on accessories (Ch 8) has been rewritten to reflect this. Our aim in this chapter has been to present the authorities in a logical fashion thus enabling the reader to approach this notoriously difficult area of the law with confidence. In addition, there is now a small but significant body of case law concerning the Fraud Act 2006 and the chapter on fraud (Ch 25) has been extensively modified to take account of it.

While all that can be given here is an overview of the changes that have been integrated into this new edition, we hope it provides an insight into the aims of *Smith and Hogan's Criminal Law: Text, Cases, and Materials* and how we have sought to achieve them. We hope we have produced a text that will instil in students an enthusiasm for the complexities of the criminal law and also assist in developing the sophisticated analytical abilities that they will be able to rely upon throughout their legal careers.

We would like to thank several people who have read drafts of chapters and made suggestions: Daniella Waddoup, Peter Yates, Tharini Sumanthiran, and Damian Warburton. Their insights were greatly appreciated. We, of course, remain responsible for the text. At OUP we have been assisted enormously by Tom Young, John Carroll, and Heather Smyth who made the publication process as painless as ever. In addition, we would like to record our huge thanks to Joy Ruskin Tompkins who copy-edited and proofread the entire manuscript while being encouraging throughout—no matter how much we tried her patience!

The manuscript was delivered in December 2013. It has been possible to take account of a few minor recent developments at proof stage. Annual updates will be available on the online page.

David Ormerod
Karl Laird
April 2014

David Ormerod writes:
The final major change which readers will note is that Karl Laird has joined me as a co-author. Karl worked as the researcher on the 13th edition of *Smith and Hogan's Criminal Law* text book. His contribution to that text was invaluable and I am delighted to welcome him as a co author of the *Text, Cases, and Materials* book. He brings with him valuable current teaching experience at the Universities of Bristol and Oxford.

Acknowledgements

Grateful acknowledgement is made to all the authors and publishers of copyright material that appear in this book, and in particular to the following for permission to reprint material from the sources indicated:

Extracts from Law Commission Reports, Criminal Law Review Commission Reports, Consultation Papers, and CPS Guidelines are Crown copyright material and are reproduced under Class Licence Number C01P0000148 with the permission of the Controller of OPSI and the Queen's Printer for Scotland. Parliamentary copyright material is reproduced with the permission of the Controller of Her Majesty's Stationery Office on behalf of Parliament.

Professor John Bell: extract from *Cambridge Law Journal*: Glanville Williams, 'Oblique Intention' (1987) 46 CLJ 417.

Hart Publishing Ltd: extracts from J. Horder: 'The Changing Face of the Law of Homicide' in J. Horder (ed): *Homicide Law in Comparative Perspective* (Hart, 2008) and S. Cunningham: 'Recklessness: Being Reckless and Acting Recklessly', 23 *King's Law Journal* (KLJ) 445 (2010).

Harvard University Press: extracts from Stuart P. Green, *Thirteen Ways to Steal a Bicycle* (HUP, 2012).

Incorporated Council of Law Reporting: extracts from the *Law Reports: Appeal Cases* (AC), and *Queen's Bench Division* (QB).

Oxford University Press: extracts from Glanville Williams: *The Mental Element in Crime* (OUP, 1966); S. P. Green: 'Six Senses of Strict Liability: A Plea for Formalism' in A. Simester (ed), *Appraising Strict Liability* (OUP, 2005); Andrew Ashworth: 'Belief and Intent in Criminal Liability' in J. Eekelaar and J. Bell (eds): *Oxford Essays in Jurisprudence* (OUP, 1987); extracts from D. Husak: 'Distraction and Negligence'; A. Simester: 'On Justifications and Excuses'; B. Mitchell: 'Years of Provocation, Followed by a Loss of Control', all in L. Zedner and J. V. Roberts (eds): *Principles and Values in Criminal Law and Criminal Justice: Essays in Honour of Andrew Ashworth* (OUP, 2012); and extract from *Current Legal Problems* (CLP): D. Ormerod: 'Making Sense of Statutory Conspiracy', CLP 185 (2006).

Prof. Paul H. Robinson: extract from P. H. Robinson, 'Four Distinctions that Glanville Williams Did Not Make: the Practical Benefits of Examining the Interrelation Among Criminal Law Doctrines', *University of Pennsylvania Faculty Scholarship*. Paper 388 (2013).

Reed Elsevier (UK) Ltd trading as LexisNexis: extracts from *All England Law Reports* (All ER) and extract from Brian Hogan: 'Omissions and the Duty Myth' in P. Smith (ed): *Criminal Law Essays in Honour of J. C. Smith* 1987 (Butterworth, LexisNexis, 1987).

Springer: extract from A. Leipold: 'A Case for Criminal Negligence' (2010) 29 *Law and Philosophy* (Law & Phil) 455.

Sweet & Maxwell Ltd: extracts from J. C. Smith: from *Justification and Excuse in the Criminal Law* (The Hamlyn Lectures, Stevens, 1989); Barbara Wootton: *Crime and the Criminal Law: Reflections of a Magistrate and a Social Scientist* (The Hamlyn Lectures, Stevens, 1963); extracts from *Criminal Law Review*: J. Chalmers and F. Leverick: 'Tracking the Creation of Criminal Offences', Crim LR 543 (2013); Lord Bingham CJ: 'Must We Wait for Ever?', Crim LR 694 (1998); J. Horder: 'A Critique of the Correspondence Principle in Criminal Law', Crim LR 759 (1955); J. Horder: 'How Culpability Can, and Cannot, be Denied in Under-age Sex Crimes', Crim LR 15 (2001); R. Buxton: 'Being an Accessory to One's Own Murder', Crim LR 275 (2012); *Mitchell and King*, Crim LR 496 (1999); J. Gobert: 'A Corporate Criminality: New Crimes for the Times', Crim LR 722 (1994); R. D. Mackay and C. Gearty: 'On Being Insane in Jersey—the Case of *Attorney General v Jason Prior*', Crim LR 560 (2001); *Sir John Smith*, Crim LR 952 (2002); Glanville Williams: 'Necessity', Crim LR 128 (1978); A. Norrie: 'The Coroners and Justice Act 2009—Partial Defences to Murder (1) Loss of Control', Crim LR 275 (2010); R. D. Mackay: 'The Coroners and Justice Act 2009—Partial Defences to Murder (2) The New Diminished Responsibility Plea', Crim LR 290 (2010); J. Horder and L. McGowan: 'Manslaughter by Causing Another's Suicide', Crim LR 1035 (2006); J. Herring: 'Mistaken Sex', Crim LR 511 (2005); Hyman Gross: 'Rape, Moralism and Human Rights', Crim LR 220 (2007); E. J. Griew: 'Dishonesty, the Objections to *Feely* and *Ghosh*', Crim LR 341 (1985); D. Ormerod: 'Case Commentary on *Dooley*', Crim LR 544 (2006); extracts from cases reported in *Criminal Law Review*; extracts from *Law Quarterly Review*: Andrew Ashworth: 'The Scope of Criminal Liability for Omissions', 105 LQR 424 (1989); Glanville Williams: 'Criminal Omissions—The Conventional View', 107 LQR 86 (1991); S. Gough: 'Intoxication and Criminal Liability: The Law Commission's Proposed Reforms', 112 LQR 335 (1996); J. Horder: 'Strict Liability, Statutory Construction, and the Spirit of Liberty', LQR 458 (2002); Robert Goff: 'The Mental Element in the Crime of Murder', 104 LQR 30 (1988); extracts from *Criminal Appeal Reports*: *R v Gibbins and Proctor*: 13 Cr App R 134, Court of Criminal Appeal (Darling, McCardie and Salter JJ) (1918); *Matthews and Alleyne*, 2 Cr App R 30, Crim LR 553, Court of Appeal, Criminal Division (Rix LJ, Crane J and Maddison HHJ) (2003); *R v Bryce*: EWCA Crim 1231, 2 Cr App R 592, Crim LR 936, Court of Appeal, Criminal Division (Potter LJ, Hooper and Astill JJ) (2004); *R v Gilmour*: 2 Cr App R 407, Court of Appeal of Northern Ireland (Carswell LCJ, Nicholson LJ and Coghlin J) (2000); *R v Becerra and Cooper*: 62 Cr App R 212, Court of Appeal, Criminal Division (Roskill and Bridge LJJ and Kilner Brown J) (1975); *R v Pommell*: 2 Cr App R 607, Court of Appeal, Criminal Division (Kennedy LJ, Steel and Hooper JJ) (1995); *R v Williams*: 78 Cr App R 276, Court of Appeal, Criminal Division (Lord Lane CJ, Skinner and McCowan JJ) (1987); *R v Martin (Anthony)*: 1 Cr App R 323, Court of Appeal, Criminal Division (Lord Woolf CJ, Wright and Grigson JJ) (2002); *Johnson*: 89 Cr App R 148 (1989); *R v Diana Richardson*: 2 Cr App R 200, Court of Appeal, Criminal Division (Otton LJ, Turner and Dyson JJ) (1998); *R v Pitchley*: 57 Cr App R 30, Court of Appeal, Criminal Division (Cairns LJ, Nield and Croom-Johnson JJ) (1972); *R v Appleyard*: 81 Cr App R 319, Court of Appeal, Criminal Division (Lord Lane CJ, Skinner and Macpherson JJ) (1985); *R v Hunt*: 66 Cr App R 105, Court of Appeal, Criminal Division (Roskill LJ, Wein and Slynn JJ) (1977); *Attorney-General's Reference (No 3 of 1992)*: 98 Cr App R 383, Court of Appeal, Criminal Division (Lord Taylor CJ, Schiemann and Wright JJ) (1993). Also extracts from *Archbold News* (Arch Rev), *European Human Rights Law Review* (EHRLR), *European Human Rights Reports* (EHRR), and *Road Traffic Reports* (RTR).

Taylor & Francis: extract from J. C. Smith: 'Responsibility in Criminal Law' in P. Bean and D. Whynes (eds): *Barbara Wootton, Essays in Her Honour* (Tavistock, Taylor & Francis Books, 1986).

Wiley-Blackwell: extracts from *Modern Law Review* (MLR): J. Chalmers and F. Leverick: 'Fair Labelling in Criminal Law' (2008) 71 MLR 217 and K. Amirthalingam: '*Caldwell* Recklessness is Dead: Long Live Mens Rea's Fecklessness' (2004) 63 MLR 491.

Every effort has been made to trace and contact copyright holders prior to going to press but this has not been possible in every case. Although we are continuing to seek the necessary permissions up to publication, if notified, the publisher will undertake to rectify any errors or omissions at the earliest opportunity.

Tables of Statutes

References in **bold** type indicate that the text is reproduced in full.

Table of Cases

Abbreviations

The following are the abbreviations used for the principal textbooks and legal journals cited in this book. References are to the latest editions, as shown below, unless it is specifically stated otherwise. The particulars of other works referred to in the text are set out in the text.

Archbold	*Criminal Pleading, Evidence and Practice* by J. F. Archbold (2014) by P. J. Richardson and others
Blackstone	*Blackstone's Criminal Practice* (2014) by D. Ormerod and Sir Anthony Hooper (eds)
Blackstone, *Commentaries*, i	*Commentaries on the Laws of England* by Sir William Blackstone, vol i (4 vols) (17th edn, 1830) by E. Christian
CFLQ	Child and Family Law Quarterly
CLJ	Cambridge Law Journal
CLP	Current Legal Problems
CLRC, Eighth Report	Criminal Law Revision Committee, Eighth Report, *Theft and Related Offences* (1966) Cmnd 2977
CLRC, Thirteenth Report	Criminal Law Revision Committee, Thirteenth Report, *Section 16 of the Theft Act 1968* (1977) Cmnd 6733
CLRC, Fourteenth Report	Criminal Law Revision Committee, Fourteenth Report, *Offences Against the Person* (1980) Cmnd 7844
CLRC, Fifteenth Report	Criminal Law Revision Committee, Fifteenth Report, *Sexual Offences* (1984) Cmnd 2913
Columbia L Rev	Columbia Law Review
Crim LR	Criminal Law Review
Criminal Law Essays	*Criminal Law: Essays in Honour of J. C.* Smith edited by P. F. Smith (1987)
Crim L & Philosophy	Criminal Law and Philosophy
E & P	International Journal of Evidence and Proof
East, I PC	*A Treatise of the Pleas of the Crown* by E. H. East, vol I (2 vols) (1803)
EHRLR	European Human Rights Law Review
Foster	*A Report on Crown Cases and Discourses on the Crown Law* by Sir Michael Foster (3rd edn, 1792) by M. Dodson
Griew, *Current Law Statutes Annotations*	*Current Law Statutes Annotations* (1981) by E. J. Griew
Hale, I PC	*The History of the Pleas of the Crown* by Sir Matthew Hale, vol i (2 vols) (1736)
Hall, *General Principles*	*General Principles of Criminal Law* (2nd edn, 1960) by J. Hall
Halsbury	*The Laws of England* by the Earl of Halsbury and Other Lawyers (5th edn, 2010–)
Harv LR	Harvard Law Review
Hawkins, I PC	*A Treatise of the Pleas of the Crown* by W. Hawkins, vol I (2 vols) (8th edn, 1795) by J. Curwood
ICCLR	International Company and Commercial Law Review
ICLQ	International and Comparative Law Quarterly
J Cr L & Cr	Journal of Criminal Law and Criminology (USA)

J Crim L	Journal of Criminal Law (English)
JR	Juridical Review
JSPTL	Journal of the Society of Public Teachers of Law
Kenny, *Outlines*	*Outlines of Criminal Law* by C. S. Kenny (19th edn, 1965) by J. W. C. Turner
KLJ	King's Law Journal
Law & Phil	Law and Philosophy
LC29	Law Com Report No 29, *Criminal Law: Report on Offences of Damage to Property* (1970)
LC76	Law Com Report No 76, *Conspiracy and Criminal Law Reform* (1976)
LC143	Law Com Report No 143, *Codification of the Criminal Law: A Report to the Law Commission* (1985) (draft Criminal Code Bill)
LC177	Law Com Report No 177, *A Criminal Code for England and Wales* (1989) (Draft Code)
LC218	Law Com Report No 218, *Legislating the Criminal Code: Offences Against the Person and General Principles* (1993)
LC237	Law Com Report No 237, *Involuntary Manslaughter* (1996)
LC276	Law Com Report No 276, *Fraud* (2002)
LC290	Law Com Report No 290, *Partial Defences to Murder* (2004)
LC300	Law Com Report No 300, *Inchoate Liability for Assisting and Encouraging Crime* (2006)
LC304	Law Com Report No 304, *Murder, Manslaughter and Infanticide* (2006)
LC305	Law Com Report No 305, *Participating in Crime* (2007)
LC314	Law Com Report No 314, *Intoxication and Criminal Liability* (2009)
LC318	Law Com Consultation Report No 318, *Conspiracy and Attempts* (2009)
LCCP 122	Law Com Consultation Paper No 122, *Legislating the Criminal Code: Offences Against the Person and General Principles* (1992)
LCCP 131	Law Com Consultation Paper No 131, *Assisting and Encouraging Crime* (1993)
LCCP 134	Law Com Consultation Paper No 134, *Consent and Offences Against the Person* (1994)
LCCP 136	Law Com Consultation Paper No 136, *The Year and A Day Rule in Homicide* (1994)
LCCP 139	Law Com Consultation Paper No 139, *Consent in the Criminal Law* (1995)
LCCP 150	Law Com Consultation Paper No 150, *Legislating the Criminal Code: Misuse of Trade Secrets* (1997)
LCCP 155	Law Com Consultation Paper No 155, *Legislating the Criminal Code: Fraud and Deception* (1999)
LCCP 173	Law Com Consultation Paper No 173, *Partial Defences to Murder* (2003)

LCCP 177	Law Com Consultation Paper No 177, *A New Homicide Act for England and Wales* (2006)
LCCP 183	Law Com Consultation Paper No 183, *Conspiracy and Attempts* (2007)
LCCP 195	Law Commission Consultation Paper No 195, *Criminal Liability in Regulatory Contexts* (2010)
LCCP 197	Law Commission Consultation Paper No 197, *Unfitness to Plead* (2010)
LCCP 200	Law Commission Consultation Paper No 200, *Simplification of Criminal Law: Kidnapping* (2011)
LCDP	Law Commission Discussion Paper, *Criminal Liability: Insanity and Automatism* (2013)
LQR	Law Quarterly Review
LS	Legal Studies, the Journal of the Society of Legal Scholars
Med Sci & L	Medicine, Science and the Law
MLR	Modern Law Review
NILQ	Northern Ireland Legal Quarterly
OJLS	Oxford Journal of Legal Studies
RCCP	Report of the Royal Commission on Capital Punishment (1953) Cmd 8932
Reshaping the Criminal Law	*Reshaping the Criminal Law: Essays in Honour of Glanville Williams* edited by P. R. Glazebrook (1978)
Russell	*Crime* by Sir W. O. Russell (12th edn, 1964) by J. W. C. Turner (2 vols)
Shute and Simester, *Criminal Law and Theory*	S. Shute and A. Simester (eds), *Criminal Law Theory: Doctrines of the General Part* (2002)
Smith, *Justification and Excuse*	*Justification and Excuse in the Criminal Law* by J. C. Smith (The Hamlyn Lectures, 1989)
Smith's Law of Theft	*The Law of Theft* (9th edn, 2007) by D. Ormerod and D. H. Williams
Smith and Hogan	*Smith and Hogan's Criminal Law* (13th edn, 2011) by D. Ormerod
Stephen, *Digest*	*A Digest of the Criminal Law* by Sir James Fitzjames Stephen (9th edn, 1950) by L. F. Struge
Stephen, HCL	*A History of the Criminal Law of England* by Sir James Fitzjames Stephen, (19th edn, 1950) by L. F. Sturge
Tadros, *Criminal Responsibility*	*Criminal Responsibility* (2005) by V. Tadros
Univ Western Aus Law Rev	University of Western Australia Law Review
Web CLI	Web Journal of Current Legal Issues
Williams, CLGP	*Criminal Law: The General Part* (2nd edn, 1961) by G. L. Williams
Williams, TBCL	*Textbook of Criminal Law* (2nd edn, 1983) by G. L. Williams
Yale LJ	Yale Law Journal

Recent Developments

You will see in chapter 14 (section 14.3.2, p 504) that we describe the *mens rea* for an attempt. At the time of writing, it seemed to be accepted that the prosecution had to prove intent as to any consequence element in the offence, but that recklessness as to a circumstance element would suffice if such a level of *mens rea* would be sufficient for the substantive offence that was being attempted. So, for example, with attempted criminal damage, it would have been sufficient to prove intent to cause damage (consequences) and recklessness as to whether the property belonged to another (circumstances), because the full offence of criminal damage requires only recklessness as to the circumstance element.

The validity of this approach was, however, doubted recently by the Court of Appeal *Pace and Rogers* [2014] EWCA Crim 186.

In response to the growing problem of metal theft, Thames Valley police undertook an investigation into scrap yards in their area. This investigation involved undercover police officers approaching scrap yard owners and offering to sell them metal that was apparently of suspicious provenance and which was presented as potentially being stolen. The metal was not in fact stolen but was the property of Thames Valley police. The appellants worked in a scrap yard and when approached by the undercover officers they agreed to buy the 'stolen' metal. They were convicted of attempting to conceal, disguise, or convert criminal property contrary to s 327(1) of the Proceeds of Crime Act 2002 (see Ch 27). The substantive offence under s 327 can be committed if D suspects that the property is from a criminal source when he conceals it etc. The defendants were charged with attempting to conceal etc. Was it necessary for the Crown to prove that they intended the metal was stolen or was it sufficient that they could prove the defendants suspected it was stolen?

The trial judge informed the jury that the metal in question was not in fact stolen, but that for the purposes of the law this did not matter. The judge directed the jury that the defendants could be guilty if they knew or suspected that the metal was stolen or had otherwise been obtained dishonestly.

The issue for the Court of Appeal was whether the attempt to commit the s 327 offence requires proof that the defendant intended or knew the property was criminal in origin although the substantive offence can be committed if the defendant merely suspects it is criminal property.

The Court of Appeal quashed the convictions and held that the trial judge's direction was defective. Davis LJ noted that to be guilty of an attempt, there must always be an intention as to the consequence element of the substantive offence, so that to be guilty of attempted murder, only intent to kill will suffice. His lordship further noted that there is uncertainty whether there must be intention as to all the elements of the actus reus of the substantive offence. Davis LJ explained how the Court of Appeal had earlier held in *Khan* ([1990] 2 All ER 783, discussed at p 502) that it sufficed for D to be reckless as to the circumstance element of rape, on the basis that this sufficed for the substantive offence. *Khan*, however, was distinguished on the grounds, inter alia, that the Court of Appeal in *Khan* had explicitly stated that it was not purporting to formulate a rule that would apply to all offences.

The Court of Appeal held

> 'Turning, then, to s.1(1) [of the Criminal Attempts Act 1981] we consider that, as a matter of ordinary language and in accordance with principle, an "intent to commit an offence" connotes an intent to commit **all the elements of the offence**. We can see no sufficient basis, whether linguistic or purposive, for construing it otherwise.' para [62] per Davis LJ (emphasis added).

This is a controversial decision. On its face, para 62 suggests that the Court is imposing a requirement of intention as to *every element* of the offence attempted. That is not a position the Court has previously adopted.

The Court draws analogy with the *mens rea* of all forms of statutory conspiracy. Under s 1(2) of the Criminal Law Act 1977 it is necessary to prove that the defendants 'intended or knew' the circumstance element of the offence they were agreeing to commit that would necessarily arise. See *Saik* [2006] UKHL 18; *Smith and Hogan's Criminal Law* (13th ed 2011), p442.

On a count of attempted money laundering, therefore, proof of suspicion was insufficient. When you are reading the chapter on attempts, consider whether it is problematic that if *Pace* is accepted as applying outside the context of money laundering, then on a count of attempted rape, the prosecution will have to prove that D intended that V would not be consenting.

1

Introduction

Unlike most jurisdictions, England and Wales has no criminal code. From very early times Parliament has created criminal offences. These have always taken effect in the context of the common law of crime, that is, the law made by the judges in the decided cases. The result is that the criminal law is spread across a huge range of statutes and decisions. No one is sure even how many criminal offences exist in English law.

J. Chalmers and F. Leverick, 'Tracking the Creation of Criminal Offences'
[2013] Crim LR 543

3,023 new offences?

In August 2006 it was claimed that the Labour government had created 3,023 offences since elected in May 1997. That figure has been regularly cited as evidence of the overuse of criminal law, and the Liberal Democrats made halting such overuse a commitment in their 2010 election manifesto. In due course, the *Coalition's Programme for Government*, published in May 2010, committed the government to 'introduc[ing] a new mechanism to prevent the proliferation of unnecessary new criminal offences'. In November 2010, the Ministry of Justice committed to creating 'a gateway to scrutinise all legislation containing criminal offences' and publishing annual statistics on the number of new offences.

According to the guidance contained in the resulting *Criminal Offences Gateway*, civil servants require 'Gateway clearance' if they propose to use legislation to create a new offence, repeal and re-enact an existing offence, amend an existing offence or create an enabling power in primary legislation providing for the creation or extension of criminal offences in secondary legislation or byelaws. The Secretary of State for Justice will approve proposals only if 'he is satisfied that the proposed offences are necessary': no test of necessity is set out, but there is a lengthy list of factors to be taken into account.

In December 2011, the Ministry of Justice published statistics on the creation of new criminal offences in England and Wales. According to these, 174 new criminal offences were created in the 12 months ending May 2011, compared to 712 in the 12 months ending May 2010.

At first sight, this suggests an impressive degree of success in stemming the tide of new offences. Matters are not, however, quite that simple. We have undertaken an independent research project examining the creation of offences over two time periods: the first 12 months of the New Labour government elected in 1997 and of the Coalition government elected in 2010. Our results are rather different. While the Ministry of Justice claims that 174 new offences applying to England and Wales were created in the first year of the Coalition government, our research produced a figure of 634. And while we have not ourselves examined the year prior to the Coalition government, our research demonstrates that the Ministry's own statistics do not provide an adequate factual basis for its claim that 2010–11 saw a 75.6 per cent fall in the number of offences created by legislation.

■ *Questions*

How many offences can you think of? Dozens? Hundreds? Can you name all 9,000+ that the criminal law assumes that you and all other people over the age of 10 know? Does it matter? Is what matters that you know where to look?

1.1 Sources of criminal law

1.1.1 Statutory offences

Whether the law relating to an offence is to be found in the common law (set out in section 1.1.2) or in a statute is frequently a matter of historical accident. The offences in statutes are not collected together as a catalogue of 'criminal legislation', and many offences appear in an otherwise unrelated statute, as for example with offences in the Companies Act 2006 or the Insolvency Act 1986.

Decided cases will be important in relation to understanding statutory and common law offences. When we seek to find the law in a statutory offence, the statute must always be the starting point but statutes have to be construed by the courts. Once the statute has been construed by a higher court it is that construction which counts. If it differs from the meaning which would naturally be put upon statute by the ordinary reader, it is the construction which prevails. The reader of s 3(1) of the Theft Act 1968 must learn that the words in that section, 'the rights of an owner', mean 'a right of an owner', because the House of Lords has so decided (see section 21.3, p 750). The Law Commission has pointed out (LC122, para 7.11) that the most important offences under the Offences Against the Person Act 1861 'have become in effect common law crimes, the context of which is determined by the case law and not by statute'. The words of the Act, when not positively misleading, are virtually irrelevant. That is an extreme case but, even in a relatively modern statute like the Theft Act 1968, the words of a section may be misleading to a reader who is unaware of the case law. Hence the emphasis put upon cases in this book.

1.1.1.1 Statutory interpretation

General principles of statutory interpretation will apply. There is a long-established principle applicable specifically in criminal law. Ambiguities in the definition of a criminal offence are to be construed in the defendant's favour in so far as that is compatible with the scope of definition:

> ...it is a universal principle that if a penal provision is reasonably capable of two interpretations, that interpretation which is most favourable to the accused must be adopted. (per Lord Reid in *Sweet v Parsley* [1970] AC 132)

This was reiterated more recently in *Hughes* [2013] UKSC 56 in which Lords Hughes and Toulson stated:

> A penal statute falls to be construed with a degree of strictness in favour of the accused. It is undoubtedly open to Parliament to legislate to create a harsh offence or penalty, just as it is open to it to take away fundamental rights, but it is not to be assumed to have done so unless that interpretation of its statute is compelled, and compelled by the language of the statute itself. The rule of construction which applies to penal legislation, and a fortiori to legislation which carries the penalty of imprisonment, is not identical to, but is somewhat analogous to, the principle of statutory interpretation known as the principle of legality.

The courts have considered how this principle relates to the general principle that where a statute is ambiguous, it is permissible to refer to the minister's statements in the parliamentary debates to determine the intended meaning: *Pepper v Hart* [1993] AC 593, HL. The courts have concluded that it is not permissible to use *Pepper v Hart* and refer to the parliamentary debates to enlarge the scope of liability, according to *Thet v DPP* [2006] EWHC 2701 (Admin). The appellant was convicted of an offence contrary to s 2(1) of the Asylum and Immigration (Treatment of Claimants, etc) Act 2004. In the course of the judgment, construing the provision, the court stated:

15. I would, however, question the use of *Pepper v Hart* in the context of a criminal prosecution. [Counsel] was not able to refer the court to any case in which *Pepper v Hart* has been used in that context. If a criminal statute is ambiguous, I would question whether it is appropriate by the use of *Pepper v Hart* to extend the ambit of the statute so as to impose criminal liability upon a defendant where, in the absence of the Parliamentary material, the court would not do so. It seems to me at least arguable that if a criminal statute is ambiguous, the defendant should have the benefit of the ambiguity.

However, in *Tabnak* [2007] EWCA Crim 380, [2007] 2 Cr App R 4 at [34], a failed asylum seeker was unwilling to provide information to enable travel documentation to be obtained to facilitate his deportation. He was convicted under s 35(3) of the Asylum and Immigration (Treatment of Claimants, etc) Act 2004. The Court of Appeal upheld his conviction. Lord Phillips CJ, *obiter*, noted that what had been said in *Thet v DPP* about the inappropriateness of invoking *Pepper v Hart* by the prosecution to admit parliamentary material in a criminal case as an aid to statutory construction, may not have the same force where a defendant in a criminal case seeks to rely on parliamentary material.

Another important feature of interpretation is that since the Human Rights Act 1998 came into force, the criminal courts have been obliged to interpret offences so as to be compatible with the rights guaranteed under the European Convention on Human Rights and Fundamental Freedoms (ECHR). Under s 3 of the 1998 Act the courts must ensure that statutes 'so far as it is possible to do so, be read and given effect in a way which is compatible with the Convention rights'. Examples of the criminal courts' approach to that duty can be seen in numerous cases. Lord Bingham summarized the position in *A-G's Reference (No 4 of 2002)* [2004] UKHL 43 at [28]:

First, the interpretative obligation under s 3 is a very strong and far reaching one, and may require the court to depart from the legislative intention of Parliament. Secondly, a Convention-compliant interpretation under s 3 is the primary remedial measure and a declaration of incompatibility under s 4 an exceptional course. Thirdly, it is to be noted that during the passage of the Bill through Parliament the promoters of the Bill told both Houses that it was envisaged that the need for a declaration of incompatibility would rarely arise. Fourthly, there is a limit beyond which a Convention-compliant interpretation is not possible, such limit being illustrated by *R (Anderson) v Secretary of State for the Home Department* [2003] 1 AC 837 and *Bellinger v Bellinger* [2003] 2 AC 467. In explaining why a Convention-compliant interpretation may not be possible, members of the committee used differing expressions: such an interpretation would be incompatible with the underlying thrust of the legislation, or would not go with the grain of it, or would call for legislative deliberation, or would change the substance of a provision completely, or would remove its pith and substance, or would violate a cardinal principle of the legislation.... All of these expressions, as I respectfully think, yield valuable insights, but none of them should be allowed to supplant the simple test enacted in the Act: 'So far as it is possible to do so...'. While the House declined to try to formulate precise rules... it was thought that cases in which s 3 could not be used would in practice be fairly easy to identify.

1.1.2 Common law offences

The general principles of criminal liability—principles dealing with whether someone has acted voluntarily, liability for omissions, definitions of terms of mens rea, criminal capacity etc—are nearly all to be found in common law, not in an Act of Parliament. The great majority of crimes, however, are now defined by statute but some very important crimes are not, including murder, manslaughter and conspiracy to defraud. These are important in terms of the seriousness and number of prosecutions which occur.

Challenges have been made in recent years to some of the best established common law offences—for example, the gross negligence manslaughter offence, *Misra* [2004] EWCA Crim 2375 (dealt with in full in section 17.3.3.1, p 633). The defence challenge to these offences is on the basis that they lack sufficient clarity and certainty of definition to be compatible with the rule of law. The challenges to the common law offences on grounds of certainty have only rarely met with success. For example, in *Misra* the challenge was to the offence of gross negligence manslaughter, which requires the jury to decide whether the defendant's negligence was so 'gross' as to deserve to be treated as criminal (dealt with in section 17.3.3, p 632). Until the jury in an individual case has returned a verdict on that matter no defendant can know whether his conduct is going to be classified as so gross as to be criminal. He might argue that he cannot know the scope of the criminal law. The Court of Appeal rejected that argument as follows:

> 63. On examination, this represents one example, among many, of problems which juries are expected to address on a daily basis. They include equally difficult questions, such as whether a defendant has acted dishonestly, by reference to contemporary standards, or whether he has acted in reasonable self-defence, or, when charged with causing death by dangerous driving, whether the standards of his driving fell far below what should be expected of a competent and careful driver. These examples represent the commonplace for juries. Each of these questions could be said to be vague and uncertain. If he made enquiries in advance, at most an individual would be told the principle of law which the jury would be directed to apply: he could not be advised what a jury would think of the individual case, and how it would be decided. That involves an element of uncertainty about the outcome of the decision-making process, but not unacceptable uncertainty about the offence itself. (per Judge LJ)

One successful challenge was in *GG* [2008] UKHL 17 where the House of Lords upheld the argument from the defence that the common law offence of conspiracy to defraud could not be used to prosecute a price-fixing arrangement in the absence of evidence of further aggravating features. The offence of conspiracy to defraud has existed for several hundred years, and has never been used to prosecute such conduct before.

The House of Lords in that case and the related appeal in *Norris v USA* [2008] UKHL 16 reiterated the importance of respect for the principle of legal certainty in common law offences (*Norris* at [52]–[62]). This echoed the comments made by Lord Bingham in *Rimmington* [2006] 1 AC 459 (below), and in *Jones* [2007] 1 AC 136. In those cases the House of Lords emphasized several principles:

> no one should be punished under a law unless it is sufficiently clear and certain to enable him to know what conduct is forbidden before he does it; and no one should be punished for any act which was not clearly and ascertainably punishable when the act was done. (at [33])

In addition, in *Jones*, Lord Bingham referred to the:

> important democratic principle in this country: that it is for those representing the people of the country in Parliament, not the executive and not the judges, to decide what conduct should be treated as lying so far outside the bounds of what is acceptable in our society as to attract criminal penalties. One would need very compelling reasons for departing from that principle. (at [29])

Even though the common law challenges have not often been successful in persuading courts to reject the application of a common law offence to given circumstances, they have encouraged the courts to acknowledge a restrictive interpretation in general. For example, in *Goldstein and Rimmington* [2005] UKHL 63 the House of Lords emphasized that the scope of a common law offence ought not to be radically enlarged. (The case involved the application of the common law offence of public nuisance (which is not dealt with in this book—for detailed analysis, see *Smith and Hogan*, Ch 32)):

There are two guiding principles: no one should be punished under a law unless it is sufficiently clear and certain to enable him to know what conduct is forbidden before he does it; and no one should be punished for any act which was not clearly and ascertainably punishable when the act was done. If the ambit of a common law offence is to be enlarged, it 'must be done step by step on a case by case basis and not with one large leap': *Clark (Mark)* [2003] EWCA Crim 991, [2003] 2 Cr App R 363, para 13.

Common law offences are generally very broadly defined. Often they have been superseded in part by statutory offences. In *Goldstein and Rimmington*, above, the legitimacy of the common law offence of public nuisance was recognized, but Lord Bingham of Cornhill made the following observation at [30]:

Where Parliament has defined the ingredients of an offence, perhaps stipulating what shall and shall not be a defence, and has prescribed a mode of trial and a maximum penalty, it must ordinarily be proper that conduct falling within that definition should be prosecuted for the statutory offence and not for a common law offence which may or may not provide the same defences and for which the potential penalty is unlimited.... *It cannot in the ordinary way be a reason for resorting to the common law offence that the prosecutor is freed from mandatory time limits or restrictions on penalty.* It must rather be assumed that Parliament imposed the restrictions which it did having considered and weighed up what the protection of the public reasonably demanded. I would not go to the length of holding that conduct may never be lawfully prosecuted as a generally-expressed common law crime where it falls within the terms of a specific statutory provision, but good practice and respect for the primacy of statute do in my judgment require that conduct falling within the terms of a specific statutory provision should be prosecuted under that provision unless there is good reason for doing otherwise. (emphasis added)

Similarly, Lord Rodger of Earlsferry stated:

53. Here, however, according to what Mr Perry [Counsel for the Crown] told the House, the Crown had deliberately chosen the common law offence in order to avoid the time-bar which Parliament had enacted and to allow the judge, if he thought fit, to impose a heavier sentence than the one permitted under statute. The issue bears some resemblance to the issue in *R v J* [2005] 1 AC 562. *There is no suggestion, of course, that the Crown acted in bad faith.* On the contrary, it is easy to understand why they did what they did. In a particular case, such as this, a time-limit which prevents prosecution once a certain time has passed since the act was committed can appear to be arbitrary and to reward an offender for concealing his offences. The sentence available under the statute may also seem inadequate to reflect the gravity of the defendant's conduct. But Parliament has deliberately chosen to intervene and to prescribe a period within which conduct of this kind can be prosecuted summarily under statute. This must be taken to reflect Parliament's judgment that, if the conduct has not been prosecuted within that time, the public interest is now against proceeding. That judgment may be based on various factors. Parliament may, for example, consider that after a certain period everyone should move on and prosecutors should turn their attention to other matters. Police and prosecution resources, it may be thought, are better spent on detecting and prosecuting recent, rather than stale, offences of this kind or recent, rather than old, incidents in a course of conduct. More serious matters should be given priority. Similarly, in the matter of sentence, Parliament has reached a view that

certain conduct is appropriately covered by an offence which can be tried only summarily and which should attract no more than a particular level of sentence. Parliament has also fixed the maximum sentence to be imposed in summary proceedings, even where the defendant is convicted of more than one charge. Again, in any particular case, the sentence available under statute may appear to the prosecutor to be inadequate. But Parliament is entitled to place an offence in what it regards as the appropriate level in the hierarchy of offences and to limit the sentencing power of a court where the accused is not tried by jury.

54. It is not for the Crown to second-guess Parliament's judgment as to any of these matters by deliberately setting out to reject the applicable statutory offences and to charge the conduct in question under common law in order to avoid the time-limits or limits on sentence which Parliament has thought appropriate. It may be that, in the light of experience, Parliament's judgment can be seen to have been flawed or to have been superseded by events. Doubtless, the prosecuting authorities have channels through which they can—and perhaps should—draw any such perceived deficiencies to the attention of the Home Secretary. It is then up to ministers and, ultimately, Parliament to decide whether the law should be changed. But, unless and until it is changed, its provisions should be respected and the Crown should not devise a strategy to avoid them.

This argument that the existence of a statutory offence precludes reliance on a common law one with which it overlaps must be kept within reasonable bounds. First, something more than mere overlap is required. In *Rimmington* there was a general offence of public nuisance which had been superseded in many instances by specific statutory wrongs. In those cases the offence of public nuisance overlapped completely with the statutory crime. Second, it is worth noting the qualification of Lord Bingham (quoted previously):

I would not go to the length of holding that conduct may never be lawfully prosecuted as a generally-expressed common law crime where it falls within the terms of a specific statutory provision, but good practice and respect for the primacy of statute do in my judgment require that conduct falling within the terms of a specific statutory provision should be prosecuted under that provision unless there is good reason for doing otherwise.

If the principle is not kept within reasonable bounds, the ramifications would be staggering. It would be wrong if serious common law offences which had partial overlap with statutory offences could not be charged.

1.1.3 EU and international law

As supranational legal regimes have begun to exert more of an influence on English criminal law, the range of sources extends ever wider. The most obvious example is European Union law, which lies behind numerous offences in English law. There is relatively little case law on EU law impacting on criminal law, but that is not to say that EU law does not have an important influence on certain areas. For example, in some aspects of cartels in competition law that are now criminalized by the Enterprise Act 2002, and in areas of VAT evasion and carousel frauds. Furthermore, in relation to regulatory offences the EU has a far more significant impact, as for example with environmental crimes.

Just how much impact EU law can have was made starkly clear due to a problem that occurred with the Video Recordings Act 1984. A defect with that Act arose because the European Commission had not originally been notified of its provisions in accordance with applicable EU law (the Technical Standards Directive, Directive 83/189 EEC). The provisions relating to video classification and distribution were unenforceable within the UK, and all prosecutions were discontinued. The Director of Public Prosecutions was informed by Barbara Follett MP, Minister for Culture and Tourism, that 'offences under the Act are unenforceable and, accordingly, all affected current prosecutions under the Act should be discontinued and future prosecutions should not be undertaken.' To remedy the defect, Parliament rushed through the Video Recordings Act 2010. However, that left the question of what to do with the convictions under the 1984 Act. In the conjoined cases of *Budimir* [2010] EWCA Crim 1486 and *Interfact Ltd v Liverpool City Council (No 2)* [2010] EWHC 1604 (Admin), the Court of Appeal, having referred to constitutional writings and a range of EU and ECHR jurisprudence, rejected the argument that the convictions were invalid because they were based on a 'law' that was not enforceable. In the view of the court, the convictions remained valid in each case. Lord Judge CJ concluded:

87.... [T]he convictions remain safe convictions.

(1) Applying principles of national law, the convictions in these cases have not given rise to any substantial injustice and therefore there are no grounds to set aside the convictions.

(2) There is no obligation on this court, either under EU law or under the European Convention on Human Rights, as given effect by the Human Rights Act 1998, to set aside the convictions.

The court also rejected challenges based on Articles 7 and 10 of the ECHR. The Supreme Court refused permission to appeal, despite the Lord Chief Justice's certified question.

■ *Question*
Do you agree with the court's assessment?

EU law aside, the English courts' approach to incorporating into domestic law offences existing at supranational level has been markedly cautious. In *Jones and others* [2006] UKHL 16 (dealt with in full in section 11.3.2.9, p 376), the defendants claimed, *inter alia*, that they were entitled to damage the property belonging to the armed forces because they were doing so to prevent the armed forces committing a crime in international law by the continued use of force in Iraq. The House of Lords rejected a claim that the crime of aggression in international law had become assimilated into English domestic law. In the course of the judgments, it was made clear that statute law was the sole source of new criminal offences and it was for those elected representatives of the country in Parliament, not the executive and not the judges, to decide what conduct should be treated as criminal. An example of a statute that incorporates into domestic law offences that exist in international law is the International Criminal Court Act 2001. As a result of the Act, genocide, crimes against humanity and war crimes are now offences in English law. Section 71 of the Coroners and Justice Act 2009 is another example of such a statute. The offences of slavery, servitude and compulsory labour are modelled to a significant extent on Article 4 of the ECHR. See section 18.7, p 670.

1.2 The label of an offence

As has already been pointed out, there exist thousands of offences in English law. Would it be possible or desirable for the criminal law to operate with fewer offences? For example, instead of having murder and the various manslaughter offences, would it be simpler to have a single offence of 'homicide'? One reason why this would not be desirable is that it would be contrary to the principle of fair labelling. Andrew Ashworth states that the concern of fair labelling is as follows:

> to see that widely felt distinctions between kinds of offences and degrees of wrongdoing are respected and signalled by the law, and that offences are subdivided and labelled so as to represent fairly the nature and magnitude of the law-breaking.

Consider the following extract.

J. Chalmers and F. Leverick, 'Fair Labelling in Criminal Law'
(2008) 71 MLR 217

Why does labelling matter?

A further preliminary question is whether the label attached by the state to an offender's conduct matters at all. The answer to this is that labelling of criminal offences clearly does matter to some extent. We have already seen that it would be impractical to operate a purely descriptive system of criminal law whereby the offender's conduct is set out in narrative form without any attempt to categorise. At the other extreme, the criminal law could dispense with description entirely, convicting offenders merely of 'an offence', and leaving all the work to be done in sentencing, regardless of whether the conduct in question involved killing, sexual assault or shoplifting. But this would be equally impractical and no rational system of criminal law could operate in this manner. Quite apart from the fact that the severity of sentencing is a very blunt tool for assessing the level of a person's wrongdoing, it may also paint an inaccurate picture – a sentence may, for example, be substantially aggravated or mitigated as a result of factors which are unrelated to and tell us nothing about the offence itself or the offender's culpability.

Given that a criminal record has a well-documented deleterious effect on employability and earning power, it would clearly be unfair on an offender for her criminal record to misrepresent her wrongdoing. Employers likewise would seem to have a legitimate interest in knowing whether a prospective employee has a criminal record, and are surely entitled to know at least whether her crime was broadly one of dishonesty, violence, sexual misconduct, or merely a minor public order offence. Such knowledge may, indeed, be essential in order to comply with statutory obligations such as those under the Protection of Children Act 1999 [Scotland], and it is possible that the employer's knowledge might be relevant to future questions of vicarious liability. Even in this broad sense, the law sometimes fails. An example is the Scottish case of *HM Advocate v Forbes*, where the accused was alleged to have broken into a flat with the intent to rape the occupant (he had removed his clothing and was carrying a tube of cream and a garment fashioned as a hood). Although Forbes was charged initially with 'housebreaking with intent to rape', the appeal court held that no such crime was recognised by Scots law, and that the appropriate charge was one of breach of the peace.

But if we accept that labelling matters at least to some degree, what is fair labelling? How narrow does the categorisation of offences need to be in order to be 'fair'? What does fairness mean in this context? Could we, as Paul Robinson has suggested, define offences in the broadest of terms (for example 'injury to a person' or 'damage to or theft of property') and leave the majority of work to be done at the sentencing stage? Or would we lose something of importance to the criminal law by doing so?

In attempting to address some of these questions, it may be productive to start by considering in more detail why labelling matters. In his original exposition of the concept in 1982, Ashworth himself said very little about why labelling is important. He dealt with the issue only towards the end of his paper and stated that, while it might be assumed that at the time of the court hearing the police, offenders, court officials and so on will be aware of the circumstances of any offence, and will not judge it purely by its legal label:

[O]nce the label is entered on the person's criminal record the passage of time will dim recollections of the precise nature of the offence and may result in the label being taken at face value. Both out of fairness to the individual and in order to ensure accuracy in our penal system, therefore, the legal designation of an offence should fairly represent the nature of the offender's criminality.

In *Principles of Criminal Law*, Ashworth is more expansive, noting essentially two reasons why fair labelling is important, namely 'proportionality' and 'maximum certainty'. In the section headed 'proportionality', it becomes clear during the course of the discussion that the main concern is actually fairness to offenders. The point being made under the heading 'maximum certainty' is less clear, but Ashworth touches upon the importance of legal definitions reflecting 'common patterns of thought in society' (although without really explaining why this matters) and the argument that broad labels give too much discretion to sentencers and to officials charged with enforcing the law.

■ *Question*

Do you agree that fair labelling is important? As you study the offences in this book, consider the extent to which they conform to the principle of fair labelling.

1.3 The Human Rights Act 1998

In addition to the primary and secondary legislation of the UK Parliament, and the decisions of the English and Welsh courts, it is increasingly important to consider other legal sources which will impact on the way that English criminal law is defined and applied. Although the ECHR impact is most significant in the context of evidence and procedure, the ECHR through the Human Rights Act also has a direct impact on the operation of the substantive criminal law in many ways. The ECHR rights will have relevance in many different offences. For example, in cases involving homicide issues under Article 2 and the right to life might be engaged, in sexual offences Article 8 and the right to respect for privacy may arise, in offences involving speech or protest Article 10 rights of freedom of expression might be engaged. In terms of the definition of crimes, the greatest impact might have been expected to be through Article 7, which proscribes retrospective criminalization, including a prohibition on criminal laws which are too vague and uncertain.

Article 7 provides:

(1) No one shall be held guilty of any criminal offence on account of any act or omission which did not constitute a criminal offence under national or international law at the time when it was committed. Nor shall a heavier penalty be imposed than the one that was applicable at the time the criminal offence was committed.

(2) This Article shall not prejudice the trial and punishment of any person for any act or omission which, at the time it was committed, was criminal according to the general principles of law recognised by civilised nations.

The European Court held in *Kokkinakis v Greece* (1994) 17 EHRR 397, and has reiterated many times since, that:

Article 7 is not confined to prohibiting the retrospective application of the criminal law to an accused's disadvantage: it also embodies, more generally, the principle that only the law can define a crime and prescribe a penalty (*nullum crimen, nulla poena sine lege*) and the principle that the criminal law must not be extensively construed to an accused's detriment, for instance by analogy . . . it follows that an offence must be clearly defined in the law. (*SW v UK* [1995] 21 EHRR 363, para 35)

The court looks to whether the individual can know from the wording of the relevant provision and, if need be, with the assistance of the courts' interpretation of it, what acts and omissions will make him criminally liable.

This is not a prohibition on the development of the common law. As the Court noted in *SW*:

> However clearly drafted a legal provision may be, in any system of law, including criminal law, there is an inevitable element of judicial interpretation. There will always be a need for elucidation of doubtful points and for adaptation to changing circumstances. Indeed, in the United Kingdom, as in the other Convention States, the progressive development of the criminal law through judicial law-making is a well entrenched and necessary part of legal tradition. Article 7 of the Convention cannot be read as outlawing the gradual clarification of the rules of criminal liability through judicial interpretation from case to case, provided that the resultant development is consistent with the essence of the offence and could reasonably be foreseen.

To date the English courts have taken a very narrow view of the protection afforded by Article 7 and have failed to accept that crimes such as manslaughter by gross negligence (see *Misra* in section 17.3.3.1, p 633), public nuisance (*Goldstein* in section 1.1.2) and encouraging or assisting offences believing one or more will be committed (see *S&H*, section 12.2.3.2, p 455) are incompatible with Article 7 on the grounds of their vagueness. That is not to say that Article 7 is redundant. In *Norris v USA* [2008] UKHL 16; *GG* [2008] UKHL 17, the House of Lords relied on Article 7 in rejecting the Crown's use of conspiracy to defraud when that offence had never previously been used to prosecute the alleged wrongdoing—price-fixing. The House acknowledged (at [55]) the 'consistent message…through cases decided from 1875 through to 1984, was that price-fixing was not of itself capable of constituting a crime…. There was no reported case, indeed, it would appear, no unreported case, no textbook, no article which suggested otherwise.' As such, it would infringe the principle of legality to impose the offence without warning. The House of Lords distinguished *SW* since in that case there was a gradual change in the law incrementally criminalizing marital rape and hence the availability of the charge had become reasonably foreseeable.

As the Human Rights Act was being implemented, leading commentators debated the likely impact the ECHR might have in producing greater certainty in the substantive criminal law. However, whether Article 7 would fulfil its promise depended to a large extent on how it was interpreted and applied by the European Court of Human Rights.

C. Murphy, 'The Principle of Legality in Criminal Law under the European Convention on Human Rights'
(2010) 2 EHRLR 192

Introduction

The core of the rule of law in criminal law can be found in art.7 of the European Convention on Human Rights (ECHR) and its requirement of *nullum crimen, noella poena sine lege*. Article 7 ECHR is a non-derogable clause, and so cannot be avoided in times of national emergency. This places it alongside the prohibitions on torture and slavery as a "higher-value" ECHR provision. The importance of the principle of legality in criminal law has been emphasised by the European Court of Human Rights. In the recent case of *Kafkaris*, the Court declared that:

'The guarantee enshrined in Article 7, which is *an essential element of the rule of law*, occupies a prominent place in the Convention system of protection…It should be construed and applied, as follows from its object and purpose, in such a way as to provide effective safeguards against arbitrary prosecution, conviction and punishment.'

Similar statements concerning the rule of law had been made in previous cases. However, despite the Court's rhetoric, art.7 ECHR is in many respects the poorer relation to the better-developed art.6 ECHR (right to a fair trial). Although the 1990s saw art.7 considered for the first time, the number of cases citing the article remains low. In a survey conducted by Greer in 2006, he noted that only nine breaches of art.7 had been identified by the Court in the years 1999–2005. By way of comparison, over 2,000 breaches of art.6 were found in the same period. In academia, the article is oft-cited but little discussed. The leading textbooks on the Convention, including those by Janis, Kay and Bradley, and Jacobs and White, each only devote a handful of pages to the clause.

The article itself is similar to its equivalent (art.15) in the International Covenant of Civil and Political Rights (ICCPR). In this study, the article is described as entailing three distinct (but overlapping) rules. First, only the law can define a crime and prescribe a penalty. Secondly, conduct may not be subject to retrospective prohibition. Thirdly, conduct may not attract a higher penalty than that provided for in law when the action took place. These three prohibitions are subject to the single explicit limitation on the rule contained in art.7(2) ECHR.10 Each aspect is considered in turn in the following discussion.

...

Accessibility and foreseeability

In *Kafkaris*, the Court noted that the definition of both the offence and the penalty must be accessible and foreseeable. These twin requirements have consistently featured in the Court's case law, even outside the context of art.7(1) ECHR. Although frequently mentioned in art.7 judgments, it is not clear if accessibility and foreseeability are related but distinct qualities, or are one and the same. Despite inconsistencies in the language used by the Court, it is possible to distinguish two different elements. First, the law must be sufficiently clear for individuals to conduct themselves in accordance with its commands (accessibility), and secondly, where there is judicial development of the law, any changes must be predictable (foreseeability).

Accessibility and foreseeability do not prevent laws from being broadly drafted where this is necessary for the law to fulfil its role. As a result, laws concerned with offences such as proselytism and terrorism may be vague, but still compliant with art.7 ECHR. Regarding the 'clarity' of the law (accessibility in the plain meaning of the word), the Court has noted that:

> 'An individual must know from the wording of the relevant provision and, if need be, with the assistance of the courts' interpretation of it, what acts and omissions will make him criminally liable and what penalty will be imposed...a law may still satisfy the requirement...where the person concerned has to take appropriate legal advice to assess, to a degree that is reasonable in the circumstances, the consequences which a given action may entail.'

The 'thin ice' principle is relevant here. Lord Morris [in *Knuller v DPP* [1973] AC 435] described this as the idea that 'those who skate on thin ice can hardly expect to find a sign which will denote the precise spot where he [*sic*] will fall in'. Despite Ashworth's claim that the 'thin ice' principle should not 'trump' the absolute art.7(1) right, the European Court seems willing to allow it to do so. In *Coeme*, it was held that 'the applicants could not have been unaware that the conduct that they were accused of might make them liable to prosecution'. Similarly in *Custers*, the Court declared that it was predictable that 'the applicants risked being sentenced to a fine'. This reference to *risk* that criminal sanctions *might* follows counteracts the foreseeability requirement. The point was put particularly clearly in *Cantoni*. The Court declared that there are always 'grey areas at the fringes of the definition [of the law]' and art.7(1) ECHR simply requires that the law is 'sufficiently clear in the large majority of cases ... the applicants must have known on the basis of their behaviour that they ran a *real risk of prosecution*'. Finally on this point, if consulting the courts is necessary for the precise meaning of the law to be determined, then art.7 ECHR must be understood as having strong links to an individual's right to legal counsel and access to justice more broadly.

The second qualitative element relates to changes to the law (foreseeability properly understood). The European Court of Human Rights has consistently held that it does not undermine the foreseeability of the law if it is adapted to reflect changing social circumstances. This change may be gradual or, in certain circumstances, may be abrupt. Gradual change is demonstrated in *SW and CR v United Kingdom*. There, the Court held that the removal of the marital rape exception by common law development was foreseeable. It held that the House of Lords judgment:

> '. . . [D]id no more than continue a perceptible line of case-law development dismantling the immunity of a husband from prosecution for rape upon his wife . . . there was an evident evolution, which was consistent with the very essence of the offence, of the criminal law through judicial interpretation towards treating such conduct generally as within the scope of the offence of rape. This evolution had reached a stage where judicial recognition of the absence of immunity had become a reasonably foreseeable development of the law.'

Despite the apparent foreseeability, *SW and CR* has been the subject of criticism. Beddard notes that in the unlikely event that the applicants had sought legal advice prior to committing the acts, the advice would most likely be that while reform was imminent, the exception was still valid law in the United Kingdom. Furthermore, such a profound change in the law of criminal liability should arguably be the province of the legislature, not the judiciary.

In the German reunification cases, the Court noted that changes to the law may be more dramatic. As discussed above, the Court held it legitimate for the unified German courts to convict based on GDR law, even where the organs of the former state would not have done so. The Court also commented on the foreseeability of the applicants' prosecution. It reiterated that the criminal law must be adapted to 'changing circumstances'. Whereas this usually happens gradually, the Court held it was 'wholly valid where, as in the present case, one State has succeeded another'. The reasons offered to sustain this conclusion were that (1) it was consistent with the system of the Convention, (2) the GDR Parliament has expressed such a wish, and (3) due to the 'pre-eminence' of the right to life in international human rights instruments. None of these reasons can truly justify what is, in essence, a retrospective change to an entire legal system. It is argued below that the marital rape and German reunification cases are better read as the 'balancing' of art.7 ECHR with the general spirit of the Convention. In other, more mundane circumstances, the European Court of Human Rights has held a dramatic departure from precedent to offend the requirement of foreseeability. In *Pessino*, a builder was prosecuted for carrying out construction in violation of a court order prohibiting him from doing so. Similar breaches of such court orders in the past had not attracted criminal liability. The abrupt change in approach by the French Court of Cassation resulted in a breach of art.7.

As the European Court of Human Rights itself has noted, the law must change to adapt to the facts of society it serves. When this occurs through the legislative process, there is at least the warning that process provides, and the democratic legitimacy derived from the institution. When criminal law is abruptly changed by courts, neither warning nor legitimacy are the same (no matter how many academics or official reports may have foreshadowed it). Article 7 requires that the guiding principle should always be the ability of individuals to plan their affairs in accordance with the law.

Murphy's characterization of Article 7 as the 'poorer relation' is borne out from an examination of domestic case law also. As has already been pointed out and will be examined later in greater detail, the Court of Appeal has given short shrift to the proposition that gross negligence manslaughter and the offence contained in s 46 of the Serious Crime Act 2007 violate Article 7.

1.4 Codification of criminal law

It was thought that the enactment of the Human Rights Act 1998 might serve as a catalyst for the implementation of the Criminal Code.

Much effort has gone into proposals to codify our criminal law—so far, in vain. Criminal Law Commissioners worked from 1833 to 1849 (and two major Bills based on their work were introduced in 1853) but made no progress, largely because of the opposition by the judges to codification of the common law. Then a judge who was also a great criminal lawyer, Sir James Fitzjames Stephen, prepared a draft code which, he said, represented the labour of many of the best years of his life and which was introduced into Parliament in 1878 and again in 1879. Again the effort failed, probably because of opposition by the judges, especially Lord Cockburn CJ.

Modified versions of Stephen's Code became the law in Canada, New Zealand and many other jurisdictions but nothing significant happened in England until 1967 when the Home Secretary of the time, Mr Roy Jenkins, made a speech in favour of codification. Almost immediately, the Law Commission, in its second programme (1968), stated its objective of a comprehensive examination of the criminal law with a view to its codification. It established a working party which produced a series of valuable papers on the general principles of criminal law. In 1980 the Commission appointed a Criminal Code Team to consider and make proposals in relation to a code. The team reported in 1985 with a draft Criminal Code Bill covering general principles of liability and offences against the person (LC 143). The generally favourable reception given to the report encouraged the Commission to proceed with the preparation of a more complete code covering, in Part I, general principles and, in Part II, the range of specific offences which would be expected in a code. A report and draft Criminal Code Bill (Draft Code, LC177) was published in 1989. The draft Bill is intended for the most part to be a restatement of the existing law but it also incorporates law reform proposals made by official bodies such as the Criminal Law Revision Committee and the Law Commission itself.

There was substantial support for codification including that from very senior judges.

The Hon Mrs Justice Arden DBE, 'Criminal Law at the Crossroads: The Impact of Human Rights from The Law Commission's Perspective and The Need for a Code'
[1999] Crim LR 439

Our criminal law is a mixed system of statutory provisions and common law. The judges can within limits keep the common law up to date. Statute law, however, has to be kept up to date by Parliament. For many years there has been legislative inertia. The situation is that there is an accumulated backlog of work for Parliament leaving large areas of criminal statutes needing reform.... The enactment of the Human Rights Act 1998 creates a new and pressing need for reform.

Lord Bingham CJ, 'Must We Wait for Ever?'
[1998] Crim LR 694

The arguments in favour of codification are what they have always been. First, it would bring clarity and accessibility to the law. As the Attorney-General put it in the House of Commons 130 years ago:

'Surely, it is a desirable thing that anybody who may want to know the law on a particular subject should be able to turn to a chapter of the Code, and there find the law he is in search of explained in a few intelligible and well-constructed sentences; nor would he have to enter upon a long examination of Russell on Crimes, or Archbold, and other text-books, because he would have a succinct and clear statement before him. (Hansard, HC, April 3, 1879, vol. 245 (3rd series), col. 316)'

Secondly, a code would bring coherence to this branch of the law. Sir John Smith expressed his general disbelief in codes—a disbelief which I for my part share—but he continued:

> 'The criminal law is entirely different. It is incoherent and inconsistent. State almost any general principle and you find one or more leading cases which contradict it. It is littered with distinctions which have no basis in reason but are mere historical accidents. I am in favour of codification of the criminal law because I see no other way of reducing a chaotic system to order, of eliminating irrational distinctions and of making the law reasonably comprehensible, accessible and certain. These are all practical objects. Irrational distinctions mean injustice. A is treated differently from B when there is no rational ground for treating him differently; and this is not justice. (Codification of the Criminal Law, Child & Co. Lecture, 1986)'

Sir John has entertained generations of students, practitioners and judges by highlighting the anomalies in our present law. As the [then] Chairman of the Law Commission has herself said, the cure now can only be achieved by codification; it cannot be provided by the courts alone. Thirdly, a code would bring greater certainty to the law, and in this of all fields the law should be so far as possible certain. The arguments for incremental development of the law, persuasive elsewhere, have no application here. It is not just that a defendant should be held punishable for an act which would not have been thought criminal when he did it; and if he is held not liable for conduct which would at that time have been thought criminal, the almost inevitable consequence is that others have been unjustly punished. Incorporation of the ECHR reinforces the need for certainty if the principle of legality is to be observed. Even the most breathless admirer of the common law must regard it as a reproach that after 700 years of judicial decision-making our highest tribunal should have been called upon time and again in recent years to consider the mental ingredients of murder, the oldest and most serious of crimes... One hopes that parliamentary time may yet be found to achieve something that has eluded our predecessors but would, I think, come to be recognised as an important milestone in our legal and public life.

A Government paper, 'Criminal Justice: The Way Ahead', included plans for 'a consolidated, modernised core criminal code'. The prospect of a single codifying statute was unrealistic. The Law Commission did, however, begin to produce a series of Bills which could have been consolidated. The Law Commission's Report (LC218), *Legislating the Criminal Code* (1993), proposed to begin with non-fatal offences against the person and contains a draft Bill covering these offences and, most importantly, some provisions governing general principles of liability which would be applicable to all offences. In February 1998 the Home Office published a Consultation Paper, 'Violence: Reforming the Offences Against the Person Act 1861' with a revised draft Bill, discussed [1998] Crim LR 317. This seemed to give real hope of a significant start on the enactment of the Code but no more was heard of the outcome of the consultation process stalled.

In more recent years the Law Commission has moved away from a programme of implementing a single code of criminal law and opted to put forward individual law reform proposals which, incrementally, will codify the criminal law. We have seen numerous examples in the last few years including the reform of incitement in the Serious Crime Act 2007, Part 2 (see Chapter 12), the Fraud Act 2006 (see Chapter 25), replacing the deception offences and the Bribery Act 2010 replacing old statutory offences of corruption.

Provisions of the Draft Code are, however, useful in understanding and scrutinizing the present law and will be found at appropriate points throughout the book.

■ *Questions*

If all of the offences known to English criminal law were printed in a single volume which was available at a reasonable price, who would buy it? Would it reduce the amount of crime? Would it enhance the quality of justice?

By 2014, the prospect of a criminal code for England and Wales has all but vanished. Indeed in its 10th Programme of Law Reform, the Law Commission removed mention of a codification project and introduced a new item, which seeks to simplify selected common law offences.

On the merits of codification generally, see G. de Búrca and S. Gardner, 'Codification of the Criminal Law' (1990) 10 OJLS 559.

FURTHER READING

P. Alldridge, 'Making Criminal Law Known' in S. Shute and A. Simester (eds), *Criminal Law Theory: Doctrines of the General Part* (2002)

R. A. Duff, 'Rule Violations and Wrong Doings' in S. Shute and A. Simester (eds), *Criminal Law Theory: Doctrines of the General Part* (2002)

Codification

S. Gardner, 'Reiterating the Criminal Code' (1992) 55 MLR 839

I. Hare, 'A Compelling Case for the Code' (1993) 56 MLR 74

On EU criminal law

G. Corstens, 'Criminal Law in the First Pillar?' (2003) 11 Eur J Crime, Crim L & Crim Justice 131

C. Harding and J. B. Banach-Gutierrez, 'The Emergent EU Criminal Policy: Identifying the Species' (2012) 37 EL Rev 758

V. Mitsilegas, *EU Criminal Law* (2009)

ECHR

B. Emmerson, A. Ashworth and A. MacDonald, *Human Rights and Criminal Justice* (3rd edn, 2012)

A. T. H. Smith, 'The Human Rights Act and the Criminal Lawyer: The Constitutional Context' [1999] Crim LR 25

On codification in other jurisdictions

P. R. Ferguson, 'Codifying Criminal Law: The Scots and English Draft Codes Compared' [2004] Crim LR 105

J. P. McCutcheon and K. Quinn, 'Codifying Criminal Law in Ireland' (1998) Statute Law Review 131

2
The elements of a crime

2.1 Actus reus and mens rea

2.1.1 Components of a crime

Anyone who thinks about it will readily appreciate that crimes ordinarily involve not merely blameworthy acts, but blameworthy mental elements on the part of defendants. Suppose I take your bicycle from the space in which you have left it, ride it home and put it in my garage. Have I stolen it? The question cannot be answered without considering my state of mind at the time of the taking. Perhaps I mistook your bicycle for my own similar model which I had left in the same area. Or perhaps I mistakenly supposed that you had said I could borrow the bicycle; or, though I knew it was your bicycle and that I was taking it without your consent, I only intended to borrow it for a day. In none of these cases have I stolen it. But, if I knew it was your bicycle and that I did not have your consent to take it and I dishonestly intended to deprive you of it permanently, I am guilty of theft. The act is the same in every case. The difference lies in the state of mind with which the act is done.

If D, driving his car, runs V down and kills him, this will be murder if D did so intending to kill V; manslaughter if, though he wished no harm to anyone, he was driving with such gross negligence as a jury thinks to deserve condemnation as that offence; causing death by careless driving if he was driving negligently; and accidental death if the collision occurred in spite of the fact that he was concentrating on what he was doing and exercising the care that a prudent and reasonably skilful driver should.

Let us take an example to explore the elements of offences. The offence of malicious wounding contrary to s 20 of the Offences Against the Person Act 1861 requires proof that the defendant caused a break in the victim's skin (both its inner and outer layers) and that the defendant intended to cause some kind of bodily harm or was malicious (reckless) as to whether it was caused (ie he saw there was a risk that his conduct would cause it but went ahead and unjustifiably took the risk).

Consider D who cuts V's stomach open with a knife. D is not necessarily guilty of wounding.

- D might lack the mental element—he might not have intended or been reckless about harming V. V might have stumbled and fallen on D, a chef holding his knife about to cut a joint of beef. D would not have the mental element for the offence of wounding and would be found not guilty.

- D might have a defence. He might have cut V's stomach open and intended to do so, but have V's consent, as where D is a surgeon operating on V in hospital.

- D might also lack criminal liability if he stabbed V with intent to cause the wound but was acting in self-defence because V was running at D with a sword.

- D might have a defence where he stabbed V in the stomach with intent to do so, but was only acting in that fashion because X was pointing a gun at D's head to make him stab V. D would then plead a defence of duress.

In a case of wounding, the proscribed conduct is unlawfully causing a wound (a break in the skin) and the proscribed mental state is that the defendant intended or was reckless (maliciously) about causing some bodily harm. The mental element defines the proscribed mental state that the defendant must have in relation to the proscribed conduct. In the previous example of the bicycle, the proscribed conduct is the appropriation (taking) of the property belonging to another and the proscribed mental element is that the taking was done dishonestly and with intention permanently to deprive the other of it.

Lawyers have long found it convenient to distinguish the mental element from the other elements for the purposes of setting out the law and have called it 'mens rea'. This phrase derives from a maxim quoted by Coke in his *Institutes* (Ch 1, fo 10), '*Actus non facit reum nisi mens sit rea*': an act does not make a man guilty of a crime unless his mind also be guilty.

The use of the expression, 'actus reus', is much more recent, having apparently been coined by Kenny in the first edition of his *Outlines of Criminal Law* in 1902 (see Hall, *General Principles*, p 222, fn 24). It is now an expression used throughout the common law world to designate the elements of an offence other than the mental element. The elements of the actus reus include elements of conduct, circumstances and, in some offences, consequences. For example, in the offence of rape, the proscribed conduct is penile penetration of the vagina, anus or mouth; the proscribed circumstances are that the victim was not consenting. With criminal damage, the proscribed conduct is the act which causes damage; the proscribed circumstances are that the damage was to property and that it belonged to another; and the proscribed consequences are that property was in fact damaged.

Most crimes require proof of a mental element of some sort. It has to be proved with the same degree of rigour as the other elements of the crime. It is possible for the courts to dispense with mens rea in whole or in part with offences of strict or absolute liability (see Chapter 7) but, except in the anomalous case of an intoxicated offender (see section 6.6, p 174), they can never dispense with the actus reus. There are no 'thought crimes'. See D. N. Husak, 'Does Criminal Liability Require an Act?' in R. A. Duff, *Philosophy and the Criminal Law* (1998). Remember that these expressions—mens rea and actus reus—are only analytical tools: they help us to identify which elements of the offence are in dispute etc. The only thing that matters in practice is whether the whole crime is committed.

Some of the controversies that will be explored in this chapter include the following:

(i)   how the elements making up a crime can differ depending on the analytical approach adopted to distinguish between actus reus and mens rea;

(ii)   the constituents of an actus reus;

(iii)   whether someone can be held criminally liable for an act that is involuntary;

(iv)   the extent to which the actus reus and mens rea must temporally coincide;

(v)   the liability of D, who intends to commit a crime in a certain way, but in fact commits it in some other way;

(vi)   whether for every element of the actus reus of an offence, there *must* be a corresponding element of mens rea.

2.1.2 Comparing approaches to analysing the elements of a crime

Courts and writers use the expressions actus reus and mens rea in different senses and it cannot be asserted that one usage is undeniably correct and others wrong. Glanville Williams (CLGP 18) writes:

... actus reus means the whole definition of the crime with the exception of the mental element—and it even includes a mental element in so far as that is contained in the definition of an act. This meaning of actus reus follows inevitably from the proposition that all the constituents of a crime are either actus reus or mens rea ...

Actus reus includes, in the terminology here suggested, not merely the whole objective situation that has to be proved by the prosecution, but also the absence of any ground of justification or excuse, whether such justification or excuse be stated in any statute creating the crime or implied by the courts in accordance with general principles (though not including matters of excuse depending on absence of mens rea). (See also, Williams, TBCL Ch 2)

This is a useful description of the concepts but it involves two points of controversy.

(1) The actus reus generally requires proof that the defendant did an act or omitted to do something he was under a duty to do. The orthodox view is that since an act is essentially a voluntary movement and not a spasm or convulsion, 'voluntariness', though a mental element, is part of the actus reus. Moreover, the word that describes the act may imply some further mental element. There are, for example, many offences where the actus reus consists of possession of prohibited articles. It has long been recognized that 'possess' imports a mental as well as a physical element. (See *Warner*, in section 7.3.2, p 197 and M. D. Dubber, 'The Possession Paradigm' in R. A. Duff and S. P. Green (eds), *Defining Crimes* (2005).) Some writers and judges have described these mental elements as part of the mens rea. However, the only thing that really matters in practice is whether they are elements of the crime. If they are, it is immaterial whether they are assigned to the actus reus or to the mens rea. It is important from a theoretical perspective, however.

(2) The second question is whether actus reus should include the absence of justification or excuse. The argument as to whether a crime ought to be subdivided can be summarized as:

- an actus reus + mens rea – defences = guilt. This is the orthodox view. According to this orthodox view a person may cause an actus reus with mens rea but not be guilty of the crime in question because of the existence of a defence.

  Using the examples of the offence of wounding discussed previously, the elements of the offence are causing a wound with intention or recklessness and the defences are consent, self-defence, duress, etc.

or

- an actus reus (including the absence of defences) + mens rea (including the absence of defences) = guilt. This is the unorthodox view.

  Applying this approach to the wounding example, discussed earlier, the elements of the offence would be recast as causing a break in the skin (without having consent or being an act in self-defence, etc) and the mental element would be recast as an intention or recklessness as to causing some bodily harm without intending or being reckless as to whether that is a justified act.

This unorthodox view seems at first to have a natural attraction. Consider, for example, the surgeon. It seems odd to say that he has committed the actus reus and mens rea of wounding and is only not guilty on the basis of a defence of consent. As a second example, take the crime of murder. The actus reus of murder may be described as the killing of a human being. If the killer, in the days when capital punishment was an available sentence, was the public executioner carrying out his duty to hang a convicted traitor it seems strange to describe this action as an actus reus and to conclude that he was only not guilty of murder by reason of a defence. There is a similar attraction to the unorthodox view where the actor knows of the circumstances which justify his action. In the case of the surgeon who performs the wounding, it might seem strange to describe his state of mind as one of a blameworthy 'mens rea'. Similarly, the public executioner did not have a 'guilty mind'. The same argument could be advanced in relation to self-defence. It may seem odd to say that D who stabs V in self-defence has performed the actus reus of wounding but can rely on the defence. It seems more natural to say that he has not performed the blameworthy act—the actus reus—in the first place. Equally, because the defendant who stabbed V in self-defence knew that he was acting in protection of himself or another, he was aware of the justifying circumstances and it seems odd to describe him as having a 'guilty mind' when he intentionally stabbed V.

Courts do sometimes adopt the unorthodox view. In *Gladstone Williams* [1983] EWCA Crim 4, (1987) 78 Cr App R 276 at 280, see section 11.6.1.1, p 415, Lord Lane CJ said: 'The mental element necessary to constitute guilt [for assault] is the intent to apply unlawful force to the victim. We do not believe that the mental element can be substantiated by simply showing an intent to apply force and no more.' If the defendant believed (though under a mistake) in circumstances which would justify the degree of force he used, in the opinion of Lord Lane, he lacked the mens rea for an assault.

However, there are powerful arguments to suggest that this unorthodox view is an illogical way of approaching things. In favour of the orthodox approach is the fact that defences also may require mental as well as external elements. For example, the partial defence of loss of control on a murder charge requires evidence not only of threatening facts or provocative things said or done but also an actual loss of self-control by D (see section 16.2, p 551). If the object of criminal law theory is clarity of exposition, there may, therefore, be something to be said for treating elements of offences and elements of defences separately. The orthodox theory advanced by Professor Lanham is the one that was adopted by the authors of the Draft Criminal Code.

There is a further illogicality in the unorthodox view. If the element of unlawfulness had to be proved as a definitional element, that is, as part of the actus reus with mens rea, the Crown would not establish a prima facie offence by proving that D intentionally stabbed V. Such wounding would not be unlawful unless the additional element of unlawfulness had to be established. It would be unlawful if it was proved to be intentionally unlawful! (See A. T. H. Smith, 'On Actus Reus and Mens Rea' in *Reshaping the Criminal Law*, p 95 and A. Simester, 'Mistakes in Defences' (1992) 12 OJLS 299.)

2.1.3 Defences as supervening elements

There are numerous possible defences to every crime but the definition of a particular crime never identifies them. For example, D who is charged with wounding might plead duress, insanity, necessity, etc. These defences are assumed to apply unless excluded. It is common to speak of 'a defence' where the defendant merely denies the existence of one or more elements of the offence—the actus reus or mens rea.

In the previous example of the wounding: in the case of the chef on whose knife V fell accidentally, D would be denying the elements of the offence; in contrast, with the example of the defendant who stabbed V because X was pointing a gun at his head, D would be pleading a defence of duress.

Sometimes the definition of the offence includes the word 'unlawfully' and this, in turn, is sometimes said to incorporate the available defences—it means 'without justification or excuse'. But many statutory definitions do not use that word and it makes no difference; the defences are still available. So it makes sense to distinguish between the elements of offences and the elements of defences.

It must be remembered that the separation of the definition of offences from that of defences is for convenience in stating the law. There is much to be said for having terms to describe the particular elements of a crime without thereby invoking all the possible defences. If the Latin expressions actus reus and mens rea are regarded merely as technical terms which do not in themselves necessarily import guilt, the difficulty of so using them disappears.

■ *Questions*

Consider the offence of wounding (discussed previously) and the defences of duress and self-defence as outlined in the discussion. What are the elements of actus reus and mens rea, and the elements of the defences? How would the elements apply in the context of: the surgeon, the chef, the person acting because he is under attack from the sword-wielding V; and the person stabbing V to avoid being shot by X?

2.2 Constituents of an actus reus

R v Dadson
(1850) 4 Cox CC 358, Court for Crown Cases Reserved

(Pollock CB, Wightman J, Williams J, Talfourd J and Martin B)

Dadson was a constable responsible for guarding a copse from which there had been thefts of wood. Dadson saw William Waters come from the copse with wood and Dadson, having called for Waters to stop, shot him when he ran off. Waters was wounded in the leg. There was no doubt that Waters was stealing, that Dadson shot him and wounded Waters with intent to do so. What Dadson did not know when he shot Waters was that because Waters had been convicted of such offences before, when he was stealing wood on this occasion Waters was actually committing a felony—a more serious classification of offence which existed at that time. A constable was allowed to use such force to prevent a felon from escaping. He was not allowed to use such force to prevent a thief who was not a felon from escaping. Dadson did not know Waters was a felon. The judge told the jury that 'shooting with intent to wound amounted to the felony charged, unless from other facts there was a justification; and that neither the belief of the prisoner that it was his duty to fire if he could not otherwise apprehend the prosecutor, nor the alleged felony, it being unknown to him, constituted such justification.' Dadson was convicted of felony. The judge sought the opinion of the senior judges as to whether this conviction was right.

[Pollock CB, delivered the judgment of the court: after stating the facts:]

We are all of opinion that the conviction is right. [Waters] not having committed a felony known to [Dadson] at the time when he fired, the latter was not justified in firing at [Waters]; and having no justifiable cause, he was guilty of shooting at [Waters] with intent to do him grievous bodily harm, and the conviction is right.

Conviction affirmed

Dadson has been the subject of much debate. Glanville Williams argues (CLGP 24) that it is wrong: that there was no actus reus—Waters was in fact a felon and therefore it was lawful to use deadly force to arrest him. Dadson had mens rea—he intentionally shot at Waters, unaware of any grounds justifying or excusing such conduct because Dadson did not know that Waters was a convicted felon—but that was immaterial if there was no actus reus.

■ *Questions*

Were all the elements of the offence proved? The Offences Against the Person Act 1828, s 12 provided that it was an offence:

... unlawfully and maliciously shoot at any person ... with intent ... to maim, disfigure or disable such person or to do some other grievous bodily harm to such person

Unless all the elements of Dadson's offence under s 12 were proved, then Dadson should have been acquitted. If they were proved, the next question is whether Dadson had made out a defence. What are the elements of the defence? If there is only one element—the arrestee was a fleeing felon who could not be stopped except by shooting—then, again, Dadson should have been acquitted because the arrestee was a felon. But the court holds that there is a second element—that the defendant knew him to be a felon. Why should the court not so decide? What are the arguments for and against?

Dadson is considered further, in section 11.6.10, p 434, in relation to the modern law of arrest. See also R. L. Christopher, 'Unknowing Justification and the Logical Necessity of the Dadson Principle in Self-Defence' (1995) 15 OJLS 229.

■ *Questions*

1. D and V are bitter enemies. D is about to shoot V who has his back turned to D. Unknown to D, V is secretly loading his gun and is about to turn round to shoot D. D shoots V and wounds him before he turns round. Can D rely on the defence of self-defence?

2. D is about to throw a petrol bomb though the window of the house belonging to V who is his worst enemy. As he creeps up to the window D is unaware of the fact that X has sent D a text message saying 'Bomb V now or I will kill your child.' D throws the petrol bomb into V's house. Can he rely on a defence of duress?

Consider again the "unorthodox" approach to analysing offences (section 2.1.2, p 17). If the definition of the offence of wounding includes the absence of self-defence (ie the element of 'unlawfulness') the accused who shot V being unaware that V was about to turn and shoot him, could not be convicted since there would be no actus reus. The justifying circumstance of which he was unaware (that V was about to kill him) would mean that the offence was not committed. This conclusion would run contrary to well-established principles.

Contrast the facts of a case like that of *Deller* (1952) 36 Cr App R 184 where D offered a car for sale, stating that he had the full legal rights to do so (and that there was no hire purchase owing on it). D thought he was lying about that: he thought the finance company was still owed money on the car. D was in fact mistaken: the finance company were not owed anything. When D said he had the right to sell the car and that there was nothing owing on it, he was telling the truth.

■ *Questions*

Was Deller guilty of an offence of making a false representation? *Should* Deller have been guilty of an offence? Would it be desirable to have a law stating: 'A person who does any act with intent thereby to commit an offence is guilty of an offence and liable to be punished as if he had committed the offence he intended to commit'? See section 14.1, p 497.

2.3 Understanding the requirement of an act

Reduced to its simplest terms, an act is merely a muscular movement—for example, the crooking of a finger. But this is a very narrow view. Reference to an "act" generally includes some of the circumstances surrounding the movement, and its consequences. For instance, if, when D crooked his finger, it was gripping the trigger of a loaded gun pointing at V's heart, to say that 'D crooked his finger' would be a most incomplete and misleading way of describing what D did. We would naturally say, 'D *shot* V', taking into account the relevant circumstances and consequences. If we say, 'D *murdered V*' we take into account still more circumstances—not only the state of mind with which D pulled the trigger, but also the absence of circumstances of justification or excuse—for example, D was not a soldier in battle shooting at an enemy, V, nor was he acting in self-defence against an aggressor who was attacking D. 'Murder', unlike 'kill', connotes a particular offence and therefore an actus reus (including the absence of excuse).

Courts rarely have to address in any detail what is meant by the act involved in a crime.

Ryan v R
(1969) 121 CLR 205, High Court of Australia

(Barwick CJ, Taylor, Menzies Windeyer and Owen JJ)

Ryan entered a service station, pointed a sawn-off rifle at the attendant and demanded money. The rifle was loaded and cocked with the safety catch off. The attendant placed money on the counter. Still pointing the rifle with one hand, Ryan attempted to tie the attendant up. When the attendant moved suddenly Ryan pressed the trigger and shot him dead. By the law of New South Wales at that time, killing, an act done in the course of committing a felony (in this case, robbery), was murder—but the act had to be a voluntary act. At his trial for murder, Ryan's defence was that he pressed the trigger involuntarily. He was convicted and his appeal to the High Court of Australia was dismissed.

[Barwick CJ, having held that a jury could not dismiss Ryan's account as incredible:]

There were therefore, in my opinion, at least four possible and distinctly different views of the discharge of the gun which, upon all the material before them, could be taken by the jury. First, the applicant's explanation could be disbelieved, and it could be concluded that he had fired the gun intentionally—that is to say, both as a voluntary act and with the intention to do the deceased harm. Second, that he fired the gun voluntarily, not intending to do any harm to the deceased but merely to frighten him as a means of self-protection. Third, that being startled, he voluntarily but in a panic, pressed the trigger but with no specific intent either to do the deceased any harm or to frighten him. Fourth, that being startled so as to move slightly off his balance, the trigger was pressed in a reflex or convulsive, unwilled movement of his hand or of its muscles. I shall later refer to these conclusions of fact as the possible views identifying each by number...

An occasion such as the fourth view of the evidence in the instant case (ante) would, in my opinion, be an instance of a deed not the result of a culpable exercise of the will to act. But such an occasion is in sharp contrast to the third view of those facts from which it needs carefully to be distinguished. If voluntariness is not conceded and the material to be submitted to the jury wheresoever derived provides a substantial basis for doubting whether the deed in question was a voluntary or willed act of the accused, the jury's attention must be specifically drawn to the necessity of deciding beyond all reasonable doubt that the deed charged as a crime was the voluntary or willed act of the accused. If it was not then for that reason, there being no defence of insanity, the accused must be acquitted... Although a claim of involuntariness is no doubt easily raised, and may involve nice distinctions, the accused, if the material adduced warrants that course, is entitled to have the issue properly put to the jury.

Windeyer J:

... The conduct which caused the death was of course a complex of acts all done by the applicant—loading the rifle, cocking it, presenting it, pressing the trigger. But it was the final act, pressing the trigger of the loaded and levelled rifle, which made the conduct lethal. When this was said to be a reflex action, the word 'reflex' was not used strictly in the sense it ordinarily has in neurology as denoting a specific muscular reaction to a particular stimulus of a physical character. The phrase was, as I understood the argument, used to denote rather the probable but unpredictable reaction of a man when startled. He starts. In doing so he may drop something which he is holding, or grasp it more firmly. Doctor Johnson in his Dictionary—and his definition has been in substance repeated by others—said that 'to start' means 'to feel a sudden and involuntary twitch or motion of the animal frame on the apprehension of danger'. The *Oxford Dictionary* speaks of a start as a 'sudden involuntary movement of the body occasioned by surprise, terror, joy or grief ...'. But assume that the applicant's act was involuntary, in the sense in which the lexicographers use the word, would that, as a matter of law, absolve him from criminal responsibility for its consequences? I do not think so. I do not think that, for present purposes, such an act bears any true analogy to one done under duress, which, although done by an exercise of the will, is said to be involuntary because it was compelled. Neither does it, I think, bear any true analogy to an act done in convulsions or an epileptic seizure, which is said to be involuntary because by no exercise of the will could the actor refrain from doing it. Neither does it, I think, bear any true analogy to an act done by a sleep-walker or a person for some other reason rendered unconscious whose action is said to be involuntary because he knew not what he was doing.

Such phrases as 'reflex action' and 'automatic reaction' can, if used imprecisely and unscientifically, be, like 'blackout', mere excuses. They seem to me to have no real application to the case of a fully conscious man who has put himself in a situation in which he has his finger on the trigger of a loaded rifle levelled at another man. If he then presses the trigger in immediate response to a sudden threat or apprehension of danger, as is said to have occurred in this case, his doing so is, it seems to me, a consequence probable and foreseeable of a conscious apprehension of danger, and in that sense a voluntary act. The latent time is no doubt barely appreciable, and what was done might not have been done had the actor had time to think. But is an act to be called involuntary merely because the mind worked quickly and impulsively?

■ **Questions**

Was Ryan's act: Voluntary? Blameworthy? Was Ryan in control of his actions? See R. A. Duff, *Answering for Crime* (2007), pp 99–106.

2.3.1 Acts and automatism

Apart from the anxieties and tensions necessarily experienced by anyone taking part in an armed robbery, Ryan was not, so far as appears, suffering from an abnormality of any kind. More commonly—at least in the reported cases—the defendant who relies upon automatism claims that he had a 'blackout' and that this was due to a condition of mind or body—a tumour on the brain, arteriosclerosis (hardening of the arteries) cutting off the supply of blood to the brain, epilepsy, hyperglycaemia (high blood sugar) caused by diabetes, hypoglycaemia (low blood sugar) caused by the administration of too much insulin to control diabetes or sleepwalking; or he may say that he was suffering from concussion following a blow on the head or that he was affected by the administration by his dentist of an anaesthetic. If the defendant was indeed in a state of automatism at the time of the alleged act as a result of any of these conditions, he cannot be guilty of the crime charged; but there is a question whether he should be simply acquitted or found not guilty by reason of insanity. The importance of this categorization is that the defendant is then liable to various types of restraint (hospital orders and supervision) which the court may impose on him.

Automatism is discussed more fully in Chapter 11. What matters for present purposes is to note that offences require proof of voluntary conduct.

2.4 Coincidence of actus reus and mens rea

In order to constitute a crime the actus reus and the mens rea must coincide (i) in point of law and (ii) in point of time.

2.4.1 Coincidence in law

All the elements of the crime charged must be proved. It is not therefore sufficient to prove that the defendant caused the actus reus of crime X with the mens rea of crime Y. Cf *Pembliton*, section 2.4.1.1, p 26.

■ *Question*

D throws a knife at V who is standing on his doorstep. V moves and the knife sticks into the door creating a large hole. What offence(s) has D committed?

It must be remembered, however, that sometimes the same mens rea is sufficient for two or more crimes; an intention to cause grievous bodily harm is a sufficient mens rea both for the offence of causing such harm with intent contrary to s 18 of the Offences Against the Person Act 1861 and for murder. Recklessness as to grievous bodily harm is sufficient for the offence of maliciously inflicting grievous bodily harm contrary to s 20 of the Offences Against the Person Act 1861 and for manslaughter.

2.4.1.1 Transferred malice

If D, with the mens rea of a particular crime, brings about the actus reus of the same crime, he is guilty of that crime even though the victim, or object, of the offence is different from that which D intended or foresaw or ought to have foreseen. This common law doctrine is restated succinctly by the Draft Code, cl 24, and appears in the following terms in the draft Criminal Law Bill, cl 32:

32. Transferred fault and defences

(1) In determining whether a person is guilty of an offence, his intention to cause, or his awareness of a risk that he will cause, a result in relation to a person or thing capable of being the victim or subject-matter of the offence shall be treated as an intention to cause or, as the case may be, an awareness of a risk that he will cause, that result in relation to any other person or thing affected by his conduct.

(2) Any defence on which a person might have relied on a charge of an offence in relation to a person or thing within his contemplation is open to him on a charge of the same offence in relation to a person or thing not within his contemplation.

By way of an example of the doctrine in operation, if D intends to kill A by shooting at him, but misses and kills B instead, D will be guilty of the murder of B even though killing B may have been the last thing D wanted. D's mens rea (intention to kill) is said to be transferred from A to

B. The reason for this is said to be that how D caused B's death is of no legal significance. Horder calls this the 'prohibited outcome' doctrine. He states that, '[s]o long as the prohibited outcome comes about (intentional killing), it matters not how or respecting whom'. See J. Horder, 'Transferred Malice and the Remoteness of Unexpected Outcomes' [2006] Crim LR 383.

In addition, if D would have been able to plead a defence for the murder of A (eg self-defence), under the doctrine this defence transfers from A to B and so D can escape liability for the murder of B.

However, it is important to appreciate the limitations of the doctrine. For example, if D shoots at V, intending to kill him, but misses and instead smashes the window of V's car, this will not suffice to make D guilty of criminal damage. D had an intention to kill, not to cause criminal damage. However, D would be guilty of criminal damage if he had an intention to smash V's window but instead smashes W's. For an example of a case that strains the boundaries of transferred malice, see *Gnango* [2011] UKSC 59. See section 8.7.8, p 275.

■ *Questions*

1. How far does the doctrine extend? D has mens rea to commit offence A and performs the actus reus of offence B. How similar must A and B be?

2. Are all forms of mens rea transferrable under the doctrine? What about gross negligence?

3. Is there really a transfer of mens rea, or is the issue simply about the scope of the offence in question? For example, if D intends to shoot A but misses and kills B, can it be said that the offence of murder is committed when D intends to kill *a* person, irrespective of whether the victim is the person whose death D desired?

Attorney-General's Reference (No 3 of 1994)
[1997] UKHL 31, House of Lords, http://www.bailii.org/uk/cases/UKHL/1997/31.html

(Lords Goff, Mustill, Slynn, Hope and Clyde)

D stabbed his girlfriend, E, whom he knew to be pregnant. E recovered; but there was evidence that the child, V, was born prematurely as a result of the wound and, as a result of the premature birth, died after 121 days. D was charged with the murder of V. The judge directed an acquittal on the ground that no conviction of murder or manslaughter was possible in law. (A foetus is not a person in law and cannot be the victim of murder or manslaughter.) On the reference by the Attorney General, the Court of Appeal held that there was evidence that D murdered V, his intent to cause grievous bodily harm (the mens rea of murder) to E being 'transferred' to V. They also held that the foetus before birth was to be regarded as an integral part of the mother, like her arm or leg; so an intention to kill or cause grievous bodily harm to the foetus was an intention to cause grievous bodily harm to a person in being, the mother.

The House held that the foetus is not a part of the mother: the mother and the foetus are two distinct organisms, living symbiotically, not a single organism with two aspects. So an intention to kill or injure the foetus is not an intention to cause GBH to a person—it is not the mens rea of murder. It was accepted that the doctrine of transferred malice was sound law.

Lord Mustill:

The sources in more recent centuries are few. Of the two most frequently cited the earlier is *R v Pembliton* (1874) LR 2 CCR 119, [1874–80] All ER Rep 1163. In the course of a fight the defendant threw a stone at others which missed and broke a window. He was indicted for that he 'unlawfully and maliciously did commit damage, injury and spoil upon a window . . .' The jury found that he did not intend to break the window. On a case stated to the Court for Crown Cases Reserved it was argued for the prosecution that 'directly it is proved that he threw a stone . . . without just cause, the offence is established'. The ancient origins of this argument need no elaboration, and indeed the report of the argument as it developed showed that it was based on a conception of general malice. The interventions in argument are instructive. After the prosecutor had relied on the fact that the prisoner was actuated by malice, Blackburn J responded (at 120): 'But only of a particular kind, and not against the person injured.' Later, in reply to a reliance on a passage from Hale, the same judge said (at 121):

> 'Lord Coke, 3 Inst., p 56, puts the case of a man stealing deer in a park, shooting at the deer, and by the glance of the arrow killing a boy that is hidden in a bush, and calls this murder; but can any one say that ruling would be adopted now?'

This most learned of judges continued:

> 'I should have told the jury that if the prisoner knew there were windows behind, and that the probable consequence of his act would be to break one of them, that would be evidence for them of malice.'

The conviction was quashed. It is sufficient to quote briefly from the judgment of Blackburn J (at 122):

> 'We have not now to consider what would be malice aforethought to bring a given case within the common law definition of murder; here the statute says that the act must be unlawful and malicious . . . The jury might perhaps have found on this evidence that the act was malicious, because they might have found that the prisoner knew that the natural consequence of his act would be to break the glass, and although that was not his wish, yet he was reckless whether he did it or not; but the jury have not so found . . .'

This decision was distinguished in *R v Latimer* (1886) 17 QBD 359, [1886–90] All ER Rep 386. Two men quarreled in a public house. One of them struck at the other with his belt. The glancing blow bounced off and struck the prosecutrix, wounding her severely. The assailant was prosecuted and convicted for having unlawfully and maliciously wounded her, contrary to s 20 of the Offences against the Person Act 1861. Counsel for the defendant relied on *R v Pembliton*. In his judgment, Lord Coleridge CJ said ((1886) 17 QBD 359 at 361, [1886–90] All ER Rep 386 at 387):

> 'It is common knowledge that a man who has an unlawful and malicious intent against another, and, in attempting to carry it out, injures a third person, is guilty of what the law deems malice against the person injured, because the offender is doing an unlawful act, and has that which the judges call general malice, and that is enough.' . . .

My Lords, I find it hard to base a modern law of murder on these two cases. The Court in *R v Latimer* was, I believe, entirely justified in finding a distinction between their statutory backgrounds and one can well accept that the answers given, one for acquittal, the other for conviction, would be the same today. But the harking back to a concept of general malice, which amounts to no more than this, that a wrongful act displays a malevolence which can be attached to any adverse consequence, has long been out of date. And to speak of a particular malice which is 'transferred' simply disguises the problem by idiomatic language. The defendant's malice is directed at one objective, and when after the event the court treats it as directed at another object it is not recognising a 'transfer' but creating a new malice which never existed before. As Dr Glanville Williams pointed out in *Criminal Law: The General Part* (2nd edn, 1961) p 184, the doctrine is 'rather an arbitrary exception to general principles'. Like many of its kind this is useful enough to yield rough justice, in particular cases, and it can sensibly be retained notwithstanding its lack of any sound intellectual basis. But it is another matter to build a new rule upon it.

I pause to distinguish the case of indiscriminate malice from those already discussed, although even now it is sometimes confused with them. The terrorist who hides a bomb in an aircraft provides an example. This is not a case of 'general malice' where under the old law any wrongful act sufficed to prove the evil disposition which was taken to supply the necessary intent for homicide. Nor is it transferred malice, for there is no need of a transfer. The intention is already aimed directly at the class of potential victims of which the actual victim forms part. The intent and the actus reus completed by the explosion are joined from the start, even though the identity of the ultimate victim is not yet fixed. So also with the shots fired indiscriminately into a crowd. No ancient fictions are needed to make these cases of murder.

[Lord Mustill said that the question of manslaughter had caused him great anxiety, but he was persuaded by the opinion of Lord Hope.

Lord Hope, having made a detailed examination of the law of involuntary manslaughter (section 17.2, p 594) concluded:]

I think, then, that the position can be summarised in this way. The intention which must be discovered is an intention to do an act which is unlawful and dangerous. In this case the act which had to be shown to be an unlawful and dangerous act was the stabbing of the child's mother. There can be no doubt that all sober and reasonable people would regard that act, within the appropriate meaning of this term, as dangerous. It is plain that it was unlawful as it was done with the intention of causing her injury. As the defendant intended to commit that act, all the ingredients necessary for mens rea in regard to the crime of manslaughter were established, irrespective of who was the ultimate victim of it. The fact that the child whom the mother was carrying at the time was born alive and then died as a result of the stabbing is all that was needed for the offence of manslaughter when the actus reus for that crime was completed by the child's death. The question, once all the other elements are satisfied, is simply one of causation. The defendant must accept all the consequences of his act, so long as the jury are satisfied that he did what he did intentionally, that what he did was unlawful and that, applying the correct test, it was also dangerous. The death of the child was unintentional, but the nature and quality of the act which caused it was such that it was criminal and therefore punishable. In my opinion that is sufficient for the offence of manslaughter. There is no need to look to the doctrine of transferred malice for a solution to the problem raised by this case so far as manslaughter is concerned.

[Lords **Goff**, **Slynn** and **Clyde** agreed with the speeches of Lords Mustill and Hope.]

■ *Questions*

1. Does the rule that an intention to cause GBH is a sufficient mens rea for murder involve a 'fiction'? No one pretends that it is an intention to kill.

2. Does the prosecution's argument involve a 'double' transfer of intent?

3. Would Lord Mustill have decided differently if D had intended to *kill* the mother, thus eliminating one of his 'fictions'? Or if D had intended (as was the fact) to cause GBH to the mother and, the child having suffered GBH as a result of the premature birth but survived, D had been charged with causing GBH to it with intent?

4. It is held that D could be guilty of manslaughter because, by the unlawful and dangerous act done to the mother, he caused the death of the child. How, if at all, does this differ from transferred malice in murder? It was an act done with the mens rea of murder; and it admittedly caused death. So why is it not murder?

5. Ashworth states that, '[a] conviction for attempt is possible in virtually all cases which fall within the doctrine of transferred liability. D will invariably have taken the sufficient steps towards committing the offence against his intended victim for there to be the *actus reus* of an attempt, and *mens rea* will be undisputed'. See A. Ashworth, 'Transferred Malice and Punishment for Unforeseen Consequences' in P. R. Glazebrook (ed), *Reshaping the Criminal Law: Essays in Honour of Glanville Williams* (1978). Is this statement accurate? Would it have been a preferable approach in these circumstances?

The Court of Appeal in the *Attorney-General's Reference* case rejected arguments advanced by Glanville Williams (i) that 'an unexpected difference of mode will be regarded as severing the chain of causation if it is sufficiently far removed from the intended mode', and (ii) that the doctrine 'should be limited to cases where the consequence was brought about by negligence in relation to the actual victim'. These arguments were not advanced in the House of Lords.

Professor Horder argues ('Transferred Malice and the Remoteness of Unexpected Outcomes from Intentions' [2006] Crim LR 383) that the correct question should have been whether murder was a representative label for D given that there was (i) an unintended victim and (ii) the death arose in a way that was not intended.

As has already been noted, it is said that defences can also be 'transferred' under the doctrine. For example, if D shoots at V and, unforeseeably, kills, and is charged with killing, X, he can rely on any defence such as self-defence, or a partial defence such as loss of control which he could have relied on had he killed, and been charged with killing, V. Cf *Gross* (1913) 23 Cox CC 455. However, Bohlander argues that *Gross* is not authority for the proposition that defences can be transferred. He states that, '[o]nce we accept that loss of control, as provocation is now to be called under the U.K. [*sic*] reform efforts in the Coroners and Justice Act 2009, is a partial defence because D is no longer able to comprehend fully the wrongness of her actions and act accordingly, we understand that *Gross* is not a case of transfer of a defense at all: just as a temporary mental disease may exempt *any and all* actions of D committed in that state from liability, a temporary loss of control exempts *any and all actions* committed under its influence'. See M. Bohlander, 'Transferred Malice and Transferred Defences' (2010) 13 NewCrimLRev 555.

Is Bohlander right? Consider D who shoots at V having lost his self-control following V's taunts which gave D a justifiable sense of being seriously wronged. D's bullet kills V, injures X and damages Z's car. Can D really plead the defence in relation to all those harms? Should he be able to? Does loss of control apply only to charges of murder as the 2009 Act states explicitly?

2.4.1.2 Correspondence principle

If an offence has an actus reus comprising elements A, B and C, to what extent is it necessary for the Crown to prove mens rea in relation to every element? In relation to criminal damage for example, the actus reus comprises conduct, in proscribed circumstances (property belonging to another), causing a result (damage). Is it sufficient that the Crown proves that D voluntarily threw a stone at the window or must it go further and show that D intended the damage to property and that he knew it was property of another?

Taking assault as a further example, D's conduct must cause V to apprehend immediate unlawful violence. D is only guilty if he intended or was reckless whether his conduct might cause V's apprehension (the result). There is a correspondence between the elements of the actus reus and mens rea. D is not liable for assault unless he has mens rea as to his conduct—he must intend to act or act voluntarily—and has mens rea as to the prohibited consequence in question (what V apprehended). There is an element of mens rea corresponding to each element of the actus reus.

■ *Questions*

Is this correspondence found in all offences? Is it desirable? What offences contravene the correspondence principle?

J. Horder, 'A Critique of the Correspondence Principle in Criminal Law'
[1995] Crim LR 759 (references omitted)

The correspondence principle (hereinafter, the 'C' principle) concerns the relationship between actus reus and mens rea. Its definition and justification are well expressed by Ashworth and Campbell ('Recklessness in Assault—And in General?' (1991) 107 L.Q.R. 187 at p.192):

> '[I]f the offence is defined in terms of certain consequences and certain circumstances, the mental element ought to correspond with that by referring to those consequences or circumstances. If a mental element as to a lesser consequence were acceptable, this would amount to constructive criminal liability.'

. . . The C principle remains very much an ideal, if anything, rather than an accurate descriptive generalisation about crimes. Even amongst crimes requiring mens rea, not all exemplify the principle to anything like the full extent. The real problem is to decide when the C principle makes sense, even as an ideal.

In this regard, Ashworth argues that the C principle is a concrete illustration of a more abstract general principle at work within the criminal law, the principle of individual autonomy. The autonomy principle dictates that people are not to be held criminally liable unless, inter alia, they can be shown to have chosen to do, or had control over the doing of, the harm or wrong in question. At first sight, the autonomy principle's emphasis on choice and control appears to provide an attractive theoretical grounding for a subjectivist understanding of the C principle. On the subjectivist view, the C principle limits criminal liability to harms or wrongs that are intended or consciously risked; and harms or wrongs intended or consciously risked would seem to be paradigm examples of things over whose occurrence one has choice or control. On closer analysis, though, it becomes clear that the C principle cannot so easily be derived theoretically from the autonomy principle. Suppose D throws a brick from a window and, in so doing, intends to, or realises that he may, hit V. In these circumstances, if V is struck by the brick, the C principle dictates that D may be held criminally liable for the striking, because D's mens rea related to that possible outcome as an element in the actus reus. Yet, at this very point, the C principle appears to part company with the autonomy principle, as stated. When D let go of the brick, he ceased to have control over events. Since the brick would have missed V if it had been blown off course, or if V had suddenly moved, the actual fact that V was struck was as much a matter of chance as of choice or control. No doubt, D is still rightly regarded as causing the striking; but no one is in control of everything they cause to occur. So, seemingly contrary to the C principle, the autonomy principle dictates that D should be held criminally liable for no more than endangering V by throwing the brick, since that action was all that D chose to do or controlled.

One might still argue that the two principles do not really conflict. Everything depends on whether the two principles are, on the one hand, what one might call 'permissive' principles or, on the other hand, 'restrictive' principles of liability. The autonomy principle appears to be broadly 'permissive' in character: if D chose to do wrong (or, say, controlled the wrongdoing of another), the imposition of criminal liability is permitted just in virtue of the choice or control. On the other hand, the C principle seems 'restrictive' in character: it restricts liability, howsoever permitted or justified by other principles, to conduct or consequences that D intended or foresaw. Seen as a restrictive principle of liability, the C principle seems to amount to no more than a hypothetical imperative: if D is to be held responsible for consequences beyond his control, he must at least have adverted to the possibility of those consequences coming about. This being so, ironically, the C principle will only make sense as an ideal in legal systems which do not respect the autonomy principle; because only then will issues arise of liability for consequences of one's conduct beyond one's control. But in spite of these difficulties, there is clearly a deeper theoretical link between the so-called autonomy principle and the C principle. Observance of the autonomy principle prevents any element of 'moral luck'—responsibility for consequences of one's conduct beyond one's control—from finding a place within the conditions of criminal liability. Observance of the C principle is meant to ensure that if a (morally unlucky) D is to be held criminally liable for the consequences of her conduct beyond her control, such liability should not be regarded as fair unless D intended to bring about, or adverted to the possibility of bringing about, those consequences. For, unless this mens rea condition is satisfied, D will not have been representatively labelled when held criminally responsible for those consequences.

... The principle of representative labelling requires that there be a close match between the label or name attached to a crime, such as 'murder' or 'manslaughter', and the nature and gravity of what the defendant has done, whether or not there was an element of chance in bringing about the outcome in question. The C principle insists that one cannot be representatively labelled as a 'murder' or as a 'manslaughterer' unless one's mens rea (intention or foresight) related to the forbidden consequence itself, the unlawful killing. As is well known, in English law both murder and manslaughter fall short of this requirement. As Ashworth puts it, speaking of murder:

> 'a person may be convicted of murder if he ... intended to cause grievous bodily harm. However, the latter species of fault breaches the principle of correspondence: the fault element does not correspond with the conduct element (which is, causing death), and so a person is liable to conviction for a higher crime than contemplated.'

Unfortunately, it is not clear that there is such a smooth connection between the C principle and the principle of representative labelling. Suppose D decides to speed unlawfully, realising that by so doing he makes it more likely that he will kill any pedestrian who steps out in front of him. A child runs out into the road, and is killed by the speed of the impact with D's car. Given that D foresaw killing as a possible consequence of his unlawful conduct, there could be no compromise of the C principle in convicting D of murder. Yet the principle of representative labelling would be compromised by a conviction for murder, because D did not intend to inflict any harm at all: intention to kill or seriously to injure is partly constitutive of the wrong of murder. The principle of representative labelling may thus insist on intention as the form of mens rea, even where the C principle is satisfied by foresight alone. A C principle theorist might reply that all this point demonstrates is that the two principles interact in the construction of criminal wrongs; but this response is unsatisfactory. A broader theory of how mens rea (and in particular, intention) can be partly constitutive of the wrongdoing in some crimes, when combined with the principle of representative labelling, threatens to make the C principle redundant in any analysis of such crimes.

... Intention rarely operates as a mere 'fault element' in the criminal law. Its main role is in changing the normative significance of conduct. If, in appropriating your property, I intend permanently to deprive you of it, that intention does not simply make me more 'at fault' in what I do. It may turn my conduct from something neutral (like putting goods in a shopping basket) into a substantive criminal offence. Intention plays the same role in all 'precursor' offences where it is the mental element, and in criminal attempts. Without the intention to commit the crime, there is not only no fault; there is simply no wrong. Unless one also insists on an intention to (try to) produce the prohibited outcome in a criminal attempt, more than merely preparatory steps taken towards the outcome merge with a different wrong: endangerment. In all these cases, of course, the C principle appears to be satisfied, since subjective mens rea will relate to the actus reus; but the appearance is misleading because the principle is doing no work. In such cases (crimes of 'specific intent'), once one has understood the role of intention in defining the limits of the criminal wrong, there is nothing left for the C principle to do. A similar point can be made about more controversial cases, where the representative labelling principle is satisfied, but the C principle is not.

Suppose D forcibly removes V's kidney during a coerced and gratuitous operation, giving no thought to whether V will survive. V dies of shock. We have seen that Ashworth draws on the C principle to argue that this kind of case is inappropriate for a murder conviction, because although D intends to inflict grievous bodily harm, he was not subjectively aware that V might die. But as the example of the speeding driver shows, even where D does realise that someone may be unlawfully killed as a result of his conduct, this is not enough in itself to constitute sufficient mens rea for murder, for the purposes of representative labelling. So, in murder cases, it turns out that the claims of the C principle are dependent for their plausibility on making the assumption that the defendant had at least an intention to inflict grievous bodily harm, in any event. Consistency with the principle of representative labelling demands no less, precisely because the present law seeks to distinguish murder from involuntary manslaughter (as representative labels) by regarding the wrong of murder as constituted by killing with no less than such an intention. The C principle only comes into play once one is already dealing with a fully constituted wrong; but in crimes of specific intent, once one has defined the wrong one may (by definition) already have accounted for the mental element. Arguably, this is true of murder. 'Murder' is a strongly evaluative label that is meant to be reserved for the worst kinds of killing. Yet, in clearly demarcating its province—for representative labelling purposes—from that of manslaughter, there need be no special theoretical link (just as there is no historical link made, in this regard, between murder and intended killing. Even if, other things being equal, an intentional killing is somehow worse than an unintentional killing brought about through (say) the intended and wrongful removal of a kidney, further argument is needed before we must accept that someone guilty of the latter act is not representatively labelled as a murderer.

... The C principle is thus a principle whose relevance, if any, is confined largely to crimes of basic intent, where mens rea plays an attributional role focused on the degree of one's fault in committing an admitted wrong. So, in cases where it is admitted that D was at fault in grievously harming V, contrary to section 20 of the Offences Against the Person Act 1861, the C principle dictates that D should not be criminally liable unless D foresaw at least the possibility of nothing less than grievous harm stemming from his or her conduct. On this view the law, which holds that it is enough to fulfil the requirements of 'malice' to show that D foresaw the possibility of no more than some physical harm, is too harsh ...

See for a different view: B. Mitchell, 'In Defence of a Principle of Correspondence' [1999] Crim LR 195 and for a response see J. Horder, 'Questioning the Correspondence Principle—A Reply' [1999] Crim LR 206.

Consider the extent to which the correspondence principle is respected in the following case.

R v Taafe
[1984] 1 All ER 747, House of Lords

(Lords Fraser, Scarman, Roskill, Bridge and Brightman)

Section 170(2) of the Customs and Excise Management Act 1979 provides:

... if any person is, in relation to any goods, in any way knowingly concerned in any fraudulent evasion or attempt at evasion:

  (a) of any duty chargeable on the goods;

  (b) of any prohibition or restriction for the time being in force with respect to the goods under or by virtue of any enactment; or

  (c) of any provision of the Customs and Excise Acts 1979 applicable to the goods, he shall be guilty of an offence under this section and may be arrested.

The defendant had committed the actus reus of the offence because he had in fact imported drugs, the importation of which was forbidden by the 1979 Act. He also had *an intention to break the law forbidding importation* because he believed (wrongly) he was importing currency and he also believed (wrongly) that the importation of currency was prohibited.

Lord Scarman:

The question is in these terms:

'When a defendant is charged with an offence, contrary to section 170(2) of the Customs and Excise Management Act 1979, of being knowingly concerned in the fraudulent evasion of the prohibition on the importation of a controlled drug—Does the defendant commit the offence where he: (a) imports prohibited drugs into the United Kingdom; (b) intends fraudulently to evade a prohibition on importation; but (c) mistakenly believes the goods to be money and not drugs; and (d) mistakenly believes that money is the subject of a prohibition against importation.'

In effect, the Recorder answered the question in the affirmative and the Court of Appeal in the negative.

. . .

[In the Court of Appeal] Lord Lane CJ construed the subsection under which the respondent was charged as creating an offence not of absolute liability but as one of which an essential ingredient is a guilty mind. To be 'knowingly concerned' meant, in his judgment, knowledge not only of the existence of a smuggling operation but also that the substance being smuggled into the country was one the importation of which was prohibited by statute. The respondent thought he was concerned in a smuggling operation but believed that the substance was currency. The importation of currency is not subject to any prohibition. Lord Lane CJ concluded ([1983] 2 All ER 625 at 628, [1983] 1 WLR 627 at 631):

'He [the respondent] is to be judged against the facts that he believed them to be. Had this indeed been currency and not cannabis, no offence would have been committed.'

Lord Lane CJ went on to ask this question:

'Does it make any difference that the [respondent] thought wrongly that by clandestinely importing currency he was committing an offence?'

The Crown submitted that it did. The court rejected the submission: the respondent's mistake of law could not convert the importation of currency into a criminal offence; and importing currency is what it had to be assumed that the respondent believed he was doing.

My Lords, I find the reasoning of Lord Lane CJ compelling. I agree with his construction of s 170(2) of the 1979 Act; and the principle that a man must be judged on the facts as he believes them to be is an accepted principle of the criminal law when the state of a man's mind and his knowledge are ingredients of the offence with which he is charged.

[The other Law Lords agreed.]

Since the act that Taffe intended to do was not actually prohibited by law—it was not an actus reus—his intention, however morally reprehensible, was not a mens rea.

If in a prosecution under s 170(2), the defendant is mistaken as to the nature of the goods, whether he is guilty will depend on the nature of the mistake. If, on the facts he believed to exist, he would be committing the actus reus of the offence charged and he was in fact committing the actus reus of the same offence, actus reus and mens rea would coincide and he would be guilty. The mistake is immaterial. For example, he believes he is smuggling a crate of Irish whisky. In fact the crate contains Scotch whisky. He believes he is importing an item on which import duty is payable and he is importing a dutiable item. He knows, because his belief and the facts coincide in this respect, that he is evading the duty chargeable on the goods in the crate. If the crate contained only an item which was not dutiable, there would be no actus reus of the full offence; but D might be guilty of an attempt. See Chapter 14.

Where D believes he is smuggling goods on which a duty must be paid but in fact the goods are not merely dutiable but completely prohibited from importation, the answer may be different. In principle, it should depend on whether the mens rea and the actus reus coincide. If s 170(2) created a single offence it should be immaterial that D thought he was committing an offence under para (a) whereas in fact he was committing an offence under para (b) because they are then the same offence—it is the same in principle as the case where D shoots to kill a person whom he believes to be a man, W, but who is in fact a woman, V. He is guilty of murder. With the mens rea of murder, he caused the actus reus of murder. The mistake is immaterial.

Whether s 170(2) creates one offence or separate offences under paras (a), (b) and (c) respectively is a question of the interpretation of the section, to which there is no certain answer.

2.4.2 Coincidence in point of time

Can D be liable for an offence if he performs the actus reus and later he forms the proscribed mental state?

■ *Questions*

1. D is driving along faultlessly and knocks down V who has suddenly stepped out into the road. On seeing who it is that he has knocked down, D is very happy since he hates V, and says 'I always wanted to kill him.' Has D committed murder?

2. D prepares a poisoned apple with the intention of giving it to his wife, V, tomorrow. V finds the poisoned apple today, eats it and dies. Is D guilty of murder? D is cleaning his gun with the intention of shooting V tomorrow. The gun goes off accidentally and kills V. Is D guilty of murder?

Fagan v Metropolitan Police Commissioner
[1968] 3 All ER 442, Queen's Bench Division

(Lord Parker CJ, Bridge and James JJ)

The defendant was directed by a police officer to park his car close to the kerb. He drove his car on to the officer's foot. The officer said, 'Get off, you are on my foot.' The defendant replied, 'Fuck you, you can wait', and turned off the ignition. He was convicted by the magistrates of assaulting the constable in the execution of his duty and his appeal was dismissed by Quarter Sessions who were in doubt whether the driving on to the foot was intentional or accidental but were satisfied that he 'knowingly, unnecessarily and provocatively' allowed the car to remain on the foot.

James J [with whom Lord Parker CJ concurred:]

...In our judgment, the question arising, which has been argued on general principles, falls to be decided on the facts of the particular case. An assault is any act which intentionally—or possibly recklessly—causes another person to apprehend immediate and unlawful personal violence. Although 'assault' is an independent crime and is to be treated as such, for practical purposes today 'assault' is generally synonymous with the term 'battery', and is a term used to mean the actual intended use of unlawful force to another person without his consent. On the facts of the present case, the 'assault' alleged involved a 'battery'. Where an assault involved a battery, it matters not, in our judgment, whether the battery is inflicted directly by the body of the offender or through the medium of some weapon or instrument controlled by the action of the offender. An assault may be committed by the laying of a hand on another, and the action does not cease to be an assault if it is a stick held in the hand and not the hand itself which is laid on the person of the victim. So, for our part, we see no difference in principle between the action of stepping on to a person's toe and maintaining that position and the action of driving a car on to a person's foot and sitting in the car while its position on the foot is maintained.

To constitute this offence, some intentional act must have been performed; a mere omission to act cannot amount to an assault. Without going into the question whether words alone can constitute an assault, it is clear that the words spoken by the appellant could not alone amount to an assault; they can only shed a light on the appellant's action. For our part, we think that the crucial question is whether, in this case, the act of the appellant can be said to be complete and spent at the moment of time when the car wheel came to rest on the foot, or whether his act is to be regarded as a con-tinuing act operating until the wheel was removed. In our judgment, a distinction is to be drawn between acts which are complete—though results may continue to flow—and those acts which are continuing. Once the act is complete, it cannot thereafter be said to be a threat to inflict unlawful force on the victim. If the act, as distinct from the results thereof, is a continuing act, there is a con-tinuing threat to inflict unlawful force. If the assault involves a battery and that battery continues, there is a continuing act of assault. For an assault to be committed, both the elements of actus reus and mens rea must be present at the same time. The 'actus reus' is the action causing the effect on the victim's mind: see the observations of Parke B, in *R v St George* [(1840) 9 C & P 483 at 490, 493]. The 'mens rea' is the intention to cause that effect. It is not necessary that mens rea should be present at the inception of the actus reus; it can be superimposed on an existing act. On the other hand, the subsequent inception of mens rea cannot convert an act which has been completed without mens rea into an assault.

In our judgment, the justices at Willesden and quarter sessions were right in law. On the facts found, the action of the appellant may have been initially unintentional, but the time came when, knowing that the wheel was on the officer's foot, the appellant (i) remained seated in the car so that his body through the medium of the car was in contact with the officer, (ii) switched off the ignition of the car, (iii) maintained the wheel of the car on the foot, and (iv) used words indicating the intention of keeping the wheel in that position. For our part, we cannot regard such conduct as mere omission or inactivity. There was an act constituting a battery which at its inception was not criminal because there was no element of intention, but which became criminal from the moment the intention was formed to produce the apprehension which was flowing from the continuing act. The fallacy of the appellant's argument is that it seeks to equate the facts of this case with such a case as where a motorist has accidentally run over a person and, that action having been completed, fails to assist the victim with the intent that the victim should suffer.

We would dismiss this appeal.

Bridge J:

I fully agree with my lords as to the relevant principles to be applied. No mere omission to act can amount to an assault. Both the elements of actus reus and mens rea must be present at the same time, but the one may be superimposed on the other. It is in the application of these principles to the highly unusual facts of this case that I have, with regret, reached a different conclusion from the majority of the court. I have no sympathy at all for the appellant, who behaved disgracefully; but I have been unable to find any way of regarding the facts which satisfied me that they amounted to the crime of assault. This has not been for want of trying; but at every attempt I have encountered the inescap-able question: after the wheel of the appellant's car had accidentally come to rest on the constable's foot, what was it that the appellant did which constituted the act of assault? However the question is approached, the answer which I feel obliged to give is: precisely nothing. The car rested on the foot by its own weight and remained stationary by its own inertia. The appellant's fault was that he omitted to manipulate the controls to set it in motion again.

Neither the fact that the appellant remained in the driver's seat nor that he switched off the ignition seem to me to be of any relevance. The constable's plight would have been no better, but might well have been worse, if the appellant had alighted from the car leaving the ignition switched on. Similarly, I can get no help from the suggested analogies. If one man accidentally treads on another's toe or touches him with a stick, but deliberately maintains pressure with foot or stick after the victim protests, there is clearly an assault; but there is no true parallel between such cases and the present case. It is not, to my mind, a legitimate use of language to speak of the appellant 'holding' or 'maintaining' the car wheel on the constable's foot. The expression which corresponds to the reality is that used by the justices in the Case Stated. They say, quite rightly, that he 'allowed' the wheel to remain.

With a reluctantly dissenting voice, I would allow this appeal and quash the appellant's conviction.

Appeal dismissed. Leave to appeal to the House of Lords refused

The courts have struggled to maintain a strict adherence to the principle that the act and mental state must coincide *exactly* in time. In several difficult circumstances, the courts have had to treat the defendant's conduct as being a continuing state of affairs.

Thabo Meli v R
[1954] 1 All ER 373, [1954] UKPC 1, Privy Council

(Lord Goddard CJ, Lord Reid and Mr L. M. D. da Silva)

The appellants, in accordance with a prearranged plan, took a man to a hut, gave him beer so that he was partially intoxicated and then struck him over the head. Believing him to be dead, they took his body and rolled it over a low cliff, dressing the scene to look like an accident. In fact the man was not dead, but died of exposure when unconscious at the foot of the cliff.

Lord Reid:

... The point of law which was raised in this case can be simply stated. It is said that two acts were done: first, the attack in the hut; and, secondly, the placing of the body outside afterwards—and that they were separate acts. It is said that, while the first act was accompanied by *mens rea*, it was not the cause of death; but that the second act, while it was the cause of death, was not accompanied by *mens rea*; and on that ground, it is said that the accused are not guilty of murder, though they may have been guilty of culpable homicide. It is said that the *mens rea* necessary to establish murder is an intention to kill, and that there could be no intention to kill when the accused thought that the man was already dead, so their original intention to kill had ceased before they did the act which caused the man's death. It appears to their Lordships impossible to divide up what was really one series of acts in this way. There is no doubt that the accused set out to do all these acts in order to achieve their plan, and as parts of their plan; and it is much too refined a ground of judgment to say that, because they were under a misapprehension at one stage and thought that their guilty purpose had been achieved before, in fact, it was achieved, therefore they are to escape the penalties of the law. Their Lordships do not think that this is a matter which is susceptible of elaboration. There appears to be no case, either in South Africa or England, or for that matter elsewhere, which resembles the present. Their Lordships can find no difference relevant to the present case between the law of South Africa and the law of England; and they are of the opinion that by both laws there can be no separation such as that for which the accused contend. Their crime is not reduced from murder to a lesser crime merely because the accused were under some misapprehension for a time during the completion of their criminal plot.

Their Lordships must, therefore, humbly advise Her Majesty that this appeal should be dismissed.

Appeal dismissed

■ *Questions*

1. In that case there was a prearranged plan. Does that matter?

2. What if the first act of the defendant was not a prearranged violent one, but an accident and his subsequent conduct caused death?

3. Arenson states that the decision in *Thabo Meli* has 'the practical effect of emasculating the doctrine of temporal coincidence beyond recognition.' Do you agree? K. Arenson, 'Thabo Meli Revisited: The Pernicious Effects of Result-Driven Decisions' (2013) 77 J Crim L 41.

R v Le Brun

[1991] 4 All ER 673, Court of Appeal, Criminal Division

(Lord Lane CJ, Auld and Judge JJ)

While the appellant and his wife were walking home at about 2 am they got into a heated argument. He hit her on the jaw, knocking her down unconscious. He then attempted to lift or drag her away from the scene but she slipped from his grasp and hit her head causing a fracture to the skull from which she died. He was charged with murder and convicted of manslaughter.

[Lord Lane CJ, delivering the judgment of the court:]

The main thrust of [the argument of Mr Wilson-Smith for the appellant] is to be found in ground 3 of the notice of appeal, which I will now read:

> 'The learned judge erred in law in directing the jury that they could convict the appellant of murder or manslaughter (depending on the intention with which he had previously assaulted the victim) if they were sure that, having committed the assault with no serious injury resulting, the appellant had accidentally dropped the victim causing her death whilst either: (a) attempting to move her to her home against her wishes, including any wishes she may have expressed prior to the previous assault, and/or (b) attempting to dispose of her body or otherwise cover up the previous assault.'

Problems of causation and remoteness of damage are never easy of solution. We have had helpful arguments from both counsel on this point, the point in the present case being, to put it in summary before coming to deal with it in more detail, that the intention of the appellant to harm his wife one way or another may have been separated by a period of time from the act which in fact caused the death, namely the fact of her falling to the ground and fracturing her skull. That second incident may have taken place without any guilty mind on the part of the appellant.

The learned editors of Smith and Hogan *Criminal Law* (6th edn, 1988 [see 13th edn, p 87]) p 320 say:

> 'an intervening act by the original actor will not break the chain of causation so as to excuse him, where the intervening act is part of the same transaction; but it is otherwise if the act which causes the *actus reus* is part of a completely different transaction. For example, D, having wounded P, visits him in hospital and accidentally infects him with smallpox of which he dies.'

The problem in the instant case can be expressed in a number of different ways, of which causation is one. Causation on the facts as the jury in this case must have found them—I say at the best from the point of view of the appellant—is in one sense clear. Death was caused by the victim's head hitting the ground as she was being dragged away by the appellant. The only remoteness was that between the initial unlawful blow and the later moment when the skull was fractured causing death.

The question can be perhaps framed in this way. There was here an initial unlawful blow to the chin delivered by the appellant. That, again on what must have been the jury's finding, was not delivered with the intention of doing really serious harm to the wife. The guilty intent accompanying that blow was sufficient to have rendered the appellant guilty of manslaughter, but not murder, had it caused death. But it did not cause death. What caused death was the later impact when the wife's head hit the pavement. At the moment of impact the appellant's intention was to remove her, probably unconscious, body to avoid detection. To that extent the impact may have been pro tanto accidental. May the earlier guilty intent be joined with the later non-guilty blow which caused death to produce in the conglomerate a proper verdict of manslaughter?

It has usually been in the context of murder that the problem has arisen in the previous decisions . . . [His lordship referred to *Thabo Meli*, earlier in this section, p 35, and to *Moore and Dorn* [1975] Crim LR 229 and continued:]

However, it will be observed that the present case is different from the facts of those two cases in that death here was not the result of a preconceived plan which went wrong, as was the case in those two decisions which we have cited. Here the death, again assuming the jury's finding to be such as it must have been, was the result of an initial unlawful blow, not intended to cause serious harm, in its turn causing the appellant to take steps possibly to evade the consequences of his unlawful act. During the taking of those steps he commits the actus reus but without the mens rea necessary for murder or manslaughter. Therefore the mens rea is contained in the initial unlawful assault, but the actus reus is the eventual dropping of the head on the ground.

Normally the actus reus and the mens rea coincide in point of time. What is the situation when they do not? Is it permissible, as the Crown contends here, to combine them to produce a conviction for manslaughter?

The answer is perhaps to be found in the next case to which we were referred, and that was *R v Church* [1965] EWCA Crim 1 [1965] 2 All ER 72, [1966] 1 QB 59. In that case the defendant was charged with the murder of a woman whose body was found in a river. The cause of death was drowning. The defendant had it seemed attacked the woman and rendered her semi-conscious. He thought she was dead and in his panic he threw her into the river. He was acquitted of murder but convicted of manslaughter . . .

[His lordship quoted from the judgment of the court given by Edmund Davies J adopting as sound Glanville Williams's view (CLGP 174) that 'If a killing by the first act would have been manslaughter, a later destruction of the supposed corpse should also be manslaughter'; and holding that, if the jury regarded the conduct of the appellant as 'a series of acts which culminated in her death . . . it mattered not whether he believed her to be alive or dead when he threw her in the river'. His lordship continued:]

It seems to us that where the unlawful application of force and the eventual act causing death are parts of the same sequence of events, the same transaction, the fact that there is an appreciable interval of time between the two does not serve to exonerate the defendant from liability. That is certainly so where the appellant's subsequent actions which caused death, after the initial unlawful blow, are designed to conceal his commission of the original unlawful assault.

It would be possible to express the problem as one of causation. The original unlawful blow to the chin was a causa sine qua non of the later actus reus. It was the opening event in a series which was to culminate in death: the first link in the chain of causation, to use another metaphor. It cannot be said that the actions of the appellant in dragging the victim away with the intention of evading liability broke the chain which linked the initial blow with the death.

In short, in circumstances such as the present, which is the only concern of this court, the act which causes death and the necessary mental state to constitute manslaughter need not coincide in point of time . . .

[Having quoted extensively from the summing-up, his lordship continued:]

The complaint made by Mr Wilson-Smith is primarily directed at the portion of that passage which we have read, namely the passage which runs: 'if he was doing that because he was determined to make her come home even though she had refused to do so...'

The argument advanced on behalf of the appellant is this. There has to be shown by the Crown in order to succeed a continuing transaction, or an unbroken chain of causation between the act which proved the mens rea and the final incident which resulted in death before it can be said that there is a sufficient connection between the mens rea and the actus reus. The mere fact that this man attempts to get his wife home when she is unconscious, it is argued, coupled with her earlier unwillingness to go home, is not enough to show a continuing transaction of an unbroken chain as has to be shown.

In every case, and this is no exception, the summing up has to be read against the background of fact which lies behind the whole of the case. Part of the background is, as we have already indicated when trying to set out the facts of the case, that the dispute between the two was certainly in part, and probably very largely, about whether she was going to go home or not...

[His lordship referred again to the summing-up and continued:]

The judge was drawing a sharp distinction between actions by the appellant which were designed to help his wife and actions which were not so designed: on the one hand that would be a way in which the prosecution could establish the connection if he was not trying to assist his wife; on the other hand if he was trying to assist his wife, the chain of causation would have been broken and the nexus between the two halves of the prosecution case would not exist....

[His lordship said that the direction given to the jury in relation to manslaughter was satisfactory.]

Appeal dismissed

There was no doubt that Le Brun caused the death of his wife (V). There was a problem of causation only if the prosecution relied upon the blow to the jaw as the cause of death. If it was, this was a straightforward case of manslaughter. V did not die of any injury directly inflicted by that blow but it rendered her unconscious. She would not have died as she did if she had not been unconscious. Was the blow then a cause of death? It is sufficient to establish liability for homicide that the act alleged is one of two or more causes of death. Was it? In *S v Masilela* 1968 (2) SA 558, AD, the appellants (DD) struck and throttled V in his house with intent to kill him. DD threw him, unconscious, on to his bed. Having ransacked the house they set it on fire. V died of carbon monoxide poisoning. They may have believed V to be dead when they started the fire. On the assumption that this was so, their convictions for murder were, nevertheless, upheld. The majority held that the strangulation injuries (which were inflicted with intent to kill) were a material and direct contributory cause of death. But for the injuries V would have had no difficulty in escaping from the fire. Hart and Honoré, *Causation in the Law* (2nd edn, 1985), p 334, refer to a German case OGHBZSt 2 (1949), 285 where D turned on the gas in the matrimonial bedroom, intending to kill his sleeping wife, V, and went away. Three hours later he returned and, believing V to be dead, turned on the gas a second time to simulate an accident. The Supreme Court of the British Zone decided that D was guilty of murder as his act on the first occasion contributed to V's death by weakening her condition. What if a third party had turned on the gas on the second occasion?

If the blow was a cause of death, did it matter whether Le Brun was trying to take his wife home against her will or was doing his best to help her? What if a passer-by had tried to carry her to get help and dropped her as Le Brun did? Does intervention by a third party 'break that chain of causation' where the accused's own act would not do so? See section 3.2.3.2, p 49.

If, on the other hand, dropping her was the sole cause of death, the 'series of acts' or transaction principle comes into play as in *Thabo Meli* (earlier in this section). Would the series of acts have come to an end if Le Brun had been attempting to get her to hospital? Or if he had thought that, whatever she had said before the blow, in the changed circumstances, she would have wished to go home?

Attorney-General's Reference (No 4 of 1980)
[1981] 2 All ER 617, Court of Appeal, Criminal Division

(Ackner LJ, Tudor Evans and Drake JJ)

In the course of an argument on the landing of a maisonette, the accused pushed the deceased, causing her to fall backwards over a handrail and head first onto the floor below. Almost immediately afterwards the accused tied a rope round the deceased's neck and dragged her upstairs by the rope. He then placed her in the bath and cut her neck with a knife to let out her blood, with the purpose of cutting up her body and disposing of it, which he then did. The body was never found. The accused was charged with manslaughter. There was evidence that the deceased died either as a result of being pushed or by being strangled by the rope or by having her throat cut, but the Crown conceded that it was impossible to prove which of those acts had caused the death. In response to a submission by the defence at the close of the Crown's case that there was no case to go to the jury, the judge decided to withdraw the case from the jury and directed an acquittal on the ground that the Crown had failed to prove the cause of the death. The Attorney General referred to the court for its opinion on the question whether, if an accused person killed another by one or other of two or more different acts, each of which was sufficient to establish manslaughter, it was necessary to prove which act caused the death in order to found a conviction.

Ackner LJ:

. . . On the above facts this reference raises a single and simple question, viz, if an accused kills another by one or other of two or more different acts each of which, if it caused the death, is a sufficient act to establish manslaughter, is it necessary in order to found a conviction to prove which act caused the death? The answer to that question is No, it is not necessary to found a conviction to prove which act caused the death. No authority is required to justify this answer, which is clear beyond argument, as was indeed immediately conceded by counsel on behalf of the accused.

What went wrong in this case was that counsel made jury points to the judge and not submissions of law. He was in effect contending that the jury should not convict of manslaughter if the death had resulted from the 'fall', because the push which had projected the deceased over the handrail was a reflex and not a voluntary action, as a result of her digging her nails into him. If, however, the deceased was still alive when he cut her throat, since he then genuinely believed her to be dead, having discovered neither pulse nor sign of breath, but frothy blood coming from her mouth, he could not be guilty of manslaughter because he had not behaved with gross criminal negligence. What counsel and the judge unfortunately overlooked was that there was material available to the jury which would have entitled them to have convicted the accused of manslaughter, whichever of the two sets of acts caused her death. It being common ground that the deceased was killed by an act done to her by the accused and it being conceded that the jury could not be satisfied which was the act which caused the death, they should have been directed in due course in the summing up, to ask themselves the following questions: (i) 'Are we satisfied beyond reasonable doubt that the deceased's "fall" downstairs was the result of an intentional act by the accused which was unlawful and dangerous?' If the answer was No, then they would acquit. If the answer was Yes, then they would need to ask themselves a second question, namely: (ii) 'Are we satisfied beyond reasonable doubt that the act of cutting the girl's throat was an act of gross criminal negligence?' If the answer to that question was No, then they would acquit, but if the answer was Yes, then the verdict would be guilty of manslaughter. The jury would thus have been satisfied that, whichever act had killed the deceased, each was a sufficient act to establish the offence of manslaughter.

The facts of this case did not call for 'a series of acts direction' following the principle in *Thabo Meli v R* (see earlier in this section, p 35).

The defendant was certainly guilty of manslaughter if he acted with the fault required on both occasions; but should he not also have been guilty if he acted with that fault on the first occasion only? If he in fact thereafter killed while disposing of what he believed to be a corpse was not this part of the 'same transaction' (*Thabo Meli*) or 'a series of acts which culminated in death' (*Church*)?

2.5 Criminal liability without an act

Being sovereign, Parliament can enact anything, even that a person commits a crime if something happens to him—for example, that he 'is found' in a particular situation.

R v Larsonneur

(1933) 24 Cr App R 74, Court of Criminal Appeal

(Lord Hewart CJ, Avory and Humphreys JJ)

L was a French citizen whose entitlement to stay in the UK was restricted so as to require: 'departure from the United Kingdom not later than the 22nd March 1933'. On that date L entered the Irish Free State (which did not constitute departure from the UK under the order). The Irish authorities deported her, escorting her to Holyhead on 20 April. British police then arrested her. On 22 April she was charged under Article 18(1)(b) of the Aliens Order 1920 (below). At trial, the jury's verdict was: 'Guilty through circumstances beyond her own control'. L was sentenced to three days' imprisonment and recommended for deportation.

By the Aliens Order 1920, Article 1(3): 'Leave shall not be given to an alien to land in the United Kingdom unless he complies with the following conditions, that is to say . . . (g) he has not been prohibited from landing by the Secretary of State.' By Article 1(4), as amended: '. . . an alien who is found in the United Kingdom at any time after the expiration of the period limited by any such condition shall for the purposes of this Order be deemed to be an alien to whom leave to land has been refused . . .'. By Article 18(1)(b), as amended: 'If any alien, having landed in the United Kingdom in contravention of art 1 of this Order, is at any time found within the United Kingdom, he shall be guilty of an offence against this Order.'

Lord Hewart CJ [delivered the judgment of the court:]

In fact, the appellant went to the Irish Free State and afterwards, in circumstances which are perfectly immaterial, so far as this appeal is concerned, came back, to Holyhead. She was at Holyhead on 21 April 1933, a date after the day limited by the condition on her passport.

In these circumstances, it seems to be quite clear that art 1(4) of the Aliens Order 1920 (as amended . . .), applies. . . . The appellant was, therefore, on 21 April 1933, in the position in which she would have been if she had been prohibited from landing by the Secretary of State and, that being so, there is no reason to interfere with the finding of the jury. She was found here and was, therefore, deemed to be in the class of persons whose landing had been prohibited by the Secretary of State, by reason of the fact that she had violated the condition on her passport.

Appeal dismissed

Larsonneur was generally condemned but defended by D. J. Lanham [1976] Crim LR 276 who considered why L should have been denied the 'most readily acceptable' of all defences, physical compulsion. He concludes:

If Miss Larsonneur had been dragged kicking and screaming from France into the United Kingdom by kidnappers and the same judgment had been given by the Court of Criminal Appeal, the defence of unforeseeable compulsion would truly have been excluded and the case would be the worst blot on the pages of the modern criminal law. But she wasn't and it wasn't and it isn't.

■ *Questions*

Did the offence consist in 'being found' or in 'landing and being found'? 'Being found' may not require a voluntary act by L, but does 'landing'?

In *Winzar v Chief Constable of Kent* (1983) The Times, 28 March, W was taken to hospital but found to be drunk and told to leave. The police were called when W remained slumped in a corridor. They took him to a police car parked in the hospital forecourt on X road. His subsequent conviction for 'being found drunk in a highway, X Road' was upheld by the Divisional Court. 'Found drunk' meant perceived to be drunk. It was enough that W was present in a highway and there perceived to be drunk. Did the police become aware of D's state in the highway?

How explicit must the statute be as to whether there is a requirement of D's voluntary conduct in the offence? In *Robinson-Pierre* [2013] EWCA Crim 2396, D was convicted of offences under s 3(1) of the Dangerous Dogs Act 1991 which provides:

If a dog is dangerously out of control in a public place, the owner . . . is guilty of an offence, or if the dog while so out of control injures any person, an aggravated offence . . .

The offence occurred when police officers executing a search warrant battered down the front door of D's home and entered. D's ferocious pit bull attacked them and pursued three more officers in the street before being destroyed by armed officers called to the scene. At trial, the judge directed the jury that D was liable without proof of fault; it was enough that D was the owner of a dog that was dangerously out of control in a public place, as D's dog clearly was. D was convicted and appealed. D argued that although s 3(1) creates a strict liability offence, a conviction under that section requires proof that D caused or contributed to the prohibited event by his voluntary act or omission. Where acts of a third party, without D's knowledge or consent, were the sole cause of the state of affairs D was not guilty: he did not do anything to bring about the prohibited state of affairs. The Crown argued that 'how a dog ends up in the factual scenario [by] which the *actus reus* engages liability is entirely irrelevant'.

The Court of Appeal in what may be a landmark case quashed the conviction. Although s 3 is an offence of strict liability, the underlying assumption of the defence provided by s 3(2) was that someone (owner or person in charge) would be in charge of the dog. It was not therefore Parliament's intention to render the owner absolutely liable in all circumstances for the existence of the prohibited state of affairs however it arose (at [40]). The court held that there must be some causal connection between having charge of the dog and the prohibited state of affairs that has arisen.

In our view, section 3(1) requires proof by the prosecution of an act or omission of the defendant (with or without fault) that to some (more than minimal) degree caused or permitted the prohibited state of affairs to come about. There had to be some causal connection between having charge of the dog and the prohibited state of affairs that had arisen (the danger in public).

The court relied on a wide range of authority including that from New Zealand and Canada. The court was also referred to the Supreme Court's recent decision in *Hughes* [2013] UKSC 56 (section 3.2.2.2, p 46) in relation to causing death by unlawful driving, but noted that the present offence was not cast in terms of causing a dangerous dog to be in a public place. Pitchford LJ stated at para 37:

we do not accept that it is the law of England and Wales that Parliament cannot provide for criminal liability when there is no causative link between the act or omission of the defendant and the prohibited event. . . . To the extent that [defence counsel] seeks to derive a principle of law that even in the case of 'absolute' liability the defendant must be shown to have *caused* the prohibited state of affairs, we disagree with him. Such a conclusion would ignore the rationale for the acceptability of some offences of strict liability. The policy behind the prohibition may be regulatory; that is, it is in the public interest to place an absolute burden on the defendant to ensure that the state of affairs prohibited does not come about; alternatively, the criminal law may create an irrebuttable presumption whose effect cannot be avoided even by proof of moral rectitude.

As the court notes, in *Smith and Hogan* it is suggested that:

as a matter of principle, even 'state of affairs' offences ought to require proof that D either caused the state of affairs or failed to terminate it or to act in order to do so when it was within his control and possible to do so.

The court took the view that:

This is a view that will have many supporters. However, we have no doubt that the supremacy of Parliament embraces the power to create 'state of affairs' offences in which no causative link between the prohibited state of affairs and the defendant need be established. The legal issue is not, in our view, whether in principle such offences can be created but whether in any particular enactment Parliament intended to create one.

FURTHER READING

A. Ashworth, 'Defining Offences Without Harm' in A. T. H. Smith (ed), *Criminal Law: Essays in Honour of J. C. Smith* (1987)

R. A. Duff, *Answering for Crime: Responsibility and Liability in the Criminal Law* (2007), pp 202–208

S. Eldar, 'The Limits of Transferred Malice' (2012) 32 OJLS 633

P. H. Robinson, 'Should the Criminal Law Abandon the Actus Reus–Mens Rea Distinction?' in S. Shute, J. Gardner and J. Horder (eds), *Action and Value in Criminal Law* (1993)

A. T. H. Smith, 'On Actus Reus and Mens Rea' in P. Glazebrook (ed), *Reshaping the Criminal Law: Essays in Honour of Glanville Williams* (1978)

P. Westen, 'The Significance of Transferred Intent' (2013) 7 Criminal Law and Philosophy 321

3
Causation

3.1 Introduction

Where the definition of a crime includes a result or consequence flowing from D's conduct, it must be proved that D caused that result. An act done with intent to cause the result may be an attempt to commit the crime but it will not be the full offence unless it actually causes it. Nor will it be sufficient that the *event* desired by D happens if it does not happen as a result of his act. So in *White* [1910] 2 KB 124, where D administered poison to V with intent to kill her and she died not of poison but of a heart attack, he was guilty of attempted murder but not of murder. It would have been different if the poison had brought about the heart attack. The death of V was the event which D desired to bring about but it was not the result of his act.

The discussion of causation usually occurs in the context of homicide, but it is an important feature in all result crimes. It is especially so in cases of strict liability where, in the absence of mens rea elements, disputes over causation become the most critical issue in determining liability. (See, for example, on environmental offences: N. Padfield, 'Clean Water and Muddy Causation' [1995] Crim LR 683.) Causation is also an important aspect of many other crimes.

Arguably, the criminal law places too much emphasis on the result occurring (which is sometimes a matter of luck) and not enough on the blameworthiness of D's conduct in seeking to bring about that result. See A. Ashworth, 'Belief Intent and Criminal Liability' in J. Eekelaar and J. Bell (eds), *Oxford Essays in Jurisprudence* (1989).

Some of the controversies that will be examined in this chapter include the following.

(i)   What should the law do where D's conduct is not the sole cause of the result? Must D be a substantial cause of the result, or does it suffice if D's contribution is more than minimal?

(ii) What should the law do where there is an intervening event between D's conduct and the result—what is necessary to break the 'chain of causation'?

(iii) To what extent can the actions of the victim break the chain of causation?

(iv) Is it possible to have a general theory of causation that is applicable across all offences?

3.2 General approach to issues of causation

We suggest that a logical approach to cases involving causation issues is as follows:

(1) Is D's conduct a 'but for' cause of the proscribed consequence ('but for' D's act would the result have occurred)?

(2) Is D's conduct potentially a relevant legal cause of the proscribed consequence:

    (a) D's conduct need not be the sole cause;

    (b) D's conduct must be a culpable cause;

   (c) D's conduct need not be a direct cause;

   (d) D's conduct must be more than merely *de minimis*?

(3) Is there any intervening act between D's conduct and the prohibited result which breaks the chain of causation? Consider the type of intervention:

   (a) naturally occurring events;

   (b) third party interventions;

   (c) the exceptional case of the medical profession;

   (d) victim's conduct.

The courts have commonly asserted that causation is simply a question of fact to be answered by the application of common sense. That is difficult to reconcile with the existence of a book, *Causation in the Law*, of over 500 pages with a 24-page table of cases by two eminent professors, Hart and Honoré. Given that it has been influential in the development of the law on causation, it is helpful to be familiar with their general approach. Hart and Honoré placed emphasis on giving causation its ordinary meaning. Their approach is based upon the distinction between normal and abnormal conditions. Only abnormal conditions can be categorized as causes; normal conditions cannot. Normal conditions are described as 'those conditions which are present as part of the usual state or mode of operation of the thing under enquiry'. They give as an example pervasive features of the environment. Therefore if a person lights a match near a haystack, setting it alight, the fact that there is oxygen in the air is a normal condition and therefore not a cause. However, the lighting of the match is abnormal and so it is right to classify it as a cause.

The difficulty of finding a practical approach to causation was recognized by the House of Lords in the *Empress* case, section 3.2.3.2, p 51. Whether that case helps to overcome the difficulty is a matter for debate.

3.2.1 'But for' causation

Consider *White* [1910] 2 KB 124. In short, D poisoned a drink with some cyanide. He placed it on a table for his mother to drink. The mother was found dead; she died from a heart attack. There was no evidence that the poisoned drink had accelerated her death in any way. D was charged with her murder. If we ask 'but for' D's act of poisoning the drink would she have died anyway, the answer is that she would. D's conduct was not therefore a cause of her death. He was acquitted of her murder but remained liable for attempting to murder her.

There is a danger with taking 'but for' causation too far and it leading to absurd results. If D invites V to dinner and V is run over by X and killed on the way to D's house, V would not have died 'but for' the invitation; but as a matter of common sense, no one would say 'D killed V', and D has not caused his death in law. The 'but for' test—or 'sine qua non' as it is sometimes called—serves to filter out irrelevant factors, but cannot be regarded as any more than a starting point in the causation inquiry.

3.2.2 Legal causes

3.2.2.1 Multiple causes

A result may have more than one cause. It is sufficient for criminal liability that D's act was one of two or more causes. If the result would not have occurred as and when it did *but for* D's act that is usually enough to fix him with responsibility for it. If V is already dying of meningitis when D strikes him and the blow accelerates V's death, D is guilty of homicide. If a fatal collision occurs because two motorists are driving dangerously and a passenger is killed, both are guilty of causing death by dangerous driving. Usually it is simply a question of fact whether the act caused the result, but the matter is more complex when an act by some other person or some event intervenes between D's act and the result (see section 3.2.3).

3.2.2.2 A culpable cause?

A person who is acting with the mental fault required for an offence may cause the forbidden result, yet there may be no connection between the fault and the result. Should he be held responsible for the result?

In *Clarke* (1990) 91 Cr App R 69, it was argued that a person who drives a car when so affected by drink that there was an obvious and serious risk that his driving would cause injury to the person or substantial damage to property was thereby guilty of reckless driving (now superseded by the offence of dangerous driving). Russell LJ responded to this argument as follows:

Suppose a person gets into a car when indisputably unfit through drink to drive it; he drives at a snail's pace and is involved in a collision that is wholly the other driver's fault; the other driver is killed. On Mr Elias's [appellant's counsel's] definition the driver drives recklessly because he is driving while unfit through drink to do so. If another road user happens to be killed, he is guilty of causing death by reckless driving. That, in our view, cannot be correct.

Obviously it is not correct; but is that because the driver is not driving recklessly or because his reckless driving did not cause the death? Consider *Crossman* [1986] RTR 49, where it was held that a lorry driver was guilty of reckless driving, however slowly and carefully he drove, if he was ignoring an obvious and serious risk that the load on his lorry was liable to fall off and cause injury. The load fell on to and killed a pedestrian and Crossman was held to be guilty of causing death by reckless driving. Assuming that Crossman was rightly held to be reckless (which he might not now be under the subjective test of recklessness, see section 5.3.1, p 130) this was right because there was a connection between the recklessness and the death. But suppose that a child had run in front of the lorry so that, notwithstanding his slow and careful driving, he could not avoid running over and killing him. Plainly he should not be held guilty of causing death by reckless driving. He was committing the offence of reckless driving when he ran over and killed the child, but the child's death was not caused by Crossman's reckless act.

Reckless driving has now been abolished but Crossman's conduct would amount to dangerous driving (see *Woodward* [1995] 2 Cr App R 388, [1995] Crim LR 487 and commentary) and, where death was caused by the insecure load, to causing death by dangerous driving. Should the reasoning of Russell LJ, in the previous extract, be applied to convict him of causing death in the hypothetical case of the child? Consider the next case, which elucidates the general approach that ought to be taken when an offence requires D to have caused a prohibited result.

R v Hughes

[2013] UKSC 56, Supreme Court, http://www.bailii.org/uk/cases/UKSC/2013/56.html

(Lords Neuberger, Mance, Kerr, Hughes and Toulson)

D was driving along a carriageway when a vehicle driven by V travelling in the opposite direction veered across the road and collided with him. V died from his injuries. It later transpired that V was driving under the influence of heroin at the time of the fatal collision. It was accepted that D's driving was faultless. However, D was driving without a full licence and did not have insurance. D was convicted of causing the death of another person by driving a motor vehicle on a road without insurance and otherwise than in accordance with a licence, contrary to s 3ZB of the Road Traffic Act 1988. The certified question for the Supreme Court to answer was: 'Is it an offence contrary to section 3ZB of the Road Traffic Act 1988 as amended by section 21(1) of the Road Safety Act 2006, committed by an unlicensed, disqualified or uninsured driver, when the circumstances are that the manner of his or her driving is faultless and the deceased was (in terms of civil law) 100% responsible for causing the fatal accident or collision?'

Lords Hughes and Toulson delivered the judgment for a unanimous court.

25. By the test of common sense, whilst the driving by Mr Hughes created the opportunity for his car to be run into by [V], what brought about the latter's death was his own dangerous driving under the influence of drugs. It was a matter of the merest chance that what he hit when he veered onto the wrong side of the road for the last of several times was the oncoming vehicle which Mr Hughes was driving. He might just as easily have gone off the road and hit a tree, in which case nobody would suggest that his death was caused by the planting of the tree, although that too would have been a sine qua non.

...

28. It follows that in order to give effect to the expression 'causes...death...by driving' a defendant charged with the offence under section 3ZB must be shown to have done something other than simply putting his vehicle on the road so that it is there to be struck. It must be proved that there was something which he did or omitted to do by way of driving it which contributed in a more than minimal way to the death. The question therefore remains what can or cannot amount to such act or omission in the manner of driving.

...

33. Juries should thus be directed that it is not necessary for the Crown to prove careless or inconsiderate driving, but that there must be something open to proper criticism in the driving of the defendant, beyond the mere presence of the vehicle on the road, and which contributed in some more than minimal way to the death. How much this offence will in practice add to the other offences of causing death by driving will have to be worked out as factual scenarios present themselves; it may be that it will add relatively little, but this is the inevitable consequence of the language used and the principles of construction explained above.

...

36. For the reasons set out, inquiry into apportionment of liability in civil terms is not appropriate to a criminal trial. But it must follow from the use of the expression 'causes...death...by driving' that section 3ZB requires at least some act or omission in the control of the car, which involves some element of fault, whether amounting to careless/inconsiderate driving or not, and which contributes in some more than minimal way to the death. It is not necessary that such act or omission be the principal cause of the death. In which circumstances the offence under section 3ZB will then add to the other offences of causing death by driving must remain to be worked out as factual scenarios are presented to the courts. In the present case the agreed facts are that there was nothing which Mr Hughes did in the manner of his driving which contributed in any way to the death. It follows that the Recorder of Newcastle was correct to rule that he had not in law caused the death by his driving. The appeal should be allowed and that ruling restored.

■ *Question*

Does the form of words used by Parliament in the section require D to be driving in a way that is 'open to criticism'?

In *Uthayakumar and Clayton* [2014] EWCA Crim 123, http://www.bailii.org/ew/cases/EWCA/Crim/2014/123.html, the appellants' convictions were quashed as a result of *Hughes*, as it was held that their respective driving was wholly without fault.

R v Dalloway

(1847) 2 Cox CC 273, Stafford Crown Court

(Erle J)

The prisoner was indicted for the manslaughter of one Henry Clarke, by reason of his negligence as driver of a cart.

It appeared that the prisoner was standing up in a spring-cart, and having the conduct of it along a public thoroughfare. The cart was drawn by one horse. The reins were not in the hands of the prisoner, but loose on the horse's back. While the cart was so proceeding down the slope of a hill, the horse trotting at the time, the deceased child, who was about three years of age, ran across the road before the horse, at the distance of a few yards, and one of the wheels of the cart knocking it down and passing over it, caused its death. It did not appear that the prisoner saw the child in the road before the accident.

Spooner, for the prosecution, submitted that the prisoner, in consequence of his negligence in not using reins, was responsible for the death of the child, but Erle J, in summing up to the jury, directed them that a party neglecting ordinary caution, and, by reason of that neglect, causing the death of another, is guilty of manslaughter; that if the prisoner had reins, and by using the reins could have saved the child, he was guilty of manslaughter; but that if they thought he could not have saved the child by pulling the reins, or otherwise by their assistance, they must acquit him.

The jury acquitted the prisoner.

■ *Questions*

1. What was the conduct that caused the death? Driving the cart? Driving the cart without holding reins?

2. D is driving his car along the road. V, a child, runs out from between parked cars and D knocks V down and injures him seriously. Expert evidence is adduced to say that D could not have stopped in time to avoid the collision. Has D caused V's serious injury? Would it make any difference if D was not watching where he was going because he was texting his girlfriend on his mobile phone?

3.2.2.3 Direct causes

The connection between D's culpable conduct and the proscribed result need not be direct. In *Mitchell* (1983) 76 Cr App R 293, CA, D entered a post office in which there was a lengthy queue. D tried to push in and an elderly man intervened and complained to D. D hit this man who fell back onto an 89-year-old lady who suffered a broken leg and died as a result of complications from that injury. D's conviction for manslaughter was upheld: 'We can see no reason of policy for holding that an act calculated to harm A cannot be manslaughter if, in fact it kills B. The criminality of the doer of the act is precisely the same . . . ,' per Staughton J at 296.

■ *Questions*

Is there any limit to this principle? D punches X, a burly man of 20, intending to cause him serious injury. X falls onto Y who lands on V who is a newborn baby and crushes V to death. Is D liable for V's murder?

3.2.2.4 *De minimis* causes

Some factual causes are so minute that they can be ignored when considering the causation inquiry. In *Kimsey* [1996] Crim LR 35, D was convicted of causing death by dangerous driving. He had been racing another car driven by the deceased, V. D argued that the reason V crashed was because of her loss of control of the car, not because of D's collision with her car. The prosecution argued that D's conduct, by racing and/or colliding and/or driving too closely had caused V's loss of control and led to her death. The Court of Appeal confirmed that the test for whether D's conduct is a cause of the prohibited result is whether the contribution made by D's conduct to the result was 'more than minute'.

This can give rise to difficult questions of degree in cases of the killing of terminally ill individuals. The question of how much acceleration of impending death needs to be established to show that D has caused V's death raises complex and controversial issues of euthanasia. There have been a number of high-profile cases in which doctors have been prosecuted for murder, or attempted murder, where they have 'eased the passing' of a terminally ill patient, often reducing life expectancy by only hours. An example was that of Dr Cox (1992) 12 BMLR 38 ('Hard cases make bad law (mercy killing and Dr Cox)' (1992) 142 NLJ 1293), and a more significant one was that of Bodkin Adams, reported at [1957] Crim LR 365. See the Law Commission's Report No 304, *Murder, Manslaughter and Infanticide* (2006), Ch 7, section 15.2.3.4, p 532, on whether a defence of mercy killing ought to be introduced into English law.

3.2.3 *Novus actus interveniens*

If D's conduct is a 'but for' cause and is not merely *de minimis*, the question will often arise as to what impact any intervening acts between D's conduct and the proscribed result have on D's liability. This commonly arises in the context of murder.

Should D remain liable for murder where he causes V some injury but before V dies:

- there is some naturally occurring event, for example lightning striking V; or
- some third party intervenes, for example D2 comes along and shoots V dead; or
- medical professionals, seeking to save V's life, blunder and accelerate his death; or
- V himself accelerates his own death?

This is a notoriously difficult area of law and the courts have struggled to produce clear principles. The diversity of factual circumstances in which interventions arise, encourages the courts to distinguish cases too readily. In addition, decisions are very heavily influenced by policy considerations, particularly since most are homicide cases in which D has performed a culpable act with mens rea. The following categories of intervening event deserve consideration.

3.2.3.1 Natural events

According to a leading American academic writer, R. M. Perkins, if D knocks down V and leaves him unconscious on the floor of a building which collapses in a sudden earthquake and kills him, D is not guilty of homicide even if it is certain that V would not have been in the building if D had not knocked him down. But if D had struck V on the seashore and left him unconscious in the path of the incoming tide, D would be responsible for V's death by drowning. (Examples given by Perkins (1946) 36 J Cr L & Cr at 393.) The seashore example was followed in *Hallett* [1969] SASR 141, on similar facts; and the court said it would have been different if the unconscious victim had been left above the high-water mark but drowned by a wholly exceptional tidal wave (tsunami) resulting from an undersea earthquake.

> ■ *Question*
>
> Suppose a hospital is struck by lightning and set on fire so that everyone in it perishes. Are all the patients who were there because they had been assaulted now the victims of homicide?

3.2.3.2 Intervening acts of others

The law struggles to distinguish precisely between voluntary and involuntary actors intervening after the defendant's conduct and before the prohibited result. It is generally accepted that where X, the intervening party, has acted in an involuntary manner, his act will not break the chain of causation, even if the act is foreseeable, and D will remain liable. On the other hand, a free, deliberate, informed act by X would break the chain of causation, whether foreseeable or not.

R v Latif; R v Shahzad
[1996] UKHL 16, House of Lords, http://www.bailii.org/uk/cases/UKHL/1996/16.html

(Lords Keith, Jauncey, Mustill, Steyn and Hoffmann)

Shahzad was in Pakistan with heroin worth £3.2m. He wanted to export it to England. Unknown to him, his principal courier, Honi, was a paid informer. With customs officials, Honi received the heroin from Shahzad and the officers arranged to export it to England. With the cooperation of the officers, Honi came to England and persuaded Shahzad to come to England. Shahzad and his accomplice, Latif, met Honi at an appointed place and received from him what they believed to be the heroin (in fact, Horlicks!).

Latif and Shahzad were convicted of being knowingly concerned in the fraudulent evasion or attempt at evasion of the prohibition of the importation of heroin, contrary to s 170(2)(b) of the Customs and Excise Management Act 1979 (set out at section 2.4.1.2, p 31). Their appeal was dismissed by the Court of Appeal ([1995] 1 Cr App R 270), who held that the words 'fraudulent evasion' extend to 'any conduct which is directed and intended to lead to the importation of goods covertly in breach of a prohibition on import'.

[Lord Steyn (with whose speech Lords Keith, Jauncey, Mustill and Hoffmann agreed) said that the prosecution did not try to support this reasoning in the House of Lords and, after reference to a commentary by Sir John Smith in [1994] Crim LR 751–752, continued:]

Counsel for the prosecution attempted to support the conviction on a different basis. He submitted that there was in truth a criminal evasion because Shahzad delivered the heroin intending that it should be imported into the United Kingdom: it was imported into the United Kingdom; and Shahzad sought to take delivery in England of the heroin. Counsel emphasized the continuing nature of the offence. He said it did not matter that the customs officers acted for their own purpose. The problem, as Sir John Smith pointed out in the note in the *Criminal Law Review*, is one of causation. The general principle is that the free, deliberate and informed intervention of a second person, who intends to exploit the situation created by the first, but is not acting in concert with him, is held to relieve the first actor of criminal responsibility: see *Hart and Honoré, Causation in the Law*, 2nd ed (1985), 325 *et seq.; Blackstone's Criminal Practice* (1995), 13–15. For example, if a thief had stolen the heroin after Shahzad delivered it to Honi, and imported it into the United Kingdom, the chain of causation would plainly have been broken. The general principle must also be applicable to the role of the customs officers in this case. They acted in full knowledge of the content of the packages. They did not act in concert with Shahzad. They acted deliberately for their own purposes whatever those might have been. In my view consistency and legal principle do not permit us to create an exception to the general principle of causation to take care of the particular problem thrown up by this case. In my view the prosecution's argument elides the real problem of causation and provides no way of solving it.

That is, however, not the end of the matter. There is another principle solution to be considered, namely the alternative argument of the prosecution in the Court of Appeal, *viz* that Shahzad was guilty of an attempted evasion under section 170(2). Initially, counsel for the prosecution did not on the hearing before your Lordships rely on this alternative argument. After your Lordships raised the question counsel for the prosecution did advance this alternative argument. On this question your Lordships heard oral submissions and subsequently received further written submissions.

Shahzad delivered the heroin to Honi in Pakistan for the purpose of exportation to the United Kingdom and subsequently Shahzad tried to collect the heroin from Honi for distribution in the United Kingdom. In these circumstances the guilt of Shahzad of an offence under that part of section 170(2) which creates the offence of an attempt at the evasion of a prohibition is plain. Counsel for Shahzad suggested that the jury might have viewed Shahzad's conduct as mere preparatory steps falling short of an attempted evasion. In my view that would have been a wholly unrealistic suggestion. In common sense and law that was only one possible answer: Shahzad committed attempts at evasion in Pakistan and in England. Indeed I am confident that counsel would not have devalued his speech to the jury with a suggestion that on the prosecution case there was no attempt at evasion. For my part I have no doubt that this case must be approached on the basis that the guilt of Shahzad of an attempt at evasion under section 170(2) cannot seriously be disputed.

Counsel for Shahzad also argued that if the movement of the heroin from Pakistan to England was not a fraudulent evasion it was impossible for Shahzad to be guilty of an offence of attempt at evasion. It will be recalled that I accepted that the customs officer, who brought the heroin to England, committed an offence under section 50(3) of the Customs and Excise Management Act 1979 and further that I assumed that the customs officer also committed an offence under section 170(2) of the same Act. In these circumstances the argument apparently falls away. In any event, Shahzad committed the attempt at evasion in Pakistan and nothing that the customs officer subsequently did could deprive Shahzad's conduct of its criminal character. And Shahzad's attempt at evasion by distribution of heroin in England was an offence. It was sufficient to prove that Shahzad intended to commit the full offence and was guilty of acts which were more than merely preparatory to the commission of the full offence.

Counsel for Shahzad further submitted that in the circumstances of this case an English court would not have had jurisdiction to try an offence of an attempt at evasion under section 170(2) in England. The attempted evasion in Pakistan, as well as the attempted evasion in England, were respectively directed at importation into the United Kingdom and associated with an importation into the United Kingdom. In these circumstances counsel's submission in regard to the attempt at evasion, which Shahzad committed in Pakistan, is destroyed by the decision of the House of Lords in *DPP v Stonehouse* [1977] 2 All ER 909, [1978] AC 55. The English courts have jurisdiction over such criminal attempts even though the overt acts take place abroad. The rationale is that the effect of the criminal attempt is directed at this country.

Appeals dismissed

The case serves as a strong authority recognizing unequivocally the orthodox position that X's act will break the chain of causation started by D where X's act is a free deliberate and informed act.

■ **Questions**

After reading *Latif*, would you consider that D could be liable for V's death where D supplies heroin to V, a sane adult, who then injects himself and dies? Is V's act a free, informed and deliberate one? See *Kennedy (No 2)* in section 3.2.3.3.

Victor Tadros, *Criminal Responsibility* (2005), poses an example (at p 179) of D stabbing V in the leg. In his first scenario D is unaware that there is a bomb nearby. It explodes killing V. D would not be liable for murder even though he stabbed with intent to kill. In the second scenario, D stabs V and leaves him, being aware that a bomb is nearby. He concludes that in this second example the bomb would not break the chain of causation because D was aware of it.

■ *Question*

To what extent is causation a matter only of looking at the actus reus of the offender?

Empress Car Co v National Rivers Authority

[1998] UKHL 5, House Lords, http://www.bailii.org/uk/cases/UKHL/1998/5.html

(Lords Browne-Wilkinson, Lloyd, Nolan, Hoffmann and Clyde)

The question was whether the company had caused the pollution of a river, contrary to what was then an offence under s 85(1) of the Water Resources Act 1991, by installing a tank of diesel oil in a position where, if the tap was turned on, the oil would flow into the river, and by omitting to provide a proper lock or other protection against misuse. The tap was turned on by a person unknown and the entire contents flowed into the river. The House upheld the conviction of the company.

Lord Hoffmann [having remarked on the many cases in which justices who have attempted to apply their common sense to the issue of causation have been reversed by the Divisional Court, went on to offer some guidance:]

The first point to emphasise is that commonsense answers to questions of causation will differ according to the purpose for which the question is asked. Questions of causation often arise for the purpose of attributing responsibility to someone, for example, so as to blame him for something which has happened or to make him guilty of an offence or liable in damages. In such cases, the answer will depend upon the rule by which responsibility is being attributed. Take, for example, the case of the man who forgets to take the radio out of his car and during the night someone breaks the quarterlight [ie side window], enters the car and steals it. What caused the damage? If the thief is on trial, so that the question is whether he is criminally responsible, then obviously the answer is that he caused the damage. It is no answer for him to say that it was caused by the owner carelessly leaving the radio inside. On the other hand, the owner's wife, irritated at the third such occurrence in a year, might well say that it was his fault. In the context of an inquiry into the owner's blameworthiness under a non-legal, commonsense duty to take reasonable care of one's own possessions, one would say that his carelessness caused the loss of the radio.

Not only may there be different answers to questions about causation when attributing responsibility to different people under different rules (in the above example, criminal responsibility of the thief, commonsense responsibility of the owner) but there may be different answers when attributing responsibility to different people under the same rule. In *National Rivers Authority v Yorkshire Water Services Ltd* [1995] 1 All ER 225, [1995] 1 AC 444 the defendant was a sewerage undertaker. It received sewage, treated it in filter beds and discharged the treated liquid into the river. One night someone unlawfully discharged a solvent called iso-octanol into the sewer. It passed through the sewage works and entered the river. The question was whether the defendant had caused the consequent pollution. Lord Mackay of Clashfern LC, with whom the other members of the House agreed, said ([1995] 1 All ER 225 at 231, [1995] 1 AC 444 at 452):

'...I am of opinion that Yorkshire Water Services having set up a system for gathering effluent into their sewers and thence into their sewage works there to be treated, with an arrangement deliberately intended to carry the results of that treatment into controlled waters, the special circumstances surrounding the entry of iso-octanol into their sewers and works do not preclude the conclusion that Yorkshire Water Services caused the resulting poisonous, noxious and polluting matter to enter the controlled waters, notwithstanding that the constitution of the effluent so entering was affected by the presence of iso-octanol.'

So in the context of attributing responsibility to Yorkshire Water Services under s 85(1) (then s 107(1)(a) of the Water Act 1989), it had caused the pollution. On the other hand, if the person who put the iso-octanol into the sewer had been prosecuted under the same subsection, it would undoubtedly have been held that he caused the pollution. . . .

I turn next to the question of third parties and natural forces. In answering questions of causation for the purposes of holding someone responsible, both the law and common sense normally attach great significance to deliberate human acts and extraordinary natural events. A factory owner carelessly leaves a drum containing highly inflammable vapour in a place where it could easily be accidentally ignited. If a workman, thinking it is only an empty drum, throws in a cigarette butt and causes an explosion, one would have no difficulty in saying that the negligence of the owner caused the explosion. On the other hand, if the workman, knowing exactly what the drum contains, lights a match and ignites it, one would have equally little difficulty in saying that he had caused the explosion and that the carelessness of the owner had merely provided him with an occasion for what he did. One would probably say the same if the drum was struck by lightning. In both cases one would say that although the vapour-filled drum was a necessary condition for the explosion to happen, it was not caused by the owner's negligence. One might add by way of further explanation that the presence of an arsonist workman or lightning happening to strike at that time and place was a coincidence. . . .

I would also wish to avoid the language of foreseeability in relation to the inquiry into causation. In deciding whether some particular factor has played so important a part that any activity by the defendant should be seen as entirely superseded as a causative element, it is not a consideration of the foreseeability, or reasonable foreseeability, of the extraneous factor which seems to me to be appropriate, but rather its unnatural, extraordinary or unusual character. Matters of fault or negligence are not of immediate relevance in the present context and the concepts particularly related to those matters should best be avoided.

■ *Questions*

Is this decision consistent with the general principle stated in *Latif,* earlier in this section (where Lord Hoffmann concurred with Lord Steyn)? *Latif* was not cited in *Empress.* Was it simply overlooked? Are the cases on this issue distinguishable?

In *Empress,* the House decided only that the justices were *entitled to find,* on the evidence, that Empress caused the pollution. But the facts were not in dispute. Could the justices have properly decided that Empress did *not* cause the pollution? Should not *the law* say either that this was the offence, or that it was not? If the factory owner does not cause the explosion where the workman deliberately drops his match into the oil drum, why did Empress cause the pollution when the unknown person turned on the tap? Can you see any difference? In both cases the intervention was 'free, deliberate and informed'. See *Pagett,* in the next extract. Could it be that the outcome in *Empress* resulted from the current concern to prevent pollution? See *Alphacell v Woodward,* in section 7.3.2, p 197.

Lord Hoffmann says that he wishes to avoid the language of foreseeability and the question he poses is therefore whether the event was 'unnatural, extraordinary or unusual'. How, if at all, does this differ from the question whether it was foreseeable?

Lord Hoffmann referred to *Stansbie v Troman* [1948] 1 All ER 599 where a decorator working alone in a house was held liable in the tort of negligence when he left the front door unlocked while he went out to buy wallpaper and a thief entered the house and stole items he found there. Cases of this kind are rarely relevant in the criminal law because the absence of mens rea means that the question of causation simply does not arise. No one would suggest that the decorator was guilty of theft (or that Lord Hoffmann's careless husband was guilty either of criminal damage to [his wife's] car or theft of her radio). But *Empress* concerned a case of strict liability where the court held that the only question was whether D 'caused' the pollution; and there is no suggestion that the word 'cause' imports any requirement of mens rea. In the rare cases where negligence is sufficient fault in the criminal law, the tort cases may be in point.

> ■ *Questions*
>
> 1. If a swimmer had swallowed the oil-polluted water and died, or a passer-by had been killed by the exploding drum, could the owner have been guilty of manslaughter by gross negligence?
>
> 2. Consider again the case of D who supplies V with a syringe of heroin and V self-injects and dies. Applying *Empress*, would V's act break the chain of causation? Always? What factors would determine whether D remained liable? See *Kennedy (No 2)* in section 3.2.3.3.

R v Pagett

[1983] EWCA Crim 1, Court of Appeal, Criminal Division, http://www.bailii.org/ew/cases/EWCA/Crim/1983/1.html

(Robert Goff LJ, Cantley and Farquharson JJ)

Pagett (P), armed with a shotgun, took a girl, Gail Kinchen (K), who was six months pregnant by him, from the home of her mother and stepfather by force, wounding the stepfather, and violently assaulting her mother. P took K to a block of flats, pursued by the police. The police called on P to come out. Eventually he did so, holding K in front of him as a shield. He approached two police officers and fired the shotgun. The officers fired back instinctively not taking any particular aim. K was struck by three bullets and died. P was convicted of, *inter alia*, manslaughter. He appealed on the ground that the judge had misdirected the jury that, on these facts, he had caused K's death.

[Robert Goff LJ delivered the judgment of the court:]

...[T]he whole subject of causation in the law has been the subject of a well-known and most distinguished treatise by Professors Hart and Honoré, *Causation in the Law*. Passages from this book were cited to the learned judge, and were plainly relied upon by him; we, too, wish to express our indebtedness to it. It would be quite wrong for us to consider in this judgment the wider issues discussed in that work. But, for present purposes, the passage which is of most immediate relevance is to be found in Chapter XII, in which the learned authors consider the circumstances in which the intervention of a third person, not acting in concert with the accused, may have the effect of relieving the accused of criminal responsibility. The criterion which they suggest should be applied in such circumstances is whether the intervention is voluntary, ie whether it is 'free, deliberate and informed.' We resist the temptation of expressing the judicial opinion whether we find ourselves in complete agreement with that definition; though we certainly consider it to be broadly correct and supported by authority. Among the examples which the authors give of non-voluntary conduct, which is not effective to relieve the accused of responsibility, are two which are germane to the present case, viz a reasonable act performed for the purpose of self-preservation, and an act done in performance of a legal duty.

There can, we consider, be no doubt that a reasonable act performed for the purpose of self-preservation, being of course itself an act caused by the accused's own act, does not operate as a *novus actus interveniens*. If authority is needed for this almost self-evident proposition, it is to be found in such cases as *Pitts* (1842) Car & M 284, and *Curley* (1909) 2 Cr App R 96. In both these cases, the act performed for the purpose of self-preservation consisted of an act by the victim in attempting to escape from the violence of the accused, which in fact resulted in the victim's death. In each case it was held as a matter of law that, if the victim acted in a reasonable attempt to escape the violence of the accused, the death of the victim was caused by the act of the accused. Now one form of self-preservation is self-defence; for present purposes, we can see no distinction in principle between an attempt to escape the consequences of the accused's act, and a response which takes the form of self-defence. Furthermore, in our judgment, if a reasonable act of self-defence against the act of the accused causes the death of a third party, we can see no reason in principle why the act of self-defence, being an involuntary act caused by the act of the accused, should relieve the accused from criminal responsibility for the death of the third party. Of course, it does not necessarily follow that the accused will be guilty of the murder, or even of the manslaughter, of the third party; though in the majority of cases he is likely to be guilty at least of manslaughter. Whether he is guilty of murder or manslaughter will depend upon the question whether all the ingredients of the relevant offence have been proved; in particular, on a charge of murder, it will be necessary that the accused had the necessary intent. . . .

No English authority was cited to us, nor we think to the learned judge, in support of the proposition that an act done in the execution of a legal duty, again of course being an act itself caused by the act of the accused, does not operate as a novus actus interveniens. . . . Even so, we agree with the learned judge that the proposition is sound in law, because as a matter of principle such an act cannot be regarded as a voluntary act independent of the wrongful act of the accused. A parallel may be drawn with the so-called 'rescue' cases in the law of negligence, where a wrongdoer may be held liable in negligence to a third party who suffers injury in going to the rescue of a person who has been put in danger by the defendant's negligent act. Where, for example, a police officer in the execution of his duty acts to prevent a crime, or to apprehend a person suspected of a crime, the case is surely a fortiori. Of course, it is inherent in the requirement that the police officer, or other person, must be acting in the execution of his duty that his act should be reasonable in all the circumstances: see section 3 of the Criminal Law Act 1967. Furthermore, once again we are only considering the issue of causation. If intervention by a third party in the execution of a legal duty, caused by the act of the accused, results in the death of the victim, the question whether the accused is guilty of the murder or manslaughter of the victim must depend on whether the necessary ingredients of the relevant offence have been proved against the accused, including in particular, in the case of murder, whether the accused had the necessary intent.

The principles which we have stated are principles of law. This is plain from, for example, the case of *Pitts* (1842) Car & M 284, to which we have already referred. It follows that where, in any particular case, there is an issue concerned with what we have for convenience called *novus actus interveniens*, it will be appropriate for the judge to direct the jury in accordance with these principles. It does not however follow that it is accurate to state broadly that causation is a question of law. On the contrary, generally speaking causation is a question of fact for the jury. Thus in, for example, *Towers* (1874) 12 Cox CC 530, the accused struck a woman; she screamed loudly, and a child whom she was then nursing turned black in the face, and from that day until it died suffered from convulsions. The question whether the death of the child was caused by the act of the accused was left by the judge to the jury to decide as a question of fact. But that does not mean that there are no principles of law relating to causation, so that no directions on law are ever to be given to a jury on the question of causation. On the contrary, we have already pointed out one familiar direction which is given on causation, which is that the accused's act need not be the sole, or even the main, cause of the victim's death for his act to be held to have caused the death.

Appeal dismissed

■ *Questions*

In what way were the police officers' acts capable of being described as 'involuntary'? What is the purpose of firearms training if officers are going to fire their weapons involuntarily?

In *Girdler* [2009] EWCA Crim 2666, http://www.bailii.org/ew/cases/EWCA/Crim/2009/2666. html, D's car collided with a taxi, driven by V1. The collision forced the taxi into the fast lane of the carriageway until it finally came to rest facing oncoming traffic. Some drivers managed to avoid the taxi, but V2 did not and died as a result of the impact. V1 was killed also. In relation to the death of V1, D was convicted of causing death by dangerous driving, contrary to s 1 of the Road Traffic Act 1988. However, the jury was unable to reach a verdict on whether D caused the death of V2. The Court of Appeal framed the issue for its consideration in the following way: 'This appeal raises the issue of what directions should be given to the jury when a defendant charged with causing death by dangerous driving in one count submits that he did not cause the death of a person, but that a driver in another vehicle, whose death the defendant is also said to have caused in another count, did.' There was also the question of whether the verdict of the two counts would have to be the same. In upholding D's conviction, Hooper LJ stated the following:

35. If the only test were to be the 'free, deliberate, and informed' test, then a driver who by his dangerous driving causes a minor accident pushing another car on to the hard shoulder would be automatically be liable for causing death by dangerous driving if the driver of a vehicle travelling at speed on the hard shoulder accidentally collided with the car on the hard shoulder whatever the circumstances, provided the jury took the view that the 'more than a trifling link' test was satisfied. In our view juries needed a tailored direction to help them decide, in the appropriate case, whether there has been a new and intervening act or event.

36. In devising such a test we remind ourselves that the offences of causing death by dangerous and careless driving will punish the conduct of a person who has not intended or necessarily foreseen the consequences of his driving. Such a person is in a very different position to a person who has intended to kill or cause serious bodily harm or who has the mens rea for manslaughter. As Lord Hoffmann said in *Environment Agency* (formerly *National Rivers Authority) v Empress Car Co (Abertillery) Ltd* [1999] 2 A.C. 22 at 29F and 31E:

[His lordship then cited a passage from *Empress Car.*]

37. What we need is a form of words which sets out a test (comparatively easy to apply) which places an outside limit on the culpability of a driver in circumstances where there is more than a trifling link between the dangerous (or careless) driving and a death. It seeks to exclude consequences which are simply 'too remote' from the driver's culpable conduct.

38. Help in devising such a test comes from the passage in Smith & Hogan to which we have made reference. In paras 4.5.6 and 4.5.6.1 (at pp.78–79) the author states that a person will not have caused something to have happened if a natural event which is not reasonably foreseeable was the immediate cause of the event. The test receives support from cl.17(2)(c) of the Draft Criminal Code for England and Wales Law Comm. No.177 (1989). It also has similarities to the test to be applied when the defendant's unlawful and violent acts are said to have caused another person to suffer injuries in the course of escaping from those acts, see *R. v Williams* (1992) 95 Cr. App. R. 1.

39. On the other hand, in the *Empress Car* case [above] which involved an offence of strict responsibility, Lord Hoffmann said (at 34E) that 'foreseeability is not the criterion for deciding whether a person caused something or not. People often cause things which they could not have foreseen'. We note that in this passage Lord Hoffmann is referring to the defendant's foresight whereas the test which we are considering is concerned with what could reasonably have been foreseen.

40. Lord Hoffmann preferred a test which made an alleged polluter liable for 'acts and events which, although not necessarily foreseeable in the particular case, are in the generality a normal and familiar fact of life' but not for 'acts or events which are abnormal and extraordinary' (at 34F). Lord Hoffmann said in his conclusions at 36B:

'If the defendant did something which produced a situation in which the polluting matter could escape but a necessary condition of the actual escape which happened was also the act of a third party or a natural event, the justices should consider whether that act or event should be regarded as a normal fact of life or something extraordinary. If it was in the general run of things a matter of ordinary occurrence, it will not negative the causal effect of the defendant's acts, even if it was not foreseeable that it would happen to that particular defendant or take that particular form. If it can be regarded as something extraordinary, it will be open to the justices to hold that the defendant did not cause the pollution.'

41. It is important to note that Lord Hoffmann was of the view that the foreseeability test was too favourable to the alleged polluter, taking into account that the offence was one of strict responsibility. Causing death by dangerous (or careless) driving are not offences of strict responsibility.

42. In practice we do not think that there is much difference in cases like the present between a reasonable foreseeability test and the test propounded by Lord Hoffmann but, on balance, we prefer the objective test of reasonable foreseeability in a case like the present where the defendant's case is that there was a new and supervening act or event. We bear in mind that Lord Bingham, in *R. v Kennedy* [2008] 1 A.C. 269, said in the passage which we have already set out in full [see section 3.2.3.3, p 58] that, 'The House was not in that decision purporting to lay down general rules governing causation in criminal law'.

43. We are of the view that the words 'reasonably foreseeable' whilst apt to describe for a lawyer the appropriate test, may need to be reworded to ease the task of a jury. We suggest that a jury could be told, in circumstances like the present where the immediate cause of death is a second collision, that if they were sure that the defendant drove dangerously and were sure that his dangerous driving was more than a slight or trifling link to the death(s) then:

'The defendant will have caused the death(s) only if you are sure that it could sensibly have been anticipated that a fatal collision might occur in the circumstances in which the second collision did occur.'

The judge should identify the relevant circumstances and remind the jury of the prosecution and defence cases. If it is thought necessary it could be made clear to the jury that they are not concerned with what the defendant foresaw.

44. We prefer such a test to the test suggested by counsel in this case.

In *DPP, ex p Jones* [2000] Crim LR 858, DC, there was evidence that M, the managing director of E Ltd, had failed to set up a safe system of work for the operation of a grab bucket crane and that a death resulting from the operation of the crane would not have occurred if such a system had been established and observed. The immediate cause of death was an inadvertent movement of the joystick of the crane by the operator, H. The court ordered the DPP to reconsider his decision not to prosecute M or E Ltd for manslaughter by gross negligence. The court clearly thought there was no evidence of a break in the chain of causation.

■ *Question*

Even if in *Jones* H's act was negligent, it was hardly 'free, deliberate and informed'. What if it had been grossly negligent (so that H would have been guilty of manslaughter)?

3.2.3.3 Drug administration cases

In a succession of cases the issue arose as to whether D who supplied V with drugs was guilty of manslaughter where V self-injects what turns out to be a fatal overdose. In *Kennedy (No 1)* [1999] Crim LR 65, the facts were agreed: K supplied heroin to MB ('the deceased'). K prepared a 'hit' of heroin for MB and gave him the syringe ready for injection. MB injected himself and returned the syringe to K. K left the room. The heroin resulted in MB's breathing being affected. Although an ambulance was summoned, the injection resulted in the death of MB. On his conviction for manslaughter, K appealed and the Court of Appeal upheld his conviction ([1999] Crim LR 65) on the basis that (i) K was a secondary party to MB's act of self-injection (this is wrong and has now been accepted to be so by the Court of Appeal—see section 8.4.1.5, p 230); (ii) that MB's act of self-injection was not a break in the chain of causation.

The idea that D was a party to V's self-injection and that V's free, informed, deliberate act did not break the chain of causation was heretical and was subjected to very strong criticism. In *Dias* [2000] 2 Cr App R 96, it was recognized, correctly, that D could not be a secondary party in these circumstances since V commits no crime in which D can assist. In *Rogers* [2003] 2 Cr App R 160, [2003] Crim LR 555, *Dias* was distinguished where D held the tourniquet for V while he injected, in those circumstances it was held that D was playing a part in the mechanics of the injection as a principal and could be liable as a principal offender. In *Finlay* [2003] EWCA Crim 3868, the Court of Appeal suggested that D could be liable provided he was a factual cause of V's death unless V's act of self-injection was extraordinary, in the sense of being outside the scope of normal occurrence. See also *Richards* [2002] EWCA Crim 3175.

In *Kennedy (No 2)* [2005] EWCA Crim 685, because subsequent decisions of the Court of Appeal cast doubt on the conclusion in *Kennedy (No 1)* the case was referred back to the Court of Appeal by the Criminal Cases Review Commission. The Court of Appeal concluded that D remains liable if the jury considers that D had been responsible for taking the action in 'joint concert' with V to enable V to inject himself. For analysis of the Court of Appeal's decision compare D. Ormerod and R. Fortson, 'Drugs Suppliers as Manslaughterers (Again)' [2005] Crim LR 819 with T. Jones, 'Causation, Homicide and the Supply of Drugs' (2006) LS 139.

The Court of Appeal certified the following question of general public importance:

When is it appropriate to find someone guilty of manslaughter where that person has been involved in the supply of a class A controlled drug, which is then freely and voluntarily self-administered by the person to whom it was supplied, and the administration of the drug then causes his death?

R v Kennedy (No 2)

[2007] UKHL 38, House of Lords, http://www.bailii.org/uk/cases/UKHL/2007/38.html

(Lords Bingham of Cornhill, Rodger of Earlsferry, Baroness Hale of Richmond, Lords Carswell and Mance)

The Committee met and considered the cause *Kennedy (On Appeal from the Court of Appeal (Criminal Division))*.

[Lord Bingham examined the scope of s 23 of the Offences Against the Person Act 1861 and turned to consider the issue of causation directly:]

14. The criminal law generally assumes the existence of free will. The law recognises certain exceptions, in the case of the young, those who for any reason are not fully responsible for their actions, and the vulnerable, and it acknowledges situations of duress and necessity, as also of deception and mistake. But, generally speaking, informed adults of sound mind are treated as autonomous beings able to make their own decisions how they will act, and none of the exceptions is relied on as possibly applicable in this case. Thus D is not to be treated as causing V to act in a certain way if V makes a voluntary and informed decision to act in that way rather than another. There are many classic statements to this effect. In his article *'Finis for Novus Actus?'* (1989) 48(3) CLJ 391, 392, Professor Glanville Williams wrote:

'I may suggest reasons to you for doing something; I may urge you to do it, tell you it will pay you to do it, tell you it is your duty to do it. My efforts may perhaps make it very much more likely that you will do it. But they do not cause you to do it, in the sense in which one causes a kettle of water to boil by putting it on the stove. Your volitional act is regarded (within the doctrine of responsibility) as setting a new "chain of causation" going, irrespective of what has happened before.'

In chapter XII of *Causation in the Law*, 2nd ed (1985), p 326, Hart and Honoré wrote:

'The free, deliberate, and informed intervention of a second person, who intends to exploit the situation created by the first, but is not acting in concert with him, is normally held to relieve the first actor of criminal responsibility.'

This statement was cited by the House with approval in *R v Latif* [1996] 1 WLR 104, 115. The principle is fundamental and not controversial.

15. Questions of causation frequently arise in many areas of the law, but causation is not a single, unvarying concept to be mechanically applied without regard to the context in which the question arises. That was the point which Lord Hoffmann, with the express concurrence of three other members of the House, was at pains to make in *Environment Agency (formerly National Rivers Authority) v Empress Car Co (Abertillery) Ltd* [1999] 2 AC 22. The House was not in that decision purporting to lay down general rules governing causation in criminal law. It was construing, with reference to the facts of the case before it, a statutory provision imposing strict criminal liability on those who cause pollution of controlled waters. Lord Hoffmann made clear that (p 29E–F) common sense answers to questions of causation will differ according to the purpose for which the question is asked; that (p 31E) one cannot give a common sense answer to a question of causation for the purpose of attributing responsibility under some rule without knowing the purpose and scope of the rule; that (p 32B) strict liability was imposed in the interests of protecting controlled waters; and that (p 36A) in the situation under consideration the act of the defendant could properly be held to have caused the pollution even though an ordinary act of a third party was the immediate cause of the diesel oil flowing into the river. It is worth underlining that the relevant question was the cause of the pollution, not the cause of the third party's act.

16. The committee would not wish to throw any doubt on the correctness of *Empress Car*. But the reasoning in that case cannot be applied to the wholly different context of causing a noxious thing to be administered to or taken by another person contrary to section 23 of the 1861 Act. In *R v Finlay* [2003] EWCA Crim 3868 (8 December 2003) V was injected with heroin and died. D was tried on two counts of manslaughter, one on the basis that he had himself injected V, the second on the basis that he had prepared a syringe and handed it to V who had injected herself. The jury could not agree on the first count but convicted on the second. When rejecting an application to remove the second count from the indictment, the trial judge ruled, relying on *Empress Car*, that D had produced a situation in which V could inject herself, in which her self-injection was entirely foreseeable and in which self-injection could not be regarded as something extraordinary. He directed the jury along those lines. The Court of Appeal upheld the judge's analysis and dismissed the appeal. It was wrong to do so. Its decision conflicted with the rules on personal autonomy and informed voluntary choice to which reference has been made above. In the decision under appeal the Court of Appeal did not follow *R v Finlay* in seeking to apply *Empress Car*, and it was right not to do so.

17. In his article already cited Professor Glanville Williams pointed out (at p 398) that the doctrine of secondary liability was developed precisely because an informed voluntary choice was ordinarily regarded as a *novus actus interveniens* breaking the chain of causation:

'Principals cause, accomplices encourage (or otherwise influence) or help. If the instigator were regarded as causing the result he would be a principal, and the conceptual division between principals (or, as I prefer to call them, perpetrators) and accessories would vanish. Indeed, it was because the instigator was not regarded as causing the crime that the notion of accessories had to be developed. This is the irrefragable argument for recognising the *novus actus* principle as one of the bases of our criminal law. The final act is done by the perpetrator, and his guilt pushes the accessories, conceptually speaking, into the background. Accessorial liability is, in the traditional theory, 'derivative' from that of the perpetrator.'

18. This is a matter of some significance since, contrary to the view of the Court of Appeal when dismissing the appellant's first appeal, the deceased committed no offence when injecting himself with the fatal dose of heroin. It was so held by the Court of Appeal in *R v Dias* [2002] 2 Cr App R 96, paras 21–24, and in *R v Rogers* [2003] EWCA Crim 945, [2003] 1 WLR 1374 and is now accepted. If the conduct of the deceased was not criminal he was not a principal offender, and it of course follows that the appellant cannot be liable as a secondary party. It also follows that there is no meaningful legal sense in which the appellant can be said to have been a principal jointly with the deceased, or to have been acting in concert. The finding that the deceased freely and voluntarily administered the injection to himself, knowing what it was, is fatal to any contention that the appellant caused the heroin to be administered to the deceased or taken by him. . . .

[His lordship considered several older cases and the Court of Appeal's decision in the present case.]

25. The answer to the certified question is: 'In the case of a fully-informed and responsible adult, never'. The appeal must be allowed and the appellant's conviction for manslaughter quashed.

Appeal allowed

■ *Question*

What is the status of *Empress* after the House of Lords' decision in *Kennedy (No 2)*? Cf the decision in the Scottish High Court: *MacAngus and Kane v HM Advocate* [2009] HCJAC 8, rejecting the approach in *Kennedy (No 2)*.

It is necessary to point out at this stage that in cases such as these, prosecutors have now taken to charging gross negligence manslaughter, rather than manslaughter by an unlawful and dangerous act, which is what Kennedy was charged with. The courts have been prepared to uphold convictions for that offence: see section 4.3.3.4 for the discussion of *Evans* [2009] EWCA Crim 650.

3.2.3.4 Intervening medical treatment

It has been noted that many of the difficult issues on causation arise in cases of homicide. In those cases a common problem is that following the defendant's infliction of injury on V, V is treated by medical professionals in a less than perfect manner. In what circumstances will the medical intervention break the chain of causation? Bear in mind that the judgments in these cases are laden with policy considerations—the courts do not want to be 'letting off' D who has, with mens rea, culpably caused some injury when V dies, particularly when the medical profession are compelled to treat V, frequently in under-resourced circumstances.

It is also important to remember that the question to focus on is whether the defendant is liable for V's death or whether there is a break in the chain of causation. The question is not whether the medical professional is criminally liable. That is a separate inquiry. There is nothing to prevent two people being independent causes of V's death and each being criminally liable. (Assassin D1 shoots V in the head and at the same time assassin D2, acting independently of D1, shoots V in the heart. Each bullet would have been sufficient to kill V. Both D1 and D2 are guilty of murder.)

In *Jordan* (1956) 40 Cr App R 152 D stabbed V. V was taken to hospital, where the wound had almost healed when a doctor administered a drug to which V was allergic. V died. The Court of Criminal Appeal held that the medical treatment and not D's act had caused the death of V. This seems to have been because the wound had virtually healed by the time V died and the treatment provided by the hospital was 'palpably wrong'. However, this case is generally thought of as exceptional. The position of the law now seems to be that medical intervention will not break the chain of causation as long as D's original act remains a significant and operative cause of V's death. This was clarified in the following case.

R v Cheshire

[1991] 3 All ER 670, Court of Appeal, Criminal Division

(Beldam LJ, Boreham and Auld JJ)

During an argument in a fish and chip shop about midnight on 9/10 December 1987 D produced a handgun and shot V in the thigh and stomach. During his treatment in hospital V developed respiratory problems and a tracheotomy tube was placed in his windpipe. He died in hospital on 15 February 1988. At the post-mortem it was found that V's windpipe had become obstructed due to narrowing near the site of the tracheotomy scar.

D was charged with murder. The pathologist who conducted the post-mortem gave evidence that the immediate cause of death was cardio-respiratory arrest 'due to a condition which was produced as a result of treatment to provide an artificial airway in the treatment of gunshot wounds of the abdomen and leg.' And he said, 'In other words, I give as the cause of death cardio-respiratory arrest due to gunshot wounds of the abdomen and leg.' For the appellant it was conceded that the sequence of events which had led to the deceased's death was not that described by the pathologist but a consultant surgeon, Mr Eadie, gave it as his opinion that by 8 February 1988 the wounds of the thigh and the abdomen no longer threatened the life of the deceased and his chances of survival were good. In his view, 'The cause of his death was the failure to recognise the reason for his sudden onset and continued breathlessness after the 8th February [and the] severe respiratory obstruction, including the presence of stridor [on 14 February] . . .'

Mr Eadie said that V would not have died if his condition had been diagnosed and properly treated. The doctors had been negligent and this was the cause of death; but they had not, in his opinion, been grossly negligent or reckless.

Judge Lowry QC directed the jury that 'the bullets caused the death, even if the treatment was incompetent, negligent. For you to find that the chain was broken, the medical treatment or lack of medical treatment must be reckless . . . Reckless conduct is where somebody could not care less. He acts or fails to act careless of the consequences, careless of the comfort or safety of another person . . .' D was convicted of murder.

[Beldam LJ, having quoted from the judgment of Robert Goff LJ in *Pagett*, in section 3.2.3.2, p 53 and his expression of indebtedness to Hart and Honoré, continued:]

We too are indebted to section IV of Chapter 12 of that work (2nd edn, 1985). Under the heading 'Doctor's or victim's negligence' the authors deal with cases in which an assault or wounding is followed by improper medical treatment or by refusal of treatment by the victim or failure on his part to take proper care of the wound or injury. The authors trace from *Hale's Pleas of the Crown* and *Stephen's Digest of the Criminal Law* the emergence of a standard set by Stephen of common knowledge or skill which they suggest appears to require proof of something more than ordinary negligence in order that one who inflicts a wound may be relieved of liability for homicide. And they refer to most American authorities as requiring at least gross negligence to negative causal connection. English decisions, however, have not echoed these words. In conclusion the authors state (at 362):

'Our survey of the place of doctor's and victim's negligence in the law of homicide, where differences of policy between civil and criminal law might be expected to make themselves felt, yields a meagre harvest. (i) On Stephen's view, which has some modern support, there is no difference between civil and criminal law as regards the effect of medical negligence: in each case gross negligence ("want of common knowledge or skill") is required to negative responsibility for death.'

Whatever may be the differences of policy between the approach of the civil and the criminal law to the question of causation, there are we think reasons for a critical approach when importing the language of the one to the other.

Since the apportionment of responsibility for damage has become commonplace in the civil law, judges have sought to distinguish the blameworthiness of conduct from its causative effect. Epithets suggestive of degrees of blameworthiness may be of little help in deciding how potent the conduct was in causing the result. A momentary lapse of concentration may lead to more serious consequences than a more glaring neglect of duty. In the criminal law the jury considering the factual question, did the accused's act cause the deceased's death, will we think derive little assistance from figures of speech more appropriate for conveying degrees of fault or blame in questions of apportionment. Unless authority suggests otherwise, we think such figures of speech are to be avoided in giving guidance to a jury on the question of causation. Whilst medical treatment unsuccessfully given to prevent the death of a victim with the care and skill of a competent medical practitioner will not amount to an intervening cause, it does not follow that treatment which falls below that standard of care and skill will amount to such a cause. As Professors Hart and Honoré comment, treatment which falls short of the standard expected of the competent medical practitioner is unfortunately only too frequent in human experience for it to be considered abnormal in the sense of extraordinary. Acts or omissions of a doctor treating the victim for injuries he has received at the hands of an accused may conceivably be so extraordinary as to be capable of being regarded as acts independent of the conduct of the accused but it is most unlikely that they will be.

We have not been referred to any English authority in which the terms of the direction which should be given to a jury in such a case have been considered. We were referred to *R v Jordan* (1956) 40 Cr App R 152 in which the appellant, who had been convicted of murder, sought leave to call further evidence about the cause of the victim's death. The application was granted and evidence was received by the court that the stab wound from which the victim died eight days later was not the cause of the victim's death. The deceased had died from the effects of sensitivity to Terramycin which had been given to him after his intolerance to it was established and in abnormal quantity. The court considered that the introduction into the system of the victim of a substance shown to be poisonous to him and in quantities which were so great as to result in pulmonary oedema leading to pneumonia were factors which ought to have been before the jury and which in all probability would have affected their decision.

R v Jordan was described in the later case of *R v Smith* [1959] 2 All ER 193, [1959] 2 QB 35 as a very particular case dependent upon its exact facts. The appellant in *R v Smith* had been convicted at court-martial of the murder of another soldier by stabbing him. The victim had been dropped twice while being taken to the medical reception station and was subsequently given treatment which was said to be incorrect and harmful. Lord Parker CJ, giving the judgment of the Court-Martial Appeal Court, rejected a contention that his death did not result from the stab wound. He said ([1959] 2 All ER 193 at 198, [1959] 2QB 35 at 42–43):

> 'It seems to the court that, if at the time of death the original wound is still an operating cause and a substantial cause, then the death can properly be said to be the result of the wound, albeit that some other cause of death is also operating. Only if it can be said that the original wounding is merely the setting in which another cause operates can it be said that the death does not result from the wound. Putting it in another way, only if the second cause is so overwhelming as to make the original wound merely part of the history can it be said that the death does not flow from the wound.'

Both these cases were considered by this Court in *R v Malcherek; R v Steel* [1981] 2 All ER 422, [1981] 1 WLR 690 in which it had been argued that the act of a doctor in disconnecting a life support machine had intervened to cause the death of the victim to the exclusion of injuries inflicted by the appellants. In rejecting this submission Lord Lane CJ, after considering *R v Jordan and R v Smith*, said ([1981] 2 All ER 422 at 428, [1981] 1 WLR 690 at 696):

'In the view of this court, if a choice has to be made between the decision in *R v Jordan* and that in *R v Smith*, which we do not believe it does (*R v Jordan* being a very exceptional case), then the decision in *R v Smith* is to be preferred.'

Later in the same judgment Lord Lane CJ said ([1981] 2 All ER 422 at 428–429, [1981] 1 WLR 690 at 696–697):

'There may be occasions, although they will be rare, when the original injury has ceased to operate as a cause at all, but in the ordinary case if the treatment is given bona fide by competent and careful medical practitioners, then evidence will not be admissible to show that the treatment would not have been administered in the same way by other medical practitioners. In other words, the fact that the victim has died, despite or because of medical treatment for the initial injury given by careful and skilled medical practitioners, will not exonerate the original assailant from responsibility for the death.'

In those two cases it was not suggested that the actions of the doctors in disconnecting the life support machines were other than competent and careful. The court did not have to consider the effect of medical treatment which fell short of the standard of care to be expected of competent medical practitioners.

A case in which the facts bear a close similarity to the case with which we are concerned is *R v Evans and Gardiner (No 2)* [1976] VR 523. In that case the deceased was stabbed in the stomach by the two applicants in April 1974. After operation the victim resumed an apparently healthy life but nearly a year later, after suffering abdominal pain and vomiting and undergoing further medical treatment, he died. The cause of death was a stricture of the small bowel, a not uncommon sequel to the operation carried out to deal with the stab wound inflicted by the applicants. It was contended that the doctors treating the victim for the later symptoms ought to have diagnosed the presence of the stricture, that they had been negligent not to do so and that timely operative treatment would have saved the victim's life. The Supreme Court of Victoria held that the test to be applied in determining whether a felonious act has caused a death which follows, in spite of an intervening act, is whether the felonious act is still an operating and substantial cause of the death.

The summing up to the jury had been based on the passage already quoted from Lord Parker CJ's judgment in *R v Smith* and the Supreme Court indorsed a direction in those terms. It commented upon the limitations of *R v Jordan* and made observations on the difference between the failure to diagnose the consequence of the original injury and cases in which medical treatment has been given which has a positive adverse effect on the victim. It concluded (at 528):

'But in the long run the difference between a positive act of commission and an omission to do some particular act is for these purposes ultimately a question of degree. As an event intervening between an act alleged to be felonious and to have resulted in death, and the actual death, a positive act of commission or an act of omission will serve to break the chain of causation only if it can be shown that the act or omission accelerated the death, so that it can be said to have caused the death and thus to have prevented the felonious act which would have caused death from actually doing so.'

Later in the judgment the court said (at 534):

'In these circumstances we agree with the view of the learned trial Judge expressed in his report to this Court that there was a case to go to the jury. The failure of the medical practitioners to diagnose correctly the victim's condition, however inept or unskilful, was not the cause of death. It was the blockage of the bowel which caused death and the real question for the jury was whether that blockage was due to the stabbing. There was plenty of medical evidence to support such a finding, if the jury chose to accept it.'

It seems to us that these two passages demonstrate the difficulties in formulating and explaining a general concept of causation but what we think does emerge from this and the other cases is that when the victim of a criminal attack is treated for wounds or injuries by doctors or other medical staff attempting to repair the harm done, it will only be in the most extraordinary and unusual case that such treatment can be said to be so independent of the acts of the accused that it could be regarded in law as the cause of the victim's death to the exclusion of the accused's acts.

Where the law requires proof of the relationship between an act and its consequences as an element of responsibility, a simple and sufficient explanation of the basis of such relationship has proved notoriously elusive.

In a case in which the jury have to consider whether negligence in the treatment of injuries inflicted by the accused was the cause of death we think it is sufficient for the judge to tell the jury that they must be satisfied that the Crown have proved that the acts of the accused caused the death of the deceased, adding that the accused's acts need not be the sole cause or even the main cause of death, it being sufficient that his acts contributed significantly to that result. Even though negligence in the treatment of the victim was the immediate cause of his death, the jury should not regard it as excluding the responsibility of the accused unless the negligent treatment was so independent of his acts, and in itself so potent in causing death, that they regard the contribution made by his acts as insignificant.

It is not the function of the jury to evaluate competing causes or to choose which is dominant provided that they are satisfied that the accused's acts can fairly be said to have made a significant contribution to the victim's death. We think the word 'significant' conveys the necessary substance of a contribution made to the death which is more than negligible.

In the present case the passage in the summing up complained of has to be set in the context of the remainder of the direction given by the judge on the issue of causation. He directed the jury that they had to decide whether the two bullets fired into the deceased on 10 December caused his death on 15 February following. Or, he said, put in another way, did the injuries caused cease to operate as a cause of death because something else intervened? He told them that the prosecution did not have to prove that the bullets were the only cause of death but that they had to prove that they were one operative and substantial cause of death. He was thus following the words used in *R v Smith*.

Appeal dismissed

■ *Questions*

In what way does a test based on 'potency' or 'independence' differ from asking whether the act of the medical professional was 'foreseeable' and 'reasonable'? To what extent is the negligence or recklessness of the medical professional important in determining whether a break in the chain of causation has occurred?

The intervening medical treatment which D alleges constitutes a break in the chain of causation may involve an omission. In *McKechnie* (1992) 94 Cr App R 51, DD beat up an elderly man, V, who suffered very serious head injuries and remained unconscious for weeks. Doctors discovered that V had a duodenal ulcer but decided that it would be too dangerous to operate because he was still unconscious from his beating. V died as a result of the ulcer bursting. DD were convicted and appealed, *inter alia*, on the direction as to causation. The Court of Appeal upheld the conviction: 'The Recorder's statement of the question of the intervening events—the doctor's decision not to operate on the duodenal ulcer because [V's] head injuries

made such an operation dangerous—properly directed the jury, not to the correctness of the
medical decision, but to its reasonableness', per Auld J at 58.

■ *Question*

What if, having been shot by D, V's wounds were healing well when he contracted MRSA in
the hospital and died? Cf *Gowans* [2003] EWCA Crim 3935 where V contracted fatal septicaemia in hospital.

3.2.3.5 The victim's conduct as a break in the chain of causation

This is, again, an area in which the courts have struggled to define any clear principles.
A number of difficult issues arise.

- To what extent does it matter that V 'acts' and exacerbates his position rather than 'omits
  to save himself'?

- If there is a principle that D 'takes his victim as he finds him' does this extend beyond
  taking V's physical infirmities (eg egg shell skull) to include also V's psychological idiosyncrasies (eg refusal to seek medical attention)?

- To what extent does D take only V's pre-existing conditions as found?

- Is the question whether V's conduct breaks the chain of causation if it is unforeseeable or
  if it is outwith a range of reasonable actions?

R v Blaue

[1975] EWCA Crim 3, Court of Appeal, Criminal Division, http://www.bailii.org/ew/cases/EWCA/
Crim/1975/3.html

(Lawton LJ, Thompson and Shaw JJ)

The appellant was convicted of manslaughter on the ground of diminished responsibility. He had
inflicted four serious stab wounds on the deceased, one of which pierced a lung. The deceased, a
Jehovah's Witness, refused to have a blood transfusion because it was contrary to her religious
beliefs, and acknowledged this refusal in writing, despite the surgeon's advice that without the
transfusion she would die. The Crown conceded at the trial that had she had the blood transfusion she would not have died. Blaue appealed on the ground, *inter alia*, that Mocatta J, following
Holland (1841) 2 Mood & R 351, in effect directed the jury to find causation proved.

[Lawton LJ delivered the judgment of the court:]

. . . In *Holland* [(1841) 2 Mood & R 351] the defendant, in the course of a violent assault, had injured one
of his victim's fingers. A surgeon had advised amputation because of danger to life through complications developing. The advice was rejected. A fortnight later the victim died of lockjaw: '. . . the real
question is', said Maule J [2 Mood & R 351 at 352], 'whether in the end the wound inflicted by the
prisoner was the cause of death?' That distinguished judge left the jury to decide that question as did
the judge in this case. They had to decide it as juries always do, by pooling their experience of life and
using their common sense. They would not have been handicapped by a lack of training in dialectics
or moral theology.

Maule J's direction to the jury reflected the common law's answer to the problem. He who inflicted
an injury which resulted in death could not excuse himself by pleading that his victim could have
avoided death by taking greater care of himself: see Hale [*Pleas of the Crown* (1800), pp 427, 428].
The common law in Sir Matthew Hale's time probably was in line with contemporary concepts of

ethics. A man who did a wrongful act was deemed *morally* responsible for the natural and probable consequences of that act. Counsel for the appellant asked us to remember that since Sir Matthew Hale's day the rigour of the law relating to homicide has been eased in favour of the accused. It has been—but this has come about through the development of the concept of intent, not by reason of a different view of causation. Well known practitioner's textbooks, such as *Halsbury's Laws* [3rd edn, vol 10, p 706] and *Russell on Crime* [(12th edn, 1964), vol 1, p 30], continue to reflect the common law approach. Textbooks intended for students or as studies in jurisprudence have queried the common law rule. See Hart and Honoré, *Causation in the Law* [(1959), pp 320, 321], and *Smith and Hogan* [*Criminal Law* (3rd edn, 1973), p 214].

The physical cause of death in this case was the bleeding into the pleural cavity arising from the penetration of the lung. This had not been brought about by any decision made by the deceased girl but by the stab wound.

Counsel for the appellant tried to overcome this line of reasoning by submitting that the jury should have been directed that if they thought the girl's decision not to have a blood transfusion was an unreasonable one, then the chain of causation would have been broken. At once the question arises—reasonable by whose standards? Those of Jehovah's Witnesses? Humanists? Roman Catholics? Protestants of Anglo-Saxon descent? The man on the Clapham omnibus? But he might well be an admirer of Eleazar who suffered death rather than eat the flesh of swine [see 2 Maccabees, ch 6, vv 18–31] or of Sir Thomas More who, unlike nearly all his contemporaries, was unwilling to accept Henry VIII as Head of the Church in England. Those brought up in the Hebraic and Christian traditions would probably be reluctant to accept that these martyrs caused their own deaths.

As was pointed out to counsel for the appellant in the course of argument, two cases, each raising the same issue of reasonableness because of religious beliefs, could produce different verdicts depending on where the cases were tried. A jury drawn from Preston, sometimes said to be the most Catholic town in England, might have different views about martyrdom to one drawn from the inner suburbs of London. Counsel for the appellant accepted that this might be so; it was, he said, inherent in trial by jury. It is not inherent in the common law as expounded by Sir Matthew Hale and Maule J. It has long been the policy of the law that those who use violence on other people must take their victims as they find them. This in our judgment means the whole man, not just the physical man. It does not lie in the mouth of the assailant to say that his victim's religious beliefs which inhibited him from accepting certain kinds of treatment were unreasonable. The question for decision is what caused her death. The answer is the stab wound. The fact that the victim refused to stop this end coming about did not break the causal connection between the act and death . . .

Appeal dismissed

■ *Questions*

1. Was not the wound a substantial and operating cause (*Smith*, section 3.2.3.4, p 62) of death? If so, did it matter whether the victim's rejection of the blood transfusion was also a cause of death?

2. Was not the victim dying of the wound when the transfusion was offered to save her?

3. Suppose that the victim had been a child who had been abducted by her parents so as to avoid the transfusion and had died. Would the defendant still have been guilty of manslaughter? Would the parents also have been guilty? See *Re S* [1993] 1 FLR 376.

In *Dear* [1996] Crim LR 595 D stabbed V with a Stanley knife after allegations that V had sexually abused D's 12-year-old daughter. V died. D claimed that V had broken the chain of causation by either reopening the wounds (suicide) or if the wounds had reopened naturally, by failing to stop the bleeding. The Court of Appeal held there was no need to inquire whether V had behaved negligently or grossly negligently:

...the cause of the deceased's death was bleeding from the artery which the defendant had severed. Whether or not the resumption or continuation of that bleeding was deliberately caused by the deceased, the jury were entitled to find that the [defendant's] conduct made an operative and significant contribution to the death.

In *D* [2006] EWCA Crim 1139 D had struck his partner a minor blow on the forehead and she had then committed suicide. This was against a lengthy background of domestic abuse amounting to psychological but not psychiatric injury by D. It was held that the infliction of mere psychological harm would not suffice to construct a manslaughter charge. However, in an *obiter dictum*, the Court of Appeal left open the possibility that a manslaughter conviction might be available:

where a decision to commit suicide has been triggered by a physical assault which represents the culmination of a course of abusive conduct, it would be possible...to argue that the final assault played a significant part in causing the victim's death.

In terms of causation, even if D's conduct in causing psychological injury was treated as a sufficient, unlawful and dangerous act, could it ever be a sufficient cause in law? There may be little doubt that in fact it operated as a cause of the suicide, but will V's actions in choosing to commit suicide break the chain of causation? Could causation have been established had the Crown relied on the unlawful act of assault? Surely there is an implicit requirement that the causation question focuses only on the unlawful act relied on by the Crown as the one that is dangerous?

Can D ever be liable for manslaughter where V has committed suicide and D's act is not at that moment a continuing and operative cause of death? Is it sufficient that V fears D's immediate attack in physical terms? Is it sufficient that V fears D's continued psychological abuse? Can suicide ever be a reasonably foreseeable response to violence or further psychological harm? Can suicide ever be within a range of reasonable responses to a threat of such harm? To what extent must D take his victim as found 'psychologically' as well as physically? Is a charge of gross negligence manslaughter preferable in these cases? See J. Horder and L. McGowan, 'Manslaughter by Causing Another's Suicide' [2006] Crim LR 1035.

Compare the approach taken in the so-called 'fright and flight' cases where V seeks to escape from D and in doing so suffers a fatal injury. In *Pitts* (1842) Car & M 284 it was held (at 284) that:

If a person, being attacked, should form an apprehension of immediate violence, an apprehension which must be well grounded and justified by the circumstances, throw himself for escape into a river, and be drowned, the person attacking him is guilty of murder.

In none of the reported 'flight' cases does it appear that the victims have chosen to commit suicide; rather, they have behaved in a dangerous fashion, being aware that their choice of escape may expose them to danger of injury or death.

In *Williams* (1992) 95 Cr App R 1 V, a hitch-hiker, leapt from a moving car and died from his injuries. The other occupants of the car were convicted of V's manslaughter, and robbery of V. On the question as to whether V had broken the chain of causation between the unlawful act of robbery and his death, the Court of Appeal (per Stuart-Smith LJ at 8) held:

The jury should consider...whether the deceased's reaction in jumping from the moving car was within the range of responses which might be expected from a victim placed in the situation which he was. The jury should bear in mind any particular characteristic of the victim and the fact that in the agony of the moment he may act without thought and deliberation.

■ *Question*

Is the correct test to apply that from *Williams* (was V's act 'daft') or that from *Blaue*?

This issue was considered more recently in *Lewis* [2010] EWCA Crim 151. D had been driving in the early hours of the morning when some students crossed the road in front of him and one struck his car. D got out of the car and on the Crown's case D then pushed one of the women students. Her brother, V, intervened. D chased V into the road, where V was hit and killed by an oncoming car. D was convicted of unlawful act manslaughter. The judge gave the jury a series of questions to assist them to reach a verdict (it is question (v) that is important here):

(i)   had D chased V by running after him;

(ii) in chasing him had D acted unlawfully by committing an assault or battery;

(iii) had V run away as a result of D's unlawful conduct;

(iv) would a sober and reasonable person have realized that D's actions would inevitably subject V to the risk of some harm;

(v)   was running away from D one of the responses which might have been expected from someone who found himself in V's situation.

D was convicted and appealed, arguing that the judge should have directed the jury that they could not convict if they found that V started running of his own volition and was unaware throughout that D was chasing him; and that the judge failed to direct the jury to consider whether V's actions in running away were foreseeable.

The Court of Appeal dismissed the appeal. In cases of death during flight from an unlawful act it had to be shown that there was cause and effect, that is, but for the unlawful act, flight and therefore death would not have taken place. Reliance was placed upon *Williams* (1992) 95 Cr App R 1. The judge's summing-up was expressed so as to give the jury the maximum assistance. Having provided directions in this manner with the explicit statement that the jury should only convict if all questions were answered positively, it was not necessary for the judge to provide the same questions couched in the reverse form for the jury to lead to acquittal.

In relation to whether V's act broke the chain of causation, Pitchford LJ stated that the judge was not bound to use the precise language of *Williams* and direct the jury to consider whether V's act was 'proportionate' or 'daft' to reinforce to them that not every flight response ought to be regarded as a foreseeable consequence of an unlawful act. The judge had directed the jury in the appropriate way by using ordinary language to explain reasonable foreseeability.

3.3 Criticisms and reform

Any law that exists on the question of causation in the criminal law is common law. Clause 17 of the Draft Criminal Code is an attempt to restate the common law principles. Whether it does so successfully is disputed but its principal critic, Glanville Williams, remarks ([1989] CLJ at 405–406) that 'it concentrates the mind wonderfully' and it at least provides a basis for discussion. Clause 17 provides:

17. Causation

(1) Subject to subsections (2) and (3), a person causes a result which is an element of an offence when—

(a) he does an act which makes a more than negligible contribution to its occurrence; or

(b) he omits to do an act which might prevent its occurrence and which he is under a duty to do according to the law relating to the offence.

(2) A person does not cause a result where, after he does such an act or makes such an omission, an act or event occurs—

(a) which is the immediate and sufficient cause of the result;

(b) which he did not foresee; and

(c) which could not in the circumstances reasonably have been foreseen.

(3) A person who procures, assists or encourages another to cause a result that is an element of an offence does not himself cause that result so as to be guilty of the offence as a principal except when—

(a) section 26(1)(c) [procuring an act by an innocent agent] applies; or

(b) the offence itself consists in the procuring, assisting or encouraging another to cause the result.

The exemption that would be created by this subsection is criticized by Glanville Williams ('*Finis* for *Novus Actus*' (1989) 48 CLJ 391) as being both too wide and too narrow.

■ *Question*

Does the Draft Code, cl 17, provide a clearer statement of the law than presently exists?

FURTHER READING

A. Ashworth, 'Defining Offences Without Harm' in P. F. Smith (ed), *Criminal Law: Essays in Honour of J. C. Smith* (1987)

R. Heaton, 'Dealing in Death' [2003] Crim LR 497

A. Norrie, 'A Critique of Criminal Causation' (1991) 54 MLR 685

A. Norrie, *Crime Reason and History* (2nd edn, 2001), Ch 7

S. Shute, 'Causation: Foreseeability v Natural Consequences' (1992) 55 MLR 584

J. Stannard, 'Criminal Causation and the Careless Doctor' (1992) 55 MLR 577

G. R. Sullivan and A. P. Simester, 'Causation Without Limits: Causing Death While Driving Without a Licence, While Disqualified, or Without Insurance' [2012] Crim LR 753

V. Tadros, *Criminal Responsibility* (2005), pp 159–185

4

Omissions

4.1 Introduction

The criminal sanction is, as we have noted, the most serious censure the State can impose on an individual and the imposition of the criminal sanction for doing nothing therefore sounds bizarre. In this chapter we examine the circumstances in which a person can be held criminally liable for not acting as well as for acting. In fact, the defendant's failure to act might not always be so easily described as 'doing nothing', and there are many situations in which the imposition of the criminal sanction is considered to be appropriate. The difficulties in this area of law are numerous and complex. They include:

- drawing distinctions between positive acts causing a prohibited result and failures to prevent a prohibited result;
- identifying circumstances in which it is appropriate to place a person under a duty to act on pain of criminal sanction for failure to do so; and
- establishing how D's failure to act can have caused a prohibited result.

Many statutes make it a specific offence to omit to do something, for example a motorist who fails to give his name and address after an accident or a company which fails to make a prescribed return under the relevant Companies Acts may be guilty of an offence. These offences, despite ascribing criminal liability to D for an omission, are uncontroversial. Most of them are of a regulatory nature. They seem to respect the principles of fair labelling and fair warning since the conviction attaches explicitly to the failure to act and not to its consequences. The controversial question is how the criminal law should deal with omissions in cases other than those where the offence is created in terms of 'failing to do x'.

How should the criminal law impose liability for omissions in relation to general offences such as murder, manslaughter and assault? The debate is a long-standing one, raising fundamental questions about the extent to which the criminal law should infringe upon the autonomy of the individual.

At *common law*, criminal liability for pure omissions is exceptional. The generally accepted definitions of most offences include a verb like 'kill', 'assault', 'damage' or 'take' which (at first sight, at least) requires an action of some kind. There are exceptions. In *Dytham* [1979] 3 All ER 641, a police officer, D, was on duty at 1 am when he saw a man, V, being ejected from a nightclub and being kicked and beaten by a number of bouncers. D took no steps to intervene. V died. D was charged with misconduct whilst acting as an officer of justice in that he deliberately failed to carry out his duties as a police constable by wilfully omitting to take any steps to preserve the peace or to protect V or to arrest or otherwise bring to justice the assailants. The conviction was upheld. (On misconduct in public office, see more generally *A-G's Reference (No 3 of 2003)* [2004] EWCA Crim 868.)

4.2 General criminal liability for omissions?

Andrew Ashworth, 'The Scope of Criminal Liability for Omissions'
(1989) 105 LQR 424

Although the paradigm of criminal liability is a prohibition on the culpable doing of a certain act, all systems of criminal law seem to include offences of omission. Some will have been drafted expressly so as to penalise an omission, e.g. 'failing to . . . ,' usually in the context of an undertaking or activity such as running a business or driving a motor vehicle. There may be other offences worded in a way which leaves open the possibility that they may be committed by omission as well as by acts. References to omissions should not, of course, be taken to imply that we may be said to omit to do everything that we do not do each day. The term 'omission' is properly applied only to failure to do things which there is some kind of duty to do, or at least things which it is reasonable to expect a person to do (on the basis of some relationship or role).

What the scope of such duties should be is therefore a major question for the legislature when considering criminal law reform and for the courts when developing the common law or interpreting statutes. Two contrasting positions may be identified, the 'conventional view' and the 'social responsibility view.' They are not polar opposites, and in a practical sense the difference between them is a matter of the extent of the duties recognised. But the two views do proceed from different theoretical foundations, and these are important when considering reasons for and against particular instances of criminal liability for omissions. What it is proposed to call the 'conventional view'—though one cannot be sure how settled or how prevalent it is—maintains that the criminal law should be reluctant to impose liability for omissions except in clear and serious cases. It is accepted that there are many activities in modern society which must, to some extent, be regulated by criminal offences, of which some will properly be offences of omission; it is also accepted that citizens have duties to support the collective good by paying taxes, etc., and that such duties may be reinforced by offences of omission; but the distinctive argument is that our duties towards other individuals should be confined to duties towards those for whom we have voluntarily undertaken some responsibility. Whereas we owe negative duties (e.g. not to kill or injure) to all people, it is right that we should owe positive duties (e.g. to render assistance, to support) only to a circumscribed group of people with whom there exists a special relationship. When supporters of the conventional view are pressed to justify this limitation, they might tend to argue that there is moral distinction between acts and omissions, maintaining that failure to perform an act with foreseen bad consequences is morally less bad than performing an act with the identical foreseen bad consequences.

. . . Adherents to the 'social responsibility view' would draw attention to the co-operative elements in social life, and would argue that it may be fair to place citizens under obligations to render assistance to other individuals in certain situations. This does not commit them to the view that the criminal law should enforce general duties to help all persons at all times. But it leads them to doubt whether the existence of some relationship or voluntary undertaking should be regarded as a precondition of criminal omissions liability. And it may also lead them to attack the argument that there is a general moral distinction between failing to perform an act with foreseen bad consequences and performing an act with identical bad consequences. All types of offence vary in their seriousness, of course, and even if it were true that on the whole omissions are less culpable than acts, it would not follow that omissions are less suitable for criminal prohibition than acts. On the 'social responsibility view,' then, there is no reason to accept the limitation imposed on omissions liability by the 'conventional view.'

. . . The conventional view embodies a minimalist stance on criminal liability for omissions. It accepts that criminal law is the sharpest end of a legal structure which aims to ensure both that respect for social values is enforced and that essential social needs are provided for. It therefore accepts criminal liability for such omissions as non-payment of taxes. But it regards it as exceptional, and as requiring special justification, for the criminal law to impose duties to assist other individuals. Apart from special relationships (such as parent-child) and other voluntarily undertaken duties, there should be no criminally enforceable duties to assist others or to perform socially useful acts.

The main buttress is an argument from individual autonomy and liberty. Each person is regarded as an autonomous being, responsible for his or her own conduct. One aim of the law is to maximise individual liberty, so as to allow each individual to pursue a conception of the good life with as few constraints as possible. Constraints there must be, of course, in modern society: but freedom of action should be curtailed only so far as is necessary to restrain individuals from causing injury or loss to others. Setting these outer limits to freedom of action is, however, much more acceptable than requiring certain actions of a citizen, especially at times and in circumstances which may be inconvenient and may conflict with one's pursuit of one's personal goals. To impose a duty to do X at a certain time prevents the citizen from doing anything else at that time, whereas the conventional prohibitions of the criminal law leave the citizen free to do whatever else is wanted apart from the prohibited conduct. Moreover, the criminal law should recognise an individual's choices rather than allowing liability to be governed by chance, and the obligation to assist someone in peril may be thrust upon a chance passer-by, who may well prefer not to become involved at all. If I am driving to a concert 50 miles away which is to feature a soloist who is being heard for the last time in this country, should I be obliged to stop and render assistance to the victims of a road accident in which I was not involved, at the risk of missing part or the whole of the concert? It is no argument to say that such a journey is always open to the possibility of chance happenings, such as engine failure in the car, a road blocked by a fallen tree, and so on, because in the case of the accident victims I am physically free to drive on to my destination whereas the other happenings amount to physical prevention, and render me incapable of reaching my destination on time. Thus it is no argument to say that all arrangements are vulnerable to chance, since the law can strive to minimise its effect and to keep individual choice as wide as possible. There is a choice whether to stop and offer assistance or to continue on my way to the concert, but an offence requiring a citizen to stop and render assistance would effectively foreclose that choice, coercing me to sacrifice the pursuit of my own interests in favour of alleviating the misfortunes of others to whom I have not voluntarily assumed any duty. By its 'chance' nature, the incidence of such a duty reduces the predictability of one's obligations and impinges on the liberty to pursue one's conception of the good life. On the conventional view, then, I deserve moral praise if I stop to assist the accident victims and thereby lose the opportunity to attend the (whole) concert, but it does not follow that I deserve blame if I do not stop. Praise may be appropriate for an act of 'saintliness' going beyond duty, whereas the duties themselves require only the basic conditions of peaceful co-existence. Stopping to help is part of the morality of aspiration, not the morality of duty.

In thus equating individual autonomy with negative liberty (i.e. liberty not to do certain acts), the conventional view rejects broad duties to others as paternalistic, and as failing to respect each individual's right to self-determination. Any obligation to help others in peril begs the question of who is to decide what 'peril' is. Individuals may choose to engage in amateur boxing or in motor cycle racing, knowing of the high risk of injury but deciding that it is worth the risk in order to enjoy the excitement of the sport. Are these boxers or motor cyclists 'in peril'? Few would extend a citizen's obligation to intervene (where it exists) to these cases, probably because the individual's decision to engage in the sport may be assumed to be an informed and settled decision. Self-determination, a value closely entwined with individual autonomy, would be impaired by the intervention of others. But what about the person who decides to commit suicide and jumps from a bridge into the River Thames? Should the passing citizen be obliged to alert the emergency services or, if the conditions are favourable, to mount a rescue attempt? The passing citizen is unlikely to know about the potential suicide's state of mind. It is known that some attempts at suicide proceed from an unbalanced state of mind, and some are merely attempts to draw attention to the person's problems rather than to relinquish life. On the conventional view these possibilities for paternalistic intervention should not be made the basis of any legal duty. If a citizen sees what appears to be an attempted suicide, the citizen's freedom from non-voluntary obligations together with the potential suicide's right to self-determination are suffi-cient to conclude the case against a duty to intervene.

A third argument looks to the social consequences of the opposite, 'social responsibility' view. Its effect in requiring each citizen to offer assistance to others in peril might on the one hand reduce the autonomy and privacy of others in pursuing their own objectives and enjoyment, however dangerous it may appear to others, and might on the other hand make citizens into busybodies who believe that they must be constantly advising others to avoid risk and danger. In other words, it might be too in-trusive and too onerous—both tendencies which go against the maximisation of liberty which is the keynote of the conventional view.

Fourthly, there is the argument that the 'social responsibility' view is unpractical because it would require each of us to avert or alleviate large numbers of situations which we know about. One strand of this argument calls attention to the problem of setting limits to the individuals duties on the social responsibility view: must I sell my car and my house, live at subsistence level and devote all my surplus earnings and time to preventing so many people from 'sleeping rough' in London, or to provide to-wards the relief of starvation in Africa? In what way do perils of these kinds differ materially from the accident victims or the person who jumps into the River Thames? A second strand of the argument is that the 'social responsibility' view may lead to the inculpation of large numbers of people, e.g. all the members of a crowd who witness someone being beaten up by others. It is excesses of this nature, in the depth and breadth of the obligations imposed, which are seen as sufficient to condemn the 'social responsibility' view as an unworkable moral or legal standard.

A fifth argument draws strength from the principle of legality: it maintains that citizens are so unaccustomed to thinking in terms of legal duties to act (as distinct from the well-known prohibi-tions) that it is unfair to impose such burdens except in circumstances which are well-defined and well-publicised. Protagonists might add that few provisions on general liability for omissions attain these standards, and that the obligation to take reasonable steps to assist a person in peril is much too uncertain to meet these standards. The social consequence is likely to be that ignorance of the law is a frequent occurrence, which cannot be good either for society or for the individuals concerned. Wide conceptions of social responsibility must therefore be rejected as a basis for criminal legislation: the conventional view, with its few well-known and voluntarily assumed duties to others, is the preferable approach.

The individualism of the conventional view doubted

The arguments for the conventional view may appear strong and practical, but they depend on a narrow, individualistic conception of human life which should be rejected as a basis for morality and (although this raises further issues) as a basis for criminal liability. Let us look again at the arguments, in turn.

The first argument, based on individual autonomy and freedom, is altogether too pure. To the extent that the conventional view relies on 'social fact' for some of its justifications, it is worth point-ing out that rarely is individual autonomy promoted as a supreme value throughout a moral or legal system. For example, paternalistic considerations are taken to outweigh it when imposing a duty to wear a seat belt in the front seat of a car: this restricts individual liberty and self-determination, and it may be justified by reference to the known dangers of travelling without a seat-belt, combined with the relatively large benefit (in the social costs of health care) reaped from such a comparatively minor infringement of freedom of action. Systems of criminal law typically include a wide range of offences which impose duties to act, in relation to taxation, motoring and business activities...

The second and third arguments for the conventional view establish, however, that limits must be set to the obligations to others if the ideal of individual autonomy is not to be submerged beneath a welter of duties imposed on each person. The resolution of these conflicts of theory and practice is no easy matter, but the 'social responsibility' view would at least start from the assumption that duties to others are not necessarily alien to individual autonomy, and would have to reconcile this with the desirability of individuals safeguarding their own interests too. This dilemma, which also underlies the fourth argument for the conventional view, demonstrates the need for principled debate about the extent of social co-operation necessary to realise individual autonomy. Those who advocate 'social responsibility' bear the heavy burden of formulating defensible and workable criteria for the imposition of duties to act. Indeed, as the fifth argument showed, attention is also necessary to the promulgation of such rules. In so far as it is true that people do not consider that they have legal duties to assist others, any legislation to introduce such duties must be phrased as precisely as possible, and must be supported by a programme of education and information. These represent considerable challenges for the 'social responsibility' view on criminal liability for omissions.

. . . On the 'social responsibility' view there are arguments for imposing certain obligations on individuals as citizens. These arguments are not founded on a simple benefit/burden calculation, that whoever takes the benefits of living in a certain society must in fairness expect to have to submit to its burdens. Such an approach leaves many unanswered questions about the quantum of burden which must be borne in order to have access to certain benefits. The reasoning is rather that the imposition of certain minimal duties shows a concern for the rights of other members of the community and therefore for the community itself, and so tends to promote the maximisation of liberty. However, the idea of maximum liberty relates to each individual as a member of the community rather than to each individual in isolation. Thus an apparent diminution of the freedom of one citizen (by requiring that citizen to take reasonable steps to prevent a harm or to call the emergency services) may be justifiable by reference to the augmentation of the freedom of another citizen (who is under attack or otherwise in danger), and such justification is in the context of striving towards a community in which the liberty of each and all can be maximised.

Once the case for imposing some citizenship duties is made out, there remain difficult questions about the proper extent and scope of these duties. Duties towards the collective good such as the duty to pay taxes may be established fairly easily, but duties towards other individuals who are strangers require further justification. It is thought that the arguments above establish the case for a duty to take steps to save other citizens in peril. It is true that this duty must be hedged about with qualifications, so as to ensure that the obligations are neither too dangerous nor too onerous for the citizen upon whom they fall. . . .

■ *Questions*

1. Do you agree that there should be a general offence of failing to save citizens in peril?

2. V is sleeping in a shop doorway. It is a bitterly cold night and V looks very pale. D is walking past the doorway and notices V. D eyes the empty vodka bottle at V's side, fears an angry and violent response if he gets involved so decides to walk by. Should D be guilty of a criminal offence if V dies? Of what offence? Manslaughter? An offence of failing to assist?

Glanville Williams, 'Criminal Omissions—The Conventional View'
(1991) 107 LQR 86

. . . Ashworth says that there is no moral difference between (i) a positive act and (ii) an omission when a duty is established. But even if this is so, he has already conceded a difference between the two when he says that an omission is culpable only when there is duty to act. The duty requirement sometimes involves considerations that are irrelevant to crimes of commission. Of course, every crime is a breach of legal duty not to commit the crime, but this is part of the meaning of the word 'crime.' The point is that no requirement of a particular duty not to act (over and above the specification of the crime) applies to wrongs of commission.

. . . First, . . . omissions liability should be exceptional, and needs to be adequately justified in each instance. Secondly, when it is imposed this should be done by clear statutory language. Verbs primarily denoting (and forbidding) active conduct should not be construed to include omissions except when the statute contains a genuine implication to this effect—not the perfunctory and fictitious implication that judges use when they are on the lawpath instead of the purely judge-path. Thirdly, maximum penalties applied to active wrongdoing should not automatically be transferred to corresponding omissions; penalties for omissions should be rethought in each case.

The case for the conventional view

The arguments for this philosophy may be briefly stated. (I would have thought them too obvious to need statement.) First, society's most urgent task is the repression of active wrongdoing. Bringing the ignorant or lethargic up to scratch is very much a secondary endeavour, for which the criminal process is not necessarily the best suited.

Secondly, our attitudes to wrongful action and wrongful inaction differ. There may be instances where our blood boils at the same temperature on account of both, but these are very exceptional. The only likely instance that comes to my mind is that of parents who are charged with killing their baby (i) by smothering it or (ii) by starving it to death. In this instance we are likely to feel more angry and sad about the slow starvation (an omission) than about the comparatively merciful infliction of death with a pillow. But on other occasions we almost always perceive a moral distinction between (for example) killing a person and failing to save his life (the former being the worse); and similarly between other acts and corresponding omissions.

This moral distinction, which we express in our language, reflects differences in our psychological approach to our own acts and omissions. We have much stronger inhibitions against active wrongdoing than against wrongfully omitting. This again is coupled with the fact that it is in every way easier not to do something (personal needs apart) than to do it. Also, a requirement to do something presupposes the ability to do it (the physical ability, and often the financial and educational ability as well), whereas almost everyone has the ability to refrain from ordinary physical acts.

Thirdly, serious crimes of commission can usually be formulated merely by stating the forbidden conduct, but laws creating crimes of omission are rarely directed against the whole world. They are intended to operate only against particular classes of person (and sometimes only for the protection of particular classes), in which case these persons must be singled out in the statement of the crime. To take an example: the courts can, in theory, punish everyone (with exceptions) who knowingly kills, but they cannot punish everyone who fails to save life, without some minimum specification of whose lives are to be saved. I cannot be made criminally responsible when I knowingly fail to save (and do not even try to save) the lives of unfortunate inhabitants of the Ganges delta who are drowned in floods; yet I could do something to help them by selling my house and giving the money to a suitable charity. Ashworth meets the point by saying that the requirement of duty 'establishes moral responsibility and delineates in time and space the number of people who may be said to have omitted'. . . . Very well, but this looks like translating law into morals rather than morals into law. Anyway, Ashworth does not propose that everything that may be regarded as a moral duty should automatically become a legal duty. So when we propose to punish omissions we are left with the problem of defining the scope of legal duty.

Fourthly, when crimes are expressed with the use of verbs implying action, it is a breach of the principle of legality to convict people of them when they have not acted; and it is unfair 'labelling' (Ashworth's expression) to convict non-doers of acts under the name of doers.

Fifthly, and perhaps most important of all, the law enforcement agencies (including the courts) have their work cut out to deal with people who offend by active conduct. The prisons, it is scarcely necessary to recall, are packed with them. To extend the campaign by attempting to punish all (or large groups of) those who contribute to the evil result by failing to co-operate in the great endeavour of producing a happier world would exceed the bounds of possibility.

Ashworth says of the conventional view that the supporting arguments 'depend on a narrow, individualistic conception of human life which should be rejected as a basis for morality and (although this raises further issues) as a basis for criminal liability' ... I leave it to the reader to judge whether the arguments as I have formulated them deserve this stricture.

In justifying the conventional view I have made no reference to the philosophy of individualism or to the autonomy principle, both of which Ashworth (erroneously I think) regards as the foundation of the conventional view. How far the State should provide financial succour and social services for those in need has nothing to do with the question whether individuals should be criminally punishable for not providing others with these advantages. To bring these considerations based on general social policy into the discussion simply muddies the waters. The same remark applies to Ashworth's support for legislation requiring the wearing of seat-belts, support which is now platitudinous, as well as being irrelevant to his attack on 'the conventional view.' The argument against treating omissions in the same way as positive acts does not go to the extent of saying that omissions running contrary to the public interest should never be punishable. Those who oppose seat belt legislation (among whom I am not to be counted) do so on the ground that it unjustifiably restricts bodily liberty, not on the ground that it wrongly punishes omissions. The legislation forbids one to drive in a car without belting up, and the forbidden conduct is a hybrid act/omission, which is legally classified as an act, not an omission.

■ *Question*

Do you find Williams' view more convincing than Ashworth's?

4.3 The present law

The courts' approach to the imposition of liability for omissions requires consideration of four issues.

(i)   Is D's conduct properly categorized as an omission, or as an act? If it can possibly be categorized as an act, the courts are likely to seek to do so to avoid complication.

(ii)   If the conduct of the accused is regarded as an 'omission' it is necessary to ask whether the particular offence is one for which an omission will be capable of grounding liability.

(iii) If an omission is a basis for liability under the offence, the question is whether D was under a duty to act. In result crimes, the result has occurred, so no one prevented it from occurring but, clearly, not everyone in the jurisdiction of the court (ie England and Wales for most offences) is liable for failing to do so. What are the criteria for selecting the culprit?

(iv)   Where the definition of the crime requires proof that D 'caused' a certain result, can he be said to have caused that result by doing nothing?

4.3.1 Act or omission?

As many of the cases in this chapter reveal, a distinction between acts and omissions is often tenuous and certainly too fine to bear the strain of distinguishing between circumstances in which there is no criminal liability and where there is liability in full measure. Some of the most striking examples of the difficulty in distinguishing acts and omissions arise in the medical context.

4.3.1.1 Act or omission—killing or failing to continue to keep alive?

■ *Questions*

V is on a life support machine which is keeping V's heart and other vital organs working. Dr X switches the machine off. V dies almost instantly.

Dr Y leaves the machine running but discontinues feeding V. V dies from starvation several days later.

Dr Z's machine is on a timer and needs to be restarted every 24 hours. Dr Z does not restart the machine and V dies almost instantly.

Has any of the doctors killed V? Assuming they had the necessary intent, could any be guilty of murder?

Dr Arthur's case

John Pearson was born at 7.55 am on 28 June 1980. It was immediately recognized that he was suffering from Down's syndrome. When his mother was informed, she rejected the baby. Dr Arthur, a highly respected consultant paediatrician, saw the parents at noon. There was a discussion as to whether the mother should keep the child. Following that discussion, Arthur wrote in his case notes: 'Parents do not wish the baby to survive. Nursing care only.' This meant that the child would be given water but no food. He entered on the treatment chart a prescription for a drug, dihydrocodeine (DF118), to be given 'as required' at four-hourly intervals by the nurse in charge. Dr Arthur was alleged to have said to a police officer '[DF118] is a sedative which stops the child seeking sustenance'. In a later written statement he said that the purpose of the drug was to reduce suffering. The baby died at 5.10 am on 1 July 1980, 57¼ hours after birth. The cause of death was stated to be broncho-pneumonia as a result of Down's syndrome.

Following an allegation that the baby had been drugged and starved to death, there was a police investigation and Arthur was charged with murder before Farquharson J and a jury at Leicester Crown Court. The prosecution alleged that death was caused by DF118 poisoning but, following defence evidence that the child might have died from inherent defects from which it was suffering before birth, the murder charge was dropped and replaced by one of attempted murder. In the course of a lengthy summing up Farquharson J directed the jury:

...the prosecution must prove not only an act which you as a jury decide is an attempt to cause the death of John Pearson, but an act accompanied by an intent that the child should die at the time the act was carried out.

[The defence say that] Arthur was not committing an act, a positive act, at all; he was simply prescribing a treatment which involved the creation of a set of circumstances whereby the child would peacefully die, and that there is all the difference in the world between the one and the other...

The prescription of that drug, dihydrocodeine, is a matter that is of consequence in this case. The importance that you attach to it is—and I must repeat—something for you to say as to whether the prosecution have, (a) proved that there was an attempt here or (b) that there was an act properly so-called on the part of Dr Arthur, as distinct from simply allowing the child to die...

Not only is it a possibility but it is a real possibility, say the defence, that in the ensuing days as [the mother] becomes more in control of herself and recovers from the trauma of giving birth to the child she could change her mind. This is a very vital part of the case because one of the main contentions of the defence here is that what was being done by Dr Arthur in prescribing this treatment had no sort of finality; it was in the nature...of a holding operation. If the mother had changed her mind then different treatment and management would have been given to the child...

However serious the case may be; however much the disadvantage of a mongol or, indeed, any other handicapped child, no doctor has the right to kill it . . .

But what has been perhaps the most agonizing part of this case is that it has become very clear, you may think, that it is a very difficult area to decide precisely where a doctor is doing an act, a positive act, or allowing a course of events or a set of circumstances to ensue . . .

If a child is born with a serious handicap—the instance we have been given is duodenal atresia where a mongol has an ill-formed intestine whereby the child will die of the ailment if he is not operated on—a surgeon may say: as this child is a mongol, handicapped in the way I have already been discussing with you, I do not propose to operate; I shall allow (and you have heard this expression several times) nature to take its course.

No one could say that the surgeon was committing an act of murder by declining to take a course which would save the child.

Equally, if a child not otherwise going to die, who is severely handicapped, is given a drug in such an excessive amount by the doctor that the drug itself will cause his death and the doctor does that intentionally it would be open to the jury to say: yes, he was killing, he was murdering the child . . .

[Dr Arthur did not give evidence. He was acquitted by the jury.]

■ *Questions*

1. Is the duty owed to a newly-born severely handicapped child different from, and of a lower order than, that owed to any other child? Consider the cases where parents and a surgeon agree that an operation to rectify an illness which would save the child's life shall not be performed (i) on a severely handicapped child, (ii) on a normal healthy child.

2. Is withholding food properly equated with not performing a surgical operation?

3. Is any of the following a 'positive act': (i) withholding food; (ii) instructing others to withhold food; (iii) administering a drug; (iv) instructing others to administer a drug?

Bland

What is the relevance of the fact that eminent paediatricians do not regard the withholding of food as a 'positive act'? Who determines the scope of the criminal law? Consider the implications of these questions in the context of the next case.

Airedale National Health Service Trust v Bland
[1992] UKHL 5, House of Lords, http://www.bailii.org/uk/cases/UKHL/1992/5.html

(Lords Keith of Kinkel, Goff of Chieveley, Lowry, Browne-Wilkinson and Mustill)

In 1989, Anthony Bland, then aged 17, was injured in the Hillsborough Stadium disaster suffering irreversible brain damage and thereafter was in a persistent vegetative state (PVS)—no cognitive function, no sight, hearing, capacity to feel pain, move his limbs or communicate in any way. Being unable to swallow, he was fed by naso-gastric tube. Repeated infections were treated by antibiotics. The consensus of medical opinion was that there was no hope of his improvement or recovery.

On the application (with the support of Bland's parents) of the Airedale NHS Trust, in whose hospital Bland was a patient, Sir Stephen Brown P granted a declaration that the Trust might lawfully (1) discontinue all life-sustaining treatment including ventilation, nutrition and hydration by artificial means and (2) discontinue medical treatment except for the purpose of enabling Bland to die peacefully with the greatest dignity and least distress. The Court of Appeal (Bingham MR, Butler-Sloss and Hoffmann LJJ) dismissed an appeal by the Official Solicitor who appealed to the House of Lords. He submitted that the withdrawal of artificial feeding would constitute murder. The House, though accepting that their decision in this civil action would not be legally binding on a criminal court, unanimously dismissed the appeal.

[Lord Keith made a speech dismissing the appeal.]

Lord Goff:

Why is it that the doctor who gives his patient a lethal injection which kills him commits an unlawful act and indeed is guilty of murder, whereas a doctor who, by discontinuing life support, allows his patient to die may not act unlawfully and will not do so if he commits no breach of duty to his patient? Professor Glanville Williams has suggested (see *Textbook of Criminal Law* (2nd edn, 1983) p 282) that the reason is that what the doctor does when he switches off a life support machine 'is in substance not an act but an omission to struggle' and that the 'omission is not a breach of duty by the doctor, because he is not obliged to continue in a hopeless case'.

I agree that the doctor's conduct in discontinuing life support can properly be categorised as an omission. It is true that it may be difficult to describe what the doctor actually does as an omission, for example where he takes some positive step to bring the life support to an end. But discontinuation of life support is, for present purposes, no different from not initiating life support in the first place. In each case, the doctor is simply allowing his patient to die in the sense that he is desisting from taking a step which might, in certain circumstances, prevent his patient from dying as a result of his pre-existing condition: and as a matter of general principle an omission such as this will not be unlawful unless it constitutes a breach of duty to the patient. I also agree that the doctor's conduct is to be differentiated from that of, for example, an interloper who maliciously switches off a life support machine because, although the interloper may perform exactly the same act as the doctor who discontinues life support, his doing so constitutes interference with the life-prolonging treatment then being administered by the doctor. Accordingly, whereas the doctor, in discontinuing life support, is simply allowing his patient to die of his pre-existing condition, the interloper is actively intervening to stop the doctor from prolonging the patient's life, and such conduct cannot possibly be categorized as an omission . . . If the justification for treating a patient who lacks the capacity to consent lies in the fact that the treatment is provided in his best interests, it must follow that the treatment may, and indeed ultimately should, be discontinued where it is no longer in his best interests to provide it. The question which lies at the heart of the present case is, as I see it, whether on that principle the doctors responsible for the treatment and care of Anthony Bland can justifiably discontinue the process of artificial feeding upon which the prolongation of his life depends.

It is crucial for the understanding of this question that the question itself should be correctly formulated. The question is not whether the doctor should take a course which will kill his patient, or even take a course which has the effect of accelerating his death. The question is whether the doctor should or should not continue to provide his patient with medical treatment or care which, if continued, will prolong his patient's life. The question is sometimes put in striking or emotional terms, which can be misleading. For example, in the case of a life support system, it is sometimes asked: should a doctor be entitled to switch it off, or to pull the plug? And then it is asked: can it be in the best interests of the patient that a doctor should be able to switch the life support system off, when this will inevitably result in the patient's death? Such an approach has rightly been criticized as misleading, for example by Professor Ian Kennedy (in his paper in *Treat Me Right, Essays in Medical Law and Ethics* (1988)), and by Thomas J in *Auckland Area Health Board v A-G* [1993] 1 NZLR 235 at 247. This is because the question is not whether it is in the best interests of the patient that he should die. The question is whether it is in the best interests of the patient that his life should be prolonged by the continuance of this form of medical treatment or care.

The correct formulation of the question is of particular importance in a case such as the present, where the patient is totally unconscious and where there is no hope whatsoever of any amelioration of his condition. In circumstances such as these, it may be difficult to say that it is in his best interests that the treatment should be ended. But, if the question is asked, as in my opinion it should be, whether it is in his best interests that treatment which has the effect of artificially prolonging his life should be continued, that question can sensibly be answered to the effect that it is not in his best interests to do so.

[Lords Lowry and Browne-Wilkinson made speeches dismissing the appeal.]

Lord Mustill:

After much expression of negative opinions I turn to an argument which in my judgment is logically defensible and consistent with the existing law. In essence it turns the previous argument on its head by directing the inquiry to the interests of the patient, not in the termination of life but in the continuation of his treatment. It runs as follows. (i) The cessation of nourishment and hydration is an omission not an act. (ii) Accordingly, the cessation will not be a criminal act unless the doctors are under a present duty to continue the regime. (iii) At the time when Anthony Bland came into the care of the doctors decisions had to be made about his care which he was unable to make for himself. In accordance with *F v West Berkshire Health Authority* [1989] 2 All ER 545, [1990] 2 AC 1 these decisions were to be made in his best interests. Since the possibility that he might recover still existed his best interests required that he should be supported in the hope that this would happen. These best interests justified the application of the necessary regime without his consent. (iv) All hope of recovery has now been abandoned. Thus, although the termination of his life is not in the best interests of Anthony Bland, his best interests in being kept alive have also disappeared, taking with them the justification for the non-consensual regime and the correlative duty to keep it in being. (v) Since there is no longer a duty to provide nourishment and hydration a failure to do so cannot be a criminal offence.

My Lords, I must recognise at once that this chain of reasoning makes an unpromising start by transferring the morally and intellectually dubious distinction between acts and omissions into a context where the ethical foundations of the law are already open to question. The opportunity for anomaly and excessively fine distinctions, often depending more on the way in which the problem happens to be stated than on any real distinguishing features, has been exposed by many commentators, including in England the authors above-mentioned, together with Smith and Hogan *Criminal Law* (6th edn, 1988) p 51, Beynon 'Doctors as murderers' [1982] Crim LR 17 and Gunn and Smith *'Arthur's* case and the right to life of a Down's syndrome child' [1985] Crim LR 705. All this being granted, we are still forced to take the law as we find it and try to make it work. Moreover, although in cases near the borderline the categorisation of conduct will be exceedingly hard, I believe that nearer the periphery there will be many instances which fall quite clearly into one category rather than the other. In my opinion the present is such a case, and in company with Compton J in *Barber v Superior Court of Los Angeles County* 147 Cal App 3d 1006 at 1017 (1983) amongst others I consider that the proposed conduct will fall into the category of omissions.

I therefore consider the argument to be soundly based. Now that the time has come when Anthony Bland has no further interest in being kept alive, the necessity to do so, created by his inability to make a choice, has gone; and the justification for the invasive care and treatment together with the duty to provide it have also gone. Absent a duty, the omission to perform what had previously been a duty will no longer be a breach of the criminal law.

■ *Questions*

1. Is there really a difference between the questions:

(a) 'is it in the best interests of the patient that he should die?' and

(b) 'is it in the best interests of the patient that his life should be prolonged by this treatment?'

2. 'How can it be lawful to allow a patient to die slowly, though painlessly, over a period of weeks from lack of food but unlawful to produce his immediate death by a lethal injection, thereby saving his family from yet another ordeal to add to the tragedy that has already struck them?'—per Lord Browne-Wilkinson—who thought this was 'undoubtedly the law'. Have you an answer?

In *Re A (children)* [2001] Fam 147, the case of the conjoined twins (section 11.5.2, p 406), Johnson J, the trial judge, held that the reasoning in *Bland* could be applied to that case. He thought that the course proposed by the doctors—to separate the twins and allow only Jodie to live—was not 'a positive act but merely the withdrawal of Mary's blood supply'. It was as if Jodie stood in the same relation to Mary as the various machines did in relation to Bland. But none of the judges in the Court of Appeal agreed—though Robert Walker LJ did say at one point that, following separation, Mary 'would die because tragically her own body, on its own, is not and never has been viable'. Ward LJ went as far as to say that the distinction between act and omission was irrelevant: 'It is important to stress that it makes no difference whether the killing is by act or by omission. That is a distinction without a difference.' He referred to the speeches of Lords Lowry, Browne-Wilkinson and Mustill in *Bland*. But was not the distinction between act and omission the foundation of the decision in *Bland*, unhappy though their lordships were with it? If Mary were not being kept alive by Jodie, it seems clear that it would not have been unlawful to omit to take steps which might briefly have prolonged her life. Yet Johnson J's conclusion was not justified. *Bland* was materially different. This was not a case of discontinuing treatment. Mary was not receiving treatment. The operation would be a positive act. It would involve the use of the scalpel and 'a number of invasions of Mary's body ... before the positive step was taken of clamping the aorta and bringing about Mary's death'.

4.3.2 Offences capable of being committed by omission

If the conduct of the defendant is regarded as an omission, the question arises whether the offence with which he is charged is one for which a conviction can be secured on the basis of an omission rather than an act. Some offences would appear not to be capable of commission by omission, as, for example, with attempted offences discussed in the next section.

4.3.2.1 Statutory interpretation

One striking example of a statutory offence turning on the word 'act' is in relation to attempts (section 14.4, p 504). The Criminal Attempts Act 1981 makes it an offence to do 'an act more than merely preparatory' to the commission of the full offence. It seems strange then to contemplate an offence of attempt by omission. In *Nevard* [2006] EWCA Crim 2896, D seriously injured his wife by striking her with an axe and a knife. He then forced her to abandon her attempt to dial 999 to call for assistance. The emergency services rang back on the number she had used, but D took the call and told them that his grandchildren must have been fooling around with the phone. The police remained suspicious so attended the scene and found D's wife, whose injuries were not fatal. D was charged with wounding with intent and with attempted murder. He pleaded guilty to the wounding. Having been directed by the judge as to the elements of attempted murder, the jury asked: 'Can you clarify whether an attempt to withhold care/emergency services constitutes attempted murder, knowing he has pleaded guilty to wounding with intent.' The trial judge's answer was:

> Obviously if a person comes across somebody who is seriously injured in the street and fails to call the emergency services, they could not be charged with attempted murder...the straight answer to the question is 'yes' and it is necessary for me to elaborate upon that. To be sure of attempted murder you must be sure that he did an act or acts with the intention of killing Mrs Nevard...The Crown's case is that he struck the blows with the axe or the axe handle. When that did not work he went and got a knife and stabbed her with that kitchen knife...and also that he slashed her arms with a Stanley knife and that when he did those acts, his intention was that she should die. Now, where the withholding of the emergency services may help you is as to what his intention was...In other words, by seeing what he did after the event you may get an insight as to what his intention was.

Nevard appealed against conviction. The Court of Appeal upheld the conviction, but suggested that the judge should have made explicit to the jury that attempting to divert the emergency services could not in itself constitute attempted murder.

■ *Questions*

Was not D's conduct in taking the return call and lying a sufficient act? He took positive steps to prevent the emergency services responding to his wife's call. If V dies because D prevents the emergency services from reaching him, or from helping him if they do arrive (eg by keeping them away at gunpoint), that must make D a substantial cause of V's death, even if D was not the one who inflicted the original injuries. If D takes such positive measures to prevent the emergency services arriving, but despite his best efforts V lives, D must surely have attempted to cause V's death. Why should D not be guilty of attempted murder?

The language of the Criminal Attempts Act may seem clear, but with other offences the position is less clear cut. Professor Glanville Williams suggested that a criminal code should state that enactments creating offences in words primarily referring to 'acts' are not to be interpreted to include mere omissions unless the enactment expressly so provides. If Parliament wishes to penalize omissions it must direct its mind to the subject and make its meaning clear. (See (1987) 7 LS 92 at 97, 'What Should the Code Do About Omissions?'.) Professor Williams concedes that 'some words can legitimately be held to "specify" both acts and omissions, even though they refer expressly to neither', instancing the word 'neglect' (at 97).

■ *Questions*

Some words certainly do describe conduct which can be performed by act or omission, as, for example, with 'obstruct'. If I am standing in a narrow passage blocking your way, and I refuse to move, does not my omission 'obstruct' you? And is not 'obstruction' a result crime, rather than a conduct crime?

Particular problems in offences against the person

Some take the view that the offences against the person are crimes of action—wounding, assaulting, battering—and should not be capable of commission by omission (see eg Wilson, *Central Theories*, p 101).

The Criminal Law Revision Committee (a reform body that was in some ways a precursor to the Law Commission) in its Fourteenth Report on Offences Against the Person identified those of its proposed offences against the person which were to be capable of being committed by omission—murder, manslaughter, causing serious injury with intent, unlawful detention, kidnapping, abduction and aggravated abduction. Other offences against the person, for example assault, would not be capable of being committed by omission. The Code team included in their Bill (LC143) a clause to give effect to this recommendation: an offence was to be capable of being committed by omission only if the enactment creating it so specified and the Code specified the chosen offences against the person. These provisions have no place in the current Draft Code. The Law Commission was persuaded by an article by Professor Glanville Williams ((1987) 7 LS 92) that it would make important changes in the law on which there had been no consultation (and which indeed had not been foreseen) and which, therefore, could not be justified. Williams pointed out that in a number of cases statutory offences had been held to be capable of being committed by omission, although there was no express provision that they might be so committed. The Code team's proposals would have reversed those cases; and no consideration had been given as to whether they ought to be reversed. The Draft Code does not specify which offences may be committed by omission. It leaves that question, as under the present law, to the courts. But cl 17(1) makes it clear that, under the Code, results 'may be caused' by omission and defines offences against the person in terms of 'causing' death (rather than 'killing') or other relevant harm. Some other offences (notably offences of damage to property) are also defined in terms of 'causing' so as to leave it fully open to the courts to decide that the offence should be capable of commission by omission if they think it appropriate.

In the Law Commission's Report No 218, *Legislating the Criminal Code: Offences Against the Person and General Principles* (1993), which deals with only non-fatal offences against the person, the Law Commission specifies which of those offences should be capable of commission by omission. It broadly follows the approach of the Criminal Law Revision Committee and specifies intentionally causing serious injury, torture, unlawful detention, kidnapping, abduction and aggravated abduction. As in the Draft Code, the draft Non-Fatal Offences Against the Person Bill makes no attempt to specify who is under a duty to act. Clause 19(1) provides:

An offence to which this section applies may be committed by a person who, with the result specified for the offence, omits to do an act that he is under a duty to do at common law.

Clause 19(1) does not apply to cl 3 (recklessly causing serious injury, which would replace s 20 of the Offences Against the Person Act 1861), cl 4 (intentionally or recklessly causing injury which would replace s 47 of the Offences Against the Person Act 1861) or cl 6 (assault) so, if the draft Bill were enacted, it would be settled that these offences could not be committed by omission. The draft Bill annexed to the Home Office Consultation Paper of February 1998 is to the same effect.

■ *Question*

Consider the following case which was much discussed in the Criminal Law Revision Committee. D, a cleaner, puts polish on the floor and then, in breach of his duty, omits to display the notice with which he has been provided warning users in the building of the dangerous state of the floor. V slips on the polish and falls. Was it a mere omission?

This floor polish example was put to the Criminal Law Revision Committee as a case of omission and was so treated by them. But one member of the committee, Glanville

Williams, had second thoughts ((1987) 7 LS at 92) about this: 'in such circumstances of act/omission the total conduct could and should be regarded as an act, so the cleaner could be guilty of the offence of causing injury recklessly...' Williams also accepts that there would not be liability if the polish was put on the floor by the cleaner but the janitor, whose duty it was to put the sign on the floor, failed to do so. Williams would convict the cleaner in the first example but acquit the janitor in the second example. He would be prepared to tolerate this fine distinction because, as he rightly says, all legal rules are capable of producing fine distinctions. This is alright if the distinction is sound in principle; but is the distinction between act/omission and omission sound? Cf *Miller* [1983] 1 All ER 978, section 4.3.3.4, p 86.

Consider the following examples: the janitor (J) has a duty to display the notice when the floor is slippery. J does not do so. V falls and (i) suffers no injury, (ii) suffers minor injury, (iii) suffers serious injury, or (iv) is killed. If J is charged with (i) assault or (ii) assault occasioning actual bodily harm or (iii) inflicting GBH or (iv) manslaughter, will the prosecution be able to establish the actus reus? Would J be likely to have the mens rea for any such offences? Is a health and safety offence a more realistic and appropriate charge?

■ *Questions*

Can these distinctions be justified? How would the current law deal with these cases?

Homicide

At common law it is established that there can be liability for murder and gross negligence manslaughter by an omission: *Gibbins and Procter* (1918) 13 Cr App R 134 in section 4.4 (murder); *Stone and Dobinson* in section 4.3.3.3 (manslaughter).

4.3.3 Who is under a duty to act?

Though an offence is capable of being committed by omission, it does not follow that everyone is under a duty to act. The courts have recognized a number of categories in which a duty to act arises, each of which is discussed in the following sections (4.3.3.1–4.3.3.4). For discussion, see L. Alexander, 'Criminal Liability for Omissions' in S. Shute and A. Simester, *Criminal Law Theory: Doctrines of the General Part* (2002).

4.3.3.1 Contract

In *Pittwood* (1902) 19 TLR 37 D, a gatekeeper on a railway line, had a contractual duty to his employer to keep the gate closed. D opened the gate and forgot to close it. V, assuming that the way was safe as the gate was open was then killed by a passing train. D's counsel argued that D only owed a duty to his employers under his contract, but the court held that a man might incur criminal liability arising from such a contract.

■ *Questions*

1. What types of contract will give rise to such a duty? Is it only contracts involving a protective or 'health and safety'-based purpose?

2. Does a lecturer owe a duty to the students in his lecture—to protect against injury from defective premises? From attack by homicidal lecture gatecrashers?

3. Aside from the difficulty of which contracts are sufficient to establish a duty, there is the question of the content and scope of the duty. If D is a lifeguard employed by the council, does his duty to save a drowning stranger in the council's pool apply when D has formally clocked off work for the day? Does D's liability under contract depend on V's knowledge that D is under contract with X (eg the council or the railway company)?

4.3.3.2 Voluntary undertakings

In *Instan* [1893] 1 QB 450 D lived with and maintained V, her aunt aged 73. For the final few days before her death V was completely incapacitated. D bought food with her aunt's money, but failed to give her any. Nor did D summon medical help. Death ensued from exhaustion and gangrene. D was convicted of manslaughter. The court affirmed her conviction. Coleridge LCJ concluded that a there was a duty—a 'legal common law duty is nothing else than the enforcing by law of that which is a moral obligation without legal enforcement'.

See further G. Mead, 'Contracting into Crime: A Theory of Criminal Omissions' (1991) 11 OJLS 147 at 168, arguing that a person who has voluntarily undertaken responsibility ought to be under a duty because:

First he is more likely to be aware that a person may be in a position of peril and in need of assistance. He will know of the vulnerability of the victim in a way that others may not. Second, he may be more capable of carrying out the required task than will a third party. We might assume that, in most cases where D undertakes to do a particular thing, he feels he has the ability to do it, whereas a third party, who has not given such an undertaking will not necessarily possess the required skills to do what is needed in order to avert danger to V. The third point is that if other people are aware of the undertaking they might feel it unproductive for them to get involved as well. They might reasonably think that they would be simply getting in the way and hinder the completion of the task in question.

■ *Questions*

1. Was D's duty in *Instan* a result of her voluntary undertaking? Her relationship? Her cohabitation? Her being paid by her aunt?

2. Is the existence of a moral duty a sufficient basis for the imposition of criminal liability?

3. If D assumes some responsibility for V, it seems less objectionable for the law to impose liability for his subsequent omissions. But what of the objections based on principles of fair labelling and fair warning? Is the scope of the duty and its content sufficiently clearly prescribed to satisfy these principled concerns?

4.3.3.3 Special relationships

Many of the cases involving relationships also involve a voluntary undertaking by the party, and it is unclear to what extent the courts would impose a duty on the basis of a relationship per se.

The most obvious type of relationship in which it has been held that a duty to act arises is that between parent and child. This is supported by statutory obligations such as the Children and Young Persons Act 1933, s 1. The failure of parents to feed and care for their children has given rise to liability for manslaughter and even in one case for murder: *Gibbins and Procter* (section 4.4, p 94). It remains unclear which other categories of relationship will give rise to such a duty.

In *Stone and Dobinson* [1977] 2 All ER 341, [1977] QB 354, CA, S and D—S's mistress—allowed S's sister, Fanny, to lodge with them. The sister became infirm while lodging with them and died of toxaemia from infected bed sores and prolonged immobilization. S and D had made only half-hearted and wholly ineffectual attempts to secure medical attention for the sister. Upholding the convictions of S and D for manslaughter, the court said:

There is no dispute, broadly speaking, as to the matters on which the jury must be satisfied before they can convict of manslaughter in circumstances such as the present. They are: (1) that the defendant undertook the care of a person who by reason of age or infirmity was unable to care for himself; (2) that the defendant was grossly negligent in regard to his duty of care; (3) that by reason of such negligence the person died. It is submitted on behalf of the appellants that the judge's direction to the jury with regard to the first two items was incorrect.

At the close of the Crown's case submissions were made to the judge that there was no, or no sufficient, evidence that the appellants, or either of them, had chosen to undertake the care of Fanny.

That contention was advanced by counsel for the appellant before this court as his first ground of appeal. He amplified the ground somewhat by submitting that the evidence which the judge had suggested to the jury might support the assumption of a duty by the appellants did not, when examined, succeed in doing so. He suggested that the situation here was unlike any reported case. Fanny came to this house as a lodger. Largely, if not entirely due to her own eccentricity and failure to look after herself or feed herself properly, she became increasingly infirm and immobile and eventually unable to look after herself. Is it to be said, asks counsel for the appellants rhetorically, that by the mere fact of becoming infirm and helpless in these circumstances, she casts a duty on her brother and Mrs Dobinson to take steps to have her looked after or taken to hospital? The suggestion is that, heartless though it may seem, this is one of those situations where the appellants were entitled to do nothing; where no duty was cast on them to help, any more than it is cast on a man to rescue a stranger from drowning, however easy such a rescue might be.

This court rejects that proposition. Whether Fanny was a lodger or not she was a blood relation of the appellant Stone; she was occupying a room in his house; Mrs Dobinson had undertaken the duty of trying to wash her, of taking such food to her as she required. There was ample evidence that each appellant was aware of the poor condition she was in by mid-July. It was not disputed that no effort was made to summon an ambulance or the social services or the police despite the entreaties of [neighbours]. A social worker used to visit [Stone]. No word was spoken to him. All these were matters which the jury were entitled to take into account when considering whether the necessary assumption of a duty to care for Fanny had been proved.

This was *not* a situation analagous to the drowning stranger. They *did* make efforts to care. They tried to get a doctor; they tried to discover the previous doctor. Mrs Dobinson helped with the washing and the provision of food. All these matters were put before the jury in terms which we find it impossible to fault. The jury were entitled to find that the duty had been assumed. They were entitled to conclude that once Fanny became helplessly infirm, as she had by 19 July, the appellants were, in the circumstances, obliged either to summon help or else to care for Fanny themselves...

■ *Questions*

Is the duty imposed because of the cohabitation? The relationship? The decision by D and S to assist Fanny? All of these? Given the limited capacity of the defendants, were their ineffectual efforts not enough to satisfy any duty that arose?

Marriage is a sufficient basis for a duty (*Hood* [2004] 1 Cr App R (S) 431), so the question surely cannot be based on blood relationships. Is the true basis of the relationship duty one of interdependence? The case law on this issue is inconsistent. In *Evans* [2009] EWCA Crim 650 (section 4.3.3.4, p 89), the Court of Appeal framed the question it had to consider—about the liability of a half-sister for her sibling's death—in the following way:

> ...notwithstanding that their relationship lacked the features of familial duty or responsibility which marked her mother's relationship with the deceased, [D] was under a duty to take reasonable steps for the safety of the deceased once she appreciated that the heroin she procured for her was having a potentially fatal impact on her health.

So it seems that half-sisters do not owe each other a duty. What about siblings that share both parents? In *Barrass* [2011] EWCA Crim 2629 D and V were siblings. V had a mild learning disorder and suffered from various physical ailments, she died in her room after a long period of self-neglect. D was convicted of gross negligence manslaughter on the following basis:

> [D] was the only person who could have alerted the authorities to her condition and he had been grossly negligent in failing to provide for her basic needs of care, warmth and clothing and to summon assistance when her condition deteriorated. As the judge was to remark in his sentencing remarks, the appellant must have entered her room every day because he had provided food to her, but the only other care he had given her, until calling for the emergency services when it was too late, was to reposition her television set.

What was D's duty founded on in this case? Was it the fact of their familial relationship or was it because there was simply no one else to care for V and alert the authorities to her condition?

■ *Questions*

1. Should a strong 14-year-old owe a duty to his ailing mother? Should a duty extend between siblings? Does a student D owe a duty to his anorexic flatmate, V, to call for medical treatment for her? To feed her?

2. What is the extent of a duty imposed by relationships? Is it a duty to do what is reasonable? What D believes to be reasonable? That which is necessary to avert the danger from V?

Note the offence under s 5 of the Domestic Violence, Crime and Victims Act 2004 relating to carers' responsibilities for death or serious injury to a child and the extension in the Domestic Violence, Crime and Victims (Amendment) Act 2012 creating a similar offence where the child or vulnerable person suffers serious injury.

4.3.3.4 Creation of a dangerous situation or 'supervening fault'

The principle for determining liability where D creates a dangerous situation was pronounced by the House of Lords in the following case.

R v Miller

[1982] UKHL 6, House of Lords, http://www.bailii.org/uk/cases/UKHL/1982/6.html

(Lords Diplock, Keith, Bridge, Brandon and Brightman)

The defendant lay on a mattress in a house in which he was a squatter and lit a cigarette. He fell asleep and woke to find the mattress on fire. He went into the next room and fell asleep. The house caught fire and £800 worth of damage was done. He was charged with arson, contrary to s 1(1) and (3) of the Criminal Damage Act 1971, in that he 'damaged by fire a house…intending to do damage to such property or recklessly as to whether such property would be damaged'. He was convicted and his appeal to the Court of Appeal was dismissed. He appealed to the House of Lords. Note that at the time of this decision the mens rea for the offence was governed by the test of recklessness in *Caldwell* (section 5.3, p 123).

Lord Diplock:

The first question is a pure question of causation; it is one of fact to be decided by the jury in a trial on indictment. It should be answered No if, in relation to the fire during the period starting immediately before its ignition and ending with its extinction, the role of the accused was at no time more than that of a passive bystander. In such a case the subsequent questions to which I shall be turning would not arise. The conduct of the parabolical priest and Levite on the road to Jericho may have been indeed deplorable, but English law has not so far developed to the stage of treating it as criminal; and if it ever were to do so there would be difficulties in defining what should be the limits of the offence.

If, on the other hand the question, which I now confine to: 'Did a physical act of the accused start the fire which spread and damaged property belonging to another?', is answered 'Yes', as it was by the Jury in the instant case, then for the purpose of the further questions the answers to which are determinative of his guilt of the offence of arson, the conduct of the accused, throughout the period from immediately before the moment of ignition to the completion of the damage to the property by the fire, is relevant; so is his state of mind throughout that period.

Since arson is a result-crime the period may be considerable, and during it the conduct of the accused that is causative of the result may consist not only of his doing physical acts which cause the fire to start or spread but also of his failing to take measures that lie within his power to counteract the danger that he has himself created. And if his conduct, active or passive, varies in the course of the period, so may his state of mind at the time of each piece of conduct. If, at the time of any particular piece of conduct by the accused that is causative of the result, the state of mind that actuates his conduct falls within the description of one or other of the states of mind that are made a necessary ingredient of the offence of arson by s 1(1) of the Criminal Damage Act 1971 (ie intending to damage property belonging to another or being reckless whether such property would be damaged), I know of no principle of English criminal law that would prevent his being guilty of the offence created by that subsection. Likewise I see no rational ground for excluding from conduct capable of giving rise to criminal liability conduct which consists of failing to take measures that lie within one's power to counteract a danger that one has oneself created, if at the time of such conduct one's state of mind is such as constitutes a necessary ingredient of the offence. I venture to think that the habit of lawyers to talk of 'actus reus', suggestive as it is of action rather than inaction, is responsible for any erroneous notion that failure to act cannot give rise to criminal liability in English law.

No one has been bold enough to suggest that if, in the instant case, the accused had been aware at the time that he dropped the cigarette that it would probably set fire to his mattress and yet had taken no steps to extinguish it he would not have been guilty of the offence of arson, since he would have damaged property of another being reckless whether any such property would be damaged.

I cannot see any good reason why, so far as liability under criminal law is concerned, it should matter at what point of time before the resultant damage is complete a person becomes aware that he has done a physical act which, whether or not he appreciated that it would at the time when he did it, does in fact create a risk that property of another will be damaged, provided that, at the moment of awareness, it lies within his power to take steps, either himself or by calling for the assistance of the fire brigade if this be necessary, to prevent or minimise the damage to the property at risk…

My Lords, in the instant case the prosecution did not rely on the state of mind of the accused as being reckless during that part of his conduct that consisted of his lighting and smoking a cigarette while lying on his mattress and falling asleep without extinguishing it. So the jury were not invited to make any finding as to this. What the prosecution did rely on as being reckless was his state of mind during that part of his conduct after he awoke to find that he had set his mattress on fire and that it was smouldering, but did not then take any steps either to try to extinguish it himself or to send for the fire brigade, but simply went into the other room to resume his slumbers, leaving the fire from the already smouldering mattress to spread and to damage that part of the house in which the mattress was.

The recorder, in his lucid summing up to the jury (they took 22 minutes only to reach their verdict), told them that the accused, having by his own act started a fire in the mattress which, when he became aware of its existence, presented an obvious risk of damaging the house, became under a duty to take some action to put it out. The Court of Appeal upheld the conviction, but its ratio decidendi appears to be somewhat different from that of the recorder. As I understand the judgment, in effect it treats the whole course of conduct of the accused, from the moment at which he fell asleep and dropped the cigarette onto the mattress until the time the damage to the house by fire was complete, as a continuous act of the accused, and holds that it is sufficient to constitute the statutory offence of arson if at any stage in that course of conduct the state of mind of the accused, when he fails to try to prevent or minimize the damage which will result from his initial act, although it lies within his power to do so, is that of being reckless whether property belonging to another would be damaged. . . .

My Lords, these alternative ways of analysing the legal theory that justifies decision which has received nothing but commendation for its accord with common sense and justice have, since the publication of the judgment of the Court of Appeal in the instant case, provoked academic controversy. Each theory has distinguished support. Professor J C Smith espouses the 'duty theory' (see [1982] Crim LR 526 at 528); Professor Glanville Williams who, after the decision of the Divisional Court in *Fagan v Metropolitan Police Comr* [set out in section 2.4.2, p 33] appears to have been attracted by the duty theory, now prefers that of the continuous act (see [1982] Crim LR 773). When applied to cases where a person has unknowingly done an act which sets in train events that, when he becomes aware of them, present an obvious risk that property belonging to another will be damaged, both theories lead to an identical result; and, since what your Lordships are concerned with is to give guidance to trial judges in their task of summing up to juries, I would for this purpose adopt the duty theory as being the easier to explain to a jury; though I would commend the use of the word 'responsibility', rather than 'duty' which is more appropriate to civil than to criminal law since it suggests an obligation owed to another person, ie the person to whom the endangered property belongs, whereas a criminal statute defines combinations of conduct and state of mind which render a person liable to punishment by the state itself.

[Lords Keith, Bridge, Brandon and Brightman agreed.]

Appeal dismissed

■ *Questions*

1. Was the defendant held liable for damaging the house by falling asleep while smoking? Or for damaging the house by failing to take reasonable steps to put out the burning bed?

2. What if the defendant had found that his 9-year-old child had set the bed on fire and had left it to burn? Or the fire had originated in an electrical fault in the wiring of the house when he switched on his electric blanket?

3. What if the defendant's fellow squatter had (i) sustained grievous bodily harm or (ii) died in the fire?

Compare the approach taken by the Divisional Court in *Fagan v Metropolitan Police Commissioner* [1968] 3 All ER 442. In that case, set out in full in section 2.4.2, p 33, D had driven onto a police officer's foot and when told of that fact by the officer had delayed in

moving his car. He was convicted by the magistrates of assaulting the constable in the execution of his duty. In the Divisional Court, it was held that:

> ... On the facts found, the action of the appellant may have been initially unintentional, but the time
> came when, knowing that the wheel was on the officer's foot, the appellant (i) remained seated in the
> car so that his body through the medium of the car was in contact with the officer, (ii) switched off the
> ignition of the car, (iii) maintained the wheel of the car on the foot, and (iv) used words indicating the
> intention of keeping the wheel in that position. For our part, we cannot regard such conduct as mere
> omission or inactivity. There was an act constituting a battery which at its inception was not criminal
> because there was no element of intention, but which became criminal from the moment the inten-
> tion was formed to produce the apprehension which was flowing from the continuing act. The fallacy
> of the appellant's argument is that it seeks to equate the facts of this case with such a case as where a
> motorist has accidentally run over a person and, that action having been completed, fails to assist the
> victim with the intent that the victim should suffer.

Bridge J dissented, holding that:

> after the wheel of the appellant's car had accidentally come to rest on the constable's foot, what was
> it that the appellant *did* which constituted the act of assault? However the question is approached,
> the answer which I feel obliged to give is: precisely nothing. The car rested on the foot by its own
> weight and remained stationary by its own inertia. The appellant's fault was that he omitted to ma-
> nipulate the controls to set it in motion again.

■ *Questions*

1. Was there a 'continuing act' in *Miller* or in *Fagan*?

2. D, a motorist, without fault on his part skids on an oil-covered surface and injures V. D
stops and sees that V is unconscious and bleeding. He could easily drive V to a nearby hospital. He drives off leaving V by the roadside. V bleeds to death. His life could have been saved
had he been driven to the hospital. Is D liable to conviction for (i) manslaughter or (ii) causing
death by dangerous driving according to *Miller*? Should it be different if D injured V by (iii)
careless driving or (iv) dangerous driving?

In *Santana–Bermudez* [2003] EWHC 2908 (Admin) S-B, a drug user, had assured a police officer about to search him that he was carrying no 'sharps'. The officer stabbed her finger on a
syringe needle in his pocket during the search. Applying *Miller*, Maurice Kay J said:

> ... where someone (by act or word or a combination of the two) creates a danger and thereby exposes
> another to a reasonably foreseeable risk of injury which materialises, there is an evidential basis for the
> actus reus of an assault occasioning actual bodily harm. It remains necessary for the prosecution to
> prove an intention to assault or appropriate recklessness.

In *Miller* it was undoubtedly the case that the dangerous situation that arose was solely attributable to D. What would be the position if D was a contributory cause, but not the sole
cause, of the dangerous situation? In *Evans* [2009] EWCA Crim 650 D supplied heroin to
her half-sister, V. Having self-injected the heroin, it became clear that V was suffering from
the symptoms of an overdose. Instead of summoning medical assistance, D stayed with V
through the night in the hope that she would recover. V died. D was found guilty of gross
negligence manslaughter. The Court of Appeal stated that D's duty to summon medical assistance did not arise from her status as V's half-sister, nor from the fact that she supplied V with
the heroin. Rather, the Court of Appeal relied on the principle first propounded in *Miller*

to find that D was under a duty to summon medical assistance and had breached that duty by failing to do so. However, it could be said that these facts are distinguishable from *Miller* on the basis that V also contributed to the creation of a dangerous situation by virtue of her choice to inject the heroin. The Court of Appeal held that:

The duty necessary to found gross negligence manslaughter is plainly not confined to cases of a familial or professional relationship between the defendant and the deceased. In our judgment, consistently with *R v Adomako* [1995] 1 AC 171 and the link between civil and criminal liability for negligence, for the purposes of gross negligence manslaughter, when a person has created or contributed to the creation of a state of affairs which he knows, or ought reasonably to know, has become life threatening, a consequent duty on him to act by taking reasonable steps to save the other's life will normally arise.

It is important to appreciate that the inclusion of the phrase 'or contributes to' arguably represents an extension of the *Miller* principle. What will remain for subsequent courts to decide is how much of a contribution D must make before the duty to act crystallizes.

■ *Questions*

1. Does the *Miller* principle apply in a case in which D has created the dangerous situation as a result of a justifiable act, rather than one of inadvertence? (See *State ex rel Kuntz v Montana Thirteenth District Court* 995 P 2d 951 (Mont, 2000). D stabbed V in self-defence but then failed to call the emergency services).

2. To alter the facts of *Miller* slightly, if X was the night watchman who let Miller sleep in the house could it be said that he has contributed to a dangerous situation and so, post-*Evans*, is under a duty?

4.3.3.5 A general duty of rescue?

Proposals have often been made for the imposition of a general duty, particularly to save others from death or serious injury. A famous early example was the proposal by Edward Livingston for his Draft Code (never enacted) for Louisiana. It was to the effect that a person shall be guilty of homicide who omits to save life which he could save 'without personal danger or pecuniary loss'. This seems at first sight to be an attractive solution to the 'child in the shallow pool' case, that is, when A walks past a child drowning in a shallow pool of water, but decides not to intervene and has not committed any offence. The Law Commissioners who in 1838 reported on the Indian Penal Code thought the proposal open to serious objection (Macaulay, *Works*, vol 7, 494.) If this were the only test of a duty it would certainly be rather inadequate; the common law duty quite properly requires the person owing it to incur 'pecuniary loss'.

A parent may be unable to procure food for an infant without money. Yet the parent, if he has the means, is bound to furnish the infant with food, and if, by omitting to do so, he voluntarily causes its death, he may with propriety be treated as a murderer. (Ibid, 494–495)

As a test for an *additional* duty its defects are less obvious; but it would, apparently, have been unacceptable to the Commissioners. They put the case of a surgeon, the only person in India who could perform a certain operation. If the operation is not performed on a particular patient he will certainly die. The surgeon could perform the operation without personal danger or pecuniary loss—in fact he will be well paid. But, for personal reasons it is extremely inconvenient for him to do so—he wishes to return to Europe or has other plans incompatible with the performance of the operation. The Commissioners thought it self-evident that he should not be guilty of murder. The example is an unusual one, highly unlikely to arise in practice, but not easy to distinguish in principle from the 'shallow pool' case. The difference, if there is one, seems to lie in the immediacy of the impending death in the shallow pool case. If Macaulay's surgeon were to witness an accident and, knowing that he was the only doctor present and that only immediate medical assistance could save an injured man's life, were to pass on because it was inconvenient to stop, it would seem less extravagant to convict him of an offence.

Macaulay excused what he thought might appear to be the excessive leniency of the Commissioners' proposals on the following grounds:

It is, indeed, most highly desirable that men should not merely abstain from doing harm to their neighbours, but should render active services to their neighbours. In general, however, the penal law must content itself with keeping men from doing positive harm, and must leave to public opinion, and to the teachers of morality and religion, the office of furnishing men with motives for doing positive good. It is evident that to attempt to punish men by law for not rendering to others all the service which it is their duty to render to others would be preposterous. We must grant impunity to the vast majority of those omissions which a benevolent morality would pronounce reprehensible, and must content ourselves with punishing such omissions only when they are distinguished from the rest by some circumstances which marks them out as peculiarly fit objects of penal legislation.

Not everyone accepts this point of view. Professor Millner (*Negligence in the Modern Law* (1967), p 33), writing in the context of the civil law of negligence, stated:

There is, however, nothing absolute about this immunity from liability, and no reason why changing attitudes should not bring some of the more callous types of indifference within the reach of the law, at least in cases where inaction amounts to calculated indifference to the fate of others, as in the case where an injured pedestrian is left to lie in the path of oncoming traffic by those who know of his plight and could remedy it; or where a person is allowed, without warning, to cross thin ice or a crumbling bridge by one who is aware that the other, in his innocence is courting disaster; or where a person who, being in a position to take *some* action, yet allows a helpless and solitary invalid to starve to death. It is hard to imagine that anyone would be affronted if the law in such cases were to raise a duty of care in favour of the victim of this kind of callous indifference to the fate of one's fellows.

For a powerful supporting argument for such liability see Ashworth (section 4.2, p 70). There is a wealth of literature on this topic; see especially J. Feinberg, *Harm to Others* (1984), Ch 4. See also M. Menlove, 'The Philosophical Foundations of a Duty to Rescue' and A. McCall Smith, 'The Duty to Rescue and the Common Law' in M. Menlove and A. McCall Smith (eds), *The Duty to Rescue: The Jurisprudence of Aid* (1993).

There is also the option of creating a specific statutory offence of the form found in many jurisdictions which criminalizes the failure to take reasonable steps to rescue. Such statutes do not impose liability for the prohibited harm that V suffers (death or injury, etc), but rather give rise to the appropriately labelled offence of failure to rescue and impose an appropriate punishment. For a valuable review of such offences, see J. T. Pardun, 'Good Samaritan Laws: A Global Perspective' (1998) 20 Loyola LA Int'l and Comparative Law J 591.

4.4 Omissions and causation

Assuming that the offence in question is one which can be interpreted so as to be committed by omission and that there is a relevant category of duty, the question remains: how can D cause any harm by omission? Stephen, in his *Digest of the Criminal Law* (4th edn, 1887), art 212, stated the general rule for offences against the person as follows: 'It is not a crime to cause death or bodily injury, even intentionally, by any omission...'

It will be noted that Stephen does not seem to have doubted that death or bodily injury may be caused by omission. He assumes that these results may be so caused, but denies that it is an offence. He gave the following famous illustration: 'A sees B drowning and is able to save him by holding out his hand. A abstains from doing so in order that B may be drowned, and B is drowned. A has committed no offence.'

Stephen went on to state exceptional cases where A would be guilty of murder—where A is B's parent, for example. If A and a stranger, C, were walking past together it is impossible to say, as a matter of fact, that A has, and that C has not, caused the death of the child, B. Either could have saved him equally easily and each deliberately refrained from doing so. The difference is that, in law, A has a duty to act but C does not.

It has been argued (Brian Hogan, 'Omissions and the Duty Myth' in *Criminal Law Essays*, p 85) that it is not true that results can be 'caused' by omission and that it ought to follow that no one should be liable for a 'result crime' because of a mere omission.

If grandma's skirts are ignited by her careless proximity to the gas oven, the delinquent grandson cannot be said to have killed her by his failure to dowse her. No sensible doctor would enter as the cause of her death, say, failure to telephone the fire brigade.... [Professor Hogan continues:]

If any proposition is self-evident (and, arguably, none is) it is that a person cannot be held to have caused an event which he did not cause. Hence my delinquent child cannot sensibly be said to have caused the death of his grandmother simply by a failure to take steps (which may or may not have been successful anyway) to prevent that death. To say to the child, 'You have killed your grandmother' would simply be untrue.

This is not to say that I am against liability for omissions. There would be nothing in principle objectionable in Parliament enacting a law which made it an offence for a member of a household to fail to take steps reasonably available to him to prevent or minimize harm to other members of the household. There are of course numerous instances where Parliament (and a handful where the common law) has penalised omissions but what is noteworthy is that the defendant is penalised for the omission but not visited with liability for the consequences of that omission....

So in no sense am I against liability for omission. I would ask only two conditions of a law punishing omissions. One is that it be clearly articulated and the other is that it seeks to punish the defendant for his dereliction and does not artificially treat him as a cause of the event he has not brought about by his conduct....

Thus far I have discussed cases where by no stretch of the imagination can it be said that the defendant has caused a result by his inaction. The question then arises whether a result may ever be caused by inaction. My answer is: No. On the other hand a result may be caused by the defendant's *conduct* and the totality of the defendant's conduct causing a result may properly include what he has not done as well as done. In such cases I doubt whether it is very, or at all, helpful to analyze each phase of the defendant's conduct as one of omission or commission. The question is simply: did the defendant's *conduct* cause the result?

Take a simple example. X, driving his car, sees Y beginning to cross the road ahead. X realizes that unless he takes some action, such as removing his foot from the accelerator to the brake or turning to left or right, he will run down Y. In fact he takes no action whatsoever and runs down Y. Charged with an offence in relation to the harm done to Y, X would surely be laughed out of court if he said: I did not do anything to cause harm to Y. We would not have the slightest difficulty in saying that X ran down Y and was the cause of the harm to Y. *R v Miller* [section 4.3.3.4, p 86] holds, and with respect rightly, that one who inadvertently (or otherwise faultlessly, presumably) starts a chain of events causing harm may be properly held liable if, having become aware that he was the cause, he fails to take steps reasonably available to him to prevent or minimize the damage that will ensue. A fortiori the driver X. There is nothing inadvertent about his causing of harm to Y. X chooses to stay with a course of conduct which he knows will cause harm to Y.

Compare the views of A. Leavens, 'A Causation Approach to Criminal Omissions' (1888) 76 Cal LR 547.

Such a view of causation is flawed because its inquiry is too limited. It depends on a definition of the status quo as the existing physical state of affairs at the precise time of the omission . . . Our everyday notions of causation, however, are not so limited because we understand that the status quo encompasses more than the physical state of affairs at a given time. Indeed, in everyday usage the status quo is taken to include expected patterns of conduct, including actions designed to avert certain unwanted results. When, for example, a driver parks a car on a steep hill, it is normal to set the parking brake and put the car in gear. If the driver forgets to do so and the car subsequently rolls down the hill, smashing into another car, we would say that the failure to park properly was a departure from the status quo. This failure, not the visibly steep hill or the predicate act of pulling the car to the curb, was the cause of the collision. Once we realize that a particular undesirable state of affairs can be avoided by taking certain precautions, we usually incorporate these precautions into what we see as the normal or at rest state of affairs. A failure to engage in the preventative conduct in these cases can thus be seen as an intervention that disturbs the status quo. When such a failure to act is a necessary condition (a 'but for' cause) of a particular harm, then that failure fairly can be said to cause that harm. In the above example, the driver's failure to park the car in a proper manner caused the accident as surely as if he had actually driven his car into the other . . .

■ **Question**

Does D kill his grandmother by failing to put out her blazing skirt?

In *Morby* (1882) 15 Cox CC 35 D was convicted of manslaughter of his son, a child under the age of 14. D knew that the child was suffering from smallpox. D did not summon a doctor because he was one of the 'Peculiar People' who did not believe in medical aid but trusted in prayer and anointment. The child died of smallpox. In the Court for Crown Cases Reserved (Lord Coleridge CJ, Grove, Stephen, Mathew and Cave JJ) D's counsel admitted that he could not contend that D was not guilty of breach of a statutory duty but argued that death was not caused by breach of that duty. Lord Coleridge CJ said:

We are all clearly of opinion that the conviction cannot be supported. The jury may have thought that, as there had been a neglect of his duty by the parent, it was right to mark their sense of it by their verdict. Nothing could be more cautious than the answers given by the medical witness to the questions put to him. It was not enough to sustain the charge of manslaughter to show that the parent had neglected to use all reasonable means of saving the life of his child; it was necessary to show that what the parent neglected to do had the effect of shortening the child's life. The utmost that the doctor would say, giving his evidence under a strong responsibility, in answer to the question, 'In your judgment, if medical advice and assistance had been called in at any stage of this disease, might the death have been averted altogether?' was, 'I cannot say that death would probably have been averted. I think it probable that life might have been prolonged. I can only say probably might, because I did not see the case during life; had I done so I might have been able to answer the question.' That evidence is far too vague to allow this conviction to stand when all that the skilled witness could say was that probably the life of the boy might have been prolonged if medical assistance had been called in.

■ *Questions*

1. Was the court in *Morby* right? If so, is this an answer to cases like Hogan's example of the
incinerated granny? The steps omitted 'may not have been successful anyway'—proof that
they would have been successful would rarely, if ever, be possible. But what if the child, observing that granny's skirt was beginning to scorch had deliberately refrained from telling
her, in the expectation—or even the hope—that it would burst into flames? *But for* the child's
omission to warn, Granny's life *would* have been saved. Is it then unreasonable to say that the
child caused her death?

2. V has a heart attack and reaches for the pills which would save his life. (i) D, a stranger,
pushes the bottle out of his reach. (ii) The bottle is just out of V's reach. D could easily give it
to him but does nothing. In both cases D wants V to die and V in fact dies. In (i) D is guilty of
murder. In (ii) he apparently commits no offence. Are the cases morally distinguishable? Is
one more deserving of punishment than the other? Should the law distinguish between them?
Can D be said to have *caused* death in (i) but not in (ii)?

R v Gibbins and Proctor
(1918) 13 Cr App R 134, Court of Criminal Appeal

(Darling, McCardie and Salter JJ)

Walter Gibbins and Edith Proctor were living together with Gibbins' daughter, Nelly, aged 7,
and other children. The children were healthy except for Nelly, who was kept upstairs apart
from the others and was starved to death. There was evidence that Proctor hated Nelly and
cursed and hit her, from which the jury could infer that she had a very strong interest in
Nelly's death. Gibbins was in regular employment, earning good wages, all of which he gave to
Proctor. According to Gibbins's counsel, it was his duty to provide the money; it was Proctor's
to provide the food. When Nelly died, Proctor told Gibbins to bury her out of sight which he
did, in the brickyard where he worked. Gibbins and Proctor were tried together and convicted
of murder of Nelly. They appealed, *inter alia*, on the ground of misdirection.

[Darling J delivering the judgment of the court:]

. . . the misdirection here complained of is on a crucial matter, where [the judge] told the jury what they
must find in order to convict either prisoner of murder. He said, 'The charge against the prisoners is,
in the first place, that they killed this child Nelly, or caused her death, by malice aforethought. That
means they intended she should die and acted so as to produce that result.' If that is a misdirection
it is one in favour of the prisoners . . . 'If you think that one or other of those prisoners wilfully and
intentionally withheld food from that child so as to cause her to weaken and to cause her grievous
bodily injury, as the result of which she died, it is not necessary for you to find that she intended or he
intended to kill the child then and there. It is enough if you find that he or she intended to set up such
a set of facts by withholding food or anything as would in the ordinary course of nature lead gradually
but surely to her death.' In our opinion that direction amply fulfils the conditions which a judge should
observe in directing the jury in such a case as this. . . .

'If the omission to provide necessary food or raiment was accompanied with an intention to cause
the death of the child, or to cause some serious bodily injury to it, then it would be malicious in the
sense imputed by this indictment, and in a case of this kind it is difficult, if not impossible, to understand
how a person who contemplated doing serious bodily injury to the child by the deprivation of food,
could have meditated anything else than causing its death.' The word used is 'contemplated', but what
has to be proved is an intention to do grievous bodily injury. In our opinion the judge left the question
correctly to the jury, and there is no ground for interfering with the convictions for those reasons.

It has been said that there ought not to have been a finding of guilty of murder against Gibbins. The court agrees that the evidence was less against Gibbins than Proctor, Gibbins gave her money, and as far as we can see it was sufficient to provide for the wants of themselves and all the children. But he lived in the house and the child was his own, a little girl of seven, and he grossly neglected the child. He must have known what her condition was if he saw her, for she was little more than a skeleton. He is in this dilemma; if he did not see her the jury might well infer that he did not care if she died; if he did he must have known what was going on. The question is whether there was evidence that he so conducted himself as to shew that he desired that grievous bodily injury should be done to the child. He cannot pretend that he shewed any solicitude for her. He knew that Proctor hated her, knew that she was ill and that no doctor had been called in, and the jury may have come to the conclusion that he was so infatuated with Proctor, and so afraid of offending her, that he preferred that the child should starve to death rather than that he should be exposed to any injury or unpleasantness from Proctor. It is unnecessary to say more than that there was evidence that Gibbins did desire that grievous bodily harm should be done to the child; he did not interfere in what was being done, and he comes within the definition which I have read, and is therefore guilty of murder.

The case of Proctor is plainer. She had charge of the child. She was under no obligation to do so or to live with Gibbins, but she did so, and receiving money, as it is admitted she did, for the purpose of supplying food, her duty was to see that the child was properly fed and looked after, and to see that she had medical attention if necessary. We agree with what Lord Coleridge CJ said in *Instan* [1893] 1 QB 450: 'There is no case directly in point, but it would be a slur upon, and a discredit to the administration of, justice in this country if there were any doubt as to the legal principle, or as to the present case being within it. The prisoner was under a moral obligation to the deceased from which arose a legal duty towards her; that legal duty the prisoner has wilfully and deliberately left unperformed, with the consequence that there has been an acceleration of the death of the deceased owing to the non-performance of that legal duty.' Here Proctor took upon herself the moral obligation of looking after the children; she was *de facto*, though not *de jure*, the wife of Gibbins and had excluded the child's own mother. She neglected the child undoubtedly, and the evidence shews that as a result the child died . . .

Appeals dismissed

■ *Questions*

1. Was Gibbins held liable for an omission upon an omission—that is, because he failed to interfere to prevent Proctor's failure to feed Nelly?

2. Proctor was not related, in blood or in law, to Nelly. Why was she under a duty to feed Nelly?

3. Can it be seriously argued (cf earlier in this section, p 92) in such a case as this that death is not *caused* by an omission? Or might the case be put on the ground that preventing Nelly from having access to the food which was sufficient to keep the other children in good health was not a mere omission but a continuing act or series of acts?

4. Does it follow from the decision that, if Nelly had not died but had sustained grievous bodily harm, the appellants would have been guilty of causing GBH with intent contrary to s 18 of the Offences Against the Person Act 1861?

In *A (children) (conjoined twins: surgical separation)* [2001] Fam 147, [2000] 4 All ER 961, section 4.3.1.1, p 80, Mary's heart and lungs were too deficient to keep her alive. She lived only because Jodie was able to circulate sufficient oxygenated blood for both of them. The evidence was that, if they were not separated, both would die. Separation would kill Mary but give Jodie a good chance of a normal life. The parents refused their consent to the operation on religious grounds.

Ward LJ: I know there is a huge chasm in turpitude between these stricken parents and the wretched parents in *R v Gibbins* (1918) 13 Cr App R 134 who starved their child to death. Nevertheless I am bound to wonder whether there is strictly any difference in the application of the principle. They know they can save her. They appreciate she will die if not separated from her twin. Is there any defence to a charge of cruelty under s 1 of the Children and Young Persons Act 1933 in the light of the clarification of the law given by *R v Sheppard* [1980] 3 All ER 889, [1981] AC 394 which in turn throws doubt on the correctness of *Oakey v Jackson* [1914] 1 KB 216? Would it not be manslaughter if Jodie died through that neglect? I ask these insensitive questions not to heap blame on the parents. No prosecutor would dream of prosecuting. The sole purpose of the inquiry is to establish whether either or both parents and doctors have come under a legal duty to Jodie, as I conclude they each have, to procure and to carry out the operation which will save her life. If so then performance of their duty to Jodie is irreconcilable with the performance of their duty to Mary. Certainly it seems to me that if this court were to give permission for the operation to take place, then a legal duty would be imposed on the doctors to treat their patient in her best interests, ie to operate upon her. Failure to do so is a breach of their duty. To omit to act when under a duty to do so may be a culpable omission. Death to Jodie is virtually certain to follow (barring some unforeseen intervention). Why is that not killing Jodie?

■ *Question*

If the parents had prevented the operation by abducting the twins and both had died, would this have been murder or manslaughter of both twins, or only of Jodie, or of neither?

FURTHER READING

L. Alexander, 'Criminal Liability for Omissions: An Inventory of Issues' in S. Shute and A. Simester (eds), *Criminal Law Theory: Doctrines of the General Part* (2002)

A. Ashworth, *Positive Obligations in Criminal Law* (2013)

P. Glazebrook, 'Criminal Omissions: The Duty Requirements in Offences Against the Person' (1960) 76 LQR 386

J. Glover, 'Not Striving to Keep Alive' in J. Glover, *Causing Death and Saving Lives* (1977)

B. Hogan, 'Omissions and the Duty Myth' in P. F. Smith (ed), *Criminal Law: Essays in Honour of J. C. Smith* (1987)

G. Hughes, 'Criminal Omissions' (1958) 67 Yale LJ 590

I. Kennedy, 'Switching Off Life Support Machines: The Legal Implications' [1977] Crim LR 443

J. Keown, 'Beyond *Bland*: A Critique of the BMA Guidance on Withholding and Withdrawing Medical Treatment' (2000) 20 LS 66

A. Simester, 'Why Omissions are Special' (1995) 1 Legal Theory 311

J. C. Smith, 'Liability for Omissions in Criminal Law' (1984) 4 LS 88

5
Fault

5.1 Introduction

There are some offences, not always minor ones, called 'offences of strict liability', where a person may be convicted although he was not at fault. Generally, however, the law requires proof of fault of some kind. Offences of strict liability are considered in Chapter 7. We saw at the outset in Chapter 2 that crime generally involves a mental element (mens rea). In offences which require proof of a result which is forbidden by the criminal law, the 'fault' or mens rea is usually the state of mind the defendant had about whether that *result* would be caused. Some offences may require proof of some proscribed *circumstance*, and the mens rea or fault is usually the state of mind the defendant had about whether that circumstance exists at the time (as with rape where D's conduct must occur in circumstances where V is not consenting and D has no reasonable belief that V is consenting).

In the present chapter we consider the different types of fault which the criminal law requires. When examining an unfamiliar offence these are usually relatively easy to identify as the same forms of mens rea are routinely included by Parliament in offences: intention, knowledge, belief, recklessness, etc. Historically Parliament used other terms such as maliciously, wilfully, etc. Although arcane sounding, they are also easy to identify when looking at the offence.

There are degrees of fault. The most blameworthy mental element is an *intention* to bring about the forbidden result or *knowledge* that a circumstance exists. Also blameworthy, but less so, is *recklessness* whether a result be caused or a circumstance exists. So, intentional killing is murder and reckless killing is manslaughter. 'Intentionally' and 'recklessly' are ordinary words of the English language but experience shows that they are capable of different meanings. The ordinary people who sit on juries, as well as philosophers, may well differ as to whether a particular state of mind constitutes intention, or recklessness, or neither of these. Many of the most important and difficult cases in recent years have been concerned with the meaning of these terms.

Sometimes the fault which must be proved is not intention or recklessness but guilty knowledge of some sort. For example, when a person is found in possession of stolen goods, say a car, he commits a crime only if he knew or believed that the car was stolen. If he bought it in perfect good faith, it is his misfortune, not his fault. He may be guilty of the tort of conversion because the car still belongs to its original owner. The tort requires no fault. He may have to return the car or account to the owner for its value and may have lost the price he paid. But the innocent buyer of stolen goods commits no crime. If, however, he knew or believed the car was stolen when he bought it, he is guilty of the crime of handling stolen goods.

What matters is whether the fault that is specified in the offence is proved. It is not a question of whether D was morally blameworthy but whether he had intention, knowledge or recklessness etc as the offence requires.

Fault is not limited to states of mind. A person who did not foresee a harmful result of his conduct obviously did not intend it but it may be that he *ought* to have foreseen the risk of causing it and avoided doing so, as a reasonably prudent person would. For some crimes, this is sufficient fault. The prosecution have to prove only that the defendant did not behave in the way a reasonable person would and, in the case of a result crime, thereby caused the proscribed result. This is negligence. There may be degrees of negligence. Any deviation from the standard of care to be expected of a reasonable person is sufficient for civil liability in the tort of negligence; but if the criminal law imposes liability for negligence, it sometimes requires 'gross' negligence—a very serious deviation from the required standard.

Some of the controversies that will be explored in this chapter include the following:

(i)   How intention is defined and in particular:

   • how judges ought to direct juries in instances when it was not D's purpose to cause the prohibited outcome;

   • the extent to which it can be said that 'oblique' intention is a form of intention at all;

   • precisely when a jury is entitled to find intention when D foresaw an outcome as virtually certain and whether it is obligated to do so.

(ii) How recklessness should be defined and in particular:

   • whether recklessness ought to be a subjective or an objective concept;

   • whether there should there be a different conception of recklessness that is dependent upon whether the offence in question is a result or conduct crime.

(iii) The appropriateness of criminalizing instances of negligence.

(iv) Whether an individual ought to be criminalized for being distracted as opposed to forgetful and vice versa.

5.2 Intention

The word 'intention' and the phrase 'with intent to' are commonly found in the definition of offences. It is important to appreciate at the outset that if a bodily movement is voluntary, it could then be said that it is intended. The concern of this chapter is whether D intended the *consequences* of a particular act. Taking criminal damage as an example, it is necessary for D's conduct to have caused damage and for D to have done so intentionally or recklessly. As with many crimes there is also a mens rea requirement as to the circumstances: in criminal damage the property damaged must belong to another and D must have intended or been reckless as to whether it did.

A number of problems arise in the application of intention, in particular: (i) how is it to be defined; (ii) can D be held to have intended result A when he sought only to achieve result B (which would almost inevitably result also in A)?

The current state of the law is:

(1)   a result is intended when it is the actor's purpose to cause it;

(2)   a court or jury *may also find* that a result is intended, though it is not the actor's purpose to cause it, when:

   (a) the result is a virtually certain consequence of that act, and

   (b) the actor knows that it is a virtually certain consequence.

There has been much controversy as to the proper legal meaning of intention. A variety of possible interpretations are possible. One of the reasons that there is still so much controversy is because the definition is central to serious offences such as murder. The courts struggle to define the boundaries of what they want that offence to include.

Two core definitions are debated. We could accept that D 'intends' a result only if:

the proscribed result is the 'purpose' or 'aim', that is, a *direct intention* of the accused;

or, in addition,

the proscribed result is foreseen by the accused as 'virtually certain' to occur or even just 'highly probable' to occur. This is called *oblique intention.*

With direct intention the focus is on D's purpose, not his desire or wish as to the consequences. D can intend by having a result as his purpose without desiring it, as where D gives V a lethal injection to put him out of his pain, but wishes he did not have to. Note also that the definition of intention is wider than 'premeditation' where that term is used to denote planning or calculated acts. Intention extends beyond those cases to include spontaneous conduct. A good way of deciding whether D had direct intention might be to ask whether D acted in order to bring about the result.

With oblique intent, the idea is that a result is intended where it is not D's *purpose* but is foreseen by him as a *probable* result of his act. This raises several problems: should it be sufficient that D foresees the result as probable? How probable must it be?

A majority of the House of Lords in *Hyam v DPP* [1975] AC 55, section 15.3.3, p 535, appeared to accept that it was sufficient to convict someone of murder (which requires proof of intent to kill or cause serious harm), if D saw either of those results as 'probable'.

In *Hyam*, D had poured petrol through her rival's letterbox in an effort to get her to leave the area so that D would have the undivided attentions of her lover. D claimed that she thought that the house was empty. It was not and children inside died. The mens rea for murder is 'malice aforethought'. At the trial Ackner J directed the jury that a person has the mens rea of murder if, when he does the act which kills, he knows that it is highly probable that he will cause death or grievous bodily harm. His direction was held by the majority of the House of Lords to be correct as a definition of the mens rea for murder. However, the House did not provide a definition of intention. The speeches of the House of Lords are confusing. Lord Hailsham, one of the majority, emphatically said that this definition of the mens rea for murder was not the test of intention. Viscount Dilhorne and Lord Cross, though disposed to think that it did amount to intention, decided only that it was a sufficient mens rea for murder. The minority thought that mens rea for murder should extend to cases where D saw it as probable that he would cause death (but not where he saw only serious harm as probable). Lord Diplock (one of the minority), however, took a view of the *ratio decidendi* different from that stated above because he said in *Whitehouse; Lemon* [1979] AC 617 at 638:

What *R v Hyam* [*Hyam v DPP*] [1975] AC 55 confirmed is that the legal definition of intention includes two states of mind (1) where D did an act because he desired it to produce that particular result and (2) D who, when he did the act, was aware that it was likely to produce that result but was prepared to take the risk that it might do so, in order to achieve some other purpose which provided his motive for doing what he did.

In the next case, *Moloney*, the House began with the assumption that the mens rea of murder is an intention to kill or to cause grievous bodily harm. Consequently, the question in issue *was* the meaning of intention. The House of Lords held that the 'golden rule' is that the judge should avoid any elaboration on what is meant by intention, instead leaving the interpretation to the jury's good sense. The House of Lords was also keen to distinguish between the

definition of intention as a matter of substantive criminal law and the evidence of such intention, which is a matter of proof. The court considered previous case law and the impact of s 8
of the Criminal Justice Act 1967:

A court or jury, in determining whether a person has committed an offence,—(a) shall not be bound
in law to infer that he intended or foresaw a result of his actions by reasons only of its being a natural
and probable consequence of those actions; but (b) shall decide whether he did intend or foresee that
result by reference to all the evidence, drawing such inferences from the evidence as appear proper in
the circumstances.

R v Moloney

[1984] UKHL 4, House of Lords, http://www.bailii.org/uk/cases/UKHL/1984/4.html

(Lord Hailsham LC, Lords Fraser, Edmund-Davies, Keith and Bridge)

The appellant (M) and his stepfather (S) drank heavily at a wedding anniversary party.
After the rest of the family had gone to bed, M and S remained and were heard laughing
and talking in an apparently friendly way until nearly 4 am when a shot rang out. M tel-
ephoned the police, saying, 'I've just murdered my father.' He stated that they had had a
disagreement as to who was quicker at loading and firing a shotgun. At S's request he got
two shotguns and cartridges. M was first to load. S said 'I didn't think you'd got the guts,
but if you have pull the trigger.' M stated 'I didn't aim the gun. I just pulled the trigger and
he was dead.'

M was convicted of murder and his appeal was dismissed by the Court of Appeal. He
appealed to the House of Lords.

Lord Hailsham LC and Lords Fraser, Edmund-Davies and Keith said that they agreed with
the speech of Lord Bridge.

[Lord Bridge, having held that the direction given by the trial judge, Stephen Brown J, was unsatisfactory and potentially misleading, continued:]

The golden rule should be that, when directing a jury on the mental element necessary in a crime of
specific intent, the judge should avoid any elaboration or paraphrase of what is meant by intent, and
leave it to the jury's good sense to decide whether the accused acted with the necessary intent, unless
the judge is convinced that, on the facts and having regard to the way the case has been presented
to the jury in evidence and argument, some further explanation or elaboration is strictly necessary
to avoid misunderstanding. In trials for murder or wounding with intent, I find it very difficult to visualise a case where any such explanation or elaboration could be required, if the offence consisted of a
direct attack on the victim with a weapon, except possibly the case where the accused shot at A and
killed B, which any first year law student could explain to a jury in the simplest of terms. Even where
the death results indirectly from the act of the accused, I believe the cases that will call for a direction
by reference to foresight of consequences will be of extremely rare occurrence. I am in full agreement
with the view expressed by Viscount Dilhorne that, in [*Hyam v DPP*] [1975] AC 55, 82 itself, if the issue
of intent had been left without elaboration, no reasonable jury could have failed to convict.

I do not, of course, by what I have said in the foregoing paragraph, mean to question the necessity,
which frequently arises, to explain to a jury that intention is something quite distinct from motive or
desire. But this can normally be quite simply explained by reference to the case before the court or, if
necessary, by some homely example. A man who, at London airport, boards a plane which he knows
to be bound for Manchester, clearly intends to travel to Manchester, even though Manchester is the
last place he wants to be and his motive for boarding the plane is simply to escape pursuit. The possibility that the plane may have engine trouble and be diverted to Luton does not affect the matter. By

boarding the Manchester plane, the man conclusively demonstrates his intention to go there, because it is a moral certainty that that is where he will arrive . . .

[Rejecting the suggestion in *DPP v Smith* that the Act, to amount to murder, must be 'aimed at' someone, Lord Bridge continued:]

But what of the terrorist who plants a time bomb in a public building and gives timely warning to enable the public to be evacuated? Assume that he knows that, following evacuation, it is virtually certain that a bomb disposal squad will attempt to defuse the bomb. In the event the bomb explodes and kills a bomb disposal expert. In our present troubled times, this is an all too tragically realistic illustration. Can it, however, be said that in this case the bomb was 'aimed' at the bomb disposal expert? . . .

Starting from the proposition established by *R v Vickers* [1957] 2 All ER 741, [1957] 2 QB 664, as modified by *DPP v Smith* [1961] AC 290 that the mental element in murder requires proof of an intention to kill or cause really serious injury, the first fundamental question to be answered is whether there is any rule of substantive law that foresight by the accused of one of those eventualities as a probable consequence of his voluntary act, where the probability can be defined as exceeding a certain degree, is equivalent or alternative to the necessary intention. I would answer this question in the negative. . . .

I am firmly of opinion [*sic*] that foresight of consequences, as an element bearing on the issue of intention in murder, or indeed any other crime of specific intent, belongs, not to the substantive law, but to the law of evidence. Here again I am happy to find myself aligned with my noble and learned friend, Lord Hailsham of St Marylebone LC, in [*Hyam v DPP*] [1974] 2 All ER 41, [1975] AC 55, where he said, at p 65: 'Knowledge or foresight is at the best material which entitles or compels a jury to draw the necessary inference as to intention.' A rule of evidence which judges for more than a century found of the utmost utility in directing juries was expressed in the maxim: 'A man is presumed to intend the natural and probable consequences of his acts.' In *DPP v Smith* [1961] AC 290 your Lordships' House, by treating this rule of evidence as creating an irrebuttable presumption and thus elevating it, in effect, to the status of a rule of substantive law, predictably provoked the intervention of Parliament by section 8 of the Criminal Justice Act 1967 [this is set out earlier.] to put the issue of intention back where it belonged, viz, in the hands of the jury, 'drawing such inferences from the evidence as appear proper in the circumstances.' I do not by any means take the conjunction of the verbs 'intended or foresaw' and 'intend or foresee' in that section as an indication that Parliament treated them as synonymous; on the contrary, two verbs were needed to connote two different states of mind.

I think we should now no longer speak of presumptions in this context but rather of inferences. In the old presumption that a man intends the natural and probable consequences of his acts the important word is 'natural'. This word conveys the idea that in the ordinary course of events a certain act will lead to a certain consequence unless something unexpected supervenes to prevent it. One might almost say that, if a consequence is natural, it is really otiose to speak of it as also being probable.

Section 8 of the Criminal Justice Act 1967 leaves us at liberty to go back to the decisions before that of this House in *DPP v Smith* [1961] AC 290 and it is here, I believe, that we can find a sure, clear, intelligible and simple guide to the kind of direction that should be given to a jury in the exceptional case where it is necessary to give guidance as to how, on the evidence, they should approach the issue of intent.

I know of no clearer exposition of the law than that in the judgment of the Court of Criminal Appeal (Lord Goddard CJ, Atkinson and Cassels JJ) delivered by Lord Goddard CJ in *R v Steane* [1947] KB 997 where he said, at p 1004:

> 'No doubt, if the prosecution prove an act the natural consequence of which would be a certain result and no evidence or explanation is given, then a jury may, on a proper direction, find that the prisoner is guilty of doing the act with the intent alleged, but if on the totality of the evidence there is room for more than one view as to the intent of the prisoner, the jury should be directed that it is for the prosecution to prove the intent to the jury's satisfaction, and if, on a review of the whole evidence, they either think that the intent did not exist or they are left in doubt as to the intent, the prisoner is entitled to be acquitted.'

In the rare cases in which it is necessary to direct a jury by reference to foresight of consequences, I do not believe it is necessary for the judge to do more than invite the jury to consider two questions. First, was death or really serious injury in a murder case (or whatever relevant consequence must be proved to have been intended in any other case) a natural consequence of the defendant's voluntary act? Secondly, did the defendant foresee that consequence as being a natural consequence of his act? The jury should then be told that if they answer yes to both questions it is a proper inference for them to draw that he intended that consequence.

Appeal allowed

■ *Questions*

1. Professor Duff has suggested that a way of testing whether D intended the outcome is to ask: would he regard himself as having failed if he did not achieve the result that he is alleged to have intended (eg death or GBH in murder)? Would that test produce results which accord with the court's decisions in any of the cases? (R. A. Duff, *Intention, Agency and Criminal Liability* (1990), p 61.)

2. Did the House of Lords provide a definition of intention? What is it? Did the House of Lords conclude that D could be said to have intended result A when he was aiming to achieve result B? If so, what state of mind must D have towards result A occurring in order to have intended it?

3. Is Lord Bridge correct that the individual at London airport who boards the plane for Manchester intends to travel to Manchester even though it might be the last place he wants to be? Does the example elucidate the meaning of intention? Consider this question in light of the following extract.

R. Buxton, 'Some Simple Thoughts on Intention'
[1988] Crim LR 484

This example has attracted a good deal of criticism: the traveller can be said to desire to travel to Manchester (in order to escape his pursuers) just as much as to intend to travel there; the traveller wanted in one sense to go to Manchester rather than remain where he was; the traveller may, consistently with Lord Bridge's account, simply have boarded the first available plane, which raises difficulties about saying that he intended to travel to *Manchester.* The first two of these complaints may turn principally on the shifting meaning of the words 'desire' and 'want,' to which we have drawn attention above; but the real trouble about the example ... is that, because it does not deal with any specifically criminal conduct, it does not focus on any defined consequence of the agent's actions as the subject of the description of his mental attitude.

  Where the same events can be categorised under a series of equally valid descriptions (taking a flight; travelling to Manchester; escaping pursuit) the layman's difficulty, raised by Lord Bridge's example, of deciding which of those descriptions relates to the agent's intention and which to his motive is solved for the criminal lawyer by the definition of the crime with which the agent is charged. If, as Dr. Williams suggests [at [1987] CLJ 433] in this context, one were dealing with an offence of taking a plane ticket with intent to travel to Manchester, it would be clear that the question was whether the agent's intention (purpose) in buying the ticket was to travel to Manchester, and equally clear that it would be no defence to such a charge that his reason or motive for that travel was to escape pursuit. But that, in itself, tells us nothing about the difference between intention and desire. What does illuminate that difference is the fact that intention in the law is confined to cases of the production by the agent of consequences specified in the definition of the crime with which he is charged, to which event or activity the language of purpose is appropriate but the language of desire may not be.

5.2.1 The extended definition of intention

Moloney tells us that in most cases the jury will need no explanation of 'intention'. However, in some cases an explanation will be needed and it is important that the law can provide a clear definition of what constitutes intention for those hard cases. We can now turn to consider the extended meaning of intention.

A result which is desired is intended, even though the actor knows that the chances of achieving it are remote. Because D *wants* to kill V, he takes great care in aiming a gun at him and pulling the trigger; but V is half a mile away and he knows his chances of hitting him are remote. Surely, he intends to kill V.

A result which is known to be an inevitable concomitant of the desired result must also be intended. A much used illustration is that of D who plants a bomb in a plane, timed to explode in mid-Atlantic and destroy the cargo in order to enable him to obtain the insurance money. D wishes the crew no ill—he would be delighted if they should, by some miracle, escape—but he knows that, if his plan succeeds, their deaths are, for all practical purposes, inevitable. It is generally agreed that D intends to kill the crew. Suppose, however, that D knows that this particular type of bomb has a 50 per cent failure rate. There is an even chance that the bomb will not go off. He still intends to destroy the cargo because that is his purpose. Does it not follow that he also intends to kill the crew? This is neither a certain result nor a desired result but it appears to be enough that it is the inevitable concomitant of a desired result. Lord Bridge's terrorist of course wants the bomb to go off. If he wants it to go off at a time when he knows the bomb squad will be attempting to defuse it the case is indistinguishable from that of the bomb in the plane; but if he is merely indifferent as to whether the squad will be working on the bomb at the time, it is difficult to see that he intends to kill or injure them.

The next House of Lords' case in the unravelling saga of the meaning of intention sought to qualify and clarify what was said in *Moloney* about the extended definition of intention.

R v Hancock and Shankland
[1985] UKHL 9, House of Lords, http://www.bailii.org/uk/cases/UKHL/1985/9.html

(Lords Scarman, Keith of Kinkel, Roskill, Brightman and Griffiths)

Hancock (H) and Shankland (S) were miners on strike from work as part of a national strike of miners which led to numerous incidents of serious violence. They objected to a miner (X) going to work. X was going to work in a taxi driven by the deceased, Wilkie (W). H and S pushed a concrete block weighing 46 lbs and a concrete post weighing 65 lbs from a bridge over the road along which X was being driven by W with a police escort. The block struck the taxi's windscreen and killed W. H and S were prepared to plead guilty to manslaughter but the Crown decided to pursue the charge of murder. The defence was that H and S intended to block the road but not to kill or do serious bodily harm to anyone. Mann J directed the jury in accordance with the *Moloney* 'guidelines' (see section 5.2, p 102).

H and S were convicted of murder. The Court of Appeal quashed their conviction. The Crown appealed to the House of Lords.

Lord Scarman [having reviewed *Moloney*:]

It is only when Lord Bridge of Harwich turned to the task of formulating guidelines that difficulty arises. It is said by the Court of Appeal that the guidelines by omitting any express reference to probability are ambiguous and may well lead a jury to a wrong conclusion. The omission was deliberate. Lord Bridge omitted the adjective 'probable' from the time-honoured formula 'foresight of the natural and probable consequences of his acts' because he thought that 'If a consequence is natural, it is really otiose to speak of it as also being probable' [1985] AC 905, 929B. But is it?

Lord Bridge of Harwich did not deny the importance of probability. He put it thus, p 925H:

'But looking on their facts at the decided cases where a crime of specific intent was under consideration, including *Hyam v DPP* [1974] 2 All ER 41, [1975] AC 55 itself, they suggest to me that the probability of the consequence taken to have been foreseen must be little short of overwhelming before it will suffice to establish the necessary intent.'

In his discussion of the relationship between foresight and intention, Lord Bridge of Harwich reviewed the case law since the passing of the Homicide Act 1957 and concluded at p 928F that 'foresight of consequences, as an element bearing on the issue of intention in murder, or indeed any other crime of specific intent, belongs, not to the substantive law, but to the law of evidence.'

He referred to the rule of evidence that a man is presumed to intend the natural and probable consequences of his acts, and went on to observe that the House of Lords in *Smith's* case [1960] 3 All ER 161, [1961] AC 290 had treated the presumption as irrebuttable, but that Parliament intervened by section 8 of the Criminal Justice Act 1967 to return the law to the path from which it had been diverted, leaving the presumption as no more than an inference open to the jury to draw if in all the circumstances it appears to them proper to draw it.

Yet he omitted any reference in his guidelines to probability. He did so because he included probability in the meaning which he attributed to 'natural'. My Lords, I very much doubt whether a jury without further explanation would think that 'probable' added nothing to 'natural'. I agree with the Court of Appeal that the probability of a consequence is a factor of sufficient importance to be drawn specifically to the attention of the jury and to be explained. In a murder case where it is necessary to direct a jury on the issue of intent by reference to foresight of consequences the probability of death or serious injury resulting from the act done may be critically important. Its importance will depend on the degree of probability: if the likelihood that death or serious injury will result is high, the probability of that result may, as Lord Bridge of Harwich noted and the Lord Chief Justice emphasised, be seen as overwhelming evidence of the existence of the intent to kill or injure. Failure to explain the relevance of probability may, therefore, mislead a jury into thinking that it is of little or no importance and into concentrating exclusively on the causal link between the act and its consequence. In framing his guidelines Lord Bridge of Harwich emphasised [1985] AC 905, 929G, that he did not believe it necessary to do more than to invite the jury to consider his two questions. Neither question makes any reference (beyond the use of the word 'natural') to probability. I am not surprised that when in this case the judge faithfully followed this guidance the jury found themselves perplexed and unsure. In my judgment, therefore, the *Moloney* guidelines as they stand are unsafe and misleading. They require a reference to probability. They also require an explanation that the greater the probability of a consequence the more likely it is that the consequence was foreseen and that if that consequence was foreseen the greater the probability is that that consequence was also intended. But juries also require to be reminded that the decision is theirs to be reached upon a consideration of all the evidence.

Accordingly, I accept the view of the Court of Appeal that the *Moloney* guidelines are defective. I am, however, not persuaded that guidelines of general application, albeit within a limited class of case, are wise or desirable.

[Lords Keith, Roskill, Brightman and Griffiths agreed.]

Appeal dismissed

■ *Questions*

How probable must the result be before D can be said to have intended it? Does it matter whether the result was probable or whether D just thought it was probable?

The next decisive step in the interpretation of the concept followed swiftly from the Court of Appeal as the Lord Chief Justice sought to clarify the meaning of intention for the assistance and guidance of the trial judges who must deal with these offences on a daily basis. The guidance is more practical than that provided by the House of Lords.

R v Nedrick
[1986] EWCA Crim 2, Court of Appeal, Criminal Division, http://www.bailii.org/ew/cases/EWCA/Crim/1986/2.html

(Lord Lane CJ, Leggatt and Kennedy JJ)

Nedrick, having threatened to 'burn out' a woman against whom he bore a grudge, poured paraffin through the letterbox of her house and set it alight. The woman's child died in the fire. Nedrick was charged with murder. The direction was given to the jury before the publication of the speeches in *Moloney*.

Lord Lane CJ:

We have endeavoured to crystallise the effect of their Lordships' speeches in *R v Moloney* and *R v Hancock* in a way which we hope may be helpful to judges who have to handle this type of case.

It may be advisable first of all to explain to the jury that a man may intend to achieve a certain result whilst at the same time not desiring it to come about.... [Lord Lane discussed Lord Bridge's illustration of the man boarding a plane at London Airport, section 5.2, p 101 and Lord Scarman's criticism of the *Moloney* guidelines in *Hancock*.]

Where the charge is murder and in the rare cases where the simple direction is not enough, the jury should be directed that they are not entitled to infer the necessary intention unless they feel sure that death or serious bodily harm was a virtual certainty (barring some unforeseen intervention) as a result of the defendant's actions and that the defendant appreciated that such was the case.

Where a man realises that it is for all practical purposes inevitable that his actions will result in death or serious harm, the inference may be irresistible that he intended that result, however little he may have desired or wished it to happen. The decision is one for the jury to be reached on a consideration of all the evidence.

Appeal allowed

Glanville Williams was critical of the direction proposed by the Court of Appeal in *Nedrick* and identified a number of problems with it.

G. Williams, 'Oblique Intention'
(1987) 46 CLJ 417

The practice proposed in one case by the Court of Appeal (referring to *Nedrick*), acting in the dim and delusive light of *Moloney*, was to tell the jury that a person may intend to achieve a certain result whilst at the same time not desiring it to come about; they must not find that he intended the result merely because he foresaw it as probable; and if he thought that the risk of its happening was very slight, then it may be easy for them to conclude that he did not intend it; they are not entitled to infer the necessary intention unless they feel sure that the result was a virtual certainty (barring some unforeseen intervention) and the defendant appreciated this. Although this mode of instruction perhaps 'works' well enough, there are several objections to it.

(1) It unnecessarily mystifies the concept of intention (as Professor J. C. Smith has pointed out). The instruction leaves the legal notion of intention unexplained, telling the jury what the definition is not, without telling them what it is. The jury are instructed that they may infer this undefined and apparently unknowable entity from given facts, without informing them what is the thing that they are supposed to be inferring.

(2) This mystery-making occurs because the instruction fails to state that intention normally involves desire (alternatively expressed as purpose), the only exception being the case of realisation

of virtual certainty. This exception apart, the test is: would the defendant have felt that he failed in his purpose if the expected result did not happen?

(3) The jury, having been told (i) that they 'must not' find intention merely because the defendant foresaw the result as probable, will be puzzled when they are then told (ii) that if the defendant foresaw a very slight risk of the result 'it may be easy' for them to conclude that he did not intend it. Proposition (ii) is merely a weaker case of (i), and in the absence of other clues to intent proposition (ii) should follow a *fortiori* from (i); they *must not*.

(4) The instruction misleadingly states that intention cannot be inferred unless the defendant appreciated that the result would be a virtual certainty. On the contrary, whenever it can be inferred from the evidence as a whole that the defendant desired the result to follow from his acts, this means that he intended it, whether he foresaw it as a virtual certainty or as any degree of probability down to an outside chance. The judges disable themselves from giving the jury this clear instruction because for obscure reasons they balk at acknowledging the significance of desire (or purpose) in the concept of intention.

■ *Questions*

1. Consider the facts of *Hyam* and those of *Nedrick*. Who was guilty of murder? Was there any difference between the blameworthiness of the two defendants?

2. Is it true that the jury is left without guidance as to the meaning of intention? If it is an ordinary word of the English language, do juries need guidance?

3. How does the *Nedrick* direction fit with the 'golden rule' that Lord Bridge propounded in *Moloney*?

The approach in *Nedrick* was finally endorsed with some minor alteration by the House of Lords to provide us with the latest judical explanation of the meaning of intention.

R v Woollin

[1998] UKHL 28, House of Lords, http://www.bailii.org/uk/cases/UKHL/1998/28.html

(Lords Browne-Wilkinson, Nolan, Steyn, Hoffmann and Hope of Craighead)

W lost his temper and threw his three-month-old son on to a hard surface, killing him. It was not alleged that W intended to kill; the issue was as to intention to cause serious harm. The appellant denied that he had any such intention.

Giving the judgment of the Court of Appeal, Roch LJ observed about *Nedrick* that:

although the use of the phrase 'a virtual certainty' may be desirable and may be necessary, it is only necessary where the evidence of intent is limited to the admitted actions of the accused and the consequences of those actions. It is not obligatory to use that phrase or one that means the same thing in cases such as the present where there is other evidence for the jury to consider.

Lord Steyn delivered the principal speech with which Lords Nolan and Hope agreed. Lords Browne-Wilkinson and Hoffmann also agreed that the appeal should be allowed.

[Lord Steyn reviewed the cases leading up to the decision in *Nedrick*:]

The direct attack on *Nedrick*

It is now possible to consider the Crown's direct challenge to the correctness of *R v Nedrick*. First, the Crown argued that *R v Nedrick* prevents the jury from considering all the evidence in the case relevant to intention. The argument is that this is contrary to the provisions of s 8 of the 1967 Act. [His lordship quoted the provisions of the Act set out in section 5.2, p 101.]

Paragraph (a) is an instruction to the judge and is not relevant to the issues on this appeal. The Crown's argument relied on para (b), which is concerned with the function of the jury. It is no more than a legislative instruction that in considering their findings on intention or foresight the jury must take into account all relevant evidence: see Professor Edward Griew 'States of mind, presumptions and inferences' in *Criminal Law: Essays in Honour of J C Smith* (1987) pp 68, 76–77. *R v Nedrick* is undoubtedly concerned with the mental element which is sufficient for murder. So, for that matter, in their different ways were *Smith, Hyam, Moloney* and *Hancock*. But, as Lord Lane CJ emphasised in the last sentence of *R v Nedrick* [1986] 3 All ER 1 at 4: 'The decision is one for the jury to be reached on a consideration of all the evidence.' *R v Nedrick* does not prevent a jury from considering all the evidence: it merely stated what state of mind (in the absence of a purpose to kill or to cause serious harm) is sufficient for murder. I would therefore reject the Crown's first argument.

In the second place the Crown submitted that *R v Nedrick* is in conflict with the decision of the House in *R v Hancock*. Counsel argued that in order to bring some coherence to the process of determining intention Lord Lane CJ specified a minimum level of foresight, namely virtual certainty. But that is not in conflict with the decision in *R v Hancock*, which, apart from disapproving Lord Bridge's 'natural consequence' model direction, approved *R v Moloney* in all other respects. And in *R v Moloney* [1985] 1 All ER 1025 at 1036 Lord Bridge said that if a person foresees the probability of a consequence as little short of overwhelming this 'will suffice to *establish* the necessary intent' (my emphasis). Nor did the House in *R v Hancock* rule out the framing of model directions by the Court of Appeal for the assistance of trial judges. I would therefore reject the argument that the guidance given in *R v Nedrick* was in conflict with the decision of the House in *R v Hancock*.

The Crown did not argue that as a matter of policy foresight of a virtual certainty is too narrow a test in murder. Subject to minor qualifications, the decision in *R v Nedrick* was widely welcomed by distinguished academic writers: see Professor J C Smith QC's commentary on *R v Nedrick* [1986] Crim LR 742 at 743–744, Glanville Williams 'The mens rea for murder: leave it alone' (1989) 105 LQR 387, J R Spencer 'Murder in the dark: a glimmer of light?' [1986] CLJ 366–367 and Ashworth *Principles of Criminal Law* (2nd edn, 1995) p 172. It is also of interest that it is very similar to the threshold of being aware that it *will* occur 'in the ordinary course of events' in the Law Commission's draft Criminal Code (see *Criminal Law: Legislating the Criminal Code: Offences against the Person and General Principles* (Law Com No 218 (1993) (Cm 2370), App A (Draft Criminal Law Bill with Explanatory Notes) pp 90–91): cf also Professor J C Smith QC 'A note on "intention" ' [1990] Crim LR 85 at 86. Moreover, over a period of 12 years since *R v Nedrick* the test of foresight of virtual certainty has apparently caused no practical difficulties. It is simple and clear. It is true that it may exclude a conviction of murder in the often cited terrorist example where a member of the bomb disposal team is killed. In such a case it may realistically be said that the terrorist did not foresee the killing of a member of the bomb disposal team as a virtual certainty. That may be a consequence of not framing the principle in terms of risk-taking. Such cases ought to cause no substantial difficulty since immediately below murder there is available a verdict of manslaughter which may attract in the discretion of the court a life sentence. In any event, as Lord Lane eloquently argued in a debate in the House of Lords, to frame a principle for particular difficulties regarding terrorism 'would produce corresponding injustices which would be very hard to eradicate' (see 512 HL Official Report (5th series) col 480). I am satisfied that the *Nedrick* test, which was squarely based on the decision of the House in *R v Moloney*, is pitched at the right level of foresight.

The argument that *Nedrick* has limited application

The Court of Appeal ([1997] 1 Cr App R 97 at 107) held that the phrase 'a virtual certainty' should be confined to cases where the evidence of intent is limited to admitted actions of the accused and the consequences of those actions. It is not obligatory where there is other evidence to consider. The Crown's alternative submission on the appeal was to the same effect. This distinction would introduce yet another complication into a branch of the criminal law where simplicity is of supreme importance. The distinction is dependent on the vagaries of the evidence in particular cases. Moreover, a jury may reject the other evidence to which the Court of Appeal refers. And in preparing his summing up a judge could not ignore this possibility. If the Court of Appeal's view is right, it might compel a judge to pose different tests depending on what evidence the jury accepts. For my part, and with the greatest respect, I have to say that this distinction would be likely to produce great practical difficulties. But, most importantly, the distinction is not based on any principled view regarding the mental element in murder. Contrary to the view of the Court of Appeal, I would also hold that s 8(b) of the 1967 Act does not compel such a result.

In my view the ruling of the court of Appeal was wrong. It may be appropriate to give a direction in accordance with *R v Nedrick* in any case in which the defendant may not have desired the result of his act. But I accept that the trial judge is best placed to decide what direction is required by the circumstances of the case.

[Lord Steyn said that the conviction of murder was unsafe and must be quashed.]

The status of *Nedrick*

In my view Lord Lane CJ's judgment in *R v Nedrick* provided valuable assistance to trial judges. The model direction is by now a tried and tested formula. Trial judges ought to continue to use it. On matters of detail I have three observations, which can best be understood if I set out again the relevant part of Lord Lane CJ's judgment. It was:

> '(A) When determining whether the defendant had the necessary intent, it may therefore be helpful for a jury to ask themselves two questions. (1) How probable was the consequence which resulted from the defendant's voluntary act? (2) Did he foresee that consequence? If he did not appreciate that death or serious harm was likely to result from his act, he cannot have intended to bring it about. If he did, but thought that the risk to which he was exposing the person killed was only slight, then it may be easy for the jury to conclude that he did not intend to bring about that result. On the other hand, if the jury are satisfied that at the material time the defendant recognised that death or serious harm would be virtually certain (barring some unforeseen intervention) to result from his voluntary act, then that is a fact from which they may find it easy to infer that he intended to kill or do serious bodily harm, even though he may not have had any desire to achieve that result ... (B) Where the charge is murder and in the rare cases where the simple direction is not enough, the jury should be directed that they are not entitled to infer the necessary intention unless they feel sure that death or serious bodily harm was a virtual certainty (barring some unforeseen intervention) as a result of the defendant's actions and that the defendant appreciated that such was the case. (C) Where a man realises that it is for all practical purposes inevitable that his actions will result in death or serious harm, the inference may be irresistible that he intended that result, however little he may have desired or wished it to happen. The decision is one for the jury to be reached on a consideration of all the evidence.' (See [1986] 3 All ER 1 at 3–4.)

First, I am persuaded by the speech of my noble and learned friend Lord Hope of Craighead that it is unlikely, if ever, to be helpful to direct the jury in terms of the two questions set out in (A). I agree that these questions may detract from the clarity of the critical direction in (B). Secondly, in their writings previously cited Glanville Williams, Professor Smith and Andrew Ashworth observed that the use of the words 'to infer' in (B) may detract from the clarity of the model direction. I agree. I would substitute the words 'to find'. Thirdly, the first sentence of (C) does not form part of the model direction. But it would always be right for the just to say, as Lord Lane CJ put it, that the decision is for the jury upon a consideration of all the evidence in the case.

■ *Questions*
1. The House rejects 'infer' in favour of 'find'. Is there any difference?
2. Has the House of Lords defined intention as a matter of criminal law? If so, what is the test that must be applied?
3. Did the House simply allow 'intention' to go undefined but accept that as a matter of evidence it can be inferred from foresight?

5.2.2 Inferring intention from foresight

The notion that intention can be inferred from foresight goes back at least to Lord Hailsham's speech in *Hyam*. In *Moloney* (section 5.2, p 101) Lord Bridge seemed to think that the notion derived support from s 8 of the Criminal Justice Act 1967. What the section says is that the court or jury must decide whether D 'did intend or foresee that result, drawing such inferences from the evidence as appear proper in the circumstances'.

'The evidence', it seems, is the nature of the act done by D and the relevant circumstances in which it was done—all objective facts. Depending on the nature of those facts, a court or jury might conclude that:

(1) D wanted to cause that result—it was his aim, object or purpose; or

(2) though he did not want to cause that result:

(a) he foresaw that he would do so—it was certain or virtually certain to happen; or

(b) he foresaw that he might—it was (i) highly probable, or (ii) probable, or at least (iii) possible.

None of these alternatives involves inferring one state of mind from another—a notion which some regard as impossible. The question in practice is whether intention should be limited to (1) and (2)(a) or extends to (2)(b)(i) or (ii) or (iii).

At one point in his speech ([1998] 4 All ER 110 (not in the previous extract)), Lord Steyn said 'The effect of the critical direction [in *Nedrick*] is that a result foreseen as virtually certain *is* an intended result' (emphasis in original). Is this what intention means in the non-legal context? Consider the following extract.

R. Goff, 'The Mental Element in the Crime of Murder'
(1988) 104 LQR 30

The narrowing down of the mental element in murder to the concept of 'intention' has generally been welcomed by jurists. But they are discovering that some cases, which they *feel* ought to be embraced within the crime of murder, do not quite fit within the concept of intention; and so they are embarking on the enterprise of illegitimately expanding the concept of intention to include these cases. The classic example of this technique is to be found in the idea of 'oblique' intent as expounded by Professor Glanville Williams in his *Textbook of Criminal Law*.

. . .

Now I have to confess that, as soon as somebody starts using an expression like 'oblique intention,' I become suspicious; because I suspect that it is only necessary to use the rather mysterious adjective 'oblique' to bring within 'intention' something which is not intention at all. And that is exactly what is happening here. For the trouble with this kind of approach is that it has distorted the plain meaning of the word. To the [example of the plane bomber] did the defendant mean to destroy the parcel? The answer is, of course, yes, he did. But to the question—did the defendant mean to kill the pilot? The answer is, no, he didn't. Indeed, if he saw the pilot safely descending by parachute, he would no doubt be delighted; and so it is absurd to say that he meant to kill him. Of course, if the pilot is killed by the explosion, I share Professor Glanville Williams' *feeling* that the defendant can properly be called a murderer; but I do not think that that result can be achieved by artificially expanding the meaning of the word 'intention.' Quite apart from anything else, it can only lead to difficulties in directing juries. In a jury system, it is far better, if you can, to use a word in its plain and ordinary meaning. And you do not intend something merely because you know that it is virtually certain to happen.

■ *Questions*

1. When a jury finds that D foresaw that the relevant result was virtually certain, by what criteria are they to decide whether to exercise their 'entitlement' to find that it amounted to intention?

See also the articles, 'After *Woollin*' [1999] Crim LR 532 by A. Norrie; M. C. Kaveny, 'Inferring Intention from Foresight' (2004) 120 LQR 81.

2. Are there advantages in having a degree of flexibility in the definition so that juries have some 'moral elbow room' to deal with difficult cases? Is certainty in definition more important than flexibility? Does it matter, when considering these issues, that these are all murder cases?

3. Is Lord Goff correct that the meaning of intention has been expanded to encompass those individuals we feel *ought* to be guilty of murder even though it might not have been their purpose to cause death or really serious harm?

The following case provides the Court of Appeal's answer to the question of whether the House of Lords had defined intention as a matter of law or merely provided guidance on what was sufficient evidence from which to infer that state of mind.

Matthews and Alleyne
[2003] 2 Cr App R 30, [2003] Crim LR 553, Court of Appeal, Criminal Division

(Rix LJ, Crane J and Maddison HHJ)

M and A were convicted of the robbery, kidnapping and murder of Jonathan. J was attacked on leaving a club in the early hours of the morning, and ultimately thrown off a bridge 25 feet high into a river 64 feet wide. J could not swim and drowned. A co-accused gave evidence that J had said he could not swim. One ground of appeal was that the judge had directed the jury that foresight of virtual certainty of consequences *was* intention.

Rix LJ [His lordship reviewed the facts and positions taken by the various co-defendants:]

25. The essential ground of appeal argued on behalf of both Alleyne and Matthews is that the judges' direction on intent was a misdirection, and that in consequence their convictions for murder are unsafe....

...

39. Mr Coker for the Crown on this appeal submits that in *Woollin* the House of Lords has finally moved away from a rule of evidence to a rule of substantive law. In this connection he drew attention to a sentence in Lord Steyn's speech at pp.17 and 93F where he says, immediately after setting out Lord Lane's observations in *Nedrick*, that the effect of the critical direction is that a result foreseen as virtually certain is an intended result.

40. We also relies on what Professor Sir John Smith has to say in his note on *R. v Woollin* [1998] Crim LR 890 and in Smith and Hogan, *Criminal Law*, 10th edition, at 70ff. Thus in the former, Professor Smith said this:

'A jury might still fairly ask: We are all quite sure that D knew that it was virtually certain that his act would cause death. You tell us we are entitled to find that he intended it. Are we bound to find that? Some of us want to and some do not. How should we decide? The implication appears to be that, even now, they are not so bound. But why not? At one point Lord Steyn says of *Nedrick* "The effect of the critical direction is that a result foreseen as virtually certain is an intended result". If that is right, the only question for the jury is, Did the defendant foresee the result as virtually certain? If he did, he intended it. That, it is submitted is what the law should be; and it now seems that we have at last moved substantially in that direction. The *Nedrick* formula, however, even as modified (entitled to find), involves some ambiguity with the hint of the existence of some ineffable, undefinable, notion of intent, locked in the breasts of the jurors.'

41. Moreover, in the latter treatise (at 72) Professor Smith cites Lord Lane speaking in the debate on the report of the House of Lords Select Committee on Murder (HL Paper, 78-I, 1989) as follows:

'in *Nedrick* the court was obliged to phrase matters as it did because of earlier decisions in your Lordships House by which it was bound. We had to tread very gingerly indeed in order not to tread on your Lordships toes. As a result, *Nedrick* was not as clear as it should have been. However, I agree with the conclusions of the committee that intention should be defined in the terms set out in para.195 of the report on p.50. That seems to me to express clearly what in Nedrick we failed properly to explain.'

42. The definition referred to, as *Smith and Hogan* goes on to explain, is that stated in cl.18(b) of the Draft Code (itself referred to by Lord Steyn in *Woollin*) as follows:

'A person acts intentionally with respect to a result when he acts either in order to bring it about or being aware that it will occur in the ordinary course of events.'

43. In our judgment, however, the law has not yet reached a definition of intent in murder in terms of appreciation of a virtual certainty. Lord Lane was speaking not of what was decided in *Nedrick* (or in the other cases which preceded it) nor of what was thereafter to be decided in *Woollin*, but of what the law in his opinion should be, as represented by the cl.18(b) definition. Similarly, although the law has progressively moved closer to what Professor Smith has been advocating (see his commentaries in the Criminal Law Review on the various cases discussed above), we do not regard *Woollin* as yet reaching or laying down a substantive rule of law. On the contrary, it is clear from the discussion in *Woollin* as a whole that *Nedrick* was derived from the existing law, at that time ending in *Moloney and Hancock*, and that the critical direction in *Nedrick* was approved, subject to the change of one word.

44. In these circumstances we think that the judge did go further than the law as it stands at present permitted him to go in redrafting the *Nedrick/Woollin* direction into a form where, as Mr Coker accepts (although we have some doubt about this), the jury were directed to find the necessary intent proved provided they were satisfied in the case of any defendant that there was appreciation of the virtual certainty of death. This is to be contrasted with the form of the approved direction which is in terms of not entitled to find the necessary intention, unless.

45. Having said that, however, we think that, once what is required is an appreciation of virtual certainty of death, and not some lesser foresight of merely probable consequences, there is very little to choose between a rule of evidence and one of substantive law. It is probably this thought that led Lord Steyn to say that a result foreseen as virtually certain is an intended result. Lord Bridge had reflected the same thought when he had said, in *R. v Moloney* (1985) 81 Cr.App.R. 93, 101, [1985] AC 905, 920C, that if the defendant there had had present to his mind, when he pulled the trigger, that his gun was pointing at his stepfathers head at a distance of six feet and its inevitable consequence, then the inference was inescapable, using words in their ordinary, everyday meaning, that he intended to kill his stepfather. Lord Lane had also spoken in *Nedrick* of an irresistible inference.

46. We also think that on the particular facts of this case, reflected in the judges directions, the question of the appellants [*sic*] intentions to save Jonathan from drowning highlight the irresistible nature of the inference or finding of intent to kill, once the jury were sure both that the defendants appreciated the virtual certainty of death (barring some attempt to save him) and that at the time of throwing Jonathan from the bridge they then had no intentions of saving him. If the jury were sure that the appellants appreciated the virtual certainty of Jonathan's death when they threw him from the bridge and also that they then had no intention of saving him from such death, it is impossible to see how the jury could not have found that the appellants intended Jonathan to die. . . .

Appeal dismissed

In *MD* [2004] EWCA Crim 1391 (at [29]), the Court of Appeal described oblique intention as:

designed to help the prosecution fill a gap in the rare circumstances in which a defendant does an act which caused death without the purpose of killing or causing serious injury, but in circumstances where death or serious bodily harm had been a virtual certainty (barring some unforeseen intervention) as a result of the defendant's action and the defendant had appreciated that such was the case. *Woollin* is not designed to make the prosecution's task more difficult. Many murderers whose purpose was to kill or cause serious injury would escape conviction if the jury was only given a *Woollin* direction. The man who kills another with a gun would be able to escape liability for murder if he could show [this seems to be an error and the court can be presumed to mean the prosecution show] that he was such a bad shot that death or serious bodily harm was not a virtual certainty or that the defendant had thought that death or serious bodily harm was not a virtual certainty.

In *Allen* [2005] EWCA Crim 1344 the Court of Appeal emphasized (at [63]) that it 'is only in an exceptional case that the extended direction by reference to foresight becomes necessary'. The further explanation must be provided only where the judge thinks it necessary to avoid misunderstanding.

When the oblique intention direction is delivered, what should a judge say to a jury who ask—'what are we seeking to "find" which may turn this state of mind of foresight of virtual certainty into one of intention?' Is the answer that they should look for some indefinable moral aspect to the state of mind?

In *Stringer* [2008] EWCA Crim 1222, M, aged 14, was alleged to have started a fire in his family home early one morning and walked off, knowing that five occupants were asleep upstairs. The issue at trial was as to the admissibility of interviews with him in which he was asked about whether he realized it was certain that people would die or be seriously injured if there was a fire started in the hallway when they were asleep. The Court of Appeal upheld the conviction:

if the jury were satisfied (as they must have been) that M started the fire after putting accelerant at the foot of the stairs, that he watched it take hold and then walked away, there could be only one answer to the question whether in fact it was a virtual certainty that somebody in the house would suffer really serious harm or death from M's actions. It would be wholly unrealistic to imagine all the occupants escaping from the house by jumping from the upstairs windows without any of them suffering any serious harm. This must have been obvious to any ordinary person at the time. Even taking account of M's age and the fact that his IQ was low/average, the inference that he must have appreciated it on that morning was also overwhelming. On the facts as the jury must have found them, the conclusion that M had the necessary intent was bound to follow.

> ■ *Question*
>
> Dan plants a bomb in a public space and sets it to detonate. He rings the local police and gives them a 15-minute warning to clear the building in which the bomb is planted. The police clear the building in 10 minutes and Victor, a bomb disposal expert, enters the building immediately to defuse the device. It explodes four minutes earlier than D had designed. The blast kills Victor and Fred, a homeless man who had been asleep under one of the seating areas in the building and who was unaware of the evacuation. How would you direct the jury on the matter of intention at Dan's trial for the murder of Victor and Fred?

5.2.3 Intention and concealed defences

In some cases, the definition or application of the concept of intention appears to provide the courts with an opportunity to apply some kind of hidden defence.

> ■ *Questions*
>
> D's house is ablaze and he is trapped on the top floor with his baby daughter V. He realizes that the flames will get to them before the emergency services are likely to arrive. In an effort to save his daughter, D throws her into the garden 40 feet below. He says he 'wanted only to save her' from certain death. Did he intend to kill or cause her serious injury? Does he deserve to be convicted if she is injured or killed?

Consider the next case and ask how can it be said that the accused had anything other than a direct intention.

R v Steane

[1947] 1 All ER 813, Court of Criminal Appeal

(Lord Goddard CJ, Atkinson and Cassels JJ)

S was convicted under the Defence (General) Regulations, reg 2A, with 'doing acts likely to assist the enemy with intent to assist the enemy'. S had made radio broadcasts for the enemy. He did so because he was threatened that if he did not he and his family would be sent to a concentration camp. S claimed he had no intention of assisting the enemy and what he did was done to save his wife and children, and that what he did could not have assisted the enemy except in a very technical sense.

[Lord Goddard CJ read the judgment of the court:]

The far more difficult question that arises, however, is in connection with the direction to the jury with regard to whether these acts were done with the intention of assisting the enemy. The case as opened, and, indeed, as put by the learned judge, appears to this court to be this: A man is taken to intend the natural consequences of his acts. If, therefore he does an act which is likely to assist the enemy, it must be assumed that he did it with the intention of assisting the enemy. Now, the first thing which the court would observe is that where the essence of an offence or a necessary constituent of an offence is a particular intent, that intent must be proved by the Crown just as much as any other fact necessary to constitute the offence. The wording of the regulation itself shows that it is not enough merely to charge a prisoner with doing an act likely to assist the enemy. He must do it with the particular intent specified in the regulation. While, no doubt, the motive of a man's act and his intention in doing the act are in law different things, it is none the less true that in many offences a specific intention is a necessary ingredient and the jury have to be satisfied that a particular act was done with that specific intent, although the natural consequences of the act might, if nothing else was proved, be said to show the intent for which it was done. To take a simple illustration, a man is charged with wounding with intent to do grievous bodily harm. It is proved that he did severely wound the prosecutor. Nevertheless, unless the Crown can prove that the intent was to do the prosecutor grievous bodily harm, he cannot be convicted of that felony. It is always open to the jury to negative by their verdict the intent and to convict only of the misdemeanour of unlawful wounding. Or again, a prisoner may be charged with shooting with intent to murder. Here, again, the prosecution may fail to satisfy the jury of the intent, although the natural consequence of firing, perhaps at close range, would be to kill. The jury can find in such a case an intent to do grievous bodily harm, or they might find that, if the person shot at was a police constable, the prisoner was not guilty on the count charging intent to murder but was guilty of intent to avoid arrest. The important thing to notice in this respect is that where an intent is charged in the indictment, the burden of proving that intent remains throughout on the prosecution. No doubt, if the prosecution prove an act the natural consequences of which would be a certain result and no evidence or explanation is given, then a jury may, on a proper direction, find that the prisoner is guilty of doing the act with the intent alleged, but if, on the totality of the evidence, there is room for more than one view as to the intent of the prisoner, the jury should be directed that it is for the prosecution to prove the intent to the jury's satisfaction, and if, on a review of the whole evidence, they either think that the intent did not exist or they are left in doubt as to the intent, the prisoner is entitled to be acquitted . . .

In this case the court cannot but feel that some confusion arose with regard to the question of intent by so much being said in the case with regard to the subject of duress. Duress is a matter of defence where a prisoner is forced by fear of violence or imprisonment to do an act which in itself is criminal. If the act is a criminal act, the prisoner may be able to show that he was forced into doing it by violence, actual or threatened, and to save himself from the consequences of that violence. There is very little learning to be found in any of the books or cases on the subject of duress and it is by no means certain how far the doctrine extends, though we have the authority both of Hale and of Fitzjames Stephen, that, while it does not apply to treason, murder and some other felonies, it does apply to misdemeanours, and offences against these regulations are misdemeanours. But here again, before any question of duress arises, a jury must be satisfied that the prisoner had the intention which is laid in the indictment. Duress is a matter of defence and the onus of proving it is on the accused.* As we have already said, where an intent is charged on the indictment, it is for the prosecution to prove it, so the onus is the other way.

Another matter which is of considerable importance in this case, but does not seem to have been brought directly to the attention of the jury, is that very different considerations may apply where the accused at the time he did the acts is in subjection to an enemy power and where he is not. British soldiers who were set to work on the Burma road or, if invasion had unhappily taken place, British subjects who might have been set to work by the enemy digging trenches would, undoubtedly, have been doing acts likely to assist the enemy. It would be unnecessary surely in their cases to consider any of the niceties of the law relating to duress, because no jury would find that merely by doing this work they were intending to assist the enemy. In our opinion, it is impossible to say that where acts were done by a person in subjection to the power of another, especially if that other be a brutal enemy, an inference that he intended the natural consequences of his acts must be drawn merely from the fact that he did them. The guilty intent cannot be presumed and must be proved. The proper direction to the jury in this case would have been that it was for the prosecution to prove the criminal intent, and that, while the jury would be entitled to presume that intent if they thought that the act was done as the result of the free, uncontrolled action of the accused, they would not be entitled to presume it if the circumstances showed that the act was done in subjection to the power of the enemy or was as equally consistent with an innocent intent as with a criminal intent, eg a desire to save his wife and children from a concentration camp. They should only convict if satisfied by the evidence that the act complained of was, in fact, done to assist the enemy and if there was doubt about the matter, the prisoner was entitled to be acquitted . . .

Appeal allowed

* NB: This *dictum* goes too far. The accused who wishes to set up duress may bear an evidential burden; but once he has introduced evidence of duress, the burden of disproving it lies on the Crown: *Gill* [1963] 2 All ER 688, [1963] 1 WLR 841.

Glanville Williams, *The Mental Element in Crime*
(1966), p 21, commenting on *Steane*

The chief English authority against the view that intention may be held to include foresight of certainty is *Steane* [in the previous extract]. Although this is frequently cited as an important authority in discussions of intention, its importance derives chiefly from its rejection of the proposition that a person is to be deemed to intend the natural consequence of his acts. The actual decision in *Steane* seems highly disputable; it could have been reached more readily and more acceptably by recognising duress as a defence. Undoubtedly the element of duress caused the Court of Criminal Appeal to be sympathetic towards the defendant; and in cases where such sympathy is absent, foresight of certainty (or knowledge of existing circumstances) is regularly taken to be equivalent to intention. Thus in *Arrowsmith v Jenkins* [1963] 2 QB 561, [1963] 2 All ER 210, the defendant's knowledge that a meeting she was addressing was obstructing the highway made her guilty of 'wilfully' obstructing the highway, even though she had no particular desire to create an obstruction as such.

Lord Denning's treatment of *Steane* in his Lionel Cohen lecture [*Responsibility before the Law* (Jerusalem, Israel, 1961)] seems hard to reconcile with his principal thesis, which is that the word 'intent' in law includes recklessness unless there is some statutory indication of a narrower meaning. I should have thought that this view would have led him to disapprove the decision in *Steane*, but Lord Denning agrees with it; and the reason he gives is that the statutory offence of doing an act likely to assist the enemy with intent to assist the enemy obviously required desire or purpose. 'This man Steane had no desire or purpose to assist the enemy. The Gestapo had said to him: "If you don't obey, your wife and children will be put in a concentration camp." So he obeyed their commands. It would be very hard to convict him of an "intent to assist the enemy" if it was the last thing he desired to do.'

I cannot myself see that the statutory language rebutted Lord Denning's wide meaning of 'intention' if there is such a wide meaning. As a matter of policy, the draftsman would surely have wished to catch the man who did an act knowing that it was likely to assist the enemy, but not caring whether it did so or not; and he has not used any language to negative this meaning except the overriding phrase 'with intent to assist the enemy', which Lord Denning does not regard as sufficient to negative recklessness. However, let me assume, with Lord Denning, that the formula is restricted to acts done with intent (in the sense of desire or purpose) to assist the enemy. Steane's predominant intent was to save his family, and in order to do that he broadcast for the enemy. On any intelligible use of language, he intentionally (purposely) broadcast. He did not broadcast by mistake or accident or in a state of automatism. If it is thought too strong to say that he desired to broadcast, at least he knew he was broadcasting, which is enough to establish wilfulness or intent. No doubt he did so reluctantly, as the lesser of two evils; but many people go to work in the morning for precisely the same reason.

But, it may be said, it is not enough to assert that Steane intentionally broadcast; what has to be established is that he intended to assist the enemy. On this, there may even be an initial doubt whether he assisted the enemy. The enemy presumably hoped and thought that the broadcasts would assist them, but it would be hard to determine whether or not the broadcasts did so. The answer to this doubt is that the notion of assisting the enemy as used in the statute is obviously not limited to acts that can be shown to have assisted the enemy to win a military victory or otherwise to have promoted their cause. It would be no defence to a traitor to show that a campaign in which he assisted the enemy turned out to be disastrous to the enemy and caused them to lose the war. 'Assisting the enemy' means assisting the enemy in the war effort, whether the outcome is successful or not, Steane's intentional participation in the enemy broadcasts was an intentional assistance to the enemy, whether or not the broadcasts in fact helped them. It could perhaps be said that Steane desired to help the enemy in this way in order to save his family; but even if this formula is objected to, he certainly knew that he was assisting the enemy's war project, and therefore intentionally assisted the enemy. The case can either be regarded as one of voluntary action in known circumstances, or as taking part in the causation of a result (the transmission of radio waves) which is foreseen as certain; on either view it is one of intention.

The concept of intention cannot distinguish between the man who assists the enemy in order to save his family and the man who assists the enemy in order to earn a packet of cigarettes. It is only the law of duress that can make a distinction. That is why Steane should have been acquitted by reason of the defence of duress, and not because he lacked intent to assist the enemy.

■ *Questions*

Was *Steane* a duress case or an intention case? Was Steane's motive relevant? Should it have been?

Steane is by no means the only case in which 'intent' is construed to mean, in effect, purpose. In *Burke* [1988] Crim LR 839, CA, it was held that a person commits an offence under the Protection from Eviction Act 1977, s 1(3) when he does an act with intent to cause a residential occupier to give up the occupation of premises although the act (storage of furniture in a bathroom), when done without any such intention, is an act which he is perfectly entitled to do. The act must be one which is 'calculated'—meaning 'likely'—to interfere with the peace or comfort of the residential occupier, but that is the sole requirement of the actus reus. The essence of the offence is the intent with which the act is done.

■ *Question*

Are the expressions 'express intent' and 'dominant intention' simply a way of describing purpose?

5.2.4 Reform of the law concerning intention

Since *Nedrick* the law concerning intention has been considered on numerous occasions by various bodies. The Law Commission Report on Codification (April 1989) proposed a definition which would apply, unless the context otherwise requires, to all code offences which require proof of intention. A Select Committee of the House of Lords on Murder and Life Imprisonment (Nathan Committee, HL Paper 78–1, 24 July 1989) recommended that, for the purposes of the law of murder (the only offence within the Committee's terms of reference), intention should be defined on the lines proposed in the Codification Report. The Law Commission recently returned to the topic in its Report No 304 on *Murder, Manslaughter and Infanticide* (2006).

The Law Commission's homicide review led them to consider a number of proposals in relation to intention. In Consultation Paper No 177, *A New Homicide Act for England and Wales* (2006), Chs 3 and 4, the Commission offered two models for consideration, one based on the clauses above, and one seeking to codify the common law position as set out in *Woollin* (section 5.2.2). The proposal to provide a definition of 'intentionally' for the offence of murder, was as follows:

Subject to the proviso set out below:

a person acts 'intentionally' with respect to a result when he or she acts either:

(1) in order to bring it about, or

(2) knowing that it will be virtually certain to occur; or

(3) knowing that it would be virtually certain to occur if he or she were to succeed in his or her purpose of causing some other result.

Proviso: a person is not to be deemed to have intended any result, which it was his or her specific purpose to avoid.

The proviso deals with the case of the baby being thrown from the window as discussed in section 5.2.3.

This proposal was criticized by commentators including Alan Norrie, 'Between Orthodox Subjectivism and Moral Contextualism' [2006] Crim LR 486 who argued that it included a concealed defence of necessity. Following consultation the Law Commission provisionally rejected the proposal to define, preferring to retain the flexibility inherent in the present law (in the moral elbow room it provides).

The Law Commission finally settled on the following recommendation (LC304, Ch 4):

We recommend that the existing law governing the meaning of intention is codified as follows:

(1) A person should be taken to intend a result if he or she acts in order to bring it about.

(2) In cases where the judge believes that justice may not be done unless an expanded understanding of intention is given, the jury should be directed as follows: an intention to bring about a result may be found if it is shown that the defendant thought that the result was a virtually certain consequence of his or her action.

This definition removes the unnecessary requirement that the result was a virtual certainty.

■ *Questions*

Would the proposal clarify the law? Would the direction to the jury in Dan's case (section 5.2.2, p 113) be any easier? See V. Tadros, 'The Homicide Ladder' (2006) 69 MLR 601 at 604.

5.3 Recklessness

Recklessness is a form of mens rea which is generally considered less blameworthy than intention. It usually describes the state of mind of someone who has seen a risk of the proscribed result arising and has gone on, unreasonably, to take the risk.

For most of the last century the law seemed settled. Consider the following extract.

R v Cunningham
[1957] QB 396, Queen's Bench Division

(Byrne, Slade and Barry JJ)

D stole a gas meter and its contents from a cellar and in so doing fractured a gas pipe. Coal gas escaped, percolated through the cellar wall to the adjoining house, and entered a bedroom where V was asleep. As a result of this, V inhaled a considerable quantity of the gas. The appellant was found guilty of <u>maliciously causing V to take a noxious thing</u>, namely, coal gas, so as thereby to endanger her life, contrary to s 23 of the Offences Against the Person Act 1861. The judge directed the jury that 'maliciously' meant 'wickedly'—that is, doing 'something which he has no business to do and perfectly well knows it'. D appealed.

Byrne J:

Before this court [counsel for D] has taken three points, all dependent upon the construction of that section. Section 23 provides: 'Whosoever shall unlawfully and maliciously administer to or cause to be administered to or taken by any other person any poison or other destructive or noxious thing, so as thereby to endanger the life of such person, or so as thereby to inflict upon such person any grievous bodily harm, shall be guilty of felony . . .'

[Counsel for D] argued, first, that mens rea of some kind is necessary. Secondly, that the nature of the mens rea required is that the appellant must intend to do the particular kind of harm that was done, or, alternatively, that he must foresee that that harm may occur yet nevertheless continue recklessly to do the act. Thirdly, that the judge misdirected the jury as to the meaning of the word 'maliciously.' He cited the following cases: *Reg. v. Pembliton, Reg. v. Latimer* and *Reg. v. Faulkner.* In reply, Mr. Snowden, on behalf of the Crown, cited *Reg. v. Martin.*

We have considered those cases, and we have also considered, in the light of those cases, the following principle which was propounded by the late Professor C. S. Kenny in the first edition of his *Outlines of Criminal Law* published in 1902 and repeated at p. 186 of the 16th edition edited by Mr. J. W. Cecil Turner and published in 1952: 'In any statutory definition of a crime, malice must be taken not in the old vague sense of wickedness in general but as requiring either (1) An actual intention to do the particular kind of harm that in fact was done; or (2) recklessness as to whether such harm should occur or not (i.e., the accused has foreseen that the particular kind of harm might be done and yet has gone on to take the risk of it). It is neither limited to nor does it indeed require any ill will towards the person injured.' The same principle is repeated by Mr. Turner in his 10th edition of *Russell on Crime* at p. 1592.

We think that this is an accurate statement of the law. It derives some support from the judgments of Lord Coleridge C.J. and Blackburn J. in Pembliton's case. In our opinion the word 'maliciously' in a statutory crime postulates foresight of consequence.

. . .

With the utmost respect to the learned judge, we think it is incorrect to say that the word 'malicious' in a statutory offence merely means wicked. We think the judge was, in effect, telling the jury that if they were satisfied that the appellant acted wickedly—and he had clearly acted wickedly in stealing the gas meter and its contents—they ought to find that he had acted maliciously in causing the gas to be taken by [V] so as thereby to endanger her life.

In our view it should have been left to the jury to decide whether, even if the appellant did not intend the injury to [V], he foresaw that the removal of the gas meter might cause injury to someone but nevertheless removed it. We are unable to say that a reasonable jury, properly directed as to the meaning of the word 'maliciously' in the context of section 23, would without doubt have convicted.

Although the definition provided by the court did not refer to the fact that the defendant must 'unjustifiably' or 'unreasonably' take the risk that he had foreseen, that was accepted to be part of this classic test of recklessness. In the last 30 years, recklessness has become one of the most hotly debated issues in criminal law in England and Wales. This followed the controversial decision in *Caldwell* (discussed in the following extract) which was much criticized but only finally overruled in the next case.

In the case of *G*, the definition of recklessness approved by Lord Bingham is that '[A] person acts . . . "recklessly" [within the meaning of s 1 of the Criminal Damage Act 1971] with respect to—(i) a circumstance when he is aware of a risk that it exists or will exist; (ii) a result when he is aware of a risk that it will occur; and it is, in the circumstances known to him, unreasonable to take the risk...' Foresight of 'a' risk of the criminal damage is sufficient, provided it was not justifiable for D to take that risk in the circumstances.

G is a landmark decision and the extract below reflects that by providing an opportunity to examine the Lords' reasoning in detail. Consider the questions interspersed throughout the speeches.

R v G and another

[2003] UKHL 50, House of Lords, http://www.bailii.org/uk/cases/UKHL/2003/50.html

(Lords Bingham of Cornhill, Browne-Wilkinson, Steyn, Hutton and Rodger of Earlsferry)

G and R, aged 11 and 12, went camping without their parents' permission. During the night they set fire to newspapers in the yard at the back of a shop and threw the lit newspapers under a wheelie bin. They left without putting out the fire. The fire spread to the wheelie bin and to the shop causing £1m worth of damage. The boys' case was that they expected the newspapers to burn themselves out on the concrete floor. Neither appreciated the risk of the fire spreading as it did. They were charged with arson contrary to s 1(1) and (3) of the 1971 Act. The judge directed the jury in accordance with *Caldwell* [1982] AC 341, expressing reservations about that being a harsh test. The Court of Appeal upheld the convictions stating that *Caldwell* had been rightly applied and certified the issue of recklessness as one of general public importance.

Lord Bingham of Cornhill:

1. My Lords, the point of law of general public importance certified by the Court of Appeal to be involved in its decision in the present case is expressed in this way:

'Can a defendant properly be convicted under s 1 of the Criminal Damage Act 1971 on the basis that he was reckless as to whether property was destroyed or damaged when he gave no thought to the risk but, by reason of his age and/or personal characteristics, the risk would not have been obvious to him, even if he had thought about it?'

The appeal turns on the meaning of 'reckless' in that section. This is a question on which the House ruled in *R v Caldwell* [1981] 1 All ER 961, [1982] AC 341, a ruling affirmed by the House in later decisions. The House is again asked to reconsider that ruling.

[His lordship referred to the facts, the trial judge's direction on the law and then examined the historical background to the 1971 Act.]

14. Enactment of the 1971 Act did not at once affect the courts' approach to the causing of unintentional damage. In *R v Briggs* [1977] 1 All ER 475, [1977] 1 WLR 605 the defendant had been charged under s 1(1) of the 1971 Act as a result of damage caused to a car and the appeal turned on the trial judge's direction on the meaning of 'reckless'. The appeal succeeded since the judge had not adequately explained that the test to be applied was that of the defendant's state of mind. The Court of Appeal (James LJ, Kenneth Jones and Peter Pain JJ) ruled ([1977] 1 All ER 475 at 477–478, [1977] 1 WLR 605 at 608):

'A man is reckless in the sense required when he carries out a deliberate act knowing that there is some risk of damage resulting from that act but nevertheless continues in the performance of that act.'

This definition was adopted but modified in *R v Parker* [1977] 2 All ER 37, [1977] 1 WLR 600 where the defendant in a fit of temper had broken a telephone by smashing the handset violently down on to the telephone unit and had been convicted under s 1(1) of the 1971 Act. The court (Scarman and Geoffrey Lane LJJ and Kenneth Jones J) ([1977] 2 All ER 37 at 39–40, [1977] 1 WLR 600 at 603–604) readily followed *R v Briggs* but held that the defendant had been fully aware of all the circumstances and that if—

'he did not know, as he said he did not, that there was some risk of damage, he was, in effect, deliberately closing his mind to the obvious-the obvious being that damage in these circumstances was inevitable.'

The court accordingly modified the *R v Briggs* definition in this way:

'A man is reckless in the sense required when he carries out a deliberate act knowing or closing his mind to the obvious fact that there is some risk of damage resulting from that act but nevertheless continuing in the performance of that act.'

This modification made no inroad into the concept of recklessness as then understood since, as pointed out by Professor Glanville Williams *Textbook of Criminal Law* (1st edn, 1978) p 79, cited by Lord Edmund-Davies in his dissenting opinion in *R v Caldwell* [1981] 1 All ER 961 at 970, [1982] AC 341 at 358:

'A person cannot, in any intelligible meaning of the words, close his mind to a risk unless he first realises that there is a risk; and if he realises that there is a risk, that is the end of the matter.'

15. The meaning of 'reckless' in s 1(1) of the 1971 Act was again considered by the Court of Appeal (Geoffrey Lane LJ, Ackner and Watkins JJ) in *R v Stephenson* [1979] 2 All ER 1198, [1979] QB 695. The defendant had tried to go to sleep in a hollow he had made in the side of a haystack. Feeling cold, he had lit a fire in the hollow which had set fire to the stack and damaged property worth £3,500. He had been charged and convicted under s 1(1) and (3) of the 1971 Act. The defendant however had a long history of schizophrenia and expert evidence at trial suggested that he may not have had the same ability to foresee or appreciate risks as the mentally normal person. Giving the reserved judgment of the court, Geoffrey Lane LJ ([1979] 2 All ER 1198 at 1201–1203, [1979] QB 695 at 700–703) reviewed the definition of recklessness in the Law Commission's Working Paper No 31, the acceptance of that definition by the leading academic authorities and the House of Lords' adoption of a subjective meaning of recklessness in tort in *British Railways Board v Herrington* [1972] 1 All ER 749, [1972] AC 877. The court thought it fair to assume that those who were responsible for drafting the 1971 Act were intending to preserve its legal meaning as described in Kenny and expressly approved in *R v Cunningham*. The court then continued:

'What then must the prosecution prove in order to bring home the charge of arson in circumstances such as the present? They must prove that (1) the defendant deliberately committed some act which caused the damage to property alleged or part of such damage; (2) the defendant had no lawful excuse for causing the damage (these two requirements will in the ordinary case not be in issue); (3) the defendant either (a) intended to cause the damage to the property, or (b) was reckless whether the property was damaged or not. A man is reckless when he carries out the deliberate act appreciating that there is a risk that damage to property may result from his act. It is however not the taking of every risk which could properly be classed as reckless. The risk must be one which it is in all the circumstances unreasonable for him to take. Proof of the requisite knowledge in the mind of the defendant will in most cases present little difficulty. The fact that the risk of some damage would have been obvious to anyone in his right mind in the position of the defendant is not conclusive proof of the defendant's knowledge, but it may well be, and in many cases doubtless will be, a matter which will drive the jury to the conclusion that the defendant himself must have appreciated the risk.'

The appeal was accordingly allowed. But the court recognised that what it called the subjective definition of recklessness produced difficulties. One of these was where a person by self-induced intoxication deprived himself of the ability to foresee the risks involved in his actions. The court suggested that a distinction was to be drawn between crimes requiring proof of specific intent and those, such as offences under s 1(1) of the 1971 Act, involving no specific intent ([1979] 2 All ER 1198 at 1204, [1979] QB 695 at 704):

'Accordingly it is no defence under the 1971 Act for a person to say that he was deprived by self-induced intoxication of the ability to foresee or appreciate an obvious risk.'

■ *Questions*

Was Stephenson capable of appreciating the risk of the harm he caused? Was Briggs? Was Parker?

[His lordship continued by discussing *R v Caldwell* [1982] UKHL 1:]

17. *R v Caldwell* [1981] 1 All ER 961, [1982] AC 341 was a case of self-induced intoxication. The defendant, having a grievance against the owner of the hotel where he worked, got very drunk and set fire to the hotel where guests were living at the time. He was indicted upon two counts of arson. The first and more serious count was laid under s 1(2) of the 1971 Act, the second count under s 1(1). He pleaded guilty to the second count but contested the first on the ground that he had been so drunk at the time that the thought there might be people in the hotel had never crossed his mind. His conviction on count 1 was set aside by the Court of Appeal which certified the following question ([1981] 1 All ER 961 at 964, [1982] AC 341 at 344):

'Whether evidence of self-induced intoxication can be relevant to the following questions-(a) Whether the defendant intended to endanger the life of another; and (b) Whether the defendant was reckless as to whether the life of another would be endangered, within the meaning of Section 1(2)(b) of the Criminal Damage Act 1971.'

In submitting that the two questions should be answered (a) Yes and (b) No, counsel for the Crown did not challenge the correctness of *R v Briggs or R v Stephenson*.

18. In a leading opinion with which Lord Keith of Kinkel and Lord Roskill agreed, but from which Lord Wilberforce and Lord Edmund-Davies dissented, Lord Diplock discounted ([1981] 1 All ER 961 at 964–965, [1982] AC 341 at 351) Professor Kenny's statement of the law approved in *R v Cunningham* as directed to the meaning of 'maliciously' in the Malicious Damage Act 1861 and having no bearing on the meaning of 'reckless' in the 1971 Act. It was, he held, no less blameworthy for a man whose mind was affected by rage or excitement or drink to fail to give his mind to the risk of damaging property than for a man whose mind was so affected to appreciate that there was a risk of damage to property but not to appreciate the seriousness of the risk or to trust that good luck would prevent the risk occurring. He observed ([1981] 1 All ER 961 at 965, [1982] AC 341 at 352):

'My Lords, I can see no reason why Parliament when it decided to revise the law as to offences of damage to property should go out of its way to perpetuate fine and impracticable distinctions such as these, between one mental state and another. One would think that the sooner they were got rid of the better.'

Reference was made to *R v Briggs*, *R v Parker* and *R v Stephenson*, but Lord Diplock saw no warrant for assuming that the 1971 Act, whose declared purpose was to revise the law of damage to property, intended 'reckless' to be interpreted as 'maliciously' had been ([1981] 1 All ER 961 at 966, [1982] AC 341 at 353). He preferred the ordinary meaning of 'reckless' which—

'surely includes not only deciding to ignore a risk of harmful consequences resulting from one's acts that one has recognised as existing, but also failing to give any thought to whether or not there is any such risk in circumstances where, if any thought were given to the matter, it would be obvious that there was. If one is attaching labels, the latter state of mind is neither more nor less "subjective" than the first. But the label solves nothing. It is a statement of the obvious; mens rea is, by definition, a state of mind of the accused himself at the time he did the physical act that constitutes the actus reus of the offence; it cannot be the mental state of some non-existent hypothetical person.'

To decide whether a person had been reckless whether harmful consequences of a particular kind would result from his act it was necessary to consider the mind of 'the ordinary prudent individual' ([1981] 1 All ER 961 at 966, [1982] AC 341 at 354). In a passage which has since been taken to encapsulate the law on this point, and which has founded many jury directions (including that in the present case) Lord Diplock then said ([1981] 1 All ER 961 at 967, [1982] AC 341 at 354):

> 'In my opinion, a person charged with an offence under s 1(1) of the 1971 Act is "reckless as to whether or not any property would be destroyed or damaged" if (1) he does an act which in fact creates an obvious risk that property will be destroyed or damaged and (2) when he does the act he either has not given any thought to the possibility of there being any such risk or has recognised that there was some risk involved and has none the less gone on to do it. That would be a proper direction to the jury; cases in the Court of Appeal which held otherwise should be regarded as overruled.'

On the facts Lord Diplock concluded ([1981] 1 All ER 961 at 967, [1982] AC 341 at 355) that the defendant's unawareness, owing to his self-induced intoxication, of the risk of endangering the lives of hotel residents was no defence if that risk would have been obvious to him had he been sober. He held ([1981] 1 All ER 961 at 967, [1982] AC 341 at 356) that evidence of self-induced intoxication was relevant to a charge under s 1(2) based on intention but not to one based on recklessness.

19. In his dissenting opinion Lord Edmund-Davies expressed ([1981] 1 All ER 961 at 969, [1982] AC 341 at 357) 'respectful, but profound, disagreement' with Lord Diplock's dismissal of Professor Kenny's statement which was—

> 'accurate not only in respect of the law as it stood in 1902 but also as it has been applied in countless cases ever since, both in the United Kingdom and in other countries where the common law prevails...'

Lord Edmund-Davies drew attention to the Law Commission's preparation of the 1971 Act and its definition of recklessness in Working Paper No 31 and continued:

> 'It was surely with this contemporaneous definition and the much respected decision of *R v Cunningham* in mind that the draftsman proceeded to his task of drafting the 1971 Act.'

He observed ([1981] 1 All ER 961 at 970, [1982] AC 341 at 358):

> 'In the absence of exculpatory factors, the defendant's state of mind is therefore all-important where recklessness is an element in the offence charged, and s 8 of the Criminal Justice Act 1967 has laid down that: "A court or jury, in determining whether a person has committed an offence,—(a) shall not be bound in law to infer that he intended *or foresaw* a result of his actions by reason only of its being a natural and probable consequence of those actions; but (b) shall decide whether he did intend *or foresee* that result by reference to all the evidence, drawing such inferences from the evidence as appear proper in the circumstances." (Emphasis added.)'

Lord Edmund-Davies differed from the majority on the relevance of evidence of self-induced intoxication: in his opinion ([1981] 1 All ER 961 at 972, [1982] AC 341 at 361) such evidence was relevant to a charge under s 1(2) whether the charge was based on intention or recklessness.

R v Lawrence

20. Judgment was given by the House in *R v Lawrence* [1981] 1 All ER 974, [1982] AC 510 on the same day as *R v Caldwell*, although only two members (Lord Diplock and Lord Roskill) were party to both decisions. The defendant had ridden a motor cycle along an urban street after nightfall and had collided with and killed a pedestrian. He had been charged and convicted under s 1 of the Road Traffic Act 1972 which made it an offence to cause the death of another person by driving a motor vehicle on a road recklessly. His appeal had succeeded on the ground of an inadequate direction to the jury. The issue on appeal to the House concerned the mental element in a charge of reckless driving.

21. Lord Hailsham of St Marylebone LC ([1981] 1 All ER 974 at 975, 978, [1982] AC 510 at 516, 520, 521), agreeing with Lord Diplock and with the majority in *R v Caldwell*, understood recklessness to evince 'a state of mind stopping short of deliberate intention, and going beyond mere inadvertence...' Lord Diplock ([1981] 1 All ER 974 at 982, [1982] AC 510 at 526) rehearsed the history of motoring offences based on recklessness beginning with s 1 of the Motor Car Act 1903 and applied essentially the same test as laid down in *R v Caldwell*, by reference to the 'ordinary prudent individual'. He formulated an appropriate jury direction to the same effect, mutatis mutandis, as that in *R v Caldwell*. But he added ([1981] 1 All ER 974 at 982, [1982] AC 510 at 527):

> 'It is for the jury to decide whether the risk created by the manner in which the vehicle was being driven was both obvious and serious and, in deciding this, they may apply the standard of the ordinary prudent motorist as represented by themselves. If satisfied that an obvious and serious risk was created by the manner of the defendant's driving, the jury are entitled to infer that he was in one or other of the states of mind required to constitute the offence and will probably do so; but regard must be given to any explanation he gives as to his state of mind which may displace the inference.'

Lord Fraser of Tullybelton, Lord Roskill and Lord Bridge of Harwich agreed with Lord Hailsham of St Marylebone LC and Lord Diplock.

■ *Question*

What was the difference between the test expressed in *Caldwell* and that in *Lawrence*?

Later cases

22. The decisions in *R v Caldwell* and *R v Lawrence* were applied by the House (Lord Diplock, Lord Keith of Kinkel, Lord Bridge of Harwich, Lord Brandon of Oakbrook and Lord Brightman) in *R v Miller* [1983] 1 All ER 978, [1983] 2 AC 161 [section 4.3.3.4, p 86], although subject to a qualification germane to the facts of that case but not to the facts of the present case ([1983] 1 All ER 978 at 983, [1983] 2 AC 161 at 179).

23. In *Elliott v C (a minor)* [1983] 2 All ER 1005, [1983] 1 WLR 939 the defendant was a 14-year-old girl of low intelligence who had entered a shed in the early morning, poured white spirit on the floor and set it alight. The resulting fire had flared up and she had left the shed, which had been destroyed. She was charged under s 1(1) of the 1971 Act and at her trial before justices the prosecution made plain that the charge was based not on intention but on recklessness. The justices sought to apply the test laid down in *R v Caldwell* [1981] 1 All ER 961, [1982] AC 341 but inferred that in his reference to 'an obvious risk' Lord Diplock had meant a risk which was obvious to the particular defendant. The justices acquitted the defendant because they found that the defendant had given no thought at the time to the possibility of there being a risk that the shed and contents would be destroyed, and this risk would not have been obvious to her or appreciated by her if she had thought about the matter ([1983] 2 All ER 1005 at 1007–1008, [1983] 1 WLR 939 at 945). The prosecutor's appeal was allowed. Glidewell J, giving the first judgment, accepted the submission that—

> 'if the risk is one which would have been obvious to a reasonably prudent person, once it has also been proved that the particular defendant gave no thought to the possibility of there being such a risk, it is not a defence that because of limited intelligence or exhaustion she would not have appreciated the risk even if she had thought about it.'

Robert Goff LJ felt constrained by the decisions of the House in *R v Caldwell*, *R v Lawrence* and *R v Miller* to agree, but he expressed his unhappiness in doing so and plainly did not consider the outcome to be just. A petition for leave to appeal against this decision was dismissed by an appeal committee.

24. The defendant in *R v Stephen Malcolm R* (1984) 79 Cr App R 334 had thrown petrol bombs at the outside wall of the bedroom of a girl who he believed had informed on him in relation to a series of burglaries. He had admitted throwing the bombs but claimed he had done so to frighten the girl and without realising that if a bomb had gone through the window it might have killed her. He was charged with arson under s 1(2) of the 1971 Act, on the basis of recklessness. At trial, it was submitted on the defendant's behalf that when considering recklessness the jury could only convict him if he did an act which created a risk to life obvious to someone of his age and with such of his characteristics as would affect his appreciation of the risk (at 337). On the trial judge ruling against that submission the defendant changed his plea and the issue in the Court of Appeal (Ackner LJ, Bristow and Popplewell JJ) was whether the ruling had been correct. The court held that it had: if the House had wished to modify the *Caldwell* principle to take account of, for instance, the age of the defendant, the opportunity had existed in *Elliott's* case and it had not been taken. Although concerned at the principle it was required to apply, the court had little doubt that on the facts of the case the answer would have been the same even if the jury had been able to draw a comparison with what a boy of the defendant's age would have appreciated.

[His lordship referred to the appeal in the driving case of *R v Reid* [1992] 3 All ER 673, [1992] 1 WLR 793.]

26. In *R v Coles* [1995] 1 Cr App R 157 a 15-year-old defendant convicted under s 1(2) of the 1971 Act on the basis of recklessness again challenged, unsuccessfully, the rule laid down by Lord Diplock in *R v Caldwell*. Since recklessness was to be judged by the standard of the reasonable, prudent man, it followed that expert evidence of the defendant's capacity to foresee the risks which would arise from his setting fire to hay in a barn had been rightly rejected.

27. In the present case the Court of Appeal (Dyson LJ, Silber J and Judge Beaumont QC) reviewed the authorities ([2002] EWCA Crim 1992 at [18], [2003] 3 All ER 206 at [18]) but was in no doubt that the *Caldwell* test had been rightly applied. It acknowledged (at [23]) that the *Caldwell* test had been criticised and had not been applied in a number of Commonwealth jurisdictions and saw great force in these criticisms but held that it was not open to the Court of Appeal to depart from it.

Conclusions

28. The task confronting the House in this appeal is, first of all, one of statutory construction: what did Parliament mean when it used the word 'reckless' in s 1(1) and (2) of the 1971 Act? In so expressing the question I mean to make it as plain as I can that I am not addressing the meaning of 'reckless' in any other statutory or common law context. In particular, but perhaps needlessly since 'recklessly' has now been banished from the lexicon of driving offences, I would wish to throw no doubt on the decisions of the House in *R v Lawrence and R v Reid*.

29. Since a statute is always speaking, the context or application of a statutory expression may change over time, but the meaning of the expression itself cannot change. So the starting point is to ascertain what Parliament meant by 'reckless' in 1971. As noted above, s 1 as enacted followed, subject to an immaterial addition, the draft proposed by the Law Commission. It cannot be supposed that by 'reckless' Parliament meant anything different from the Law Commission. The Law Commission's meaning was made plain both in its report (Law Com No 29) and in Working Paper No 23 which preceded it. These materials (not, it would seem, placed before the House in *R v Caldwell*) reveal a very plain intention to replace the old-fashioned and misleading expression 'maliciously' by the more familiar expression 'reckless' but to give the latter expression the meaning which *R v Cunningham* [1957] 2 All ER 412, [1957] 2 QB 396 and Professor Kenny had given to the former. In treating this authority as irrelevant to the construction of 'reckless' the majority fell into understandable but clearly demonstrable error. No relevant change in the mens rea necessary for proof of the offence was intended, and in holding otherwise the majority misconstrued section 1 of the Act.

30. What conclusion is by no means determinative of this appeal. For the decision in *R v Caldwell* was made more than 20 years ago. Its essential reasoning was unanimously approved by the House

in *R v Lawrence*. Invitations to reconsider that reasoning have been rejected. The principles laid down have been applied on many occasions, by Crown Court judges and, even more frequently, by justices. In the submission of the Crown, the ruling of the House works well and causes no injustice in practice. If Parliament had wished to give effect to the intention of the Law Commission it has had many opportunities, which it has not taken, to do so. Despite its power under *Practice Statement (Judicial Precedent)* [1966] 3 All ER 77, [1966] 1 WLR 1234 to depart from its earlier decisions, the House should be very slow to do so, not least in a context such as this.

31. These are formidable arguments, deployed by Mr Perry with his habitual skill and erudition. But I am persuaded by Mr Newman QC for the appellants that they should be rejected. I reach this conclusion for four reasons, taken together.

32. First, it is a salutary principle that conviction of serious crime should depend on proof not simply that the defendant caused (by act or omission) an injurious result to another but that his state of mind when so acting was culpable. This, after all, is the meaning of the familiar rule *actus non facit reum nisi mens sit rea*. The most obviously culpable state of mind is no doubt an intention to cause the injurious result, but knowing disregard of an appreciated and unacceptable risk of causing an injurious result or a deliberate closing of the mind to such risk would be readily accepted as culpable also. It is clearly blameworthy to take an obvious and significant risk of causing injury to another. But it is not clearly blameworthy to do something involving a risk of injury to another if (for reasons other than self-induced intoxication (see *DPP v Majewski* [1976] 2 All ER 142, [1977] AC 443)) one genuinely does not perceive the risk. Such a person may fairly be accused of stupidity or lack of imagination, but neither of those failings should expose him to conviction of serious crime or the risk of punishment.

33. Secondly, the present case shows, more clearly than any other reported case since *R v Caldwell* [1981] 1 All ER 961, [1982] AC 341, that the model direction formulated by Lord Diplock (see [18], above) is capable of leading to obvious unfairness. As the excerpts quoted above reveal, the trial judge regretted the direction he (quite rightly) felt compelled to give, and it is evident that this direction offended the jury's sense of fairness. The sense of fairness of 12 representative citizens sitting as a jury (or of a smaller group of lay justices sitting as a bench of magistrates) is the bedrock on which the administration of criminal justice in this country is built. A law which runs counter to that sense must cause concern. Here, the appellants could have been charged under s 1(1) of the 1971 Act with recklessly damaging one or both of the wheelie-bins, and they would have had little defence. As it was, the jury might have inferred that boys of the appellants' age would have appreciated the risk to the building of what they did, but it seems clear that such was not their conclusion (nor, it would appear, the judge's either). On that basis the jury thought it unfair to convict them. I share their sense of unease. It is neither moral nor just to convict a defendant (least of all a child) on the strength of what someone else would have apprehended if the defendant himself had no such apprehension. Nor, the defendant having been convicted, is the problem cured by imposition of a nominal penalty.

34. Thirdly, I do not think the criticism of *R v Caldwell* expressed by academics, judges and practitioners should be ignored. A decision is not, of course, to be overruled or departed from simply because it meets with disfavour in the learned journals. But a decision which attracts reasoned and outspoken criticism by the leading scholars of the day, respected as authorities in the field, must command attention. One need only cite (among many other examples) the observations of Professor John Smith [1981] Crim LR 392 at 393–396 and Professor Glanville Williams 'Recklessness Redefined' (1981) 40 CLJ 252. This criticism carries greater weight when voiced also by judges as authoritative as Lord Edmund-Davies and Lord Wilberforce in *R v Caldwell* itself, Robert Goff LJ in *Elliott v C (a minor)* [1983] 2 All ER 1005, [1983] 1 WLR 939 and Ackner LJ in *R v Stephen Malcolm R* (1984) 79 Cr App R 334. The reservations expressed by the trial judge in the present case are widely shared. The shop floor response to *R v Caldwell* may be gauged from the editors' commentary, to be found in *Archbold's Pleading, Evidence and Practice in Criminal Cases* (41st edn, 1982) pp 1009–1010 (para 17–25). The editors suggested that remedial legislation was urgently required.

35. Fourthly, the majority's interpretation of 'reckless' in s 1 of the 1971 Act was, as already shown, a misinterpretation. If it were a misinterpretation that offended no principle and gave rise to no injustice there would be strong grounds for adhering to the misinterpretation and leaving Parliament to correct it if it chose. But this misinterpretation is offensive to principle and is apt to cause injustice. That being so, the need to correct the misinterpretation is compelling.

36. It is perhaps unfortunate that the question at issue in this appeal fell to be answered in a case of self-induced intoxication. For one instinctively recoils from the notion that a defendant can escape the criminal consequences of his injurious conduct by drinking himself into a state where he is blind to the risk he is causing to others. In *R v Caldwell* it seems to have been assumed (see [18], above) that the risk would have been obvious to the defendant had he been sober. Further, the context did not require the House to give close consideration to the liability of those (such as the very young and the mentally handicapped) who were not normal, reasonable adults. The overruling by the majority of *R v Stephenson* [1979] 2 All ER 1198, [1979] QB 695 does however make it questionable whether such consideration would have led to a different result.

37. In the course of argument before the House it was suggested that the rule in *R v Caldwell* might be modified, in cases involving children, by requiring comparison not with normal, reasonable adults but with normal, reasonable children of the same age. This is a suggestion with some attractions but it is open to four compelling objections. First, even this modification would offend the principle that conviction should depend on proving the state of mind of the individual defendant to be culpable. Second, if the rule were modified in relation to children on grounds of their immaturity it would be anomalous if it were not also modified in relation to the mentally handicapped on grounds of their limited understanding. Third, any modification along these lines would open the door to difficult and contentious argument concerning the qualities and characteristics to be taken into account for purposes of the comparison. Fourth, to adopt this modification would be to substitute one misinterpretation of s 1 for another. There is no warrant in the Act or in the *travaux préparatoires* which preceded it for such an interpretation.

38. A further refinement, advanced by Professor Glanville Williams (1981) 40 CLJ 252 at 270–271, adopted by the justices in *Elliott's* case and commented upon by Robert Goff LJ in that case is that a defendant should only be regarded as having acted recklessly by virtue of his failure to give any thought to an obvious risk that property would be destroyed or damaged, where such risk would have been obvious to him if he had given any thought to the matter. This refinement also has attractions, although it does not meet the objection of principle and does not represent a correct interpretation of the section. It is, in my opinion, open to the further objection of over-complicating the task of the jury (or bench of justices). It is one thing to decide whether a defendant can be believed when he says that the thought of a given risk never crossed his mind. It is another, and much more speculative, task to decide whether the risk would have been obvious to him if the thought had crossed his mind. The simpler the jury's task, the more likely is its verdict to be reliable. Robert Goff LJ's reason for rejecting this refinement ([1983] 2 All ER 1005 at 1011–1012, [1983] 1 WLR 939 at 950) was somewhat similar.

39. I cannot accept that restoration of the law as understood before *R v Caldwell* would lead to the acquittal of those whom public policy would require to be convicted. There is nothing to suggest that this was seen as a problem before *R v Caldwell*, or before the 1971 Act. There is no reason to doubt the common sense which tribunals of fact bring to their task. In a contested case based on intention, the defendant rarely admits intending the injurious result in question, but the tribunal of fact will readily infer such an intention, in a proper case, from all the circumstances and probabilities and evidence of what the defendant did and said at the time. Similarly with recklessness: it is not to be supposed that the tribunal of fact will accept a defendant's assertion that he never thought of a certain risk when all the circumstances and probabilities and evidence of what he did and said at the time show that he did or must have done.

40. In his printed case, Mr Newman advanced the contention that the law as declared in *R v Caldwell* was incompatible with art 6 of the European Convention for the Protection of Human Rights

and Fundamental Freedoms 1950 (as set out in Sch 1 to the Human Rights Act 1998). While making no concession, he forbore to address legal argument on the point. I need say no more about it.

41. For the reasons I have given I would allow this appeal and quash the appellants' convictions. I would answer the certified question obliquely, basing myself on cl 18(c) of the Criminal Code Bill annexed by the Law Commission to its report *A Criminal Code for England and Wales* (1989) (Law Com no 177) vol 1, Report and Draft Criminal Code Bill):

> '[A] person acts . . . "recklessly" [within the meaning of s 1 of the 1971 Act] with respect to-(i) a circumstance when he is aware of a risk that it exists or will exist; (ii) a result when he is aware of a risk that it will occur; and it is, in the circumstances known to him, unreasonable to take the risk . . .'

Lord Steyn: . . .

45. In my view the very high threshold for departing from a previous decision of the House has been satisfied in this particular case. In summary I would reduce my reasons to three propositions. First, in *R v Caldwell* the majority should have accepted without equivocation that before the passing of the 1971 Act foresight of consequences was an essential element in recklessness in the context of damage to property under s 51 of the Malicious Damage Act 1861. Secondly, the matrix of the immediately preceding Law Commission recommendations shows convincingly that the purpose of s 1 of the 1971 Act was to replace the out of date language of 'maliciously' causing damage by more modern language while not changing the substance of the mental element in any way. Foresight of consequences was to remain an ingredient of recklessness in regard to damage to property. Thirdly, experience has shown that by bringing within the reach of s 1(1) cases of inadvertent recklessness the decision in *R v Caldwell* became a source of serious potential injustice which cannot possibly be justified on policy grounds. . . .

52. In the case before the House the two boys were 11 and 12 respectively. Their escapade of camping overnight without their parents' permission was something that many children have undertaken. But by throwing lit newspapers under a plastic wheelie-bin they caused £1m of damage to a shop. It is, however, an agreed fact on this appeal that the boys thought there was no risk of the fire spreading in the way it eventually did. What happened at trial is highly significant. The jury were perplexed by the *Caldwell* directions which compelled them to treat the boys as adults and to convict them. The judge plainly thought this approach was contrary to common sense but loyally applied the law as laid down in *R v Caldwell*. The view of the jurors and the judge would be widely shared by reasonable people who pause to consider the matter. The only answer of the Crown is that where unjust convictions occur the judge can impose a lenient sentence. This will not do in a modern criminal justice system. Parliament certainly did not authorise such a cynical strategy.

53. Ignoring the special position of children in the criminal justice system is not acceptable in a modern civil society. In 1990 the United Kingdom ratified the United Nations *Convention on the Rights of the Child* (New York, 20 November 1989; TS 44 (1992); Cm 1976) (the UN convention) which entered into force on 15 January 1992. Article 40(1) provides:

> 'States Parties recognize the right of every child alleged as, accused of, or recognized as having infringed the penal law to be treated in a manner consistent with the promotion of the child's sense of dignity and worth, which reinforces the child's respect for the human rights and funda-mental freedoms of others and which takes into account the child's age and the desirability of promoting the child's reintegration and the child's assuming a constructive role in society.' (My emphasis.)

This provision imposes both procedural and substantive obligations on state parties to protect the special position of children in the criminal justice system. For example, it would plainly be contrary to art 40(1) for a state to set the age of criminal responsibility of children at, say, five years. Similarly, it is contrary to art 40(1) to ignore in a crime punishable by life imprisonment, or detention during Her

Majesty's pleasure, the age of a child in judging whether the mental element has been satisfied. It is true that the UN convention became binding on the United Kingdom after *R v Caldwell* was decided. But the House cannot ignore the norm created by the UN convention. This factor on its own justified a reappraisal of *R v Caldwell*.

■ *Questions*

Is there a strong argument for having a special test of recklessness for children? What about adults with mental or physical incapacity?

---

54. If it is wrong to ignore the special characteristics of children in the context of recklessness under s 1 of the 1971 Act, an adult who suffers from a lack of mental capacity or a relevant personality disorder may be entitled to the same standard of justice. Recognising the special characteristics of children and mentally disabled people goes some way towards reducing the scope of s 1 of the 1971 Act for producing unjust results which are inherent in the objective mould into which the *Caldwell* analysis forced recklessness. It does not, however, restore the correct interpretation of s 1 of the 1971 Act. The accepted meaning of recklessness involved foresight of consequences. This subjective state of mind is to be inferred 'by reference to all the evidence, drawing such inferences from the evidence as appear proper in the circumstances' (per Lord Edmund-Davies [1981] 1 All ER 961 at 970, [1982] AC 341 at 358, citing s 8 of the Criminal Justice Act 1967). That is what Parliament intended by implementing the Law Commission proposals.

55. This interpretation of s 1 of the 1971 Act would fit in with the general tendency in modern times of our criminal law. The shift is towards adopting a subjective approach. It is generally necessary to look at the matter in the light of how it would have appeared to the defendant. Like Lord Edmund-Davies I regard s 8 of the 1967 Act, as of central importance. There is, however, also a congruence of analysis appearing from decisions of the House. In *Director of Public Prosecutions v Morgan* [1975] 2 All ER 347, [1976] AC 182 [[1975] UKHL 3] the House ruled that a defence of mistake must be honestly rather than reasonably held. In *Beckford v R* [1987] 3 All ER 425 at 432, [1988] AC 130 at 145 per Lord Griffiths [section 11.6.1, p 414], the House held that self-defence permits a defendant to use such force as is reasonable in the circumstances as he honestly believed them to be. *B (a minor) v Director of Public Prosecutions* [2000] 1 All ER 833, [2000] 2 AC 428 concerned the offence contrary to s 1(1) of the Children Act 1961 [see section 7.3.1, p 185]. The House held that the accused's honest belief that a girl was over 14 need not be based on reasonable grounds. Lord Nicholls of Birkenhead observed ([2000] 1 All ER 833 at 837, [2000] 2 AC 428 at 462):

> 'Considered as a matter of principle, the honest belief approach must be preferable. By definition the mental element in a crime is concerned with a subjective state of mind, such as intent or belief.'

To same effect is *R v K* [2001] UKHL 41, [2001] 3 All ER 897, [2002] 1 AC 462 [section 7.3.1, p 185] where it was held that while a girl under the age of 16 cannot in law consent to an indecent assault, it is a defence if the defendant honestly believed she was over 16. It is true that the general picture is not entirely harmonious. Duress requires reasonable belief (see Lord Lane CJ in *R v Graham* [1982] 1 All ER 801 at 806, [1982] 1 WLR 294 at 300, approved by the House of Lords in *R v Howe* [1987] 1 All ER 771, [1987] AC 417; *R v Martin* [1989] 1 All ER 652). Duress is a notoriously difficult corner of the law. However, in *R v Graham* [1982] 1 All ER 801 at 806, [1982] 1 WLR 294 at 300 [section 11.3.3, p 377] Lord Lane CJ stated that in judging the accused's response the test is:

> '...have the prosecution made the jury sure that a sober person of reasonable firmness, sharing the characteristics of the defendant, would not have responded to whatever he reasonably believed [the threatener] said or did by taking part in the [offence].' (My emphasis.)

The age and sex of the defendant (but possibly no other characteristics) are relevant to the cogency of the threat (see *R v Bowen* [1996] 4 All ER 837, [1997] 1 WLR 372). In regard to provocation a wider view of the impact on defendant has prevailed (see *R v Smith* [2000] 4 All ER 289, [2001] 1 AC 146 (by a three to two majority)).

56. These developments show that what Lord Diplock described in *R v Caldwell* [1981] 1 All ER 961 at 966, [1982] AC 341 at 353 as an 'esoteric meaning' of recklessness was also consistent with the general trend of the criminal law.

Conclusion on *Caldwell*

57. The surest test of a new legal rule is not whether it satisfies a team of logicians but how it performs in the real world. With the benefit of hindsight the verdict must be that the rule laid down by the majority in *R v Caldwell* failed this test. It was severely criticised by academic lawyers of distinction. It did not command respect among practitioners and judges. Jurors found it difficult to understand: it also sometimes offended their sense of justice. Experience suggests that in *R v Caldwell* the law took a wrong turn.

58. That brings me to the question whether the subjective interpretation of recklessness might allow wrongdoers who ought to be convicted of serious crime to escape conviction. Experience before *R v Caldwell* did not warrant such a conclusion. In any event, as Lord Edmund-Davies explained ([1981] 1 All ER 961 at 970, [1982] AC 341 at 358), if a defendant closes his mind to a risk he must realise that there is a risk and, on the evidence, that will usually be decisive. One can trust the realism of trial judges, who direct juries, to guide juries to sensible verdicts and juries can in turn be relied on to apply robust common sense to the evaluation of ridiculous defences. Moreover, the endorsement by Parliament of the Law Commission proposals could not seriously have been regarded as a charter for the acquittal of wrongdoers.

59. In my view the case for departing from *R v Caldwell* has been shown to be irresistible.

60. I agree with the reasons given by Lord Bingham of Cornhill. I have nothing to add to his observations on self-induced intoxication.

Appeal allowed

■ Questions

Should a person be held to be reckless only if:

(i) he was aware of a risk of the proscribed result and unreasonably took the risk; or

(ii) he was aware of a risk of the proscribed result or if not aware personally he would have been aware of it if *he* had given thought to the matter (compare *Briggs* and *Stephenson* referred to in Lord Bingham's judgment) and unreasonably took it; or

(iii) he was aware of a risk of the proscribed result or if not aware personally a person of his age and with his relevant characteristics who gave thought to the matter would have been aware of one (see the rejected argument in *Stephen Malcolm R*) and unreasonably took the risk; or

(iv) he was aware of a risk of the proscribed result or if not aware personally a reasonably prudent person who gave thought to the matter would have been aware of it and D took that risk?

Into which category above would the defendants in *G* fit?

The House of Lords in *G* made clear that the principle espoused in *Caldwell* was unacceptable for serious crimes (see in particular Lord Bingham at [32]). In this respect the House of Lords was endorsing its commitment to subjectivism (oddly enough it has done so at a time when Parliament keeps creating serious offences based on objective fault elements, as in sexual offences).

The law is returned to what it was intended to be. Recklessness in criminal damage is to be construed in a subjective sense—by looking to the state of mind of the individual defendant.

■ *Question*

Should the law be stricter still and require foresight of a 'substantial' or 'real' risk?

5.3.1 Subjective recklessness of general application

Although explicitly a decision on the criminal damage offences, G is, it seems, being accepted as providing the correct test for recklessness in any offence for which that state of mind suffices as the fault element. In *A-G's Reference (No 3 of 2003)* [2004] EWCA Crim 868, [2004] 2 Cr App R 23 the defendant police officers had arrested V who had been injured in a fight and had become abusive and aggressive towards hospital staff when receiving treatment. Following medical confirmation that V was fit to be detained, he was placed partially face down wearing handcuffs in the custody suite but developed breathing difficulties and died. The officers were charged with gross negligence manslaughter and misconduct in a public office. They were acquitted on the judge's direction because (i) there was a lack of causation on the gross negligence counts, and (ii) there was insufficient evidence of recklessness for a conviction for misconduct. On the reference by the Attorney General, the court considered the subjective approach to recklessness pronounced in G. The Crown sought to restrict the impact of G in two ways. First, it was argued that the House of Lords expressly limited its conclusions on recklessness to criminal damage. It was argued that in conduct crimes such as misconduct in public office, the issue of recklessness ought to be focused on the misconduct itself, not on the likelihood of any result being caused. The Crown argued that the prosecution ought to succeed on proof that there has been misconduct by the defendant and he was '*indifferent*' as to whether the acts or omissions constituting the misconduct may have any consequences. The court rejected any such limitation on the subjective approach in G. Secondly, the Crown argued that in crimes in which liability arises because of a duty situation, an objective test of recklessness ought to apply so that those who do not advert to the risk of harm to particular individuals ought to be found reckless. The Court of Appeal rejected the argument. The court considered the House of Lords' interpretation of 'wilful neglect' in the case of duty as in *Sheppard* [1981] AC 394 (dealing with child neglect), and emphasized that in its view *Sheppard* imposed a subjective test in which the characteristics of the individual defendant were to be taken into consideration. The Court of Appeal's conclusion was (at para 7) that *Sheppard* 'did not impose a lower duty on the prosecution than G'. For the purposes of wilful neglect or misconduct it was necessary for the offender to have subjective awareness of the duty to act or a subjective recklessness as to the existence of the duty.

5.3.1.1 Foresight of a risk

In *Brady* [2006] EWCA Crim 2413, D was drunk when he climbed on railings at a nightclub and fell onto the dance floor below causing serious injuries to V who was dancing there. Directing the jury as to recklessness, the judge had said, 'where there is no issue of intoxication [see section 6.3, p 151] the test requires that the defendant should be aware of a risk and go on to take it, the risk being of injury'. He then directed the jury on recklessness in the context of voluntary intoxication, saying, 'if the defendant had been sober and in good mental shape would he have realised that some injury... might result from his actions in what he was doing in the condition he was in that night'. D's first ground of appeal was that the effect of the decision in *G and R* [2003] UKHL 50 required the jury to be directed that the Crown had to establish that D had foreseen 'an obvious and significant risk' of injury to another by his actions, or else that he would have done so had he been sober. The Court of Appeal held *G* does not require proof that D had foreseen 'an obvious and significant risk' in order to establish that he had acted recklessly; and it followed that there was no need for a trial judge directing a jury as to recklessness to qualify the word 'risk' by the words 'obvious and significant'. However, the Court of Appeal allowed the appeal, because the judge had failed to direct the jury as to recklessness in sufficiently clear and careful terms. The judge had directed the jury that the only issue for them was one of recklessness, when in fact it had been necessary for him to direct the jury as to recklessness in the different contexts of whether the appellant had deliberately jumped from the railings or whether he had accidentally fallen. Further, it was not sufficiently clear from the judge's directions that the test of recklessness was not an objective one.

See also *Booth* [2006] EWHC 192 (Admin), where D damaged V's car when he was knocked down by V. D was convicted of criminal damage since he was reckless as to the damage having seen the risk of being knocked down and closed his mind to that risk.

■ *Question*

Must D be aware of the risk of causing the exact harm that the law prohibits, or is it sufficient if D has a general sense that his conduct is risky?

5.3.2 *Caldwell*

Although the decision in *Caldwell* has now been overruled and is to be regarded as wrong as regards its conclusions on recklessness, it deserves further consideration. For criticism of *Caldwell* see commentary [1981] Crim LR 393; E. Griew, 'Reckless Damage and Reckless Driving—Living with *Caldwell* and *Lawrence*' [1981] Crim LR 743; G. Syrota, 'A Radical Change in the Law of Recklessness' [1982] Crim LR 97; and Glanville Williams, 'Recklessness Redefined' (1981) 40 CLJ 252. See also J. McEwan and St John Robilliard, 'Recklessness: The House of Lords and the Criminal Law' (1981) 1 LS 267 and the response of G. Williams (1982) 2 LS 189.

The majority in *Caldwell* had ruled:

> a person charged with an offence under s 1(1) of the 1971 Act is 'reckless as to whether or not any property would be destroyed or damaged' if (1) he does an act which in fact creates an obvious risk that property will be destroyed or damaged and (2) when he does the act he either has not given any thought to the possibility of there being any such risk or has recognised that there was some risk involved and has none the less gone on to do it.

■ *Questions*

1. Was recklessness under the *Caldwell* definition a 'state of mind'? Was it really mens rea? Glanville Williams wrote that to describe giving no thought as a state of mind was 'an abuse of language' (1981) 40 CLJ 252.

2. Might it be said that Lord Diplock was reckless in producing his model direction by failing to refer to the Law Commission work on the definition intended for the 1971 Act?!

Caldwell recklessness was described by some as a form of negligence. It was pointed out by critics of the *Caldwell/Lawrence* test of recklessness that the only thing that prevented it from being a straightforward gross negligence test was that a person who did give thought to the possibility of there being a risk and concluded, grossly negligently, that there was no risk, was not guilty of recklessness under either of Lord Diplock's alternatives. This escape hole became known as 'the lacuna'. Some writers disputed whether it existed at all; but its existence was essential if any credence was to be given to Lord Diplock's insistence that he was describing two 'states of mind'. good illustration of the so-called lacuna is to be found in the facts of *Crossman* (1986) 82 Cr App R 333, [1986] Crim LR 406 though the point of law was not taken. D, a lorry driver, rejected the advice of the loaders of a piece of heavy machinery on his lorry that it was unsafe unless chained and sheeted. D said it was 'as safe as houses'. When he drove away, the load fell off and killed a pedestrian. D's defence, that reckless driving must have something to do with the handling or control of the vehicle, was rejected. He then pleaded guilty to causing death by reckless driving. The same point was taken on appeal and the appeal was dismissed. But could D be said to have failed to give thought to the possibility of there being any risk when that possibility had been drawn to his attention, considered and rejected by him? And could he be said to have recognized that there was some risk involved if he really believed that the load was 'as safe as houses'? Should not the case have gone to the jury with a direction that, if D believed, or may have believed, that the load was as safe as houses, recklessness was not proved? He may have been grossly negligent in forming his opinion. If so, he would now be guilty of causing death by dangerous driving and his liability for manslaughter would depend on whether his negligence created a risk to life, bad enough, in the opinion of the jury, to deserve condemnation as that offence. In *Reid* [1992] 3 All ER 673, HL, the House acknowledged the lacuna. Lord Browne-Wilkinson agreeing with Lords Ackner and Goff, said 'There may be cases where, despite the defendant being aware of the risk and deciding to take it, he does so because of a reasonable misunderstanding, sudden disability or emergency which renders it inappropriate to characterise his conduct as being reckless.' See L. Leigh, 'Recklessness after *Reid*' (1993) 56 MLR 208.

5.3.3 Objective recklessness and its merits

One of the interesting aspects of *Caldwell* was that it caused commentators to consider important questions about what the approach to recklessness *ought* to be.

■ **Questions**

Should what matters be D's *attitude* to the risk of harm rather than his foresight of it? Which test—*Caldwell* or *G*—better reflects that? See further, D. Birch [1988] Crim LR 4.

In *Caldwell* (section 5.3.2, p 121), Lord Diplock had suggested that there is no difference in culpability between a defendant who has given no thought to the possibility that there might be a risk and one who knows there is a risk and decides to take it. Do you agree? Consider the case of the South Wales bus driver who in 1982 attempted to drive his 13ft 9in double-decker under a railway bridge 10ft 6in high, killing six people and injuring several others. (See *The Times*, 7 October 1982, 2 November 1982 and 13 January 1983.) It appears that he had driven the route regularly for ten years but had never taken a double-decker on the route before. When he hit the bridge he thought, 'My God, a double-decker.' He knew he was driving a double-decker because, only two stops before the crash, he had told passengers boarding the bus that there was plenty of room upstairs. But, as he approached the bridge, he had apparently forgotten that he was driving a double-decker. It was stated at the inquest that the Director of Public Prosecutions did not consider there was evidence for a charge of manslaughter or causing death by dangerous (meaning, presumably 'reckless', dangerous driving having been, at that time, abolished) driving. The driver subsequently pleaded guilty to driving without due care and attention.

Although *G* was a unanimous decision, Lord Rodger was clearly not as committed to the subjectivist approach to recklessness as his brethren:

Lord Rodger of Earlsferry:

65. It is no secret that, for a long time, many of the leading academic writers on English criminal law have been 'subjectivists'. By that I mean, at the risk of gross over-simplification, that they have believed that the criminal law should punish people only for those consequences of their acts which they foresaw at the relevant time. Those who subscribe to that philosophy will tend to approve the concept of recklessness in *R v Cunningham* [1957] 2 All ER 412, [1957] 2 QB 396. The late Professor Glanville Williams and the late Professor John Smith, who were members of the influential Criminal Law Revision Committee, were two of the most distinguished proponents of such views. . . .

68. It is equally clear that other views are not only possible but have actually been adopted by English judges at different times over the centuries. Their judgments reveal many strands of thinking (see J Horder 'Two Histories and Four Hidden Principles of Mens Rea' (1997) 113 LQR 95). There is therefore no reason to treat the concept of recklessness expounded in *R v Cunningham* either as being the quintessence of the historic English criminal law on the point or as necessarily providing the best solution in all circumstances. Indeed in *R v Stephenson* [1979] 2 All ER 1198, [1979] QB 695, a case on s 1(1) of the 1971 Act, Geoffrey Lane LJ recognised that the subjective approach was problematical in certain situations. Having made it quite clear that in his view the test of recklessness under the 1971 Act remained subjective and that the knowledge or appreciation of risk of some damage must have entered the defendant's mind, he commented ([1979] 2 All ER 1198 at 1204, [1979] QB 695 at 704):

> 'There is no doubt that the subjective definition of "recklessness" does produce difficulties. One of them which is particularly likely to occur in practice is the case of the person who by self-induced intoxication by drink or drugs deprives himself of the ability to foresee the risks involved in his actions. Assuming that by reason of his intoxication he is not proved to have foreseen the relevant risk, can he be said to have been "reckless"? Plainly not, unless cases of self-induced intoxication are an exception to the general rule. In our judgment the decision of the House of Lords in *Director of Public Prosecutions v Majewski* ([1976] 2 All ER 142, [1977] AC 443) makes it clear that they are such an exception.'

In *R v Caldwell* just the kind of problem envisaged by Geoffrey Lane LJ arose: the defendant said that he was so drunk that it did not occur to him that there might be people in the hotel whose lives might be endangered if he set fire to it. Part of what Lord Diplock did to confront the kind of difficulty identified by Geoffrey Lane LJ was to adopt a wider definition of recklessness that covered culpable inadvertence. In so doing, as the House now holds, he misconstrued the terms of the 1971 Act.

69. It does not follow, however, that Lord Diplock's broader concept of recklessness was undesirable in terms of legal policy. On the contrary, there is much to be said for the view that, if the law is to operate with the concept of recklessness, then it may properly treat as reckless the man who acts without even troubling to give his mind to a risk that would have been obvious to him if he had thought about it. This approach may be better suited to some offences than to others. For example, in the context of reckless driving the House endorsed and re-endorsed a more stringent version (see *R v Lawrence* [1981] 1 All ER 974, [1982] AC 510; *R v Reid* [1992] 3 All ER 673, [1992] 1 WLR 793). I refer in particular to the discussion of the policy issues by Lord Goff of Chieveley in *R v Reid* [1992] 3 All ER 673 at 686–689, [1992] 1 WLR 793 at 808–812. Moreover, the opposing view, that only advertent risk-taking should ever be included within the concept of recklessness in criminal law, seems to be based, at least in part, on the kind of thinking that the late Professor Hart demolished in his classic essay, 'Negligence, Mens Rea and Criminal Responsibility' (1961), reprinted in HLA Hart *Punishment and Responsibility* (1968) pp 136–157.

70. Because the decision in *R v Caldwell* involved this legitimate choice between two legal policies, I was initially doubtful whether it would be appropriate for the House to overrule it. An alternative way to allow the appeal by reanalysing Lord Diplock's speech and overruling *Elliott v C (a minor)* [1983] 2 All ER 1005, [1983] 1 WLR 939 might well have been found. But, for the reasons that I have already indicated, I have come to share your Lordships' view that we should indeed overrule *R v Caldwell* and set the law back on the track that Parliament originally intended it to follow. If Parliament now thinks it preferable for the 1971 Act to cover culpably inadvertent as well as advertent wrongdoers, it can so enact. The Law Commission recognised that, if codifying the law, Parliament might wish to adopt that approach (see A Criminal Code for England and Wales (1989) (Law Com no 177) vol 2, Commentary on Draft Criminal Code Bill, p 366 (para 8.21), pp 446–447 (para 17.6)).

■ *Questions*

Do you agree that 'there is much to be said for the view that, if the law is to operate with the concept of recklessness, then it may properly treat as reckless the man who acts without even troubling to turn *his* mind to a risk that would have been obvious to him if he had thought about it?'

See the excellent article by J. Horder, 'Two Histories and Four Hidden Principles of *Mens Rea*' (1997) 113 LQR 95.

Was the House of Lords right to reject a modified position of the *Caldwell* approach to deal only with cases involving children? Why should the law tolerate a child's incapacities any more than those of an adult with a relevant disability? On recklessness and *G*, see the excellent discussion by H. Keating, 'Reckless Children' [2007] Crim LR 546. Professor Keating conducted empirical work, based on hypothetical scenarios similar to those in *G*. These revealed that 69 per cent of members of the public *do* regard behaviour such as that of the boys as criminally blameworthy. Most of those believed that boys of that age (11 and 12) were old enough to have realized the risks involved. Do you agree?

Perhaps the definition of recklessness ought to depend upon the nature of the offence? Consider the following extract.

S. Cunningham, 'Recklessness: Being Reckless and Acting Recklessly' (2010) 23 KLJ 445

The key to the mistakes made by the courts is that they tried to find a definition of recklessness to apply to both conduct crimes and result crimes. Reckless driving is a conduct crime. It does not require any concrete harm to have been caused by the blameworthy conduct of the offender, since it exists to punish those who take risks and to regulate the dangerous activity of driving. Non-aggravated criminal damage [ie cases in which D does not intend or is reckless as to whether the life of another will be endangered. See Chapter 28] and offences against the person such as assault are result crimes, which require a specific harm to have been caused as part of the *actus reus* of the offence. These two different types of crime should have been dealt with in entirely different ways by the courts, given their different natures.

...

Examples of conduct crimes (reckless driving, child neglect, rape, aggravated criminal damage) all involve the creation of risks. But all of these activities are in themselves hazardous occupations if not carried out with care. The underlying risk is always present in that: driving is inherently dangerous; caring for a child can easily end in tragedy if sufficient attention is not paid to the child's needs; there is the possibility of interfering with another's autonomy; damage to property can easily create danger of at least injury to others. [Cunningham then quotes an article on the psychology of risk, before continuing:]

If someone is engaging in hazardous conduct, where the potential for risk exists, the question of whether she has foreseen that a risk might materialise is not relevant. The salient point is that she must take care in engaging in the activity to try to minimise the possibility of the potential risk occurring. If she fails to take sufficient care, creating a risk from a hazardous situation, she becomes blameworthy, whether or not she adverts to the risk. She carried out the hazardous activity in a reckless manner if she fails to take care, thereby creating a risk which should have been avoided.

An objective test of *mens rea* is appropriate in relation to conduct crimes, because D is partaking in a dangerous activity and so *should* pay attention to the risks and is blameworthy if she does not. D ought to make her knowledge of a risk 'explicit', to use another term employed by Duff, by making herself alert to the potential risks involved in the activity and calling her latent knowledge to mind. If she fails to do so she is blameworthy and should attract criminal condemnation. On the other hand, in relation to result crimes we start from the position that a particular proscribed harm has been caused, and need to work our way from there in order to determine whether D's state of mind is sufficiently blameworthy in relation to that harm in order to attract criminal liability. A different test from that employed in relation to conduct crimes is appropriate.

■ *Questions*

Is Cunningham correct that whether recklessness is understood in an objective or subjective sense should be contingent upon whether the offence in question is a result crime as opposed to a conduct crime? Is it really true to say that conduct crimes necessarily involve D partaking in a hazardous activity? What about fraud?

Although it is true that the House of Lords in *G* affirmed the prominence of subjectivism, there are those who argue that this has the potential to create a disparity between the legal test of mens rea and the community's sense of moral wrong.

K. Amirthalingham, '*Caldwell* Recklessness is Dead: Long Live Mens Rea's Fecklessness' (2004) 63 MLR 491

An assumption in this paper is that criminal liability requires moral blameworthiness, which is provided by proof of mens rea. It is beyond the scope of a case note to expand on this argument, which although not universally accepted nevertheless commands some support. Briefly, blameworthiness goes beyond mere conduct responsibility; it is a normative inquiry as to whether the person deserves to be labeled and punished as a criminal. The blameworthiness of an accused is not determined merely by inquiring whether there existed a 'subjective' mens rea; it requires an additional crucial step of asking whether the 'mens was rea'. This inquiry involves an 'objective' element and includes inadvertence within mens rea. Even if one does not accept the moral blameworthiness thesis and adopts Hart's view that mens rea is merely about ensuring that the accused had a fair opportunity to exercise his or her physical and mental capacities to avoid infringing the law, a similar conclusion as to inadvertence is reached. As Hart himself says, 'it does not appear unduly harsh, or a sign of archaic or unenlightened conceptions of responsibility, to include gross, unthinking carelessness among the things for which we blame and punish'. Criminal fault is a composite of subjective and objective elements. Orthodox theory however insists on an artificial bifurcation and the inquiry into blameworthiness is hijacked by the futile exercise of labeling fault as subjective or objective. *R v G* regretfully preserves this unhelpful predilection.

The earlier mens rea term of 'maliciously' was inherently normative as it connoted wickedness or wrongfulness. Thus, a person who acted maliciously could be fairly said to be blameworthy or culpable. The modern subjective concepts of intention and recklessness however are in reality limited to attributing the conduct, not blameworthiness, to the accused. One cannot determine blameworthiness or culpability without reference to some external standard. This calls for a degree of objective evaluation, which is shunned by the subjectivists. The exclusion of objective fault from mens rea is based on the misguided belief that there is such a thing as purely subjective fault.

That the law has never attempted anywhere a purely subjective test is at once apparent. If we speak of legal fault, we mean only that the actor's conduct has departed from the standards of the community because the actor is different from others in one of two respects. He may differ from the community in his ideas of the relative values of different interests, or may fall below the community standard in the exercise of his will. . . . Thus 'fault' becomes a failure to exercise the will or the improper exercise of it with reference to a standard will and a standard valuation of desirables and undesirables. There is no subjective legal fault. What often escapes the subjectivists' consciousness is the fact that objective evaluation of blameworthiness is an integral part of the criminal law; it is just dealt with separately in the form of various defences such as mistake, duress, provocation, self defence and necessity. It is when these 'excusing' factors overlap with mens rea that courts are forced into a subjective approach, thus disabling the normative subjective/objective balance that has been developed within the existing structure of the criminal law. Incorporating an objective evaluation of blameworthiness within the doctrine of mens rea need not be seen as a radical proposition.

Mens rea is presently treated as a unitary concept, which is wholly subservient to subjectivism. It is suggested that a dualistic model be preferred, where the 'mens' and the 'rea' are separate. The 'mens' is the subjective mental element that attributes responsibility for the conduct and consequence to the accused; and the 'rea' is the normative evaluation of that mental element, which attributes moral blameworthiness to the accused. Instead of asking whether there was 'mens rea', the question would be whether the 'mens was rea'.

With recklessness, the 'rea' question in many cases will be whether the accused should have foreseen certain additional consequences of his intentional or foreseeable conduct. Andrew Ashworth has argued that every individual has certain duties of citizenship, one of which is to abide by the law and to know and understand the law. The theory was offered to recognise certain mistakes of law as capable of excusing the accused; in such cases one could fairly say that the 'mens' was not 'rea'. Similarly one can argue that as members of a community, there is a duty to consider obvious risks attending one's conduct. A failure to advert would therefore be culpable and an accused could not argue that his mental state was free from blame; in such cases the 'mens' would be 'rea'.

Caldwell fell into error by using an objective test to determine the existence, rather than the quality, of the relevant mental state. This was flawed because it was not the accused's mental state that was being judged. A subjective test is necessary to establish the existence of a relevant mental state—the 'mens'. This ensures individual responsibility; it takes into account the accused's personal capacity so it cannot be said that the accused him or herself did not have a fair opportunity to avoid criminal liability. It is only in determining the blameworthiness of the accused's mental state—the 'rea'—that some objectivity is necessary. This approach still honours the goal of subjectivism, as it is the accused's mental state that is at issue; unlike liability for negligence, where it is purely the accused's conduct that is at issue. Expanding negligence is not appropriate because it does not reflect the 'evil mind' that is the touchstone of criminal liability and that which distinguishes it from civil liability. The House of Lords in *R* v *G* was willing to overturn an established, time-tested authority in order to nurture a criminal law doctrine of fault that fairly attributes blameworthiness to the accused and accords with the community's sense of fairness and justice. On the facts, the purely subjective approach to mens rea was apposite, but it would be a mistake to pretend that a purely subjective doctrine is the salve to our mens rea woes. Lord Rodger of Earlsferry acknowledged this in his opinion where he expressed the view that Lord Diplock's broader concept of recklessness, encompassing an objective element was not undesirable in terms of legal policy; and further, held that inadvertence need not necessarily be excluded from recklessness.

■ *Questions*

Is it possible to have a purely subjective notion of fault? Must there not always be some element of objectivity incorporated within it? Consider the following case.

In *Seray-Wurie v DPP* [2012] EWHC 208 (Admin) D was charged with criminal damage after using black marker pen to write on two parking notices placed by the management company in the residential estate where he lived. On appeal from the magistrates' court, the Crown Court directed itself that when it comes to recklessness D must be aware that there is a risk of a certain result occurring and that in those circumstances it was unreasonable to take that risk. It found that D was aware that there was a risk that his writing on the notices would cause damage to them. The basis for this was that D was an intelligent man and that he must have appreciated it because any normal person would have done. D appealed his conviction by way of case stated to the Divisional Court and argued that although he accepted writing on the parking notices with a black marker pen, he did not intend to cause damage to them, nor was he reckless as to whether damage would be caused. In upholding D's conviction, Lloyd Jones J held as follows.

I accept that if the Crown Court had concluded that the requirement of recklessness was satisfied because the risk would have been obvious to a reasonable person that would have been the application of an objective test and would, after G, be wrong in law. However, it is clear from the transcript of the judgment that the Crown Court did not fall into that error. On the contrary, in deciding whether the appellant was aware of the risk of damage the Crown Court took into account the circumstances known to the appellant and found that the evidence led it to the sure conclusion that, despite his assertion to the contrary, he did appreciate that there was a risk of damage. The Crown Court did not make a finding of objective recklessness, that is, it did not conclude that damage was not foreseen but that it ought to have been foreseen. It concluded that it was sure that the appellant appreciated that damage was likely to result. The court made a finding as to the subjective state of mind of the appellant. In coming to that conclusion it was entitled to consider how obvious was the risk. As [counsel for the Crown] puts it, the more obvious the risk the less inclined a tribunal will be to accept that a defendant was not aware of it, absent any characteristics of a defendant that would affect his ability to appreciate the risk. However, the test applied remains the subjective test. (at para [21])

Look again at paragraph [39] of Lord Bingham's judgment in *G*. Does the subjective approach place too much reliance on jurors' ability to identify and disregard specious claims by defendants that they did not appreciate the existence of the risk? How are juries to distinguish between genuine and false denials in circumstances other than when D is a child or suffers from some kind of objectively identifiable cognitive incapacity? To get round this, does the approach of the Divisional Court seem to reverse the burden of proof?

5.4 Malice

Many old statutes use the word 'maliciously' to describe the mental element required. 'Malice' was not given its natural meaning of 'spitefully' or 'with ill-will'. Professor C. S. Kenny in his *Outlines of Criminal Law* (1902) stated the general proposition that:

in any statutory definition of a crime, 'malice' must . . . be taken—not in its vague common law sense as 'wickedness' in general, but—as requiring an actual intention to do the particular kind of harm that in fact was done (or at least a recklessness as to doing it). (15th edn, p 189)

In the famous case of *Cunningham* [1957] 2 All ER 412, section 5.3, D, in order to steal money from a gas meter, ripped the meter away from the supply pipes and released a cloud of noxious coal gas into the house next door. D was charged with *maliciously* administering a noxious substance (the gas) to the neighbour so as thereby to endanger her life, contrary to s 23 of the Offences Against the Person Act 1861. The Court of Criminal Appeal stated that:

in any statutory definition of a crime 'malice' must be taken not in the old vague sense of 'wickedness' in general, but as requiring either (1) an actual intention to do the particular *kind* of harm that in fact was done, or (2) recklessness as to whether such harm should occur or not (i.e. the accused has foreseen that the particular kind of harm might be done, and yet has gone on to take the risk of it). (*Outlines of Criminal Law*, 1902)

The House of Lords confirmed that interpretation in *Savage; Parmenter* [1991] 4 All ER 698. Malice is a form of subjective fault. See further section 18.1.1.3.

5.5 Knowledge

Some of the cases discussed previously raise a more general problem about knowledge in the criminal law: at what point must D know the risk and must it be at the forefront of his mind before he can be said to know it? Does a person 'know' a fact which is not present to his mind at the relevant moment, though he is quite capable of recalling it—as the bus driver recalled that he was driving a double-decker at the moment of impact? Professor Glanville Williams at one time thought he does. The following passage in the first edition of his *Textbook* (p 79) does not appear in the second edition but it is not clear whether he changed his mind. He was discussing *Parker* (discussed in Lord Bingham's speech in *G* see section 5.3, p 119). D, in a telephone kiosk, being frustrated by his inability to get through, twice slammed the telephone down on to its cradle. On the second occasion he smashed it. Charged with criminal damage, he said that he did not realize at the time he acted that he was likely to break the telephone. The Court of Appeal held he was rightly convicted because 'a man is reckless when he carried out the deliberate act knowing or closing his mind to the obvious fact that there is some risk of damage resulting from that act, but nevertheless continued the performance of that act.'

The case was such a paradigm of recklessness that the appeal might well have been dismissed on the ground that no miscarriage of justice had actually occurred, even if the direction was regarded as misleading. Parker must have slammed the receiver down extremely hard to break the plastic, and it is impossible to believe that he did not know the risk of damaging it. It is a misunderstanding of the legal requirement to suppose that this knowledge of risk must be a matter of conscious awareness at the moment of the act. We grow up in a world in which we come to know, from the earliest age, that things are broken by rough treatment. Some things are more resistant than others: one could, in a temper, kick a farm tractor or the wheel of a lorry without doing damage. But is there anyone who does not know that a telephone receiver can be damaged by being violently slammed down? The fact that it is slammed down because of a feeling of frustration is nothing to the purpose.

If this is right, what was all the fuss over *DPP v Smith* (section 15.3.1, p 533) about? Smith, rightly suspected by a police officer of having stolen goods in his car, drove off at speed with the officer hanging on to the car and pursued an erratic course until he was thrown off in the path of an oncoming vehicle and killed. The whole incident lasted about 10 seconds: [1961] AC at 298 and 302. The Court of Criminal Appeal, whose judgment seems now to be rehabilitated (section 15.3.1, p 533), thought the relevant question was as to the state of mind of the defendant during those 10 seconds of panic. But if when Smith was sitting quietly at home, relaxed in his armchair, someone had said to him, 'Jim, if you were to drive off in your car at top speed in a busy street with a copper clinging to the bonnet, do you think it is likely that he would suffer serious injury?' would not his reply have been an unprintable affirmative? The Court of Appeal in that case, however, thought that the relevant question was what Smith thought in a moment of panic and the 10 seconds which the whole episode occupied.

In some offences knowledge appears as the explicit mens rea requirement. The definition of the term was subjected to scrutiny in the House of Lords in two cases dealing with money laundering and conspiracies to launder money. The judicial view is clear: knowledge is true belief and one cannot know something or a circumstance that has yet to occur. As the Canadian Supreme Court explained in *USA v Dynar* [1997] 2 SCR 462:

> In the Western legal tradition, knowledge is defined as *true* belief: 'The word "know" refers exclusively to true knowledge; we are not said to "know" something that is not so'.

This view was endorsed in the House of Lords in two more recent cases. In *Montila* [2004] 1 WLR 3141 the House accepted (at [27]) that:

> A person cannot know that something is A when in fact it is B. The proposition that a person knows that something is A is based on the premise that it is true that it is A. The fact that the property is A provides the starting point. Then there is the question whether the person knows that the property is A.

Subsequently, in *Saik* [2006] UKHL 18, the House of Lords concluded:

> the word 'know' should be interpreted strictly and not watered down. In this context knowledge means true belief.

See, generally, S. Shute, 'Knowledge and Belief in the Criminal Law' in S. Shute and A. Simester (eds), *Criminal Law Theory: Doctrines of the General Part* (2002), Ch 8 and see G. R. Sullivan, 'Knowledge, Belief and Culpability', ibid, Ch 9.

5.5.1 'Wilful blindness'

A requirement of knowledge has frequently been held to be satisfied by proof of what is sometimes called 'wilful blindness'.

It has indeed been stated in the House of Lords, in *Westminster City Council v Croyalgrange Ltd* [1986] 2 All ER 353 at 359, that:

> it is always open to the tribunal of fact, when knowledge on the part of a defendant is required to be proved, to base a finding of knowledge on evidence that the defendant had deliberately shut his eyes to the obvious or refrained from inquiry because he suspected the truth but did not want to have his suspicions confirmed.

In so far as this states a universal rule, it goes too far. In handling stolen goods (Chapter 27) a person is not taken to 'know' that the goods are stolen merely because he suspects that they may be stolen and asks no questions because he prefers not to know.

In the seminal case on the subject, *Roper v Taylor's Garage* [1951] 2 TLR 284 at 288, Devlin J emphasized:

> a vast distinction between a state of mind which consists of deliberately refraining from making inquiries, the result of which a person does not care to have [wilful blindness], and a state of mind which is merely neglecting to make such inquiries as a reasonable and prudent person would make [constructive knowledge].

Other judicial definitions have variously incorporated elements of:

(i)   a deliberate or intentional refusal to investigate the circumstances suspected;

(ii) an opportunity to investigate them;

(iii) an absence of doubt as to outcome or at least an awareness by D of the likely outcome of investigation and that the outcome would not be one D desired if he investigated his suspicions;

(iv) a causal link between the refusal to investigate and the assumed likely outcome.

The core elements appear to be a degree of awareness of the likely existence of the prohibited circumstances coupled with a blameworthy conscious refusal to enlighten oneself.

Academic opinion seems united in requiring proof of more than mere suspicion. See M. Wasik and M. P. Thompson, 'Turning a Blind Eye as Constituting Mens Rea' (1981) 32 NILQ 324 at 337–341. Glanville Williams described it in terms of suspicion *plus* a deliberate omission to inquire: CLGP (1953), p 127, para 41. However described, the second limb of the test ensures that the defendant must have possessed more than a state of awareness of the risk—he must demonstrate a blameworthiness that justifies treating his state of mind as akin to actual knowledge.

Wilful blindness is distinct from recklessness because, while recklessness involves knowledge of a danger *or risk* and persistence in a course of conduct which creates *a risk* that the prohibited result will occur, wilful blindness arises where a person who has become aware of the need for some inquiry declines to make the inquiry because he does not wish to know the truth. He would prefer to remain ignorant.

Wilful blindness does not include negligence: *Flintshire County Council v Reynolds* [2006] EWHC 195 (Admin) confirmed that negligence is not a form of 'knowledge'. In *Flintshire* (at [17]), it was emphasized that a person who has 'constructive notice' may be negligent as to the relevant facts, but is not to be taken to have knowledge of them.

5.5.2 Knowledge distinguished from belief

The relationship between knowledge and belief is examined in close detail in the context of handling stolen goods (see Chapter 27). According to the Court of Appeal in *Hall* (1985) 81 Cr App R 260 at 264, [1985] Crim LR 377:

> Belief, of course, is something short of knowledge. It may be said to be the state of mind of a person who says to himself: 'I cannot say I know for certain that [the circumstance exists] but there can be no other reasonable conclusion in the light of all the circumstances, in the light of all that I have heard and seen'.

In *Moys* (1984) 79 Cr App R 72, the court suggested simply that the question whether D knew or believed that the proscribed circumstance existed is a subjective one and that suspicion, even coupled with the fact that D shut his eyes to the circumstances, is not enough.

5.5.3 Knowledge distinguished from suspicion/reasonable grounds to suspect

There are many serious offences with low-level mens rea requirements such as 'suspicion' and 'having reasonable grounds to suspect'. The money laundering offences in the Proceeds of Crime Act 2002 and offences in the Terrorism Acts are some of the clearest examples. In the mens rea hierarchy, suspicion comes below belief (which is below knowledge).

5.5.3.1 Suspicion

In *Da Silva* [2006] EWCA Crim 1654, 'suspicion' was held to impose a subjective test: D's suspicion need not be based on 'reasonable grounds'. D must think that there is a possibility, which is more than fanciful, that the relevant facts exist. Use of words like 'fleeting thought' and 'inkling' is apt to mislead. The court held (at [16]) that the:

> essential element in the word 'suspect' and its affiliates, in this context, is that the defendant must think that there is a possibility, which is more than fanciful, that the relevant facts exist. A vague feeling of unease would not suffice. But the statute does not require the suspicion to be 'clear' or 'firmly grounded and targeted on specific facts', or based upon 'reasonable grounds'.

The court adopted the dictionary definitions, which are consistent with the previous judicial interpretations of the concept of suspicion in the related field of criminal procedure such as that of Lord Devlin in *Hussien v Chang Fook Kam* [1970] AC 942 at 948:

> Suspicion in its ordinary meaning is a state of conjecture or surmise where proof is lacking: 'I suspect but I cannot prove'. Suspicion arises at or near the starting point of an investigation of which the obtaining of prima facie proof is the end.

5.5.3.2 Reasonable grounds to suspect

In *Saik* [2006] UKHL 18 (a case on former offences of money laundering) the House of Lords held that the mens rea element 'reasonable grounds to suspect', also found in many of the current money laundering offences, includes a requirement that the defendant had actual suspicion. Lord Hope concluded at [52]–[55] that:

> the first requirement contains both a subjective part—that the person suspects—and an objective part—that there are reasonable grounds for the suspicion.

It had previously been widely assumed that this mens rea element was a purely objective one, requiring proof only that the reasonable person would have formed the suspicion on the facts available, irrespective of whether the individual defendant formed such suspicion himself.

■ *Question*

Should 'suspicion' be a sufficient basis of fault for serious offences?

5.6 Negligence

Recklessness is the conscious taking of an unjustifiable risk, while negligence is the inadvertent taking of an unjustifiable risk. If D is aware of the risk and decides to take it, he is reckless; if he is unaware of the risk, but ought to have been aware of it, he is negligent. Where D did consider whether or not there was a risk and concluded, wrongly and unreasonably, that there was no risk, or so small a risk that it would have been justifiable to take it, he is negligent.

Before *Caldwell*, and now under the present law since *G* overruled *Caldwell*, a clear line is drawn by judges between recklessness and negligence. Recklessness is advertent risk-taking. Negligence is inadvertent risk-taking. In both cases the risk is an unreasonable risk that a prudent person would not take. The reckless person is aware of the risk, while the negligent person ought to have been aware of it but is not. Thus for Jerome Hall (GPCL 114–115):

Recklessness is like [intentionality] in that the actor is conscious of a forbidden harm, he realizes that his conduct increases the risk of its occurrence, and he has decided to create that risk;

whereas—

. . . negligence implies inadvertence, ie that the defendant was completely unaware of the dangerousness of his behaviour although actually it was unreasonably increasing the risk of the occurrence of an injury.

Similarly, for Dr J. W. C. Turner (writing as editor of *Russell on Crime* (12th edn), pp 41–42) a reckless person is one who:

acts with full knowledge that he is taking the chance that this secondary result will follow . . . His precise mental attitude will be one of two kinds (a) he would prefer that the harmful result should not occur, or (b) he is indifferent as to whether it does or does not occur. Whichever it may be the common law makes no distinction in his liability.

Whereas (p 43):

Negligence . . . in this connection connotes *inadvertence* . . .

Glanville Williams (CLGP 100) wrote:

Responsibility for some crimes may be incurred by the mere neglect to exercise due caution, where the mind is not actively but negatively or passively at fault. This is inadvertent negligence. Since advertent negligence has a special name (recklessness) it is convenient to use 'negligence' generally to mean inadvertent negligence.

While *Caldwell* was a binding authority, this distinction between advertent and inadvertent risk-taking was no longer synonymous with the distinction between recklessness and negligence. Inadvertent risk-taking arising from a failure to give thought to the existence of a risk amounted to *Caldwell* recklessness. The only distinction between *Caldwell* recklessness and negligence lay in the existence of the so-called 'lacuna' discussed previously (section 5.3.2, p 132).

Given the importance of whether a defendant is reckless or negligent, it might be thought that there would exist a sophisticated body of literature on the distinction between the two. This does not appear to be the case; a lacuna that Douglas Husak has described as 'scandalous'. See D. Husak, 'Negligence, Belief and Criminal Liability: The Special Case of Forgetting' (2011) 5 Crim L & Philosophy 199. In 'Distraction and Negligence' in L. Zedner and J. V. Roberts (eds), *Principles and Values in Criminal Law and Criminal Justice: Essays in Honour of Andrew Ashworth* (2012), the question Husak poses is: when D creates a condition that becomes risky because he forgets he has created it, under what circumstances can D be described as reckless as opposed to negligent? A similar question exists in relation to cases of distraction. Consider the following extract. Although Husak is discussing the law in the United States, his analysis is applicable to the law of England and Wales also.

The practical importance of the distinction between recklessness and negligence requires us to contrast these two culpable states carefully. As a matter of definition, the contested issue is easily described. In many jurisdictions in the United States recklessness—which nearly everyone concedes to be a mode of culpability—is distinguished form negligence—which is highly controversial—by a single factor: the presence or absence of *conscious awareness* of a substantial and unjustifiable risk the defendant disregards. If the defendant *is* aware of the risk, he is reckless. If he is *not* aware, he is negligent as long as he *should* have been aware; that is, if a reasonable person in his situation *would* have been aware of the risk. As commentators such as Ashworth have insisted, the normative basis for holding persons to the standard of the reasonable person presupposes that they possess the mental and physical capacities to have taken the necessary precautions. Thus the blameworthiness in negligence, according to Ashworth, consists in 'the culpability of unexercised capacity'. Both the specification of these capacities as well as the reliability of the evidence that given defendants possess or lack them can be problematic, but I will not pursue these familiar difficulties here. Instead, I seek to clarify the concept of *awareness* that is central in contrasting uncontested from highly disputably impositions of blame and penal liability.

When *is* a person *aware* of something? In particular, when is a person aware of a risk? My answer is speculative and tentative. The Model Penal Code provides some guidance in its definition of knowledge, which it equates with awareness. Thus I will tentatively suppose as a matter of positive law in the United States that the contrast between recklessness and negligence depends on whether or not the defendant *knows* he is creating a risk. Pursuant to this supposition, the negligent defendant, unlike the reckless defendant, does not know he is creating a risk, even though a reasonable person in his situation would have known. One might suspect that this definition would not succeed in advancing this enquiry, since we are just as likely to be uncertain about whether or not a given defendant knows he is imposing a risk.

Husak's conclusion is that the case for a finding of recklessness when distracted is generally stronger than in cases of forgetting. One of the reasons for this, according to Husak, is that while people do not usually choose to forget, the same is not true in cases of distraction.

Except in highly unusual circumstances, people do not choose to forget. The same cannot be said for distraction. We tend to distinguish situations in which the distracting event is initiated by the defendant from those in which it has an external source. A driver can become distracted from the road by a billboard depicting her favourite movie star, for example. In this latter case, the distraction seems less voluntary and merely negligent, rather than reckless. Of course, the distinction between voluntary and non-voluntary distraction is probably a continuum allowing for borderline cases that elude simple categorization. Still, sympathy for distracted drivers erodes when we learn the source of their distraction is internal and governed by choice. If distraction *happens* to someone, rather than being the result of something that one actively *does*, we cannot impose liability through what might be called a 'culpability in causing' or 'tracing' rationale: when someone is culpable for causing the conditions in which he alleges his culpability is reduced, we tend to hold him culpable for those latter conditions.

...

These considerations reveal an important point about judgments about recklessness and negligence: examples of distraction or forgetfulness should not be treated alike. Not all cases of distraction are reckless and not all cases of forgetfulness are merely negligent. Instead, the relevance of further details about particular examples indicates that our judgments about blame and liability are highly fact sensitive and do not admit of general resolution. Commentators should stop pretending that we can sort all cases of distraction and / or forgetting into simple categories. Sweeping generalizations about the blame or liability of forgetful or distracted persons should be avoided.

■ *Questions*

Was the forgetful bus driver, considered at section 5.3.3, p 132, reckless or negligent? Should his liability depend upon whether he forgot he was driving a double-decker bus at the time as opposed to being distracted by something he saw on the road?

Although negligence is undoubtedly recognized as a form of mens rea, there are those who believe that it does not demonstrate sufficient culpability to justify the imposition of criminal sanction.

L. Alexander and K. Kessler Ferzan with S. Morse, *Crime and Culpability:*
A Theory of Criminal Law
(2009), p 70

I. Why Negligence Is Not Culpable

Essentially, those who deem negligence to be culpable argue that failure to advert to a risk that one had a fair chance to perceive (had one tried) is culpable, even though it does not entail a conscious choice to produce or to unreasonably risk harm.

We disagree. The world is full of risks to which we are oblivious. Or, more accurately, because risk is an epistemic, not ontic, notion, [meaning that it is one contingent upon knowledge rather than one based upon factual existence] we frequently believe we are creating a certain level of risk when someone in an epistemically superior position to ours would assess the risk to be higher or lower than we have estimated. Sometimes the epistemically superior position is the product of better information: for example the doctor knows that what we believe is just a mole is in fact a life-threatening melanoma. At other times, we have failed to notice something that another might have noticed, or we have forgotten sometime that another might have remembered. Once in a while, our lack of information, failure to notice, failure to make proper inferences from what information we do have, or forgetfulness results in our underestimating the riskiness of our conduct and causing harm.

We are not morally culpable for taking risks of which we are unaware. At any point in time we are failing to notice a great many things, we have forgotten a great many things, and we are misinformed or uninformed about many things. An injunction to notice, remember, and be fully informed about anything that bears on risks to others is an injunction no human being can comply with, so violating this injunction reflects no moral defect. Even those most concerned with the well-being of others will violate this injunction constantly.

The argument the authors make is that people can and often do make momentary mistakes, and that acts of clumsiness or stupidity hardly seem like the sort of things for which people should be held criminally liable. Consider, however, the following response.

A. Leipold, 'A Case for Criminal Negligence'
(2010) 29 Law & Phil 455

Let's begin with the strong argument. A claim that negligence isn't enough starts at the bottom of a large hill, because our willingness to impose serious sanctions on a negligent actor is deeply rooted. We do not think it especially unfair to fire someone from their job, drive them out of business, or make them pay huge sums of money (including punitive damages) for gross inattention to detail. And of course descriptively, criminal liability has always been, and often still is, based on negligent behavior. So at the outset there is nothing intuitively shocking about treating someone as a criminal when they engage in a 'gross deviation from the standard of care that a reasonable person would observe in the actor's situation'.

The authors respond that whatever the criminal law is doing now with negligence is flawed, because it is not based on truly blameworthy acts. The core problem with negligence, they say, is that 'an injunction to notice... and to be fully informed about *everything* that bears on risks to others is an injunction no human can comply with, so violating this injunction reflects no moral defect'. And apparently we are all sinners, because 'even those most concerned with the well being of others will violate this injunction constantly'.

I would agree that *if* the negligence standard really required us to be fully informed about everything that bears on the risk of harm to others, it should have no place in the criminal law (or maybe the civil law, for that matter). But it doesn't, and as a result, I do not think that negligence requires an impossible degree of attentiveness, nor do I think people are constantly violating its commands.

As Eric Johnson and others have nicely pointed out, the Model Penal Code does not require me to know *everything* on pain of being found negligent, but instead, asks (a) what things did I know at the time I acted? and (b) within that universe of facts, was my failure to perceive a risk a gross departure from what a reasonable person would perceive? This is the plain import of the requirement that we evaluate the actor's riskcreating behavior 'under the circumstances known to him'. Consider the case of the pedestrian talking on a cell phone who blindly steps off the curb, causing the oncoming driver to swerve and nearly crash. The pedestrian is surely acting carelessly and stupidly, but nothing in the negligence standard makes him liable for negligent homicide simply because he was not fully informed that the swerving driver was rushing a sick friend to the hospital, and the near-accident so unnerved the driver that he drove too slowly and failed to get medical attention in time.

Stated differently, nothing in the negligence standard requires unrealistic perceptiveness or care. Nor is criminal negligence, properly defined, so widespread that everyone is routinely exceeding its limits, making it unfair to sanction the few unlucky souls who happen to get caught. Criminal negligence is explicitly relative—it only reaches those departures from the attentiveness that an ordinary person would observe. (The authors, of course, offer sharp and valid criticisms of the reasonable person standard, but that is a different point.) We know that ordinary people sometimes forget to lock up the cleaning supplies, sometimes take their eye off the road for just a moment, and do not always rotate their tires every 5,000 miles to prevent uneven tread wear that can lead to a blowout. On the other hand, those who take these behaviors to extreme degrees—taking your eye off the road for 40 seconds to send a text message—have so far departed from a reasonable standard of care that a jury can justifiably characterize it as a moral defect.

■ **Questions**

Should negligence be a sufficient fault for criminal offences? If so, should it constitute the mens rea for only those crimes that are of least seriousness?

There is also uncertainty as to what extent it is necessary in an evaluation of negligence to take account of the defendant's characteristics.

In *RSPCA v C* [2006] EWHC 1069 (Admin), it was held that the question whether a juvenile (aged 15) was negligent in not taking an injured cat to the vet should be judged by the standards of a reasonable girl of *her* age. Cf *Price* [2014] EWCA Crim 229 (negligence in the military).

■ **Questions**

Which other characteristics ought to be taken into account? Is age a unique factor?

In *C* [2001] Crim LR 845, the defendant, who was a paranoid schizophrenic, had performed the conduct for the offence of stalking by sending offensive letters to his MP, on at least two occasions. He was convicted and appealed on the basis that the judge should have directed the jury to consider his mental disorder as a relevant condition of the hypothetical reasonable person in s 1(2) of the Protection from Harassment Act 1997. The Protection from Harassment Act 1997, s 1(1)(b) read with s 1(2), imposes a requirement that the course of conduct (which is alleged to amount to harassment) must be one which D knew *or ought to have known* amounts to harassment. That is a statutory crime of negligence. The test of whether he knew or ought to have known is, under s 1, whether a reasonable person *in possession of the same information* as D would think the course of conduct did amount to harassment. The Court of Appeal held that s 1(2) involved a purely objective test relating to the reasonable person and reasonable conduct. D's illness was not relevant to that question. Section 1(2) seeks to endow the reasonable person with knowledge of circumstances that would render otherwise seemingly innocuous conduct harassing.

■ *Question*

D1 knows that previous advances towards V have been rejected and continues to send gifts. D2 who suffers from schizophrenia has previously been rebuffed in his advances to V but continues to send her flowers. Are D1 and D2 guilty of harassment?

See more generally on negligence as an element of harassment, under the Protection from Harassment Act 1997, E. Finch, 'Stalking the Perfect Stalking Law: An Evaluation of the Efficacy of the Protection from Harassment Act 1997' [2002] Crim LR 703 at 714.

Section 2A of the Road Traffic Act 1991 contains the offence of dangerous driving. The offence contains two limbs. First, D's driving must have fallen far below what would be expected of a competent and careful driver and, secondly, it would have been obvious to the competent and careful driver that driving in this way would be dangerous. This is a statutory offence of negligence. Section 2A(3) states: 'in determining for the purposes of those subsections what would be expected of, or obvious to, a competent and careful driver in a particular case, regard shall be had not only to the circumstances of which he could be expected to be aware but also to any circumstances shown to have been within the knowledge of the accused.' In *Bannister* [2009] EWCA Crim 1571, D was an advanced police driver who was convicted of dangerous driving after losing control of his car and crashing it into a copse of trees having driven at 113 mph in wet conditions. On appeal D contended that, by virtue of s 2A(3), the jury should have been directed that they could take into account his advanced driving skills in evaluating whether he was driving dangerously. The Court of Appeal rejected this argument and held that such an interpretation of s 2A would detract from its objective nature.

■ *Questions*

Does s 2A(3) necessarily import a subjective element into the offence? Would this be consistent with how negligence has been interpreted outside the context of dangerous driving?

FURTHER READING

Intention

R. A. Duff, 'The Obscure Intentions of the House of Lords' [1986] Crim LR 771

J. Horder, 'Intention in the Criminal Law—A Rejoinder' (1995) MLR 678

I. Kugler, *Direct and Oblique Intention in the Criminal Law* (2002)

N. Lacey, 'A Clear Concept of Intention' (1993) 56 MLR 621

N. Lacey, 'In(de)terminable Intentions' (1995) 58 MLR 692

A. W. Norrie, 'Oblique Intention and Legal Politics' [1989] Crim LR 793

A. Pedain, 'Intention and the Terrorist Example' [2003] Crim LR 579

J. C. Smith, 'A Note on Intention' [1990] Crim LR 85

J. C. Smith, 'Intention in Criminal Law' (1974) 27 CLP 93

V. Tadros, *Criminal Responsibility* (2005), Ch 8

G. Williams, 'The Mens Rea for Murder—Leave it Alone' (1989) 105 LQR 387

Recklessness

J. Brady, 'Recklessness, Negligence, Indifference and Awareness' (1980) 43 MLR 381

D. Kimel, 'Inadvertent Recklessness in Criminal Law' (2004) 120 LQR 548

V. Tadros, 'Recklessness and the Duty to Take Care' in S. Shute and A. Simester (eds),

Criminal Law Theory: Doctrines of the General Part (2002)

Knowledge

E. Griew, 'Consistency, Communication and Codification—Reflections on Two Mens Rea Words' in P. R. Glazebrook (ed), *Reshaping the Criminal Law* (1978), p 57

S. Shute, 'Knowledge and Belief in the Criminal Law' in S. Shute and A. Simester (eds), *Criminal Law Theory: Doctrines of the General Part* (2002), p 171

G. R. Sullivan, 'Knowledge, Belief and Culpability' in S. Shute and A. Simester

(eds), *Criminal Law Theory: Doctrines of the General Part* (2002), p 207

M. Wasik and M. P. Thompson, 'Turning a Blind Eye as Constituting Mens Rea' (1981) 32 NILQ 328

Negligence

H. L. A. Hart, 'Negligence Mens Rea and Criminal Responsibility' in *Punishment and Responsibility* (1968)

A. P. Simester, 'Can Negligence be Culpable' in J. Horder (ed), *Oxford Essays in Jurisprudence* (2000)

6

Intoxication

6.1 Introduction

Many offences are committed by persons who are intoxicated by alcohol or other drugs. Many of these offences would not have been committed if the offender had not been intoxicated. Alcohol weakens the restraints and inhibitions which normally govern a person's conduct. It also impairs perception and judgement so that a drunken person is liable to be involved in incidents which would not happen if he were sober. See, generally, G. Dingwall, *Alcohol and Crime* (2005).

It has never been a defence for a person simply to say, however truthfully, that he would not have committed the offence if he had not been drunk—that 'it was the drink that did it'. If that is all, his intoxicated condition is, at most, a matter to be taken into account in imposing sentence. The fact that he had been drinking may sometimes mitigate the gravity of the offence, and sometimes—as in dangerous driving—it may aggravate it.

> ■ *Question*
> Consider, when you have read the materials in this chapter, whether it would be preferable if English criminal law managed without any special rules of substantive law on intoxication and left it as a matter to be considered in sentencing in all cases?

Special rules of substantive law are generally accepted to be necessary to deal with those cases in which the definition of the offence includes a subjective mental element and the defendant claims that he lacked that mental element because he was intoxicated—that is, he failed to foresee a result which he would have foreseen had he been sober or he made a mistake of fact which he would not have made when sober. In such cases if he is, or may be, telling the truth and the mistake or failure to foresee negatives the mens rea of the offence, the prosecution has not proved its case. However, the inquiry into the defendant's blameworthiness must proceed further in such cases. If the intoxication is 'involuntary'—for example, the defendant was unaware that his lemonade had been heavily laced with vodka—he will be acquitted. Where the intoxication is voluntary the law has never allowed this defence in all cases. With voluntary intoxication a distinction is made between:

- offences requiring 'specific intent'. Intoxication is an answer to these charges if because of the intoxication D lacked mens rea;

- offences of basic intent. The defendant will be convicted of the offence of basic intent even though the mental element, which must be proved in the case of all sober defendants, has not been proved against him. This is known, after the leading case, as 'the *Majewski* approach';

- offences requiring only negligence as a fault element. Mistakes caused by D's voluntary intoxication are not an answer to offences requiring negligence because they amount to a failure to comply with the standard of conduct which the law requires. The reasonable, prudent person is not voluntarily intoxicated. *A fortiori*, such mistakes and failures are not an answer to offences of strict liability, not requiring fault.

6.1.1 Structured approach to the issues

As the very basic outline in Figure 6.1 demonstrates, cases involving intoxication may usefully be approached by considering several questions in sequence.

(i) Is the intoxication *voluntary or involuntary*? If involuntary, and D lacks mens rea at the time of the actus reus, D is to be acquitted of any mens rea crime. But a drunken intent is still an intent, so the negation of mens rea must be total.

(ii) If the intoxication is voluntary, the next issue is whether the crime charged is one of *'specific'* intent or *'basic'* intent. The courts have failed to distinguish these with any principled precision, but as a working rule, crimes with mens rea of intent are specific intent and those of recklessness or negligence are basic intent. If the crime is one of specific intent and D was voluntarily intoxicated so that he lacked the mens rea for the crime, he should be acquitted of that crime.

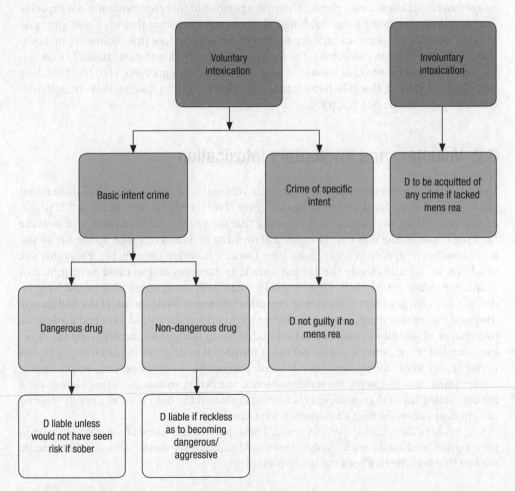

Figure 6.1 Approach to cases involving intoxication

(iii) If the intoxication is voluntary and the crime is one of basic intent, the next question is whether the *drug* involved is one *of a dangerous nature* (ie one known to create states of unpredictability or aggression). If so, in assessing D's guilt, the jury or magistrates should ignore his intoxication in considering whether he was reckless as to the harm caused/whether he was negligent as to the harm caused. If the drug is one of a non-dangerous form (eg a soporific drug such as valium) D will be guilty of the crime charged if he was reckless as to becoming unpredictable or aggressive by taking that drug.

The operation of these questions which focus on the three key distinctions drawn in the law may be illustrated by a hypothetical case. D stabbed his friend, V, believing, because he was intoxicated, that he was stabbing a theatrical dummy. Suppose that V had survived and D had been charged with wounding with intent to cause GBH, contrary to the Offences Against the Person Act 1861 (OAPA), s 18. The intoxication was voluntary—it was not a case of D's drink being laced or of D taking prescribed medicines in accordance with the medical instructions. The crime under s 18 involves an 'intent to cause GBH' and is a specific intent crime and, as D obviously had no such intent, he must be acquitted. If D, however is charged instead with unlawful and malicious wounding, contrary to the OAPA, s 20, his voluntary intoxication is no excuse to s 20 which is a basic intent crime. Section 20 requires proof that the accused was aware that his act might cause physical harm to a person but that requirement is not a specific intent. D, believing that he was stabbing a dummy, was not aware that his act might cause physical harm to any person: but, since his lack of awareness arose from voluntary intoxication, he may be liable to conviction. The final question is whether the intoxicant D took was one commonly known to create states of unpredictability or aggression. If so (eg if the drug was alcohol, LSD, etc), D will be liable for the s 20 offence. This approach follows from the decision in *Majewski*, section 6.3, p 151.

6.2 Voluntary and involuntary intoxication

In most cases the intoxication will be entirely voluntary. Kenny gives a vivid illustration (also referred to by Lord Denning in *Gallagher* [1961] 3 All ER 299, section 6.5, p 172) of a nurse who got so drunk at a christening that she put the baby on the fire in mistake for a log of wood. She was clearly capable of forming an intent to make up the fire so she must have been *capable* of forming an intent to kill, however improbable it was that she would do so. Equally clearly she did not form that intention and so must be acquitted of murder: *Pordage* [1975] Crim LR 575. Being voluntarily intoxicated, she would have no defence to a charge of manslaughter or any other offence of basic intent. If she had merely dropped the supposed log, causing the baby a slight injury, she would have had no defence to a charge of assault occasioning actual bodily harm (also basic intent). Suppose, however, that her intoxication was due, not to her too liberal indulgence in the champagne, but to her orange juice having been heavily laced, without her knowledge, with vodka (involuntary intoxication). Even if she was *capable* of committing an assault, is there any ground for convicting her of that offence? Or of manslaughter, if the baby died as a result of being dropped, or put on the fire? Cf *Goring* [1999] Crim LR 670.

Hughes LJ in *Coley* [2013] EWCA Crim 223 held that where D knew of the effects of mixing prescription medication with alcohol, this would constitute voluntary intoxication despite the fact that the drug had been medically prescribed.

> ■ *Questions*
>
> 1. Should D's intoxication be regarded as involuntary where he knew he was drinking alcohol, but underestimated the strength of the alcohol (*Allen* [1988] Crim LR 698)?
>
> 2. What of D who becomes intoxicated through taking brandy administered to D after an accident? Is this involuntary intoxication?

See J. Horder, 'Pleading Involuntary Lack of Capacity' (1993) 52 CLJ 298; R. Smith and L. Clements, 'Involuntary Intoxication, the Threshold of Inhibition and the Instigation of Crime' (1995) 46 NILQ 210.

6.3 'Specific' and 'basic' intent

The distinction between the two categories has a profound importance and yet has never been adequately explained by the courts.

The distinction drawn by the courts could be interpreted as meaning:

(i)   that all offences for which the mens rea is predominantly that of intention or knowledge are to be treated as specific intent crimes, and all offences for which the predominant fault element is of recklessness, or negligence or in which liability is strict, are basic intent offences; or

(ii)   that specific intent offences are those for which the mens rea goes beyond the immediate actus reus. For example, in a crime such as causing criminal damage with intent or recklessness to endanger life, the mens rea goes beyond the immediate act of causing criminal damage. There is an ulterior intent, and the offence is therefore one of specific intent. This approach means that offences for which the mens rea involves nothing more than recklessness can still be categorized as ones of specific intent. For example, reckless criminal damage being reckless as to whether life is endangered; or

(iii) that crimes of specific intent are those for which the defendant must act 'purposively.'

The leading authority on the distinction between specific and basic intent is *Majewski*.

Director of Public Prosecutions v Majewski
[1976] UKHL 2, House of Lords, http://www.bailii.org/uk/cases/UKHL/1976/2.html

(Lord Elwyn-Jones LC, Lords Diplock, Simon of Glaisdale, Kilbrandon, Salmon, Edmund-Davies and Russell of Killowen)

The appellant was convicted on three counts of assault occasioning actual bodily harm and on three counts of assault on a police constable in the execution of his duty. The evidence which was largely undisputed showed that the offences were committed in the Bull public house in Basildon and that during a fierce struggle Majewski shouted at the police: 'You pigs, I'll kill you all, you fucking pigs, you bastards.' He had consumed large quantities of drugs and alcohol shortly before the offences. He was a drug addict, and admitted that he had previously 'gone paranoid' but said that this was the first time he had 'completely blanked out'. He claimed not to have known what he was doing. The medical evidence suggested that such a state, called 'pathological intoxication', was possible but unlikely: it was quite possible for an intoxicated person to know what he was doing at the time and to suffer an 'amnesic patch' later. Judge Petre directed the jury to 'ignore the subject of drink and drugs as being in any way a defence' to the assaults. An appeal to the House of Lords was unanimously dismissed.

Lord Elwyn-Jones LC:

... If a man consciously and deliberately takes alcohol and drugs not on medical prescription, but in order to escape from reality, to go 'on a trip', to become hallucinated, whatever the description may be, and thereby disables himself from taking the care he might otherwise take and as a result by his subsequent actions causes injury to another—does our criminal law enable him to say that because he did not know what he was doing he lacked both intention and recklessness and accordingly is entitled to an acquittal?

Originally the common law would not and did not recognise self-induced intoxication as an excuse. Lawton LJ [[1975] 3 All ER 296 at 305, 306] spoke of the 'merciful relaxation' to that rule which was introduced by the judges during the 19th century, and he added:

'Although there was much reforming zeal and activity in the 19th century Parliament never once considered whether self-induced intoxication should be a defence generally to a criminal charge. It would have been a strange result if the merciful relaxation of a strict rule of law had ended, without any Parliamentary intervention, by whittling it away to such an extent that the more drunk a man became, provided he stopped short of making himself insane, the better chance he had of an acquittal ... The common law rule still applied but there were exceptions to it which Lord Birkenhead LC [*DPP v Beard*] tried to define by reference to specific intent.'

There are, however, decisions of eminent judges in a number of Commonwealth cases in Australia and New Zealand (but generally not in Canada nor in the United States), as well as impressive academic comment in this country, to which we have been referred, supporting the view that it is illogical and inconsistent with legal principle to treat a person who of his own choice and volition has taken drugs and drink, even though he thereby creates a state in which he is not conscious of what he is doing, any differently from a person suffering from the various medical conditions like epilepsy or diabetic coma and who is regarded by the law as free from fault. However, our courts have for a very long time regarded in quite another light the state of self-induced intoxication. The authority which for the last half century has been relied on in this context has been the speech of Lord Birkenhead LC in *DPP v Beard* [[1920] AC 479 at 494, [1920] All ER Rep 21 at 25]:

'Under the law of England as it prevailed until early in the nineteenth century voluntary drunkenness was never an excuse for criminal misconduct; and indeed the classic authorities broadly assert that voluntary drunkenness must be considered rather an aggravation than a defence. This view was in terms based upon the principle that a man who by his own voluntary act debauches and destroys his will power shall be no better situated in regard to criminal acts than a sober man.'

Lord Birkenhead LC made an historical survey of the way the common law from the 16th century on dealt with the effect of self-induced intoxication on criminal responsibility. This indicates how, from 1819 on, the judges began to mitigate the severity of the attitude of the common law in such cases as murder and serious violent crime when the penalties of death or transportation applied or where there was likely to be sympathy for the accused, as in attempted suicide. Lord Birkenhead LC [[1920] AC 479 at 499, 500, [1920] All ER Rep 21 at 27, 28] concluded that (except in cases where insanity was pleaded) the decisions he cited:

'establish that where a specific intent is an essential element in the offence, evidence of a state of drunkenness rendering the accused incapable of forming such an intent should be taken into consideration in order to determine whether he had in fact formed the intent necessary to constitute the particular crime. If he was so drunk that he was incapable of forming the intent required he could not be convicted of a crime which was committed only if the intent was proved.... In a charge of murder based upon intention to kill or to do grievous bodily harm, if the jury are satisfied that the accused was, by reason of his drunken condition, incapable of forming the intent to kill or to do grievous bodily harm ... he cannot be convicted of murder. But nevertheless unlawful homicide has been committed by the accused, and consequently he is guilty of unlawful homicide without malice aforethought, and that is manslaughter: per Stephen J in *Doherty's* case [(1887) 16 Cox CC 306 at 307]. [He concluded the passage:] the law is plain beyond all question that in cases falling short of insanity a condition of drunkenness at the time of committing an offence causing death can only, when it is available at all, have the effect of reducing the crime from murder to manslaughter.'

From this it seemed clear—and this is the interpretation which the judges have placed on the decision during the ensuing half-century—that it is only in the limited class of cases requiring proof of specific intent that drunkenness can exculpate. Otherwise in no case can it exempt completely from criminal liability . . .

[His lordship discussed *A-G for Northern Ireland v Gallagher* (section 6.5, p 172) and *Bratty v A-G for Northern Ireland* (section 10.4.1, p 327).]

The seal of approval is clearly set on the passage of the *Beard* decision. In no case has the general principle of English law as described by Lord Denning in *Gallagher's* case and exposed again in *Bratty's* case [[1963] AC 386, [1961] 3 All ER 523] been overruled in this House and the question now to be determined is whether it should be.

I do not for my part regard that general principle as either unethical or contrary to the principles of natural justice. If a man of his own volition takes a substance which causes him to cast off the restraints of reason and conscience, no wrong is done to him by holding him answerable criminally for any injury he may do while in that condition. His course of conduct in reducing himself by drugs and drink to that condition in my view supplies the evidence of mens rea, of guilty mind certainly sufficient for crimes of basic intent. It is a reckless course of conduct and recklessness is enough to constitute the necessary mens rea in assault cases: see *Venna* [[1975] 3 All ER 788 at 793] per James LJ. The drunkenness is itself an intrinsic, an integral part of the crime, the other part being the evidence of the unlawful use of force against the victim. Together they add up to criminal recklessness. On this I adopt the conclusion of Stroud [[1920] 36 LQR at 273] that:

'It would be contrary to all principle and authority to suppose that drunkenness (and what is true of drunkenness is equally true of intoxication by drugs) can be a defence for crime in general on the ground that "a person cannot be convicted of a crime unless the *mens was rea*". By allowing himself to get drunk and thereby putting himself in such a condition as to be no longer amenable to the law's commands, a man shows such regardlessness as amounts to mens rea for the purpose of all ordinary crimes.'

This approach is in line with the American Model Code [s 2.08(2)]:

'When recklessness establishes an element of the offence, if the actor, due to self-induced intoxication, is unaware of a risk of which he would have been aware had he been sober, such unawareness is immaterial.'

Acceptance generally of intoxication as a defence (as distinct from the exceptional cases where some additional mental element above that of ordinary mens rea has to be proved) would in my view undermine the criminal law and I do not think that it is enough to say, as did counsel for the appellant, that we can rely on the good sense of the jury or of magistrates to ensure that the guilty are convicted. It may well be that Parliament will at some future time consider, as I think it should, the recommendation in the Butler Committee Report on Mentally Abnormal Offenders [(1975) Cmnd 6244] that a new offence of 'dangerous intoxication' should be created. But in the meantime it would be irresponsible to abandon the common law rule, as 'mercifully relaxed', which the courts have followed for a century and a half . . .

The final question that arises is whether s 8 of the Criminal Justice Act 1967 has had the result of abrogating or qualifying the common law rule. That section emanated from the consideration the Law Commission gave to the decision of the House in *DPP v Smith* [[1961] AC 290, [1960] 3 All ER 161]. Its purpose and effect was to alter the law of evidence about the presumption of intention to produce the reasonable and probable consequences of one's acts. It was not intended to change the common law rule. In referring to 'all the evidence' it meant all the *relevant* evidence. But if there is a substantive rule of law that in crimes of basic intent, the factor of intoxication is irrelevant (and such I hold to be the substantive law), evidence with regard to it is quite irrelevant. Section 8 does not abrogate the substantive rule and it cannot properly be said that the continued application of that rule contravenes the section. For these reasons, my conclusion is that the certified question should be answered Yes, that there was no misdirection in this case and that the appeal should be dismissed.

My noble and learned friends and I think it may be helpful if we give the following indication of the general lines on which in our view the jury should be directed as to the effect on the criminal responsibility of the accused of drink or drugs or both, whenever death or physical injury to another person results from something done by the accused for which there is no legal justification and the offence with which the accused is charged is manslaughter or assault at common law or the statutory offence of unlawful wounding under s 20, or of assault occasioning actual bodily harm under s 47 of the Offences against the Person Act 1861.

In the case of these offences it is no excuse in law that, because of drink or drugs which the accused himself had taken knowingly and willingly, he had deprived himself of the ability to exercise self-control, to realise the possible consequences of what he was doing or even to be conscious that he was doing it. As in the instant case, the jury may be properly instructed that they 'can ignore the subject of drink or drugs as being in any way a defence to' charges of this character.

[Lord Diplock said that he agreed with the speech of Lord Elwyn-Jones LC.]

Lord Simon:

... The best description of 'specific intent' in this sense that I know is contained in the judgment of Fauteux J in *George* [(1960) 128 CCC 289 at 301]:

> 'In considering the question of mens rea, a distinction is to be made between (i) intention as applied to acts considered in relation to their purposes and (ii) intention as applied to acts apart from their purposes. A general intent attending the commission of an act is, in some cases, the only intent required to constitute the crime while, in others, there must be, in addition to that general intent, a specific intent attending the purpose for the commission of the act.'

In short, where the crime is one of 'specific intent' the prosecution must in general prove that the purpose for the commission of the act extends to the intent expressed or implied in the definition of the crime ...

As I have ventured to suggest, there is nothing unreasonable or illogical in the law holding that a mind rendered self-inducedly insensible (short of *M'Naghten* [*M'Naghten's case* (1843) 10 Cl & Fin 200, [1843–60] All ER Rep 229 [section 10.5, p 334] insanity), through drink or drugs, to the nature of a prohibited act or to its probable consequences is as wrongful a mind as one which consciously contemplates the prohibited act and foresees its probable consequences (or is reckless whether they ensue). The latter is all that is required by way of mens rea in a crime of basic intent. But a crime of specific intent requires something more than contemplation of the prohibited act and foresight of its probable consequences. The mens rea in a crime of specific intent requires proof of a purposive element. This purposive element either exists or not; it cannot be supplied by saying that the impairment of mental powers by self-induced intoxication is its equivalent, for it is not. So that the 19th century development of the law as to the effect of self-induced intoxication on criminal responsibility is juristically entirely acceptable; and it need be a matter of no surprise that Stephen stated it without demur or question.

[Lord Kilbrandon said that he agreed with the speech of Lord Elwyn-Jones.]

Lord Salmon:

... an assault committed accidentally is not a criminal offence. A man may, eg, thoughtlessly throw out his hand to stop a taxi, or open the door of his car and accidentally hit a passer-by and perhaps unhappily cause him quite serious bodily harm. In such circumstances, the man who caused the injury would be liable civilly for damages but clearly he would have committed no crime. It is, I agree, possible to commit assault and other crimes of violence recklessly, not caring whether or not what you do causes injury. There are no doubt some contexts, eg, commercial contracts in which the words 'very carelessly' and 'recklessly' are synonymous, but I do not think that this is usually true in the context of the criminal law, except perhaps in the case of manslaughter. I do not, however, wish to take up your Lordships' time in discussing this topic further for it is hardly relevant to the question before this House.

There are many cases in which injuries are caused by pure accident. I have already given examples of such cases: to these could be added injuries inflicted during an epileptic fit, or whilst sleep-walking, and in many other ways. No one, I think, would suggest that any such case could give rise to criminal liability.

It is argued on behalf of the appellant that a man who makes a vicious assault may at the material time have been so intoxicated by drink or drugs that he no more knew what he was doing than did any of the persons in the examples I have given and that therefore he too cannot be found guilty of a criminal offence.

To my mind there is a very real distinction between such a case and the examples I have given. A man who by voluntarily taking drink and drugs gets himself into an aggressive state in which he does not know what he is doing and then makes a vicious assault can hardly say with any plausibility that what he did was a pure accident which should render him immune from any criminal liability. Yet this in effect is precisely what counsel for the appellant contends that the learned judge should have told the jury.

A number of distinguished academic writers support this contention on the ground of logic. As I understand it, the argument runs like this. Intention, whether special or basic (or whatever fancy name you choose to give it), is still intention. If voluntary intoxication by drink or drugs can, as it admittedly can, negative the special or specific intention necessary for the commission of crimes such as murder and theft, how can you justify in strict logic the view that it cannot negative a basic intention, eg, the intention to commit offences such as assault and unlawful wounding? The answer is that in strict logic this view cannot be justified. But this is the view that has been adopted by the common law of England, which is founded on common sense and experience rather than strict logic. There is no case in the 19th century when the courts were relaxing the harshness of the law in relation to the effect of drunkenness on criminal liability in which the courts ever went so far as to suggest that drunkenness, short of drunkenness producing insanity, could ever exculpate a man from any offence other than one which required some special or specific intent to be proved ...

[Lord Edmund-Davies and Lord Russell of Killowen made speeches dismissing the appeal.]

Appeal dismissed

■ *Questions*

1. Which of the three interpretations of the meaning of specific intent listed at the beginning of this section, p 151, did the House of Lords adopt? Did different members adopt different interpretations?

2. Is the decision confined to the case where 'a man consciously and deliberately takes alcohol and drugs ... in order to escape from reality, to go "on a trip", to become hallucinated ...'? Or does it also apply to cases of ordinary social drinking?

3. Which of the following crimes are specific intent: (i) murder, (ii) rape (see section 20.2.1, p 701), (iii) reckless criminal damage being reckless as to life endangerment (see section 28.3.4, p 918)?

6.3.1 Prior fault

The approach taken in *Majewski* can be explained in terms of 'prior fault'. There is a degree of fault in the accused's decision to become so heavily intoxicated, and that fault, albeit well before he commits any criminal acts, is sufficient to provide the necessary blameworthiness for the offence, even though at the time of the criminal conduct the accused does not have the relevant mens rea for the offence because he is too intoxicated to form it. For example, in a case of wounding contrary to s 20 OAPA where at the time D stabs V he is so intoxicated that he thinks he is stabbing a theatrical dummy, D has no intention to stab a human being at the time nor can he be said to be reckless about that since he has not foreseen the risk that his action will result in a wounding of a human being. The reason for that lack of mens rea required is that he is too intoxicated to form it. Following *Majewski*, D's decision to take the intoxicating substances to the extent that he becomes dangerous in his actions involves an element of fault on D's part. That prior fault compensates for the lack of fault at the time of the stabbing and justifies D's conviction.

■ *Questions*

1. Is it justifiable to convict on the ground that D was reckless at the time he took the intoxicant? See S. Gough, section 6.3.2.2, p 145.

2. What was D reckless about at that time of becoming intoxicated? Is that the same type of fault as the fault required for the offence of wounding? Over how long a period can we transfer the prior fault in intoxication to the subsequent criminal acts?

R v Kingston

[1994] UKHL 9, House of Lords, http://www.bailii.org/uk/cases/UKHL/1994/9.html

(Lords Keith, Goff, Browne-Wilkinson, Mustill and Slynn)

D was a man with a sexual interest in under-age boys, but had never before committed any offences against children. D was engaged in a business dispute with X who knew of D's sexual interest in children. X invited D round to his flat and laced his drink with a drug that he knew would lower D's inhibitions. Also present at the flat was a 15-year-old boy who was unconscious due to his having taken a drink which X laced with a soporific drug. Once D's inhibitions were lowered, he committed indecent assault on the boy. X video recorded the offences for the purposes of blackmailing D. Having rejected D's argument that he lacked the necessary mens rea on the general principle that an intoxicated mens rea is still a mens rea, Lord Mustill thought it necessary to consider the law laid down in *Majewski*. He concluded that, as in other common law jurisdictions, evidence of voluntary intoxication is excluded, except in 'specific intent' cases, as a matter of policy. He continued:

There remains the question by what reasoning the House [in *Majewski*] put this policy into effect. As I understand it two different rationalisations were adopted. First that the absence of the necessary consent is cured by treating the intentional drunkenness (or more accurately, since it is only in the minority of cases that the drinker sets out to make himself drunk, the intentional taking of drink without regard to its possible effects) as a substitute for the mental element ordinarily required by the offence. The intent is transferred from the taking of drink to the commission of the prohibited act. The second rationalisation is that the defendant cannot be heard to rely on the absence of the mental element when it is absent because of his own voluntary acts. Borrowing an expression from a far distant field it may be said that the defendant is estopped from relying on his self-induced incapacity.

Your Lordships are not required to decide how these two explanations stand up to attack, for they are not attacked here. The task is only to place them in the context of an intoxication which is not voluntary.

Taking first the concept of transferred intent, if the intoxication was not the result of an act done with an informed will there is no intent which can be transferred to the prohibited act, so as to fill the gap in the offence. As regards the 'estoppel' there is no reason why the law should preclude the defendant from relying on a mental condition which he had not deliberately brought about. Thus, once the involuntary nature of the intoxication is added the two theories of *Majewski* fall away, and the position reverts to what it would have been if *Majewski* had not been decided, namely that the offence is not made out if the defendant was so intoxicated that he could not form an intent. Thus, where the intoxication is involuntary *Majewski* does not *subtract* the defence of absence of intent; but there is nothing in *Majewski* to suggest that where intent is proved involuntary intoxication *adds* a further defence.

Lord Mustill considered authorities in other jurisdictions. In particular he discussed a number of Scottish decisions involving involuntary intoxication. These make it clear that, in Scotland, a defence is made out if it is 'based … on an inability to form mens rea due to some factor which was outwith the accused's control and which he was not bound to foresee'; or if he was 'suffering from a total alienation of reason rendering him incapable of controlling or appreciating what he was doing'. These and the other *dicta* all require an inability to form the intent.

■ **Question**

Should excuse be limited to situations of inability, or should it extend to the case where a person capable of forming an intent fails to do so because he is involuntarily intoxicated? For more on what an excuse is, see section 11.8, p 437.

6.3.2 Distinguishing between offences of specific and basic intent

6.3.2.1 The orthodox application of *Majewski*

In *Caldwell* [1982] AC 34 1 at 968 (section 5.3, p 121), Lord Diplock said:

… classification into offences of specific and basic intent is irrelevant where being reckless whether a particular harmful consequence will result from one's act is a sufficient alternative mens rea.

This was right when, under the *Caldwell* interpretation of recklessness, there was an obvious risk and the defendant had not given any thought to the possibility of it. However intoxicated he was, he had the fault required for the crime and was liable. D might say that he did consider whether there was a risk and decided there was none. He was then not *Caldwell* reckless. But, if he would have appreciated the existence of the risk had he been sober, he will still be liable because of *Majewski*. Since G [2003] UKHL 50, overruling *Caldwell*, the application of intoxication to *Caldwell* recklessness need no longer be considered. Until recently *Majewski* was understood to mean that any offence which may be committed by recklessness would be regarded as 'an offence of basic intent'. That was a simple and workable model.

6.3.2.2 A reinterpretation of *Majewski*?

The Court of Appeal has recently suggested a fundamental reinterpretation of *Majewski* based on Lord Simon's speech in that case.

R v Heard

[2007] EWCA Crim 125, Court of Appeal, Criminal Division, http://www.bailii.org/ew/cases/EWCA/Crim/2007/125.html

(Hughes LJ, Henriques and Field JJ)

D, while drunk, exposed his penis and rubbed it against the thigh of a police officer. D had no recollection of the incident. D relied on his voluntary intoxication as negating his mens rea of an intention to touch for the purposes of the Sexual Offences Act 2003, s 3(1)(a). The trial judge ruled that the intentional touching element of the offence required proof of a basic intent, and that it followed that voluntary intoxication was not a defence. The offence is defined as follows:

3. Sexual assault

(1) A person (A) commits an offence if—

    (a) he intentionally touches another person (B),

    (b) he touching is sexual,

    (c) does not consent to the touching, and

    (d) does not reasonably believe that B consents.

(2) Whether a belief is reasonable is to be determined having regard to all the circumstances, including any steps A has taken to ascertain whether B consents.

(3) Sections 75 and 76 apply to an offence under this section.

Applying the established interpretation of *Majewski*, on a charge such as that under s 3 with the requirement of an 'intentional' touching, it was arguable at least that the crime would be one of specific intent. The effect of that categorization would be that if D sought to rely on his voluntary intoxication to deny that he had the mens rea for the offence, the Crown would be obliged to prove that he formed the intent, despite his intoxication. The circumstances where a sufficient degree of intoxication would arise to negative mens rea, certainly in cases of intoxication by alcohol, would be limited in practice.

[**Hughes LJ** set out the facts and the judge's direction to the jury:]

9. The appellant contends that . . . the offence is . . . one requiring proof of a specific intent and the jury should have been directed to consider whether the drink which the appellant had taken meant that he did not have the intention to touch. The Crown on the other hand contends that the offence is one of basic intent and that evidence of self-induced intoxication is simply irrelevant. . . .

11. In a little more detail, Mr Stern's argument for the appellant runs like this:

    i)   The correct reading of *DPP v Majewski* and subsequent cases is that voluntary intoxication is incapable of being a defence only where recklessness suffices as the mens rea of the offence; it is such offences which are properly described as those of 'basic intent'.

    ii)   The present offence is one for which reckless touching will not suffice; only intentional touching will do.

    iii)   Therefore this is an offence of specific and not of basic intent. Voluntary intoxication is a relevant factor to consider when asking whether the appellant did or did not have the intention to touch required by the section.

12. For the Crown, Mr Perry's argument, similarly summarised, runs as follows:

    iv)   The *Majewski* concept of crimes of basic intent, in which voluntary intoxication cannot be advanced as a defence, is not limited to those where recklessness suffices; the correct distinction is between crimes requiring ordinary intent (where voluntary intoxication cannot be relied upon), and those requiring specific or purposive intent (where it can).

    v)   There is however no universally logical test for distinguishing between crimes in which voluntary intoxication can be advanced as a defence and those in which it cannot; there is a large element of policy; categorisation is achieved on an offence by offence basis.

    vi)   Before the Sexual Offences Act 2003, indecent assault could only be committed by intentional touching; yet voluntary intoxication was not a defence, as it was also not to rape. The decisions of *Woods* (1982) 74 Cr App R 312 and *R v C* [1992] Crim LR 642 are relied upon. The new Act was not intended to change the law in this respect; on the contrary its object was to improve the protection of potential victims of sexual interference. To treat sexual assault as a crime of specific intent would mean treating similarly the very many other sexual offences created by the 2003 Act which are structured in the same way, including rape (section 1), assault by penetration (section 2) and most of the child sex offences. In sexual assault (and in rape and other similar offences) a defendant's belief in consent is said by the statute to provide a defence only if it is reasonable, and that must mean that a drunken belief cannot be relied upon.

vii) Where it applies, the rule that voluntary intoxication cannot be relied upon is a rule of substantive law; accordingly in sexual assault and other similarly structured sexual offences under the 2003 Act voluntarily taken intoxicants are simply to be ignored for all purposes when considering whether the offence has been committed.

viii) Although the requirement that the touching be intentional means that it must be deliberate, if accident is suggested the question whether what happened was accidental or not must be answered as if the defendant had been sober, even though he was not.

Discussion

...

14. The first thing to say is that it should not be supposed that every offence can be categorised simply as either one of specific intent or of basic intent. So to categorise an offence may conceal the truth that different elements of it may require proof of different states of mind. In the law of rape, as it stood immediately before the passing of the Sexual Offences Act 2003, rape was sexual intercourse with a woman who did not in fact consent, by a man who either knew she did not or was reckless as to whether she did. No-one doubted that the act of intercourse could only be committed intentionally. But when it came to the defendant's state of mind as to the woman's lack of consent, either knowledge or recklessness sufficed for guilt: section 1 Sexual Offences (Amendment) Act 1976. Many other examples of the point could be cited. The current legislative practice of itemising separately different elements of offences created by statute, which is much exhibited in the Sexual Offences Act 2003, may occasionally have the potential to complicate matters for a jury, but it demonstrates the impossibility of fitting an offence into a single pigeon-hole, whether it be labelled 'basic intent' or 'specific intent'.

15. The offence of sexual assault, with which this case is concerned, is an example. The different elements of the offence, identified in paragraphs (a) to (d) of section 3, do not call for proof of the same state of mind. Element (a), the touching, must by the statute be intentional. Element (b), the sexual nature of the touching, takes one to section 78. By that section the primary question is a purely objective one, as set out in s 78(a). If, however, the act itself is objectively equivocal, the *purpose* of the Defendant may be a relevant consideration, as provided by s 78(b), and that must be a reference to his own (subjective) purpose. The state of mind in a defendant which must be proved in relation to element (c), the absence of consent, is expressly stipulated by element (d) and by s 3(2), and the stipulation is in terms which make it clear that the test is substantially objective; a belief in consent which was induced largely by drink would be most unlikely to be reasonable. It is accordingly of very limited help to attempt to label the offence of sexual assault, as a whole, one of either basic or specific intent, because the state of mind which must be proved varies with the issue. For this reason also, it is unsafe to reason (as at one point the Crown does) directly from the state of mind required in relation to consent to the solution to the present question.

16. Since it is only the touching which must be intentional, whilst the sexual character of the touching is, unless equivocal, to be judged objectively, and a belief in consent must be objectively

reasonable, we think that it will only be in cases of some rarity that the question which we are posed in this appeal will in the end be determinative of the outcome.

17. We do not think that it determines this appeal. On the evidence the Appellant plainly did intend to touch the policeman with his penis. That he was drunk may have meant either:

ix) That he was disinhibited and did something which he would not have done if sober; and/or

x)   That he did not remember it afterwards.

But neither of those matters (if true) would destroy the intentional character of his touching. In the homely language employed daily in directions to juries in cases of violence and sexual misbehaviour, 'a drunken intent is still an intent.' And for the memory to blot out what was intentionally done is common, if not perhaps quite as common as is the assertion by offenders that it has done so. In the present case, what the appellant did and said at the time, and said in interview afterwards, made it perfectly clear that this was a case of drunken intentional touching. Although the Judge directed the jury that drink was no defence, he also directed the jury that it must be sure that the touching was deliberate. That amounted to a direction that for conviction the appellant's mind (drunken or otherwise) had to have gone with his physical action of touching. Mr Stern realistically conceded that he could not hope to improve upon that direction.

18. We do not attempt the notoriously unrealistic task of foreseeing every possible permutation of human behaviour which the future may reveal. But it nevertheless seems to us that in the great majority of cases of alleged sexual assault, or of comparable sexual crimes, as in the present case, the mind will have gone with the touching, penetration or other prohibited act, albeit in some cases a drunken mind.

19. It is, however, possible to envisage the exceptional case in which there is a real possibility that the intoxication was such that the mind did not go with the physical act. In *R v Lipman* (1969) 55 Cr App R 600 the defendant contended that when he killed his victim by stuffing bedclothes down her throat he was under the illusion, induced by hallucinatory drugs voluntarily taken, that he was fighting for his life against snakes. If an equivalent state of mind were (assumedly genuinely) to exist in someone who committed an act of sexual touching or penetration, the question which arises in this appeal would be directly in point.

20. A different situation was also put to us in the course of argument. Its formulation probably owes much to Professor Ormerod's current edition of *Smith and Hogan's Criminal Law* (11th edition, page 624). It is that of the intoxicated person whose control of his limbs is unco-ordinated or impaired, so that in consequence he stumbles or flails about against another person, touching him or her in a way which, objectively viewed, is sexual—for example because he touches a woman on her private parts. Can such a person be heard to say that what happened was other than deliberate when, if he had been sober, it would not have happened?

21. In the present case the Judge directed the jury that drunkenness was not a defence, although coupling with it the direction that the touching must be deliberate. Whether or not the jury's decision was likely to be that the appellant had acted intentionally (albeit drunkenly), the Judge had to determine whether or not it was necessary for the jury to investigate the suggestion that the appellant was so drunk that his mind did not go with his act. That question may also face judges and juries, as it seems to us, in many cases where a defendant wishes to contend that he was thus intoxicated, and scientific or medical evidence can say no more than that in an extreme case drink or drugs are capable of inducing a state of mind in which a person believes that what he is doing is something different to what he in fact does. In those circumstances, and in deference to the full argument which we have heard, we have concluded that we should address the issue, rather than confine ourselves to saying that this conviction is safe.

22. We are in the present case concerned with element (a), the touching. The Act says that it must be intentional. We regard it as clear that a reckless touching will not do. The Act plainly proceeds upon

the basis that there is a difference between 'intentionally' and 'recklessly'. Where it wishes to speak in terms of recklessness, the Act does so: see for example sections 63(1), 69(1)(c) & (2)(c) and 70(1)(c). It is not necessary to decide whether or not it is possible to conceive of a reckless, but unintentional, sexual touching. Like their Lordships in *R v Court* [1989] 1 AC 28, we think that such a possibility is a remote one, but we are unable wholly to rule it out. One theoretical possible example might be a Defendant who intends to avoid (just) actual physical contact, but realises that he may touch and is reckless whether he will.

23. Because the offence is committed only by intentional touching, we agree that the Judge's direction that the touching must be deliberate was correct. To flail about, stumble or barge around in an unco-ordinated manner which results in an unintended touching, objectively sexual, is not this offence. If to do so when sober is not this offence, then nor is it this offence to do so when intoxicated. It is also possible that such an action would not be judged by the jury to be objectively sexual, on the basis that it was clearly accidental, but whether that is so or not, we are satisfied that in such a case this offence is not committed. The intoxication, in such a situation, has not impacted on intention. Intention is simply not in question. What is in question is impairment of control of the limbs. Accordingly we reject Mr Perry's submission number (v).... We would expect that in some cases where this was in issue the Judge might well find it useful to add to the previously-mentioned direction that 'a drunken intent is still an intent', the corollary that 'a drunken accident is still an accident'. To the limited, and largely theoretical, extent that a reckless sexual touching is possible the same would apply to that case also. Whether, when a defendant claims accident, he is doing so truthfully, or as a means of disguising the reality that he intended to touch, will be what the jury has to decide on the facts of each such case.

24. The remaining question is whether the Judge was also correct to direct the jury that drunkenness was not a defence.

25. We do not agree with Mr Stern's submission for the appellant that the fact that reckless touching will not suffice means that voluntary intoxication can be relied upon as defeating intentional touching. We do not read the cases, including *DPP v Majewski*, as establishing any such rule. As we shall show, we would hold that it is not open to a defendant charged with sexual assault to contend that his voluntary intoxication prevented him from intending to touch. The Judge was accordingly correct, not only to direct the jury that the touching must be deliberate, but also to direct it that the defence that voluntary drunkenness rendered him unable to form the intent to touch was not open to him. Our reasons are as follows.

26. In *Majewski* the rival contentions before the House of Lords were these. For the appellant it was contended that if intoxication affected the mind of the defendant it was illogical and unethical to distinguish between its effect on one state of mind and on another; it was capable of destroying any state of mind which is required as a component of a criminal offence. There was thus, it was argued, no permissible distinction between offences of basic intent and those of specific intent. The Crown contended that that distinction had nevertheless represented the law of England for many years. The House upheld the Crown's contention. It did so in the full knowledge that it was not perfectly logical. It so held, in large measure, on grounds of policy. As was observed by several of their Lordships, historically the law of England regarded voluntary intoxication as an aggravation rather than a potential excuse and the development of the law had been by way of a partial, but only a partial, relaxation of that common law rule where a specific intent was required. Both Lord Elwyn-Jones LC (at 471H) and Lord Edmund-Davies (at 494F) approved what Lawton LJ had said in the Court of Appeal: [His lordship referred to the speeches in *Majewski* (section 6.3, p 151).]

27. Mr Stern's proposition that *Majewski* decides that it is only where recklessness suffices that voluntary intoxication cannot be relied upon derives from a part of the speech of Lord Elwyn-Jones LC in *Majewski* and some observations, *obiter*, of Lord Diplock in the subsequent case of *R v Caldwell* [1982] AC 341.

[His lordship referred to the passage in Lord Elwyn Jones' speech (section 6.3, p 152).]

28. In *Caldwell*, Lord Diplock added this, at page 355F

'The speech of Lord Elwyn-Jones LC in *Reg v Majewski* . . . is authority that self-induced intoxication is no defence to a crime in which recklessness is enough to constitute the necessary mens rea . . . Reducing oneself by drink or drugs to a condition in which the restraints of reason and conscience are cast off was held to be a reckless course of conduct and an integral part of the crime.'

[His lordship described the facts of *Caldwell*.]

. . .

30. There are a number of difficulties about extracting Mr Stern's proposition [for the defence] from the passages cited.

xi) Lord Elwyn-Jones was addressing the submission made on behalf of the appellant in *Majewski* that it was unprincipled or unethical to distinguish between the effect of drink upon the mind in some crimes and its effect upon the mind in others. In rejecting that submission, and upholding the distinction between crimes of basic and of specific intent, he was drawing attention to the fact that a man who has got himself into a state of voluntary intoxication is not, by ordinary standards, blameless. Both the Lord Chancellor and others of their Lordships made clear their view that to get oneself into such a state is, viewed broadly, as culpable as is any sober defendant convicted of a crime of basic intent, whether because he has the basic intent or because he is reckless as to the relevant consequence or circumstance. Throughout *Majewski* it is clear that their Lordships regarded those latter two states of mind as equivalent to one another for these purposes. It therefore does not follow from the references to recklessness that the same rule (that voluntary intoxication cannot be relied upon) does not apply also to basic intent; on the contrary, it seems to us clear that their Lordships were treating the two the same.

xii) The new analysis of recklessness in *Caldwell* may have led readily to the proposition that voluntary intoxication is broadly equivalent to recklessness, thus defined. But that analysis and definition of recklessness have now been reversed by the House of Lords in *R v G* [2004] 1 AC 1034. As now understood, recklessness requires actual foresight of the risk.

xiii) Since the majority in *Caldwell* held that it was enough for recklessness that the risk was obvious objectively (thus, to the sober man) no question of drink providing a defence could arise; it follows that the explanation of *Majewski* which was advanced was plainly *obiter*.

xiv) Lord Diplock's proposition in *Caldwell* attracted a vigorous dissent from Lord Edmund-Davies, who, like Lord Diplock, had been a party to *Majewski*, and with whom Lord Wilberforce agreed. They dissented not only from the new definition of recklessness, but also from the analysis of *Majewski*. Their view was that arson being reckless as to the endangering of life is an offence of specific, not of basic, intent; that would seem to have been because the state of mind went to an ulterior or purposive element of the offence, rather than to the basic element of causing damage by fire.

xv) There were, moreover, many difficulties in the proposition that voluntary intoxication actually supplies the mens rea, whether on the basis of recklessness as re-defined in *Caldwell* or on the basis of recklessness as now understood; if that were so the drunken man might be guilty simply by becoming drunk and whether or not the risk would be obvious to a sober person, himself or anyone else. That reinforces our opinion that the proposition being advanced was one of broadly equivalent culpability, rather than of drink by itself supplying the mens rea.

31. It is necessary to go back to *Majewski* in order to see the basis for the distinction there upheld between crimes of basic and of specific intent. It is to be found most clearly in the speech of Lord Simon, at pages 478B to 479B. Lord Simon's analysis had been foreshadowed in his speech in *DPP v Morgan* [1976] AC 182, 216 (dissenting in the result), which analysis was cited and approved in *Majewski* by Lord

Elwyn-Jones (at 471). It was that crimes of specific intent are those where the offence requires proof of purpose or consequence, which are not confined to, but amongst which are included, those where the purpose goes beyond the actus reus (sometimes referred to as cases of 'ulterior intent').

[His lordship referred to Lord Simon's quotation from Fauteux J in *Reg v George* (1960) 128 Can CC 289 at 301 (section 6.3, p 154):]

That explanation of the difference is consistent with the view of Lord Edmund-Davies that an offence contrary to s 1(2)(b) Criminal Damage Act is one of specific intent in this sense, even though it involves no more than recklessness as to the endangering of life; the offence requires proof of a state of mind addressing something beyond the prohibited act itself, namely its consequences. We regard this as the best explanation of the sometimes elusive distinction between specific and basic intent in the sense used in *Majewski*, and it seems to us that this is the distinction which the Judge in the present case was applying when he referred to the concept of a 'bolted-on' intent. By that test, element (a) (the touching) in sexual assault contrary to s 3 Sexual Offences Act 2003 is an element requiring no more than basic intent. It follows that voluntary intoxication cannot be relied upon to negate that intent.

32. We therefore accept Mr Perry's submission number (i). We also, however, recognise the accuracy of submission number (ii). There is a great deal of policy in the decision whether voluntary intoxication can or cannot be relied upon. We have already referred to one of several passages in *Majewski* where the rule is firmly grounded upon common sense, whether purely logical or not. We agree that it is unlikely that it was the intention of Parliament in enacting the Sexual Offences Act 2003 to change the law by permitting reliance upon voluntary intoxication where previously it was not permitted. *R v Woods*, relied upon by the Crown, does not entirely resolve the question which we are now addressing. What was there decided was that a defendant charged with rape could not rely on voluntary drunkenness when the question was whether he was reckless as to whether the woman consented. By the statute then in force, the presence or absence of reasonable grounds for belief in consent was made a factor to be taken into account. There are now separate, and differently expressed, statutory provisions as to belief in consent, which make it clear that belief must not only be held in fact but be objectively reasonable.

Appeal dismissed

■ **Question**

If not every offence could be categorized simply as either one of 'specific intent' or of 'basic intent', what is this other category that exists?

The court's reinterpretation of *Majewski* aligning specific intent with an ulterior mens rea produces difficulties, as illustrated by two examples each producing unsatisfactory results. Consider a character who, like *Lipman* (1969) 55 Cr App R 600, CA (section 6.4, p 169) becomes so heavily intoxicated on LSD that he genuinely has no appreciation of the circumstances or consequences surrounding his physical actions. D might be so intoxicated that he thinks he is stroking an animal at the centre of the earth when in fact he is stroking a woman's breast. On the court's approach, since the offence is one of 'basic' intent this actor will be guilty. But it is submitted that in such a case it would be difficult in any ordinary sense of the word to say that D 'intended' to touch V sexually as s 3 requires. Nor can his conduct properly be described as 'accidental'.

In contrast consider someone who is heavily intoxicated, fooling around with his mates in a pub and who pretends to strike the bottom of a woman who is bending over to reach to the bar and who cannot see him. He aims to avoid contact by stopping his hand short, thereby amusing his mates in the process. His intoxication causes him to misjudge the distance and he ends up patting her on the bottom. It is submitted that it would be a misuse of the word 'intention' to say that he had intended to touch her sexually. He intends to move his arm and intends to come close to touching her, but specifically does not intend to in fact touch her. He is reckless about that consequence: he has seen the risk and gone on to take it. But recklessness will not do under s 3, as the court acknowledges. Hughes LJ concludes that D must in these circumstances be acquitted, but does so (at [23]) by describing D's conduct as 'accidental'.

■ *Question*

Does this broad application of the word 'accidental' which results in acquittal undermine the whole protective purpose of the law's approach to intoxication and basic intent?

Will the court's *obiter* rejection of the orthodox interpretation of *Majewski* be applied throughout the criminal law? There are several reasons why it is respectfully submitted that this would be undesirable. First, it is more difficult to apply: looking for the 'bolt on' element of additional mens rea in a crime in order to categorize it appropriately is less straightforward than asking simply whether it was one for which recklessness suffices. Second, looking for this ulterior mens rea creates no fewer anomalies than the established interpretation of *Majewski*: murder should be a specific intent offence but where is the 'bolt on' intent beyond that to kill? Indeed this was one of the principal bases on which *Majewski* was criticized; cf G. Williams, *Textbook of Criminal Law* (1978), p 429. Third, the complexity will be exacerbated by the fact that an offence can be one of specific intent even if it contains no element of intent at all—provided there is an ulterior mens rea: reckless criminal damage being reckless as to whether life is endangered thereby would be a crime of specific intention. Finally, despite its obscure exposition in the House of Lords, and its unsatisfactory theoretical underpinnings, the *Majewski* approach had subsequently been knocked into pragmatic shape: it was an established and universally applied test. Those virtues ought not to be undervalued.

In *Heard*, Hughes LJ, as he then was, suggested that a charge of aggravated arson based on reckless criminal damage being reckless that life is thereby endangered, is a crime of specific intent. His lordship returned to this issue in *Coley* [2013] EWCA Crim 223 where his lordship referred to the basic intent principle and continued:

> There remains some room for doubt as to whether the aggravated offence of reckless arson, charged in the present case, is governed by this principle or should be regarded as an offence of specific intent—see for example the (dissenting) opinion of Lord Edmund-Davies in *Caldwell* at 361D and the passing *obiter* reference in *R v Heard* [2008] QB 43 at [31], where, however, the offence under consideration (sexual assault) was one requiring not recklessness but (basic) intent. We see some force in the argument that voluntary intoxication ought not to be a defence to an offence involving recklessness, even subjective recklessness; it may fall for decision in a later case whether Lord Lane's view in *Stephenson* correctly represents the law now that *Caldwell* recklessness has passed away.

■ *Question*

On the basis of the law as stated in *Majewski* and *Heard*, are the following offences ones of basic or specific intent: (i) murder; (ii) intentionally causing GBH with intent to resist arrest; (iii) rape; (iv) criminal damage being reckless as to life endangerment?

The courts do not seem to have produced the greatest clarity in distinguishing between basic and specific intention. Have the academics done any better?

S. Gough, 'Intoxication and Criminal Liability: The Law Commission's Proposed Reforms' (1996) 112 LQR 335 at 342 (references omitted)

...

The Specific-Basic Distinction

The origins of the terminology of 'specific intent'

The distinction between offences of specific and basic intent has been a persistent headache for criminal lawyers, especially over the last two or three decades. The terminology of 'specific' intent is traceable to the mid nineteenth century. Patterson J. spoke in *Cruse* (1838) [8 C & P 541] of intoxication's ability to defeat the 'positive intention' required by murder, while in *Monkhouse* (1849) [4 Cox CC 55.] Coleridge J. noted that drunkenness would not lead to an acquittal unless, inter alia, it deprived the defendant of 'the power of forming any specific intention.' Most importantly, Lord Birkenhead L.C. referred to specific intent in *D.P.P. v. Beard* (1920):

> 'Where a specific intent is an essential element in the offence, evidence of a state of drunkenness rendering the accused incapable of forming such an intent should be taken into consideration in order to determine whether he had in fact formed the intent necessary to constitute the particular crime.' [[1920] AC 479 at 499]

Yet these cases gave no indication that a 'specific intent' was different from an ordinary intent. Indeed, other intoxication cases of the period omit any reference to 'specific' intent and speak simply of intoxication's ability to negate intent [*Meakin* (1836) 7 C & P 297]. *Beard* is particularly confusing in that, having used the language of 'specific intent' in the first half of his opinion, Lord Birkenhead switches to the language of intent simpliciter in the second half [[1920] AC 479 at 504–505]. In short, the terms 'intent' and 'specific intent' seem to have been used interchangeably.

Why, then, did some judges use the term 'specific intent' instead of just 'intent'? In answering this question we must bear in mind the 19th and early 20th century approach to mens rea. Stephen, writing in the late 19th century, points to 'malice' as a sufficient mental element for most offences. The word carried its common meaning of moral depravity or 'wickedness' [*General View of the Criminal Law of England* (1863), p 82], and there is no indication that any subjective mental state was required. This is confirmed by Harris who, writing around the same time, noted that

> 'Malice is found not only in cases: i) Where the mind is actively or positively in fault, as where there is a deliberate design to defraud, but also: ii) Where the mind is passively or negatively to blame, that is, where there is culpable or criminal inattention or negligence.' [S. F. Harris, *Principles of the Criminal Law* (1st edn, 1877), p 14.]

In any event, as Harris pointed out, many offences would have been satisfied even in the absence of malice:

> 'When the law expressly declares an act to be criminal, the question of intention or malice need not be considered; at least, except by the judge in estimating the amount of punishment.' [ibid]

Early 20th century criminal lawyers paint a similar picture [Kenny, *Outlines* (1st edn, 1902)].

Intoxicatedly inadvertent behaviour would have been perfectly consistent with liability for an offence with a mental element of malice or less. As Kenny noted around the turn of the century, '[D's] mens rea in allowing himself to become intoxicated is sufficient to supply the ordinary mental element of guilt to any criminal act which may ensue from it.' [p 60] The key words here are 'ordinary mental element'. Some offences, as Kenny later points out, required mental elements that were out of the ordinary. In these cases intoxication might, depending on the nature of the mental element required, operate to negate liability for that offence:

> '[Intoxication] may disprove the presence of some additional mens rea that is essential to the definition of some particular crime. It may, for instance, disprove the presence of murderous malice, or of an intent to do grievous bodily harm, or of an intent to commit a felony.' [p 61]

Here, then, is an explanation for the occasional use of words like 'specific' or 'positive' in the early cases. The ordinary mental element required by offences at this time was 'malice', a form of negligence that intoxication would obviously not negate. There were, though, a few offences that specifically (or positively or explicitly) required specific (or particular or positive) mental states. Depending on their exact nature, these extra mental requirements might be incompatible with extreme intoxication. In other words, 'specificity' was not a characteristic of the intent required by an offence, although 'specifically requiring intent' might be a characteristic of offences themselves.

The specific-basic distinction in modern law

The casually used terminology of specific intent has been pressed into service in modern law to ensure that the kinds of offences that would have allowed liability for (objective) intoxicated wrongdoing in the past can continue to do so despite their more recent subjectivist overhaul. In simple terms, where the offence is one of 'specific intent', the defendant cannot be liable unless he acted with the necessary mental state. It makes no difference that his lack of mens rea was the result of intoxication. On the other hand, where, apart from his mental state, the defendant satisfies the conditions of liability for an offence that is not one of 'specific intent' (that is, of a 'basic intent' offence), he will (effectively) be held liable irrespective of his lack of mens rea. However, this explanation leaves at least two questions unanswered. How can modern offences that ostensibly require a subjective mens rea be satisfied by inadvertent intoxicated wrongdoing? And why is it that only some (ostensibly) subjective offences can be treated in this way while other (actually) subjective offences cannot?

There have been several attempts to explain the mechanism by which intoxicated wrongdoing satisfies the requirements of subjective offences. The Law Commission [Law Com No 229, *Legislating the Criminal Code: Intoxication and Criminal Liability* (1995)] considered two approaches, one that treats intoxicated wrongdoing as a substitute for subjectively reckless wrongdoing and another that presumes that there is subjectively reckless wrongdoing where intoxicated wrongdoing is shown to be present. Neither approach is particularly attractive. Intoxicated wrongdoing is not a direct alternative to subjectively reckless wrongdoing, and that is a good reason for not presuming it to be. Rather, there are differences between the two types of wrongdoing that may need to be reflected in different sentences or—and this is the important point—in different offence headings.

Considerations of fair labelling, the set of principles governing the assimilation of particular types of wrongdoing under particular offence headings, have driven the specific-basic distinction into the law. Intoxicated wrongdoing is not equivalent to subjective wrongdoing, but where it is perceived to share the salient characteristics of the wrong or family of wrongs associated with a particular offence heading, including any characteristics given salience by being specified in the offence heading itself, there will be little objection to assimilating it under that heading. Any remaining differences between the two types of wrongdoing will be minor enough to be taken into account at the sentencing stage. There are, on the other hand, some offence headings that do not exhibit this degree of flexibility. Killing in drunken inadvertence, for example, while it is a very serious form of wrongdoing, could hardly be considered equivalent to the specific and serious wrongs normally associated with murder. Or, at least, to treat it as murder would so broaden the types of wrongdoing associated with that offence as to risk diluting the special opprobrium attaching to it. Similarly, where a heading gives salience to particular characteristics of the wrongs prohibited by explicitly specifying them—wounding with intent to do grievous bodily harm, for example—it would be paradoxical to use it to convict the unthinking drunken wounder whose wrongdoing exhibits no such characteristic.

This is not to say that the specific-basic distinction can be explained solely in terms of fair label-ling. The common law judges have had to work with existing offence headings and there are certain types of intoxicated wrongdoing that do not fit particularly neatly under any of these. Where such wrongdoing is considered relatively venial, the temptation may be to sacrifice the conviction of de-serving offenders in order to preserve the coherence of the law's labelling scheme. Perhaps thought-less drunken trespass or appropriation ought to be criminal, but it would seem wrong to deal with such offenders under the ancient and emotive headings of burglary and theft, and in the absence of appropriate existing offence headings they go free. Where the intoxicated wrongdoing is considered more serious, by contrast, the temptation may be to sacrifice the principles of fair labelling in order to secure the conviction of deserving offenders. The classification of rape as a basic intent offence may be an example of this type of compromise. There are serious doubts whether the rapist who drunkenly believes his victim to be consenting should be dealt with under the same opprobrious heading as the advertent rapist who knowingly risks that they are not. Since there is no other appropriate offence heading, though, it is better to convict the intoxicated individual under the rape heading than to ac-quit completely.

Objections to the specific-basic distinction

I should mention three objections that might be raised against this approach to the specific-basic distinction.

(1) It may be objected that the process of tacitly extending offences to cover closely related but not explicitly prohibited wrongs is contrary to the rule of law (in that it involves retrospective crim-inalisation and judicial legislation) or that it is impractical (in that its role in securing the conviction of a handful of admittedly deserving individuals does not justify the complexity and difficulty that it introduces). Such objections are not particularly persuasive. Judicial extension of offences to cover closely related types of wrongdoing is not confined to the intoxication rules: it is a common tech-nique used to give flexibility to offence headings, to circumvent the letter of the law and give effect to its spirit.... Consider also the non-contemporaneity cases like *Church* [[1966] 1 QB 59]. *Thabo Meli* [[1954] 1 WLR 228] (and, it may be added, *Gallagher* [[1963] AC 349]). The defendants had all com-mitted wrongs similar to the central wrong prohibited by murder save only that their behaviour did not satisfy the contemporaneity requirements of that offence. That is, while they had intended to kill and had caused death, the acts causing death had not involved an intent to kill. The instinct of the courts in each case was to ignore the minor difference between the actual and the required wrongdoing and convict under the murder heading. To the extent that it would be undesirable to rewrite the law in these various respects and allow plainly culpable individuals to get off scot-free, perhaps it is not the specific-basic distinction that we should be rethinking but our assumptions about the practical and constitutional difficulties presented by the current intoxication rules.

(2) A second objection rejects the specific-basic distinction as unprincipled because it cannot be reduced to a neat general formula. Many people have attempted to find such a formula—some have tried to identify specific intent with ulterior intent, others with purpose, others with subjective reck-lessness. All of these enterprises make the mistake, identified above, of assuming 'specificity' to be a quality of the mental elements required by certain offences and, as a result, they all fail to capture the common law distinction. Some of them require counterintuitive amendments to the accepted catego-risations of offences as specific or basic—under the 'purpose' of 'ulterior intent' approaches, for ex-ample. Murder would have to be reclassified as a basic intent offence because neither of those mental states is necessary for its commission. Others overconfidently classify as specific or basic offences like rape over which the common law has understandably dithered.

In fact, to search for a neat reduction of the specific-basic distinction is to misunderstand its nature. 'Specific intent offence' is an (inapt) label given to offences which, for the kinds of reasons already discussed, cannot appropriately be extended to cover inadvertent intoxicated wrongdoing. We do not expect a general formula to tell us whether a certain offence heading should cover a certain objectively reckless wrong, subjectively reckless wrong, intentional wrong, or wrong characterised by a special quality like dishonesty or indecency. It is similarly misguided to expect a general theory to tell us whether a particular offence heading should cover a given intoxicated wrong.

...

(3) Finally, many have wanted to deal with intoxicated wrongdoing under a special heading ('dangerous intoxication', for example) rather than, as at present, under ordinary offences. While there may be an argument to be made along these lines, it is difficult to imagine that it would be very persuasive. In particular, it seems implausible to claim, as advocates of a new offence must be claiming, that the reasons against grouping intoxicated vandals alongside advertent vandals under the existing criminal damage heading are more powerful than the reasons against grouping intoxicated vandals alongside intoxicated killers under some new offence. The underlying mistake is the assumption that wrongs should be grouped primarily according to their mental components and with little reference to their other characteristics. Not only have offence labels always reflected the non-mental characteristics of the wrongs they prohibit, but in many cases such characteristics are the only basis for a labelling distinction—consider the separate classification of murder as opposed to section 18 wounding, or of common assault as opposed to section 47 actual bodily harm, or of attempted offences as opposed to completed offences. Why should we apologise for distinguishing between intoxicated killers and intoxicated vandals on the same grounds? All this being said, it is doubtful how many of the advocates of a new offence realise they are making this implausible argument. Most of them are, I suspect, motivated by a vague and unfocused objection to objective liability per se. The attempt to reconcile such extreme subjectivist views with an uneasy acceptance that it would not be right or, at least, not politically acceptable for intoxicated offenders to get off leads to the rather sloppy conclusion that there should be a special offence—a criminal law ghetto in which the slightly fishy intoxicated wrongs are kept separate from 'proper' (subjective) criminal wrongdoing.

The introduction of one bland offence heading to cover all criminal intoxicated wrongdoing may well be undesirable, but we should not rule out the possibility that a range of narrowly circumscribed new offences should be introduced to cover forms of intoxicated wrongdoing that are difficult to categorise at present. On the other hand, there are dozens of other considerations bearing on whether such reforms should be introduced. Should the law be made even more complex? How far would the new offences be open to abuse? How, for example, would deterrence and respect for the law be affected if enough real rapists were able to bluff themselves into a new 'forcible intercourse' category designed to catch inadvertent offenders? Even leaving these difficulties aside, though, it is hard to accept that very many intoxicated wrongs sit uncomfortably under their existing basic intent offence headings. Even if we were given carte blanche to rewrite the specific-basic distinction and to introduce new offences where necessary, I doubt that we would want to change very much. Certainly, it seems unlikely that we would want to bring intoxicated killers under any other category than manslaughter, or intoxicated vandals under any other category than criminal damage or intoxicated wounders under any other categories than unlawful wounding or assault occasioning actual bodily harm.

See also J. Horder, 'Crimes of Ulterior Intent' in A. Simester and A. T. H. Smith (eds), *Harm and Culpability* (1996) and J. Horder, 'The Classifications of Crimes and the Special Part' in R. A. Duff and S. P. Green (eds), *Defining Crimes: Essays on the Special Part of the Criminal Law* (2005).

■ *Question*

Would it be better to have an offence of 'committing [the actus reus of offence X] while intoxicated'? See R. Williams, 'Voluntary Intoxication—A Lost Cause?' (2013) 129 LQR 264.

6.4 Voluntary intoxication leading to a loss of mens rea

The rules are clear: if the case is one of voluntary intoxication, the defendant can rely on his intoxication as an excuse only to a crime of specific intent (eg murder), but not one of basic intent (eg manslaughter). In some instances D's voluntary intoxication is so great that he becomes an automaton. However D cannot plead automatism to a crime of basic intent if he induced that state through his voluntary consumption of alcohol or drugs (*Coley* [2013] EWCA Crim 223).

R v Lipman

[1970] 1 QB 152, Court of Appeal, Criminal Division

(Widgery and Fenton Atkinson LJJ, James J)

Both the applicant, L, and the victim, V, were drug addicts and both took a quantity of LSD in V's room. The next morning L (who was a US citizen) hurriedly left the country. V's landlord found her dead in her room the following day. She had suffered two blows on the head causing haemorrhage of the brain, but she died of asphyxia as a result of some eight inches of sheet having been crammed into her mouth. L was eventually tracked down and arrested. He explained how after taking LSD with V he had the illusion of descending to the centre of the earth and being attacked by snakes, with which he had fought. He killed the victim in the course of this experience, but he said he had no knowledge of what he was doing and no intention to harm her. He was charged with murder, but the jury evidently accepted that he lacked the necessary intention to kill or to do grievous bodily harm, as to manslaughter. Milmo J directed the jury that L 'would be guilty of manslaughter if the jury were to find either—(1) that he must have realized before he got himself into the condition he did by taking the drugs, that acts such as those he subsequently performed and which resulted in the death, were dangerous; or (2) that the taking of the drugs which the defendant took that night was dangerous and that the [defendant] must have realized that by taking them he was incurring a risk of some harm, not necessarily serious harm, to some other person or persons; or (3) that in taking these drugs in the circumstances in which he took them, the [defendant] was grossly negligent and reckless and this involves the jury considering whether or not he thought that what he was doing was safe so far as other people were concerned.' (See [1970] 1 QB 152.)

The jury found the defendant not guilty of murder but guilty of manslaughter by reason of grounds (1) and (3) above. The defendant appealed.

[**Widgery LJ** delivered the judgment of the court:]

In this court counsel for the applicant contends that . . . the jury should have been directed further that it was necessary for the Crown to prove that the applicant had intended to do acts likely to result in harm, or foresaw that harm would result from what he was doing.

For the purposes of criminal responsibility we see no reason to distinguish between the effect of drugs voluntarily taken and drunkenness voluntarily induced. As to the latter there is a great deal of authority. [His lordship quoted from the speeches of Lord Birkenhead in *Beard*'s case and Lord Denning in *Bratty*'s case (see section 10.4.1, p 327) and *Gallagher*'s case (see section 6.5, p 172)].

These authorities show quite clearly, in our opinion, that it was well established that no specific intent was necessary to support a conviction for manslaughter based on killing in the course of an unlawful act and that, accordingly, self-induced drunkenness was no defence to such a charge.

[His lordship cited the facts and a passage from the judgment of Edmund Davies J, section 17.2.3, p 599, noting that the appellant was arguing that some intention or foresight was an essential element of manslaughter as defined in *Church*.]

In our judgment, there is a flaw in the applicant's argument; and the flaw lies in the assumption that *Church* introduced a new element of intent or foreseeability into this type of manslaughter. All that the judgment in *Church* says in terms is that whereas, formerly, a killing by any unlawful act amounted to manslaughter, this consequence does not now inexorably follow unless the unlawful act is one in which ordinary sober and responsible people would recognise the existence of risk. The development recognised by *Church* relates to the type of act from which a charge of manslaughter may result, not in the intention (real or assumed) of the prisoner. It is perhaps unfortunate that a reference to mens rea, which had been found unhelpful by Lord Atkin, was repeated in *Church*, and to give it the effect now contended for would be contrary to *DPP v Beard* and the other authorities which we have cited. The decision in *Church* was referred to in this court later in *Lamb* [see section 17.2.1.1, p 595] where the accused had pointed a revolver at the victim in the belief, as he said, that there was no round in the chamber, but the revolver had fired and the victim was killed. It was pointed out in this court that no unlawful act on the part of the prisoner had been proved in the absence of the necessary intent to constitute an assault. But this is intention of a different kind. Even if intent has to be proved to constitute the unlawful act, no specific further intent is required to turn that act into manslaughter. Manslaughter remains a most difficult offence to define because it arises in so many different ways and, as the mental element (if any) required to establish it varies so widely, any general reference to mens rea is apt to mislead.

We can dispose of the present application by reiterating that when the killing results from an unlawful act of the accused no specific intent has to be proved to convict of manslaughter, and self-induced intoxication is accordingly no defence. Since in the present case the acts complained of were obviously likely to cause harm to the victim (and did, in fact, kill her) no acquittal was possible and the verdict of manslaughter, at the least, was inevitable.

Appeal dismissed

■ *Questions*

1. Why is it relevant whether a person knows it is dangerous to cram eight inches of bedsheet into a woman's mouth if he has no idea that he is going to do, or is doing, such an act?

2. According to (i) Milmo J's summing up and (ii) the Court of Appeal, was the act for which Lipman was responsible (iii) the taking of the drugs or (iv) the acts done?

3. The court concedes, 'even if intent has to be proved to constitute the unlawful act...' Was any intent proved with respect to the unlawful acts done?

In *Coley* [2013] EWCA Crim 223 Hughes LJ stated that the line between voluntary intoxication and insanity may in some cases be difficult to draw with precision. His lordship stated that, 'it would be perfectly legitimate to say of a very drunken man that his mind had become detached from reality by the intoxication'. Some such extreme cases will turn on whether there was a disease of the mind, see section 10.5.1, p 343.

6.4.1 Voluntary intoxication by dangerous drugs

In the case where D has become voluntarily intoxicated and the offence with which he is charged is one of basic intent, there remains one important issue to consider—whether the substance ingested is dangerous, that is, commonly known to create states of unpredictability or aggression. Even if the drug is not one that is commonly known to create such states, D may nevertheless be liable if he mixes it with alcohol and has been warned against doing so (*Coley* [2013] EWCA Crim 223).

R v Hardie

[1984] 3 All ER 848, Court of Appeal, Criminal Division, http://www.bailii.org/ew/cases/EWCA/Crim/1984/2.html

(Parker LJ, Stuart-Smith and McCowan JJ)

The defendant's relationship with the woman with whom he was living broke down and she left him. He became upset and took several tablets of valium, a sedative drug, belonging to the woman. Later he started a fire in the bedroom of the flat while the woman and her daughter were in the sitting room. Charged with an offence under the Criminal Damage Act 1971, s 1(2), he argued that the effect of the drug was to prevent him having the mens rea. The judge directed the jury that this could be no defence because the drug was self-administered. The defendant appealed on grounds of misdirection.

Parker LJ:

. . . in *R v Bailey* [1983] 2 All ER 503, [1983] 1 WLR 760 this court had to consider a case where a diabetic had failed to take sufficient food after taking a normal dose of insulin and struck the victim over the head with an iron bar. The judge directed the jury that the defence of automatism, ie that the mind did not go with the act, was not available because the incapacity was self-induced. It was held that this was wrong on two grounds: (a) because on the basis of *DPP v Majewski* it was clearly available to the offence embodying specific intent and (b) because although self-induced by the omission to take food it was also available to negative the other offence which was of basic intent only.

Having referred to *DPP v Majewski* and *R v Lipman* Griffiths LJ, giving the considered judgment of the court, said ([1983] 2 All ER 503 at 507, [1983] 1 WLR 760 at 764–765):

'It was submitted on behalf of the Crown that a similar rule should be applied as a matter of public policy to all cases of self-induced automatism. But it seems to us that there may be material distinctions between a man who consumes alcohol or takes dangerous drugs and one who fails to take sufficient food after insulin to avert hypo-glycaemia. It is common knowledge that those who take alcohol to excess or certain sorts of drugs may become aggressive or do dangerous or unpredictable things; they may be able to foresee the risks of causing harm to others, but nevertheless persist in their conduct. But the same cannot be said, without more, of a man who fails to take food after an insulin injection. If he does appreciate the risk that such a failure may lead to aggressive, unpredictable and uncontrollable conduct and he nevertheless deliberately runs the risk or otherwise disregards it, this will amount to recklessness. But we certainly do not think that it is common knowledge, even among diabetics, that such is a consequence of a failure to take food; and there is no evidence that it was known to this appellant. Doubtless he knew that if he failed to take his insulin or proper food after it he might lose consciousness, but as such he would only be a danger to himself unless he put himself in charge of some machine such as a motor car, which required his continued conscious control. In our judgment, self-induced automatism, other than that due to intoxication from alcohol or drugs, may provide a defence to crimes of basic intent. The question in each case will be whether the prosecution has proved the necessary element of recklessness. In cases of assault, if the accused knows that his actions or inaction are likely to make him aggressive, unpredictable or uncontrolled with the result that he may cause some injury to others and he persists in the action or takes no remedial action when he knows it is required, it will be open to the jury to find that he was reckless.'

In the present instance the defence was that the valium was taken for the purpose of calming the nerves only, that it was old stock and that the appellant was told it would do him no harm. There was no evidence that it was known to the appellant or even generally known that the taking of valium in the quantity taken would be liable to render a person aggressive or incapable of appreciating risks to others or have other side effects such that its self-administration would itself have an element of recklessness. It is true that valium is a drug and it is true that it was taken deliberately and not taken on medical prescription, but the drug is, in our view, wholly different in kind from drugs which are liable to cause unpredictability or aggressiveness. It may well be that the taking of a sedative or soporific drug will, in certain circumstances, be no answer, for example in a case of reckless driving, but if the effect of a drug is merely soporific or sedative the taking of it, even in some excessive quantity, cannot in the ordinary way raise a conclusive presumption against the admission of proof of intoxication for the purpose of disproving mens rea in ordinary crimes, such as would be the case with alcoholic intoxication or incapacity or automatism resulting from the self-administration of dangerous drugs.

In the present case the jury should not, in our judgment, have been directed to disregard any incapacity which resulted or might have resulted from the taking of valium. They should have been directed that if they came to the conclusion that, as a result of the valium, the appellant was, at the time, unable to appreciate the risks to property and persons from his actions they should then consider whether the taking of the valium was itself reckless. We are unable to say what would have been the appropriate direction with regard to the elements of recklessness in this case for we have not seen all the relevant evidence, nor are we able to suggest a model direction, for circumstances will vary infinitely and model directions can sometimes lead to more rather than less confusion. It is sufficient to say that the direction that the effects of valium were necessarily irrelevant was wrong.

Appeal allowed

■ *Questions*

1. Are drugs to be divided into two categories—(i) alcohol and 'dangerous' drugs which attract the operation of *Majewski* and (ii) other drugs which do not?

2. Which category does cannabis fall into?

3. Is it permissible for the court to apply a 'conclusive presumption' of recklessness in the light of the Criminal Justice Act 1967, s 8, section 5.2.2, p 109?

4. *In Chaulk* (2008) 223 CCC (3d) 174, the Nova Scotia Court of Appeal held that the test for self-induced intoxication is that D voluntarily consumed a substance, which he knew *or ought to* have known was an intoxicant, and the risk of becoming intoxicated was *or should have been* within his contemplation. There was held to be no need to prove that that the substance was illegal or that D knew precisely what the substance was. Do you agree with that approach?

6.5 Drinking 'with intent': Dutch courage

In some cases, the defendant forms the intention to commit the crime and then intoxicates himself to strengthen his resolve to go through with it. Should this be a defence?

Attorney-General for Northern Ireland v Gallagher
[1961] 3 All ER 299, House of Lords, http://www.bailii.org/uk/cases/UKHL/1961/2.html

(Lords Reid, Goddard, Tucker, Denning and Morris of Borth-y-Gest)

G had a grievance against his wife because she had been instrumental in getting him detained in a mental hospital. He had made up his mind to kill her and bought a knife for that purpose. He also drank most of a bottle of whisky—'either to give himself Dutch courage to do the deed or to drown his conscience after it'—and killed her. He raised pleas of insanity and intoxication. The Court of Criminal Appeal in Northern Ireland quashed the conviction for murder because the trial judge, in their view, had directed the jury to apply the *M'Naghten* test (section 10.5, p 334) not to the time when the accused killed his wife but to the morning of that day, before he opened the bottle of whisky.

[Lord Tucker, with whom Lords Goddard and Reid agreed, held that the jury had not been misdirected.]

Lord Denning:

. . . My Lords, this case differs from all others in the books in that the respondent, whilst sane and sober, before he took to the drink, had already made up his mind to kill his wife. This seems to me to be far worse—and far more deserving of condemnation—than the case of a man who, before getting drunk, has no intention to kill, but afterwards in his cups, whilst drunk, kills another by an act which he would not dream of doing when sober. Yet, by the law of England, in this latter case his drunkenness is no defence even though it has distorted his reason and his will-power. So why should it be a defence in the present case? And is it made any better by saying that the man is a psychopath? The answer to the question is, I think, that the case falls to be decided by the general principle of English law that, subject to very limited exceptions, drunkenness is no defence to a criminal charge nor is a defect of reason produced by drunkenness. This principle was stated by Sir Matthew Hale in his Pleas of the Crown, Vol 1, p 32, in words which I would repeat here:

> 'This vice [drunkenness] doth deprive men of the use of reason, and puts many men into a perfect, but temporary frenzy . . . by the laws of England such a person shall have no privilege by this voluntary contracted madness, but shall have the same judgment as if he were in his right senses.'

This general principle can be illustrated by looking at the various ways in which drunkenness may produce a defect of reason: (a) It may impair a man's powers of perception so that he may not be able to foresee or measure the consequences of his actions as he would if he were sober. Nevertheless, he is not allowed to set up his self-induced want of perception as a defence. Even if he did not himself appreciate that what he was doing was dangerous, nevertheless, if a reasonable man in his place, who was not befuddled with drink, would have appreciated it, he is guilty; see *Meade* [[1909] 1 KB 895], as explained in *DPP v Beard* [see section 6.3, p 152]. (b) It may impair a man's power to judge between right or wrong, so that he may do a thing when drunk which he would not dream of doing while sober. He does not realise he is doing wrong. Nevertheless, he is not allowed to set up his self-induced want of moral sense as a defence. In *Beard's* case Lord Birkenhead LC distinctly ruled that it was not a defence for a drunken man to say he did not know he was doing wrong. (c) It may impair a man's power of self-control so that he may more readily give way to provocation than if he were sober. Nevertheless, he is not allowed to set up his self-induced want of control as a defence. The acts of provocation are to be assessed, not according to their effect on him personally, but according to the effect they would have on a reasonable man in his place. [His lordship referred to the old law on provocation—see now section 16.2, p 551.]

. . .

I would allow this appeal and restore the conviction of murder.

Appeal allowed

Archbold (1992 edn), para 17-147, commenting on *Gallagher*'s case stated:

> If A with the intention of killing B enrages a gorilla with the result that the gorilla in fact kills B, A is clearly guilty of murder and, under the old law, as a principal . . . What difference does it make if for the gorilla he substitutes himself?

■ *Question*

What if Gallagher, getting up in the night to relieve himself, had blundered drunkenly into the grandfather clock on the landing and knocked it down the stairs, killing his wife who had just arrived home?

6.6 Intoxication and defences

We have seen (section 2.1.3, p 19) that, just as a state of mind is a necessary element in the definition of an offence, so also it is a necessary element in some defences. Just as intoxication may cause a person to *lack* the mens rea of an *offence* so it may cause him to *have* the necessary mental element of a *defence*. It is necessary for a defendant who relies on self-defence to offer evidence that he believed he was being attacked in such a way as to justify or excuse the force which he used to defend himself. What if that belief was mistaken—he was not under attack at all—and the mistake was made because he was drunk at the time? The issue is whether intoxication is always to be ignored when explaining the seemingly incredible mistake which the accused is relying on. The position can be summarized as follows:

- as a matter of policy the courts have taken the approach of treating as irrelevant a defendant's mistaken beliefs in facts that would, if true, provide grounds for a defence where the basis for the mistake is one of self-induced intoxication. However, while this is true of some defences, for example self-defence, it is questionable whether it is true of others, such as loss of control or necessity;
- if D is pleading self-defence he is to be treated as being aware of anything which he would have been aware of had he not been intoxicated.

These principles are derived from the following cases.

R v O'Grady
[1987] 3 All ER 420, Court of Appeal, Criminal Division, http://www.bailii.org/ew/cases/EWCA/Crim/1987/2.html

(Lord Lane CJ, Boreham and McCowan JJ)

The defendant (O) and his friend, the deceased (M), had been drinking heavily and fell asleep in O's flat. O said that he awoke to find M hitting him, that M had a piece of glass in one hand and that he, O, picked up a piece of glass and hit M. M died of the injury caused. At the invitation of counsel for the prosecution, Judge Underhill gave the following additional direction to the jury:

It might be a view that you might take, I know not, that this defendant thought he was under attack from the other man mistakenly and made a mistake in thinking that he was under attack because of the drink that was in him. If he made such a mistake in drink he would nevertheless be entitled to defend himself even though he mistakenly believed that he was under attack. He would be entitled in those circumstances to defend himself. But if in taking defensive measures, then he went beyond what is reasonable either because of his mind being affected by drink or for any other reason, then the defence of self-defence would not avail him because, as I told you earlier on, you are entitled to defend yourself if it is necessary so to do, but the defensive measures that you take must be reasonable ones and not go beyond what is reasonable.

O was convicted of manslaughter and appealed on the grounds, *inter alia*, that the judge was wrong to limit the reference to mistake as to the *existence* of an attack and should have included a reference to the possibility of a mistake as to the *severity* of it; and that the judge had 'in effect divorced the reasonableness of the appellant's reaction from the appellant's state of mind at the time'.

Lord Lane CJ [having said that the court had found no case directly in point which was binding:]

As McCullough J [the single judge, giving leave to appeal] pointed out helpfully in his observations for the benefit of the court:

'Given that a man who *mistakenly* believes he is under attack is entitled to use reasonable force to defend himself, it would seem to follow that, if he is under attack and mistakenly believes the attack to be more serious than it is, he is entitled to use reasonable force to defend himself against an attack of the severity he believed it to have. If one allows a mistaken belief induced by drink to bring this principle into operation, an act of gross negligence (viewed objectively) may become lawful even though it results in the death of the innocent victim. The drunken man would be guilty of neither murder nor manslaughter.'

How should the jury be invited to approach the problem? One starts with the decision of this court in *R v Williams* [1987] 3 All ER 411, namely that where the defendant might have been labouring under a mistake as to the facts he must be judged according to that mistaken view, whether the mistake was reasonable or not. It is then for the jury to decide whether the defendant's reaction to the threat (real or imaginary) was a reasonable one. The court was not in that case considering what the situation might be where the mistake was due to voluntary intoxication by alcohol or some other drug.

We have come to the conclusion that, where the jury are satisfied that the defendant was mistaken in his belief that any force or the force which he in fact used was necessary to defend himself and are further satisfied that the mistake was caused by voluntarily induced intoxication, the defence must fail. We do not consider that any distinction should be drawn on this aspect of the matter between offences involving what is called specific intent, such as murder, and offences of so called basic intent, such as manslaughter. Quite apart from the problem of directing a jury in a case such as the present where manslaughter is an alternative verdict to murder, the question of mistake can and ought to be considered separately from the question of intent. A sober man who mistakenly believes he is in danger of immediate death at the hands of an attacker is entitled to be acquitted of both murder and manslaughter if his reaction in killing his supposed assailant was a reasonable one. What his intent may have been seems to us to be irrelevant to the problem of self-defence or no. Secondly, we respectfully adopt the reasoning of McCullough J already set out.

This brings us to the question of public order. There are two competing interests. On the one hand the interest of the defendant who has only acted according to what he believed to be necessary to protect himself, and on the other hand that of the public in general and the victim in particular who, probably through no fault of his own, has been injured or perhaps killed because of the defendant's drunken mistake. Reason recoils from the conclusion that in such circumstances a defendant is entitled to leave the court without a stain on his character. . . .

We have therefore come to the conclusion that a defendant is not entitled to rely, so far as self-defence is concerned, on a mistake of fact which has been induced by voluntary intoxication.

As already indicated, the judge's addendum to his summing up, which he made at the suggestion of prosecuting counsel, was unnecessary and erred in favour of the appellant.

The appeal against conviction is accordingly dismissed.

Appeal dismissed

■ *Questions*

1. As O was appealing from a conviction of manslaughter, could the opinion of the court as to the correct direction on a charge of murder be any more than an *obiter dictum*?

2. The court was much influenced by its assumption that, if the drunken mistake founded a defence to murder, it also founded a defence to manslaughter. Was this assumption correct? See later in this section. Was McCullough J right to say that, if the appellant's arguments were right, 'an act of gross negligence (viewed objectively) may become lawful even though it results in the death of an innocent victim'? Why is it not manslaughter simply because it is a case of causing death by gross negligence?

The proposition in *O'Grady* that a drunken mistake could not found a defence of self-defence on a murder charge was subjected to heavy criticism.

The Law Commission, in declining to follow that proposition in the Draft Code said (LC177, para 8.42):

> ...it would, we believe, be unthinkable to convict of murder a person who thought, for whatever reason, that he was acting to save his life and who would have been acting reasonably if he had been right.

The Court of Appeal, however, continued to think the unthinkable in *O'Connor* [1991] Crim LR 135. They were aware of the heavy criticism of *O'Grady* but declared that the case was binding on them. This too appears to be *obiter*, being unnecessary to the decision because O'Connor's conviction of murder was quashed on the ground that the judge omitted to direct the jury that voluntary intoxication could have prevented the appellant from forming the specific intent to kill or cause GBH.

In *Hatton* [2005] EWCA Crim 2951, the Court of Appeal confirmed that the decision in *O'Grady* applied equally to cases of manslaughter and murder: a defendant seeking to rely on self-defence could not rely on a mistake induced by voluntary intoxication. H, who had drunk more than 20 pints of beer, killed V, who was found with at least seven blows from a sledgehammer. H stated that he could not recall V's death but that he had a vague recollection that a stick fashioned in the shape of a Samurai sword had been involved. H said that he believed that V had hit him with the stick and that he must have believed that V was attacking him. H wished to raise self-defence based on his own mistaken belief that he thought he was being attacked by an SAS officer (as V had earlier pretended to be) with a sword. The judge ruled, following *O'Grady*, that it was not open to H to rely on a mistake induced by drunkenness. H argued that if he had mistaken the nature of the attack because of intoxication, he was entitled in law to have defended himself in a manner that was reasonable having regard to his drunken perception of the danger he faced and the jury should have been directed accordingly. H argued that the discussion of the matter in *O'Grady* was *obiter dicta* because it related to manslaughter only and not murder. The Court of Appeal held that *O'Grady* was applicable to both murder and manslaughter.

The Criminal Justice and Immigration Act 2008, s 76, now confirms this approach:

> (4) If D claims to have held a particular belief as regards the existence of any circumstances—
>
>   (a) the reasonableness or otherwise of that belief is relevant to the question whether D genuinely held it; but
>
>   (b) if it is determined that D did genuinely hold it, D is entitled to rely on it for the purposes of subsection (3), whether or not—
>
>   (i) it was mistaken, or
>
>   (ii) (if it was mistaken) the mistake was a reasonable one to have made.
>
> (5) But subsection (4)(b) does not enable D to rely on any mistaken belief attributable to intoxication that was voluntarily induced.

If H had not mentioned the drink and had said simply that he made a genuine though unreasonable mistake that he was under attack, he would have been entitled to rely on that mistake and following *Williams* he could be acquitted. He might have been convicted of manslaughter if the mistake was one which was so unreasonable as to be grossly negligent.

If H had not mentioned the mistake and had simply relied on the level of intoxication as an excuse, saying that he did not have the mens rea for murder at the time of the killing, following *Majewski* he would be acquitted of murder and at worst convicted of manslaughter.

When H relies on the intoxication to explain the mistake he made and make it more believable that he made such a mistake, he is convicted of murder!

■ *Questions*

1. How can H be in a worse position by combining two pleas which, individually, would have at worst led to a manslaughter conviction?

2. D is charged with murder. He hit V in the face with a beer glass, causing a cut from which V bled to death. D says (i) he was acting in self-defence and (ii) he had no intent to cause death or GBH. V was not in fact attacking him but D says that, in his drunken condition, (iii) he believed V was attacking him with a broken glass so as to threaten his life; (iv) he forgot he had a glass in his own hand. Following *O'Grady* and *O'Connor*, so far as (i) is concerned, the jury must treat D as if he were not drunk (would he have known that he was not being attacked if he had not been drunk?), whereas for (ii) they must take his drunkenness into account. His drunkenness is relevant to the question (iv) whether he knew he had a glass in his own hand (because that goes to specific intent) but not to the question (iii) whether he believed there was a glass in V's hand (because that goes to self-defence). Can this be justified?

Jaggard v Dickinson
[1980] 3 All ER 716, Queen's Bench Division

(Donaldson LJ and Mustill J)

The defendant lived in a house belonging to her friend. Making her way home drunk, she went by mistake to the wrong house, found it locked and did damage by breaking in. She was charged with an offence under s 1(1) of the Criminal Damage Act 1971. She relied on s 5(2) of the Act, section 28.2.5, p 903, saying that she believed that her friend would have consented to her doing the damage in the circumstances. The magistrates held that this drunken belief could not be a defence.

Mustill J:

... It is convenient to refer to the exculpatory provisions of s 5(2) as if they created a defence whilst recognising that the burden of disproving the facts referred to by the subsection remains on the prosecution. The magistrates held that the appellant was not entitled to rely on s 5(2) since the belief relied on was brought about by a state of self-induced intoxication.

In support of the conviction counsel for the respondent advanced an argument which may be summarised as follows. (i) Where an offence is one of 'basic intent', in contrast to one of 'specific intent', the fact that the accused was in a state of self-induced intoxication at the time when he did the acts constituting the actus reus does not prevent him from possessing the mens rea necessary to constitute the offence: see *DPP v Morgan* [1975] UKHL 3, *DPP v Majewski* [section 6.3, p 151], (ii) Section 1(1) of the 1971 Act creates an offence of basic intent: see *R v Stephenson* [1979] 2 All ER 1198, [1979] QB 695. (iii) Section 5(3) has no bearing on the present issue. It does not create a separate defence, but is no more than a partial definition of the expression 'without lawful excuse' in s 1(1). The absence of lawful excuse forms an element in the mens rea: see *R v Smith* [1974] 1 All ER 632 at 636, [1974] QB 354 at 360 [section 28.2.4, p 898]. Accordingly, since drunkenness does not negative mens rea in crimes of basic intent, it cannot be relied on as part of a defence based on s 5(2).

Whilst this is an attractive submission, we consider it to be unsound, for the following reasons. In the first place, the argument transfers the distinction between offences of specific and of basic intent to a context in which it has no place. The distinction is material where the defendant relies on his own drunkenness as a ground for denying that he had the degree of intention or recklessness required in order to constitute the offence. Here, by contrast, the appellant does not rely on her drunkenness to displace an inference of intent or recklessness; indeed she does not rely on it at all. Her defence is founded on the state of belief called for by s 5(2). True, the fact of the appellant's intoxication was relevant to the defence under s 5(2) for it helped to explain what would otherwise have been inexplicable, and hence lent colour to her evidence about the state of her belief. This is not the same as using drunkenness to rebut an inference of intention or recklessness. Belief, like intention or recklessness, is a state of mind; but they are not the same states of mind.

It was, however, urged that we could not properly read s 5(2) in isolation from s 1(1), which forms the context of the words 'without lawful excuse' partially defined by s 5(2). Once the words are put in context, so it is maintained, it can be seen that the law must treat drunkenness in the same way in relation to lawful excuse (and hence belief) as it does to intention and recklessness, for they are all part of the mens rea of the offence. To fragment the mens rea, so as to treat one part of it as affected by drunkenness in one way and the remainder as affected in a different way, would make the law impossibly complicated to enforce.

If it had been necessary to decide whether, for all purposes, the mens rea of an offence under s1(1) extends as far as an intent (or recklessness) as to the existence of a lawful excuse, I should have wished to consider the observations of James LJ, delivering the judgment of the Court of Appeal in *R v Smith* [1974] 1 All ER 632 at 636, [1974] QB 354 at 360. I do not however find it necessary to reach a conclusion on this matter and will only say that I am not at present convinced that, when these observations are read in the context of the judgment as a whole, they have the meaning which the respondent has sought to put on them. In my view, however, the answer to the argument lies in the fact that any distinctions which have to be drawn as to the relevance of drunkenness to the two subsections arises from the scheme of the 1971 Act itself. No doubt the mens rea is in general indivisible, with no distinction being possible as regards the effect of drunkenness. But Parliament has specifically isolated one subjective element, in the shape of honest belief, and has given it separate treatment and its own special gloss in s 5(3). This being so, there is nothing objectionable in giving it special treatment as regards drunkenness, in accordance with the natural meaning of its words.

Appeal allowed

■ *Questions*

1. Would the defendant have been liable if she had believed (through intoxication or otherwise) that the house was her own? Cf *Smith* [1974] QB 354, section 28.2.4, p 898. Would it be sensible for the law to distinguish between the two cases?

2. Is there a distinction between using intoxication to rebut an inference of recklessness and to rebut evidence of belief? What if the belief is that there is no risk?

3. Did *Smith*, section 28.2.4, p 898, decide that the absence of lawful excuse forms an element in the mens rea?

In *Richardson and Irwin* [1999] 1 Cr App R 392, [1999] Crim LR 494, it was held, following *Aitken* (1992) 95 Cr App R 304, C-MAC, that a drunken belief that the victim of 'horseplay' was consenting to a dangerous act was a defence to a charge of unlawfully and maliciously inflicting GBH contrary to s 20 of the Offences Against the Person Act 1861. In *Aitken* the court considered the Judge-Advocate's direction under two heads, 'Unlawfully' and 'Maliciously'. They discussed intoxication only under 'maliciously', and the effect of the alleged belief in consent only under 'unlawfully', as if belief went to the issue of actus reus rather than mens rea. But, where actual consent would be a defence (as appears to be the case here), the absence of a belief that the victim consents is an element in the mens rea. Section 20 being an offence of basic intent, D would not have been allowed to rely on his intoxication to show he did not foresee that he might cause any injury. Why should he be able to rely on it to show belief in consent? Is this another instance of the fragmentation of mens rea which Mustill J thought Parliament required him to tolerate in *Jaggard v Dickinson*, in the previous extract, p 177? But Parliament has said nothing about the absence of consent in the s 20 offence. Was it necessary or desirable to differentiate between the two elements of mens rea?

6.7 Reform of the law

The Law Commission published its latest proposals in Report No 314, *Intoxication and Criminal Liability* (2009), http://lawcommission.justice.gov.uk/docs/lc314_Intoxication_and_Criminal_Liability.pdf.

In relation to voluntary intoxication the Law Commission recommend that a statutory form of the *Majewski* rule be enacted:

There should be a general rule that

(1) if D is charged with having committed an offence as a perpetrator;

(2) the fault element of the offence is not an integral fault element (for example, because it merely requires proof of recklessness); and

(3) D was voluntarily intoxicated at the material time;

then, in determining whether or not D is liable for the offence, D should be treated as having been aware at the material time of anything which D would then have been aware of but for the intoxication. (para 3.35)

In addition, it is proposed that:

If the subjective fault element in the definition of the offence, as alleged, is one to which the justification for the *Majewski* rule cannot apply, then the prosecution should have to prove that D acted with that relevant state of mind. (para 3.42)

'Specific intent' type offences are excluded from this rule:

The following subjective fault elements should be excluded from the application of the general rule and should, therefore, always be proved:

(1) intention as to a consequence;

(2) knowledge as to something;

(3) belief as to something (where the belief is equivalent to knowledge as to something);

(4) fraud; and

(5) dishonesty. (para 3.46)

■ *Questions*

1. Does this replicate the *Majewski* rule as you understand it?
2. Would this clarify the law?

In relation to mistakes, the Law Commission recommended that:

> D should not be able to rely on a genuine mistake of fact arising from self-induced intoxication in sup-
> port of a defence to which D's state of mind is relevant, regardless of the nature of the fault alleged.
> D's mistaken belief should be taken into account only if D would have held the same belief if D had not
> been intoxicated. (para 3.53)

But if the offence charged:

> requires proof of a fault element of failure to comply with an objective standard of care, or requires no
> fault at all, D should be permitted to rely on a genuine but mistaken belief as to the existence of a fact,
> where D's state of mind is relevant to a defence, only if D would have made that mistake if he or she
> had not been voluntarily intoxicated.

In relation to involuntary intoxication the Law Commission proposed as a general rule that:

> D's state of involuntary intoxication should be taken into consideration:
>
>   (1) in determining whether D acted with the subjective fault required for liability, regardless of the
>   nature of the fault element; and
>
>   (2) in any case where D relies on a mistake of fact in support of a defence to
>
> which his or her state of mind is relevant. (para 3.121)

Significantly, the Commission sought to provide a non-exhaustive list of situations which
would count as involuntary intoxication:

>   (1) the situation where an intoxicant was administered to D without D's consent;
>
>   (2) the situation where D took an intoxicant under duress;
>
>   (3) the situation where D took an intoxicant which he or she reasonably believed was not an
>   intoxicant;
>
>   (4) the situation where D took an intoxicant for a proper medical purpose.
>
> D's state of intoxication should also be regarded as involuntary if, though not entirely involuntary, it
> was *almost* entirely involuntary. (paras 3.125–3.126)

■ *Question*

Would this clarify the law on involuntary intoxication?

FURTHER READING

S. Gough, 'Surviving without *Majewski*'
[2000] Crim LR 719

P. Handler, 'Intoxication and Criminal
Responsibility in England, 1819–1920'
(2013) 33 OJLS 243

J. Horder, 'Pleading Involuntary Lack of
Capacity' (1993) 52 CLJ 298

A. C. E. Lynch, 'The Scope of Intoxication'
[1982] Crim LR 139

G. Orchard, 'Surviving without *Majewski*'
[1993] Crim LR 426

R. Smith and L. Clements, 'Involuntary
Intoxication, the Threshold of Inhibition
and the Instigation of Crime' (1995) 46
NILQ 210

7
Strict liability

7.1 Introduction

A crime is one of strict liability if there is any one or more elements of the actus reus which do not require proof of fault—intention, knowledge, recklessness, belief, suspicion or even negligence. The imposition of strict liability is seen as a direct conflict with the primacy of the requirement of fault—mens rea—in criminal offences. Although the courts have recently reaffirmed the significance of the mens rea principle, there are now so many strict liability offences in English criminal law that in practical terms strict liability is of enormous importance.

This chapter focuses on identifying the circumstances in which an offence will be construed as one of strict liability—that is, where the Crown will not have to establish mens rea in relation to every element of the actus reus. It may be surprising to find that offences of great seriousness carrying heavy penalties and with serious social stigma have been interpreted as ones of strict liability. For example, the House of Lords has held that in sexual offences involving children under 13, liability as to age is strict. D aged 14 has sexual intercourse with V aged 12. V consents to the act. V has told D that she is 13. D has no reason to disbelieve her. He is guilty of an offence under s 5 of the Sexual Offences Act 2003 of having sex with a child under 13 carrying a maximum sentence of life imprisonment even though he had no idea V was under 13. See *G*, section 7.6.1, p 202.

The controversies that will be examined in this chapter include the following:

(i) the presumption of mens rea, that is, unless Parliament has indicated otherwise, the appropriate mental element is an unexpressed ingredient of every statutory offence;

(ii) how to ascertain whether an offence is in fact one of strict liability;

(iii) whether strict liability infringes Article 6 of the ECHR;

(iv) the merits of strict liability offences.

7.2 What does strict liability mean?

There is a degree of confusion over the meaning of strict liability, which is both disappointing and surprising. It is commonly said that, in offences of strict liability, 'no mens rea' need be proved. Indeed, it was held in *Sandhu* [1997] Crim LR 288, that mens rea not only need not, but must not, be proved. As the cases in this chapter will show, strict liability usually means that no mens rea need be proved with respect to one or more elements of the offence. It does not mean that no mental element whatever need be proved. Lord Edmund-Davies in *Whitehouse; Lemon* [1979] 1 All ER 898 at 920 cited the statement in *Smith and Hogan* (see 9th edn, 1999, p 98) that 'an offence is regarded—and properly regarded—as one of strict liability if no mens rea need be proved as to a single element in the actus reus'. Care has to be taken with the definition. The single element to which no mens rea attaches is usually one of crucial importance so the effect is that a person with no moral culpability may be convicted.

S. P. Green, 'Six Senses of Strict Liability: A Plea for Formalism'
in A. Simester (ed), *Appraising Strict Liability* (2005) (references omitted)

1. Six Senses of Strict Criminal Liability

In this section, I consider the various ways in which the term 'strict liability' has been used in the criminal law literature. Six different senses of the term will be identified: (1) offences that contain at least one material element for which there is no corresponding *mens rea* element; (2) statutory schemes that bar the use of one or more *mens-rea*-negating defences; (3) procedural devices that require a defendant's intent to be presumed from other facts; (4) offences that require a less serious form of *mens rea* than has traditionally been required by the criminal law; (5) offences that require a less serious form of harmfulness than has traditionally been required by the criminal law; and (6) offences that require a less serious form of wrongfulness than has traditionally been required by the criminal law.

Offences Omitting Requirement of Mens Rea

The most common use of the term 'strict liability' in the criminal law—and the only one, ultimately, that I can recommend—is to refer to offences that contain at least one material element for which there is no corresponding *mens rea* requirement. By *mens rea*, I mean the requirement that a defendant perform a voluntary physical act with intent, purpose, knowledge, belief, recklessness, negligence, or some other prescribed mental state. Thus, strict liability in this first sense is simply criminal liability in the absence of intent, purpose, knowledge, and the like. . . . [Within this category] several clarifications are in order. First, we can distinguish between offences for which no *mens rea* is required with respect to any material element (referred to here as 'pure' strict liability), and offences for which no *mens rea* is required with respect to at least one element but is required with respect to at least one other element (referred to as 'impure' strict liability). [See *Larsonneur*, section 2.5, p 40.]

. . . [S]tatutory rape is properly viewed as a strict liability offence because, although the defendant must be shown to have engaged intentionally in sexual intercourse with an under-age person, the offence does not require that the defendant know that the victim was under age [see the Sexual Offences Act 2003, s 5, section 7.6.1, p 201]. That is, a defendant may be convicted of statutory rape even though he reasonably but mistakenly believed that the victim was old enough to consent to intercourse. Secondly, within the category of impure strict liability, we can distinguish between 'constructive' and 'non-constructive' strict liability. [Unlawful act manslaughter involves constructive strict liability in that what must usually be proved is *mens rea* as to some crime—ie the intentional commission of an offence but no mens rea as to death, see section 17.2.1.1, p 595.] The *mens rea* required for non-constructive forms of strict liability (such as statutory rape) is not *mens rea* as to a crime. Indeed, it is not *mens rea* as to any form of wrongdoing. Rather, it is simply *mens rea* as to some defining element, such as, in the case of selling adulterated food or drugs, knowledge that one has sold food or drugs. Thus, once we consider non-constructive forms of strict liability, we can see how much broader the class of impure strict liability is than the class of pure strict liability. Thirdly, there are some offences that, while they do not require proof of *mens rea*, do allow the defendant to offer a defence of 'due diligence' [see section 7.8.2, p 211]. Because such offences omit the requirement of *mens rea*, they should be regarded as imposing strict liability in this first sense identified; although, as we shall see below, they might not satisfy the requirements of so-called 'substantive' strict liability. Fourthly, we can distinguish between offences that do not require a showing of *mens rea*, but do allow the assertion of affirmative defences such as mistake of fact; and offences that not only do not require a showing of *mens rea* but also prohibit the assertion of affirmative defences (this latter kind of strict liability is usually referred to as 'absolute liability').

In addition, following the Model Penal Code's culpability scheme, we can distinguish among strict liability with respect to a (1) conduct element, (2) result element, and (3) attendant circumstance element. Driving an automobile above the speed limit is an example of an offence that typically imposes strict liability with respect to the defendant's conduct. The prosecution need not prove that the defendant intended to drive above the speed limit, or even that he believed that he was driving in such a manner, in order for liability to be imposed. [Unlawful act manslaughter] is an example of an offence that imposes strict liability with respect to a result element. The defendant need not intend, or even believe, that his conduct might result in death in order for liability to be imposed. Statutory rape imposes strict liability with respect to an attendant circumstance—namely, the circumstance of whether the . . . victim is below the statutory age. Once again, the defendant need not be aware that the attendant circumstance existed. . . .

[Green describes each of the other five uses of the term strict liability and continues:]

Formal versus Substantive Strict Liability

A number of commentators have distinguished broadly between two different senses of the term 'strict liability': (1) 'formal' strict liability (also referred to as 'narrow', 'legal', or 'elemental' strict liability); and (2) 'substantive' strict liability (also referred to as 'broad' or 'moral' strict liability). In order to determine whether a statute involves strict liability in the substantive sense, we need to apply a normative test; that is, we need to ask whether, under such a regime, a defendant can be convicted without a showing of moral 'fault'. By contrast, determining whether a criminal statute involves strict liability in the formal sense can supposedly be determined by a 'mechanical' test without consideration of the statute's deeper moral content, simply by asking whether the offence requires a showing of some form of mental element.

Of the six kinds of strict liability identified in the previous section, only the first—omission of the *mens rea* requirement—qualifies as formal. The other five—barring *mens-rea*-negating defences; presuming intent; and reducing the level of required culpability, harmfulness, or wrongfulness—are all substantive. Thus, the position that I am advocating in this chapter can be reframed as follows: The term 'strict liability' should be used solely in its formal or legal sense, and not in its substantive or moral sense . . .

[Green offers:] five reasons for eschewing the substantive senses of strict liability and adhering strictly to its formal sense: First, moving away from the substantive sense of strict liability and towards a formalistic approach is consistent with an important parallel trend in the criminal law away from the broad, 'blameworthiness' sense of *mens rea* and towards its narrow, 'elemental' sense. Secondly, there are significant, perhaps irresoluble, difficulties in determining whether an offence entails substantive strict liability. Thirdly, talking about strict liability in the substantive sense contributes to a mistaken impression of moral equivalence among different forms of what I shall refer to as 'moral deficiency' in the criminal law. Fourthly, talking about strict liability in the substantive sense creates confusion in determining whether a statute should be interpreted as omitting *mens rea*. Finally, talk of substantive strict liability leads to a miscalculation of the extent of the overcriminalization problem.

7.2.1 Strict liability and moral fault

It is important to recall that mens rea is not synonymous with moral fault (see *Kingston* [1994] UKHL 9, section 6.2, p 156). See also the arguments advanced by Stuart Green (in the previous extract, p 182). To found the determination of an offence as one of strict liability or mens rea on the basis of moral fault would be fraught with difficulty and lead to inconsistency and incoherence. In cases in which the courts find that the presumption of mens rea has been rebutted so that an offence is one of strict liability, that does not suggest that the offender is morally at fault or otherwise.

A defendant might be found to be guilty of a serious crime to which strict liability applies, without having any moral fault. A modern example of a long line of cases imposing liability without fault is *Pharmaceutical Society of Great Britain v Storkwain Ltd* [1986] 2 All ER 635, [1986] 1 WLR 903, HL (discussed by B. S. Jackson in '*Storkwain*: A Case Study in Strict Liability and Self Regulation' [1991] Crim LR 892). The Medicines Act 1968, s 58(2), provides that no person shall sell by retail specified medicinal products except in accordance with a prescription given by an appropriate medical practitioner. The defendant supplied specified drugs on prescriptions purporting to be signed by Dr Irani. The prescriptions were forged. There was no finding that the defendants acted dishonestly, improperly or even negligently. So far as appeared, the forgery was sufficient to deceive the sellers without any shortcoming on their part. Yet the House of Lords held that the Divisional Court had rightly directed the magistrate to convict.

The House discerned the intention of Parliament to create an offence of strict liability from the facts that (i) express requirements of mens rea are to be found in other sections of the Act but not in s 58(2)(a), and (ii) exercising a power under the Act, the Minister had provided for an exemption where the seller, having exercised all due diligence, believes on reasonable grounds that the product is not a 'prescription only' medicine. Storkwain of course knew that the medicine was 'prescription only', but believed on reasonable grounds that the prescription was valid. The Minister had not provided an exemption for that. For criticism, see [1986] Crim LR at 814.

■ *Questions*

1. How does the exercise of powers by a Minister after the Act has been passed reveal the intention of Parliament in passing it?

2. What more could the pharmacist have done? Is it fair to criminalize his conduct? Would the knowledge of the potential for criminal liability in such circumstances deter you from being a pharmacist?

It is important to appreciate that where an offence is interpreted to be one of strict liability, subject to any due diligence defence as discussed in section 7.8.2, p 211 the fact that the defendant could not have avoided the prescribed harm even if he had tried to will not absolve him of liability.

7.3 When will strict liability be imposed?

Most offences are now defined by statute. It is therefore a question of statutory construction whether the external elements of the offence require proof of mental elements and, if so, what each mental element is. Often the definition uses a word or a phrase—'knowingly', 'with intent to', 'recklessly', 'wilfully', 'dishonestly', and so on—which gives guidance to the court. Often the definition uses a verb or noun which imports a mental element of some kind—'permits' and 'possesses', are examples—so that there cannot be an actus reus without that mental element.

However, it does not follow that, simply because Parliament has not used a word or phrase importing a mental element, the court will necessarily find that mens rea is not required. On the contrary, the courts have frequently asserted that there is a presumption in favour of mens rea which must be rebutted by the prosecution; but the application of this presumption has been far from consistent.

All earlier cases must now be reconsidered in the light of the two leading cases, *B (a minor) v DPP* [2000] UKHL 13 and *K* [2002] 1 AC 642, which follow. The presumption of mens rea is reasserted with particular emphasis. It applies to all statutory offences, unless excluded expressly or by necessary implication. According to Lord Steyn, 'It can only be displaced by specific language, ie, an express provision or a necessary implication.' What distinguishes these from earlier pronouncements is not only the fact they are two unanimous decisions of the House of Lords but also the fact that they effectively overrule *Prince* (1875) LR 2 CCR 154, regarded as the leading case on strict liability for 125 years, and many cases which applied it. (Prince was convicted of taking a girl under 16 out of the possession of her parents although he believed on reasonable grounds that she was 18. Liability as to her age was held to be strict.) The principles stated by the House are not limited to age-related elements of the actus reus; there is a presumption of mens rea in respect of every element of the actus reus unless displaced.

7.3.1 The presumption of mens rea

The first question in determining whether an offence is one of strict liability is to consider whether the statute imposes a requirement of mens rea expressly or by necessary implication. The House of Lords reasserted the primacy of the presumption of mens rea in *B v DPP*. The decision was controversial since it involved an offence designed to protect young children against sexual predators. Consider the merits of the options open to the House of Lords:

- liability as to V's age should be strict and D can be convicted even if he was unaware of V's age;
- the prosecution must prove that D did not have a genuine and reasonable belief as to V's age; and
- the prosecution must prove that D did not have a genuine belief in V's age.

B (a minor) v Director of Public Prosecutions
[2000] UKHL 13, House of Lords, http://www.bailii.org/uk/cases/UKHL/2000/13.html

(Lord Irvine LC, Lords Mackay, Nicholls, Steyn and Hutton)

The Indecency with Children Act 1960, s 1(1) provided that 'Any person who commits an act of gross indecency with or towards a child under 14 [subsequently raised to 16, see now the Sexual Offences Act 2003, s 8, section 20.3.1, p 734] or who incites a child under that age to such an act with him or another' is guilty of an offence. The offence at the time of this case was punishable with two years' imprisonment on indictment. B, a boy of 15, was sitting next to a 14-year-old girl on a bus and asked her to give him what he described as a 'shiner', meaning not a black eye, but an act of oral sex. He was charged with inciting her, contrary to the 1960 Act. On a preliminary point of law, a magistrates' court ruled that s 1(1) imposed strict liability and that a mistaken belief, however reasonable, that the child was 14 or over, was no defence. B then pleaded guilty. On an appeal by way of case stated to the Divisional Court, Brooke LJ, Rougier and Tucker JJ delivered judgments, reluctantly dismissing the appeal. B appealed to the House of Lords.

[Lords Irvine, for the reasons given by Lord Nicholls, and Mackay, for the reasons given by Lords Nicholls, Steyn and Hutton, agreed that the appeal should be allowed.]

Lord Nicholls of Birkenhead:

My Lords, an indecent assault on a woman is a criminal offence. So is an indecent assault on a man. Neither a boy nor a girl under the age of 16 can, in law, give any consent which would prevent an act being an assault. These offences have existed for many years. . . .

Following a report of the Criminal Law Revision Committee in August 1959 (*First Report (Indecency with Children)* (Cmnd 835)), Parliament enacted the Indecency with Children Act 1960. Section 1(1) of this Act makes it a criminal offence to commit an act of gross indecency with or towards a child under the age of 14, or to incite a child under that age to such an act. The question raised by the appeal concerns the mental element in this offence so far as the age ingredient is concerned.

The answer to this question depends upon the proper interpretation of the section. There are, broadly, three possibilities. The first possible answer is that it matters not whether the accused honestly believed that the person with whom he was dealing was over 14. So far as the age element is concerned, the offence created by s 1 of the 1960 Act is one of strict liability. The second possible answer is that a necessary element of this offence is the absence of a belief, held honestly and on reasonable grounds by the accused, that the person with whom he was dealing was over 14. The third possibility is that the existence or not of reasonable grounds for an honest belief is irrelevant. The necessary mental element is simply the absence of an honest belief by the accused that the other person was over 14.

The common law presumption

As habitually happens with statutory offences, when enacting this offence Parliament defined the prohibited conduct solely in terms of the proscribed physical acts. Section 1(1) says nothing about the mental element. In particular, the section says nothing about what shall be the position if the person who commits or incites the act of gross indecency honestly but mistakenly believed that the child was 14 or over.

In these circumstances the starting point for a court is the established common law presumption that a mental element, traditionally labelled mens rea, is an essential ingredient unless Parliament has indicated a contrary intention either expressly or by necessary implication. The common law presumes that, unless Parliament indicated otherwise, the appropriate mental element is an unexpressed ingredient of every statutory offence. On this I need do no more than refer to Lord Reid's magisterial statement in the leading case of *Sweet v Parsley* [1969] 1 All ER 347 at 349–350, [1970] AC 132 at 148–149:

'...there has for centuries been a presumption that Parliament did not intend to make criminals of persons who were in no way blameworthy in what they did. That means that, whenever a section is silent as to mens rea, there is a presumption that, in order to give effect to the will of Parliament, we must read in words appropriate to require mens rea ...it is firmly established by a host of authorities that mens rea is an essential ingredient of every offence unless some reason can be found for holding that that is not necessary.'

Reasonable belief or honest belief

The existence of the presumption is beyond dispute, but in one respect the traditional formulation of the presumption calls for re-examination. This respect concerns the position of a defendant who acted under a mistaken view of the facts. In this regard, the presumption is expressed traditionally to the effect that an honest mistake by a defendant does not avail him unless the mistake was made on reasonable grounds. Thus, in *R v Tolson* (1889) 23 QBD 168 at 181, [1886–90] All ER Rep 26 at 34 Cave J observed:

'At common law an honest and reasonable belief in the existence of circumstances, which, if true, would make the act for which a prisoner is indicted an innocent act has always been held to be a good defence. This doctrine is embodied in the somewhat uncouth maxim "*actus non facit reum, nisi mens sit rea.*" Honest and reasonable mistake stands in fact on the same footing as absence of the reasoning faculty, as in infancy, or perversion of that faculty, as in lunacy...So far as I am aware it has never been suggested that these exceptions do not equally apply in the case of statutory offences unless they are excluded expressly or by necessary implication.'

The other judges in that case expressed themselves to a similar effect. In *Bank of New South Wales v Piper* [1897] AC 383 at 389–390 the Privy Council likewise espoused the 'reasonable belief' approach: '...the absence of mens rea really consists in an honest and reasonable belief entertained by the accused of facts which, if true, would make the act charged against him innocent.'

In *Sweet v Parsley* Lord Diplock referred to a general principle of construction of statutes creating criminal offences, in similar terms:

> '...a general principle of construction of any enactment, which creates a criminal offence [is] that, even where the words used to describe the prohibited conduct would not in any other context connote the necessity for any particular mental element, they are nevertheless to be read as subject to the implication that a necessary element in the offence is the absence of a belief held honestly and on reasonable grounds in the existence of facts which, if true, would make the act innocent.' (See [1969] 1 All ER 347 at 361, [1970] AC 132 at 163.)

The 'reasonable belief' school of thought held unchallenged sway for many years. But over the last quarter of a century there have been several important cases where a defence of honest but mistaken belief was raised. In deciding these cases the courts have placed new, or renewed, emphasis on the subjective nature of the mental element in criminal offences. The courts have rejected the reasonable belief approach and preferred the honest belief approach. When mens rea is ousted by a mistaken belief, it is as well ousted by an unreasonable belief as by a reasonable belief. In the pithy phrase of Lawton LJ in *R v Kimber* [1983] 3 All ER 316 at 319, [1983] 1 WLR 1118 at 1122 it is the defendant's belief, not the grounds on which it is based, which goes to negative the intent. This approach is well encapsulated in a passage in the judgment of Lord Lane CJ in *R v Williams* [1987] 3 All ER 411 at 415:

> 'The reasonableness or unreasonableness of the defendant's belief is material to the question of whether the belief was held by the defendant at all. If the belief was in fact held, its unreasonableness, so far as guilt or innocence is concerned, is neither here nor there. It is irrelevant. Were it otherwise, the defendant would be convicted because he was negligent in failing to recognise that the victim was not consenting ... and so on.'

Considered as a matter of principle, the honest belief approach must be preferable. By definition the mental element in a crime is concerned with a subjective state of mind, such as intent or belief. To the extent that an overriding objective limit ('on reasonable grounds') is introduced, the subjective element is displaced. To that extent a person who lacks the necessary intent or belief may nevertheless commit the offence. When that occurs the defendant's 'fault' lies exclusively in falling short of an objective standard. His crime lies in his negligence. A statute may so provide expressly or by necessary implication. But this can have no place in a common law principle, of general application, which is concerned with the need for a mental element as an essential ingredient of a criminal offence.

The traditional formulation of the common law presumption, exemplified in Lord Diplock's famous exposition in *Sweet v Parsley*, cited above, is out of step with this recent line of authority, in so far as it envisages that a mistaken belief must be based on reasonable grounds. This seems to be a relic from the days before a defendant in a criminal case could give evidence in his own defence. It is not surprising that in those times juries judged a defendant's state of mind by the conduct to be expected of a reasonable person. ...

[Lord Nicholls discussed *DPP v Morgan* [1976] AC 182], *Kimber* [1983] 3 All ER 316, *Williams*, section 11.6.1.1, p 414 and *Blackburn v Bowering*, section 18.2.1.4, p 651.]

The Crown advanced no suggestion to your Lordships that any of these recent cases was wrongly decided. This is not surprising, because the reasoning in these cases is compelling. Thus, the traditional formulation of the common law presumption must now be modified appropriately. Otherwise the formulation would not be an accurate reflection of the current state of the criminal law regarding mistakes of fact. Lord Diplock's dictum in *Sweet v Parsley* [1969] 1 All ER 347 at 361, [1970] AC 132 at 163 must in future be read as though the reference to reasonable grounds were omitted.

I add one further general observation. In principle, an age-related ingredient of a statutory offence stands on no different footing from any other ingredient. If a man genuinely believes that the girl with whom he is committing a grossly indecent act is over 14, he is not intending to commit such an act with a girl under 14. Whether such an intention is an essential ingredient of the offence depends upon a proper construction of s 1 of the 1960 Act. I turn next to that question.

The construction of s 1 of the Indecency with Children Act 1960

In s 1(1) of the 1960 Act Parliament has not expressly negatived the need for a mental element in respect of the age element of the offence. The question, therefore, is whether, although not expressly negatived, the need for a mental element is negatived by necessary implication. 'Necessary implication' connotes an implication which is compellingly clear. Such an implication may be found in the language used, the nature of the offence, the mischief sought to be prevented and any other circumstances which may assist in determining what intention is properly to be attributed to Parliament when creating the offence.

I venture to think that, leaving aside the statutory context of s 1, there is no great difficulty in this case. The section created an entirely new criminal offence, in simple unadorned language. The offence so created is a serious offence. The more serious the offence, the greater is the weight to be attached to the presumption, because the more severe is the punishment and the graver the stigma which accompany a conviction. Under s 1 conviction originally attracted a punishment of up to two years' imprisonment. This has since been increased to a maximum of ten years' imprisonment. The notification requirements under Pt 1 of the Sex Offender's Act 1997 now apply, no matter what the age of the offender: see Sch 1, para 1(1)(b). Further, in addition to being a serious offence, the offence is drawn broadly ('an act of gross indecency'). It can embrace conduct ranging from predatory approaches by a much older paedophile to consensual sexual experimentation between precocious teenagers of whom the offender may be the younger of the two. The conduct may be depraved by any acceptable standard, or it may be relatively innocuous behaviour in private between two young people. These factors reinforce, rather than negative, the application of the presumption in this case.

The purpose of the section is, of course, to protect children. An age ingredient was therefore an essential ingredient of the offence. This factor in itself does not assist greatly. Without more, this does not lead to the conclusion that liability was intended to be strict so far as the age element is concerned, so that the offence is committed irrespective of the alleged offender's belief about the age of the 'victim' and irrespective of how the offender came to hold this belief.

Nor can I attach much weight to a fear that it may be difficult sometimes for the prosecution to prove that the defendant knew the child was under 14 or was recklessly indifferent about the child's age. A well-known passage from a judgment of that great jurist, Sir Owen Dixon, in *Thomas v R* (1937) 59 CLR 279 at 309, bears repetition:

> 'The truth appears to be that a reluctance on the part of courts has repeatedly appeared to allow a prisoner to avail himself of a defence depending simply on his own state of knowledge and belief. The reluctance is due in great measure, if not entirely, to a mistrust of the tribunal of fact—the jury. Through a feeling that, if the law allows such a defence to be submitted to the jury, prisoners may too readily escape by deposing to conditions of mind and describing sources of information, matters upon which their evidence cannot be adequately tested and contradicted, judges have been misled into a failure steadily to adhere to principle. It is not difficult to understand such tendencies, but a lack of confidence in the ability of a tribunal correctly to estimate evidence of states of mind and the like can never be sufficient ground for excluding from inquiry the most fundamental element in a rational and humane criminal code.'

Similarly, it is far from clear that strict liability regarding the age ingredient of the offence would further the purpose of s 1 more effectively than would be the case if a mental element were read into this ingredient. There is no general agreement that strict liability is necessary to the enforcement of the law protecting children in sexual matters. For instance, the draft Criminal Code Bill prepared by the Law Commission in 1989 (*A Criminal Code of England and Wales* (Law Com No 177)) proposed a compromise solution. Clauses 114 and 115 of the Bill provided for committing or inciting acts of gross indecency with children aged under 13 or under 16. Belief that the child is over 16 would be a defence in each case: see vol 1, report and draft Criminal Code Bill, p 81.

Is there here a compellingly clear implication that Parliament should be taken to have intended that the ordinary common law requirement of a mental element should be excluded in respect of the age ingredient of this new offence? Thus far, having regard especially to the breadth of the offence and the gravity of the stigma and penal consequences which a conviction brings, I see no sufficient ground for so concluding.

Indeed, the Crown's argument before your Lordships did not place much reliance on any of the matters just mentioned. The thrust of the Crown's argument lay in a different direction: the statutory context. This is understandable, because the statutory background is undoubtedly the Crown's strongest point. The Crown submitted that the law in this field has been regarded as settled for well over 100 years, ever since the decision in *R v Prince* (1875) LR 2 CCR 154, [1874–80] All ER Rep 881. That well known case concerned the unlawful abduction of a girl under the age of 16. The defendant honestly believed she was over 16, and he had reasonable grounds for believing this. No fewer than 15 judges held that this provided no defence. Subsequently, in *R v Maughan* (1934) 24 Cr App Rep 130 the Court of Criminal Appeal (Lord Hewart CJ, Avory and Roche JJ) held that a reasonable and honest belief that a girl was over 16 could never be a defence to a charge of indecent assault. The court held that this point had been decided in *R v Forde* [1923] 2 KB 400, [1923] All ER Rep 477. The court also observed that in any event the answer was to be found in *R v Prince*. Building on this foundation Mr Scrivener QC submitted that the 1956 Act was not intended to change this established law, and that s 1 of the 1960 Act was to be read with the 1956 Act. The preamble to the 1960 Act stated that its purpose was to make 'further' provision for the punishment of indecent conduct towards young people. In this field, where Parliament intended belief as to age to be a defence, this was stated expressly: see, for instance, the 'young man's defence' in s 6(3) of the 1956 Act.

This is a formidable argument, but I cannot accept it. I leave on one side Mr O'Connor QC's sustained criticisms of the reasoning in *R v Prince* and *R v Maughan*. Where the Crown's argument breaks down is that the motley collection of offences, of diverse origins, gathered into the 1956 Act displays no satisfactorily clear or coherent pattern. If the interpretation of s 1 of the 1960 Act is to be gleaned from the contents of another statute, that other statute must give compelling guidance. The 1956 Act as a whole falls short of this standard. So do the two sections, ss 14 and 15, which were the genesis of s 1 of the 1960 Act.

Accordingly, I cannot find, either in the statutory context or otherwise, any indication of sufficient cogency to displace the application of the common law presumption. In my view the necessary mental element regarding the age ingredient in s 1 of the 1960 Act is the absence of a genuine belief by the accused that the victim was 14 years of age or above. The burden of proof of this rests upon the prosecution in the usual way. If Parliament considers that the position should be otherwise regarding this serious social problem, Parliament must itself confront the difficulties and express its will in clear terms. I would allow this appeal.

I add a final observation. As just mentioned, in reaching my conclusion I have left on one side the criticisms made of *R v Prince* and *R v Maughan*. Those cases concerned different offences and different statutory provisions. The correctness of the decisions in those cases does not call for decision on the present appeal. But, without expressing a view on the correctness of the actual decisions in those cases, I must observe that some of the reasoning in *R v Prince* is at variance with the common law presumption regarding mens rea as discussed above. To that extent, the reasoning must be regarded as unsound.

Appeal allowed

■ *Question*

Was B's conduct blameworthy irrespective of the age of the person to whom he spoke?
See the comments of Jeremy Horder later in this section, p 193.

In a commentary in [2000] Crim LR 404 it was suggested by J. C. Smith that B's case would
have far-reaching consequences. The editors of *Archbold* (2001 edn, para 17-12), however,
'submitted that this significantly overstates its significance because it is far from clear what it
decides other than in relation to the particular offence with which their Lordships were concerned'. Then came the following case in which the House of Lords reaffirmed the view in *B*
again in a case involving sexual offences designed to protect children.

R v K

[2001] UKHL 41, House of Lords, http://www.bailii.org/uk/cases/UKHL/2001/41.html

(Lords Bingham, Nicholls, Steyn, Hobhouse and Millett)

K, aged 26, was charged with indecent assault on a girl C, aged 14, contrary to the Sexual
Offences Act 1956, s 14(1) [see now the offence of sexual assault under the Sexual Offences Act
2003, s 3, section 20.2.3, p 749]. K claimed that C consented and that she had told him she was
16 and that he had had no reason to disbelieve her. At trial it was argued that the prosecution
had to prove that at the time of the incident K did not honestly believe that C was 16 or over.
The Court of Appeal certified the following point of law of general public importance:

(a) Is a defendant entitled to be acquitted of the offence of indecent assault on a complainant
under the age of 16 years, contrary to s 14(1) of the 1956 Act, if he may hold an honest belief
that the complainant in question was aged 16 years or over?

(b) If yes, must the belief be held on reasonable grounds?'

Lord Bingham of Cornhill:

Section 14 of the 1956 Act is in these terms:

'(1) It is an offence, subject to the exception mentioned in subsection (3) of this section, for a person
to make an indecent assault on a woman.

(2) A girl under the age of sixteen cannot in law give any consent which would prevent an act being
an assault for the purposes of this section.

(3) Where a marriage is invalid under section two of the Marriage Act 1949, or section one of the
Age of Marriage Act 1929 (the wife being a girl under the age of sixteen), the invalidity does not
make the husband guilty of any offence under this section by reason of her incapacity to consent
while under that age, if he believes her to be his wife and has reasonable cause for the belief.

(4) A woman who is a defective cannot in law give any consent which would prevent an act being
an assault for the purposes of this section, but a person is only to be treated as guilty of an indecent assault on a defective by reason of that incapacity to consent, if that person knew or had
reason to suspect her to be a defective.'

This section is matched by a parallel section, s 15, which makes it an offence for a person to make an
indecent assault on a man. Subsections (2) and (3) of s 15 are to the same effect, in relation to men, as
sub-ss (2) and (4) in relation to women.

   If the provisions of s 14 were part of a single, coherent legislative scheme and were read without
reference to any overriding presumption of statutory interpretation, there would be great force in
the simple submission which Mr Scrivener, resisting this appeal on behalf of the Crown, based upon

them: sub-ss (3) and (4) define circumstances in which a defendant's belief, knowledge or suspicion exonerate a defendant from liability for what would otherwise be an indecent assault; if it had been intended to exonerate a defendant who believed a complainant to be 16 or over, this ground of exoneration would have been expressed in sub-s (2); the omission of such a provision makes plain that no such ground of exoneration was intended.

It is, however, plain that s 14 was not part of a single, coherent legislative scheme. The 1956 Act was a consolidation Act. Its provisions derived from diverse sources. The rag-bag nature of the 1956 Act and its predecessor statutes has been the subject of repeated comment: see, for example, the observations of the draftsman of the Offences Against the Person Act 1861 Act quoted in *B (a minor) v DPP* [2000] 1 All ER 833 at 848, [2000] 2 AC 428 at 473; the criticisms of Lord Nicholls of Birkenhead in the same case (see [2000] 1 All ER 833 at 841, [2000] 2 AC 428 at 465); the description of the Act by Professor Lacey as 'a patchwork of pre-existing offences' in 'Beset by Boundaries: The Home Office Review of Sex Offences' [2001] Crim LR 3; the recognition of the Home Office in 'Setting the Boundaries: Reforming the law on sex offences; Vol 1, p 35, para 3.2.3 (July 2000) that the present legislation 'does not form a coherent code'.

[His lordship then referred to the offences under the old legislation and how they were criticized on the basis that they did not afford adequate protection to children]

Neither in s 14 nor elsewhere in the 1956 Act is there any express exclusion of the need to prove an absence of genuine belief on the part of a defendant as to the age of an underage victim. Had it been intended to exclude that element of mens rea it could very conveniently have been so provided in or following sub-s (2).

For reasons already given, significance cannot be attached to the inclusion of grounds of exoneration in sub-ss (3) and (4) and the omission of such a ground from sub-s (2), although sub-ss (3) and (4) do reflect parliamentary recognition that a defendant should not be criminally liable if he misapprehends a factual matter on which his criminal liability depends. There is nothing in the language of this statute which justifies, as a matter of necessary implication, the conclusion that Parliament must have intended to exclude this ingredient of mens rea in s 14 any more than in s 1. If the effect of the presumption is read into s 14, with reference to the defendant's belief as to the age of the victim, no absurdity results. With the wisdom of hindsight it can be seen that Avory J was right to hold, in *R v Forde*, that the statutory defence in s 2 of the 1922 Act could not be read into s 1 of that Act, but he was wrong in failing to apply to s 1 of the 1922 Act the overriding presumption referred to in [17] above. He may, no doubt, have been misled by the now discredited authority of *R v Prince* (1875) LR 2 CCR 154, [1874–80] All ER Rep 881, which although not apparently cited will have been very familiar to him.

I consider that [the trial judge] reached the right conclusion. The Court of Appeal gave more weight to the re-enactment of the relevant provisions in 1956 than was appropriate for a consolidation Act.

I would accordingly give an affirmative answer to the first certified question. It is common ground that a negative answer should be given to the second question. In giving those answers I would make the following concluding points: (1) Nothing in this opinion has any bearing on a case in which the victim does not in fact consent. While s 14(2) provides that a girl under the age of 16 cannot in law give any consent which would prevent an act being an assault, she may in fact (although not in law) consent. If it is shown that she did not consent, and that the defendant did not genuinely believe that she consented, any belief by the defendant concerning her age is irrelevant, since her age is relevant only to her capacity to consent. (2) While a defendant's belief need not be reasonable provided it is honest and genuine, the reasonableness or unreasonableness of the belief is by no means irrelevant. The more unreasonable the belief, the less likely it is to be accepted as genuine (see *R v Gladstone Williams* [1987] 3 All ER 411 at 415.) (3) Although properly applied to s 1 of the 1960 Act and s 14 of the 1956 Act, the presumption cannot be applied to ss 5 and 6 of the 1956 Act. Those sections as a pair derive directly from corresponding sections in the 1871 Act, as demonstrated above. The statutory or young man's defence was introduced into what is now s 6. Its omission from what is now s 5 is plainly deliberate. A genuine belief that a child three years under the age of consent was over that age would in any event defy credulity. Section 6(3) of the 1956 Act plainly defines the state of knowledge which will exonerate a defendant accused under that section, and this express provision necessarily excludes the more general presumption. (4) Nothing in this opinion should be taken to minimise the potential seriousness of the offence of indecent assault. While some instances of the offence may be relatively minor, others may be scarcely less serious than rape itself. This is reflected in the maximum penalty, now increased to ten years' imprisonment, and the mandatory requirement that those convicted be subject to the notification requirements of the Sex Offenders Act 1997. These considerations make it more rather than less important that, in any forthcoming recasting of the law on sexual offences, the *mens rea* requirement should be defined with extreme care and precision. Parliament is sovereign and has the responsibility to decide where the boundaries of criminal activity should be drawn. . . . I would allow this appeal.

[Lord Nicholls agreed, Lords Steyn and Hobhouse made concurring speeches.]

Lord Millett:

My Lords, I have had the advantage of reading in draft the speech of my noble and learned friend Lord Bingham of Cornhill, with which I agree. For the reasons he gives I would allow the appeal and answer the certified questions as he proposes.

I do so without reluctance but with some misgiving, for I have little doubt that we shall be failing to give effect to the intention of Parliament and will reduce s 14 of the Sexual Offence Act 1956 to incoherence. The section creates a single offence of indecent assault. It is intended for the protection of women. Subsection (2) and the first part of sub-s (4) extend the scope of the section. They are intended to protect women who are particularly vulnerable and who by reason of age or mental infirmity may be prevailed upon to give their consent to what would otherwise be an indecent assault. Subsection (3) and the proviso to sub-s (4) afford the defendant a limited defence based on the defendant's state of mind.

The need for such a defence in the case of a woman with impaired mental faculties is obvious. Her mental state may well not be apparent, and it would be manifestly unjust to deny a defence where the defendant believed that she was normal and had no reason to suspect that she was not. The absence of a similar proviso to sub-s (2), while suggesting that no similar defence is intended in the case of underage girls, does not lead inevitably to that conclusion. But sub-s (3) is a different matter. Introduced when the age of marriage was raised to 16, its policy is self-evident. There is no need to extend the scope of the section, designed to protect women from assault and young girls from exploitation, to a girl whom the defendant believes he has married. In such a case the defendant has not taken advantage of her age for his own sexual gratification. On the contrary, he is labouring under the belief that he has undertaken a lifelong responsibility towards her.

Yet sub-s (3) requires the defendant's mistaken belief in the subsistence of a valid marriage to be reasonable as well as honest. To afford a defendant who has not married the girl a more generous defence than one who believes he has is grotesque. It cannot have been the intention of Parliament, either in 1929 when it introduced the sub-s (3) defence, or when it consolidated the law in 1956. Parliament must have known that it was a commonplace for men to be convicted of the offence despite their genuine belief that the girl was over 16, a matter which went to mitigation but not defence. Parliament not only viewed this state of affairs with equanimity, but on the earlier occasion at least legislated on a basis which made no sense unless this was the law.

But the age of consent has long since ceased to reflect ordinary life, and in this respect Parliament has signally failed to discharge its responsibility for keeping the criminal law in touch with the needs of society. I am persuaded that the piecemeal introduction of the various elements of s 14, coupled with the persistent failure of Parliament to rationalise this branch of the law even to the extent of removing absurdities which the courts have identified, means that we ought not to strain after internal coherence even in a single offence. Injustice is too high a price to pay for consistency.

Appeal allowed

Lord Bingham observes that a man who has sexual intercourse with a girl aged 12 is unlikely to be able plausibly to assert that he believed her to be 16 but (i) it is not impossible, (ii) that does not affect the principle, and (iii) the 'man'—who may be a boy—may easily have believed her to be 13 or 14. See the discussion, section 7.6.1, p 202, of the mens rea in relation to the corresponding offences under the Sexual Offences Act 2003.

■ *Questions*

Did not Lord Millett acknowledge the truth—that the House, having lost patience with Parliament, was ignoring its plain intention? Can this be justified? Is it a breach of the constitutional principle that Parliament is sovereign?

In *Kumar* [2005] Crim LR 470, [2004] EWCA Crim 3207, K's conviction for buggery, contrary to the Sexual Offences Act 1956, s 12, following consensual anal intercourse with the 14-year-old complainant was quashed by the Court of Appeal. It was held that the mental element had not been excluded expressly from s 12 by any compellingly clear or truly necessary implication, and that such a construction did not give rise to any internal inconsistency. Buggery stemmed from a common law offence and was unlike the age-based offences in the 1956 Act.

The cases of *B* and *K* met with warm approval from some (Sir John Smith at [2000] Crim LR 403 and [2001] Crim LR 993), and harsh criticism from others (eg P. Glazebrook, 'How Old Did *You* Think She Was?' (2001) 60 CLJ 26).

J. Horder, 'How Culpability Can, and Cannot, be Denied in Under-age Sex Crimes'
[2001] Crim LR 15 (references omitted)

... The decision of the House of Lords [in *B*], a decision that flies in the face of Legislation and case law across much of the rest of the common law world (e.g. *R. v. Hess; R. v. Nguyen* [1990] 2 S.C.R. 906), can be attributed more or less directly to the pervasive influence of a subjectivist understanding of the so-called 'correspondence principle' in criminal law theory. According to subjectivists, this theory requires that defendants should not in general be held criminally liable unless they intended to bring about, or realised that they might bring about, the forbidden consequences in the forbidden circumstances. Here is *Smith and Hogan*'s statement of this article of faith:

> 'An ideal rule would seem to be [one] requiring intention or recklessness as to all the elements in the actus reus. Presumably, no element is included in the definition of an actus reus unless it contributes to the heinousness of the offence. If the accused is blamelessly inadvertent with respect to any one element in the offence ... is it then proper to hold him responsible for it?' (J. C. Smith and B. Hogan, *Criminal Law* (9th ed), (1999, Butterworths), p. 72).

... The so-called 'ideal rule' entails that where D believes that any element of the actus reus is absent, no matter how morally insignificant it may have been to the crime's definition, he or she is not criminally culpable. Applying the 'ideal rule' to section 1(1), the House of Lords concerned itself exclusively with whether D realised that V might be, as section 1(1) demands, aged under 14. That concern is with the wrong issue. Whether V is aged just under or over 14 years is, for the purposes of section 1(1), in itself a matter of moral insignificance, in spite of its legal import. There is no moral distinction to be drawn between a case in which a man invites a girl aged just under 14 to commit an act of gross indecency, and a case in which a man does the same to a girl aged just over 14. Even supposing it to be a true belief, a belief that V is aged 14 has—in and of itself (an important qualification, as we shall see)—no bearing on what D is morally permitted to do, in so far as inciting acts of gross indecency with young girls is concerned. It follows that a mistaken belief that V is aged 14 has no moral bearing on whether D is to be blamed for engaging in the actus reus, by (as in the instant case) inciting an act of gross indecency with a young girl. If one accepts this, and accepts (as the House of Lords appears to do) that a concern for mens rea is a concern about moral culpability, then one ought also to accept that under section 1(1) D's belief that V is aged 14 has, by itself, no legal bearing on his culpability. And the logic of the argument dictates that this will remain true, however reasonable D's belief about V's age may have been. Once these points have been accepted it becomes possible to focus on the main issue, overlooked by the House of Lords. This is the need to identify an element of the actus reus, bearing on D's liability, that does have practical moral significance. Once one has identified such an element it will follow, on now generally accepted legal principles, that a belief that it is absent is also a matter of practical moral significance, and hence a basis for denying culpability (mens rea) even when the actus reus was fulfilled. . . .

2. The Irrationality of the Subjectivist Approach to B's Belief

. . . Suppose D, an adult paedophile, invites V, who is in fact 13, to commit an act of gross indecency with him. D believes V is over 14. D's belief is based, however, solely on an inference drawn from the character of previous sexual experiences he has had with V, as compared to his numerous sexual experiences with other children both younger and older than V. The law as it stands after *B. (A Minor) v. DPP* would acquit D in this example, even though it was nothing more than his experience as a paedophile that led him to believe that V was over 14. . . .

3. Law, Morality and the Significance of Age

. . . Take a case in which D has sexual intercourse with the 15-year-old V, reasonably believing that she is 16, and is charged with having had sexual intercourse with an under-age girl contrary to section 6 of the Sexual Offences Act 1956. As is well-known, the Statute provides for a denial of mens rea in only very limited circumstances. There is a case, however, for the general availability of a defence of lack of mens rea, where D honestly (and, I would add reasonably) believed that V was 16. That exact age, as the age of consent, is a guiding reason, giving those over that age permission to engage in consensual sexual intercourse. The stipulation of exactly 16 as the age of consent is in law what I earlier referred to as an example of determination. Moral reason suggests that the law should protect those whose mental, social and moral development is below that at which the full significance to the giving of consent to sexual activity is appreciated. And in practice (or as we assume), it is best to do this through a general prohibition on sexual advances towards those below a certain age, even though different individuals' mental, social and moral development may proceed at somewhat different rates. Moral and practical thinking of this kind does not, however, dictate any particular age (within the bounds of reason) at which the general prohibition cuts in: that is where the stipulative role of determination in law comes into play. Even so, unlike (say) the fixing of a speed limit at exactly 50 or 70, the legal settlement of the age of consent as 16 is neither arbitrary nor (now) without moral significance, whatever the position may have been when the law was changed to raise the age of consent from 13 to 16 in 1885. It is not just that birthdays are commonly regarded across cultures as having in themselves a moral and social significance that would make the setting of the age of consent at, say, 15 and a half far more arbitrary. It is that, as the Home Office Consultation Paper puts it, 'The present age of sixteen is well established, well understood and well supported'; it has, in other words 'gathered moral import with age, and . . . contribute[d] to structuring people's moral thinking' (see note 1). In this regard, I venture to suggest that what distinguishes the age of 16 from the age of 14, the age at issue in section 1 of the ICA 1960, is that the age of 14 has little or no moral resonance, and has not structured people's moral thinking in any significant way. This is the thought that lies behind my earlier suggestion that a mistaken belief that V is aged 14 is a mistake about a matter of moral indifference, unlike a mistaken belief that V is aged 16.

...The criteria relevant to culpability ought only to be those which relate to guiding moral reasons for the actions in question; and D's belief that V is aged 14 is not such a guiding reason. It is not in itself a moral reason for doing as he does...

A subjectivist might reply in the following way. The subjectivist might say, in relation to section 1(1), that a belief about V's age can operate as a guiding reason, for D him or herself. D, a paedophile, might have a self-imposed restriction that he seeks to have sexual relations only with children over 14 because it would be 'going too far' to interfere with children under that age. If he then incites a child who is in fact aged under 14, but whom he believes to be 14, should this belief not operate as a denial of *mens rea*? The problem with this subjectivist reply, is that it only gains plausibility by making it open to defendants themselves to determine the standards by which their culpability is judged. On the contrary, putting aside cases where D's lack of capacity is in issue, culpability is rightly assessed by reference to general, not individual standards....

■ *Question*

Is the moral culpability of D who has consensual sexual intercourse with V, aged 12, greater if he knows her to be under 13 or does it not matter what he thinks about her age? Consider the offences under the Sexual Offences Act 2003, ss 5–16, sections 20.3.1 and 20.3.2, p 736.

7.3.1.1 Application of *B v DPP* and *K*

The offences in issue in *B v DPP* [2000] UKHL 13 and *K* [2002] 1 AC 642 have been replaced by those in the Sexual Offences Act 2003, which itself contains numerous strict liability offences (see Chapter 20). The cases remain important authorities on the presumption of mens rea generally. It would be misleading, however, to think that since *B* and *K* the courts have consistently rejected strict liability; far from it. There are numerous instances of provisions being interpreted as imposing strict liability, see, for example, *Mohammed* [2002] EWCA Crim 1856, 2 WLR 1050 (materially contributing to insolvency by gambling carrying two years' imprisonment) and *Matudi* [2004] EWCA Crim 697 (importing prohibited animal products). In *Jackson* [2006] EWCA Crim 2380, the Court of Appeal held that the offence of unlawful low flying contrary to the Air Force Act 1955, s 51, was one of strict liability. In *Deyemi* [2007] EWCA Crim 2060, possession of an electronic stun gun was held to constitute possession of a firearm where D was unaware it was a weapon: liability was strict. In those cases, the court had found the presumption rebutted by necessary implication having regard to well-established criteria: the words of the statute, seriousness of the offence, stigma attaching, legislative purpose, statutory context, ease of proof, etc. These are all discussed in the next section.

What *B* and *K* should do is cause the courts to revisit decisions in which particular statutes and words in statutes were previously found to impose strict liability. In *Cambridgeshire CC v Associated Lead Mills Ltd* [2005] EWHC 1627 (Admin), although Kennedy LJ was prepared to uphold a conviction based on a strict interpretation of the term 'use' on the basis of previous case law, Walker J, having regard to the discussion of the 'revitalised presumption' in *B* and *K* questioned whether even the offence based on 'use' is to be construed as one of strict liability.

The Supreme Court recently relied on *K* and *B* in *Brown* [2013] UKSC 43. The court held that the offence of having unlawful carnal knowledge of a girl under the age of 14 years contrary to s 4 of the Criminal Law Amendment Acts (Northern Ireland) 1885–1923 was an offence of strict liability. Lord Kerr stated that the same policy considerations which were at issue in *G* [2008] UKHL 37 applied to the facts of this case, namely protecting young girls. See section 7.6.1, p 202.

7.3.2 Factors relevant to determining strict liability

The identification of offences of strict liability, or, more precisely, the identification of the element or elements in the offence which will attract strict liability remains a difficult problem.

The factors commonly cited as influencing the decision whether the presumption of mens rea is rebutted in any case include:

(1) the use of verbs and adverbs importing a mental element—knowingly, wilfully, etc;

(2) the social context of the crime:

    (a) whether it is a 'real crime' or a quasi-crime or regulatory offence;

    (b) whether the crime is one of general or special prohibition—the latter making it more likely that the presumption will be rebutted;

    (c) the ease with which those affected by the regulation might comply;

    (d) the social danger involved;

(3) the severity of the punishment.

In *Gammon (Hong Kong) Ltd v A-G of Hong Kong* [1984] UKPC 17, Lord Scarman attempted to give some guidance by listing five criteria:

(1) there is a presumption of law that mens rea is required before a person can be held guilty of a criminal offence; (2) the presumption is particularly strong where the offence is 'truly criminal' in character; (3) the presumption applies to statutory offences, and can be displaced only if this is clearly or by necessary implication the effect of the statute; (4) the only situation in which the presumption can be displaced is where the statute is concerned with an issue of social concern; public safety is such an issue; (5) even where a statute is concerned with such an issue, the presumption of mens rea stands unless it can be shown that the creation of strict liability will be effective to promote the objects of the statute by encouraging greater vigilance to prevent the commission of the prohibited act.

This must now be read in the light of *B* and *K*.

Lord Scarman says that the presumption which always favours mens rea is particularly strong where the offence is truly criminal. The presumption can only be displaced where the statute is concerned with an issue of social concern. Even here the presumption in favour of mens rea remains unless it can be shown that the creation of strict liability will be effective to promote the objects of the statute by creating greater vigilance. Can all this be reconciled with the assertion by Lord Steyn in *K* that the presumption 'can only be displaced by specific language, ie, an express provision or a necessary implication'? Up to an uncertain point it is possible to identify offences, or elements in offences, which were, and perhaps still are, likely to attract strict liability. Usually, though by no means invariably, the offence is one created in a statute which seeks to regulate the activities of a particular class of persons such as licensees, or the sellers of food and drugs, or employers in industry and commerce. Hence the expression 'regulatory offences', namely, offences which are meant to regulate the carrying on of particular activities. It might be convenient, it would certainly be simpler, if all such offences could be classified as offences of strict liability but it is not as straightforward as that. Parliament is (or the Parliamentary draftsmen are) unhelpful in that the use of a mens rea word (eg 'knowingly' or 'permitting') in one provision and its absence in another provision (or sometimes in the same provision) appears to be haphazard and without any underlying rationale.

It is difficult to discern from the cases to what extent, if at all, the courts openly express one dominant feature (statutory construction, real or quasi-crime, social context, penalty, etc) as the basis for imposing or refusing to impose strict liability.

Some famous examples of the courts addressing whether the offence before them was one of strict liability include the following.

Cundy v Le Cocq [1884] 13 QBD 207, Queen's Bench Division: the court held that the offence under the Licensing Act 1872, s 13, was one of strict liability. D, being the keeper of licensed premises, unlawfully sold intoxicating liquor to a drunken person. It was proved that there had been a sale of intoxicating liquor and that the person served was drunk. Neither D nor his servants had noticed that the person served was drunk; that person had been quiet and had done nothing to indicate insobriety.

■ *Questions*

Why is it appropriate to interpret this as a strict liability offence? Because it has a low penalty? Because it is not 'real crime'? Because it might promote more vigilant landlords? What more could the publican have done?

Alphacell Ltd v Woodward [1972] UKHL 4, http://www.bailii.org/uk/cases/UKHL/1972/4. html: D was a company that caused large quantities of polluted material to flow into a river. The pumps that D had installed at his plant to prevent this failed to work on the day in question because they were blocked by debris. D had regularly inspected the mechanism and no debris had been in them when the pumps were inspected a few days before the overflow. D was found guilty of the offence under the Rivers (Prevention of Pollution) Act 1951 which criminalizes a person who 'causes or knowingly permits to enter a stream any poisonous, noxious or polluting matter'. The House of Lords upheld the conviction. There was no mens rea as to the form of the offence based on 'causing' pollution.

■ *Questions*

1. Was the case then, one of strict liability? But could this be said of the *Empress Car* case [1998] 1 All ER, section 3.2.3.2, p 51?

2. Is the case a good illustration of the argument that strict liability crimes are more efficient methods of punishment? Is it fair to treat it as a crime of strict liability because it is not 'real crime'?

See further G. Richardson, 'Strict Liability for Regulatory Crime: The Empirical Research' [1987] Crim LR 295, who reports that 'the majority of enforcement officers regard [strict liability] with favour and urge its retention' (at 303). In regulatory offences this claim that 'negotiated compliance' by a regulatory authority is more efficient is often advanced. See J. Rowan-Robinson, P. Q. Watchman and C. R. Barker, 'Crime and Regulation' [1988] Crim LR 211.

Warner v Metropolitan Police Commissioner [1968] 2 All ER 356, House of Lords: D was convicted of possessing drugs. He was found in possession of two boxes. One box contained perfume (which D was in the habit of selling), the other 20,000 tablets containing a prohibited drug. D claimed he thought both boxes contained perfume and he had not looked inside them. Lord Guest concluded: 'There are therefore, three requisites of possession. First, there must be actual or potential physical control, secondly physical control is not possession, unless accompanied by intention, hence, if a thing is put into a hand of a sleeping person, he had not possession of it. Thirdly, the possibility and intention must be visible or evidenced by external signs, for if the thing shows no signs of being under the control of anyone, it is not possessed'. A person must know he is in possession of the thing but there is no need to prove awareness that it is a drug. See now the Misuse of Drugs Act 1971, s 28.

■ *Questions*

1. Why does the offence of possession of these articles need to be interpreted so strictly?

2. D is found carrying a sealed package which contains heroin. How would the judges have dealt with him if he believed: (i) the box was empty; (ii) the box contained aspirin, or sweets, or jewellery, or stolen jewellery, or explosives, or something, but he had no idea what?

Gregor [2011] EWCA Crim 1712: G was convicted of possessing an altered firearm (sawn-off shotgun) without a firearm certificate and of possessing a firearm when prohibited. G and his mother had been observed going into a wood and on emerging an hour later when their car was stopped, a sawn-off shotgun was found in the boot. G claimed that he had found a package whilst walking in the woods. He realized it was a firearm and had taken it back to the car intending to keep it. However, his mother persuaded him to hand it into the police and they were on their way to the local police station when they were stopped. At trial for the possession offences, the judge ruled that s 1(1) of the Firearms Act 1968 created an absolute offence (ie one with no mens rea and no defences: see section 7.4, p 200) and that G's mental state was irrelevant. There being no defence to the charge, G thereupon pleaded guilty. The judge considered G's version of events at a Newton hearing (a hearing of facts to determine sentence) and found that G had not come across the gun by chance and that he had not proposed immediately to take it to the police. G appealed arguing that the judge was wrong to conclude that s 1(1) created an absolute offence and, in the alternative, that the guilty plea was entered on a flawed basis since the defence of duress of circumstances should have been available to him. The Court of Appeal upheld the conviction. The offence was one of 'strict' liability rather than one of 'absolute' " liability. As the Lord Chief Justice stated at [10]:

it was wrong for him to describe the offence as one of absolute liability. To be in possession of a firearm without a firearm certificate is an offence of strict liability. The authorities are consistent and numerous. They are conveniently summarised in *R v Zahid* [2010] EWCA Crim 2158, adopting *R v Deyemi and Edwards* [2008] 1 Cr App R 25.

Price [2006] EWCA Crim 3363: D was convicted of distributing an indecent photograph of a child contrary to s 1(1)(b) of the Protection of Children Act 1978. D gave a work colleague a CD-ROM containing indecent images of children. D claimed that he did not know the CD-ROM contained indecent images. On appeal, D sought to argue that the offence was only committed when an individual *knowingly* distributed indecent images of children. The Court of Appeal rejected this argument. It was clear that Parliament had intended to create a strict liability offence in order to discourage the careless transmission of pornographic material of this nature. In addition, the court observed that if D's contention were accepted, it would leave no room for the operation of the statutory defence in s 1(4).

J. Horder, 'Strict Liability, Statutory Construction, and the Spirit of Liberty'
[2002] LQR 458 (references omitted)

In interpreting the scope of criminal offences created by statute, English courts have always claimed to take very seriously a responsibility to protect personal liberty. Lord Goddard C.J. once explained how it is that the courts have sought to do this in a principled way:

'It is of the utmost importance for the protection of the liberty of the subject that a court should always bear in mind that, unless a statute, either clearly or by necessary implication, rules out *mens rea* as a constituent part of a crime, the court should not find a man guilty of an offence against the criminal law unless he has a guilty mind.' [*Brend v. Wood* (1946) 62 T.L.R. 462 at p. 463]

In a broad sense, it is simply more 'just' that criminal conviction should generally follow only when the mens was rea; but fault requirements focused on whether defendants knew (or could have known) that they might be engaged in acts or omissions amounting to an offence also minimise the encroachment on liberty involved in criminalisation. Such requirements can ensure that those who did all that could reasonably have been done to avoid falling foul of the criminal law will remain free from its clutches....

The courts' understanding of personal liberty emerges from what they regard as a key distinction between 'real' and 'regulatory' crime, between *mala in se*, crimes that are said to be 'truly criminal' in character, and *mala prohibita*, crimes said to be focussed on 'regulation of a particular activity involving potential danger'. On a number of important occasions, the House of Lords has implied mens rea requirements into a criminal statute because that statute was concerned with wrongdoing conviction for which carries great stigma with it (such as sex-related or drug-related criminal wrongdoing). Such wrongdoing is conceived of as being 'truly criminal'. On other occasions, the House of Lords has refused to imply mens rea requirements into a criminal statute, because that statute concerned conduct prohibited solely because it exemplified bad (risky; unsafe) practice in a context in which there are public or industry standards of good practice. Such conduct is made criminal only as an aid to regulation, and conviction is not thought to attract stigma. The difference in approach towards the two kinds of cases reflects an underlying assumption that liberty is at stake, and must hence be protected by an implication of mens rea, only in cases involving 'truly criminal' wrongdoing, wrongdoing conviction for which attracts stigma.

There is certainly an important kind of liberty, freedom from undeserved stigma, at stake in cases involving 'truly criminal' wrongdoing. Conviction for some statutory crimes (such as sex-related crimes) carries with it a tendency, to use the older language of libel law, to vilify someone, and bring him or her into hatred, contempt and ridicule. Someone exposed to such a risk clearly has his or her prospects for autonomous life significantly reduced. Quite apart from whatever adverse official consequences of conviction that there may be, one's plans, projects, relationships, and so forth, that can be successfully pursued only in common with others may be undermined by widespread distrust or disregard fomented amongst those others by knowledge of one's conviction. Accordingly, a determination to imply (in the absence of legislative provision to the contrary) mens rea requirements in statutory provisions creating such crimes ensures—assuming that the courts imply the right kind of mens rea requirements—that adverse consequences of this kind are not undeservedly imposed.

When it comes to the interpretation of criminal statutes and the possible imposition of strict liability, however, there may be a different but equally important kind of liberty at stake in many 'regulatory' criminal cases, whether or not conviction in such cases attracts stigma. The imposition of strict liability in a 'regulatory' context may seriously threaten the participation of individuals in activities of intrinsic worth to their pursuit of an autonomous life. To give some examples from the case law, for the butcher, baker, pharmacist, corner-shop owner, farmer, dogowner, antique gun collector or amateur radio broadcaster, there is what has been termed an 'action' reason, and not (or not just) an 'outcome' reason, to participate in their livelihood or hobby respectively. In other words, for such people it is engaging in the activity itself or, in some occupational cases, engaging in the role that one's activities give one (say, within the local community), rather than simply securing a given outcome (say, profit) of the activity, that contributes to their wellbeing and hence to their individual autonomy. As Raz puts it, 'freedom [autonomy] consists in the pursuit of valuable forms of life, and ... its *value* derives from the value of that pursuit' (my emphasis) [J. Raz, *The Morality of Freedom* (1986) at p 395]. Moreover, for Raz, forms of life include 'socially defined and determined pursuits and activities', meaning recognised and socially organised hobbies as well as (say) occupations serving the community.

By using the deterrent weapon of strict liability to convict people of a criminal offence when, perhaps by unhappy mischance, they have fallen into bad practice in the pursuit of an intrinsically valuable activity, in Raz's sense, the courts are ignoring the importance of action-reasons to people's freedom, and posing undue threats to their prospects for an autonomous life. A more nuanced approach to criminal statutes and to strict liability is hence required, if the courts' claim to be champions of personal liberty is to be comprehensively vindicated. First, the courts should seek to distinguish between statutes dealing with activities with largely instrumental value—like transport—where strict liability may in principle be more easily justified, and statutes dealing with activities that may have intrinsic value for the participants. Secondly, where the latter are in issue, the courts must further consider whether the outcome-value of strict liability is so overwhelming that even considerations of personal autonomy must give way to it. This second stage may look much like the familiar contrast between 'the policy of objective liability' (supporting strict liability) and 'the principle of mens rea,' in statutory interpretation; but it should in fact give the courts considerably less scope to find strict liability justified than the familiar contrast does. This is because the courts would no longer treat the question whether to imply a culpability requirement as a simple matter of balancing conflicting outcome-reasons: i.e. the outcome reasons that favour such an implication (less chance of conviction, and greater scope to err for defendants), as against the outcome reasons that militate in favour of strict liability (greater deterrent effect; more chance of conviction). The courts would also be asking whether those falling foul of the statute's criminal provisions will, when they do so, be likely to have been engaged in activities whose intrinsic value lies in their being constitutive of an autonomous life. Taking this question seriously ought, at the very least, to lead to a new class of cases in which strict liability is, on the grounds of liberty, found to be an implication that is unwarranted despite the social concerns that justified criminalisation in the first place.

■ *Questions*

Should Parliament be obliged to make clear, in unambiguous language, when it is declaring an offence to be one of strict liability?

Is there an argument for creating two categories of offence—'real' crimes and 'violations'—to which different rules apply?

For theoretical analysis of the arguments for the imposition of strict liability, particularly in cases of quasi-criminal regulations, see A. Simester, 'Is Strict Liability Always Wrong?' in A. Simester (ed), *Appraising Strict Liability* (2005). He draws on the distinction between formal strict liability (where one element of the actus reus has no mens rea attaching to it which is the sense in which strict liability is used in this chapter) and substantive strict liability (where D who is completely blameless can nevertheless be convicted). Simester argues (at p 24) that:

   (i)   substantive strict liability is always wrong in stigmatic crimes;

   (ii) substantive strict liability may not be wrong in quasi criminal regulations;

   (iii) in some circumstances, formal strict liability may not be wrong in stigmatic crimes.

■ *Questions*

What are stigmatic crimes? Is Storkwain's crime a stigmatic one (see section 7.2.1, p 184)?

7.4 Strict liability and defences

If an offence is one of strict liability it might be thought that it is not therefore possible to plead a defence, either originating in statute or common law, to negate liability. However this is not the case, as liability is not 'absolute'. For example, the Divisional Court accepted in *Santos v CPS* [2013] EWHC 550 (Admin) that necessity could be pleaded as a defence to the strict liability offences of riding a motorcycle without insurance and protective headgear. In addition, it was explicitly stated in the earlier case of *Martin* [1988] EWCA Crim 2 that duress can be pleaded as a defence to a crime of strict liability. There does seem to be uncertainty over whether insanity is available as a defence. In *DPP v H* [1997] 1 WLR 1406 McGowan LJ doubted whether the defence was available because, 'the [insanity] defence is based on an absence of mens rea but none is required for the offence of driving with an excess of alcohol.' However, the insanity defence is not predicated upon a denial of mens rea but rather a denial of moral responsibility for committing the actus reus of the offence, so the validity of this authority seems to be rather questionable. See section 10.4, p 326.

7.5 Strict liability, mens rea and the burden of proof

Another aspect of the imposition of strict liability to consider is the relationship with the burden of proof in the criminal trial. In the famous case of *Woolmington v DPP* [1935] AC 462, Viscount Sankey stated that the 'golden thread' of English criminal law is that it is the duty of the prosecution to prove the defendant's guilt. Nevertheless, in some instances it would seem more just for the defence to be left to prove on the balance of probabilities that D did not have the requisite mens rea as to a particular element of the actus reus rather than impose strict liability in relation to it. The following offences are ones in which it has been held that it is more just for D to prove that he did not have the requisite mens rea as to an element of the actus reus:

- offences affecting the environment: *Alphacell Ltd v Woodward* [1972] 2 All ER 475. If liability were not strict it is argued that it would be difficult to prove any mens rea in such cases;
- drugs offences: *Warner v Metropolitan Police Commissioner* [1968] 2 All ER 356. Liability is usually strict as to awareness of possession of the drug to avoid defendants making spurious claims about the origin of the articles in their possession or what they thought they were;
- firearms offences: *Williams* [2012] EWCA Crim 2162. Liability as to the article being a weapon is strict; it is for D to prove the defence in s 5 of the Firearms Act 1968.

7.6 Strict liability offences and the ECHR

The arguments relating to the relationship between the burden of proof and the imposition of strict liability were clearly fuelled by the arrival of the Human Rights Act. It has been argued that the imposition of strict liability might engage, for example:

- Article 3 (freedom from inhuman or degrading treatment). Was the criminal trial for sexual offending degrading treatment in *R v K*, section 7.3.1.1?
- Article 8 (respect for privacy). Are the Article 8 rights of a 15-year-old who has sex with a consenting 12-year-old who told him she was 13 infringed when he is sent to prison for up to a maximum of life imprisonment? See *G* in the following section, p 202.

See G. R. Sullivan, 'Strict Liability for Criminal Offences in England and Wales following Incorporation into English Law of the ECHR' in A. Simester (ed), *Appraising Strict Liability* (2005), p 206.

Since the Human Rights Act does not empower courts to 'strike down' statutes, the challenge is not of the same magnitude as that in, for example, the United States, where it is possible for some strict liability offences to be held to be unconstitutional (R. A. Duff, 'Strict Liability, Legal Presumptions and the Presumption of Innocence' in A Simester (ed), *Appraising Strict Liability* (2005), p 125).

7.6.1 Strict liability and Article 6

A major controversy has been whether strict liability offences infringe the presumption of innocence guaranteed under Article 6(2) of the European Convention. Some commentators argued that strict liability offences may offend against Article 6(2) because once the prohibited act is proved, D is 'presumed' to be liable. See, for example, V. Tadros and S. Tierney, 'The Presumption of Innocence and the Human Rights Act' (2004) 67 MLR 402. Some commentators argued that the effect of the presumption and the imposition of strict liability is the same, but this functional equivalence was keenly disputed by others (see P. Roberts, 'Strict Liability and the Presumption of Innocence' in A. Simester (ed), *Appraising Strict Liability* (2005), p 151). Most commentators regarded the argument based on Article 6(2) as a weak one. As Professor Ashworth explained:

> it is wrong to convict people of serious offences without proof of culpability, and that is a separate argument from the presumption of innocence. It is not an argument about evidence and procedure at all but an argument about the proper preconditions of criminal liability. (A. Ashworth, 'Four Threats to the Presumption of Innocence' (2006) E & P 241 at 252–253)

The English courts agreed, drawing a distinction between the protection afforded under Article 6(2) which was procedural and the imposition of strict liability in substantive criminal law, and holding, in cases such as *Barnfather v Islington LBC* [2003] EWHC 418 (Admin), that Article 6(2) is restricted to providing procedural protection and does not render the imposition of strict liability incompatible with Article 6(2). As Lord Bingham stated in *Sheldrake* [2005] 1 AC 246 at [21] (emphasis added):

> The overriding concern is that a trial should be fair, and the presumption of innocence is a fundamental right directed to that end. The Convention does not outlaw presumptions of fact or law but requires that these should be kept within reasonable limits and should not be arbitrary. *It is open to states to define the constituent elements of a criminal offence, excluding the requirement of mens rea.* But the substance and effect of any presumption adverse to a defendant must be examined, and must be reasonable. Relevant to any judgment on reasonableness or proportionality will be the opportunity given to the defendant to rebut the presumption, maintenance of the rights of the defence, flexibility in application of the presumption, retention by the court of a power to assess the evidence, the importance of what is at stake and the difficulty which a prosecutor may face in the absence of a presumption.

The issue came before the House of Lords for direct consideration in the case of *G*.

R v G and another
[2008] UKHL 37, House of Lords, http://www.bailii.org/uk/cases/UKHL/2008/37.html

(Lords Hoffmann, Hope, Carswell, Baroness Hale and Lord Mance)

G, who was aged 15, pleaded guilty to rape of a child under 13 (Sexual Offences Act 2003, s 5). Section 5 of the Sexual Offences Act 2003 provides:

> (1) A person commits an offence if —
>
>   (a) he intentionally penetrates the vagina, anus or mouth of another person with his penis; and
>
>   (b) the other person is under 13.
>
> (2) A person guilty of an offence under this section is liable, on conviction on indictment, to imprisonment for life.

G's basis of plea was that V consented and that he reasonably believed her to be older than 13, because she had so informed him. The Court of Appeal upheld his conviction and confirmed that s 5 creates an offence of strict liability to which belief in consent or the age of the victim has no application. The actus reus of the offence is vaginal, anal or oral sexual intercourse with a victim under 13, whether the victim consented or not. Section 5 created an offence even where the defendant reasonably believed that the child was 16 or over. The presumption of mens rea was negatived by necessary implication, arising from the contrast of the express references to reasonable belief that a child was 16 or over, in other sections—s 9 of the 2003 Act—and the absence of any such reference in relation to children under 13. G appealed. The Court of Appeal dismissed the appeal against conviction but allowed an appeal against sentence and substituted a conditional discharge. It certified two questions as being of general public importance:

(1) May a criminal offence of strict liability violate article 6(1) and/or 6(2)...?

(2) Is it compatible with a child's rights under article 8 ... to convict him of rape contrary to section 5 ... in circumstances where the agreed basis of plea establishes that his offence fell properly within the ambit of section 13 ...?

G appealed to the House of Lords.

[Lord Hoffmann stated the facts and continued:]

3. The mental element of the offence under section 5, as the language and structure of the section makes clear, is that penetration must be intentional but there is no requirement that the accused must have known that the other person was under 13. The policy of the legislation is to protect children. If you have sex with someone who is on any view a child or young person, you take your chance on exactly how old they are. To that extent the offence is one of strict liability and it is no defence that the accused believed the other person to be 13 or over.

4. Article 6(1) provides that in the determination of his civil rights or any criminal charge, everyone is entitled to a 'fair and public hearing' and article 6(2) provides that everyone charged with a criminal offence 'shall be presumed innocent until proved guilty according to law'. It is settled law that Article 6(1) guarantees fair procedure and the observance of the principle of the separation of powers but not that either the civil or criminal law will have any particular substantive content: see *Matthews v Ministry of Defence* [2003] UKHL 4; [2003] 1 AC 1163. Likewise, article 6(2) requires him to be presumed innocent of the offence but does not say anything about what the mental or other elements of the offence should be. In the case of civil law, this was established (after a moment of aberration) by *Z v United Kingdom* (2002) 34 EHRR 3. There is no reason why the reasoning should not apply equally to the substantive content of the criminal law. In *R v Gemmell* [2002] EWCA Crim 1992; [2003] 1 Cr App R 343, 356, para 33 Dyson LJ said:

'The position is quite clear. So far as Article 6 is concerned, the fairness of the provisions of the substantive law of the Contracting States is not a matter for investigation. The content and interpretation of domestic substantive law is not engaged by Article 6.'

5. The only authority which is said to cast any doubt upon this proposition is the decision of the Strasbourg court in *Salabiaku v France* (1988) 13 EHRR 379 and in particular a statement in paragraph 28 (at p.388) that 'presumptions of fact or of law' in criminal proceedings should be confined 'within reasonable limits'. No one has yet discovered what this paragraph means but your Lordships were referred to a wealth of academic learning which tries to solve the riddle.

6. My Lords, I think that judges and academic writers have picked over the carcass of this unfortunate case so many times in attempts to find some intelligible meat on its bones that the time has come to call a halt. The Strasbourg court, uninhibited by a doctrine of precedent or the need to find a

ratio decidendi, seems to have ignored it. It is not mentioned in *Z v United Kingdom* (2002) 34 EHRR 3. I would recommend your Lordships to do likewise. For my part, I would simply endorse the remarks of Dyson LJ in *R v Gemmell* [2003] 1 Cr App R 343, 356 . . .

[His lordship dismissed the Article 8 argument.]

Lord Hope of Craighead:

. . .

Article 6(2)

24. Mr Owen's primary submission was that the offence which section 5 creates, interpreted as one of strict liability, is incompatible with article 6(2) of the Convention, which provides that everyone charged with a criminal offence shall be presumed innocent until proved guilty according to law. He sought support for this argument in the observations of the European Court in *Salabiaku v France* (1988) 13 EHRR 379. In paras 27–28 of its judgment the court said:

> '27. As the Government and the Commission have pointed out, in principle the Contracting States remain free to apply the criminal law to an act where it is not carried out in the normal exercise of one of the rights protected under the Convention and, accordingly, to define the con-stituent elements of the resulting offence. In particular, and again in principle, the Contracting States may, under certain conditions, penalise a simple or objective fact as such, irrespective of whether it results from criminal intent or from negligence. Examples of such offences may be found in the laws of the Contracting States.
>
> . . . 28 . . . Presumptions of fact or of law operate in every legal system. Clearly, the Convention does not prohibit such presumptions in principle. It does, however, require the Contracting States to remain within certain limits in this respect as regards criminal law. . . .
>
> Article 6(2) does not therefore regard presumptions of fact or of law provided for in the crim-inal law with indifference. It requires States to confine them within reasonable limits which take into account the importance of what is at stake and maintain the rights of the defence.'

25. Mr Owen sought to apply what he described as the reasonable limits test to the offence that section 5 creates. The effect of any offence of strict liability, he said, was to create a presumption that the accused had done something of which he was innocent. So the creation of strict criminal liability will always engage a consideration of compatibility with the presumption of innocence in article 6(2). The conduct to which the appellant had pleaded guilty in this case was morally blameless, as the com-plainant willingly agreed to have sexual intercourse with him. It was difficult to distil from *Salabiaku* a clear principle that strict criminal liability was always free from regulation under article 6(2). The European Court said in para 27 that the Contracting States could penalise a simple or objective fact as such irrespective of whether there was criminal intent. But it had made it clear that it could only do so under certain conditions. This was to be read as applying not just to matters of procedure. The substance of an offence could be examined too, and it would violate article 6(2) if it failed properly to recognise that the accused is to be presumed innocent until proven guilty of the conduct which it was intended to deter.

. . .

27. This argument seems me to read far too much into the wording of article 6(2) and to the Court's reasoning in *Salabiaku*. Article 6(2), like article 6(3), must be read in the context of article 6(1). The article as a whole is concerned essentially with procedural guarantees to ensure that there is a fair trial, not with the substantive elements of the offence with which the person has been charged. As has been said many times, article 6 does not guarantee any particular content of the individual's civil rights. It is concerned with the procedural fairness of the system for the administration of justice in the contracting states, not with the substantive content of domestic law: *Matthews v Ministry of Defence*

[2003] 1 AC 1163, para 3, per Lord Bingham of Cornhill, paras 30–35 per Lord Hoffmann, para 142, per Lord Walker of Gestingthorpe; *R (Kehoe) v Secretary of State for Work and Pensions* [2005] UKHL 48; [2006] 1 AC 42, para 41. The approach which the article takes to the criminal law is the same. Close attention is paid to the requirements of a fair trial. But it is a matter for the contracting states to define the essential elements of the offence with which the person has been charged. So when article 6(2) uses the words 'innocent' and 'guilty' it is dealing with the burden of proof regarding the elements of the offence and any defences to it. It is not dealing with what those elements are or what defences to the offence ought to be available.

28. The observations in paras 27–28 of *Salabiaku* are not inconsistent with this analysis. As the Court of Appeal noted in para 31 of its decision, that case was decided, in accordance with the practice of the Strasbourg court, on its own facts. The principles which it was seeking to enunciate are set out in rather general terms, which that court has not so far attempted to enlarge upon. But the key to a proper understanding of the passage as a whole is to be found in the first sentence of para 27. It contains a clear affirmation of the principle that the contracting states are free to apply the criminal law to any act, so long as it is not one which is carried out in the exercise of one of the rights protected under the Convention. Accordingly they are free to define the constituent elements of the offence that results from that act. So when the court said in the next sentence that the contracting states may 'under certain conditions' penalise a simple or objective fact as such, irrespective of whether it results from criminal intent or negligence, it was reaffirming the same principle. As in the previous sentence, the certain conditions that are referred to indicate that objection could be taken if the offence was incompatible with other articles of the Convention. But they have no wider significance. If there is no such incompatibility, the definition of the constituents of the offence is a matter for domestic law.

29. *Salabiaku* is not easy to construe, as my noble and learned friend Lord Hoffmann points out. But I do not agree with him that we should simply ignore it. Read in the way I have indicated, it continues to offer guidance about the extent of the guarantee that is afforded by article 6(2). Dyson LJ's remarks in *R v Gemmell* [2003] 1 Cr App R, 343, 356, para 33 with which I too agree, are consistent with that guidance. The substantive content of the criminal law does not raise issues of fairness of the kind to which that article is directed.

30. I would therefore respectfully endorse the conclusion which the Court of Appeal drew from the reasoning in *Salabiaku*. It said in para 33:

'An absolute offence may subject a defendant to conviction in circumstances where he has done nothing blameworthy. Prosecution for such an offence and the imposition of sanctions under it may well infringe articles of the Convention other than article 6. The legislation will not, however, render the trial under which it is enforced unfair, let alone infringe the presumption of innocence under article 6(2).'

It follows that I would not attach the significance to the decision in *Hansen v Denmark* that Mr Owen sought to attach to it. The offence in that case was one of strict liability. But, as the court noted, the burden of proof of all its elements was throughout on the prosecution. As it said, there was nothing to indicate that the courts in fulfilling their functions started from the assumption that the applicant was liable. This passage in its judgment is consistent with the view that article 6(2) does not proscribe offences of strict liability, so long as the prosecution bears the burden of proof of all the elements that constitute the offence.

31. That requirement is plainly met in this case. So I would hold that section 5 of the 2003 Act is not incompatible with article 6(2) of the Convention and that the prosecutor's act in prosecuting the appellant under that section was not unlawful in that respect.

[Lord Mance and Baroness Hale concurred with Lords Hoffmann and Hope on the Article 6 issues. Lord Carswell addressed only the Article 8 issue.]

■ *Questions*

1. Was G blameworthy?

2. Did G deserve the label 'statutory rapist'?

3. What differences are there in legislating to provide:

(a) it is an offence to touch a person under 13 sexually even if the defendant is unaware that the person is under 13; and

(b) if a person under 13 is touched sexually by the defendant, he is presumed to have known that she was under 13 unless he proves the contrary.

G appealed to the European Court of Human Rights. In *G v UK* (2011) 53 EHRR SE25 it was held that the complaint was inadmissible and so the case never reached the Court for a full hearing. There was no potential violation of Article 6.

28. The Court notes that Parliament created the offence under s.5 of the 2003 Act in order to protect children from sexual abuse. As the domestic courts confirmed, the objective element (actus reus) of the offence is penile penetration, by any person old enough for criminal responsibility, of the vagina, anus or mouth of a child aged 12 or under. The subjective element (mens rea) is intention to penetrate. Knowledge of, or recklessness as to, the age of the child or as to the child's unwillingness to take part in the sexual activity are not elements of the offence.

29. In the instant case, the prosecution was required to prove all the elements of the offence beyond reasonable doubt. The Court does not consider that Parliament's decision not to make available a defence based on reasonable belief that the complainant was aged 13 or over can give rise to any issue under art.6(1) or (2) of the Convention. Section 5 of the 2003 does not provide for presumptions of fact or law to be drawn from elements proved by the prosecution. The principle considered in *Salabiaku* therefore has no application here.

It was held that Article 8 was engaged but that it was inarguable that there was an infringement of the right to respect for private and family life.

37. It remains for the Court to determine whether the continued prosecution, conviction and sentencing of the applicant were 'necessary in a democratic society' within the meaning of the second paragraph of art.8. The Court recalls that, according to its established case law, the notion of necessity implies that the interference corresponds to a pressing social need and, in particular, that it is proportionate to the legitimate aim pursued. In determining whether an interference is 'necessary in a democratic society', the Court will take into account that a margin of appreciation is left to the national authorities (see, among many authorities, *Laskey* at [42]).

38. The scope of this margin of appreciation is not identical in each case and will vary according to the context. Thus, where the activities at stake involve an intimate aspect of private life, the margin allowed to the state is generally narrow (see, *mutatis mutandis*, *Dudgeon* at [52]; and *ADT v United Kingdom* (2001) 31 E.H.R.R. 33 at [37]). On the other hand, in this case the countervailing public interest was the need to protect the complainant and other children in her position against premature sexual activity, exploitation and abuse. As the domestic courts pointed out, the state is under a positive obligation under art.8 to protect vulnerable individuals from sexual abuse (*X v Netherlands*; compare *KA v Belgium*). The Court has found that the contracting states enjoy a wide margin of appreciation as regards the means to ensure adequate protection against rape (*MC v Bulgaria* (2005) 40 E.H.R.R. 20 at [154]). Given the nature of the public interest at stake, the Court concludes that the state authorities' margin of appreciation in the present case must be wide.

39. As Baroness Hale observed, the consequences of penetrative sex for a child of 12 or under may be very harmful. The Court does not consider that the national authorities can be said to have

exceeded the margin of appreciation available to them by creating a criminal offence which is called 'rape' and which does not allow for any defence based either on apparent consent by the child or on the accused's mistaken belief about the child's age. Nor does the Court consider that the authorities exceeded their margin of appreciation by deciding to prosecute the applicant for this offence, particularly since the legislation permitted for a broad range of sentences and the mitigating circumstances in the applicant's case were taken into account by the Court of Appeal.

7.7 The merits of strict liability

The potential merits of imposing strict liability have long been debated. For a collection of essays considering the topic, see A. Simester, *Appraising Strict Liability* (2005). The core arguments are neatly encapsulated in the following essay from Lady Wootton over 50 years ago.

Barbara Wootton, *Crime and the Criminal Law*
(1963), p 48

Nothing has dealt so devastating a blow at the punitive conception of the criminal process as the proliferation of offences of strict liability; and the alarm has forthwith been raised. Thus Dr J Ll J Edwards has expressed the fear that there is a real danger that the 'widespread practice of imposing criminal liability independent of any moral fault' will result in the criminal law being regarded with contempt. 'The process of basing criminal liability upon a theory of absolute prohibition', he writes, 'may well have the opposite effect to that intended and lead to a weakening of respect for the law' [J Ll J Edwards, *Mens Rea in Statutory Offences* (1955), p 247]. Nor, in his view, is it an adequate answer to say that absolute liability can be tolerated because of the comparative unimportance of the offences to which it is applied and because, as a rule, only a monetary penalty is involved; for, in the first place, there are a number of important exceptions to this rule (drunken driving for example); and, secondly, as Dr Edwards himself points out, in certain cases the penalty imposed by the court may be the least part of the punishment. A merchant's conviction for a minor trading offence may have a disastrous effect upon his business.

  Such dislike of strict liability is not by any means confined to academic lawyers. In the courts, too, various devices have been used to smuggle mens rea back into offences from which, on the face of it, it would appear to be excluded. To the lawyer's ingenious mind the invention of such devices naturally presents no difficulty. Criminal liability, for instance, can attach only to voluntary acts. If a driver is struck unconscious with an epileptic seizure, it can be argued that he is not responsible for any consequences because his driving thereafter is involuntary: indeed he has been said not to be driving at all. If on the other hand he falls asleep, this defence will not serve since sleep is a condition that comes on gradually, and a driver has an opportunity and a duty to stop before it overpowers him. Alternatively, recourse can be had to the circular argument that anyone who commits a forbidden act must have intended to commit it and must, therefore, have formed a guilty intention. As Lord Devlin puts it, the word 'knowingly' or 'wilfully' can be read into acts in which it is not present; although as his Lordship points out this subterfuge is open to the criticism that it fails to distinguish between the physical act itself and the circumstances in which this becomes a crime [Lord Devlin, *Samples of Law Making* (1962), pp 71–80]. All that the accused may have intended was to perform an action (such as firing a gun or driving a car) which is not in itself criminal. Again, in yet other cases such as those in which it is forbidden to permit or to allow something to be done the concept of negligence can do duty as a watered down version of *mens rea* for how can anyone be blamed for permitting something about which he could not have known?

All these devices, it cannot be too strongly emphasised, are necessitated by the need to preserve the essentially punitive function of the criminal law. For it is not, as Dr Edwards fears, the criminal law which will be brought into contempt by the multiplication of offences of strict liability, so much as this particular conception of the law's function. If that function is conceived less in terms of punishment than as a mechanism of prevention these fears become irrelevant. Such a conception, however, apparently sticks in the throat of even the most progressive lawyers. Even Professor Hart, in his Hobhouse lecture on *Punishment and the Elimination of Responsibility* [H. L. A. Hart, *Punishment and the Elimination of Responsibility* (1962), pp 27, 28] seems to be incurably obsessed with the notion of punishment, which haunts his text as well as figuring in his title. Although rejecting many traditional theories, such as that punishment should be 'retributive' or 'denunciatory', he nevertheless seems wholly unable to envisage a system in which sentence is not automatically equated with 'punishment'. Thus he writes of 'values quite distinct from those of retributive punishment which the system of responsibility does maintain, and which remain of great importance even if our aims in punishing are the forward-looking aims of social protection'; and again 'even if we *punish* men not as wicked but as nuisances . . .' while he makes many references to the principle that liability to punishment must depend on a voluntary act. Perhaps it requires the naïveté of an amateur to suggest that the forward-looking aims of social protection might, on occasion, have absolutely no connection with punishment.

If, however, the primary function of the courts is conceived as the prevention of forbidden acts, there is little cause to be disturbed by the multiplication of offences of strict liability. If the law says that certain things are not to be done, it is illogical to confine this prohibition to occasions on which they are done from malice aforethought; for at least the material consequences of an action, and the reasons for prohibiting it, are the same whether it is the result of sinister malicious plotting, of negligence or of sheer accident. A man is equally dead and his relatives equally bereaved whether he was stabbed or run over by a drunken motorist or by an incompetent one; and the inconvenience caused by the loss of your bicycle is unaffected by the question whether or no the youth who removed it had the intention of putting it back, if in fact he had not done so at the time of his arrest. It is true, of course, as Professor Hart has argued [op cit, pp 29, 30], that the material consequences of an action by no means exhaust its effects. 'If one person hits another, the person struck does not think of the other as *just* a cause of pain to him . . . If the blow was light but deliberate, it has a significance for the person struck quite different from an accidental much heavier blow.' To ignore this difference, he argues, is to outrage 'distinctions which not only underlie morality, but pervade the whole of our social life'. That these distinctions are widely appreciated and keenly felt no one would deny. Often perhaps they derive their force from a purely punitive or retributive attitude; but alternatively they may be held to be relevant to an assessment of the social damage that results from a criminal act. Just as a heavy blow does more damage than a light one, so also perhaps does a blow which involves psychological injury do more damage than one in which the hurt is purely physical.

The conclusion to which this argument leads is, I think, not that the presence or absence of the guilty mind is unimportant, but that mens rea has, so to speak—and this is the crux of the matter—*got into the wrong place*. Traditionally, the requirement of the guilty mind is written into the actual definition of a crime. No guilty intention, no crime, is the rule. Obviously this makes sense if the law's concern is with wickedness: where there is no guilty intention, there can be no wickedness. But it is equally obvious, on the other hand, that an action does not become innocuous merely because whoever performed it meant no harm. If the object of the criminal law is to prevent the occurrence of socially damaging actions, it would be absurd to turn a blind eye to those which were due to carelessness, negligence or even accident. The question of motivation is *in the first instance* irrelevant.

But only in the first instance. At a later stage, that is to say, after what is now known as a conviction, the presence or absence of guilty intention is all-important for its effect on the appropriate measures to be taken to prevent a recurrence of the forbidden act. The prevention of accidental deaths presents different problems from those involved in the prevention of wilful murders. The results of the actions of the careless, the mistaken, the wicked and the merely unfortunate may be indistinguishable from one another, but each case calls for a different treatment. Tradition, however, is very strong, and the notion that these differences are relevant only after the fact has been established that the accused committed the forbidden act seems still to be deeply abhorrent to the legal mind. Thus Lord Devlin, discussing the possibility that judges might have taken the line that all 'unintentional' criminals might be dealt with simply by the imposition of a nominal penalty, regards this as the 'negation of law'. 'It would' [Lord Devlin, *Samples of Law Making* (1962), p 73], he says, 'confuse the function of mercy which the judge is dispensing when imposing the penalty with the function of justice. It would have been to deny to the citizen due process of law because it would have been to say to him, in effect: Although we cannot think that Parliament intended you to be punished in this case because you have really done nothing wrong, come to us, ask for mercy, and we shall grant mercy.... In all criminal matters the citizen is entitled to the protection of the law...and the mitigation of penalty should not be adopted as the prime method of dealing with accidental offenders.'

Within its own implied terms of reference the logic is unexceptionable. If the purpose of the law is to dispense punishment tempered with mercy, then to use mercy as a consolation for unjust punishment is certainly to give a stone for bread. But these are not the implied terms of reference of strict liability. In the case of offences of strict liability the presumption is not that those who have committed forbidden actions must be punished, but that appropriate steps must be taken to prevent the occurrence of such actions.

The counter arguments were put with characteristic clarity by Sir John Smith over 20 years later.

J. C. Smith, 'Responsibility in Criminal Law'
in P. Bean and D. Whynes (eds), *Barbara Wootton: Essays in Her Honour* (1986), p 149

Judging the intentions of others

The law relating to responsibility, Lady Wootton rightly says, 'presumes an ability to make judgments about other men's intentions and the degree of their iniquity, the validity of which cannot ever be objectively demonstrated' (Wootton 1981: 64). It is certainly true that the doctrine of *mens rea* does presume this ability. If the presumption is baseless the doctrine is a sham and should be abolished as soon as possible. It should not be accepted that it is baseless, however, because its validity cannot be 'objectively demonstrated', in the way that the rules of science may be demonstrated in a laboratory. We can often be as certain that a man had a particular state of mind as we can be certain of anything. Does any rational being doubt that armed men who enter a bank and demand money at gunpoint intend to steal, that they dishonestly intend to appropriate property belonging to the bank and permanently to deprive the bank of it? That a man who lies in wait for a girl in a dark lane, knocks her down, and has sexual intercourse with her, intends to have sexual intercourse with her without her consent? That a man who applies a loaded shotgun to another's knee and pulls the trigger intends to cause grievous bodily harm? In such cases we can be just as certain that the defendant had the intention as that he did the act. That, indeed, is what the law requires. The judge tells the jury that they must be convinced not only that the defendant did the act, but that he did it with *mens rea*. Evidence is always admissible to challenge the inference and, if it casts doubt on even the most overwhelming inference of *mens rea*, the defendant is entitled to be acquitted.

Moreover, Lady Wootton herself assumes that these matters would be taken into account at the sentencing stage. 'The prevention of accidental death presents different problems from those involved in the prevention of wilful murders' (1981: 48). But it is no easier to answer the question at the one stage than the other. While we retain our present procedures it will be the magistrates who will have to answer the question at whatever point it arises. In the Crown Court it becomes a question of whether the matters which really determine the fate of the defendant are to be decided by the judge or by the jury. It would not be appropriate here to attempt to assess the relative virtues of the judge and jury in matters of fact-finding; but there would certainly be grave disquiet in many quarters if the jury were relegated to the role of answering only the question, 'Did he do it?'.

No doubt there is a greater difficulty in answering the second point: can we properly assess the degree of iniquity? We can, however, assess reasonably objectively the gravity of the harm caused; and, if the defendant chose to cause that harm, or to take a risk of causing it, this seems to afford a reasonable measure by which to assess 'iniquity'. This assumes that the defendant could and did choose.

[Having discussed *Tolson*, section 7.3.1, p 186, and *Ball* (1966) 50 Cr App R 266.] This brings me to what I regard as the major difficulty in Lady Wootton's theory. It is essentially a practical one. The only question for the court of trial is to be 'Did he do it?' Whether he did it intentionally, recklessly, negligently, or by sheer accident is irrelevant. In any event the person who did it is to be passed on to the 'sentencer' who will consider what should be done to ensure that he does not do it again. Now if the court of trial has to disregard the question of fault, so too surely do the police and the prosecuting authority (or whatever takes its place). If we allow the police or prosecutor to decide to proceed or not on the basis of whether or not the defendant was at fault, we do indirectly what we will not permit to be done directly. We allow the crucial decision which is now made formally and openly on proper evidence in court to be made informally, privately, and on whatever evidence the prosecutor, in his wisdom, or lack of it, considers relevant. The logic of the system requires the prosecution of *all* cases because even if the forbidden result has resulted from 'sheer accident', the sentencer is under a duty to consider whether there is anything to be done to ensure that the 'offender' does not have such accidents again. Everyone who causes an injury to another person, everyone who damages another's property, could, and should, be brought to court. Every buyer or seller of goods who makes an innocent misrepresentation, every bona-fide purchaser of goods in fact stolen, the surgeon whose patient dies on the operating table, the Good Samaritan who innocently gives help to a person escaping after committing an arrestable offence—all these have brought about the harm which it is the object of the law to prevent; so they should be subject to process of law so as to ensure that they do not cause the harm again. The business of the courts would be enormously multiplied. And to what purpose? What is to be done with all those who (like Ball and Mrs Tolson) have behaved reasonably and have had the misfortune to cause the forbidden result by sheer accident—except to tell them to continue to behave reasonably?

It is reasonably safe to assume that what would in fact happen is that, however illogically, the fault test would be applied at the police or prosecution stage. This would be prompted, not only by the natural sense of justice of those operating the system, but also by their realization of the futility of invoking legal process against one who has behaved entirely reasonably.

A further practical difficulty is that the system would put enormous discretion into the hands of the sentencer. He would apparently have the same power in law over one who caused death accidentally as over a murderer. It is difficult to believe that such a large discretion would be tolerable. It would dilute, if not destroy, the criminal law as a moral force and that at a time when the decline of religious belief has, as Lady Wootton herself says, created a dangerous vacuum. The shift from punishment to prevention may be intended to remove the moral basis of the law; but if, as some believe, one of the major reasons why people do not commit crimes is the sense of guilt which attaches to them, should not the aim be to enhance the sense of guilt rather than otherwise? To remove the element of fault is to empty the law of moral content. If murder were, in law, no different from accidental death, should we be so inhibited from committing murder as most of us are?

■ *Questions*

Does the bereaved relative of a victim of a murder feel differently from the bereaved victim of a causing death by careless driving? Do the relative's perceptions matter? Would you rather have the determination of the offender's 'fault' decided by the jury or by the judge at sentencing?

7.8 Compromise positions on strict liability

7.8.1 The 'halfway house'

Many common law countries have developed a so-called 'halfway house' between strict liability and a full mens rea requirement. It takes various forms but, in general, the effect is that the prosecution has to prove the commission of the actus reus but then the onus shifts to the defendant to prove, on the balance of probabilities, that he did not have mens rea and was not negligent. Sometimes it does not go so far but imposes a merely evidential burden on the defendant. See, for example, *City of Sault Ste Marie* (1978) 85 DLR 3d 161 at 181, where the Canadian Supreme Court acknowledged a defence for the defendant to:

avoid liability by proving that he took all reasonable care. This involves consideration of what a reasonable man would have done in the circumstances. The defence would be available if the accused reasonably believed in a mistaken set of facts which, if true, would render the act or omission innocent, or if he took all reasonable steps to avoid the particular event.

Lord Cooke, a distinguished New Zealand judge who sees merit in the halfway house, noted in his Hamlyn lectures that the doctrine had made no headway in England. Subsequently, the theory was rejected in *B (a minor) v DPP* and not referred to in *K*. It seems that it has no future in England unless included in the statute in question.

Hostility to statutory reverse onuses, following the enactment of the Human Rights Act 1998 (cf *Lambert* [2001] UKHL 37) makes it even less likely that the courts will depart from the *Woolmington* principle unless statute requires, and the European Convention permits, them to do so.

See also the comparative study by J. Spencer and A. Pedain, 'Approaches to Strict and Constructive Liability in Continental Criminal Law' in A. Simester (ed), *Appraising Strict Liability* (2005) noting that a reason for continental systems avoiding strict liability is that their procedures allow for proof more easily than the strict adversarial system in England.

7.8.2 Due diligence defences

It is common for the drastic effect of a statute imposing strict liability to be mitigated by the provision of a statutory 'due diligence' defence. Such defences usually impose on the defendant a burden of proving both that he had no mens rea and that he took all reasonable precautions and exercised all due diligence to avoid the commission of an offence. Such provisions are a distinct advance on unmitigated strict liability; but they are still a deviation from the fundamental principle that the prosecution must prove the whole of their case.

See for discussion, D. Parry, 'Judicial Approaches to Due Diligence' [1995] Crim LR 695; C. Manchester, 'Knowledge Due Diligence and Strict Liability in Regulatory Offences' [2006] Crim LR 213.

In some recent cases the courts have held that although liability is strict as to an element of the offence, so mens rea is irrelevant in that sense, it can be relevant when considering the due diligence defence.

An example is the case of *Unah* [2011] EWCA Crim 1837. U was convicted of possession of a false identity document contrary to s 25(5) of the Identity Cards Act 2006.

Section 25(5) of the Identity Cards Act 2006 (now replaced by the Identity Documents Act 2010) provided:

> (5) It is an offence for a person to have in his possession or under his control, without reasonable excuse—
>
>   (a) an identity document that is false;
>
>   (b) an identity document that was improperly obtained;
>
>   (c) an identity document that relates to someone else...

U was a Nigerian national with indefinite leave to remain in the UK. U had presented documents at a job centre interview including her current Nigerian passport, an expired Nigerian passport and a document evidencing her indefinite leave to remain. The expired passport was a false one. U's current Nigerian passport was legitimate. U claimed that she had believed that the false passport was a legitimate one. She had obtained that passport, now acknowledged to be false, by completing the appropriate forms and paying the appropriate fee, and had done so with the help of a friend who regularly travelled to the UK. At trial, U accepted that she had had the passport in her possession and that the biographical page was counterfeit, but claimed that she had not known or believed that the identity document was false and, therefore, she had a reasonable excuse. As a preliminary matter, the judge ruled that the offence under s 25(5) was one of strict liability and that the defendant had no defence in law to the charge. The trial judge ruled that the defence of 'reasonable excuse' applied where a defendant could justify his or her possession or control of the false document, for example where a person found a document and took it to the police to be handed in, or where a police officer confiscated the document. It was not possible for U to claim that her lack of knowledge of the falsity of the document was a 'reasonable excuse'. U pleaded guilty on re-arraignment and appealed against conviction. The Court of Appeal allowed the appeal. In determining whether an excuse was reasonable, reference to the circumstances in which a document had been obtained, which had caused a defendant to believe it was genuine, were relevant to the jury's consideration.

> A belief that a document is genuine might, for example, explain why it has not been thrown away or handed in to the police. It is capable of providing an explanation for the possession of the document. Of course, there may be circumstances where the explanation as to why the defendant has the document in his or her possession is simply not believed by the jury, or it may be that the jury accepts the explanation advanced but does not consider that it is reasonable in all the circumstances. But the concept of reasonable excuse is potentially a broad one, and we do not see why the circumstances in which the document was obtained, and which may cause the defendant to believe that it was genuine, should be ignored when considering whether an excuse for possessing it is reasonable or not. (at [5])

The court had regard to the other offences created under s 25 as an aid to the construction of subs (5). Section 25(5) does not contain the words 'with the requisite intention' as found in s 25(1). That suggested that the fact that a defendant did not have the knowledge or belief that a document was false was not in itself an excuse. The Court of Appeal accepted that there was no justification to imply those words into the s 25(5) offence: it is not necessary for the Crown to prove that D knew he had the document or that he knew it was false. However, the reasonable excuse defence could apply where a defendant denied either knowing possession and/or knowledge of the falsity of the document. The defence would not, however, be satisfied by a defendant merely claiming a lack of knowledge; something more was required.

Note that the Identity Documents Act 2010 repealed the Identity Cards Act 2006, although ss 25 and 26 (possession of false identity documents etc) and s 38 of the 2006 Act are replaced by very similar (but not identical) provisions contained in ss 4 to 10 of the new Act.

See also the similar approach to defences based on reasonable excuse in *JB v CPS* [2012] EWHC 72 (Admin).

7.9 Reform

The Law Commission suggested in its draft Criminal Code Bill, cl 20:

(1) Every offence requires a fault element of recklessness with respect to each of its elements other than fault elements, unless otherwise provided.

(2) Subsection 1 does not apply to pre-Code offences....

The recklessness referred to is *Cunningham*, not *Caldwell*, recklessness.

The Law Commission considered a suggestion that the presumption in favour of mens rea should be displaceable only by an *express* provision requiring some fault other than recklessness, or stating that no fault is required. But, said the Commission, 'We do not think that this would be appropriate. We are mindful of the constitutional platitude pointed out by Lord Ackner in *Hunt* [1987] AC 352 at 380, that the courts must give effect to what Parliament has provided not only expressly but also by necessary implication. If the terms of a future enactment creating an offence plainly implied an intention to displace the presumption created by clause 20(1), the courts would no doubt feel obliged to give effect to that intention even if the present clause were to require express provision for the purpose.'

In 2010 the Law Commission published a consultation paper *Criminal Liability in Regulatory Contexts* (CP195) in which it considered the use of criminal offences against business enterprises. As part of its examination of this branch of the criminal law, consideration was given to the prevalence of strict liability in so-called 'regulatory offences'. The Law Commission made the following proposals and posed the following questions.

CONCLUSION

6.92 In an ideal world, criminal offences created by statute would always indicate when fault need not be proved, or if it needs to be proved what kind of fault (or defence) is involved. Since there are so many criminal offences under statute that fall short of the ideal, we believe that, subject to some possible exceptions, the courts should be given the power to apply a defence of due diligence in all the circumstances to statutory offences that would otherwise involve strict liability with no adequate defence. This approach has the advantage of leaving the strict basis of liability in the relevant provision intact. That means the courts will no longer need to search for what may be non-existent Parliamentary intention respecting fault requirements and will no longer need to decide whether a presumption that fault must be proved applies, and if so, whether the presumption has been displaced.

6.93 Clearly, the courts would not apply the defence of due diligence where to do so would defeat the purpose of the statute. A related point is that we would expect the courts not to apply it if, despite the absence of a requirement for proof of a positive fault requirement, there are specific defences applicable to the offence that mean the fairness objective has been met. Even where the courts did apply it, the burden of proof, on the balance of probabilities, would be on the defendant to establish that due diligence in the circumstances had been shown.

6.94 We believe that the introduction of the power to apply the defence has the potential to secure the fairness objective in a greater range of cases than at present. Moreover, unlike the presumption that fault must be proved, it can secure the fairness objective in a way that is sensitive to the differences between the capacities and resources of defendants to organise their affairs in such a way that offences are not committed in the course of business.

PROPOSALS AND QUESTIONS

6.95 We provisionally propose that:

Proposal 14: The courts should be given a power to apply a due diligence defence to any statutory offence that does not require proof that the defendant was at fault in engaging in the wrongful conduct. The burden of proof should be on the defendant to establish the defence.

6.96 If proposal 14 is accepted, we also provisionally propose that:

Proposal 15: The defence of due diligence should take the form of showing that due diligence was exercised in all the circumstances to avoid the commission of the offence.

6.97 However, we recognise that consultees may prefer this defence to have the same wording and to impose the same standards as the most commonly encountered statutory form of the defence. Accordingly, we ask following question:

Question 1: Were it to be introduced, should the due diligence defence take the stricter form already found in some statutes, namely, did the defendant take all reasonable precautions and exercise all due diligence to avoid commission of the offence?

6.98 We ask the further question:

Question 2: If the power to apply a due diligence defence is introduced, should Parliament prevent or restrict its application to certain statutes, and if so which statutes?

FURTHER READING

A. Ashworth, 'Should Strict Criminal Liability be Removed from All Imprisonable Offences?' in A. Ashworth, *Positive Obligations in Criminal Law* (2013)

P. Brett, 'Strict Responsibility: Possible Solutions' (1974) 37 MLR 417

J. Horder, 'Strict Liability, Statutory Construction and the Spirit of Liberty' (2002) 118 LQR 458

L. H. Leigh, *Strict and Vicarious Liability* (1982)

A. Simester (ed), *Appraising Strict Liability* (2005)

8
Parties to offences

8.1 Introduction

In this chapter we consider the way in which the criminal law applies to those who are responsible for assisting or encouraging crimes. Vast numbers of crimes are carried out by people acting together and it is essential that the criminal law has effective rules in place to deal with the conduct of all who are involved. The way that English and Welsh law has done so, historically, has been to treat the person who assists as guilty in the same manner and for the same offence as the person who most directly commits the crime. The person who provides the gun to the murderer is prosecuted as a murderer himself and is liable to the same punishment as the person who pulls the trigger.

In this chapter, we will consider those who assisted or encouraged the commission of an offence *that was completed or attempted*. In Chapter 12 we consider the responsibility of those who have assisted or encouraged irrespective of whether the crime that they assisted or encouraged was in fact carried out or even attempted.

Suppose that Dawn visits Peter, a 'contract killer', and tells him that she wants him to kill her husband, Victor. Dawn is now liable to conviction for assisting or encouraging Peter to commit murder under the Serious Crime Act 2007, s 44. That crime is committed as soon as Dawn's words are spoken. It would make no difference if Peter said he would have nothing to do with the proposal (see Chapter 13). If Peter agrees to commit the murder, the pair of them are guilty of conspiracy to murder. Conspiracy to commit a crime is another distinct offence, committed as soon as the agreement is made. It would make no difference to liability for conspiracy (though it would affect the sentence) that, immediately afterwards, they thought better of it and decided to abandon the plan (see Chapter 14).

If Peter goes ahead and kills Victor he is guilty of murder. He is the 'principal offender'. Dawn is also guilty of murder. She is an 'accessory' sometimes also known as a 'secondary party' or 'accomplice'. She may be miles away at the time but she is equally responsible in law with Peter for Peter's act. Suppose that Peter has taken into his confidence two friends, Carl, who lent him a gun with which to shoot Victor, and Eric who drove him to Peter's house and kept watch outside while Peter did the deed inside. Carl and Eric are also guilty of the murder of Victor. They are also accessories. Dawn, Peter, Carl and Eric are all equally liable to be convicted of murder and liable to the same punishment—which, for murder, must be life imprisonment. In the case of crimes other than murder, where the judge has a discretion in imposing sentence, the permissible maximum is the same for all; but sentences may vary according to the responsibility of each party. The principal is not necessarily the most blameworthy. An accessory such as Dawn may be the 'mastermind' and the dominant personality and her sentence is likely to reflect that.

In this chapter we examine the nature and extent of liability for secondary participation in a crime. As the previous example shows, secondary participation is closely interrelated with assisting and encouraging under the Serious Crime Act 2007 and conspiracy; but as they are distinct crimes they are considered separately, along with the crime of attempt with which they are closely associated, in Chapters 12 to 14.

The controversies that will be examined in this chapter include:

(i)   the conceptual basis for secondary liability;

(ii) what is meant by 'aiding, abetting, counselling and procuring';

(iii) the mens rea necessary to establish secondary liability;

(iv) the elements of 'joint enterprise' liability;

(v)   the Supreme Court's decision in *Gnango*.

8.2 The derivative nature of secondary liability

The distinctive feature of secondary liability is that, subject to one exception discussed in section 8.4.1.4, p 225, it is derivative: the liability of Dawn, Carl and Eric 'derives' from that of Peter. It is only when Peter performs the conduct element of the offence of murder that the liability of the others *as accessories* is triggered.

When Peter points the gun at Victor, Dawn, Carl and Eric have done everything necessary to become accessories to murder, but whether they do so depends on whether Peter pulls the trigger. If he changes his mind at the last moment none of them would be guilty of murder, for no murder has been committed. The liability of the secondary party derives from the *guilt* of the principal, not from his *conviction*. If, after killing Victor, Peter kills himself, or goes abroad and is never heard of again, Dawn, Carl and Eric may still be convicted as accessories to the murder Peter committed. If, at their trial, it is proved that Peter (who is absent and not on trial) committed the murder and that they played the parts described, Peter's absence and the fact that he is not convicted are immaterial. We consider later the merits of a scheme based on inchoate liability (where the liability of Dawn, Carl and Eric would arise irrespective of whether Peter committed murder) rather than derivative secondary liability.

Over the centuries, a wide variety of verbs were used by the courts and by Parliament to describe the acts which amount to secondary participation. In modern times, however, they have been generally, though not invariably, limited to the following four: 'aid, abet, counsel or procure'. The common law rules of secondary participation apply automatically to every offence unless expressly or impliedly excluded. When Parliament creates a new offence it does not usually provide that anyone who aids, abets, counsels or procures it will be guilty. There is no need to do so. The common law rule is now embodied in statute law.

Accessories and Abettors Act 1861

8. Abettors in misdemeanours

Whosoever shall aid, abet, counsel, or procure the commission of any indictable offence, whether the same be an offence at common law or by virtue of any Act passed or to be passed, shall be liable to be tried, indicted, and punished as a principal offender.

Magistrates' Courts Act 1980

44. Aiders and abettors

(1) A person who aids, abets, counsels or procures the commission by another person of a summary offence shall be guilty of the like offence and may be tried (whether or not he is charged as a principal) either by a court having jurisdiction to try that other person or by a court having by virtue of his own offence jurisdiction to try him.

(2) Any offence consisting in aiding, abetting, counselling or procuring the commission of an offence triable either way (other than an offence Listed in Schedule 1 to this Act) shall by virtue of this sub-section be triable either way.

8.3 Distinguishing principals, innocent agents and accessories

Notwithstanding the provisions of the Accessories and Abettors Act and the Magistrates' Courts Act as set out above, it is sometimes necessary to distinguish between the principal and secondary parties:

(i) in the case of all offences of strict liability because, even in these cases, secondary parties must be proved to have mens rea although the principal need not;

(ii) in all cases where the offence is so defined that it can be committed as a principal only by a member of a specified class (eg only a man can commit rape as a principal because the definition of the offence is that a man penetrates *with his penis*);

(iii) where vicarious liability is in issue. In some offences vicarious liability may be imposed for the act of another who is a principal or does the act of a principal; but there is no vicarious liability for the act of a secondary party.

8.3.1 Principal

Where there are several participants in a crime we define the principal as the participant 'whose act is the most immediate cause of the actus reus'. With offences in which there is no result or consequence to be proved, the principal offender is perhaps more accurately the person who engages in the conduct element of the actus reus. Thus, in murder for example, he is the person who, with mens rea, fires the gun or administers the poison which causes death; in theft, the person who, with mens rea, appropriates the thing which is stolen, etc. The extent to which it could be argued that the Supreme Court in *Gnango* [2011] UKSC 59 widened the scope of who can be considered a principal will be considered in section 8.7.8, p 275.

8.3.2 Joint principal offenders

There may be two or more principal offenders in the same crime. If D1 and D2 make an attack on V intending to murder him and the combined effect of their blows is to kill him, both are guilty of murder as joint principal offenders; *Macklin and Murphy's Case* (1838) 2 Lew CC 225.

■ *Question*

Consider whether Gibbins in *Gibbins and Proctor* (1918) 13 Cr App R 134, section 4.4, p 94, was a joint principal or an accessory.

The position is different if D causes another person, X (who is fully aware of the circumstances and consequences of what he is being persuaded to do, so is not an *innocent* agent, see section 8.3.4), by persuasion or otherwise, to commit the offence. That does not amount to D causing the actus reus. X's voluntary intervening conduct 'breaks the chain of causation' so that D is not a principal offender. X will be liable as the principal offender. D may be liable (i) under the Serious Crime Act 2007, ss 44–46 (see Chapter 12), depending on his mens rea, or (ii) as a secondary party.

8.3.3 Principal or accessory?

It has always been sufficient to secure a conviction that the prosecution can prove that the defendant was either the principal or a secondary party. For example, in *Gianetto* [1997] 1 Cr App R 1, it was sufficient for the prosecution to allege that the defendant killed his wife or that he was an accessory to her death (by contracting a killer to do so). The prosecution could not be sure whether D was the principal offender or a secondary party, but could establish beyond doubt that he was involved in plotting her killing. Provided the defendant knows the allegation he has to meet—in terms of the part he is alleged to have played—in most cases the Crown need not specify whether he was a principal or accessory. This is because he is charged and prosecuted in the same way, and liable to the same penalty, regardless of whether he was in fact the principal or accessory. However, this must be distinguished from the case where there are two defendants and it cannot be proven which defendant committed the principal offence. In *Banfield* [2013] EWCA Crim 1394, the Court of Appeal reaffirmed that if all that can be proven is that the principal offence was committed by either D1 or D2, and it cannot be shown that whichever was not the principal must have been assisting, then both must be acquitted. For example, V is killed and only D and P had access to V at that time. It could have been P alone, D alone, D assisting P or P assisting D, but unless the Crown can establish in relation to each defendant that they were involved in some capacity, they must both be acquitted.

8.3.4 Innocent agents

It may be that the person whose act is the most immediate cause of the actus reus is not a participant in the crime at all. For example, D and E prepare a letter bomb addressed to V and D posts it. The letter passes through several hands in the Post Office and is put through V's letterbox by F, an unsuspecting postman. V opens it and is injured or killed. F's act is the most immediate cause of the killing but F is not a participant in the crime. Obviously D is the principal. F and the other Post Office employees who handled the letter are described as 'innocent agents'.

A person might be an innocent agent because:

(i)   he is under 10 years of age and therefore under the age of criminal responsibility; or

(ii) he does the act or acts without the fault required for the offence; or

(iii) he has a defence.

Our postman falls into category (ii). A 9-year-old child who is persuaded to smother a baby would be an example of category (i). A person (X) who is compelled by another (D) by threats of death to wound a third person (Y) would be an example of (iii). If charged with wounding, X would have the defence of duress. If Y died of his wounds and D and X were charged with murder, X would now be the alleged principal and D the alleged accessory because duress is not a defence to murder.

The Law Commission proposes replacing the common law innocent agency doctrine with a new statutory offence; see section 8.10, p 297, and R. D. Taylor, 'Procuring, Causation, Innocent Agency and the Law Commission' [2008] Crim LR 32.

See, generally, P. Alldridge, 'The Doctrine of Innocent Agency' (1990) 2 Crim L Forum 45; G. Williams, 'Innocent Agency and Causation' (1992) 3 Crim L Forum 289.

We return to discuss a complexity with innocent agents and procuring at section 8.4.1.4, p 225.

8.4 Liability as an accessory

The accessory is liable for the principal's offence and prosecuted as a principal, but there is no secondary liability in the abstract. D cannot be an accessory per se; he must be an accessory to a specific crime—murder, theft, etc. In approaching the secondary party's liability, it is logical to begin by identifying the principal and the crime the principal is alleged to have committed. It is then necessary to turn to the accomplice's liability. His offence of secondary liability has its own actus reus and mens rea which must be proved before he can be convicted as an accomplice.

8.4.1 Actus reus: aiding, abetting, counselling or procuring

Section 8 of the 1861 Act describes the actus reus of the secondary party as aiding, abetting, counselling or procuring. It is enough that D did one of the four things—aided, abetted, counselled or procured.

One of the disadvantages in having the law relating to accessories based on a statute dating from 1861 and on the common law development since that date is that the principles of liability are not as clearly expressed as they might be. The language is also archaic, adding to the ambiguity and inaccessibility of the law.

Attorney-General's Reference (No 1 of 1975)
[1975] EWCA Crim 1, Court of Appeal, Criminal Division, http://www.bailii.org/ew/cases/EWCA/Crim/1975/1.html

(Lord Widgery CJ, Bristow and May JJ)

Lord Widgery CJ [delivered the following judgment of the court:]

This case comes before the court on a reference from the Attorney General under s 36 of the Criminal Justice Act 1972, and by his reference he asks the following question:

> 'Whether an accused who surreptitiously laced a friend's drinks with double measures of spirits when he knew that his friend would shortly be driving his car home, and in consequence his friend drove with an excess quantity of alcohol in his body and was convicted of the offence under the Road Traffic Act 1972, s 6(1) is entitled to a ruling of no case to answer on being later charged as an aider and abettor, counsellor and procurer, on the ground that there was no shared intention between the two, that the accused did not by accompanying him or otherwise positively encourage the friend to drive, or on any other ground.'

The language in the section which determines whether a 'secondary party', as he is sometimes called, is guilty of a criminal offence committed by another embraces the four words 'aid, abet, counsel or procure'. The origin of those words is to be found in s 8 of the Accessories and Abettors Act 1861 which provides:

> 'Whosoever shall aid, abet, counsel, or procure the commission of any misdemeanor, whether the same be a misdemeanor at common law or by virtue of any Act passed or to be passed, shall be liable to be tried, indicted, and punished as a principal offender.'

. . .

Of course it is the fact that in the great majority of instances where a secondary party is sought to be convicted of an offence there has been a contact between the principal offender and the secondary party. Aiding and abetting almost inevitably involves a situation in which the secondary party and the main offender are together at some stage discussing the plans which they may be making in respect of the alleged offence, and are in contact so that each knows what is passing through the mind of the other.

In the same way it seems to us that a person who counsels the commission of a crime by another, almost inevitably comes to a moment when he is in contact with that other, when he is discussing the offence with that other and when, to use the words of the statute, he counsels the other to commit the offence.

The fact that so often the relationship between the secondary party and the principal will be such that there is a meeting of minds between them caused the trial judge in the case from which this reference is derived to think that this was really an essential feature of proving or establishing the guilt of the secondary party and, as we understand his judgment, he took the view that in the absence of some sort of meeting of minds, some sort of mental link between the secondary party and the principal, there could be no aiding, abetting or counselling of the offence within the meaning of the section.

So far as aiding, abetting and counselling is concerned we would go a long way with that conclusion. It may very well be, as I said a moment ago, difficult to think of a case of aiding, abetting or counselling when the parties have not met and have not discussed in some respects the terms of the offence which they have in mind. But we do not see why a similar principle should apply to procuring. We approach s8 of the 1861 Act on the basis that the words should be given their ordinary meaning, if possible. We approach the section on the basis also that if four words are employed here, 'aid, abet, counsel or procure', the probability is that there is a difference between each of those four words and the other three, because, if there were no such difference, then Parliament would be wasting time in using four words where two or three would do. Thus, in deciding whether that which is assumed to be done under our reference was a criminal offence we approach the section on the footing that each word must be given its ordinary meaning.

To procure means to produce by endeavour. You procure a thing by setting out to see that it happens and taking the appropriate steps to produce that happening. We think that there are plenty of instances in which a person may be said to procure the commission of a crime by another even though there is no sort of conspiracy between the two, even though there is no attempt at agreement or discussion as to the form which the offence should take. In our judgment the offence described in this reference is such a case.

If one looks back at the facts of the reference: the accused surreptitiously laced his friend's drink. This is an important element and, although we are not going to decide today anything other than the problem posed to us, it may well be that in similar cases where the lacing of the drink or the introduction of the extra alcohol is known to the driver quite different considerations may apply. We say that because where the driver has no knowledge of what is happening, in most instances he would have no means of preventing the offence from being committed. If the driver is unaware of what has happened, he will not be taking precautions. He will get into his car seat, switch on the ignition and drive home and, consequently, the conception of another procuring the commission of the offence by the driver is very much stronger where the driver is innocent of all knowledge of what is happening, as in the present case where the lacing of the drink was surreptitious.

The second thing which is important in the facts set out in our reference is that following and in consequence of the introduction of the extra alcohol, the friend drove with an excess quantity of alcohol in his blood. Causation here is important. You cannot procure an offence unless there is a causal link between what you do and the commission of the offence, and here we are told that in consequence of the addition of this alcohol the driver, when he drove home, drove with an excess quantity of alcohol in his body.

Giving the words their ordinary meaning in English, and asking oneself whether in those circumstances the offence has been procured, we are in no doubt that the answer is that it has. It has been procured because, unknown to the driver and without his collaboration, he has been put in a position in which in fact he has committed an offence which he never would have committed otherwise. We think that there was a case to answer and that the trial judge should have directed the jury that an offence is committed if it is shown beyond reasonable doubt that the accused knew that his friend was going to drive, and also knew that the ordinary and natural result of the additional alcohol added to the friend's drink would be to bring him above the recognised limit of 80 milligrammes per 100 millilitres of blood.

It was suggested to us that, if we held that there may be a procuring on the facts of the present case, it would be but a short step to a similar finding for the generous host, with somewhat bibulous friends, when at the end of the day his friends leave him to go to their own homes in circumstances in which they are not fit to drive and in circumstances in which an offence under the Road Traffic Act 1972 is committed. The suggestion has been made that the host may in those circumstances be guilty with his guests on the basis that he has either aided, abetted, counselled or procured the offence.

The first point to notice in regard to the generous host is that that is not a case in which the alcohol is being put surreptitiously into the glass of the driver. That is a case in which the driver knows perfectly well how much he has to drink and where to a large extent it is perfectly right and proper to leave him to make his own decision.

Furthermore, we would say that if such a case arises, the basis on which the case will be put against the host is, we think, bound to be on the footing that he has supplied the tool with which the offence is committed. This of course is a reference back to such cases as those where oxyacetylene equipment was bought by a man knowing it was to be used by another for a criminal offence [*Bainbridge*, section 8.5.2.3, p 248]. There is ample and clear authority as to the extent to which supplying the tools for the commission of an offence may amount to aiding and abetting for present purposes.

Accordingly, so far as the generous host type of case is concerned we are not concerned at the possibility that difficulties will be created, as long as it is borne in mind that in those circumstances the matter must be approached in accordance with well-known authority governing the provision of the tools for the commission of an offence, and never forgetting that the introduction of the alcohol is not there surreptitious, and that consequently the case for saying that the offence was procured by the supplier of the alcohol is very much more difficult.

Our decision on the reference is that the question posed by the Attorney-General should be answered in the negative.

Determination accordingly

The court holds that Parliament must have intended the four words, 'aid, abet, counsel and procure' to have different meanings, but the court did not have the advantage of an exposition of the history of secondary participation and might have arrived at a different conclusion if it had. See J. C. Smith, 'Aid, Abet, Counsel or Procure' in *Reshaping the Criminal Law*, p 120. The Code Team and the Law Commission thought that the scope of secondary participation as defined in the case law is accurately described by three words, 'procure, assist, or encourage'.

■ *Questions*

Professor Kadish, with whom Glanville Williams agrees, thinks that only two types of activity are involved—'intentionally influencing the decision of the primary party to commit the crime, and intentionally helping the primary actor to commit the crime': *Blame and Punishment: Essays in Criminal Law* (1987), pp 135, 151.

Does this formula adequately cover a case like the *A-G's Reference*? See discussion at [1991] Crim LR 765 and 930.

Lord Widgery's generous host fills the guest's glass as rapidly as the guest empties it and may be aware that the guest, who has come alone in his car, will drive home with an excess of alcohol. Does the host cause this result? Does he cause it by *endeavour*? Lord Widgery said that 'to procure means to produce by *endeavour*'. What is the significance of the words, 'by endeavour'?

Williams, TBCL 339, writes: 'In so far as *Attorney-General's Reference* purports to decide that merely causing an offence can be said to be a procuring of it, it should be regarded as too incautious a generalisation.'

Despite the decision that all four words have different meanings, they may be used together to charge a person who is alleged to have participated in an offence otherwise than as a principal offender (ie D can be charged with having aided, abetted, counselled or procured, etc). As long as the evidence establishes that D's conduct satisfied one of the words, that is enough. However, where the prosecution chooses only one term—for example, 'procures'—it is necessary to prove that D's conduct fits that term.

8.4.1.1 Aiding

The natural meaning of the word would be to describe someone who helped perhaps by acting as a lookout while P burgled premises or by supplying the assassin, P, with a gun. It was generally accepted that D could still be liable even though D's aid need not have actually helped P. Perhaps D supplied P with a gun to murder V, but P chose to use a knife instead. D should still be liable for aiding murder. Consider however the next case.

R v Bryce
[2004] EWCA Crim 1231, [2004] 2 Cr App R 592, [2004] Crim LR 936, Court of Appeal, Criminal Division, http://www.bailii.org/ew/cases/EWCA/Crim/2004/1231.html

(Potter LJ, Hooper and Astill JJ)

D was convicted of murder as an aider and abettor. In the course of a drug dealers' dispute D assisted X, who was acting on the orders of another, Black, by transporting X and a gun to a caravan near V's home so that X could carry out the murder. Twelve hours after D had left X at the scene, he shot V with the gun. D assisted in disposing of evidence after the killing. D's appeal was focused on the issue of causation—that what D did was too remote in time and place to the killing and that at that stage when D assisted, X had not yet formed the intention to commit any criminal offence.

Potter LJ:

72. So far as causation is concerned . . . , in order to establish the liability of a secondary party, the precise extent to which it is necessary to prove a causative link between the act of assistance alleged against the secondary party and the substantive crime committed by the perpetrator is by no means clearly established in our criminal law. In the case of one charged with 'procuring' an offence, it is clear that a causal link must indeed be demonstrated. In *Attorney General's Reference (No. 1 of 1975)* [1975] QB 773, [1975] 2 All ER 684 the court stated at 780B

'You cannot procure an offence unless there is a causal link between what you do and the commission of the offence.'

Further, in no less an authority than Stephen's *Digest* (4th ed) Art 39, it is stated that, not only one who procures but one who 'counsels' or 'commands' is liable, and by implication only liable, when the crime committed by the perpetrator

'. . . is committed in consequence of such counselling, procuring, or commandment.'

73. It has been held that 'counselling' need not be the cause of the commission of the offence in the sense of showing that, without such counselling, the offence would not have been committed: see *A-G v Able* [1984] QB 795, [1984] 1 All ER 277 at 812. It has also been held that proffered advice or encouragement which has no effect on the mind of the perpetrator is not counselling: *R v Clarkson* [1971] 3 All ER 344, [1971] 1 WLR 1402. Nonetheless, for secondary party liability there must be some causal connection between the act of the secondary party relied on and the commission of the offence by

the perpetrator. In *R (on the application of Morgan) v Assistant Recorder of Kingston-upon-Hull* Lord Parker CJ, in distinguishing the offence of incitement from the liability of an accomplice, observed:

'It is of the essence of the offence established by "counselling, procuring or commanding" that, *as a result* of the counselling, procuring or commanding, something should have happened which constituted either the full offence or the attempt . . .' (emphasis added)

74. On the other hand, it seems clear that the requirement for a causal connection is given a wide interpretation where a secondary party prior to the crime has counselled or assisted the perpetrator in actions taken by him which are directed towards the commission of the crime eventually committed. In *Attorney General's Reference (No.1 of 1975)*, when considering the word 'counsel' and giving it its ordinary meaning of 'advise, solicit or something of that sort', this court stated:

'There is no implication in the word itself that there should be any causal connection between counselling and the offence. [But] there must clearly be, first, contact between the parties, and, second, a connection between the counselling and the murder. So long as there is counsel-ling . . . so long as the principal offence is committed by the one counselled and so long as the one counselled is acting within the scope of his authority . . . we are of the view that the offence is made out.'

75. It thus appears that in such circumstances liability will be established unless:

'Considered as a matter of causation there . . . [is] . . . an overwhelming supervening event which is of such a character that it will relegate into history matters which would otherwise be looked upon as causative factors'

per Lord Parker CJ in *R v Anderson and Morris* [1966] 2 QB 110, [1966] 2 All ER 644 at 120, when considering the question of the liability of an accomplice for acts of a perpetrator which have gone beyond the parties' common purpose. Absent some such 'overwhelming supervening event', if the secondary party is to avoid liability for assistance rendered to the perpetrator in respect of steps taken by the perpetrator towards the commission of the crime, only an act taken by him which amounts to countermanding of his earlier assistance and a withdrawal from the common purpose will suffice.

■ *Question*

Can there be a case of aiding, abetting or counselling where the parties have not met and have not discussed the offence? Cf *Mohan v R* [1967] 2 All ER 58, [1967] 2 AC 187, PC.

8.4.1.2 Abetting

Where D did not 'procure' the commission of the offence and did not 'aid' the principal, the prosecution may rely on the fact that he encouraged ('abetted') its commission. The natural meaning of 'abet' is 'to incite, instigate or encourage'. It is probably not necessary to prove that P was influenced in any way by D, but he must at least be aware that he has the authority, encouragement, or approval of D to do the relevant acts.

■ *Questions*

To what extent must D realize that his conduct is encouraging or may have the effect of encour-aging the actions of P? Can there be encouragement without D agreeing with P what he will do?

If X and Y agree to race in a dangerous manner in cars on the highway and one of them runs down and kills a pedestrian, both are guilty of causing death by dangerous driving and pos-sibly of manslaughter. It is immaterial that it is impossible to identify the actual killer: the one who did not kill was an accessory and may be indicted and convicted as a principal: *Swindall and Osborne* (1846) 2 Car & Kir 230, 175 ER 95. Williams (TBCL 360) suggests that this result depends on the agreement to race. He contrasts the following case:

> D1, driving a car, passes D2. D2, angered by this, accelerates to pass D1; and so a kind of competition develops between the two drivers, and each drives at a negligent speed. A pedestrian is killed by one of the drivers, it is not known which. Only the driver who killed the pedestrian is guilty of manslaughter; and if his identity cannot be established, neither driver can be convicted of this crime. Here neither driver wished the other to drive at speed or intended to give him encouragement in the affair. Knowingly causing another person to act is not sufficient to constitute incitement to do it.

Perhaps it is not sufficient to constitute *incitement* (now an offence under the Serious Crime Act 2007, s 44) but it does not necessarily follow that it is insufficient to constitute aiding and abetting. If D1 and D2 are passing and repassing each must know that his conduct is an encouragement to the other.

It does not matter in such cases that there is no prior agreement between the parties. In *Turner* [1991] Crim LR 57, the court accepted that there was no suggestion that there had been any prior arrangement to race. L lost control, collided with an oncoming car and killed his own passenger. He had pleaded guilty to causing death by reckless driving. The prosecution's case against T was that he aided and abetted L. T's appeal against conviction for causing death by reckless driving was dismissed. The jury had been properly directed that they had to be sure, first, that L and T were racing and, secondly, that the racing was a cause of the passenger's death.

■ Questions

If two drivers are racing (whether by prior agreement or not) does it necessarily follow that each is encouraging the other to drive dangerously? Or should the jury be directed that they must be sure that the principal was in fact encouraged, and the alleged abettor knew that he was encouraging him?

8.4.1.3 Counselling

D might also commit the actus reus of being a secondary party by counselling the principal offender. To 'counsel' means to advise or solicit or encourage.

R v Calhaem
[1985] 2 All ER 266, Court of Appeal, Criminal Division

(Parker LJ, Tudor Evans J and Sir John Thompson)

The prosecution alleged that Calhaem (C) hired Zajac (Z) to murder Mrs Rendell (R), C's rival for the affections of her solicitor. Z, the principal witness for the prosecution, testified to the hiring and said that he went to R's house, armed but with no intention of killing her; that he intended only to act out a charade so that C and R would think an attempt had been made; but that, when R screamed, he went berserk and killed her. It was argued, *inter alia*, that the judge had misdirected the jury by not telling them that, as in the case of procuring, the counselling by C must have been a 'substantial cause' of the killing. C's appeal was dismissed.

[Parker LJ, having cited *A-G's Reference (No 1 of 1975)*, section 8.4.1, continued:]

> We must therefore approach the question raised on the basis that we should give to the word 'counsel' its ordinary meaning, which is, as the judge said, 'advise', 'solicit', or something of that sort. There is

no implication in the word itself that there should be any causal connection between the counselling and the offence. It is true that, unlike the offence of incitement at common law, the actual offence must have been committed, and committed by the person counselled. To this extent there must clearly be, first, contact between the parties, and, second, a connection between the counselling and the murder. Equally, the act done must, we think, be done within the scope of the authority or advice, and not, for example, accidentally when the mind of the final murderer did not go with his actions. For example, if the principal offender happened to be involved in a football riot in the course of which he laid about him with a weapon of some sort and killed someone who, unknown to him, was the person whom he had been counselled to kill, he would not, in our view, have been acting within the scope of his authority; he would have been acting entirely outside it, albeit what he had done was what he had been counselled to do.

■ *Question*

What is the difference between 'connection' and 'cause'?

It is clearly the law that an attempt to counsel does not amount to counselling. Proffered advice or encouragement which has no effect on the mind of the principal offender is not counselling. There is, however, no need for the prosecution to prove that D's counselling was a cause of the commission of the offence by P.

To what extent can D be liable for counselling P if P goes beyond anything D had envisaged or sought to encourage? Note that the secondary liability is derivative (section 8.2, p 216) so the liability of D is only triggered once the full offence is committed by P. By contrast, with inchoate liability, D can be liable for his particular act of encouragement irrespective of what, if anything, P goes on to do.

8.4.1.4 Procuring

The final way in which the defendant can act as an accessory is as a procurer. The Court of Appeal in *A-G's Reference (No 1 of 1975)*, section 8.4.1, p 219, explained that 'To procure means to "produce by endeavour." You cannot procure an offence unless there is a causal link between what you do and the commission of the offence.'

Can D be guilty of procuring P to commit only the conduct element of the offence?

As we saw in section 8.3.4 when discussing innocent agents, if Dawn causes a 9-year-old, or the postman (who acts without the fault required for the offence), or an insane person (who has a defence) to do the act which kills or causes GBH, she causes the harm in law as well as in fact and is liable accordingly as the principal. Once the causation element is satisfied, she fits the definition of the offence. She has herself done what the law forbids.

But it is not every offence which can be committed through an agent. Consider bigamy. D, knowing that P's wife is alive, tells P that she is dead and persuades him to marry V. P has committed the actus reus of bigamy ('being married, marries') but is not guilty of that offence because he lacks mens rea. D has knowingly caused the commission of the actus reus but is it possible to say that he has himself committed it? D may be a bachelor but, whether he is or not, can it be said that he has, by his actions, 'married'? Is bigamy—except in the case of a proxy marriage—a crime which is capable of commission through an innocent agent? Consider the following case. *Millward* provides a mechanism for convicting D of procuring an actus reus by P even if P does not commit the full offence.

R v Millward

[1994] Crim LR 527, Court of Appeal, Criminal Division

(McCowan LJ, Scott Baker and Blofeld JJ)

H and M were charged with causing death by reckless driving. H was the driver and M was charged as an aider, abettor, counsellor, or procurer. The alleged recklessness was not in the manner of the driving but in taking the vehicle, a tractor with a defective towing mechanism, on the road. The trailer became detached and collided with an oncoming vehicle, causing death. The jury acquitted H and convicted M who appealed, arguing that the actus reus of the offence was never committed.

McCowan LJ:

We have been referred to a number of authorities.... The first is the case of *Thornton v Mitchell* [1940] 1 All ER 339. In that case a bus driver was charged with driving without due care and attention and driving without reasonable consideration for other road users contrary to section 12 of the Road Traffic Act 1930. The conductor was charged with aiding and abetting the offences. The bus had to be reversed. It was the duty of the conductor to signal to the driver that the road was clear, because the driver could not see. The conductor erroneously signalled that it was clear. Unfortunately, two pedestrians were knocked down and the injuries to one of them proved fatal. The driver of the bus was acquitted of the two charges against him, but the conductor was convicted. It was held that the conductor could not be convicted of aiding and abetting the principal in what the principal was not doing. He could not be convicted as a principal because, on the particular wording of section 12, only the driver could be guilty of the principal offence.

It seems to us that the ratio of this case is that the driver did not commit the *actus reus* of the offence of careless driving. He had driven with due care and attention. He had relied on the conductor's signals.

...*R v Cogan and Leak* [1975] 2 All ER 109, [1976] QB 217 ... in the view of this court, provides the greatest assistance as regards this appeal. In that case, Cogan was charged with the rape of Leak's wife. Leak was charged with aiding and abetting, counselling and procuring Cogan to commit the rape. Both men were convicted. The material facts can be summarised as follows. Leak took Cogan back to his house and told his wife that Cogan wanted to have sexual intercourse with her and he was going to see that she did. Leak's wife was unwilling but frightened of Leak. She did have intercourse with Cogan and did not struggle, although she was sobbing throughout the whole incident. Leak's statement amounted to a confession that he had procured Cogan to have sexual intercourse with his wife. Cogan was convicted upon the basis that although he genuinely believed that Leak's wife was consenting, he had no reasonable grounds for that belief. On the state of the law as perceived at that time, Cogan was, on that basis, guilty of rape. But between the trial and the appeal the case of *R v Morgan* was decided by the House of Lords. In *Morgan* it was held that the all important matter was the defendant's genuine belief, and not whether there were reasonable grounds for it. Cogan's conviction was therefore quashed and Leak contended that his conviction could not stand following Cogan's acquittal.

Certain passages in that authority are of importance. Lawton LJ, giving the judgment of the court, said at 223C:

'Her ravishment had come about because Leak had wanted it to happen and had taken action to see that it did by persuading Cogan to use his body as the instrument for the necessary physical act. In the language of the law the act of sexual intercourse without the wife's consent was the actus reus: it had been procured by Leak who had the appropriate mens rea, namely, his intention that Cogan should have sexual intercourse with her without her consent. In our judgment it is irrelevant that the man whom Leak had procured to do the physical act himself did not intend to have sexual intercourse with the wife without her consent. Leak was using him as a means to procure a criminal purpose.

> . . . [The 1861 Act] allowed Leak to be tried and punished as a principal offender. In our judg-
> ment he could have been indicted as a principal offender. It would have been no defence for him
> to submit that if Cogan was an "innocent" agent, he was necessarily in the old terminology of
> the law a principal in the first degree, which was a legal impossibility as a man cannot rape his
> own wife during cohabitation. The law no longer concerned itself with niceties of degrees in
> participation in crime; but even if it did Leak would still be guilty. The reason a man cannot by his
> own physical act rape his wife during cohabitation is because the law presumes consent from the
> marriage ceremony . . .'

The law on that has since changed.

> 'Had Leak been indicted as a principal offender, the case against him would have been clear be-
> yond argument. Should he be allowed to go free because he was charged with "being aider and
> abettor to the same offence"? If we are right in our opinion that the wife had been raped (and
> no one outside a court of law would say that she had not been), then the particulars of offence
> accurately stated what Leak had done, namely, he had procured Cogan to commit the offence.
> This would suffice to uphold the conviction. We would prefer, however, to uphold it on a wider
> basis. In our judgment convictions should not be upset because of mere technicalities of plead-
> ing in an indictment. Leak knew what the case against him was and the facts in support of that
> case were proved. But for the fact that the jury thought that Cogan in his intoxicated condition
> might have mistaken the wife's sobs and distress for expressions of her consent, no question
> of any kind would have arisen about the form of pleading. By his written statement Leak virtu-
> ally admitted what he had done. As Judge Chapman said in *R v Humphreys* [1965] 3 All ER 689,
> 692: "It would be anomalous if a person who admitted to a substantial part in the perpetration
> of a misdemeanour as aider and abettor could not be convicted on his own admission merely be-
> cause the person alleged to have been aided and abetted was not or could not be convicted." In
> the circumstances of this case it would be more than anomalous: it would be an affront to justice
> and to the common sense of ordinary folk. It was for these reasons that we dismissed the appeal
> against conviction.'

In our judgment, what is of particular relevance in this case, as emerges from the case of *Cogan and Leak*, is whether the actus reus has been committed by the principal offender. In the present case Hodgson, the co-defendant, was acquitted because he lacked, in the view of the jury, the necessary element of mens rea.

Mr MacDonald [for the appellant] seeks to distinguish *Cogan and Leak* on two grounds. In the first place, he says that in this area of the law each case has to be decided and dealt with upon its own facts. Secondly, he says that *Cogan* was in reality a case of aiding and abetting rather than of pro-curing. He contends that this is an important distinction. He says too that in that case Leak was present and that he could not, in such circumstances, have been convicted in his absence. In our view, whilst there may in many cases be an overlap between aiding and abetting, on the one hand, and counsel-ling or procuring on the other, we do not think that that is of any significance in this case. Essentially, it would seem to us, the case of *Cogan and Leak* was a case of procuring, as indeed is the present case. In this court's view, it is impossible to find any significant distinction between the case of *Cogan and Leak* and the present case.

Support is to be found in *Blackstone's Criminal Practice* 3rd edn 1993, p 69 where the author says, having made earlier reference to *Cogan and Leak*:

> 'There is some debate over the precise principle involved in these cases but everyone agrees that
> the result is just. To say that the liability is really that of a principal acting through an innocent
> agent can cause problems where the accused lacks some characteristic essential for liability as a
> principal, for example, if in *Cogan* it had been a woman, rather than Mrs Leak's husband, who
> had terrorised her into submitting to intercourse. The definition of rape in the Sexual Offences
> Act 1956, s 1, requires it to be committed by a man, whereas there is no problem in convicting a
> person as accessory to an offence which he or she cannot commit as a principal (see *Ram* (1893)

17 Cox CC 609, woman as accessory to rape). Thus it is probably preferable to adopt the principle that an accessory can be liable provided that there is the actus reus of the principal offence even if the principal offender is entitled to be acquitted because of some defence personal to himself. It may well be, however, that this principle is limited to cases where the accessory has procured the *actus reus* (ie, has caused it to be committed as in the case of *Bourne* and *Cogan*). This would also be consistent with the position stated above that procuring does not mean a common intention between the accessory and the principal, whereas other forms of aiding and abetting generally do. If the principal lacks the *mens rea* of the offence there can hardly be a common intention that it should be committed. But this is not required for procuring.'

In our view, that passage from *Blackstone* correctly sets out the law. It is necessary to refer briefly to one further authority. That is the case of *R v Calhaem* [section 8.4.1.3, p 224] . . .

[McCowan LJ quoted from the judgment and continued:]

Then this sentence appears:

'Of course, the law is that the offence must have been committed before anyone can be convicted as an abettor or counsellor of it.'

We do not think that too much should be read into those words of Parker LJ in that case. In the first place, what the case was concerned with was causal connection. But it may well be that what he was in reality saying was that before anyone can be convicted as abettor or counsellor, the actus reus of the offence must be committed. In any event, the earlier decision in *Cogan and Leak* does not appear to have been referred to, or considered at all, by the court in *Calhaem*.

In this court's view, it is the authority of *Cogan and Leak* that is relevant to the decision that we have to make. In this court's view, the actus reus in the present case was the taking of the vehicle in the defective condition on to the road so as to cause the death of the little boy. It was procured by this appellant. The requisite mens rea was, in our judgment, present on the jury's fihat is relevant to the decision that we have to make. In this court's view, the actus reus in the present case was the taking of the vehicle in the

Appeal dismissed

The principle in *Millward* can apply only where there has been at least the actus reus performed by P. Causing death by reckless driving, which was the offence in issue in that case, has since been replaced by the offence of causing death by dangerous driving. The actus reus of the new offence is more precisely defined and it includes the situation where 'it would be obvious to a competent and careful driver that driving the vehicle in its current state would be dangerous.' In *Loukes* [1996] 1 Cr App R 444, [1996] Crim LR 341, the propeller shaft of a tipper truck broke while it was being driven on a motorway, causing the truck to crash into a car and kill its driver. The judge directed the jury to acquit the driver of causing death by dangerous driving: there was no evidence on which a jury could find that it would have been obvious to a competent and careful driver that driving the vehicle in its current state would be dangerous. The judge directed that the appellant, L, who was responsible for the maintenance of the vehicle could be guilty as a secondary party to the offence. His conviction was quashed: there was no actus reus by the driver, so L could not be held to have procured one. See commentary on *Loukes* [1996] 1 Cr App R 444, [1996] Crim LR 341.

Millward was followed in *Wheelhouse* [1994] Crim LR 756 where P and W were charged with burglary by stealing a car from V's garage. P took the car and it was alleged that W procured him to do so. The jury acquitted P, probably because they thought that W may have persuaded P that the car belonged to him, and convicted W. W's appeal was dismissed. But was it necessary to invoke the controversial decision in *Millward*?

It is necessary to invoke the *Millward* principle only where the crime is one which is incapable of being committed by an innocent agent, like rape, bigamy or a driving offence.

To be clear, if D has caused P to perform the actus reus with P having an innocent state of mind, D will either be liable as a principal because P is an innocent agent or D will be liable for procuring P's actus reus if the offence is one that P cannot commit as a principal in person.

The question of whether D can be guilty of procuring P's actus reus had been much discussed long before *Millward*. In *Bourne* (1952) 36 Cr App R 125, CCA, a man was held guilty of aiding and abetting his wife to commit buggery with a dog, although she could not have been convicted because she was acting under duress by him. Cross ((1953) 68 LQR 354) argued that the decision was correct in principle because 'The wife committed the actus reus with the mens rea required by the definition of the crime in question and the husband participated in that mens rea.' The wife had mens rea because she knew exactly what she was doing. That would not explain *Cogan and Leak*, cited in *Millward*, where Cogan may have believed that Mrs Leak was consenting to the sexual intercourse, in which case he committed the actus reus *without* mens rea. Lawton LJ gave two reasons:

(i) that Leak might have been convicted as a principal; but everything that Leak did could have been done by a woman and it would be nonsense to say that a woman could be guilty of rape (which requires penile penetration) as a principal; and

(ii) that Leak had procured the *crime of rape* (cf Glanville Williams, TBCL 371–372)—'no one outside a court of law would say that Mrs Leak had not been [raped]', but Lawton LJ was *in* a court of law.

It would take a bold person to tell Mrs Leak that she had not been raped; but, if Cogan thought she was consenting, she had not been raped by him. A similar argument could be advanced by someone who had had a valuable possession taken: they might think it has been stolen but if the person who took it did so mistaking it for his own similar article there was no theft. However, rightly or wrongly, the second reason given by the court in *Cogan and Leak* was that Leak had procured not merely the actus reus, but the offence, of rape by Cogan.

■ *Question*

Was either *ratio decidendi* of *Cogan and Leak*—(i) L was a principal, or (ii) L procured the commission of *the offence*—applicable to *Millward*?

The theory (advanced in every edition of *Smith and Hogan*), that procuring the actus reus of an offence is sufficient to make D liable for P's conduct, is criticized by S. Kadish (*Blame and Punishment: Essays in Criminal Law* (1987), p 180) saying that it 'at least technically ... amounts to creating a new crime'. The Law Commission (*Assisting and Encouraging Crime*, Consultation Paper No 131 (1993), para 4.207), writing before *Millward*, was also sceptical:

A prime danger of such a rule is that, in its anxiety to meet cases of the type just discussed (including *Bourne* and *Cogan and Leak*) it will reach too far.

■ *Questions*

1. Is the principle in *Millward* limited to procurers, as distinct from aiders, abettors and counsellors—who assist or encourage but do not, by their own acts, *cause*, the commission of the offence by another?

2. X, a married man, believes on reasonable grounds that his wife, Y, is dead. D knows she is alive. D persuades X to marry Z. E and F also know that Y is alive. E acts as best man at the wedding and F gives the bride away. Are D, E and F guilty of bigamy? Or is only D guilty?

We have considered the exceptional possibility of procuring an actus reus under *Millward*. A related problem on which there is little authority is that of the person who intentionally causes another to commit a crime by providing him with a motive. Sir James Fitzjames Stephen writing in the nineteenth century thought that if A told B of facts which gave B a motive to murder C and B did so, 'it would be an abuse of language to say that A had killed C, though no doubt he has been the remote cause of C's death'. He discusses Shakespeare's play, *Othello*. Iago wanted Othello to murder his wife, Desdemona, and caused him to do so by persuading him that Desdemona was committing adultery with his lieutenant, Cassio. Stephen remarks:

I am inclined to think that Iago could not have been convicted as an accessory before the fact to Desdemona's murder, but for one single remark—'do it not with poison, strangle her in her bed'.

Sanford Kadish (*Blame and Punishment: Essays in Criminal Law* (1987), p 166) disagrees with this reasoning, pointing out that it is not necessary to prove that a secondary party to murder 'killed', only that his actions make him responsible for killing by another. Iago has certainly in fact caused Othello's act but, as Othello is the principal, Iago is not regarded in law as having caused Desdemona's death. But this is true of secondary parties generally. Is there any reason why, if these facts were proved, Iago should not be held liable as an accessory, even if he had never expressly encouraged Othello to kill? Did he not procure the killing by endeavour?

Of course Iago was telling Othello a pack of lies and Kadish thinks the problem is different if the alleged accessory was telling the truth. Lies are evidence, or corroboration, of the intent. Suppose Desdemona really had been up to no good with Cassio and Iago had told Othello no more than the truth, but with the same object of provoking him into killing her.

8.4.1.5 Actus reus of secondary parties—further issues

We have now considered all four forms of actus reus of accessories – aiding, abetting, counselling and procuring. We must deal with three other issues.

- Does the accessory's actus reus (aiding, abetting, counselling or procuring) have to cause P's offence?

- Does the accessory's liability only arise from his acts or can the actus reus (aiding, abetting, counselling or procuring) be satisfied by an omission?

- Can the actus reus of the secondary party be satisfied by proof of mere presence when P is committing the offence?

Accessories and causation

Suppose that Dawn hires Peter to beat up Victor and Peter does so. Section 18 of the Offences Against the Person Act 1861 provides that:

Whosoever shall unlawfully and maliciously . . . cause any grievous bodily harm to any person . . . with intent . . . to do some grievous bodily harm to any person . . . shall be liable to imprisonment for life.

Peter has committed this offence as a principal and Dawn who counselled and procured him to do so is liable as a secondary party. But why is not Dawn a principal? Has she not *caused* grievous bodily harm to Victor with intent—the very thing which the statute forbids? The beating up occurred only because she hired Peter to do it. In a very real sense Dawn did cause GBH to Victor; but in law she is not regarded as having caused the harm. The intervening voluntary act by Peter breaks the chain of causation. If this were not so, the legal distinction between principals and secondary parties would break down because in many, though not all, cases of secondary liability the secondary party, like Dawn in the example, *in fact* is a cause of the actus reus.

In *Kennedy (No 2)* [2007] UKHL 38 (section 3.2.3.3, p 57), the House of Lords reaffirmed this fundamental principle. Lord Bingham stated that:

17. . . . Professor Glanville Williams pointed out (at p 398) [in *'Finis* for *Novus Actus?'* (1989) 48 CLJ 391] that the doctrine of secondary liability was developed precisely because an informed voluntary choice was ordinarily regarded as a *novus actus interveniens* breaking the chain of causation:

> 'Principals cause, accomplices encourage (or otherwise influence) or help. If the instigator were regarded as causing the result he would be a principal, and the conceptual division between principals (or, as I prefer to call them, perpetrators) and accessories would vanish. Indeed, it was because the instigator was not regarded as causing the crime that the notion of accessories had to be developed. This is the irrefragable argument for recognising the *novus actus* principle as one of the bases of our criminal law. The final act is done by the perpetrator, and his guilt pushes the accessories, conceptually speaking, into the background. Accessorial liability is, in the traditional theory, 'derivative' from that of the perpetrator.'

Despite this, judges have sometimes stated that the basis of secondary liability is that D has caused P to commit the principal offence. For example, in *Mendez* [2010] EWCA Crim 516 Toulson LJ stated that:

18. At its most basic level, secondary liability is founded on a principle of causation, that a defendant (D) is liable for an offence committed by a principal actor (P) if by his conduct he has caused or materially contributed to the commission of the offence (with the requisite mental element); and a person who knowingly assists or encourages another to commit an offence is taken to have contributed to its commission.

If this were correct it would have the potential to collapse the distinction between principals and accessories demanded by *Kennedy*. Toulson LJ qualified this *dicta* somewhat in the subsequent case of *Stringer* [2011] EWCA Crim 1396:

48. It is well established that D's conduct need not cause P to commit the offence in the sense that 'but for' D's conduct P would not have committed the offence: see *R v Mendez*, para 23. But it is also established by the authorities referred to in *R v Mendez* that D's conduct must have some relevance to the commission of the principal offence; there must, as it has been said, be some connecting link. The moral justification for holding D responsible for the crime is that he has involved himself in the commission of the crime by assistance or encouragement, and that presupposes some form of connection between his conduct and the crime. The Law Commission observed in *Participating in Crime*, para 2.33:

> 'However, the precise nature of this sufficient connection is elusive. It is best understood, at least where D's conduct consists of assistance, as meaning that D's conduct has made a contribution to the commission of the offence.'

In 'Sir Michael Foster, Professor Williams and Complicity in Murder' (in D. Baker and J. Horder (eds), *The Sanctity of Life and the Criminal Law: The Legacy of Glanville Williams* (2013)) Sir Roger Toulson expanded upon what he meant by this in the following terms.

It is plainly right and just that there should have to be some 'connecting link'. It would be morally repugnant to find a person guilty of murder for behaving in a way which on a fair view was unconnected with the crime. However, I would regard it as morally and pragmatically justifiable to hold that where P commits an offence with D's knowing assistance or encouragement, D is taken to have contributed to the offence, even if his assistance or encouragement may have been inessential. This analysis involves a concept of causation which is appropriate to the context. I do not see an alternative foundation on which secondary liability can satisfactorily be said to rest. The verdict of a jury that X murdered Y carries with it a necessary judgment that X was in some way responsible for Y's death.

Although there must be some 'connecting link' between D's act and P's commission of the offence, that is different from saying that D must have caused it.

Accessories and omissions

Can the secondary party be liable for aiding, abetting, counselling or procuring by omission or inactivity?

D can be liable as an accessory to P where the law imposes a *duty* on D to act. Thus, a husband who stands by and watches his wife drown their children is guilty of abetting the homicide.

D can also be liable as an accessory to P's crime if D has a *power or right to control* the actions of another and he deliberately refrains from exercising it, his inactivity *may* be a positive encouragement to the other to perform an illegal act, and, therefore, an aiding and abetting. If a licensee of a public house stands by and watches his customers drinking after hours (principal offence committed by them), he is guilty of aiding and abetting them in doing so: *Tuck v Robson* [1970] 1 All ER 1171.

In *Du Cros v Lambourne* [1907] KB 40, D was charged with driving his Mercedes motor car at a speed dangerous to the public (about 50 mph), contrary to s 8 of the Motor Car Act 1903. A number of witnesses testified that D was driving the car but D and three other persons gave evidence that it was being driven by Miss Victoria Godwin, a 'certified expert motor-car driver'. The Court of Quarter Sessions were satisfied that, whether D or Godwin was driving, he must have known that the speed at which the car was being driven was very dangerous to the public, having regard to the locality and all the circumstances of the case. If Godwin was driving, she was doing so with the consent and approval of D, who was the owner and in control of the car and was sitting by her side, and he could and ought to have prevented her driving at such excessive and dangerous speed, but instead he allowed her to do so and did not interfere in any way. They held that it was therefore unnecessary to decide whether D was himself driving or not. The Divisional Court (Alverstone LCJ, Ridley and Darling JJ) agreed. Alverstone LCJ said:

It is impossible to come to any other conclusion than that the court was satisfied that the appellant was doing acts which would amount to aiding, abetting, counselling or procuring.

Darling J said (1906) 21 Cox CC 311 at 316, that allowing Godwin to drive:

...was precisely the same thing as if he did it himself. He had authority and power to interfere but he did not do so although he knew the car was being driven at excessive speed. It seems to me that it is a misuse of language to say that he was not driving the motor-car.

But Darling J evidently had second thoughts because this passage does not appear in his revised judgment in [1907] 1 KB 40 at 46. Were his lordship's second thoughts best?

In *Webster* [2006] EWCA Crim 415, the Court of Appeal approved *Du Cros v Lambourne*, holding that:

a defendant might be convicted of aiding abetting dangerous driving if the driver drives dangerously in the owner's presence *and with the owner's consent and approval*.

Webster emphasizes that it must be proved that D knew of those features of P's driving which rendered it dangerous and failed to take action within a reasonable time. The court in *Webster* recognized the need to establish not only knowledge of the dangerous driving but knowledge at a time when there was an opportunity to intervene. 'In pursuance of this... approach, we conclude that the prosecution had to prove that [D] knew that [P] was, by virtue of the speed the vehicle was travelling, driving dangerously at a time when there was an opportunity to intervene. It was [D's] failure to take that opportunity and, exercise his right as owner of the vehicle, which would lead to the inference that he was associating himself with the dangerous driving.'

■ *Questions*

If the Crown can prove that it must have been either D or P who was driving but not which, can both D and P be convicted of dangerous driving? What if it was D's car?

Mere presence at the scene as a sufficient actus reus for secondary liability

In most cases, there is some conduct on the part of D which is clearly evidence of his assisting or encouraging P, over and above D's 'mere' presence. In some rare cases, however, the question arises whether D can be held to be aiding and abetting, counselling or procuring simply by being there.

Can mere voluntary presence, without anything more, satisfy the conduct element of secondary liability? What about presence with an intention to encourage satisfy the conduct element of secondary liability? Consider the following cases.

R v Allan

[1963] 2 All ER 897, Court of Criminal Appeal

(Edmund Davies, Marshall and Lawton JJ)

The appellants were convicted of making an affray at common law (see now s 3 of the Public Order Act 1986) and appealed on the ground of misdirection.

Edmund Davies J:

In effect, it amounts to this: that the learned judge ... directed the jury that they were in duty bound to convict an accused who was proved to have been present and witnessing an affray if it was also proved that he nursed an intention to join in if help was needed by the side which he favoured, and this notwithstanding that he did nothing by words or deeds to evince his intention and outwardly played the role of a purely passive spectator. It was said that, if that direction is right, where A and B behave themselves to all outward appearances in an exactly similar manner, but it be proved that A had the intention to participate if needs be, whereas B had no such intention, then A must be convicted of being a principal in the second degree to the affray, whereas B should be acquitted. To do that, it is objected, would be to convict A on his thoughts, even though they found no reflection in his actions. For the Crown, on the other hand, it is contended that the direction was unimpeachable, and that, in the given circumstances, a jury doing its duty would be bound to convict A of aiding and abetting in an affray, even though he uttered no word of encouragement and acted throughout in exactly the same manner as all the other spectators of what was happening.

Applying [passages in *Coney*] to the direction in the present case, we have come to the conclusion that, in effect, the trial judge here dealt with facts which, at most, might provide some evidence of encouragement as amounting to conclusive proof of guilt. The jury were in terms told that a man who chooses to remain at a fight, nursing the secret intention to help if the need arose, but doing nothing to evince that intention, *must* in law be held to be a principal in the second degree and that, on these facts being proved, the jury would have no alternative but to convict him. In our judgment, that was a misdirection. As Cave J said in *Coney* [(1882) 8 QBD 534 at 540], 'Where presence is prima facie not accidental it is evidence, but no more than evidence, for the jury', and it remains no more than evidence for the jury even when one adds to presence at an affray a secret intention to help. No authority in support of the direction given in the present case has been cited to us. The passage in *Young* [(1838) 8 C & P 644 at 652] cited in *Coney* [(1882) 8 QBD 534 at 541], is incomplete, and reference to the report itself makes clear that Vaughan J was there dealing with presence at a fight as the result of a previous arrangement. The only other case cited by the Crown, *Wilcox v Jeffery* [later in this section, p 235] turned on special facts very different from the present, and is one from which we think no general principle can be deduced. In the present case, the trial judge dealt with matters of evidence from which encouragement (and, therefore, guilty participation) might be inferred if—but only if—the jury thought fit to do so as necessarily amounting in law to proof that guilt was established. In our judgment, this amounted to a misdirection, and one, unfortunately, of a basic kind.

Appeals allowed

■ *Questions*

1. Did Allan intend that the principal would be assisted or encouraged?
2. Did Allan do any act of assistance or encouragement? What?

Mere presence at the scene of a crime is *capable* of constituting encouragement or assistance, but a person is not necessarily guilty as a secondary party merely because he is present and does nothing to prevent the crime

R v Clarkson and Carroll

[1971] 3 All ER 344, Courts-Martial Appeal Court

(Megaw LJ, Geoffrey Lane and Kilner Brown JJ)

The appellants, soldiers, entered a room in their barracks in which a girl was being raped by other soldiers. They were charged with aiding and abetting the rape. There was no evidence that either had done any act or uttered any word which involved direct physical participation or verbal encouragement. They appealed on the ground of misdirection by the judge-advocate.

Megaw LJ [delivered the judgment of the court:]

Coney [(1882) 8 QBD 534] decided that non-accidental presence at the scene of the crime is not conclusive of aiding and abetting. The jury has to be told by the judge, or as in this case the court-martial has to be told by the judge-advocate, in clear terms what it is that has to be proved before they can convict of aiding and abetting; what it is of which the jury or the court-martial, as the case may be, must be sure as matters of inference before they can convict of aiding and abetting in such a case where the evidence adduced by the prosecution is limited to non-accidental presence. [His lordship quoted from *Coney* (1882) 8 QBD 534 at 557, 558.] It is not enough, then, that the presence of the accused has, in fact, given encouragement. It must be proved that he *wilfully* encouraged. In such a case as the present, more than in many other cases where aiding and abetting is alleged, it was essential that that element should be stressed; for there was here at least the possibility that a drunken man with his self-discipline loosened by drink, being aware that a woman was being raped, might be attracted to the scene and might stay on the scene in the capacity of what is known as a voyeur; and, while his presence and the presence of others might in fact encourage the rapers or discourage the victim, he himself, enjoying the scene or at least standing by assenting, might not intend that his presence should offer encouragement to rapers and would-be rapers or discouragement to the victim; he might not realise that he was giving encouragement; so that, while encouragement there might be, it would not be a case in which, to use the words of Hawkins J [(1882) 8 QBD 534 at 558] the accused person wilfully encouraged. [His lordship quoted *Allan*, the previous extract, p 233.]

　　From that it follows that mere intention is not in itself enough. There must be an intention to encourage; and there must also be encouragement in fact, in cases such as the present case.

Appeals allowed

> ■ *Question*
>
> D, a student, continues to share a room with P whom D knows to be in unlawful possession of drugs. Is D aiding abetting P's drug possession? Consider the next case.

Wilcox v Jeffery

[1951] 1 All ER 464, King's Bench Division

(Lord Goddard CJ, Humphreys and Devlin JJ)

Lord Goddard CJ:

This is a case stated by the metropolitan magistrate at Bow Street Magistrates' Court before whom the appellant, Herbert William Wilcox, the proprietor of a periodical called *Jazz Illustrated*, was charged on an information that 'on 11 December 1949, he did unlawfully aid and abet one Coleman Hawkins in contravening art 1(4) of the Aliens Order 1920, by failing to comply with a condition attached to a grant of leave to land, to wit, that the said Coleman Hawkins should take no employment paid or unpaid while in the United Kingdom, contrary to art 18(2) of the Aliens Order 1920'. Under the Aliens Order, art 1(1), it is provided that

> '...an alien coming...by sea to a place in the United Kingdom—(a) shall not land in the United Kingdom without the leave of an immigration officer...'

It is provided by art 1(4) that:

> 'An immigration officer, in accordance with general or special directions of the Secretary of State, may, by general order or notice or otherwise, attach such conditions as he may think fit to the grant of leave to land, and the Secretary of State may at any time vary such conditions in such manner as he thinks fit, and the alien shall comply with the conditions so attached or varied...'

If the alien fails to comply, he is to be in the same position as if he has landed without permission, ie he commits an offence.

The case is concerned with the visit of a celebrated professor of the saxophone, a gentleman by the name of Hawkins who was a citizen of the United States. He came here at the invitation of two gentlemen of the name of Curtis and Hughes, connected with a jazz club which enlivens the neighbourhood of Willesden. They, apparently, had applied for permission for Mr Hawkins to land and it was refused, but, nevertheless, this professor of the saxophone arrived with four French musicians. When they came to the airport, among the people who were there to greet them was the appellant. He had not arranged their visit, but he knew they were coming and he was there to report the arrival of these important musicians for his magazine. So, evidently, he was regarding the visit of Mr Hawkins as a matter which would be of interest to himself and the magazine which he was editing and selling for profit. Messrs Curtis and Hughes arranged a concert at the Princes Theatre, London. The appellant attended that concert as a spectator. He paid for his ticket. Mr Hawkins went on the stage and delighted the audience by playing the saxophone. The appellant did not get up and protest in the name of the musicians of England that Mr Hawkins ought not to be here competing with them and taking the bread out of their mouths or the wind out of their instruments. It is not found that he actually applauded, but he was there having paid to go in, and, no doubt, enjoying the performance, and then, lo and behold, out comes his magazine with a most laudatory description, fully illustrated, of this concert. On those facts the magistrate has found that he aided and abetted.

Reliance is placed by the prosecution on *Coney* [see the previous extract, p 234].

There was not accidental presence in this case. The appellant paid to go to the concert and he went there because he wanted to report it. He must, therefore, be held to have been present, taking part, concurring, or encouraging, whichever word you like to use for expressing this conception. It was an illegal act on the part of Hawkins to play the saxophone or any other instrument at this concert. The appellant clearly knew that it was an unlawful act for him to play. He had gone there to hear him, and his presence and his payment to go there was an encouragement. He went there to make use of the performance, because he went there, as the magistrate finds and was justified in finding, to get 'copy' for his newspaper. It might have been entirely different, as I say, if he had gone there and protested, saying: 'The musicians' union do not like you foreigners coming here and playing and you ought to get off the stage'. If he had booed, it might have been some evidence that he was not aiding and abetting. If he had gone as a member of a *claque* to try to drown the noise of the saxophone, he might very likely be found not guilty of aiding and abetting. In this case it seems clear that he was there, not only to approve and encourage what was done, but to take advantage of it by getting 'copy' for his paper. In those circumstances there was evidence on which the magistrate could find that the appellant aided and abetted, and for these reasons I am of opinion that the appeal fails.

Humphreys J:

I agree that there was evidence sufficient to justify the finding of the magistrate.

Devlin J:

I agree, and I wish to add only a word on the application of *Coney*. Counsel for the appellant sought to distinguish that case on the facts inasmuch as in *Coney* the performance, which was a prize fight, was illegal from beginning to end, whereas in the case we are considering the bulk of the concert was quite legal, the only part of the performance which was illegal being that which involved Mr Hawkins. That, however, is not, in my judgment, a distinction which affects the application to this case of the principle in *Coney*. It may well be that if a spectator goes to a concert he may explain his presence during an illegal item by saying that he hardly felt it necessary to get up and go out and then return when the performance resumed its legality, if I may so call it. It is conceivable that in such circumstances (and I should wish to consider it further if it ever arose) the presence of a person during one item might fall within the accidental or casual class was envisaged by Cave J. Here there was abundant evidence, apart from the mere fact of the appellant's presence, that he was making use of this item in the performance and that his attendance at that item was, therefore, deliberate. In those circumstances I think the principle in *R v Coney* applies, and that the magistrate was justified in drawing the inference which he did draw.

Appeal dismissed with costs

Would liability really depend on whether Wilcox applauded Hawkins?

■ **Question**

Bert and Ernie go to a pub on Saturday night. They know that during the evening an obscene performance lasting half an hour will be given by Vikki on the pole-dancing stage. Bert, who only drinks lemonade, goes because he relishes an obscene show. Ernie, who is not interested in the show, is only there for the beer. The licensee is convicted of keeping a disorderly house. Are Bert and Ernie guilty of abetting him?

8.5 Mens rea of the secondary party

The mens rea requirements of the secondary party are complex, but can be summarized in the following way:

(i) the secondary party must intend to assist or encourage the principal offender's conduct, or in the case of procuring, to bring the offence about; and

(ii) the secondary party must have knowledge as to the essential elements of the principal's offence (including any facts as to which the principal bears strict liability). This includes an awareness that the principal might act with mens rea.

The law is so lacking in clarity that the Law Commission was able to identify no fewer than four possible statements of the principles in the case law (see LC305, para 1.16).

8.5.1 Accessory's intention

It must be proved that D intended to do the acts which he knew to be capable of assisting or encouraging the commission of the crime. There are two elements—an intention to perform the act capable of encouraging or assisting and an intention, or a belief, that that act will be of assistance. Where D supplies a weapon to P, which P uses in a murder, proof of his intention will turn on whether D meant to hand it over (as opposed to accidentally leaving it and P discovering it) and whether D intended that this handing over would assist P.

Should intention to assist or encourage include oblique intention (ie does it suffice that D foresees that it is virtually certain that his act will assist P), or must it be D's purpose to assist P? Consider the next case.

National Coal Board v Gamble
[1958] 3 All ER 203, Queen's Bench Division

(Lord Goddard CJ, Slade and Devlin JJ)

The offence in question was one of using a motor lorry on a road with a load weighing more than that permitted, in contravention of the Motor Vehicles (Construction and Use) Regulations 1955, regs 68 and 104. The lorry was driven by Mallender, who was allowed to leave the NCB depot when it was overladen. Mallender's employers were convicted of the offence as principals. The Board was convicted of having aided, abetted, counselled and procured the commission of the offence by allowing the lorry to leave when overladen. They appealed by way of case stated. The facts appear sufficiently in the judgment of Devlin J.

[Lord Goddard delivered judgment dismissing the appeal.]

Devlin J:

A person who supplies the instrument for a crime or anything essential to its commission aids in the commission of it; and if he does so knowingly and with intent to aid, he abets it as well and is therefore guilty of aiding and abetting. I use the word 'supplies' to comprehend giving, lending, selling or any other transfer of the right of property. In a sense a man who gives up to a criminal a weapon which the latter has a right to demand from him aids in the commission of the crime as much as if he sold or lent the article, but this has never been held to be aiding in law (see *Lomas* (1913) 110 LT 239, and *Bullock* [1955] 1 All ER 15, [1955] 1 WLR 1). The reason, I think, is that in the former [*sic*, presumably 'latter' is intended] case there is in law a positive act and in the latter [*sic*, presumably 'former' is intended] only a negative one. In the transfer of property there must be either a physical delivery or a positive act of assent to a taking; but a man who hands over to another his own property on demand, although he may physically be performing a positive act, in law is only refraining from detinue [a tort now abolished]. Thus in law the former act is one of assistance voluntarily given and the latter is only a failure to prevent the commission of the crime by means of a forcible detention, which would not even be justified except in the case of felony. Another way of putting the point is to say that aiding and abetting is a crime that requires proof of mens rea, that is to say, of intention to aid as well as of knowledge of the circumstances, and that proof of the intent involves proof of a positive act of assistance voluntarily done. These considerations make it necessary to determine at what point the property in the coal passed from the Coal Board and what the Coal Board's state of knowledge was at that time. If the property had passed before the Coal Board knew of the proposed crime, there was nothing they could legally do to prevent the driver of the lorry from taking the overloaded lorry out on to the road. If it had not, then they sold the coal with knowledge that an offence was going to be committed.

[His lordship referred to the factual circumstances of the contract between the Coal Board and the Central Electricity Authority and the manner in which the lorry on the relevant occasion was overladen but the driver, M, was nevertheless given a ticket to leave the premises by the weighbridge operator Haslam. Haslam had informed Mallender that his load was nearly four tons overweight. Haslam asked Mallender whether he intended taking the load and Mallender said he would risk it; he then took the weight ticket from Haslam and left the colliery.]

In these circumstances prima facie the property in the coal passed on delivery to the carrier in accordance with r5 of s18 of the Sale of Goods Act 1893. If the delivery was complete after loading and before weighing, the Coal Board had not until after delivery any knowledge that an offence had been committed; but where weighing is necessary for the purpose of the contract, as for example in order to ascertain the price of an instalment, the property does not pass until the weight has been agreed. . . .

It was contended on behalf of the Coal Board that Haslam had no option after weighing but to issue the ticket for the amount then in the lorry. I think that this contention is unsound. In the circumstances of this case the loading must be taken as subject to adjustment; otherwise, if the contract were for a limited amount, the seller might make an over-delivery or an under-delivery which could not thereafter be rectified and the carrier might be contractually compelled to carry away a load in excess of that legally permitted. I think that the delivery of the coal was not completed until after the ascertained weight had been assented to and some act was done signifying assent and passing the property. *The property passed when Haslam asked Mallender whether he intended to take the load and Mallender said he would risk it and when the mutual assent was, as it were, sealed by the delivery and acceptance of the weight ticket. Haslam could, therefore, after he knew of the overload have refused to transfer the property in the coal.* [emphasis added]

This is the conclusion to which the justices came. Counsel for the Coal Board submits that it does not justify a verdict of guilty of aiding and abetting. He submits, first, that even if knowledge of the illegal purpose had been acquired before delivery began, it would not be sufficient for the verdict; and secondly, that if he is wrong about that, the knowledge was acquired too late, and the Coal Board was not guilty of aiding and abetting simply because Haslam failed to stop the process of delivery after it had been initiated.

On his first point counsel submits that the furnishing of an article essential to the crime with knowledge of the use to which it is to be put does not of itself constitute aiding and abetting; there must be proved in addition a purpose or motive of the defendant to further the crime or encourage the criminal. Otherwise, he submits, there is no mens rea.

I have already said that in my judgment there must be proof of intent to aid. I would agree that proof that the article was knowingly supplied is not conclusive evidence of intent to aid. *Fretwell* ((1862) Le & Ca 161) is authority for that. *Steane* [section 5.2.3, p 113] in which the defendant was charged with having acted during the war with intent to assist the enemy contrary to the defence regulations then in force, makes the same point. But prima facie—and *Steane* makes this clear also—a man is presumed to intend the natural and probable consequences of his acts and the consequence of supplying essential material is that assistance is given to the criminal. It is always open to the defendant, as in *Steane* to give evidence of his real intention; but in this case the defence called no evidence. The prima facie presumption is therefore enough to justify the verdict, unless it is the law that some other mental element besides intent is necessary to the offence.

This is what counsel for the Coal Board argues, and he describes the additional element as the purpose or motive of encouraging the crime. No doubt evidence of an interest in the crime or of an express purpose to assist it will greatly strengthen the case for the prosecution, but an indifference to the result of the crime does not of itself negative abetting. *If one man deliberately sells to another a gun to be used for murdering a third, he may be indifferent whether the third man lives or dies and interested only in the cash profit to be made out of the sale, but he can still be an aider and abettor.* [emphasis added] To hold otherwise would be to negative the rule that mens rea is a matter of intent only and does not depend on desire or motive.

. . .

[His lordship referred to cases supporting this view.]

The case chiefly relied on by counsel for the Coal Board was *Coney* ((1882) 8 QBD 534). In this case the defendants were charged with aiding and abetting an illegal prize fight at which they had been present. The judgments all refer to 'encouragement', but it would be wrong to conclude from that that proof of encouragement is necessary to every form of aiding and abetting. Presence on the scene of the crime without encouragement or assistance is no aid to the criminal; the supply of essential material is. Moreover, the decision makes it clear that encouragement can be inferred from mere presence. Cave J, who gave the leading judgment, said of the summing up (ibid, at p 543):

> 'It may mean either that mere presence unexplained is evidence of encouragement, and so of guilt, or that mere presence unexplained is conclusive proof of encouragement, and so of guilt. If the former is the correct meaning, I concur in the law so laid down, if the latter, I am unable to do so.'

This dictum seems to me to support the view which I have expressed. If voluntary presence is prima facie evidence of encouragement and therefore of aiding and abetting, it appears to me to be a fortiori that the intentional supply of an essential article must be prima facie evidence of aiding and abetting.

As to counsel for the Coal Board's alternative point, I have already expressed the view that the facts show an act of assent made by Haslam after knowledge of the proposed illegality and without which the property would not have passed. If some positive act to complete delivery is committed after knowledge of the illegality, the position in law must, I think, be just the same as if the knowledge had been obtained before the delivery had been begun. Of course, it is quite likely that Haslam was confused about the legal position and thought that he was not entitled to withhold the weight ticket. There is no mens rea if the defendant is shown to have a genuine belief in the existence of circumstances which, if true, would negative an intention to aid; see *Wilson v Inyang* ([1951] 2 KB 799, [1951] 2 All ER 237). This argument, however, which might have been the most cogent available to the defence, cannot now be relied on, because Haslam was not called to give evidence about what he thought or believed. . . .

[Slade J dissented, holding that an aider and abettor must be shown to have assisted or encouraged and that 'assist' and 'encourage' necessarily import motive. There was no evidence that Haslam was inspired by a desire to encourage Mallender to commit the offence.]

Appeal dismissed

The crucial question was when the property in the coal passed. Was it when loaded into the lorry or when the lorry was weighed? If the property had already passed by the time it was weighed, could the NCB be liable? If the property passed at the time the lorry was weighed, could the NCB have stopped the lorry leaving and by not stopping the lorry could they be held to have aided and abetted? If so, what mens rea must they have?

■ *Questions*

1. Does D have to have a purposive intent to assist P or will an oblique intention suffice?

2. Did those watching the rape in *Clarkson and Carroll* (section 8.4.1.5) have a direct intent to assist or encourage? Did they intend to encourage or were they merely reckless as to their presence having that effect?

3. D sells P poison which P says he will use to murder V. D thinks that there is a 50 per cent chance that P will do so. Has D aided and abetted murder? Consider the implications of the decision in *Gamble* for those selling goods—knives, guns, weedkiller, etc.

Confirmation of the sufficiency of oblique intent as a mens rea for an accessory is found in a more recent case.

R v Bryce
(section 8.4.1.1, p 222), http://www.bailii.org/ew/cases/EWCA/Crim/2004/1231.html

Potter LJ [stated the facts and the grounds of appeal:]

41. The required mens rea is the same for aiding, abetting counselling and procuring: see *R v Rook* [1993] 2 All ER 955 and [1993] Crim LR 698 and commentary thereto. . . .

42. . . . [I]t is necessary to show firstly that the act which constitutes the aiding, abetting etc was done intentionally in the sense of deliberately and not accidentally and secondly that the accused knew it to be an act capable of assisting or encouraging the crime. In this case, as in most cases, the first requirement will not be in issue. The act of taking X to the caravan with the gun was obviously done deliberately. However, on the defence which the appellant sought to advance through his counsel, the second requirement was implicitly in issue in that Mr Foy wished to submit to the jury that the appellant's actions were intended to impede rather than assist.

43. . . . [I]t is now well established that it is not necessary to prove that the secondary party at the time of the act of aiding, abetting etc intended the crime to be committed.

44. As Devlin J said in *National Coal Board v Gamble* [1958] 3 All ER 203, [1959] 42 CAR 240 at 250:

> 'If one man deliberately sells to another a gun to be used for murdering a third, he may be indifferent whether the third man lives or dies and interested only in the cash profit to be made out of the sale, but he can still be an aider and abetter.'

45. Thus, if it is proved that the defendant intended to do the acts of assistance or encouragement, it is no defence that he hoped that events might intervene to prevent the crime taking place. So, where the defendant drove the perpetrator to a place where he knew that the perpetrator intended to murder a policeman, his intentional driving of the car to that place amounted to an aiding and abetting of the offence despite his unwillingness that the killing should take place: see *Lynch v DPP for Northern Ireland* [1975] AC 653, [1975] 1 All ER 913, at 678 . . .

. . .

60. We have already seen that Devlin J, in *National Coal Board v Gamble* referred to an intent to aid and that in *Maxwell*, Sir Robert Lowry CJ referred to intentionally lending his assistance in order that the crime shall be committed, in a passage cited with approval by Lloyd LJ in *Rook*. Although in *Rook* the endorsement of the passage from *Smith and Hogan* and of the written direction includes no

reference to intent to assist, the Court had earlier approved the direction that the appellant must have done the various things 'intending to assist [the principals] to commit a murder.'

61. In *Criminal Law Theory and Doctrine*, Simester and Sullivan, 2000 the authors state that a secondary party must intend 'that his conduct will help or encourage P's actions' (page 198). 'It is the assistance, not the ultimate crime, that must be intended by' the secondary party.

62. *Blackstone's Criminal Practice 2004* (paragraph A 5.4, page 73) relying upon the passage from Devlin J in *National Coal Board v Gamble* which we have already cited, also states that there must be an intention to aid. The authors consider the case of *Lynch*:

'Thus in *DPP for Northern Ireland v Lynch* [1975] AC 653 the accused's alleged opposition to the principal offence did not preclude a finding that he intended to aid.'

63. The authors then consider the authorities such as *R. v Woollin* [1999] AC 82 which decide that a person may still intend to do something even though he does not desire it. The authors continue:

'*Gillick v West Norfolk and Wisbech Area Health Authority* [1986] AC 112 is an example of a type of case where the uncertainties of the precise meaning of intention effectively confer a perhaps welcome discretion on whether to impose responsibility. That case concerned, inter alia, the question of whether a doctor giving contraceptive advice or treatment to a girl under the age of 16 could be liable as accessory to a subsequent offence of unlawful sexual intercourse committed by the girl's sexual partner. The House of Lords held that generally this would not be the case (the action was a civil one for a declaration) since the doctor would lack the necessary intention (even though he realised that his actions would facilitate such intercourse). One rationale for the decision would be that a jury would not infer intention in such circumstances if they thought that the doctor was acting in what he considered to be the girl's best interests.

Similar reasoning could be applied to a troublesome group of cases involving the supply of articles for use in crime which the recipient already has some sort of civil right to receive. The general position seems to be that this is not aiding and abetting (see, for example, *Lomas* (1913) 9 Cr App R 220 concerning the return of a jemmy to its owner) because the alleged accessory does not intend to aid the offence but rather merely to comply with his supposed civil-law duties. Critics of this general position rightly point out that it can hardly apply to a person returning a revolver to its owner knowing that he is then going to use it to carry out a murder. But here a jury probably would infer intention to aid from the accused knowledge of the effects of his action, and the flexibility of the notion of intention enables an appropriate solution to be found to situations for which it is difficult to formulate precise rules in advance.

It is particularly important to stress the need for an intention to aid where the accused may not personally appreciate the natural and probable consequences of his action as in *Clarkson* [1971] 1 WLR 1402 where there was 'at least the possibility that a drunken man with his self-discipline loosened by drink . . . might not intend that his presence should offer encouragement to rapers; . . . he might nor realise that he was giving encouragement' (at p. 1406). The reference to intoxication underlines the fact that complicity normally requires intention rather than recklessness (*Blakely v DPP* [1991] Crim LR 763) and that, for the purposes of the Majewski rule (*DPP v Majewski* [1977] AC 443: see A3.10), complicity can be regarded as requiring specific intent.'

. . . [His lordship referred to *Powell* and *Daniels* (section 8.8.3) and rejected that decision as being of assistance.]

67. We return to *Lynch*. . . . The second certified question was:

'Where a person charged with murder as an aider and abettor is shown to have intentionally done an act which assists in the commission of the murder with knowledge that the probable result of his act, combined with the acts of those whom his act is assisting, will be the death or serious bodily injury of another, is his guilt thereby established *without the necessity of proving his willingness to participate in the crime*?' (emphasis added)

68. The emphasised words show that the second question was concerned with whether the secondary party must intend the crime to be committed. We have already set out the view of Lord Morris on that issue (see paragraph 45 above).

69. Lord Simon said at 698F that the majority in the Court of Appeal had held, rightly in his view, that the mens rea 'did not involve 'a specific intent'. Lord Simon continued at 698G–699B:

'As Devlin J said in *National Coalboard v Gamble* [1959] 1 QB 11, 20:

A person who supplies the instrument for a crime or anything essential to its commission aids in the commission of it; and if he does so knowingly and with intent to aid, he abets it as well and is therefore guilty of aiding and abetting.

The actus reus is the supplying of an instrument for a crime or anything essential for its commission. On Devlin J's analysis the mens rea does not go beyond this. The act of supply must be voluntary (in the sense I tried to define earlier in this speech), and it must be foreseen that the instrument or other object or service supplied will probably (or possibly and desiredly) be used for the commission of a crime. The definition of the crime does not in itself suggest any ulterior intent; and whether anything further in the way of mens rea was required was precisely the point at issue in *Gamble's* case. Slade J thought the very concept of aiding and abetting imported the concept of motive. But Lord Goddard CJ and Devlin J disagreed with this. So do I. Slade J thought that abetting involved assistance or encouragement, and that both implied motive. So far as assistance is concerned, this is clearing not so. One may lend assistance without any motive, or even with the motive of bringing about a result directly contrary to that in fact assisted by one's effort.'

70. Despite that passage, it seems to us, as to the authors *of Blackstone* (paragraph 63 above) that *Lynch* is not authority for the proposition that there does not have to be an intent to assist. We do not think that those words of Lord Simon were intended to go further than the words of Devlin J which he was approving. *Lynch* was concerned primarily with duress and secondly with whether it was necessary to show that the secondary party intended the commission of the crime committed by the perpetrator.

71. [In basic accessory liability cases] where a defendant, D, is charged as the secondary party to an offence committed by P in reliance on acts which have assisted steps taken by P in the preliminary stages of a crime later committed by P in the absence of D, it is necessary for the Crown to prove intentional assistance by D in the sense of an intention to assist (and not to hinder or obstruct) P in acts which D knows are steps taken by P towards the commission of the offence. Without such intention the mens rea will be absent whether as a matter of direct intent on the part of D or by way of an intent sufficient for D to be liable on the basis of 'common purpose' or 'joint enterprise'. Thus, the prosecution must prove:

  (a) an act done by D which in fact assisted the later commission of the offence,

  (b) that D did the act deliberately realising that it was capable of assisting the offence,

  (c) that D at the time of doing the act contemplated the commission of the offence by A ie he foresaw it as a 'real or substantial risk' or 'real possibility' and,

  (d) that D when doing the act intended to assist A in what he was doing.

Mere recklessness, still less negligence, whether assistance is given, is probably not enough. D's realization that he may have left his gun cupboard unlocked and that his son has a disposition to commit armed robbery, is probably not sufficient to fix D with liability for the armed robbery and homicide which the son commits using one of D's guns.

8.5.2 Accessory's knowledge of facts relating to P's crime

In addition to proof of intention, there is a further, yet more complex, element of the secondary party's mens rea: he must have knowledge of, or at least turn a blind eye to, the essential elements of the principal offence. He need not actually know that an offence has been committed, because he may not know that the facts constitute an offence and ignorance of the law is not a defence.

Johnson v Youden
[1950] 1 All ER 300, King's Bench Division

(Lord Goddard CJ, Humphreys and Lynskey JJ)

It was an offence under the Building Materials and Housing Act 1945, s 7, for a builder to sell a house at a price in excess of that fixed by the local authority in the licence to build the house. The three respondents, partners in a firm of solicitors, were charged with aiding and abetting a builder in an offence under this section and were acquitted. The prosecutor appealed.

Lord Goddard CJ:

...In this case the builder had a licence which entitled him to sell the house for £1,025. He induced a railway porter to agree to buy the house for £1,275, ie £250 more than the controlled price, and he instructed a firm of solicitors, in which the three respondents are partners, to act as his solicitors for the sale. The builder was charged with an offence against s 7(1) of the Act of 1945 and was convicted, but the three respondents were acquitted on charges of aiding and abetting him.

In regard to the respondents, the justices found that, until 6 April 1949, none of them knew anything about the extra £250 which the builder was receiving, and that the first two respondents, Mr Henry Wallace Youden and Mr George Henry Youden, did not know about it at any time, as the builder deliberately concealed the fact and even refused to give the purchaser a receipt for that £250. The justices, therefore, were right, in our opinion, in dismissing the information against the first two respondents on the ground that they could not be guilty of aiding and abetting the commission of the offence as they did not know of the matter which constituted the offence. If they had known that the builder was receiving the extra £250 and had continued to ask the purchaser to complete, they would have committed an offence by continuing to assist the builder to offer the property for sale, contrary to the provisions of s 7(1) of the Act of 1945, and, as ignorance of the law is no defence, they would have been guilty of the offence even if they had not realised that they were committing an offence, but a person cannot be convicted of aiding and abetting the commission of an offence if he does not know of the essential matters which would constitute the offence.

[The court held that in respect of the third partner the evidence was that correspondence from the builder gave him awareness of the additional £250 which ought not to have been charged. With that awareness he nevertheless arranged for the completion of the sale].

He was, therefore, clearly aiding and abetting the builder in the offence which the builder was committing.

Humphreys J:

I agree.

Lynskey J:

I also agree.

Appeal dismissed in respect of the first two respondents and allowed in respect of the third respondent. Case remitted to the justices with a direction to convict the third respondent. No order as to costs

8.5.2.1 'Knowledge'

This is a particularly difficult mens rea to establish. D does not 'know' (ie have true belief) of the circumstances unless he has first-hand knowledge of that fact. In view of the practical difficulties in proving D's knowledge as to future events, the courts have interpreted 'knowledge' as equivalent to D foreseeing (or in some cases turning a blind eye to) the likelihood of the essential matters. In *Bryce*, the court applied a slightly different formula, holding that it was sufficient that D did the act of assistance by transporting P to the scene, and at the time of doing that act 'contemplated a real possibility' of the commission of an offence of the type that P committed. Potter LJ in *Bryce* explained:

46. . . . As was stated by Lord Goddard CJ in *Johnson v Youden* [1950] 1 KB 544, [1950] 1 All ER 300 at 446:

'Before a person can be convicted of aiding and abetting the commission of an offence he must at least know the essential matters which constitute that offence.'

He went on to say:

'He need not actually know that an offence has been committed, because he may not know that the facts constitute an offence and ignorance of the law is not a defence. If a person knows all the facts and is assisting another person to do certain things, and it turns out that the doing of those things constitutes an offence, the person who is assisting is guilty of aiding an abetting that offence.'

This statement was approved by the House of Lords in *Maxwell v DPP for Northern Ireland* [1978] 3 All ER 1140, (1979) 68 Crim App R 128 HL.

47. Sir Robert Lowry CJ in *Maxwell* (supra) at 140–141 stated:

'[The secondary party's] guilt springs from the fact that he contemplates the commission of one (or more) of a number of crimes by the principal and he intentionally lends his assistance in order that such a crime shall be committed. In other words, he knows that the principal is committing or about to commit one of a number of specified illegal acts and with that knowledge helps him to do so.'

48. But does the secondary party actually have to know that the crime will be committed, as this passage suggests, or is something less sufficient? Lord Simon in *Lynch* 698G–699B cited Devlin J in *National Coalboard v Gamble* [1959] 1 QB 11, [1958] 3 All ER 203, 20 and continued:

'The act of supply must be voluntary (in the sense I tried to define earlier in this speech), and it must be *foreseen* that the instrument or other object or service supplied will *probably (or possibly and desiredly)* be used for the commission of a crime.' (Emphasis added)

49. Those words were uttered in respect of a person participating at the time of the commission of the offence by the actual perpetrator. However, in the context of a person charged as an accessory who has rendered assistance prior to the commission of the crime by the perpetrator, the circumstances in respect of which knowledge is sufficient for liability may go wider than that of the specific crime actually committed. This is because, as pointed out in *Blackstone's Criminal Practice* (2004) at A6.5 (p.75), it is inappropriate and unworkable to require knowledge of the essential matters constituting the offence in a situation where the offence is yet to be committed in the future or by a person of whose precise intentions the accused cannot be certain in advance. It is thus sufficient for the accused to have knowledge of the type of crime in contemplation. Thus where a person supplies equipment to be used in the course of committing an offence of a particular type, he is guilty of aiding and abetting the commission of any such offence committed by the person to whom he supplies the equipment, providing that he knows the purpose to which the equipment is to be put or realises that there is a real possibility that it will be used for that purpose and the equipment is actually used for that purpose: see *R v Bullock* [1955] 1 All ER 15, 38 Crim App R 151 and *R v Bainbridge* [1960] 1 QB 129, [1959] 3 All ER 200.

. . . [His lordship considered *Rook*.]

58. *Rook* is, in our view, authority for the proposition that it is not necessary to show that the secondary party intended the commission of the principal offence and that it is sufficient if the secondary party at the time of his actions relied on as lending assistance or encouragement contemplates the commission of the offence, that is knows that it will be committed or realises that it is a real possibility that it will be committed.

■ *Question*

Is the mens rea described in *Bryce* what you understand to be a test of knowledge?

Consider the next case where the principal offenders were drinkers in a bar who were drinking after-hours. The question was whether the licensee could be liable for aiding and abetting the drinkers despite having taken all steps to prevent them drinking after-hours. Knowledge cannot be imputed to D.

Ferguson v Weaving

[1951] 1 All ER 412, King's Bench Division

(Lord Goddard CJ, Hilbery and Devlin JJ)

The respondent was the licensee of a hotel with several rooms in which intoxicating liquor was served. She was charged with aiding, abetting, counselling and procuring customers to consume liquor after hours, contrary to the Licensing Act 1921, s 4(b), and acquitted. She had given signals to indicate the approach, and arrival, of closing time. (The law did not then allow 'drinking-up time'.) Waiters, in breach of the instructions given by the respondent, failed to collect glasses from the offending customers in the concert room. She was performing her duties in another part of the hotel; and the magistrate found that she had done everything she could to see that the requirements of the law were complied with. The prosecutor appealed.

Lord Goddard CJ [reading the judgment of the court:]

. . . In this case there is no substantive offence in the licensee at all. The substantive offence is committed only by the customers. She can aid and abet the customers if she knows that the customers are committing the offence, but we are not prepared to hold that knowledge can be imputed to her so as to make her, not a principal offender, but an aider and abettor. So to hold would be to establish a new principle in criminal law and one for which there is no authority. If Parliament had desired to make a licensee guilty of an offence by allowing persons to consume liquor after hours it would have been perfectly easy so to provide in the section. A doctrine of criminal law that a licensee who has knowledge of the facts is liable as [an accessory] is no reason for holding that, if she herself had no knowledge of the facts but someone in her employ and to whom she may have entrusted the management of the room did know them, this makes her an aider and abettor. As no duty is imposed on her by the section to prevent the consumption of liquor after hours there was no duty in this respect that she could delegate to her employees. While it may be that the waiters could have been prosecuted for aiding and abetting the consumers, as to which we need express no opinion, we are clearly of opinion that the respondent could not be. To hold the contrary would, in our opinion, be an unwarranted extension of the doctrine of vicarious responsibility in criminal law. The appeal will be dismissed with costs.

Appeal dismissed

■ *Question*

If the Licensing Act had made it an offence for a licensee to permit liquor to be consumed after-hours, would Weaving have been guilty of that offence?

8.5.2.2 'Knowledge' or 'recklessness' as to the essential elements?

Although the courts have adopted a broad interpretation of the knowledge that D must have as to P's crime, there are also circumstances in which recklessness or belief as to an essential element of P's crime may be sufficient mens rea for D. Consider the next case.

Blakely and Sutton v Director of Public Prosecutions
[1991] RTR 405, Queen's Bench Division

(Bingham LJ and McCullough J)

Blakely (B) was associating with Taft (T), a married man who was in the process of divorcing his wife. T sometimes spent the night with B. On 26 October 1988 T met B in a pub and told her that at the end of the evening he intended to drive home to his wife. B was upset. She knew that, when T intended to drive home, it was his invariable practice to drink two pints of beer and, thereafter, tonic water. After T had drunk his two pints, at Sutton's (S's) suggestion, B and S added vodka to T's tonic water. B intended to tell T what she had done when the time came for him to leave. B and S believed that T would not be willing to drive with an excess of alcohol. At closing time T went to the lavatory and then drove off before B and S could tell him what they had done. T was charged with, and pleaded guilty to, driving with an excess of alcohol. B and S were convicted by the justices, and on appeal by the Crown Court, of jointly aiding, abetting, counselling, procuring or commanding T to commit the offence.

The judge directed the justices that the defendants would be guilty of procuring if the jury were satisfied so as to be sure that the defendants deliberately set out to cause T to consume an amount of alcohol in excess of the level permitted for drivers and did so (the circumstance element of P's crime); and that in doing so they either knew that he would drive or were reckless as to whether or not he would drive (the conduct element of P's crime). The judge adopted the definition of 'recklessness' given by Lord Diplock in *Lawrence* (section 5.3, p 122) which has now been superseded, but the discussion of whether recklessness suffices is still relevant.

B and S appealed by way of case stated.

McCullough J concluded that the judge had been wrong: the liability of a secondary party depended on proof that the accused contemplated that his act would or might bring about, or assist the commission of, the principal offence. He must have been prepared nevertheless to do his own act, and he must have done that act intentionally.

In relation to those accused only of 'procuring' and perhaps also those accused only of 'counselling and commanding', it may be, as the judgment of Lord Goddard CJ in *Ferguson v Weaving* [1951] 1 KB 814, 819 would permit and as the judgment of Lord Widgery CJ in *A-Gs Reference (No 1 of 1975)* [1975] RTR 473, 477H–J strongly suggests, that it is necessary to prove that the accused intended to bring about the principal offence. The present case does not, however, require this to be decided.

...

Finally, I must deal with an alternative submission advanced by Mr McCahill. It is that since (i) the defendants laced Taft's drink with the intention of putting his blood-alcohol level over the statutory limit, (ii) at that time they knew that Taft intended to drive, and (iii) it was in consequence of their action that, when he drove, his blood-alcohol level was over the limit, it follows that they procured his offence.

I cannot accept this. The facts that Mr McCahill Lists omit the defendants' belief that when they, as they intended, told Taft what they had done he would not be prepared to drive. Mr McCahill seeks to relegate this important fact to oblivion by labelling it a 'secret hope' and saying that it derived from their motive, which was that he should spend the night with Blakely rather than drive home. This, in my view, is unrealistic. I accept that their motive was that he should spend the night with Blakely, but their intention to prevent him from driving was just as real as their knowledge that he intended to drink so little that he would be able lawfully to drive. On the facts which they found the court may well have convicted the defendants on the basis that they gave no thought to the risk that, despite their intention to tell him that they had laced his drink, he might nevertheless drive. On my understanding of the law that would have been wrong.

Appeal allowed

D's awareness of the risk of P committing the offence in this case relates to the conduct element of P's offence (driving).

Compare that with the case of *Carter v Richardson* [1974] RTR 314 which was concerned only with the circumstance element of P's offence (being over the limit).

The facts were that Carter was supervising Collin, a learner driver, whose blood-alcohol level exceeded the prescribed limit. Carter was a principal in the second degree (ie an accessory). The argument in the magistrates' court seems to have turned on whether there had to be evidence that Carter knew the exact amount of alcohol in the driver's blood or whether it was enough that he knew that the driver had consumed such a quantity of alcohol that the level in his blood must have been above the prescribed limit. The justices preferred the latter view and Carter was convicted.

Lord Widgery CJ held that they were right.

The word 'reckless' appears only once in the judgments. In *Carter v Richardson* [1974] RTR 314 Lord Widgery CJ said, at p 317H:

Going on through the justices' case, we find that they give as their opinion that: '...it was impossible for the defendant to know exactly how many milligrammes of alcohol there were in a millilitre of Collin's blood and that it sufficed that an aider and abettor was aware that the principal had consumed an excessive amount of alcohol or was reckless as to whether he had done so'—I pause there to say that for my part I think that is a correct statement of the law.'

This passage, however, stands alone. Everywhere else in his judgment Lord Widgery CJ spoke in terms of Carter's 'knowledge' or 'awareness': see the following, at p 318A, D–F:

The justices were right if they took the view that it was sufficient if the defendant was aware that the principal offender had consumed excessive alcohol...What is apparent from the case is that the justices saw fit to draw the inference that the defendant knew that Collin had had too much to drink, if I may put it in the colloquial sense...In my judgment they were perfectly entitled on the primary facts found to draw the further inference not only that the defendant knew that Collin had been drinking, but that the defendant knew that Collin had been drinking to such an extent that it was probable that his blood-alcohol content was over the limit. If that is established then the offence is established.

MacKenna J, who agreed with the judgment of Lord Widgery CJ, said, at p 318H:

...the justices were entitled to infer that he, when the car was stopped, either knew that Collin had too much alcohol in his blood or at least believed that it was probable that he had.

May J said no more than that he agreed.

In *Blakely* the court's test is drafted in terms of foresight of risk that an offence *might* be committed, which is a more relaxed test than foresight that an offence is probably being or will probably be committed.

The Draft Code, cl 27, which was intended to restate these two decisions, provided that:

a person is guilty of an offence as an accessory if:

(a) he intentionally procures or assists or encourages the act which constitutes or results in the commission of the offence by the principal; and

(b) he knows that, or (where recklessness suffices in the case of the principal) is reckless with respect to, any circumstance that is an element of the offence...

Carter would be guilty under this provision because he intentionally assisted or encouraged the act of driving (conduct), being reckless whether the driver had an excess of alcohol in his blood (circumstances).

Blakely, while she intended the *circumstance* (the excess of alcohol), did not intentionally procure the *act of driving* because her aim was to prevent T from driving.

■ *Questions*

Was the Code right? Or should it be the law that Blakely was guilty if she knew there was a risk that T might drive with excess alcohol?

In *Webster* [2006] EWCA Crim 415, the Court of Appeal allowed an appeal where D had been driving a vehicle and had then allowed P to drive, knowing that P was drunk. P drove dangerously and a passenger, V, was killed. P was charged with causing death by dangerous driving and D with aiding and abetting that crime. The court held that to establish secondary liability against D the prosecution had to prove that D did foresee that P was likely to drive dangerously, but it is not sufficient to prove that D *ought to have foreseen* that P would drive dangerously. The court went on (at [25]–[26]) to note the practical difficulties involved:

Generally the prosecution will be able to prove the actual state of mind of the defendant, absent any confession, by reference to what must have been obvious to him from all the surrounding circumstances. But it is important to distinguish between that which must have been obvious to a defendant and what the defendant foresaw. In most cases there will be no space between the two concepts; if the prosecution can prove what must have been obvious, it will generally be able to prove what the defendant did foresee. But the danger of eliding the two concepts, namely what the defendant did foresee and what he must have foreseen, is that it might suggest that it is sufficient to prove what the defendant ought to have foreseen. That is not enough. It is the defendant's foresight that the principal was likely to commit the offence which must be proved and not merely that he ought to have foreseen that the principal was likely to commit the offence.

The meaning of 'knowledge' has clearly been diluted to an incredible extent in this context. However, the courts are not, however, prepared to regard D's negligence as to the circumstances of P's crime as a sufficient mens rea: *Webster*. This is so even if P's crime is one of strict liability: *Callow v Tillstone* (1900) 83 LT 411.

8.5.2.3 Knowledge of the type of crime is sufficient

If D aids, abets, counsels or procures P to commit a crime of a certain 'type', neither party specifying any particular victim, time or place, D may be convicted as a secondary party to any crime of that type which P commits.

R v Bainbridge
[1959] 3 All ER 200, Court of Criminal Appeal

(Lord Parker CJ, Byrne and Winn JJ)

B was convicted of being accessory to office-breaking. The Stoke Newington branch of the Midland Bank was broken into by cutting the bars of a window, the doors of the strong room and of a safe inside the strong room. They were opened by means of oxygen cutting equipment and nearly £18,000 was stolen. B had bought the cutting equipment six weeks earlier. The prosecution alleged that he bought it on behalf of one or more of the thieves and that he knew that it was going to be used, if not against that branch, for the purposes of breaking and entering premises.

Lord Parker CJ [delivered the following judgment of the court:]

The appellant's case, as given in his evidence, was this: 'True, I had bought this equipment from two different firms. I had gone there with a man called Shakeshaft to buy it for him. As a result of conversation which I had with him, I was suspicious that he wanted it for something illegal. I thought it was for breaking up stolen goods which Shakeshaft had received, and, as the result, in making those purchases I gave false names and addresses; but I had no knowledge that the equipment was going to be used for any such purpose as that for which it was used.'

The complaint here is that Judge Aarvold, who tried the case, gave the jury a wrong direction in regard to what it was necessary for them to be satisfied of in order to hold the appellant guilty of being an accessory before the fact. The passages in question are these:

'To prove that, the prosecution have to prove these matters; first of all, they have to prove that the felony itself was committed. Of that there is no doubt. That is not contested. Secondly, they have to prove that the [appellant] knew that a felony of that kind was intended and was going to be committed, and with that knowledge he did something to help the felons commit the crime. The knowledge that is required to be proved in the mind of [the appellant] is not the knowledge of the precise crime. In other words, it need not be proved that he knew that the Midland Bank, Stoke Newington branch, was going to be broken and entered, and money stolen from that particular bank, but he must know the type of crime that was in fact committed. In this case it is a breaking and entering of premises and the stealing of property from those premises. It must be proved that he knew that that sort of crime was intended and was going to be committed. It is not enough to show that he either suspected or knew that some crime was going to be committed, some crime which might have been a breaking and entering or might have been disposing of stolen property or anything of that kind. That is not enough. It must be proved that he knew that the type of crime which was in fact committed was intended.'

There are other passages to the same effect; in particular, when the jury returned for further directions before they came to their verdict, the learned judge said this:

'If in fact, before it has happened, [the appellant], knowing what is going to happen, with full knowledge that a felony of that kind is going to take place, deliberately and wilfully helps it on its way, he is an accessory . . . If he was not present he would not be guilty as a principal, but then you would have to decide whether he helped in purchasing this equipment for Shakeshaft knowing full well the type of offence for which it was going to be used, and, with that knowledge, buying it and helping in that way.'

Counsel for the appellant, who argued this case very well, contended that that direction was wrong. As he put it, in order that a person should be convicted of being accessory before the fact, it must be shown that, at the time when he bought the equipment in a case such as this, he knew that a particular crime was going to be committed; and by 'a particular crime' counsel meant that the premises in this case which were going to be broken into were known to the appellant and contemplated by him, and not only the premises in question but the date when the crime was going to occur; in other words, that he must have known that on a particular date the Stoke Newington branch of the Midland Bank was intended to be broken into.

The court fully appreciates that it is not enough that it should be shown that a person knew that some illegal venture was intended. To take this case, it would not be enough if the appellant knew—he says that he only suspected—that the equipment was going to be used to dispose of stolen property. That would not be enough. Equally, this court is quite satisfied that it is unnecessary that knowledge of the intention to commit the particular crime which was in fact committed should be shown, and by 'particular crime' I am using the words in the same way as that in which counsel for the appellant used them, namely, on a particular date and particular premises.

It is not altogether easy to lay down a precise form of words which will cover every case that can be contemplated. But, having considered the cases and the law, this court is quite clear that the direction of Judge Aarvold in this case cannot be criticised. Indeed, it might well have been made with the passage in Foster's *Crown Cases* (3rd edn) (1792) at p 369, in mind, because there the learned author says:

> 'If the principal totally and substantially varieth, if being solicited to commit a felony of one kind he *wilfully and knowingly* committeth a felony of another, *he* will stand single in that offence, and the person soliciting will not be involved in his guilt. For on *his* part it was no more than a fruitless ineffectual temptation.'

The converse of course is that, if the principal does not totally and substantially vary the advice or the help and does not wilfully and knowingly commit a different form of felony altogether, the man who has advised or helped, aided or abetted, will be guilty as an accessory before the fact.

Judge Aarvold in this case, in the passages to which I have referred, makes it clear that there must be not merely suspicion but knowledge that a crime of the type in question was intended, and that the equipment was bought with that in view. In his reference to the felony of the type intended it was, as he states, the felony of breaking and entering premises and the stealing of property from those premises. The court can see nothing wrong in that direction.

Appeal dismissed

■ **Questions**

1. What is a 'type' of crime? Violent? Dishonest? Sexual? How many types of crime are there in English law?

2. Is this case authority for the proposition that the supplier of equipment for use in committing a particular type of crime is liable for *all* crimes of that type which are committed by the person supplied, using that equipment? Does the fact that the equipment was left behind suggest that it was for use on one occasion only?

8.5.2.4 Knowledge of one of a number of crimes sufficient

Particular difficulties arise where D is aware that P is going to commit an offence, but is not sure which of a number of offences it will be. The House of Lords added to the principle in *Bainbridge* to meet this problem in the following case.

Director of Public Prosecutions for Northern Ireland v Maxwell
[1978] 3 All ER 1140, House of Lords

(Viscount Dilhorne, Lords Hailsham of St Marylebone, Edmund-Davies, Fraser of Tullybelton and Scarman)

The appellant, a member of the Ulster Volunteer Force, proscribed in Northern Ireland, had guided terrorists to the Crosskeys Inn by leading them there in his car. The trial judge found that the appellant knew there was to be 'an attack on the Crosskeys bar, not a casual or social visit or mere reconnaissance' and that 'the attack would be one of violence in which people would be endangered or premises seriously damaged'. However, the appellant did not know precisely what offence was to be committed. Although the appellant was charged as a principal in the offence of planting a pipe bomb in the Crosskeys Inn, contrary to the Explosive Substances Act 1883, s 3(1)(a), the true nature of his role was that of an aider and abettor. He appealed against conviction on the ground that he must be shown to have known the type of crime intended to be committed and the kind of means of offence being carried to the scene.

Lowry LCJ [delivering the judgment of the Court of Criminal Appeal in Northern Ireland:]

... Suppose the intending principal offender (whom I shall call 'the principal') tells the intended accomplice (whom I shall call 'the accomplice') that he means to shoot A or else leave a bomb at A's house and the accomplice agrees to drive the principal to A's house and keep watch while there, it seems clear that the accomplice would be guilty of aiding and abetting whichever crime the principal committed, because he would know that one of two crimes was to be committed, he would have assisted the principal and he would have intended to assist him. Again, let us suppose that the principal tells the accomplice that the intention is to murder A at one house but, if he cannot be found or the house is guarded, the alternative plan is to go to B's house and leave a bomb there or thirdly to rob a particular bank (or indeed murder somebody, or bomb somebody's house or rob any bank, as to which see *Bainbridge* ([1960] 1 QB 129, [1959] 3 All ER 200)) and requests the accomplice to make a reconnaissance of a number of places and report on the best way of gaining access to the target. The accomplice agrees and makes all the reconnaissances and reports, and the principal then, without further communication, selects a target and commits the crime. It seems clear that, whichever crime the principal commits, all the ingredients of the accomplice's guilt are present. In each of these examples the accomplice knows exactly what is contemplated and the only thing he does not know is to which particular crime he will become an accessory when it is committed. His guilt springs from the fact that he contemplates the commission of one (or more) of a number of crimes by the principal and he intentionally lends his assistance in order that such a crime will be committed. In other words, he knows that the principal is committing or about to commit one of a number of specified illegal acts and with that knowledge he helps him to do so.

The situation has something in common with that of two persons who agree to rob a bank on the understanding, either express or implied from conduct (such as the carrying of a loaded gun by one person with the knowledge of the other), that violence *may* be resorted to. The accomplice knows, not that the principal will shoot the cashier, but that he may do so; and if the principal does shoot him, the accomplice will be guilty of murder. A different case is where the accomplice has only offence A in contemplation and the principal commits offence B. Here the accomplice, although morally culpable (and perhaps guilty of conspiring to commit offence A), is not guilty of aiding and abetting offence B.

The principle with which we are dealing does not seem to us to provide a warrant, on the basis of combating lawlessness generally, for convicting an alleged accomplice of *any* offence which, helped by his preliminary acts, a principal may commit. The relevant crime must be within the contemplation of the accomplice and only exceptionally would evidence be found to support the allegation that the accomplice had given the principal a completely blank cheque. . . .

The facts found here show that the appellant, as a member of an organisation which habitually perpetrates sectarian acts of violence with firearms and explosives, must, as soon as he was briefed for his role, have contemplated the bombing of the Crosskeys Inn as not the only possibility but one of the most obvious possibilities among the jobs which the principals were likely to be undertaking and in the commission of which he was intentionally assisting. He was therefore in just the same situation, so far as guilty knowledge is concerned, as a man who had been given a list of jobs and told that one of them would be carried out. And so he is guilty of the offence alleged against him in count 1 . . .

[The court certified the following point of law of general importance:

> 'If the crime committed by the principal, and actually assisted by the accused, was one of a number of offences, one of which the accused knew the principal would probably commit, is the guilty mind which must be proved against an accomplice thereby proved against the accused?'

The House of Lords dismissed the appeal. All of their lordships approved the judgment of Lowry LCJ. **Lord Edmund-Davies** said that to do more than approve it would be a sleeveless errand; but he agreed with the view (below) of Viscount Dilhorne.]

Viscount Dilhorne:

...No objection could be taken to the form of these counts as by statute [Accessories and Abettors Act 1861, s 8; Criminal Law Act 1967, s 1(2)] aiders and abettors can be charged as principals, but the particulars to each count give no indication of the case the prosecution intended to present and which the appellant had to meet. In the particulars to the first count, he is charged with placing the bomb in the Crosskeys Inn; in the particulars to the second with having had it in his possession or under his control. The prosecution did not attempt to prove that he had placed the bomb or that he had been present when the bomb was put in the inn, nor was any attempt made to establish that at any time he had the bomb in his possession or under his control. It is desirable that the particulars of the offence should bear some relation to the realities and where, as here, it is clear that the appellant was alleged to have aided and abetted the placing of the bomb and its possession or control, it would in my opinion have been better if the particulars of offence had made that clear.

Lord Scarman [having quoted from the judgment of Lowry LCJ:]

Lowry LCJ continues:

> 'The relevant crime must be within the contemplation of the accomplice and only exceptionally would evidence be found to support the allegation that the accomplice had given the principal a completely blank cheque.'

The principle thus formulated has great merit. It directs attention to the state of mind of the accused: not what he ought to have in contemplation, but what he did have. It avoids definition and classification, while ensuring that a man will not be convicted of aiding and abetting any offence his principal may commit, but only one which is within his contemplation. He may have in contemplation only one offence, or several; and the several which he contemplates he may see as alternatives. An accessory who leaves it to his principal to choose is liable, provided always the choice is made from the range of offences from which the accessory contemplates the choice will be made. Although the court's formulation of the principle goes further than the earlier cases, it is a sound development of the law and in no way inconsistent with them. I accept it as good judge-made law in a field where there is no statute to offer guidance.

Appeal dismissed

In *Taylor, Harrison and Taylor* [1998] Crim LR 582, the court said that it was the 'proper practice, urged by the House of Lords [in *Maxwell*, above], but almost universally ignored, that where the allegation is one of secondary liability, and there is information available to the prosecution that indicates that, that allegation should be specifically set out in the particulars'.

8.5.2.5   D not liable for P's crime if P makes change of substance to what was agreed

Where D knows that the offence by P that D is assisting or encouraging is to be committed against a particular victim or in respect of a particular item of property, D will be liable provided P does not *deliberately* choose a different victim or item. This is described by Hawkins (at 2 PC c 29, s 21):

But if a man command another to commit a felony on a particular person or thing and he do it on another; as to kill A and he kill B or to burn the house of A and he burn the house of B or to steal an ox and he steal an horse; or to steal such an horse and he steal another; or to commit a felony of one kind and he commit another of a quite different nature; as to rob J S of his plate as he is going to market, and he break open his house in the night and there steal the plate; it is said that the commander is not an accessory because the act done varies in substance from that which was commanded.

As the second part of that quotation makes clear, the principle applies where there is a substantial variation from the proposed course of conduct, even if the victim and item are the same.

Hawkins also stated (at s 20):

[I]f the felony committed be the same in substance with that which was intended, and variant only in some circumstance, as in respect of the time or place, at which, or the means whereby it was effected, the abettor of the intent is altogether as much an accessory as if there had been no variance at all between it and the execution of it; as where a man advises another to kill such a one in the night, and he kills him in the day, or to kill him in the fields, and he kills him in the town, or to poison him, and he stabs or shoots him.

■ *Question*

D has a grievance against V. P offers to set fire to V's house. D accepts the offer and gives P V's address. P goes to V's house, changes his mind, and sets fire to V's Mercedes instead. D did not know that V owned such a car. Is D liable as an accessory to arson?

This category of case must be distinguished from those in which P's change of plan is not a deliberate one. The doctrine of transferred malice applies to secondary parties as it does to principal offenders (see section 2.4.1.1, p 24). Where P, intending to follow D's advice to kill V, mistakes X for V and kills X, D is guilty as a secondary party, and P as a principal offender, of murder. If D advises P to burn V's house and P does so but the flames spread and burn Y's house, D as well as P is guilty of arson of Y's house: D as accessory and P as principal.

In *Saunders and Archer* (1573) 2 Plowd 473, P intended to murder his wife. Following the advice of D, P gave her a poisoned apple to eat. She ate a little of it and gave the rest to their child. P loved the child, yet he stood by and watched it eat the poison, of which it soon died. It was held that P was guilty of murder of the child, but the judges agreed that D, who, of course, was not present when the child ate the apple, was not an accessory to this murder. If P had been absent when the child ate the apple it is thought that this would have been a case of transferred malice and D would have been liable; but P's presence and failure to act made the killing of the child, in effect, a deliberate, and not an accidental, departure from the agreed plan.

8.5.2.6 Summary of the 'knowledge' requirement

The case law set out previously establishes that D must know the 'essential matters which constitute P's offence'. D need not know that the essential elements of P's conduct constitute a crime since ignorance of the criminal law is no defence. In summary:

- D must know the conduct element of P's offence, although not all of the details of when, where, etc the commission of the actus reus will occur;

- D must foresee the possibility (not necessarily a probability) of the consequences of P's crime occurring;

- D must know/foresee that P will act with mens rea. Thus, if D knows/foresees that P might beat V up, but does not know/foresee that P will perform that action with the intention of killing or causing V grievous bodily harm, D will not have 'knowledge' of the 'essential matters' comprising the principal offence of murder. Note that D need not have the same mens rea as P. P must have the mens rea for the principal offence; D must have knowledge/foresight of P's mens rea. The difficulties involved in proving one person's contemplation of another's state of mind are obvious.

8.6 Can an accessory be liable for a more serious offence than the principal?

We have examined the actus reus and mens rea element of the secondary party. Are there any limits of the offences for which D can be liable as an accessory?

R v Burke and Clarkson

[1986] UKHL 4, House of Lords, http://www.bailii.org/uk/cases/UKHL/1986/4.html

(Lord Hailsham LC, Lords Bridge, Brandon, Griffiths and Mackay)

The Crown alleged that Burke shot a man (Botton) dead because Clarkson told him to do so to prevent Botton testifying against C at a forthcoming trial. Clarkson denied having any involvement. Burke's defence was that he had agreed to shoot Botton only out of fear of Clarkson; but that in the event the gun went off accidentally and the killing was unintentional and therefore only manslaughter. Both were convicted of murder. The judge directed that if Burke was guilty only of manslaughter and not murder, then Clarkson could be found guilty at worst of manslaughter. Burke's appeal arguing that this was a misdirection was dismissed by the Court of Appeal. The question certified for the House of Lords was 'can one who incites or procures by duress another to kill or be a party to a killing be convicted of murder if that other is acquitted by reason of duress?'

[Lords Hailsham, Bridge, Brandon and Griffiths dismissed the appeal.]

Lord Mackay:

In the view that I take on the first question the second question does not properly arise. However, I am of opinion that the Court of Appeal reached the correct conclusion on it as a matter of principle.

Giving the judgment of the Court of Appeal Lord Lane CJ said ([1986] 1 All ER 833 at 839–840, [1986] QB 626 at 641–652):

'The judge based himself on a decision of this court in *R v Richards (Isabelle)* [1973] 3 All ER1088, [1974] QB 776. The facts in that case were that Mrs Richards paid two men to inflict injuries on her husband which she intended should "put him in hospital for a month". The two men wounded the husband but not seriously. They were acquitted of wounding with intent but convicted of unlawful wounding. Mrs Richards herself was convicted of wounding with intent, the jury plainly, and not surprisingly, believing that she had the necessary intent, though the two men had not. She appealed against her conviction on the ground that she could not properly be convicted as accessory before the fact to a crime more serious than that committed by the principals in the first degree. The appeal was allowed and the conviction for unlawful wounding was substituted. The court followed a passage from *Hawkins's Pleas of the Crown* (2 Hawk PC (8th edn) p442): "I take it to be an uncontroverted rule that [the offence of the accessory can never rise higher than that of the principal]; it seeming incongruous and absurd that he who is punished only as a partaker of the guilt of another, should be adjudged guilty of a higher crime than the other." James LJ, delivering the judgment in *R v Richards* [1973] 3 All ER 1088 at 1092, [1974] QB 776 at 780, had this to say: "If there is only one offence committed, and that is the offence of unlawful wounding, then the person who has requested that offence to be committed, or advised that that offence be committed, cannot be guilty of a graver offence than that in fact which was committed." The decision in *R v Richards* has been the subject of some criticism (see for example Smith and Hogan *Criminal Law* (5th edn, 1983) p140). Counsel before us posed the situation where A hands a gun to D informing him that it is loaded with blank ammunition only and telling him to go and scare X by discharging it. The ammunition is in fact live (as A knows) and X is killed. D is convicted only of manslaughter, as he might be on those facts. It would seem absurd that A should thereby escape conviction for murder. We take the view that *R v Richards* was incorrectly decided, but it seems to us that it cannot properly be distinguished from the instant case.'

I consider that the reasoning of Lord Lane CJ is entirely correct and I would affirm his view that, where a person has been killed and that result is the result intended by another participant, the mere fact that the actual killer may be convicted only of the reduced charge of manslaughter for some reason special to himself does not, in my opinion, in any way result in a compulsory reduction for the other participant.

The House had decided that duress could never be a defence to murder so the question certified could not arise. If duress were a defence to murder, the supposed killer would be guilty of no offence and it seems perfectly obvious that the duressor would be guilty of murder through an innocent agent.

Question 2 did not raise the question posed by *Richards* and by Burke's defence (above) but Lord Mackay, probably *obiter*, affirmed the Court of Appeal's opinion on that issue. Probably everyone will agree with the court's example of the loaded gun.

■ *Question*

How can the accessory be liable for a more serious offence than the principal if secondary liability is 'derivative' as we explained at the outset?

Academics have struggled to identify a coherent basis for liability being imposed on the accessory for a graver crime than that for which the principal is liable. See Kadish, *Blame and Punishment: Essays in Criminal Law* (1987), p 183 and compare Glanville Williams (TBCL, 373).

■ *Questions*

1. Is it significant that the actions of the two men in *Richards* were 'fully voluntary'? They knew perfectly well what they were doing.

2. D sends a letter bomb through the post to V. E, the postman, notices wires sticking out of the envelope and is aware that letter bombs have been sent recently by terrorists with fatal results. He thinks, 'This could be a letter bomb—but I'm in a hurry—I'll risk it' and pushes the envelope through V's letterbox. It explodes and kills V. If E is guilty of manslaughter, can D be convicted of murder?

8.6.1 Can D be liable as an accessory to a crime committed on himself?

The traditional approach to this question was found in the case of *Tyrell* [1894] 1 QB 710.

Section 5 of the Criminal Law Amendment Act 1885 made it an offence for a man to have carnal knowledge of a girl over the age of 12 and under the age of 16. The defendant, a girl whose age fell within that bracket, was convicted of (i) aiding, abetting, counselling and procuring the commission of that offence by a man upon herself and (ii) of inciting the man to commit the same offence. On appeal these convictions were robustly quashed. Lord Coleridge CJ, giving the leading judgment, said at p 712:

The Criminal Law Amendment Act 1885 was passed for the purpose of protecting women and girls against themselves. At the time it was passed there was a discussion as to what point should be fixed as the age of consent. That discussion ended in a compromise, and the age of consent was fixed at sixteen. With the object of protecting women and girls against themselves the Act of

Parliament has made illicit connection with a girl under that age unlawful; if a man wishes to have such illicit connection he must wait until the girl is sixteen, otherwise he breaks the law; but it is impossible to say that the Act, which is absolutely silent about aiding or abetting, or soliciting or inciting, can have intended that the girls for whose protection it was passed should be punishable under it for the offences committed upon themselves. I am of the opinion that this conviction ought to be quashed.

Glanville Williams relied on this case to identify a principle that he described as the 'victim rule':

...where the courts perceive that the legislation is designed for the protection of a class of persons. Such people should not be convicted as accessories to an offence committed in respect of them when they co-operate in it. Nor should they be convicted as conspirators. ('Victims and Other Exempt Parties in Crime' (1990) 10 LS at p 245)

The rule was restated in the Supreme Court in *Gnango* (discussed in full in section 8.7.8, p 275). It was held that the *Tyrell* principle only applies when an offence is intended to protect a particular class of vulnerable people.

53. We can see no reason why this court should consider extending the common law so as to protect from conviction any defendant who is, or is intended to be, harmed by the crime that he commits, or attempts to commit. Such an extension would defeat the intention of Parliament in circumscribing the victim rule in section 51 of the 2007 Act. In *R v Brown (Anthony)* [1994] 1 AC 212 sado-masochists were held to have been rightly convicted of causing injury to others who willingly consented to the injuries that they received. There would have been no bar to conviction of the latter of having aided and abetted the infliction of those injuries upon themselves. It is no doubt appropriate for prosecuting authorities to consider carefully whether there is justification for prosecuting anyone as party to a crime where he is the victim, or intended victim of that crime, but that is not to say that the actual or intended victim of a crime should on that ground alone be absolved from criminal responsibility in relation to it. As Lord Lane CJ observed in *Attorney-General's Reference (No 6 of 1980)* [1981] QB 715, 719: 'it is not in the public interest that people should try to cause, or should cause, each other actual bodily harm for no good reason.'

■ *Questions*

A and B are outside a pub one night and get into a fight, with each punching the other on the nose. Could A and B now be guilty not only of assault occasioning actual bodily harm for the blow inflicted on the other, but also of aiding and abetting their own ABH? Do you think this odd?

8.7 Joint enterprise or 'parasitic accessorial liability'

'Joint enterprise' liability arises where D and P agree to commit an offence (offence A) or share an intention to commit an offence (offence A), and in the course or furtherance of that offence P goes beyond what was agreed to, what was part of the common intention and commits another offence (offence B).

For example, D and P agree to burgle V's house. D knows that P has a violent temper and often carries a knife. D foresees that P might intentionally use it to do GBH or kill. D and P commit the burglary (whether with D as an accessory or as a joint principal with P) and in the course of the burglary P kills the householder with the knife. P is guilty of murder. D is now also guilty of murder applying the doctrine of joint enterprise or 'parasitic accessorial liability'.

To take another example, D and P agree to go shoplifting. D foresees that P might turn violent if challenged. They set out on their shoplifting spree (with D as either an accessory or a joint principal in the theft) and P commits GBH on the shop owner to snatch the goods from him. P is guilty of GBH and robbery and D becomes liable for those offences also by the doctrine of joint enterprise or 'parasitic accessorial liability' as it is sometimes known.

This section of the chapter considers to what extent D can be liable as a secondary party for the acts of P which are collateral to the crime that they had agreed or for which D shared P's purpose. Although the term 'joint enterprise' has become commonplace to denote a distinct doctrine separate from the principles governing 'basic' accessorial liability (ie aiding, abetting, counselling and procuring in a single crime), the term 'parasitic accessorial liability' will be used here instead. The reason for this is that the courts have now accepted that there is no doctrine of joint enterprise which exists separately from basic accessorial liability; it is merely the application of those principles. In *Stringer* [2011] EWCA Crim 1396, Toulson LJ stated:

> 57. Joint enterprise is not a legal term of art. In *R v Mendez* [2011] QB 876, the court favoured the view that joint enterprise as a basis of secondary liability involves the application of ordinary principles; it is not an independent source of liability. Participation in a joint criminal adventure involves mutual encouragement and assistance.

8.7.1 General principles

This is a particularly difficult area of law. In summary, the requirements for parasitic accessorial liability are as follows:

- D and P have a common purpose to commit a crime (with D either as an accessory to P committing crime A or as joint principals);
- D *foresees* when embarking on the joint venture to commit crime A that in the course or furtherance of the commission of crime A, P *might* commit crime B and that P might have the mens rea for that offence when P did so;
- In the course or furtherance of crime A, P commits crime B and does so in a manner not fundamentally different from the way that D foresaw he might;
- D was continuing to participate at the time P committed crime B.

8.7.2 Common purpose

D must share P's purpose that 'crime A' is committed before the parasitic liability principles can apply.

In *Gnango* (section 8.7.8) D had voluntarily engaged in an exchange of gunfire with an opponent (P) in a public place. One of P's shots, aimed at D, killed a passer-by. D was convicted of possessing a firearm with intent to endanger life, attempted murder and, by way of joint enterprise, the murder of the passer-by.

In the Supreme Court, Lord Phillips, Judge and Wilson define parasitic liability as arising where: (i) D and P have a common intention to commit crime A, (ii) P, as an incident of committing crime A, commits crime B, and (iii) D had foreseen the possibility that P might do so (at [41]). That view is endorsed by Lord Clarke at [78], Lord Dyson at [95] and Lord Kerr at [114].

■ *Questions*

Taking a practical example of the difficulty in requiring proof of common purpose, it is not obvious what the difference is in terms of responsibility of the following defendants:

Case 1: D shares P's common purpose to commit robbery. He loans P a gun, for the usual hire fee, to commit the crime and foresees that P might, in the course of the robbery intentionally commit GBH or kill. D is liable for murder if P does murder in the course of the robbery.

Case 2: D does not share P's purpose that robbery of V should be committed. He nevertheless wants the cash that P offers for loan of the gun. D lends P the gun. D is liable as a secondary party to robbery. If D foresees that P might, in the course of the robbery intentionally commit GBH or kill, D is *not* liable for murder if P does murder in the course of the robbery.

Note that it is clear that D's liability for P's commission of crime B does not turn on D sharing P's purpose that offence B is committed. In parasitic liability, D's liability for the murder turns on whether he *foresaw* that P might intentionally commit it.

8.7.3 D's foresight of P's crime

D must foresee that P might commit crime B and have the mens rea for that crime at the time he does so.

This element is the reason why this area of law most commonly presents problems in murder cases. D and P set out with a shared purpose to rob V or to burgle or to commit public order offences and at the scene P goes beyond what was agreed or what was part of their shared purpose and kills V. In these cases it is now well established that D can be liable for murder if he was party to a joint enterprise with P and D foresees as a possibility that P might intentionally kill or commit GBH. D's mens rea is far lower than that of P. To be guilty of murder, P must intend to kill or do GBH. For D to be guilty of murder (and sentenced to life imprisonment) as a secondary party, D need only foresee that P might intentionally cause GBH with intent.

R v Powell; R v English
[1997] UKHL 57, House of Lords, http://www.bailii.org/uk/cases/UKHL/1997/57.html

(Lords Goff, Jauncey, Mustill, Steyn and Hutton)

P and D went with another man to the house of a drug dealer for the purpose of buying drugs but the drug dealer was shot dead at the door. It was not clear who had shot the drug dealer but P and D were convicted of murder on the basis of the Crown's case that if the third man had fired the gun, they knew that he was armed with a gun and realized that he might use it to kill or cause really serious injury to the drug dealer. P and D appealed against their convictions to the Court of Appeal, which dismissed the appeals and P and D appealed to the House of Lords.

In the second appeal, E and W took part in a joint attack on a police officer in which they both caused injury with wooden posts but the police officer died from fatal stab wounds inflicted by W. E was convicted of murder, the judge having directed the jury to do so if they found that he had joined in an unlawful attack realizing at the time that there was a substantial risk that W might kill the police officer during the attack or at least cause some really serious injury to him. E and W appealed to the Court of Appeal, which dismissed the appeals and E appealed to the House of Lords.

[Lord Goff and Lord Jauncey agreed with the speech of Lord Hutton.

Lord Mustill concurred in the reasoning of Lord Steyn and Lord Hutton.

Lord Steyn agreed with the speech of Lord Hutton and continued:]

There are two separate but complementary legal concepts at stake. The first is the mental element sufficient for murder, ie an intention to kill or to cause really serious bodily injury. Only if this element is proved in respect of the primary offender, and if the other ingredients of murder are proved, does the second concept arise for consideration, viz the criminal liability of accessories to a joint criminal enterprise. Under the accessory principle criminal liability is dependent on proof of subjective foresight on the part of a participant in the criminal enterprise that the primary offender might commit a greater offence, that being in these cases foresight that the primary offender might commit murder as defined in law.

The thrust of both appeals was to challenge the existing law and practice regarding the second concept. The appeals under consideration relate to charges of murder. But there is no special rule regarding the criminal liability of accessories in cases of murder. The principle governing the criminal liability of accessories applies across the spectrum of most criminal offences. Any alteration in the accessory principle, as presently understood, would have to apply to most criminal offences. That does not mean that the arguments advanced on behalf of the appellants are unsound. But it underlines the sweeping impact of the changes to the existing law and practice necessarily involved in an acceptance of the submissions made on behalf of the appellants in these appeals.

The established principle is that a secondary party to a criminal enterprise may be criminally liable for a greater criminal offence committed by the primary offender of a type which the former foresaw but did not necessarily intend. The criminal culpability lies in participating in the criminal enterprise with that foresight. Foresight and intention are not synonymous terms. But foresight is a necessary and sufficient ground of the liability of accessories. That is how the law has been stated in two carefully reasoned decisions of the Privy Council (see *Chan Wing-siu v R* [1984] 3 All ER 877, [1985] AC 168 and *Hui Chi-ming v R* [1991] 3 All ER 897, [1992] 1 AC 34). In a valuable article Professor Sir John Smith has recently concluded that there is no doubt that this represents English law (see 'Criminal Liability of Accessories: Law and Law Reform' (1997) 113 LQR 453 at 455). And Lord Hutton has demonstrated in his comprehensive review of the case law that the law is as stated in the two Privy Council decisions. That does not mean that the established principle cannot be re-examined and, if found to be flawed, reformulated. But the existing law and practice forms the starting point.

Counsel for the appellants argued that the secondary party to a criminal enterprise should only be guilty of a murder committed by the primary offender if the secondary party has the full mens rea sufficient for murder, ie an intent to kill or to cause really serious bodily harm. Their arguments fell into three parts, namely: (1) that there is a disharmony between two streams of authority; (2) that the accessory principle involves a form of constructive criminal liability; and (3) that it is anomalous that a lesser form of culpability is sufficient for a secondary party than for the primary offender. The first part of the argument centred on the scope of decisions of the House of Lords in *R v Moloney* [section 5.2, p 100] and *R v Hancock* [section 5.2.1, p 103]. Those decisions distinguish between foresight and intention and require in the case of murder proof of intention to kill or cause serious bodily injury. But those decisions were intended to apply to a primary offender only. The liability of accessories was not in issue. Plainly the House did not intend in those decisions to examine or pronounce on the accessory principle. The resort to authority must therefore fail.

That brings me to the second argument. If the application of the accessory principle results in a form of constructive liability that would be contrary to principle and it would be a defect in our criminal law. But subject to a qualification about the definition of the mens rea required for murder to which I will turn later, I would reject the argument that the accessory principle *as such* imposes a form of constructive liability. The accessory principle requires proof of a subjective state of mind on the part of a participant in a criminal enterprise, viz foresight that the primary offender might commit a different and more serious offence. Professor Sir John Smith explained how the principle applies in the case of murder ((1997) 113 LQR 453 at 464):

[His lordship then quoted an extract from Professor Smith's article.]

The foresight of the secondary party must be directed to a real possibility of the commission by the primary offender in the course of the criminal enterprise of the greater offence. The liability is imposed because the secondary party is assisting in and encouraging a criminal enterprise which he is aware might result in the commission of a greater offence. The liability of an accessory is predicated on his culpability in respect of the greater offence as defined in law. It is undoubtedly a lesser form of mens rea. But it is unrealistic to say that the accessory principle as such imposes constructive criminal liability.

At first glance, there is substance in the third argument that it is anomalous that a lesser form of culpability is required in the case of a secondary party, viz foresight of the possible commission of the greater offence, whereas in the case of the primary offender the law insists on proof of the specific intention which is an ingredient of the offence. This general argument leads, in the present case, to the particular argument that it is anomalous that the secondary party can be guilty of murder if he foresees the possibility of such a crime being committed while the primary can only be guilty if he has an intent to kill or cause really serious injury. Recklessness may suffice in the case of the secondary party but it does not in the case of the primary offender. The answer to this supposed anomaly, and other similar cases across the spectrum of criminal law, is to be found in practical and policy considerations. If the law required proof of the specific intention on the part of a secondary party, the utility of the accessory principle would be gravely undermined. It is just that a secondary party who foresees that the primary offender might kill with the intent sufficient for murder, and assists and encourages the primary offender in the criminal enterprise on this basis, should be guilty of murder. He ought to be criminally liable for harm which he foresaw and which in fact resulted from the crime he assisted and encouraged. But it would in practice almost invariably be impossible for a jury to say that the secondary party wanted death to be caused or that he regarded it as virtually certain. In the real world proof of an intention sufficient for murder would be well nigh impossible in the vast majority of joint enterprise cases. Moreover, the proposed change in the law must be put in context. The criminal justice system exists to control crime. A prime function of that system must be to deal justly but effectively with those who join with others in criminal enterprises. Experience has shown that joint criminal enterprises only too readily escalate into the commission of greater offences. In order to deal with this important social problem the accessory principle is needed and cannot be abolished or relaxed. For these reasons, I would reject the arguments advanced in favour of the revision of the accessory principle.

Lord Hutton [having comprehensively reviewed the authorities, concluded that it is sufficient to found a conviction for murder for a secondary party to have realized that in the course of the joint enterprise the primary party might kill with intent to do so or with intent to cause grievous bodily harm and that, accordingly, the appeals of Powell and Daniels must be dismissed:]

Mr Sallon QC, for the appellant, advanced to your Lordships' House the submission (which does not appear to have been advanced in the Court of Appeal) that in a case such as the present one where the primary party kills with a deadly weapon, which the secondary party did not know that he had and therefore did not foresee his use of it, the secondary party should not be guilty of murder. He submitted that to be guilty under the principle stated in *Chan Wing-siu v R* the secondary party must foresee an act of the type which the principal party committed, and that in the present case the use of a knife was fundamentally different to the use of a wooden post.

My Lords, I consider that this submission is correct. It finds strong support in the passage of the judgment of Lord Parker CJ in *R v Anderson and Morris* [1966] 2 All ER 644 at 648, [1966] 2 QB 110 at 120 which I have set out earlier, but which it is convenient to set out again in this portion of the judgment:

'It seems to this court that to say that adventurers are guilty of manslaughter when one of them has departed completely from the concerted action of the common design and has suddenly formed an intent to kill and has used a weapon and acted in a way which no party to that common design could suspect is something which would revolt the conscience of people today.'

The judgment in *Chan Wing-siu v R* [1984] 3 All ER 877 at 880, [1985] AC 168 at 175 also supports the argument advanced on behalf of the appellant because Sir Robin Cooke stated: 'The case must depend rather on the wider principle whereby a secondary party is criminally liable for *acts by the primary offender of a type* which the former foresees but does not necessarily intend.' (My emphasis).

There is also strong support for the appellant's submission in the decision of Carswell J (as he then was), sitting without a jury in the Crown Court in Northern Ireland, in *R v Gamble* [1989] NI 268. In that case, the four accused were all members of a terrorist organisation, the Ulster Volunteer Force, who had a grievance against a man named Patton. The four accused entered upon a joint venture to inflict punishment upon him, two of them, Douglas and McKee, contemplating that Patton would be subjected to a severe beating or to 'kneecapping' (firing a bullet into his kneecap). In the course of the attack upon him Patton was brutally murdered by the other two accused. His throat was cut with a knife with great force which rapidly caused his death. In addition he was shot with four bullets, and two of the bullet wounds would have been fatal had his death not been caused by the cutting of his throat. Douglas and McKee had not foreseen killing with a knife or firing of bullets into a vital part of the body. It was argued, however, on behalf of the prosecution that the joint enterprise of committing grievous bodily harm, combined with the rule that an intent to cause such harm grounded a conviction for murder in respect of a resulting death, was sufficient to make the two accused liable for murder notwithstanding that they had not foreseen the actions which actually caused death. After citing the relevant authorities Carswell J rejected this argument and stated (at 283–284):

'When an assailant "kneecaps" his victim, ie discharges a weapon into one of his limbs, most commonly into the knee joint, there must always be the risk that it will go wrong and that an artery may be severed or the limb may be so damaged that gangrene sets in, both potentially fatal complications. It has to be said, however, that such cases must be very rare among victims of what is an abhorrent and disturbingly frequent crime. Persons who take a part in inflicting injuries of this nature no doubt do not generally expect that they will endanger life, and I should be willing to believe that in most cases they believe that they are engaged in a lesser offence than murder. The infliction of grievous bodily harm came within the contemplation of Douglas and McKee, and they might therefore be regarded as having placed themselves within the ambit of life-threatening conduct. It may further be said that they must be taken to have had within their contemplation the possibility that might be put at risk. The issue is whether it follows as a consequence that they cannot be heard to say that the murder was a different crime from the attack which they contemplated, and so cannot escape liability for the murder on the ground that it was outside the common design. To accept this type of reasoning would be to fix an accessory with consequences of his acts which he did not foresee and did not desire or intend. The modern development of the criminal law has been away from such an approach and towards a greater emphasis on subjective tests of criminal guilt, as Sir Robin Cooke pointed out in *Chan Wing-Siu*. Although the rule remains well entrenched that an intention to inflict grievous bodily harm qualifies as the mens rea of murder, it is not in my opinion necessary to apply it in such a way as to fix an accessory with liability for a consequence which he did not intend and which stems from an act which he did not have within his contemplation. I do not think that the state of the law compels me to reach such a conclusion, and it would not in my judgment accord with the public sense of what is just and fitting.'

In my opinion, this decision was correct in that a secondary party who foresees grievous bodily harm caused by kneecapping with a gun should not be guilty of murder where, in an action unforeseen by the secondary party, another party to the criminal enterprise kills the victim by cutting his throat with a knife. The issue (which is one of fact after the tribunal of fact has directed itself, or has been directed, in accordance with the statement of Lord Parker CJ in *R v Anderson and Morris* [1966] 2 All ER 644 at 648, [1966] 2 QB 110 at 120) whether a secondary party who foresees the use of a gun to kneecap, and death is then caused by the deliberate firing of the gun into the head or body of the victim, is guilty of murder is more debatable although, with respect, I agree with the decision of Carswell J on the facts of that case.

Accordingly, in the appeal of English, I consider that the direction of the learned trial judge was defective (although this does not constitute a criticism of the judge . . .

Powell's and Daniels' appeals dismissed

English's appeal allowed

■ *Questions*

1. D will be liable for P's further offences of murder, provided that D contemplated that P might perform the conduct element of that offence with the relevant mens rea for the offence. Should D be labelled and sentenced as a murderer in such circumstances?

2. Do you agree with Lord Steyn that liability is not constructive?

8.7.3.1 D's liability for unforeseen consequences

Consider the case where D is liable for *an act* done by P in the course of a joint enterprise; he is liable for the unforeseen consequences of that act to the same extent as P, subject to a fundamental change of plan by P. D foresees that P may do an act with intent to cause GBH—P does so and, unforeseen by either, the act causes death—both are guilty of murder. If D foresees that P may do an act with intent to cause ABH and P does so, both are guilty of manslaughter if, unforeseen and unforeseeably, the act causes death.

■ *Questions*

What of D who instructs P to carry a shotgun to frighten V, but P uses it to shoot V dead at point-blank range? Is D liable for murder? For manslaughter? What is the act that D must have foreseen—the firing of a shotgun in V's presence or the shooting *at* V?

8.7.3.2 Unforeseen consequences of foreseen acts done in the course of a joint enterprise

Consider the case where D and P independently intend the same result, but it is not proved that each intends to assist or encourage the other. Neither is liable for acts done by the other which, though he might be pleased by the result, he did not assist or encourage the other to commit: *Petters and Parfitt* [1995] Crim LR 501. If, in such a case, it is not possible to prove which caused the injury or death, neither can be convicted. If, however, D intentionally assists P, even without P's knowledge, it seems that D will be liable for any crime committed by P which D foresaw P might commit while doing the act assisted.

8.7.4 Crime B must be committed

It is crucial that the prosecution prove that crime B was committed, even if they cannot identify the principal offender. If the offence is committed by a group, as it often is in the case of joint enterprise murders, the fact that the jury cannot be sure which of the members of a group delivered the fatal blow does not prevent murder convictions for all or any members. This was confirmed by the House of Lords in *Rahman* [2008] UKHL 45.

In *ABCD* [2010] EWCA Crim 1622, Hughes LJ stated:

It is not, of course, necessary for the guilt of D that P be identified. In a multi-handed assault it will often be the case that no-one can say whose hand did the act which proved fatal. But what is necessary is that someone (identified or not) be shown to have committed murder.

In many instances of common enterprise murder there will be no doubt about there having been murder by someone. As we have said, many of the reported cases concern the use by P (whether identified or not) of a knife to stab or a gun to shoot. In such cases there is little doubt that P committed murder in stabbing or shooting, for such acts carry by themselves the almost inevitable intention to kill or to cause grievous bodily harm. But it is not quite so clear where there is no lethal weapon and the common purpose is to administer a beating. If death ensues, that may well justify the conclusion that someone at least acted with the necessary murderous intent, viz to kill or to do grievous bodily harm, but it does not necessarily do so. The issue may in some cases be a live one. The mere fact that the injuries proved fatal is a powerful pointer to their having been inflicted, by one or more of the assailants, with intent at least to do grievous bodily harm. But as everyone knows, death may sometimes result where the intent of the assailant(s) has been no more than to cause some, not serious, injury; that is the basis of many convictions for manslaughter.

8.7.5 P's act fundamentally different from that D contemplated

Several questions arise from the decisions in *Powell* and *English*.

(i)   When exactly does the 'fundamentally different' qualification bite?

(ii)   What part does P's mens rea play in deciding whether P's acts are sufficiently fundamentally different so as to take his conduct outside the joint enterprise and lead to D's acquittal for P's crime?

(iii)   What types of conduct by P will constitute a 'fundamental' change so that D is absolved of responsibility for P's crime?

(iv)   If P's act is fundamentally different, does D escape all liability?

Many of these issues were considered in *Rahman* [2008] UKHL 45 (see the following sections).

Before considering the implications of that decision, it is important to appreciate that 'fundamental difference' is not a separate doctrine per se. Recall that parasitic accessorial liability depends upon D's foresight of P's mens rea and the manner in which P might commit offence B, for example murder. Given that this is the case, the fundamental difference 'rule' is not really a rule, but is the corollary of the requirement that D must, in murder, have at least contemplated that P might kill or do GBH with intent in the *manner* in which he did.

8.7.5.1 When can D rely on a fundamentally different act by P?

The first difficult question is in what circumstances D is precluded from claiming that P's conduct amounts to a 'fundamentally different' act. As a matter of principle, the law would be too generous to D if that plea could be advanced in any case. For example, where D intends that P will kill V with intent, it would be wrong for D to be entitled to base an excuse on P's decision to kill with a knife rather than with a gun as D contemplated.

In *Rahman* [2008] UKHL 45, the appellants were each convicted of murder. V had sustained a fatal stab wound from a knife during an attack on him by a number of men, many of whom were armed with blunt instruments. The Crown alleged that each of the Ds had been a party to a joint enterprise to inflict unlawful violence on V. It could not be proved which person had inflicted the fatal blow. Each D denied possession of a knife and each asserted that he had not foreseen, believed, known or realized that anyone else in the group had a knife.

Each D claimed that the person who had inflicted the wound, whoever that was, had been acting outside the scope of any joint enterprise to attack.

On appeal to the House of Lords, the House also upheld the convictions, but Lord Brown made a significant change to the availability of the fundamentally different qualification. His lordship restated the law (at [68]) as follows:

> If D realises (without agreeing to such conduct being used) that P may kill or intentionally inflict serious injury, but nevertheless continues to participate with P in the venture, that will amount to a sufficient mental element for D to be guilty of murder if P, with the requisite intent, kills in the course of the venture *unless (i) P suddenly produces and uses a weapon of which D knows nothing and which is more lethal than any weapon which D contemplates that P or any other participant may be carrying and (ii) for that reason P's act is to be regarded as fundamentally different from anything foreseen by D.* (The italicised words are in the original and designed to reflect the *English* qualification).

Lord Neuberger agreed (at [72]) as did Lord Scott (at [31]) (although Lord Scott earlier in that paragraph stated that if the death of V is a foreseeably possible consequence D should be liable no matter what weapon was used).

According to this majority view, D is now in some cases able to rely on the *English* qualification where he foresaw that P might kill with intent.

■ *Questions*

Is this too generous to D? If D has committed himself to a venture foreseeing that P might kill with intent should it matter what *method* of killing D foresaw?

More recently in *Mendez* [2010] EWCA Crim 516 the Court of Appeal sought to clarify what was said in *Rahman*. It did so by stating that emphasis ought to be placed on whether the act of P was more life-threatening than anything foreseen by D.

> In cases where the common purpose is not to kill but to cause serious harm, D is not liable for the murder of V if the direct cause of V's death was a deliberate act by P which was of a kind (a) unforeseen by D and (b) likely to be altogether more life-threatening than acts of the kind intended or foreseen by D. The reference to 'a deliberate act' is to the quality of the act—deliberate and not by chance—rather than to any consideration of P's intention as to the consequences. (at [44]–[47])

The focus on the life-threatening nature of P's act is also evident when the court discusses the application of the fundamental difference 'rule' and weapons:

> what matters is not simply the difference in weapon but the way in which it is likely to be used and the degree of injury which it is likely to cause. (at [42])

Although the Court of Appeal said in *Mendez* that it was not its goal to place a gloss on the words of the House of Lords in *Rahman*, is this nevertheless what it has done? Is this to be welcomed?

8.7.5.2 Change of mens rea by P as a fundamentally different act

This was directly in issue in *Rahman*. D claimed that because he only foresaw that P might kill with intent to do GBH, if P killed with intent to kill (as was inferred from the depth of the penetration with the knife), that constituted a fundamental change by P. The House of Lords unanimously rejected this basis of the appeal. If P killed with intent to kill and D foresaw that P might at most intentionally cause really serious injury, the greater mens rea P actually held does not make his act fundamentally different so as to bring it within the *English* qualification and absolve D of liability.

Lord Bingham's reasons for rejecting the defence argument were twofold.

24. Authority apart, there are in my view two strong reasons, one practical, the other theoretical, for [rejecting] the contention. The first is that the law of joint enterprise in a situation such as this is already very complex, as evidenced by the trial judge's direction and the Court of Appeal's judgment on these appeals, and the appellants' submission, if accepted, would introduce a new and highly undesirable level of complexity. Given the fluid, fast-moving course of events in incidents such as that which culminated in the killing of the deceased, incidents which are unhappily not rare, it must often be very hard for jurors to make a reliable assessment of what a particular defendant foresaw as likely or possible acts on the part of his associates. It would be even harder, and would border on speculation, to judge what a particular defendant foresaw as the intention with which his associates might perform such acts. It is safer to focus on the defendant's foresight of what an associate might do, an issue to which knowledge of the associate's possession of an obviously lethal weapon such as a gun or a knife would usually be very relevant.

25. Secondly, the appellants' submission, as it seems to me, undermines the principle on which, for better or worse, our law of murder is based. In the prosecution of a principal offender for murder, it is not necessary for the prosecution to prove or the jury to consider whether the defendant intended on the one hand to kill or on the other to cause really serious injury. That is legally irrelevant to guilt. The rationale of that principle plainly is that if a person unlawfully assaults another with intent to cause him really serious injury, and death results, he should be held criminally responsible for that fatality, even though he did not intend it. If he had not embarked on a course of deliberate violence, the fatality would not have occurred. This rationale may lack logical purity, but it is underpinned by a quality of earthy realism. To rule that an undisclosed and unforeseen intention to kill on the part of the primary offender may take a killing outside the scope of a common purpose to cause really serious injury, calling for a distinction irrelevant in the case of the primary offender, is in my view to subvert the rationale which underlies our law of murder.

There would also be the complication of identifying P's intent at relevant points in time in the criminal enterprise (Lord Brown at [70]). Lord Bingham's second reason is one of principle: in a murder trial it is legally irrelevant whether the killer intended to kill or cause really serious injury. This harsh rule is underpinned by a 'quality of earthy realism' (at [25]). Lord Bingham concludes such a distinction should not affect the liability of the secondary party. Lord Neuberger (at [83]–[87]) offers some principled arguments supporting this view.

The Court of Appeal emphasized in *Mendez* [2010] EWCA Crim 516 that D can only plead fundamental difference when he does not share a common purpose with P to kill. If D and P share a common purpose to kill, then D cannot escape liability for murder if P goes on to fulfil that common purpose by committing murder in a way unforeseen by D.

■ *Question*

Do you agree that because the mens rea for the principal in murder draws no distinction between intent to kill and to cause serious injury, it is irrelevant to secondary liability?

Care should, it is submitted, be taken with some of the broad pronouncements in the speeches. D's foresight of P's mens rea does matter in a joint enterprise. D must contemplate that P might perform the act of killing or causing serious injury with the requisite intent for murder. What is irrelevant is whether D contemplates that P's mens rea will be of an intent to kill or an intent to cause serious injury.

8.7.5.3 What types of conduct by P will constitute a 'fundamental' change?

A great many of the joint enterprise cases turn on the question of whether D knew that P was carrying the weapon he used to cause injury or death. If D did know, that is cogent evidence that he knew that there was a risk that P might commit the crime charged. If D did not know, that is evidence in his favour. In circumstances in which the *English* qualification is available, the Court of Appeal had left the issue of whether P's conduct was fundamentally different to be determined by the jury. Lord Bingham in *Rahman* (at [26]) describes 'fundamentally different' as having a 'plain meaning' and suggests that it is 'not a term of art'.

Lord Brown's redefinition of the test at [68] in *Rahman* (section 8.7.5.1, p 263) makes a significant change by restricting the availability of the exception to cases where D was unaware of the weapon which P uses to kill V. The courts have not previously gone as far as holding that as a matter of law D is precluded from relying on the *English* qualification if he was aware that P had the weapon.

■ *Questions*

1. As a matter of principle, this poses problems: why should D who is aware that P has a weapon but does not foresee the possibility that P might use it be in a worse position than D who is unaware of the weapon? In practical terms, the ramifications of this restriction are significant.

2. What of cases where D is aware that P is vicious with his fist, but on this occasion uses a shod foot to kick V to death?

Since a change of P's mens rea will not render his acts fundamentally different, only changes in his conduct may do so. Beyond that, the position is far from clear. Different views were advanced in the House of Lords in *Rahman*. According to some Lords, an act can be fundamentally different only by a change of weapon or the use of a weapon when none at all was contemplated (see Lord Rodger at [47]; Lord Brown at [68]; Lord Neuberger at [88]—although his lordship is more flexible at [102]). With respect, it is doubtful whether that can be right. In *A-G's Reference (No 3 of 2004)* [2005] EWCA Crim 1882, the fundamental change was P firing the very weapon of which D was aware *at* V rather than *near* V. Further ambiguity remains because, although a change of weapon is a necessary requirement of the *English* qualification, it is not, it seems, a sufficient one. There is the further requirement that the weapon used by P must be different from that which D foresaw might be used *and* more 'lethal' (see Lord Brown at [68]). Things become even more complex when regard is had to Lord Brown's third requirement—that *because of* the change of weapon and its more lethal nature, P's act may be regarded as fundamentally different. Thus, not every killing by P with an unforeseen weapon of a more lethal nature will necessarily amount to a fundamentally different act.

■ *Questions*

Should the fundamental change test be about:

(i) a change of weapon to a more lethal weapon? What is a more lethal weapon, a stick or a knife?

(ii) a change of conduct and the manner of P performing the conduct?

In *Gamble* [1989] NI 268, D was not guilty of murder when P had gone beyond the agreed knee-capping and killed V by cutting his throat. This was regarded as a fundamental change.

■ *Question*

Do you agree with the decision?

In *Rahman*, Lord Bingham (at [29]) regarded P's change in *Gamble* from gun to knife as sufficient, the carrying of the latter to a knee-capping being 'potentially even more sinister' than a gun. Lords Bingham and Rodger regarded the throat-cutting (at [29]) as 'of an entirely different character in an entirely different context'. In contrast, Lords Scott, Brown and Neuberger in *Rahman* query the correctness of the decision.

In *Mendez*, Lord Justice Toulson stated:

D is not liable for the murder of V if the direct cause of V's death was a deliberate act by P which was of a kind (a) unforeseen by D and (b) likely to be altogether more life-threatening than acts of the kind intended or foreseen by D.

■ *Questions*

Is slitting someone's throat with a knife (killing with intent) fundamentally different from knee-capping them (GBH with intent) bearing in mind that the change of mens rea is not sufficient following *Rahman* to constitute a fundamental change? Would it be fundamental applying *Rahman*? Would it be applying *Mendez*?

Consider *Rafferty* [2007] EWCA Crim 1846, in which D and his co-defendants, P1 and P2, attacked V. D punched V twice. He then left the scene with V's cash card and headed for an ATM. Meanwhile, P1 and P2 continued the attack on V, escalating the violence by kicking him in the head and finally drowning him in the sea. D returned to find V dead. Was the act which caused the death of V fundamentally different from that which D had foreseen? In this case the cause of death was drowning (importantly, the experts all agreed that V would probably have made a recovery from the other injuries, but that is not to say that the kicking and punching do not remain causes of death in law). The crucial question is then whether D realized that one of the attackers might intentionally do this act, that is, the drowning. The answer to that would seem to be that he did not. The act of drowning was accepted to be of a fundamentally different nature to P1 and P2's act which D foresaw. The Court of Appeal, rightly, does not go as far as to say that drowning will always be fundamentally different from an attack with fists, etc. Everything will turn on the facts and circumstances of the attack.

■ *Question*

Why was the drowning fundamentally different from what D foresaw (GBH by kicking)?

There is another way of analysing this case. D's liability might be described as being in two stages. He was a party to a joint enterprise to rob. There is no doubt that V was robbed of his cash card and that D was a party to the violence used to appropriate that property. D does not withdraw from that enterprise when he goes off to fulfil a part of the plan by withdrawing money from an ATM with V's cash card. He intended to return with the money to distribute it.

■ *Questions*

Has the robbery been completed by the time D walks off with the card? Can D be liable for the death of V on the basis of the acts he performed as part of the original joint enterprise robbery?

8.7.5.4 If P's act is 'fundamentally different', does D escape all liability for homicide?

In cases such as *Rafferty*, D would remain liable for the injury he inflicted on V and his part in the robbery. The question remains whether if the act of drowning was regarded as fundamentally different so that, following *English*, D is not liable for murder, D should remain liable for manslaughter.

R v Gilmour

[2000] 2 Cr App R 407, Court of Appeal of Northern Ireland

(Carswell LCJ, Nicholson LJ and Coghlin J)

According to G, whose admissions were the only evidence of his part in the incident, he was roused from his bed by M and P ('the principals'), whom he knew to be members of the UVF, who told him to drive them to what turned out to be the scene of the crime, 'which he did not do willingly'. There, a 1-litre whisky bottle containing petrol was thrown by M or P through the ground-floor window of a house in which six people were asleep. A fierce fire quickly developed with thick smoke. Three adults escaped but three young boys were killed by carbon monoxide poisoning. The judge (sitting in a Diplock court, ie one without a jury) was satisfied, having regard to the nature of the bottle from which the bomb was constituted, that those who made and threw it had an actual intention to kill. He was satisfied that G knew that M intended to use a petrol bomb and to cause really serious injury. He convicted all three of murder. G appealed.

Carswell LCJ [rejected an attack on the judge's conclusion as to the intention of M and P and continued:]

There is, however, more substance in the next submission, that the proof is insufficient that the appellant realised that those who threw the petrol bomb intended at least grievous bodily harm to the occupants of the house. Throwing petrol bombs at dwelling houses is regrettably common and always contains an element of potential danger to the occupants. It is right to say, however, that it has fortunately been only a rare consequence that occupants have been injured in such attacks, and the majority of them appear, so far as judicial notice can take us, to cause only minor fires. There is not in our view sufficient evidence to conclude that the appellant was aware that the petrol was contained in an unusually large bottle, which might be expected to cause a larger conflagration and result in greater danger to the occupants. On the evidence he realised at a late stage that a petrol bomb attack was about to take place, and his intention was formed in that short period before he co-operated in driving the principals away from the scene. It would be difficult to attribute to him with any degree of certainty an intention that the attack should result in more than a blaze which might do some damage, put the occupants in fear and intimidate them into moving from the house. The principals and the appellant did have a grudge against Colm Quinn, but there is not sufficient evidence to establish that they expected him to be sleeping in the house that night. Nor do we think that the talk that Colm Quinn was 'going to be used as a Guy Fawkes' is enough to establish beyond reasonable doubt that the appellant intended that those who were in occupation should suffer injuries in the fire. We therefore do not consider that the judge's finding that he appreciated that the principals intended to inflict grievous bodily harm can be supported as a safe conclusion of fact.

We conclude accordingly that the appellant's conviction for murder cannot be sustained. Nor can his conviction on counts 4, 5 and 6, each of which involves an intention to commit grievous bodily harm. The issue then is whether he can be found guilty of manslaughter on the first three counts, on the basis that if the principals had thrown the petrol bomb into the house without the intention of killing or inflicting grievous bodily harm on any person they would have properly been convicted of that offence. It was argued on behalf of the appellant that if he did not share the intention of the principals he should not be found guilty of either murder or manslaughter, in the same way as if the principals go outside the contemplated acts involved in the joint enterprise the accessory cannot be convicted of either offence: see our recent decision in *Crooks* [1999] NI 226, following the principles laid down in *R v Powell and English* [1998] 1 Cr App R 261, [1999] AC 1.

The issue is discussed in Blackstone's *Criminal Practice*, 2000 ed, para A5.5 at p 75, in which the example is posed where the principal and accessory agree that the principal will post an incendiary device to the victim, the accessory contemplating only superficial injuries but the principal foreseeing and hoping that the injuries will be serious or fatal. The principal will be guilty of murder and the accessory will not. The editors conclude that the accessory should in such a case be convicted of manslaughter, because the act done by the principal is precisely what was envisaged.

In our opinion this is the correct principle to apply in the present case. The appellant foresaw that the principals would carry out the act of throwing a petrol bomb into the house, but did not realise that in so doing they intended to kill or do grievous bodily harm to the occupants. To establish that a person charged as an accessory to a crime of specific intent is guilty as an accessory it is necessary to prove that he realised the principal's intention: see *Hyde* (1991) 92 Cr App R 131, 135, [1991] 1 QB 134, 139, *per* Lord Lane CJ, approved by Lord Hutton in *R v Powell and English* [1998] 1 Cr App R 261, 283, [1999] AC 1, 27–28. The line of authority represented by such cases as *Anderson and Morris* (1966) 50 Cr App R 216, [1966] 2 QB 110, approved in *R v Powell and English*, deals with situations where the principal departs from the contemplated joint enterprise and perpetrates a more serious act of a different kind unforeseen by the accessory. In such cases it is established that the accessory is not liable at all for such unforeseen acts. It does not follow that the same result should follow where the principal carries out the very act contemplated by the accessory, though the latter does not realise that the principal intends a more serious consequence from the act.

We do not consider that we are obliged by authority to hold that the accessory in such a case must be acquitted of manslaughter as well as murder. The cases in which an accessory has been found not guilty both of murder and manslaughter all concern a departure by the principal from the *actus reus* contemplated by the accessory, not a difference between the parties in respect of the *mens rea* of each. In such cases the view has prevailed that it would be wrong to hold the accessory liable when the principal committed an act which the accessory did not contemplate or authorise. We do not, however, see any convincing policy reason why a person acting as an accessory to a principal who carries out the very deed contemplated by both should not be guilty of the degree of offence appropriate to the intent with which he so acted. It is of course conceivable, as is suggested in *Blackstone, loc cit*, that in some cases the nature of the principal's *mens rea* may change the nature of the act committed by him and take it outside the type of act contemplated by the accessory, but it does not seem to us that the existence of such a possibility affects the validity of the basic principle which we have propounded.

A verdict of guilty of manslaughter on this basis was upheld by the Court of Appeal in *Stewart and Schofield* [1995] 1 Cr App R 441, [1995] 3 All ER 159. The judgment has been strongly criticised by Sir John Smith in [1995] Crim LR 296 and [1995] Crim LR 422 and in Smith & Hogan, *Criminal Law*, 9th edn, 1999 p 145. Even if there may be ground for criticism of some of the propositions enunciated in the Court's judgment, the principle accepted as its basis is in our view sustainable.

We accordingly allow the appeal, substitute a verdict of not guilty of murder but guilty of manslaughter on counts 1 to 3 and set aside the verdicts of guilty on counts 4 to 6.

Appeal allowed

■ *Questions*

1. Was there any evidence that G shared the common purpose of M and P to throw a petrol bomb? Was his purpose in 'unwillingly' driving the car to and from the scene proved to be other than that of avoiding unpleasant consequences to himself or his family?

2. Was he properly regarded as a party to a joint enterprise? Does it—should it—make any difference? Did he not know he was aiding and abetting a joint enterprise?

3. Was the throwing of the unusually large bottle fundamentally different from the throwing of an ordinary bottle which, it appears, is unlikely to cause any injury? Should not the judge have asked himself this question? In an English court (ie with a jury), would not a judge have been obliged to leave it to the jury?—*Powell and English*, section 8.7.3, p 258.

4. E administers to V a particular drug, XYZ, which E knows is certain to kill, and is assisted or encouraged by D who knows the drug is XYZ but believes the only effect of XYZ will be to give V a headache. V is killed. Is D guilty of manslaughter? Was the administration by E the 'very deed' contemplated by P?

Cf commentary at [2000] Crim LR 763, discussion of *Gilmour* at [2001] Crim LR 333–335 and *Day* [2001] Crim LR 984.

8.7.5.5 D's liability for manslaughter if P is convicted of murder

Suppose the jury find that P murdered V but that D did not foresee that P might kill or cause really serious harm. D did, however, foresee that P might cause V some lesser form of harm. Should D escape liability altogether or can he be found guilty of manslaughter? That was the issue the Court of Appeal had to decide in the following case.

R v Carpenter
[2011] EWCA Crim 2568, Court of Appeal, Criminal Division, http://www.bailii.org/ew/cases/EWCA/Crim/2011/2568.html

(Richards LJ, Keith and Nicol JJ)

D was the mother of P. P got into a dispute with V and they decided to settle things by having a 'fair-play fight'. The families of P and V gathered and, in the course of the fight, P stabbed V with a knife he had brought with him. D and P were charged with murder. The Crown's case was that D had been aware that her son was carrying a knife when she accompanied him to the fight and that she lent him assistance by restraining V's mother from assisting him. P was guilty of murder. At D's trial, the judge directed the jury that if they acquitted her of murder, they could nevertheless convict her of manslaughter if they found that she had known that her son was carrying a knife and had foreseen that he might use it to cause some injury or harm falling short of killing or causing really serious injury. The jury acquitted D of murder but convicted her of manslaughter. D appealed on the basis that the judge should not have directed the jury that they could convict her of manslaughter if they acquitted her of murder.

Discussion

15. In our judgment, [counsel for D's] submissions run contrary to a clear and well established line of authority in this court; and whilst they gain superficial support from passages of the judgment in *R v Mendez* [2011] QB 876, that case does not in reality represent a departure from the established line of authority and does not provide the defendant with any assistance.

   16. For the line of authority against [counsel for D's] submissions, it is sufficient to go back to *R v Day (M)* [2001] EWCA Crim 1594; [2001] Crim LR 984. In that case there were three defendants alleged to have participated in a joint enterprise to attack the deceased. Two of them had been convicted of

murder, whereas the third, Marc Day, had been convicted of manslaughter. It was argued that since the other two defendants had been convicted of murder on a joint enterprise basis, Marc Day could only have been guilty if he participated in the joint enterprise to inflict grievous bodily harm with intent, and in that case he would have been guilty of murder. If his state of mind was only to intend some harm and he did not foresee the infliction of grievous bodily harm by the others, then he was not a participant in the joint enterprise in question and he should have been acquitted. In rejecting that argument, Laws LJ, giving the judgment of the court, said [2001] EWCA Crim 1594 at [52]–[53]:

'52. As regards the second point, it is not part of the law of joint enterprise that a secondary party, B, must share the mens rea of the principal offender, A—see *R v Slack* [1989] QB 775 and *R v Hyde* [1991] 1 QB 134 where it was made clear that foresight of what the principal may do is sufficient mens rea for the accessory even if there is no actual agreement between him and the principal. In *R v Powell (Anthony)* [1999] 1 AC 1 itself a major question was whether a secondary party in a murder case must be shown to have been actuated by the mens rea required in the principal offender, and the question was answered in the negative. The subject matter of a joint enterprise is not a state of mind or intention but an objective act which it is contemplated will or might be done.

'53. That proposition we think provides the key to the right result in a class of case which is not, so far as counsel's researches have revealed, distinctly the subject of any authority. Suppose that the participants in a joint enterprise all propose or foresee the same kind of violence being inflicted on their victim, let it be punching with the possibility of kicking to follow. On that they are at one. But two of them harbour a subjective intention to inflict really serious injury by means of such violence. The third harbours only, or foresees or intends only, that some harm might be done. One of those actuated by an intent to do grievous bodily harm punches or kicks the victim just as all three foresaw. The victim falls and suffers a subdural haemorrhage and dies. The principal is guilty of murder as he had the mens rea required. So also is the accessory who, like him, intended or contemplated the infliction of the serious injury. What of the third adventurer? Mr Fitzgerald submits he must escape altogether because he did not foresee a murderous state of mind would be harboured by his fellows. Yet if his fellows had entertained only an intention to do some harm and otherwise the facts were the same, all three would be guilty of manslaughter. It does not seem to us that that can be right. In such a case there was a joint enterprise to inflict some harm, and that is not negated by the larger intentions of the other two adventurers. In our judgment in such a case there is no reason why the participants should not be convicted and sentenced appropriately as their several states of mind dictate.'

17. In *R v A* [2011] QB 841, a case concerning the liability of secondary parties for murder, Hughes LJ, giving the judgment of the court, drew a distinction, at para 27, between a case where D2 foresees that D1 will cause death by acting with murderous intent (in which case D2 has associated himself with a foreseen murder) and a case where all that D2 foresees is that death may be caused without that intention (in which case he has associated himself not with a foreseen murder but with foreseen manslaughter). He then cited a substantial part of the passage we have quoted above from *R v Day (M)*, before concluding, at para 28:

'Thus this court proceeded upon the basis that the second participant was guilty of murder because he at least foresaw the deliberate infliction of GBH, whereas the third was not because he did not. That is precisely the law as we have endeavoured to state it. This court was not beginning to say that D2 could be guilty of murder without foresight that D1 might act with murderous intent.'

The focus was of course on secondary liability for murder, but there was not the slightest suggestion of disagreement with the conclusion reached in *R v Day (M)* that the participant who lacked the requisite state of mind for murder might none the less be guilty of manslaughter.

18. To similar effect as *R v Day (M)* [2001] Crim LR 984 is the judgment in *R v Yemoh* [2009] EWCA Crim 930; [2009] Crim LR 888, albeit *R v Day (M)* does not appear to have been cited to the court

in *R v Yemoh*. The case concerned a knife killing in which joint enterprise was alleged. One of the defendants had been convicted of murder, the others of manslaughter. In broad terms, therefore, the case had a degree of factual similarity to the present case. One of the arguments advanced on behalf of those convicted of manslaughter was that the judge had been wrong to direct the jury that a defendant would be guilty of manslaughter if it was proved that he participated in the attack and that when he did so

> 'he knew that the knifeman had a knife or other sharp implement and intended to use it to cause some injury or harm, but falling short of killing or causing really serious bodily harm, or he realised that that person might use the weapon to cause some injury, falling short of really serious harm.'

In rejecting the defendant's submissions Hooper LJ, giving the judgment of the court, said, at paras 125–126:

> '125. This submission cannot succeed in the light of the decision of the House of Lords in *R v Rahman* [2009] AC 129, upholding the decision of the Court of Appeal. In *R v Rahman* it was argued that the fact that the stabber intended to kill (or may have intended to kill) took (or could take) the stabber's actions out of the scope of the common design because what the stabber did was 'fundamentally different' from what the defendants had intended or foreseen. All that they had intended or foreseen was the infliction of serious bodily harm. That argument was rejected.
>   '126. The argument presented in this case on behalf of those convicted of manslaughter is only a slight variation on this argument. If a defendant knowing that the stabber had a knife intends the stabber to cause some injury to the deceased or realises that he might cause some injury, then the fact that the stabber stabbed the deceased intending to kill him is not 'fundamentally different' from what the defendant had intended or foreseen. Counsel could point to no authority to the effect that the fundamentally different rule in manslaughter cases is different to the rule as it applies to murder cases. It follows that, in so far as this argument is concerned, there was no misdirection and it also follows that the judge was entitled if not obliged to leave manslaughter to the jury.'

19. Mr Raggatt directed our attention to what is said about *R v Yemoh* in *Smith & Hogan's Criminal Law*, 13th ed (2011), pp 225–226:

> 'In *R v Yemoh* the Court of Appeal confirmed that P's greater mens rea from that which D foresaw will not prevent D being guilty of manslaughter. D, a member of the gang, knew that another member of the gang, P, had a knife and intended that other to cause some injury to V or realized that he might cause some injury. The fact that P stabbed V *intending to kill* (ie with graver mens rea) did not absolve D. If D intended or foresaw that one of the group might cause non-serious injury, D remains liable for manslaughter even if P kills with intent to kill or do grievous bodily harm, unless P's manner of doing so is fundamentally different from that D foresaw.'

20. To similar effect is the commentary in *Archbold's Criminal Pleading, Evidence and Practice*, 2011 ed, para 19-26, referring inter alia to *R v Day (M)* [2001] Crim LR 984, *R v Rahman* [2009] AC 129 and *R v Yemoh* [2009] Crim LR 888.

21. All this is fundamentally at odds with the case advanced by Mr Tedd on the present appeal. Mr Tedd submitted, however, that it cannot stand with *R v Mendez* [2011] QB 876, which does not appear to have been cited to the court in *R v A* [2011] QB 841 (nor indeed in *R v Yemoh*) and which we should now follow.

[The Court of Appeal held that *Mendez* was not authority for the proposition that manslaughter was not an alternative to murder on the facts of the case. The following reasons were given.]

29. First, the context was very different. The underlying issue was whether use of a knife to stab the deceased was fundamentally different from anything the secondary party foresaw, so as to fall outside the scope of the joint enterprise, where there was evidence that he foresaw the use of violence and of weapons (fist, foot, pieces of wood and/or metal bars) but not that he foresaw the use of a knife. The particular test of liability for murder set out and approved at paras 45 and 47, and against

which the judge's directions to the jury were tested, was directed to that issue. The court was not considering a case where the use of a knife to do some harm was foreseen but the secondary party did not share or foresee the murderous intention with which the principal actually used the knife.

30. What the court said about the unavailability of manslaughter as a possible verdict has to be read in that context: it was directed to a case where use of a knife was not foreseen, rather than to a case where use of a knife was foreseen but the secondary party did not share or foresee the intention with which it was used. This can be seen very clearly from the passage in *R v Powell (Anthony)* [1999] 1 AC 1, para 22 which the court evidently had in mind when stating that *R v Reid (Barry)* 62 Cr App R 109 no longer represented the law because the House of Lords had adopted a different analysis of *R v Anderson; R v Morris* [1966] 2 QB 110. The passage is in the speech of Lord Hutton [1999] 1 AC 1, 30:

> 'Accordingly, in the appeal of English, I consider that the direction of the trial judge was defective... because in accordance with the principle stated by Lord Parker CJ in *R v Anderson* [1966] 2 QB 110, 120B he did not qualify his direction on foresight of really serious injury by stating that if the jury considered that the use of the knife by Weddle was the use of a weapon and an action on Weddle's part which English did not foresee as a possibility, then English should not be convicted of murder. As the unforeseen use of the knife would take the killing outside the scope of the joint venture the jury should also have been directed, as the Court of Criminal Appeal held in *R v Anderson*, that English should not be found guilty of manslaughter.
> 'On the evidence the jury could have found that English did not know that Weddle had a knife. Therefore the judge's direction made the conviction unsafe and in my opinion his appeal should be allowed and the conviction for murder quashed.'

31. It follows that what was said in *R v Mendez* [2011] QB 876 about the unavailability of a verdict of manslaughter has no bearing on the issue in the present case. The court was simply not addressing a situation where, as here, use of a knife was foreseen but it was not intended or foreseen that the knife would be used with the intention to kill or cause really serious harm. It is therefore unsurprising that cases such as *R v Day (M)* [2001] Crim LR 984 and *R v Yemoh* [2009] Crim LR 888 are not referred to in the judgment and do not appear to have been cited to the court: the issue in those cases did not arise for consideration in *R v Mendez* [2011] QB 876.

32. If, contrary to our reading of the judgment, anything said in *R v Mendez* is to be taken as applying to the availability of a verdict of manslaughter in circumstances such as those of the present case, what was said was plainly *obiter* (the case was concerned with liability for murder, not for manslaughter) and was expressed without consideration of the *R v Day (M)* line of authority, and in our view it cannot displace that line of authority.

33. Accordingly, we take the view that the *R v Day (M)* line of authority remains good law. Its application is determinative of this appeal. We are satisfied that the alternative of manslaughter was properly left to the jury and that there was no material error in the judge's directions. It might have been better for him to give the jury a separate 'route to verdict' in respect of the defendant, rather than directing them to make the appropriate substitutions in the 'route to verdict' in respect of her husband, but the jury can have been left in no doubt as to the test they had to apply and there is nothing to cast doubt on the safety of the defendant's conviction.

8.7.6 D was continuing to participate at the time P committed crime B

In *Willett* [2010] EWCA Crim 1620, D was convicted of murder. D and P set out to steal from V's van. D went to the van and P remained in the getaway vehicle. D was disturbed by the owner. D ran to the car and P drove off. As they turned the corner, V blocked their path. P knocked him down, killing him. D was at least an accessory to theft. D would only be liable for P's act of murder if D either (i) gave direct assistance or encouragement to that act of murder or (ii) having participated in the theft, D foresaw that P might commit at least GBH with intent when driving away and continued to participate in the criminal venture. In this case, the Court of Appeal concluded that D could not have foreseen that P might drive at V until a few seconds before (when they turned the corner). It was necessary therefore for the Crown to prove that D actively assisted or encouraged. The court concluded that D's act of continuing to sit in the passenger seat could not of itself amount to assistance or encouragement. There was, however, evidence from a witness to whom D had confessed his encouragement from which a jury could reasonably conclude that he had participated in and given encouragement to the murder. The Court of Appeal held that the trial judge had erred in leaving the jury with the option of convicting on the basis of D's presence in the car alone.

8.7.7 D's liability for manslaughter when P is liable for unlawful act manslaughter

If P commits unlawful act manslaughter (see section 17.2, p 594), what must D foresee before he will be guilty of the offence also? Unlawful act manslaughter requires proof that P performed (i) an intentional unlawful act, (ii) in circumstances that a reasonable person would see posed a risk of some harm to someone, and (iii) that unlawful act caused death. Apart from having to intend to perform the act, P's liability is strict. What about D who is an accessory? What must D foresee about P's act and mens rea?

In *Bristow and Bristow* [2013] EWCA Crim 1540, V ran an off-road vehicle repair business from a secluded farm. The only access to the farm was by a single lane track and entry to the lane from the main road was gained through a metal gate. The defendants entered the premises with the aim of stealing the valuable equipment which V had stored there. The defendants bypassed the metal gate by driving down a ditch to the side of it. Evidence indicated that V had probably intervened while the burglary was taking place. His cause of death was injury consistent with having been struck and/or run over by one or more of the vehicles at the scene. The Crown's case was unlawful act manslaughter, the unlawful act in question being the burglary of the farm. Although the Crown could not say who was driving the vehicle or vehicles that had struck V, it was asserted that each D took part in the burglary and in doing so, in the particular circumstances, each D foresaw a real possibility that someone intervening at the scene might suffer harm as a result of the carrying out of the burglary, including harm caused during their escape from the scene. The defendants were found guilty. In summing-up the judge had told the jury that if a defendant, instead of trying to escape, drove deliberately and needlessly out of his way intending to run down and kill V, that would be outside the scope of a joint venture. On appeal, counsel for the defendants argued that if the driver of a vehicle, in seeking to escape, drove with an intention to kill or do grievous bodily harm, that went outside the scope of the joint enterprise so that the other defendants could not in any event be found guilty. The Court of Appeal rejected this.

41. As to [counsel for the defendants] additional point relating to an asserted misdirection concerning a driver who in the course of escape drove the vehicle with murderous intent, we reject it. The decisions of this court in *R v Carpenter* [2011] EWCA Crim 2568 (a case of manslaughter), and of the House of Lords in *R v Rahman & Others* [2009] 1 Cr App R 1 (a case of murder), demonstrate that the test of an accessory's liability is one of foresight, namely foresight of what the principal might do, rather than foresight of the intention with which the principal might perform such acts. Accordingly, the argument advanced by [counsel for the defendants] against conviction must fail in the case of all appellants, including Terrence Bristow, who is equally affected by it.

Despite what the Court of Appeal states, it is clear that a long line of authority establishes that D must foresee not only what P might do, but also that P might have the requisite mens rea for the offence in question. This case is important in two respects. First of all, it establishes that D can still be liable on the basis of parasitic accessorial liability despite P's change of mens rea, provided that P is still acting within the scope of their joint venture. Secondly, and more importantly, the case demonstrates how the principles of parasitic accessorial liability will operate when the offence in question is a constructive one, such as unlawful act manslaughter. The defendant whose case the jury were considering must (i) have participated in the burglary and foreseen the circumstances in which it would take place. If that was proved, the question was whether a reasonable person would realize that the manner of committing the burglary might cause a risk of some harm to someone. If that was established, and the cause of death was the commission of the burglary, the defendant would be guilty of unlawful act manslaughter unless the principal had carried out the burglary in a fundamentally different manner. There is no mens rea as to death for P that needs to be proved, so no mens rea for D as to P's mens rea.

■ **Questions**

Do you think that in cases of constructive crime convicting D on the basis of parasitic accessorial liability extends the scope of the law too far?

D and P set out to steal cable from a railway by cutting the live cable to sell it. D is in the pick-up truck ready to pull the cable away at the top of the embankment. P cuts it with cable cutters leaving it live and exposed. V, a railway worker, is electrocuted when he attends the scene to investigate. P is guilty of unlawful act manslaughter. What would the jury need to be sure of for D to be guilty of manslaughter?

8.7.8 The Supreme Court's decision in *Gnango*

In one respect, the case of *Gnango* [2011] UKSC 59 is one of the most important criminal law cases to have been decided for some time. However, in many others it may have very little impact on the law as it relates to parasitic accessorial liability. The facts can be stated simply, but what the majority of the Supreme Court decided is far from simple. V was a nurse walking home from work through an estate in south London. D was engaged in a dispute over money with a man who came to be known in the course of proceedings as 'Bandana Man' (BM). D and BM happened to come across one another in the estate through which V was walking. Both men fired shots at one another from firearms they had been carrying with them. One of the shots that BM aimed at D missed him and instead hit V, killing her. BM was never identified sufficiently clearly for anyone to be charged. The Crown sought to charge D with not only the attempted murder of D, but also with the murder of V. Establishing BM's liability for the murder of V would have been straightforward, relying upon the doctrine of transferred malice. However, establishing D's liability is more difficult. At D's trial, the Crown sought to base D's liability for the murder of V on two grounds:

(i) that D had aided and abetted the shooting by BM with intent to kill. This was rejected by the trial judge; it could not be said that D encouraged BM to fire back at him. In addition, the trial judge stated that accepting this line of argument would necessitate D being guilty of aiding and abetting his own attempted murder, which would be a 'real oddity'; or

(ii) that the gunfight was a joint enterprise between D and BM and that each foresaw that in the course of it the other might shoot, with intent to kill or do really serious bodily injury, and might kill someone other than the immediate target of his shot. The trial judge accepted this argument and held that it could be said that there was a joint enterprise to commit affray by the use of unlawful violence, it being a question for the jury whether death by gunshot was within the contemplation of the parties to the affray.

D was convicted on the basis of (ii) and appealed. D's argument on appeal was that there could be no joint enterprise when he and BM were engaged in individual, diametrically opposed missions. Each had an intention to harm a specific individual. D's aim was to hit BM; BM's aim was to hit D. In the absence of a common purpose, there could be no joint enterprise. The Court of Appeal ([2010] EWCA Crim 1691) quashed D's conviction on the basis that there was no common purpose between D and BM.

59. What is at issue here is secondary liability. The essence of secondary liability is that the parties are acting *together* or, as it is often put, *in concert*. For what we have described as the third type of joint enterprise liability [i.e. parasitic accessorial liability] they must be acting together or in concert in crime A, here affray. Two people who voluntarily engage in fighting each other might, exceptionally, be acting together or in concert, but ordinarily they are not. It is not realistic to say that they acted in concert to cause fear; they acted independently and antagonistically in a manner which did so. Absent a shared purpose to shoot *and be shot at*, the submission made by the appellant was correct that there was no room on the facts for any other common purpose. The jury was never asked to confront the question whether the shared common purpose was not only to shoot, but to be shot at.

The Crown appealed to the Supreme Court, which restored D's conviction. However, the individual justices did so for divergent reasons and it is therefore helpful to examine their judgments separately.

If (1) D1 and D2 voluntarily engage in fighting each other, each intending to kill or cause grievous bodily harm to the other and each foreseeing that the other has the reciprocal intention, and if (2) D1 mistakenly kills V in the course of the fight, in what circumstances, if any, is D2 guilty of the offence of murdering V?

Lords Phillips and **Judge** (with whom **Lord Wilson** agreed):

[Their lordships agreed with the Court of Appeal that D could not be guilty of murder on the basis of parasitic accessorial liability as there was no common purpose between him and BM. Instead, their lordships relied upon the conventional principles of secondary liability.]

55. If the defendant aided, abetted, counselled and procured Bandana Man to shoot at him he was, on my analysis, guilty of aiding and abetting the attempted murder of himself. Had he been killed by Bandana Man, he would have been a party to his own murder. Although he had not intended that Bandana Man should succeed in hitting him, complicity in his attempt to do so would have rendered him a party to the successful achievement of that attempt. As it was, Bandana Man accidentally shot [V]. Under the doctrine of transferred malice he was liable for her murder. Under the same doctrine, the defendant, if he had aided abetted, counselled and procured the attempt, was party to the murder that resulted. Does it follow that, having regard to the terms of the judge's directions, the jury must have been satisfied that the defendant had aided, abetted, counselled and procured Bandana Man to shoot at him with murderous intent? If so, his conviction can stand. If not, the Court of Appeal correctly quashed it.

56. In his ruling that there was a case to go to the jury the judge ruled that it could not be said that the defendant actively encouraged Bandana Man to shoot at him. He could not be said to have encouraged Bandana Man to fire at him, although he might have provoked this. Perhaps it was with this passage of his ruling in mind that the Court of Appeal observed at para 59 that the jury was never

asked to confront the question whether the shared common purpose was not only to shoot but be shot at. In the next paragraph the Court of Appeal observed that the judge was, in effect, leaving to the jury a limited common purpose—limiting it to an exchange of gun fire which did not extend to the gunman being hit.

57. Having carefully considered the passages in the judge's summing up that we have set out at para 23 above we do not consider that they support the Court of Appeal's conclusion. It may well be that the intention of the judge was to direct the jury to consider whether there was a common intention to have an affray that fell short of an intention to shoot at each other and be shot at. For the reasons that we have given this would have been an incredible scenario. Either there was no joint plan or agreement at all, or there was a common intention to shoot at one another, which can only mean to shoot and be shot at. What matters, however, is not the route that the judge considered would lead to a conviction, but the direction that he gave to the jury. He directed the jury that, in order to convict they had to be satisfied that there was a plan or agreement to 'have a shoot out...whether made beforehand...or made on the spur of the moment when they saw each other and fired at each other from the steps and the car park respectively'.

58. This direction did not permit the jury to convict if they believed that one of the protagonists might have been the aggressor and the other merely responding in self defence. It was an unequivocal direction that the jury could convict only if they were satisfied that the protagonists had formed a mutual plan or agreement to have a gun fight in which each would attempt to kill or seriously injure the other. If the jury were satisfied of this, the consequence in law was that each of the protagonists was party, not merely to his own attempt to kill or seriously injure the other, but to the other's attempt to kill or seriously injure him. Contrary to the finding of the Court of Appeal, the direction of the judge required the jury to consider whether they were satisfied that the defendant and Bandana Man had a common plan or agreement to shoot at each other and be shot at. If they were so satisfied, and their verdict indicates that they were, this was a proper basis for finding that the defendant was guilty of murder.

In order to come to this conclusion, their lordships had to bypass the so-called '*Tyrell* principle', discussed at section 8.6.1, p 255. As has already been discussed, their lordships held that this principle only applies when the offence in question is intended to protect a specified class of person. Since murder is not such an offence, it was held that the '*Tyrell* principle' was of no application.

Lord Brown's judgment is the most explicit in recognizing the role that policy played in the outcome of this appeal.

Lord Brown:

68. Although the facts of this case are more fully described in Lord Phillips of Worth Matravers PSC's judgment, the appeal to my mind must necessarily be decided by reference to the bare scenario already outlined, not the many surrounding details that can all too easily obscure rather than clarify the real issue arising. And to my mind the all-important consideration here is that both A and B were intentionally engaged in a potentially lethal unlawful gunfight (a 'shoot-out' as it has also been described) in the course of which an innocent passer-by was killed. The general public would in my opinion be astonished and appalled if in those circumstances the law attached liability for the death only to the gunman who actually fired the fatal shot (which, indeed, it would not always be possible to determine). Is he alone to be regarded as guilty of the victim's murder? Is the other gunman really to be regarded as blameless and exonerated from all criminal liability for that killing? Does the decision of the Court of Appeal here, allowing A's appeal against his conviction for murder, really represent the law of the land?

[His lordship agreed that D's conviction for murder ought to be restored, but on the basis that D and BM were joint principals in the murder of V. After the paragraph extracted above, Lord Brown continued:]

69. To my mind the answer to these questions is a plain 'no'. Realistically this case is indistinguish-able from the succession of authorities establishing criminal liability on the part of anyone who willingly involves himself in the use of unlawful violence between protagonists intent on killing or seriously injuring each other, be they duellers, prize-fighters or sado-masochists: see respectively *R v Young and Webber* (1838) 8 C & P 644, *R v Coney* (1882) 8 QBD 534 and *R v Brown (Anthony)* [1994] 1 AC 212. It is the very purpose of those engaging in these various activities that injuries will occur. The suggestion that certain of the perpetrators of such consensual violence, merely because they are also its prospective victims, cannot be liable for it, whether as principals or accessories by virtue of the deci-sion in *R v Tyrrell* [1894] 1 QB 710 (discussed by Lord Phillips PSC and Lord Judge CJ at para 18 of their judgment), cannot be right. The principle underlying criminal liability for duelling, prize-fighting and so forth is not to be understood simply as the protection of those most directly at risk of the injuries intended. Rather it is the protection of society generally from the damaging consequences of such injuries and the discouragement of violent conduct as a whole. Another powerful illustration of the principle (discussed by Lord Phillips PSC and Lord Judge CJ at para 52) is the law with regard to suicide (modified although that now is).

70. Such being the rationale for criminal liability in this line of cases, how could the principle not encompass also the present case? In so far as there are factual differences between this case and an old-fashioned duel—most notably the absence here of the civilities and formalities characterising a duel and the spur of the moment nature (if such it was) of the decision here to engage in a gunfight (ie to shoot and, inevitably, be shot at)—none of these suggest any lesser criminality for whatever injuries may result than in the case of a duel itself. Quite the contrary, indeed. The public interest in criminalis-ing the violence engaged in is yet more obvious: here there were others about so that the risk of harm was by no means confined merely to the protagonists themselves.

71. For my part I am not disposed to analyse A's liability for C's murder here in accessory terms—as the aider or abetter, counsellor or procurer of B's attempt to kill him (A himself) whose liability for C's death thus arises, *R v Tyrrell* constituting no obstacle, under the doctrine of transferred malice. Rather it seems to me that A is liable for C's murder as a principal—a direct participant engaged by agreement in unlawful violence (like a duel, a prize-fight or sado-masochism) specifically designed to cause and in fact causing death or serious injury. But whichever analysis is adopted, A's liability for C's murder seems to me clear and I would regard our criminal law as seriously defective were it otherwise.

You will recall from the earlier analysis that the principal is the individual who most directly causes the actus reus of the offence in question. So the principal in this case was the one whose act most directly caused the death of V, but was that not BM? How can it therefore be said that D and BM were joint principals?

Like Lord Brown, Lord Clarke restored D's murder conviction on the basis that he and BM were joint principals.

Lord Clarke:

78. As Lord Phillips PSC and Lord Judge CJ have explained, the judge had ruled that it was open to the jury to find that the defendant and Bandana Man were engaged on a joint enterprise to commit an affray and that, if the jury found that the defendant foresaw that Bandana Man might shoot and kill an innocent passer-by this would found a verdict of murder on the part of the defendant. I agree with Lord Phillips PSC and Lord Judge CJ (at para 42) that no issue of what they call parasitic accessory liability could arise here because it cannot be said that the two protagonists had a joint intention to commit vio-lence of a type that fell short of the violence committed. Either they had no common intention, or the common intention was to have a shoot-out, which involved each necessarily accepting that the other would shoot at him with the intention to kill or cause serious injury. It was thus open to the jury to find that there was an agreement to that effect which may have been made on the spur of the moment but was in any event made before Bandana Man shot and killed the victim, Miss Pniewska.

79. My only concern has been whether, in the light of the judge's ruling, he intended to direct the jury that they could convict if the common intention fell short of an intention to shoot and be shot at. However, I agree with the conclusion of Lord Phillips PSC and Lord Judge CJ at para 57 that it is not realistic to think that the jury could have found such a common intention and with their conclusion at para 58 that the direction the judge in fact gave was an unequivocal direction that the jury could only convict if they were sure that the protagonists had formed a mutual plan or agreement to have a gun fight in which each would attempt to kill or seriously injure the other. It follows that I would not accept the conclusions of the Court of Appeal to the contrary.

80. At paras 55–60 Lord Phillips PSC and Lord Judge CJ return to the relevance of aiding and abetting. For the reasons I have given, I do not think that this is a case of aiding and abetting. It is a case of an agreement to shoot and be shot at just like the agreement between the principal protagonists to a duel. It does not seem to me that any assistance is to be gained by a consideration of the position of the seconds at a duel or of those present at a duel or a prize fight.

81. In reaching these conclusions, I entirely agree with Lord Brown JSC's conclusions at paras 69–71. Like him, I am not disposed to analyse the defendant's liability for murder in accessory terms but as a principal to a joint enterprise (that is an agreement) to engage in unlawful violence specifically designed to cause death or serious injury, where death occurs as a result. I would be inclined to describe this as a form of principal and not secondary liability, but if it is a form of secondary liability, so be it. I also agree with Lord Brown JSC that such a conclusion is consistent with public policy and, for the reasons he gives at para 72, does not extend criminal responsibility for death as widely as the Court of Appeal envisaged at paras 74 and 75 of their judgment.

■ *Question*

Do you think that Lords Brown and Clarke have potentially created a significant enlargement of the class of principal offenders? It seems that if their reasoning were to be followed in future cases all parties to an agreement to commit a serious offence may be principals when one of the parties causes a harm during the course of the criminal endeavour.

Lord Dyson did not believe there to be any differences of substance between principals and secondary parties and was willing to restore D's conviction based on either of these two grounds.

Lord Dyson:

102. In his summing up, the judge did not direct the jury on aiding and abetting. He did not ask them in terms to consider whether, by shooting back, the defendant encouraged Bandana Man in turn to shoot back at him with intent to do so. In view of his ruling, these omissions on the part of the judge were not by an oversight: they were quite deliberate. But the question is whether, although the issue of aiding and abetting by encouragement was not before the jury in terms, they showed by their verdict on the issue that was before them (parasitic accessory liability) that they were sure that the defendant and Bandana Man had a common purpose to shoot and be shot at and encouraged each other to give effect to that purpose.

103. This question has caused me considerable anxiety, not least because (i) this was a murder charge, (ii) a finding of aiding and abetting by encouragement did not accord with this careful judge's assessment of the facts and (iii) he did not direct the jury explicitly on the aiding and abetting issue. But I have been persuaded by the reasoning of Lord Phillips PSC and Lord Judge CJ that the jury must nevertheless have been satisfied that there was an agreement between the defendant and Bandana Man to shoot and be shot at and that they encouraged each other to carry that agreement into effect. The jury were directed that they had to be sure that the defendant and Bandana Man planned to use

unlawful violence towards each other 'by having a shootout whether that plan was made beforehand and the meeting was pre-arranged or was made on the spur of the moment when they saw each other and fired at each other from the steps and the car respectively'. The judge gave the standard direction for joint enterprise (in the context of parasitic accessory liability) that the offence (in this case affray by gunfight) had to be the joint commission of an offence by two or more people who are 'in it together as part of a joint plan'. In my view, a shootout *pursuant to a plan* must mean an exchange of fire pursuant to an agreement to shoot and be shot at; and persons who *agree* to shoot at each other must by virtue of their agreement intend to encourage each other to do so. It differs from a simple exchange of fire. Nor is it relevant that each of the participants hopes that his shot will prove fatal and that there will be no return of fire. The fact that the jury convicted the defendant of the murder of [V] following the judge's directions must mean that, if they had been asked in terms whether the defendant and Bandana Man (i) agreed to shoot and be shot at and (ii) thereby encouraged each other to that end (intending to do so), they would have answered both questions in the affirmative. In other words, the jury showed by their verdict that they considered that this was analogous to a duel.

104. I would, therefore, uphold the conviction on the basis that the jury must have been satisfied that the defendant aided and abetted the murder of [V] by encouraging Bandana Man to shoot at him in the course of the planned shootout.

Liability as a joint principal

105. This is the route favoured by Lord Brown and Lord Clarke JJSC and accepted as an alternative by Lord Phillips PSC and Lord Judge CJ. They say that the defendant is liable by reason of his participation 'by agreement in unlawful violence specifically designed to cause and causing death or serious injury'. For the reasons that I have given, I am persuaded that the jury must have been sure that Bandana Man and the defendant exchanged fire pursuant to an agreement to have a shoot out, ie an agreement to shoot and be shot at. That is why in my view Lord Phillips PSC and Lord Judge CJ are right to say that in this case the difference between holding the defendant liable as a principal to an agreed joint activity rather than as an accessory is not a difference of substance. Either way, the Crown had to prove that the defendant and Bandana Man agreed to shoot and be shot at with the necessary intent. It follows that, for the reasons I have given, the jury must have been sure that the defendant participated with Bandana Man in an agreed shoot out or agreement to shoot and be shot at with the necessary intent. Accordingly, if the jury had been asked whether the defendant was guilty of the murder of [V] on the basis that he had acted in concert with Bandana Man in shooting at each other pursuant to an agreement to shoot and be shot at, in my view, in the light of the terms of the summing up, they would have answered that question in the affirmative. I would, therefore, uphold the conviction on this basis too.

■ *Question*

Does it matter whether D is liable as a principal or as a secondary party?

Lord Kerr was the only justice to dissent. His lordship's judgment is worth an extended analysis for the way in which it exposes the flaws in the reasoning of the various majority judgments.

Lord Kerr:

118. The judge told the jury that the prosecution case was that there was a plan on the part of Gnango and [BM] to have what he described as a 'shoot-out':

'Now here it is said by the prosecution that Bandana Man and the defendant planned to use unlawful violence towards [one] another by having a shoot-out, whether that plan was made beforehand and the meeting was pre-arranged or was made on the spur of the moment when they saw each other and fired at each other from the steps and the car respectively.'

119. A little later in his charge he gave this critical direction:

'If you are sure that Bandana Man and the defendant joined together to commit such unlawful violence by having a gunfight, whether pre-planned or whether on the spur of the moment on the top of the steps and the side of the car, and that this joint enterprise came into being before Magda was killed by a shot from Bandana Man, then the defendant would be guilty of murder also, along with Bandana Man.'

120. At para 58 Lord Phillips PSC and Lord Judge CJ have said that this amounted to an unequivocal direction that the jury could only convict if they were satisfied that Gnango and [BM] had planned to have a gun fight in which each would attempt to kill or seriously injure the other. He suggests that if the jury was satisfied of this, it meant in law that both were party not merely to his own attempt to kill or seriously injure the other but to the other's attempt to kill or seriously injure him. Lord Dyson JSC expressed essentially the same view at para 102 where he said:

'In my view, a shootout *pursuant to a plan* must mean an exchange of fire pursuant to an agreement to shoot and be shot at; and persons who *agree* to shoot at each other must by virtue of their agreement intend to encourage each other to do so.'

121. The terms of any 'plan' are critical to any conclusion that the parties to it must be taken to have encouraged each other to shoot. But an anterior question must be addressed. Can it be said that solely because there was an exchange of fire, this must be on foot of a plan? Agreement to shoot it out with an opponent, if reached in advance, would be such a plan although there is no evidence that this is what happened here. But where there has been what has been described as a 'spontaneous agreement' to engage in a shoot-out, the question arises whether this can truly be said to be the product of an agreement in any real sense. Is it not at least as likely to be the result of a sudden, simultaneously reached, coincident intention by the two protagonists to fire at each other? I do not consider that because there was a shoot-out (whatever that term may mean) and because the jury were asked to consider that Gnango and [BM] 'joined together . . . to commit . . . unlawful violence', by returning a verdict of guilty, the jury must be taken to have concluded that there was a plan in the sense of an agreement between them.

122. But even if the jury's verdict can be taken as evidence of their conclusion that there had been a plan or agreement between Gnango and [BM], does it follow that an element of that plan *must* be that they agreed to be shot at, as well as to shoot? Agreeing to a shoot-out does not necessarily mean agreeing to be shot at. This is particularly so where the plan takes the form of (and here it could only take the form of) an instantaneous meeting of minds between Gnango and [BM] on their first catching sight of each other on the occasion of the gunfight. That type of situation is quite different from a duel where participants meet at a pre-arranged place and an appointed time. The essence of a duel conducted with firearms is that there should be an exchange of fire. The parties to the duel anticipate—and may be said to impliedly consent to—being fired on as well as firing. But there is no basis on which to infer that such was the intention of the two protagonists here, much less to conclude that the jury's verdict can only be consistent with such implicit intention on the part of Gnango and [BM]. It is at least just as likely that neither agreed to be fired on and that both hoped that they would avoid that unpleasant eventuality by hitting the target with their own shot. Put shortly, when the only material that the jury had to go on was that there was a shoot-out, it is, in my view, impossible to conclude that the finding of guilt can only be explained on the basis that it had been proved that there was a plan between Gnango and [BM] to shoot and be shot at.

123. Even if it were possible so to conclude, however, it does not follow that this amounted to an intention on the part of Gnango or [BM] to assist or encourage each other to shoot. One might be alive to the very real risk that firing, if the target was not hit, would prompt return fire, but that is a

significantly different thing from saying that this was encouragement to fire back. Being prepared to run the risk does not equate with encouraging an opponent to fire at you. Before, therefore, one could be confident that the jury's verdict meant that they had found it established that Gnango had intended to encourage [BM] to fire, it would have been necessary for them to receive directions about that vital component of aiding and abetting. As the judge said, when ruling that he would not allow this to go to the jury as a possible basis of liability, 'on the evidence, the defendant fired at Bandana Man in the hope of killing him or causing him grievous bodily harm, frightening him, or arguably, in self-defence'. Being shot at was hardly likely to have been a desired outcome on the part of Gnango. Intending to encourage B to fire at him was even less likely.

. . .

125. It is, of course, true that, in considering whether there was an intention to encourage, intent must be clearly distinguished from desire or motive. In a trilogy of cases, *R v Moloney* [1985] AC 905; *R v Hancock* [1986] AC 455 and *R v Woollin* [1999] 1 AC 82 the House of Lords held that intention is not restricted to consequences that are wanted or desired, but includes consequences which a defendant might not want to ensue, but which the jury find (a) are the virtually certain result of the defendant's actions (barring some unforeseen intervention); and (b) are consequences which the defendant appreciated were virtually certain to occur. Before such an oblique intention could form the basis of a jury's verdict, of course, precise directions to this effect would have to be given. In the absence of a specific direction on Gnango's intention to encourage B to shoot at him, I do not consider that the verdict of the jury can be upheld on the basis that it was founded on their conclusion that he either had the requisite intention or that the virtually certain result of his firing at B was that he would return fire and that Gnango knew that this was virtually certain to occur.

Liability as a joint principal

127. It is important at the start of this discussion to recognise the clear distinction that must be drawn between the concepts of joint principal liability and joint enterprise. Joint principal offending is a species of primary liability. In *Smith & Hogan's Criminal Law*, 13th ed (2011), p 215, para 8.5.1.1, the following definition of joint principals is given: 'D1 and D2 are joint principal offenders where each does an act which is a cause of the actus reus.' Unlike the position in a joint enterprise, no common purpose is required in order to render those who cause or contribute to a cause of the actus reus guilty as joint principals. What is required is that each must contribute by his own act to the commission of the offence with the necessary mens rea.

128. By contrast, the doctrine of joint enterprise arises in situations where there are two offences, the first being that which has been jointly embarked on and the second the unplanned but foreseen offence committed by one of the participants alone. It is therefore *par excellence* a species of secondary liability as Hughes LJ explained in *R v A* [2011] QB 841, para 37 where he said:

> 'It is necessary to remember that guilt based upon common enterprise is a form of *secondary* liability. The principle is that D2 is implicated in the guilt of D1 not only for the agreed crime A but for the further crime B which he foresaw D1 might commit in the course of A. This form of liability therefore arises only where D1 has committed the further crime B.'

129. The two models are therefore, if not mutually exclusive, at least conceptually distinct. To speak of joint principal offenders being involved in a joint enterprise is, at least potentially, misleading. The essential ingredient for joint principal offending is a contribution to the cause of the actus reus. If this is absent, the fact that there is a common purpose or a joint enterprise cannot transform the offending into joint principal liability.

130. The actus reus in this case was the killing of [V]. To be guilty of that offence as a joint principal, it would have to be shown that Gnango caused or contributed to a cause of her death. With great respect to the views of Lord Brown of Eaton-under-Heywood and Lord Clarke of Stone-cum-Ebony

JJSC, it is not sufficient that he be shown to be engaged by agreement in violence designed to cause death or serious injury. The crucial question is whether he caused or contributed to the death of the victim. This is not an issue which was put to the jury and a conclusion as to whether Gnango's actions caused or contributed to [V]'s death cannot be inferred from their verdict.

131. In any event, major difficulties of proof lie in the way of a case that Gnango's actions were an effective cause of the killing of the victim. As a thesis it depends on the proposition that [BM] fired the fatal shot because he was caused to do so by Gnango firing on him. That proposition faces the immediate problem that [BM] fired on Gnango first. It is, one might suppose, possible to assert that, notwithstanding this, [BM]'s continued firing at Gnango was caused by the latter's return of fire. But that claim encounters the difficulty that was identified by Lord Bingham of Cornhill in *R v Kennedy (No 2)* [2008] AC 269, para 14 where he said:

> 'The criminal law generally assumes the existence of free will. The law recognises certain excep-
> tions, in the case of the young, those who for any reason are not fully responsible for their
> actions, and the vulnerable, and it acknowledges situations of duress and necessity, as also of
> deception and mistake. But, generally speaking, informed adults of sound mind are treated as au-
> tonomous beings able to make their own decisions how they will act . . . Thus D is not to be treated
> as causing V to act in a certain way if V makes a voluntary and informed decision to act in that
> way rather than another. There are many classic statements to this effect. In his article 'Finis for
> Novus Actus?' [1989] CLJ 391, 392, Professor Glanville Williams wrote: "I may suggest reasons to
> you for doing something; I may urge you to do it, tell you it will pay you to do it, tell you it is your
> duty to do it. My efforts may perhaps make it very much more likely that you will do it. But they
> do not cause you to do it, in the sense in which one causes a kettle of water to boil by putting it
> on the stove. Your volitional act is regarded (within the doctrine of responsibility) as setting a new
> 'chain of causation' going, irrespective of what has happened before." In chapter XII of *Causation
> in the Law*, 2nd ed (1985), p 326, Hart & Honoré wrote: "The free, deliberate, and informed inter-
> vention of a second person, who intends to exploit the situation created by the first, but is not
> acting in concert with him, is normally held to relieve the first actor of criminal responsibility." This
> statement was cited by the House with approval in *R v Latif* [1996] 1 WLR 104, 115. The principle
> is fundamental and not controversial.'

132. If [BM] fired at Gnango first, it seems to me highly questionable (at least) that Gnango's returning fire *caused* [BM] to fire again. The first shot surely betokened an intention on the part of [BM] to
fire at and to hit Gnango, irrespective of whether Gnango fired back. It might be said, to borrow the
words of Professor Glanville Williams, that Gnango's firing on B made it much more likely that B would
fire again, but that is not enough to show that B was caused to fire because of Gnango's shot. I do not
consider, therefore, that Gnango can be guilty of the murder of [V] as a joint principal.

■ *Question*

Do you find Lord Kerr's reasoning compelling?

The decision in *Gnango* has proved to be controversial. Consider the criticisms made in the following extract and whether you agree with them.

R. Buxton, 'Being an Accessory to One's Own Murder'
[2012] Crim LR 275

The brocard of aiding, etc. is the antique, though at the date of *Gnango* still binding, wording of s.8
of the Accessories and Abettors Act 1861. In modern times, the substantive law there assumed is
expressed in terms of assisting or encouraging the principal. The present case could hardly be said
to be one of assistance, but G's participation in the affray was held by the Supreme Court to have

amounted to encouragement of BM: even though that had not been the view of the trial judge who had heard the evidence. But, assuming for the moment that that (factual) conclusion was open to the Supreme Court, various issues still remain.

First, the conclusion that G encouraged BM is a conclusion as to the objective nature of G's conduct as seen by the court. It says nothing as to G's state of mind: whether he intended to encourage BM, or realised that his participation in the shoot-out would have that effect. What is required of the accessory in terms of intention or (subjective) recklessness as to encouragement is a much debated question in the law of secondary liability. It might have been said in *Gnango*, had this issue ever been considered, that G must have appreciated that by participating in the shoot-out he was egging BM on to respond. But the Court of Appeal, when rejecting the argument based on affray, pointed out that the participants did not act in concert, but independently and antagonistically, without a shared purpose to shoot and be shot at. That state of mind does not drive one to think that G had in his mind the encouragement of BM; and if BM's reaction had been not to fire back but to throw down his weapon and run away, G would scarcely have thought that he had failed in his objective.

Secondly, assuming nonetheless that G did encourage BM, and had the necessary mental realisation of that process of encouragement, what was it that G encouraged BM to do? Plainly G did not intend to encourage BM to kill him, or to inflict grievous bodily harm, the two alternative limbs of the actus reus of murder, the crime that he was convicted of encouraging. The most that could be said was that G encouraged BM into a course of conduct that he realised carried a risk, perhaps a high risk, of BM murdering G. In the ordinary case, foresight that the principal offence might be committed is enough to inculpate an accessory. But it is much less obvious that that general approach should be applied to a case where the alleged accessory, although appreciating a risk that the principal offence may occur, specifically does not wish it to occur. True it is that where D does an act that he knows will assist P to commit a foreseen crime, it is no defence that he is indifferent as to whether or not the crime is in fact committed; nor indeed that he only assisted reluctantly and in respect of a crime that commission of which horrified him. But those cases, and the general line of authority in this area, concern *assistance*. There it can be said that the only issue is whether, objectively, an act is one that assists in the commission of the principal crime; and once the factual act of assistance is established the secondary party's reluctance or regret is nothing to the point. But we are concerned with whether G's actions could be said to amount to 'encouragement' in the first place. It is much less clear that D can be said to *encourage* P to produce consequence *x* when consequence *x* is exactly what D does not want to occur.

This point can be put in another way. As Professor Ormerod points out in a valuable note on the decision of the Court of Appeal, the requirement in law that G should have intended to encourage BM can, in relation to encouragement to kill or wound G, be supplied by 'oblique' intention. But he cites Professor Smith for the view that, even if there is a possibility or likelihood of collateral outcome *x* arising from D's conduct, it does not make good sense to say that D intended outcome *x*, whether in the sense of direct or of oblique intention, when it was his purpose to avoid that outcome. We respectfully agree.

These problems are not directly confronted in the judgments of the Supreme Court, but as we have seen the substance of them is sought to be met by holding that G was complicit in BM's *attempted* murder; so that when that attempt succeeded G was equally complicit in the result. It may indeed be more plausible to say that G encouraged BM to try to kill him, hoping that he would not succeed, than it is to say that G encouraged BM to kill him *tout court*. There are, however, serious difficulties about rationalising the case in those terms, which are not confronted in the judgments in the Supreme Court.

What G was charged with was assisting and encouraging murder, not attempted murder. First, to make that charge good it had to be established that G encouraged the commission of the actus reus of the principal crime. The actus reus of murder necessarily includes causing the death of the victim. If the Supreme Court, understandably, drew back from finding that G encouraged BM to kill him, by the same token they could only conclude that G encouraged attempted murder, and not the murder with which he was charged. Secondly, G was convicted by the Supreme Court on the basis of transferred malice, that BM's intent towards G was still operative when he killed MP. It is, however, elementary that transferred malice requires that D, with the mens rea of a particular crime, causes the actus reus of the same crime. If, as the Supreme Court found, he had the mens rea of attempted murder in relation to G that could not be translated into the mens rea of the different crime of the actual murder of MP.

Joint principalship

Lord Brown and Lord Clarke put the liability of G not on accessoryship but on the basis that G and BM were joint principals in the murder of MP. The 'shoot-out' involved a joint exercise in unlawful violence, designed to cause death or serious injury. If death in fact resulted, both of them were equally liable for it, no matter who fired the fatal shot. If that approach were correct it is difficult to see why it was not used to try to rescue the case on joint enterprise, the assumed joint intention to cause death being a much more plausible candidate as a criminal joint enterprise than was the affray that was relied on both in the Court of Appeal and in the Supreme Court. But as a case of *principalship* the analysis presents a serious difficulty.

For a party to be a (joint) principal he must be shown to have contributed by his own act to the causation of the actus reus. Therefore, did G 'cause' BM to shoot MP? That issue is not addressed in the context of joint principalship by any of the judges, Lords Brown, Clarke and Dyson, who favoured that solution, but Lords Clarke and Dyson considered causation as a separate and freestanding possible head of liability. Lord Clarke at [91] held on the basis of tort authority that the act of BM in firing back would not have broken the chain of causation between G's firing and the death of MP, but that since little or no argument had been addressed on the subject the court could not proceed on that basis. Lord Dyson, relying principally on the speech of Lord Bingham in *Kennedy*, was strongly inclined to think that the voluntary and informed act of BM in firing would have broken the chain of causation, though he was still able (puzzlingly) to support the conviction on the basis of joint principalship. Lord Kerr, who rejected the case of joint principalship, did so because of the difficulty of fixing G with causal responsibility for the death, again relying on *Kennedy*.

The approach in terms of joint principalship is, therefore, at best difficult. It is also a matter of some concern that all of Lords Phillips, Judge, Wilson and Dyson thought that it was of little or no moment whether the accused was inculpated on the basis of accessory liability or on the basis of joint principalship. But while principalship requires causation of the actus reus to be demonstrated, accessoryship does not. Since the doctrines are different, with different rules, fidelity to the principles that govern criminal liability requires the court to decide which chapter of the law it is proceeding under, and to follow the rules that apply to that chapter. It is quite true that *Smith & Hogan* draw attention to the practice of charging an offender under s.8 without particularising whether he is indicted as an accessory or as a principal, and that at [63] of its judgment the Supreme Court relied on observations in *Giannetto* to the effect that where a person is charged under s.8 but it is not clear whether he was a principal or an accessory, the jury on convicting him can be assumed to have been unanimous that he was at least an accessory. But that solution is not available when, as in the present case, the ambiguous charge is relied on to convict of commission of the offence as a principal, rather than the lesser included offence of accessoryship. Where the two routes to a conviction depend on different analyses of complex facts, the prosecution at the trial should be required to nail its colours to one or other of those different theories. The fair charging rules in art.6(3)(a) of the European Convention require no less.

Suicide; and a reality check

Two further points demonstrate the uncomfortable nature of G's conviction.

First, it is a fundamental tenet of the common law that an accessory commits the same crime as his principal; and s.8 of the 1861 Act requires him to be tried, indicted and punished as a principal offender. Thus, if BM had not killed MP but wounded G, a properly drawn count would on the law as laid down by the Supreme Court have said that BM and G on October 2, 2007 unlawfully and maliciously wounded G. And if it had been G and not MP who was killed, and BM had been available to be charged, in order to reflect the whole case as seen by the Supreme Court the count should have read that BM and G on October 2, 2007 murdered G. That in relation to G is *felo de se*, which amounts to suicide. But since the Suicide Act 1961, suicide is no longer a crime. The doctrine of transferred malice therefore not only transferred BM's intent from G to MP, but also turned a man who otherwise would have been a suicide into a murderer.

Secondly, amongst the many qualities of the judges of the Queen's Bench Division is a strong awareness of arguments that, however they may be theoretically tortured out of general principles formulated in cases with very different facts, do not in the circumstances to which they are sought to be applied stand the test of practical reality. That was the quality displayed by Cooke J. when he said that it would be a real oddity for a victim of an attempted murder to be a secondary party to that attempt. His instinct should have been respected.

See for further comment, G. Virgo, 'Joint Enterprise Liability is Dead: Long Live Accessorial Liability' [2012] Crim LR 850; P. Mirfield, 'Guilt by Association: A Reply to Professor Virgo' [2013] Crim LR 577; G. Virgo, 'A Reply' [2013] Crim LR 584.

8.7.9 Reform of parasitic accessorial liability in murder

The law in relation to parasitic accessorial liability is one of the most difficult in English criminal law. It has been subjected to scrutiny by law reform agencies on numerous occasions.

The Ministry of Justice published its Consultation Paper on *Murder, Manslaughter and Infanticide: Proposals for Reform of the Law* (2008) including recommendations on complicity (see http://webarchive.nationalarchives.gov.uk/20110218135832/http:/justice.gov.uk/consultations/docs/murder-manslaughter-infanticide-consultation.pdf).

The Consultation Paper represents the latest phase in the homicide law reform project begun by the Law Commission. It draws not only on the Law Commission Report No 304, *Murder, Manslaughter and Infanticide* (2006), but also the Law Commission's Report No 305, *Participating in Crime* (2007). The recommendation is to create a new statutory offence of murder for those who intentionally assist or encourage that offence (cl 1) and a statutory offence of murder where P is guilty of manslaughter owing to a lack of mens rea and D assisted or encouraged intending P to kill or cause serious injury (cl 2). In cases of joint criminal venture, the recommendation adopts the Law Commission proposal to retain a broader offence (cl 3). On the fundamentally different rule, the Government believes that statutory reform is desirable, proposing a more flexible statutory rule based on whether P's act was 'within the scope of the joint criminal venture'. This would be the case where the act did not go 'far beyond that which was planned, agreed to or foreseen by the secondary party' (para 101). The fundamentally different qualification would only be available where D has not foreseen death of V as a possibility, and even when it applies it will result in a manslaughter conviction (cl 4). Do you think these proposals would clarify the law?

In 2012 the Justice Committee of the House of Commons heard evidence on how joint enterprise operated in practice. The Committee concluded that the uncertainty bedevilling this area of law was unacceptable and called for the Government to enshrine the common law in legislation. The Committee recommended that the Government consult on the Law Commission's proposals that were contained in the Report No 305 *Participating in Crime* (see section 8.10, p 297) and to use them as a basis for reform. So far no legislation has been forthcoming. It also recommended that the Director of Public Prosecutions issue guidance on the use of joint enterprise when charging. This guidance was published later in 2012 and is available at https://www.cps.gov.uk/legal/assets/uploads/files/Joint_Enterprise.pdf.

8.8 Defences peculiar to secondary parties

A secondary party can rely on the defences that are available generally—duress, infancy, insanity, etc—and in addition there are specific defences made available to secondary parties.

8.8.1 The defence of withdrawal

Recall that liability as a secondary party is derivative on P's liability. Until P's conduct is performed and the crime is attempted or committed, D has no secondary liability. There is an opportunity for withdrawal. This contrasts with inchoate liability where D's liability is complete as soon as he has performed the acts of assistance or encouragement (under the Serious Crime Act 2007, see Chapter 12) or formed the agreement in a conspiracy (Chapter 13) or done the acts more than merely preparatory to the commission of the offence in attempt (Chapter 14). In inchoate offences there is no scope for a plea of withdrawal; it is too late. How, if at all, can a person who is about to become a secondary party to an offence withdraw so as to avoid liability when the crime is committed?

R v Becerra and Cooper

(1975) 62 Cr App R 212, Court of Appeal, Criminal Division

(Roskill and Bridge LJJ and Kilner Brown J)

B, C and G broke into a house with intent to steal from the householder, an old lady, F. While G was holding a pillow over F's face, B cut the telephone wires with a knife with a 3½ inch blade. B then gave the knife to C. The burglars were surprised by the appearance of a man, V, the tenant of a flat in the house. B called out 'Come on, let's go' and, followed by G, climbed out of a window and ran away. C tried the back door but it was locked and, being confronted by V, stabbed and killed him. B and C were convicted of murder and appealed.

Roskill LJ [having held that there was evidence to support the jury's finding of a common design to cause death or serious bodily harm if it was necessary to do so in order to carry out the theft, turned to the argument that B had effectively withdrawn from any common design:]

It is necessary, before dealing with that argument in more detail, to say a word or two about the relevant law. It is a curious fact, considering the number of times in which this point arises where two or more people are charged with criminal offences, particularly murder or manslaughter, how relatively little authority there is in this country upon the point. But the principle is undoubtedly of long standing.

Perhaps it is best first stated in *Saunders and Archer* (1573) 2 Plowd 473 (in the eighteenth year of the first Queen Elizabeth) at p 476, in a note by *Plowden*, thus: '... for if I command one to kill JS and before the Fact done I go to him and tell him that I have repented, and expressly charge him not to kill JS and he afterwards kills him, there I shall not be Accessory to this Murder, because I have countermanded my first Command, which in all Reason shall discharge me, for the malicious Mind of the Accessory ought to continue to do ill until the Time of the Act done, or else he shall not be charged; but if he had killed JS before the Time of my Discharge or Countermand given, I should have been Accessory to the Death, notwithstanding my private Repentance'.

The next case to which I may usefully refer is some 250 years later, but over 150 years ago. *Edmeads* (1828) 3 C & P 390, where there is a ruling of Vaughan B at a trial at Berkshire Assizes, upon an indictment charging Edmeads and others with unlawfully shooting at game keepers. At the end of his ruling the learned Baron said on the question of common intent, at p 392, 'that is rather a question for the jury; but still, on this evidence, it is quite clear what the common purpose was. They all draw up in lines, and point their guns at the game keepers, and they are all giving their countenance and assistance to the one of them who actually fires the gun. If it could be shewn that either of them separated himself from the rest, and showed distinctly that he would have no hand in what they were doing, the objection would have much weight in it.'

I can go forward over 100 years. Mr Owen (to whose juniors we are indebted for their research into the relevant Canadian and United States cases) referred us to several Canadian cases, to only one of which it is necessary to refer in detail, a decision of the Court of Appeal in British Columbia in *Whitehouse* (alias *Savage*) [1941] 1 WWR 112. I need not read the headnote. The Court of Appeal held that the trial judge concerned in that case, which was one of murder, had been guilty of misdirection in his direction to the jury on this question of 'withdrawal'. The matter is, if I may most respectfully say so, so well put in the leading judgment of Sloan JA, that I read the whole of the passage at pp 115 and 116:

> 'Can it be said on the facts of this case that a mere change of mental intention and a quitting of the scene of the crime just immediately prior to the striking of the fatal blow will absolve those who participate in the commission of the crime by overt acts up to that moment from all the consequences of its accomplishment by the one who strikes in ignorance of his companions' change of heart? I think not. After a crime has been committed and before a prior abandonment of the common enterprise may be found by a jury there must be, in my view, in the absence of exceptional circumstances, something more than a mere mental change of intention and physical change of place by those associates who wish to dissociate themselves from the consequences attendant upon their willing assistance up to the moment of the actual commission of that crime. I would not attempt to define too closely what must be done in criminal matters involving participation in a common unlawful purpose to break the chain of causation and responsibility. That must depend upon the circumstances of each case but it seems to me that one essential element ought to be established in a case of this kind: Where practicable and reasonable there must be timely communication of the intention to abandon the common purpose from those who wish to dissociate themselves from the contemplated crime to those who desire to continue in it. What is "timely communication" must be determined by the facts of each case but where practicable and reasonable it ought to be such communication, verbal or otherwise, that will serve unequivocal notice upon the other party to the common unlawful cause that if he proceeds upon it he does so without the further aid and assistance of those who withdraw. The unlawful purpose of him who continues alone is then his own and not one in common with those who are no longer parties to it nor liable to its full and final consequences.'

The learned judge then went on to cite a passage from 1 Hale's *Pleas of the Crown* 618 and the passage from *Saunders and Archer* (supra) to which I have already referred.

In the view of each member of this court, that passage, if we may respectfully say so, could not be improved upon and we venture to adopt it in its entirety as a correct statement of the law which is to be applied in this case.

The last case, an English one, is *Croft* (1944) 29 Cr App R 169, [1944] 1 KB 295; a well known case of a suicide pact where, under the old law, the survivor of a suicide pact was charged with and convicted of murder. It was sought to argue that he had withdrawn from the pact in time to avoid liability (as the law then was) for conviction for murder.

The Court of Criminal Appeal, comprising Lawrence J (as he then was), Lewis and Wrottesley JJ dismissed the appeal and upheld the direction given by Humphreys J to the jury at the trial. Towards the end of the judgment Lawrence J said, at p 173 (pp 297 and 298): '...counsel for the appellant complains—although I do not understand that the point had ever been taken in the court below—that the summing-up does not contain any reference to the possibility of the agreement to commit suicide having been determined or countermanded. It is true that the learned judge does not deal expressly with that matter except in a passage where he says: Even if you accept his statement in the witness-box that the vital and second shot was fired when he had gone through that window, he would still be guilty of murder if she was then committing suicide as the result of an agreement which they had mutually arrived at that should be the fate of both of them, and it is no answer for him that he altered his mind after she was dead and did not commit suicide himself.... the authorities, such as they are, show in our opinion, that where a person has acted as an accessory before the fact, in order that he should not be held guilty as an accessory before the fact, he must give express and actual countermand or revocation of the advising, counselling, procuring, or abetting which he had given before.'

It seems to us that those authorities make plain what the law is which has to be applied in the present case.

We therefore turn back to consider the direction which the learned judge gave in the present case to the jury and what was the suggested evidence that Becerra had withdrawn from the common agreement. The suggested evidence is the use by Becerra of the words 'Come on let's go,' coupled, as I said a few moments ago, with his act in going out through the window. The evidence, as the judge pointed out, was that Cooper never heard that nor did the third man. But let it be supposed that that was said and the jury took the view that it was said.

On the facts of this case, in the circumstances then prevailing, the knife having already been used and being contemplated for further use when it was handed over by Becerra to Cooper for the purpose of avoiding (if necessary) by violent means the hazards of identification, if Becerra wanted to withdraw at that stage, he would have to 'countermand', to use the word that is used in some of the cases or 'repent' to use another word so used, in some manner vastly different and vastly more effective than merely to say 'Come on, let's go' and go out through the window.

It is not necessary, on this application, to decide whether the point of time had arrived at which the only way in which he could effectively withdraw, so as to free himself from joint responsibility for any act Cooper thereafter did in furtherance of the common design, would be physically to intervene so as to stop Cooper attacking Lewis, as the judge suggested, by interposing his own body between them or somehow getting in between them or whether some other action might suffice. That does not arise for decision here. Nor is it necessary to decide whether or not the learned judge was right or wrong, on the facts of this case, in that passage which appears at the bottom of p 206, which Mr Owen criticised: 'and at least take all reasonable steps to prevent the commission of the crime which he had agreed the others should commit.' It is enough for the purposes of deciding this application to say that under the law of this country as it stands, and on the facts (taking them at their highest in favour of Becerra), that which was urged as amounting to withdrawal from the common design was not capable of amounting to such withdrawal. Accordingly Becerra remains responsible, in the eyes of the law, for everything that Cooper did and continued to do after Becerra's disappearance through the window as much as if he had done them himself.

Cooper being unquestionably guilty of murder, Becerra is equally guilty of murder. Mr Owen's careful argument must therefore be rejected and the application by Becerra for leave to appeal against conviction fails.

Appeal dismissed

■ *Questions*

What could Beccarra have done? To avoid liability, must Beccarra:

(i)   make clear he is withdrawing?

(ii) do all he can to negate the effects of his contribution to the crime? or

(iii) do all he reasonably can to stop Cooper?

In *Mitchell and King* [1999] Crim LR 496, an unplanned fight broke out in and around a restaurant. One person was killed. The appellants were convicted of murder, alleged to have been committed in the course of a joint enterprise. M claimed that if there was such an enterprise, he had withdrawn from it before the fatal act. The judge directed the jury by reading the passage from *Whitehouse*, in the previous extract. Quashing M's conviction, Otton LJ said:

The case from which this passage is taken concerned pre-planned violence. It is not necessary when the violence is spontaneous. Although absent any communication, it may, as a matter of evidence, be easier to persuade a jury that a defendant, who had previously participated, had not in fact withdrawn. Such considerations are clearly relevant in such cases, but less so when violence has erupted spontaneously.

Secondary participation consists in assisting or encouraging the principal offender in the commission of the crime. A party who withdraws from an enterprise, spontaneous or not, usually ceases to assist but he does not necessarily cease to encourage. Suppose that P is encouraged in the fight because he knows D is in there with him. If D decides he has had enough and quietly slopes off without attracting P's attention, the external element of secondary participation still continues. D's encouragement of P is still operative. Does mere withdrawal then relieve D of responsibility? A person who has done an act which makes him potentially liable for a crime cannot relieve himself of responsibility by a mere change of mind. Once the arrow is in the air, it is no use wishing to have never let it go. The archer is guilty of homicide when the arrow gets the victim through the heart. The withdrawer, it is true, does not merely change his mind: he withdraws—but is that relevant if the withdrawal has no more effect on subsequent events than the archer's repentance?

Commenting on *O'Flaherty* [2004] 2 Cr App R 20, Professor Ashworth observes (at [2004] Crim LR 751):

Why should withdrawal be a defence? The main reason must be that a person who aids, abets, counsels or procures at first but then has a voluntary change of mind, before the full offence is completed, is significantly less culpable than an accomplice who continued to support the commission of the offence throughout. The withdrawing accomplice remains liable for what was done up to that point, but not for what was done thereafter. This desert-based rationale must be linked to the nature of the accomplice's contribution to the principal offence, and the requirements of withdrawal should similarly depend on that contribution. In other words, the further D has gone in supporting the commission of the offence, the more it is right to expect by way of withdrawal (*cf.* K.J.M. Smith, 'Withdrawal in Complicity: A Restatement of Principles' [2001] Crim.L.R. 769). On this approach, then, the law should 'reward' the withdrawing accomplice by providing the possibility of a defence, though strictly circumscribed (mitigation of sentence will provide for those whose purported withdrawal is insufficiently definite). Others prefer to say that the defence is necessary to provide an incentive for accomplices to withdraw, although the language of incentives is really only apposite if people in that situation are aware of the legal rule. But much also depends on whether the rationale for accessorial liability lies primarily in the culpability of the accomplice or in the causal contribution to the principal offence, since withdrawal may negative culpability for subsequent acts but not (in some instances) sever the causal contribution to subsequent acts. Judicial discussion of complicity is suffused with references to 'joint enterprise' and 'common enterprise', and the significance of this decision is to demonstrate the shortcomings of expressing cases of complicity in that way. The language of joint enterprise assumes some kind of plan to commit an offence, however hastily or informally conceived. One then moves from the idea of a plan to the notion of withdrawing from the plan. However, many of the cases coming before the courts concern violence erupting outside a pub, club or sporting venue, where some people join in, some stay on the fringes, and others walk away. Thus, in *Mitchell and King* [1999] Crim.L.R. 496, Otton L.J. said (at para.6): 'Communication of withdrawal is a necessary condition for dissociation from preplanned violence. It is not necessary when the violence is spontaneous. Although absent any communication it may, as a matter of evidence, be easier to persuade a jury that a defendant, who had previously participated, had not in fact withdrawn. Such considerations are clearly relevant in such cases, but less so when the violence has erupted spontaneously.' Otton L.J. drew this distinction between planned and spontaneous offences without reliance on any authority. In this case, Mantell L.J. followed the *Mitchell and King* approach, but translated it into the language of joint enterprise. Thus, the jury must be satisfied 'that the fatal injuries were sustained when the joint enterprise was continuing and that the defendant was still acting within that joint enterprise' (at [64]); and 'in a case of spontaneous violence such as this where there has been no prior agreement, the jury will usually have to make inferences as to the scope of the joint enterprise from the knowledge and actions of individual participants' (at [65]). It is doubtful whether it is helpful to translate the events into a joint enterprise and then, as it were, translate them back in order to make sense of the roles of individual participants. This was a spontaneous chain of events. Sir John Smith doubted whether the fact that an attack arose spontaneously should lead to an alteration of the requirements for withdrawal: is it right to allow withdrawal without communication, he asked, 'if A was encouraged by B's participation and was unaware that B had withdrawn?' (Smith and Hogan, *Criminal Law* (10th ed., 2002), p.177). The answer depends, surely, on the rationale. If the foundations of complicity and of withdrawal lie chiefly in B's culpability, a definite withdrawal from spontaneous violence (even if not accompanied by communication) should suffice. But if the foundations lie chiefly in B's contribution to A's offence, B's withdrawal in those circumstances may (as Sir John hinted) be no more effective than an uncommunicated withdrawal from a non-spontaneous offence. On the facts of this case, two of the men (R and T) participated in the initial attack but then broke off from the group and did not accompany them into the next street. They did not 'communicate' their withdrawal to anyone. But it was a spontaneous attack, and they had probably not signalled their arrival either, other than by physical participation. Should we speculate on whether the group of attackers who went into the next street were still being encouraged by the belief that the two men were with them, when they were not? Surely the two men's act of leaving should be sufficient to dissociate them from subsequent events, in the absence of any kind of plan to which they had all assented. They were culpable for what they had done up to that point, but not in respect of anything thereafter. The attackers had eyes and ears, and had no reason to believe that the two were still supporting them. But O'Flaherty's position was held to be different because he did follow the attackers into the next street and he was present, holding a cricket bat, when the fatal attack took place. He did not participate actively in the fatal attack, but neither he did he do anything amounting to withdrawal. It is then a question of fact whether his series of actions amounted to aiding and abetting murder, resulting in the mandatory sentence of life imprisonment.

In *Grundy* [1977] Crim LR 543, D had supplied E, a burglar, with information which was presumably valuable to E in committing the burglary in question; but, for two weeks before E did so, D had been trying to stop him breaking in. It was held that there was evidence of an effective withdrawal which should have been left to the jury. In *Whitefield* (1984) 79 Cr App R 36, [1984] Crim LR 97, there was evidence that D had served unequivocal notice on E that, if he proceeded with a burglary they had planned together, he would do so without D's aid or assistance. It was held that the jury should have been told that, if they accepted this evidence, there was a defence. Cf *McPhillips* (1990) 6 BNIL, section 13.4.6.2, p 478, where an uncommunicated intention to frustrate an agreement to commit murder, to which D was a party, was a defence to a charge of conspiracy to murder and *Rook* [1993] 2 All ER 955, [1993] Crim LR 698.

The principles which apply appear from the case law to be as follows:

- withdrawal will operate only exceptionally: *Mitchell* [1990] Crim LR 496;
- a change of mind by D is insufficient; there must be physical acts demonstrating disengagement: *Bryce* [2004] EWCA Crim 1231;
- the same principles apply whether the offence involves spontaneous or planned violence: *Robinson* [2000] EWCA Crim 8. In *Mitchell* [1990] Crim LR 496, it was emphasized that with spontaneous violence the issue was not whether there had been communication

of withdrawal but whether the original joint venture was still continuing at the time of the principal's act. This was followed in *O'Flaherty* [2004] 2 Cr App R 20, where the question was 'whether a particular defendant disengaged before the fatal injury or injuries were caused';

- D must communicate the withdrawal to P unequivocally unless physically impossible in the circumstances: *Robinson*;

- D's withdrawal before P's act must be 'unequivocal': *O'Flaherty*;

- whether D is still a party to the joint enterprise is a question of fact and degree for the jury to determine: *O'Flaherty*;

- D throwing down his weapon and walking away *may* be enough: *O'Flaherty*;

- where D is one of the instigators of the attack, more may be needed to demonstrate withdrawal: *Gallant* [2008] EWCA Crim 1111;

- a judge need not direct on withdrawal in every case (eg it is unnecessary where D denies that there was a joint enterprise: *Gallant*).

■ *Questions*

Is withdrawal:

(i) a defence that operates only where D brings to an end the actus reus of assisting or encouraging P?;

(ii) a defence that operates because D's withdrawal negates his mens rea of intention to assist or encourage?; or

(iii) a defence operating despite the presence of D's continuing actus reus and mens rea as a secondary party?

Which should it be?

R v Bryce
(section 8.4.1.1, p 222), http://www.bailii.org/ew/cases/EWCA/Crim/2004/1231.html

75.... if the secondary party is to avoid liability for assistance rendered to the perpetrator in respect of steps taken by the perpetrator towards the commission of the crime, only an act taken by him which amounts to countermanding of his earlier assistance and a withdrawal from the common purpose will suffice. Repentance alone, unsupported by action taken to demonstrate withdrawal will be insufficient. Thus, if the secondary party had the necessary mens rea at the time of the act of rendering his advice or assistance, the fact that his mind is 'innocent' at the time when the crime is committed is no defence: see *R v Becerra* (1975) 62 Crim App R 212. In that case it was stated that any communication of withdrawal by the secondary party to the perpetrator must be such as to serve 'unequivocal notice' upon the other party to the common unlawful cause that, if he proceeds upon it, he does so without the further aid and assistance of the withdrawing party: c.f. the position in *R v Whitefield* (1984) 79 Crim App R 36, [1984] Crim LR 97.

See further, D. Lanham, 'Accomplices and Withdrawal' (1981) 97 LQR 575; K. J. M. Smith, 'Withdrawal in Complicity: A Restatement of Principles' [2001] Crim LR 769.

8.8.2 A defence for victims alleged to be parties

Where an offence is created for the protection of a class of persons, a member of the class who is the victim of such an offence cannot be convicted either of inciting or aiding, abetting, counselling or procuring its commission, even though he has done acts which would usually amount to such an offence. However, see section 8.7.8 for the discussion of *Gnango* and the reduction in the scope of this defence.

8.8.3 A defence for an accessory who acts under legal duty?

In *Garrett v Arthur Churchill (Glass) Ltd* [1970] 1 QB 92, [1969] 2 All ER 1141, D, who as an agent of P had bought a goblet, was held guilty of being knowingly concerned in the exportation of goods without a licence, when, on P's instructions, he delivered P's own goblet to P's agent who was to take it to the United States. Parker LCJ ([1969] 2 All ER at 1145) said:

> albeit there was a legal duty in ordinary circumstances to hand over the goblet to the owners once the agency was determined, I do not think that an action would lie for breach of that duty if the handing over would constitute the offence of being knowingly concerned in its exportation.

In *Lomas* (1913) 9 Cr App R 220, the accused was held to be not guilty of aiding and abetting a burglary by returning to the burglar, King, a jemmy which the accused had borrowed from him.

■ *Question*

D agrees: (a) to sell, (b) to let on hire, his car to E. D knows that E intends to drive the car himself and—(i) has no licence to drive, or (ii) has no insurance against third party risks, or (iii) is disqualified, or (iv) is subject to epileptic seizures. Is D liable for offences that E commits by driving the car?

8.9 Derivative versus inchoate liability

As we noted at the start of this chapter, the derivative basis for liability is in contrast to the inchoate offences under Part 2 of the 2007 Act and in conspiracy and attempt. See D. Lanham, 'Primary and Derivative Criminal Liability: An Australian Perspective' [2000] Crim LR 707 and Law Commission Report No 300, *Inchoate Liability for Assisting and Encouraging Crime* (2006) and Report No 305, *Participating in Crime* (2007), Ch 3.

Returning to the example at the start, Dawn who hired Peter as a contract killer would be liable for an inchoate offence (ss 44 to 46 of the Serious Crime Act 2007) as soon as she tried to persuade Peter. She would be liable irrespective of whether he went on to commit the offence. Similarly, Carl and Eric would be liable for their acts of assistance or encouragement as soon as those were performed, irrespective of whether Peter went on to commit the offence. The argument for imposing liability at that stage is that the blameworthiness of D, C and E is not affected by what happens later. That is entirely in the hands of Peter.

In its Report in 1993 the Law Commission proposed to replace all derivative secondary liability with inchoate liability. Would that be a better system?

In its later Report No 300 in 2006, the Law Commission rejected its provisional proposals from 1993, citing the arguments of those who responded to the original proposals in 1993:

2.7 Those respondents who provided an analysis of whether inchoate liability should supplant secondary liability focused on:

(1) forensic considerations,

(2) public acceptability,

(3) condemnation and labelling,

(4) the connection between D's conduct and the offence committed by P.

Forensic considerations

2.8 By virtue of section 8 of the Accessories and Abettors Act 1861, a person who is an accessory can be charged, indicted and punished as a principal offender. This means that the prosecution can obtain a conviction even if it cannot be proved whether the accused was a principal offender or an accessory provided that he or she must have been one or the other. For example, suppose that D1 and D2 are jointly charged with burglary. It is known that one of them entered the premises while the other kept watch. D1 and D2 can each be convicted of burglary despite the prosecution being unable to prove who entered the premises (the principal offender) and who kept watch (the accessory).

2.9 This is of considerable assistance to the prosecution in cases where it is difficult or impossible to prove the precise role of the various parties. In addition, the prosecution does not have to specify in advance whether the allegation is that an accused was a principal offender or an accessory. . . .

2.10 Some respondents felt that these forensic advantages would be jeopardised by adopting a scheme consisting solely of inchoate offences. They felt that such a scheme would adversely affect the law's ability to accurately attribute criminal liability in those cases where it is impossible to be sure who was the principal offender and who was the accessory.

Public acceptability

2.11 Professor Sir John Smith said that the public attaches enormous importance to the consequences that result from a criminal act and that Parliament reacts accordingly. He provided this example:

Example 2C

D gives instructions to P, whom D believes to be a 'contract killer' to kill D's partner, V.

Under the proposals in the [1993 Paper], D would be guilty of the same offence, assisting murder, *irrespective* of whether P decided to kill V or instead to report D to the police.

2.12 Professor Smith doubted whether the public would consider that outcome to be acceptable. He said that society expects an offender to be convicted of and punished for offences that reflect not only his moral culpability but also the harm caused by his or her conduct. Thus, the maximum term of imprisonment for causing dangerous driving is two years but when death is caused the offence becomes causing death by dangerous driving and the maximum term of imprisonment increases to 14 years.

2.13 The Society of Public Teachers of Law agreed. In its view, in a case such as example 2C, should P go on to kill V, it would be unrealistic to attribute responsibility for V's death solely to P given that D would have played a prominent part in bringing about V's death.

Condemnation, culpability and labelling

2.14 There was criticism that the proposals in the CP would not adequately fulfil the condemnatory and labelling function of the law. In particular, they would not adequately connect an accused with the consequences of his or her offence. . . .

2.15 A specific criticism was that to de-couple an accessory's liability from the harmful consequences of the principal's conduct would be particularly anomalous where the culpability of the former exceeds that of the latter. Professor Sir John Smith provided the following example:

Example 2D

D, a gang leader, sends out his subordinate P to detonate a bomb. P does so without warning in a busy shopping centre. The explosion results in the deaths of 20 people.

2.16 Professor Sir John Smith said that, under the proposals in the CP, P would be liable for 20 murders but D merely for one offence of encouraging murder. The anomaly would be even more striking if D had compelled P to carry out the act by holding P's partner, Z, as a hostage and threatening to kill Z because duress is no defence to murder.

2.17 Sometimes, death is an unexpected and unforeseen consequence:

Example 2E

D encourages P to inflict grievous bodily harm on V. P does so. Normally V's injuries would not prove fatal. However, medical complications set in and V dies.

Under the current law, both D and P are guilty of murder. Under the proposals in the CP, P would be guilty of murder but D would be guilty only of encouraging P to cause grievous bodily harm with intent.

2.18 Professor Sir John Smith agreed that it is arguable that in example 1E neither D nor P should be held responsible for the unintended and unforeseen consequences. However, the proposals in the [1993 paper] lead to a conclusion that he thought even less acceptable, namely that P is held responsible for those consequences whereas D, the more culpable party, is not held responsible.

The connection between D's conduct and P's offence

2.19 In the [1993 paper], the Commission said that D's liability for encouraging or assisting P to commit an offence should be inchoate because it was impossible to connect D to P's offence. Professor K J M Smith questioned this assertion: . . .

> it has always been implied in the concept of complicity that an accessory's involvement . . . did make some difference to the outcome, and, as a consequence of this, accessories have been implicitly linked to the harm element in the principal offence. No other plausible explanation exists for complicity's tenacious, fundamental requirement of the commission of the principal offence. . . . In sum then, under existing doctrine, the accessory's liability is derivative or parasitic of a principal offence and its harm content. Rather than relying solely on the accessory's mental culpability, unlike inchoate liability, complicity responsibility also implicitly draws on the attributable harm of the principal offence.

CONCLUSION

2.20 We acknowledge that it is possible to preserve some of the forensic benefits of the current law in a scheme consisting solely of inchoate offences. This could be achieved by a statutory provision stating that if the prosecution can prove that D must have been either the principal offender or the encourager/assister, D can be convicted of the inchoate offence.

2.21 However, such a provision would not meet the criticism that the proposals in the [1993] paper would not accurately label and condemn D for his or her conduct:

Example 2F

D gives P chocolates to give to V. V eats them and dies because they are poisoned. D knew the chocolates were poisoned and would kill anyone who ate them.

Under the proposals in the CP, D would be guilty of murder if P was unaware that the chocolates were poisoned because P would be an innocent agent and D would be considered to have perpetrated the offence as a principal offender. However, if P knew that the chocolates were poisoned, P would be guilty of murder but D would be guilty of assisting murder.

2.22 Example 2F illustrates why it would be wrong to abolish secondary liability. It cannot be right that D is guilty of murder if P is unaware that the chocolates are poisoned but only of assisting murder if P is aware that the chocolates are poisoned. D's conduct and state of mind are identical in each case. Further, whereas examples 2D and 2E might be thought to reveal problems with specific aspects of the law of murder that might be better resolved by reforming those aspects, the anomaly in example 2F is not the product of any defects in the law of murder.

2.23 We believe that if P commits an offence that it was D's intention P should commit, account should be taken of D's connection with the harm that results from P committing the offence. D's state of mind in intending that the offence should be committed connects D to the offence and the resulting harm in a morally significant way that can only be properly reflected by convicting D of the offence rather than encouraging or assisting the commission of the offence. In as much as there is a difference in the culpability of P and D, this can be reflected in the nature or severity of the punishment each is to receive for his or her involvement.

2.24 Further, we also believe that if P in the course of a joint venture commits a collateral offence that D foresaw that P might commit, account should be taken of D's connection with the harm that results from P committing the offence. It is true that D does not intend that P should commit the collateral offence and may even be opposed to the commission of the offence. However, D, by participating in the joint venture, contributes to the circumstances giving rise to the commission of the collateral offence. Further, by contemplating the collateral offence as a possible incident of the unlawful venture and nevertheless deciding to participate, D consciously accepts the risk that such an offence might be committed.

2.25 We acknowledge that the retention of secondary liability may sometimes result in D being liable for unexpected consequences. However, this will usually be the result of anomalies in the substantive law that the doctrine of secondary liability must accommodate. The doctrine of secondary liability is of general application, applying to many different offences whether or not those offences are well structured, well defined or even consistent with one another. Removing D's, but not P's, liability for unforeseen consequences, would simply create a new anomaly.

2.26 One aim of the proposals in the CP was to simplify the law by creating a clear distinction between the liability of the principal offender and the liability of the accessory. We now believe that this simplicity comes at too high a price. If P commits an offence that D either intended should be committed or believed might be committed in the course of a joint venture, there are compelling reasons for convicting D of the offence should P commit it. We now believe that to confine D's liability in such cases to that of encouraging or assisting the offence would be to confine it too narrowly.

■ *Question*

Do you agree with the consultees' arguments for rejecting the shift to inchoate liability?

See the following section, p 297, and Chapter 12 for the scheme the Law Commission did recommend, which relies heavily on wide inchoate offences whilst retaining a narrower form of secondary liability.

See also Law Commission Report No 305, *Participating in Crime* (2006), para 3.3.

8.10 Reform

Law Commission Report No 305, *Participating in Crime*
(2007)

AN OUTLINE OF THE SCHEME THAT WE ARE RECOMMENDING IN THIS REPORT

The overall structure

1.46 In place of the common law rules of secondary liability and innocent agency, we are recommending a statutory scheme.... The scheme consists of three conceptually distinct forms of liability:

Type 1: secondary liability

1.47 First, D would be liable, provided he or she satisfies the requisite fault element, for an offence that P commits with D's encouragement or assistance (clause 1 of the Bill). Secondly, D would be liable, provided he or she satisfies the requisite fault element, for any offences committed pursuant to a joint criminal venture (clause 2 of the Bill).

CLAUSE 1 OF THE BILL

1.48 Under clause 1 of the Bill, D would be liable for a principal offence committed by P if D assisted or encouraged P to perpetrate the conduct element of the principal offence and *intended* that the conduct element should be perpetrated. This would have the effect of narrowing the scope of secondary liability in cases where D and P are not parties to a joint criminal venture.

   1.49 For the purposes of clause 1, D 'intends' only if he or she acts in order that the conduct element of the principal offence is perpetrated. In our use and understanding of the word 'intention', we adopt the common law meaning. This means that if D foresaw as a virtual certainty P engaging in the conduct element of the offence, that would be evidence from which the jury or magistrates could (but would not have to) find that D intended the perpetration of the conduct element.

CLAUSE 2 OF THE BILL

1.50 Clause 2 would govern D's liability where D and P have formed a joint criminal venture. This will cover both agreed offences and collateral offences committed by P in the course of the joint criminal venture.

   1.51 In relation to clause 2, D would be liable for any offence committed by P provided that its commission fell within the scope of the joint venture. A joint criminal venture is formed when the parties agree to commit an offence or when they share with each other a common intention to commit an offence. D would be liable for any offence (agreed or collateral) that he or she foresaw might be committed as a possible result of the venture. The mere fact that D was not present when the offence was committed or that he or she would rather that it was not committed would not in itself preclude a jury finding that the offence fell within the scope of the joint venture.

Type 2: innocent agency

1.52 We are recommending that the common law doctrine of innocent agency should be replaced by a statutory regime. D would be liable for an offence as a principal offender if he or she intentionally caused P, an innocent agent, to commit the conduct element of an offence but P does not commit the offence because P:

   (1) is under the age of 10 years;

   (2) has a defence of insanity; or

   (3) acts without the fault required to be convicted of the offence;

Type 3: causing the commission of a no-fault offence

1.54 We are recommending the creation of a new statutory offence of causing another person to commit a no-fault offence. Accordingly, under this form of liability, D would be convicted as a principal offender rather than, as under the current law, a secondary party to the no-fault offence committed by P.

Summary

1.55 Much more so than at common law, the scheme emphasises the derivative nature of secondary liability. Subject to a very limited number of exceptions, D would incur secondary liability only if P commits a principal offence. The exceptions relate to where P does not commit an offence because he or she has a complete defence, for example duress, or a partial defence to murder, for example provocation.

1.56 Our scheme confines secondary liability to cases where D has assisted or encouraged P and/or has formed a joint criminal venture with P. Under the current law, D can incur secondary liability by 'procuring' P to commit an offence. Under our recommendations, 'procuring' will cease to be a basis of secondary liability. Instead, procuring in the sense of intentionally causing a person to do a criminal act will result in D incurring liability as a principal offender.

Limitations on liability and defences

The Tyrrell exemption

1.57 Under the current law, if an offence is enacted to protect a category of persons and D falls within that category, D cannot be convicted of committing the offence as a secondary party (or of inciting P to commit the offence). This is known as the *Tyrrell* exemption. In *Tyrrell*, P, an adult, had unlawful sexual intercourse with D, a child aged between 13 and 16. It was alleged that D had encouraged P to commit the offence. Despite this, the court held that D could not be liable as a secondary party because the primary offence was intended to protect 'victims from themselves'. Our scheme preserves and refines the common law *Tyrrell* exemption.

1.58 We are recommending that D should not be held liable as a secondary party or as a principal offender by virtue of innocent agency if:

(1) the principal offence is one that exists for the protection of a particular category of person;

(2) D falls within that category; and

(3) D is the victim of the principal offence.

Acting to prevent the commission of an offence or to prevent or limit the occurrence of harm

1.59 We are recommending that if D is charged with committing an offence as a secondary party, it should be a defence if D proves on the balance of probabilities that he or she acted in order to prevent the commission of an offence or the occurrence of harm and that it was reasonable to act as D did.

. . .

AN OVERVIEW OF INCHOATE AND SECONDARY LIABILITY FOR ASSISTING AND ENCOURAGING CRIME

1.60 It is important that the recommendations in this report are read in the light of the recommendations that we made in the first report [now implemented in Part 2 of the Serious Crime Act 2007—see Chapter 12]. In this section, we provide a brief outline of the overall scheme.

D's liability where P does not commit the principal offence

1.61 D's liability would always be inchoate. D would commit an inchoate offence of encouraging or assisting P to commit an offence:

(1) if D does an act capable of encouraging or assisting P to commit an offence:

(a) intending to assist or encourage P to perpetrate the conduct element of the offence ('the clause 1 inchoate offence'); or

(b) believing that his or her act will assist or encourage P to perpetrate the conduct element and that P will perpetrate it ('the clause 2 inchoate offence');

AND

(2) if the principal offence requires proof of fault:

(a) D believes that P will perpetrate the conduct element with the fault element required to be convicted of the offence; or

(b) D's own state of mind is such that were he to perpetrate the conduct element, he would do so with the requisite fault.

Specific defences

1.62 Where D's liability is grounded on the clause 2 inchoate offence, it would be a defence if D acted reasonably in the circumstances. The burden of proof would be on D to demonstrate that he or she had acted reasonably. The defence would not be available to the clause 1 inchoate offence.

D's liability where P does commit the principal offence

Clause 1

1.63 Beyond inchoate liability, D would be liable for P's offence as a secondary party provided that D intended P to engage in the conduct element of the offence and:

(1) D believed that P would perpetrate the conduct element with the fault required to be convicted of the offence; or

(2) D's state of mind was such that, had he or she perpetrated the conduct element, it would have been with the fault required for conviction of the offence.

1.64 Accordingly, if D indifferently assisted or encouraged P to commit an offence, D would no longer be a secondary party to P's offence. However, if D believed that P would commit the principal offence, D would commit the clause 2 inchoate offence of assisting or encouraging P to commit the principal offence believing D would commit it.

1.65 Accordingly, there is scope for the clause 2 inchoate offence to apply even if P does commit or attempt to commit the principal offence. However, for the clause 2 inchoate offence to apply, D must believe that P *will* commit the principal offence. This means that if D believes that P might commit the principal offence, D will not incur either secondary or inchoate liability in respect of the principal offence.

Clause 2

1.66 D would be liable for any offence committed by P that was within the scope of the joint criminal venture. It would be a question of fact and degree whether the offence committed by P was within the scope of the venture. The fact that D was opposed to the commission of the offence would not in itself prevent the tribunal of fact from finding that the offence was within the scope of the venture.

General defences

1.67 There would be two defences to both inchoate and secondary liability. The first would be where D acted reasonably in order to prevent the commission of an offence or to limit the occurrence of harm. The burden of proof would be on D to establish the defence. The second would be where the principal offence was one which existed for the protection of a particular category of person and D was both a member of that category and the victim of the offence (or would have been had the principal offence been committed).

For critical comment on the proposals, see W. Wilson, 'A Rational Scheme of Liability for Participation in Crime' [2008] Crim LR 3, suggesting the proposals generally 'succeed admirably'; cf G. R. Sullivan, 'Participating in Crime' [2008] Crim LR 19, suggesting the proposals on joint ventures show a disregard for the 'minimum standards of clarity and comprehensibility' and R. D. Taylor, 'Procuring, Causation, Innocent Agency and the Law Commission' [2008] Crim LR 32, who is also critical of the complexity and incoherence of the proposals. See also J. Horder, *Homicide and the Politics of Law Reform* (2012), Ch 6 for a response to Sullivan's criticisms.

■ *Question*
Would the scheme represent an improvement on the existing law?

FURTHER READING

P. Alldridge, 'The Doctrine of Innocent Agency' (1990) 2 Crim L Forum 45

D. Baker, 'Liability for Encouraging One's Own Murder, Victims, and Other Exempt Parties' (2012) 23 KLJ 256

I. H. Dennis, 'The Mental Element for Accessories' in P. Smith (ed), *Essays in Honour of J. C. Smith* (1987)

I. H. Dennis, 'Intent and Complicity—A Reply' [1988] Crim LR 649

J. Herring, 'Victims as Defendants: When Victims Participate in Crimes against Themselves' in A. Reed and M. Bohlander (eds), *Participation in Crime: Domestic and Comparative Perspectives* (2013)

P. Mirfield, 'Guilt by Association: A Reply to Professor Virgo' [2013] Crim LR 577

A. Simester, 'The Mental Element in Complicity' (2006) 122 LQR 578

G. R. Sullivan, 'Intent, Purpose and Complicity' [1988] Crim LR 638

G. R. Sullivan, 'Accessories and Principles after *Gnango*' in A. Reed and M. Bohlander (eds), *Participation in Crime: Domestic and Comparative Perspectives* (2013)

G. Williams, 'Innocent Agency and Causation' (1992) 3 Crim L Forum 289

9
Liability of corporations

9.1 Introduction

This chapter deals with the potential criminal liability of organizations. The main focus is on corporations, which include public limited companies (plc) and private limited companies (Ltd) as well as limited liability partnerships (LLP). The criminal law has developed special rules and procedures to deal with the fact that corporations have a separate legal identity. They are treated in law as having a legal personality distinct from the natural persons—members, directors, employees etc—who make up the corporation. That presents the opportunity, in theory, of imposing liability on the corporation separately from any criminal liability which might be imposed on the individual members for any wrongdoing.

The chapter will address particular ways in which organizations and their members might be held liable in criminal law. These include:

    (i)   personal liability of individuals within an organization;

    (ii)   vicarious liability;

    (iii) corporate liability:

- by breaching a statutory duty imposed on the organization;
- by committing strict liability offences;
- by being liable for the acts of individuals under the identification doctrine;
- the specific statutory liability of organizations for homicide under the Corporate Manslaughter and Corporate Homicide Act 2007;

    (iv) liability of unincorporated associations.

9.2 Personal liability

Individuals who are directors, managers, employers etc can be prosecuted for their personal wrongdoing just like any other human being. For example, the managing director of a film company who makes films which involve indecent images of children or extreme pornography (contrary to the Criminal Justice and Immigration Act 2008, s 63) will be at risk of personal prosecution. An employee sales person who commits offences of driving carelessly while on company business, or frauds etc will be personally liable. The general principles of criminal liability which are described throughout this book will apply.

If a corporation is found criminally liable, an individual employee or director etc can also be liable as a secondary party to the corporation's wrongdoing under s 8 of the Accessories and Abettors Act 1861 (see Chapter 8). Occasionally Parliament precludes such liability, as for example with the corporate manslaughter offence (see section 9.5). Sometimes a provision will create an offence that a corporation can be guilty of committing and simultaneously creates an additional form of liability that an officer of the company can be liable for. An example of such a provision is the Regulatory Reform (Fire Safety) Order 2005 which imposes liability on a director for conniving or being party to the company's neglect. It was confirmed in *Wilson* [2013] EWCA Crim 170 that provisions such as these are not discrete offences but forms of secondary liability.

Many statutes, particularly those dealing with regulatory offences, create offences that can be committed by the specified person (eg the employer) in person. If the specified person is in breach of that duty, he commits the actus reus of the offence and, if it imposes strict liability, he is personally guilty of the offence. A good example is the Health and Safety at Work etc Act 1974. By s 3(1) the Act imposes on every employer a duty 'to conduct his undertaking in such a way as to ensure, so far as is reasonably practicable' that persons not in his employment are not exposed to risk. In *British Steel plc* [1995] 1 WLR 1356, [1995] Crim LR 654, D's subcontractor, negligently conducting D's undertaking, caused V's death. D had not ensured as far as was, in the opinion of the court, reasonably practicable, that persons were not exposed to risk and D was therefore guilty. D was liable for his own failure to ensure that there was no risk of such a thing happening. This was a case of personal liability being imposed by the statute. D was not being held liable for the acts of the independent contractor who caused death but for the breach of his own personal duty to protect against the harm.

9.3 Vicarious liability

Vicarious liability is a mechanism commonly used in the civil law to impose liability on employers for the acts of their employees. Employers are generally liable for the tortious acts of their employees committed in the course of their employment. In tort law, this makes good sense because an employee will rarely have the means adequately to compensate a person to whom he has caused a serious injury, so the loss will lie with the innocent victim unless the employer can be required to pay. As between the victim and the employer, it is thought right that the employer should bear the loss, even though he may personally be blameless. The primary function of the criminal law, however, is not the compensation of the victim but the punishment of the wrongdoer—and the grounds for punishing the blameless employer are tenuous at best. The employee's wrongful act is sometimes a crime as well as a tort. It may be theft, fraud, assault or even manslaughter and the employee is of course liable to conviction of the crime. The employer, even though responsible for the act in the civil law and liable to pay compensation, is not criminally liable. Criminal liability is of a personal nature. That is the general rule and, with the exception of the anomalous offence of public nuisance, now the universal rule at common law; but in statutory offences there are exceptions, or apparent exceptions, to it. These tend to arise in areas of law regulating sales or licensing. It is easy to see how this might be useful where, for example, a major store has sold an 18-rated DVD to a child, *Tesco Stores Ltd v Brent London Borough Council* [1993] 2 All ER 718, [1993] Crim LR 624, DC, or a waiter in a restaurant (in breach of the licence) serves alcohol to someone who is not dining but merely on the premises, *Vane v Yiannopoullos* [1964] 3 All ER 820, HL. We do not discuss the forms of vicarious liability further here. See *Smith and Hogan* (13th edn), p 273.

9.4 Liability of a corporation

A corporation is a legal person, for example a limited company, a person distinct from the persons who are members of it. The corporation, as distinct from its members, has no physical existence. It exists only in law. It cannot therefore act or form an intention except through its members. But a corporation can incur legal liabilities, both civil and criminal.

9.4.1 Crimes a corporation cannot commit

A corporation cannot commit a crime for which it cannot be sentenced. So it cannot commit murder, as a principal or an accessory, because the mandatory sentence is life imprisonment and a corporation is incapable of being imprisoned. Nearly all crimes can be punishable by a fine so this is not a serious limitation on the scope of criminal liability. There are other offences which it is extremely unlikely that an official of a corporation could commit within the scope of his employment; for example, bigamy, rape, incest and perjury (cf *Re Odyssey (London) Ltd v OIC Run Off Ltd* (2000) The Times, 3 March, CA (Civ Div)).

The fact that a corporation cannot commit the offence as a principal does not mean, however, that it is incapable of committing it as an accessory. It is difficult to imagine a case in which a company could be held liable as a principal for dangerous driving but it may certainly be convicted as a secondary party: *Robert Millar (Contractors) Ltd* [1970] 1 All ER 577, [1970] 2 QB 54.

■ *Question*

The manager of ABC Dating Co, a marriage advisory bureau, arranged a marriage which he knew to be bigamous. Is the company guilty?

9.4.2 The liability of corporations for statutory offences

When Parliament creates an offence the statute usually provides that it is an offence for 'a person' to do or omit to do the act in question; and the Interpretation Act 1978, s 5, provides: 'In any Act, unless the contrary intention appears, words and expressions listed in Schedule 1 to this Act are to be construed according to that Schedule.'

Schedule 1 provides: '"Person" includes a body of persons corporate or unincorporate. [1889].'

By Schedule 2, para 4(1)(a), the date, '[1889]', means that the definition of 'person' applies to Acts passed after 1889. Schedule 2, para 4(5) provides: 'The definition of 'person', so far as it includes bodies corporate, applies to any provision of an Act whenever passed relating to an offence punishable on indictment or on summary conviction.'

The effect is that, where it is a statutory offence for 'a person' to do or not do something, that offence may (unless the contrary intention appears) be committed by a corporation, whatever the date of the statute, and by an unincorporate body if the statute was passed after 1889. A contrary intention may appear because, for example, the actus reus is incapable of being committed by a corporation.

9.4.2.1 Breach of statutory duty

A corporation, as distinct from its employees or managers etc, can be criminally liable for offences laid down by Parliament as applying specifically to corporations. A corporation is a legal person but it has no physical existence. As a legal entity, a corporation may be placed under a duty by Parliament to comply with a particular regulation and the failure to do so may result in criminal liability.

9.4.2.2 Strict liability offences

Offences of strict liability can be committed by a corporation. Since there is no need for proof of mens rea, there is no difficulty in establishing any fault on the part of the corporation. Corporate liability for strict liability offences is in theory no different from strict liability imposed on human actors. No more need be said about this form of liability. It was considered in full in Chapter 7.

9.4.3 The identification doctrine?

In criminal law the corporation can be held to be *personally* liable because the acts in the course of the corporation's business of those officers who control its affairs (in the Draft Code called 'controlling officers'), and the intentions with which those acts are done, are deemed to be the acts and intentions of the corporation. This is so in respect of common law as well as statutory offences. A corporation may therefore be a party to a common law conspiracy and may commit manslaughter. A corporation is not criminally liable for the acts of its members or employees who are not controlling officers, unless it is an offence to which the rules of vicarious liability considered previously apply—for example, it is a case of selling in breach of a statutory provision. In the case of other offences, the question is often whether the status of the individual perpetrator is that of a controlling officer.

In *H. L. Bolton (Engineering) Co Ltd v T. J. Graham & Sons Ltd* [1956] 3 All ER 624, [1957] 1 QB 159 Denning LJ likened a company to a human body: 'It has a brain and nerve centre which controls what it does. It also has hands which hold the tools and act in accordance with directions from the centre.'

Where a corporation is charged with an offence which can be committed only personally and not vicariously, a crucial question is whether the person who did the relevant acts was 'the directing mind and will of the company'. If he is, the company has done those acts. If he is not, there may be a question whether the company should nevertheless be held liable for them. In *Meridian Global Funds Management Asia Ltd v Securities Commission* [1995] 3 WLR 413, PC, http://www.bailii.org/uk/cases/UKPC/1995/1995_26.htm, the Board recognized that the liability of a company under the identification doctrine turns on the rules by which the corporation operates, its structure, the language of the offence etc. Contrast was made between the two previous leading cases. Lord Hoffmann described them:

Tesco v Nattrass [1972] AC 153, http://www.bailii.org/uk/cases/UKHL/1971/1.html:

Tesco were prosecuted for displaying a notice that goods were being 'offered at a price less than that at which they were in fact being offered...'. Its supermarket in Northwich had advertised that it was selling certain packets of washing powder at the reduced price of 2s 11d, but a customer who asked for one was told he would have to pay the normal price of 3s 11d. This happened because the shop manager had negligently failed to notice that he had run out of the specially marked low-price packets. Section 24(1) provided a defence for a shopowner who could prove that the commission of the offence was caused by 'another person' and that: 'He took all reasonable precautions and exercised all due diligence to avoid the commission of such an offence by himself or any person under his control.' The company was able to show that it owned hundreds of shops and that the board had instituted systems of supervision and training which amounted, on its part, to taking reasonable precautions and exercising all due diligence to avoid the commission of such offences in its shops. The question was: whose precautions counted as those of the company? If it was the board, then the defence was made out. If they had to include those of the manager, then it failed. The House of Lords held that the precautions taken by the board were sufficient for the purposes of section 24(1) to count as precautions taken by the company and that the manager's negligence was not attributable to the company. It did so by examining the purpose of section 24(1) in providing a defence to what would otherwise have been an absolute offence: it was intended to give effect to 'a policy of consumer protection which does have a rational and moral justification': per Lord Diplock, at pp194–195. This led to the conclusion that the acts and defaults of the manager were not intended to be attributed to the company....

Re Supply of Ready Mixed Concrete (No 2) [1995] 1 AC 456:

A restrictive arrangement in breach of an undertaking by a company to the Restrictive Practices Court was made by executives of the company acting within the scope of their employment. The board knew nothing of the arrangement; it had in fact given instructions to the company's employees that they were not to make such arrangements. But the House of Lords held that for the purposes of deciding whether the company was in contempt, the act and state of mind of an employee who entered into an arrangement in the course of his employment should be attributed to the company. This attribution rule was derived from a construction of the undertaking against the background of the Restrictive Trade Practices Act 1976: such undertakings by corporations would be worth little if the company could avoid liability for what its employees had actually done on the ground that the board did not know about it.

In *Great Western Trains Co* (30 June 1999, unreported), Scott Baker J ruled that the only basis on which a corporation might be liable under the directing mind and will doctrine was by identifying some one person within the company whose gross negligence was that of the company itself. As no such person was identified he directed a verdict of not guilty. The Attorney General referred the case to the Court of Appeal. In *Attorney-General's Reference (No 2 of 1999)* [2000] 2 Cr App R 207, the Court of Appeal agreed with the trial judge.

Unless an identified individual's conduct, ... can be attributed to the company the company is not, in the present state of the common law, liable.

For an example of the Court of Appeal taking a strict approach to *Meridian*, see *St Regis Paper Co* [2011] EWCA Crim 2527. (However, it is arguable that in that case rather than relying upon the identification doctrine, D's conviction could have been upheld on the basis of vicarious liability). For an example of the identification doctrine applying in relation to recklessness, see *X Ltd* [2013] EWCA Crim 818.

9.5 Corporate manslaughter

Various disasters each with large loss of life—in particular the *Herald of Free Enterprise* ferry disaster (*P & O European Ferries (Dover) Ltd* (1990) 93 Cr App R 72), and various rail crashes (Southall, Ladbrooke Grove, Paddington, Hatfield)—all reinforced the public desire for legislation fixing the corporation with liability.

The Law Commission Report No 237 (1996) made recommendations for a corporate manslaughter offence. See H. Keating, 'The Law Commission Report on Involuntary Manslaughter: (1) The Restoration of a Serious Crime' [1998] Crim LR 535; A. McColgan, 'Heralding Corporate Liability' [1994] Crim LR 547. See also S. Field and N. Jorg, 'Corporate Liability and Manslaughter: Should We Be Going Dutch?' [1991] Crim LR 156 and C. Wells, 'The Corporate Manslaughter Proposals: Pragmatism, Paradox or Peninsularity' [1996] Crim LR 545 at 553.

The Law Commission Report was followed by a Home Office Consultation Paper *Reforming the Law on Involuntary Manslaughter: The Government's Proposals* (2000). After considerable delay a Bill appeared in 2005 as a commitment to a manifesto promise of the Labour Government. Following a Report of the Home Affairs and Work and Pensions Committees in 2005, the Government finally responded in March 2006 with another Bill which, after much controversy in Parliament, became the present Act.

9.5.1 The Corporate Manslaughter and Corporate Homicide Act 2007

The Act abolishes gross negligence manslaughter as far as it applies to corporations and other bodies to which the 2007 Act applies (s 20). An organization can, although this is much less likely, be convicted of unlawful act manslaughter in appropriate circumstances (eg where D is the manager of a company who encourages employee X to set fire to the company premises in an insurance scam which leads to the death of V on the premises). The corporation may also be liable as an accessory to the principal individual offender in other homicide offences such as causing death by dangerous driving.

9.5.1.1 The offence

The offence of corporate manslaughter is triable only on indictment (s 1(6)). The offence is defined in s 1.

> (1) An organisation to which this section applies is guilty of an offence if the way in which its activities are managed or organised—
>
>   (a) causes a person's death, and
>
>   (b) amounts to a gross breach of a relevant duty of care owed by the organisation to the deceased.
>
> . . .
>
> (3) An organisation is guilty of an offence under this section only if the way in which its activities are managed or organised by its senior management is a substantial element in the breach referred to in subsection (1).
>
> (4) For the purposes of this Act—
>
>   (a) 'relevant duty of care' has the meaning given by section 2, read with sections 3 to 7;
>
>   (b) a breach of a duty of care by an organisation is a 'gross' breach if the conduct alleged to amount to a breach of that duty falls far below what can reasonably be expected of the organisation in the circumstances;
>
>   (c) 'senior management', in relation to an organisation, means the persons who play significant roles in—
>
>   (i) the making of decisions about how the whole or a substantial part of its activities are to be managed or organised, or
>
>   (ii) the actual managing or organising of the whole or a substantial part of those activities.
>
> (5) The offence under this section is called—
>
>   (a) corporate manslaughter, in so far as it is an offence under the law of England and Wales or Northern Ireland; . . .
>
> (6) An organisation that is guilty of corporate manslaughter or corporate homicide is liable on conviction on indictment to a fine.

The offence mirrors many of the core aspects of gross negligence manslaughter. The crucial difference is that 'rather than being contingent on the guilt of one or more individuals, liability for the new offence depends on a finding of gross negligence in the way in which the activities of the organisation are run.'

Determining whether liability arises under the Act is best approached by asking:

- Is the organization one to which the Act applies?
- Is a relevant duty owed to the victim?
- Was the breach of the duty by the organization as a result of the way the activities are managed or organized?
- Was a substantial element of the breach of the duty due to the way the senior management managed or organized activities?
- Was the breach of the duty a gross one?
- Was V's death caused by the breach of the duty?

9.5.1.2 Who can be liable?

The Act provides that individuals cannot be liable as a secondary party to an offence of corporate manslaughter (s 18(1)). Individuals within companies can, of course, still be prosecuted for gross negligence manslaughter as principal offenders subject to what has been said previously.

The Act extends to 'organizations' rather than merely corporations. Section 1(2) defines the organizations to which the new offence applies:

(2) The organisations to which this section applies are—

(a) a corporation;

(b) a department or other body listed in Schedule 1;

(c) a police force;

(d) a partnership, or a trade union or employers' association, that is an employer.

The list of organizations to which the offence applies can be further extended by secondary legislation, for example to further types of unincorporated association, subject to the affirmative resolution procedure (s 21). Schedule 1 lists the Government departments to which the offence applies.

By s 11:

(1) An organisation that is a servant or agent of the Crown is not immune from prosecution under this Act for that reason.

(2) For the purposes of this Act—

(a) a department or other body listed in Schedule 1, or

(b) a corporation that is a servant or agent of the Crown,

is to be treated as owing whatever duties of care it would owe if it were a corporation that was not a servant or agent of the Crown.

In the course of debates in the House of Lords it was emphasized how important the extension of the offence to public bodies is:

there is no reason why the death of an individual in one situation should be considered less of a death, or less deserving of justice, merely because that situation was presided over by government officials as opposed to privately employed foremen. Indeed, it is all the more of a tragedy and contravention of the natural principle of justice where the state itself acts with such gross negligence that the very lives of its own citizens are forfeit. (Hansard HL, 15 January 2007, col GC189 (Lord Hunt))

9.5.1.3 Is there a duty on the organization?

By s 2:

(1) A 'relevant duty of care', in relation to an organisation, means any of the following duties owed by it under the law of negligence—

(a) a duty owed to its employees or to other persons working for the organisation or performing services for it;

(b) a duty owed as occupier of premises;

(c) a duty owed in connection with—

(i) the supply by the organisation of goods or services (whether for consideration or not),

(ii) the carrying on by the organisation of any construction or maintenance operations,

(iii) the carrying on by the organisation of any other activity on a commercial basis, or

(iv) the use or keeping by the organisation of any plant, vehicle or other thing;

> (d) a duty owed to a person who, by reason of being a person within subsection (2), is someone for whose safety the organisation is responsible.
>
> [Subsection (2) lists the organizations referred to in (d) above, and is discussed in full below.]
>
> (3) Subsection (1) is subject to sections 3 to 7.
>
> . . .
>
> (7) In this section—'construction or maintenance operations' means operations of any of the following descriptions—
>
> > (a) construction, installation, alteration, extension, improvement, repair, maintenance, decoration, cleaning, demolition or dismantling of—
> >
> > > (i)   any building or structure,
> > >
> > > (ii) anything else that forms, or is to form, part of the land, or
> > >
> > > (iii) any plant, vehicle or other thing;
> >
> > (b) operations that form an integral part of, or are preparatory to, or are for rendering complete, any operations within paragraph (a);

The duties reflect the duties of care arising at common law. The duty is that owed in the common law of negligence or, where applicable, the statutory duty which has superseded the common law duty. This is made clear by s 2(4):

> A reference in subsection (1) to a duty owed under the law of negligence includes a reference to a duty that would be owed under the law of negligence but for any statutory provision under which liability is imposed in place of liability under that law.

Some common law duties which have been superseded by statute are expressly incorporated within s 2(1) by s 2(7), for example the Occupiers' Liability Act 1957. Section 2(4) does not therefore apply to occupiers' liability since the statutory duty of care is already included as part of 'the law of negligence' by virtue of s 2(7) and thus can be a relevant duty of care under the Act. Section 2(4) is, however, applicable to preserve a (fault-based) duty of care for these purposes in cases where the law of negligence has been superseded by a statutory provision imposing strict liability. The Explanatory Notes give the example of the Carriage by Air Act 1961.

Who decides on the duty question?

Given the potential breadth of the categories of duty and examination of the common law which might be necessary to determine whether a duty does exist, it is reassuring to see that the question whether a duty of care is owed is a question of law. It is for the judge to decide: s 2(5). Moreover, 'the judge must make any findings of fact necessary to decide that question'. This latter provision about the judge finding facts is highly unusual.

The scope of the duty

> (6) For the purposes of this Act there is to be disregarded—
>
> > (a) any rule of the common law that has the effect of preventing a duty of care from being owed by one person to another by reason of the fact that they are jointly engaged in unlawful conduct;
> >
> > (b) any such rule that has the effect of preventing a duty of care from being owed to a person by reason of his acceptance of a risk of harm.

Section 2(6) makes it clear that the duty of care will not be excluded by *ex turpi causa* and *volenti* doctrines. This is potentially very important. The scope of liability at common law is restricted in practice by the operation of these doctrines. However, the reason that they are excluded as defences or limits on criminal liability in this context is easy enough to deduce.

The duty in relation to detained individuals

The most controversial category is that relating to duties arising from detention.

Section 2(2) contains the list of people for whom a duty is owed on the basis that they comprise those for whose safety the organization is responsible, as referred to in s 2(1)(d). It provides:

(2) A person is within this subsection if—

(a) he is detained at a custodial institution or in a custody area at a court, a police station or customs premises;

(aa) he is detained in service custody premises;

(b) he is detained at a removal centre or short–term holding facility;

(c) he is being transported in a vehicle, or being held in any premises, in pursuance of prison escort arrangements or immigration escort arrangements;

(d) he is living in secure accommodation in which he has been placed;

(e) he is a detained patient.

Lord Ramsbotham, former Chief Inspector of Prisons, was successful in the House of Lords in amending the Bill to include what is now s 2(1)(d). There was considerable Government opposition and the Bill almost lapsed. Several powerful speeches were made arguing for the extension of liability to cover deaths in custody. The final compromise was that commencement of s 2(1)(d) would require the further approval of both Houses of Parliament, by way of the affirmative resolution procedure. This approval was subsequently given and the provisions have been in force since 1 September 2011.

■ *Questions*

1. McKay, a prison governor, allows the state of his prison to fall into disrepair. Fletcher, an inmate, is killed when a brick falls on his head in the exercise yard. Godber is distraught at the loss of his cellmate. His mental condition is acknowledged by the prison doctor to be serious and there is concern that he may be suicidal. The prison warder, Mr Barraclough, fails to keep regular watch on Godber and he commits suicide in his cell. Does the prison authority have any criminal liability for these deaths?

2. Would it make any difference if Mr McKay were unable to perform the repairs owing to budget cuts imposed on him by central government? See later s 3 in section 9.5.5.1.

9.5.2 The breach of the duty by the organization must be as a result of the way the activities are managed or organized

The second element of the offence is designed to ensure that the focus is on the management failure. The old limitations of the identification doctrine are gone. This test is not linked to a particular level of management but considers how an activity was managed within the organization as a whole. It will now be possible to aggregate the shortcomings of a wide variety of individuals within the organization to prove a failure of management *by the organization*. The language is designed to reflect the concentration of things done consistently with the organization's culture and policies more generally.

■ *Question*
What difficulties might there be in proving this?

9.5.2.1 Senior managers
Under s 1(3), the offence is committed by an organization *only* if:

the way in which its activities are managed and organised *by its senior management* is a substantial element in the breach referred to in subsection (1).

By s 1(4)(c) the senior managers are:

(c) 'senior management', in relation to an organisation, means the persons who play significant roles in—

(i) the making of decisions about how the whole or a substantial part of its activities are to be managed or organised, or

(ii) the actual managing or organising of the whole or a substantial part of those activities.

This extends beyond the narrow category of senior individuals who would be caught at common law by the identification doctrine being the directing mind and will.

■ *Questions*
1. Is the test too restrictive? Will companies seek to avoid this by nominating people in less senior positions to take responsibility for all health and safety policies?
2. Is this a clearer test than that of the controlling officer in *Meridian*?

9.5.2.2 Senior managers were a substantial element in the breach
The senior managers' management and organization must be a 'substantial element' in the breach of duty leading to death. Two important consequences flow from this aspect of the offence. First, since the senior managers' involvement need only be a substantial element in the organization etc, the involvement and conduct of others—'non-senior managers' who are involved in the management and organization of activities—is also relevant. Secondly, when assessing the management failure the contribution of these individuals who are not senior management can be taken into account even if their involvement is 'substantial' provided it is not so great as to render the senior managers' involvement something less than substantial.

■ *Questions*
Can there be more than one substantial element causing a result? If so, will this not be a relatively easy element for the prosecution to establish?

9.5.3 A 'gross' breach of duty?
This element of the offence is clearly designed to echo the gross negligence manslaughter offence at common law. Section 1(4)(b) provides a more detailed explanation of the concept:

(b) a breach of a duty of care by an organisation is a "gross" breach if the conduct alleged to amount to a breach of that duty falls far below what can reasonably be expected of the organisation in the circumstances.

The language chosen is similar to that proposed by the Law Commission as a suitable form of words to replace gross negligence. The test retains a degree of circularity, although not to the extent of that in the common law offence of gross negligence manslaughter (see section 17.3.3.1, p 630).

9.5.3.1 Determining the grossness of the breach

The question is one for the jury. By s 8:

(1) This section applies where—

   (a) it is established that an organisation owed a relevant duty of care to a person, and

   (b) it falls to the jury to decide whether there was a gross breach of that duty.

(2) The jury must consider whether the evidence shows that the organisation failed to comply with any health and safety legislation that relates to the alleged breach, and if so—

   (a) how serious that failure was;

   (b) how much of a risk of death it posed.

(3) The jury may also—

   (a) consider the extent to which the evidence shows that there were attitudes, policies, systems or accepted practices within the organisation that were likely to have encouraged any such failure as is mentioned in subsection (2), or to have produced tolerance of it;

   (b) have regard to any health and safety guidance that relates to the alleged breach.

(4) This section does not prevent the jury from having regard to any other matters they consider relevant.

(5) In this section 'health and safety guidance' means any code, guidance, manual or similar publication that is concerned with health and safety matters and is made or issued (under a statutory provision or otherwise) by an authority responsible for the enforcement of any health and safety legislation.

Note that the jury 'must' consider these issues. Note also that the jury is obliged to consider whether the 'organization' complied, not just whether its senior management complied. Section 8(3) emphasizes that the jury may have reference to general organizational and systems failures. This section has been influenced, as has much of this Act, by the Australian legislation and academic comment in Australia. See B. Fisse and J. Braithwaite, *Corporations, Crime and Accountability* (1993). The inability to consider the corporation's policies under the old law was a source of common complaint. How the 'attitudes etc' are proved is a different matter. There is the potential for lengthy arguments and evidence comparing practices across the particular sector or industry. Imagine a prosecution of a rail company and the potential for it to adduce evidence of safety procedures and policies across the sector to demonstrate the quality of its own.

■ *Questions*

In the Zeebrugge case, should the jury have heard about the practices of other cross-channel ferry companies? Would that help to determine liability? Does it matter that the other companies also operated negligently?

9.5.4 Causing death

There must be a death of a person. Causation must be established in accordance with orthodox principles, see Chapter 3.

9.5.5 Excluded liability

The most important aspect of the legislation is not the scope of the relevant duty and of potential liability under s 1 and s 2, but rather what the Government excluded from the scope of liability under ss 3 to 7. The excluded categories of duty are considerable. The different categories and sub-categories of duty also make the interpretation of whether a duty is owed rather more complex.

9.5.5.1 Public policy

The broadest exclusion comes in s 3(1) and deals with decisions of public policy taken by public authorities.

> Any duty of care owed by a public authority in respect of a decision as to matters of public policy (including in particular the allocation of public resources or the weighing of competing public interests) is not a 'relevant duty of care'.

■ *Question*

To what extent will the criminal courts be willing to engage in detailed evaluations of the common law on this issue?

Section 3(2) provides a less extensive exclusion in relation to things done 'in the exercise of an exclusively public function':

> (2) Any duty of care owed in respect of things done in the exercise of an exclusively public function is not a 'relevant duty of care' unless it falls within section 2(1)(a), (b) or (d).
>
> ...
>
> (4) In this section—
>
>   'exclusively public function' means a function that falls within the prerogative of the Crown or is, by its nature, exercisable only with authority conferred—
>
>   (a) by the exercise of that prerogative, or
>
>   (b) by or under a statutory provision;
>
>   'statutory function' means a function conferred by or under a statutory provision.

The duty of care owed as employer or occupier or custodian under s 2(1)(a), (b) or (d) still applies in these circumstances. This exclusion relates only to the public functions involved in s (2)(1)(c), such as the supply of goods or services, construction work or the use of vehicles etc.

9.5.5.2 Military activities: s 4

Many of the activities performed by the armed forces will be excluded by virtue of s 3(2) (see the previous extract). Section 3(2) does not prevent liability arising as an employer or occupier. Section 4 goes further by providing a total exclusion for some active service-type activities.

9.5.5.3 The police: s 5

The exemptions provided for police activities are also complex. Two categories exist. Section 5(1) and (2) create a total exemption, that is, no relevant duty arises for some types of policing activity. In short, these are where there are operations in relation to terrorism or civil unrest.

In other circumstances, by s 5(3) a 'relevant duty of care' is owed where the organization is acting as employer, occupier or custodian (ie s 2(1)(a), (b) or (d)). This exemption will exclude circumstances where a member of the public has been killed in the pursuit of law enforcement activities.

9.5.5.4 Emergency services: s 6

In the law of tort, considerable difficulties have arisen in identifying the scope of the duty of care owed by the emergency and rescue services in the course of performing rescue activity. Section 6 puts beyond doubt that the corporate manslaughter offence does not apply generally to these agencies when responding to emergencies. The emergency services may still be liable for a death arising from their status as employer or occupier even where the death arises in the course of an emergency. The exemption also does not apply to duties that do not relate to *the way in which* a body responds to an emergency, for example duties to maintain vehicles in a safe condition. Such duties will be capable of engaging the offence. The exemption does not extend to medical treatment itself, or to decisions about this (other than decisions that establish the priority for treating patients). Matters relating to the organization and management of medical services will therefore be within the ambit of the offence (s 6(4)).

9.5.5.5 Child protection and probation: s 7

Section 7 applies in relation to the duty of care that a local authority or other public authority owes in respect of the exercise of its functions under Parts 4 and 5 of the Children Act 1989 and in relation to probation.

9.5.6 Penalty

An organization guilty of the offence is liable to an unlimited fine (s 1(6)). In *Cotswold Geotechnical Holdings Ltd* [2011] EWCA Crim 1337, the Court of Appeal upheld the imposition of a fine that had the effect of putting the defendant company into liquidation. Such a situation was 'unavoidable and inevitable'. In addition to a fine, the court has power on the application of the prosecution to impose a remedial order against an organization convicted of corporate manslaughter requiring it to take specified steps to remedy: the breach; any matter appearing to have resulted from it and to have been a cause of the death; or any health and safety deficiency in the 'organisation's policies, systems or practices' appearing to be indicated by the breach (s 9(1) and (2)). This provision is also heavily influenced by Australian experience.

Any such order must be on 'such terms (whether those proposed or others) as the court considers appropriate having regard to any representations made, and any evidence adduced, in relation to that matter by the prosecution or on behalf of the organisation' (s 9(2)).

Section 9(4) provides for the form of a remedial order. It must specify a period within which the remedial steps are to be taken and may require the organization to supply evidence of compliance. Periods specified may be extended or further extended by order of the court on an application made before the end of that period or extended period.

An organization which fails to comply with a remedial order commits an offence triable only on indictment and punishable with an unlimited fine (s 9(5)). There appears to be nothing to prevent the conviction of a director as an accessory to this offence.

■ *Questions*

What basis should be used for determining the level of fine to be imposed? Annual profits? If a global corporation, say a petrochemical company, with a turnover of billions of pounds is fined say £100m for causing a number of deaths on one of its oil rigs, who will bear the cost? Is it worth imposing the fine on the company if it is to be borne by thousands of innocent motorists who pay the additional cost for fuel?

The Sentencing Council has published a definitive guideline on sentencing for corporate manslaughter and health and safety offences causing death. It applies to sentences imposed on or after 15 February 2010.

In addition, the court has power to impose a 'publicity order' under s 10 'requiring the organisation to publicise in a specified manner' its conviction, specified particulars, the amount of any fine and the terms of any remedial order. The Corporate Manslaughter and Corporate Homicide Act 2007 (Commencement No 2) Order 2010 (SI 2010 No 276) brought s 10 of the Act into force on 15 February 2010. Before imposing such an order the court must ascertain the views of any relevant enforcement authority as it considers appropriate, and have regard to any representations made by the prosecution or the organization. Section 10(3) provides for the form of a remedial order. It must specify a period within which the publicity order must be complied with and may require the organization to supply evidence of compliance. An organization which fails to comply with an order commits an offence triable only on indictment and punishable with an unlimited fine (s 10(4)).

Section 10 was added to the Bill during its passage in the House of Lords. It is clearly predicated on the assumption (probably correct) that large organizations are more concerned about adverse publicity than a fine.

■ *Question*

What type of publicity order would be appropriate in a case such as the Zeebrugge ferry disaster if that had led to prosecutions under the 2007 Act?

9.6 Unincorporated associations

Criminal liability of unincorporated associations involves quite separate principles from those relating to corporations. Subject to important exceptions, unincorporated associations are not regarded as having legal personality. There are numerous statutory offences which are expressly applicable to associations. In relation to all other statutes creating criminal offences (since 1889) the question whether the unincorporated association is subject to prosecution turns on s 5 of and Schedule 1 to the Interpretation Act 1978: 'In any Act, unless the contrary intention appears', . . . ' "Person" includes a body of persons corporate or unincorporate.'

In *L* [2008] EWCA Crim 1970 the chairman and treasurer of a golf club with 900 members were prosecuted for polluting a watercourse by an escape of heating oil from the premises caused directly by an independent contractor. The question arose as to whether it was correct to prosecute the individuals rather than the association. The trial judge ruled that the club should itself have been charged. The prosecution conceded that this would have been a better approach. The Court of Appeal disagreed.

Hughes LJ explained that in determining whether 'person' includes a body of persons corporate or unincorporate or whether 'a contrary intention appears' there is no form of words applied universally:

there is no doubt that several statutes do make specific provision for the criminal liability of unincorporated associations. However, on inspection, these provisions vary so greatly that there is no settled policy which can be discerned from them, and we find it impossible to draw from them any general proposition that there is a form of enactment which is to be expected if an unincorporated association is to be criminally liable, and of which the absence signals a contrary intention for the purposes of section 5 of the Interpretation Act. (at [22])

Different considerations apply in mens rea offences and those at common law. Where individual members of an unincorporated association are prosecuted, it is not on the basis of some form of vicarious liability.

Vicarious liability, when it exists, arises out of the employment by the defendant of another person to act for him. There is no sense in which the chairman, treasurer, or any other member of this club employed the club to do anything for them. The criminal liability of the members of the club, including the chairman and the treasurer, is primary liability, not vicarious liability. (at [34])

■ *Questions*

Which of the 900 golf club members could be prosecuted for the leakage from the oil pipe caused directly by the act of the independent contractor? Those who hired him? The committee? All members? The richest, that is, those most likely to be able to pay the fine?

9.7 Why convict corporations at all?

What is the purpose of imposing criminal liability upon a corporation? It is a creature of the law with no physical existence. It cannot suffer imprisonment or any kind of physical punishment. It can be fined but the fine does not have the effects it does upon a human being. The corporation cannot go cold or hungry or feel the loss of the luxuries of life. It cannot feel shame, remorse or repentance. It is as devoid of moral as of physical sensations. Of course, its officers can suffer like other persons, but the penalties of the criminal law can be imposed on them without making the corporation liable. The imposition of a fine may affect a company's shareholders by reducing their dividends, but in the case of large companies this is likely to be imperceptible, except in the case of a quite exceptionally large fine. (See for a full discussion of fines: M. Jefferson, 'Corporate Criminal Liability: The Problem of Sanctions' (2001) J Crim L 235.) In any case, the shareholders rarely have any effective control over the day-to-day operation of the company's business and so, morally, may well be thought to have no responsibility for the company's transgressions. Moreover, many corporations do not have shareholders. A heavy fine on the University of Poppleton could adversely affect only the staff and students and the research and other activities of the university.

On the other hand, it is clear that the officers of corporations do care about a criminal conviction of the corporation. It is something they are anxious to avoid. Sometimes directors go to expensive efforts to get the company's conviction quashed. Obviously, directors are worried not about the trivial amount of the fine, but about the effect of the conviction on the standing and reputation of the company. The conviction of the company has an effect on the public mind that the conviction of individual officers does not. If directors are so very concerned about the effect of a conviction, is it not likely that they will make strenuous efforts to avoid contravention of the criminal law? And if they do, has not the law achieved its purpose? Do we need to look for any further justification?

But there is another aspect. The victims of corporate wrongdoing may have a powerful urge to punish the corporation. Press reports suggest that the indignation of many of those bereaved by the Zeebrugge ferry disaster was directed not so much at individual officers as at the shipping company itself. It is perhaps significant that the corporation was prosecuted not merely for regulatory offences but for the common law crime of manslaughter, punishable in the case of a human being with life imprisonment. When the prosecution of the company failed, the prosecution of individual officers was discontinued—though the grounds for dismissal of the charge against the company did not necessarily remove the basis of the case against some of the officers. Similar reactions against corporations have been observed in other disasters, such as the Southall rail crash. Although Great Western Trains was fined as much for its offence under the Health and Safety at Work Act as it would have been on conviction for manslaughter, public disquiet at its acquittal of homicide was unabated. The satisfaction of the demand for retribution by those injured by crime has long been recognized as a proper ground for the imposition of punishment.

■ *Questions*

1. Is it a sufficient ground for the imposition of criminal liability on a corporation that strong public feeling demands that corporate wrongdoing should be publicly condemned by the courts? If that feeling exists, does it matter whether it is rational or irrational?

2. To what extent is our decision whether to criminalize corporate wrongs conditioned by how that can be done within the existing legal framework?

J. Gobert, 'A Corporate Criminality: New Crimes for the Times'
[1994] Crim LR 722

The subject of corporate criminality is ripe for systematic review by Parliament. Liability should not depend upon the identification of those persons responsible for the crime in question, a task which is difficult at best; let alone on the determination of the perpetrators' status within the company, as required under *Nattrass*. Instead, a model of 'corporate fault' should be adopted [J. Gobert, 'Corporate Criminality: Four Models of Fault' (1994) 14 LS 393]. A company should be criminally liable where a crime is authorised, permitted or tolerated as a matter of company policy or de facto practice. In this situation liability should be for the substantive offence which has occurred.

The difficulty with formulating liability in these terms is one of proof. A prosecutor may search in vain for a company policy which authorises, permits, or tolerates criminal behaviour. Far more likely to be found is a pro forma resolution which prohibits crimes by company personnel or which exhorts employees to conduct themselves in accord with the highest ethical standards. To pierce this different type of corporate veil, another form of criminal liability is needed. The focus would be on the creation of risks likely to lead to the occurrence of serious harm. If the harm in fact materialised, the company's liability would be for the failure to prevent the harm rather than for the substantive crime itself. Penalties would not necessarily be identical to those for the substantive offence, although some overlap might be desirable to cover cases where it was both foreseeable and virtually inevitable that the corporate failure would lead to the actual harm which occurred.

...The crux of the liability proposed in this article...is a failing on the company's part, but it is that failing in and of itself which would constitute the offence. That the risk created did not eventuate would not necessarily be fatal to a prosecution, although it might be of evidentiary significance as to whether there actually was a danger. The proposed liability is predicated on an implied duty on the part of a company to prevent crime. From where might such a duty arise? The state allows companies to carry on a business for profit under the protective umbrella of its laws. Its courts provide relief from the unfair practices of competitors, and a mechanism for securing debts owed to the company.

In exchange for being able to operate within this legal structure, created and enforced by the state, comes a corresponding duty not to conduct its business in a way which exposes innocent individuals to the dangers of harms proscribed by that same state's criminal laws [L. Leigh, 'The Criminal Liability of Corporations and Other Groups' (1977) 9 Ottawa L Rev 247 at 287].

Furthermore, a company is free to choose the business which it enters into, and the methods by which it conducts that business. From these choices it derives its profit. Often the nature of a company's activities engenders risks to the public. A company that creates a situation of danger, or places an employee in a better position to perpetrate a crime than he or she would otherwise have been in, has an obligation to take steps to prevent criminal harm from occurring. What this means in practical terms is that companies have a duty to promulgate and adopt policies directed towards the prevention of crime and, more intangibly but no less importantly, to establish a corporate ethos which gives appropriate place to protecting the public from crimes which might occur in the course of the company's business.

As for mens rea in the corporate context, this construct may confound rather than promote reasoned analysis. Again it may prove helpful to return to basics, and ask what function mens rea is designed to serve. In instrumental terms mens rea provides a useful tool for identifying defendants who have acted in a blameworthy manner and for assessing the degree of their culpability. Without a concept of mens rea, it might be argued, companies that have done their best to prevent harm might be convicted of crime. Not so. Mens rea is one way, but not the only way, of getting at the issue of blameworthiness.

An alternative, arguably more apropos in the corporate context, is to ask whether the company could have taken steps to identify and avoid the occurrence of harm, whether it was reasonable for it to do so, and whether it in fact did so. In other words, instead of requiring the Crown to prove mens rea, it should be a defence for the company to prove due diligence. Such a defence is not unknown in English law. On occasion Parliament has incorporated it into a statute (Weights and Measures Act 1985, s. 34). What is envisaged here, however, is more broadly conceived, across-the-board defence which would protect a corporate defendant from liability where the company has made a conscientious and reasonable effort to prevent the substantive crime which has occurred (American Law Institute, Model Penal Code, s. 2.07(5). [See also Note, 'Developments in the Law—Corporate Crime: Regulating Corporate Behaviour Through Criminal Sanctions' (1979) 92 Harv LR 1127 at 1257–1259.]

As the company is in the best position to know what it has done to protect against the commission of a crime, the burden of establishing due diligence should be on it. The burden should not be simply that of presenting evidence in the first instance but should extend to convincing the trier of fact by a balance of probabilities that it acted with due diligence. More severe a burden would be too onerous, and any less a burden would put the Crown in the position of having to disprove due diligence when records and other relevant evidence lay buried within a mountain of files controlled by the defendant. The burden should not be subject to discharge by mere proof of an unawareness of the dangers on the part of management without also a showing that it was not reasonable to expect the company to have been aware of the risks [C. Wells, 'Corporations: Culture, Risk and Criminal Liability' [1993] Crim LR 551).] Nor should it be enough for the company to establish that its mode of operation conformed to that which was prevalent in the industry. Although compliance with an industry wide standard may be evidence of due diligence, the possibility must nonetheless be entertained that the entire industry has acted in a culpable manner.

How much must a company do in order to satisfy the demands of due diligence? No simple answer is possible or even desirable. The likelihood of harm and the extent of harm, should the risk which has been created eventuate, will need to be balanced against the social utility of the activity in question and the practicability and cost of eliminating risk. A company will have to demonstrate that it took reasonable and appropriate steps under the circumstances to prevent harm from occurring. . . .

At some point the question of corporate criminality becomes one of political will. There is an understandable legislative ambivalence about addressing corporate crime that is not present when the offender is an individual. The typical murder or theft has no social redeeming value, and there are few compunctions about imprisoning the perpetrator of such a crime. A company, on the other hand, often contributes to the public welfare through the products it manufactures. Through the taxes it pays and its employment of workers it promotes the economic well-being of the nation. It is not so obviously in the government's interest to jeopardise its own financial position by discouraging corporate activity that might border on the criminal. . . .

A fair yet firm approach to corporate crime is called for. Regulatory offences lack the muscle to provide a sufficient disincentive from activities which are profitable but which may entail the commission of criminal offences, and the *Nattrass* approach to conventional criminal law may simply encourage devolved decision-making as a means of avoiding liability. The role of corporate policy (or absence thereof) in the bringing about of the crime warrants close examination, and the Crown should not be satisfied with the scapegoat prosecutions of individuals. The law needs to be restructured so that companies that do not take seriously their responsibilities to society are sanctioned, and those which do are not inadvertently drawn into the net of the criminal law. Much more than it has to date, the law must grapple with the questions of when it can be said that a company has acted in a blameworthy manner and what consequences attach to a showing of such blameworthiness.

■ *Question*

To what extent does the 2007 Act allow the jury to take account of corporate attitudes and policies in determining guilt for manslaughter?

FURTHER READING

Corporate liability

D. Bergman, *The Case for Corporate Responsibility* (2000)

N. Cavanagh, 'Corporate Criminal Liability: An Assessment of the Models of Fault' (2011) 75 J Crim L 414

C. Clarkson, 'Kicking Corporate Bodies and Damning their Souls' (1996) 59 MLR 557

J. Gobert, 'Corporate Criminality: Four Models of Fault' (1994) 14 LS 393

J. Gobert and M. Punch, *Rethinking Corporate Crime* (2003)

R. Grantham, 'Corporate Knowledge: Identification or Attribution?' (1996) 59 MLR 732

G. R. Sullivan, 'Expressing Corporate Guilt' (1995) 15 OJLS 281

C. Wells, *Corporations and Criminal Responsibility* (2nd edn, 2001)

Corporate manslaughter

S. Field and L. Jones, 'Five Years On: The Impact of the Corporate Manslaughter and Corporate Homicide Act 2007: Plus ça change?' [2013] ICCLR 239

P. R. Glazebrook, 'A Better Way of Convicting Businesses of Avoidable Deaths and Injuries' (2002) 61 CLJ 405

J. Gobert, 'Corporate Killing at Home and Abroad: Reflections on the Government Proposals' (2002) 118 LQR 72

J. Horder, 'Corporate Manslaughter and Public Authorities' in *Homicide and the Politics of Law Reform* (2012)

H. Keating, 'The Law Commission Report on Involuntary Manslaughter: (1) The Restoration of a Serious Crime' [1998] Crim LR 535

D. Ormerod and R. Taylor, 'The Corporate Manslaughter and Corporate Homicide Act 2007' [2008] Crim LR 589

10
Mental conditions

10.1 Introduction

The mental condition of a person (D) accused of crime may be relevant at three stages of criminal proceedings:

- pre-trial where D's mental condition is so bad that he cannot be brought to court;
- at trial where D's mental condition is such that he is unfit to be tried; and
- at trial where D is fit to be tried, but pleads that at the time of the offence he was insane or sane automaton.

In each case we have to consider in what circumstances it is appropriate, fair and just to subject someone with a mental condition to a criminal trial. We must also consider to what extent it is fair and just to deny a suspect a right to a trial by hospitalizing him or detaining him in some other way without having established his guilt for the crime alleged beyond a reasonable doubt. These issues are difficult enough. In addition we have to consider the stark differences between the legal understanding of mental disorder and definitions of insanity applied in the criminal courts as compared to the approach of the medical professions. The categories of individual which are treated in law as being insane would shock and offend the lay person. In fact, the manner in which the criminal law deals with those suffering from a mental disorder is unsatisfactory, archaic and lacking in modern medical foundation. Note that the discussion of diminished responsibility is reserved until Chapter 16. Diminished responsibility is only available as a plea to a charge of murder.

The controversies that will be examined in this chapter include:

(i)   when an individual can be regarded as mentally incapable of being tried;

(ii) the relationship between insane and sane automatism;

(iii) the extent to which the insanity defence reflects modern psychiatric practice;

(iv) whether the lack of direct correlation between the medical and legal definitions of 'insanity' infringes the European Convention on Human Rights (ECHR);

(v)   how the insanity defence ought to be reformed.

10.2 Fitness to plead

When D is brought up for trial, it may then be asserted by D, or the prosecution, or the judge, that he is 'unfit to plead'—that is, incapable, because of a disability, of being properly tried. In *M* [2003] EWCA Crim 3452, the trial judge ruled that the defendant had to have sufficient ability in relation to six things: (i) to understand the charges, (ii) to understand the plea, (iii) to challenge jurors, (iv) to instruct counsel and his solicitor, (v) to understand the course of the trial, and (vi) to give evidence if he chooses.

> ### ■ *Questions*
> Are these the most pertinent questions? Is it appropriate to try D when he is suffering from some impairment that inhibits his competence to run the best trial in his defence?

The number of people pleading unfitness continues to rise. See R. D. Mackay, B. Mitchell and L. Howe, 'A Continued Upturn in Unfitness to Plead—More Disability in Relation to the Trial under the 1991 Act' [2007] Crim LR 530, revealing an increase from 50 unfitness findings in 1997 to a peak of 80 in 1999. See for further information on the prevalence of the plea, the Law Commission *Analysis of Reponses* to its Consultation Paper No 195 at http://lawcommission. justice.gov.uk/docs/cp197_unfitness_to_plead_analysis-of-responses.pdf.

Since the Domestic Violence, Crime and Victims Act 2004, s 22, the issue of whether D is fit to be tried is now to be determined by a court without a jury. The procedure is set out in the Criminal Procedure (Insanity) Act 1964 as amended:

- if D is found by the trial judge, sitting alone, to be fit to plead the trial proceeds with a jury;
- if he is found unfit by the trial judge a jury is empanelled to determine whether he has 'done the act or made the omission charged'. If not, he is simply acquitted; if he is found by the jury to have 'done the act or made the omission charged' he may be dealt with under the powers in s 5 of the 1964 Act (section 10.2.1, p 325).

The first question is: what does unfitness mean?

R v Podola
[1959] 3 All ER 418, Court of Criminal Appeal

(Lord Parker CJ, Hilbery, Donovan, Ashworth and Paull JJ)

Podola was charged with murder. He raised a preliminary issue that he was unfit to plead owing to loss of memory of events prior to and including the time of the alleged homicide. Edmund Davies J ruled that there was an onus of proof on a balance of probabilities on the defendant to establish his unfitness. The jury found that the defendant was not suffering from a genuine loss of memory. The trial proceeded and Podola was found guilty of capital murder. The case was referred to the Court of Appeal under a power then available to the Home Secretary.

Lord Parker CJ:

In our judgment the right principles may be stated as follows:

1. In all cases in which a preliminary issue as to the accused person's sanity is raised, whether that issue is contested or not, the jury [now the judge sits alone] should be directed to consider the whole of the evidence and to answer the question 'Are you satisfied on that evidence that the accused person is insane so that he cannot be tried on the indictment?' If authority were needed for the principle, it is to be found in the very words of the section itself, quoted above.

2. If the contention that the accused is insane is put forward by the defence and contested by the prosecution, there is in our judgment a burden on the defence of satisfying the jury of the accused's insanity. In such a case, as in other criminal cases in which the onus of proof rests on the defence, the onus is discharged if the jury are satisfied on the balance of probabilities that the accused's insanity has been made out.

3. Conversely, if the prosecution alleges and the defence disputes insanity, there is a burden on the prosecution of establishing it. . . .

It is not suggested in this case that the appellant could not plead to the indictment, or that he did not know that he had the right of challenge, or that he could not follow the evidence given, but counsel for the appellant submitted strongly that, where there was the partial obliteration of memory alleged in this case, a prisoner could not make a proper defence and could not 'comprehend' the details of the evidence within the meaning of the words used in *Pritchard* [(1836) 7 C & P 303 at 304]. So far as 'making a proper defence' is concerned, it is important to note that the words do not stand alone, but form part of a sentence the whole of which is 'whether he is of sufficient intellect to comprehend the course of proceedings on the trial, so as to make a proper defence'. In other words this passage itself defines what Alderson B meant by 'making a proper defence'. As to the word 'comprehend' we do not think that this word goes further in meaning than the word 'understand'. In our judgment the direction given by Alderson B is not intended to cover and does not cover a case where the prisoner can plead to the indictment and has the physical and mental capacity to know that he has the right of challenge and to understand the case as it proceeds

[His lordship then referred to two Scottish cases and concluded:]

It is true that in the case of a deaf mute the word 'insane' does not strictly apply, but . . . the practice of including as coming within the word the case of persons who, from mental or physical infirmity cannot follow what is happening in a case is in accordance with reason and common sense. We cannot see that it is in accordance either with reason or common sense to extend the meaning of the word to include persons who are mentally normal at the time of the hearing of the proceedings against them and are perfectly capable of instructing their solicitors as to what submission their counsel is to put forward with regard to the commission of the crime . . .

Appeal dismissed

■ *Questions*

1. Is a person fit to be tried if he is perfectly capable and aware at the time of trial but, because of mental disability, is unable to remember anything at all about the period of the alleged crime? Is he capable of instructing his lawyers as to any defence which may in fact exist?

2. Is the effect of *Podola*'s case that a person may be convicted although a court was not satisfied that he was capable of making out a proper defence at his trial?

If D suffers from a disability that renders him unfit to be tried, it is for the jury to determine whether the evidence satisfies them that D 'did the act or made the omission charged against him as the offence'. This is known as a 'trial of the facts' and is determined by a jury. The procedure is now set out in s 4 and s 4A of the Criminal Procedure (Insanity) Act 1964 as amended.

If before the court has begun to decide on whether D did the acts alleged, D is found to have recovered so as to be fit to stand trial, the court should revisit the question of fitness to plead. This reflects the important principle that D should, wherever possible, have an opportunity to contest his guilt in a normal criminal trial: *R (Hasani) v Blackfriars CC* [2005] EWHC 3016 (Admin).

■ *Questions*

1. How do the jury decide if D has 'done the act' alleged?

2. In respect of any crime that is charged the 'act' must be identified and the jury's attention focused on it. What is the 'act'?

In *Egan* (1996) 35 BMLR 103, [1997] Crim LR 225, Ognall J said of s 4A(2)(b): 'we are satisfied, and indeed both counsel agree, that although the words "the act" are used in the relevant legislation, the phrase means neither more or less than proof of all the necessary ingredients of what otherwise would be an offence, in this case theft'. There is no doubt that this was the meaning intended by the Butler Committee on Mentally Abnormal Offenders on whose recommendation the section was based: (1975) Cmnd 6244, para 1024, 'Trial of the facts'. But it is certainly not the natural meaning of the words 'the act' and it is not the meaning intended by the Home Office minister who introduced the Bill in the House of Commons—and therefore probably not the meaning intended by Parliament. See R. D. Mackay and G. Kearns, 'The Trial of the Facts and Unfairness to Plead' [1997] Crim LR 644.

■ *Questions*

Can the act in an offence include the mens rea? Or defences?

See the discussion of actus reus and mens rea above (Chapter 2) and consider the next case.

R v Antoine

[2000] UKHL 20, House of Lords, http://www.bailii.org/uk/cases/UKHL/2000/20.html

(Lords Nicholls, Mackay, Nolan, Hope and Hutton)

A was charged with murder and found unfit to plead by reason of disability. A jury was empanelled to determine whether A 'had done the act…charged against him as an offence'. The judge rejected a submission that A was entitled to rely on diminished responsibility as a defence and the jury found that A had done the act of murder. The Court of Appeal dismissed A's appeal. In the House of Lords all their lordships agreed with the speech of Lord Hutton.

Lord Hutton:

The purpose of s 4A, in my opinion, is to strike a fair balance between the need to protect a defendant who has, in fact, done nothing wrong and is unfit to plead at his trial and the need to protect the public from a defendant who has committed an injurious act which would constitute a crime if done with the requisite mens rea. The need to protect the public is particularly important where the act done has been one which caused death or physical injury to another person and there is a risk that the defendant may carry out a similar act in the future. I consider that the section strikes this balance by distinguishing between a person who has not carried out the actus reus of the crime charged against him and a person who has carried out an act (or made an omission) which would constitute a crime if done (or made) with the requisite mens rea. As Judge LJ stated:

'Where on an indictment for rape it is proved that sexual intercourse has taken place without the consent of the woman, and the defendant has established insanity, he should not be entitled to an acquittal on the basis that he mistakenly, but insanely, understood or believed that she was consenting'. [See *A-G's Reference (No 3 of 1998)* [1999] 3 All ER 40 at 48, [1999] 3 WLR 1194 at 1202; see now *Braham* [2013] EWCA Crim 3, section 20.2.1.6, p 727.]

A number of learned authors have commented that it is difficult in some cases to distinguish precisely between the actus reus and the mens rea and that the actus reus can include a mental element. In Smith and Hogan *Criminal Law* p 28, Professor Sir John Smith states:

'It is not always possible to separate actus reus from mens rea. Sometimes a word which describes the actus reus, or part of it, implies a mental element.'

In his speech in *DPP for Northern Ireland v Lynch* [1975] 1 All ER 913 at 933, [1975] AC 653 at 688 Lord Simon of Glaisdale recognised the difficulties arising from what he termed 'the chaotic terminology' relating to the mental element in crime. Nevertheless, he recognised that actus reus and mens rea are useful terms and said:

> 'Both terms have, however, justified themselves by their usefulness; and I shall myself employ them in their traditional senses—namely, actus reus to mean such conduct as constitutes a crime if the mental element involved in the definition of the crime is also present (or, more shortly, conduct prohibited by law); and mens rea to mean such mental element, over and above volition, as is involved in the definition of the crime.' [See [1975] 1 All ER 913 at 934, [1975] AC 653 at 690.]

Therefore, I consider that the ruling of the Court of Appeal in *A-G's Reference (No 3 of 1998)* was correct.

In their full and helpful submissions counsel raised a further issue on which they invited the guidance of your Lordships. The issue is this. If, on a determination under s 4A(2), the jury are only concerned to decide whether the defendant did the 'act' and are not required to consider whether the defendant had the requisite mens rea for the offence, should the jury nevertheless decide that the defendant did not do the 'act' if the defendant would have had an arguable defence of accident or mistake or self-defence which he could have raised if he had not been under a disability and the trial had proceeded in the normal way. The difficulty inherent in this issue is that such defences almost invariably involve some consideration of the mental state of the defendant. Thus in *Palmer v R* [1971] 1 All ER 1077 at 1088, [1971] AC 814 at 832 when considering self-defence, Lord Morris of Borth-y-Gest referred to the defendant doing 'what he honestly and instinctively thought was necessary' to defend himself. But on the determination under s 4A(2) the defendant's state of mind is not to be considered. How then is this difficulty to be resolved? I would hold that it should be resolved in this way. If there is objective evidence which raises the issue of mistake or accident or self-defence, then the jury should not find that the defendant did the 'act' unless it is satisfied beyond reasonable doubt on all the evidence that the prosecution has negatived that defence. For example, if the defendant had struck another person with his fist and the blow had caused death, it would be open to the jury under s 4(A)(4) to acquit the defendant charged with manslaughter if a witness gave evidence that the victim had attacked the defendant with a knife before the defendant struck him. Again, if a woman was charged with theft of a handbag and a witness gave evidence that on sitting down at a table in a restaurant the defendant had placed her own handbag on the floor and, on getting up to leave, picked up the handbag placed beside her by a woman at the next table, it would be open to the jury to acquit.

But what the defence cannot do, in the absence of a witness whose evidence raises the defence, is to suggest to the jury that the defendant may have acted under a mistake, or by accident, or in self-defence, and to submit that the jury should acquit unless the prosecution satisfies them that there is no reasonable possibility that that suggestion is correct. I consider that the same approach is to be taken if defence counsel wishes to advance the defence that the defendant, in law, did not do the 'act' because his action was involuntary, as when a man kicks out and strikes another in the course of an uncontrollable fit brought about by a medical condition. In such a case there would have to be evidence that the defendant suffered from the condition.

The defence of provocation to a charge of murder is only relevant when the jury are satisfied that the defendant had the requisite mens rea for murder, and I wish to reserve my opinion on the question whether, on a determination under s 4A(2), it would be open to the defence to call witnesses to raise the issue of provocation. [See now the defence of loss of control section 16.2.]

As I have observed at the commencement of this judgment, it was the co-accused of the appellant who killed the victim by stabbing him and it appears that the appellant was charged as a principal in the second degree. No issue was raised before the Crown Court judge or before the Court of Appeal or your Lordships in relation to the fact that the appellant was the secondary party, no doubt because it was clear that by his own actions in preventing the victim from leaving and in striking him the appellant had played a part in the killing. However, on a determination under s 4A(2) where the defendant had been charged with participation in a murder as a secondary party and another person had carried out the actual killing, difficult questions could arise as to the meaning of the word 'act' in such a situation and as to the matters which the jury would have to consider, and I express no opinion on such questions in this judgment.

Therefore, for the reasons which I have given, I would dismiss the appeal.

Appeal dismissed

■ *Questions*

Are not the 'defences' of mistake and accident simply pleas that mens rea has not been proved? If those 'defences' are allowed to be considered on a trial of the facts, what has become of the ruling that 'the act' means the actus reus?

Can the defences of diminished responsibility and loss of control which reduce murder to manslaughter be equated for the purpose of this issue with complete defences? In *Grant* [2002] Crim LR 404, it was held that provocation which was intimately bound up with the defendant's state of mind could not sensibly be considered in the context of s 4A. Provocation presupposed that all the elements of murder, including the intent to kill or cause grievous bodily harm, were present. See the commentary at 406. See below, Chapter 16, on diminished responsibility and the new defence of loss of control.

Concerns were raised as to the compatibility of the procedure under s 4A of the Act with Article 6 of the ECHR (section 7.6.1, p 202). In *H* [2003] UKHL 1 the House of Lords managed to avoid this issue. Their lordships did so by finding that s 4A did not, as a matter of domestic law, involve the determination of a criminal charge within the meaning of Article 6 of the ECHR.

In *B* [2012] EWCA Crim 770, a 24-year-old man with Asperger's was convicted of two counts of voyeurism. The mothers of two 6-year-old boys had seen B lying on his back looking under the dividers between cubicles in changing rooms watching their sons while they were naked. At trial, the judge found B to be unfit to be tried. The issue arose as to what the 'act' was in the offence of voyeurism. The judge ruled that it was the physical act of 'observing' the boys in their state of undress in a private place, but that it was not also necessary to establish that B acted 'for the purpose of sexual gratification'. That element would be required to prove the full offence, but not on a s 4A hearing. On appeal, the Court of Appeal quashed the finding. It was held that in determining under the Criminal Procedure (Insanity) Act 1964, s 4A(2), whether a defendant who was unfit to stand trial was guilty of voyeurism, the jury had to be satisfied that he had deliberately observed another person doing a private act *for the purpose of his own sexual gratification*. It was not necessary to be sure of the accused's knowledge that the person observed does not consent to being observed for the purposes of the accused's sexual gratification. Having regard to the 'social mischiefs' which the voyeurism offence was created to tackle, the court held (at [65]) that:

the link between deliberate observation and the purpose of sexual gratification of the observer is central to the statutory offence of voyeurism. To use Lord Hutton's phrase, it is that purpose which turns the deliberate observation of another doing an intimate act (such as undressing) in private into an 'injurious act' . . . If that is so, then we must conclude that, in the case of an offence of voyeurism under section 67(1) of the [Sexual Offences Act 2003], the relevant '*act . . . charged as the offence*' of the purposes of section 4A(2) is that of deliberate observation of another doing a private act where the observer does so for the specific purpose of the observer obtaining sexual gratification. That omnibus activity is the 'injurious act'. Although the activity has two components, they are indissoluble; together they are the relevant '*act*'.

The court acknowledges the criticism and potential irony that the s 4A procedure, which aims to protect defendants with a disability from a full criminal trial and an inquiry into their mental state which they cannot defend (in the sense that they are unfit to be tried and so cannot give instructions to their lawyers and cannot, save in exceptional circumstances, give evidence) means that the system might place them in a worse position than they would otherwise be (at [57]).

On ECHR concerns with the operation of the procedure, see E. Baker, 'Human Rights and McNaughten and the 1991 Act' [1994] Crim LR 84; R. D. Mackay, 'On Being Insane in Jersey Part Two' [2002] Crim LR 728; 'On Being Insane in Jersey Part Three—the Case of the *Attorney General v O'Driscoll*' [2004] Crim LR 219. For reform options, see the Law Commission Consultation Paper No 197 (2010) which provisionally proposes a shift to a test based on whether D is capable of participating effectively in his trial.

10.2.1 Disposal

Since the 1991 Act, a person who is found unfit to plead but not to have done the act or made the omission charged simply goes free unless there is a civil power of detention applicable. Where he is found to be unfit *and* to have done the act or made the omission a wider range of disposals is now generally available. The Domestic Violence, Crime and Victims Act 2004, s 24, inserts a new s 5 into the 1964 Act, so that in any case other than one of a fixed sentence, the court may now make:

(i)   a hospital order (with or without a restriction order);

(ii) a supervision order; or

(iii) an order for absolute discharge.

10.3 The relationship between automatism and insanity

If at trial D is found fit to plead, or that issue is not raised, he may claim that his mental condition at the time of the alleged offence was such that he was not responsible for his actions. D may plead insanity (one form of which is insane automatism). Alternatively, D may plead that he was in a state of sane automatism.

10.3.1 Distinguishing sane and insane automatism

The law draws a fundamental distinction between pleas of a lack of control which amount to 'insane' and 'non-insane' automatism. It is an unsatisfactory distinction which turns on whether the cause is an 'internal' or an 'external' factor. If the automatism is caused by an internal factor, the plea is, in law, one of not guilty by reason of insanity. If the automatism is caused by an external factor, it is a simple plea of not guilty.

10.3.1.1 Sane automatism

If the defendant's ability to control his movement is impaired because of an external factor such as the taking of medicines, drugs, a blow to the head, etc his defence is one of automatism.

(i)   The defendant bears only an evidential burden: he does not have to prove anything, but must introduce such evidence as might leave a reasonable jury in reasonable doubt whether he was in the state alleged.

(ii) If the automatism is self-induced, the defendant's liability will turn on the principles explained in Chapter 6 on intoxication. That will depend on whether the offence is one of specific or basic intent and whether the substance ingested is one commonly known to create states of automatism and whether D was aware of that. See section 6.3.2, p 157.

(iii) If the automatism is not self-induced the verdict will be one of outright acquittal.

10.3.1.2 Insanity/insane automatism

A plea that D was suffering from some mental incapacity caused by some internal malfunctioning of some element his body (diabetes, epilepsy, sleepwalking, etc) is one of insanity—it is a 'disease of the mind' (see section 10.5.1, p 337):

(i) the burden of proof (on the balance of probabilities) is on the defence;

(ii) it must be supported by the written or oral evidence of two or more registered medical practitioners at least one of whom is 'duly approved': Criminal Procedure (Insanity and Unfitness to Plead) Act, 1991, s 1 (section 10.5, p 337); and

(iii) if the defence succeeds, the defendant will be found not guilty by reason of insanity but will not necessarily walk free. He may be made the subject of a hospital order or other measure authorized by the Criminal Procedure (Insanity) Act 1964 s 5(2), as amended, see section 10.8, p 350).

10.4 Automatism

The Law Commission recently identified different categories of automatism. See Discussion Paper: *Insanity and Automatism* (2013), Ch 5.

> 1. Automatism arising from a 'disease of the mind' (eg epilepsy). If successful, this results in a special verdict irrespective of the charge.

This is dealt with later in the section on insanity.

> 2. Automatism arising from the accused ingesting or taking substances (for example, the accused who, having taken insulin, suffers a hypoglycaemic episode). This results in a complete acquittal unless the accused was at fault in inducing or failing to avoid the loss of control. If the accused was at fault, either because he foresaw the likelihood of a loss of control and unreasonably failed to avert it or because he took a drug commonly known to create loss of control, he or she will be liable for any offences of basic intent charged. A recent example of this is the case of *C* [[2007] EWCA Crim 1862 at [16]] in which it was said that for the automatism defence to succeed, the accused, who claimed a hypoglycaemic attack, would have to show an evidential basis for a conclusion that he was 'totally unable to control the car due to an unforeseen hypoglycaemic attack' and 'that he could not reasonably have avoided the attack, by advance testing, and that there were no advance warnings during the course of his drive'.

This has been the subject of discussion in Chapter 6. This is another aspect of the prior fault doctrine.

> 3. Automatism arising from some external physical factor other than the accused taking substances (for example, the accused has been stung by a wasp while driving, or struck by a stone thrown up from the road surface causing a reflex action). A person suffering a blow to the head causing concussion is another example. If successful, this leads to a not guilty verdict for any offence charged.

This is the subject matter of this section.

10.4.1. Automatism defined

Unfortunately, the courts have failed to provide a clear definition of sane automatism.

Bratty v Attorney-General for Northern Ireland

[1963] AC 386, [1961] 3 All ER 523, House of Lords, http://www.bailii.org/uk/cases/UKHL/1961/3.html

(Viscount Kilmuir LC, Lords Tucker, Denning, Morris of Borth-y-Gest and Hodson)

The accused killed a girl whom he was driving in his car by taking off her stocking and strangling her with it. He gave evidence that a 'blackness' came over him and said 'I didn't know what I was doing. I didn't realise anything.' There was evidence that he might have been suffering from psychomotor epilepsy which could cause ignorance of the nature and quality of acts done. At the trial, the defences of automatism and insanity were raised. The trial judge rejected the defence of insanity. The Court of Criminal Appeal in Northern Ireland dismissed an appeal against conviction for murder. On appeal to the House of Lords the House discussed the difference between sane and insane automatism.

[Viscount Kilmuir LC made a speech dismissing the appeal. Lord Tucker agreed.]

Lord Denning:

My Lords, in *Woolmington v Director of Public Prosecutions* Viscount Sankey LC said:

> 'When dealing with a murder case the Crown must prove (a) death as the result of a voluntary act of the accused and (b) malice of the accused.'

The requirement that it should be a voluntary act is essential, not only in a murder case, but also in every criminal case. No act is punishable if it is done involuntarily: and an involuntary act in this context—some people nowadays prefer to speak of it as 'automatism'—means an act which is done by the muscles without any control by the mind such as a spasm, a reflex or a convulsion; or an act done by a person who is not conscious of what he is doing such as an act done whilst suffering from concussion or whilst sleep-walking. [But see *Burgess*, section 10.5.1, p 340.] The point was well put by Stephen J in 1889:

> '...can anyone doubt that a man who, though he might be perfectly sane, committed what would otherwise be a crime in a state of somnambulism, would be entitled to be acquitted? And why is this? Simply because he would not know what he was doing';

The term 'involuntary act' is, however, capable of wider connotations: and to prevent confusion it is to be observed that in the criminal law an act is not to be regarded as an involuntary act simply because the doer does not remember it. When a man is charged with dangerous driving, it is no defence for him to say 'I don't know what happened. I cannot remember a thing': see *Hill v Baxter* [[1958] 1 QB 277, [1958] 1 All ER 193]. Loss of memory afterwards is never a defence in itself, so long as he was conscious at the time; see *Russell v HM Advocate* [1946 JC 37]; *Podola* [see section 10.2, p 320]. Nor is an act to be regarded as an involuntary act simply because the doer could not control his impulse to do it. When a man is charged with murder, and it appears that he knew what he was doing, but that he could not resist it, then his assertion 'I couldn't help myself' is no defence in itself: see *A-G for South Australia v Brown* [[1960] AC 432, [1960] 1 All ER 734]: though it may go towards a defence of diminished responsibility, in places where that defence is available, see *Byrne* [see section 16.3, p 577]: but it does not render his act involuntary so as to entitle him to an unqualified acquittal. Nor is an act to be regarded as an involuntary act simply because it is unintentional or its consequences are unforeseen. When a man is charged with dangerous driving, it is no defence for him to say, however truly, 'I did not mean to drive dangerously'. There is said to be an absolute prohibition against that offence, whether he had a guilty mind or not (see *Hill v Baxter* per Lord Goddard CJ), but even though it is absolutely prohibited, nevertheless he has a defence if he can show that it was an involuntary act in the sense that he was unconscious at the time and did not know what he was doing (see *HM Advocate v Ritchie* [1926 JC 45], *Minor* [(1955) 15 WWRNS 433] and *Cooper v McKenna, ex p Cooper* [[1960] Qd R 406]).

Another thing to be observed is that it is not every involuntary act which leads to a complete acquittal. Take first an involuntary act which proceeds from a state of drunkenness. If the drunken man is so drunk that he does not know what he is doing, he has a defence to any charge, such as murder or wounding with intent, in which a specific intent is essential, but he is still liable to be convicted of manslaughter or unlawful wounding for which no specific intent is necessary; see *Beard's* case [see section 6.3, p 152]. Again, if the involuntary act proceeds from a disease of the mind, it gives rise to a defence of insanity, but not to a defence of automatism. Suppose a crime is committed by a man in a state of automatism or clouded consciousness due to a recurrent disease of the mind. Such an act is no doubt involuntary, but it does not give rise to an unqualified acquittal, for that would mean that he would be let at large to do it again. The only proper verdict is one which ensures that the person who suffers from the disease is kept secure in a hospital so as not to be a danger to himself or others. That is, a verdict of guilty but insane.

Once you exclude all the cases I have mentioned, it is apparent that the category of involuntary acts is very limited. So limited indeed that until recently there was hardly any reference in the English books to this so-called defence of automatism. There was a passing reference to it in 1951 in *Harrison-Owen* [[1951] 2 All ER 726] where a burglar, who broke into houses, said he did not know what he was doing. I should have thought that, in order to rebut this defence, he could have been cross-examined about his previous burglaries: but the Court of Criminal Appeal ruled otherwise. I venture to doubt that decision. The next is the singular case of *Charlson* [[1955] 1 All ER 859]. Stanley Charlson, a devoted husband and father, hit his ten-year-old son on the head with a hammer and threw him into the river and so injured him. There was not the slightest cause for the attack. He was charged with causing grievous bodily harm with intent, and with unlawful wounding. The evidence pointed to the possibility that Charlson was suffering from a cerebral tumour in which case he would be liable to a motiveless outburst of impulsive behaviour over which he would have no control at all. Now comes the important point—no plea of insanity was raised, but only the defence of automatism. Barry J directed the jury in these words [[1955] 1 All ER 859 at 864]:

> 'If he did not know what he was doing, if his actions were purely automatic and his mind had no control over the movement of his limbs, if he was in the same position as a person in an epileptic fit and no responsibility rests on him at all, then the proper verdict is "not guilty" ...'

On that direction the jury found him not guilty. In striking contrast to *Charlson* is *Kemp*. A devoted husband of excellent character made an entirely motiveless and irrational attack on his wife. He struck her violently with a hammer. He was charged with causing her grievous bodily harm. It was found that he suffered from hardening of the arteries which might lead to a congestion of blood in the brain. As a result of such congestion, he suffered a temporary lack of consciousness, so that he was not conscious that he picked up the hammer or that he was striking his wife with it. It was therefore an involuntary act. Note again the important point—no plea of insanity was raised but only the defence of automatism. Nevertheless, Devlin J put insanity to the jury. He held that hardening of the arteries was a 'disease of the mind' within the M'Naghten rules and he directed the jury they ought so to find. They accordingly found Kemp guilty but insane.

My Lords, I think that Devlin J was quite right in *Kemp* in putting the question of insanity to the jury, even though it had not been raised by the defence. When it is asserted that the accused did an involuntary act in a state of automatism, the defence necessarily puts in issue the state of mind of the accused man: and thereupon it is open to the prosecution to show what his true state of mind was. The old notion that only the defence can raise a defence of insanity is now gone ...

It is to be noticed that in *Charlson and Kemp* the defence raised only automatism, not insanity. In the present case the defence raised both automatism and insanity. And herein lies the difficulty because of the burden of proof. If the accused says he did not know what he was doing, then, so far as the defence of automatism is concerned, the Crown must prove that the act was an involuntary act; see *Woolmington's* case. But so far as the defence of insanity is concerned, the defence must prove that the act was an involuntary act due to disease of the mind; see *M'Naghten's Case*. This apparent incongruity was noticed by Sir Owen Dixon, Chief Justice of the High Court of Australia, in an address which is to be found in 31 Australian Law Journal 255 and it needs to be resolved. The defence here say: Even though we have not proved that the act was involuntary, yet the Crown have not proved that it was a voluntary act: and that point at least should have been put to the jury.

My Lords, I think that the difficulty is to be resolved by remembering that, whilst the *ultimate* burden rests on the Crown of proving every element essential in the crime, nevertheless in order to prove that the act was a voluntary act, the Crown is entitled to rely on the presumption that every man has sufficient mental capacity to be responsible for his crimes: and that if the defence wish to displace that *presumption* they must give some evidence from which the contrary may reasonably be inferred...To use the words of Devlin J the defence of automatism 'ought not to be considered at all until the defence has produced at least prima facie evidence', see *Hill v Baxter* [[1958] 1 QB 277 at 285, [1958] 1 All ER 193 at 196]; and the words of North J in New Zealand 'unless a proper foundation is laid', see *Cottle* [[1958] NZLR 999 at 1025]. The necessity of laying this proper foundation is on the defence: and if it is not so laid, the defence of automatism need not be left to the jury, any more than the defence of drunkenness (*Kennedy v HM Advocate* [1944 JC 171]) provocation (*Gauthier* [(1943) 29 Cr App R 113]) or self-defence (*Lobell* [[1957] 1 QB 547, [1957] 1 All ER 734]) need be.

What, then, is a proper foundation? The presumption of mental capacity of which I have spoken is a provisional presumption only. It does not put the legal burden on the defence in the same way as the presumption of sanity does. It leaves the legal burden on the prosecution, but nevertheless, until it is displaced, it enables the prosecution to discharge the ultimate burden of proving that the act was voluntary. Not because the presumption is evidence itself, but because it takes the place of evidence. In order to displace the presumption of mental capacity, the defence must give sufficient evidence from which it may reasonably be inferred that the act was involuntary. The evidence of the man himself will rarely be sufficient unless it is supported by medical evidence which points to the cause of the mental incapacity. It is not sufficient for a man to say 'I had a black-out': for 'black-out' as Stable J said in *Cooper v McKenna, ex p Cooper* [[1960] Qd R 406 at 419] 'is one of the first refuges of a guilty conscience, and a popular excuse'. The words of Devlin J in *Hill v Baxter* [[1958] 1 QB 277 at 285, [1958] 1 All ER 193 at 197] should be remembered:

> 'I do not doubt that there are genuine cases of automatism and the like, but I do not see how the layman can safely attempt without the help of some medical or scientific evidence to distinguish the genuine from the fraudulent.'

When the only cause that is assigned for an involuntary act is drunkenness, then it is only necessary to leave drunkenness to the jury, with the consequential directions, and not to leave automatism at all. When the only cause that is assigned for it is a disease of the mind, then it is only necessary to leave insanity to the jury, and not automatism. When the cause assigned is concussion or sleepwalking, there should be some evidence from which it can reasonably be inferred before it should be left to the jury. If it is said to be due to concussion, there should be evidence of a severe blow shortly beforehand. If it is said to be sleepwalking, there should be some credible support for it. His mere assertion that he was asleep will not suffice. Once a proper foundation is thus laid for automatism, the matter becomes at large and must be left to the jury. As the case proceeds, the evidence may weigh first to one side and then to the other: and so the burden may appear to shift to and fro. But at the end of the day the legal burden comes into play and requires that the jury should be satisfied beyond reasonable doubt that the act was a voluntary one... There was [in the present case] no evidence of automatism apart from insanity. There was therefore no need for the judge to put it to the jury... I would therefore dismiss the appeal.

[Lord Morris of Borth-y-Gest made a speech dismissing the appeal with which Lord Hodson agreed.]

Appeal dismissed

10.4.2 What level of automatism negates liability?

In *A-G's Reference (No 2 of 1992)* (1993) 99 Cr App R 429, [1994] Crim LR 692, D, a professional lorry driver, was charged with causing death by reckless driving. He had driven for six hours out of 12 (but breached no regulation) when he drove at 40 mph about half a mile along the hard shoulder of a motorway and ran into the back of a stationary van which had broken down, pushing it into the recovery vehicle. On the evidence of an expert witness, Professor Brown, that D was 'driving without awareness' the judge left automatism to the jury who acquitted. The Attorney General referred the case to the Court of Appeal who ruled that automatism ought not to have been left to the jury.

Lord Taylor CJ:

Mr Pert QC [for D] . . . conceded that despite Professor Brown's phrase 'driving without awareness,' the Professor's description of the condition shows that it amounts only to reduced or imperfect awareness. There remains the ability to steer the vehicle straight. There is also usually a capacity to react to stimuli appearing in the road ahead. In the present case the respondent admitted he had actually seen the flashing lights a quarter of a mile from the scene.

Mr Pert confined his argument to the question whether Professor Brown's evidence properly raised the issue of automatism, which is the sole point of the reference. . . .

[Lord Taylor referred to the cases (above) distinguishing between 'internal' and 'external' causes and continued:]

Here, Mr Pert argues that the precipitating cause of the condition described by Professor Brown was the external factor of motorway conditions. However that may be, the proper approach is that prescribed by Lord Lane CJ in *Burgess* at pages 43 and 96C as follows:

'Where the defence of automatism is raised by a defendant, two questions fall to be decided by the judge before the defence can be left to the jury. The first is whether a proper evidential foundation for the defence of automatism has been laid. The second is whether the evidence shows the case to be one of insane automatism, that is to say a case which falls within the *M'Naghten* Rules, or one of non-insane automatism.'

The first of those questions is the one raised by this reference. In our judgment the 'proper evidential foundation' was not laid in this case by Professor Brown's evidence of 'driving without awareness.' As the authorities cited above show the defence of automatism requires that there was a total destruction of voluntary control on the defendant's part. Impaired, reduced or partial control is not enough. Professor Brown accepted that someone 'driving without awareness' within his description, retains some control. He would be able to steer the vehicle and usually to react and return to full awareness when confronted by significant stimuli.

Accordingly, in our judgment the learned recorder ought not to have left the issue of automatism to the jury in this case and the answer to the point of law as formulated is: no.

■ *Questions*

Should a person who is so exceptionally susceptible to these conditions that he is in fact reduced to a state of automatism and causes injury or damage, remain free from any restraint to do it again? Do you think that the fact that the alleged automatism arose in the context of the driving had any influence on the court's reasoning? Why?

In *Coley* [2013] EWCA Crim 223, Hughes LJ (at [22]) confirmed that the requirement in automatism of a total loss of control was not restricted to road traffic cases:

> Automatism, if it occurs, results in a complete acquittal on the grounds that the act was not that of the defendant at all. It has been variously described. The essence of it is that the movements or actions of the defendant at the material time were wholly involuntary. The better expression is complete destruction of voluntary control: *Watmore v Jenkins* [1962] 2 QB 572 and *Attorney-General's Reference (No 2 of 1992)* [1994] QB 91. Examples which have been given in the past include the driver attacked by a swarm of bees or the man under hypnosis. 'Involuntary' is not the same as 'irrational'; indeed it needs sharply to be distinguished from it.

10.4.3 The difficulty in distinguishing external and internal causes

The law draws the crucial distinction between insanity and sane automatism on the basis of the internal or external cause of the defendant's loss of control. Can that distinction be drawn in such a way that it applies logically and fairly? Consider the next two cases. Why is one classified as automatism and one insanity? Which defendant is more culpable for losing control? Is one defendant more likely than the other to suffer a similar episode and pose a risk of future harm?

R v Quick and Paddison

[1973] 3 All ER 347, Court of Appeal, Criminal Division, http://www.bailii.org/ew/cases/EWCA/Crim/1973/1.html

(Lawton LJ, Mocatta and Milmo JJ)

The appellants were nurses employed at a mental hospital. They were convicted of assault occasioning actual bodily harm to a paraplegic patient at the hospital. Quick called medical evidence to show that he was diabetic and that at the time of the alleged assault he was suffering from hypoglycaemia and was unaware of what he was doing. He submitted that the evidence established a defence of automatism. Bridge J ruled that the defence raised was one of insanity, whereupon Quick changed his plea to guilty. Paddison was convicted by the jury on the basis that he had abetted Quick. Quick appealed on the ground that the judge's ruling was wrong and that a diabetic in a temporary and reversible condition of hypoglycaemia was not, while in that condition, suffering from any defect of reason from disease of the mind.

> [Lawton LJ, delivering the judgment of the court, reviewed the evidence and the decisions in *Bratty, Kemp, Hill v Baxter* [1958] 1 All ER 193, [1958] 1 QB 277 and *Kay v Butterworth* (1945) 173 LT 191, and continued:]
>
> In this quagmire of law seldom entered nowadays save by those in desperate need of some kind of defence, *Bratty v A-G for Northern Ireland* provides the only firm ground. Is there any discernible path? We think there is—judges should follow in a common sense way their sense of fairness. This seems to have been the approach of the New Zealand Court of Appeal in *Cottle* [[1958] NZLR 999] and of Sholl J in *Carter* [[1959] VR 105]. In our judgment no help can be obtained by speculating (because that is what we would have to do) as to what the judges who answered the House of Lords' questions in 1843 [see section 10.5, p 334] meant by disease of the mind, still less what Sir Matthew Hale meant in the second half of the 17th century [(1682) Vol I, Ch IV] . . . Our task has been to decide what the law means now by the words 'disease of the mind'. In our judgment the fundamental concept is of a malfunctioning of the mind caused by disease. A malfunctioning of the mind of transitory effect caused by the application to the body of some external factor such as violence, drugs, including anaesthetics,

alcohol and hypnotic influences cannot fairly be said to be due to disease. Such malfunctioning, unlike that caused by a defect of reason from disease of the mind, will not always relieve an accused from criminal responsibility. A self-induced incapacity will not excuse (see *Lipman* [see section 6.4, p 169]) nor will one which could have been reasonably foreseen as a result of either doing, or omitting to do something, as for example, taking alcohol against medical advice after using certain prescribed drugs, or failing to have regular meals whilst taking insulin. From time to time difficult borderline cases are likely to arise. When they do, the test suggested by the New Zealand Court of Appeal in *Cottle* is likely to give the correct result, viz can this mental condition be fairly regarded as amounting to or producing a defect of reason from disease of the mind?

In this case Quick's alleged mental condition, if it ever existed, was not caused by his diabetes but by his use of the insulin prescribed by his doctor. Such malfunctioning of his mind as there was, was caused by an external factor and not by a bodily disorder in the nature of a disease which disturbed the working of his mind. It follows in our judgment that Quick was entitled to have his defence of automatism left to the jury and that Bridge J's ruling as to the effect of the medical evidence called by him was wrong. Had the defence of automatism been left to the jury, a number of questions of fact would have had to be answered. If he was in a confused mental condition, was it due to a hypoglycaemic episode or to too much alcohol? If the former, to what extent had he brought about his condition by not following his doctor's instructions about taking regular meals? Did he know that he was getting into a hypoglycaemic episode? If Yes, why did he not use the antidote of eating a lump of sugar as he had been advised to do? On the evidence which was before the jury Quick might have had difficulty in answering these questions in a manner which would have relieved him of responsibility for his acts. We cannot say, however, with the requisite degree of confidence, that the jury would have convicted him. It follows that his conviction must be quashed on the ground that the verdict was unsatisfactory.

Appeals allowed

What would have been the result if the court had found that it was the diabetes and not the insulin which caused the automatism? Compare the next case.

R v Hennessy

(1989) 89 Cr App R 10, Court of Appeal, Criminal Division, http://www.bailii.org/ew/cases/EWCA/Crim/1989/1.html

(Lord Lane CJ, Rose and Pill JJ)

H, a diabetic, was charged with taking a conveyance and driving while disqualified. His defence was that at the relevant time he had failed to take his proper dose of insulin due to stress, anxiety and depression and consequently was suffering from hyperglycaemia (excessive blood sugar) and was in a state of automatism. The trial judge ruled that the condition, if it existed, was caused by diabetes, a disease, so that the defence was one of insanity under the *M'Naghten* Rules. H then pleaded guilty. He appealed arguing that the judge's ruling was wrong and that his depression and marital troubles were a sufficiently potent external factor to override the effect of the diabetic shortage of insulin. The Court of Appeal held this was an insanity plea.

Lord Lane CJ quoted from the judgment of Devlin J in *Hill v Baxter* [1958] 1QB 277 at 285:

'I have drawn attention to the fact that the accused did not set up a defence of insanity. For the purposes of the criminal law there are two categories of mental irresponsibility, one where the disorder is due to disease and the other where it is not. The distinction is not an arbitrary one. If disease is not the cause, if there is some temporary loss of consciousness arising accidentally, it is reasonable to hope that it will not be repeated and that it is safe to let an acquitted man go entirely free. But if disease is present the same thing may happen again, and therefore, since 1800, the law has provided that persons acquitted on this ground should be subject to restraint.'

That is the submission made by Mr Owen as a basis for saying the judge's decision was wrong and that this was a matter which should have been decided by the jury.

In our judgment, stress, anxiety and depression can no doubt be the result of the operation of external factors, but they are not, it seems to us, in themselves separately or together external factors of the kind capable in law of causing or contributing to a state of automatism. They constitute a state of mind which is prone to recur. They lack the feature of novelty or accident, which is the basis of the distinction drawn by Lord Diplock in *R v Sullivan* (below). It is contrary to the observations of Devlin J, to which we have just referred in the case of *Hill v Baxter* (supra). It does not, in our judgment, come within the scope of the exception 'some external physical factor such as a blow on the head or the administration of an anaesthetic.' . . .

Appeal dismissed

Law Commission, *Criminal Liability: Insanity and Automatism: Discussion Paper* (2013)

The Commission criticizes the failure to distinguish logically between insanity and sane automatism. (Footnotes omitted.)

1.41 [The law] has adopted a distinction between whether the cause of the accused's lack of control was due to an 'internal factor' (ie some malfunctioning of the person's body) or an 'external factor' (such as a blow to the head). Involuntary conduct caused by an 'internal factor' is classed as insanity and that leads to the special verdict. Involuntary conduct caused by an 'external factor' is classed as (sane) automatism, leading to a simple acquittal. This leads to illogical results. The 'line drawn between sane and insane automatism can never make medical sense'. It 'makes illogical, hair-splitting distinctions inevitable, allowing some an outright acquittal while condemning others to plead guilty or take the risk of a special verdict', . . .

[The Commission describes the cases of *Hennessy* and *Quick*.]

1.43 The upshot is that a diabetic who, without fault, fails to take insulin and then commits an allegedly criminal act would be treated as insane. In contrast, a diabetic who took insulin in accordance with a medical prescription would be acquitted if he or she was an automaton at the time of committing an allegedly criminal act, whether that was because he or she had an unexpected reaction to the insulin or because having taken the insulin he or she failed to eat through no fault of their own. As Professor Ashworth has written:

There can be no sense in classifying hypoglycaemic states as automatism and hyperglycaemic states as insanity, when both states are so closely associated with such a common condition as diabetes.

1.44 Beyond its application to diabetes, another basis for criticism is that with some conditions, both internal and external factors may operate simultaneously, as in sleepwalking or hypnosis: some people are more susceptible to sleep disorders, but then there may be an external trigger (an interruption to sleep) which also plays a part in loss of capacity.

1.45 A yet further difficulty with this boundary between internal (insanity) and external (automatism) has arisen in so-called 'psychological blow' cases where the accused enters into a dissociative state following a traumatic event.

The Commission identified a further situation in which automatism might arise but which would not fall within the insanity plea nor easily be described as an external cause case.

5.13 An example might be where an accused, who is driving, experiences a sudden cramp in his leg, causing him to press on the accelerator and crash the car. There is no external factor which triggers the symptom—it has a purely internal cause—yet there has been no impairment of the accused's mental functioning and the effect is purely physical. There is therefore no disease of the mind in the sense adopted in *Sullivan* [section 10.5.1, p 337] which could found a defence of [insanity]. This results in a complete acquittal unless the defendant was at fault in inducing or failing to avoid the loss of control.

5.14 Such a case has never, to our knowledge, been directly considered by the courts. We take the view that if one were to arise, it would be treated as sane automatism. This is supported by a non-binding comment about self-induced automatism in *Quick*, where Lord Justice Lawton says:

> A self-induced incapacity will not excuse . . . nor will one which could reasonably have been fore-
> seen as a result of either doing something, or omitting to do something, as, for example, taking
> alcohol against medical advice after taking certain prescribed drugs, or failing to have regular
> meals while taking insulin.

5.15 We recognise that this departs from the orthodox understanding of the internal/external distinction, but we think that this must be the present state of the law. This is because the defendant in the cramp example above cannot be categorised either as having a disease of the mind (so that he could be included within the insane automatism category), nor as being incapacitated due to any external cause. He must, therefore, fall into the sane automatism category, but with an internal cause.

■ *Question*

Does this demonstrate simply that the decisions are based on policy about how likely a condition is to recur and affect a defendant?

10.5 Insanity: the *M'Naghten* Rules

If D pleads insanity, the *M'Naghten* Rules apply. The result of a finding of insanity is a 'special verdict' of not guilty by reason of insanity.

■ *Question*

Might there be cases where a person would rather plead guilty than have a defence if that meant being labelled 'insane'? On the frequency of insanity pleas, see R. D. Mackay, B. Mitchell and L. Howe, 'Yet More Facts About the Insanity Defence' [2006] Crim LR 399; R. D. Mackay, 'Ten More Years of the Insanity Defence' [2012] Crim LR 946.

Astonishingly, the law governing a plea of insanity is to be found in the opinion of the Law Lords over 170 years ago.

M'Naghten's Case
(1843) 10 Cl & Fin 200, http://www.bailii.org/uk/cases/UKHL/1843/J16.html

M'Naghten was charged with the murder by shooting of Edward Drummond. He pleaded not guilty. Medical evidence was called on his behalf to prove that he was not, at the time of committing the act, in a sound state of mind. The evidence was to the effect that persons of otherwise sound mind might be affected by morbid delusions and that M was in that condition; that a person labouring under a morbid delusion might have a moral perception of right and wrong, but that in the case of M it was a delusion which carried him away beyond the power of his own control, and left him with no such perception; and that he was not capable of exercising any control over acts which had connection with his delusion: that it was the nature of the disease with which M was affected to go on gradually until it had reached a climax, when it burst forth with irresistible intensity: that a man might go on for years quietly, though at the same time under its influence, but would all at once break out into the most extravagant and violent paroxysms.

Some of the witnesses who gave this evidence had previously examined M, while others had never seen him until he appeared in court and formed their opinions on hearing the evidence given by other witnesses.

[Tindal CJ directed the jury:]

The question to be determined is whether at the time the act in question was committed, the prisoner had or had not the use of his understanding, so as to know that he was doing a wrong or wicked act. If the jurors should be of opinion that the prisoner was not sensible, at the time he committed it, that he was violating the laws of both God and man, then he would be entitled to a verdict in his favour: but if, on the contrary, they were of opinion that when he committed the act he was in a sound state of mind, then their verdict must be against him.

Verdict, Not guilty, on the ground of insanity

This verdict was made the subject of debate in the House of Lords and it was determined to take the opinion of all the judges on the law governing such cases The judges attended on two occasions and, on the second occasion, five questions were put to them.

[Maule J having referred to the difficulty which he felt about answering hypothetical questions on which he had heard no argument and his fear that the answers might embarrass the administration of criminal justice, stated that he would have been glad if his learned brethren would have joined him in praying their lordships to excuse them from answering the questions Maule J then offered his own answers.]

Tindal CJ:

The first question proposed by your Lordships is this: 'What is the law respecting alleged crimes committed by persons afflicted with insane delusion in respect of one or more particular subjects or persons: as, for instance, where at the time of the commission of the alleged crime the accused knew he was acting contrary to law, but did the act complained of with a view, under the influence of insane delusion, of redressing or revenging some supposed grievance or injury, or of producing some supposed public benefit?'

In answer to which question, assuming that your Lordships' inquiries are confined to those persons who labour under such partial delusions only, and are not in other respects insane, we are of opinion that, notwithstanding the party accused did the act complained of with a view, under the influence of insane delusion, of redressing or revenging some supposed grievance or injury, or of producing some public benefit, he is nevertheless punishable according to the nature of the crime committed, if he knew at the time of committing such crime that he was acting contrary to law; by which expression we understand your Lordships to mean the law of the land.

Your Lordships are pleased to inquire of us, secondly, 'What are the proper questions to be submitted to the jury, where a person alleged to be afflicted with insane delusion respecting one or more particular subjects or persons, is charged with the commission of a crime (murder, for example), and insanity is set up as a defence?' And, thirdly, 'In what terms ought the question to be left to the jury as to the prisoner's state of mind at the time when the act was committed?' And as these two questions appear to us to be more conveniently answered together, we have to submit our opinion to be, that the jurors ought to be told in all cases that every man is to be presumed to be sane, and to possess a sufficient degree of reason to be responsible for his crimes, until the contrary be proved to their satisfaction; and that *to establish a defence on the ground of insanity, it must be clearly proved that, at the time of the committing of the act, the party accused was labouring under such a defect of reason, from disease of the mind, as not to know the nature and quality of the act he was doing; or, if he did know it, that he did not know he was doing what was wrong.* [Emphasis added.] The mode of putting the latter part of the question to the jury on these occasions has generally been, whether the accused at the time of doing the act knew the difference between right and wrong: which mode, though rarely, if ever, leading to any mistake with the jury, is not, as we conceive, so accurate when put generally and in the abstract, as when put with reference to the party's knowledge of right and wrong in respect to the very act with which he is charged. If the question were to be put as to the knowledge of the accused solely and exclusively with reference to the law of the land, it might tend to confound the jury, by inducing them to believe that an actual knowledge of the law of the land was essential in order to lead to a conviction; whereas the law is administered upon the principle that everyone must be taken conclusively to know it, without proof that he does know it. If the accused was conscious that the act was one which he ought not to do, and if that act was at the same time contrary to the law of the land, he is punishable; and the usual course therefore has been to leave the question to the jury, whether the party accused had a sufficient degree of reason to know that he was doing an act that was wrong: and this course we think is correct, accompanied with such observations and explanations as the circumstances of each particular case may require.

The fourth question which your Lordships have proposed to us is this: 'If a person under an insane delusion as to existing facts, commits an offence in consequence thereof, is he thereby excused?' To which question the answer must of course depend on the nature of the delusion: but, making the same assumption as we did before, namely, that he labours under such partial delusion only, and is not in other respects insane, we think he must be considered in the same situation as to responsibility as if the facts with respect to which the delusion exists were real. For example, if under the influence of his delusion he supposes another man to be in the act of attempting to take away his life, and he kills that man, as he supposes, in self-defence, he would be exempt from punishment. If his delusion was that the deceased had inflicted a serious injury to his character and fortune, and he killed him in revenge for such supposed injury, he would be liable to punishment.

The question lastly proposed by your Lordships is: 'Can a medical man conversant with the disease of insanity, who never saw the prisoner previously to the trial, but who was present during the whole trial and the examination of all the witnesses, be asked his opinion as to the state of the prisoner's mind at the time of the commission of the alleged crime, or his opinion whether the prisoner was conscious at the time of doing the act that he was acting contrary to law, or whether he was labouring under any and what delusion at the time?' In answer thereto, we state to your Lordships, that we think the medical man, under the circumstances supposed, cannot in strictness be asked his opinion in the terms above stated, because each of those questions involves the determination of the truth of the facts deposed to, which it is for the jury to decide, and the questions are not mere questions upon a matter of science, in which such evidence is admissible. But where the facts are admitted or not disputed, and the question becomes substantially one of science only, it may be convenient to allow the question to be put in that general form, though the same cannot be insisted on as a matter of right.

Trial of Lunatics Act 1883, s 2 (as amended)

2. Special verdict where accused found guilty, but insane at date of act or omission charged, and orders thereupon

(1) Where in any indictment or information any act or omission is charged against any person as an offence, and it is given in evidence on the trial of such person for that offence that he was insane, so as not to be responsible, according to law, for his action at the time when the act was done or omission made, then, if it appears to the jury before whom such person is tried that he did the act or made the omission charged, but was insane as aforesaid at the time when he did or made the same, the jury shall return a special verdict that the accused is not guilty by reason of insanity.

(2)–(4) [Repealed.]

Criminal Procedure (Insanity and Unfitness to Plead) Act 1991

1. Acquittals on grounds of insanity

(1) A jury shall not return a special verdict under section 2 of the Trial of Lunatics Act 1883 (acquittal on ground of insanity) except on the written or oral evidence of two or more registered medical practitioners at least one of whom is duly approved.

[Section 1(2) contains provisions respecting proof of an offender's mental condition.]

> ■ *Question*
>
> What status has the opinion of a number of members of the House of Lords not sitting in a judicial capacity as in *M'Naghten*?

If D pleads insanity the prosecution must prove that the accused performed the act alleged. There is then a burden on the accused to prove:

(1) that he suffered from *a disease of the mind*;

(2) that the disease of the mind caused a defect of reason such that:

(a) he did not know the *nature and quality of his act*; or

(b) he *did not know it was 'wrong'*.

If the defence succeeds (D must prove the balance of probabilities), D will be found Not Guilty by Reason of Insanity.

The court will then have 'disposal' options (since D is not guilty he is not 'sentenced') of either a hospital order with or without restriction, supervision order or absolute discharge.

10.5.1 Disease of the mind

What types of malfunctioning of the mind will amount to a disease of the mind to constitute insanity?

In *Kemp* [1957] 1 QB at 407, [1956] 3 All ER at 253, D made an entirely motiveless and irrational attack on his wife with a hammer. He was charged with causing GBH to her with intent to murder her. It appeared that he suffered from arteriosclerosis which caused a congestion of blood in his brain. As a result, he suffered a temporary lapse of consciousness during which he made the attack. It was conceded that D did not know the nature and quality of his act and that he suffered from a defect of reason but it was argued on his behalf that this arose not from any mental disease, but from a purely physical one. It was argued that if a physical disease caused the brain cells to degenerate (as in time, it might), then it would be a disease of the mind; but until it did so, it was said, this temporary interference with the working of the brain was like a concussion or something of that sort and not a disease of the mind. Devlin J rejected this argument and held that D was suffering from a disease of the mind. He said:

The law is not concerned with the brain but with the mind, in the sense that 'mind' is ordinarily used, the mental faculties of reason, memory and understanding. If one reads for 'disease of the mind' 'disease of the brain,' it would follow that in many cases pleas of insanity would not be established because it could not be proved that the brain had been affected in any way, either by degeneration of the cells or in any other way. In my judgment the condition of the brain is irrelevant and so is the question of whether the condition of the mind is curable or incurable, transitory or permanent.

The definition encompasses mental conditions suffered by large numbers of the population.

R v Sullivan

[1983] 2 All ER 673, House of Lords

(Lords Diplock, Scarman, Lowry, Bridge and Brandon)

The accused suffered from epilepsy which was controlled by medication. One day when visiting his 86-year-old neighbour he had a seizure and kicked a fellow visitor aged 80 around the head and body. He had no recollection of the incident. He was charged with maliciously inflicting GBH and intentionally causing GBH under ss 20 and 18 of the Offences Against the Person Act 1861.

Lord Diplock [His lordship stated that the judge had ruled that he would direct the jury that, if they accepted this evidence, they would be bound to return a verdict of not guilty by reason of insanity, whereupon the appellant changed his plea to guilty of assault occasioning actual bodily harm and was sentenced to three years' probation. He reviewed the *M'Naghten* Rules and *Bratty*, section 10.4.1, p .327 and continued:]

In the instant case, as in *Bratty's* case, the only evidential foundation that was laid for any finding by the jury that the appellant was acting unconsciously and involuntarily when he was kicking Mr Payne was that when he did so he was in the post-ictal stage of a seizure of psychomotor epilepsy. The evidential foundation in the case of Bratty, that he was suffering from psychomotor epilepsy at the time he did the act with which he was charged, was very weak and was rejected by the jury; the evidence in the appellant's case, that he was so suffering when he was kicking Mr Payne, was very strong and would almost inevitably be accepted by a properly directed jury. It would be the duty of the judge to direct the jury that if they did accept the evidence the law required them to bring in a special verdict and none other. The governing statutory provision is to be found in s 2 of the Trial of Lunatics Act 1883. This says 'the jury *shall* return a special verdict'.

My Lords, I can deal briefly with the various grounds on which it has been submitted that the instant case can be distinguished from what constituted the ratio decidendi in *Bratty's* case, and that it falls outside the ambit of the M'Naghten Rules.

First, it is submitted the medical evidence in the instant case shows that psychomotor epilepsy is not a disease of the mind, whereas in *Bratty's* case it was accepted by all the doctors that it was. The only evidential basis for this submission is that Dr Fenwick said that in medical terms to constitute a 'disease of the mind' or 'mental illness', which he appeared to regard as interchangeable descriptions, a disorder of brain functions (which undoubtedly occurs during a seizure in psychomotor epilepsy) must be prolonged for a period of time usually more than a day, while Dr Taylor would have it that the disorder must continue for a minimum of a month to quality for the description 'a disease of the mind'.

The nomenclature adopted by the medical profession may change from time to time; Bratty was tried in 1961. But the meaning of the expression 'disease of the mind' as the cause of 'a defect of reason' remains unchanged for the purposes of the application of the M'Naghten Rules. I agree with what was said by Devlin J in *R v Kemp* [1956] 3 All ER 249 at 253, [1957] 1QB 399 at 407 that 'mind' in the M'Naghten Rules is used in the ordinary sense of the mental faculties of reason, memory and understanding. If the effect of a disease is to impair these faculties so severely as to have either of the consequences referred to in the latter part of the rules, it matters not whether the aetiology of the impairment is organic, as in epilepsy, or functional, or whether the impairment itself is permanent or is transient and intermittent, provided that it subsisted at the time of commission of the act. The purpose of the legislation relating to the defence of insanity, ever since its origin in 1880, has been to protect society against recurrence of the dangerous conduct. The duration of a temporary suspension of the mental faculties of reason, memory and understanding, particularly if, as in the appellant's case, it is recurrent, cannot on any rational ground be relevant to the application by the courts of the M'Naghten Rules, though it may be relevant to the course adopted by the Secretary of State, to whom the responsibility for how the defendant is to be dealt with passes after the return of the special verdict of not guilty by reason of insanity.

To avoid misunderstanding I ought perhaps to add that in expressing my agreement with what was said by Devlin J in *R v Kemp*, where the disease that caused the temporary and intermittent impairment of the mental faculties was arteriosclerosis, I do not regard that judge as excluding the possibility of non-insane automatism, for which the proper verdict would be a verdict of not guilty, in cases where temporary impairment not being self-induced by consuming drink or drugs, results from some external physical factor such as a blow on the head causing concussion or the administration of an anaesthetic for therapeutic purposes. I mention this because in *R v Quick* [1973] 3 All ER 347, [1973] QB 910 Lawton LJ appears to have been inconsistent with the speeches in this House in *Bratty's* case, where *R v Kemp* was alluded to without disapproval by Viscount Kilmuir LC and received the express approval of Lord Denning. The instant case, however, does not in my view afford an appropriate occasion for exploring possible causes of non-insane automatism.

The only other submission in support of the appellant's appeal which I think it necessary to mention is that, because the expert evidence was to the effect that the appellant's acts in kicking Mr Payne were unconscious and thus 'involuntary' in the legal sense of that term, his state of mind was not one dealt with by the M'Naghten Rules at all, since it was not covered by the phrase 'as not to know the nature and quality of the act he was doing'. Quite apart from being contrary to all three speeches in this House in *Bratty's* case, the submission appears to me, with all respect to counsel, to be quite unarguable. Dr Fenwick himself accepted it as an accurate description of the appellant's mental state in the post-ictal stage of a seizure. The audience to whom the phrase in the M'Naghten Rules was addressed consisted of peers of the realm in the 1840s when a certain orotundity of diction had not yet fallen out of fashion. Addressed to an audience of jurors in the 1980s it might more aptly be expressed as: he did not know what he was doing.

My Lords, it is natural to feel reluctant to attach the label of insanity to a sufferer from psychomotor epilepsy of the kind to which the appellant was subject, even though the expression in the context of a special verdict of not guilty by reason of insanity is a technical one which includes a purely temporary and intermittent suspension of the mental faculties of reason, memory and understanding resulting from the occurrence of an epileptic fit. But the label is contained in the current statute, it has appeared in this statute's predecessors ever since 1800. It does not lie within the power of the courts to alter it. Only Parliament can do that. It has done so twice; it could do so once again.

Sympathise though I do with the appellant, I see no other course open to your Lordships than to dismiss this appeal.

[The other Law Lords agreed.]

Appeal dismissed

■ *Questions*

Would any doctor describe Sullivan as insane? Should the law be permitted to be so out of step with medical understanding and definitions?
Can Sullivan's act be described as anything other than purposeful?

The *M'Naghten* Rules extend the definition of insanity to epileptics (*Sullivan* [1984] AC 156, diabetics (*Hennessy* [1989] 2 All ER 9, section 10.4.3, p 332), pre-menstrual syndrome sufferers (*Smith* [1982] Crim LR 531 and see V. St John, 'Premenstrual Syndrome in the Criminal Law' [1997] Auckland Uni LR 331).

Even sleepwalking is classified as insane as the next case demonstrates.

R v Burgess
[1991] 2 All ER 769, Court of Appeal, Criminal Division

(Lord Lane CJ, Roch and Morland JJ)

Burgess and his friend and neighbour, Miss Curtis, spent an evening at her flat watching video tapes. She fell asleep. While she was asleep he hit her over the head with a bottle and the video recorder and then grasped her round the throat. When she cried out he appeared to come to his senses and showed great anxiety over what he had done. He was charged with wounding with intent. His defence was that he lacked the mens rea because he was sleepwalking which, he argued, was *sane* automatism. The judge ruled that, assuming that he was not conscious at the time of the act, the medical evidence was evidence of insanity. He was found not guilty by reason of insanity and ordered to be detained in a secure hospital. He appealed on the ground that the judge's ruling was wrong.

[Lord Lane CJ delivering the judgment of the court:]

The appellant plainly suffered from a defect of reason from some sort of failure (for lack of a better term) of the mind causing him to act as he did without conscious motivation. His mind was to some extent controlling his actions, which were purposive rather than the result simply of muscular spasm, but without his being consciously aware of what he was doing. Can it be said that that 'failure' was a *disease* of the mind rather than a defect or failure of the mind not due to disease? That is the distinction, by no means always easy to draw, upon which this case depends, as others have depended in the past.

One can perhaps narrow the field of inquiry still further by eliminating what are sometimes called the 'external factors' such as concussion caused by a blow on the head. There were no such factors here. Whatever the cause may have been, it was an 'internal' cause. The possible disappointment or frustration caused by unrequited love is not to be equated with something such as concussion. On this aspect of the case, we respectfully adopt what was said by Martin JA giving the judgment of the court in the Ontario Court of Appeal in *R v Rabey* (1977) 17 OR (2d) 1 at 17, 22, which was approved by a majority in the Supreme Court of Canada (see [1980] SCR 513 at 519) (where the facts bore a similarity to those in the instant case although the diagnosis was different):

'Any malfunctioning of the mind, or mental disorder having its source primarily in some subjective condition or weakness internal to the accused (whether fully understood or not), may be a "disease of the mind" if it prevents the accused from knowing what he is doing, but transient disturbances of consciousness due to certain specific external factors do not fall within the concept of disease of the mind . . . In my view, the ordinary stresses and disappointments of life which are the common lot of mankind do not constitute an external cause constituting an explanation for a malfunctioning of the mind which takes it out of the category of a "disease of the mind". To hold otherwise would deprive the concept of an external factor of any real meaning.'

[His lordship quoted from the speech of Lord Diplock in *Sullivan*, section 10.5.1, p 338, and that of Lord Denning in *Bratty*, section 10.4.1, p 327, concluding with Lord Denning's opinion that 'any mental disorder which has manifested itself in violence and is prone to recur is a disease of the mind. At any rate it is the sort of disease for which a person should be detained in hospital rather than be given a qualified acquittal.' Lord Lane continued:]

It seems to us that if there is a danger of recurrence that may be an added reason for categorising the condition as a disease of the mind. On the other hand, the absence of the danger of recurrence is not a reason for saying that it cannot be a disease of the mind. Subject to that possible qualification, we respectfully adopt Lord Denning's suggested definition.

There have been several occasions when during the course of judgments in the Court of Appeal and the House of Lords observations have been made, obiter, about the criminal responsibility of sleepwalkers, where sleepwalking has been used as a self-evident illustration of non-insane automatism.

[His lordship referred to Lord Denning's remarks and his reference to Stephen J in *Bratty*, section 10.4.1, p 327 and continued:]

We have also been referred to a Canadian decision, *R v Parks* (1990) 56 CCC (3d) 449. In that case the defendant was charged with murder. The undisputed facts were that he had, whilst according to him he was asleep, at night driven his motor car some 23 km to the house of his wife's parents where he had stabbed and beaten both his mother-in-law and his father-in-law. His mother-in-law died as a result and his father-in-law sustained serious injuries. A number of defence witnesses, including experts in sleep disorders, gave evidence to the effect that sleepwalking is not regarded as a disease of the mind, mental illness or mental disorder, and the trial judge directed the jury that if the accused was in a state of somnambulism at the time of the killing, then he was entitled to be acquitted on the basis of non-insane automatism. The defendant was acquitted of the murder of his mother-in-law and subsequently acquitted of the attempted murder of his father-in-law.

The Crown Court appealed from the accused's acquittal and it was held by the Ontario Court of Appeal that the appeal should be dismissed. The court concluded that sleep is a normal condition and 'the impairment of the respondent's faculties of reason, memory and understanding was caused not by any disorder or abnormal condition but by a natural, normal condition—sleep (at 465–66).' [The Crown's further appeal to the Supreme Court of Canada was dismissed, distinguishing *Burgess* (1992) 95 DLR (4th) 27.]

We accept of course that sleep is a normal condition, but the evidence in the instant case indicates that sleepwalking, and particularly violence in sleep, is not normal...[*Parks*] apart, in none of the other cases where sleepwalking has been mentioned, so far as we can discover, has the court had the advantage of the sort of expert medical evidence which was available to the judge here.

One turns then to examine the evidence upon which the judge had to base his decision and for this purpose the two medical experts called by the defence are the obvious principal sources. Dr d'Orban in examination-in-chief said:

'On the evidence available to me, and subject to the results of the tests when they became available, I came to the same conclusion as Dr Nicholas and Dr Eames, whose reports I had read, and that was that [the appellant's] actions had occurred during the course of a sleep disorder.'

He was asked, 'Assuming this is a sleep associated automatism, is it an internal or external factor?' He answered: 'In this particular case, I think that one would have to see it as an internal factor.'

Then in cross-examination:

'Q. Would you go so far as to say that it was liable to recur? *A.* It is possible for it to recur, yes.
Judge Lewis. Is this a case of automatism associated with a pathological condition or not?
A. I think the answer would have to be Yes, because it is an abnormality of the brain function, so it would be regarded as a pathological condition.'

Dr Eames in cross-examination agreed with Dr d'Orban as to the internal rather than the external factor. He accepted that there is a liability to recurrence of sleepwalking. He could not go so far as to say that there is no liability of recurrence of serious violence but he agreed with the other medical witnesses that there is no recorded case of violence of this sort recurring.

The prosecution, as already indicated, called Dr Fenwick, whose opinion was that this was not a sleepwalking episode at all. If it was a case where the appellant was unconscious of what he was doing, the most likely explanation was that he was in what is described as a hysterical dissociative state. That is a state in which, for psychological reasons, such as being overwhelmed by his emotions, the person's brain works in a different way. He carries out acts of which he has no knowledge and for which he has no memory. It is quite different from sleepwalking.

He then went on to describe features of sleepwalking. This is what he said.

'Firstly, violent acts in sleepwalking are very common. In just an exposure of one day to a sleepwalking clinic, you will hear of how people are kicked in bed, hit in bed, partially strangled—it is usually just arms round the neck, in bed, which is very common. Serious violence fortunately is rare. Serious violence does recur, or certainly the propensity for it to recur is there, although there are very few cases in the literature—in fact I know of none—in which somebody has come to court twice for a sleepwalking offence. This does not mean that sleepwalking violence does not recur; what it does mean is that those who are associated with the sleeper take the necessary precautions. Finally, should a person be detained in hospital? The answer to that is: Yes, because sleepwalking is treatable. Violent night terrors are treatable. There is a lot which can be done for the sleepwalker, so sending them to hospital after a violent act to have their sleepwalking sorted out, makes good sense.'

Dr Fenwick was also of the view that in certain circumstances hysterical dissociative states are also subject to treatment.

It seems to us that on this evidence the judge was right to conclude that this was an abnormality or disorder, albeit transitory, due to an internal factor, whether functional or organic, which had manifested itself in violence. It was a disorder or abnormality which might recur, though the possibility of it recurring in the form of serious violence was unlikely. Therefore, since this was a legal problem to be decided on legal principles, it seems to us that on those principles the answer was as the judge found it to be. It does however go further than that. Dr d'Orban as already described, stated it as his view that the condition would be regarded as pathological. Pathology is the science of diseases. It seems therefore that in this respect at least there is some similarity between the law and medicine.

The judge was alive to the apparent incongruity of labelling this sort of disability as insanity. He drew attention, as we would also wish to do, to the passage of the speech of Lord Diplock in *R v Sullivan* [1983] 2 All ER 673 at 678, [1984] AC 156 at 173 [cited in section 10.5.1, p 338].

This appeal must accordingly be dismissed.

Appeal dismissed

■ *Questions*

1. Was Burgess' act purposeful? Is it fair and just to treat sleepwalkers as insane?

See the excellent discussion of voluntariness and sleepwalking: I. Ebrahim et al, 'Violence Sleepwalking and the Criminal Law: (1) The Medical Aspects' [2005] Crim LR 601; W. Wilson et al, 'Violence Sleepwalking and the Criminal Law: (2) The Legal Aspects' [2005] Crim LR 614.

2. D hates his wife V. He would like to kill her. D visits a hypnotist, X, and asks the hypnotist to suggest to him, D, that he should go home and kill V. X does so and D goes home and kills V while still in the hypnotic trance. Is D guilty of murder? Is X guilty of any crime?

Cf C. Finkelstein, 'Involuntary Crimes, Voluntarily Committed' in S. Shute and A. Simester (eds), *Criminal Law Theory*, 143.

3. Are sufferers of these conditions rightly regarded as 'insane'?

Cf A. Loughnan, 'Manifest Madness: Towards a New Understanding of the Insanity Defence' (2007) 70 MLR 379, arguing that the way in which insanity is defined for the criminal law describes forms of 'manifest madness' familiar to the lay person. See also A. Loughnan, *Manifest Madness: Mental Incapacity in the Criminal Law* (2012). In addition, see the Law Commission Discussion Paper on Insanity and Automatism (2013) proposing a new defence of Not Criminally Responsible by Reason of Recognised Medical Condition. The Commission proposal would treat all medical conditions as potentially relevant to that new defence, provided they caused a total loss of control. See section 10.9, p 351.

The treatment of sleepwalking as insanity has led some first instance judges to allow a defence of sane automatism to be run to avoid that conclusion. See *Lowe* (2005, unreported), discussed in W. Wilson et al, 'Violence, Sleepwalking and the Criminal Law' [2005] Crim LR 601 and 614; *Pooley* (2007, unreported), discussed in R. D. Mackay and B. Mitchell, 'Sleepwalking, Automatism and Insanity' [2006] Crim LR 901.

10.5.1.1 Intoxication as a disease of the mind?

R v Coley

[2013] EWCA Crim 223, Court of Appeal, Criminal Division, http://www.bailii.org/ew/cases/EWCA/Crim/2013/223.html

(Hughes LJ, Hickinbottom and Holroyde JJ)

In a series of three conjoined appeals, the Court of Appeal considered aspects of the insanity defence. D was charged with attempted murder. One evening he dressed up in combat gear and broke into his neighbour's house. He was carrying what was called a 'Rambo knife'. D stabbed the neighbour repeatedly before escaping the house. D then went to his own house where he was calmed by his father and waited for the police. D was heard to say that he thought he had done something very wrong. D's evidence was that he had 'blacked out' and had no recollection of the stabbing. D was a heavy user of cannabis and had been so for some time. Three psychiatrists testified that D was not suffering from an underlying mental illness but that there was a real possibility that he had suffered a 'brief psychotic episode' induced by the cannabis. The judge declined to leave the issues of insanity and automatism to the jury. D was convicted of attempted murder and appealed.

13. The judge ruled that insanity was not available on the evidence. He held that this was a case of voluntary intoxication, rather than insanity. The possible abnormality of mind could not be classified as insanity in law because it arose from an external and not an internal cause and was self induced. It was a temporary malfunctioning of the mind caused by the application to the body of illegal drugs, and that did not constitute insanity within the M'Naghten rules He relied upon the principled limitation imposed by the law on the extent to which voluntary intoxication can be a defence to criminal charges He also relied on the decision of this court in *R v Quick* [1973] QB 910.

14. [Counsel for D] contends that this was not a case of intoxication but rather had passed to a recognised condition of mental illness, namely a psychotic episode, no matter how transient. He contends that insofar as *Quick* holds otherwise, it is wrong and inconsistent with the law's recognition of the difference between intoxication or drunkenness *simpliciter*, on the one hand, and a disease of the mind induced by drunkenness on the other.

15. We agree that the law has long recognised the distinction which [counsel for D] identifies between intoxication and a disease of the mind induced by intoxicants. That distinction can be found in many cases. [Counsel for D] rightly identifies one of the earliest in the direction of Stephen J to the jury in *R v Davis* (1881) 14 Cox CC 563, which was approved by Lord Birkenhead LC giving the sole speech in the famous intoxication case of *Beard* (1920) 14 Cr App R 160 at 194:

'But drunkenness is one thing and the diseases to which drunkenness leads are different things, and if a man by drunkenness brings on a state of disease which causes such a degree of madness, even for a time, as would have relieved him from responsibility if it had been caused in any other way, then he would not be criminally responsible'.

We also agree that, as Lord Birkenhead also made clear, insanity which is temporary is as much insanity as that which is long-lasting or permanent. *Davis* was a case of a defendant suffering (temporarily) from *delirium tremens*. That, self evidently, is not intoxication. It is, if anything, the opposite. It is a condition brought about by the protest of the brain and nerve receptors against the *removal* of intoxicants to which the body has become accustomed.

16. We do not doubt that the possible state of mind in which this defendant stabbed the man next door can properly be called a mental abnormality (or, in the nineteenth century language of *M'Naghten*, a defect of reason) which is recognised medically by psychiatrists As a matter of fact, some care may need to be exercised in discovering exactly how the expressions 'psychosis' or 'psychotic' are used, which was not much explored in the evidence in this case, save to explain that the doctors were speaking of a state in which the mind becomes detached, to a greater or lesser extent, from reality. Generally, as we understand it, these expressions are more often encountered as descriptions of symptoms than as constituting a mental illness in their own right. The underlying cause of such symptoms may vary. Well understood ones certainly include schizophrenia and bi-polar disorder, which are no doubt mental disorders or illnesses Another well known possible cause of psychotic symptoms is drug abuse, which is not a mental disorder. But with that caveat, we agree that to speak of a psychotic episode is no doubt to speak of a temporary abnormality of the brain or mind and thus of a defect of reason for the purposes of the *M'Naghten* rules

17. However, the key thing to understand is that whether there is or is not a 'disease of the mind' for the purpose of the *M'Naghten* rules is, and has to be, a question of law and not of medical usage. It makes excellent sense for medical people to classify a great variety of conditions as recognised medically. It enables statistics to be gathered, resources allocated, diagnoses understood with reasonable consistency and treatment to be advised: see the discussion in the slightly different context of diminished responsibility in *R v Dowds* [2012] EWCA Crim 281. But the law has to cope with the synthesising of the law of insanity with the law of voluntary intoxication. The first calls for a special verdict of acquittal and very particular means of disposal. The latter is generally no defence at all, but may be relevant to whether the defendant formed a specific intention, if the offence in question is one which requires such: *DPP v Majewski* [1977] AC 443. In most, but not all, intoxication cases, the intoxication will be possibly relevant to a serious offence allegedly committed but will afford no defence to a lesser offence constituted by the same facts: for example causing grievous bodily harm with intent (s 18) and causing grievous bodily harm without such intent (s20), or of course murder and manslaughter. In the development of the common law, intoxication was historically regarded chiefly as an aggravation of offending, rather than as an excuse for it. For all the reasons explained in *Majewski*, the law refuses as a matter of policy to afford a general defence to an offender on the basis of his own voluntary intoxication. The pressing social reasons for maintaining this general policy of the law are certainly no less present in modern conditions of substance abuse than they were in the past.

18. The precise line between the law of voluntary intoxication and the law of insanity may, we do not doubt, be difficult to identify in some borderline cases But the present case falls comfortably on the side of the line covered by voluntary intoxication. It matters not that the condition of the defendant as observed in the aftermath of his attack on the neighbour was not that of conventional intoxication, in the sense that he was not, for example, staggering or unable to speak clearly. If the doctors were right about his state of mind, his mind was to an extent detached from reality by the direct and acute effects on it of the ingestion of cannabis Every intoxicated person has his mind affected, and to an extent disordered, by the direct and acute effects of the ingestion of intoxicants; all intoxication operates through the brain. Not infrequently it would be perfectly legitimate to say of a very drunken man that his mind had become detached from reality by the intoxication; that is obviously true, for example, of the drunken man who suffers delusions as a result of the drink, but the proposition is not limited to that case. In order to engage the law of insanity, it is not enough that there is an effect on the mind, or, in the language of the *M'Naghten* rules, a 'defect of reason'. There must also be what the law classifies as a disease of the mind. Direct acute effects on the mind of intoxicants, voluntarily taken, are not so classified. That is the distinction drawn by Stephen J in *Davis* and maintained ever since. In the slightly different legal context of diminished responsibility a similar distinction is recognised: see *R v Wood* [2008] EWCA Crim 1305. [Counsel for D's] superficially simple argument amounts to treating every 'defect of reason' as a 'disease of the mind', but that is not the law.

The Court of Appeal recognized that in some instances distinguishing between voluntary intoxication and insanity may not be clear. Even if the effect of the intoxication is to induce a state where the mind becomes detached from reality (a defect of reason), this will not necessarily qualify as insanity. In addition to a 'defect of reason' (which the Court of Appeal emphasized is a question of law) there must be what the law classifies as a 'disease of the mind'. If D's defect of reason arises only from his having voluntarily consumed intoxicants, that is not recognized by the law as a disease of the mind. However, if D's chronic substance misuse causes him to have a disease of the mind (eg alcohol dependence syndrome), and that causes a defect of reason, he will have a defence of insanity. In this case, D had suffered from a brief psychotic episode brought on by his voluntary intoxication. That was not insanity; it was not a case of a disease of the mind caused by the prolonged misuse. Much will turn on the evidence of the experts, but remember these are questions of law, not medicine or psychiatry.

Once a disease of the mind is established, the question is whether D falls into one of the two categories of insanity: not knowing the nature of the act or not knowing it was wrong.

10.5.2 Not knowing the nature and quality of the act

R v Clarke

[1971] EWCA Crim 5, Court of Appeal, Criminal Division, http://www.bailii.org/ew/cases/EWCA/Crim/1971/5.html

(Lord Widgery CJ, Sachs LJ and Ackner J)

C selected various items in a supermarket and put them into the wire basket provided. Before she went to the checkout, she transferred three items into her own bag so that, when she presented the basket, these items were not in it and were not paid for. She was charged with stealing them. Her defence was that she had no intent to steal. She suffered from diabetes and had various domestic problems. There was evidence that, prior to the alleged theft, she had behaved absent-mindedly in the home. She said that she must have put the articles in her bag in a moment of absent-mindedness. Her doctor and a consultant psychiatrist were called and testified that she was suffering from depression which one of them accepted to be a minor mental illness which could produce absent-mindedness consistent with her story.

Ackner J:

Unfortunately the medical witnesses were pressed to, what it seems to us, an unreasonable degree to explain the workings of this particular illness. The psychiatrist stated that what happens in these cases is 'that there is a patchy state of affairs, and the consciousness, if you like, goes off at times and comes on again, changing every few minutes and not in proper control of the patient'.

The effect of this evidence on the assistant recorder was to convince him that the defence was in truth a defence of 'not guilty by reason of insanity' under the *M'Naghten* rules [section 10.5, p 334]. He was undoubtedly influenced to this decision by the evidence that the depression was an illness which he translated as meaning also a disease and by the fact that on the medical evidence, as he understood it, a possible explanation was that there had been a total lack of consciousness at the moment when the offence was committed. In order to sustain a defence under the *M'Naghten* rules it is necessary to show that the party accused was labouring under such a defect of reason from the *disease of the mind as not to know the nature and quality of the act he was doing* or if he did know, that he did not know that what he was doing was wrong.

It may be that on the evidence in this case the assistant recorder was entitled to the view that the appellant suffered from a disease of the mind but we express no concluded view on that. However, in our judgment the evidence fell very far short either of showing that she suffered from a defect of reason or that the consequences of that defect in reason, if any, were that she was unable to know the nature and quality of the act she was doing. The *M'Naghten* rules relate to accused persons who by reason of a disease of the mind are deprived of the power of reasoning. They do not apply and never have applied to those who retain the power of reasoning but who in moments of confusion or absent-mindedness fail to use their powers to the full. The picture painted by the evidence was wholly inconsistent [*sic*] with this being a woman who retained her ordinary powers of reason but who was momentarily absent-minded or confused and acted as she did by failing to concentrate properly on what she was doing and by failing adequately to use her mental powers.

Because the assistant recorder ruled that the defence put forward had to be put forward as a defence of insanity, although the medical evidence was to the effect that it was absurd to call anyone in the appellant's condition insane, defending counsel felt constrained to advise the appellant to alter her plea from not guilty to guilty so as to avoid the disastrous consequences of her defence, as wrongly defined by the assistant recorder, succeeding. Thus the appellant in this case ultimately pleaded guilty solely by reason of the assistant recorder's ruling.... The conviction is accordingly quashed.

Appeal allowed

■ *Questions*

Was Mrs Clarke insane as a matter of law? As a matter of psychiatry?

10.5.3 Not knowing that the act is 'wrong'

Does the defendant have to prove that he did not know that the act was legally wrong or morally wrong?

■ *Question*

Consider D who claims that God told him to kill prostitutes because they are evil. D says he knows that this is murder, but thought it was morally right. Is he insane?

R v Windle

[1952] 2 All ER 1, Court of Criminal Appeal

(Lord Goddard CJ, Jones and Parker JJ)

W was convicted of murdering his wife. He was described as being of 'weak character' married to a woman 18 years older than himself and in an unhappy marriage. Medical opinion was that his wife was mentally ill and was always talking about committing suicide. W became obsessed with this and discussed it with his workmates until they were tired of hearing him, and on one occasion, just before this crime was committed, one of them said 'Give her a dozen aspirins.' W gave his wife 100 aspirin tablets. She took them and died; W told the police that he 'supposed he would be hanged for it'.

At the trial W pleaded insanity. There was some evidence that W suffered from some defect of reason or disease of the mind. The defence expert said it was a form of communicated insanity known as *folie à deux* which arises when a person is in constant attendance on a person of unsound mind.

[Lord Goddard CJ delivered the following judgment of the court: his lordship quoted the *M'Naghten* Rules.]

The argument in this appeal really has been concerned with what is meant by the word 'wrong'. The evidence that was given on the issue of insanity was that of the doctor called by the appellant and that of the prison doctor who was called by the prosecution. Both doctors expressed without hesitation the view that when the appellant was administering this poison to his wife he knew he was doing an act which the law forbade. I need not put it higher than that. It may well be that in the misery in which he had been living with this nagging and tiresome wife who constantly expressed the desire to commit suicide, he thought she was better out of the world than in it. He may have thought it was a kindly act to put her out of her sufferings or imagined sufferings, but the law does not permit such an act as that. There was some exceedingly vague evidence that the appellant was suffering from a defect of his reason owing to his communicated insanity, and, if the only question in the case had been whether the appellant was suffering from a disease of the mind, that question must have been left to the jury because there was some evidence of it, but that was not the question. The question, as I endeavoured to point out in giving judgment in *Rivett* [(1950) 34 Cr App R 87], in all these cases is one of responsibility. A man may be suffering from a defect of reason, but, if he knows that what he is doing is wrong—and by 'wrong' is meant contrary to law—he is responsible. Counsel for the appellant suggested that the word 'wrong' as it is used in the *M'Naghten* rules did not mean contrary to law, but had some qualified meaning—morally wrong—and that, if a person was in a state of mind through a defect of reason that he thought that what he was doing, although he knew it was wrong in law, was really beneficial, or kind, or praiseworthy, that would excuse him.

Courts of law, however, can only distinguish between that which is in accordance with the law and that which is contrary to law. There are many acts which, we all know, to use an expression to be found in some of the old cases, are contrary to the law of God and man. In the Decalogue are the commandments: 'Thou shall not kill' and 'Thou shall not steal'. Such acts are contrary to the law of man and they are contrary to the law of God. In regard to the Seventh Commandment: 'Thou shall not commit adultery', it will be found that, so far as the criminal law is concerned, though that act is contrary to the law of God, it is not contrary to the law of man.

The test must be whether an act is contrary to law. In *Rivett* I referred to the Trial of Lunatics Act 1883, s 2(1) of which provides: [His lordship quoted the provision in section 10.5, p 336.]

I emphasise again that the test is responsibility 'according to law'. . . . Devlin J was right to withdraw the case from jury. This appeal fails.

Appeal dismissed

In *Johnson* [2007] EWCA Crim 1978, the Court of Appeal held that whilst there is an argument for extending the scope of the defence of insanity to include acts which the defendant knew to be legally wrong, but thought were morally justified, the law remained as settled in *Windle*.

It appears that Johnson was unfortunate to have had legal and medical practitioners who applied the strict letter of the law. Professor Mackay's research has revealed that in practice the narrow *Windle* definition is often ignored and little distinction is made between a lack of awareness of legal and moral wrong concluding that: 'in many of the [cases] the "wrongness" limb was interpreted to cover whether the defendant thought his/her actions were legally/morally justified, and/or whether the actions were in perceived self defence of themselves or others, in the sense of protecting their physical or spiritual well-being.' See R. Mackay, B. Mitchell, and L. Howe, 'Yet More Facts About the Insanity Plea' [2006] Crim LR 399.

Law reformers and academic commentators have repeatedly suggested that the narrow approach in *Windle* ought to be reconsidered. The Butler Committee, 'The Report of the Committee on Mentally Abnormal Offenders' (1975) Cmnd 6244, observed (at para 18.8) that:

knowledge of the law is hardly an appropriate test on which to base ascription of responsibility to the mentally disordered. It is a very narrow ground of exemption since even persons who are grossly disturbed generally know that murder and arson are crimes.

The Law Commission also proposes changing this element of the defence in its 2013 Discussion Paper. Similarly, Professor Mackay criticizes *Windle* for its 'extremely narrow cognitive approach towards the rules ensuring that their application would be restricted to fundamental or extreme intellectual defects' in *Mental Condition Defences in the Criminal Law* (1995), p 97.

See R. D. Mackay, B. J. Mitchell and L. Howe, 'Yet More Facts about the Insanity Defence' [2006] Crim LR 399, discussing research which suggests that there continues to be a gradual increase in the use of the defence, with the 'wrongness limb' of *M'Naghten* being used more commonly than the 'nature and quality limb'.

■ *Question*

Is the test under-inclusive because it focuses so heavily on the cognitive state of the accused (has he appreciated the nature or wrongness) rather than on whether he had the capacity to be held responsible? See V. Tadros, *Criminal Responsibility*, Ch 12.

10.6 Insanity and self-defence

What is the law if D suffers from an insane delusion that he is being attacked by evil spirits and uses the force that he honestly believes is necessary to repel them? Can D plead self-defence when it transpires that the evil spirits are in fact police officers or is insanity his only available defence? The Court of Appeal considered this issue in *Oye* [2013] EWCA Crim 1725. As we explore in the next chapter, self-defence has two limbs. The first is whether D genuinely believed it was necessary to use force. This is a subjective test. The second limb requires an assessment of the reasonableness of the degree of force used. While the requirement that the use of force be reasonable imports an objective evaluation, it is important to bear in mind that s 76(3) and (4) of the Criminal Justice and Immigration Act 2008 mandates that the assessment of the reasonableness of the force used is to be decided by reference to the circumstances as D believed them to be. So, is the reasonableness of D's actions to be judged by reference to what his insane delusions told him was necessary? The Court of Appeal rejected this proposition.

R v Oye

[2013] EWCA Crim 1725, Court of Appeal, Criminal Division, http://www.bailii.org/ew/cases/EWCA/Crim/2013/1725.html

(Davis LJ, Keith and Lewis JJ)

Davis LJ:

44. From this background, and from the provisions of s 76(3) in particular, one can now appreciate the nature of the main argument advanced on behalf of the appellant. In essence—although rather masked in the very long and elaborate written grounds—what it comes to is this. Here not only was the agreed psychiatric evidence to the effect that the appellant acted as he did thinking that he had to defend himself by reason of his insane delusions but also it was positively accepted by the Crown at trial that that was so and that he was indeed suffering from an insane delusion that evil spirits were intent on harming him. That was this the basis on which the trial proceeded. As we have said, [counsel for the Crown] also confirmed that the Crown did not dispute that in the circumstances the first limb

of self-defence had been made out (or rather, could not be disproved by the prosecution). [Counsel for D] thus submitted that *in the circumstances as the appellant believed them to be* the prosecution could not, on the evidence prove that the degree of force used was unreasonable or disproportionate in those circumstances. That his belief in those circumstances derived from his insane delusion, it was submitted, was immaterial. The point was that it was his genuine, if insanely deluded belief.

45. If this is right, the potential implication for other cases are most disconcerting. It could mean that the more insanely deluded a person may be in using violence in purported self-defence, the more likely that an entire acquittal may result. It could mean that an individual who for his own benefit and protection may require hospital treatment or supervision gets none. It could mean that the public is exposed to possible further violence from an individual with a propensity for suffering insane delusions, without any intervening preventative remedies being available to the courts in the form of hospital or supervision orders. Thus, whatever the purist force in the argument, there are strong policy objections to the approach advocated on behalf of the appellant.

46. In our view it is not right.

47. The position remains, as we think plain from the provisions of s 76 of the 2008 Act, that the second limb of self-defence does include an objective element by reference to reasonableness, even if there may also be a subjective element: see in particular s 76(6) and see also the decision in *R v Keane & McGrath* [2011] EWCA Crim 2514. An insane person cannot set the standards of reasonableness as to the degree of force used by reference to his own insanity. In truth, it makes little sense to talk of the reasonable lunatic as it did, in the context of cases on provocation, to talk of the reasonable glue-sniffer.

The Court of Appeal observed that the wording of s 76(3) could be interpreted widely so as to bear the meaning contended for by D but that this would entail changing the common law, whereas s 76(9) states that the purpose of the 2008 Act is merely to 'clarify' it. The approach in *Oye* was followed by the Court of Appeal in *Press* [2013] EWCA Crim 1849 where the defence was one of sane automatism brought about by D's PTSD from his military service.

10.7 Insanity and the ECHR

Most of the modern reported cases concerning the *M'Naghten* Rules have been concerned with the question whether the accused's alleged condition was the result of a 'disease of the mind' or some other cause, see section 10.5.1, p 337.

The focus on the definition *in legal terms* with no direct correlation with medical definitions renders this aspect of the test potentially incompatible with Article 5(1)(e) of the ECHR where it results in D's loss of liberty.

R. D. Mackay and C. Gearty, 'On Being Insane in Jersey—the Case of
Attorney General v Jason Prior'
[2001] Crim LR 560

1. The M'Naghten Rules and the Human Rights Act

... the way in which the English courts have interpreted 'disease of the mind' to include conditions such as diabetic hyperglycaemia and epilepsy does seem to run counter to the *Winterwerp* requirement that there must be objective medical expertise supporting the fact that the accused is of unsound mind. In this connection it is of particular importance to note that the objective medical evidence that is required, relates not to whether the accused suffered from hyperglycaemia or epilepsy, but to the fact of mental disorder. A lack of such objective medical expertise supporting the fact that the accused is suffering from a true mental disorder in these diabetes and epilepsy cases seems to present an insuperable problem from a Convention perspective. Further, in the recent decision of the European Court of Human Rights in *Varbanov v. Bulgaria* [5 October 2000, Application No 00031365/96], it was stated in a case dealing with the lawfulness of detention under article 5(1)(e), that 'the medical assessment must be based on the actual state of mental health of the person concerned and not solely on past events. A medical opinion cannot be seen as sufficient to justify deprivation of liberty if a significant period of time has elapsed'. This additional requirement presents a further problem in so far as the defence of insanity relates to the accused's state of mind at the time of the commission of the offence.

As far as English law is concerned there is nothing in the relevant statutory provisions under the 1964 and 1991 Acts to prevent the detention in hospital of a defendant based solely on the fact that the was legally insane at the time of the commission of the offence rather than on his present mental state. It appears that the same is true of the law in Jersey. The fact that English law has introduced flexibility of disposal under the Criminal Procedure (Insanity and Unfitness to Plead) Act 1991 fails to answer this point for two reasons. First, the 1991 Act retains compulsory detention in cases where the sentence is fixed by law, which means a court has no opportunity, but to hospitalise the defendant even in cases where this may not be appropriate. Secondly, in those cases where a court is able to choose how to dispose of a defendant found not guilty by reason of insanity, although in exercising a choice between guardianship, a supervision and treatment order or absolute discharge the court must decide which one 'is most suitable in all the circumstances of the case (see below)' the same requirement does not apply to the making of an admission order to hospital. This means that there is nothing in the statute to prevent a court making such an admission order although by the time of the trial the accused is mentally well and does not require in-patient treatment...

See further R. D. Mackay, 'On Being Insane in Jersey Part Two' [2002] Crim LR 728; 'On Being Insane in Jersey Part Three—the Case of the *Attorney General v O'Driscoll*' [2004] Crim LR 219.

10.8 Disposal of persons unfit to plead or not guilty by reason of insanity

Until 1991 a person found not guilty by reason of insanity, like a person found unfit to plead, had to be ordered to be detained indefinitely in a mental hospital. Defendants who may in truth have been not guilty by reason of insanity sometimes preferred to plead guilty rather than incur the stigma of the insanity label and indefinite detention. Cf *Sullivan* [1984] AC 156, section 10.5.1, p 338. The stigma remains but indefinite detention is no longer the necessary result of a finding either of unfitness to plead or a verdict of not guilty by reason of insanity, except in a case where the sentence is fixed by law—in practice, murder. Defendants may be more ready to raise the defence of insanity in future.

Criminal Procedure (Insanity) Act 1964
(Sections substituted by the Criminal Procedure (Insanity and Unfitness to Plead) Act 1991)

5. Powers to deal with persons not guilty by reason of insanity or unfit to plead etc

(1) This section applies where—
  (a) a special verdict is returned that the accused is not guilty by reason of insanity; or
  (b) findings have been made that the accused is under a disability and that he did the act or made the omission charged against him.

(2) The court shall make in respect of the accused—

    (a) a hospital order (with or without a restriction order);

    (b) a supervision order; or

    (c) an order for his absolute discharge.

(3) Where—

    (a) the offence to which the special verdict or the findings relate is an offence the sentence for which is fixed by law, and

    (b) the court have power to make a hospital order,

the court shall make a hospital order with a restriction order (whether or not they would have power to make a restriction order apart from this subsection).

10.9 Reform of the law

The Law Commission has recently undertaken a review of this area of the law and made the following proposals (Discussion Paper, *Criminal Liability: Insanity and Automatism* (2013)).

Proposal 1

10.6 We provisionally propose that the common law rules on the defence of insanity be abolished. [4.158]

Proposal 2

10.7 We provisionally propose the creation of a new statutory defence of not criminally responsible by reason of recognised medical condition. [4.159]

Conclusion 1

10.1 We provisionally conclude that there should be a defence which allows for a special verdict where the case is not proved against the accused because of his or her mental disorder as well as where it is proved because of the mental disorder. [2.34]

In short the new law would involve the following elements:

(1) A total loss of a relevant capacity.

10.8 The party seeking to raise the new defence must adduce expert evidence that at the time of the alleged offence the defendant wholly lacked the capacity:

    (i) rationally to form a judgment about the relevant conduct or circumstances;

    (ii) to understand the wrongfulness of what he or she is charged with having done; or

    (iii) to control his or her physical acts in relation to the relevant conduct or circumstances as a result of a qualifying recognised medical condition. [4.160]

(2) The total loss of a relevant capacity must not arise from the defendant's prior fault—if it does the rules on intoxication govern liability.

(3) The total loss of capacity must arise from a recognized medical condition—not merely those which are mental illnesses.

(4) The recognized medical condition must be one that is a 'qualifying' recognized medical condition in law. The proposal is that certain medical conditions will not be qualifying ones (that question being one of law):

We provisionally propose that certain conditions would not qualify. These include acute intoxication or any condition which is manifested solely or principally by abnormally aggressive or seriously irresponsible behaviour. [4.161]

(5) The burden of proof would then be on the prosecution:

If sufficient evidence is adduced on which, in the opinion of the court, a properly directed jury could reasonably conclude that the defence might apply, the defence should be left to the tribunal of fact to consider. The prosecution then bears the burden of disproving the defence beyond reasonable doubt. [4.163]

(6) The verdict.

10.2 We provisionally conclude that there should be a special verdict in those cases of total lack of criminal capacity resulting from a recognised medical condition (provided the other criteria of the defence are met) without limiting it to mental disorders [2.63]

10.12 The jury (or magistrates) shall return a special verdict of 'not criminally responsible by reason of recognised medical condition' unless satisfied beyond reasonable doubt that the accused did not suffer a complete loss of capacity by reason of a qualifying recognised medical condition. [4.164]

10.13 We provisionally propose that the special verdict of 'not criminally responsible' may only be returned where evidence on the accused's medical condition has been received from two or more experts, one of whom is a registered medical practitioner. [4.165]

(7) Disposal.

Proposal 10

10.15 We provisionally propose that the following disposals should be available following a special verdict of 'not criminally responsible by reason of recognised medical condition': a hospital order (with or without a restriction), supervision order, or an absolute discharge. [4.167]

In addition to its proposals for reform of the insanity defence, the Law Commission also made proposals as to how the defence of automatism could also be improved. The two new defences would be mutually exclusive.

THE REFORMED AUTOMATISM DEFENCE

General features

5.108 As with the defence of recognised medical condition, the reformed automatism defence would be available in respect of all offences. No distinction would be drawn between charges of basic and specific intent.

5.109 The reformed automatism defence would not lead to a special verdict. If successful, this defence would result in a simple acquittal.

5.110 It would not be available where the loss of capacity was due to a recognised medical condition. In practice, therefore, the defence of automatism is likely to be applicable in relation to automatic reflex reactions, or to transient states or circumstances; if a person's condition persists and worsens it might then qualify as a recognised medical condition.

No prior fault

5.111 If the accused's loss of capacity to control his or her actions is due to something he or she culpably did or failed to do (as provided for by the common law), then the defence of automatism should not be available to him or her. In this respect we are not proposing any change to the law.

Denial of actus reus or of mens rea?

5.112 As we have seen above, commentators do not agree as to whether the defence of automatism is a denial of the actus reus or of the mens rea, and at least one commentator would see it as a denial that there has been any voluntary act. Our proposed defence allows that there is an act but provides that D is not guilty if that act occurs in particular circumstances.

Total loss of control or loss of effective control?

5.113 As we discuss above, the essence of the defence of automatism lies in a lack of capacity to control one's actions (or inactions). The loss of ability to control the body may be accompanied by loss of consciousness, but that is not an essential feature. The next question is what degree of lack of control should be required for a defence of automatism.

5.114 We note in Appendix A that there is potential for confusion about the precise meaning of 'voluntary' and 'involuntary', so we do not propose to put the defence in terms of loss of voluntary control. (In the draft Criminal Code we thought the word 'involuntary' was best avoided, because of 'the variable use to which it tends to be put'.)

5.115 As noted, the case law on the current defence of (sane) automatism requires there to be a 'total destruction of voluntary control' on the part of the accused, even if only for a short time, in order for a plea of automatism to succeed. The draft Code referred instead to a person being deprived of 'effective control'. It did so because the authors believed that a person in the position of the defendant in *Broome v Perkins* should not be convicted. In *Broome v Perkins* the accused had suffered an episode of hypoglycaemia and had driven five or six miles in that state, driving erratically and causing a collision. The Divisional Court held that the defence of automatism was not open to him because on the evidence he must have had control for at least some of the journey. Under our proposals someone in this position would rely on the defence of not criminally responsible by reason of recognised medical condition.

5.116 Was the draft Criminal Code right to shift the requirement from total loss of control to loss of effective control? Ashworth has written that in this respect the draft Code 'rightly recognizes that total absence of control should not be required, but it therefore leaves us with a test dependent on a judgment of degree and value ("effective"), and does so without identifying the relevance of the defendant's capacity rather than awareness and "choice" '. We noted above that the cases seemed to set a higher standard where the offence was a driving offence, and that this might be for reasons of policy, namely, the need to avoid the risk of dangerous drivers being acquitted. That risk was mitigated by requiring the driver to show total loss of control. If, however, the requirement were only for loss of the capacity for effective control, then it would be a more flexible standard for the courts to define, one which could accommodate a greater variety of situations We suspect the courts would interpret the notion of loss of effective control as amounting to something close to total loss of control in driving cases, but the more flexible standard would not require them to do so in every case.

5.117 There is, however, a risk that a defence in terms where the accused says he or she was deprived of 'effective control' will lead to litigation about what amounts to 'effective control'. That will have significant implications in cost and delay at trial.

Conclusion

5.118 Our provisional conclusion is that the defence of automatism should require the accused to have a total loss of capacity to control his or her physical actions We are not limiting the new defence to cases of unconsciousness

The Commission's new scheme for the defences is represented in Figure 10.1.

■ *Question*

Would these proposals represent an improvement on the current law?

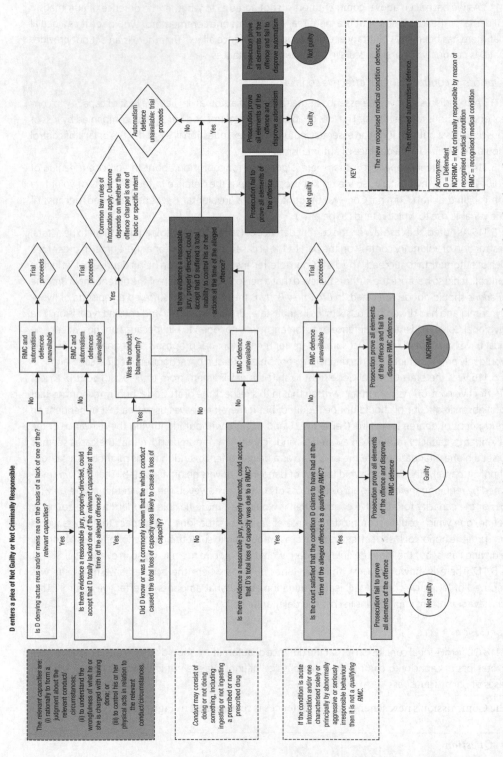

Figure 10.1 Steps a court would take where a defendant enters a plea by reason of a recognized medical condition

10.10 Diminished responsibility

For the purposes of the law of murder only, a much broader category of mental abnormality may, since the Homicide Act 1957, afford a defence. See section 16.3, p 577.

FURTHER READING

A. Duff, 'Fitness to Plead and Fair Trials' [1994] Crim LR 419

P. Fennell, 'The Criminal Procedure (Insanity and Unfitness to Plead) Act 1991' (1992) 55 MLR 547

D. Grubin, 'What Constitutes Unfitness to Plead' [1993] Crim LR 748

R. D. Mackay, *Mental Condition Defences in Criminal Law* (1998)

R. D. Mackay and W. Brookbanks, 'Protecting the Unfit to Plead' [2005] JR 173

R. D. Mackay and G. Kearns, 'The Trial of the Facts and Unfitness to Plead' [1997] Crim LR 644

R. D. Mackay and G. Kearns, 'More Facts(s) about the Insanity Defence' [1999] Crim LR 714

R. D. Mackay and M. Reuber, 'Epilespy and the Defence of Insanity—Time for a Change' [2007] Crim LR 782

R. D. Mackay, B. Mitchell and L. Howe, 'A Continued Upturn in Unfitness to Plead— More Disability in Relation to the Trial under the 1991 Act' [2007] Crim LR 530

S White, 'The Criminal Procedure (Insanity and Unfitness to Plead) Act 1991' [1992] Crim LR 4

W. Wilson et al, 'Violence, Sleepwalking and the Criminal Law' [2005] Crim LR 601 and 614

11
General defences

11.1 Introduction

In this chapter we are concerned with defences in the strictest sense of the word. The defendant is not denying that he committed the actus reus with mens rea. He is asserting the existence of other facts which, he claims, justify or excuse his doing what would otherwise be a crime. Following *Woolmington* [1935] AC 462 the defendant does not have to prove the existence of those facts. If there is some evidence of them, the onus is on the prosecution to disprove one or more of them. This means that in a criminal trial, although the Crown will bear the legal burden of proving the offence against the defendant (if they fail to do so the defendant is acquitted), the defendant will often bear an evidential burden in relation to defences he wishes to run. The evidential burden does not oblige D to prove the particular defence in order to be acquitted. It is not a legal burden. It obliges the defendant to 'raise evidence' of the defence in order to get it on its feet. Once the defendant has raised the defence it is for the Crown to disprove it; the Crown has the legal burden of proving that the defence was not applicable on the facts. The defence succeeds if, on consideration of the whole of the evidence, the jury think it reasonably possible that all the elements of the defence were present. If so, the prosecution has not proved beyond reasonable doubt that the defendant is guilty. Taking a simple example, if D is charged with murdering V and he pleads self-defence, the Crown must establish that D caused the death of V under the Queen's Peace, intending to kill or cause at least GBH. If D raises his defence of self-defence by identifying evidence in support of that defence, the Crown must then rebut it by proving that D was not acting in self-defence when he killed V.

The controversies that will be examined in this chapter include the following:

(i)   whether the fact of childhood constitutes a defence;

(ii) the extent to which duress can negate criminal liability;

(iii) whether necessity ought to be a defence;

(iv) whether recent legislative developments have rendered self-defence unduly complex;

(v)   the distinction between justifications and excuses and whether these classifications have any practical import.

11.2 The incapacity of children

> ■ *Question*
>
> From what age should children be subject to prosecution and punishment for acts which constitute criminal offences under English criminal law?

11.2.1 Children under 10 years

Children and Young Persons Act 1933, s 50

50. Age of criminal responsibility

It shall be conclusively presumed that no child under the age of ten years can be guilty of any offence.

There may be the clearest evidence that a young child satisfied the actus reus and mens rea of the offence but once it is shown that he was, or may have been, under the age of 10 at the time of the act, no criminal proceedings may follow.

11.2.2 Children aged 10–13

At common law there was a rebuttable presumption that these children were *doli incapax*, incapable of forming a criminal state of mind. The presumption was rebutted only if the prosecution proved beyond reasonable doubt not only that the child caused the actus reus, but also that he knew the particular act was 'seriously wrong' (as opposed to merely naughty or mischievous). That presumption was removed by the Crime and Disorder Act 1998, s 34:

The rebuttable presumption of criminal law that a child aged ten or over is incapable of committing an offence is hereby abolished.

The House of Lords concluded in *T* [2009] UKHL 20 that the clear intention of Parliament was to abolish the concept of *doli incapax*. This means that a child over 10 can be convicted of an offence, provided they have the necessary mens rea.

Although the defence of *doli incapax* is no longer available to 10–13-year-olds, the criminal law has recently begun to recognize the need for a child defendant to be able to participate effectively in proceedings (*T & V v UK* (2000) 30 EHRR 121). Where there is evidence that he cannot, at the judge's discretion the process should switch to determining as a matter of fact whether the child performed the act alleged (cf the unfitness to plead process discussed in Chapter 10). If even that cannot be achieved, a stay of proceedings for abuse of process will be granted as a last resort. (That is an order from the court that the prosecution is to be stopped with immediate effect.)

The age of criminal responsibility in England is set at a remarkably low level, and many have called for it to be raised. The issue of the appropriate age of criminal responsibility is a complex one with political and human rights dimensions.

■ *Questions*

1. At what age do you think a child should be held criminally responsible for his actions in English law?

2. Is it safe to assume that all those children aged between 10 and 14 who commit criminal acts understand that what they are doing is criminal? If not, is it fair to convict them?

3. Consider facts similar to those in *G* [2008] UKHL 37 (section 7.6.1, p 202). Would every 13-year-old boy engaging in penetrative sexual activity with his 'consenting' 12-year-old girlfriend realize that his conduct was seriously wrong and that he would be convicted and labelled as a rapist?

11.3 Duress by threats or circumstances

It is now established that two forms of duress are recognized by the criminal law. The first, duress by threats, has existed for centuries but, until modern times, made very rare appearances in the law reports. In the last 50 years, the law has developed relatively quickly and is now reasonably well defined. However, several areas of uncertainty remain. Much more recent is the recognition of the existence of the related defence of duress of circumstances, the first case *Willer* (1986) 83 Cr App R 225, section 11.4.1, p 392, appearing in the law reports in 1986, the first use of the phrase by the courts in 1988 (*Conway* [1989] QB 290, section 11.4.1, p 392) and its recognition as a general defence in 1995 (*Pommel* [1995] 2 Cr App R 607, section 11.4.1, p 396).

The typical case of duress by threats is that where D is told, 'Do this (the crime charged) or else…' D yields to the threat and does the criminal act he was told to do. Duress of circumstances may arise more widely, when no one is telling the accused to commit the crime. The effect of the threat, however, may be the same. For example, D who is disqualified from driving:

(i)　is told by a menacing gang of youths, 'Drive the car or we will kill you';

(ii)　sees the same gang bearing down on him with shouts of 'Kill him' and the only way he can escape is to drive the car.

In both cases D intentionally commits the actus reus of the offence of driving while disqualified and in both cases he does so in order to save his life from the same menace. If he has a defence in the one case, he ought to have a defence in the other. The close relationship is illustrated by the fact that in *Willer* the court was concerned with a case of type (ii) (circumstances) but it showed no awareness of this and relied on the law relating to duress by threats. In *Martin*, section 11.4.1, p 395, by contrast the court decided the case as one of duress by circumstances, whereas closer inspection would have revealed that it was duress by threats.

The principles applicable to the two types of duress are probably the same and the cases below, though mainly concerned with duress by threats, also state the law for duress of circumstances. They are considered here together, with some further discussion of duress of circumstances, section 11.4, p 392.

11.3.1 Overview of the current law

R v Hasan

[2005] UKHL 22, House of Lords, http://www.bailii.org/uk/cases/UKHL/2005/22.html

(Lords Bingham of Cornhill, Steyn, Rodger of Earlsferry, Baroness Hale of Richmond and Lord Brown of Eaton-under-Heywood)

H was charged with aggravated burglary and pleaded duress. He claimed that he had been coerced into committing the burglary by S, a drug dealer with a reputation for violence, who had threatened that H and his family would be harmed if H did not commit the crime. H claimed that he had had no chance to escape and go to the police.

Lord Bingham of Cornhill [his lordship dealt with the facts of the case and other unrelated issues]:

17. The common sense starting point of the common law is that adults of sound mind are ordinarily to be held responsible for the crimes which they commit. To this general principle there has, since the 14th century, been a recognised but limited exception in favour of those who commit crimes because

they are forced or compelled to do so against their will by the threats of another. Such persons are said, in the language of the criminal law, to act as they do because they are subject to duress.

18. Where duress is established, it does not ordinarily operate to negative any legal ingredient of the crime which the defendant has committed. Nor is it now regarded as justifying the conduct of the defendant, as has in the past been suggested: *Attorney-General v Whelan* [1934] IR 518, 526; Glanville Williams, *Criminal Law, The General Part* (2nd edn, 1961), p 755. Duress is now properly to be regarded as a defence which, if established, excuses what would otherwise be criminal conduct: *Director of Public Prosecutions for Northern Ireland v Lynch* [1975] AC 653, 671, 680, 710–711; *Hibbert v The Queen* (1995) 99 CCC (3d) 193, paras 21, 38, 47, per Lamer CJC.

19. Duress affords a defence which, if raised and not disproved, exonerates the defendant altogether. It does not, like the defence of provocation to a charge of murder, serve merely to reduce the seriousness of the crime which the defendant has committed. And the victim of a crime committed under duress is not, like a person against whom a defendant uses force to defend himself, a person who has threatened the defendant or been perceived by the defendant as doing so. The victim of a crime committed under duress may be assumed to be morally innocent, having shown no hostility or aggression towards the defendant. The only criminal defences which have any close affinity with duress are necessity, where the force or compulsion is exerted not by human threats but by extraneous circumstances, and, perhaps, marital coercion under section 47 of the Criminal Justice Act 1925.

Where the evidence in the proceedings is sufficient to raise an issue of duress, the burden is on the prosecution to establish to the criminal standard that the defendant did not commit the crime with which he is charged under duress: *R v Lynch*, above.

[His lordship referred to Law Commission proposals.]

The prosecution's difficulty is of course the greater when, as is all too often the case, little detail of the alleged compulsion is vouchsafed by the defence until the trial is under way.

21. Having regard to these features of duress, I find it unsurprising that the law in this and other jurisdictions should have been developed so as to confine the defence of duress within narrowly defined limits. Most of these are not in issue in this appeal, but it seems to me important that the issues the House is asked to resolve should be approached with understanding of how the defence has developed, and to that end I shall briefly identify the most important limitations:

(1) Duress does not afford a defence to charges of murder (*R v Howe* [1987] AC 417), attempted murder (*R v Gotts* [1992] 2 AC 412) and, perhaps, some forms of treason (Smith & Hogan, *Criminal Law*, 10th edn, 2002, p 254). The Law Commission has in the past (eg. in 'Criminal Law. Report on Defences of General Application' (Law Com No 83, Cm 556, 1977, paras 2.44–2.46)) recommended that the defence should be available as a defence to all offences, including murder, and the logic of this argument is irresistible. But their recommendation has not been adopted, no doubt because it is felt that in the case of the gravest crimes no threat to the defendant, however extreme, should excuse commission of the crime....

(2) To found a plea of duress the threat relied on must be to cause death or serious injury. In *Alexander MacGrowther's Case* (1746) Fost. 13, 14, 168 ER 8, Lee CJ held:

'The only force that doth excuse, is a force upon the person, and present fear of death.'

But the Criminal Law Commissioners in their Seventh Report of 1843 (p 31, article 6) understood the defence to apply where there was a just and well-grounded fear of death or grievous bodily harm, and it is now accepted that threats of death or serious injury will suffice: *R v Lynch*, above, p 679; *R v Abdul-Hussain* (Court of Appeal (Criminal Division), 17 December 1998, unreported).

(3) The threat must be directed against the defendant or his immediate family or someone close to him: *Smith & Hogan*, above, p 258. In the light of recent Court of Appeal decisions such as *R v Conway* [1989] QB 290 and *R v Wright* [2000] Crim LR 510, the current (April 2003) specimen direction of the Judicial Studies Board suggests that the threat must be directed, if not to the defendant or a member

of his immediate family, to a person for whose safety the defendant would reasonably regard himself as responsible. The correctness of such a direction was not, and on the facts could not be, in issue on this appeal, but it appears to me, if strictly applied, to be consistent with the rationale of the duress exception.

(4) The relevant tests pertaining to duress have been largely stated objectively, with reference to the reasonableness of the defendant's perceptions and conduct and not, as is usual in many other areas of the criminal law, with primary reference to his subjective perceptions. It is necessary to return to this aspect, but in passing one may note the general observation of Lord Morris of Borth-y-Gest in *R v Lynch*, above at p 670:

> '...it is proper that any rational system of law should take fully into account the standards of honest and reasonable men. By those standards it is fair that actions and reactions may be tested.'

(5) The defence of duress is available only where the criminal conduct which it is sought to excuse has been directly caused by the threats which are relied upon.

(6) The defendant may excuse his criminal conduct on grounds of duress only if, placed as he was, there was no evasive action he could reasonably have been expected to take. It is necessary to return to this aspect also, but this is an important limitation of the duress defence and in recent years it has, as I shall suggest, been unduly weakened.

(7) The defendant may not rely on duress to which he has voluntarily laid himself open. The scope of this limitation raises the most significant issue on this part of this appeal, and I must return to it. [See section 11.3.2.5, p 364.]

...22. For many years it was possible to regard the defence of duress as something of an anti-quarian curiosity, with little practical application. Sir James Stephen, with his immense experience, never knew or heard of the defence being advanced, save in the case of married women, and could find only two reported cases: *A History of the Criminal Law of England* (1883), vol II, p 106. Edwards, drawing attention to the absence of satisfactory modern authority, inferred that the defence must be very rare: 'Compulsion, Coercion and Criminal Responsibility' (1951) 14 MLR 297. Professor Hart described duress as a defence of which little is heard: *Punishment and Responsibility* (1960), p 16. This has changed. As Dennis correctly observed in 'Duress, Murder and Criminal Responsibility' (1980) 96 LQR 208,

> 'In recent years duress has become a popular plea in answer to a criminal charge.'

This is borne out by the steady flow of cases reaching the appellate courts over the past 30 years or so, and by the daily experience of prosecutors. As already acknowledged, the House is not invited in this appeal to recast the law on duress. It can only address, piecemeal, the issues which fall for decision. That duress is now regularly relied on as a complete defence to serious criminal charges does not alter the essential task which the House must undertake, but does give it additional practical importance. I must acknowledge that the features of duress to which I have referred in paras 18 to 20 above incline me, where policy choices are to be made, towards tightening rather than relaxing the conditions to be met before duress may be successfully relied on. In doing so, I bear in mind in particular two observations of Lord Simon of Glaisdale in *R v Lynch* above....

> '...your Lordships should hesitate long lest you may be inscribing a charter for terrorists, gang-leaders and kidnappers.' (p 688).
> 'A sane system of criminal justice does not permit a subject to set up a countervailing system of sanctions or by terrorism to confer criminal immunity on his gang.' (p 696).

The restriction on pleading duress to charges of murder and attempted murder is considered in section 11.3.5, p 381.

11.3.2 The nature of the threat

There are a number of issues to consider in relation to the nature of the threat and its sufficiency to found the defence of duress or duress of circumstances.

(i)   Is there a threat of death or serious injury?

(ii)   Against whom must the threat be made?

(iii)   Must the threat emanate from a source external to D?

(iv)   Must the threat of death or serious injury be the sole cause of D committing the crime?

(v)   Can D rely on a threat he has 'courted'?

(vi)   How immediate must the threat of death or serious injury be?

(vii)   Need the duressor specify a particular crime that D must commit?

(viii) Need there be a threat in fact, or is it sufficient that D believes in one?

(ix)   Must the threat be criminal?

11.3.2.1 A threat of death or serious injury

In *DPP for Northern Ireland v Lynch* [1975] AC 653, D was charged with helping others to murder a police officer in Northern Ireland. D drove the gunmen to and from the crime. D pleaded duress as he was ordered to drive the car by a gunman known for his ruthlessness. On the issue of what constitutes a sufficient threat, the House of Lords concluded, per Lord Simon, at 686:

> The type of threat which affords a defence must be one of human physical harm, (including possibly, imprisonment) so that threat of injury [*sic*] to property is not enough . . .

Threats of a non-violent nature, no matter how overwhelming, will not suffice. In *Singh* [1973] 1 All ER 122, D was trafficking in illegal immigrants and pleaded duress based on the threats of blackmail against him. The Court of Appeal held, per Lawton LJ, at 126:

> the submission on duress which counsel for the appellant . . . made was old but wrong. He asked us to say that a man who commits a crime at the request of a blackmailer whom he fears can plead duress. He cannot. Duress arises from threats of violence not exposure.

The Court of Appeal has consistently resisted attempts to widen the scope of the defence by permitting it to be pleaded in circumstances where D fears something less than death or serious injury. For example, in *Vinh van Dao* [2012] EWCA Crim 1717 DD were convicted of cultivating cannabis and sought to plead duress. The trial judge rejected the submission that a threat of false imprisonment was sufficient to permit them to raise the defence. The Court of Appeal, relying on Lord Bingham's judgment in *Hasan* accepted, *obiter*, that this approach was the correct one. Gross LJ stated as follows:

> 44. In our judgment, even if only provisionally, policy considerations point strongly towards confining the defence of duress to threats of death or serious injury and against extending the defence to treat threats of false imprisonment as sufficing. Our reasons follow.
>
> 45. First, there are the difficulties of proof alluded to by Lord Bingham in [*Hasan*], at [20]. These should not be underestimated. If once the evidence is sufficient to permit the defence to be raised, the burden is on the prosecution to disprove it to the criminal standard. In practical terms, the defence may consist of little more than assertions, only expanded upon at trial. It would be all too easy to assert a threat of false imprisonment, especially if it is unnecessary for any such assertion to be underpinned by a threat of death or serious injury.

46. Secondly, having regard to Lord Simon of Glaisdale's words of warning as to the ramifications of the defence of duress, highlighted by Lord Bingham in [*Hasan*] at [22] and set out above, it must be right to hesitate before permitting a widening of the defence and thus its more ready availability.

47. Thirdly, with respect to Mr. Unwin, we are not persuaded that the other limitations of the defence would furnish a sufficient safeguard against unwarranted over-reliance on the defence, if once broadened to encompass the threat of false imprisonment without the threat of death or serious injury.

48. Fourthly, confining the defence within its present relatively narrow limits does not preclude doing justice when sentencing, to reflect a defendant's true culpability—even if, on the facts, falling short of the requirements for reliance on duress: see [*Hasan*] at [22].

49. Accordingly, the policy considerations, foreshadowed in authority, point strongly towards confining the threats necessary to establish duress to those of death or serious injury. For completeness, we are not at all persuaded that it would be illogical to draw the line there but, however that may be, we would in this area place the requirements of practical policy ahead of those of strict logic. All that said, as already explained, our view remains provisional rather than final.

In *Ashley* [2012] EWCA Crim 434, A had retracted a complaint of rape made against her husband (H). A then reasserted that she had been raped and issued proceedings for a non-molestation order in the county court. A was charged with perverting the course of justice by falsely retracting a true allegation of rape. The Court of Appeal considered (i) A's argument that she had a duress defence to perverting the course of justice on account of the domestic violence H subjected her to and (ii) that the prosecution should not have proceeded. In dismissing her appeal, the Court of Appeal held that the defence was subject to clear limitations. There had to be a threat of death or serious injury, which would include rape, and those threats could not be reasonably evaded. It was emphasized that the limitations of the defence of duress should not be eroded. On the facts, A had never suggested to her legal advisers or to the police that when she falsely retracted her truthful complaints she was acting under the threat of violence from H. See Laura Hoyano's case comment on *Ashley* [2013] Crim LR 242.

If she had been threatened by him with violence if she did not withdraw the complaint, as it seems to us, it is unconceivable that she would not have said so at the time. If she was asserting that he forced a retraction by raping her or threatening to rape her, there was no reason why she should not also have explained her retraction of the rapes by reference to any such threats. (at [64] per Lord Judge CJ)

■ *Questions*

1. Is a threat of damage to property, or of blackmail, sometimes as effective on D's will as a threat of violence? Should the law in each case balance the harm threatened against the seriousness of the crime committed?

2. If the harm D caused by submitting to the threat was clearly less than that which would have been inflicted had he defied it, should he be allowed a defence? What of D who commits a serious crime when faced with a threat of serious injury? What is 'serious injury' for these purposes? Can it depend on the crime D has committed when faced with the threat?

11.3.2.2 Against whom must the threat be made?

The Law Commission recommended (LC281 (1993), paras 28.1 et seq) that there should be no formal limitation to any class of persons against whom the threat must be directed. The relationship between D and the person threatened should be only one of the circumstances to be taken into account in determining whether the threat was one which D could reasonably be expected to resist (on which, see section 11.3.5, p 381). In *Shayler* [2001] 1 WLR 2206, the Lord Chief Justice at [49], approving a statement of Rose LJ in *Hussain*, stated that:

> the evil must be directed towards the defendant or a person or persons for whom he has responsibility or, we would add, persons for whom the situation makes him responsible; ...[this extends], by way of example, [to] the situation where the threat is made to set off a bomb unless the defendant performs the unlawful act. The defendant may have not have had any previous connection with those who would be injured by the bomb but the threat itself creates the defendant's responsibility for those who will be at risk if he does not give way to the threat.

■ *Question*

If a bank robber threatens to shoot a customer in the bank unless D, the clerk, hands him the keys, does D have a defence of duress to a charge of being an accessory to the robbery?

11.3.2.3 The threat must be an extraneous one

The threat must have some source extraneous to the defendant himself. In *Rodger and Rose* [1998] 1 Cr App R 143, D who was serving a life sentence was informed that his tariff had been substantially increased. He broke out of prison and raised duress as a defence to the charge of prison-breaking. It was conceded for the purpose of the appeal that he broke out because he had become suicidal and would have committed suicide had he not done so. There was a threat to his life, but since the threat did not come from an extraneous source, it was no defence. To allow it, said the court, 'could amount to a licence to commit crime dependent on the personal characteristics and vulnerability of the offender'. See also *Quayle* [2005] EWCA Crim 1415 (section 11.5.4, p 408 in relation to duress of circumstances/necessity).

11.3.2.4 Duress and mixed motives

There may be several threats, one capable of amounting to duress, the others not: 'Do it or you will be made bankrupt, your adultery will be revealed to your wife and you will be maimed'; or there may be a threat capable of amounting to duress coupled with a promise: 'Do it and there is £100,000 for you; don't do it and you will be shot.'

■ *Question*

Should duress only serve as a defence if it is the sole cause of the crime?

In *Valderrama-Vega* [1985] Crim LR 220, D was charged with importing cocaine from Colombia. His defence was (i) that he and his family had been subjected to threats of death or injury by a Mafia-type organization in Colombia; (ii) that he was heavily indebted and under severe financial pressure; and (iii) that he had been threatened with disclosure of his homosexual inclinations. Neither (ii) nor (iii) could amount to duress. The jury were directed that duress was a defence only if D acted *solely* as the result of threats of death or serious injury. Though D's conviction was upheld, it was held that the use of the word 'solely' was wrong: it 'might have led the jury to convict even though they believed that [D] would not have acted as he did in the absence of threats to his life, if there were other motives or reasons for his actions...'.

In *Ortiz* (1986) 83 Cr App R 173, also concerning a Colombian importer of cocaine who apparently had substantial financial inducements to commit the crime, the judge told the jury to write down the elements of the defence: 'Did he act solely as a result of threats [of death or serious injury].... The important word is "solely" so you can underline that.' The Court of Appeal, dismissing his appeal, held that:

Whatever may be the theoretical justification for such an argument [that a person may commit a crime partly because of threats and partly because of another motive, for example greed], it is difficult to conceive of a situation where a man could reasonably say that he committed a criminal act because his will was overborne by the threats made to him and also because he wanted to make money. Inevitably, one would suppose the jury, in those circumstances, would reject the claim that he acted under duress. The essence of the defence is that the will of the subject of the threats is no longer under his own control because of the fear engendered by those threats. There is no room for other motives for his acts.

■ *Questions*

1. What if D would not have done it for the money alone. He would have resisted the threats but for the offer of the money; but the combination of the money and the threats was irresistible?
2. What if D would have done it for the money alone but was terrified by the threat and would have yielded to it even if no money had been on offer?

Consider also *DPP v Bell* [1992] RTR 335, [1992] Crim LR 176, DC. Bell had been drinking and was over the limit. He admitted that he intended to drive home. A fracas occurred and, fearing serious personal injury, he ran to his car pursued by others and drove off. The Crown Court allowed his appeal against conviction for driving with an excess of alcohol on the ground of duress (sc, of circumstances) and an appeal by way of case stated was dismissed. It had been found as a fact that he drove because of terror and whether he would have driven if there had been no threats was a hypothetical question. He might have changed his mind or been persuaded by his passengers not to drive.

■ *Question*

What if the Crown Court had found as a fact that Bell would have driven home with an excess of alcohol anyway?

11.3.2.5 The (risk of the) threat must not be one D has 'courted'

This element operates as a further important limitation on the defence, and one that has become increasingly important as the courts have sought to prevent the defence being too readily available to those involved in drug-related and terrorist crime, in particular where their involvement demonstrates a degree of prior culpability. The problem commonly arises where D has joined a criminal organization and, having committed a crime as part of that organization or on behalf of it, D pleads that members of the organization threatened death or serious injury to him/others unless he committed the crime.

■ *Questions*

What limitations might be placed on the defence to meet these concerns? What if D has not voluntarily joined the organization? Perhaps he was under duress to join? To what type of risk must D be exposing himself? Must D be aware of the risk that he is exposing himself to or is it sufficient that he ought to have been aware? Must D be aware of the type of crime he might be compelled to commit?

R v Hasan
(section 11.3.1, p 358), http://www.bailii.org/uk/cases/UKHL/2005/22.html

[Lord Bingham referred to the certified question:]

'Whether the defence of duress is excluded when as a result of the accused's voluntary association with others:

(i) he foresaw (or possibly should have foreseen) the risk of being subjected to any compulsion by threats of violence, or

(ii) only when he foresaw (or should have foreseen) the risk of being subjected to compulsion to commit criminal offences, and, if the latter,

(iii) only if the offences foreseen (or which should have been foreseen) were of the same type (or possibly of the same type and gravity) as that ultimately committed.'

The Crown contend for answer (i) in its objective form. The defendant commends the third answer, omitting the first parenthesis.

30. In their definition of duress the Criminal Law Commissioners of 1879 included a proviso:

'Provided also, that he [the defendant] was not a party to any association or conspiracy the being party to which rendered him subject to such compulsion.'

A qualification to very similar effect is to be found in the criminal codes of [many jurisdictions.] But its implications were not for many years examined in the British courts.

31. The issue might have been raised in *R v Lynch*, [section 11.3.2.1] where the appellant claimed to have been press-ganged by the IRA, but the argument in that case was largely directed to the question whether the defence of duress was open to a defendant charged as a secondary party to murder. It was in *R v Fitzpatrick* [1977] NI 20, another IRA case, that the Court of Criminal Appeal in Northern Ireland had occasion to consider the matter in depth. The ratio of the decision is found in the judgment of the court delivered by Lowry LCJ at p 33:

'A person may become associated with a sinister group of men with criminal objectives and co-ercive methods of ensuring that their lawless enterprises are carried out and thereby voluntarily expose him-self to illegal compulsion, whether or not the group is or becomes a proscribed organization . . . if a person voluntarily exposes and submits himself, as the appellant did, to illegal compulsion, he cannot rely on the duress to which he has voluntarily exposed himself as an excuse either in respect of the crimes he commits against his will or in respect of his continued but unwilling association with those capable of exercising upon him the duress which he calls in aid.'

32. That statement was no doubt drafted with the peculiar character of the IRA in mind. *R v Sharp* [1987] QB 853 arose from criminal activity of a more routine kind committed by a gang of robbers. The trial judge's direction which was challenged on appeal is fully quoted in *R v Shepherd* (1987) 86 Cr App R 47, 51, and was to this effect:

'. . . but in my judgment the defence of duress is not available to an accused who voluntarily exposes and submits himself to illegal compulsion.

It is not merely a matter of joining in a criminal enterprise; it is a matter of joining in a criminal enterprise of such a nature that the defendant appreciated the nature of the enterprise itself and the attitudes of those in charge of it, so that when he was in fact subjected to compulsion he could fairly be said by a jury to have voluntarily exposed himself and submitted himself to such compulsion.'

The Court of Appeal (Lord Lane CJ, Farquharson and Gatehouse JJ) upheld that direction in *R v Sharp*, expressing the principle at p 861:

'. . . where a person has voluntarily, and with knowledge of its nature, joined a criminal organisation or gang which he knew might bring pressure on him to commit an offence and was an active member when he was put under such pressure, he cannot avail himself of the defence of duress.'

In *R v Shepherd*, above, the criminal activity was of a less serious kind: the question which the jury should have been (but were not) directed to consider (p 51) was 'whether the appellant could be said to have taken the risk of P's violence simply by joining a shoplifting gang of which he [P] was a member'.

33. *R v Ali* is summarised at [1995] Crim LR 303, but the ratio of the decision more clearly appears from the transcript of the judgment given by the Court of Appeal (Lord Taylor of Gosforth CJ, Alliott and Rix JJ) on 14 November 1994. The appellant claimed to have become involved in drug dealing and to have become indebted to his supplier, X, who (he said) had given him a gun and told him to obtain the money from a bank or building society the following day, failing which he would be killed. The appellant accordingly committed the robbery of which he was convicted. In directing the jury on the defence of duress advanced by the defendant the trial judge had said:

> 'The final question is this: did he, in obtaining heroin from Mr X and supplying it to others for gain, after he knew of Mr X's reputation for violence, voluntarily put himself in a position where he knew that he was likely to be forced by Mr X to commit a crime?'

It was argued by the appellant that the judge should have said 'forced by Mr X to commit armed robbery', but this was rejected, and the court held that by 'a crime' the jury could only have understood the judge to be referring to a crime other than drug dealing. The principle stated by the court on p 7 of the transcript was this:

> 'The crux of the matter, as it seems to us, is knowledge in the defendant of either a violent nature to the gang or the enterprise which he has joined, or a violent disposition in the person or persons involved with him in the criminal activity he voluntarily joined. In our judgment, if a defendant voluntarily participates in criminal offences with a man "X", whom he knows to be of a violent disposition and likely to require him to perform other criminal acts, he cannot rely upon duress if "X" does so.'

(In this case, it would seem that the defence of duress should in any event have failed, for lack of immediacy, since the threat was not to be executed until the following day, and therefore the defendant had the opportunity to take evasive action).

34. In its Working Paper No 55 of 1974, the Law Commission in para 26 favoured

> 'a limitation upon the defence [of duress] which would exclude its availability where the defendant had joined an association or conspiracy which was of such a character that he was aware that he might be compelled to participate in offences of the type with which he is charged.'

This reference to 'offences of the type with which he is charged' was, in substance, repeated in the Law Commission's 'Report on Defences of General Application' (Law Com No 83) of 1977, paras 2.38 and 2.46(8). . . . But there was no warrant for this gloss in any reported British authority until the Court of Appeal (Roch LJ, Richards J and Judge Colston QC) gave judgment in *R v Baker and Ward* [1999] 2 Cr App R 335. The facts were very similar to these in *R v Ali*, above, save that the appellants claimed that they had been specifically instructed to rob the particular store which they were convicted of robbing. The trial judge had directed the jury (p 341):

> 'A person cannot rely on the defence of duress if he has voluntarily and with full knowledge of its nature joined a criminal group which he was aware might bring pressure on him of a violent kind or require him if necessary to commit offences to obtain money where he himself had defaulted to the criminal group in payment to the criminal group.'

This was held to be a misdirection (p 344):

> 'What a defendant has to be aware of is the risk that the group might try to coerce him into committing criminal offences of the type for which he is being tried by the use of violence or threats of violence.'

At p 346 this ruling was repeated:

> 'The purpose of the pressure has to be to coerce the accused into committing a criminal offence of the type for which he is being tried.'

The appeals were accordingly allowed and the convictions quashed.

35. Counsel for the defendant in the present case contends (as the Court of Appeal accepted) that this ruling was correct and that the trial judge in the present case misdirected the jury because he did not insist on the need for the defendant to foresee pressure to commit the offence of robbery of which he was convicted.

In *R v Heath* (Court of Appeal: Kennedy LJ, Turner and Smedley JJ, 7 October 1999, [2000] Crim LR 109) the appellant again claimed that he had become indebted to a drug supplier, and claimed that he had been compelled by threats of physical violence to collect the consignment of drugs which gave rise to his conviction. His defence of duress failed at trial, rightly as the Court of Appeal held. In its judgment, Kennedy LJ said:

'The appellant in evidence conceded that he had put himself in the position where he was likely to be subjected to threats. He was therefore, in our judgment, not entitled to rely on those same threats as duress to excuse him from liability for subsequent criminal conduct.'

The court found it possible to distinguish *R v Baker and Ward*, observing:

'It is the awareness of the risk of compulsion which matters. Prior awareness of what criminal activity those exercising compulsion may offer as a possible alternative to violence is irrelevant.'

[His lordship referred to *R v Harmer* (Court of Appeal: May LJ, Goldring and Gross JJ, 12 December 2001 [2002] Crim LR 401) . . . in which the court concluded:]

'We cannot accept that where a man voluntarily exposes himself to unlawful violence, duress may run if he does not foresee that under the threat of such violence he may be required to commit crimes. There is no reason in principle why that should be so.'

37. The principal issue between the Crown on one side and the appellant and the Court of Appeal on the other is whether *R v Baker and Ward* correctly stated the law. To resolve that issue one must remind oneself of the considerations outlined in paras 18–22 [extracted at section 11.3.1, p 358] above. The defendant is seeking to be wholly exonerated from the consequences of a crime deliberately committed. The prosecution must negative his defence of duress, if raised by the evidence, beyond reasonable doubt. The defendant is, *ex hypothesi*, a person who has voluntarily surrendered his will to the domination of another. Nothing should turn on foresight of the manner in which, in the event, the dominant party chooses to exploit the defendant's subservience. There need not be foresight of coercion to commit crimes, although it is not easy to envisage circumstances in which a party might be coerced to act lawfully. In holding that there must be foresight of coercion to commit crimes of the kind with which the defendant is charged, *R v Baker and Ward* mis-stated the law.

There remains the question, which the Court of Appeal left open in para 75 of their judgment, whether the defendant's foresight must be judged by a subjective or an objective test: i.e. does the defendant lose the benefit of a defence based on duress only if he actually foresaw the risk of coercion or does he lose it if he ought reasonably to have foreseen the risk of coercion, whether he actually foresaw the risk or not? I do not think any decided case has addressed this question, and I am conscious that application of an objective reasonableness test to other ingredients of duress has attracted criticism: see, for example, Elliott, 'Necessity, Duress and Self-Defence' [1989] Crim LR 611, 614–615, and the commentary by Professor Ashworth on *R v Safi* [2003] Crim LR 721, 723. The practical importance of the distinction in this context may not be very great, since if a jury concluded that a person voluntarily associating with known criminals ought reasonably to have foreseen the risk of future coercion they would not, I think, be very likely to accept that he did not in fact do so. But since there is a choice to be made, policy in my view points towards an objective test of what the defendant, placed as he was and knowing what he did, ought reasonably to have foreseen. I am not persuaded otherwise by analogies based on self-defence or provocation for reasons I have already given. The policy of the law must be to discourage association with known criminals, and it should be slow to excuse the criminal conduct of those who do so. If a person voluntarily becomes or remains associated with others engaged in criminal activity in a situation where he knows or ought reasonably to know that he may be the subject of compulsion by them or their associates, he cannot rely on the defence of duress to excuse any act which he is thereafter compelled to do by them. It is not necessary in this case to decide whether or to what extent that principle applies if an undercover agent penetrates a criminal gang for bona fide law enforcement purposes and is compelled by the gang to commit criminal acts.

39. I would answer this certified question by saying that the defence of duress is excluded when as a result of the accused's voluntary association with others engaged in criminal activity he foresaw or ought reasonably to have foreseen the risk of being subjected to any compulsion by threats of violence.

In *Ali* [2008] EWCA Crim 716, the Court of Appeal applied the full rigour of Lord Bingham's objective approach in *Hasan*, and arguably went further, holding that if D has joined with others whom he ought to have realized might subject him to threats of violence, he is denied the defence of duress. The defence is lost irrespective of whether he has joined an existing criminal gang or not. D was convicted of the robbery at knifepoint of a vehicle owner. His plea of duress had been rejected at trial on the basis that D had voluntarily joined with the alleged duressor, BH, a co-accused in the robbery. D knew that BH carried a knife and had been warned not to associate with BH. The Court of Appeal upheld the conviction. In *Hasan*, Lord Bingham answered the certified question by saying that:

the defence of duress is excluded when as a result of the accused's voluntary association *with others engaged in criminal activity* he foresaw or ought reasonably to have foreseen the risk of being subjected to any compulsion by threats of violence. (emphasis added)

The italicized words might suggest that the defence is only lost where D joins a criminal gang. The Court of Appeal in *Ali* rejected any such limitation, drawing on the approval by Lord Bingham of the trial judge's direction in *Hasan* (quoting it at [14] in *Hasan*):

Did the defendant voluntarily put himself in the position, in which he knew he was likely to be subjected to threats? You look to judge that in all the circumstances . . . It is for you to decide. It is right to say he says he did stop associating but [the duressor] kept finding him. It may not be wholly straightforward. It is for you to consider and it is a relevant consideration because if someone voluntarily associates with the sort of people who he knows are likely to put pressure on him, then he cannot really complain, if he finds himself under pressure. If you are sure that he did voluntarily put himself in such a position, the defence fails and he was guilty. If you are not sure and you have not been sure about all of the other questions, then you would find him not guilty.

Although most of the old reported authorities involve D joining a criminal gang, the defence is denied in much broader circumstances: whenever D *ought to* have foreseen a risk of threats.

■ *Question*

D is a drug addict. He associates with X, a drug dealer. Will D have any opportunity to rely on a defence of duress if X subsequently threatens D with serious injury or death unless D commits crimes to acquire money to pay his debts for drugs bought?

R v Hasan
(section 11.3.1, p 358), http://www.bailii.org/uk/cases/UKHL/2005/22.html

Baroness Hale's minority speech in *Hasan* adopts a more subjective approach, suggesting that the defence is denied only where D has himself foreseen a risk that he will be compelled by threats of violence to commit crime. It is submitted that this is a preferable approach to that in *Ali*.

Baroness Hale [her ladyship referred to the Law Commission's Report, *Legislating the Criminal Code: Offences against the Person and General Principles* (Law Com No 218, 1993) (published when her Ladyship was a Law Commissioner) in which the Commission had recommended placing the burden on the accused:]

...I remain attracted by the Law Commission's proposals. The real reasons for the unpopularity of the defence are those given by Lord Lane CJ in Howe: that it is readily raised by the least deserving of people but difficult for the prosecution to disprove. We are told by Mr Perry [for the Crown] that, perhaps because of advances in forensic science which have made crimes easier to detect and more difficult to defend, duress is now very frequently raised, often late in the day, by defendants up and down the country.

73. If we are not to have legislation to alter the burden of proof, and I agree that it is not open to us to do it ourselves, then I understand your lordships' desire to maintain the objective standards set by Lord Lane in *Graham*. But it seems to me that the best counter to Lord Lane's concerns is the *Fitzpatrick* doctrine [that a defendant is denied the defence of duress if he courted the risk of being threatened] which is the issue in this case. Logically, if it applies, it comes before all the other questions raised by the defence: irrespective of whether there was a threat which he could not reasonably be expected to resist, had the defendant so exposed himself to the risk of such threats that he cannot now rely on them as an excuse? If even on his own story he had done so, then the defence can be withdrawn from the jury without more ado; if that issue has to be left to the jury, but they resolve it against him, there is no need for them to consider the other questions.

...

The foreseeable risk should be one of duress: that is, of threats of such severity, plausibility and immediacy that one might be compelled to do that which one would otherwise have chosen not to do. The battered wife knows that she is exposing herself to a risk of unlawful violence if she stays, but she may have no reason to believe that her husband will eventually use her broken will to force her to commit crimes. For the same reason, I would say that it must be foreseeable that duress will be used to compel the person to commit crimes of some sort. I have no difficulty envisaging circumstances in which a person may be coerced to act lawfully. The battered wife knows very well that she may be compelled to cook the dinner, wash the dishes, iron the shirts and submit to sexual intercourse. That should not deprive her of the defence of duress if she is obliged by the same threats to herself or her children to commit perjury or shoplift for food.

78. But this brings me to a concern which I have had throughout this case. It is one thing to deny the defence to people who choose to become members of illegal organisations, join criminal gangs, or engage with others in drug-related criminality. It is another thing to deny it to someone who has a quite different reason for becoming associated with the duressor and then finds it difficult to escape. I do not believe that this limitation on the defence is aimed at battered wives at all, or at others in close personal or family relationships with their duressors and their associates, such as their mothers, brothers or children. The Law Commission's Bills all refer to a person who exposes himself to the risk 'without reasonable excuse'. The words were there to cater for the police infiltrator (see Law Com No 83, para 2.37) but they are also applicable to the sort of association I have in mind. The other elements of the defence, narrowly construed in accordance with existing authority, are more than adequate to keep it within bounds in such cases.

■ *Question*
Do you agree with Baroness Hale's approach?

11.3.2.6 How immediate must the threat be?

> ■ *Questions*
>
> 1. Should the defence be denied to D who has an opportunity to avoid the threat by taking evasive action? Only if D had no opportunity to avoid the threat? Only if he had no *reasonable* opportunity? Only if he believed he had no opportunity?
> 2. Should a failure for D to seek help from the police to protect him from the threats automatically deny him a defence of duress?

R v Hudson and Taylor

[1971] EWCA Crim 2, Court of Appeal, Criminal Division, http://www.bailii.org/ew/cases/EWCA/Crim/1971/2.html

(Lord Parker CJ, Widgery LJ and Cooke J)

The accused, H and T, were girls aged 17 and 19. They were the main prosecution witnesses at the trial of W, on a charge of wounding. They both failed to identify W and testified that they did not know him. W was acquitted. H and T were tried for perjury and admitted that their evidence was false. H said that she had been approached and warned that she would be 'cut up' if she 'told on' W. H passed this on to T, who had also been warned by other girls. The accused were frightened and decided to tell lies to avoid the consequences. Their decision was confirmed when, on arriving in court, they saw one of the threatening men in the public gallery.

The recorder directed that the defence of duress was not open because there was no present immediate threat capable of being carried out there and then, since the accused were in court in the presence of the judge and the police. On appeal, the Crown argued that the ruling could be upheld on the additional ground that the accused should have neutralized the threat by seeking police protection when they came to court or beforehand.

[Lord Widgery CJ, having stated the facts, continued:]

This appeal raises two main questions; first, as to the nature of the necessary threat and, in particular, whether it must be 'present and immediate'; secondly, as to the extent to which a right to plead duress may be lost if the accused has failed to take steps to remove the threat as, for example, by seeking police protection.

It is essential to the defence of duress that the threat shall be effective at the moment when the crime is committed. The threat must be a 'present' threat in the sense that it is effective to neutralise the will of the accused at that time. Hence an accused who joins a rebellion under the compulsion of threats cannot plead duress if he remains with the rebels after the threats have lost their effect and his own will has had a chance to re-assert itself (*McGrowther's case* [(1746) Fost 13] and *A-G v Whelan* [[1934] IR 518]). Similarly a threat of future violence may be so remote as to be insufficient to over-power the will at the moment when the offence was committed, or the accused may have elected to commit the offence in order to rid himself of a threat hanging over him and not because he was driven to act by immediate and unavoidable pressure. In none of these cases is the defence of duress available because a person cannot justify the commission of a crime merely to secure his own peace of mind.

When, however, there is no opportunity for delaying tactics, and the person threatened must make up his mind whether he is to commit the criminal act or not, the existence at that moment of threats sufficient to destroy his will ought to provide him with a defence even though the threatened injury may not follow instantly, but after an interval. This principle is illustrated by *Subramaniam v Public Prosecutor* [[1956] 1 WLR 965], when the appellant was charged in Malaya with unlawful possession of ammunition and was held by the Privy Council to have a defence of duress, fit to go to the jury, on his plea that he had been compelled by terrorists to accept the ammunition and feared for his safety if the terrorists returned.

In the present case the threats of Farrell were likely to be no less compelling, because their execution could not be effected in the court room, if they could be carried out in the streets of Salford the same night. Insofar, therefore, as the recorder ruled as a matter of law that the threats were not sufficiently present and immediate to support the defence of duress we think that he was in error. He should have left the jury to decide whether the threats had overborne the will of the appellants at the time when they gave the false evidence.

Counsel for the Crown, however, contends that the recorder's ruling can be supported on another ground, namely, that the appellants should have taken steps to neutralise the threats by seeking police protection either when they came to court to give evidence, or beforehand. He submits on grounds of public policy that an accused should not be able to plead duress if he had the opportunity to ask for protection from the police before committing the offence and failed to do so. The argument does not distinguish cases in which the police would be able to provide effective protection, from those when they would not, and it would, in effect, restrict the defence of duress to cases where the person threatened had been kept in custody by the maker of the threats, or where the time interval between the making of the threats and the commission of the offence had made recourse to the police impossible. We recognise the need to keep the defence of duress within reasonable bounds but cannot accept so severe a restriction on it. The duty, of the person threatened, to take steps to remove the threat does not seem to have arisen in an English case but in a full review of the defence of duress in the Supreme Court of Victoria (*Hurley and Murray* [[1967] VR 526]), a condition of raising the defence was said to be that the accused 'had no means, with safety to himself, of preventing the execution of the threat'.

In the opinion of this court it is always open to the Crown to prove that the accused failed to avail himself of some opportunity which was reasonably open to him to render the threat ineffective, and that on this being established the threat in question can no longer be relied on by the defence. In deciding whether such an opportunity was reasonably open to the accused the jury should have regard to his age and circumstances, and to any risks to him which may be involved in the course of action relied on.

In our judgment the defence of duress should have been left to the jury in the present case, as should any issue raised by the Crown and arising out of the appellants' failure to seek police protection. The appeals will, therefore, be allowed and the convictions quashed.

Appeals allowed

In *Cole* [1994] Crim LR 582, D was convicted of robbing two building societies and pleaded duress on the basis that he had been threatened by money lenders to whom he was in debt. The Court of Appeal held that a plea of duress was not available as the money lenders had not stipulated that he commit robbery to meet their demands. There was not the degree of immediacy and directness required between the peril threatened and the offence charged.

In *Abdul-Hussain* [1999] Crim LR 570, the appellants were convicted of hijacking, contrary to the Aviation Security Act 1982, s 1(1). They were Shiite Muslims from Southern Iraq, living in Sudan and they feared return by the Sudanese authorities to Iraq, followed by torture and probable death. Using imitation hand grenades and plastic knives, they hijacked an aircraft bound for Amman and eventually landed in England. The judge withdrew the defence of duress from the jury.

Following *Hudson and Taylor*, in the previous extract, p 370, the Court of Appeal in *Abdul-Hussain* held that the defence should have been left to the jury. While the threat must be 'imminent', it need not be 'immediate'; nor need the reaction be 'spontaneous'. The appellants were in no immediate danger of death or serious bodily harm, but there was evidence that the threat was hanging over them, that it was 'imminent'. In *Abdul-Hussain*, the court gave a vivid and persuasive example to support its decision.

If Anne Frank had stolen a car to escape from Amsterdam and been charged with theft, the tenets of English law would not, in our judgment, have denied her a defence of duress of circumstances, on the ground that she should have waited for the Gestapo's knock on the door.

In *Hasan* (section 11.3.1, p 358), the trial judge had directed the jury that, 'The third question is: Could the defendant have avoided acting as he did without harm coming to his family? . . . If you are sure that he could have avoided acting as he did without harm coming to his family, again the defence fails and he is guilty.' In the House of Lords, Lord Bingham observed that:

24. [T]he Court of Appeal held that the judge had misdirected the jury on question 3 because, it was held, there was no suggestion that the defendant could have taken evasive action. This may, or may not, on the facts, be so, and this suggested misdirection does not feature in the question on duress certified for the opinion of the House the third question put by the judge, and regularly put in such cases, whether or not correctly put on the facts of this case, in my opinion focuses attention on a cardinal feature of the defence of duress, and I would wish to warn against any general notion that question 3 'collapses' into [the question about whether D has responded reasonably to the threat as he reasonably perceives it to be; see section 11.3.4, p 378].

[His lordship referred to the position in other jurisdictions.]

26. The recent English authorities have tended to lay stress on the requirement that a defendant should not have been able, without reasonably fearing execution of the threat, to avoid compliance. Thus Lord Morris of Borth-y-Gest in *R v Lynch*, above, at p 670, emphasised that duress

'must never be allowed to be the easy answer of those who can devise no other explanation of their conduct nor of those who readily could have avoided the dominance of threats nor of those who allow themselves to be at the disposal and under the sway of some gangster-tyrant.'

Lord Simon of Glaisdale gave as his first example of a situation in which a defence of duress should be available (p 687):

'A person, honestly and reasonably believing that a loaded pistol is at his back which will in all probability be used if he disobeys'

In the view of Lord Edmund-Davies (p 708) there had been

'for some years an unquestionable tendency towards progressive latitude in relation to the plea of duress.'

27. In making that observation Lord Edmund-Davies did not directly criticise the reasoning of the Court of Appeal in its then recent judgment in *R v Hudson and Taylor* [1971] 2 QB 202, but that was described by Professor Glanville Williams as 'an indulgent decision' (*Textbook of Criminal Law*, 2nd edn, 1983, p 636), and it has in my opinion had the unfortunate effect of weakening the requirement that execution of a threat must be reasonably believed to be imminent and immediate if it is to support a plea of duress. [His lordship referred to the decision in *Hudson and Taylor* extracted at the beginning of this section.]

The Court of Appeal placed reliance on the decision of the Privy Council in *Subramaniam v Public Prosecutor* [1956] 1 WLR 965. That case, however, involved a defendant who sought at trial to advance a defence of duress under a section of the Penal Code of the Federated Malay States which provided that, with certain exceptions 'nothing is an offence which is done by a person who is compelled to do it by threats, which, at the time of doing it, reasonably cause the apprehension that instant death to that person will otherwise be the consequence'.

The appeal was allowed because evidence relied on by the appellant to show that he had had a reasonable apprehension of instant death was wrongly excluded. It is hard to read that decision as authority for the Court of Appeal's conclusion. I can understand that the Court of Appeal in *R v Hudson and Taylor* had sympathy with the predicament of the young appellants but I cannot, consistently with principle, accept that a witness testifying in the Crown Court at Manchester has no opportunity to avoid complying with a threat incapable of execution then or there. When considering necessity in *R v Cole* [1994] Crim LR 582, 583, Simon Brown LJ, giving the judgment of the court, held that the peril relied on to support the plea of necessity lacked imminence and the degree of directness and immediacy required of the link between the suggested peril and the offence charged, but in *R v Abdul-Hussain*, above, the Court of Appeal declined to follow these observations to the extent that they were inconsistent with *R v Hudson and Taylor*, by which the court regarded itself as bound.

28. The judge's direction on question 3 was modelled on the JSB specimen direction current at the time, and is not in my opinion open to criticism. It should however be made clear to juries that if the retribution threatened against the defendant or his family or a person for whom he reasonably feels responsible is not such as he reasonably expects to follow immediately or almost immediately on his failure to comply with the threat, there may be little if any room for doubt that he could have taken evasive action, whether by going to the police or in some other way, to avoid committing the crime with which he is charged.

■ *Questions*

1. Following *Hasan*, would Anne Frank have been best advised to wait until the Gestapo knocked at the door to be able to plead duress when charged with stealing a car to escape to freedom?

2. Should the defence be available where D has not taken the opportunity to seek official protection? The draft Criminal Law Bill, cl 25(2), provides, as one of the conditions of the defence, that D does the act 'because he knows or believes... (c) that there is no other way of preventing the threat being carried out.' Is that a satisfactory solution?

More recently, in *Batchelor* [2013] EWCA Crim 2638 the Court of Appeal reiterated the criticisms that were made of *Hudson and Taylor* in *Hasan*. Elias LJ noted that D could have gone to the police at any time over a period of two and a half years. His lordship stated:

The law requires a certain degree of fortitude to be shown by victims in circumstances such as these. The teenaged girls were no doubt in genuine and real fear of their safety in *Hudson*, but that was not a justification for applying the defence of duress because they had the opportunity to avoid complying with the threat. The CACD in that case had allowed its sympathy to distort legal principles. Were we to accede to this appeal, then even assuming that the account of the intimidation was true, we would be doing the same thing. (at [15])

11.3.2.7 Must the threat be backed by a demand to commit a nominated crime?

In the paradigmatic case of duress, the defendant will have been told by the threatening party 'perform this crime or else'. In *Cole* [1994] Crim LR 582, A's defence to robbing two building societies was that moneylenders to whom he owed money had threatened him, his girlfriend and his child. The defence of duress by threats did not apply because the moneylenders did not stipulate that he commit robbery to meet their demands. Simon Brown LJ: 'In our judgment it is plain that the defence of duress by threats can only apply when the offence charged (the offence which the accused asserts he was constrained to commit) is the very offence which was nominated by the person making the threat, ie when the accused was required by the threat to commit the offence charged....' Subsequently, in *Ali* [1995] Crim LR 303, D, a heroin addict, was convicted of robbing a building society and claimed that his supplier, X, who had a reputation for violence, had demanded repayment of money D owed him. Further, that X had provided D with a gun and told D to get the money by the following day from a bank or a building society. The Court of Appeal upheld his conviction but appeared to accept that a threat is capable of amounting to duress when the duressee is charged with robbing a particular building society not specified by the duressor. In view of the strict approach taken to the issue of immediacy in *Hasan*, doubt must be cast on *Ali*.

11.3.2.8 The defendant must believe that there is a threat; it need not exist in fact

There is no requirement for there to be a threat in fact. It is sufficient that D believes that there is a threat of the relevant gravity. If the defence was only available where there was a threat in fact, D could not plead duress where threatened with an unloaded gun, nor where D escaped from prison erroneously believing it to be on fire. This would be unduly restrictive. If the threat did in fact exist, it would be wholly irrelevant if D was unaware of it. It becomes relevant only if, and to the extent that, D is aware of it.

■ *Questions*

Is the existence of the threat any more relevant when D knows of it than when he mistakenly believes in it? Is not his culpability determined exclusively by his state of mind? Is there a case for requiring D's belief to be reasonable in order to deny the defence to those suffering from irrational fears?

R v Safi and others

[2003] EWCA Crim 1809, [2003] Crim LR 721, Court of Appeal, Criminal Division

(Longmore LJ, Hooper and Cox JJ)

Afghan members of the Organization of Young Intellectuals of Afghanistan (the 'Organization') hijacked a plane which ultimately landed at Stansted. The defence said that the Taliban had discovered that the Organization was its political opponent, and had arrested and tortured four of its members who between them knew the names of the appellants and most of the other members of the Organization. The defendants claimed that their fear of persecution at the hands of the Taliban constituted a defence of duress (of circumstances). The trial judge directed that the defence failed unless there was evidence that there was in fact, or might in fact have been, an imminent peril to the defendants or their families. S appealed on the basis that the defence should be available if he *reasonably* believed that if he had not acted in the way he had, he (and/or the family) would have been killed or seriously injured.

Lord Justice Longmore [his lordship stated the facts and the grounds of appeal and discussed the inconsistent directions given at the first trial and on the retrial. His lordship then revisited *Graham* where Lord Lane CJ, delivering the judgment of the court, set out how a jury should be directed:]

'The Crown having conceded that the issue of duress was open to the appellant and was raised on the evidence, the correct approach on the facts of this case would have been as follows: (1) Was the defendant, or may he have been, impelled to act as he did because, *as a result of what he reasonably believed [the duressor] had said or done*, he had good cause to fear that if he did not so act [the duressor] would kill him or (if this is to be added) cause him serious physical injury? (2) If so, have the prosecution made the jury sure that a sober person of reasonable firmness, sharing the characteristics of the defendant, would not have responded *to whatever he reasonably believed [the duressor] said or did* by taking part in the killing? The fact that a defendant's will to resist has been eroded by the voluntary consumption of drink or drugs or both is not relevant to this test.' (Emphasis added.)

The passages we have [italicized] show that the defendant's conduct is to be judged by what he reasonably believed [the duressor] had said or done both in the first and second questions. It can, no doubt, be said that Lord Lane CJ's formulation of the first part of the direction was *obiter*, but on any view it was carefully considered and must have been intended as a guide for judges who had to direct juries on the defence of duress in future. Moreover, the directions which Lord Lane CJ stated should be given to the jury were approved by Lord Mackay in the House of Lords in *R v Howe* [1987] AC 417, 459 as 'entirely correct'. They have subsequently been followed more than once by the Court of Appeal. In *R v Conway* [1989] QB 290, 298C Lord Woolf giving the judgment of the court said that 'the approach must be that indicated by Lord Lane CJ in *Graham*'. *Conway* was itself approved and followed in *R v Martin* (1989) 88 Cr App R 343.

[The court referred to other cases with contradictory approaches:]

Although it is true that the Crown in *Graham* conceded that duress did arise on the facts and although it is true that the court was critical of that concession, that criticism does not, in our view, undermine the considered direction which Lord Lane CJ thought it right to formulate. It is clear that it is the defendant's reasonable belief in relation to the words or conduct said to constitute the threat for the purpose of the defence of duress that is critical; that is separate from the fact that the defendant must also have 'good cause' to fear death or physical injury. Mr Houlder QC for the Crown submitted that what Lord Lane CJ meant to convey was that there had to be an actual threat *and* the defendant had, reasonably, to believe that there was such a threat. But we cannot so read Lord Lane's words; indeed, if there was a threat in fact, it would be superfluous to superimpose a further requirement that the defendant must reasonably believe there to be a threat. It cannot, moreover, be right to disregard a considered decision as to the appropriate direction to be given to a jury, even if there is, in the background, a dubious concession on the facts by the Crown. The decision was intended to be a guide for future cases and should be so regarded.

Mr Houlder's submission is, in any event, not without its practical difficulties. If a defendant commits a crime as a result of a gun being pointed at him, would it be open to the Crown to prove there was no threat in fact, because the gun was not loaded? If a prisoner escapes from prison thinking there is a fire and he does not intend to 'stay to be burnt' (to adopt the Tudor example cited in *Southwark LBC v Williams* [1971] 1 Ch 734, 746), can the Crown prove there was no fire in fact so that, however reasonable the prisoner's belief may be, he is guilty of the offence of escape from lawful custody? In the present case itself, the judge's ruling led to the Crown calling evidence from the Home Office to prove that there was, in fact, no risk of the defendants' return to Afghanistan from England. The defence, by way of riposte, called evidence from Mr Ian Macdonald QC to show that such risk did, in fact, exist. None of this evidence was necessary in the first trial.

If, moreover, Mr Houlder's submission were correct, hearsay evidence of the existence of a threat would, strictly, be inadmissible. Yet in cases of duress it is routinely admissible as evidence of the defendant's state of mind.... To adopt Rose LJ V-P's example [in *Abdul-Hussain* [1999] Crim LR 570, section 11.3.2.6, p 371], if Anne Frank would have been entitled to invoke the defence of duress before the Gestapo knocked on her door, it might very well be because a sympathiser had informed her that the Gestapo were on their way.

Appeals allowed

The court was clearly concerned by the anxiety that its judgment created a terrorists' or hijackers' charter. It stated:

In the light of some of the newspaper comments on the announcement of our decision, we think it right to add that we do not for a moment accept that the success of this appeal is a charter for future hi-jackers. The only reason why this appeal has succeeded is that there was a misdirection in relation to the law as explained to the jury. An earlier jury was given a direction that, in one respect may have been too generous to the defendants, and was unable to agree. We have every confidence that future juries given a correct direction, in accordance with the law set out in *R v Graham* in 1982, will convict in appropriate cases and acquit, if it is right to do so.

The decision clearly does not give carte blanche to hijackers. It decides only that the defence of duress was wrongly explained to the jury. If the defence was left to the jury, they would have had to consider whether the hijacking was a reasonable and proportionate response to the threat—an objectivexquestion. The onus would of course have been on the prosecution to prove that it was not; but is not hijacking such a dangerous and terrifying operation that the prosecution might well have succeeded?

11.3.2.9 Need the threats constitute a crime?

In *Jones and others* [2004] EWCA Crim 1981 (affirmed on other grounds in the House of Lords [2006] UKHL 16), Ds were charged with conspiracy to commit criminal damage at an RAF base. Their defences were duress/necessity, lawful excuse under the Criminal Damage Act 1971, s 5(2)(b), and the prevention of crime under the Criminal Law Act 1967, s 3. Each of these defences was predicated on the argument that the UK was engaged in an unlawful act of war against Iraq. At a preliminary hearing, Grigson J ruled that the issue of the legality of the war could not be adjudicated on/decided by domestic courts as the UK Government was exercising its prerogative powers relating to foreign policy. His lordship made further rulings in relation to the defences. The Court of Appeal held that the defence of duress of circumstances was potentially a domestic law (ie not international law) defence to a domestic law offence, but no domestic crime was committed by the UK Government. The executive's action in declaring and waging war was, in itself, a lawful exercise of its powers under the prerogative. The trial court would therefore have to consider the extent to which necessity might afford a defence to the defendants in the light of their beliefs on that basis.

D. Ormerod in the Criminal Law Review ([2005] Crim LR 122) observes:

The conclusion is that no 'domestic crime' is involved by the UK's act of war on Iraq. From that the court concludes that the defences of duress and necessity are unavailable. With respect, it is not clear that this follows. Taking first the defence of duress of circumstances, the requirement is that D (or those he acts to protect) faces an imminent threat of death or serious injury. That does not require that the death or serious injury threatened against him/them is criminal in origin. D might plead the defence where he steals V's car to take to safety his family when they are faced with a threat of death from a looming cloud of noxious gas that has escaped from a factory without criminal fault. The jury, in evaluating the reasonableness of D's response must surely have regard to the type of threat D faces. How can the jury assess the proportionality of D's actions in ignorance of the lawfulness of the action D is responding to?

Turning to necessity, there is no requirement that there is a threat of death or serious injury, nor even a criminal act facing D or those he seeks to protect. The court's suggestion that necessity is only a 'domestic defence to a domestic crime' is, it is submitted, far too narrow. Clearly it is its operation as a domestic defence that matters, but since there is not an offence, let alone a domestic one, how can it be limited to acts against domestic crimes? Admittedly, even on a more liberal interpretation of the defence of necessity, it is not clear that the defence would be available to Ds in the present case since the jury would have to be convinced that the actions were reasonable and proportionate to protect people for whom Ds could reasonably regard themselves as being responsible.

11.3.3 Evaluating D's perception of the threat

■ *Questions*

1. Must the defendant *reasonably* believe that he or someone for whom he is responsible is under an immediate threat of death or serious injury, etc (and he has not voluntarily exposed himself to a risk of threats)?

2. Is it enough that D genuinely, though mistakenly, believes he is under threat?

R v Graham
[1982] 1 All ER 801, Court of Appeal, Criminal Division

(Lord Lane CJ, Taylor and McCullough JJ)

The appellant (G) was a homosexual living in 'a bizarre ménage à trois' with his wife (W) and another homosexual, King (K). G suffered from an anxiety state. He was taking valium which, according to medical evidence, would make him more susceptible to bullying. K was a violent man and had in 1978 tipped G and W off a settee because they were embracing and K was jealous. G knew K had been guilty of other acts of violence. On 27 June 1980 K attacked W with a knife. W then went to G's mother's home. G and K stayed, drinking heavily, while G also took valium. K suggested getting rid of the wife once and for all. G induced her to return by pretending that he had cut his wrists. She knelt beside him as he lay face down on the floor pretending to be seriously hurt. K put a kettle flex round her neck, saying, 'What's it like to know you are going to die?' She put up her hands to the flex. K told G to pull on one end of the flex. He did so, he said, only because he was afraid of K. The plug which he was pulling came off the flex, leaving it in doubt whether his act made any contribution to W's death. G was convicted of murder.

Lord Lane CJ [first dealt with the fact that the Crown at the trial conceded that, on those facts, it was open to the defence to raise the issue of duress to murder. That aspect of the law is now governed by the decision in *Howe* (section 11.3.5, p 382)]:

As a matter of public policy, it seems to us essential to limit the defence of duress by means of an objective criterion formulated in terms of reasonableness. Consistency of approach in defences to criminal liability is obviously desirable. Provocation and duress are analogous. [NB: provocation has since been replaced with a defence of loss of control discussed in Chapter 16.] In provocation the words or actions of one person break the self-control of another. In duress the words or actions of one person break the will of another. The law requires a defendant to have the self-control reasonably to be expected of the ordinary citizen in his situation. It should likewise require him to have the steadfastness reasonably to be expected of the ordinary citizen in his situation. So too with self-defence, in which the law permits the use of no more force than is reasonable in the circumstances. And, in general, if a mistake is to excuse what would otherwise be criminal, the mistake must be a reasonable one.

It follows that we accept counsel for the Crown's submission that the direction in this case was too favourable to the appellant. The Crown having conceded that the issue of duress was open to the appellant and was raised on the evidence, the correct approach on the facts of this case would have been as follows: (1) was the defendant, or may he have been, impelled to act as he did because, as a result of what he reasonably believed King had said or done, he had good cause to fear that if he did not so act King would kill him or (if this is to be added) cause him serious physical injury? (2) if so, have the prosecution made the jury sure that a sober person of reasonable firmness, sharing the characteristics of the defendant, would not have responded to whatever he reasonably believed King said or did by taking part in the killing? The fact that a defendant's will to resist has been eroded by the voluntary consumption of drink or drugs or both is not relevant to this test.

Appeal dismissed

D's perception of a threat of death or serious injury must be reasonable.

> ■ *Question*
>
> To what extent do a defendant's personal incapacities affect the requirements that the perception of the threat of death or serious injury and the commission of the crime must be reasonable?

In *Graham*, Lord Lane, equating duress with self-defence in this respect, thought that in self-defence the law permits only force that is reasonable in the circumstances and that only a reasonable mistake would excuse. But less than two years later in *Gladstone Williams* (1987) 78 Cr App R 276, section 11.6.1.1, p 415, Lord Lane himself took a different view regarding self-defence, holding that an unreasonable belief might excuse if it was honestly held. In *Gladstone Williams*, Lord Lane followed *Kimber* [1983] 3 All ER 316, [1983] 1 WLR 1118, a case of indecent assault, where Lawton LJ appreciated the general effect of *DPP v Morgan* [1976] AC 182. Should this have required a change of mind by Lord Lane regarding duress as well? In *DPP v Rogers* [1998] Crim LR 202, DC, the court seems to have mistakenly assumed that the Law Commission recommendation for reform of the law (Law Com No 218, pp 49–51) had been implemented. *Abdul-Hussain*, however, confirms that it is still the law that a defendant cannot rely on an unreasonable mistake of fact in order to found a defence of duress of either variety. See also *Safi* (section 11.3.2.8).

11.3.4 Evaluating D's response to the perceived threat

As we saw in *Graham*, if the jury think that D may reasonably have held the belief alleged and that that belief may have given him good cause to fear, the next question is whether 'a sober person of reasonable firmness sharing the characteristics of the defendant' would have responded as he did.

> ■ *Questions*
>
> 1. What characteristics of the individual defendant are relevant?
> 2. What if D has irrational fears or is simply more timid than most? Should he be able to rely on a defence of duress based on implausible threats?

A weak will and irresolution are not relevant. In *Bowen* [1996] 2 Cr App R 157, [1996] Crim LR 577, CA, it was held that a low IQ was not a relevant characteristic:

> We do not see how low IQ, short of mental impairment or mental defectiveness, can be said to be a characteristic that makes those who have it less courageous and less able to withstand threats and pressure.

The Court of Appeal reviewed the cases and confirmed the following principles.

(1) The mere fact that the accused is more pliable, vulnerable, timid or susceptible to threats than a normal person are not characteristics with which it is legitimate to invest the reasonable/ordinary person for the purpose of considering the objective test.

(2) The defendant may be in a category of persons who the jury may think less able to resist pressure than people not within that category. Obvious examples are age,

where a young person may well not be so robust as a mature one; possibly sex, though many women would doubtless consider they had as much moral courage to resist pressure as men; pregnancy, where there is added fear for the unborn child; serious physical disability, which may inhibit self protection; recognized mental illness or psychiatric condition, such as post-traumatic stress disorder leading to learned helplessness. (See the case of *GAC*, later in this section, p. 381.)

(3) Characteristics which may be relevant in considering loss of control, because they are a 'circumstance' relevant to something other than D's general capacity for tolerance and self restraint, will not necessarily be relevant in cases of duress.

(4) Characteristics due to self-induced abuse, such as alcohol, drugs or glue-sniffing, cannot be relevant.

(5) Psychiatric evidence may be admissible to show that the accused is suffering from some mental illness, mental impairment or recognized psychiatric condition, provided persons generally suffering from such conditions may be more susceptible to pressure and threats and thus to assist the jury in deciding whether a reasonable person suffering from such a condition might have been impelled to act as the defendant did. It is not admissible simply to show that in the doctor's opinion an accused, who is not suffering from such illness or condition, is especially timid, suggestible or vulnerable to pressure and threats. Nor is medical opinion admissible to bolster or support the credibility of the accused.

(6) Where counsel wishes to submit that the accused has some characteristic which falls within point (2), this must be made plain to the judge.

(7) In the absence of some direction from the judge as to what characteristics are capable of being regarded as relevant, the direction approved in *Graham* without more will not be as helpful as it might be, since the jury may be tempted, especially if there is evidence, as there was in this case, relating to suggestibility and vulnerability, to think that these are relevant. In most cases it is probably only the age and sex of the accused that is capable of being relevant. If so, the judge should, as he did in this case, confine the characteristics in question to these (per Stuart Smith LJ at 166–167).

If the defendant with low IQ is no less able to resist pressure than a person with average IQ, there is no need to afford him any special treatment. But the court said that persons suffering from a 'recognised mental illness or psychiatric condition, such as post traumatic stress disorder leading to learned helplessness' (see *Emery* (1992) 14 Cr App R (S) 394, later in this section, p 380) are a category whose condition should be taken into account. Certainly this is so on the subjective issue, that is, whether D's will was in fact 'overborne'; but the question is whether they can be taken into account in applying the objective test. In *Hurst* [1995] 1 Cr App R 82 at 90, Beldam LJ said 'we find it hard to see how the person of reasonable firmness can be invested with the characteristics of a person who lacks reasonable firmness'.

In duress only characteristics affecting the gravity of the threat would be relevant. Such characteristics, depending on the circumstances, might include age, sex, pregnancy, physical disability—anything which made the threat more frightening. Cf the defence of loss of control in Chapter 16. The divergence between the two defences has been created by s 54(3) of the Coroners and Justice Act 2009. See section 16.2.9. Characteristics which made it harder for D to resist it, making him a person of less than reasonable firmness—and that would seem to include 'recognized psychiatric conditions'—would not be relevant. Though this was not what the Law Commission intended, their recommendation, if enacted, might be construed to reach this result. The threat must be one which:

in all the circumstances (including any of his personal characteristics *which affect its gravity*) he cannot reasonably be expected to resist. (emphasis added)

A further difficulty is that, according to one expert opinion, there are no recognized criteria identifying a group whose ability to withstand threats is reduced and that the test in *Bowen* is unworkable: A. Buchanan and G. Virgo, 'Duress and Mental Abnormality' [1999] Crim LR 517 at 529. However, the courts continue to apply it. In *Rogers* [1999] 9 *Archbold News* 1, CA, it was held that the appellant's history of 'Asperger Syndrome and other co-morbid conditions which would have made him peculiarly amenable [to threats]' should have been taken into account. On the other hand, in *Hegarty* [1994] Crim LR 353 evidence that the defendant was 'emotionally unstable' and 'in a grossly elevated neurotic state' was not to be taken into account in applying the objective test. In *Hurst* (earlier in this section) the judge refused to admit the evidence of a psychiatrist of the effect of sexual abuse upon the defendant as a child. It was held that he was right to do so, even if it indicated that D, due to her experiences, suffered from a personality defect which made her lack the firmness and resolution to be expected of someone of her age and sex.

Horder [1994] Crim LR 334 is also critical of this aspect of the Law Commission's proposal. He puts the case of a practising paedophile who has been threatened with serious injury unless he has intercourse with a child: 'The fact that he is inured to intercourse with children might well be something that made it less reasonable to expect him to resist the threat.' But does the fact that D is a paedophile affect the 'gravity of the threat'? The threat to beat him up might be more terrifying because D is small, or a haemophiliac, or otherwise physically vulnerable; but is it any more terrifying because he happens to be a paedophile? The fact that D is a 'racist' may cause him more readily to succumb to a demand that he assault a person of a different race; but does it affect the gravity of a threat to slash his face if he does not do so? Are not paedophilia and racism irrelevant by any test?

The Law Commission recently confirmed that in its view:

in deciding whether a person of reasonable firmness might have acted as the defendant did, the jury should be able to take into account all the circumstances of the defendant, including his or her age but not any other characteristics which bear upon his or her capacity to withstand duress. (LC304, para 6.86)

■ *Question*

If the threats are sufficient to wear down the will of even a defendant of ordinary fortitude, will they suffice for the defence of duress whoever the defendant is?

A simple threat to twist an arm is one thing. A threat to twist an arm after 24 hours of continuous arm-twisting is quite another. The person of reasonable fortitude who would certainly resist the former may well succumb to the latter. Attention cannot reasonably be confined to the final act which caused the defendant to give way. In *Emery* (1992) 14 Cr App R (S) 394, D relied unsuccessfully on duress to a charge of cruelty to a child. The Court of Appeal held that expert medical evidence admitted at the trial was allowed to go too far but that it would have been properly admitted if it had been confined to 'an expert account of the cause of the condition of dependent helplessness, the circumstances in which it might arise and what level of abuse would be required to produce it.' Lord Taylor CJ said:

The question for the doctors was whether a woman of reasonable firmness with the characteristics of Miss Emery, if abused in the same manner which she said, would have had her will crushed so that she could not have protected the child.

Obviously a woman of reasonable firmness suffering from a condition of dependent helplessness would be a contradiction in terms.

■ *Questions*

Is the point that the alleged history of violence said to have produced that condition is all part of the duress? Does the jury have to envisage an ordinary woman who is of reasonable firmness before the history of violence begins and consider whether, by the time of the alleged offence, her will would have been so overborne that she would be unable to resist the threat?

In *Emery*, the ill-treatment of the child was an ongoing state of affairs. If the defendant was a person of reasonable firmness when she began to commit the crime she was presumably then liable and continued to be liable for acts done up to the point when it became unreasonable to expect her to escape from or resist the threat. After that point, she had the defence but only in respect of acts done to the child thereafter. If she had a defence to the cruelty offences would she not, once reduced to 'dependent helplessness', also have had a defence to any other crimes committed in response to her oppressor's threats—for example, to rob a bank or to inflict grievous bodily harm? In *GAC* [2013] EWCA Crim 1472, the Court of Appeal dealt with G's claim of duress to a charge of importing drugs. G claimed that she had not been in a position to plead duress at trial as she was a victim of domestic violence at the hands of X who was responsible for making her import the drugs. There was evidence of X's violence to her and expert psychiatric reports that G was suffering from battered woman syndrome (BWS) and was in a state of 'learned helplessness' at the time. The court held that duress by threats may be available in such a case. The court accepted that the approach to the BWS claim for duress was counter-intuitive. A woman who was claiming BWS would be relying on her learned helplessness which would itself have produced inconsistencies in her accounts and may result in her withdrawing allegations of violence committed against her. Duress was not available on the evidence in this case because, although G suffered some violence at the hands of X, it was not of the kind that might raise the possibility of duress. The court noted that not every woman who suffered from domestic violence went on to suffer from BWS, and not every woman who suffered from BWS could claim the defence of duress. The question was whether the BWS was so severe that D's will was overborne; in this case, the evidence did not suggest that it was.

11.3.5 To which crimes is duress available?

■ *Questions*

1. If D reasonably perceives himself or someone for whom he is responsible to be under an immediate threat of death or serious injury, is it reasonable for him to commit any crime in response? Even murder?

2. Should it make any difference whether D commits the crime as a principal or a secondary party?

In the 1970s, the House of Lords held, in *Lynch v DPP* [1975] 1 All ER 913, that duress could operate as a defence to murder where D acted as a secondary party in the killing. In the Privy Council in *Abbott v The Queen* [1976] 3 All ER 340 a few months later, the Board held that duress was no defence to murder committed as a principal offender. The confusion was resolved and the law settled by the House of Lords in the following case.

R v Howe and Bannister; R v Burke and Clarkson
[1987] 1 All ER 771, House of Lords

(Lord Hailsham LC, Lords Bridge, Brandon, Griffiths and Mackay)

There were two separate cases conjoined on appeal before the House of Lords.

(1) The appellants, Howe and Bannister, were charged with murder together with Murray and Bailey who pleaded guilty. The four of them drove Elgar, to whom Murray had offered a job, to a remote spot. Murray told the appellants that Elgar was a 'grass' and they were going to kill him. Both appellants kicked and punched Elgar and he was finally strangled by Bailey. The appellants said they attacked Elgar only because they believed they would receive the same treatment if they did not. Very similar events resulted in the death of another man, Pollitt. The appellants appealed against their conviction for murder on the ground, *inter alia*, that the judge had misdirected the jury that the defence of duress was not available to a person charged as a principal in the first degree to murder (ie the killer).

(2) Burke shot a criminal, Botton, on the doorstep of Botton's house. The prosecution alleged that he had done this at the request of Clarkson who was anxious to prevent Botton giving evidence against him. Clarkson's defence was that he had nothing to do with the shooting. Burke's defence was that he had agreed to shoot Botton only out of fear of Clarkson; but that, in the event, the gun went off accidentally and the killing was unintentional and therefore only manslaughter. See section 17.2, p 594. Burke appealed on the ground, *inter alia*, that the judge had misdirected the jury in not leaving the defence of duress to them on the murder charge. The appeals were dismissed by the Court of Appeal.

One of the questions certified for the House of Lords was:

Is duress available to a person charged with murder as principal in the first degree (the actual killer)?

The House dismissed the appeal, holding that the defence of duress is not available to a person charged with murder whether as principal or as accessory.

[**Lord Hailsham** and **Lord Bridge** made speeches dismissing the appeal.]

Lord Brandon [expressed his agreement with Lord Mackay:]

I cannot pretend, however, that I regard the outcome as satisfactory. It is not logical, and I do not think it can be just, that duress should afford a complete defence to charges of all crimes less grave than murder, but not even a partial defence to a charge of that crime. I say nothing as to treason, for that is not here in issue. I am persuaded, nevertheless, to agree with my noble and learned friend by three considerations. Firstly, it seems to me that, so far as the defence of duress is concerned, no valid distinction can be drawn between the commission of murder by one who is a principal in the first degree and one who is a principal in the second degree. Secondly, I am satisfied that the common law of England has developed over several centuries in such a way as to produce the illogical, and as I think unjust, situation to which I have referred. Thirdly, I am convinced that, if there is to be any alteration in the law on such an important and controversial subject, that alteration should be made by legislation and not by judicial decision.

[**Lord Griffiths** made a speech dismissing the appeal.]

Lord Mackay:

The question whether duress is available as a defence in law to a person charged with murder as a principal in the first degree (the actual killer) has not been the subject of a previous decision of this

House. The matter received consideration in this House in *Lynch v DPP for Northern Ireland* [[1975] 1 All ER 913] It was accepted by the majority of the House in *Lynch's* case that at that time the balance of such judicial authority as existed was against the admission of the defence of duress in cases of . . . murder [as a principal offender]. The writers were generally agreed in saying that the defence was not available in murder although later writers appear to have said so following Hale. The references are *Hale's Pleas of the Crown* (I Hale PC (1736) 51, 434); *East's Pleas of the Crown* (I East PC (1803) 294); *Blackstone's Commentaries on the Laws of England* (4 Bl Corn (1809 edn) 30); Glanville Williams *Criminal Law: The General Part* (2nd edn, 1961) p 759, para 247; *Russell on Crime* (12th edn, 1964) vol 1, pp 90–91; Smith and Hogan *Criminal Law* (3rd edn, 1973) pp 166–167. . . .

Counsel for Burke, Bannister and Howe in his very detailed and careful submission accepted this position as reflecting the law up to the time of *Lynch's* case. Since that time, on this question there has been the decision of the Privy Council in *Abbott v R* [1976] 3 All ER 140, [1977] AC 755, a majority decision in which the minority consisted of Lord Wilberforce and Lord Edmund-Davies, who, along with Lord Morris, had constituted the majority in *Lynch's* case. Counsel for these appellants submitted that your Lordships should hold that the reasoning of the majority in *Lynch's* case should be applied and extended to cover the present cases. . . .

The first question, accordingly, that arises in this appeal is whether any distinction can be made between this case and *Lynch's* case.

[His lordship quoted from the speeches in *Lynch's* case.]

In my opinion, it is plain from these quotations that the majority of this House in *Lynch's* case, and particularly Lord Morris, were reaching a decision without committing themselves to the view that the reasoning which they had used would apply to an actual killer.

While therefore *Lynch's* case was decided by reasoning which does not extend to the present case, the question remains whether there is a potential distinction between this case and *Lynch's* case by which to determine whether or not the defence of duress should be available. I consider that *Smith and Hogan* were perfectly right in the passage cited from that work by Lord Edmund-Davies to which I have already referred. ['The difficulty about adopting a distinction between the principal and secondary parties as a rule of law is that the contribution of the secondary party to the death may be no less than that of the principal': 3rd edn, 1973, p 166.] I have not been able to find any writer of authority that is able to give rational support for the view that the distinction between principals in the first degree and those in the second degree is relevant to determine whether or not duress should be available in a particular case of murder. . . .

I believe that the discussions of this matter have shown that at one extreme, namely that of the person who actually kills by a deliberate assault on a person who is then present, there is a fair body of support for the view either that the defence of duress should not be allowed or that the practical result will be, even if it is allowed, that it will never be established, while there is also strong support for the view that at the other extreme minor participation which the law regards as sufficient to impute criminal guilt should be capable of being excused by the defence of duress.

So far, I have not found any satisfactory formulation of a distinction which would be sufficiently precise to be given practical effect in law and at the same time differentiate between levels of culpability so as to produce a satisfactory demarcation between those accused of murder who should be entitled to resort to the defence of duress and those who were not.

The House is therefore, in my opinion, faced with the unenviable decision of either departing altogether from the doctrine that duress is not available in murder or departing from the decision of this House in *Lynch's* case. While a variety of minor attacks on the reasoning of the majority were mounted by counsel for the Crown in the present case, I do not find any of these sufficiently important to merit departing from *Lynch's* case on these grounds. I do, however, consider that, having regard to the balance of authority on the question of duress as a defence to murder prior to *Lynch's* case, for this House now to allow the defence of duress generally in response to a charge of murder would be to effect an important and substantial change in the law. In my opinion too, it would involve a departure from the decision in the famous case of *R v Dudley and Stephens* (1884) 14 QBD 273, [1881–5] All ER Rep 61. The justification for allowing a defence of duress to a charge of murder is that a defendant should be excused who killed as the only way of avoiding death himself or preventing the death of some close relation such as his own well-loved child. This essentially was the dilemma which Dudley and Stephens faced and in denying their defence the court refused to allow this consideration to be used in a defence to murder. If that refusal was right in the case of Dudley and Stephens it cannot be wrong in the present appeals. Although the result of recognising the defence advanced in that case would be that no crime was committed and in the case with which we are concerned that a murder was committed and a particular individual was not guilty of it (subject to the consideration of the second certified question) that does not distinguish the two cases from the point of view now being considered.

To change the law in the manner suggested by counsel for the appellants in the present case would, in my opinion, introduce uncertainty over a field of considerable importance.

So far I have referred to the defence of duress as if it were a precisely defined concept, but it is apparent from the decisions that it is not so. [His lordship referred to difficulties with the defence identified by Lord Simon in *Lynch*'s case [1975] AC 653 at 686, [1975] 1 All ER 913 at 931.]

To say that a defence in respect of which so many questions remain unsettled should be introduced in respect of the whole field of murder is not to promote certainty in the law.

[His lordship referred to the fact that the Law Commission had made reform recommendations in 1985.]

I notice that in the Law Commission report dated 28 March 1985 (Law Com no 143), which contains a report to the Law Commission in respect of the codification of the criminal law by a team from the Society of Public Teachers of Law, doubt is expressed on the soundness of this recommendation in Law Com no 83. This particular matter does not arise in the circumstances of the present case, but the great difficulty that has been found in obtaining a consensus of informed opinion on it is just one illustration of the uncertain nature of what would be introduced into this most important area of the criminal law if the defence of duress were to be available.

Since the decision in *Lynch*'s case the Law Commission have published in their report (Law Com no 83), to which I have referred, the result of an extensive survey of the law relating to duress and have made recommendations on it which have been laid before Parliament. In my opinion the problems which have been evident in relation to the law of murder and the availability of particular defences is not susceptible of what Lord Reid described as a solution by a policy of make do and mend (see *Myers v DPP* [1965] AC 1001 at 1002, [1964] 2 All ER 881 at 886). While I appreciate fully the gradual development that has taken place in the law relating to the defence of duress, I question whether the law has reached a sufficiently precise definition of that defence to make it right for us sitting in our judicial capacity to introduce it as a defence for an actual killer for the first time in the law of England. Parliament, in its legislative capacity, although recommended to do so by the report of the Law Commission, has not taken any steps to make the defence of duress available generally to a charge of murder even where it has the power to define with precision the circumstances in which such a defence would be available.

It has also been suggested for consideration whether, if the defence of duress is to be allowed in relation to murder by the actual killer, the defence should have the effect, if sustained, of reducing the crime to that of manslaughter by analogy with the defence of provocation. Provocation itself was introduced into the law by judicial decision in recognition of human frailty, although it is now the subject of a statutory provision (see the Homicide Act 1957, s 3) and it was suggested that the same approach might be taken now with regard to duress.... [See now loss of control discussed in Chapter 16.]

In my opinion we would not be justified in the present state of the law in introducing for the first time into our law the concept of duress acting to reduce the charge to one of manslaughter even if there were grounds on which it might be right to do so. On that aspect of the matter the Law

Commission took the view that where the defence of duress had been made out it would be unjust to stigmatise the person accused with a conviction and there is clearly much force in that view.

The argument for the appellants essentially is that, *Lynch's* case having been decided as it was and there being no practical distinction available between *Lynch's* case and the present case, this case should be decided in the same way. The opposite point of view is that, since *Lynch's* case was concerned not with the actual killer but with a person who was made guilty of his act by the doctrine of accession, the correct starting point for this matter is the case of the actual killer. In my opinion this latter is the correct approach. The law has extended the liability to trial and punishment faced by the actual killer to those who are participants with him in the crime and it seems to me, therefore, that, where a question as important as this is in issue, the correct starting point is the case of the actual killer. It seems to me plain that the reason that it was for so long stated by writers of authority that the defence of duress was not available in a charge of murder was because of the supreme importance that the law afforded to the protection of human life and that it seemed repugnant that the law should recognise in any individual in any circumstance, however extreme, the right to choose that one innocent person should be killed rather than another. In my opinion that is the question which we still must face. Is it right that the law should confer this right in any circumstances, however extreme? While I recognise fully the force of the reasoning which persuaded the majority of this House in *Lynch's* case to reach the decision to which they came in relation to a person not the actual killer, it does not address directly this question in relation to the actual killer. I am not persuaded that there is good reason to alter the answer which Hale gave to this question. No development of the law or progress in legal thinking which has taken place since his day has, to my mind, demonstrated a reason to change this fundamental answer. In the circumstances which I have narrated of a report to Parliament from the Law Commission concerned, inter alia, with this very question, it would seem particularly inappropriate to make such a change now. For these reasons, in my opinion, the first certified question should be answered in the negative.

It follows that, in my opinion, the House should decline to follow the decision in *Lynch's* case.

Appeals dismissed

Lord Hailsham criticized what he took to be the view of the majority in *Lynch* and the minority in *Abbott* that 'the ordinary man of reasonable fortitude is not to be supposed to be capable of heroism if he is asked to take an innocent life rather than sacrifice his own'.

See K. J. M. Smith, 'Must Heroes Behave Heroically?' [1989] Crim LR 622 and 'Duress and Steadfastness: In Pursuit of the Unintelligible' [1999] Crim LR 363.

■ *Questions*

1. Should a person be liable to conviction for murder for failing to be a hero?

2. Are there no circumstances in which a person of reasonable fortitude would submit to threats and kill?

3. If duress were a defence to murder, would a person have a defence if he submitted to threats which would not prevail upon a person of reasonable fortitude?

Lord Hailsham also thought that a man who takes the life of another to save his own cannot claim that he is choosing the lesser of two evils.

■ *Question*

Suppose that D is told, 'Kneecap X'—that is, cause him serious bodily harm—'or you, your wife and family will all be killed'. If D does as he is told, and X dies, could not D, being charged with murder, claim that he chose the lesser of two evils?

The argument that Parliament had not acted on the recommendation of the Law Commission some years earlier that the defence of duress should be extended to murder is a weak one. In *Hasan*, Lord Bingham referred to the Law Commission's view:

The Law Commission has in the past (eg. in 'Criminal Law. Report on Defences of General Application' (Law Com No 83, Cm 556, 1977, paras 2.44–2.46)) recommended that the defence should be available as a defence to all offences, including murder, and the logic of this argument is irresistible.

■ *Question*

Is it a good argument against allowing the defence of duress to murder that in 'hard cases' no prosecution will be brought (the 'duressee' may be a prosecution witness on the trial of the duressor) or that, if he is prosecuted and convicted of murder (and sentenced to life imprisonment), he will soon be let out (on licence for the rest of his life, of course)?

Wilson [2007] EWCA Crim 1251 illustrates the now well-established principle that duress cannot be a defence to a charge of murder, even if the person seeking to rely on that defence is a child and even if his alleged role in the murder was that of a secondary party acting out of fear of an adult perpetrator. The 13-year-old defendant in this case was not able to plead duress, but argued instead that he had 'not known what he was doing in that his mind did not go with his actions'. His police interview did not support this defence, but suggested that he acted under duress from his father—the very defence he was precluded from running. The Court of Appeal observed that there 'might be grounds for criticising' a rule that denied a child any defence to a charge of murder on the ground of adult or parental duress, but had no choice but to apply the law as it stood.

■ *Question*

Could D have pleaded simply a lack of intention? Whether a defence of duress would have been accepted had the alleged offence been something other than murder remains a matter for speculation.

The Law Commission has recommended on more than one occasion that duress become a defence to murder—with the burden of proof on the accused. See Law Com Report No 304, *Murder, Manslaughter and Infanticide* (2006), Ch 6. The Law Commission had provisionally proposed that duress would only be a partial defence to what would in their proposed scheme be first degree murder, reducing the crime to one of second degree murder (LCCP 177, para 7.32). In its final report, the Commission rejected that option and rejected a number of other options for reform (LC304). The Law Commission preferred the option that duress should be a full defence to first degree murder, second degree murder and attempted murder:

The argument that duress should be a full defence to first degree murder has a moral basis. It is that the law should not stigmatise a person who, on the basis of a genuine and reasonably held belief, intentionally killed in fear of death or life threatening injury in circumstances where a jury is satisfied that an ordinary person of reasonable fortitude might have acted in the same way. If a reasonable person might have acted as D did, then the argument for withholding a complete defence is undermined. In the words of Professor Ormerod, 'if the jury find that the defendant has, within the terms of the defence, acted reasonably, it seems unfair to treat him as a second degree murderer or even a manslaughterer'.

6.44 Further, the option also accords with the way that duress operates as a complete defence in relation to other offences and it is, therefore, conducive to coherence and consistency as we pointed out above.

6.45 One respondent who favoured duress being a partial defence to first degree murder did so because he thought that this was the best way of accommodating each side in the moral debate. We see the force of this argument. However, we believe that if the arguments of principle and morality point decidedly in one direction, our recommendation should reflect what we believe to be a principled approach rather than one based on a desire to accommodate the different viewpoints.

6.46 An important counter-argument is that the law rightly attaches special sanctity to innocent human life and that this should preclude duress ever being a full defence to first degree murder. We now depart from this view, in so far as we believe that the 'sanctity of life' argument was not meant to deal with examples such as ten year olds or peripheral secondary parties becoming involved in killing under duress. The 'sanctity of life' argument may be more confusing than illuminating in this context.

. . .

6.52 We also think it important to bear in mind the stringent qualifying conditions that attach to the defence. In particular, the majority of the House of Lords in [*Hasan*] were firmly of the view that the defence ought not to be available to D if he or she saw or ought to have foreseen the risk of being subjected to any compulsion by threats of violence. We believe that this will serve to exclude the most unmeritorious cases where the defence should simply not be available. It is true that it will not in itself exclude all undeserving cases but we believe that juries should be trusted not to accept the defence in undeserving cases.

6.53 Above all, we believe that it is essential to recognise and accord proper weight to the fact that for the defence to succeed, a jury must form a judgement that a reasonable person in D's position might have committed first degree murder. If a jury forms that judgement, we believe that D should be completely exonerated despite having intentionally killed. . . .

6.76 We recommend that for duress to be a full defence to [our recommendation for] first degree murder, second degree murder and attempted murder, the threat must be one of death or life-threatening harm. (footnotes omitted)

The Law Commission also rejected any distinction based on whether or not the defendant acted in response to a threat against his or her own person. Similarly, the Commission rejected a distinction in application of the defence between principal offenders and secondary parties.

■ *Question*

Should the burden of proof be reversed where D pleads duress to murder?

Lord Bingham in *Hasan* at [20], section 11.3.1, p 358, expressed reservation as to whether the reverse burden would withstand scrutiny by the House of Lords.

It took many years and many cases to establish the generality of the principle in *Woolmington* [1935] AC 462, that the burden of disproving defences which have been properly raised is, with the anomalous exception of insanity, on the prosecution. The case for shifting the onus of proof of duress (whether by threats or of circumstances) to the defendant was very fully argued by the Law Commission in Law Com Report No 218, *Legislating the Criminal Code* (1993), pp 59–62, and again in Law Com Report No 304, *Murder, Manslaughter and Infanticide* (2006), Ch 6.

■ *Questions*

1. If duress is no defence to murder, what about attempted murder or s 18 of the Offences Against the Person Act 1861?

2. Can it be justifiable that a person who is acquitted on grounds of duress of an offence under the Offences Against the Person Act 1861, s 18 (section 18.4.3, p 659) should become guilty of murder if his victim subsequently dies? How can it be that the act which was excusable as long as the victim lived became inexcusable when he died?

R v Gotts

[1992] 1 All ER 832, House of Lords

(Lords Keith, Templeman, Jauncey, Lowry and Browne-Wilkinson)

Gotts, aged 16, seriously injured his mother with a knife. He pleaded not guilty to a charge of attempted murder. He sought to adduce evidence that he was acting under duress because his father had threatened to shoot him unless he killed her. The judge ruled that the evidence was inadmissible since duress was not a defence to a charge of attempted murder.

Gotts then pleaded guilty and was put on probation for three years. His appeal against conviction, on the ground that the judge's ruling was wrong, was dismissed by the Court of Appeal [1991] 1 QB 660, [1991] 2 All ER 1. He appealed to the House of Lords.

[**Lord Keith** (dissenting) said that he agreed with Lord Lowry and would allow the appeal. (1) There was much to be said in favour of the view that the defence was withheld only in the case of murder and treason. (2) Murder is a crime in a category of its own. (3) He found it difficult to accept that a person acting under duress had a truly evil intent. (4) It was unsatisfactory that a defence should be available on a charge of wounding with intent to cause GBH and not on a charge of attempted murder—there being in many cases a nice question whether an offence was the one or the other. The issue was much better left to Parliament.]

[**Lord Templeman** agreed with Lord Keith that the matter would be best decided by Parliament but he would dismiss the appeal for the reasons given by Lord Jauncey.]

Lord Jauncey [having reviewed the authorities and arguments continued:]

As the question is still open for decision by your Lordships it becomes a matter of policy how it should be answered. It is interesting to note that there is no uniformity of practice in other common law countries. The industry of Mr Miskin who appeared with Mr Farrer disclosed that in Queensland, Tasmania, Western Australia, New Zealand and Canada duress is not available as a defence to attempted murder but that it is available in almost all the states of the United States of America. The reason why duress has for so long been stated not to be available as a defence to a murder charge is that the law regards the sanctity of human life and the protection thereof as of paramount importance. Does that reason apply to attempted murder as well as to murder? As Lord Griffiths pointed out in the passage to which I have just referred—an intent to kill must be proved in the case of attempted murder but not necessarily in the case of murder. Is there logic in affording the defence to one who intends to kill but fails and denying it to one who mistakenly kills intending only to injure? If I may give two examples. (1a) A stabs B in the chest intending to kill him and leaves him for dead. By good luck B is found whilst still alive and rushed to hospital where surgical skill saves his life. (1b) C stabs D intending only to injure him and inflicts a near identical wound. Unfortunately D is not found until it is too late to save his life. I see no justification or logic or morality for affording a defence of duress to A who intended to kill when it is denied to C who did not so intend. (2a) E plants in a passenger aircraft a bomb timed to go off in mid-flight. Owing to bungling it explodes while the aircraft is still on the ground with the result that some 200 passengers suffer physical and mental injuries of which many are permanently disabling, but no one is killed. (2b) F plants a bomb in a light aircraft intending to disable the pilot before it takes off but in fact it goes off in mid-air killing the pilot who is the sole occupant of the airplane. It would in my view be both offensive to common sense and decency that E if he established duress should be acquitted and walk free without a stain on his character notwithstanding the appalling results which he has achieved, whereas F who never intended to kill should, if convicted in the absence of the defence, be sentenced to life imprisonment as a murderer.

It is of course true that withholding the defence in any circumstances will create some anomalies but I would agree with Lord Griffiths that nothing should be done to undermine in any way the highest duty of the law to protect the freedom and lives of those that live under it (see [1987] 1 All ER 771 at 789, [1987] AC 417 at 444). I can therefore see no justification in logic, morality or law in affording to an attempted murderer the defence which is withheld from a murderer. The intent required of an attempted murderer is more evil than that required of a murderer and the line which divides the two offences is seldom, if ever, of the deliberate making of the criminal. A man shooting to kill but missing a vital organ by a hair's breadth can justify his action no more than can the man who hits that organ. It is pure chance that the attempted murderer is not a murderer and I entirely agree with what Lord Lane CJ said ([1991] 2 All ER 1 at 8, [1991] 1QB 660 at 667): '... the fact that the attempt failed to kill should not make any difference.'

For the foregoing reasons I have no doubt that the Court of Appeal reached the correct conclusion and that the appeal should be dismissed.

Lord Lowry [having reviewed the authorities and arguments continued:]

If the common law has had a policy towards duress heretofore, it seems to have been to go by the result and not primarily by the intent and, if a change of policy is needed with regard to criminal liability, it must be made prospectively by Parliament and not retrospectively by a court.

I am not influenced in favour of the appellant by the supposed illogicality of distinguishing between attempted murder on the one hand and conspiracy and incitement to murder on the other and I agree on this point with the view of Lord Lane CJ: short of murder itself, attempted murder is a special crime. But I am not swayed in favour of the Crown by the various examples of the anomalies which are said to result from holding that the duress defence applies to attempted murder. As Lord Lane CJ said, it would be possible to suggest anomalies wherever the line is drawn (see [1991] 2 All ER 1 at 8, [1991] 1QB 660 at 667). The real logic would be to grant or withhold the duress defence universally.

Attempted murder, however heinous we consider it, was a misdemeanour. Until 1861 someone who shot and missed could suffer no more than two years' imprisonment and I submit that, when attempted murder became a felony, that crime, like many other serious felonies, continued to have available the defence of duress.

My Lords, having considered all the arguments on either side, I am of the opinion that your Lordships *are* constrained by a common law rule (though not by judicial authority) from holding that the defence of duress does not apply to attempted murder. Accordingly, I would allow the appeal, quash the conviction and set aside the probation order but, in the special circumstances of this case, I would not propose that a new trial be ordered.

[**Lord Browne-Wilkinson** said that the speeches of Lord Jauncey and Lord Lowry both demonstrated that it was uncertain whether duress is a defence to attempted murder. Their lordships had to clarify the position. He could see no logical or policy ground for distinguishing between the case of the successful and unsuccessful would-be murderer and would dismiss the appeal. He hoped that Parliament would consider the whole question of duress as a defence to all crimes with particular reference to the question whether duress is not better regarded as a mitigating factor than as a defence.]

Appeal dismissed

It would certainly be illogical to allow duress as a defence to attempted murder when it is not a defence to murder; but, as Lord Lowry shows, it is equally illogical to allow duress to be a defence to a charge of causing GBH with intent when it is not a defence to the murder which might be charged if the victim were to die of the GBH. As long as duress is not a defence to murder, the only question is where is the illogical line to be drawn? As far as logic goes, it might as well be under murder as under attempted murder. In Lord Lowry's view, under murder would be the appropriate place, the reason for the exclusion of the defence being 'the stark fact of death'.

Although duress is not a defence to attempted murder, the question arose whether it should be for conspiracy. In *Gotts* [1992] AC 412, as has already been pointed out, the House of Lords, by a majority, decided that the defence of duress was not open to the accused on a charge of attempted murder either. The House of Lords affirmed the decision of the Court of Appeal (in which the judgment of the court was given by Lord Lane CJ) [1991] 1 QB 660. In the Court of Appeal in *Gotts*, Lord Lane said at 668:

> We note the suggestion that if attempt is excluded the same should apply to conspiracy and other kindred offences. We consider there is a legitimate distinction to be drawn. Conspiracy, incitement and so on are, generally speaking, a stage further away from the completed offence than is the attempt. Wherever the line is drawn it would be possible to suggest anomalies.

The only member of the House of Lords in *Gotts* to deal with the argument was Lord Lowry in his dissent (see his lordship's judgment in the earlier extract). The Law Commission in Report No 218, *Legislating the Criminal Code: Offences Against the Person and General Principles* (2003) Cm 2370 recommended that duress be a defence to all crimes, but in the course of the discussion, referred to the statement of Lord Lane in *Gotts* and commented:

> 32.3 As to conspiracy and kindred offences, we respectfully agree with the Court of Appeal that to exclude the defence of duress in a case of attempted murder because the accused has done an act intending that it should cause death, thus fulfilling the *mens rea* for murder itself, does not demand, either as a matter of logic or of policy, that other offences preliminary to murder, where the accused has *not* done such an act, should also be excluded from the ambit of duress. Indeed, if the reason for excluding the defence in the completed offence of murder is that the accused had the *mens rea* for murder, that reasoning shows that the exclusion of the defence in murder is, at least so far as logic is concerned, inconsistent with the basic rationale of the law of duress.

In *Ness* [2011] Crim LR 645 it was held that the defence was available on a charge of conspiracy to murder. For the many who regard it as undesirable that duress is unavailable as a defence to murder, the refusal to extend that harsh doctrine yet further will be welcome. There is no question that it produces illogicality. Consider D1 who under the threat of serious injury or death from D2, a terrorist leader, agrees that bombs should be detonated on the Underground. If D1's bomb fails to detonate he will be guilty of attempted murder if charged but not of conspiracy to murder. The way to avoid the illogicality of the distinctions between murder, attempt and conspiracy is to allow the duress defence to be pleaded to any of them.

■ *Questions*

1. Should the defence be reformed so as to be available to murder and attempted murder?

2. Is there a principled basis for permitting duress as a defence to conspiracy to murder, but not attempted murder?

The judges in *Howe* and in *Gotts* and more recently in *Hasan* seem generally to accept that the time is ripe for Parliament to consider the defence of duress and to decide whether it should exist at all and, if so, what its extent should be. Lord Lowry says, 'The real logic would be to grant or withhold the duress defence universally.'

In 2006, the Law Commission recommended that duress becomes a full defence to attempted murder (LC304):

6.70 Since we are recommending that duress should be a full defence to [our recommendation for] first degree murder, it would be anomalous were we to recommend otherwise in relation to second degree murder and attempted murder.

6.71 We recommend that duress, if successfully pleaded, should be a full defence to second degree murder and attempted murder.

6.72 We believe that our recommendations that duress should be a full defence to first degree murder, second degree murder and attempted murder are conducive to achieving clarity and coherence. However, we have rejected other options not merely because we think that they are intellectually untidy. Ultimately, the function of the criminal law is not to produce intellectual tidiness for its own sake but, rather, to do practical justice as it would be seen by ordinary members of the public. We do not believe that the options that we have rejected would achieve that result. We believe that the recommendations we are making would do so.

11.4 Duress of circumstances

The elements of the defence of duress of circumstances are almost identical to those for duress. The significant difference is that with duress of circumstances, it is sufficient that D perceives the threat of death or serious injury, to himself or someone for whom he is responsible, to arise from the circumstances at the time of the crime. There need not be another person whom the defendant believes is threatening such violence.

Curiously, all the early cases on duress of circumstances related to driving offences but *Pommel*, section 11.4.1, p 396, acknowledged that the defence of duress of circumstances applies generally (although it is not strictly a duress case at all), and this is confirmed by *Abdul-Hussain*, section 11.3.2.6, p 371. It applies to all offences except murder, attempted murder and some forms of treason. There is a tentative suggestion in *Abdul-Hussain* that it does not apply to conspiracy; but the defence of duress by threats was held applicable (though not made out on the facts) to a charge of conspiracy to defraud in *Verrier* [1965] Crim LR 732.

■ *Questions*

If duress is a defence to doing something, must it not also be defence to agreeing to do it? Otherwise, might not two duressees find themselves effectively deprived of the defence, whereas, in exactly similar circumstances, one would not?

11.4.1 Relationship with duress by threats

R v Conway
[1988] EWCA Crim 1, Court of Appeal, Criminal Division, http://www.bailii.org/ew/cases/EWCA/Crim/1988/1.html

(Woolf LJ, McCullough and Auld JJ)

A passenger in the appellant's car, Tonna, had been the target of an attack on another vehicle a few weeks earlier when another man was shot and Tonna was chased and narrowly escaped. On the occasion which was the subject of the present appeal, two young men in civilian clothes came running towards the appellant's parked car and Tonna shouted hysterically, 'Drive off.' The appellant drove off because he said he feared a fatal attack on Tonna. His car was chased by the two men in an unmarked vehicle and he drove in a manner which would undoubtedly be normally regarded as reckless. He was convicted of reckless driving. The two young men were police officers who knew Tonna was the subject of a bench warrant (ie an arrest warrant issued by a judge) but the appellant said he did not know this until after the incident. It was accepted at the trial that the case could not be distinguished from *Denton* (1987) 85 Cr App R 246 where the trial judge refused to leave the defence of necessity to the jury and an appeal was dismissed.

Woolf J:

In *R v Denton* the court went on to comment on another recent decision of this court, *R v Willer* (1986) 83 Cr App Rep 225. In *R v Willer* the appellant had been convicted of reckless driving. As he drove up a narrow road he was confronted with a gang of shouting and bawling youths, 20 to 30 strong. He heard one of them shouting, 'I'll kill you, Willer,' and another threatening to kill his passenger. He stopped and tried to turn the car around. The youths surrounded him. They banged on the car. One of the youths dived on the passenger who was sitting in the back and, in the words of Watkins LJ (at 226):

> 'The appellant realised that the only conceivable way he could somehow escape from this formidable gang of youths, who were obviously bent on doing further violence, was to mount the pavement on the right-hand side [of the road] and on the pavement to drive through a small gap into the front of the shopping precinct (which he did at about 10 miles per hour).'

Subsequently he returned, driving back very slowly, because he realised one of his passengers was missing from the car. Throughout this period there was still a youth fighting with one of his rear passengers in the car, so the appellant drove to the local police station and reported the matter. During the course of the trial Willer changed his plea after a ruling that he was not entitled to rely on the defence of necessity. In dealing with this change of plea, Watkins LJ said (at 227):

> 'Returning to how the appellant came to change his plea, one begins with the reasons advanced by the assistant recorder for declaring that the defence of necessity was not available to the appellant. He seems to have based himself upon the proposition, though saying that necessity was a defence known to English law, that it was not, albeit available to the appellant in respect of the journey through the gap into the car park in front of the shopping precinct, available to him upon the return journey because he was not at that stage being besieged by the gang of youths. We feel bound to say that it would have been for the jury to decide, if necessity could have been a defence at all in those circumstances, whether the whole incident should be regarded as one, or could properly be regarded as two separate incidents so as to enable them to say that necessity applied in one instance but not in the other. For that reason alone the course adopted by the assistant recorder was we think seriously at fault. Beyond that upon the issue of necessity we see no need to go for what we deem to have been appropriate in these circumstances to raise as a defence by the appellant was duress. The appellant in effect said: "I could do no other in the face of this hostility than to take the right turn as I did, to mount the pavement and to drive through the gap out of further harm's way, harm to person and harm to my property." Thus the defence of

duress, it seems to us, arose but was not pursued. What ought to have happened therefore was that the assistant recorder upon those facts should have directed that he would leave to the jury the question as to whether or not upon the outward or the return journey, or both, the appellant was wholly driven by force of circumstance into doing what he did and did not drive the car otherwise than under that form of compulsion, ie under duress.'

It will be noted from the passage in Watkins LJ's judgment that in *R v Willer* it was apparently accepted by the assistant recorder and counsel that there could be a defence of necessity to reckless driving. This may explain why the report does not suggest that any authorities were cited to the Court of Appeal, although apparently authorities, including American and Australian authorities, were cited to the assistant recorder.

It is convenient to refer to the 'duress' of which Watkins LJ spoke as 'duress of circumstances'. In *R v Denton* (1987) 85 Cr App Rep 246 at 248, in relation to *R v Willer*, the court said:

'This authority might be taken to suggest that the court assumed that on the facts of the case the defence of necessity could have been raised to a charge of reckless driving. We do not think this authority goes so far. We think it shows that the court doubted whether necessity as a defence could have been raised on the facts of that case but the court saw no need to decide whether such a defence existed as a matter of law. The court said a very different defence was available, which was duress, which should have been left to the jury. It should be observed that where the head-note says ((1986) 83 Cr App Rep 225) "Further the judge erred in ruling that the defence of necessity was not available to the defendant" it is referring to the argument advanced by the appellant and not to the decision of the appellate court.'

The judgment in *R v Denton*, while making this reservation on the decision in *R v Willer* so far as the defence of necessity is concerned, made no similar reservation with regard to what was said in *R v Willer* as to duress. In *R v Willer* there were a number of grounds on which this court disapproved of the way in which the case had been dealt with in the Crown Court. However, in relation to duress we regard the decision as binding on this court.

We have, in addition, had the advantage of having been referred to such other authorities as there are on the subject. In particular, we have been referred to the views of Professor Glanville Williams in his *Textbook of Criminal Law* (2nd edn, 1983) p 517 and Smith and Hogan *Criminal Law* (6th edn, 1988) p 224. We have also been referred to the Law Commission's Report on Defences of General Application (Law Com no 83 (1977)), which recommended that 'there should be no general defence of necessity and if any such general defence exists at common law, it should be abolished'. This conclusion was in striking contrast to the commission's provisional proposals in its Working Paper no 55 (1974), to which we were also referred. We have also seen the Law Commission's report on the Codification of the Criminal Law (Law Com no 143 (1985)), which took the view that necessity should remain as a defence at common law, in so far as it is one already. It appears that it is still not clear whether there is a general defence of necessity or, if there is, what are the circumstances in which it is available.

We conclude that [the defence is only available to] a charge of reckless driving where the facts establish 'duress of circumstances', as in *R v Willer*, ie where the defendant was constrained by circumstances to drive as he did to avoid death or serious bodily harm to himself or some other person.

As the learned editors point out in Smith and Hogan *Criminal Law* (6th edn, 1988) p 225, to admit a defence of 'duress of circumstances' is a logical consequence of the existence of the defence of duress as that term is ordinarily understood, ie 'do this or else'. This approach does no more than recognise that duress is an example of necessity. Whether 'duress of circumstances' is called 'duress' or 'necessity' does not matter. What is important is that, whatever it is called, it is subject to the same limitations as the 'do this or else' species of duress. As Lord Hailsham LC said in his speech in *R v Howe* [1987] AC 417 at 429, [1987] 1 All ER 771 at 777:

'There is, of course, an obvious distinction between duress and necessity as potential defences: duress arises from the wrongful threats or violence of another human being and necessity arises from any other objective dangers threatening the accused. This, however, is, in my view a distinction without a relevant difference, since on this view duress is only that species of the genus of necessity which is caused by wrongful threats. I cannot see that there is any way in which a person of ordinary fortitude can be excused from the one type of pressure on his will rather than the other.'

No wider defence to reckless driving is recognised. Bearing in mind that reckless driving can kill, we cannot accept that Parliament intended otherwise. When Parliament intended a wider defence it made express provision. Section 36(3) of the Road Traffic Act 1972, in relation to the lesser offence of driving motor vehicles elsewhere than on roads, provides:

'A person shall not be convicted of an offence under this section with respect to a vehicle if he proves to the satisfaction of the court that it was driven in contravention of this section for purposes of saving life or extinguishing a fire or meeting any other like emergency.'

It follows that a defence of 'duress of circumstances' is available only if from an objective stand-point the defendant can be said to be acting in order to avoid a threat of death or serious injury. The approach must be that indicated by Lord Lane CJ in *R v Graham* [1982] 1 All ER 801. Lord Lane CJ, in a passage of his judgment approved by the House of Lords in *R v Howe*, said [... The passage is set out in section 11.3.3, p 377].

Adopting the approach indicated by Lord Lane CJ, and not that argued by counsel, which involved a subjective element, we ask ourselves whether the judge in the Crown Court should have left the defence of 'duress of circumstances' to the jury, notwithstanding the submission made by his counsel that it was 'impossible to run the defence of necessity . . . or indeed leave it to the jury.'

On the facts alleged by the appellant we are constrained to hold that the judge was obliged to do so, notwithstanding the appellant's counsel's submission at the hearing. The judge was referred to both *R v Denton* and *R v Willer*, and it appears that the explanation for counsel not relying on *R v Willer* is that he was wrongly of the view that the facts of this case are indistinguishable from those in *R v Denton*. However, in fact, as indicated by the judge, his client's defence was that he drove as he did because he was in fear for his life and that of Tonna. Although it is unlikely that the outcome of the jury's deliberations would have been any different, they should have been directed as to the possibility that they could find the appellant not guilty because of duress of circumstances, although they were otherwise satisfied that he had driven recklessly.

The jury not having received this direction, this is not a case in which we can properly apply the proviso. On the facts the non-direction related in reality to the appellant's only conceivable defence, and, although unlikely, it is just possible that the jury, if properly directed, would have found the appellant not guilty because of this defence.

Accordingly, we allow this appeal and quash the conviction.

J. C. Smith, *Justification and Excuse in the Criminal Law*
(The Hamlyn Lectures, 1989), discussing *Conway*

It seems probable, therefore, that duress of circumstances, like duress by threats, is a defence to crimes generally, but not a defence to murder, or perhaps attempted murder. It applies not only to an act done for the preservation of one's own life and safety but also to an act done to protect another— probably any other person who is in peril. It does not appear that there was any relationship between Conway and Tonna, other than that of driver and passenger. The case is therefore of considerable importance. Consider the following hypothetical case put by Lord Denning in *Buckoke v Greater London Council* [1971] 2 All ER 254, CA:

'A driver of a fire engine with ladders approaches the traffic lights. He sees 200 yards down the road a blazing house with a man at an upstairs window in extreme peril. The road is clear in all directions. At that moment the lights turn red. Is the driver to wait for 60 seconds or more, for the lights to turn green? If the driver waits for that time, the man's life will be lost.'

Lord Denning accepted the opinion of both counsel in that case that the driver would commit an offence if he crossed the red light. Necessity would be no answer to a charge of breaking the Road Traffic Regulations. But would it be the same now that the courts have discovered the defence of duress of circumstances? The threat to the fictional man at the upstairs window seems to be no less than the threat to the passenger in Conway's car. The necessity for immediate action is no less. If we have to look for some relationship between the defendant and the person rescued, that between a fireman and a person imperilled by a fire is surely enough—the fireman probably has a duty to do all that he lawfully and reasonably can to rescue any member of the public. But it is thought that the better view is that no special relationship is necessary. Suppose that Mr Tonna had leapt into the car of a perfect stranger, screaming that he was about to be shot. Would not the stranger be excused, no less than Mr Conway, for any infringement of the letter of the law which reasonably appeared to him to be necessary to save a man from being murdered? Should a private citizen, driving a van with a long ladder, be less deserving of excuse than a fireman because he crossed the red light to make a rescue? I submit, not.

Perhaps Lord Denning would not be displeased by this result. He was applying the law as he believed it then to be; but he said of his hypothetical fire engine driver who crossed the red light: he 'should not be prosecuted. He should be congratulated.' It has always seemed to me very odd that the great Master of the Rolls should find that this conduct was both a breach of the criminal law and a case for congratulation. Plainly, he thought that, from a moral point of view, the driver's conduct was not only excusable but justifiable.

■ *Questions*

1. Is there any good reason to treat the defences of duress by threats and duress of circumstances differently?

2. In *Willer, Conway* and *Martin* (in the following extract), the threat came from the actions of human beings. In *Buckoke* [1971] Ch 655, it came from a fire. Is that a material difference? Should the result have been any different in *Willer* or *Conway* if the threat had come from a wall of floodwater, a runaway lorry or a herd of charging bulls?

The definition of the defence in terms similar to those for duress by threats was confirmed in the following case.

R v Martin (CM)

[1988] EWCA Crim 2, Court of Appeal, Criminal Division, http://www.bailii.org/ew/cases/EWCA/Crim/1988/2.html

(Lord Lane CJ, Simon Brown and Roch JJ)

M was convicted of driving while disqualified. He alleged that his stepson overslept so that he was bound to be late for work and at risk of losing his job unless driven there. M's wife, who had suicidal tendencies, was in a distraught state and threatened to commit suicide if M did not drive the boy to work. A doctor had made a statement that it was likely that she would have carried out her threat. M said he drove because he genuinely and reasonably believed she would carry out her threat if he did not. The judge ruled that these facts, if proved, would constitute no defence to the charge, whereupon M pleaded guilty and appealed.

Simon Brown J [having referred to *Conway*, at the beginning of this section, p 392]:

The principles may be summarised thus: first, English law does, in extreme circumstances, recognise a defence of necessity. Most commonly this defence arises as duress, that is pressure on the accused's will from the wrongful threats or violence of another. Equally however it can arise from other objective dangers threatening the accused or others. Arising thus it is conveniently called 'duress of circumstances'.

Second, the defence is available only if, from an objective standpoint, the accused can be said to be acting reasonably and proportionately in order to avoid a threat of death or serious injury.

Third, assuming the defence to be open to the accused on his account of the facts, the issue should be left to the jury, who should be directed to determine these two questions: first, was the accused, or may he have been, impelled to act as he did because as a result of what he reasonably believed to be the situation he had good cause to fear that otherwise death or serious physical injury would result; second, if so, would a sober person of reasonable firmness, sharing the characteristics of the accused, have responded to that situation by acting as the accused acted? If the answer to both those questions was Yes, then the jury would acquit; the defence of necessity would have been established.

That the defence is available in cases of reckless driving is established by *R v Conway* itself and indeed by an earlier decision of the court in *R v Willer*. *R v Conway* is authority also for the proposition that the scope of the defence is no wider for reckless driving than for other serious offences. As was pointed out in the judgment, 'reckless driving can kill'.

We see no material distinction between offences of reckless driving and driving whilst disqualified so far as the application and scope of this defence is concerned. Equally we can see no distinction in principle between various threats of death; it matters not whether the risk of death is by murder or by suicide or indeed by accident. One can illustrate the latter by considering a disqualified driver being driven by his wife, she suffering a heart attack in remote countryside and he needing instantly to get her to hospital.

It follows from this that the judge quite clearly did come to a wrong decision on the question of law, and the appellant should have been permitted to raise this defence for what it was worth before the jury.

Appeal allowed

Martin lays down the clearest definition of the defence of duress of circumstances. It was unclear, however, whether the defence was available only in respect of road traffic offences (where it is frequently pleaded) or of wider application. The case of *Pommell* was the first to confirm its general application.

R v Pommell

[1995] 2 Cr App R 607, Court of Appeal, Criminal Division

(Kennedy LJ, Steel and Hooper JJ)

Pommell was found by police at 8.00 am lying in bed with a loaded sub-machine gun against his leg. He said that between 12.30 and 1.00 am, 'I took it off a geezer who was going to do some people some damage with it.' He said that he removed the loaded gun but put it back when he decided to wait until morning to get his brother to hand the gun in to the police. He kept the gun in bed because he did not want his girlfriend to see it. The trial judge ruled that his failure to go to the police immediately deprived him of any defence of necessity that might otherwise have been available. He appealed against conviction for possessing a prohibited weapon and ammunition without a licence, arguing that this ruling was wrong.

Kennedy LJ:

There is an obvious attraction in the argument that if A finds B in possession of a gun which he is about to use to commit a crime, and if A is then able to persuade B to hand over the gun so that A may hand it to the police, A should not immediately upon taking possession of the gun become guilty of a criminal offence. However, if that is right, then in 1974, at least in the result, the case of *Woodage v Moss* [1974] 1 All ER 584, DC, was wrongly decided.

The strength of the argument that a person ought to be permitted to breach the letter of the criminal law in order to prevent a greater evil befalling himself or others has long been recognised (see, for example, *Stephen's Digest of Criminal Law*), but it has, in English law, not given rise to a recognised general defence of necessity, and in relation to the charge of murder, the defence has been specifically held not to exist (see *Dudley and Stephens* (1884) 14 QBD 273). Even in relation to other offences, there are powerful arguments against recognising the general defence. As Dickson J said in the Supreme Court of Canada in *Perka v R* (1984) 13 DLR (4th) 1, at p14:

> ' "... no system of positive law can recognise any principle which would entitle a person to violate the law because on his view the law conflicted with some higher social value". The Criminal Code has specified a number of identifiable situations in which an actor is justified in committing what would other-wise be a criminal offence. To go beyond that and hold that ostensibly illegal acts can be validated on the basis of their expediency, would import an undue subjectivity into the criminal law. It would invite the courts to second-guess the Legislature and to assess the relative merits of social policies underlying criminal prohibitions.'

However, that does not really deal with the situation where someone commendably infringes a regulation in order to prevent another person from committing what everyone would accept as being a greater evil with a gun. In that situation it cannot be satisfactory to leave it to the prosecuting authority not to prosecute, or to individual courts to grant an absolute discharge. The authority may, as in the present case, prosecute because it is not satisfied that the defendant is telling the truth, and then, even if he is vindicated and given an absolute discharge, he is left with a criminal conviction which, for some purposes, would be recognised as such.

It was, as it seems to us, to meet this difficulty that the limited defence of duress of circumstances has been developed in English law in relation to road traffic offences.

[Kennedy LJ discussed the cases, including *DPP v Jones* [1990] RTR 33, and continued commenting on the case of *Bell*] Professor Sir John Smith has written:

> 'All the cases so far have concerned road traffic offences but there are no grounds for supposing that the defence is limited to that kind of case. On the contrary, the defence, being closely related to the defence of duress by threats, appears to be general, applying to all crimes except murder, attempted murder and some forms of treason, ...': see [1992] Crim LR 176.

We agree.

...

That leads us to the conclusion that in the present case the defence was open to the appellant in respect of his acquisition of the gun ... That leaves the question as to his continued possession of the gun thereafter. In our judgment, the test laid down in *Martin* [earlier in this section, p 395], is not necessarily the appropriate test for determining whether a person continues to have a defence available to him. For example, a person takes a gun off another in the circumstances in which this appellant says he did and then locks it away in a safe with a view to safeguarding it while the police are informed. When the gun is in the safe, the test laid down in *Martin* may not be satisfied: there would then be no immediate fear of death or serious injury. In our judgment, a person who has taken possession of a gun in circumstances where he has the defence of duress by circumstances must 'desist from committing the crime as soon as he reasonably can' (Smith and Hogan, *Criminal Law* (7th edn) p239). This test is similar to the test in *Jones*, to which we have already referred. In deciding whether a defendant acted reason-ably, regard would be had to the circumstances in which he finds himself. Can it be said, in this case, that there was no evidence upon which a jury could have reached the conclusion that the appellant did desist, or may have desisted, as soon as he reasonably could? In answering this question, the jury would have to have regard to the delay that had occurred between, on the appellant's account, his acquisition of the gun and ammunition at 12.30 to 1 am, and the arrival of the police some hours later. The appellant has offered an explanation for that delay but, as it seems to us, the defence of duress of circumstances could not avail him once a reasonable person in his position would have known that the duress, in this case the need to obtain and retain the firearm, had ceased. In the present case the judge said that the failure of the appellant to go immediately to the police 'robs him of a defence'. We accept that in some cases a delay, especially if unexplained, may be such as to make it clear that any duress must have ceased to operate, in which case the judge would be entitled to conclude that even on the defendant's own account of the facts, the defence was not open to him. There would then be no reason to leave the issue to the jury. However, the situation does not seem to us to have been sufficiently clear cut to make that an appropriate step in the present case. In the first place, the delay of a few hours overnight might not be regarded as being unduly long and, secondly, the defendant did offer an explanation for it, therefore, in our judgment, the proposed defence should have been left to the jury.

We have considered whether the reloading of the gun and the fact that the appellant had the gun in his bed deprived him of the defence. Must a person who has acquired a gun in circumstances in which he has the defence of duress of circumstances not only desist from committing the offence as soon as he reasonably can but, in the meanwhile, act in a reasonable manner with the gun? The answer is that if he does not do so, it will be difficult for the court to accept that he desisted from committing the offence as soon as he reasonably could. Therefore, in our judgment, the acts of reloading and putting the gun in the bed do not of themselves deprive him of the defence, but are matters which may be taken into account by the jury in deciding the issues to which we have already made reference.

Appeal against conviction allowed

Retrial ordered

■ *Questions*

Was Pommell acting under duress of circumstances? Was there an immediate threat to him or another? Is this case best seen as one of necessity?

11.5 Necessity

Duress of circumstances was treated by the courts in *Conway* and *Martin* as a defence of necessity. As noted previously, the effect, logically, should have been to extend the defence to some cases where it was previously thought not to apply, as in the conduct of Lord Denning's hypothetical fireman in *Buckoke*'s case. It could also have had the effect of limiting the defence by importing the restrictions which seem to have become established on the defence of duress by threats—the limitation to threats of death or GBH and the objective tests of *reasonable* belief in facts creating the necessity, *good* cause for fear and the response of a person of *reasonable* firmness. The courts have limited the duress of circumstances defence by restricting it in the same terms of duress by threats. There is, however, a separate defence of necessity at common law which is not restricted in that way. It is rarely successful and its limits are not clearly defined in the case law.

It is important to appreciate that the availability of a plea of necessity to a statutory offence will turn on the particular statutory scheme. In *CS* [2012] EWCA Crim 389 it was held that no defence of necessity was available to a parent charged under s 1 of the Child Abduction Act 1984 who believed (without foundation) that the child's father posed a risk of sexually abusing her. The statutory scheme, with the requirement for court orders to sanction one parent taking a child from the other, made it 'impossible to see how, within the legislative scheme, the legislature could have contemplated that a parent could have the defence of necessity available in respect of the offence of removing a child from England and Wales where the whole purpose of making removal an offence was to reinforce the objective of retaining the child within England and Wales so the child could be subject to the protection of the court' (at [13] per Sir John Thomas P). The court left open the question whether the defence of necessity is different from that of duress of circumstances (at [15]).

11.5.1 The scope of the necessity defence

Consider whether the following case shows that necessity is a wider defence than duress of circumstances.

F v West Berkshire Authority
[1989] 2 All ER 545, House of Lords

(Lords Bridge, Brandon, Griffiths, Goff and Jauncey)

F, aged 36, a female patient in a psychiatric hospital, suffered from a very serious mental disability. She had formed a sexual relationship with a male patient. Medical evidence was that, from a psychiatric point of view, it would be disastrous if she became pregnant. There were serious objections to all ordinary methods of contraception. She was incapable of giving consent to a sterilization operation. Her mother, acting as her next friend, obtained a declaration that the absence of her consent would not make sterilization an unlawful act. The Court of Appeal dismissed an appeal by the Official Solicitor who appealed to the House of Lords. The appeal was dismissed. The operation was lawful because it was in the best interests of the patient. The decision of the House must now be read with the Mental Capacity Act 2005 in mind.

Lord Brandon:

At common law a doctor cannot lawfully operate on adult patients of sound mind, or give them any other treatment involving the application of physical force however small (which I shall refer to as 'other treatment'), without their consent. If a doctor were to operate on such patients, or give them other treatment, without their consent, he would commit the actionable tort of trespass to the person. There are, however, cases where adult patients cannot give or refuse their consent to an operation or other treatment. One case is where, as a result of an accident or otherwise, an adult patient is unconscious and an operation or other treatment cannot be safely delayed until he or she recovers consciousness. Another case is where a patient, though adult, cannot by reason of mental disability understand the nature or purpose of an operation or other treatment. The common law would be seriously defective if it failed to provide a solution to the problem created by such inability to consent. In my opinion, however, the common law does not fail. In my opinion, the solution to the problem which the common law provides is that a doctor can lawfully operate on, or give other treatment to, adult patients who are incapable, for one reason or another, of consenting to his doing so, provided that the operation or other treatment concerned is in the best interests of such patients. The operation or other treatment will be in their best interests if, but only if, it is carried out in order either to save their lives or to ensure improvement or prevent deterioration in their physical or mental health.

Different views have been put forward with regard to the principle which makes it lawful for a doctor to operate on or give other treatment to adult patients without their consent in the two cases to which I have referred above. The Court of Appeal in the present case regarded the matter as depending on the public interest. I would not disagree with that as a broad proposition, but I think that it is helpful to consider the principle in accordance with which the public interest leads to this result. In my opinion, the principle is that, when persons lack the capacity, for whatever reason, to take decisions about the performance of operations on them, or the giving of other medical treatment to them, it is necessary that some other person or persons, with the appropriate qualifications, should take such decisions for them. Otherwise they would be deprived of medical care which they need and to which they are entitled.

In many cases, however, it will not only be lawful for doctors, on the ground of necessity, to operate on or give other medical treatment to adult patients disabled from giving their consent: it will also be their common law duty to do so.

Lord Goff:

On what principle can medical treatment be justified when given without consent? We are searching for a principle on which, in limited circumstances, recognition may be given to a need, in the interests of the patient, that treatment should be given to him in circumstances where he is (temporarily or permanently) disabled from consenting to it. It is this criterion of a need which points to the principle of necessity as providing justification.

That there exists in the common law a principle of necessity which may justify action which would otherwise be unlawful is not in doubt. But historically the principle has been seen to be restricted to two groups of cases, which have been called cases of public necessity and cases of private necessity. The former occurred when a man interfered with another man's property in the public interest, for example (in the days before we could dial 999 for the fire brigade) the destruction of another man's house to prevent the spread of a catastrophic fire, as indeed occurred in the Great Fire of London in 1666. The latter cases occurred when a man interfered with another's property to save his own person or property from imminent danger, for example when he entered on his neighbour's land without his consent in order to prevent the spread of fire onto his own land.

There is, however, a third group of cases, which is also properly described as founded on the principle of necessity and which is more pertinent to the resolution of the problem in the present case. These cases are concerned with action taken as a matter of necessity to assist another person without his consent. To give a simple example, a man who seizes another and forcibly drags him from the path of an oncoming vehicle, thereby saving him from injury or even death, commits no wrong. But there are many emanations of this principle, to be found scattered through the books. These are concerned not only with the preservation of the life or health of the assisted person, but also with the preservation of his property (sometimes an animal, sometimes an ordinary chattel) and even to certain conduct on his behalf in the administration of his affairs. Where there is a pre-existing relationship between the parties, the intervener is usually said to act as an agent of necessity on behalf of the principal in whose interests he acts, and his action can often, with not too much artificiality, be referred to the pre-existing relationship between them. Whether the intervener may be entitled either to reimbursement or to remuneration raises separate questions which are not relevant to the present case.

We are concerned here with action taken to preserve the life, health or well-being of another who is unable to consent to it. Such action is sometimes said to be justified as arising from an emergency; in Prosser and Keeton *Torts* (5th edn, 1984) p 117 the action is said to be privileged by the emergency. Doubtless, in the case of a person of sound mind, there will ordinarily have to be an emergency before such action taken without consent can be lawful; for otherwise there would be an opportunity to communicate with the assisted person and to seek his consent. But this is not always so; and indeed the historical origins of the principle of necessity do not point to emergency as such as providing the criterion of lawful intervention without consent. The old Roman doctrine of *negotiorum gestio* presupposed not so much an emergency as a prolonged absence of the *dominus* from home as justifying intervention by the *gestor* to administer his affairs. The most ancient group of cases in the common law, concerned with action taken by the master of a ship in distant parts in the interests of the ship-owner, likewise found its origin in the difficulty of communication with the owner over a prolonged period of time, a difficulty overcome today by modern means of communication. In those cases, it was said that there had to be an emergency before the master could act as agent of necessity; though the emergency could well be of some duration. But, when a person is rendered incapable of communication either permanently or over a considerable period of time (through illness or accident or mental disorder), it would be an unusual use of language to describe the case as one of 'permanent emergency', if indeed such a state of affairs can properly be said to exist. In truth, the relevance of an emergency is that it may give rise to a necessity to act in the interests of the assisted person without first obtaining his consent. Emergency is however not the criterion or even a prerequisite; it is simply a frequent origin of the necessity which impels intervention. The principle is one of necessity, not of emergency.

Appeal dismissed

In *F*'s case the doctor performing the operation would have been guilty of criminal offences of assault and wounding in the absence of some defence. The majority of their lordships were content that the operation was in the best interests of the patient and in the public interest. But there is no authority for any such general defence to crime and tort. Lords Brandon and Goff searched for a principle underlying the conclusion reached by all their lordships and found it in the defence of necessity. In contrast, in the case of *Gillick v West Norfolk and Wisbech Area Health Authority* [1985] 1 All ER 553, [1986] AC 112 none of the House of Lords relied on necessity in deciding that a doctor may engage in conduct which was prima facie, aiding and abetting an offence. The question was: 'whether a doctor may ever, in any circumstances, lawfully give contraceptive advice or treatment to a girl under the age of sixteen without her parent's consent'.

Under the Sexual Offences Act 1956, a man who had intercourse with a girl under 16 committed an offence, but the girl was guilty of no offence, even though she may have incited, aided, abetted, counselled and procured the man to commit it. The provision of contraceptive advice or treatment encourages or facilitates the commission of the offence by removing the inhibition of the risk of an unwanted pregnancy (see now the defence in the Sexual Offences Act 2003, s 73, section 20.3.1, p 734). The doctor therefore appeared to be a party to the offence, no less than one who supplies equipment to a burglar, knowing that it will facilitate the commission by him of burglaries. The House (Lords Brandon and Templeman dissenting) nevertheless held the question should be answered in the affirmative. According to Lord Fraser the doctor acts lawfully if he is satisfied:

(1) that the girl (although under 16 years of age) will understand his advice; (2) that he cannot persuade her to inform her parents or to allow him to inform the parents that she is seeking contraceptive advice; (3) that she is very likely to begin or to continue having sexual intercourse with or without contraceptive treatment; (4) that unless she receives contraceptive advice or treatment her physical or mental health or both are likely to suffer; (5) that her best interests require him to give her contraceptive advice, treatment or both without the parental consent.

Lord Scarman said:

He may prescribe only if she has the capacity to consent or if exceptional circumstances exist which justify him in exercising his clinical judgment without parental consent. The adjective 'clinical' emphasises that it must be a medical judgment based on what he honestly believes to be necessary for the physical, mental and emotional health of his patient. The bona fide exercise by a doctor of his clinical judgment must be a complete negation of the guilty mind which is an essential ingredient of the criminal offence of aiding and abetting the commission of unlawful sexual intercourse.

Lord Templeman dissented only on the ground that the treatment or advice must be given with the concurrence of the girl's parents. He said:

Section 6 of the Sexual Offences Act 1956 does not, however, in my view, prevent parent and doctor from deciding that contraceptive facilities shall be made available to an unmarried girl under the age of 16 whose sexual activities are recognised to be uncontrolled and uncontrollable. Section 6 is designed to protect the girl from sexual intercourse. But if the girl cannot be deterred then contraceptive facilities may be provided, not for the purpose of aiding and abetting an offence under s 6 but for the purpose of avoiding the consequences, principally pregnancy, which the girl may suffer from illegal sexual intercourse where sexual intercourse cannot be prevented.

Lord Brandon thought the contraceptive advice was always unlawful, whether the parents concurred in it or not, because it necessarily encouraged the commission of the offence.

Notwithstanding *dicta* in the case, the basis for the doctor's immunity does not appear to be lack of the requisite intention because he knows that he is encouraging the commission of the offence and it is no answer for an alleged aider and abettor to say 'It would have happened anyway'. What is the basis of the immunity if not necessity? (See commentary at [1986] Crim LR 114.)

■ *Question*

What if the doctor prescribed contraception after the girl told him that she would not have intercourse without it (see Lord Fraser in the earlier extract) but she says that abstinence is making her ill, and he honestly believed that it was necessary for her physical, mental and emotional health (see Lord Scarman in the earlier extract)?

There may be other cases in the medical field where a defence of necessity is the underlying but unexpressed justification or excuse for certain practices. A more dramatic example is the case of *Mrs S* [1994] 4 All ER 671, where Stephen Brown P granted a declaration that it was lawful for surgeons to carry out a caesarean operation upon a woman without her consent in an attempt to save the life of her unborn child. The woman, who was competent to make the decision and who was supported by her husband, had refused to submit to the operation because of the nature of her religious beliefs. The evidence of the surgeon was that it was a matter of life and death for both the mother and child and a matter of minutes rather than hours. The operation was carried out but the child died. The life of the mother was saved. Professor Ian Kennedy is reported in *The Times* to have said of the 'epoch-making' decision:

It has massive implications for the status of women in regarding them as chattels and ambulatory wombs. It is so potentially intrusive as to reduce women back to the status of slaves.

■ *Questions*

Do you agree? Suppose that the surgeon had decided there was no time to go to court and that, if the child was to have a chance of survival, the operation must be carried out immediately. If he had done so and been prosecuted for assault or wounding, should he have had a defence of duress of circumstances?

11.5.2 Necessity as a defence to murder?

R v Dudley and Stephens
[1881–5] All ER Rep 61, Queen's Bench Division

(Lord Coleridge CJ, Grove and Denman JJ, Pollock and Huddleston BB)

The two accused, with a third man and the deceased, a 17-year-old boy, were cast away in an open boat, 1,600 miles from land. When they had been eight days without food and six days without water, the accused killed the boy, who was weak and unable to resist but did not assent to being killed. The men fed upon his body and blood for four days until they were picked up by a passing vessel. At the trial for murder, the jury found by a special verdict that if the men had not fed upon the boy they would probably not have survived the four days; that the boy was likely to have died first; that at the time of the act there was no reasonable prospect of relief; that it appeared to the accused that there was every probability that they would die of starvation unless one of the castaways was killed; that there was no appreciable chance of saving life except by killing; but that there was no greater necessity for killing the boy than any of the three men. The finding of the jury was referred to the Queen's Bench Division for its decision.

Lord Coleridge CJ [having referred to the special verdict, continued:]

...this is clear, that the prisoners put to death a weak and unoffending boy upon the chance of preserving their own lives by feeding upon his flesh and blood after he was killed, and with a certainty of depriving him of any possible chance of survival. The verdict finds in terms that: 'if the men had not fed upon the body of the boy, they would probably not have survived...' and that 'the boy, being in a much weaker condition, was likely to have died before them'. They might possibly have been picked up next day by a passing ship; they might possibly not have been picked up at all; in either case it is obvious that the killing of the boy would have been an unnecessary and profitless act. It is found by the verdict that the boy was incapable of resistance, and, in fact, made none; and it is not even suggested that his death was due to any violence on his part attempted against, or even so much as feared by, them who killed him....

[His lordship dealt with objections taken by counsel for the prisoners which do not call for report, and continued:]

First, it is said that it follows, from various definitions of murder in books of authority—which definitions imply, if they do not state, the doctrine—that, in order to save your own life you may lawfully take away the life of another, when the other is neither attempting nor threatening yours, nor is guilty of any illegal act whatever towards you or anyone else. But, if these definitions be looked at, they will not be found to sustain the contention. The earliest in point of date is the passage cited to us from Bracton, who wrote in the reign of Henry III.... But in the very passage as to necessity, on which reliance has been placed, it is clear that Bracton is speaking of necessity in the ordinary sense, the repelling by violence—violence justified so far as it was necessary for the object—any illegal violence used towards oneself. If, says Bracton (Lib iii, *Art De Corona*, cap 4, fol 120), the necessity be *'evitabilis et evadere posset absque occisione, tunc erit reus homicidii'*—words which show clearly that he is thinking of physical danger, from which escape may be possible, and that *'inevitabilis necessitas'*, of which he speaks as justifying homicide, is a necessity of the same nature.

It is, if possible, yet clearer that the doctrine contended for receives no support from the great authority of Lord Hale. It is plain that in his view the necessity which justifies homicide is that only which has always been, and is now, considered a justification. He says (I Hale, PC 491):

'In all these cases of homicide by necessity, as in pursuit of a felon, in killing him that assaults to rob, or comes to burn or break a house, or the like, which are in themselves no felony.'

Again, he says that the necessity which justifies homicide is of two kinds:

'(1) That necessity which is of private nature; (2) That necessity which relates to the public justice and safety. The former is that necessity which obligeth a man to his own defence and safeguard; and this takes in these inquiries: 1. What may be done for the safeguard of a man's own life;'

and then follow three other heads not necessary to pursue. Lord Hale proceeds (I Hale PC 478):

'1. As touching the first of these, viz, homicide in defence of a man's own life, which is usually styled *se defendendo*.'

It is not possible to use words more clear to show that Lord Hale regarded the private necessity which justified, and alone justified, the taking the life of another for the safeguard of one's own to be what is commonly called self-defence. But if this could be even doubtful upon Lord Hale's words, Lord Hale himself has made it clear, for, in the chapter in which he deals with the exemption created by compulsion or necessity, he thus expresses himself (I Hale PC 51):

> 'If a man be desperately assaulted, and in peril of death, and cannot otherwise escape, unless to satisfy his assailant's fury he will kill an innocent person then present, the fear and actual force will not acquit him of the crime and punishment of murder if he commit the fact, for he ought rather to die himself than to kill an innocent; but if he cannot otherwise save his own life, the law permits him in his own defence to kill the assailant, for, by the violence of the assault and the offence committed upon him by the assailant himself, the law of nature and necessity hath made him his own protector *cum debito moderamine inculpatae tutelae*.'

But, further still, Lord Hale, in the following chapter (I Hale PC 54), deals with the position asserted by the casuists, and sanctioned, as he says by Grotius and Puffendorf, that in a case of extreme necessity, either of hunger or clothing,

> 'theft is no theft, or at least not punishable as theft, and some even of our own lawyers have asserted the same; but I take it that here in England that rule, at least by the laws of England, is false, and, therefore, if a person, being under necessity for want of victuals or clothes, shall upon the account clandestinely and *animo furandi* steal another man's goods, it is a felony and a crime by the laws of England punishable with death.'

If, therefore, Lord Hale is clear, as he is, that extreme necessity of hunger does not justify larceny, what would he have said to the doctrine that it justified murder?

It is satisfactory to find that another great authority, second probably only to Lord Hale, speaks with the same unhesitating clearness on this matter. [His lordship referred to *Foster's Discourse on Homicide*, Ch 3, and other authorities.]

There remains the authority of Stephen J who both in his *Digest* (art 32) and in his *History of the Criminal Law* (vol 2, p 108) uses language perhaps wide enough to cover this case. The language is somewhat vague in both places, but it does not in either place cover this case of necessity, and we have the best authority for saying that it was not meant to cover it. If it had been necessary we must with true deference have differed from him; but it is satisfactory to know that we have, probably at least, arrived at no conclusion in which, if he had been a member of the court, he would have been unable to agree. Neither are we in conflict with any opinion expressed upon this subject by the learned persons who formed the commission for preparing the Criminal Code. They say on this subject:

> 'We are not prepared to suggest that necessity should in every case be a justification; we are equally unprepared to suggest that necessity should in no case be a defence. We judge it better to leave such questions to be dealt with when, if ever, they arise in practice by applying the principles of law to the circumstances of the particular case.'

It would have been satisfactory to us if these eminent persons could have told us whether the received definitions of legal necessity were, in their judgment, correct and exhaustive, and, if not, in what way they should be amended; but as it is we have, as they say, 'to apply the principles of law to the circumstances of this particular case.'

It is admitted that the deliberate killing of this unoffending and unresisting boy was clearly murder, unless the killing can be justified by some well-recognised excuse admitted by the law. It is further admitted that there was in this case no such excuse, unless the killing was justified by what has been called necessity. But the temptation to the act which existed here was not what the law has ever called necessity. Nor is this to be regretted. Though law and morality are not the same, and though many things may be immoral which are not necessarily illegal, yet the absolute divorce of law from morality would be of fatal consequence, and such divorce would follow if the temptation to murder in this case were to be held by law an absolute defence of it. It is not so.

To preserve one's life is generally speaking, a duty, but it may be the plainest and the highest duty to sacrifice it. War is full of instances in which it is a man's duty not to live, but to die.... It is not correct, therefore, to say that there is any absolute and unqualified necessity to preserve one's life.... It is enough in a Christian country to remind ourselves of the Great Example which we profess to follow.

It is not needful to point out the awful danger of admitting the principle which has been contended for. Who is to be the judge of this sort of necessity? By what measure is the comparative value of lives to be measured? Is it to be strength, or intellect, or what? It is plain that the principle leaves to him who is to profit by it to determine the necessity which will justify him in deliberately taking another's life to save his own. In this case the weakest, the youngest, the most unresisting was chosen. Was it more necessary to kill *him* than one of the grown men? The answer be, No....

There is no path safe for judges to tread but to ascertain the law to the best of their ability, and to declare it according to their judgment, and if in any case the law appears to be too severe on individuals, to leave it to the Sovereign to exercise that prerogative of mercy which the Constitution has entrusted to the hands fittest to dispense it. It must not be supposed that, in refusing to admit temptation to be an excuse for crime, it is forgotten how terrible the temptation was, how awful the suffering, how hard in such trials to keep the judgment straight and the conduct pure. We are often compelled to set up standards we cannot reach ourselves, and to lay down rules which we could not ourselves satisfy. But a man has no right to declare temptation to be an excuse, though he might himself have yielded to it, nor allow compassion for the criminal to change or weaken in any manner the legal definition of the crime....

[The Lord Chief Justice thereupon passed sentence of death in the usual form. The prisoners were afterwards respited and their sentence commuted to one of six months' imprisonment without hard labour.]

Judgment for the Crown

■ *Questions*

1. Should it be a defence that many lives would be saved by the sacrifice of one?

2. The Model Penal Code, §3.02 provides: 'recognizing that the sanctity of life has a supreme place in the hierarchy of values, it is nonetheless true that conduct that results in taking life may promote the very value sought to be protected by the law of homicide.' Is this what the judges should have recognized in *Dudley and Stephens*?

3. What if, instead of choosing to kill and eat the cabin boy, the crew had drawn lots and it was cabin boy who happened to draw the shortest lot? Would this have impacted upon the court's reasoning? Should it have?

4. A is injured and needs an immediate blood transfusion to save his life. B is the only person who can be found locally with the same rare blood group. He refuses to give any blood. May B be overpowered and the blood taken without his consent?

5. Should the criminal law set up standards reasonable people cannot reach?

See further on *Dudley and Stephens*, A. W. B. Simpson, *Cannibalism and the Common Law* (1984).

Re A (children) (conjoined twins: separation)

[2000] EWCA Civ 254, Court of Appeal, Civil Division, http://www.bailii.org/ew/cases/EWCA/Civ/2000/254.html

(Ward, Brooke and Robert Walker LJJ)

Brooke LJ:

Necessity: modern academic writers

At the coroner's inquest conducted in October 1987 into the Zeebrugge disaster, an army corporal gave evidence that he and dozens of other people were near the foot of a rope ladder. They were all in the water and in danger of drowning. Their route to safety, however, was blocked for at least ten minutes by a young man who was petrified by cold or fear (or both) and was unable to move up or down. Eventually the corporal gave instructions that the man should be pushed off the ladder, and he was never seen again. The corporal and many others were then able to climb up the ladder to safety.

In his third lecture, 'Necessity and Duress', Professor Smith [Hamlyn Lectures (published under the title *Justification and Excuse in the Criminal Law* (1989)] evinced the belief at pp 77–78 that if such a case ever did come to court it would not be too difficult for a judge to distinguish *R v Dudley and Stephens*. He gave two reasons for this belief. The first was that there was no question of choosing who had to die (the problem which Lord Coleridge had found unanswerable in *R v Dudley and Stephens*) because the unfortunate young man on the ladder had chosen himself by his immobility there. The second was that unlike the ship's boy on the Mignonette, the young man, although in no way at fault, was preventing others from going where they had a right, and a most urgent need, to go, and was thereby unwittingly imperilling their lives.

I would add that the same considerations would apply if a pilotless aircraft, out of control and running out of fuel, was heading for a densely populated town. Those inside the aircraft were in any event 'destined to die'. There would be no question of human choice in selecting the candidates for death, and if their inevitable deaths were accelerated by the plane being brought down on waste ground, the lives of countless other innocent people in the town they were approaching would be saved.

It was an argument along these lines that led the rabbinical scholars involved in the 1977 case of conjoined twins to advise the worried parents that the sacrifice of one of their children in order to save the other could be morally justified. George J Annas *Siamese Twins: Killing One to Save the Other* (Hastings Center Report, April 1987) p 27, described how they—

> 'reportedly relied primarily on two analogies. In the first, two men jump from a burning aeroplane. The parachute of the second man does not open, and as he falls past the first man, he grabs his legs. If the parachute cannot support them both, is the first man morally justified in kicking the second man away to save himself? Yes, said the rabbis, since the man whose parachute didn't open was "designated for death". The second analogy involves a caravan surrounded by bandits. The bandits demand a particular member of the caravan be turned over for execution; the rest will go free. Assuming that the named individual has been "designated for death", the rabbis concluded it was acceptable to surrender him to save everyone else. Accordingly, they concluded that if a twin A was "designated for death" and could not survive in any event, but twin B could, surgery that would kill twin A to help improve the chance of twin B was acceptable.'

There is, however, no indication in the submission we received from the Archbishop of Westminster that such a solution was acceptable as part of the philosophy he espoused. The judge's dilemma in a case where he or she is confronted by a choice between conflicting philosophies was thoughtfully discussed by Simon Gardner in his article 'Necessity's Newest Inventions' (1991) 11 OJLS 125. He explored the possibility of rights-based justifications based on a principle that otherwise unlawful actions might be justified where the infraction was calculated to vindicate a right superior to the interest protected by the rule, but he was perplexed by the idea that judges in a democracy could make their own decisions as to what was right and what was wrong in the face of established law prohibiting the conduct in question. The whole article requires careful study, but its author concluded that in jurisdictions where rights were guaranteed, the judicial vindication of a guaranteed right would be seen as protecting democracy rather than contravening it. This consideration does not, however, assist us in a case where there are conflicting rights of apparently equal status and conflicting philosophies as to the priority, if any, to be given to either.

Before I leave the treatment afforded to the topic of necessity by modern academic writers of great distinction (there is a valuable contemporary summary of the issues in Smith and Hogan's *Criminal Law* (9th edn, 1999) pp 245–252 [13th edn, 2011, pp 365–375]), I must mention the section entitled 'Justifications, Necessity and the Choice of Evils' in *Principles of Criminal Law* (3rd edn, 1999) by Professor Andrew Ashworth. After referring to the facts of the Zeebrugge incident he said at pp 153–154:

> 'No English court has had to consider this situation, and it is clear that only the strongest prohibition on the taking of an innocent life would prevent a finding of justification here: in an urgent situation involving a decision between n lives and $n + 1$ lives, is there not a strong social interest in preserving the greater number of lives? Any residual principle of this kind must be carefully circumscribed; it involves the sanctity of life, and therefore the highest value with which the criminal law is concerned. Although there is a provision in the Model Penal Code allowing for a defence of "lesser evil", it fails to restrict the application of the defence to cases of imminent threat, opening up the danger of citizens trying to justify all manner of conduct by reference to overall good effects. The moral issues are acute: "not just anything is permissible on the ground that it would yield a net saving of lives". Closely connected with this is the moral problem of "choosing one's victim", a problem which arises when, for example, a lifeboat is in danger of sinking, necessitating the throwing overboard of some passengers, or when two people have to kill and eat another if any of the three is to survive. To countenance a legal justification in such cases would be to regard the victim's rights as morally and politically less worthy than the rights of those protected lives saved and deaths avoided in the aggregate but must somehow attempt to come to grips with the nature of the rights and duties being assessed. This would seem to be consistent with Lord Coleridge's conclusion that necessity can provide no justification for the taking of a life, such an act representing the most extreme form of rights violation. As discussed above, if any defence for such a homicidal act is to succeed, it would have to be framed as an excuse grounded on self-preservation. It could not possibly be declared by the court to be rightful.'

See Richard Huxtable, 'Separation of Conjoined Twins: What Next for English Law?' [2002] Crim LR 459; J. Rogers, 'Necessity, Private-Defence and the Killing of Mary' [2001] Crim LR 515.

■ *Questions*

1. Was the corporal in Zeebrugge guilty of murder under the law as stated in *Dudley and Stephens*?

2. According to a report in *The Times*, 5 May 1998, the commander of an Australian naval ship 'took the decision to save the rest of his crew by sealing four sailors in the blazing engine room, consigning them to certain death, after rescuers were beaten back by the flames'. Was the officer guilty of murder of the four sailors? If he had refused to seal the engine room and the four had escaped but the ship had been lost with most of the crew, would he have been guilty of any offences? Can it be the law that both of the alternative courses amount to crimes? If the officer's belief that the only way to save the ship and crew was to sacrifice the four men was reasonable, is it conceivable that he would be convicted of murder?—or any crime?

3. Consider the case of conjoined twins who have only one heart. The heart cannot be divided, as some other organs can. It cannot support both twins and, if nothing is done, both will soon die. Should that be allowed to happen if one can be saved by being given the heart? Will the inevitable death of the other be murder? Should it make any difference that one is (i) slightly stronger, (ii) very much stronger, than the other? Or that one is a boy and the other a girl and the parents dearly want a boy and are not interested in a girl (or vice versa)?

4. Is it lawful for a military aircraft to shoot down a hijacked passenger aircraft, killing all the passengers and crew where the hijackers on board are piloting the plane on a suicide mission towards a skyscraper in the city? See M. Bohlander, 'In Extremis: Hijacked Airplanes, Collateral Damage and the Limits of the Criminal Law' [2006] Crim LR 579, and the letter by D. Ormerod [2006] Crim LR referring to the Sixth Report of the Parliamentary Defence and Security Committee (2002).

11.5.3 Necessity and killing to alleviate pain

In the case of *Bodkin Adams* ([1957] Crim LR 365, (1957) The Times, 9 April), Devlin J directed the jury that there is no special defence justifying a doctor in giving drugs which shorten life in the case of severe pain: 'If life were cut short by weeks or months it was just as much murder as if it were cut short by years.' He went on:

> But that does not mean that a doctor aiding the sick or dying has to calculate in minutes or hours, or perhaps in days or weeks, the effect on a patient's life of the medicines which he administers. If the first purpose of medicine—the restoration of health—can no longer be achieved, there is still much for the doctor to do, and he is entitled to do all that is proper and necessary to relieve pain and suffering even if measures he takes may incidentally shorten life.

In September 1992, Dr Nigel Cox was convicted of attempted murder and sentenced to 12 months' imprisonment suspended for a year after he had administered potassium chloride to a patient, B, a 70-year-old woman, in order to terminate the great pain from which she was suffering. B died within five minutes of the injection. She had pleaded with Dr Cox to end her life. He was not charged with murder because it was impossible to prove the cause of death. In this case, painkilling drugs were no longer effective to relieve B's suffering. Dr Cox decided to give the injection of potassium chloride which had the effect of stopping her heart. He said: 'I seemed to have no more options left. She was going to die very soon in any case. I was faced with a choice of several evils. I chose what seemed to me the least evil with respect to [B] at that time.' An expert medical witness at a subsequent General Medical Council hearing said that Dr Cox's mistake was to give potassium chloride; a large dose of sedative, causing B to lapse into a coma, would have fallen on the right side of the law ((1992) The Times, 18 November).

■ *Questions*

What is the difference between administering potassium chloride in order to end pain and administering the sedative to do so, if the doctor knows that the sedative will also shorten life? Is it that the purpose of the doctor in the former case is to kill in order to relieve pain whereas in the latter his purpose is to relieve pain? Is this a valid distinction?

Dr Moor's Case (Hooper J) ('The Trial of Dr David Moor' by Anthony Arlidge QC [2000] Crim LR 31 and comment by J. C. Smith at 41) seems to confirm that there is a special doctor's defence: although satisfied that he knew his act would accelerate death significantly, the jury is not entitled to convict him of murder if they think his purpose was, or may have been, to give treatment which, in the circumstances as he understood them, he believed to be proper treatment to relieve pain. This seems to be, in substance, an application of the doctrine of double effect.

The Court of Appeal, in *R (Nicklinson) v Ministry of Justice* [2013] EWCA Civ 961, has recently reiterated that necessity cannot be pleaded as a defence to murder, in this case in the context of euthanasia. It was held that whether the defence ought to be available on a charge of murder is a matter for Parliament, not the courts. See F. Stark, 'Necessity and *Nicklinson*' [2013] Crim LR 949.

11.5.3.1 The doctrine of double effect

This is a philosophical or theological rather than a legal doctrine which applies where a person knows that his act will inevitably have two immediate consequences, one good and one bad. If he acts with the sole purpose of bringing about the good consequence, he is not to be blamed for bringing about the bad one. According to Glanville Williams, *The Sanctity of Life in the Criminal Law* (1957), p 184, 'it is allowed to be used only when both effects are the immediate result of the act'. The doctrine is not applied if the good effect is the result of the bad one for this would be to admit the unacceptable proposition that the end justifies the means.

Ward LJ in *Re A (children) (conjoined twins: surgical separation)* [2000] EWCA Civ 254 readily accepted that the doctrine could apply to the doctor administering drugs to a patient for the sole purpose of relieving pain, knowing that the effect would be to accelerate the patient's death, but thought it could not apply in the case before him where the good effect was on one patient and the bad effect on another. Brooke LJ also thought that:

> ...the doctrine of double effect could have no possible application in this case because...by no stretch of the imagination it could be said that the surgeons would be acting in Mary's best interests when they prepared an operation which benefit Jodie but kill Mary.

This is difficult to follow since the doctrine presupposes one bad as well as one good consequence. Although Robert Walker LJ thought the operation would be in the best interests of both twins, he recognized that to kill Mary, merely because it was in her best interests to die, would have been murder and, if it was murder, it could hardly be regarded, in law, as other than an evil consequence, albeit an evil consequence which would not be unlawful because it was not 'the purpose or intention of the surgery'.

> ■ *Questions*
>
> Did not Ward and Brooke LJJ in substance apply the doctrine of double effect (at least as it is described by Glanville Williams) in *Re A*? Was their purpose not to bring about the good result—the healthy survival of Jodie while simultaneously causing the (as they acknowledged) bad result, killing Mary?

11.5.4 Evaluating the objective threat D faces

R v Quayle and Other Appeals; Attorney-General's Reference (No 2 of 2004); R v Ditchfield
[2005] EWCA Crim 1415, Court of Appeal, Criminal Division, http:www.bailli.org/ew/cases/EWCA/Crim/2005/1415.html

(Mance LJ, Newman and Fulford JJ)

The court heard a number of appeals against conviction and a reference by the Attorney General because they raised similar issues, in particular whether the common law defence of 'necessity by circumstance' (*sic*) should be left to the jury in respect of offences of: (i) possession, cultivation or production of cannabis where the accused had genuinely and reasonably believed that the activities were *necessary* to avoid him suffering pain arising from a pre-existing medical condition or from conventional medicine to which he or she would otherwise resort to reduce the pain; and (ii) importation or possession with intent to supply cannabis for the purpose of alleviating the same type of pain suffered by others in such a predicament.

In rejecting the availability of a defence of necessity to each case, the Court of Appeal summarized a number of principles relating to that defence.

Lord Justice Mance:

[His lordship referred to the facts and legislative framework under the Misuse of Drugs Act 1971 for prescription of drugs and licensing of production, cultivation, supply and possession. His lordship also set out in detail a reply to a report dated 4 November 1998 of the House of Lords Select Committee on Science and Technology, 'Cannabis, the Scientific and Medical Evidence' (9th Report, 1997–98, HL Paper 151, Session 1997–98).]

. . . The primary case advanced on behalf of Messrs Quayle, Wales [who were cultivating the drug for personal use to ease their pain with various illnesses] and Kenny [who was in possession and was supplying to those who preferred to use cannabis rather than conventional medicines to ease pain] is that their cultivation or preparation (and use and possession) of cannabis were all excusable in law since they genuinely and reasonably believed that these activities were necessary to avoid them suffering serious injury or pain, and that the charges against them should have been left to the jury on that basis; alternatively, that, if such activities were only excusable in law if necessary to avoid serious injury (as distinct from pain), the judge should also have left the jury to consider the charges on that basis. In this context, Mr Fitzgerald submits that, on the evidence, it was open to the jury to conclude that pain may involve or lead to psychological injury and/or that the alternative analgesic drugs may themselves cause 'serious injury'. . . .

In the cases of Messrs Taylor and Lee [who were importing with a view to distributing to those who would use the drug as a painkiller], the contention is that the judge's ruling in each case wrongly prevented the jury considering a defence of necessity, to the effect that they acted as they did in the interests of others towards whom they reasonably regarded themselves as responsible and who they genuinely and reasonably feared would suffer serious pain and/or (if required) serious injury if they did not receive the cannabis being imported or supplied. The successful defence of Mr Ditchfield was to that effect.

[His lordship considered the degree of threat in cases such as *F*, *Bourne*, etc in this section.]

In the light of these authorities, we are not persuaded by Mr Fitzgerald's attempts to derive from individual authorities in different areas a coherent over-arching principle applicable in all cases of necessity. Such an attempt appears to us to pay too little attention to the particular context of individual decisions, and not to correspond with the case by case approach suggested by the authorities. However, there is a recognised defence of duress by threats, to which it is clear that the defence of necessity by circumstances bears a close affinity. Save that, in the present cases at least, the offences in question are not readily seen as involving any individual victim, the arguments which Lord Bingham mentioned in *Hasan* in favour of a confined definition appear to us applicable to any defence of necessity by circumstances.

Apart from the general considerations addressed . . . above, there are also detailed requirements of any defence of necessity which are indicated by the common law authorities and which the present cases in our view lack.

Extraneous circumstances. Lord Bingham spoke in *Hasan* of the need for 'a just and well-founded fear', while accepting that threats of death or serious injury will suffice. He noted that the relevant requirements had been defined objectively, and went on (with the majority of the House) to apply the same approach when he decided that the defence was not available if the defendant ought reasonably to have foreseen the risk of coercion. It is by 'the standards of honest and reasonable men' therefore that the existence or otherwise of such a fear or such threats falls to be decided. We have observed that Lord Bingham did not address or comment on the case of *Safi*, in which this court held that what matters is not whether there was actually a threat of torture, but whether there was a reasonable perception of such a threat. But that still involves an objective test based on external events, conduct or words about which evidence would have to be produced or given. It is also notable that Lord Bingham described the criminal defence which he thought had a close affinity with duress by threats as 'necessity. . . by extraneous circumstances'.

There is therefore considerable authority pointing towards a need for extraneous circumstances capable of objective scrutiny by judge and jury and as such, it may be added, more likely to be capable of being checked and, where appropriate, met by other evidence. Lord Bingham's dictum fits in this regard with dicta in *Abdul-Hussain*, the decision in *Rodger & Rose* and Lord Woolf's dicta in *Shayler* speaking of a 'fundamental ingredient' of 'some external agency' as well as with the non-counsel decision in *Brown*.

The appellants' objection to any such distinction is that it means, for example, that the commission of an offence could be excused if it was to avoid the realisation of a danger of one's wife committing suicide (cf *Martin*), but not if in that case it had been the wife herself who, realising that she would commit suicide unless she drove her son to school, had driven while disqualified (cf *Rodger & Rose*). Likewise, they suggest, the distinction could deny a defence of necessity to a person at risk of serious injury or perhaps pain, but allow it potentially to a parent or carer responsible for the well-being of such a person; and in circumstances like those in *Rodger & Rose*, a compassionate warder with responsibility for the prisoner, could release the prisoner, if he was able to detect the risk of suicide in time; while in cases such as the present, a person in or at risk of serious injury or pain could not himself engage in cultivation, possession or use of cannabis for medical purposes, but a parent or carer responsible for his upkeep could cultivate or obtain and administer cannabis to him or her for such purposes. The appellants suggest that none of these distinctions can stand scrutiny, so that *Rodger & Rose* must be regarded as a special case based on policy considerations.

■ *Question*

Is the court's decision on this issue based on anything other than policy?

[His lordship continued:]

On the authorities . . . the requirement of an objectively ascertainable extraneous cause has a considerable, and in our view understandable, basis. It rests on the pragmatic consideration that the defence of necessity, which the Crown would carry the onus to disprove, must be confined within narrowly defined limits or it will become an opportunity for almost untriable and certainly peculiarly difficult issues, not to mention abusive defences. On that basis, we consider that the Crown's first narrow point, namely that, for the defence of necessity of circumstances to be potentially available, there must be extraneous circumstances capable of objective scrutiny by judge and jury, is valid.

Pain. It is, however, submitted on behalf of Messrs. Quayle, Wales and Kenny that any such test is satisfied in all their cases both because of the objectively ascertainable facts giving rise to the pain they suffer actually, or would suffer if they were not to use cannabis, whether from their afflictions or from taking alternative lawful medicaments, and because pain is capable of some degree of objective scrutiny and is not wholly subjective. In addressing this submission, we do not gain any real assistance from cases from other areas of the law, where distinctions may or may not have been drawn between injury and harm or pain.

The reason why we would not accept the submission is that the law has to draw a line at some point in the criteria which it accepts as sufficient to satisfy any defence of duress or necessity. Courts and juries have to work on evidence. If such defences were to be expanded in theory to cover every possible case in which it might be felt that it would be hard if the law treated the conduct in question as criminal, there would be likely to be arguments in considerable numbers of cases, where there was no clear objective basis by reference to which to test or determine such arguments. It is unlikely that this would lead overall to a more coherent result, or even necessarily to a more just disposition of any individual case. There is, on any view, a large element of subjectivity in the assessment of pain not directly associated with some current physical injury. The legal defences of duress by threats and necessity by circumstances should in our view be confined to cases where there is an imminent danger of physical injury. In reaching these conclusions, we recognise that hard cases can be postulated, but these, as Lord Bingham said, can and should commonly be capable of being dealt with in other ways. The nature of the sentences passed in the cases before us is consistent with this.

■ *Question*

Can pain or the threat of pain be equated with an extraneous threat of serious harm?

Imminence and immediacy. . . . In each of these three cases, the defendant was taking a deliberately considered course of conduct over a substantial period of time, involving continuous or regular breaches of the law. In each case, the defendant was not the immediate sufferer and had every opportunity to reflect and to desist. The compassionate grounds which may well have motivated Mr Taylor and Ms Lee and which the jury evidently accepted did motivate Mr Ditchfield cannot avoid the fact that they deliberately chose to act contrary to the law on a continuous basis.

We note in passing that the court in *Southwark L.B.C. v. Williams* refused to recognise a defence of necessity raised by squatters in answer to a claim to recover possession of properties owned by the council. The evidence was that there were no homes for the squatters, they had been living in 'quite deplorable conditions' and the empty council properties in which they then squatted had been vandalised by the council to make them unfit for habitation, but that they had entered and lived there in an orderly way and repaired them after entry. Nevertheless, the court upheld summary possession orders, 'for the sake of law and order', as Lord Denning put it, and because the circumstances 'do not . . . constitute the sort of emergency to which the plea [of necessity] applies', as Edmund Davies LJ said. Megaw LJ agreed with both judgments on this aspect. The case is an old one, and the law has developed, so that we need not consider it further. But the underlying theme, that a continuous and deliberate course of otherwise unlawful self-help is unlikely to give rise to the defence has itself, in our view, continuing relevance.

. . . Where there is no imminent or immediate threat or peril, but only a general assertion of an internal motivation to engage in prohibited activities in order to prevent or alleviate pain, it is also difficult to identify any extraneous or objective factors by reference to which a jury could be expected to measure whether the motivation was such as to override the defendant's will or to force him to act as he did. If the response is that the defendant was not forced, but chose to act as he did, then the considerations mentioned in the previous paragraph apply.

■ *Questions*

1. Have the courts now merged the defences of duress and necessity completely? Were these individuals compelled to claim to be under a threat of death or serious injury simply to attempt to fit into the duress of circumstances defence?

2. The court's language is in terms of necessity, but does it not narrow that defence by the requirements of duress of circumstances?

In *Altham* [2006] EWCA Crim 07, the Court of Appeal rejected the argument in an appeal similar to *Quayle* that the State prosecuting sufferers in circumstances of their cultivation or possession for private use infringed Article 3 of the European Convention on Human Rights (ECHR) by subjecting the sufferers to torture or inhuman or degrading treatment.

11.5.5 Relationship between defences of duress and necessity

In *Shayler*, the Court of Appeal (Woolf LCJ, Wright and Leveson JJ) (reported sub nom *S (D)* in [2001] Crim LR 986) discussed the relationship between duress of circumstances and necessity. The House of Lords ([2002] 2 All ER 477) held that no question of duress or necessity arose and that it was 'a little unfortunate' that these topics had been discussed by the trial judge and the Court of Appeal. Lord Bingham (at [15]) and Lord Hutton (at [117]) made it clear that they did not necessarily agree with all that was said about these defences. The Court of Appeal's remarks are therefore *obiter* but, coming from a strong court, of some weight. Woolf LCJ said that *Abdul-Hussain* (section 11.3.2.6, p 371) reflected other decisions 'which have treated the defences of duress and necessity as being part of the same defence and the extended form of the defence [ie, duress of circumstances] as being different labels for essentially the same thing'. The case are unclear about whether they are separate.

■ *Question*

What are the courts so worried about in having a separate defence of necessity?

(i) It seems to be settled that duress cannot be a defence to murder or attempted murder (*Howe and Bannister*, section 11.3.5, p 382, *Gotts*, section 11.3.5, p 388) but is it not now reasonably clear that, following *Re A (children) (conjoined twins)*, necessity may in some circumstances be a defence?

(ii) The only occasion for a defence of duress of either variety is imminent threat of death or GBH. But is necessity so limited? Should it not be a defence to a charge of battery that D was pushing a child to save him from some quite minor injury or even damage to his clothing?

(iii) Necessity is a defence only if the evil which D seeks to avoid is greater than that which he knows he is causing. But if D yields to torture which no ordinary person could be expected to resist, should he not be excused, however grave the consequences of his capitulation?

(iv) It seems that necessity may create a duty to act—cf *Re A* and *F v West Berkshire Health Authority*, section 11.5.1, p 399—but can duress ever do so?

If Parliament were to abolish the defence of duress by threats, thereby remedying the present inconsistencies, what would become of duress of circumstances? Since the latter has developed by analogy to the former, it would be logical to decide that they stand or fall together. It would certainly be very strange if the main growth were cut down and the off-shoot left standing. It is not clear what effect this would have on the defence of necessity, which certainly exists though its limits are uncertain. It would be absurd to provide that threats of, or the imminence of, death or serious bodily harm should never be a defence if other less serious threats or dangers might; so the logical implication might be the abolition of any existing defence of necessity as well. This was at one time proposed by the Law Commission but the proposal attracted such powerful criticism that it was soon withdrawn.

11.6 The use of force in public or private defence

Force causing personal injury, damage to property or even death may be justified or excused because the force was reasonably used in the defence of certain public or private interests. Public and private defence is therefore a general defence to any crime of which the use of force is an element or which is alleged to have been committed by the use of force. It is clear that the burden of disproving claims of public or private defence rests on the prosecution.

The common law governing self-defence had evolved to a clear position. Private or 'self'-defence at common law coexisted and often overlapped with the statutory plea under the Criminal Law Act 1967, s 3, which applies only where D uses force in the prevention of a crime. In the last few years Parliament has intervened so that we now have a common law defence 'clarified' in the Criminal Justice and Immigration Act 2008 existing alongside s 3 for cases where D is using force to prevent crime and a supposedly different test to be applied where D's use of force was against a trespasser in a dwelling.

All these defences based on use of force can be conveniently described in terms of trigger and response:

- the trigger being D's belief that the circumstances render it reasonable for him to use force; and

- the response being the proportionality of the amount of force he uses.

At common law it was clear that for the trigger element of the defence it is sufficient that D genuinely though mistakenly and unreasonably believes that there is a need for force. For the response element of the defence, the degree of force used must, in the opinion of the jury, be reasonable based on the facts as D believed them to be. For example, if D believed that he was being attacked with a deadly weapon and he used only such force as was reasonable to repel such an attack, he has a defence to any charge of an offence arising out of his use of that force. It is immaterial that he was mistaken. Indeed, it is immaterial that he was unreasonably mistaken. Section 76 of the Criminal Justice and Immigration Act 2008 now confirms this established common law principle.

11.6.1 The belief in the need to use force

11.6.1.1 The common law test of D's belief in the need for some force

At common law, D could rely on self-defence where he had a genuine belief in the need for the use of force.

R v Williams

(1987) 78 Cr App R 276, Court of Appeal, Criminal Division

(Lord Lane CJ, Skinner and McCowan JJ)

One M saw a youth rob a woman in a street. He caught the youth and held him, but the latter broke from M's grasp. M caught the youth again and knocked him to the ground. The appellant, who had only seen the later stages of the incident was told by M that he, M, was arresting the youth for mugging a woman. M said that he was a police officer, which was untrue, so when asked by the appellant for his warrant card, he could not produce one. A struggle followed and the appellant assaulted M by punching him in the face and was charged with assault occasioning actual bodily harm contrary to section 47 of the Offences against the Person Act 1861. His defence was that he honestly believed that the youth was being unlawfully assaulted by M. The jury was directed that, on the assumption that M was acting lawfully, the appellant's state of mind on the issue of defence of another was to be determined by whether the appellant had an honest belief based on reasonable grounds that reasonable force was necessary to prevent a crime. The appellant was convicted and appealed on the ground that the judge had misdirected the jury. Held, that the jury should have been directed that, first, the prosecution had the burden of proving the unlawfulness of the appellant's actions; secondly, if the appellant might have been labouring under a mistake as to facts, he was to be judged according to his mistaken view of the facts, whether or not the mistake was, on an objective view, reasonable or not. The reasonableness or unreasonableness of the appellant's belief was material to the question whether the belief was held by him at all. If the belief was held, its unreasonableness, so far as guilt or innocence was concerned, was irrelevant. Accordingly, the appeal must be allowed and the conviction quashed.

[In the course of his judgment Lord Lane CJ, discussing the offence of assault, said ([1987] 3 All ER 411 at 414):]

The mental element necessary to constitute guilt is the intent to apply unlawful force to the victim. We do not believe that the mental element can be substantiated by simply showing an intent to apply force and no more.

This decision was approved in the Privy Council in the following case.

Beckford v R

[1987] 3 All ER 425, Privy Council, http://www.bailii.org/uk/cases/UKPC/1987/1.html

(Lords Keith, Elwyn-Jones, Templeman, Griffiths and Oliver)

The appellant, a police officer, while investigating a report that a man was terrorizing his family, shot and killed a man who ran out of the back of the house. There was a conflict of evidence as to the circumstances. At the trial of the appellant for murder, the judge directed the jury that he was entitled to be acquitted on the ground of self-defence if he had a reasonable belief that his life was in danger or that he was in danger of serious bodily harm. He appealed to the Court of Appeal in Jamaica on the ground that the jury should have been told that he had a defence if he had an honest belief in the danger, even if it was unreasonable. The appeal was dismissed. He appealed to the Privy Council.

Lord Griffiths:

The common law recognises that there are many circumstances in which one person may inflict violence on another without committing a crime, as for instance in sporting contests, surgical operations or, in the most extreme example, judicial execution. The common law has always recognised as one of these circumstances the right of a person to protect himself from attack and to act in the defence of others and if necessary to inflict violence on another in so doing. If no more force is used than is reasonable to repel the attack such force is not unlawful and no crime is committed. Furthermore, a man about to be attacked does not have to wait for his assailant to strike the first blow or fire the first shot: circumstances may justify a pre-emptive strike.

It is because it is an essential element of all crimes of violence that the violence or the threat of violence should be unlawful that self-defence, if raised as an issue in a criminal trial, must be disproved by the prosecution. If the prosecution fail to do so the accused is entitled to be acquitted because the prosecution will have failed to prove an essential element of the crime, namely that the violence used by the accused was unlawful.

If then a genuine belief, albeit without reasonable grounds, is a defence to rape because it negatives the necessary intention, so also must a genuine belief in facts which if true would justify self-defence be a defence to a crime of personal violence because the belief negatives the intent to act unlawfully. Their Lordships therefore approve the following passage from the judgment of Lord Lane CJ in *R v Williams* [1987] 3 All ER 411 at 415 as correctly stating the law of self-defence:

> 'The reasonableness or unreasonableness of the defendant's belief is material to the question of whether the belief was held by the defendant at all. If the belief was in fact held, its unreasonableness, so far as guilt or innocence is concerned, is neither here nor there. It is irrelevant. Were it otherwise, the defendant would be convicted because he was negligent in failing to recognise that the victim was not consenting or that a crime was not being committed and so on. In other words the jury should be directed, first of all, that the prosecution have the burden or duty of proving the unlawfulness of the defendant's actions, second, that if the defendant may have been labouring under a mistake as to the facts he must be judged according to his mistaken view of the facts and, third, that that is so whether the mistake was, on an objective view, a reasonable mistake or not. In a case of self-defence, where self-defence or the prevention of crime is concerned, if the jury come to the conclusion that the defendant believed, or may have believed, that he was being attacked or that a crime was being committed, and that force was necessary to protect himself or to prevent the crime, then the prosecution have not proved their case. If, however, the defendant's alleged belief was mistaken and if the mistaken belief was an unreasonable one, that may be a powerful reason for coming to the conclusion that the belief was not honestly held and should be rejected. Even if the jury come to the conclusion that the mistake was an unreasonable one, if the defendant may genuinely have been labouring under it, he is entitled to rely on it.'

Looking back, *DPP v Morgan* can now be seen as a landmark decision in the development of the common law, returning the law to the path on which it might have developed but for the inability of an accused to give evidence on his own behalf. Their Lordships note that not only has this development the approval of such distinguished criminal lawyers as Professor Glanville Williams and Professor Smith (see *Textbook of Criminal Law* (2nd edn, 1983) pp 137–138 and Smith and Hogan *Criminal Law* (5th edn, 1983) pp 329–330) but it also has the support of the Criminal Law Revision Committee (see 14th Report on Offences Against the Person (1980) (Cmnd 7844) and of the Law Commission (see Codification of the Criminal Law (1985) (Law Com no 143)).

There may be a fear that the abandonment of the objective standard demanded by the existence of reasonable grounds for belief will result in the success of too many spurious claims of self-defence. The English experience has not shown this to be the case. The Judicial Studies Board, with the approval of the Lord Chief Justice, has produced a model direction on self-defence which is now widely used by judges when summing up to juries. The direction contains the following guidance:

> 'Whether the plea is self-defence or defence of another, if the defendant may have been labouring under a mistake as to the facts, he must be judged according to his mistaken belief of the facts: that is so whether the mistake was, on an objective view a reasonable mistake or not.'

Their Lordships have heard no suggestion that this form of summing up has resulted in a disquieting number of acquittals. This is hardly surprising, for no jury is going to accept a man's assertion that he believed that he was about to be attacked without testing it against all the surrounding circumstances. In assisting the jury to determine whether or not the accused had a genuine belief the judge will of course direct their attention to those features of the evidence that make such a belief more or less probable. Where there are no reasonable grounds to hold a belief it will surely only be in exceptional circumstances that a jury will conclude that such a belief was or might have been held.

Their Lordships therefore conclude that the summing up in this case contained a material misdirection and they answer question 1(a) by saying that the test to be applied for self-defence is that a person may use such force as is reasonable in the circumstances as he honestly believes them to be in the defence of himself or another.

Appeal allowed. Conviction quashed

11.6.1.2 The statutory 'clarification'

76 Reasonable force for purposes of self-defence etc.

(1) This section applies where in proceedings for an offence—

    (a) an issue arises as to whether a person charged with the offence ('D') is entitled to rely on a defence within subsection (2), and

    (b) the question arises whether the degree of force used by D against a person ('V') was reasonable in the circumstances.

(2) The defences are—

    (a) the common law defence of self-defence;

    (aa) the common law defence of defence of property; and

    (b) the defences provided by section 3(1) of the Criminal Law Act 1967

(3) The question whether the degree of force used by D was reasonable in the circumstances is to be decided by reference to the circumstances as D believed them to be, and subsections (4) to (8) also apply in connection with deciding that question.

(4) If D claims to have held a particular belief as regards the existence of any circumstances—

    (a) the reasonableness or otherwise of that belief is relevant to the question whether D genuinely held it; but

    (b) if it is determined that D did genuinely hold it, D is entitled to rely on it for the purposes of subsection (3), whether or not—

        (i) it was mistaken, or

        (ii) (if it was mistaken) the mistake was a reasonable one to have made.

(5) But subsection (4)(b) does not enable D to rely on any mistaken belief attributable to intoxication that was voluntarily induced.

In *Keane* [2010] EWCA Crim 2514, Hughes LJ made the following observations on the operation of s 76.

4. The law of self-defence is not complicated. It represents a universally recognised commonsense concept. In our experience juries do not find that commonsense concept at all difficult to understand. The only potential difficulty for a judge is that he needs to remember the potential possibility of what lawyers would call a subjective element at an early stage of the exercise, whilst the critical question of the reasonableness of the response is, in lawyer's expressions, an objective one. In using those lawyer's terms we do not for a moment suggest that it is helpful to use them in a summing-up.

5. It is however very long established law that there are usually two and sometimes three stages into any enquiry into self-defence. There may be more, but these are the basic building blocks of a large proportion of the cases in which it is raised:

1. If there is a dispute about what happened to cause the defendant to use the violence that he did, and there usually is such a dispute, then the jury must decide it, attending of course to the onus and standard of proof.

2. *If* the defendant claims that he thought that something was happening which the jury may find was not happening, then the second question which arises is what did the defendant genuinely believe was happening to cause him to use the violence that he did? That question does not arise in every case. If it does arise then whether his belief was reasonable or not, providing it is genuinely held, he is to be judged on the facts as he believed them to be unless his erroneous belief is the result of voluntarily taken drink or drugs, in which event it is to be disregarded.

3. Once it has thus been decided on what factual basis the defendant's actions are to be judged, either because they are the things that actually happened and he knew them or because he genuinely believed in them even if they did not occur, then the remaining and critical question for the jury is: was his response reasonable, or proportionate (which means the same thing)? Was it reasonable (or proportionate) in all the circumstances? Unlike the earlier stages which may involve the belief of the defendant being the governing factor, the reasonableness of his response on the assumed basis of fact is a test solely for the jury and not for him. In resolving it the jury must usually take into consideration what are often referred to as the 'agony of the moment' factors. That means that the jury must be reminded when it arises, as it very often does, that there is in a confrontation no opportunity for the kind of hindsight or debate which can take place months afterwards in court. The defendant must act on the instant at any rate in a large number of cases. If he does so, and does no more than seems honestly and instinctively to be necessary, that is itself strong evidence that it was reasonable. It is strong evidence, not conclusive evidence. Whilst the jury's attention must be directed to these factors if they arise, the jury must also be made to understand that the decision of what is a reasonable response is not made by the defendant, it is made by the jury. We should perhaps add that 'in all the circumstances' means what it says. There can be no exhaustive catalogue of the events, human reactions and other circumstances which may affect the reasonableness or proportionality of what the defendant did. That is explicitly recognised by section 76(8).

6. The single judge invited the court to consider whether the statutory formulation of the law in section 76 might have contributed to any degree of confusion and debate which ensued before the judge in the second of our cases. We do not think in fact that section 76 contributed significantly to the debate in question, nor to such degree of confusion as there was. For the avoidance of doubt, it is perhaps helpful to say of section 76 three things: (a) it does not alter the law as it has been for many years; (b) it does not exhaustively state the law of self-defence but it does state the basic principles; (c) it does not require any summing-up to rehearse the whole of its contents just because they are now contained in statute. The fundamental rule of summing-up remains the same. The jury must be told the law which applies to the facts which it might find; it is not to be troubled by a disquisition on the parts of the law which do not affect the case.

■ *Question*

How if at all does the Criminal Justice and Immigration Act 2008, s 76, 'clarify' the common law principle as laid down in *Beckford*?

For many years the courts stated that a defendant could rely on a public or private defence only if he believed *on reasonable grounds* in the circumstances which entitled him to take the defensive action—for example, a belief that he faced certain death at the hands of an aggressor unless he took the action in question was no defence to a charge of murder unless the belief was based on reasonable grounds. As we have seen, in *Gladstone Williams*, section 11.6.1.1, p 415, the Court of Appeal held that this was an incorrect statement of the common law and that the only question was whether the belief was honestly held. The view that only reasonable mistakes of fact can excuse has now been comprehensively repudiated by the House of Lords: *B (a minor) v DPP* and *K*, section 7.3.1, p 185.

On the other hand, we have also seen that in the common law of duress the courts still insist that the defence is open only to one who believes on reasonable grounds in the threat of death or grievous bodily harm: *Graham*, approved in *Howe*, section 11.3.5, p 381.

Not everyone agrees with the 'subjective' approach to self-defence. The Australian courts continue to require reasonable grounds for a defence of self-defence, an approach which is defended by S. M. H. Yeo, *Compulsion in the Criminal Law* (1990), pp 200–219. A distinction is made between elements of offences (as to which a subjective test is appropriate) and defence elements, where the test is objective. The distinction is related to the theory of justification and excuse. Yeo puts the case of 'a person who is unnaturally apprehensive or cowardly which leads her to honestly but unreasonably believe that she is being attacked. Without the limitation of reasonable belief, such a person can react violently with impunity. And she can do so time and again if that is her inclination.'

■ *Questions*

1. Is this a valid objection to the subjective test?

2. Will jurors see through spurious claims of self-defence?

3. Does s 76 of the 2008 Act make it more or less likely that those who take the law into their own hands will be convicted?

11.6.2 Evaluating the reasonableness of the force used

11.6.2.1 The common law test for assessing the amount of force D used

Owino [1996] 2 Cr App R 128, [1995] Crim LR 743 confirms explicitly that, 'a person may use such force as is (objectively) reasonable in the circumstances as he (subjectively) believes them to be'. See also *DPP v Armstrong-Braun* [1999] Crim LR 416.

R v Martin (Anthony)

[2002] 1 Cr App R 323, Court of Appeal, Criminal Division

(Lord Woolf CJ, Wright and Grigson JJ)

M lived alone in an isolated farmhouse ('Bleak House'). Two men, evidently burglars, broke a window and entered the house at night. M shot them both with a pump-action shotgun and one died. M's defence of self-defence was rejected by the jury who convicted him of murder. He appealed on various grounds. It was held that he was not entitled to rely on the evidence of two psychiatrists, not called at the trial, to the effect that he was suffering from an abnormality of mind, a long-standing personality disorder; and that the breaking into his house would be perceived by him as being a greater threat to his safety than it would in the case of a normal person.

Lord Woolf CJ:

Mr Wolkind [for the appellant] relied on the recent decision of the House of Lords in *R v Smith (Morgan)* [2001] 1 Cr App Rep 31 [2001] 1 AC 146. This was also a provocation case that Mr Wolkind contended could be applied to the similar issues which arise when a defendant relies on self-defence. In that case Smith was relying upon evidence that he suffered from clinical depression. There was no dispute that the evidence was admissible and relevant on the issue as to whether he was provoked, the subjective issue. The problem was whether the evidence was admissible as being relevant on the objective issue of loss of self-control. As to this the majority of their Lordships came to the conclusion that the jury were entitled to take into account some characteristic, whether temporary or permanent, which affected the degree of control which society could reasonably expect of a defendant and which it would be unjust not to take into account.

Is the same approach appropriate in the case of self-defence? There are policy reasons for distinguishing provocation from self-defence. Provocation only applies to murder, but self-defence applies to all assaults. In addition, provocation does not provide a complete defence; it only reduces the offence from murder to manslaughter. There is also the undoubted fact that self-defence is raised in a great many cases resulting from minor assaults and it would be wholly disproportionate to encourage medical disputes in cases of that sort. Lord Hobhouse in his dissenting speech in *Smith* recognised that in relation to self-defence, too generous an approach as to what is reasonable could result in an 'exorbitant defence' (para. 186). Lord Hoffmann also appeared conscious of this. As a matter of principle we would reject the suggestion that the approach of the majority in *Smith* in relation to provocation should be applied directly to the different issue of self-defence.

We would accept that the jury are entitled to take into account in relation to self-defence the physical characteristics of the defendant. However, we would not agree that it is appropriate, except in exceptional circumstances which would make the evidence especially probative, in deciding whether excessive force has been used to take into account whether the defendant is suffering from some psychiatric condition....

[Having rejected the defence of self-defence, the court quashed the conviction for murder and substituted a conviction for manslaughter on the ground of diminished responsibility. NB: the defence of provocation has been replaced by that of loss of control—see Chapter 16.]

In *Shaw v R* [2002] 1 Cr App R 77, [2002] Crim LR 140, PC, D appealed against his conviction for murder in Belize, having unsuccessfully raised self-defence. It was common ground that the applicable law was as stated in Smith and Hogan, *Criminal Law* (9th edn), p 253, and as it was put by D's counsel: '... you will judge him as he saw it and only as he saw it'. The Board (Lords Bingham, Hoffmann, Cooke and Scott, and Sir Patrick Russell), applying the common law of England and Belize framed the two essential questions for the jury:

(1) Did the appellant honestly believe or may he have believed that it was necessary to defend himself?

(2) If so, and taking the circumstances *and the danger* as the appellant honestly believed them to be, was the amount of force which he used reasonable?

■ *Questions*

1. Note the words, 'the danger as the appellant honestly believe[d] [it] to be'. If that is right, was the expert evidence properly excluded on the issue of self-defence in *Martin (Anthony)*?

2. Does s 76 put the decision of the Privy Council in *Shaw* on a statutory footing?

11.6.2.2 The statutory 'clarification'

Criminal Justice and Immigration Act 2008, s 76(3)

The question whether the degree of force used by D was reasonable in the circumstances is to be decided by reference to the circumstances as D believed them to be, and subsections (4) to (8) also apply in connection with deciding that question.

It is important to point out that although the reasonableness of the force used is to be evaluated by reference to the circumstances as D believed them to be, not all circumstances are permitted to be considered. In *Oye* [2013] EWCA Crim 1725 (see section 10.4, p 349) the Court of Appeal held that the reasonableness of D's actions was not to be judged according to what his delusions caused him to believe was necessary, namely that he was repelling an attack by evil spirits (who were in fact police officers). Davis LJ stated that: 'An insane person cannot set the standards of reasonableness as to the degree of force used by reference to his own insanity.' It was held that the statutory 'clarification' did not mandate a wholly subjective test. In the subsequent case of *Press* [2013] EWCA Crim 1849, Pitchford LJ explained the ratio of *Oye* in these terms: 'in the assessment of reasonableness of force used in self defence, an honest and instinctive belief in the necessity for the force used, formed because the defendant was acting under an insane delusion as to the nature of the threat, was to be left out of account.' The Act now makes clear that there is no duty on D to retreat, but the possibility that D could have retreated is to be considered as a relevant factor in deciding whether the degree of force was reasonable in the circumstances as he saw them.

■ *Questions*

1. Would Martin have been any more likely to be acquitted under s 76 of the 2008 Act than at common law?

2. Does s 76 clarify the law in respect of the characteristics of the accused which may be taken into account in evaluating his plea of self-defence?

11.6.3 'Householder' cases

Section 76 as amended by the Crime and Courts Act 2013 provides:

(5A) In a householder case, the degree of force used by D is not to be regarded as having been reasonable in the circumstances as D believed them to be if it was grossly disproportionate in those circumstances.

(6) In a case other than a householder case, the degree of force used by D is not to be regarded as having been reasonable in the circumstances as D believed them to be if it was disproportionate in those circumstances.

(6A) In deciding the question mentioned in subsection (3), a possibility that D could have retreated is to be considered (so far as relevant) as a factor to be taken into account, rather than as giving rise to a duty to retreat.

(7) In deciding the question mentioned in subsection (3) the following considerations are to be taken into account (so far as relevant in the circumstances of the case)—

(a) that a person acting for a legitimate purpose may not be able to weigh to a nicety the exact measure of any necessary action; and

(b) that evidence of a person's having only done what the person honestly and instinctively thought was necessary for a legitimate purpose constitutes strong evidence that only reasonable action was taken by that person for that purpose.

(8) Subsections (6A) and (7) are not to be read as preventing other matters from being taken into account where they are relevant to deciding the question mentioned in subsection (3).

(8A) For the purposes of this section 'a householder case' is a case where—

(a) the defence concerned is the common law defence of self defence,

(b) the force concerned is force used by D while in or partly in a building, or part of a building, that is a dwelling or is forces accommodation (or is both),

(c) D is not a trespasser at the time the force is used, and

(d) at that time D believed V to be in, or entering, the building or part as a trespasser.

(8B) Where—

(a) a part of a building is a dwelling where D dwells,

(b) another part of the building is a place of work for D or another person who dwells in the first part, and

(c) that other part is internally accessible from the first part, that other part, and any internal means of access between the two parts, are each treated for the purposes of subsection (8A) as a part of a building that is a dwelling.

(8C) Where—

(a) a part of a building is forces accommodation that is living or sleeping accommodation for D,

(b) another part of the building is a place of work for D or another person for whom the first part is living or sleeping accommodation, and

(c) that other part is internally accessible from the first part, that other part, and any internal means of access between the two parts, are each treated for the purposes of subsection (8A) as a part of a building that is forces accommodation.

(8D) Subsections (4) and (5) apply for the purposes of subsection (8A)(d) as they apply for the purposes of subsection (3).

(8E) The fact that a person derives title from a trespasser, or has the permission of a trespasser, does not prevent the person from being a trespasser for the purposes of subsection (8A).

(8F) In subsections (8A) to (8C)—

'building' includes a vehicle or vessel, and

'forces accommodation' means service living accommodation for the purposes of Part 3 of the Armed Forces Act 2006 by virtue of section 96(1)(a) or (b) of that Act.

(9) This section, except so far as making different provision for householder cases, is intended to clarify the operation of the existing defences mentioned in subsection (2).

(10) In this section—

(a) 'legitimate purpose' means—

(i) the purpose of self-defence under the common law,

(ia) the purpose of defence of property under the common law, or

(ii) the prevention of crime or effecting or assisting in the lawful arrest of persons mentioned in the provisions referred to in subsection (2)(b);

(b) references to self-defence include acting in defence of another person; and

(c) references to the degree of force used are to the type and amount of force used.

The Ministry of Justice produced guidance on the operation of the section.

If the case is 'a householder case', as defined in s 8A of the Act, the degree of force D used is not to be regarded as having been reasonable in the circumstances as D believed them to be if it was grossly disproportionate in those circumstances. This is intended to provide a degree of 'heightened protection' for householders. In a Ministry of Justice circular, this new element of the defence was explained in the following terms:

8. The provisions in section 43 of the Crime and Courts Act also amend section 76 of the 2008 Act. These changes go further than clarifying existing law; they strengthen the law in relation to householders who are defending themselves from intruders in their homes.

9. Section 43 adds new subsection (5A) to section 76 of the 2008 Act. The effect of subsection (5A) is that householders who use a disproportionate level of force to protect themselves or others in their homes will not automatically be regarded as having acted unlawfully and treated as criminals. The use of grossly disproportionate force will continue to be unlawful however.

10. The provision does *not* give householders free rein to use disproportionate force in every case they are confronted by an intruder. The new provision must be read in conjunction with the other elements of section 76 of the 2008 Act. The level of force used must still be reasonable in the circumstances as the householder believed them to be (section 76(3)). Section 76(7) says if people only do what they honestly and instinctively thought was necessary for a legitimate purpose, this will be strong evidence that only reasonable action was taken for that purpose.

11. The key change introduced by section 43 is that if householders act honestly and instinctively to protect themselves or their loved ones from intruders using force that was reasonable in the circumstances as they saw them, they will not be guilty of an offence if the level of force turns out to have been disproportionate in those circumstances. The provision is designed to give householders greater latitude in terrifying or extreme situations where they may not be thinking clearly about the precise level of force that is necessary to deal with the threat faced.

12. The court will need to consider the individual facts of each case, including the personal circumstances of the householder and the threat (real or perceived) posed by the offender. There are no hard and fast rules about what types of force might be regarded as 'disproportionate' and 'grossly disproportionate'. The following example is included for illustrative purposes only and prosecutors and the court would need to come to its own view, taking into account all of the evidence available and individual circumstances of the cases.

'A householder is woken during the night by the sound of breaking glass downstairs. His wife and children have also woken up and are very frightened. The householder goes downstairs to investigate and meets an intruder armed with a knife in the hallway. The intruder had broken a glass panel in the front door to enter the property. A scuffle ensues and the householder wrestles the knife from the intruder's hand and it drops to the floor. Having dropped his weapon and with the mother and children screaming upstairs, the intruder realises he has met his match and turns to flee through the open door. With adrenaline pumping and heart pounding, the householder instinctively punches the intruder on the back of the head as he leaves. He falls awkwardly and is knocked unconscious.'

13. In this case, the householder arguably did not need to strike the intruder again; he had already dropped the knife and was turning to make his escape. The level of force used in that split second was on one view disproportionate to the threat posed by the intruder in that instant. Section 43 of the Crime and Courts Act means that the householder would not be guilty of an offence in these circumstances, providing the court were satisfied that the use of force was reasonable in the circumstances as he saw them.

14. It is important to note, however, that new subsection (5A) adds that the use of grossly disproportionate force will never be lawful. This is to ensure, for example, that violent and/or calculated acts of revenge or retribution do not go unpunished. In the example given above, had the householder kicked and punched the intruder repeatedly or picked up the knife that had been dropped and stabbed him with it knowing full well that he was already unconscious, such an action is more likely to be considered as grossly disproportionate.

■ *Questions*

1. Does this make the defence even more complex? Was this amendment necessary? Will it have any practical effect?

2. If D confronts V in the garden, is this a 'householder case'? What about in the garden shed?

11.6.4 Use of force in making arrest or preventing crime

Criminal Law Act 1967, s 3

(1) A person may use such force as is reasonable in the circumstances in the prevention of crime, or in effecting or assisting in the lawful arrest of offenders or suspected offenders or of persons unlawfully at large.

(2) Sub-section (1) above shall replace the rules of the common law on the question when force used for a purpose mentioned in the sub-section is justified by that purpose.

Section 3 operates only where D responds to prevent a 'crime'. In *Jones and others* [2006] UKHL 16 (section 11.3.2.9, p 376), the House of Lords concluded that the concept of 'crime' in this context can only have been intended to mean a 'domestic' crime (ie not a crime only in international law). The Criminal Law Revision Committee (CLRC) explained the proposed s 3 in very broad terms:

[T]he court, in considering what was reasonable force, would take into account all the circumstances, including in particular the nature and degree of force used, the seriousness of the evil to be prevented and the possibility of preventing it by other means; but there is no need to specify in the clause the criteria for deciding the question. Since the clause is framed in general terms, it is not limited to arrestable or any other class of offences, though in the case of very trivial offences it would very likely be held that it would not be reasonable to use even the slightest force to prevent them. (Cmnd 2659, para 23)

Section 3 excuses only the use of force. In *Blake v DPP* [1993] Crim LR 586, D, demonstrating against the Iraqi war, wrote with a felt pen on a concrete pillar near the Houses of Parliament. He was charged with criminal damage and argued that his act was justified by, *inter alia*, s 3. The court held that his act was 'insufficient to amount to the use of force within the section'.

The defence is only available if the defendant uses force to prevent crime, or to effect or assist in the lawful arrest of offenders or suspected offenders. It is no defence therefore if D drives dangerously, where he is intent only on ascertaining the registration number of a car D believed had earlier crashed into his. This point was made clear in *Bailey* [2013] EWCA Crim 378.

■ *Questions*

1. If D in *Blake* had used a chisel to inscribe his protest on the pillar, would he have been able to rely on s 3? Would he have been able to rely on the common law defence?

2. If D is attacked by a child under 10 or an insane person, can he use reasonable force to defend himself and rely on s 3?

One issue that remained uncertain until relatively recently is whether it is necessary for D to have a reasonable belief that force was necessary in the prevention of crime or whether it suffices that D's belief is honest. In *Morris* [2013] EWCA Crim 436, D was a taxi driver who mistakenly thought a passenger, X, was attempting to make off without payment. D mounted the pavement to prevent X from committing the offence and X was injured. The judge ruled that the offence of making off without payment would have been committed as soon as X left the taxi, so by the time D drove onto the pavement he could not have been acting in the prevention of crime as the offence had already been committed. Therefore D could only rely on second limb of s 3(1), that he was using force in effecting or assisting the lawful arrest of an offender. What D had forgotten was that there was another individual in the back of the taxi, Y, who was intending to pay the fare. The judge ruled that D had to have a reasonable belief that the use of force was necessary. D was convicted. In rejecting the approach adopted by the trial judge, Leveson LJ stated:

19. The use of reasonable force in self defence or in defence of another person is lawful. The essence of these defences is the honestly held belief of the defendant as to the facts (but not the law: see *R. v Jones (Margaret)* [2006] UKHL 16; [2006] 2 Cr. App. R. 9 (p.136); [2007] 1 A.C. 136; [2006] 2 W.L.R. 772 per Lord Bingham of Cornhill at [24] and Lord Hoffmann at [72]). In relation to use of force in the prevention of crime (such as to prevent an unlawful attack on another), the defence is afforded by s.3 of the Criminal Justice Act 1967. If honest belief affords a defence under s.3 in those circumstances, it must equally do so for a person who claims to have used reasonable force to prevent the commission of a crime other than a crime of violence against another.

20. Accordingly, if, as the appellant contended in this case, he honestly believed that the men were making off without payment, he was entitled to use reasonable force in order to prevent the commission of that offence; the jury would thus be required to consider whether driving on to the pavement (howsoever that occurred) was the reasonable exercise of the use of force. The difficulty with the way in which the judge put the case was that his direction required the jury to consider whether the appellant had reasonable grounds to believe that it was necessary to arrest [X] to prevent him making off before a constable could assume responsibility for him. If they concluded that he did not have reasonable grounds (perhaps because he should have realised the fourth man was still in the cab), they never get to the question of the use of reasonable force.

21. The judge did not deal with the possibility that the jury could conclude that the appellant was acting to prevent crime because he concluded, as a matter of law, that once the passengers had moved away from the window of the taxi (ie where they should have paid the fare), they had 'made off'. He thereby failed to ensure that the jury focused on what the appellant honestly (i.e. genuinely) believed were the facts before using their conclusions as to that belief to go on to decide whether he may have had reasonable grounds for suspecting that an offence was being committed (or had been committed such that he had a reasonable belief that an arrest was necessary) and crucially, whether the force used may have been reasonable. This approach is consistent with *R. v Faraj* [2007] EWCA Crim 1033; [2007] 2 Cr. App. R. 25 (p.322).

22. In the circumstances, we accept the submission that there was an error of law in the direction of law that the jury were given. Although we have real reservations about the question whether a jury properly directed could ever have concluded that the use of force in this case was or may have been reasonable and, thus, that the offence of dangerous driving was not made out, in the light of the failure to focus on the honest belief of the appellant, we conclude that the conviction is unsafe.

Private defence and the prevention of crime are sometimes indistinguishable. If D goes to the defence of E whom V is trying to murder, he is exercising the right of private defence but he is also seeking to prevent the commission of a crime. It would be absurd to ask D whether he was acting in defence of E or to prevent murder being committed and preposterous that the law should differ according to his answer.

11.6.5 Defence against attacks on property

11.6.5.1 Common law

R v Hussey

(1924) 18 Cr App R 160, Court of Criminal Appeal

(Lord Hewart CJ, Avory and Salter JJ)

Appeal against conviction and sentence.

H was convicted of unlawful wounding, and was sentenced to 12 months' imprisonment with hard labour. H had rented a room at Brixton from a Mrs West. Mrs West purported to give him oral notice to quit. H contended that was not valid notice. West and two others armed with a hammer, a spanner, a poker and a chisel, tried to force their way into the room. H had barricaded himself in. H fired a gun through a break in the door wounding two of the three. The appeal against conviction was based on the question whether the defence was available that H's use of violence was necessary to protect his life and that of his wife and children. He appealed.

The Lord Chief Justice:

No sufficient notice had been given to appellant to quit his room, and therefore he was in the position of a man defending his house. In *Archbold's Criminal Pleading, Evidence and Practice*, 26th edn, p 887, it appears that:

> 'In defence of a man's house, the owner or his family may kill a trespasser who would forcibly dispossess him of it, in the same manner as he might, by law, kill in self-defence a man who attacks him personally; with this distinction, however, that in defending his home he need not retreat, as in other cases of self-defence, for that would be giving up his house to his adversary.'

That is still the law, but not one word was said about that distinction in the summing-up, which proceeded on the foundation that the defence was the ordinary one of self-defence. The jury, by their verdict, negatived felonious intent, and with a proper direction they might have come to a different conclusion. This appeal must therefore be allowed.

Conviction quashed

In *Faraj* [2007] EWCA Crim 1033, the Court of Appeal considered the defence of protection of property where D had made a mistake in thinking that a gas repair man, Mr Haq, was a burglar. Faraj detained him and threatened him with a knife. Tuckey LJ stated:

We can see no reason why a house-holder should not be entitled to detain someone in his house whom he genuinely believes to be a burglar. He would be acting in defence of his property by doing so. Here full effect can be given to the defendant's belief however unreasonable it may be. But this defence, like self defence, has its limits. The householder must honestly believe that he needs to detain the suspect and must do so in a way which is reasonable. So if the appellant believed that Mr Haq was a burglar he would be entitled to be judged on this basis even if his belief was unreasonable. If all that he had done was to detain Mr Haq for the purposes of establishing his identity it is most unlikely that he would be found to have acted unreasonably. Whether his use of a knife to do so was reasonable is another matter which, like everything else, would be for the jury to decide.

   Should there be some free standing right to detain which is not subject to the limits which arrest and defence of property are, as [counsel] contends? We do not think so. The law has always jealously guarded the right to freedom of movement. Any restriction of that right has to be justified and confined within established limits. In the event we think that in the circumstances of this case defence of property gave the appellant sufficient protection.

■ *Questions*

1. Hussey was acting in the defence of his home. Was he also acting in the prevention of crime? Should it make any difference to the amount of force he might lawfully use? Would it have been different if the assailants had intended not to dispossess Hussey but to gatecrash a party he was giving?

2. Could it be reasonable to stand and fight in defence of the home when it would be unreasonable to stand and fight if the attack was directed at the defendant's person?

3. Al and Ben try to burst open the door of Dan's ground-floor room, intending to tar-and-feather him. Dan could easily escape through the window. He fires a shotgun through the door and wounds Al. Is he guilty of unlawful wounding?

11.6.5.2 Statutory impact

The s 76 provisions apply where D was using force to protect property, but the heightened householder test does not.

11.6.6 Defending oneself against non-criminal acts?

11.6.6.1 Common law

In *A (children) (conjoined twins)*, section 11.5.2, p 402, Ward LJ said:

> The reality here—harsh as it is to state it, and unnatural as it is that it should be happening—is that Mary is killing Jodie. That is the effect of the incontrovertible medical evidence and it is common ground in the case. Mary uses Jodie's heart and lungs to receive and use Jodie's oxygenated blood. This will cause Jodie's heart to fail and cause Jodie's death as surely as a slow drip of poison. How can it be just that Jodie should be required to tolerate that state of affairs? One does not need to label Mary with the American terminology which would paint her to be 'an unjust aggressor', which I feel is wholly inappropriate language for the sad and helpless position in which Mary finds herself. I have no difficulty in agreeing that this unique happening cannot be said to be unlawful. But it does not have to be unlawful. The six-year-old boy indiscriminately shooting all and sundry in the school playground is not acting unlawfully for he is too young for his acts to be so classified. But is he 'innocent' within the moral meaning of that word as used by the Archbishop? I am not qualified to answer that moral question because, despite an assertion—or was it an aspersion—by a member of the Bar in a letter to *The Times* that we, the judges, are proclaiming some moral superiority in this case, I for my part would defer any opinion as to a child's innocence to the Archbishop [of Westminster] for that is his territory. If I had to hazard a guess, I would venture the tentative view that the child is not morally innocent. What I am, however, competent to say is that *in law* killing that six-year-old boy in self-defence of others would be fully justified and the killing would not be unlawful. I can see no difference in essence between that resort to legitimate self-defence and the doctors coming to Jodie's defence and removing the threat of fatal harm to her presented by Mary's draining her life-blood. The availability of such a plea of quasi self-defence, modified to meet the quite exceptional circumstances nature has inflicted on the twins, makes intervention by the doctors lawful.

The common law therefore seems to follow the Draft Criminal Code, cl 44 which, having provided that a person does not commit an offence by using necessary and reasonable force to protect himself or another from unlawful force or unlawful personal harm, goes on:

> (3) For the purpose of this section, an act is 'unlawful' although a person charged with an offence in respect of it would be acquitted on the ground only that—
>
>   (a) he was under 10 years of age; or
>
>   (b) he lacked the fault required for the offence or believed that an exempting circumstance existed; or
>
>   (c) he acted in pursuance of a reasonable suspicion; or
>
>   (d) he acted under duress, whether by threats or circumstances; or
>
>   (e) he was in a state of automatism or suffering from severe mental illness or severe mental handicap.

11.6.7 Availability of defences to initial aggressor.

11.6.7.1. What if D is the initial aggressor?

In *Rashford* [2005] EWCA Crim 3377, [2006] Crim LR547, the Court of Appeal made it clear that D does not lose the opportunity to rely on self-defence even if he was the initial aggressor, if the person whom he attacks not only defends himself but goes over to the offensive. This seems right, subject to the restriction that it should not be available where D deliberately provoked the attack with the intention of killing purportedly in self-defence.

In *Hichins* [2011] EWCA Crim 1626 it was recognized that self-defence and the defence under s 3 of the Criminal Law Act 1967 extended to the use of force against an innocent third party where such force was used to prevent a crime from being committed against someone else. Examples of the defence arising included a police constable bundling a man out of the way to get to another man who was about to detonate an explosive device, and where, for example, a person knocked car keys out of the hands of a third party to prevent the keys being given to a drunk person who was attempting to drive. However, facts giving rise to such a defence would be rare and the degrees of likelihood, and the imminence of the commission of a crime, were important factors to be borne in mind.

11.6.7.2 Section 76 and the duty to retreat

The Act now explicitly states that there is no duty to retreat.

(6A) In deciding the question mentioned in subsection (3), a possibility that D could have retreated is to be considered (so far as relevant) as a factor to be taken into account, rather than as giving rise to a duty to retreat.

11.6.8 The effect of a successful plea

If D pleads the defence successfully it results in an acquittal for all crimes. The Crown must disprove the defence to the criminal standard. Does this mean that the grossly mistaken killer will be completely acquitted? Not necessarily. Gross negligence is now acknowledged to be a sufficient fault for manslaughter (section 17.3, p 615) so why should not the grossly negligent mistake, resulting as it does in death, be a ground of liability in itself? See also *O'Grady* [1987] QB 995, section 6.6, p 174. In the case of non-fatal offences, the grossly negligent mistake would exempt the defendant entirely; but this is consistent with the present law, that causing non-fatal injuries by gross negligence is not an offence.

If D has a belief in force, but has used excessive force even on the facts as he believed them to be, the self-defence plea fails completely and D is convicted.

Many have argued that in such cases, where the charge is murder, D should have a partial defence.

R v Clegg

[1995] 1 All ER 334, House of Lords, http://www.bailii.org/uk/cases/UKHL/1995/1.html

(Lords Keith, Browne-Wilkinson, Slynn, Lloyd and Nicholls)

C was a soldier on patrol in the course of his duties in Northern Ireland in 1990. A car approached the patrol at speed. C fired three shots at the windscreen and a fourth after the car had passed him. The last shot killed the passenger. C was charged with murder. His defence was that he fired in defence of himself and a fellow soldier. C was convicted of murder and his appeal was dismissed by the Court of Appeal of Northern Ireland. He appealed to the House of Lords.

[Lord Lloyd said that the first question (whether, when force used in self-defence is excessive, the law allows a verdict of manslaughter instead of murder), did not arise since the danger had passed when C fired the fourth and fatal shot; but that it was convenient to deal with it. Having discussed the Report of the Royal Commission of 1879, he continued:]

There does not appear to have been any development in the law until *R v Howe* (1958) 100 CLR 448, decided by the High Court of Australia in 1958. There was an extensive citation of all the authorities in this corner of the law going back to *Cook*'s Case (1639) Cro Car 537, 79 ER 1063. The decision of the court is well summarised in the following paragraph of the headnote:

> 'Where a plea of self-defence to a charge of murder fails only because the death of the deceased was occasioned by the use of force going beyond what was necessary in the circumstances for the protection of the accused or what might reasonably be regarded by him as necessary in the circumstances, it is, in the absence of clear and definite decision, reasonable in principle to regard such a homicide as reduced to manslaughter.'

Twelve years later the same point came before the Privy Council on appeal from the Supreme Court of Jamaica (see *Palmer v R* [1971] 1 All ER 1077, [1971] AC 814). Lord Morris of Borth-y-Gest, giving the opinion of the Privy Council, declined to follow *R v Howe* (1958) 100 CLR 448, preferring the decision of the West Indian Federal Supreme Court in *De Freitas v R* (1960) 2 WIR 523.

After setting out the elements of the defence of self-defence, he said ([1971] 1 All ER 1077 at 1088, [1971] AC 814 at 832):

> '...if the prosecution have shown that what was done was not done in self-defence then that issue is eliminated from the case. If the jury consider that an accused acted in self-defence or if the jury are in doubt as to this then they will acquit. The defence of self-defence either succeeds so as to result in an acquittal or it is disproved in which case as a defence it is rejected.'

In other words, there is no half-way house. There is no rule that a defendant who has used a greater degree of force than was necessary in the circumstances should be found guilty of manslaughter rather than murder.

In 1971 a Court of Appeal consisting of Edmund Davies LJ and Lawton and Forbes JJ approved and followed *Palmer v R* in *R v McInnes* [1971] 3 All ER 295 at 301:

> 'But where self-defence fails on the ground that the force used went clearly beyond that which was reasonable in the light of the circumstances as they reasonably appeared to the accused, is it the law that the inevitable result must be that he can be convicted of manslaughter only, and not of murder? It seems that in Australia that question is answered in the affirmative...but not, we think, in this country. On the contrary, if self-defence fails for the reason stated, it affords the accused no protection at all.'

Of course, as the court pointed out, the verdict may be reduced from murder to manslaughter on other grounds, for example, if the prosecution fail to negative provocation, where it arises, or fail to prove the requisite intent for murder. But so far as self-defence is concerned, it is all or nothing. The defence either succeeds or it fails. If it succeeds, the defendant is acquitted. If it fails, he is guilty of murder.

In a subsequent case in Australia, *Viro v R* (1978) 141 CLR 88, the High Court decided by a bare majority over a strong dissent by Barwick CJ to follow *R v Howe* (1958) 100 CLR 448 in preference to *Palmer v R*. Mason J suggested that in self-defence cases juries should be directed in accordance with six propositions which he formulated at the end of his judgment, and which, in his view, best accorded 'with acceptable standards of culpability'. But the propositions proved to be unworkable in practice. Juries found difficulty in applying, or perhaps even understanding them. As a result, a Full Court of seven judges was convened to reconsider the position in *Zecevic v DPP (Victoria)* (1987) 162 CLR 645. The High Court decided by a majority of five to two to revert to the law as stated in *Palmer v R* and *R v McInnes*, and declined to follow *R v Howe* and *Viro v R*. Wilson, Dawson and Toohey JJ said (at 665):

'Believing, as we do, that the law as we have set it out is dictated by basic principle upon a matter of fundamental importance, it is unthinkable that the Court should abdicate its responsibility by declining to declare it accordingly. It has the virtue of being readily understandable by a jury. It restores consistency to the law relating to self-defence whether raised in a case of homicide or otherwise. Finally, it has the effect of expressing the common law in terms which are in accord with the views expressed in *Palmer* (adopted in England in *McInnes*) and which are generally consonant with the law in the code States.'

[Lord Lloyd went to hold that the degree of permissible force, and the consequence of the use of excessive force, is the same, whether the force be used in self-defence or in the prevention of crime; and in the circumstances of this case, it made no difference that C was a member of the security forces, acting in the course of his duty. There is no defence of superior orders.]

Appeal dismissed

Lord Lloyd said that the question whether the law should be changed to allow a conviction of manslaughter was, in truth, part of the wider question whether the mandatory sentence for murder should still be maintained. But is not that a different question? Members of the CLRC who were in favour of the abolition of the mandatory life sentence nevertheless thought that the defences of diminished responsibility and provocation reducing murder to manslaughter should be maintained: Fourteenth Report ((1980) Cmnd 7844), para 56. Similarly, the recommendations of the Committee that killing by excessive force in self-defence should be manslaughter and not murder was quite independent of the question of the mandatory life sentence. The Select Committee of the House of Lords on Murder and Life Imprisonment (HL Paper 78-1, session 1988–89, para 83) agreed with the CLRC's opinion; and the Select Committee's own recommendation for a defence to murder of excessive self-defence was coupled with its principal recommendation that the mandatory life sentence should be abolished: 'If murder is to be reserved for those homicides most deserving of stigma this does not seem to be one of them', para 88.

Noting that the House had, by a majority, extended the defence of duress to a charge of aiding and abetting murder in *Lynch v DPP for Northern Ireland*, section 11.3.5, p 383, Lord Lloyd remarked that the difference is that duress is a matter of common law, whereas in the use of force to prevent crime 'Parliament has already taken a hand by enacting section 3 of the 1967 [Criminal Law] Act. Parliament did not, in doing so, see fit to create a qualified defence in cases where the defendant uses excessive force in preventing crime.' Does not this overlook the fact that, notwithstanding the title of the Act, the law stated in s 3 is primarily civil law? It states when force may be used—when its use is lawful, so that it is neither a tort nor a crime. It says nothing at all about defences to crime, which is a different question as is demonstrated by *Gladstone Williams*, section 11.6.1.1, p 415 and its successors.

A person who uses force which is *unreasonable* in the circumstances to prevent crime and who cannot therefore justify his actions under s 3 nevertheless has a defence to a criminal charge if the force would have been reasonable if the circumstances had been as he mistakenly (and even unreasonably) believed them to be. The questions whether the use of force is justified under s 3 and whether the user has a defence to a criminal charge are not the same. See generally, J. C. Smith, 'Using Force in Self-Defence and the Prevention of Crime' (1994) 47 CLP 101.

A holding that the user of excessive force is guilty only of manslaughter and not of murder would have been in no sense inconsistent with s 3. See further, J. Rogers, 'Justifying the Use of Firearms by Policemen and Soldiers: A Response to the Home Office's Review of the Law on the Use of Lethal Force' (1998) 18 LS 486 and S. Skinner, 'Citizens in Uniform: Public Defence, Reasonableness and Human Rights' [2000] PL 266.

The Law Commission (Report No 290, *Partial Defences to Murder* (2004)) concluded that no new partial defence to murder should be created for the defendant who kills by using excessive force. In its more recent proposals in Report No 304, *Murder, Manslaughter and Infanticide* (2006), the Law Commission confirmed this view. A defendant will, in appropriate circumstances, be able to advance a 'pure' self-defence plea and the new broader provocation-based plea. Under the proposed scheme, if the jury rejects the self-defence plea, they might still return a manslaughter verdict on the application of the new defence.

Note that where D loses self-control and kills because of a fear of serious violence from V, D is entitled to plead the loss of self-control defence under ss 54 to 56 of the Coroners and Justice Act 2009, and if successful will be convicted of manslaughter only. See Chapter 16.

11.6.9 ECHR limits to self defence

The Human Rights Act has prompted many to ask whether the protection English law affords to a victim of a defendant acting in 'self-defence'/'private defence' is compatible with Article 2. The fact that D is entitled to an acquittal if he held a genuine though unreasonable belief in the need for violence is argued to be too generous to D, and results in the UK providing inadequate protection for its citizens' lives under Article 2. See A. Ashworth, 'Human Rights: Case Commentary on *Andronicou and Constantinou v. Cyprus*' [1998] Crim LR 823. See also A. Ashworth, 'The European Convention and Criminal Law' in J. Beatson, *The Human Rights Act and the Criminal Justice and Regulatory Process* (1999); F. Leverick, *Killing in Self-Defence* (2006); B. Sangero, *Self Defence in Criminal Law* (2006).

Article 2 of the ECHR provides that:

(1) Everyone's right to life shall be protected by law. No-one shall be deprived of his life intentionally save in the execution of a sentence of a court following his conviction of a crime for which this penalty is provided by law.

(2) Deprivation of life shall not be regarded as inflicted in contravention of this article when it results from the use of force which is no more than absolutely necessary:

(a) in defence of any person from unlawful violence;

(b) in order to effect a lawful arrest or to prevent the escape of a person lawfully detained;

(c) in action lawfully taken for the purpose of quelling a riot or insurrection.

F. Leverick, 'Is English Self-Defence Law Incompatible with Article 2 of the ECHR' [2002] Crim LR 347 concludes that:

English law is contrary to Article 2 of the ECHR. The reason for this claim is that, in allowing the unreasonably mistaken defendant to escape punishment in this way, English law fails to respect the right to life of the person who, through no fault of their own, is mistaken for an attacker. An examination of relevant case law leads to the conclusion that the substance of English law does indeed contravene Article 2. It had been suggested that because killing in self-defence is not an intentional killing, Article 2 does not apply. Regardless of the theoretical merits of this suggestion, it can be dismissed as it has consistently been held that self-defensive killing does fall to be assessed under Article 2. Further, an examination of relevant cases shows that the court has consistently required that a mistaken belief in the need to use self-defensive force be based on good reasons. It is also clear, from cases such as *A v. United Kingdom* and *X and Y v. Netherlands*, that a violation of the Convention can take place when there has been a failure on the part of the State to provide a criminal law sanction that protects its citizens from the violent acts of other individuals, regardless of whether these individuals were State officials or private citizens. This is not to say that the Convention would necessarily require English law to convict the unreasonably mistaken self-defender of murder. It may be that a conviction for a lesser offence, such as manslaughter, is sufficient. Consideration of the degree of punishment appropriate in such circumstances is outside the scope of this paper. The point is that English law as it stands at present contains no sanctions whatsoever for the defendant who deprives another of her life in the unreasonable belief that she was an attacker.

Sir John Smith responded [2002] Crim LR 952:

The established English law is that, where a person is charged with a crime requiring mens rea and alleged to be committed by the use of force when acting in public or private defence, he is to be judged on the facts as he honestly believed them to be, whether reasonably or not. If, in light of the supposed circumstances, it was reasonable to use that degree of force, he is not guilty of such a criminal offence. It has been suggested by no less an authority than Professor Andrew Ashworth [Commentary on *Andronicou and Constantinou v Cyprus* [1998] Crim L R 823–825] that this may be incompatible with Article 2 (Right to Life) of the ECHR—that the Article requires a criminal sanction where a person kills on the basis of an erroneous and unreasonable belief. I have argued otherwise and have recently written [[2001] Crim L R 400 at 402–403] that the point appears to be settled for English law by the decision in *Re A (children) (conjoined twins): surgical separation* [section 11.5.2]...Article [2] proscribes only intentional killing, which means by an act done with the purpose of killing. The doctors in that case intended to kill within the meaning of the common law of murder because they knew that death was certain to result from their act but they did not act with the purpose of killing, so the Article was inapplicable.

Fiona Leverick criticises my argument and states that I cite no authority for my view. If that were so, I would indeed be remiss, but I thought, and think, it is obvious that my authority was the very decision for the Court of Appeal on which I was commenting. The judgments of the three Lords Justices, though arriving at the same result, differ in some important respects. But they appear to be unanimously of the opinion that 'intentionally' in the Article means 'with the purpose of' [Brooke LJ at 1050a–e and Robert Walker LJ at 1067–1068]; and this ruling is the ratio decidendi of the court on this issue. For the purposes of the English law of murder, the doctors intended to kill baby Mary but, as their only purpose was to save the life of twin Jodie, they were not killing Mary intentionally within the meaning of the Article.

Ms Leverick states that my argument 'can be fairly easily dismissed' from an examination of the case law on Article 2 and goes on to discuss a series of decisions of the European Court of Human Rights ('ECtHR'). But, while an English court must 'take into account' any judgment of the ECtHR, such a judgment is not binding but only persuasive—as, of course, Ms Leverick knows. I was, and am, discussing English law and, if there is an inconsistency between the interpretation put on the Convention by the English courts and that which appears to be put on it by the ECtHR, it is the English court's ruling which prevails and represents the law of England.

It appears that the court in *Re A* received extensive written and oral argument on the issue of Article 2 and that relevant decisions of the ECtHR were cited. I do not venture into this arena, but, if the court's interpretation of those decisions differs from that of Ms Leverick, it is the court's interpretation which must prevail. She cites some European decisions delivered after *Re A* but, however persuasive they might be, they cannot affect the authority of *Re A* unless and until an English court decides otherwise.

...So I adhere firmly to my view that, until the House of Lords or Parliament decide otherwise, Re A decides that Article 2 has no application to a person acting bona fide in self-defence and that is the law of England.

What if the Article does require a criminal sanction?

Ms Leverick concedes that the Convention would not necessarily require English law to convict the unreasonably mistaken self-defender of murder:

'It may be that a conviction for a lesser offence, such as manslaughter, is sufficient . . . The point is that English law as it stands at present contains no sanction whatsoever for the defendant who deprives another of her life in the unreasonable belief that she was an attacker.'

This is an understandable view because there is no direct authority that the unreasonably mistaken killer in self-defence is guilty of a crime. However, I do not believe it is the law and I have so argued long before the question of compatibility with the ECHR arose.

Where the force used was reasonable in the circumstances which the defendant believed to exist. The defendant is not guilty of murder but the question whether he may be guilty of manslaughter at common law does not appear to have been raised in any case.

Where the evidence suggests that the defendant was acting under a mistaken belief, a jury should be directed that, if the force used was reasonable in the circumstances as he honestly believed them to be, then they must acquit him of murder. But, if they do so acquit him, they must go on to consider whether (i) in the actual circumstances, the force used was unreasonable and, if it was, (ii) whether the defendant, in making the mistake, was guilty of gross negligence, so bad as in their judgment to amount to a crime. If they are sure that he was, then they should convict him of manslaughter . . .

Ms Leverick concentrates on private defence but suggests that the incompatibility argument may be 'especially compelling' where force is used in the prevention of crime and section 3 of the Criminal Law Act 1967 is in issue because 'section 3 of the Human Rights Act 1998 requires primary legislation to be read and given effect in a way which is compatible with Convention rights'. But a person who uses more than reasonable force in the prevention of crime is in breach of section 3. He is acting unlawfully, whatever his honest belief. Section 3 can hardly be said to be incompatible with the Convention but, notwithstanding the title of the Act, this section does not say anything about the criminal law. When the defendant is charge with a criminal offence, it is the criminal law which is in issue. The court is not construing section 3. The requirements of mens rea are the same, whether it is public or private defence which is in issue.

See Fiona Leverick's further response at [2002] Crim LR 963.

■ *Question*

Do you find Sir John's argument persuasive?

In the most recent pronouncement from the English court, it has been accepted that the current rules of English law on the use of potentially lethal force by the police are not incompatible with the European Convention. In judicial review proceedings, in *R (Bennett) v HM Coroner for Inner London* [2006] EWHC 196 (Admin), a coroner's decision not to leave unlawful killing as a possible verdict for the jury was challenged. B's son had died as a result of being shot by a police officer. A witness had told the police that the deceased was carrying a gun and two firearms officers attended the scene. In 30 seconds, one officer fired six shots, four of which struck the deceased in the back and side and one of which was fatal. At the inquest, the coroner decided not to leave a verdict of unlawful killing to the jury and the jury returned a verdict of lawful killing. B sought judicial review on the ground that the coroner's direction on self-defence had failed to pay heed to Article 2. In the High Court, Collins J held, having regard to the case law, that:

the European Court of Human Rights has considered what English law requires for self defence, and has not suggested that there is any incompatibility with Article 2. In truth, if any officer reasonably decides that he must use lethal force, it will inevitably be because it is absolutely necessary to do so. To kill when it is not absolutely necessary to do so is surely to act unreasonably. Thus, the reasonableness test does not in truth differ from the Article 2 test as applied in *McCann*.

The Court of Appeal upheld that decision ([2007] EWCA Civ 617). The basis of appeal was principally that it had been a misdirection not to direct the jury to consider whether the officer's claim to have acted in self-defence was reasonable in the light of the requirement in the relevant ACPO manual to reassess at all times whether it was 'absolutely necessary' to shoot.

■ *Questions*

1. Could it be lawful to use lethal force to protect your house against a burglar?

2. Does the Criminal Justice and Immigration Act 2008, s 76, render English law less likely to be challenged under Article 2?

3. D, a police officer, shoots V whom D reasonably suspects to be a suicide bomber. D shoots him repeatedly in the head so that there is no risk that any suicide bomb can be activated by some slight movement. V is in fact not a terrorist but an innocent man. Is D liable for murder? See also J. Rogers, 'Shoot, Identify and Repent?' (2005) 155 NLJ 1273.

11.6.10 Unknown circumstances of justification or excuse

In *Dadson* (1850) 2 Den CC 35 (section 2.2, p 20), we saw that circumstances which would have justified or excused D's conduct in shooting at V if he had been aware of them were no defence because D was unaware that those circumstances existed. The majority of the CLRC were satisfied that the principle of that case was correct and it was embodied in their recommendation in their Fourteenth Report as to the law of private defence.

In *Gladstone Williams*, discussed in section 11.6.1.1, p 415, the Court of Appeal held that the recommendation was a true statement of the common law and therefore it now is the law, being persuasively confirmed by   (section 11.6.1.1, p 415). An arrest can be lawful only if the arrestor is in a position to state a valid ground for arrest. Dadson was not in that position. 'I arrest you on the ground that you have stolen wood from the copse' would not satisfy the common law or s 28 of the Police and Criminal Evidence Act. Stealing the wood was not a felony but an offence punishable only on summary conviction by a fine of £5 with no power to arrest the offender.

■ *Questions*

1. Does the Criminal Justice and Immigration Act 2008, s 76, clarify the position in English law on the use of force to a threat of which D is unaware?

2. How would you draft a clause to insert into that section to improve matters?

3. D shoots V dead. Unknown to D at the time that he shot V, V was about to take aim to shoot him (D) with intent to kill. What is D's criminal liability? What should it be?

11.7 Judicial development of defences

Glanville Williams, 'Necessity'
[1978] Crim LR 128

[Having pointed out that a purpose of codification is to enable the citizen to know what conduct is penalized, the writer continues:]

It by no means follows that it should be any part of the purpose of a code to get rid of open-ended defences, or to fetter the power of the courts to create new defences in the name of the common law. That the courts have power to enlarge defences is sometimes denied by the judges, just as they deny in terms their power to enlarge offences; but history records some examples of the former activity as well as innumerable examples of the latter.

The Draft Code of 1879 recognised this distinction of policy. It contained two sections (5 and 19), one removing the power of the judges to create new crimes and the other preserving judicial creativity in respect of justifications and excuses. The proposal was immediately criticised by Cockburn LCJ on the ground that the arguments for exhaustive codification of offences applied equally to defences. Stephen, the architect of the code, replied to this criticism in a notable article. [See the *Nineteenth Century* for January 1880, pp 152–157. I am indebted to Sir Rupert Cross for calling my attention to this article.] He first distinguished two meanings of the term 'common law': a body of relatively fixed principles result-ing from judicial decisions, and the qualified power of the judges to make new law under the fiction of declaring existing law, or in other words 'not a part of the law actually existing, but law which has only a potential existence—that which, if the case should ever occur, the judges would declare to be the law.' Stephen thought it justifiable to save the common law in the second sense in respect of defences, though not in respect of offences. The central passage of his argument is worth quoting rather fully.

'It appears to me that the two proposed enactments stand on entirely different principles. After the experience of centuries, and with a Parliament sitting every year, and keenly alive to all mat-ters likely to endanger the public interest, we are surely in a position to say the power of declaring new offences shall henceforth be vested in Parliament only. The power which has at times been claimed for the judges of declaring new offences cannot be useful now, whatever may have been its value in earlier times.

On the other hand it is hardly possible to foresee all the circumstances which might possibly jus-tify or excuse acts which might otherwise be crimes. A long series of authorities have settled certain rules which can be put into a distinct and convenient form, and it is of course desirable to take the opportunity of deciding by the way minor points which an examination of the authorities shows to be still open. In this manner rules can be laid down as to the effect of infancy, insanity, compulsion, and ignorance of law, and also as to the cases in which force may lawfully be employed against the person of another; but is it therefore wise or safe to go so far as to say that no other circumstances than those expressly enumerated shall operate by way of excuse or justification for what would otherwise be a crime? To do so would be to run a risk, the extent of which it is difficult to estimate, of producing a conflict between the Code, and the moral feelings of the public. Such a conflict is upon all possible grounds to be avoided. It would, if it occurred, do more to discredit codification than anything which could possibly happen, and it might cause serious evils of another kind. Cases sometimes occur in which public opinion is at once violently excited and greatly divided, so that con-duct is regarded as criminal or praiseworthy according to the sympathies of excited partisans. If the Code provided that nothing should amount to an excuse or justification which was not within the express words of the Code, it would, in such a case, be vain to allege that the conduct of the accused person was justifiable; that, but for the Code, it would have been legally justifiable; that every legal analogy was in its favour; and that the omission of an express provision about it was probably an oversight. I think such a result would be eminently unsatisfactory. I think the public would feel that the allegations referred to ought to have been carefully examined and duly decided upon.

To put the whole matter very shortly, the reason why the common law definitions of offences should be taken away, whilst the common law principles as to justification and excuses are kept alive, is like the reason why the benefit of a doubt should be given to a prisoner. The worst result that could arise from the abolition of the common law offences would be the occasional escape of a person morally guilty. The only result which can follow from preserving the common law as to justification and excuse is, that a man morally innocent, not otherwise protected, may avoid punishment. In the one case you remove rusty spring-guns and man-traps from unfrequented plantations, in the other you decline to issue an order for the destruction of every old-fashioned drag or lifebuoy which may be found on the banks of a dangerous river, but is not in the inventory of the Royal Humane Society. This indeed does not put the matter strongly enough. The continued existence of the undefined common law offences is not only dangerous to individuals, but may be dangerous to the administration of justice itself. By allowing them to remain, we run the risk of tempting the judges to express their disapproval of conduct which, upon political, moral, or social grounds, they consider deserving of punishment, by declaring upon slender authority that it constitutes an offence at common law; nothing, I think, could place the bench in a more invidious position, or go further to shake its authority . . .

Besides the well-known matters dealt with by the Code, there are a variety of speculative questions which have been discussed by ingenious persons for centuries, but which could be raised only by such rare occurrences that it may be thought pedantic to legislate for them expressly beforehand, and rash to do so without materials which the course of events has not provided. Such cases are the case of necessity (two shipwrecked men on one plank), the case of a choice of evils (my horses are running away, and I can avoid running over A only by running over B), and some others which might be suggested.

Any ingenious person may divert himself, as Hecato did, by playing with such questions. The Commission acted on the view that in practice the wisest answer to all of them is to say, 'When the case actually happens it shall be decided'; and this is effected by the preservation of such parts of the common law as to justification and excuse as are not embodied in the Code. Fiction apart, there is at present no law at all upon the subject, but the judges shall make one under the fiction of declaring it, if the occasion for doing so should ever arise.'

■ *Question*

Should we leave it to Parliament to create offences and the courts defences?

In *Kingston* [1995] 2 AC 355, section 6.2, p 156, although counsel was not disposed to argue the point, Lord Mustill considered ([1994] 3 All ER at 370) whether the House might take the 'bold step' of recognizing a new defence of involuntary intoxication. He suspected that no new general defence had been created in modern times (but what about duress of circumstances?), adding:

Nevertheless, the criminal law must not stand still, and if it is both practical and just to take this step, and if judicial decision rather than legislation is the proper medium, then the courts should not be deterred simply by the novelty of it.

Having examined the nature of the proposed defence, Lord Mustill found that it ran into difficulties at every turn. Involuntary intoxication was best left to be taken into account in sentencing; but the question of a new defence was one which the Law Commission might usefully consider.

F v West Berkshire Health Authority, section 11.5.1, p 399, *Gillick*'s case, section 11.5.1, p 401 and *Re A (children) (conjoined twins)*, section 11.5.2, p 406, may perhaps be regarded as applications of the common law power in relation to necessity.

11.8 Justifications and excuses

It is said by philosophers who take an interest in this particular area of the law that there exists a dichotomy in criminal defences between excuses and justifications. It is sometimes claimed that 'actors are excused; acts are justified'. However, what does this mean and are these distinctions valid? Andrew Simester argues that there are four types of 'exculpatory defence', encompassing three types of excuse. These are distinct from non-exculpatory defences, such as diplomatic immunity, which immunize the defendant from the jurisdiction of the court but do not negate the wrongfulness of his act. Simester states that there exist justifications and three different classes of excuse. First of all, there are 'irresponsibility defences', which are predicated on a denial of the defendant's responsibility for doing the prohibited act. These defences, such as insanity or the incapacity of children, recognize D's inadequacy as an agent capable of moral responsibility. The second type of excuses are 'rationale-based excuses'. These are different from irresponsibility defences, which ask whether D was morally *responsible* for the act, by asking whether D was morally *culpable* for the act. The exculpatory power of these defences depends on the nature and seriousness of D's action, as well as upon the circumstances in which it was committed: they ask *why* D did the act. The final category articulated by Simester is mistake-based. These can be mistakes as to actus reus, for example where D thought he was shooting a deer but it turned out to be a human being. In this case, the mistake as to actus reus would result in D denying that he had the requisite mens rea to make him guilty of homicide. In the following extract, Simester seeks to disaggregate the distinctions between these types of defence.

A. Simester, 'On Justifications and Excuses'
in L Zedner and J. V. Roberts (eds), *Principles and Values in Criminal Law and Criminal Justice: Essays in Honour of Andrew Ashworth* (2012)

2. Distinguishing Justification and Excuse

A justified action is a morally appropriate response to the circumstances and is, for that reason, permissible. D has a justification when his reasons for [doing the prohibited act] are sufficient to defeat those that militate against [doing the prohibited act], that [doing the prohibited act] is morally permitted. Permitted, not tolerated. Douglas Husak suggests that 'an act is permissible when it is tolerated'. That may be true—legally speaking. Not morally. Something that is morally permissible does not call for toleration, because there is nothing wrong with it. One can only tolerate something that one considers to be wrongful. Justified [wrongdoing] is not like that. It may be harmful is some way. It may generate reasons for regret. But where it is morally justified, [doing the prohibited act] is not, all things considered, wrongful.

Notice that the foregoing definition takes account of D's own reasons. In putting it this way, I am embracing a thesis that, for reasons of space, cannot be defended here: that justification depends upon D's actual or 'subjective' reasons for [doing the prohibited act] and not solely upon any guiding—'objective' reasons that are in fact available to justify [doing the prohibited act]. Hence it is not sufficient that [the wrongdoing] be justifi*able* in the circumstances. D's own reasons must themselves be valid, and sufficient, for D's act of [wrongdoing] to be justi*fied*.

For convenience, let me call this the motivational thesis. While controversial, its validity will be assumed here. In any case, that debate concerns the scope of reasons eligible to justify D's [wrongdoing]. The important point to start with is that, whatever reasons are treated as eligible, justification requires those reasons to be sufficient. They must pass an evaluative, objective, test of whether, taken as a whole, they supply D with good reasons to [do the prohibited act]. Overall, they must defeat, or at least match, the reasons D has not to [do the prohibited act]. They must make it morally okay—or as Greenawalt puts it, warranted—to [do the prohibited act].

No such requirement exists for excuses. That said, there is a tendency to relegate excuses to a catch-all dustbin. Expressed more generally, D can be said to have an excuse if the reasons why he [does the prohibited act] are such that he is not culpable for doing so. Unfortunately, while that definition is appealingly simple, it can be applied more-or-less to all four kinds of exculpatory defences we identified earlier, and certainly to justifications. No surprise, then, that writers tend to add a proviso that excused conduct is unjustified, or that they sometimes conflate irresponsibility defences with rationale-based excuses.

Excuses differ from irresponsibility defences in that they address D's own reasons for action, not his capacity for reasoning. D's [wrongdoing] is excusable if, in choosing to [do the prohibited act] he exhibits no shortcoming of a kind that grounds blame—no shortfall of the character or moral judgment that we should expect of an ordinary, decent person. D need not be perfect. We all have limitations, even decent folk. Exoneration requires only that the limitations explaining why D [did the prohibited act] be normal ones, ones that do not reflect badly on D. Perhaps supererogation [ie an act going beyond the call of duty] was possible. Perhaps D could have exhibited abnormal levels of altruism, etc, and refrained from [committing the prohibited act]. But blame does not turn on D's failure to merit praise. It requires that he fall short, not of standards of perfection, but of standards of reasonableness. And excuses require only that his failings be, so to speak, understandable or reasonable ones.

Like justifications, and unlike the irresponsibility defences, all rationale-based excuses therefore require that D's reasons for [committing the prohibited act] be subjected to evaluative assessment. Moreover, the assessment is not relativized to any personal limitations of virtue that the defendant might have. The difference lies in the conclusion of that assessment. When justified, there is no moral error—it is morally okay for D to [do the prohibited act]. In the case of excuse, D is not culpable for [wrongdoing] even though [wrongdoing] might not be okay. Any moral error by D is understandable, the kind of error that a decent person might well make.

■ *Questions*

Which categories do the defences discussed in this chapter fall into? Do you think it matters?

Glanville Williams ([1982] Crim LR 732) expressed the view that while the distinction between excuses and justifications was of theoretical significance, it was of no practical significance. He stated:

What is the difference between a justification and an excuse? Very little. They are both defenses in the full sense, leading to an acquittal. However, when the act is not justified but only excused it is still regarded as being in some tenuous way wrong, for certain collateral purposes.

This assertion has recently been challenged by Paul Robinson, who uses the following, vivid examples to illustrate his point.

P. H. Robinson, 'Four Distinctions that Glanville Williams Did Not Make: The Practical Benefits of Examining the Interrelation Among Criminal Law Doctrines'
in D. J. Baker and J. Horder (eds), *The Sanctity of Life and the Criminal Law: The Legacy of Glanville Williams* (2013)

A third example of the practical importance of these general defense distinctions is seen in the problem of ambiguous acquittals that arises when these distinctions are not recognized. Note that justification and excuse defences say directly opposite things about the defendant's conduct: a justification defense announces that the conduct is condoned; an excuse defense announces that the conduct is condemned. Where these two kinds of general defences are not distinguished, as in a general verdict of acquittal, it is easy for an excuse to be mistaken for a justification.

Recall the Rodney King case in which, after a long car chase, officers surrounded Rodney King and continued to beat him. The jury acquitted the officers, and riots in Los Angeles followed. The jury acquittal may well have been on the theory that the adrenaline build-up during the long car chase, the lack of adequate training to deal with the circumstances, as well as the lack of good supervision on the scene, meant that the conduct was not justified—it was excessive—but that the defendants did not deserve to be punished for it. In other words, the striking conduct on the tape is an example of conduct that we would not want repeated in the same circumstances in the future, but it is not to be punished in this instance because the officers were blameless for it. Yet with an ambiguous general verdict of acquittal, people in the community could easily have come to the conclusion that the conduct they saw on the tape was conduct that the criminal law was condoning (as objectively justified), and that could be quite upsetting. It is easy enough to construct a more nuanced verdict system of a 'no violation' verdict and a 'blameless violation' verdict, but such a solution would be ineffective where the doctrine does not distinguish between (objective) justifications and excuses.

A fourth illustration of practical value concerns what one might call post-acquittal collateral consequences. For a justification defense, there ought to be none. What the defendant did was the right thing to do, which others can do in similar situations in the future. For an excuse defense, one might want to at least ask the question whether the cause of the excusing conditions is recurring. We already do this with insanity acquittals, by having a special verdict for 'not guilty by reason of insanity', which is commonly followed by an examination to determine whether civil commitment is appropriate. But there may be any number of situations that give rise to excuse defenses that would benefit from future civil supervision or even just education. Non–exculpatory defenses present an even stronger case for the possible need for collateral consequences. It may well be that we want to give the serial child molester a double jeopardy defense for the case at hand, but that does not mean that we should not be sure that he is denied a license to drive school buses.

■ *Question*

Do you agree with Robinson that there are practical ramifications that follow from whether a defence is classified as an excuse or a justification?

FURTHER READING

P. Alldridge, 'Developing the Defence of Duress' [1986] Crim LR 433

A. Ashworth, 'Criminal Liability in a Medical Context: The Treatment of Good Intentions' in A. Simester and A. T. H. Smith (eds), *Harm and Culpability* (1996)

R. Christopher, 'Unknowing Justification and the Logical Necessity of the *Dadson* Principle in Self Defence' (1995) 15 OJLS 229

C. Clarkson, 'Necessary Action: A New Defence' [2004] Crim LR 81

I. H. Dennis, 'Duress Murder and Criminal Responsibility' (1980) 106 LQR 208

J. Dressler, 'Justifications and Excuses: A Brief Review of the Concepts and the Literature' (1987) 33 Wayne L Rev 1155

J. Dressler, 'Reflections on *Dudley and Stephens* and Killing the Innocent: Taking a Wrong Conceptual Path' in J. Horder and D. Baker (eds), *The Sanctity of Life and the Criminal Law: The Legacy of Glanville Williams* (2013)

D. W. Elliott, 'Necessity, Duress and Self-Defence' [1989] Crim LR 611

S. Gardner, 'Necessity's Newest Invention' (1991) 11 OJLS 125

P. Glazebrook, 'The Necessity Plea in English Criminal Law' (1972) 30 CLJ 87

J. Loveless, 'Domestic Violence, Coercion and Duress' [2010] Crim LR 93

P. H. Robinson, 'Criminal Law Defenses: A Systematic Analysis' (1982) 82 Columbia L Rev 199

J. Rogers, 'Necessity, Private Defence and the Killing of Mary' [2001] Crim LR 515

W. Wilson, 'The Structure of Defences' [2005] Crim LR 125

12

Assisting and encouraging: Serious Crime Act 2007, Part 2

12.1 Introduction

In the next three chapters we consider inchoate liability. In everyday language if something is described as being 'inchoate' it has just begun and so is not fully formed. Inchoate liability can thus be contrasted with secondary liability, which was considered in Chapter 8. In secondary liability D has aided, abetted, counselled or procured P to commit an offence P has in fact committed. In contrast, with inchoate liability D is punished for his conduct that has not in fact led to the commission of a full offence by D or P. The caveat that must be added to this is that there is now an overlap between inchoate liability and secondary liability due to the reforms introduced by the Serious Crime Act 2007, as will be explained in this chapter.

At common law the offence of incitement was a form of inchoate offence. The definition was accepted to be that a person was guilty of an offence if (i) he incited another to do or cause to be done an act or acts which, if done, would involve the commission of the offence or offences by the other; and (ii) he intend or believed that the other, if he acted as incited, should or would do so with the fault required for the offence or offences. The offence was commonly used to prosecute those who were instigating others to commit crimes even though the person incited did not go on to commit the offence; for example where D encouraged P, an undercover police officer, to attack D's wife for a fee to be paid by D.

The common law was said to be problematic. For example, the Law Commission stated that the fault element of the offence had been distorted by decisions of the Court of Appeal that had focused too much on the state of mind of P rather than D. The common law was eventually replaced with the offences contained in Part 2 of the Serious Crime Act 2007.

The offences in Part 2 are extremely complex and care must be taken when examining the Act to ensure that the elements of each offence are understood.

12.2 The Serious Crime Act 2007, Part 2

The Serious Crime Act 2007, Part 2 followed the Law Commission recommendation to abolish the common law offence of incitement (s 59). It is replaced with three new offences. These are committed where:

- D does an act that is *capable* of encouraging or assisting *intending* to encourage or to assist another, P, to commit an offence (s 44);

- D does an act that is *capable* of encouraging or assisting *believing* that the offence by P will be committed and D *believes* that his act will encourage or assist its commission (s 45); and

- D does an act that is *capable* of encouraging or assisting the commission of one or more of a number of offences and he *believes* (i) that one or more of those offences will be committed (without having any belief as to which particular crime); and (ii) that his act will encourage or assist the commission of one or more of them (s 46).

Understanding and applying the provisions is rendered more difficult because they were designed as only part of the package of secondary and inchoate liability which the Law Commission devised. The Law Commission's recommendations in Report No 300 which have been enacted were designed to be supplemented with the recommendations in Report No 305 where the Law Commission advances a new scheme to deal with all aspects of secondary liability. These have not been enacted. As such, the law has been left in rather an imbalanced state. The Law Commission deliberately designed the inchoate offences in the 2007 Act to be of wide application because it was also recommending that the offences to replace secondary liability would be much narrower than under present law.

The 2007 Act offences are criticized as being too complex, over broad and impractical: see D. Ormerod and R. Fortson, 'The Serious Crime Act 2007 Part 2' [2009] Crim LR 389.

(iv) Breadth of inchoate liability

Aside from the potential for the offences to overlap significantly with the principal offence and supersede secondary liability, their breadth raises concerns even in terms of the appropriate limits of inchoate liability. We are not seeking here to revisit the academic debate on the appropriateness of inchoate liability generally. Nor on the significance which the law ought to attach to the infliction of harm in the form proscribed in the principal/substantive offence as opposed to the willingness of an offender to try to bring it about by his efforts. Our point is simply this: Pt 2 creates broad offences whereby liability can be imposed for conduct far removed from what might typically be regarded as the offence 'paradigm' of blameworthy wrongdoing resulting in a proscribed harm. As Professor Ashworth has succinctly stated, 'as the form of criminal liability moves further away from the infliction of harm, so the grounds of liability should become more narrow'. We submit that this is certainly not the case with the offences under ss.45–46. Indeed, all the Pt 2 offences focus on D's conduct in acts capable of assisting or encouraging P, but the imposition of criminal responsibility on D for that conduct is twice removed from the principal offence. Inchoate liability can be founded on the actions of the accused alone, far removed from the commission of the principal offence, and in the case of ss.45 and 46 in particular, on proof of mens rea requirements of less than purpose or intent. There is the stark risk of over-criminalisation.

■ *Question*

As you proceed through the chapter, consider whether you agree with the above analysis.

The 2007 Act offences are unduly complex. This is particularly true in respect of the s 46 offence. They necessitate close analysis of the substantive offence which it is alleged D has assisted or encouraged P to commit. D's liability will turn on whether D's conduct was capable of assisting or encouraging P in terms of the conduct, circumstances and consequence elements of P's anticipated substantive offence but, of course, the offence by P need not have been committed. The 2007 Act offences also require that D has mens rea about what mens rea P will have if P carries out the anticipated offence.

12.2.1 Intentional assisting or encouraging

Serious Crime Act 2007, s 44

(1) A person commits an offence if—

(a) he does an act capable of encouraging or assisting the commission of an offence; and

(b) he intends to encourage or assist its commission.

(2) But he is not to be taken to have intended to encourage or assist the commission of an offence merely because such encouragement or assistance was a foreseeable consequence of his act.

Section 44 is triable in the same way as the 'anticipated offence' (s 55 (1)): that offence which D is intentionally assisting or encouraging P to commit but which P does not in fact need to commit. Where the anticipated offence is murder, the sentence on conviction under s 44 is a maximum of life: s 58(1). Where the anticipated offence is any offence other than murder the maximum sentence is that available for the full anticipated offence if it had been committed: s 58(2).

The offence is inchoate. As the Law Commission suggested:

... If D sells P a weapon that D intends P will use to murder V, D has done everything that that he or she intends to do. Nothing more turns on D's subsequent conduct whereas P has yet to take the step of attempting to commit the offence. (LC300, para 4.25)

■ *Questions*

D sends an email to P telling him to murder all 'unbelievers':

(a) P does not receive the email;

(b) P receives the email and ignores it because he was going to kill V, an 'unbeliever', in any event;

(c) P is so persuaded by the email that he commits murder when previously he had no intention of doing do.

1. Is D guilty of an offence under s 44? What is the maximum sentence for his conduct?

2. Is D also guilty of aiding and abetting under the Accessories and Abettors Act 1861, s 8? If so, which offence would you choose to prosecute and why?

3. What if P had intended to kill V but had only succeeded in wounding him? For what offences would D be liable (i) under s 44 or (ii) as an accessory?

4. Since the offence is committed at the time when D emails P, there is no scope for a defence of withdrawal. Should there be?

The facts of one of the conjoined appeals against sentence in *Blackshaw* [2011] EWCA Crim 2312 provides a stark example of this offence in operation and also demonstrates the forms of behaviour that may now potentially come within the scope of the offences in Part 2 of the 2007 Act. There were a number of conjoined appeals against sentence after convictions arising from the riots that broke out in various British cities in the summer of 2011. D set up a Facebook page entitled 'The Warrington Riots', which was available for public viewing. On this webpage D included a photograph of police officers in riot equipment in a 'stand off position' with a group of rioters. He also included a photograph of himself and others in a pose described by police as 'gangster-like'. D sent messages via Facebook to 400 contacts inviting them to meet at a local venue. Forty-seven people confirmed their intention to attend the meeting. Concerned citizens of Warrington who saw or heard about D's Facebook page contacted the police. Before the police could close the website down, D retracted his invitation and stated online that it was all a joke. D was arrested and pleaded guilty to intentionally encouraging or assisting the commission of an offence contrary to s 44 of the Serious Crime Act 2007. The offence which D pleaded guilty to intentionally assisting or encouraging was riot. D was sentenced to four years' imprisonment and the Court of Appeal upheld D's sentence. In doing so, Lord Judge CJ stated:

72. When dealing with these two appeals we are, of course, conscious of the fact that in the end no actual harm in the streets of Northwich and Warrington actually occurred. It is not however accurate to suggest that neither crime had any adverse consequences. We know for a certainty that in each case a number of decent citizens were appalled by what they had read, and given the widespread rioting throughout the country, which at that time was spiralling out of control, we have no doubt that some, at least, of them were put in fear. In any event the fact that no rioting occurred in the streets of Northwich or Warrington owed nothing to either defendant. The reality was that armed with information from members of the public who were disturbed at the prospect, the police were able to interfere and bring the possibility of riot to an end.

73. We are unimpressed with the suggestion that in each case the defendant did no more than make the appropriate entry in his Facebook. Neither went from door to door looking for friends or like-minded people to join up with him in the riot. All that is true. But modern technology has done away with the need for such direct personal communication. It can all be done through Facebook or other social media. In other words, the abuse of modern technology for criminal purposes extends to and includes incitement of very many people by a single step. Indeed it is a sinister feature of these cases that modern technology almost certainly assisted rioters in other places to organise the rapid movement and congregation of disorderly groups in new and unpoliced areas.

■ *Questions*

1. Do you think that D's criminality justified the imposition of a four-year custodial sentence?

2. Should D have been able to plead a defence of withdrawal?

3. Could D have argued that his entire course of conduct, including his withdrawal of the invitation to meet, was reasonable and so avoided liability by pleading the defence in s 50? See section 12.2.1.3, p 448 for discussion of this defence.

12.2.1.1 Actus reus

D's conduct must be 'capable' of 'assisting or encouraging'. The focus is on D's conduct, not P's. D's conduct can include a 'course of conduct' (s 67) as where D supplies a number of articles to P over time. Section 67 provides that 'a reference in this Part to an act includes a reference to a course of conduct, and a reference to doing an act is to be read accordingly'.

There is no requirement that D's act does in fact encourage or assist P or anyone. Perhaps D's email in the earlier example is not received by P. P might ignore D's assistance or encouragement, or find it of no encouragement or assistance at all. It is arguable that there is not even any need for P to be aware of D's acts which were intended to assist or encourage him.

What does capable of encouraging mean?

Under the common law offence of incitement, a very broad view was taken of what might amount to encouragement. For example, in *Invicta Plastics Ltd v Clare* [1976] RTR 251, the defendant company manufactured a device called 'Radatec' which made a noise when approaching a police radar trap. The company advertised the device in a motoring magazine. The advertisement stated, 'You ought to know more about Radatec. Ask at your accessory shop or write for name of nearest stockist…' It depicted a view of a road and a speed limit sign through a car windscreen

THE SERIOUS CRIME ACT 2007, PART 2

with the device attached. In response to a request by the prosecutor, the company sent him a stockist's name and a leaflet which included the words: 'The majority of [such] transmissions are not intended for public use and therefore their deliberate reception is illegal unless licensed by the Post Office.... However, no licence is required to receive [other such] transmissions. It is illegal to employ the Radatec specifically for the reception of, for instance, police radar transmissions.' The defendants were convicted by the justices of inciting readers of the magazine and of the leaflet to contravene the Wireless Telegraphy Act 1949, s 1(1), which forbade the use of any wireless telegraphy apparatus except under a licence. On appeal, Park J referred to the fact that:

When summing up to the jury on a case of incitement, judges sometimes use such words as 'incitement involves the suggestion to commit the offence' or 'a proposal to commit the offence' or 'persuasion or inducement to commit the offence' which the defendant is alleged to have incited. But Lord Denning MR considered the meaning of 'incitement' in *Race Relations Board v Applin* [1973] QB 815, 825G, where he said:

'Mr Vinelott suggested that to "incite" means to urge or spur on by advice, encouragement, and persuasion, and not otherwise. I do not think the word is so limited, at any rate in this context. A person may "incite" another to do an act by threatening or by pressure, as well as persuasion.'

Accordingly, the justices had to decide whether, in the context, the advertisement amounted to an incitement to the readers of the magazine to commit the offence...

I think that it is necessary to look at the advertisement as a whole. Approaching it in this way, I have come to the conclusion that the company did incite a breach of the Act by means of the advertisement. I think, therefore, that the justices were right to convict the company of this offence.

■ *Question*

Would the manufacturers of the device be liable under s 44 of the 2007 Act?

The scope of the actus reus under s 44 is extended further by s 65.

(1) A reference in this Part to a person's doing an act that is capable of encouraging the commission of an offence includes a reference to his doing so by threatening another person or otherwise putting pressure on another person to commit the offence.

(2) A reference in this Part to a person's doing an act that is capable of encouraging or assisting the commission of an offence includes a reference to his doing so by—

(a) taking steps to reduce the possibility of criminal proceedings being brought in respect of that offence;

■ *Questions*

1. Alf owns a fancy dress shop. Ben comes into the shop asking for a police uniform costume. Alf overhears Ben talking to Charles on his mobile phone about their planned robbery of the local bank and how Ben will be able to assist the getaway if he gets the police uniform. Alf hates the local bank manager who recently denied Alf a loan. He provides the most realistic uniform for Ben that he can. Is Alf liable for any offence?

2. On a separate occasion, Dara enters Alf's shop and asks to hire a burkha. Alf recognizes Dara from the television news alerts about a person who is suspected of murder and who is trying to flee the country. Alf provides the burkha to Dara. Is Alf liable under s 44 of the 2007 Act? For what exactly?

The actus reus extends further still by s 65(2)(b) whereby:

> ... doing an act that is capable of encouraging or assisting the commission of an offence includes a reference to his doing so by—
>
> ...
>
> (b) failing to take reasonable steps to discharge a duty.
>
> (3) But a person is not to be regarded as doing an act that is capable of encouraging or assisting the commission of an offence merely because he fails to respond to a constable's request for assistance in preventing a breach of the peace.

■ *Questions*

D, a night-time security guard at the bank is so bored with his job that he forgets to set the alarm. P burgles the bank. Is D liable under s 44? For what offence?

The actus reus is extended yet further by s 66 of the 2007 Act:

> If a person (D1) arranges for a person (D2) to do an act that is capable of encouraging or assisting the commission of an offence, and D2 does the act, D1 is also to be treated for the purposes of this Part as having done it.

■ *Questions*

1. D1 supplies a gun to D2 to supply to P to kill V. P receives the gun and shoots at but misses V. Who is guilty of what?

2. Don, a police officer, encourages P, a drug dealer, to sell drugs to V. P ignores the request. Is Don guilty of an offence? See s 50 in section 12.2.1.3, p 448.

The offence is extended not only against D who does an act capable of assisting or encouraging, but also to P. The Law Commission gave the following example:

> P asks D to supply him or her with an article so that P can commit an offence, P is doing an act capable of encouraging D to do an act capable of assisting P to commit an offence. In other words, if D supplies the article to P, not only is D committing the [s 45] offence but, by encouraging D to commit the [s 45] offence, P is committing the [s 44] offence. (LC300, para 4.26)

If D's act is capable of encouraging or assisting the commission of a number of offences, then by s 49(2), s 44 will apply separately in relation to each offence that he intends to encourage or assist to be committed. If D provides P with a gun which he intends P to use in threatening a number of debtors, D will be liable for each offence or robbery, blackmail, etc which P commits provided that it was D's purpose to assist those offences.

12.2.1.2 Mens rea

There are four elements of mens rea to be proved under s 44 of the 2007 Act.

Intention to do acts capable of assisting or encouraging

There must be an intention to do the act which is *capable* of encouraging or assisting. In the previous example with the email, D must intend to do the act by which he intends P to be encouraged or assisted in the murder. This element means that D is not liable if he recklessly leaves open his gun cupboard allowing P to take a gun to shoot V.

Intention to assist or encourage

D must intend to encourage or assist. Section 44(2) makes clear that this is not satisfied by proof that the encouragement was a foreseeable consequence of D's intentional acts; oblique intention has no part to play here.

■ *Questions*

1. Why is it necessary for D to have as his purpose that P will be assisted or encouraged?

2. In the example above, if P killed V would D be liable as an accessory?

If D's act is capable of encouraging or assisting the commission of a number of offences then, by s 49(2), s 44 will apply separately in relation to *each* offence that he intends to encourage or assist to be committed.

■ *Question*

D provides P with a gun which he intends P to use in threatening a number of D's debtors. Will D be liable for each offence or robbery, blackmail, etc which P commits or for each one that D intended that he commits?

D's mens rea as to P's mens rea

Where the anticipated crime is one of mens rea, D must believe or be reckless as to whether P *will* (not might) perform the conduct element for the anticipated offence and that P will at that time act with the prescribed mens rea. Section 47(5)(a) provides that it must be proved that:

(i)   D believed that, were the act to be done, it would be done with that fault;

(ii) D was reckless as to whether or not it would be done with that fault; or

(iii) D's state of mind was such that, were he to do it, it would be done with that fault;

■ *Question*

D encourages P to touch V sexually. What would the prosecution have to prove for D to be liable under s 44 for encouraging the offence? (The mens rea of the offence under the Sexual Offences Act 2003, s 3, is an intention to touch a person sexually, see section 20.2.3, p 729.)

Section 47(5)(a)(iii) deals with the cases where D would have mens rea if *he* committed the anticipated crime even though he does not believe and is not reckless as to whether P would have it.

■ *Questions*

D encourages P to rape V. P has sex with V but lacks mens rea for rape because he reasonably believed V was consenting. Can D be guilty of encouraging rape? See s 47(6)). What if D is a woman?

D's mens rea as to consequences and circumstances of P's offence

D must also have mens rea as to the consequences and circumstances, if any, of the anticipated offence.

By s 47(5)(b) if the offence is one requiring proof of particular circumstances or consequences (or both), it must be proved that:

(i) D believed [or intended] that, were the act to be done, it would be done in those circumstances or with those consequences; or

(ii) D was reckless as to whether or not it would be done in those circumstances or with those consequences.

■ *Questions*

The offence of criminal damage is committed where a person intentionally or recklessly damages property belonging to another. D encourages P to throw a stone at a window. What must the prosecution prove to establish D's guilt under s 44? What if the window was P's and D did not know that?

12.2.1.3 Defences and exemptions to s 44

The standard defences that are discussed in Chapters 10 and 11 will apply. If, when he hands P a weapon, D is insane or acting in self-defence he will be entitled to an acquittal. By s 47(2), 'If it is alleged under section 44(1)(b) that a person (D) intended to encourage or assist the commission of an offence, it is sufficient to prove that he intended to encourage or assist the doing of an act which would amount to the commission of that offence.' It is therefore no defence that D is unaware that the conduct by P that D is intentionally encouraging or assisting would be criminal. It is no defence for D to claim that no offence is actually committed by P: s 49(1).

Reasonable conduct

It is a defence for D to prove on the balance of probabilities that he acted reasonably.

Serious Crime Act 2007, s 50

(1) A person is not guilty of an offence under this Part if he proves—

(a) that he knew certain circumstances existed; and

(b) that it was reasonable for him to act as he did in those circumstances.

(2) A person is not guilty of an offence under this Part if he proves—

(a) that he believed certain circumstances to exist;

(b) that his belief was reasonable; and

(c) that it was reasonable for him to act as he did in the circumstances as he believed them to be.

(3) Factors to be considered in determining whether it was reasonable for a person to act as he did include—

(a) the seriousness of the anticipated offence (or, in the case of an offence under section 46, the offences specified in the indictment);

(b) any purpose for which he claims to have been acting;

(c) any authority by which he claims to have been acting.

It is not enough that D thinks that his conduct is reasonable; it must be found to be reasonable by the jury. Three specific examples of the defence in operation were offered by the Law Commission:

D, a motorist, changes motorway lanes to allow a following motorist (P) to overtake, even though D knows that P is speeding; D, a reclusive householder, bars his front door to a man trying to get into his house to escape from a prospective assailant (P); D, a member of a DIY shop's check-out staff, believes the man (P) purchasing spray paint will use it to cause criminal damage. (LC300, para A.63)

■ *Questions*

1. Fagin runs a pawnbroker shop. He buys lots of goods cheaply from all sorts of unsavoury characters. Oliver repeatedly brings in good-quality iPods to trade in for cash. Fagin is not sure about the provenance of the iPods but he keeps buying them from Oliver. He is charged with assisting or encouraging Oliver to steal iPods. Fagin pleads that he considered his behaviour was reasonable because he has to make a living.

2. D belongs to a fundamentalist religious organization. D encourages P to kill those who oppose his views. D claims that his religion demands that he behave in this way. Does he have a defence under s 50?

Under the common law offence of incitement, in *Marlow* [1997] Crim LR 897, M, under a pseudonym, wrote a book on the cultivation and production of cannabis which was advertised in *Private Eye* and sold some 500 copies. He was convicted of a specific statutory incitement contrary to s 19 of the Misuse of Drugs Act 1971 ('It is an offence to incite or attempt to incite another person to commit [an offence under any other provision of this Act]'). This is retained by the 2007 Act. M's defence was that the book was no more than a scientific exposition of the subject and was not reasonably capable of being regarded as incitement. M was convicted and pursued his case to the European Court of Human Rights claiming that his Article 10 rights of freedom of expression had been infringed. The Court declared the application inadmissible ([2001] EHRLR 444).

■ *Questions*

Would Marlow be at risk of conviction under s 44? Would he have a defence under s 50? Would he have a claim that his Article 10 rights were infringed by s 44 of the 2007 Act?

Under the common law offence of incitement, in *Shaw* [1994] Crim LR 365 D, an employee of a car-leasing company, persuaded K, another employee of the company, to obtain cheques from the company by falsely accepting bogus invoices, supplied by D as real invoices for real work done by real garages. He was charged with inciting K to obtain property by deception. His defence was that his purpose was not to make a profit but to demonstrate to his employers how easy it was to circumvent their security arrangements. He did not tell K his purpose, but eventually he would have done so. D's appeal was allowed. Would D have a defence under s 50?

Defences for victims

The *Tyrrell* ([1894] 1 QB 710) principle is put in statutory form. D will have a defence if he is a 'victim'. Section 51 provides that a person does not commit an offence if:

(1) ...

    (a) he falls within the protected category; and

    (b) he is the person in respect of whom the protective offence was committed or would have been if it had been committed.

(2) 'Protective offence' means an offence that exists (wholly or in part) for the protection of a particular category of persons ('the protected category').

■ *Questions*

1. D, aged 12, encourages P, aged 15, to have sex with her. Is D guilty of an offence of encouraging P to engage in sexual activity with a child under 13?

2. D's mother, E, allows D, aged 12, to have her boyfriend P, aged 15, over to stay and to sleep in D's room. Is E liable for an offence?

3. D, an adult, asks P, also an adult, to beat him for his sexual gratification. Is D guilty of an offence under s 44? Since *Gnango* [2011] UKSC 59 (see section 8.6.1, p 256), D would be guilty of aiding and abetting his own ABH.

12.2.1.4 What crimes are capable of being assisted or encouraged?

The 2007 Act describes D's conduct in terms of acts capable of encouraging or assisting the commission of '*an offence*'. Read literally, this is wide enough to mean that D can be liable under s 44 for assisting or encouraging substantive crimes, attempts and conspiracies.

Assisting or encouraging attempts or conspiracies

The Law Commission proposed that D should be liable for the inchoate offence of doing an act, which is capable of encouraging or assisting D2 to *attempt* to commit an offence, but *only if* it was his *direct intention* that P should do so (LC300, para 7.23). Under s 44, D can be convicted of an offence if he performs acts capable of assisting or encouraging P to *attempt* to commit an offence.

Under the Criminal Law Act 1977, s 5(7), it was no offence to incite a conspiracy but the Law Commission in Report No 300 recommended that D should be liable for acts capable of encouraging or assisting P to *conspire* to commit an offence, but only if it was D's *direct intention* that P should do so. D can be liable under s 44 where he does acts capable of assisting or encouraging P1 and P2 to *conspire* to commit an offence. Section 5(7) of the Criminal Law Act 1977 is repealed (Serious Crime Act 2007, Schedule 6, Part 2, para 54). The 2007 Act does not repeal s 1(4)(b) of the Criminal Attempts Act 1981 which precludes there being an offence of attempting to aid, abet, etc. The failure to repeal this provision has been criticized in the following terms (M. Bohlander, 'The Conflict Between the Serious Crime Act 2007 and Section 1(4)(b) Criminal Attempts Act 1981—A Missed Repeal?' [2010] Crim LR 483):

> So, on the one hand, it still is conceptually not possible to attempt to aid, abet, counsel or procure, in other words doing acts capable of encouraging or assisting another's offence under s.1(4)(b) of the Criminal Attempts Act 1981. Even if D were to commit acts that are more than merely preparatory to encouraging and assisting P to commit an offence, liability would be excluded under s.1(4)(b). On the other hand, however, ss.44 et seq. of the Serious Crime Act 2007 would appear to cover exactly this sort of behaviour. We need to remember that for s.44 to be triggered, it is not even necessary that P himself does any act that is more than merely preparatory. At the very least s.44 clashes conceptually with s.1(4)(b); the latter would now appear to be mostly devoid of substance and creates confusion with the Serious Crime Act 2007.

Assisting or encouraging the act of assisting or encouraging

D can be liable for performing acts capable of encouraging or assisting P1 to encourage or assist P2. If D supplies a weapon to P1 knowing that the weapon will be passed to P2 to perpetrate a murder, D is liable under s 44. As the Law Commission explained (at para 7.15), 'If it is D's intention that P should encourage or assist X, his or her conduct should not be considered too remote from the principal offence merely because, were P to encourage or assist X, P would not intend X to commit the principal offence.' Does this form of 'double' inchoate liability extend the ambit of the criminal law too far?

Attempting or conspiring to commit: s 44

D's acts need only be capable of assisting or encouraging. The possibility of attempting to assist or encourage arises where, for example, D is about to post the letter to P containing details of how to break into V's safe. There seems to be nothing wrong in principle with liability for conspiracy: D1 agreeing with D2 that D1 will perform acts capable of assisting or encouraging P to commit an offence against V. For example, D1 and D2, serious drug villains, agree that D1 should supply a local hoodlum with a weapon so that he will kill V, a competitor in the local drug market.

■ *Question*

What if D1 cannot get hold of D2: is he attempting to conspire with D2 to assist or encourage P?

12.2.2 Section 45

By s 45 of the Act a person commits an offence if:

> (a) he does an act capable of encouraging or assisting the commission of an offence; and
>
> (b) he believes—
>
>> (i)   that the offence will be committed; and
>>
>> (ii) that his act will encourage or assist its commission.

D supplies a gun to P, *believing* that P would use it to commit a murder. D would not be liable for assisting or encouraging unless P committed the murder. D would not be liable for conspiring with P unless there was a common agreement. Under the law before the Serious Crime Act 2007, D could not have been charged with incitement unless there was encouragement rather than pure assistance. Under s 45, D can now be convicted of the inchoate offence of assisting or encouraging the commission of a crime, even if P does not commit the crime.

The s 45 offence is triable in the same way as the 'anticipated offence' (ie that P would commit if he did as D believed): s 55(1). Where the anticipated offence is murder, the maximum sentence on conviction under s 45 is life: s 58(1). Where the anticipated offence is any offence other than murder the maximum sentence is that available for the full anticipated offence if it had been committed: s 58(2).

By way of an example, in *Woodford* [2013] EWCA Crim 1098, D hired a van for C to use. In addition, D had booked passage on a ferry for C to travel from the continent to Dover. He also provided him with a satnav for use on the trip. C was stopped by the UK Border Agency at Dover and in the back of the van there was found a significant quantity of a powder commonly known to be used as a cutting agent in the supply of heroin. C was arrested. Two months later D contacted police and told them that the van was his and the powder was for use on his mother's lawn. D was also arrested. D was convicted of encouraging or assisting the commission of an offence of supplying a controlled drug of Class A, heroin, believing that the offence would be committed, contrary to s 45 of the 2007 Act.

■ *Questions*

1. Could D and C have been guilty of conspiracy? If so, why were they not charged with this offence?

2. On these facts, do you believe that there was sufficient evidence to infer that D believed that the offence of supplying heroin would be committed? What if D testified that he had not found anyone to supply heroin and that, as a consequence, he was going to spread the powder on his mother's lawn?

12.2.2.1 Actus reus

D's conduct needs only to be *capable* of assisting or encouraging (as with s 44). There is no requirement that P is actually encouraged or assisted nor that P commits the offence. D's conduct can be a 'course of conduct': s 67. Conduct capable of assisting or encouraging includes threats or putting pressure on another person: s 65(1). The extended definitions from s 65 (see section 12.2.1.1) apply as in s 44 (taking steps to reduce the possibility of criminal proceedings being brought, and failing to fulfil a duty) and failing to assist a police officer preventing a breach of the peace does not. If D arranges for P to do an act capable of encouraging or assisting X and P does that act, D is treated as also having done it: s 66.

12.2.2.2 Mens rea

Serious Crime Act 2007, s 47

(3) If it is alleged under section 45(b) that a person (D) believed that an offence would be committed and that his act would encourage or assist its commission, it is sufficient to prove that he believed—

 (a) that an act would be done which would amount to the commission of that offence; and

 (b) that his act would encourage or assist the doing of that act.

 …

(5) In proving for the purposes of this section whether an act is one which, if done, would amount to the commission of an offence—

 (a) if the offence is one requiring proof of fault, it must be proved that—

  (i) D believed that, were the act to be done, it would be done with that fault;

  (ii) D was reckless as to whether or not it would be done with that fault; or

  (iii) D's state of mind was such that, were he to do it, it would be done with that fault; and

 (b) if the offence is one requiring proof of particular circumstances or consequences (or both), it must be proved that—

  (i) D believed that, were the act to be done, it would be done in those circumstances or with those consequences; or

  (ii) D was reckless as to whether or not it would be done in those circumstances or with those consequences.

Belief that acts will assist or encourage

D must be proved to have *believed* that his act *will* (not might) encourage or assist P in his performance of the conduct element of the offence.

> **■ Questions**
>
> D supplies P with poison believing that P will use it to kill his wife as he previously threatened. Is D liable under s 45? What for exactly?

Belief that offence will be committed

Under s 45, D must believe that an act will be done which 'would amount to the commission' of the anticipated offence. In the previous example, D must believe that P will use the poison to cause GBH or death.

D's mens rea as to P's mens rea

Where the anticipated crime is one of mens rea, say murder, D must believe or be reckless as to whether P would perform the conduct element of the offence with the prescribed mens rea for that offence with which he, P, would be charged: s 47(5).

> **■ Question**
>
> D supplies the poison to P believing he will use it to kill V. What more must the prosecution prove about D's mens rea in order to convict him under s 45?

D's mens rea as to circumstances and consequences

D must also have mens rea as to the consequences and circumstances of the offence he anticipates by P: s 47(5)(b).

> **■ Questions**
>
> D encourages P to touch V sexually. Is D liable if he believes that P will sexually touch V with intent (which is the mens rea required under the Sexual Offences Act 2003, s 3)? If V is 12, what mens rea must D have as to V's age if he is to be prosecuted under the 2007 Act? (Liability as to age is strict under the Sexual Offences Act 2003, s 7, see section 20.3.1, p 735.)

12.2.2.3 Defences and exemptions to s 45

There is no defence that the anticipated offence did not occur. It is a defence for D to prove that he acted reasonably under s 50. D cannot be liable if he is a 'victim': s 51. These defences are considered in section 12.2.1 when discussing s 44.

12.2.2.4 To which offences does s 45 not apply?

D cannot be convicted under s 45 for:

- assisting or encouraging offences listed in Schedule 3 to the 2007 Act (offences listed in Parts 1 to 3 include (*inter alia*) those under the Offences Against the Person Act 1861, s 4; the Official Secrets Act 1920, s 7; the Misuse of Drugs Act 1971, ss 19 and 20; the Immigration Act 1971, ss 25 and 25B; the Computer Misuse Act 1990, s 3A(1), (2) and (3); the Terrorism Act 2000, s 59; the Terrorism Act 2006, ss 1(2), 2(1), 5, 6(1) and (2); the Perjury Act 1911, s 7(2); the Criminal Law Act 1967, ss 4(1) and 5(1); the Criminal Law Act 1977, ss 1(1), 5(2) and (3); the Criminal Attempts Act 1981, s 1(1); and the Public Order Act 1986, ss 12(6), 13(9) and 14(6). Also covered are offences of attempt under special statutory provisions (see the Criminal Attempts Act 1981, s 3);

- doing an act capable of encouraging/assisting P to encourage or assist X;

- encouraging or assisting a conspiracy to commit an offence, on mere belief that the offence (conspiracy) will be committed: Schedule 3, para 32;

- doing an act that is capable of encouraging or assisting P to attempt to commit an offence, on a mere belief that the attempt will be committed: Schedule 3, para 33; or

- encouraging or assisting P to do act which is capable of assisting X to commit a crime: s 49(4).

12.2.3 Section 46

By s 46 of the 2007 Act, D is guilty of this offence if:

. . .

   (a) he does an act capable of encouraging or assisting the commission of one or more of a number of offences; and

   (b) he believes—

      (i)   that one or more of those offences will be committed (but has no belief as to which); and

      (ii) that his act will encourage or assist the commission of one or more of them.

 (2) It is immaterial for the purposes of subsection (1)(b)(ii) whether the person has any belief as to which offence will be encouraged or assisted.

It is not necessary for the prosecution to specify in the indictment every offence that D potentially might have encouraged or assisted, but the indictment must specify all the offences which the Crown allege D contemplated might be committed: s 46(3). Note that an offence charged under s 46 is triable only on indictment: s 55(5).

D supplies a knife which is capable of encouraging or assisting the commission of one or more of a number of offences (eg one or more robberies or murders). D is liable under s 46 if:

- D *believes* that one or more such offences *will* be committed (even if it cannot be proved that D had a belief or intent as to which *one* will be committed); and

- D believes that his act of supplying the knife to P *will* encourage or assist the commission of at least one of those offences; and

- D believes, or is reckless as to whether, when P is to perform the conduct element of the offence, P will do so with the mens rea required for that offence (or D's state of mind is sufficient itself as such that, were he to do it, it would be done with the fault required); and

- D believes or is reckless as to whether, were the conduct to be done by P, it would be done in those circumstances or with those consequences, if any, of which the offence requires proof.

■ *Questions*

D is a member of an extreme racist gang. He receives an email inviting him to attend a meeting at which 'radical action' has been promised. He is unsure whether this will involve just the usual speeches and rhetoric or whether the leaders might engage in something more serious as they have been promising. He thinks that they might go through with some of the earlier threatened action to: (i) graffiti the local synagogue, (ii) attack the owner of the local curry house who is from Bangladesh, (iii) look for local black youths to fight with and possibly kill.

D replies saying that he will be there and that he hopes that this time they mean 'radical *action*' not words. The meeting takes place but D is unable to attend. Has D committed an offence? How is the judge to sentence D (on the basis of the appropriate sentence for (i) criminal damage, (ii) assault, (iii) murder)?

12.2.3.1 Actus reus

D's conduct needs only to be *capable* of assisting or encouraging. There is no requirement that the conduct does in fact encourage or assist P or anyone. As under s 44 and s 45, D's conduct can be a 'course of conduct'; it can be satisfied by threats or putting pressure on another person (s 65). The extended definitions from s 65 apply so that D is liable if he takes steps to reduce the possibility of criminal proceedings being brought, or fails to fulfil a duty, but failing to assist a police officer preventing a breach of the peace does not. Under s 66, if D arranges for P to do an act capable of encouraging or assisting X and P does that act, D is treated as also having done it.

12.2.3.2 Mens rea

There are no fewer than five elements of mens rea to be proved.

D's belief that he will assist or encourage

D must believe that his act will encourage or assist one or more of the offences. It is not necessary that the Crown establish a belief as to which offence will be committed.

■ *Questions*

D believes that the knife he provides to P will be used to rob V. P uses it to kill V. Can D be liable under s 46? For what exactly?

D's belief as to offences

D must believe that one or more of the offences *will* be committed. It is sufficient that D believes that the offence, or one of the offences, will be committed if certain conditions apply (s 49(7)).

■ *Questions*

D believes that the knife he provides to P will be used to rob V if V refuses to hand over his iPod. P uses it to kill V. Can D be liable under s 46? For what exactly?

D's belief as to one of a number of offences

If the allegation is that D believed one or more of a number of offences would be committed and that his act would encourage or assist the commission of one or more of them, by s 47(4), it is sufficient to prove that D believed:

(a) that one or more of a number of acts would be done which would amount to the commission of one or more of those offences; and

(b) that his act would encourage or assist the doing of one or more of those acts.

The aim of the provision is to allow for a conviction where although it cannot be proved that D had a belief or intent as to which *crime* will be committed, it can be proved that D *believes* that one or more such offences *will* be committed. However, the section refers to the 'act' of P.

■ *Questions*

D provides P with a can of petrol believing that P will use it to start a fire. P uses the petrol to burn his own possessions. Has D committed the s 46 offence? Has P committed a crime (if the property is his own)? Does that matter?

D's mens rea as to P's mens rea

Where the anticipated crime is one of mens rea, D must believe or be reckless as to whether P would act with the mens rea for one of the anticipated offences with which he would be charged. Section 47(5) provides:

> (5) In proving for the purposes of this section whether an act is one which, if done, would amount to the commission of an offence—
>
> (a) if the offence is one requiring proof of fault, it must be proved that—
>
>   (i) D believed that, were the act to be done, it would be done with that fault;
>
>   (ii) D was reckless as to whether or not it would be done with that fault; or
>
>   (iii) D's state of mind was such that, were he to do it, it would be done with that fault; and
>
> (b) if the offence is one requiring proof of particular circumstances or consequences (or both), it must be proved that—
>
>   (i) D believed that, were the act to be done, it would be done in those circumstances or with those consequences; or
>
>   (ii) D was reckless as to whether or not it would be done in those circumstances or with those consequences.
>
> (6) For the purposes of subsection (5)(a)(iii), D is to be assumed to be able to do the act in question.

■ *Questions*

D encourages P to commit sexual touching of V or to rape her. What beliefs must D hold about P's anticipated conduct to be liable under s 46 of the 2007 Act? What are the anticipated offences? What mens rea of P would be required? What mens rea must D have as to P's mens rea?

D's mens rea as to circumstances and consequences of P's act

If the offence is one requiring proof of particular circumstances or consequences (or both) D must also have mens rea as to the consequences and circumstances of one of the anticipated offences: s 47(5).

■ *Questions*

D, aged 15, encourages his friend P, aged 14, to sexually touch or have sexual intercourse with V, aged 12. Is D liable for an offence under s 46? What mens rea must D have as to the anticipated offences? (Rape of a child under 13 involves proof of an intentional act of penetration but liability is strict as to the child's age. Sexual touching of a child under 13 requires proof of an intentional sexual touching but liability as to the age of the child is strict, see section 20.3.1, p 734.)

There have been two cases examining the proper interpretation of s 46. They are unusual as they concern the same defendant and in the most recent case the Court of Appeal has effectively overturned the earlier one. In *S & H* [2011] EWCA Crim 2872, D was convicted of supplying various chemical cutting agents believing that they would assist in the supply of Class A or Class B drugs, contrary to s 46 of the Serious Crime Act 2007. D argued that the offence in s 46 was so vague and uncertain that it rendered it contrary to Article 7 of the European Convention on Human

Rights. The Court of Appeal rejected this argument and went on to examine the mens rea of the s 46 offence. The question the Court of Appeal addressed was whether it suffices for D to believe that one of the offences A, B or C may be committed, although he does not know which one, or whether in a case where a single count particularizes offences A, B and C, D must believe that all the particularized offences will be committed. The Court of Appeal considered that the latter interpretation was the most appropriate one. The practical consequence of the judgment was that when D is charged with an offence contrary to s 46, each separate offence, A, B and C, which his act is capable to assisting or encouraging must be charged as a separate count on the indictment. Some commentators were critical of this decision. For example, Graham Virgo in 'Encouraging or Assisting More Than One Offence' (2012) 2 Arch Rev 6 stated as follows:

As a consequence of this ruling, it was held that, when the defendant is charged with an offence contrary to s.46, each offence which the defendant's act is capable of encouraging or assisting (known as the reference offence) must be charged as a separate count. Further, for each count it must be shown that the defendant believed that that particular offence will be committed with the necessary fault. The application of this decision can be tested by considering the facts of *Blackshaw*, modified slightly. A defendant has posted a message on Facebook inviting those who read the message to meet the next day at a designated spot in order to wreak havoc in a named town. Posting such a message is capable of encouraging a variety of crimes, including burglary, riot and criminal damage. It could include many other offences as well, such as affray, violent disorder, theft or robbery, but it was recognised in *S and H* that not every possible reference offence needs to be charged. The defendant is likely, therefore, to be charged with encouraging the commission of offences contrary to s.46 and each count would designate a separate reference offence which was capable of being encouraged by his conduct. So, the first count would identify burglary as the relevant offence. The defendant would only be guilty of encouraging this offence if he believed both that burglary will be committed and that the message on Facebook will encourage the offence to be committed. But such a defendant would be unlikely to believe that burglary will necessarily be committed. Much more likely is the belief that an offence will be committed and that this might be burglary. Similarly, with the separate counts of riot and criminal damage.

It follows that the typical case of a defendant who contemplates a variety of offences being assisted or encouraged by his act and believes that only one of them will be committed, but is unsure which, cannot be guilty of the s.46 offence and so cannot be guilty of any offence under the Serious Crime Act. Further, the conviction of the defendant in *Blackshaw* is now suspect, since it is not apparent that he believed that any of the reference offences of burglary, riot or criminal damage would necessarily be committed. The decision of the Court of Appeal in *S and H* has one further implication. In the modified *Blackshaw* scenario, the defendant would have to be charged with three separate counts, relating to each reference offence which is considered to be capable of being encouraged by the defendant's act. The defendant will only be guilty of each count if he believes that the particular reference offence will be committed and that his act will encourage that offence. But this is also what must be proved for the s.45 offence. It follows that there is no longer any need to charge the defendant under s.46 at all. Section 46 has been rendered effectively redundant by *S and H*. It would still be possible to use s.46 where the act is capable of encouraging or assisting a number of offences and the defendant believes that one particular offence will necessarily be committed, but there is no reason why this cannot be charged under s.45, since the defendant will have done an act which is capable of assisting or encouraging a particular crime, even though it is capable of encouraging or assisting other crimes, and the defendant believes that the particular crime will be committed and that his act will encourage or assist its commission. Indeed, the statute states that, where a person's act is capable of encouraging or assisting a number of offences, the s.45 offence applies separately in respect of each offence which the defendant believes will be encouraged or assisted: s.49(2)(b).

■ *Questions*

Was the effect of the Court of Appeal's decision to render the offence in s 46 redundant? If so, might this be desirable?

This is not the end of the saga, however. The Court of Appeal considered the safety of D's conviction again in *Sadique* [2013] EWCA Crim 1150. The judgment of Lord Judge CJ differs from that of his brethren in the earlier case.

30. As we have already explained, the 2007 Act created three distinct offences. It is not open to the court to set one or other of them aside and the legislation must be interpreted to give effect to the creation by statute of the three offences. It may well be that the common law offence of inciting someone else to commit an offence was less complex. It may equally be that the purpose of the legislation could have been achieved in less tortuous fashion. Nevertheless these three distinct offences were created by the 2007 Act, with none taking priority over the other two. S.46 creates the offence of encouraging or assisting the commission of one or more offences. Its specific ingredients and the subsequent legislative provisions underline that an indictment charging a s.46 offence of encouraging one or more offences is permissible.

31. This has the advantage of reflecting practical reality. A defendant may very well believe that his conduct will assist in the commission of one or more of a variety of different offences by another individual without knowing or being able to identify the precise offence or offences which the person to whom he offers encouragement or assistance intends to commit, or will actually commit. As Professor Virgo explains in his most recent article, the purpose of the s.46 was 'to provide for the relatively common case where a defendant contemplates that one of a variety of offences might be committed as a result of his or her encouragement'. We entirely agree.

32. *DPP v Maxwell* [1978] 1 WLR 1350 provides a clear example of how the s.46 offence should operate. Maxwell was a member of the Ulster Volunteer Force who agreed to drive his own car and lead a second car containing three or four other men to a remote public house. Having guided them to the scene, he drove slowly passed the public house, and then returned home. The car containing the gang of men stopped, one of the occupants got out, and ran towards the public house, where he threw a pipe bomb containing explosives into the hall way. As it happened the attack failed. He was convicted as an accomplice of doing an act with intent to cause an explosion by a bomb, and with possession of a bomb, both offences contrary to the Explosives Substances Act 1883. On appeal to the House of Lords it was submitted that Maxwell could not properly be convicted of aiding and abetting the commission of these crimes because he did not know the form the attack would take, or of the presence of the bomb in the car containing the gang.

33. The appeal was dismissed. Maxwell could properly be convicted of aiding and abetting the commission of these offences provided he contemplated the commission of one of a limited number of crimes by the principals and intentionally lent his assistance in the commission of such crimes. It was irrelevant that when he lent his assistance Maxwell did not know which of those particular crimes the principal intended to commit, or indeed the precise target or weapons which the gang would use. In short, save that the broad purpose of the gang he led to the site was encompassed in the concept of terrorism, Maxwell did not know (or believe) which particular offence that gang was intent on perpetrating.

34. In our judgment the ingredients of the s.46 offence, and the ancillary provisions, and s.58(4)–(7) in particular, underline that an indictment charging a s.46 offence by reference to one or more offences is permissible, and covers the precise situation for which the legislation provides. Before the appellant in the present case could be convicted, the jury had to be satisfied that (a) he was involved in the supply of the relevant chemicals and (b) that, if misused criminally, the chemicals were capable of misuse by others to commit offences of supplying or being concerned in the supply

of, or being in possession with intent to supply class A and/or class B drugs. None of this would be criminal unless it was also proved (c) that at the time when the relevant chemicals were being supplied, the appellant believed that what he was doing would encourage or assist the commission of one or more of these drug related offences and (d) that he also believed that this was the purpose, or one of the purposes, for which the chemicals would be used by those to whom he supplied them. If those ingredients were established, as the chemicals could be used for cutting agents for class A drugs or class B drugs, or both, it was not necessary for the Crown to prove that he had a specific belief about the particular drug related offence which those he was encouraging or assisting would or did commit.

35. So far as the defendant in Maxwell's position was concerned, s.46 remains apt to cover the encouragement or assistance he offered, not only when the explosive device was actually thrown (when he might equally have been convicted as an accomplice) but also if the plans were not brought to fruition, because of a sudden change of plan so that the device was hurled at a police officer rather than thrown into the public house, or even if the presence of a large number of police officers at the locality led the terrorist gang to drive away without any explosive being thrown at all.

The Court of Appeal effectively adopted the interpretation of s 46 which had previously been rejected. While some welcome this decision (see Virgo (2013) 7 Arch Rev 4) the outcome is not one that all commentators welcome. See Rudi Fortson QC's case comment at [2014] Crim LR 60.

■ *Questions*

D supplied X with a crowbar and is charged with doing an act capable of assisting or encouraging the commission of murder, burglary and criminal damage believing that one or more of those offences will be committed but having no belief as to which. If D is convicted, is there the possibility that four members of the jury were sure that in supplying X with the crowbar D believed that criminal damage would be committed, another four were sure that D believed that burglary would be committed, while the final four jurors were sure that D believed that murder would be committed? Is it fair to convict D? Of what? How is the judge to approach the task of sentencing D? Section 58(4)–(7) states that the maximum sentence when D is found guilty under s 46 is the same as the offence which D believed might be committed that carries the longest sentence. If there is the possibility that not all the jurors were sure that D believed that murder would be committed, do you think it fair that D potentially receives a life sentence?

12.2.3.3 Defences

There is no defence that the anticipated offences did not occur: s 47(4). It is a defence for D to prove that he acted reasonably under s 50. D cannot be liable if he is a 'victim': s 51. These are discussed earlier in the chapter.

12.2.3.4 Which offences are capable of being assisted or encouraged?

In deciding under s 46 whether an act is capable of encouraging or assisting the commission of one or more of a number of offences, listed offences in Schedule 3 (see section 12.2.2.4). D cannot be liable for encouraging or assisting:

- P to commit a statutory incitement of X;
- P to attempt to commit an offence;

- P to do an act which is capable of assisting X to commit a crime; or
- conspiracy to commit an offence.

12.3 Impossibility and the Serious Crime Act 2007

What if D believes he is doing an act capable of assisting or encouraging murder, intending to assist or encourage, but in fact the substantive offence in question is impossible to commit because V is already dead? The 2007 Act makes no reference to the position regarding impossibility. The Law Commission believed that impossibility would be no defence and that this has been achieved by its silence. The Law Commission gave the following example.

if D . . . provides P with a weapon believing that P will use it to attack V1 (intending to kill V1), D is guilty of assisting murder irrespective of whether P uses the weapon to attack anyone. Were P to attack and murder V2, instead of V1, D would be equally guilty of encouraging or assisting murder. If P attacked V2 because V1 was already dead at the time that D provided the weapon, D would still be guilty of encouraging or assisting murder. It may have been impossible for V1 to be murdered but, nonetheless, D had done an act capable of encouraging or assisting the conduct element of murder, namely an attack on any human being.

Although this example may seem straightforward, less clear is the case where D's act, which he thinks is capable of assisting or encouraging, is in fact incapable of doing so.

12.4 The possibility of reform?

In addition to the criticisms of Part 2 that have been made by academics and the judiciary, the House of Commons Justice Committee had the following to say.

26. We expect the Ministry to consider the effect of the Court of Appeal's 2013 judgment in the case of *Sadique* upon its analysis of Part 2 of the SCA. In the light of this fresh judgment (upon which, at the time of preparing this report, there were no academic articles), we make no conclusions or recommendations in relation to the contents of Part 2, save that we concur with the academics who told us that the sections are complex and difficult to understand for lawyers, let alone for defendants, jurors and other lay-people working in the criminal justice system. We consider that the Court of Appeal's use of the word 'tortuous' in the 2013 *Sadique* judgment is entirely apt to describe the complexity and prolixity of Part 2 of the SCA.

. . .

31. In relation to the SCA, as stated above, we are concerned about the complexity of the provisions, and the difficulties that academics, lawyers and judges have found in interpreting the provisions. At the same time, we accept that there are, as yet, relatively few cases, and that the latest judgment in the case of *Sadique* may allow the legislation to settle into accepted use and interpretation. *We recommend that the Ministry conduct a further and full post-legislative assessment of Part 2 in 2016. If, in the meantime, the number of appeals on Part 2 increases, we expect the Ministry to consider bringing forward legislative proposals for revising, or even replacing, Part 2 to meet the purpose of the legislation in a less tortuous fashion.*

Available in full at http://www.publications.parliament.uk/pa/cm201314/cmselect/cmjust/639/63904.htm.

■ *Question*

Do you agree that Part 2 ought to be revised, or even completely replaced?

FURTHER READING

D. Baker, 'Complicity, Proportionality and the Serious Crime Act 2007' (2011) 14 New Crim L Rev 403

J. Child, 'Exploring the *Mens Rea* Requirements of the Serious Crime Act 2007: Assisting and Encouraging Offences' (2012) 76 J Crim L 220

J. Child and A. Hunt, 'Mens Rea and the General Inchoate Offences: Another New Culpability Framework' (2012) 63 NILQ 247

R. Fortson and D. Ormerod, 'The Serious Crime Act 2007 Part 2' [2009] Crim LR 389

Law Commission Consultation Paper No 131, *Assisting and Encouraging Crime* (1993)

Law Commission Report No 300, *Inchoate Liability for Assisting and Encouraging* (2005)

F. Stark, 'Encouraging or Assisting Clarity?' (2013) 72 CLJ 497

13
Conspiracy

13.1 Introduction

Conspiracy is a form of inchoate offence based on agreement to commit a crime. It is committed as soon as A and B agree to commit a criminal offence as, for example, where A and B agree to burgle a house next week. The crime is committed and is not undone even if they immediately regret it and abandon the plan. Their repentance would mitigate the sentence but would have no effect on liability to conviction.

At common law, unlike incitement and attempt, conspiracy was not limited to cases where the defendants had in view the commission of a crime. Conspiracy was defined at common law as an agreement to do an unlawful act or to do a lawful act by unlawful means; and the word 'unlawful' included not only all crimes but also some torts, fraud, the corruption of public morals and the outraging of public decency, whether or not the acts in question amounted to crimes when done by an individual. The scope of criminal liability was excessive. The common law of conspiracy has been greatly modified by statute and the law is now found principally in the Criminal Law Act 1977.

Some of the controversies that will be examined in this chapter include the following:

(i)   whether it is necessary and/or desirable to criminalize conspiracies;

(ii) the extent to which there can be a conspiracy under the 1977 Act if the parties have only agreed to commit the substantive offence subject to some condition;

(iii) what must be agreed and who must intend what to happen for a crime of conspiracy;

(iv) the mens rea of statutory conspiracies;

(v)   whether common law conspiracies are so vague as to infringe the rule of law.

13.2 Rationale of offence

Where D1 and D2 agree to graffiti V's house, a conspiracy to commit criminal damage is complete even though they have never been near the house and have taken no further steps to perpetrate that crime. Although no one would doubt that the substantive offence of criminal damage should exist to protect against harm to property, the question is whether the mere agreement to do so ought also to constitute a crime. Some argue that the conduct involved in the agreement represents a different 'wrong' or 'harm' from the commission of the criminal damage itself, but is it a sufficiently serious wrong to warrant criminalization? See the discussion in Law Commission Consultation Paper No 183, *Conspiracy and Attempts* (2007), section 13.4.6.1, p 476, Ch 2 and I. Dennis, 'The Rationale of Criminal Conspiracy' (1977) 93 LQR 39. These are not mere 'academic' anxieties: when the Law Commission began its study of the subject in 1970, one of the first questions posed to Glanville Williams was 'Do We Need an Offence of Conspiracy At All?' (D. Hodgson, 'Law Commission No 76: A Case Study in Criminal Law Reform' in *Reshaping the Criminal Law*.

There are numerous arguments, many of considerable merit, which cannot be dealt with in full here; however, it is possible to give a flavour of the diversity and ingenuity of the objections to what is an offence of considerable pedigree, and significant practical value:

- it criminalizes conduct before it has been confirmed to constitute a harm or real threat of harm—even earlier than an attempt in which an overt act of more than mere preparation is required;
- it allows for the punishment of conduct by two which would not be criminal if performed by a sole actor; and
- procedurally, it allows the Crown to avoid specificity in the case and carries with it the disadvantages inherent in joint trials.

There are equally respectable counter-arguments defending the need for conspiracy:

- the offence allows for the intervention of the police authorities at an early stage of the enterprise and this better protects society against the commission of the substantive crime;
- conspiracy is important in deterring not only the commission of the substantive crime but the planning and collaboration in crime generally. This differs from attempt where no distinct harm, and hence no distinct deterrence, is involved in the performance of an act more than merely preparatory to the offence;
- there is a unique and distinct harm involved in the preparedness to collaborate in criminal activity. As the US Supreme Court has observed:

For two or more to . . . combine together to commit . . . a breach of the criminal laws is an offense of the gravest character, sometimes quite outweighing, in injury to the public, the mere commission of the contemplated crime. It involves deliberate plotting to subvert the laws, educating and preparing the conspirators for further and habitual criminal practices. And it is characterized by secrecy, rendering it difficult of detection, requiring more time for its discovery and adding to the importance of punishing it when discovered. (*US v Rabinowich* 238 US 78 at 88 (1915))

- collaboration may increase the likelihood of commission of the offence and perhaps even an increased level of harm if committed. (This must surely depend on the type of crime. Counter-arguments are that the collaboration may also render conspiracies weaker since they are more susceptible to a disclosure of information or one party reneging. On the psychological and economic strengths of conspiracies, see N. Katyal, 'Conspiracy Theory' (2003) 112 Yale LJ 1307);
- conspiracy allows the true nature of the criminality of a group of individuals to be the focus of a prosecution; and
- arguably, conspiracy better respects the principle of fair labelling since the description of D's conduct accurately reflects his personal behaviour.

■ *Questions*

1. Is a crime of conspiracy necessary bearing in mind that a defendant can be charged with attempt as soon as he goes beyond acts of mere preparation towards the commission of the offence?

2. To what extent is it desirable and/or possible to have an offence of conspiracy focused on the mere fact of agreement and collaboration?

3. To what extent must the conspiracy offence depend on the detail of the substantive offence that is the object of the conspiracy?

13.3 Statutory and common law conspiracy

13.3.1 Statutory conspiracy

The Criminal Law Act 1977 created a new offence of statutory conspiracy. Section 1 of that Act (as amended) provides:

1. The offence of conspiracy

(1) Subject to t he following provisions of this Part of this Act, if a person agrees with any other person or persons that a course of conduct shall be pursued which, if the agreement is carried out in accordance with their intentions, either:

(a) will necessarily amount to or involve the commission of any offence or offences by one or more of the parties to the agreement, or

(b) would do so but for the existence of facts which render the commission of the offence or any of the offences impossible, he is guilty of conspiracy to commit the offence or offences in question.

(2) Where liability for any offence may be incurred without knowledge on the part of the person committing it of any particular fact or circumstance necessary for the commission of the offence, a person shall not be guilty of conspiracy to commit that offence by virtue of subsection (1) above unless he and at least one other party to the agreement intend or know that that fact or circumstance shall or will exist at the time when the conduct constituting the offence is to take place.

(3) [*Repealed.*]

(4) In this Part of this Act 'offence' means an offence triable in England and Wales.

[Section 1A Conspiracies to commit offences outside the United Kingdom, is omitted.]

Statutory conspiracy is not limited to agreements to commit a statutory crime—agreements to commit the common law offences, such as murder or cheating the revenue, are charged under this offence—rather, the term 'statutory conspiracy' is used to distinguish it from common law conspiracies. An agreement to commit a crime is now a statutory conspiracy, regulated by the 1977 Act instead of the common law.

The penalty for statutory conspiracy is provided by s 3 of the Act—broadly, the conspiracy is punishable in the same manner as the crime the offenders have conspired to commit.

Section 1(1)(b) deals with the issue of 'impossible' conspiracies. The effect of the provision is that the parties to the conspiracy will be judged on the facts as they believed them to be, not what they were in reality. For example, if A and B agree to kill C, but unbeknownst to them C is already dead, the fact of C's death will not preclude A and B being guilty of conspiracy to commit murder.

13.3.2 Common law conspiracies

It is an offence triable only on indictment to agree:

(i) to defraud, whether or not the fraud amounts to a crime;

(ii) to do an act which tends to corrupt public morals or outrage public decency, whether or not the act amounts to a crime.

The 1977 Act has no part to play in the prosecution of such offences.

It is the ultimate aim of the Law Commission to limit conspiracy to agreements to commit crimes. It was thought, however, that the complete abolition of common law conspiracy would leave some unacceptable gaps in the law and that, pending the enactment of some new but undefined substantive offences, it was necessary to ensure that conspiracies to defraud, to corrupt public morals and to outrage public decency continue to be punishable. In the case of conspiracy to defraud, there is an overlap with the statutory conspiracy offence and either can be charged: see s 12 of the Criminal Justice Act 1987.

13.4 The elements of statutory conspiracy

The elements of the offence can be broken down as follows:

(i) an agreement;

(ii) a course of conduct;

(iii) necessarily involving the commission of a criminal offence;

(iv) the crime is to be committed by one of the parties to the conspiracy;

(v) intention;

(vi) knowledge or intention as to proscribed circumstances.

13.4.1 An agreement

The offence is complete once a concluded agreement (going beyond mere negotiation) exists. In *Saik* [2006] UKHL 18 (extracted in section 13.4.7, p 482) Lord Nicholls stated that, 'The offence therefore lies in making an agreement. Implicitly, the subsection requires also that the parties intend to carry out their agreement. The offence is complete at that stage. The offence is complete even if the parties do not carry out their agreement. The offence is complete even if the substantive offence is not thereafter committed by any of the conspirators or by anyone else'. Once there is an agreement, it (and therefore the criminal conspiracy) subsists until the agreement is performed or abandoned: *DPP v Doot* [1973] AC 807. During this time anyone joining the enterprise, knowing of the criminal purpose, becomes a party to the conspiracy, even if they were not party to the original agreement: *Zezev* [2002] EWHC Admin 589. It is not necessary for all the parties to know each other or even to know what other parties exist: *Meyrick* (1929) 21 Cr App R 94. In that case the Ds had each been involved in the bribery of a police officer in Soho. Their individual agreements with the police officer enabled them to contravene the licensing laws. A number of the defendants appealed against their conviction on the ground that all those involved in the conspiracy had never even met each other. Their appeals were dismissed.

> Lord Hewart CJ:
>
> It seems to us that it was clearly put to the jury that in order to find these persons, or any of them, guilty of the conspiracy charged . . . it was necessary that the prosecution should establish, not indeed that the individuals were in direct communication with each other, or directly consulting together, but that they entered into an agreement with a common design. Such agreements may be made in various ways. There may be one person, to adopt the metaphor of counsel, round whom the rest revolve. The metaphor is the metaphor of the centre of the circle and the circumference. There may be a conspiracy of another kind, where the metaphor would be rather that of a chain; A communicates with B, B with C, C with D, and so on to the end of the list of conspirators. What has to be ascertained is always the same matter: is it true to say, in the words already quoted, that the acts of the accused were done in pursuance of a criminal purpose held in common between them?

But there must be a criminal purpose that the parties to the conspiracy share as their common purpose: *Griffiths* [1966] 1 QB 589: D conspired with each of a number of farmers to defraud the Ministry of Agriculture; but it was not shown to be one conspiracy and therefore was not chargeable as such. In some instances it is alleged that there are several separate conspiracies: D with A; D with B; D with C, etc. In others, it is alleged that there is a single conspiracy between D, A, B and C. In such a case, it is essential that all members of the conspiracy have a shared common purpose; not a series of separate parallel purposes.

It is clear that in these so-called 'wheel conspiracies', the conspiracy may revolve around some third party, X, who is in touch with each of D1, D2 and D3, though they are not in touch with one another. Provided that the result is that they have a common design—for example, to rob a particular bank—D1, D2 and D3 may properly be indicted for conspiring together though they have never been in touch with one another until they meet in the dock. The same is true of a chain conspiracy where D1 communicates with D2, D2 with D3, etc.

The issue of whether there was one conspiracy as opposed to multiple conspiracies arose recently in *Shillam* [2013] EWCA Crim 160. It was alleged that R was the central character in supplying cocaine and that S and X were regular purchasers from him for onward sale. The evidence showed that R was in regular contact with S, but not with any other alleged conspirator, X. All three were convicted of conspiracy to supply cocaine. The judge directed the jury that they had to be sure that in the case of each defendant he had agreed with at least one other person to supply cocaine to someone else. The jury asked whether the conspiracy had to be between any two of the three defendants or whether it sufficed that it was between one of them and persons unknown. The judge directed the jury that the latter sufficed. S appealed and argued that the judge's direction meant that the jury could convict the defendants without them necessarily being sure that they were all party to the same conspiracy. The Court of Appeal agreed that the judge had misdirected the jury. Toulson LJ stated that:

19. Conspiracy requires a single joint design between the conspirators within the terms of the indictment. . . . the evidence may prove the existence of a conspiracy of narrower scope and involving fewer people than the prosecution originally alleged, in which case it is not intrinsically wrong for the jury to return guilty verdicts accordingly, but it is always necessary that for two or more persons to be convicted of a single conspiracy each of them must be proved to have shared a common purpose or design.

20. In the present case the prosecution's argument was in effect that there was a 'wheel' or 'chain' conspiracy with Robb at its centre or head; but in such a case, although each conspirator need not necessarily know of the identity or even the existence of all the other conspirators, there must be a shared criminal purpose or design in which all have joined, rather than merely similar or parallel ones.

[His lordship then quoted a passage from *Smith and Hogan's Criminal Law* p 427 before continuing:]

22. The judge's summing up did not address that issue. On the contrary, he directed the jury that for a defendant to be convicted it was sufficient to show that he had agreed with another person, whether identified or unknown, for the supply of cocaine within the period of the indictment. This left it open to the jury to convict all three defendants of the conspiracy charged against them, if satisfied that the appellant and [X] had each made arrangements with Robb to buy cocaine from him, whether or not the appellant or [X] was party to a wider design. This was wrong.

23. Since Robb was put by the prosecution as the head of the alleged conspiracy, and the involvement of the appellant and [X] was with him, the jury should have been directed to consider first the case in relation to Robb. As to that, there was a strong case that he masterminded the acquisition and processing of the drugs for onward distribution, and that this must have involved the knowing participation of others, so rendering him guilty of the conspiracy charged. The jury should next have been told that if they were not sure of Robb's guilt, they should also acquit the other defendants; but that if they were sure of his guilt, they must then consider whether the prosecution had proved as against each of the other defendants that they shared a common purpose or design (as distinct from separate but similar designs) so as to be a party to the *same* conspiracy, i.e. a conspiracy wider than the supply of cocaine to that particular defendant.

■ *Questions*

1. How realistic is it to say that D1 and D2 are in agreement on something if they have never met or communicated together?

2. Are the terms 'wheel' and 'chain' conspiracy helpful or might they be misleading? Consider Rudi Fortson's criticisms in his case comment on *Shillam* at [2013] Crim LR 592.

13.4.2 Course of conduct

The parties must agree 'that a course of conduct shall be pursued which...will necessarily amount to or involve the commission of any offence...by one or more parties to the agreement'. A 'course of conduct' is an ambiguous phrase. It might mean that A and B need only have agreed on (i) the actual physical acts which they propose shall be done (eg putting poison in V's tea); or (ii) that they have agreed on the act and consequences which they intend to follow from their conduct and the relevant circumstances which they know, or believe, or intend, to exist (eg V will die).

'Course of conduct' must include the contemplated result. If A and B agree to kill V by shooting him, this is surely conspiracy to murder even though B knows that he is a rotten shot and may well miss his target. They agree *and* intend to kill. Their objective *is* the intended result, and the agreed course of conduct is merely the means (however flawed) towards that intended end.

As for relevant circumstances, it would again seem absurd not to include these as requirements of the 'course of conduct'. If D1 and D2 agree to have intercourse with a person, V, their liability for conspiracy to rape a child under 13 contrary to the Sexual Offences Act 2003, s 5, must depend on their agreed course of conduct including the proscribed *circumstance* of the child's age.

13.4.3 'Necessarily amount to or involve the commission of any offence... by one or more parties to the agreement'

D1 and D2 agree to marry next Tuesday, knowing that D1's wife is alive. Have they conspired to commit bigamy? Will their agreement necessarily amount to or involve the commission of an offence? Before next Tuesday, D1's wife may die. These events may be unlikely, but they are possible, and therefore it cannot be said that the going through the marriage ceremony will *necessarily* amount to, or involve, the offence of bigamy.

■ *Questions*

D1 and D2 agree to receive goods from X. They believe they will be stolen goods. Have D1 and D2 conspired to receive stolen goods? What if the goods are no longer stolen by the time they receive them?

One way the courts tried to get round this difficulty was to take an expansive reading of the mens rea and construe 'course of conduct' to include material circumstances which the parties *believe* will (not may) exist. The main difficulty about this approach is s 1(2) of the Act. This provides that a person is not guilty of conspiracy to commit an offence unless he '*intends or knows*' that circumstances necessary for the commission of the offence shall or will exist at the time when the conduct constituting the offence is to take place. In the examples just given, D cannot 'know' that the circumstances will exist because, as we have seen, they may not do so; this was confirmed in *Saik* [2006] UKHL 18 (extracted in section 13.4.7, p 482) and implicitly in the House of Lords in *Montilla* [2004] UKHL 50 and it seems strange to say that D 'intends' that they shall exist when D has, and knows he has, no control over their existence. D 'believes' they will exist; but s 1(2) does not use that word.

The Law Commission has described the problem in the following terms:

1.26 So far as it relates to the conduct or consequence elements of an offence, the 'necessary in-volvement' requirement is an important safeguard against overextension of the law of conspiracy. If D1 and D2 agree on a course of conduct that, if carried out in accordance with their intentions, merely 'might' involve criminal conduct or consequences, that agreement should not amount to a criminal conspiracy. D1 and D2 may, for example, agree to drive as fast as possible from London to Manchester, realising that there is a risk of causing death by dangerous driving in so doing. Whatever one may think of their agreement, it is not an agreement to cause death by dangerous driving and is hence not a criminal conspiracy. It is only if causing death by dangerous driving would necessarily be involved in what D1 and D2 plan to do that there is a conspiracy contrary to the 1977 Act.

1.27 If a substantive offence itself requires proof of actual knowledge of particular facts or circum-stances, then section 1(1)(a) appears to require proof of such knowledge on a charge of conspiracy to commit that substantive offence. (LCCP 183)

13.4.3.1 Conditional intentions

It is necessary to consider whether there can be a conspiracy if there is an agreement between D1 and D2 subject to some condition existing before the crime will be committed.

> ■ *Question*
>
> D1 and D2 agree to rob a bank if the coast is clear. Have they agreed on a course of conduct that will necessarily involve the commission of an offence?

Lord Nicholls in *Saik*, at [18], stated:

An intention to do a prohibited act is within the scope of section 1(1) even if the intention is expressed to be conditional on the happening, or non-happening of some particular event.... A conspiracy to rob a bank tomorrow if the coast is clear when the conspirators reach the bank is not, by reason of this qualification, any less a conspiracy to rob.... Fanciful cases apart, the conditional nature of the agree-ment is insufficient to take the conspiracy outside section 1(1).

The problem frequently arises in the context of money laundering. There is commonly an agreement between D1 and D2 to deal with certain quantities of cash if and when they arrive from X, but D1 and D2 do not know of the precise provenance of the cash. It may represent the proceeds of criminal conduct, but it may not. Dealing with criminal property is a money laundering offence under the Proceeds of Crime Act 2002 (see section 27.10, p 888). Is agree-ing to deal with cash in these circumstances a conspiracy to launder money?

See further, D. Ormerod, 'Making Sense of Statutory Conspiracy' [2006] CLP 185:

...

Distinguishing types of 'conditional' intentions

Academic writing has produced a diverse range of classifications and terminology in this area, but three broad categories are accepted.

- We will do 'x' if 'y'.

Kenneth Campbell in his useful analysis of the concepts ['Conditional Intention' [1982] 2 LS 77, 84–85] describes these as 'non-comprehensive conditional intentions.' The defendant's state of mind is declared only in relation to one possible eventuality.

If D1 and D2 declare 'we will transfer the money if it is clean money', there is no declared intention about what course of conduct they would adopt if the money is illicit. This is not, it is submitted, a sufficient state of mind to constitute an intention to launder money. D1 and D2 have, implicitly, seen the risk that the money will be illicit, but have not declared an intention to deal with criminal money. It cannot be said that D1 and D2 have agreed on a course of conduct that will *necessarily* involve them in the commission of an offence if carried out in accordance with their intentions. In fact, acting in accordance with their declared intentions, all we can assert is that they will not commit a money laundering offence.

If the statement is 'we will transfer money if it is criminal', clearly this is a sufficient intention to constitute a conspiracy to launder money. The other eventuality—what they would do if the money is legitimate—is neither here nor there. D1 and D2 have declared an intention to pursue a course of conduct which if carried out in accordance with their intentions (which here must be taken to mean including those circumstances that they anticipate and accept) will necessarily involve a criminal offence. There will be few such cases.

- We will do 'x' only if 'y'

Campbell calls these 'comprehensive conditional intentions.' They differ significantly from the previous category because D1 and D2 have declared intentions as to their course of conduct in both eventualities: where *y* materialises and not.

The money laundering duo might say: 'we will transfer the money *only if* the money is clean, if it is not we will not transfer it'. There is no intention to pursue a course of conduct that will necessarily involve the commission of an offence. There can be no liability for conspiracy. Alternatively, the duo might say 'we will transfer the money only if the money is criminal.' This would obviously constitute an intention to launder. D1 and D2 would have agreed on a course of conduct which if carried out in accordance with their intentions (again, this must include the circumstances they anticipate and accept) will necessarily involve them in the commission of a criminal offence. These will be rare, in the money laundering context at least. It may be that they are more frequent in other examples—the paedophile might say 'I will touch the girl sexually only if she is under 13'; or the thief—'I will steal only if there is something worth stealing'.

. . .

- To do 'x' even if 'y'

Campbell calls these unconditional intentions. They are generally regarded as a form of direct intention. Taking the money laundering duo as an example, let us imagine that D1 and D2 say 'we know that the monies involved in our business might be criminal, we do not know for sure that they will be, but our business is transferring money and we agree that we will pursue such conduct *even though* some of the monies we transfer are criminal.' Their agreement could be reconstructed as one which includes a confirmed intention:

'we intend to pursue a course of conduct (transferring money) which is not criminal money and if certain circumstances transpire (the money is criminal), we intend nevertheless to pursue a course of conduct (transferring money).'

The agreement will, if completed in accordance with one of their intentions, necessarily involve the commission of a crime.

How would this approach work with other problems postulated above:

D1 and D2 agree to pursue a course of conduct (touching a person in a sexual manner) they foresee that the victim might be under 13. They agree to continue if she is under 13. This could be seen as an agreement to touch a person *even if* she is under 13 if that circumstance arises. On that agreement they will necessarily commit an offence: their agreements include one to touch a child sexually if she is under 13.

> D1 and D2 agree to pursue a course of conduct (damaging property) they foresee that the property might not belong to D1. They agree to continue *even if* that may be the case. Their agreements include one intentionally to damage property if it belongs to another.

Consider the following two examples provided by the Court of Appeal in *Reed* [1982] Crim LR 819:

> In the first, A and B agree to drive from London to Edinburgh in a time which can be achieved without exceeding the speed limits, but only if the traffic they encounter is exceptionally light. Their agreement will not necessarily involve the commission of any offence even if it is carried out in accordance with their intentions, and they do arrive from London to Edinburgh within the agreed time. Accordingly, the agreement does not constitute the offence of statutory conspiracy or indeed of any offence. In the second example, A and B agree to rob a bank, if when they arrive at the bank it seems safe to do so. Their agreement will necessarily involve the commission of an offence of robbery if it is carried out in accordance with their intentions. Accordingly, they are guilty of the statutory offence of conspiracy.

In *Reed*, A and B were held guilty of conspiring to aid and abet suicide where they agreed that A would visit individuals contemplating suicide and either discourage them or actively help them, depending on his assessment of the appropriate course of action. In *Jackson* [1985] Crim LR 442, CA, D and E agreed to shoot their friend V in the leg if he was convicted of the burglary for which he was on trial. (They believed he would thereby receive a lighter sentence.) V was shot and disabled. D and E were convicted of conspiring to pervert the course of justice. They appealed on the ground that their agreement did not necessarily involve the commission of a crime, as everything depended on a contingency—V being convicted. The court held:

> Planning was taking place for a contingency and if that contingency occurred the conspiracy would necessarily involve the commission of an offence. 'Necessarily' is not to be held to mean that there must inevitably be the carrying out of an offence. It means, if the agreement is carried out in accordance with the plan, there must be the commission of the offence referred to in the conspiracy count.

■ *Questions*

1. Is the distinction to be drawn on the basis of whether the commission of the crime is the direct object or incidental to the agreement? Is that a workable solution in practice?

2. Can these cases be better dealt with as each involving two agreements? In *Reed*, for example: an agreement to drive to Edinburgh and an agreement to speed if traffic is heavy? The latter necessarily involves the commission of a crime subject to a condition, but that does not preclude a conspiracy. Similarly, image D1 and D2 who agree to burgle 20 Acacia Avenue unless there are police outside when they arrive to do so—this is a completed conspiracy, their reservation does not preclude liability.

In *O'Hadhmaill* [1996] Crim LR 509, it was held that an agreement by members of the IRA during the period of the IRA ceasefire to make bombs with a view to causing explosions if, but only if, the ceasefire came to an end, was a conspiracy to cause an explosion. Is this an agreement subject to a reservation, or contingency?

■ *Questions*

Are burglars guilty of conspiracy to murder if they set out to commit burglary, having agreed that, if it is necessary to do so in order to complete the burglary or to escape, they will shoot to kill? Will their agreement 'necessarily' involve murder?

13.4.3.2 'Either or' conspiracies

It is possible to enter an agreement to commit offence A *or* offence B, but such an agreement in law constitutes a conspiracy to commit offence A *and* offence B. An agreement to rob the first person who comes around the corner if it is a man constitutes a conspiracy to rob. Similarly an agreement to rape the first person to come around the corner if it is a woman constitutes a conspiracy to rape. Thus, an agreement to rob the first person who comes around the corner if it is a man, but to rape if it is a woman, is an agreement to commit only one of two offences, but it is an agreement which in law amounts to a conspiracy to do both. The condition precedent of the one offence excludes the commission of the other, but at the time of the agreement the relevant facts are unknown and it seems that the parties therefore agree to commit robbery or rape as the prevailing circumstances permit.

The courts have concluded that if conspirators agree that they will steal a particular item and that they will, if necessary, either commit burglary or robbery to obtain that item, that will amount to an agreement to commit the offences of theft, burglary *and* robbery: *A-G's Reference (No 4 of 2003)* [2004] EWCA Crim 1944 at [14]; *Suchedina* [2006] EWCA Crim 2543.

13.4.4 Crime to be committed by one or more of the parties to the conspiracy

An agreement will amount to a statutory conspiracy only if carrying it out will necessarily amount to or involve the commission of an offence *by one or more of the parties to the conspiracy*.

In *Hollinshead* [1985] 1 All ER 850 at 857, the defendants had agreed to supply 'black boxes' to a man (in fact an undercover policeman) who was expected to resell them to persons unknown who would use them to defraud electricity boards. (The black box reverses the flow of current so as to make it appear that less electricity has been used. It has no other use.) The Court of Appeal held that there could be no conspiracy where the fraud contemplated was to be carried out, not by any party to the agreement, but by a third party.

13.4.5 'Crime' to be committed by a conspirator must be a substantive crime

The Court of Appeal in *Hollinshead* also held that the offence of conspiracy under s 1 of the Criminal Law Act 1977 requires D1 and D2 to reach an agreement that will involve 'a course of conduct' amounting to or involving 'the commission of an offence'. It was not enough that D1 and D2 had agreed on a course of conduct that would aid and abet X to commit an offence. D1 and D2 had to have agreed on a 'course of conduct' that would amount to a crime. Their agreed course of conduct was selling the equipment. That was not a crime. The prosecution obtained leave to appeal to the House of Lords.

R v Hollinshead
[1985] 2 All ER 769, House of Lords

(Lords Fraser, Diplock, Roskill, Bridge and Brandon)

Lord Roskill [having examined cases on conspiracy to defraud]:

...The Court of Appeal was of the opinion that...s 1(1) of the 1977 Act did not, on its true construction, make a charge of conspiracy to aid, abet, counsel or procure possible in law. The foundation for this view is a passage in Smith and Hogan *Criminal Law* (5th edn, 1983) pp 234–235, which is quoted in full in the judgment by Hodgson J and with which the Court of Appeal expressed complete agreement (see [1985] 1 All ER 850 at 857–858, [1985] 2 WLR 761 at 770–771).

My Lords, I do not find it necessary to consider whether or not this view is correct for this reason. Even if such a charge of conspiracy to aid, abet, counsel or procure were possible in law, I can see no evidence whatever that the respondents ever agreed so to aid, abet, counsel or procure or indeed did aid, abet, counsel or procure those who as the ultimate purchasers or possessors of the black boxes were destined to be the actual perpetrators of the intended frauds on electricity boards. It follows that on no view could the respondents have been convicted on count 1 even if that count were sustainable in law. This last question is obviously one of some difficulty and a case in which that question arose for direct decision is likely to be a rarity. I suggest that in any future case in which that question does arise it should be treated as open for consideration de novo, as much may depend on the particular facts of the case in question.

[Lords Fraser, Diplock, Bridge and Brandon agreed.]

Appeal allowed

■ *Question*

Lord Roskill said that he could see no evidence whatever of an agreement to aid, abet, etc. Yet he also held that 'the manufacture and sale was for the dishonest purposes of enabling those black boxes to be used by persons other than the respondents to the detriment of the intended victim'. If that is not aiding, etc what is?

In *Kenning* [2008] EWCA Crim 1534, Lord Phillips CJ has confirmed the conclusion of the Court of Appeal. The appellants were convicted of 'conspiracy to aid and abet the production of cannabis'. K and F ran a shop selling hydroponic equipment, cannabis seeds and cultivation literature. Undercover officers had gathered evidence of K and F offering advice on cannabis cultivation and anti-detection measures. However, the equipment K and F sold to the officers could have been used for growing legal plants. The judge directed the jury that the offence of aiding, abetting, counselling or procuring the commission of an offence could be made out even if the latter offence was never in fact committed. The appellants submitted that the offence of conspiring to aid and abet was unknown to law. In the Court of Appeal, Lord Phillips CJ quashed the conviction, confirming that there was no such offence as conspiracy to aid and abet:

We endorse the court's conclusion [in *Hollinshead*] that an agreement to aid and abet an offence is not in law capable of constituting a criminal conspiracy under section 1(1) of the 1977 Act.

If 'course of conduct' is construed more broadly to include P's use of the equipment in growing the cannabis there is still no offence. The agreement must be as to 'the commission of any offence by *one or more of the parties*' to the agreement'. P (the grower) is not a party to the agreement. But do the words 'commission of any offence' include *participation* in the offence as a secondary party? Since all the parties to a conspiracy to commit an offence will be guilty of that offence if it is committed, but s 1(1) contemplates that it may be *committed* by only one of them, it is clear that 'commission' means commission by a principal. An agreement to aid and abet an offence is not a conspiracy under the Act. This is desirable, as it ensures that the boundaries of the criminal law are not extended too far and that the law of conspiracy is consistent with that of attempts, as by s 1(4)(b) of the Criminal Attempts Act 1981 it is not an offence to attempt to aid and abet. See also recently *Dang* [2014] EWCA Crim 348.

13.4.6 Intention and conspiracy

Part I of the Criminal Law Act 1977 was based on the Law Commission Report, *Conspiracy and Criminal Law Reform* (LC76 (1976)), and that includes a full discussion of the mental element to be required for conspiracy (paras 1.25–1.41). The Law Commission's conclusion on the common law was that:

... it is reasonably clear from such authority as there is that what the law requires before a charge of conspiracy can be proved against a defendant is that *he should intend to bring about any consequences prohibited by the offence* and should have full knowledge of all the circumstances or facts which need to be known to enable him to know that the agreed course of conduct will result in a crime. [emphasis added]

The Commission thought that this was what the law ought to be: 'We think that the law should require full intention and knowledge before a conspiracy can be established.' Their recommendation (5), para 7.2 reads:

A person should be guilty of conspiracy if he agrees with another person that an offence shall be committed. *Both must intend that any consequence in the definition of the offence will result* and both must *know* of the existence of any state of affairs which it is necessary for them to know in order to be aware that the course of conduct agreed upon will amount to the offence. [emphasis added]

The Report included a draft Bill, implementing the Commission's intentions. Clause 1, which became s 1 of the 1977 Act, included the phrase, 'in accordance with their intentions', which was discussed by the House of Lords in the next case.

13.4.6.1 Intention to carry out the agreement

R v Anderson
[1985] 2 All ER 961, House of Lords

(Lords Scarman, Diplock, Keith, Bridge and Brightman)

The appellant was remanded in custody with Ahmed Andaloussi. He confidently expected to be released on bail but Andaloussi was awaiting trial for very serious drug offences. The appellant agreed with Andaloussi's brother Mohamed and Mohamed Assou to participate in a scheme to effect Andaloussi's escape from prison. Anderson agreed to supply diamond wire capable of cutting through metal bars to be smuggled into prison. He received £2,000 on account. Anderson admitted that he intended to supply the wire on payment of a further £10,000 but claimed to the police that he would then have left for Spain and taken no further part in the scheme, which he believed could not possibly succeed. At his trial for conspiracy to commit the crime of escape, Anderson claimed that he lacked the mental element. That plea was rejected by the trial judge and the Court of Appeal. That court held (i) that a person who agrees with two or more others, who do intend to carry out the agreement, but who has a secret intention himself to participate only in part, is guilty of an offence under the Criminal Law Act 1977, s 1(1); and (ii) if he is not guilty as a principal offender, then he may be convicted of aiding and abetting the conspiracy. He appealed to the House of Lords and both points of law were certified for decision.

Lord Bridge:

The 1977 Act, subject to exceptions not presently material, abolished the offence of conspiracy at common law. It follows that the elements of the new statutory offence of conspiracy must be ascertained purely by interpretation of the language of s 1(1) of the 1977 Act. For purposes of analysis it is perhaps convenient to isolate the three clauses each of which must be taken as indicating an essential ingredient of the offence as follows: (1) 'if a person agrees with any other person or persons that a course of conduct shall be pursued' (2) 'which will necessarily amount to or involve the commission of any offence or offences by one or more of the parties to the agreement' (3) 'if the agreement is carried out in accordance with their intentions'.

Clause (1) presents, as it seems to me, no difficulty. It means exactly what it says and what it says is crystal clear. To be convicted, the party charged must have agreed with one or more others that 'a course of conduct shall be pursued'. What is important is to resist the temptation to introduce into this simple concept ideas derived from the civil law of contract. Any number of persons may agree that a course of conduct shall be pursued without undertaking any contractual liability. The agreed course of conduct may be a simple or an elaborate one and may involve the participation of two or any larger number of persons who may have agreed to play a variety of roles in the course of conduct agreed.

Again, clause (2) could hardly use simpler language. Here what is important to note is that it is not necessary that more than one of the participants in the agreed course of conduct shall commit a substantive offence. It is, of course, necessary that any party to the agreement shall have assented to play his part in the agreed course of conduct, however innocent in itself, knowing that the part to be played by one or more of the others will amount to or involve the commission of an offence.

It is only clause (3) which presents any possible ambiguity. The heart of the submission for the appellant is that in order to be convicted of conspiracy to commit a given offence the language of clause (3) requires that the party charged should not only have agreed that a course of conduct shall be pursued which will necessarily amount to or involve the commission of that offence by himself or one or more other parties to the agreement, but must also be proved himself to have intended that the offence should be committed. Thus, it is submitted here that the appellant's case that he never intended that Andaloussi should be enabled to escape from prison raised an issue to be left to the jury, who should have been directed to convict him only if satisfied that he did so intend. I do not find it altogether easy to understand why the draftsman of this provision chose to use the phrase 'in accordance with their intentions'. But I suspect the answer may be that this seemed a desirable alternative to the phrase 'in accordance with its terms' or any similar expression, because it is a matter of common experience in the criminal courts that the 'terms' of a criminal conspiracy are hardly ever susceptible of proof. The evidence from which a jury may infer a criminal conspiracy is almost invariably to be found in the conduct of the parties. This was so at common law and remains so under the statute. If the evidence in a given case justifies the inference of an agreement that a course of conduct should be pursued, it is a not inappropriate formulation of the test of the criminality of the inferred agreement to ask whether the further inference can be drawn that a crime would necessarily have been committed if the agreed course of conduct had been pursued in accordance with the several intentions of the parties. Whether that is an accurate analysis or not, I am clearly driven by consideration of the diversity of roles which parties may agree to play in criminal conspiracies to reject any construction of the statutory language which would require the prosecution to prove an intention on the part of each conspirator that the criminal offence or offences which will necessarily be committed by one or more of the conspirators if the agreed course of conduct is fully carried out should in fact be committed. A simple example will illustrate the absurdity to which this construction would lead. The proprietor of a car hire firm agrees for a substantial payment to make available a hire car to a gang for use in a robbery and to make false entries in his books relating to the hiring to which he can point if the number of the car is traced back to him in connection with the robbery. Being fully aware of the circumstances of the robbery in which the car is proposed to be used he is plainly a party to the conspiracy to rob. Making his car available for use in the robbery is as much a part of the relevant agreed course of conduct as the robbery itself. Yet, once he has been paid, it will be a matter of complete indifference to him whether the robbery is in fact committed or not. In these days of highly organised crime the most serious statutory conspiracies will frequently involve an elaborate and complex agreed course of conduct in which many will consent to play necessary but subordinate roles, not involving them in any direct participation in the commission of the offence or offences at the centre of the conspiracy. Parliament cannot have intended that such parties should escape conviction of conspiracy on the basis that it cannot be proved against them that they intended that the relevant offence or offences should be committed.

There remains the important question whether a person who has agreed that a course of conduct will be pursued which, if pursued as agreed, will necessarily amount to or involve the commission of an offence is guilty of statutory conspiracy irrespective of his intention, and, if not, what is the mens rea of the offence. I have no hesitation in answering the first part of the question in the negative. There may be many situations in which perfectly respectable citizens, more particularly those concerned with law enforcement, may enter into agreements that a course of conduct shall be pursued which will involve commission of a crime without the least intention of playing any part in furtherance of the ostensibly agreed criminal objective, but rather with the purpose of exposing and frustrating the criminal purpose of the other parties to the agreement. To say this is in no way to encourage schemes by which police act, directly or through the agency of informers, as agents provocateurs for the purpose of entrapment. That is conduct of which the courts have always strongly disapproved. But it may sometimes happen, as most of us with experience in criminal trials well know, that a criminal enterprise is well advanced in the course of preparation when it comes to the notice either of the police or of some honest citizen in such circumstances that the only prospect of exposing and frustrating the criminals is that some innocent person should play the part of an intending collaborator in the course of criminal conduct proposed to be pursued. The mens rea implicit in the offence of statutory conspiracy must clearly be such as to recognise the innocence of such a person, notwithstanding that he will, in literal terms, be obliged to agree that a course of conduct be pursued involving the commission of an offence.

I have said already, but I repeat to emphasise its importance, that an essential ingredient in the crime of conspiring to commit a specific offence or offences under s1(1) of the 1977 Act is that the accused should agree that a course of conduct be pursued which he knows must involve the commission by one or more of the parties to the agreement of that offence or those offences. But, beyond the mere fact of agreement, the necessary mens rea of the crime is, in my opinion, established if, and only if, it is shown that the accused, when he entered into the agreement, intended to play some part in the agreed course of conduct in furtherance of the criminal purpose which the agreed course of conduct was intended to achieve. Nothing less will suffice; nothing more is required.

Applying this test to the facts which, for the purposes of the appeal, we must assume, the appellant, in agreeing that a course of conduct be pursued that would, if successful, necessarily involve the offence of effecting Andaloussi's escape from lawful custody, clearly intended, by providing diamond wire to be smuggled into the prison, to play a part in the agreed course of conduct in furtherance of that criminal objective. Neither the fact that he intended to play no further part in attempting to effect the escape, nor that he believed the escape to be impossible, would, if the jury had supposed they might be true, have afforded him any defence.

[Lords Scarman, Diplock, Keith and Brightman agreed.]

Appeal dismissed

The Law Commission in its more recent Consultation Paper No 183 described the decision in the following terms:

1.38 Section 1(1) of the 1977 Act appears unambiguously to require that for a person to be convicted of conspiracy he or she must intend that the conduct element of the principal offence be perpetrated and that the consequence element (if any) of the substantive offence materialise. However, the well-known and much criticised decision of the House of Lords in *Anderson* detracts from the clarity of this position. On the one hand, it requires that D must intend 'to play some part in the agreed course of conduct.' On the other hand, it does not require that D should intend that the agreement be carried through to completion. In both respects, the decision is troublesome.

First, there is no reason, in terms of statutory language or policy, for insisting that D must intend to play some part in implementing the agreement. If D1 and D2 agree to murder V, D1 ought to be convicted of conspiracy to murder even if it was not his or her intention to play any part in V's murder. Secondly, an agreement to commit an offence implies an intention that it should be committed, as section 1(1) of the 1977 Act seems to make clear. The idea of a conspiracy that the conspirators agree to take part in but which none intends to see carried out is very unsatisfactory.

In the light of the controversy surrounding the decision in *Anderson* it is worth pointing out that the decision has been marginalized somewhat. For example, in *Yip Chiu-Ching* [1995] 1 AC 111, Lord Griffiths stated that, 'The crime of conspiracy requires an agreement between two or more persons to commit an unlawful act with the intention of carrying it out. It is the intention to carry out the crime that constitutes the necessary *mens rea* for the offence.' This is contrary to what Lord Bridge had earlier held in *Anderson*. Although the Privy Council was considering common law conspiracy, there is no principled reason why there ought to be a distinction between the two types of conspiracy in relation to this issue.

As will be discussed in section 13.7, the effect of the Law Commission's recommendations would be to overturn the decision in *Anderson*.

■ *Questions*

1. Is there any warrant in the words of the Act for the opinion that a person is guilty of conspiracy only if he intended to play some part in the furtherance of the criminal purpose?

2. A incites B to murder C and B agrees to do so. A intends to do nothing more. Is this a conspiracy to murder?

The Court of Appeal had insisted that there must be two parties who do intend to carry out the agreement. The House of Lords disagreed.

■ *Questions*

D1 and D2 agree to kill V. What if only D1 intends to carry out the agreement? What if neither D1 nor D2 intend to do so?

Consider Parliament's intention in section 13.4.6.

13.4.6.2 Can there be a conspiracy without intent to carry out the agreement?

R v Edwards

[1991] Crim LR 45, Court of Appeal, Criminal Division

(Russell LJ, Drake and Morland JJ)

The case involved an undercover investigation into drug dealing. Two undercover agents, C and A, contacted E on 19 April and expressed interest in one pound of amphetamine and that they might be interested in purchasing up to one kilogram of that drug. E said there would be no problem and quoted £1,600 for a pound. C agreed that price but said he would expect discount on future purchases. E promised delivery of the pound of drugs at his house in a week's time. C and A returned a week later to take delivery but E told them they would have to go to Huntingdon to collect, saying, 'It's all set up.' All three went to Huntingdon and E visited his sister's house on 26 April. After 20 minutes, E returned to say, 'I'm sorry, she hasn't got it all.' He was then arrested. There was evidence that what was available at the Huntingdon house was not amphetamine but a milder drug, not controlled in the same way as amphetamine, namely ephedrine.

E and his sister, N, were charged *inter alia* with conspiring between 18 and 22 April 1989 to supply amphetamine to persons unknown.

E appealed, arguing that C and A were agents provocateurs and that consequently the evidence of the officers should have been excluded under the Police and Criminal Evidence Act 1984, s 78 (evidence, the admission of which 'would have such an adverse effect on the fairness of the proceedings that the court ought not to admit it'). It was submitted that, but for the enticement, the offence charged would not have occurred.

Russell LJ:

The contrary argument to that is of course to this effect. The whole scenario demonstrated that this was not, on the part of this appellant, an isolated incident into which he was enticed by the invitations of the police officers. Because of the way in which the appellant behaved, because of his reaction to the police officer's request, because of his familiarity with what might be termed as the drugs scene, evidenced by his acknowledgment of drug slang, because of his agreement to accept a discount upon the price in respect of future supplies, it is manifestly plain that this appellant, at the time he was approached by the police officers was already an established drug dealer and what happened involving the police officers was simply an isolated manifestation of a much wider conspiracy involving his co-defendants to which the appellant was a party. . . .

[Having discussed and approved the summing up:]

We are abundantly satisfied that it would be an abuse of language to say here that these officers in the circumstances of this case were enticing the appellant to commit an isolated offence. We are abundantly satisfied that when the officers came on the scene there was ample evidence to demonstrate that he was already established in the type of conspiracy which formed the subject-matter of count 1 in this indictment. Accordingly we take the view that there is no merit in the submission, however admirably it has been made by Mr Gold, that there was here evidence that the undercover officers were agents provocateurs. . . .

Mr Gold [for the appellant] . . . points out accurately that it was important that the jury should understand . . . that they should convict on count 1 only if they were sure that the appellant intended to supply amphetamine.

Appeal dismissed

■ *Questions*

1. What if E and N had been charged with conspiring to supply C and A with one pound of amphetamine? Would C and A then have been agents provocateurs? Would the same evidence then have had an adverse effect on the fairness of the proceedings which it did not have when the charge was of a conspiracy to supply goods to persons unknown—that is, a continuing conspiracy to supply any suitable customers who presented themselves? Cf commentary at [1991] Crim LR 46.

2. E had agreed to supply amphetamine. According to Lord Bridge in *Anderson*, did it matter if he never intended to supply amphetamine? Ought it to matter?

Does it matter that D1 in a two-person conspiracy did not intend that the offence would be carried out? What if D1 intended to warn the police before the object of the agreement could be carried out. Does D1 still intend the result for the purposes of conspiracy? Consider the next case.

R v McPhillips

[1990] 6 BNIL, Court of Appeal of Northern Ireland (unreported)

(Lord Lowry CJ, O'Donnell and Kelly LJJ)

About 11 pm on 10 October 1985 the police stopped a car driven by Drumm, going towards the Seagoe Hotel. McPhillips was in the front passenger seat. Behind the driver's seat was a bomb containing four kilograms of explosive. It was a device of considerable power, capable of causing a significant explosion. In a statement, McPhillips admitted that the bomb was to be placed on the flat roof of the Seagoe Hotel where a disco was taking place. He said that it had been decided by Drumm and other accomplices that the best time for the bomb to go off would be 1 am as the disco was going on until 1.30 am. McPhillips and Drumm were charged with (1) conspiracy to murder, (2) conspiracy to cause an explosion, and (3) offences under the Explosive Substances Act 1883. At the trial, McPhillips accepted that he was a party to the plan to cause the explosion and pleaded guilty to counts (2) and (3). He pleaded not guilty to conspiracy to murder. He said, and the trial judge believed him, that he intended to give a warning to the police in time for the dance hall to be cleared. The judge held that, notwithstanding McPhillips's intention to give a warning, he was guilty as an aider and abettor of conspiracy to murder. He appealed on the ground that this ruling was wrong.

Lord Lowry CJ:

To be guilty at common law of conspiracy to murder the accused must agree with another that murder will be committed and must intend that this will happen. The guilty act is the agreement that the crime contemplated will be committed; the guilty mind is the intention that that crime will be committed. . . . In regard to the offence of statutory conspiracy section 1(1) 'assumes the existence of an intention of the parties to carry out the agreement': Smith and Hogan, *Criminal Law*, 6th edition, p 259. The wording of the identical Article 9(1) [applicable in Northern Ireland] makes this clear: the agreed course of conduct was the planting of a 'no warning' bomb at the Seagoe Hotel and persons who had agreed to that course of conduct intending it to be carried out would be guilty of conspiracy to murder because, if the agreement had been carried out in accordance with their intentions it would (unless all the patrons of the disco had gone home or had a miraculous escape) necessarily involve the commission of murder. But, on the facts found here, this result would not have been in accordance with the intention of the appellant. Therefore he was not guilty of conspiracy to murder. So, although by going to the Seagoe in Drumm's car, the appellant up to a point acted in accordance with the agreed course of conduct (and was thereby guilty of conspiracy to cause an explosion), he was not guilty as an alleged conspirator in respect to count 1. This result is consistent with the doctrine that, if a joint enterprise goes beyond the agreed or authorised act, a party to that enterprise is not guilty beyond the acts which he agreed to or authorised. To put the matter simply, there must be a common criminal design and, in order to be guilty of a conspiracy to carry out that design, the accused must be a party to the design. That condition is not satisfied in this case.

The Crown's alternative proposition is that the appellant was guilty of aiding and abetting a conspiracy to murder on the part of the conspirators and was therefore liable to be tried, indicted and punished (as happened in the instant case) as a principal offender. The need, and the ability, to rely on this proposition must stem from the hypothesis that the appellant was not a party to the conspiracy to murder, and that hypothesis (having regard to the appellant's ostensible acquiescence in the murder plan) must be based on the fact that the appellant did not intend or authorise the commission of murder. But how then, say the appellant's counsel, did he aid and abet a conspiracy to murder? The Crown's answer is that the appellant assisted the conspirators by his presence when the murder plan was devised and by accompanying Drumm in the car which was conveying the bomb to the intended scene of the crime, and counsel relies on the following passage in the judgment of the learned trial judge.

The common law offence of aiding and abetting involves an act of assisting the principal (actus reus) and a guilty intention (mens rea) that the crime will be committed. This intention is not to be confused with purpose, motive or desire (although those elements may be and often are present) but can be inferred from, and has been in the recent past wrongly identified with, the probability, overwhelming probability or certainty (known to the aider and abettor) that the crime will be committed. Conspiracy is a crime which it is possible to aid and abet and thus the ingredients of aiding and abetting a conspiracy remain as we have described them: a person aids and abets a conspiracy to commit a crime when, not being a party to the conspiracy (otherwise he would be a principal offender) and knowing of the agreement and at least its general object, he assists the principal offenders (by an actus reus, such as supplying a vehicle or a weapon) with the guilty intention (mens rea) that the object of the conspiracy should be achieved . . . the decisive point here is that, whether the test is based on *Hyam* or on *Hancock*, the fact that the appellant had the intention, which he could reasonably have expected to implement, that murder would not take place destroys the possibility of finding the necessary mens rea on his part.

The appellant's acts and intentions were sufficient to render him guilty of conspiracy to cause an explosion, and the same acts are relied on to prove him guilty of aiding and abetting the conspiracy to murder. This overlooks the fact that his intentions differed between causing an explosion and aiding the commission of a murder. The law relating to joint criminal enterprises, which was reviewed at length by Sir Robin Cooke in *Chan Wing-Siu v R* [1985] AC 168, [1984] 3 All ER 877, provides a ready answer. The action proposed by the conspirators, namely, to plant a bomb with no warning (and thereby to extend a property damaging explosion into a murder) was something which the appellant did not authorise and had actually made up his mind to prevent. And the fact that the extension of the crime involved a negative, that is, a failure to warn, cannot obscure the reality that this proposed failure was to be an aggravation of the crime, since the distinction between a warning bomb and a no warning bomb is well understood.

[Lord Lowry discussed the decision of the Court of Appeal in *Anderson*, section 13.4.6.1, p 474, and continued:]

So far as concerns the hearing before the House of Lords, we find it necessary only to recall what Lord Bridge of Harwich, who delivered the leading speech, said in *R v Anderson* [1986] AC 27, [1985] 2 All ER 961, at p 39D of the former report:

'I have said already, but I repeat to emphasise its importance, that an essential ingredient in the crime of conspiring to commit a specific offence or offences under section 1(1) of the Act of 1977 is that the accused should agree that a course of conduct be pursued which he knows must involve the commission by one or more of the parties to the agreement of that offence or those offences.'

It is obvious, for the reasons already given, that, so far as count 1 is concerned, the conduct of the appellant does not satisfy that test. It is equally clear that *R v Anderson* [1986] AC 27, [1985] 2 All ER 961, is not an authority for the proposition that someone who at all times intends to frustrate the commission of the crime 'agreed upon' is guilty of conspiracy to commit that crime or of aiding and abetting such a conspiracy.

[Lord Lowry referred to Lord Bridge's *dictum* in *Anderson* concerning the person who joins a criminal conspiracy with the object of frustrating it and continued:]

In the different circumstances of this case, the same principle applies: the appellant was not guilty of conspiracy to murder either as a principal offender or as an accomplice because his mind did not go with his acts, but on the contrary was directed towards frustrating the conspiracy to murder. The mere fact that the appellant had already committed terrorist offences and was a member of a terrorist organisation does not disable him from relying on the absence of the necessary intent and the principle enunciated in *R v Fitzpatrick* [1977] NI 20, is not in point.

While the conviction on counts 2 and 3 will stand, the conviction appealed against in relation to count 1 must therefore be quashed.

■ *Questions*

1. Is Lord Lowry's judgment consistent with Lord Bridge's opinion in *Anderson* that it is not necessary to prove that a principal conspirator intended that the criminal offence be committed?

2. Is *Anderson* distinguishable on the ground that McPhillips intended, so far as murder was concerned, to frustrate the enterprise?

3. When McPhillips joined in the agreement to plant a no-warning bomb and helped to carry out the initial stages of the plan, did he not intentionally aid and abet the continuance of the ongoing conspiracy to murder?

13.4.6.3 Must D play some part in the agreed course of conduct?

R v Siracusa
[1989] Crim LR 712, Court of Appeal, Criminal Division

(O'Connor LJ, Boreham and Ian Kennedy JJ)

The appellant was convicted of conspiracies to commit offences against the Customs and Excise Management Act 1979, s 170(2)(b), section 2.4.1.2, p **. The judge directed the jury as follows:

What matters is whether you are satisfied that he agreed with any other defendant or any other named conspirator that a course of conduct should be pursued which, if carried out in accordance with their intentions, would amount to this offence by any of those other persons, because if it does, then he is guilty of conspiracy, whether he himself has actively done anything in order to bring about the objects of that conspiracy, because the reason, as you will appreciate, is that the nub of the offence of conspiracy consists of the agreement to do the unlawful act, and that may mean that you are doing it yourself actively or that you are agreeing that somebody else should do it actively. In either event, you are guilty of the conspiracy.

The appeals against conviction were dismissed.

[O'Connor LJ, referring to *Anderson*, section 13.4.6.1, p 474 said:]

We think it obvious that Lord Bridge cannot have been intending that the organiser of a crime who recruited others to carry it out would not himself be guilty of conspiracy unless it could be proved that he intended to play some active part himself thereafter. Lord Bridge had pointed out [section 13.4.6.1, p 473] that 'in these days of highly organised crime the most serious statutory conspiracies will frequently involve an elaborate and complex agreed course of conduct in which many will consent to play necessary but subordinate roles not involving them in any direct participation in the commission of the offence or offences at the centre of the conspiracy'.

The present case is a classic example of such a conspiracy. It is the hallmark of such crimes that the organisers try to remain in the background and more often than not are not apprehended. Secondly, the origins of all conspiracies are concealed and it is usually quite impossible to establish when or where the initial agreement was made, or when or where other conspirators were recruited. The very existence of the agreement can only be inferred from overt acts. Participation in a conspiracy is infinitely variable: it can be active or passive. If the majority shareholder and director of a company consents to the company being used for drug smuggling carried out in the company's name by a fellow director and minority shareholder, he is guilty of conspiracy. Consent, that is the agreement or adherence to the agreement, can be inferred if it is proved that he knew what was going on and the intention to participate in the furtherance of the criminal purpose is also established by his failure to stop the unlawful activity. Lord Bridge's dictum does not require anything more.

Appeal dismissed

■ **Questions**

1. What *did* Lord Bridge mean in *Anderson*?

2. In *King* [2012] EWCA Crim 805, Pitchford LJ stated that, 'It is a controversial question whether the defendant must harbour an intention to participate in the conduct which constitutes the substantive offence', but declined to settle the issue one way or the other. Should the Court of Appeal now overturn *Siracusa*?

3. If the key element of conspiracy is agreement, is the requirement that D intended to play some part not superfluous?

13.4.7 Knowledge or intention as to circumstances

Section 1(2) of the Criminal Law Act 1977 provides:

Where liability for any offence may be incurred without knowledge on part of the person committing it of any particular fact or circumstance necessary for the commission of the offence, a person shall nevertheless not be guilty of conspiracy to commit that offence by virtue of subsection (1) above unless he and at least one other party to the agreement intend or know that that fact or circumstance shall or will exist at the time when the conduct constituting the offence is to take place.

This deals with the case where the parties are charged with conspiracy to commit an offence which imposes strict liability, or is satisfied by recklessness as to some fact or circumstance. The subsection makes clear that a party to the agreement is not guilty of conspiracy unless he, and at least one other party, 'intend or know that the fact or circumstance shall or will exist.' It appears, then, that the prosecution must prove intention or knowledge as to every fact or circumstance in the actus reus of the crime it is agreed will be committed. This is an exceptionally strict requirement since mens rea at common law was generally satisfied by proof of recklessness. It is stricter than is required by the related offence of attempt; see section 14.2, p 497.

Consider D1 who agrees to help D2 move out of his flat. D2 is unsure whether the cabling he has installed for his hi-fi now belongs to him or to his landlord. D1 and D2 confer together and are uncertain, but agree, nevertheless, to remove it knowing their actions will result in damage to the cabling in the process. They therefore have an intention to cause damage, and are reckless as to whether the property belongs to another. The substantive offence of criminal damage requires that D intends or is reckless as to the causing of damage (the result), *and* that D knows or is reckless as to whether the property belongs to another (circumstance). If D1 and D2 went ahead, they would have sufficient mens rea to be convicted of the substantive offence. As for the conspiracy, in the *actual* circumstances that exist, the carrying out of the agreement 'will necessarily amount' to criminal damage; but, on an orthodox reading of s 1(2), it is not a conspiracy to commit criminal damage. It would not be criminal damage in the circumstances which the parties *intend, or know, shall or will exist*. Ds are merely reckless as to the circumstance. Recklessness as to the circumstance of the actus reus (property belonging to another) is not a sufficient mens rea on a charge of conspiracy to commit a crime (criminal damage) even where it is a sufficient mens rea for the crime itself.

The problem became an acute one in prosecutions for money laundering where persons agree to transfer money. This gave rise to a problem: D1 and D2 might agree to transfer money not being certain whether it was criminal property. How can the defendants have the requisite mens rea within s 1(2)? The requirement is that D (and one other party) *knows or intends* the relevant circumstances for the commission of the offence (that the money will be from a criminal source when they transfer it). D1 and D2 may believe or suspect that the money is criminal, but can they know that unless they were involved in generating it by committing the crime themselves? A person who believes that there is a 50/50 chance that something is so can hardly be said to 'know' that it is so; and 'intend' appears to be irrelevant where the parties know they have no control over the existence of the fact or circumstance— as here. See D. Ormerod, 'Making Sense of Statutory Conspiracies' [2006] CLP 185 (section 13.4.3.1, p 468).

A further problem identified was that on a literal reading, intention or knowledge as to all the circumstances of the actus reus is to be required *only* where the agreement is to commit a crime which may be committed with recklessness or strict liability as to a material circumstance. On this reading, intention or knowledge would *not* be required where the substantive offence *does* require knowledge. Section 1(2) would therefore have imposed a more onerous mens rea for conspiracy to commit crimes of strict liability than for conspiracy to commit crimes which in substantive form require proof of knowledge or intention as to circumstances.

These issues were addressed by the House of Lords in the following case:

R v Saik

[2006] UKHL 18, House of Lords, http://www.bailii.org/uk/cases/UKHL/2006/18.html

(Lords Nicholls of Birkenhead, Steyn, Hope of Craighead, Baroness Hale of Richmond and Lord Brown of Eaton-under-Heywood)

Saik was charged with conspiracy to launder money. He operated a bureau de change in London. At his trial he pleaded that he did not know the money that he was to transfer in that office was the proceeds of crime. He only suspected this was so. He was convicted (in fact he pleaded because of a misunderstanding about the scope of the offence) of conspiracy and appealed on the basis that he could not know that the money he was agreeing to transfer was criminal property. Although a mens rea of reasonable grounds for suspicion is enough for the substantive offence of laundering money, Saik argued it was not enough for the conspiracy to commit that offence.

The House of Lords accepted that s 1(2) was to be read as applicable even 'where liability for an offence may be incurred without knowledge [etc]'. Section 1(2) applies to all offences and to all ingredients of an offence where the existence of a particular fact or circumstance was at issue. The requirement under s 1(2) is for 'knowledge' which means 'true belief'. It is not enough to show that D suspected the relevant circumstance.

Lord Nicholls of Birkenhead:

The statutory offence of criminal conspiracy

[His lordship referred to s 1 of the 1977 Act.]

The offence therefore lies in making an agreement. Implicitly, the subsection requires also that the parties intend to carry out their agreement. The offence is complete at that stage. The offence is complete even if the parties do not carry out their agreement. The offence is complete even if the substantive offence is not thereafter committed by any of the conspirators or by anyone else.

4. Thus under this subsection the mental element of the offence, apart from the mental element involved in making an agreement, comprises the intention to pursue a course of conduct which will necessarily involve commission of the crime in question by one or more of the conspirators. The conspirators must intend to do the act prohibited by the substantive offence. The conspirators' state of mind must also satisfy the mental ingredients of the substantive offence. If one of the ingredients of the substantive offence is that the act is done with a specific intent, the conspirators must intend to do the prohibited act and must intend to do the prohibited act with the prescribed intent. A conspiracy to wound with intent to do grievous bodily harm contrary to section 18 of the Offences of the Person Act 1861 requires proof of an intention to wound with the intent of doing grievous bodily harm. The position is the same if the prescribed state of mind regarding the consequence of the prohibited act is recklessness. Damaging property, being reckless as to whether life is endangered thereby, is a criminal offence: Criminal Damage Act 1971, section 1(2). Conspiracy to commit this offence requires proof of an intention to damage property, and to do so recklessly indifferent to whether this would endanger life.

5. An intention to do a prohibited act is within the scope of section 1(1) even if the intention is expressed to be conditional on the happening, or non-happening, of some particular event. The question always is whether the agreed course of conduct, if carried out in accordance with the parties' intentions, would necessarily involve an offence. A conspiracy to rob a bank tomorrow if the coast is clear when the conspirators reach the bank is not, by reason of this qualification, any less a conspiracy to rob. In the nature of things, every agreement to do something in the future is hedged about with conditions, implicit if not explicit. In theory if not in practice, the condition could be so far-fetched that it would cast doubt on the genuiness of a conspirator's expressed intention to do an unlawful act. If I agree to commit an offence should I succeed in climbing Mount Everest without the use of oxygen, plainly I have no intention to commit the offence at all. Fanciful cases apart, the conditional nature of the agreement is insufficient to take the conspiracy outside section 1(1).

6. Section 1(2) qualifies the scope of the offence created by section 1(1). This subsection is more difficult. Its essential purpose is to ensure that strict liability and recklessness have no place in the offence of conspiracy. [His lordship quoted the section.]

7. Under this subsection conspiracy involves a third mental element: intention or knowledge that a fact or circumstances necessary for the commission of the substantive offence will exist. Take the offence of handling stolen goods. One of its ingredients is that the goods must have been stolen. That is a fact necessary for the commission of the offence. Section 1(2) requires that the conspirator must intend or know that this fact will exist when the conduct constituting the offence takes place.

8. It follows from this requirement of intention or knowledge that proof of the mental element needed for the commission of a substantive offence will not always suffice on a charge of conspiracy to commit that offence. In respect of a material fact or circumstance conspiracy has its own mental element. In conspiracy this mental element is set as high as 'intend or know'. This subsumes any lesser mental element, such as suspicion, required by the substantive offence in respect of a material fact or circumstances. In this respect the mental element of conspiracy is distinct from and supersedes the mental element in the substantive offence. When this is so, the lesser mental element in the substantive offence becomes otiose on a charge of conspiracy. It is an immaterial averment. To include it in the particulars of the offence of conspiracy is potentially confusing and should be avoided.

9. The phrase 'fact or circumstance necessary for the commission of the offence' is opaque. Difficulties have sometimes arisen in its application. The key seems to lie in the distinction apparent in the subsection between 'intend or know' on the one hand and any particular 'fact or circumstance necessary for the commission of the offence' on the other hand. The latter is directed at an element of the actus reus of the offence. A mental element of the offence is not itself a 'fact or circumstance' for the purposes of the subsection. . . .

[His lordship then reviewed the law reform process culminating in the enactment of s 1(2) and continued:]

13. The rationale underlying this approach is that conspiracy imposes criminal liability on the basis of a person's intention. This is a different harm from the commission of the substantive offence. So it is right that the intention which is being criminalised in the offence of conspiracy should itself be blameworthy. This should be so, irrespective of the provisions of the substantive offence in that regard.

14. Against that background I turn to some issues concerning the scope and effect of section 1(2). The starting point is to note that this relieving provision is not confined to substantive offences attracting strict liability. The subsection does not so provide. Nor would such an interpretation of the subsection make sense. It would make no sense for section 1(2) to apply, and require proof of intention or knowledge, where liability for the substantive offence is absolute but not where the substantive offence has built into it a mental ingredient less than knowledge, such as suspicion.

15. So much is clear. A more difficult question arises where an ingredient of the substantive offence is that the defendant must *know* of a material fact or circumstance. On its face section 1(2) does not apply in this case. The opening words of section 1(2), on their face, limit the scope of the subsection to cases where a person may commit an offence *without* knowledge of a material fact or circumstance.

16. Plainly Parliament did not intend that a person would be liable for conspiracy where he lacks the knowledge required to commit the substantive offence. That could not be right. Parliament could not have intended such an absurd result. Rather, the assumption underlying section 1(2) is that, where knowledge of a material fact is an ingredient of a substantive offence, knowledge of that fact is also an ingredient of the crime of conspiring to commit the substantive offence.

17. There are two ways this result might be achieved. One is simply to treat section 1(2) as inapplicable in this type of case. This would mean that the knowledge requirement in the substantive offence would survive as a requirement which must also be satisfied in respect of a conspiracy. In the same way as a conspirator must intend to do the prohibited act with any specific intent required by the substantive offence, so he must intend to do the prohibited act having the knowledge required by the substantive offence. Accordingly, on this analysis, where knowledge of a fact is an ingredient of the substantive offence, section 1(2) is not needed.

18. The other route is to adopt the interpretation of section 1(2) suggested by Sir John Smith. The suggestion is that section 1(2) applies in such a case despite the opening words of the subsection. Section 1(2) is to be read as applicable *even* 'where liability for an offence may be incurred without knowledge [etc]'. It is difficult to see what other function the word 'nevertheless' has in the

subsection. This may seem a slender peg on which to hang a conclusion of any substance, but it is enough: see 'Some Answers' [1978] Crim LR 210.

19. The first route accords more easily with the language of section 1(2), but I prefer the second route for the following reason. A conspiracy is looking to the future. It is an agreement about future conduct. When the agreement is made the 'particular fact or circumstance necessary for the commission' of the substantive offence may not have happened. So the conspirator cannot be said to *know* of that fact or circumstance at that time. Nor, if the happening of the fact or circumstance is beyond his control, can it be said that the conspirator *will* know of that fact or circumstance.

20. Section 1(2) expressly caters for this situation. The conspirator must 'intend or know' that this fact or circumstance 'shall or will exist' when the conspiracy is carried into effect. Although not the happiest choice of language, 'intend' is descriptive of a state of mind which is looking to the future. This is to be contrasted with the language of substantive offences. Generally, references to 'knowingly' or the like in substantive offences are references to a past state of affairs. No doubt this language could be moulded appropriately where the offence charged is conspiracy. But the more direct and satisfactory route is to regard section 1(2) as performing in relation to a conspiracy the function which words such as 'knowingly' perform in relation to the substantive offence. That approach accords better with what must be taken to have been the parliamentary intention on how the phrase 'intend or know' in section 1(2) would operate in this type of case. Thus on a charge of conspiracy to handle stolen property where the property has not been identified when the agreement is made, the prosecution must prove that the conspirator *intended* that the property which was the subject of the conspiracy *would* be stolen property.

21. In my view, therefore, the preferable interpretation of section 1(2) is that the subsection applies to all offences. It applies whenever an ingredient of an offence is the existence of a particular fact or circumstance. The subsection applies to that ingredient . . .

25. Does 'know' in this context have the meaning attributed to it in the *Montila* case when considering the substantive offence? If it does, the identified property to which the conspiracy related must actually be or represent the proceeds of crime, and the conspirator must be aware of this. Or does 'know' in this context mean 'believe', as seems to be suggested in *R v Ali* [2006] 2 WLR 316, 335, para 98? On the ordinary use of language a person cannot 'know' whether property is the proceeds of crime unless he participated in the crime. He can only believe this is so, on the basis of what he has been told. Adopting this approach would mean that, so far as section 93C is concerned, equating knowledge with belief in the case of identified property would achieve a measure of symmetry with the requirement of intention in the case of unidentified property. It would mean that in both cases what matters is the conspirator's state of mind: the actual provenance of the property would not be material.

26. I do not think the latter approach can be accepted. The phrase under consideration ('intend or know') in section 1(2) is a provision of general application to all conspiracies. In this context the word 'know' should be interpreted strictly and not watered down. In this context knowledge means true belief. . . .

Lord Hope [discussed the scope of s 1(2) and continued:]

75. . . . A conspiracy is complete when the agreement to enter into is formed, even if nothing is done to implement it. Implementation gives effect to the conspiracy, but it does not alter its essential elements. The statutory language adopts this approach. It assumes that implementation of the agreement lies in the future. The question whether its requirements are fulfilled is directed to the stage when the agreement is formed, not to the stage when it is implemented.

76. First there is section 1(1). It refers to (i) an agreement, (ii) a course of conduct to be pursued under that agreement and (iii) the fact that, if the agreement is carried out as intended, it 'will necessarily' amount to or involve the commission of an offence by one or more of the parties to the agreement. Let us assume that there are two parties to the agreement: parties X and Y. X is in possession

of cash which he knows is the proceeds of crime (A). Y does not know the cash is A, which it is. But he suspects that it is A, and he has reasonable grounds for his suspicion. The agreement is that X will hand over the cash to Y, and that Y will immediately convert it into a different currency. If the agreement is carried out as they intend, the cash will be converted. The conversion of cash which is A by someone who knows that it is A is an offence contrary to section 93C(2). X knows that the cash is A. So the carrying out of the agreement between X and Y in accordance with their intentions will necessarily amount to the commission of an offence by X. This is enough to satisfy section 1(1)(a). But the carrying out of the agreement will also necessarily amount to the commission of an offence by Y. The cash will be A, because that is the fact known to X. And the conversion of cash which is in fact A by someone who has reasonable grounds to suspect that it is A is an offence under section 93C(2)....

78. ... Section 1(2) tells us that a person shall not be guilty of the conspiracy to commit that offence by virtue of subsection (1) unless he and at least one other party to the agreement 'intend or know' that the fact necessary for the commission of the offence—that the cash is A—'shall or will exist' at the time when the cash is converted into a different currency. There is no problem about X, of course. He knows that the cash which he will hand over to Y is A. He knows that it will be A when the conduct takes place—when it is converted into a different currency. But what about Y? He suspects that the cash is A. But he does not know that it is, or that it will be when it is handed over to him and he converts it. Can it be said that he intends that it should be A, when he does not know what he will be dealing with? Solving this problem is not easy because the word 'intend' in section 1(2) refers to the existence of a fact or a circumstance, not to the consequences of giving effect to the agreement. But the words 'shall or will' indicate that nothing short of intention or knowledge as to its existence will do.

79. I think that the answer to this question will depend on the facts. It could be said of Y that he knows enough about the purpose of the transaction because of the grounds for his suspicion for it not to matter whether he will be able to tell by looking at the cash that it is in fact the proceeds of crime. It may be open to the Crown to prove that Y knew very well what the purpose of the agreement was—that he knew that the cash was to be converted to assist someone to avoid prosecution for an offence or the making or enforcement of a confiscation order, which is what section 93C(2) refers to. It might be going too far to say that he knew that the cash would be A when he came to deal with it. But it could be inferred that he intended that the cash would be A, because he knew that that was the only purpose of the transaction.

80. But in this case all we know is that the appellant suspected that the money 'was' the proceeds of crime. The appellant must be dealt with according to the terms of his plea. We cannot say that he was wilfully blind as to the purpose of the agreement, because that is not what he admits to. He suspected that he was being asked to convert the proceeds of criminal conduct. But he did not know that this was the origin of the money that was actually being given to him. He was prepared to go ahead and convert the money without knowing that it was in fact the proceeds of crime. It would not be quite right to say that he was reckless. All he was to do was simply to convert money from one currency into another—an everyday transaction which involves no risk to anyone. But he was willing to go ahead with this without troubling to find out whether or not what he was proposing to do was criminal. A person who is in that state of mind cannot be said to intend that the fact or circumstance that makes his act criminal should exist. That being the position I would hold that, although he was suspicious, the appellant cannot be said to have intended that the money should be the proceeds of crime when he came to deal with it.

...

Baroness Hale:

99. ... B is not guilty of conspiracy unless both he and A 'intend or know' that the money is the proceeds of crime. A knows that it is. B does not. But does he *intend* that it will be? Is a conditional intent

of the 'even if' kind sufficient for the purpose of section 1(2) as many think that it is for the purpose of section 1(1)? My Lords, I cannot see why it should be sufficient for the one but not for the other. The main objection in both cases is that it could be seen as 'a recklessness formula in disguise', a phrase taken from Professor David Ormerod's most helpful Current Legal Problems lecture, 'Making Sense of *Mens Rea* in Statutory Conspiracies' (2006) CLP [185], to which I am much indebted. Even the late Professor JC Smith seems to have regretted that the Law Commission, in their determination to exclude recklessness, might have 'thrown out the baby, conditional intention, with the bathwater, recklessness' (see '*Mens Rea* in Statutory Conspiracy: Some Answers' [1978] Crim LR 210, at 212). My Lords, I do not think that they did. The dividing line between them may be narrow, but it is discernible. Once again, it is important to distinguish between what happens when the substantive offence is committed—when the men have intercourse with the woman whether or not she consents—and what happens when they agree to do so. When they agree, they have thought about the possibility that she may not consent. They have agreed that they will go ahead *even if at the time when they go ahead they know that she is not consenting*. If so, that will not be recklessness; that will be intent to rape. Hence they are guilty of conspiracy to rape.

100. So if, in our example, the conspirator agrees to launder the money even if at the time he does so he is told that it is in fact the proceeds of crime, then he does indeed intend that fact to be the case when he does the deed. The fact that he is equally happy to convert the money even if it is not the proceeds of crime makes no difference. So perhaps the real question for the jury is, 'what would he have done if, when the money came in, someone had let him know the truth?' Would he have said, 'take it away'? Or would he have said 'hand it over'?

101. In my view, this provides an entirely principled and sensible way of making sense of the language of section 1(1) and (2) of the 1977 Act.

Appeal allowed

■ **Questions**

Consider the impact of the decision on a prosecution for conspiracy to handle stolen goods in which:

(i)   the property which D is to be invited to handle has already been stolen at the time of the offer to D for him to receive it and it is 'identified property' (D1 and D2 agree that they will receive the property which E has stolen and which he shows to them). Is this a knowledge case?

(ii) the property has yet to be stolen (D1 and D2 agree that they will receive the property E has suggested to them he will steal later that week). Is the mens rea one of intention or knowledge as to the status of the property?

The majority concluded that knowledge under s 1(2) was not akin to a conditional intention. Baroness Hale dissented on this point. The point did not arise for consideration since the Crown had not shown more than that the defendants had agreed to transfer cash being suspicious as to its criminal provenance. They had not gone further and established that the defendants had agreed that even if the property was criminal, as they suspected, they would launder it nevertheless. It is submitted that it is still open to the courts to accept that such an agreement is a conspiracy to launder.

The House of Lords' decision made it much more difficult to secure prosecutions because the mens rea requirement of intention or knowledge as to circumstances is a demanding one. The Law Commission examined the possibility of reform and published its recommendations in 2009.

Law Commission Report No 318, *Conspiracy and Attempts*
(2009)

IS IT NECESSARY TO GO BEYOND WHAT WAS SAID IN *SAIK* ABOUT CONDITIONAL INTENT?

2.110 In our view, the answer to this question is 'no'. The draft Bill makes this explicit.

2.111 In the passage from the speech of Lord Nicholls just cited, Lord Nicholls says that only in 'fanciful' cases will the conditional nature of an intent have a bearing on whether or not proof of that intent will suffice as proof of fault for the purposes of liability for conspiracy. However, the current edition of *Smith and Hogan* casts some doubt on how 'fanciful' a case may have to be to take it outside section 1(1). In *O'Hadhmaill*, some IRA members agreed to make bombs during a ceasefire period, with the intention of causing explosions if the ceasefire period came to an end. The Court of Appeal found that proof of this 'conditional' intention to cause explosions was enough to satisfy the requirements of a criminal conspiracy. Of this result, *Smith and Hogan* says:

> The [decision] may be criticised on the basis that the satisfaction of the condition may be too dependent on DD's own subsequent evaluation of the circumstances to be said to represent a true intention . . . In *O'Hadhmaill*, the question arises whether the ceasefire could be regarded as a fact or circumstance that was clearly determinable without reverting to D's opinion.

2.112 In our view, *O'Hadhmaill* was correctly decided. The triggering of the condition, in D's conditional intention, may often depend on some element of evaluation. To elaborate on Lord Nicholls example, if D1 and D2 decide to go ahead with a robbery only if the coast is clear, whether the coast is 'clear' may depend on an element of evaluation or opinion. For D1, the coast being clear may mean that there must be no security personnel in sight at all, whereas for D2 it may mean only that there is no reason to think that the police are there waiting for them. For D1, the coast may still be clear even if there is someone who has spent the night under cover of the bank entrance way and is causing a slight obstruction, whereas perhaps for D2 the coast would not be 'clear' in such circumstances. Unless such differences of opinion or evaluation prevent D1 and D2 reaching an agreement to rob in the first place (which they clearly do not), then they are, and should be, irrelevant to their liability.

2.113 Deep conceptual waters can be avoided in this context if it is kept in mind that an 'intention' to do something need not involve a high-level commitment, unlike a pledge, vow or oath. In this context, an 'intention' is nothing more than a (possibly, quite weak) provisional conclusion reached in reasoning about action. It is a decision to do something, unless reconsideration (whether or not involving new factors) at some point leads the person who has the intention to abandon or modify it.

2.114 Such considerations or factors may be factually determinable ('will there or will there not be a police officer outside the bank?'), or wholly evaluative ('will I still feel like going through with it when I get to the bank?'). In itself, uncertainty bearing on the fulfilment of conditions need not negate the existence of a conditional intention to do something. This will only happen if the uncertainty prevents the formation of the intention at the relevant time *at all* ('whether I agree to rob the bank depends on how I feel about it when I wake up on the morning in question').

■ *Question*

Consider how wide the conspiracy offence would become.

13.5 Exemptions from liability for conspiracy

Section 2 of the Criminal Law Act 1977 provides:

2. Exemptions from liability for conspiracy

(1) A person shall not by virtue of section 1 above be guilty of conspiracy to commit any offence if he is an intended victim of that offence.

(2) A person shall not by virtue of section 1 above be guilty of conspiracy to commit any offence or offences if the only other person or persons with whom he agrees are (both initially and at all times during the currency of the agreement) persons of any one or more of the following descriptions, that is to say:

(a) his spouse [or civil partner];

(b) a person under the age of criminal responsibility; and

(c) an intended victim of that offence or of each of those offences.

(3) A person is under the age of criminal responsibility for the purposes of subsection (2)(b) above so long as it is conclusively presumed, by virtue of section 50 of the Children and Young Persons Act 1933, that he cannot be guilty of any offence.

In relation to s 2(1) and s 2(2)(c), see *Tyrrell*, discussed in section 12.2.1.3, p 449.

■ *Questions*

Is D guilty of conspiracy if he agrees: (i) with Poppy, a 15-year-old girl, to have sexual intercourse with her, (ii) with Poppy to take indecent images of her at her request?

D and his fiancée, Penny, carry on a business as suppliers of prohibited drugs. On 1 April 2012 they get married. On 5 April, Al, an undercover officer, enquires about drugs and they agree to supply him. Is Al an 'agent provocateur'? (See *Edwards* [1991] Crim LR 45, section 13.4.6.2, p 447.)

Are any of these exemptions justifiable in the twenty-first century? For proposed reform, see the Law Commission report in section 13.7, p 494.

13.6 Common law conspiracies

13.6.1 Conspiracy to defraud

It is generally accepted that there are two categories of conspiracy to defraud. The first relates to injury to economic interests, the second to inducing a person to act contrary to his duty. The second category, as well as the first, is relevant to commercial fraud because its most likely application is to inducing acts which will lead to economic gain, such as obtaining an export licence. The nearest approach to a definition of the first category of conspiracy to defraud is the statement by Lord Dilhorne with which all their lordships agreed in *Scott v Metropolitan Police Comr* [1975] AC 819 at 840, HL:

. . . it is clearly the law that an agreement by two or more by dishonesty to deprive a person of something which is his or to which he is or would be or might be entitled and an agreement by two or more by dishonesty to injure some proprietary right of his, suffices to constitute the offence of conspiracy to defraud.

(At 839 Lord Dilhorne put it slightly differently—'might *but for the perpetration of the fraud* be entitled' (emphasis added).)

Under the second category, a person is defrauded if he is deceived into acting contrary to his duty. An agreement by deception to induce a public official to issue an export licence (*Board of Trade v Owen* [1957] AC 602, HL) or a national insurance number to a person not entitled to one (*Moses* [1991] Crim LR 617) is a conspiracy to defraud the official. These examples are all concerned with public officials performing public duties. Lord Diplock, in *Scott*, said that the offence was limited to such cases. In *Wai Yu-tsang v R* [1991] 4 All ER 664 at 670, however, the Privy Council disapproved of Lord Diplock's *dictum* in *Scott*, pointing out that he alone took this point in that case. But no reference was made in *Wai* to *Withers* [1975] AC 842, HL, where Lords Simon and Kilbrandon seem to have been of the same mind as Lord Diplock. However that may be, the Privy Council considered that:

> ...the cases concerned with persons performing public duties are not to be regarded as a special category...but rather as exemplifying the general principle that conspiracies to defraud are not restricted to cases of intention to cause the victim economic loss. On the contrary they are to be understood in the broad sense described by Lord Radcliffe and Lord Denning in *Welham's* case [1961] AC 103.

Lord Denning said in *Welham*: 'If anyone may be prejudiced in any way by the fraud, that is enough'; and Lord Radcliffe said 'What it [the law] has looked for in considering the effect of cheating on another person and so in defining the criminal intent is the prejudice of that person; what *Blackstone's Commentaries* (4 Bl Com (18th ed) 247) called "to the prejudice of another man's right".'

So it appears that conspiracy to defraud is an agreement dishonestly to do *any* act prejudicial to another. Dishonesty is the concept formulated in *Ghosh* [1982] QB 1053, section 21.6, p 772. In *Withers* the House of Lords rid the law of an offence of public mischief (an act prejudicial to the public) and conspiracy to effect a public mischief. Nevertheless, we are left with conspiracy to defraud which is extremely broad.

Everything depends on whether the jury consider the agreement to be dishonest.

The Law Commission has been struggling for over 20 years with the problem of replacing common law conspiracy to defraud either with a series of specific offences of dishonesty or a general fraud offence.

Law Commission Report No 276, *Fraud*
(2002) (references omitted)

PART III

DEFECTS OF THE PRESENT LAW

...

Conspiracy to defraud

An anomalous crime

3.2 The concept of fraud, for the purposes of conspiracy to defraud, is wider than the range of conduct caught by any of the individual statutory offences involving dishonest behaviour. Thus it can be criminal for two people to agree to do something which it would not be unlawful for one person to do.

3.3 This anomaly has an historical basis. Before the Criminal Law Act 1977, a criminal conspiracy could be based on an agreement to commit an unlawful but non-criminal act, such as a tort or breach of contract. It appears that the justification for this was that there was a greater danger from people acting in concert than alone. As Professor Andrew Ashworth has explained:

> In legal terms, the reasoning seemed to be that acts which were insufficiently antisocial to justify criminal liability when done by one person could become sufficiently antisocial to justify criminal liability when done by two or more people acting in agreement. Such a combination of malefactors might increase the probability of harm resulting, might in some cases increase public alarm, and might in other cases facilitate the perpetration and concealment of the wrong.

3.4 The 1977 Act was the implementation of our Report on Conspiracy and Criminal Law Reform, which 'emphatically' concluded that the object of a conspiracy should be limited to the commission of a substantive offence and that there should be no place in a criminal code for a law of conspiracy extending beyond this ambit. An agreement should not be criminal where that which it was agreed should be done would not amount to a criminal offence if committed by one person.

3.5 This Commission has repeated its adherence to this principle in subsequent reports and we believe it commands very wide support. *Either* conspiracy to defraud is too wide in its scope (in that it catches agreements to do things which are rightly not criminal) *or* the statutory offences are too narrow (in that they fail to catch certain conduct which should be criminal)—*or*, which is our view, the problem is a combination of the two. On any view, the present position is anomalous and has no place in a coherent criminal law.

The definition of 'to defraud'

3.6 As we stated in paragraphs 2.4 to 2.6, the cases on the meaning of 'to defraud' have given it a broad meaning, so that any dishonest agreement to make a gain at another's expense could form the basis of conspiracy to defraud. We take the view that this definition is *too* broad. In a capitalist society, commercial life revolves around the pursuit of gain for oneself and, as a corollary, others may lose out, whether directly or indirectly. Such behaviour is perfectly legitimate. It is only the element of 'dishonesty' which renders it a criminal fraud. In other words, that element 'does all the work' in assessing whether particular facts fall within the definition of the crime.

3.7 In most cases it will be self-evident that the conduct alleged, if proved, would be dishonest, and the question will be whether that conduct has been proved. Nonetheless, in some cases, the defence will argue that the alleged conduct was not dishonest. There is no statutory definition of dishonesty, so the issue is determined with reference to *Ghosh*. In that case it was held that the fact-finders must be satisfied (a) that the defendant's conduct was dishonest according to the ordinary standards of reasonable and honest people, *and* (b) that the defendant must have realised that it was dishonest according to those standards (as opposed to his or her own standards).

3.8 Activities which would otherwise be legitimate can therefore become fraudulent if a jury is prepared to characterise them as dishonest. Not only does this delegate to the jury the responsibility for defining what conduct is to be regarded as fraudulent, but it leaves prosecutors with an uncommonly broad discretion when they are deciding whether to pursue a conspiracy to defraud case. If, for example, the directors of a company enter into 'industrial espionage' in order to gain the edge over a competitor, they could potentially be prosecuted for conspiracy to defraud, despite the absence of any statutory offence governing such activities. As *Smith and Hogan* states, the offence opens 'a very broad vista of potential criminal liability'.

3.9 In effect, conspiracy to defraud is a 'general dishonesty offence', subject only to the irrational requirement of conspiracy.

The Fraud Act failed to follow through the Law Commission's intention of abolition. The Government was concerned that if the common law offence of conspiracy to defraud was abolished, there might be unforeseen lacunae in the protection offered by the criminal law against fraudulent conduct.

The advantages and dangers of the use of conspiracy to defraud are clearly encapsulated in the following statement taken from the inquiry initiated by the Attorney General following the collapse of the Jubilee Line case:

Conspiracy to defraud at common law is an extremely useful weapon for a fraud prosecutor and frequently a course of offending cannot be adequately reflected in an indictment without recourse to it. For example, such a charge avoids the difficulties associated with 'specimen' counts of substantive offences. Not surprisingly, it is frequently used and is the main charge in most SFO prosecutions. However, it can sometimes be resorted to in an attempt to sidestep significant difficulties in the proof of any substantive offence and bridge the gaps in an investigation which has failed to prove more specific offences of dishonesty. Furthermore, as happened in this case, the use of the charge, because of its great breadth, can make potentially relevant a very large body of documentary and other evidence which would not be relevant or admissible in relation to specific statutory offences.

■ *Question*

Is an offence which is so vague compatible with Article 7 of the European Convention on Human Rights? See section 1.3, p 9 for an overview of Article 7.

13.6.2 Corruption of public morals and outraging public decency

Shaw v Director of Public Prosecutions
[1961] 2 All ER 446, House of Lords, http://www.bailii.org/uk/cases/UKHL/1961/1.html

(Viscount Simonds, Lords Reid, Tucker, Morris of Borth-y-Gest and Hodson)

The appellant published a booklet entitled 'The Ladies' Directory' with the object of enabling prostitutes to ply their trade. The booklet contained names and addresses and sometimes photographs of prostitutes and in some cases abbreviations indicating the type of conduct in which the woman would indulge. The women paid for the advertisements to be inserted. Shaw was convicted on three counts: (i) conspiracy to corrupt public morals; (ii) living wholly or in part on the earnings of prostitution, contrary to s 30(1) of the Sexual Offences Act 1956; and (iii) publishing an obscene article contrary to s 2(1) of the Obscene Publications Act 1959. His appeal to the Court of Criminal Appeal was dismissed. That court held that conduct calculated and intended to corrupt public morals was an indictable misdemeanour at common law and that it followed that an agreement to do so was a conspiracy; s 2(4) of the Obscene Publications Act 1959 did not prohibit the prosecution of the appellant for conspiracy because that offence consisted in an agreement to corrupt, and did not 'consist of the publication' of the booklets. The appellant appealed against his conviction on the first and second counts.

The following extracts from the speeches of their lordships relate only to the conspiracy charge.

[Viscount Simonds, having asserted that, contrary to the appellant's submission, conspiracy to corrupt public morals is an offence known to the common law, continued:]

Need I say, my Lords, that I am no advocate of the right of the judges to create new criminal offences? . . .

But I am at a loss to understand how it can be said either that the law does not recognise a conspiracy to corrupt public morals or that, though there may not be an exact precedent for such a conspiracy as this case reveals, it does not fall fairly within the general words by which it is described. I do not propose to examine all the relevant authorities. That will be done by my noble and learned friend. The fallacy in the argument that was addressed to us lay in the attempt to exclude from the scope of general words acts well calculated to corrupt public morals just because they had not been committed or had not been brought to the notice of the court before. It is not thus that the common law has developed. We are, perhaps, more accustomed to hear this matter discussed on the question whether such and such a transaction is contrary to public policy. At once the controversy arises. On the one hand it is said that it is not possible in the twentieth century for the court to create a new head of public policy, on the other it is said that this is but a new example of a well-established head. In the sphere of criminal law, I entertain no doubt that there remains in the courts of law a residual power to enforce the supreme and fundamental purpose of the law, to conserve not only the safety and order but also the moral welfare of the state, and that it is their duty to guard it against attacks which may be the more insidious because they are novel and unprepared for. That is the broad head (call it public policy if you wish) within which the present indictment falls. It matters little what label is given to the offending act. To one of your Lordships it may appear an affront to public decency, to another, considering that it may succeed in its obvious intention of provoking libidinous desires, it will seem a corruption of public morals. Yet others may deem it aptly described as the creation of a public mischief or the undermining of moral conduct. The same act will not in all ages be regarded in the same way. The law must be related to the changing standards of life, not yielding to every shifting impulse of the popular will but having regard to fundamental assessments of human values and the purposes of society. Today a denial of the fundamental Christian doctrine, which in past centuries would have been regarded by the ecclesiastical courts as heresy and by the common law as blasphemy, will no longer be an offence if the decencies of controversy are observed. When Lord Mansfield, speaking long after the Star Chamber had been abolished, said [in *Delaval* (1763) 3 Burr 1434 at 1438] that the Court of King's Bench was the custos morum of the people and had the superintendency of offences *contra bonos mores*, he was asserting, as I now assert, that there is in that court a residual power, where no statute has yet intervened to supersede the common law, to superintend those offences which are prejudicial to the public welfare. Such occasions will be rare, for Parliament has not been slow to legislate when attention has been sufficiently aroused. But gaps remain and will always remain since no one can foresee every way in which the wickedness of man may disrupt the order of society. Let me take a single instance to which my noble and learned friend, Lord Tucker, refers. Let it be supposed that, at some future, perhaps, early, date homosexual practices between adult consenting males are no longer a crime. Would it not be an offence if, even without obscenity, such practices were publicly advocated and encouraged by pamphlet and advertisement? Or must we wait until Parliament finds time to deal with such conduct? I say, my Lords, that, if the common law is powerless in such an event, then we should no longer do her reverence. But I say that her hand is still powerful and that it is for Her Majesty's judges to play the part which Lord Mansfield pointed out to them.

The appeal on both counts should, in my opinion, be dismissed.

[Lord Reid made a dissenting speech.]

[Lords Tucker, Morris and Hodson made speeches dismissing the appeal.]

Appeal dismissed

■ *Questions*

Is it appropriate that such vague common law offences are retained? Are they compatible with Article 10 of the European Convention on Human Rights guaranteeing a right to freedom of expression?

In *Knuller v DPP* [1973] AC 435 the House of Lords clarified a number of points in relation to the offence. The appellants published a magazine, the *International Times*, which contained on inner pages columns of advertisements headed 'Males'. Most of these advertisements solicited homosexual acts. In upholding the appellants' convictions, the House of Lords held that it suffices to make out the offence if the material corrupts the morals of such members of the public as may be influenced by the matter published, rather than the public at large. It was also confirmed that it is for the jury to decide whether or not advertisements were, by present-day standards, corrupting of public morals.

As the Court of Appeal confirmed in *Gibson* [1991] 1 All ER 439 that there is a common law offence of outraging public decency, any conspiracies ought to be charged as statutory conspiracies.

■ *Question*

Would these offences withstand challenge in Strasbourg?

13.6.3 Impossibility

There is an important distinction between common law and statutory conspiracies in relation to the issue of impossibility. As has already been pointed out, impossibility is not a defence when considering statutory conspiracies. The same is not true, however, of common law conspiracies. In *DPP v Nock* [1978] AC 979 the House of Lords held that when two or more persons agree upon a course of conduct with the object of committing a criminal offence, but, unknown to them, it is impossible to achieve that object by that course of conduct, they do not commit the crime of conspiracy. However, this principle only applies where the conspiracy could never be achieved. For example, if A and B intend to defraud V, but unbeknownst to them V is already dead, there can be no conspiracy to defraud him.

13.7 Reform of conspiracy

The Law Commission in its Report No 318, *Conspiracy and Attempts*, made the following recommendations:

CONSPIRACY

9.1 We recommend that a conspiracy must involve an agreement by two or more persons to engage in the conduct element of an offence and (where relevant) to bring about any consequence element of the substantive offence.

9.2 We recommend that a conspirator must be shown to have intended that the conduct element of the offence, and (where relevant) the consequence element (or other consequences), should respectively be engaged in or brought about.

9.3 We recommend that an alleged conspirator must be shown at the time of the agreement to have been reckless whether a circumstance element of a substantive offence (or other relevant circumstance) would be present at the relevant time, when the substantive offence requires no proof of fault, or has a requirement for proof only of negligence (or its equivalent), in relation to that circumstance.

9.4 We recommend that where a substantive offence has fault requirements not involving mere negligence (or its equivalent), in relation to a fact or circumstance element, an alleged conspirator may be found guilty if shown to have possessed those fault requirements at the time of his or her agreement to commit the offence.

9.5 We recommend that it should be possible for a defendant to deny that he or she possessed the fault element for conspiracy because of intoxication, whether voluntary or involuntary, even when the fault element in question is recklessness (or its equivalent).

9.6 We recommend that agreements comprising a course of conduct which, if carried out, will amount to more than one offence with different fault as to circumstance elements or to which different penalties apply, should be charged as more than one conspiracy in separate counts on an indictment.

9.7 We recommend that the present requirement for the Director of Public Prosecutions to give consent if proceedings to prosecute a conspiracy to commit a summary offence are to be initiated need not be retained.

9.8 We recommend that the immunity for spouses and civil partners provided for by section 2(2)(a) of the Criminal Law Act 1977 should be abolished.

9.9 We recommend that the present exemption for a non-victim co-conspirator should be abolished but that the present exemption for a victim (D) should be retained if:

(a) The conspiracy is to commit an offence that exists wholly or in part for the protection of a particular category of persons;

(b) D falls within the protected category; and

(c) D is the person in respect of whom the offence agreed upon would have been committed.

9.10 We recommend that the rule that an agreement involving a person of or over the age of criminal responsibility and a child under the age of criminal responsibility gives rise to no criminal liability for conspiracy should be retained.

9.11 We recommend that the defence of acting reasonably provided for by section 50 of the Serious Crime Act 2007 should be applied in its entirety to the offence of conspiracy.

The Commission also made recommendations about liability for conspiracy where the agreement or the commission of the substantive offence did not all take place within England and Wales.

■ *Questions*

1. Consider the recommendation in para 9.1. Does this mean that to be guilty of conspiracy every party to the agreement must intend to play a part in the crime? Will D1, who is the gang boss, escape liability as it is clear that he never intended to play a part personally, he was just agreeing with his gang members what crimes they would commit? Is the offence rendered redundant in relation to the cases in which it is often so useful?

2. Consider paras 9.3 and 9.4. How would these recommendations work with an offence such as money laundering where the mens rea for the substantive offence requires proof of suspicion as to the circumstance element—that the money is criminal property?

FURTHER READING

L. Alexander and K. Kessler, 'Mens Rea and Inchoate Crimes' (1997) 87 J Cr L & Cr 1138

I. Dennis, 'The Rationale of Criminal Conspiracy' (1977) 93 LQR 39

D. Hodgson, 'Law Commission No 76: A Case Study in Criminal Law Reform' in P. R. Glazebrook (ed), Reshaping the Criminal Law: Essays in Honour of Glanville Williams (1978)

P. E. Johnson, 'The Unnecessary Crime of Conspiracy' (1973) 61 Cal L Rev 1137

N. Katyal, 'Conspiracy Theory' (2003) 112 Yale LJ 1307

P. Marcus, 'Conspiracy: The Criminal Agreement in Theory and in Practice' (1977) 65 Georgetown LJ 925

D. Ormerod, 'Making Sense of Statutory Conspiracies' [2006] CLP 185

A. Reed, 'Conspiracy to Defraud: The Threshold Standardisation' (2012) 76 J Crim L 373

14
Attempt

14.1 Introduction

As the discussion of earlier issues, particularly actus reus (Chapter 2) and causation (Chapter 3) has highlighted, there are often problems in proving that a defendant is guilty of a particular crime even though he has engaged in blameworthy conduct with a blameworthy state of mind. Take the case of *White* [1910] 2 KB 124 (section 3.2.1, p 44) as an example. D had placed the poison in the drink for his mother to take and he intended her to take it. After he placed the poison, she was found dead. D could not be found guilty of her murder because she had died of natural causes—he had not caused her death. Few people would argue that D should escape liability in such circumstances. It is therefore necessary that the criminal law has an appropriate offence to tackle such conduct. The answer lies in the crime of attempts. White was guilty of attempting to murder his mother. The same can be said of people like Deller ((1952) 36 Cr App R 184, section 2.2, p 21) who when selling his car to V made a statement to V, intending to deceive V. D thought his statement was false but it turned out to be true. D had not deceived V since D told the truth. He had attempted to deceive V.

For the rationale of a law of attempts, see section 14.7, p 522.

Some of the controversies examined in this chapter include the following:

(i) the precise mens rea for attempt: whether in addition to intending any result required for the crime, D must also intend the circumstances of the substantive offence in order to be guilty of attempting it;

(ii) how far D's acts must go towards committing the substantive offence before he will be guilty of an attempt;

(iii) whether the law criminalizes D who attempts to commit an offence even though on the facts it would have been impossible for him to commit the substantive offence;

(iv) reasons as to why it is appropriate to criminalize attempts to commit crimes.

14.2 Definition

The common law of attempts was abolished for all purposes by s 6 of the Criminal Attempts Act 1981. The present law of attempts to commit crime is to be found entirely in the 1981 Act. Section 1 provides:

1. Attempting to commit an offence

(1) If, with intent to commit an offence to which this section applies, a person does an act which is more than merely preparatory to the commission of the offence, he is guilty of attempting to commit the offence.

[Subsections (1A) and (1B) which relate to attempts to commit an offence under the Computer Misuse Act 1990 are omitted.]

(2) A person may be guilty of attempting to commit an offence to which this section applies even though the facts are such that the commission of the offence is impossible.

(3) In any case where:

(a) apart from this subsection a person's intention would not be regarded as having amounted to an intent to commit an offence; but

(b) if the facts of the case had been as he believed them to be, his intention would be so regarded,

then, for the purposes of subsection (1) above, he shall be regarded as having had an intent to commit that offence.

(4) This section applies to any offence which, if it were completed, would be triable in England and Wales as an indictable offence, other than:

(a) conspiracy (at common law or under section 1 of the Criminal Law Act 1977 or any other enactment);

(b) aiding, abetting, counselling, procuring or suborning the commission of an offence:

(c) offences under section 4(1) (assisting offenders) or 5(1) (accepting or agreeing to accept consideration for not disclosing information about an offence) of the Criminal Law Act 1967.

Section 1A, which extends jurisdiction to certain attempts to commit offences which, if completed, would not be triable in England and Wales, is omitted here. The method of trial of, and the penalties for, offences of attempt are provided by s 4:

4. Trial and penalties

(1) A person guilty by virtue of section 1 above of attempting to commit an offence shall:

(a) if the offence attempted is murder or any other offence the sentence for which is fixed by law, be liable on conviction on indictment to imprisonment for life; and

(b) if the offence attempted is indictable but does not fall within paragraph (a) above, be liable on conviction on indictment to any penalty to which he would have been liable on conviction on indictment of that offence; and

(c) if the offence attempted is triable either way, be liable on summary conviction to any penalty to which he would have been liable on summary conviction of that offence.

It is submitted that the most logical way of applying the law in relation to attempts is to:

(i)   identify the substantive offence that it is alleged D is attempting. There is no attempt in the air—there must be an attempted offence (murder, rape, robbery, burglary, etc);

(ii) identify what the elements of the actus reus of that substantive offence are (killing, having non-consensual sex, etc);

(iii) assess whether D intended any consequence elements of the substantive offence and intended or was at least reckless as to the relevant circumstances elements if appropriate; and

(iv) assess what acts D performed and whether they are more than mere preparatory to the commission of the substantive offence.

The first two steps relate to the elements of the substantive crime. Our analysis in this chapter therefore begins with step (iii).

14.3 Mens rea

As with all inchoate offences—that is, those in which the substantive offence has not been committed—the mens rea element assumes an elevated significance because the actus reus may be something relatively innocuous, and in order to ensure that the criminal law does not extend too wide, the offence must only catch those who are truly deserving of criminal punishment. The essence of an attempt to do something is that D is trying to do it and wants it to happen. Taking *White* as an example, D's act of putting poison in V's drink was dangerous, but might have been done accidentally, or negligently eg if the poison was stored in an old jar similar to that D used for sugar). In those circumstances most people would agree that it would not be appropriate to convict D of attempted murder.

14.3.1 Defining intention

It will be noted that s 1(1) of the Act begins with the words, 'If, with intent to commit an offence to which this section applies…' In *Whybrow* (1951) 35 Cr App R 141, Lord Goddard held that in attempt, the intent is 'the principal ingredient of the crime'. The Act offers no definition of 'intent' but in *Pearman* (1984) 80 Cr App R 259, [1984] Crim LR 675, the Court of Appeal could see no reason why the Act should have altered the common law in this respect and applied *Mohan*.

R v Mohan

[1975] 2 All ER 193, Court of Appeal, Criminal Division

(James LJ, Talbot and Michael Davies JJ)

The appellant was convicted of attempting by 'wanton driving to cause bodily harm' to be done to a police constable. The judge directed the jury that it must be proved that the appellant 'must have realised at the time that he was driving that such driving… was likely to cause bodily harm if he went on, or he was reckless as to whether bodily harm was caused. It is not necessary to prove an intention actually to cause bodily harm.'

[James LJ, giving the judgment of the court, said:]

The first question we have to answer is: what is the meaning of 'intention' when that word is used to describe the mens rea in attempt? It is to be distinguished from 'motive' in the sense of an emotion leading to action: it has never been suggested that such a meaning is appropriate to 'intention' in this context. It is equally clear that the word means what is often referred to as 'specific intent' and can be defined as 'a decision to bring about a certain consequence' or as the 'aim'. In *Hyam* [section 15.3.3, p 535] Lord Hailsham cited with approval the judicial interpretation of 'intention' or 'intent' applied by Asquith LJ in *Cunliffe v Goodman* [1950] 2 KB 237 at 253. 'An intention to my mind connotes a state of affairs which the party intending—I will call him X—does more than merely contemplate: it connotes a state of affairs which, on the contrary, he decides so far as in him lies to bring about and which, in point of possibility, he has a reasonable prospect of being able to bring about by his own act of volition.'

If that interpretation of 'intent' is adopted as the meaning of mens rea in the offence of attempt it is not wide enough to justify the direction in the present case. The direction, taken as a whole, can be supported as accurate only if the necessary mens rea includes not only specific intent but also the state of mind of one who realises that, if his conduct continues, the likely consequence is the commission of the complete offence and who continues his conduct in that realisation, or the state of mind of one who, knowing that continuation of his conduct is likely to result in the commission of the complete offence, is reckless as to whether or not that is the result.

[His lordship considered *Hyam* (section 15.3.3, p 535) and continued:]

We do not find in the speeches of their Lordships in the case of *Hyam* anything which binds us to hold that mens rea in the offence of attempt is proved by establishing beyond reasonable doubt that the accused knew or correctly foresaw that the consequences of his act unless interrupted would 'as a high degree of probability', or would be 'likely' to, be the commission of the complete offence. Nor do we find authority in that case for the proposition that a reckless state of mind is sufficient to constitute the mens rea in the offence of attempt. Prior to the enactment of the Criminal Justice Act 1967, s 8, the standard test in English Law of a man's state of mind in the commission of an act was the foreseeable or natural consequence of the act. Therefore it could be said that when a person applied his mind to the consequences that did happen and foresaw that they would probably happen he intended them to happen, whether he wanted them to happen or not. So knowledge of the foreseeable consequence could be said to be a form of 'intent'. [His lordship read s 8 (section 5.2, p 100).]

Thus, upon the question whether or not the accused had the necessary intent in relation to a charge of attempt, evidence tending to establish directly, or by inference, that the accused knew or foresaw that the likely consequence, and, even more so, the highly probable consequence, of his act—unless interrupted—would be the commission of the completed offence, is relevant material for the consideration of the jury. In our judgment, evidence of knowledge of likely consequences, or from what knowledge of likely consequences can be inferred, is evidence by which intent may be established but it is not, in relation to the offence of attempt, to be equated with intent. If the jury find such knowledge established they may and, using common sense, they probably will find intent proved, but it is not the case that they must do so.

An attempt to commit crime is itself an offence. Often it is a grave offence. Often it is as morally culpable as the completed offence which is attempted but not in fact committed. Nevertheless it falls within the class of conduct which is preparatory to the commission of a crime and is one step removed from the offence which is attempted. The Court must not strain to bring within the offence of attempt conduct which does not fall within the well established bounds of the offence. On the contrary, the Court must safeguard against extension of those bounds save by the authority of Parliament. The bounds are presently set requiring proof of specific intent, a decision to bring about, in so far as it lies within the accused's power, the commission of the offence which it is alleged the accused attempted to commit, no matter whether the accused desired that consequence of his act or not.

In the present case the final direction was bad in law. Not only did the judge maintain the exclusion of 'intent' as an ingredient of the offence in Count 2 but he introduced an alternative basis for a conviction which did not and could not constitute the necessary mens rea . . .

Appeal on count 2 allowed

■ *Question*

The substantive crime of murder involves proof that D's conduct resulted in death. The mens rea for the attempt is therefore that D intended to cause V's death. Nothing less will do. What do you understand intention to mean following the decision in *Mohan*?

Consider the following example provided by Glanville Williams, *The Mental Element in Crime* (1966), p 24:

. . . P and D are walking at the edge of a cliff; they both see a watch lying on the path in front of them, and both plunge forward to get it. P is the more powerful and swifter man and will inevitably reach the watch first unless D takes extreme measures. D therefore gives P a sudden and treacherous push which he intends to result in P's falling over the cliff. He knows full well that if he is successful in his plan, P will certainly be killed.... There is no reason why D should not be guilty of attempted murder.

■ **Questions**

Do you agree with Williams? What is D's purpose?

See K. J. Arenson, 'The Pitfalls in the Law of Attempt: A New Perspective' (2005) J Crim Law 146.

In *Walker and Hayles* (1989) 90 Cr App R 226, [1990] Crim LR 44, on a charge of attempted murder the judge's direction that it was sufficient that the defendant foresaw that there was 'a very high degree of probability' that he would cause death was upheld. The Court of Appeal, when upholding the conviction for murder in *Woollin*, section 5.2.1, p 106, said they were 'fortified' by that decision. The House of Lords quashed Woollin's conviction, insisting that nothing less than foresight of virtual certainty would suffice. If that is so for murder, should it not be so, *a fortiori*, for attempted murder—and attempts generally?

■ **Questions**

Should foresight of virtual certainty be sufficient mens rea for attempt? Does not attempting mean *trying* to achieve a result—having the *purpose* of doing so?

In many instances intention in attempt is equated with the defendant 'trying' to commit the substantive offence. Is this an accurate description of the mens rea? Is there a difference between (i) trying to do something and (ii) trying to succeed?

See J. Hornby, 'On What's Intentionally Done' in S. Shute, J. Gardner and J. Horder, *Action and Value in Criminal Law* (1993), p 60 and J. Horder, 'Varieties of Intention, Criminal Attempts and Endangerment' (1994) 14 LS 335. See also Law Commission Consultation Paper No 183, suggesting that D having a conditional intent will suffice: para 16.68.

14.3.2 Intention and circumstances

It is clear that, on a charge of attempt, intention is required as to any result/consequence element in the definition of the actus reus of the substantive offence even though intention as to that result is not required on a charge of committing the complete crime. In *Mohan*, it was necessary to prove that the defendant intended to cause bodily harm. The Law Commission in its most recent Report proposed to retain this rule: Law Com No 318, para 2.46.

But there has been much controversy over the question whether, on a charge of attempt, intention is required as to a circumstance in the actus reus, where, on a charge of committing the complete crime, recklessness as to that circumstance would suffice.

For example, in criminal damage, the offence comprises elements of actus reus: causing damage (consequence) to property (circumstance) belonging to another (circumstance). The mens rea for the substantive crime requires proof of D's intention or recklessness as to the element of damage and as to the circumstances. On a charge of attempted criminal damage, it is necessary to prove that D intended the consequence (damage), but is it sufficient that he was reckless as to whether the property belonged to another (circumstances)?

The Law Commission, when drafting the report which led to the 1981 Act thought that a distinction between consequences and circumstances would be unworkable and recommended that intention should be required as to all the elements in the definition of the offence.

The Criminal Attempts Act 1981 (see section 14.2, p 498) does not deal with the matter expressly. It simply requires 'intent to commit [the] offence'.

The question then is as to the proper construction of the Criminal Attempts Act 1981, s 1. Consider the next case where the offence was attempted rape. The substantive offence of rape requires no proof of any consequence, but does requires proof of a circumstance (the lack of V's consent): does attempted rape require proof of intention that V will not consent?

R v Khan
[1990] 2 All ER 783, Court of Appeal, Criminal Division

(Russell LJ, Rose and Morland JJ)

After a disco, a 16-year-old girl accompanied five youths in a car to a house where they were joined by other youths. Three youths succeeded in having sexual intercourse with her. Four others, the appellants, tried to do so but failed. The girl did not consent to any sexual activity. The appellants were convicted of attempted rape and appealed. It was argued that the judge had misdirected the jury by telling them that, even if a defendant did not know the girl was not consenting, he was guilty of attempted rape if he tried unsuccessfully to have sexual intercourse, being reckless whether she consented or not—that is, it was sufficient that he could not care less whether she consented or not. (At that time, D was guilty of rape if he intended to have sex with V without her consent or was reckless (did not care less) whether she consented.)

Russell LJ:

In our judgment an acceptable analysis of the offence of rape [as defined under the 1956 Act, see now the definition in s 1 of the Sexual Offences Act 2003, section 20.2.1, p 701] as is as follows: (1) the intention of the offender is to have sexual intercourse with a woman; (2) the offence is committed if, but only if, the circumstances are that (a) the woman does not consent *and* (b) the defendant knows that she is not consenting or is reckless as to whether she consents.

Precisely the same analysis can be made of the offence of attempted rape: (1) the intention of the offender is to have sexual intercourse with a woman; (2) the offence is committed if, but only if, the circumstances are that (a) the woman does not consent *and* (b) the defendant knows that she is not consenting or is reckless as to whether she consents.

The only difference between the two offences is that in rape sexual intercourse takes place whereas in attempted rape it does not, although there has to be some act which is more than preparatory to sexual intercourse. Considered in that way, the intent of the defendant is precisely the same in rape and in attempted rape and the mens rea is identical, namely an intention to have intercourse plus a knowledge of or recklessness as to the woman's absence of consent. No question of attempting to achieve a reckless state of mind arises; the attempt relates to the physical activity; the mental state of the defendant is the same. A man does not recklessly have sexual intercourse, nor does he recklessly attempt it. Recklessness in rape and attempted rape arises not in relation to the physical act of the accused but only in his state of mind when engaged in the activity of having or attempting to have sexual intercourse.

If this is the true analysis, as we believe it is, the attempt does not require any different intention on the part of the accused from that for the full offence of rape. We believe this to be a desirable result which in the instant case did not require the jury to be burdened with different directions as to the accused's state of mind, dependent on whether the individual achieved or failed to achieve sexual intercourse.

We recognise, of course, that our reasoning cannot apply to all offences and all attempts. Where, for example as in causing death by reckless driving or reckless arson, no state of mind other than recklessness is involved in the offence, there can be no attempt to commit it.

In our judgment, however, the words 'with intent to commit an offence' to be found in s 1 of the 1981 Act mean, when applied to rape, 'with intent to have sexual intercourse with a woman in circumstances where she does not consent and the defendant knows or could not care less about her absence of consent'. The only 'intent', giving that word its natural and ordinary meaning, of the rapist is to have sexual intercourse. He commits the offence because of the circumstances in which he manifests that intent, ie when the woman is not consenting and he either knows it or could not care less about the absence of consent.

Accordingly, we take the view that in relation to the four appellants the judge was right to give the directions that he did when inviting the jury to consider the charges of attempted rape.

Appeals against conviction dismissed

Thus, the court held that recklessness as to the circumstance of consent is a sufficient mens rea for the attempt. As a general principle, it seems that recklessness as to a circumstance element of the actus reus of the full offence will be a sufficient mens rea for attempts where recklessness as to that circumstance is a sufficient mens rea for the full offence.

■ *Question*

Dan is sick of the piles of old papers lying around in the office he shares with his colleague, Victor. He takes the papers out into the garden at the back of the offices and tries to set fire to them. He cannot get his cigarette lighter to work so he gives up on the plan. Some of the papers later turn out to be Victor's papers. Is Dan guilty of attempting to damage Victor's papers?

The decision in *Khan* was limited to rape but it was followed in *A-G's Reference (No 3 of 1992)* (1993) 98 Cr App R 383, [1994] Crim LR 348, section 28.2.4, p 898, where the offence charged was attempted arson, being reckless whether life be endangered, contrary to the Criminal Damage Act 1971, s 1(2) (section 28.2.4, p 898). The court stated a general principle:

. . . a defendant, in order to be guilty of an attempt, must be in one of the states of mind required for the commission of the full offence, and did [*sic*] his best, so far as he could, to supply what was missing from the completion of the offence. It is the policy of the law that such people should be punished notwithstanding that in fact the intentions of such a defendant have not been fulfilled.

This is an important case and should not be overlooked. Four issues arise from the decision and the *dictum*.

(1) The decision goes beyond *Khan* because in this case the recklessness related not to a circumstance but to a result. The result which must occur for the full offence is arson and D did intend that. Section 1(2) of the Criminal Damage Act is exceptional in this respect. This is a problem that can arise when seeking to determine what the mens rea for attempting a particular offence actually is (step (ii) in section 14.2). Sometimes there can be confusion as to whether an element of an offence is a circumstance as opposed to a result. If the element is treated as a circumstance and for the substantive offence recklessness as to that circumstance suffices, then recklessness will also suffice for attempting the offence. This case demonstrates the mischief that can result when a result is confused with a circumstance, as it has arguably led to an extension of the law that goes far beyond what Parliament ever intended. However, there are those who argue that the case is consistent with *Khan* because they believe that the requirement that D was reckless to whether life was endangered actually related to a circumstance. See 'Attempted Aggravated Criminal Damage—"with intent to commit (the) offence"' (1994) 1 Arch News 4.

(2) Secondly, the statement is overbroad. Read literally, this approach would lead to the conviction for attempt of D who is merely reckless as to a consequence element of the offence provided he had an intention as to the relevant missing circumstance element(s). This is clearly not what the Act was intended to mean.

(3) The principle stated in *A-G's Reference* would introduce strict liability into the law of attempts. Section 9 of the Sexual Offences Act 2003 makes it an offence to touch sexually a child under 16, but if V is aged over 12 and under 16 D is only guilty if he has no belief that she is over 16. If D tries to touch sexually a girl, V, whom he believes on reasonable grounds to be aged 16 but who is in fact only 12, he would be guilty of an attempt to commit the offence under s 7 of the Sexual Offences Act 2003. He has the state of mind required for the commission of the full offence (an intention to touch a person, who is in fact, whether he knows it or not, under the age of 13); and he has done his best 'to supply [in the quaint language of the court] what was missing from the commission of the full offence'—sexual touching. There is a logical argument in favour of such an extension of inchoate liability: J. C. Smith (1957) 70 Harv LR 422 at 433 and [1962] Crim LR 135, but it goes beyond anything actually decided and beyond any recommendation of the Law Commission.

(4) Finally, at the time of the *A-G's Reference*, it was settled that *Caldwell* recklessness was sufficient for the full offence under the Criminal Damage Act and the court held that this was also the right test on the attempt charge. Advertent recklessness (*Cunningham/G* recklessness) has long been thought to be an acceptable mens rea as to circumstances in attempt because it is a true state of mind. However, a person may be *Caldwell* reckless even if the possibility of the relevant risk (danger to life) never enters his head. Arguably, this is an unacceptable extension of liability for an inchoate offence. The point does not appear to have been considered explicitly by the court. Given the overruling of *Caldwell* [1982] UKHL 1 in *G* [2003] UKHL 50 (section 5.3, p 119), the issue assumes less significance in relation to criminal damage, but if it is interpreted more broadly so that recklessness, negligence or even strict liability as to a circumstance suffice, it remains of fundamental importance. For criticism see also Law Commission Consultation Paper No 183, paras 14.42 et seq. However, the Court of Appeal in *Pace and Rogers* [2014] EWCA Crim 186 has recently cast doubt on the validity of this approach.

On current interpretation the mens rea for attempt requires proof of intent as to consequences, recklessness as to a circumstances may suffice if that is the mens rea of the substantive offence, but any lesser mens rea should not be sufficient.

14.4 Actus reus

The actus reus of attempt cannot be defined with the same precision as the actus reus of a substantive offence. It can take as many forms as there are substantive offences. It may, moreover, be an objectively innocent act. D puts sugar in V's tea. There is nothing wrong with that—V likes sweet tea. But D believes, mistakenly, that the sugar is arsenic and intends to kill V. He is guilty of attempted murder, the actus reus of the attempt being that objectively innocent act. With *Deller*, the actus reus was telling the truth!

It will be recalled that Lord Goddard in *Whybrow*, section 14.3.1, p 499, described the intent as the principal ingredient of the offence of attempt. It is not, however, the only ingredient. Something must be done to put the intent into execution. The question is, how much? The law has always distinguished mere acts of preparation from attempts. It was said at common law that the act had to be sufficiently proximate to the complete offence. The doctrine of proximity excluded from liability acts which some thought should entail guilt. The 1981 Act (see section 14.2, p 497), following the recommendations of the Law Commission, makes no attempt to state a test of proximity. It merely requires that the act done by the defendant should be 'more than merely preparatory to the commission of the offence'.

R. A. Duff, *Criminal Attempts* (1996), p 386 observes:

What relates an agent's conduct to the commission of an offence is partly her intention to commit that offence, but it also matters how close she has come to fully actualizing that intent. The conduct of someone who has so far only reconnoitered a building from which he plans to steal, for example, or only obtained a poison with which he intends to kill someone, is still 'remote' from the commission of theft (or burglary) or murder. We could not yet count her actions as essentially larcenous or murderous, or as attacks on property or life; there is still too wide a gap between what she has actually done and the commission, of the intended offence.

This is not to say that we should see her conduct simply as, for instance, 'walking round a building', or 'buying arsenic', which are indeed remote from the commission of the theft or murder that she intends to commit; we understand it, and respond to it, as by her intention, and her commission of the crime has so far only a shadowy existence in the public world: it exists in thought (in her intention), but has yet to acquire any very concrete existence in her actions. As her criminal enterprise advances, and her criminal intention is further actualized in action, her prospective commission of the crime becomes less shadowy, more concrete as an active engagement in the world. Her actions connect her more closely to the commission of the crime, and in the end that crime becomes something she is doing, rather than merely something she is intending or preparing to do.

Why should this matter? Why should we demand not merely conduct undertaken with intent to commit an offence (and perhaps corroborative of that intent), but conduct which comes close to the actual commission of the offence? An initial answer is that the law should leave intending criminals a *locus poenitentiae*: the chance to decide for themselves to abandon their criminal enterprises. This matters, because the law should treat and address its citizens as responsible agents. The central value to which this answer appeals is that of individual freedom to determine one's own actions.

■ *Questions*

Should it be necessary to prove that:

(i) D had performed the last act short of committing the full offence (crooking the finger round the trigger of the gun and aiming before pulling the trigger)?

(ii) D had commenced the final stages of the conduct necessary to complete the commission of the full offence (set out armed on his way to the place where the assassination of V would take place)?

The only well-settled rule of common law was that if D had done the last act which, as he knew, was necessary to achieve the consequence alleged to be attempted, he was guilty. Every act preceding the last one might quite properly be described as 'preparatory'. The assassin crooks his finger round the trigger *preparatory* to pulling it. If every preparatory act were to be regarded as outside the scope of the offence, the effect of the Act would be to narrow the scope of the offence beyond that of the common law position. It was well recognized at common law that some prior acts were sufficiently proximate. Though it has been argued that the word 'merely' does no more than add emphasis (E. Griew, annotations to *Current Law Statutes Annotations*), it seems that it has a key role. In *Tosti* [1997] Crim LR 746 it was held that the appellant, 'had committed acts which were preparatory, but not merely so'. Therefore, not all preparatory acts are excluded; only those that are *merely* preparatory; and it is thought that the assassin's crooking of the finger, though preparatory, would not be regarded as *merely* preparatory. The reason, it appears, is that he is now engaged in the commission of the offence—as Rowlatt J put it in *Osborn* (1919) 84 JP 63, he is 'on the job'.

Whether the act is more than merely preparatory is a question of fact: s 4(4). In a jury trial it is for the judge to decide whether there is sufficient evidence to support such a finding. In *A-G's Reference (No 1 of 1992)* [1993] 2 All ER 190, [1993] Crim LR 274, the point of law referred was 'Whether, on a charge of attempted rape, it is incumbent on the prosecution, as a matter of law, to prove that the defendant physically attempted to penetrate the woman's vagina with his penis.' The court answered 'no'. It is sufficient that there is evidence of intent to rape and of acts which a jury could properly regard as more than merely preparatory to the commission of the offence—for example, in that case, the respondent's acts of dragging V up some steps, lowering his trousers and interfering with her private parts. (Note that under the Sexual Offences Act 2003, s 1, the offence is extended to include penile penetration of the vagina, anus or mouth of the complainant.)

■ *Questions*

As rape consists in the physical penetration of a person's vagina, anus or mouth by a man's penis, how can there be an attempt to commit rape if there is no attempt by the man to penetrate the orifice? Is it not a contradiction in terms to say:

(i)   he did not attempt to penetrate her, but

(ii) he did attempt to rape her?

To take an analogous case, can there be an attempt to commit murder if there is no attempt to kill? Can we properly say:

(i)   D did not attempt to kill V, but

(ii) he did attempt to murder him?

Is the solution for the courts to give the word 'attempt' a particular meaning for the purposes of the Criminal Attempts Act so that it captures conduct which would not be considered an attempt in the ordinary meaning of the word? Or is it that the ordinary meaning is wider than the court appears to allow? For example, *was* the defendant, lowering his trousers and interfering with V's private parts with intent to penetrate her, attempting to do so in the ordinary meaning of the word? Cf commentary [1993] Crim LR 276.

The Court of Appeal has considered what is meant by 'more than merely preparatory' in numerous cases, but it is difficult to discern how the court determines whether this requirement was made out on the facts of each case. Clarkson argues that most of the cases can be explained on the basis that there is only an attempt if there has been a 'confrontation' between D and the victim, be it an actual person or property. See C. Clarkson, 'Attempt: The Conduct Requirement' (2009) 29 OJLS 25. Examine the following cases and consider the extent to which Clarkson's attempt at (partially) rationalizing the case law is successful.

R v Gullefer

[1990] 3 All ER 882, Court of Appeal, Criminal Division

(Lord Lane CJ, Kennedy and Owen JJ)

Gullefer jumped on to the track at a greyhound-racing stadium and waved his arms in order to distract the dogs during the running of a race. He later admitted that he hoped that the stewards would declare 'no race' so that he would recover from a bookmaker the stake he had placed on a dog that was losing in the race. He was convicted of attempted theft of his stake from the bookmaker under the Criminal Attempts Act 1981, s 1(1), and appealed to the Court of Appeal.

[Lord Lane CJ, having cited ss 1(1) and 4(3) of the 1981 Act:]

Thus the judge's task is to decide whether there is evidence on which a jury could reasonably come to the conclusion that the defendant had gone beyond the realm of mere preparation and had embarked on the actual commission of the offence. If not, he must withdraw the case from the jury. If there is such evidence, it is then for the jury to decide whether the defendant did in fact go beyond mere preparation. That is the way in which the judge approached this case. He ruled that there was sufficient evidence. Counsel for the appellant submits that he was wrong in so ruling.

The first task of the court is to apply the words of the 1981 Act to the facts of the case. Was the appellant still in the stage of preparation to commit the substantive offence, or was there a basis of fact which would entitle the jury to say that he had embarked on the theft itself? Might it properly be said that when he jumped on to the track he was trying to steal £18 from the bookmaker?

Our view is that it could not properly be said that at that stage he was in the process of committing theft. What he was doing was jumping onto the track in an effort to distract the dogs, which in its turn, he hoped, would have the effect of forcing the stewards to declare 'no race', which would in its turn give him the opportunity to go back to the bookmaker and demand the £18 he had staked. In our view there was insufficient evidence for it to be said that he had, when he jumped onto the track, gone beyond mere preparation.

So far at least as the present case is concerned, we do not think that it is necessary to examine the authorities which preceded the 1981 Act, save to say that the sections we have already quoted in this judgment seem to be a blend of various decisions, some of which were not easy to reconcile with others.

However, in deference to the arguments of counsel, we venture to make the following observations. Since the passing of the 1981 Act, a division of this court in *R v Ilyas* (1983) 78 Cr App R 17 has helpfully collated the authorities. As appears from the judgment in that case, there seem to have been two lines of authority. The first was exemplified by the decision in *R v Eagleton* (1855) Dears CC 376, 515, [1843–60] All ER Rep 363. That was a case where the defendant was alleged to have attempted to obtain money from the guardians of a parish by falsely pretending to the relieving officer that he had delivered loaves of bread of the proper weight to the outdoor poor, when in fact the loaves were deficient in weight.

Parke B, delivering the judgment of the court of nine judges, said ((1855) Dears CC 376, 515 at 538, [1843–60] All ER Rep 363 at 367):

'Acts remotely leading towards the commission of the offence are not to be considered as attempts to commit it, but acts immediately connected with it are; and if, in this case, after the credit with the relieving officer for the fraudulent overcharge, any *further step* on the part of the defendant had been necessary to obtain payment, as the making out a further account or producing the vouchers to the Board, we should have thought that the obtaining credit in account with the relieving officer would not have been sufficiently proximate to the obtaining the money. But, on the statement in this case, no other act on the part of the defendant would have been required. It was the last act, *depending on himself*, towards the payment of the money, and therefore it ought to be considered as an attempt.' (Parke B's emphasis.)

Lord Diplock in *DPP v Stonehouse* [1977] 2 All ER 909 at 917, [1978] AC 55 at 68, having cited part of that passage from *R v Eagleton* (1855) Dears CC 376, 515, [1843–60] All ER Rep 363, added: 'In other words the offender must have crossed the Rubicon and burnt his boats.'

The other line of authority is based on a passage in *Stephen's Digest of the Criminal Law* (5th edn, 1894) art 50:

'An attempt to commit a crime is an act done with intent to commit that crime, and forming part of a series of acts which would constitute its actual commission if it were not interrupted.'

As Lord Edmund-Davies points out in *DPP v Stonehouse* [1977] 2 All ER 909 at 933, [1978] AC 55 at 85–86, that definition has been repeatedly cited with judicial approval: see Byrne J in *Hope v Brown* [1954] 1 All ER 330 at 332, [1954] 1 WLR 250 at 253 and Lord Parker CJ in *Davey v Lee* [1967] 2 All ER 423 at 425, [1968] 1 QB 366 at 370. However, as Lord Parker CJ in the latter case points out, *Stephen's* definition falls short of defining the exact point of time at which the series of acts can be said to begin.

It seems to us that the words of the 1981 Act seek to steer a midway course. They do not provide, as they might have done, that the *R v Eagleton* test is to be followed, or that, as Lord Diplock suggested, the defendant must have reached a point from which it was impossible for him to retreat before the actus reus of an attempt is proved. On the other hand the words give perhaps as clear a guidance as is possible in the circumstances on the point at which *Stephen's* 'series of acts' begins. It begins when the merely preparatory acts come to an end and the defendant embarks on the crime proper. When that is will depend of course on the facts in any particular case.

Appeal allowed

■ **Questions**

1. What if the declaration of 'no race' would have led (or the defendant believed it would have led) to the automatic refund of his stake?

2. It was not necessary to decide whether the successful completion of Gullefer's plan would have amounted to theft; but would it have done? Cf commentary [1987] Crim LR 196.

R v Jones (Kenneth)
[1990] 3 All ER 886, Court of Appeal, Criminal Division

(Taylor LJ, Mars-Jones and Waite JJ)

Jones got into a car driven by his ex-mistress's new lover, Foreman. Jones was wearing overalls and a crash helmet with the visor down and carrying a bag containing a loaded sawn-off shotgun. He had bought the gun and sawn off the barrel a few days earlier. Jones pointed the gun at Foreman at a range of 10 to 12 inches and said, 'You are not going to like this', or similar words. Foreman grabbed the end of the gun and, after a struggle, escaped unharmed. The safety catch on the gun was on and it was unclear whether Jones's finger was ever on the trigger. Jones was charged with attempted murder. It was submitted that there was no case to go to the jury because Jones had at least three acts to do before murder could be committed—(i) to remove the safety catch, (ii) to put his finger on the trigger, and (iii) to pull it. The judge rejected the submission, the jury convicted of attempted murder, and Jones appealed to the Court of Appeal on the ground that the case should have been withdrawn.

[Taylor LJ, having cited the last paragraph of the extract from Lord Lane CJ's judgment in *Gullefer*, in the previous extract:]

We respectfully adopt those words. We do not accept counsel's contention that s 1(1) of the 1981 Act in effect embodies the 'last act' test derived from *R v Eagleton*. Had Parliament intended to adopt that test, a quite different form of words could and would have been used.

It is of interest to note that the 1981 Act followed a report from the Law Commission on *Attempt, and Impossibility in Relation to Attempt, Conspiracy and Incitement* (Law Com No 102). At para 2.47 the report states:

'The definition of sufficient proximity must be wide enough to cover two varieties of cases; first, those in which a person has taken all the steps towards the commission of a crime which he believes to be necessary as far as he is concerned for that crime to result, such as firing a gun at another and missing. Normally such cases cause no difficulty. Secondly, however, the definition must cover those instances where a person has to take some further step to complete the crime, assuming that there is evidence of the necessary mental element on his part to commit it; for example, when the defendant has raised the gun to take aim at another but has not yet squeezed the trigger. We have reached the conclusion that, in regard to these cases, it is undesirable to recommend anything more complex than a rationalisation of the present law.'

In para 2.48 the report states:

'The literal meaning of "proximate" is "nearest, next before or after (in place, order, time, connection of thought, causation, etc)". Thus, were this term part of a statutory description of the actus reus of attempt, it would clearly be capable of being interpreted to exclude all but the "final act"; this would not be in accordance with the policy outlined above.'

Clearly, the draftsman of s 1(1) must be taken to have been aware of the two lines of earlier authority and of the Law Commission's report. The words 'an act which is more than merely preparatory to the commission of the offence' would be inapt if they were intended to mean 'the last act which lay in his power towards the commission of the offence'.

Looking at the plain natural meaning of s 1(1) in the way indicated by Lord Lane CJ, the question for the judge in the present case was whether there was evidence from which a reasonable jury, properly directed, could conclude that the appellant had done acts which were more than merely preparatory. Clearly his actions in obtaining the gun, in shortening it, in loading it, in putting on his disguise and in going to the school could only be regarded as preparatory acts. But, in our judgment, once he had got into the car, taken out the loaded gun and pointed it at the victim with the intention of killing him there was sufficient evidence for the consideration of the jury on the charge of attempted murder. It was a matter for them to decide whether they were sure that those acts were more than merely preparatory. In our judgment, therefore, the judge was right to allow the case to go to the jury, and the appeal against conviction must be dismissed . . .

Appeal dismissed

■ *Questions*

In *Jones* there was an attempt although Jones may have had as many as three more acts to do. How many acts did Gullefer still have to do? Is it helpful to count the acts to be done? Or are *time* and *place* more important? Is it significant that Jones (i) was in the place where the crime was to be committed (see also *Campbell* (1990) 93 Cr App R 350, later in this section) and (ii) would have committed it within seconds if the victim had not escaped?

In *Boyle and Boyle* (1986) 84 Cr App R 270, [1987] Crim LR 111, CA, persons who damaged a house door with a view to entering premises were held to have done an act more than merely preparatory to burglary. The court said that in deciding whether an act is more than merely preparatory it was entitled to look at the law before 1981. Was the court right?

In *Campbell* (1990) 93 Cr App R 350, [1991] Crim LR 268, C was arrested within a yard of the door of a post office. He was wearing a crash helmet and gloves and carrying an imitation gun and a threatening note. He admitted that he intended to use the note to frighten the person behind the counter in the post office to hand over money. He claimed he had changed his mind and decided not to carry out the robbery but was arrested before he could leave. His conviction for attempted robbery was quashed: a number of acts remained undone and he had not even gained entry to the place where he could be in a position to perform an act which could properly be said to be an attempt. He was convicted of the offence of carrying an imitation firearm.

■ *Questions*

How should the police deal with a man whom they believe to be armed and about to enter and rob a post office? Should they arrest him on the ground that he is, or they have reasonable ground for suspecting that he is, about to commit an offence? Or should they wait until he demands money at the counter of the post office, so that they are sure he has committed attempted robbery?

In *Geddes* [1996] Crim LR 894, D was found in the boys' toilet of a school, equipped in such a way as to suggest strongly that his purpose was kidnapping. His conviction for attempted false imprisonment was quashed. Even clear evidence of what D had in mind 'did not throw light on whether he had begun to carry out the commission of the offence'. The offence would now be one of trespass with intent to commit a sex offence contrary to the Sexual Offences Act 2003, s 63. *Tosti* [1997] Crim LR 746, where the accused were examining a door to decide how best to break in, was held to fall on the other side of the line: there was sufficient evidence of attempted burglary—that is, of an attempt to enter. In *Bowles and Bowles* [2004] EWCA Crim 1608, the Court of Appeal held that there was no case to answer in respect of a count of attempting to make a false instrument (a last will and testament) with intent, where DDs' acts of drafting the document and placing it in a drawer for safe keeping were no more than preparatory acts within the Criminal Attempts Act 1981, s 1(1).

In *Mason v DPP* [2009] EWHC 2198 (Admin), D was convicted of attempting to drive while over the limit. D opened the door of his car with the key in his hand, intending to drive off, but was robbed of his keys before he could get into the car. D argued that this was merely a preparatory act and so he was not guilty of attempting to drive while over the limit. The Divisional Court agreed and stated that this case was similar to *Campbell*. It was held that D could not be regarded as embarking on the 'crime proper' until he did something which was part of the actual process of putting the car in motion. Turning on the engine would be such a step, but simply opening the car door was held to be insufficient. In another case involving an attempt to commit a road traffic offence, *Moore v DPP* [2010] EWHC 1822 (Admin), Toulson LJ observed that the law relating to attempts is 'not satisfactory'. His lordship emphasized that the fact an act is preparatory does not mean it cannot constitute an attempt. The act in question must be *merely* preparatory. His lordship went on to question whether use of the phrase 'on the job' is helpful given that it does not elucidate when the 'job' begins. A better exposition of what is meant by 'more than merely preparatory' was said to be the following paragraph taken from the Law Commission's most recent consultation paper.

> To elaborate further, preparatory conduct by D which is sufficiently close to the final act to be properly regarded as part of the execution of D's plan can be an attempt... In other words, it covers the steps immediately preceding the final act necessary to effect D's plan and bring about the commission of the intended offence.

As has already been pointed out, it is difficult to discern from the case law what test ought to be applied in order to determine whether what D has done is more than merely preparatory to the commission of the substantive offence. This can lead to cases the outcomes of which are hard to reconcile with each other. For example, in *Ferriter* [2012] EWCA Crim 2211, D was charged with attempted rape. D had been in a bar drinking all night and was the last customer present before it closed. V was the barmaid who was waiting for D to finish his drink so that she could lock up. D went behind the bar to where V was standing and confronted her face to face. A struggle ensued during which V ended up on the floor with D on top of her. It was V's evidence that he attempted to pull down her trousers a number of times. V eventually managed to break free and ran for help. D was charged and convicted of attempted rape. On appeal, D's contention was that there was insufficient evidence from which the jury could have been sure that he intended to commit rape. The Court of Appeal agreed and quashed his conviction. However, the court went on to find that D undoubtedly had a sexual motive and so substituted a conviction for sexual assault. D's actions had gone beyond mere preparation and into the commission of that substantive offence. In *Dagnall* [2003] EWCA Crim 2441, D had also been convicted of attempted rape. D and V were waiting at a bus stop. D began to talk to V in a way she found uncomfortable, so she walked to another bus stop. D followed V, walked up beside her and told her that he wanted to 'fuck her'. D told V that he would take her to a dark road where he would remove her trousers. V told D that this was not going to happen and she ran off. However, D grabbed V by the hair and pulled her towards him before pushing her up against a fence, declaring his intention to rape her if she would not have intercourse with him willingly. The ordeal then came to an end when a police car arrived. The Court of Appeal upheld D's conviction as his acts had been more than merely preparatory to the commission of rape. Latham LJ stated that 'In what [D] did he had virtually succeeded in achieving all that he needed. He had overcome [V's] resistance and it was only, it would appear, the arrival of the police car that prevented the ultimate offence from taking place.' This was because D had indicated to V that his intention was to rape her and he had seized her by force.

■ *Questions*

1. Should Dagnall's conviction for attempted rape have been upheld? What test was the court applying to determine whether his actions were more than merely preparatory? Could it be said that the court was swayed more by D's declared intention than what he actually did? If the actus reus of rape is penile penetration of the vagina, anus or mouth and V's lack of consent, should more not have been necessary before D was found guilty of attempted rape?

2. Should Ferriter's conviction for attempted rape have been substituted for one of sexual assault? Are the facts of the two cases sufficiently distinguishable to justify the different outcomes?

Fletcher (G. Fletcher, *Rethinking Criminal Law* (1978)) breaks down the rationales for criminalizing attempts into objectivist and subjectivist theories. This has implications for what the actus reus of attempts ought to be. Adopting an objectivist approach, D, by intending to commit the crime and committing acts closely connected to it, has crossed a moral threshold. There is thus a similarity between D's moral culpability in having attempted to commit the crime and the moral culpability that would attach if D had succeeded in committing it. D's actions must evince an unequivocal commitment to bringing about the substantive offence. The corollary of this is that the actus reus of an attempt will not be made out until D has come close to committing the offence. On the other hand, a subjectivist approach focuses on D's state of mind. All that is required to make D guilty of an attempt on this approach is some action that corroborates D's intention to commit the substantive offence. This means that the law can intervene much earlier than the objectivist approach would permit. The actus reus of an attempt is thus made out much earlier in time.

> ■ *Question*
>
> Do the cases examined above evince the adoption by courts in England of an objectivist or subjectivist approach, or an ad hoc mixture of both?

14.4.1 Omission

It is generally thought that the Criminal Attempts Act 1981, s 1(1), section 14.2, p 497 ('does an act'), rules out attempts by omission, although it was in fact the intention of the Government that in some cases attempt by omission should be an offence.

In *Nevard* [2006] EWCA Crim 2896, D seriously injured his wife by striking her with an axe and a knife. He then forced her to abandon her attempt to dial 999 to call for assistance. The emergency services rang back on the number she had used, but D took the call and told them that his grandchildren must have been fooling around with the phone. The police remained suspicious so attended the scene and found D's wife, whose injuries were not fatal. D was charged with wounding with intent and with attempted murder. He pleaded guilty to the wounding. The jury asked:

Can you clarify whether an attempt to withhold care/emergency services constitutes attempted murder, knowing he has pleaded guilty to wounding with intent?

The trial judge's answer was:

The Crown's case is that he struck the blows with the axe or the axe handle. When that did not work he went and got a knife and stabbed her with that kitchen knife . . . and also that he slashed her arms with a Stanley knife and that when he did those acts, his intention was that she should die. Now, where the withholding of the emergency services may help you is as to what his intention was. . . . In other words, by seeing what he did after the event you may get an insight as to what his intention was.

The judge instructed the jury to regard D's conduct in preventing the emergency services as an element of the overall evidence of D's intention to kill. The Court of Appeal upheld the conviction, but suggested that the judge should have made explicit to the jury that attempting to divert the emergency services could not in itself constitute attempted murder.

> ■ *Question*
>
> Was not D's conduct in taking the return call and lying to the emergency services a sufficient 'act'?

14.4.2 Abetting an attempt is, but attempting to abet is not, an offence

Section 1(4)(b) of the Criminal Attempts Act is unsatisfactorily worded. As interpreted in *Dunnington* [1984] QB 472 it provides that attempting to commit a crime is itself a crime, so it can be aided and abetted like any other crime; but aiding and abetting is not, as such, an offence, so there can be no attempt to 'commit' it. Bohlander argues that the enactment of the Serious Crime Act 2007 means that this section ought to have been repealed. He argues that under s 44 of the 2007 Act, D can intentionally do an act that would otherwise fall within the ambit of s 1(4)(b). To address this paradox, Bohlander proposes two options. Either the principle that the more recent law implicitly repeals a previous law that regulates the same matter (the *lex posterior* principle) ought to apply, or the legislature expressly repeals or amends s 1(4)(b) to bring it in line with the Serious Crime Act 2007. He prefers the latter option. See M. Bohlander, 'The Conflict Between the Serious Crime Act 2007 and Section 1(4)(b) Criminal Attempts Act 1981—A Missed Repeal?' [2010] Crim LR 483. For the contrary view, see J. J. Child, 'The Differences Between Attempted Complicity and Inchoate Assisting and Encouraging—A Reply to Professor Bohlander' [2010] Crim LR 924.

14.5 Impossibility and attempts

In attempts we are not concerned with whether the substantive offence has occurred. This leads to some challenging questions: for example, does the English law of attempt criminalize the person who takes his own umbrella believing it is that of another person? The House of Lords addressed this issue in two cases. In the earlier case, *Anderton v Ryan* [1985] AC 560, the House of Lords held that the impossibility of committing the substantive offence was a defence to a charge of attempting to commit it. In that case, there could be no attempt to handle stolen goods if the goods D intended to handle were not in fact stolen. The view was heavily criticized by Glanville Williams. See G. Williams, 'The Lords and Impossible Attempts, or Quis Custodiet Ipsos Custodes?' (1986) 45 CLJ 33. The House of Lords soon changed its mind in the following case.

R v Shivpuri

[1986] UKHL 2, House of Lords, http://www.bailii.org/uk/cases/UKHL/1986/2.html

(Lord Hailsham LC, Lords Elwyn-Jones, Scarman, Bridge and Mackay)

S was arrested by customs officials while in possession of a suitcase. He admitted that he knew that it contained prohibited drugs. Analysis showed that the material in the suitcase was not a prohibited drug but vegetable matter akin to snuff. S was convicted under the Criminal Attempts Act 1981, s 1(1) (section 14.2, p 497), of attempting to commit the offence of being knowingly concerned in dealing with and harbouring prohibited drugs contrary to the Customs and Excise Management Act 1979, s 170(1)(b). He appealed on the ground that because the substance was not a prohibited drug he had not done an act which was 'more than merely preparatory to the commission of the offence' as required by the 1981 Act. The Court of Appeal dismissed his appeal.

[Lord Bridge, having cited the Criminal Attempts Act 1981, s 1 (section 14.2, p 497), continued:]

Applying this language to the facts of the case, the first question to be asked is whether the appellant intended to commit the offences of being knowingly concerned in dealing with and harbouring drugs of class A or class B with intent to evade the prohibition on their importation. Translated into more homely language the question may be rephrased, without in any way altering its legal significance, in the following terms: did the appellant intend to receive and store (harbour) and in due course pass on to third parties (deal with) packages of heroin or cannabis which he knew had been smuggled into England from India? The answer is plainly Yes, he did. Next, did he, in relation to each offence, do an act which was more than merely preparatory to the commission of the offence? The act relied on in relation to harbouring was the receipt and retention of the packages found in the lining of the suitcase. The act relied on in relation to dealing was the meeting at Southall station with the intended recipient of one of the packages. In each case the act was clearly more than preparatory to the commission of the intended offence; it was not and could not be more than merely preparatory to the commission of the actual offence, because the facts were such that the commission of the actual offence was impossible. Here then is the nub of the matter. Does the 'act which is more than merely preparatory to the commission of the offence' in s 1(1) of the 1981 Act (the *actus reus* of the statutory offence of attempt) require any more than an act which is more than merely preparatory to the commission of the offence which the defendant intended to commit? Section 1(2) must surely indicate a negative answer; if it were otherwise, whenever the facts were such that the commission of the actual offence was impossible, it would be impossible to prove an act more than merely preparatory to the commission of that offence and sub-ss (1) and (2) would contradict each other.

This very simple, perhaps over-simple, analysis leads me to the provisional conclusion that the appellant was rightly convicted of the two offences of attempt with which he was charged. But can this conclusion stand with *Anderton v Ryan*? The appellant in that case was charged with an attempt to handle stolen goods. She bought a video recorder believing it to be stolen. On the facts as they were to be assumed it was not stolen. By a majority the House decided that she was entitled to be acquitted. I have re-examined the case with care. If I could extract from the speech of Lord Roskill or from my own speech a clear and coherent principle distinguishing those cases of attempting the impossible which amount to offences under the statute from those which do not, I should have to consider carefully on which side of the line the instant case fell. But I have to confess that I can find no such principle.

Running through Lord Roskill's speech and my own in *Anderton v Ryan* is the concept of 'objectively innocent' acts which, in my speech certainly, are contrasted with 'guilty acts'. A few citations will make this clear. Lord Roskill said ([1985] 2 All ER 355 at 364, [1985] AC 560 at 580):

'My Lords, it has been strenuously and ably argued for the respondent that these provisions involved that a defendant is liable to conviction for an attempt even where his actions are innocent but he erroneously believes facts which, if true, would make those actions criminal, and further, that he is liable to such a conviction whether or not in the event his intended course of action is completed.'

He proceeded to reject the argument. I referred to the appellant's purchase of the video recorder and said ([1985] 2 All ER 355 at 366, [1985] AC 560 at 582): 'Objectively considered, therefore, her purchase of the recorder was a perfectly proper commercial transaction.'

A further passage from my speech stated ([1985] 2 All ER 355 at 366, [1985] AC 560 at 582–583):

'The question may be stated in abstract terms as follows. Does s 1 of the 1981 Act create a new offence of attempt where a person embarks on and completes a course of conduct, which is objectively innocent, solely on the ground that the person mistakenly believes facts which, if true, would make that course of conduct a complete crime? If the question must be answered affirmatively it requires convictions in a number of surprising cases: the classic case, put by Bramwell B in *R v Collins* (1864) 9 Cox CC 497 at 498, of the man who takes away his own umbrella from a stand, believing it not to be his own and with intent to steal it; the case of the man who has consensual intercourse with a girl over 16 believing her to be under that age; the case of the art dealer who sells a picture which he represents to be and which is in fact a genuine Picasso, but which the dealer mistakenly believes to be a fake. The common feature of all these cases, including that under appeal, is that the mind alone is guilty, the act is innocent.'

I then contrasted the case of the man who attempts to pick the empty pocket, saying ([1985] 2 All ER 355 at 367, [1985] AC 560 at 583):

'Putting the hand in the pocket is the guilty act, the intent to steal is the guilty mind, the offence is appropriately dealt with as an attempt, and the impossibility of committing the full offence for want of anything in the pocket to steal is declared by [sub-s (2)] to be no obstacle to conviction.'

If we fell into error, it is clear that our concern was to avoid convictions in situations which most people, as a matter of common sense, would not regard as involving criminality. In this connection it is to be regretted that we did not take due note of para 2.97 of the Law Commission Report, Criminal Law: Attempt and Impossibility in Relation to Attempt, Conspiracy and Incitement (1980) (Law Com no 102) which preceded the enactment of the 1981 Act, which reads:

'If it is right in principle that an attempt should be chargeable even though the crime which it is sought to commit could not possibly be committed, we do not think that we should be deterred by the consideration that such a change in our law would also cover some extreme and exceptional cases in which a prosecution would be theoretically possible. An example would be where a person is offered goods at such a low price that he believes that they are stolen, when in fact they are not; if he actually purchases them, upon the principles which we have discussed he would be liable for an attempt to handle stolen goods. Another case which has been much debated is that raised in argument by Bramwell B in *Reg v Collins*. If A takes his own umbrella, mistaking it for one belonging to B and intending to steal B's umbrella, is he guilty of attempted theft? Again, on the principles which we have discussed he would in theory be guilty, but in neither case would it be realistic to suppose that a complaint would be made or that a prosecution would ensue.'

The prosecution in *Anderton v Ryan* itself falsified the Commission's prognosis in one of the 'extreme and exceptional cases'. It nevertheless probably holds good for other such cases, particularly that of the young man having sexual intercourse with a girl over 16, mistakenly believing her to be under that age, by which both Lord Roskill and I were much troubled.

However that may be, the distinction between acts which are 'objectively innocent' and those which are not is an essential element in the reasoning in *Anderton v Ryan* and the decision, unless it can be supported on some other ground, must stand or fall by the validity of this distinction. I am satisfied on further consideration that the concept of 'objective innocence' is incapable of sensible application in relation to the law of criminal attempts. The reason for this is that any attempt to commit an offence which involves 'an act which is more than merely preparatory to the commission of the offence' but which for any reason fails, so that in the event no offence is committed, must *ex hypothesi*, from the point view of the criminal law, be 'objectively innocent'. What turns what would otherwise, from the point of view of the criminal law, be an innocent act into a crime is the intent of the actor to commit an offence. I say 'from the point of view of the criminal law' because the law of tort must surely here be quite irrelevant. A puts his hand into B's pocket. Whether or not there is anything in the pocket capable of being stolen, if A intends to steal his act is a criminal attempt; if he does not so intend his act is innocent. A plunges a knife into a bolster in a bed. To avoid the complication of an offence of criminal damage, assume it to be A's bolster. If A believes the bolster to be his enemy B and intends to kill him, his act is an attempt to murder B; if he knows the bolster is only a bolster, his act is innocent. These considerations lead me to the conclusion that the distinction sought to be drawn in *Anderton v Ryan* between innocent and guilty acts considered 'objectively' and independently of the state of mind of the actor cannot be sensibly maintained.

Another conceivable ground of distinction which was to some extent canvassed in argument, both in *Anderton v Ryan* and in the instant case, though no trace of it appears in the speeches in *Anderton v Ryan*, is a distinction which would make guilt or innocence of the crime of attempt in a case of mistaken belief dependent on what, for want of a better phrase, I will call the defendant's dominant intention. According to the theory necessary to sustain this distinction, the appellant's dominant intention in *Anderton v Ryan* was to buy a cheap video recorder; her belief that it was stolen was merely incidental. Likewise in the hypothetical case of attempted unlawful sexual intercourse, the young man's dominant intention was to have intercourse with the particular girl; his mistaken belief that she was under 16 was merely incidental. By contrast, in the instant case the appellant's dominant intention was to receive and distribute illegally imported heroin or cannabis.

While I see the superficial attraction of this suggested ground of distinction, I also see formidable practical difficulties in its application. By what test is a jury to be told that a defendant's dominant intention is to be recognised and distinguished from his incidental but mistaken belief? But there is perhaps a more formidable theoretical difficulty. If this ground of distinction is relied on to support the acquittal of the appellant in *Anderton v Ryan*, it can only do so on the basis that her mistaken belief that the video recorder was stolen played no significant part in her decision to buy it and therefore she may be acquitted of the intent to handle stolen goods. But this line of reasoning runs into head-on collision with s 1(3) of the 1981 Act. The theory produces a situation where, apart from the subsection, her intention would not be regarded as having amounted to any intent to commit an offence. Section 1(3)(b) then requires one to ask whether, if the video recorder had in fact been stolen, her intention would have been regarded as an intent to handle stolen goods. The answer must clearly be Yes, it would. If she had bought the video recorder knowing it to be stolen, when in fact it was, it would have availed her nothing to say that her dominant intention was to buy a video recorder because it was cheap and that her knowledge that it was stolen was merely incidental. This seems to me fatal to the dominant intention theory.

I am thus led to the conclusion that there is no valid ground on which *Anderton v Ryan* can be distinguished. I have made clear my own conviction, which as a party to the decision (and craving the indulgence of my noble and learned friends who agreed in it) I am the readier to express, that the decision was wrong. What then is to be done? If the case is indistinguishable, the application of the strict doctrine of precedent would require that the present appeal be allowed. Is it permissible to depart from precedent under the 1966 *Practice Note* ([1966] 3 All ER 77) notwithstanding the especial need for certainty in the criminal law? The following considerations lead me to answer that question affirmatively. Firstly, I am undeterred by the consideration that the decision in *Anderton v Ryan* was so recent. The 1966 Practice Statement is an effective abandonment of our pretention to infallibility. If a serious error embodied in a decision of this House has distorted the law, the sooner it is corrected the better. Secondly, I cannot see how, in the very nature of the case, anyone could have acted in reliance on the law as propounded in *Anderton v Ryan* in the belief that he was acting innocently and now find that, after all, he is to be held to have committed a criminal offence. Thirdly, to hold the House bound to follow *Anderton v Ryan* because it cannot be distinguished and to allow the appeal in this case would, it seems to me, be tantamount to a declaration that the 1981 Act left the law of criminal attempts unchanged following the decision in *Haughton v Smith* [1975] AC 476. Finally, if, contrary to my present view, there is a valid ground on which it would be proper to distinguish cases similar to that considered in *Anderton v Ryan*, my present opinion on that point would not foreclose the option of making such a distinction in some future case.

I cannot conclude this opinion without disclosing that I have had the advantage, since the conclusion of the argument in this appeal, of reading an article by Professor Glanville Williams entitled 'The Lords and Impossible Attempts, or *Quis Custodiet Ipsos Custodes*?' [1986] CLJ 33. The language in which he criticises the decision in *Anderton v Ryan* is not conspicuous for its moderation, but it would be foolish, on that account, not to recognise the force of the criticism and churlish not to acknowledge the assistance I have derived from it.

I would answer the certified question in the affirmative and dismiss the appeal.

[**Lord Hailsham LC**, having stated that, save for one relatively minor point, he agreed with Lord Bridge, continued:]

I must add, however, that, even had I not been able to follow my noble and learned friend in interring *Anderton v Ryan* [later in this extract] by using the 1966 Practice Statement, I would still have dismissed the instant appeal by distinguishing its facts from that case. Shortly, my reasoning would have been that the appellant was guilty on the clear wording of s 1(1) and (2) of the 1981 Act and that no recourse was therefore necessary to the wording of s 1(3), which if so would be irrelevant.

[His lordship set out the provisions of the Act.]

I would have arrived at this conclusion by asking myself three simple questions to which the answers could only be made in one form. They are: *Question 1*. What was the intention of the appellant throughout? *Answer*. His intention throughout was to evade and defeat the customs authorities of the United Kingdom. He had no other intention. His motive was gain (the bribe of £1,000). But as

I pointed out in *Hyam v DPP* [1974] 2 All ER 41 at 5, [1975] AC 55 at 73 motive is not the same thing as intention. *Question 2*. Is the knowing evasion of the United Kingdom customs in the manner envisaged in the appellant's intent an offence to which s 1 of the 1981 Act applies? *Answer*. Yes: see s 1(4). *Question 3*. Did the appellant do an act which was more than preparatory to the commission of the offence? *Answer*. Yes, for the reasons stated in the relevant paragraphs of my noble and learned friend Lord Bridge's speech.

In this connection I do not feel it would have been necessary to invoke the doctrine of dominant and subordinate intention referred to by my noble and learned friend. The sole intent of the instant appellant from start to finish was to defeat the customs prohibition. In *Anderton v Ryan* the only intention of Mrs Ryan was to buy a particular video cassette recorder at a knock-down price, and the fact that she believed it to be stolen formed no part of that intention. It was a belief, assumed to be false and not an intention at all. It was a false belief as to a state of fact, and, if it became an intention, it was only the result of the deeming provisions of s 1(3). Whether or not *Anderton v Ryan* was correctly decided, one has to go to s 1(3) to decide whether Mrs Ryan had committed a criminal attempt under the Act as the result of her belief, assumed to be false, that the video cassette recorder had in fact been stolen.

[Lord Mackay agreed with disposal of the appeal proposed by Lord Bridge; but agreed with Lord Hailsham on the 'relatively minor point' referred to by him.]

[Lord Elwyn-Jones said that he would have been content to dismiss the appeal by distinguishing *Anderton v Ryan*, as Lord Hailsham had done; but he agreed with Lord Bridge and would dismiss the appeal for the reasons given by him.]

[Lord Scarman agreed with Lord Bridge.]

[A second ground of appeal, that is, that the judge was wrong to direct the jury that it was immaterial that the appellant did not know precisely what the prohibited goods were, was also rejected: although s 170(1)(b) created a number of separate offences, the only mens rea necessary was the knowledge that the thing was a controlled drug.]

Appeal dismissed

■ *Questions*

1. Does the decision in *Shivpuri* offend the principle of legality (no one shall be convicted of doing something which has not been declared by the law to be an offence)? Cf [1984] Crim LR 584 and [1985] Crim LR 504 at 505 and B. Hogan, 'The Principle of Legality' (1986) 136 NLJ 267. (Note also Article 7 of the European Convention on Human Rights, section 1.3, p 10.)

2. D and E agree that they will use D's tools to break into V's safe and steal a diamond. D tries to do so. It is quite impossible to break into the safe with those tools. Of what offences are D and E guilty? Does it matter whether the diamond exists? What if D attempts to break open the safe, but it is empty?

3. D, 16, has sex with V. She consents. He thinks she is only 12, she is in fact 16. Has D attempted to rape a child under 13?

4. D hates his neighbour, V, and plans to kill him. In order to effectuate his plan, D makes a voodoo doll of V and stabs it through the heart. D believes that this will kill V. Is D guilty of attempted murder? Should he be? If D is not guilty, could the reason be that he has not increased the risk that harm will be caused to V? However, are there not other impossible attempts that only pose a minimal risk of harm but that intuition tells us nevertheless ought to be criminalized?

14.6 Reform

The Law Commission published a Consultation Paper No 183, *Conspiracy and Attempts* (2007) (see also the Law Commission Report No 318 on *Conspiracy and Attempts* (2009)).

WHAT IS WRONG WITH ATTEMPTS

Background

12.12 ... The offence was drafted to cover the sort of conduct associated with 'trying' to commit an intended offence; but it was also designed to encompass earlier preparatory acts—acts sufficiently proximate to a completed attempt to justify the imposition of criminal liability.

12.13 However, as a mechanism for determining the criminal liability of persons who take proximate steps towards trying to commit an offence, we believe this inchoate offence is unsatisfactory. We believe that a change of approach, through legislative intervention, is necessary.

12.14 First of all, in the absence of clear, consistent guidelines the 'more than merely preparatory' test of proximity has proved to be too vague and uncertain a basis for a court to determine whether an attempt has been committed. . . .

12.15 Secondly, because of the absence of any clear, consistent guidance, the Court of Appeal has had to determine where the line between mere preparation and attempt is to be drawn. As a result too much emphasis has on occasion been placed on the offence's label ('attempt')—and therefore on the notion of 'trying' to commit an offence. Too little regard has correspondingly been paid to the underlying rationale for the offence. Under our provisional proposals, clarity would be introduced to the law of attempt in this respect, because the offence of 'attempt' would be confined to the last acts D needs to do to bring about the commission of the offence. The key distinction would become one between 'mere' preparation and 'criminal' preparation, for the purposes of that proposed new offence.

12.16 In that regard, we take the view that there are a number of sound policy reasons for imposing criminal liability for some preparatory conduct occurring before D actually completes or all-but completes an attempt to commit another offence. These are:

(1) the need for effective intervention by the police;

(2) the desirability of imposing criminal liability in relation to conduct associated with a sufficiently vivid danger of intentional harm; and

(3) the high moral culpability associated with preparatory acts closely linked in time with (what would be) the last act towards the commission of an intended offence.

12.17 The case of *Geddes* [explained in section 14.4, p 510] provides perhaps the most worrying example of the Court of Appeal's restrictive approach to the offence of attempt. In our view, it gives rise to the accusation that the criminal law does not adequately protect the public in the way that it interprets that offence. Unfortunately, *Geddes* is not an isolated example.

12.18 Another troubling example is *Campbell* [section 14.4, p 509]. In that case D's conviction for attempted robbery was quashed even though he had been apprehended with an imitation firearm as he came within a metre of the door of a post office he intended to rob, with the aid of a threatening note for the cashier. The Court of Appeal's view was that there was no evidence on which a jury could 'properly and safely' find that D's acts were more than merely preparatory. . . .

12.24 Our third reason for believing section 1(1) of the 1981 Act to be unsatisfactory is that it would appear omissions are currently excluded from the scope of the offence. We take the view that there is no reason in principle, or indeed as a matter of policy, why attempts should be limited to the commission of positive acts, particularly as the Crown must always prove D's intention. If D deliberately starves his or her baby to death, this is murder even though the death is achieved through 'doing nothing' rather than by a positive act of killing. Suppose, however, that someone overhears D admitting that he or she is endeavouring to starve his or her baby to death and has already denied the baby food for a couple of days. We believe it would be wrong if D could avoid liability for attempted murder in such circumstances, but it may well be that this is the present legal position.

12.25 Our fourth reason relates to the current requirement that the jury should be directed to determine whether D's proven or admitted conduct amounts to an 'attempt' for the purposes of the 1981 Act, even when the trial judge has already made a ruling on this issue. This is difficult to reconcile with the general division of roles between judge and jury in criminal proceedings. More worryingly, lay triers of fact may have an insufficient understanding of the scope of the offence, or of the policy considerations underpinning it, to be able to apply it in the way it was intended to be applied. The present test may give rise to inconsistent or perverse verdicts. . . .

12.26 Finally, there is a lack of clarity in relation to the fault element required for circumstance elements of an attempt to commit an offence. It may be that inchoate liability can now arise for attempting an (indictable) offence of strict liability regardless of whether the accused 'intended' to do anything unlawful (and even regardless of whether he or she had any culpable state of mind at all). . . .

12.27 We believe it is of crucial importance that the law should properly address the relationship between the various stages in the run up to the commission of an intended offence. There are in effect three such stages:

(1) Stage 1: the preliminary preparatory steps taken by D;

(2) Stage 2: the 'on the job' preparatory steps taken by D (that is, the preparatory acts immediately preceding the (attempted) commission of an intended offence);

(3) Stage 3: conduct beyond what would ordinarily be regarded as 'on the job' preparation, where D is attempting to commit the intended offence.

12.28 For the criminal law to deal properly with this area, a number of questions need to be answered:

(1) Should criminal attempt be restricted, to a specific kind of behaviour prior to the commission of a substantive offence, namely last acts needing to done by D to commit the offence?

(2) If so, should there also be a separate offence of 'preparation' (or additions to the existing battery of offences of preparation) to cover:

(a) some or all of the types of preparatory conduct which were originally intended to fall within the scope of the present offence of attempt; or

(b) an even wider band of preparatory conduct?

(3) Alternatively, should section 1(1) of the 1981 Act be retained but remodelled so that its label and/or definition accord more visibly with the true scope of the offence as intended by Parliament that is, an offence extending back beyond the notion of trying or endeavouring to commit an offence?

(4) If so, should there be a further general offence of 'preparation' (or additions to the existing battery of offences of preparation) to cover other preparatory conduct warranting criminal liability?

[The Commission proposed models of the offence.]

Option 1: two offences (without elaboration)

12.35 There would be a narrower general offence of 'attempt' limited in scope to cases of completed or all-but completed attempt where the offender is engaged in the last acts needed to bring about the commission of the offence. However, there would also be a new general offence of 'criminal preparation' (with intent) limited in scope to the narrow band of preparatory acts immediately preceding an attempt (that is, stage 2). This option would expressly declare through the definition given to 'criminal preparation' that the broad interpretation of the present offence of attempt is correct, contrary to the restrictive approach of the Court of Appeal in *Geddes*. However, individuals whose conduct goes no further than stage 2 would no longer be labelled as 'attemptors'.

12.36 The definition of 'criminal preparation' would not be elaborated upon in the relevant legislation. Additional guidance for the courts would, however, be provided in the form of examples set out in our final report. . . .

Option 2: two offences (with statutory examples)

12.38 This approach would follow option 1 in all respects, save for one key difference. Specific examples of 'criminal preparation' would be provided in the legislation to guide the courts in their interpretation of the offence and their understanding of the types of conduct falling within stage 2 (paragraph 12.27 above). No such examples would be provided for the new, narrower offence of 'attempt' because, being limited to last acts needing to be done by D to bring about the commission of the crime, there would be no ambiguity as to its scope.

Examples of criminal preparation

12.39 Irrespective of whether option 1 or option 2 is preferred, we believe that the new general offence of criminal preparation should encompass the following situations:

(1) D gains entry into a building, structure, vehicle or enclosure or (remains therein) with a view to committing the intended offence there and then or as soon as an opportunity presents itself.

(2) D examines or interferes with a door, window, lock or alarm or puts in place a ladder or similar device with a view there and then to gaining unlawful entry into a building, structure or vehicle to commit the intended offence within.

(3) D commits an offence or an act of distraction or deception with a view to committing the intended offence there and then.

(4) D, with a view to committing the intended offence there and then or as soon as an opportunity presents itself:

    (a) approaches the intended victim or the object of the intended offence, or

    (b) lies in wait for an intended victim, or

    (c) follows the intended victim.

Option 3: the minimalist approach

12.40 Under this approach, there would continue to be a single inchoate offence of 'attempt', as currently defined, and its breadth would continue to be controlled by interpretations of section 1(1) of the 1981 Act given by the Court of Appeal.

12.41 However, on the assumption that the courts may come to the definitive conclusion that 'attempt' is to be interpreted narrowly, in line with the Court of Appeal's judgment in *Geddes*, the battery of specific statutory offences of preparation would be carefully reviewed with a view to eliminating anomalies. Our approach would be predicated on the desirability of ensuring that individuals who reach stage 2 (paragraph 12.27 above) in their plan to commit an intended offence do not escape all criminal liability.

■ *Question*

In its provisional proposals the Law Commission favoured option 1. Do you agree?

Additional proposals

12.43 We also provisionally propose the following:

Proposal 18: Fault

(1) 'Intention' in the two proposed offences should bear its normal meaning, namely that given to it by the House of Lords in *Woollin*, but should also encompass so-called conditional intent;

(2) Intention in the sense just given should be required for the conduct elements and (if any) consequence elements of an offence of attempt or of criminal preparation, but not for the circumstance elements (if any);

(3) If the completed offence requires recklessness, negligence or no fault as to a circumstance element, the fault requirement in relation to an attempt to commit that offence, or in relation to the offence of criminal preparation, should be subjective recklessness;

(4) If the completed offence requires a higher degree of fault in relation to a circumstance element than recklessness (such as knowledge), then that higher degree of fault should also be required in relation to the circumstance element on a charge of attempt or of criminal preparation.

Proposal 19: Omissions

12.44 The two proposed offences should be drafted to cover omissions where, as a matter of law, the intended offence is capable of being committed by an omission.

Proposal 20: The roles of judge and jury

12.45 The procedural rule under the 1981 Act, that it is for the jury to determine not only whether D acted in the way the Crown alleges but also whether that proven conduct amounts to the commission of an attempt, should be abolished in relation to the proposed offences.

Proposal 21: Application to summary offences

12.46 It should be permissible to prosecute D for attempting or preparing to commit a summary offence.

12.47 However, we ask whether the consent of the Director of Public Prosecutions should be required in such cases.

■ *Questions*

Do you think that having crimes of criminal preparation and attempt would be confusing? Would it encourage the courts to extend liability to acts of the accused that are even further remote from the substantive crime and earlier than the current law of attempts?

The Consultation Paper was followed by a Report (No 318). The recommendations made in relation to the law of attempt were far less ambitious:

ATTEMPTS

9.17 We recommend that the Criminal Attempts Act 1981 be amended to provide that, for the purposes of section 1(1), an intent to commit an offence includes a conditional intent to commit it. **(Recommendation 17, paragraph 8.106)**

9.18 We recommend that for substantive offences which have a circumstance requirement but no corresponding fault requirement, or which have a corresponding fault requirement which is objective (such as negligence), it should be possible to convict D of attempting to commit the substantive offence only if D was subjectively reckless as to the circumstance at the relevant time. **(Recommendation 18, paragraph 8.133)**

9.19 We recommend that where a substantive offence has fault requirements not involving mere negligence (or its equivalent) in relation to a fact or circumstance, it should be possible to convict D of attempting to commit the substantive offence if D possessed those fault requirements at the relevant time. **(Recommendation 19, paragraph 8.137)**

9.20 We recommend that the Criminal Attempts Act 1981 be amended so that D may be convicted of attempted *murder* if (with the intent to kill V) D failed to discharge his or her legal duty to V (where that omission, unchecked, could have resulted in V's death).

14.7 Why have a crime of attempt?

Does the criminal law need a crime of attempt:

   (i)   To allow the investigating agency to intervene before the harm involved in the substantive offence is caused? If so, is the law defined with sufficient clarity to optimize the opportunity for the police to act in a preventative role?

  (ii)   To reflect the moral wrongdoing of one who has tried to commit a crime? Is that moral wrongdoing any less than one who succeeds in the commission of the substantive crime?

Andrew Ashworth, 'Belief and Intent in Criminal Liability' in J. Eekelaar and J. Bell (eds), *Oxford Essays in Jurisprudence* (1987), p 16 asks:

Is A, who shoots at X intending to kill him but misses because X unexpectedly moves, any less culpable than B who shoots at Y intending to kill him and does so? An external description of both sets of events would probably not suggest that they have 'done' the same thing, whereas an account which paid more attention to the actor's point of view and to matters which lay within the actor's control would suggest that they both intended and tried, to the same extent, to do the same thing. The argument here is that, because of the element of uncertainty in the outcome of things which we try to do, it would be wrong for assessments of culpability to depend on the occurrence or non-occurrence of the intended consequences. 'Success or failure . . . makes no difference at all to [an agent's] moral status in relation to his original act. His original act, strictly considered, was simply his trying and that is what moral assessment must concern itself with' (Winch, *Ethics and Action*, 1972, p.139) . . . Moral blame and criminal liability should be based so far as possible on choice and control, on the trying and not what actually happened thereafter. What are the reasons for wishing to reduce the influence of chance upon criminal liability? It cannot be doubted that luck plays a considerable part. Actual results also play a considerable part in judgments of others, and tend to dominate assessments in such fields as business, sport, and education. Those who try hard but are unsuccessful often receive less recognition than those who achieve goals (no matter how little effort they put into it). But these are not moral assessments of the individual and their characters. If one turns to moral and social judgments, it is doubtful whether outcomes should be proper criteria. It may be desirable overall to have fewer bad outcomes and more good outcomes in society, but that does not lead to the conclusion that moral praise and blame should be allocated solely according to result. Indeed, a bad outcome stemming from a good intent may be a better predictor of good outcomes than a good outcome born of a bad intent. From time to time we may praise someone for producing a good result, even though it was not what he was trying to do, but this is more a reflection of our pleasure at the outcome than an assessment of his conduct and character. If we turn to blaming, is it not unacceptable to blame people for causing results irrespective of whether they were caused intentionally, negligently, or purely accidentally? Blaming is a moral activity which is surely only appropriate where the individual had some choice or control over the matter. For this reason the criminal law should seek to minimize the effect of luck upon the incidence and scale of criminal liability.

Compare the view of J. C. Smith, 'The Element of Chance in Criminal Liability' [1971] Crim LR 63:

... great significance is still attached to the harm done, as distinct from the harm intended or foreseen. Perhaps the significance of the harm done derives from our emotional reaction to the acts of others. If one of my small boys, not looking what he is doing, throws a stone which just misses the dining room window, I shall be very cross with him; but if the stone breaks the dining room window, I shall be absolutely furious. His behaviour is just as bad and just as dangerous in the one case as in the other; but my indignation is much greater in the case where he has caused the harm than in that where he has not.

It might fairly be answered that the criminal law should be rational and not based on emotional reactions. Is not this naked retribution—and a very crude form of retribution, the degree of punishment being based not on the moral culpability but on the harm done?

On the other hand, it is certain that the legislator cannot afford to ignore altogether the reactions—even the irrational reactions—of ordinary people, in the interests of logic and consistency. Stephen J., the great criminal law judge of the nineteenth century thought that the gratification of public sentiment was a proper purpose of the criminal law ... He thought there was nothing irrational in basing liability on the harm done:

'If two persons are guilty of the very same act of negligence, and if one of them causes thereby a railway accident, involving the death and mutilation of many persons, whereas the other does no injury to anyone, it seems to me that it would be rather pedantic than rational to say that each had committed the same offence, and should be subjected to the same punishment. In one sense, each has committed an offence, but the one has had the bad luck to cause a horrible misfortune, and to attract public attention to it, and the other the good fortune to do no harm. Both certainly deserve punishment, (*History of the Criminal Law*, Vol. III, pp. 311 et seq.)'

■ *Question*

Would a crime of endangerment offer a partial solution to this problem?

More recently, Gideon Yaffe has based a complex and detailed theory of attempts upon the 'Transfer Principle'.

G. Yaffe, *Attempts*
(2010), p 21

When the legislature defines a crime—when it specifies a punishment for a person shown beyond reasonable doubt to have acted in a certain way in certain circumstances and with certain results—it succeeds in defining a second crime as well, namely the crime of attempting to commit the crime defined. The legislature could choose specifically not to proscribe the attempt to commit a crime defined, but in the absence of an explicit statement to that effect, by defining the crime the legislature grants the state the power to punish also for the attempt. We seem to accept, that is, the following principle: '*If a particular form of conduct is legitimately criminalized, then the attempt to engage in that form of conduct is also legitimately criminalized.*' Call this 'The Transfer Principle', since, under it, the legitimacy of criminalization transfers from completion to attempt. In accepting the Transfer Principle, the criminal law reflects a deeply entrenched principle of moral thought: if you shouldn't do something, then you shouldn't try to do it either. Moral prohibition, like justifiable criminalization, seems to transfer from completion to attempt.

CHAPTER 14. ATTEMPT

Generally, it is through appeal to the Transfer Principle that attempts become crimes. The legislature might have a long debate about whether to pass a law making a certain kind of behavior a crime. But it does not then have a separate debate about whether to criminalize attempts to engage in that kind of behavior. Rather, when the law is passed, the attempt, too, has *ipso facto* become a crime. The Transfer Principle, then, is of great practical importance: it serves as a silent premise in the legislature's reasoning about what to criminalize. As such, it is in need of justification. Why do we think that justifiable criminalization transfers automatically from completed crimes to our efforts to engage in them? The principle is in particularly pressing need of justification, given that the first thing (although not necessarily the only thing) that one would cite in defense of criminalizing many completions—think of murder, rape, or robbery—is the harm that such acts cause. But attempts often cause no harm at all. What, then, justifies the Transfer Principle?

Yaffe goes on to consider two rationales that might justify his 'transfer principle', but rejects them both. The first is based on the intuitively appealing notion that when a type of act is wrong, then so is the attempt of it. Yaffe rejects this argument on the basis that for it to be true, completion and attempt must be equally and equivocally wrong. However, since the law criminalizes both 'last act' and non-last act attempts and an individual who engages in a non-last act attempt can be acting while conceiving of the possibility that he will not go through with his plan, non-last act attempts are not as wrong as completed crimes. The second argument rejected by Yaffe is based on the notion that criminalization of attempts is justified on the basis of risk suppression. There are two facets to this argument, both of which are rejected. It could be said that by trying, but failing, to commit the substantive offence, the defendant has demonstrated that he is dangerous and there is therefore a risk that there will be a completed crime on some later occasion. Alternatively, it could be said that the defendant has risked the completion of the crime on the occasion when he failed. The probability that the crime would be committed is higher given the fact that the defendant has attempted it. Both of these arguments are rejected on the basis that the law does not just criminalize those attempts that created a risk, but it also criminalizes attempts to commit a crime even though there was no possibility that the crime could be committed. Of course, Yaffe is here referring to the fact that the law criminalizes impossible attempts.

The justification Yaffe offers for his 'transfer principle' is that completed crimes and attempts share features that warrant the criminalization of each. He states that, 'both reflect corruption in the modes of recognition and response to legal reasons employed by the actor, and...these modes of recognition and response to reasons play a role in guiding the actor's conduct.' This simply means that D is someone who displays a disregard for the proscriptions of the criminal law. Yaffe assumes that the mens rea elements of a completed crime are indicators of modes of recognition and response to criminal legal reasons of defendants who complete crimes and that the corresponding intention of the person who attempts a crime is an indicator of the same or worse modes.

■ *Questions*

1. Do you find Yaffe's rejection of the risk suppression and moral equivalence justifications compelling?

2. Husak argues that the Transfer Principle cannot solely be descriptive but must be prescriptive also, in that it also influences what the content of the law is. This is because existing law does recognize exceptions to the Transfer Principle. Some offences should not allow attempt liability because this would constitute double or even triple inchoate liability, for example aiding an attempt. Are all instances of double inchoate liability unjustifiable? See D. Husak, 'Why Punish Attempts at All? Yaffe on "The Transfer Principle" (2012) 6 Crim L & Philosophy 399.

FURTHER READING

C. Clarkson, 'General Endangerment Offences: The Way Forward?' (2005) Univ Western Aus Law Rev 131

R. A. Duff, *Criminal Attempts* (1996)

P. Glazebrook, 'Should We Have a Law of Attempted Crime' (1969) 85 LQR 28

J. Horder, 'Varieties of Intention, Criminal Attempts and Endangerment' (1994) 14 LS 335

J. Hornby, 'On What's Intentionally Done' in S. Shute, J. Gardner and J. Horder (eds), *Action and Value in Criminal Law* (1993), p 60

K. J. M. Smith, 'Proximity in Attempt: Lord Lane's Midway Course' [1991] Crim LR 576

J. Stannard, 'Making Up for the Missing Element: A Sideways Look at Attempts' (1987) 7 LS 194

G. R. Sullivan, 'Intent, Subjective Recklessness and Culpability' (1992) 12 OJLS 380

15
Murder

15.1 Introduction

The classic definition of the offence, still in use today, derives from a book from the seventeenth century. That definition provided by Coke is:

> Murder is when a man of sound memory, and of the age of discretion, unlawfully killeth within any county of the realm any reasonable creature *in rerum natura* under the king's peace, with malice aforethought, either expressed by the party or implied by law, [so as the party wounded, or hurt, etc die of the wound or hurt, etc within a year and a day after the same]. (Coke 3 Inst 47)

Attorney-General's Reference (No 3 of 1994)
[1997] UKHL 31, House of Lords, http://www.bailii.org/uk/cases/UKHL/1997/31.html

[Lord Mustill (at 938):]

My Lords, murder is widely thought to be the gravest of crimes. One could expect a developed system to embody a law of murder clear enough to yield an unequivocal result on a given set of facts, a result which conforms with apparent justice and has a sound intellectual base. This is not so in England, where the law of homicide is permeated by anomaly, fiction, misnomer and obsolete reasoning.

The Law Commission has described murder as a 'rickety structure set upon shaky foundations'. Law Commission Consultation Paper No 177, *A New Homicide Act for England and Wales* (2005) (LCCP 177), para 1.4. See section 15.4.1, p 545.

Murder carries a mandatory sentence of life imprisonment; it has the most serious stigma of any offence and yet it is still defined only at common law. It is no surprise then that the Law Commission proposed reform. See LCCP 177 and Law Commission Report No 304, *Murder Manslaughter and Infanticide* (2006) (LC 304), section 15.4.2, p 546. Reform is no easy task. One of the reasons that the offence is so difficult to define satisfactorily is that the offence must deal with some fundamental questions.

The controversies that will be examined in this chapter include the following:

(i)   when does life begin and end for the purposes of the law of murder;

(ii) should an intention to cause really serious harm suffice as the mens rea for murder;

(iii) how might this area of the law be reformed so as to reflect generally recognized principles of the criminal law?

15.2 The actus reus of murder

The actus reus of murder and manslaughter is generally the same. It is the unlawful killing of any person 'under the Queen's Peace'. Each word merits close attention.

> ■ *Question*
> In what circumstances might it be lawful to kill with intention to kill?

15.2.1 Causing death

It must be proved that the defendant caused the death of the deceased person. Most of the problems in relation to causation arise in the context of homicide. The leading cases have been considered in Chapter 3, and reference may be made to these.

In homicide, it is important not to lose sight of the fact that what must be caused is some acceleration of death: everyone must die sooner or later. It follows that every killing is merely an acceleration of death; and it makes no difference for this purpose that the victim is already suffering from a fatal disease or injury or is under sentence of death.

15.2.2 Year and a day rule

At common law, homicide was committed only if the death occurred within a year and a day of the act causing death (see D. Yale, 'A Year and A Day in Homicide' (1989) 48 CLJ 202, and on the reform see Law Commission Consultation Paper No 136, *The Year and a Day Rule in Homicide* (1994) (LCCP 136). That rule was abolished by the Law Reform (Year and a Day Rule) Act 1996. If an act can be shown to be the cause of death, it may now be murder, or any other homicide offence, or suicide, however much time has elapsed between the act and the death. In some cases, for example where three years or more separate D's act and V's death, the consent of the Attorney General is needed to prosecute for murder.

15.2.3 A person 'in being'

The victim of homicide must have been born and not have died before the defendant's act took effect. Although this principle is discussed here exclusively in connection with homicide, it is probably applicable to offences against the person generally.

15.2.3.1 Birth

If the child has 'an existence independent of its mother' it is capable of being murdered. To have such an existence the child must have been wholly expelled from its mother's body and be alive. The cord and afterbirth need not have been expelled from the mother nor severed from the child. The tests of independent existence which the courts have accepted are that the child should have an independent circulation, and that it should have breathed after birth. But there are difficulties about both these tests. There are very few modern cases on the point.

In *Re A (children) (conjoined twins: surgical separation)* [2000] EWCA Civ 254, section 11.5.2, p 406, the court was satisfied that Mary was 'a reasonable creature in being', having an existence independent of her mother, although she was wholly dependent on Jodie for her continued existence. Mary thus came under the protection of the law of murder.

Brooke LJ:

Advances in medical treatment of deformed neonates suggest that the criminal law's protection should be as wide as possible, and a conclusion that a creature in being was not reasonable would be confined only to the most extreme cases of which this is not an example. Whatever might have been thought of as [mere 'monsters'] by Bracton, Coke, Blackstone, Locke and Hobbes, different considerations would apply today. This proposition might be tested in this way: suppose an intruder broke into the hospital and stabbed twin M causing her death. Clearly it could not be said that his actions would be outside the limit of the law of homicide.

Modern English statute law has mitigated the prospective burden that might otherwise fall on the parents of severely handicapped children and their families if they are willing to avail themselves of its protection at any time up to the time the child (or children) is born. [His lordship considered the Abortion Act 1997, s 1(1)(d), as substituted by the Human Fertilisation and Embryology Act 1990, s 37(1), and continued:] Once a seriously handicapped child is born alive, the position changes, and it is as much entitled to the protection of the criminal law as any other human being.

■ *Questions*

Should the status quo be altered? In *Iby* [2005] NSWCCA 178, discussed at [2005] Crim LR 742, the conclusion was that the decision of viability be left largely to the jury.

Is this a sensible suggestion? Will it promote certainty and consistency in the law?

15.2.3.2 Killing or injuring the foetus

There is, predictably, great controversy about defining the point at which a foetus becomes a human or, in this particular context, about defining the point at which the foetus deserves the protection of the criminal law of homicide.

- It is not murder to kill a foetus in the womb or in the process of leaving the womb.
- If the foetus is not capable of being born alive, the offence of destruction under the Offences Against the Person Act 1861 (OAPA), s 58 may have been committed.
- Where the foetus is capable of being born alive and is killed, it is an offence under the Infant Life (Preservation) Act 1929.

■ *Questions*

Should it be murder to destroy a foetus with intent to do so? From what point in gestation? From conception? From the point at which the foetus is *capable* of living an independent existence, that is, is viable?

In *A-G's Reference (No 3 of 1994)* [1997] UKHL 31, section 15.1, p 526, D stabbed his pregnant girlfriend. At that point in time it was not appreciated that the stab wound had penetrated the abdomen of the foetus. D pleaded guilty to the offence of wounding. The girlfriend gave birth to a 'grossly premature' daughter. The stabbing had in fact injured the foetus. The daughter survived for 120 days; her death was attributable to her being grossly premature. The defendant was charged with murder. The trial judge ruled that there could be no conviction for either murder or manslaughter. The Attorney General referred the issue to the Court of Appeal which held that since the foetus was a part of the mother, the defendant's intent to cause at least serious injury to the mother was sufficient to found liability for murder in respect of the child. On appeal to the House of Lords, Lord Mustill regarded the following as established rules:

Lord Mustill:

... 1. it is sufficient to raise a prima facie case of murder (subject to entire or partial excuses such as self-defence or provocation) for it to be proved that the defendant did the act which caused the death intending to kill the victim or to cause him at least grievous bodily harm. Although it will be necessary to look at the reasoning which founded this rule, it is undeniably a part of English law: see *R v Vickers* [1957] 2 All ER 741, [1957] 2 QB 664; *Hyam v DPP* [1974] 2 All ER 41, [1975] AC 55 and *R v Cunningham* [1981] 2 All ER 863, [1982] AC 566. Thus, if M had died as a result of the injuries received B would have been guilty of murdering her, even though in the everyday sense he did not intend her death.

2. If the defendant does an act with the intention of causing a particular kind of harm to X, and unintentionally does that kind of harm to Y, then the intent to harm X may be added to the harm actually done to Y in deciding whether the defendant has committed a crime towards Y. This rule is usually referred to as the doctrine of 'transferred malice', a misleading label but one which is too firmly entrenched to be discarded. Nor would it be possible now to question the rule itself, for although the same handful of authorities are called up repeatedly in the texts they are constantly cited without disapproval ... [See section 2.4.1.1, p 24.]

3. Except under statute an embryo or foetus *in utero* cannot be the victim of a crime of violence. In particular, violence to the foetus which causes its death *in utero* is not a murder. The foundation authority is the definition by Sir Edward Coke of murder by reference to the killing of 'a reasonable creature, in *rerum natura*' (see 3 Co Inst (1680) 50). The proposition was developed by the same writer into examples of prenatal injuries as follows:

> 'If a woman be quick with childe, and by a potion or otherwise killeth it in her wombe; or if a man beat her, whereby the child dieth in her body, and she is delivered of a dead childe; this is a great misprision, and no murder ...'

It is unnecessary to look behind this statement to the earlier authorities, for its correctness as a general principle, as distinct from its application to babies expiring in the course of delivery or very shortly thereafter, has never been controverted. It can, for example, be found in 4 Bl Com (1830) 198, *Stephen Digest of the Criminal Law* (1877) p 138, *Smith and Hogan Criminal Law* (8th edn, 1996) p 338 and in many other places over the years.

4. The existence of an interval of time between the doing of an act by the defendant with the necessary wrongful intent and its impact on the victim in a manner which leads to death does not in itself prevent the intent, the act and the death from together amounting to murder, so long as there is an unbroken causal connection between the act and the death.

5. Violence towards a foetus which results in harm suffered after the baby has been born alive can give rise to criminal responsibility even if the harm would not have been criminal (apart from statute) if it had been suffered *in utero*. Once again, the rule founds on a statement of Coke, following immediately after the passage above quoted:

> '... if the childe be born alive, and dieth of the potion, battery, or other cause, this is murder: for in law it is accounted a reasonable creature, *in rerum natura*, when it is born alive.' (See 3 Co Inst 50.)

This view did not at first command universal acceptance, largely on the practical ground that medical science did not then permit a clear proof of causal connection, but it was adopted in early Victorian times by the *Fourth Report of the Commissioners on Criminal Law* (1839), British Parliamentary Papers (1839) vol 19, pp 235, 266 and the Second Report of the Commissioners for Revising and Consolidating Criminal Law (1846), British Parliamentary Papers (1846) vol 24, pp 107, 127 and never substantially doubted since. In *R v West* (1848) 2 Car & Kir 784, 175 ER 329, a case to which I must briefly return, the rule was extended to a situation such as the present where the assault caused the death, not through injury to the child, but by causing the child to be born prematurely. In *R v Senior* (1832) 1 Mood CC 346, 168 ER 1298 the principle was applied to manslaughter, where death resulted from gross negligence by a midwife before the child had been fully born. Since the principle is not disputed I will not cite the numerous references to it by institutional writers during the past three centuries...

■ *Questions*

1. D intended to stab the girlfriend. He intended to cause her at least GBH. If he had missed and stabbed V standing next to the girlfriend and V had died, would D have been guilty of murder?

2. Should D be guilty of murdering the child which was born and died as a result of the injury D inflicted?

15.2.3.3 Article 2 and the right to life

The European Court of Human Rights (ECtHR) has declined to decide directly whether the foetus is protected by the right to life in Article 2. In *Vo v France* [2004] 2 FCR 577, a doctor negligently caused fatal injury to a viable foetus after mistaking the mother's identity for that of another patient. The French Criminal Court acquitted him on the basis that the foetus was not a human being for the purposes of the offence. On application to the ECtHR, the Court ruled that the issue of life's commencement and its protection by criminal law was within the margin of appreciation extended to the Member States. The Court acknowledged (at [80]) that in:

the circumstances examined to date by the Convention institutions—that is, in the various laws on abortion—the unborn child is not regarded as a 'person' directly protected by Article 2 of the Convention and that if the unborn do have a 'right' to 'life', it is implicitly limited by the mother's rights and interests. The Convention institutions have not, however, ruled out the possibility that in certain circumstances safeguards may be extended to the unborn child... It is also clear from an examination of these cases that the issue has always been determined by weighing up various, and sometimes conflicting, rights or freedoms claimed by a woman, a mother or a father in relation to one another or vis-à-vis an unborn child.

The Grand Chamber of the ECtHR in *A, B and C v Ireland* (2011) 53 EHRR 13 confirmed (at [222]) that:

it was neither desirable nor possible to answer the question of whether the unborn was a person for the purposes of Article 2 of the Convention, so that it would be equally legitimate for a State to choose to consider the unborn to be such a person and to aim to protect that life.

15.2.3.4 Death

Defining the point in time at which life ends so that the person is no longer the subject of the protection of the law of homicide is also difficult.

Criminal Law Revision Committee, Fourteenth Report

37. We have considered whether there should be a statutory definition of death. A memorandum issued by the honorary secretary of the Conference of Medical Royal Colleges and Faculties in the United Kingdom on 15 January 1979 refers to an earlier report of the Conference which expressed their unanimous opinion that 'brain death' could be diagnosed with certainty. The memorandum states that the report published by the Conference has been widely accepted and says that the identification of brain death means that a patient is truly dead, whether or not the function of some organs,

such as a heart beat, is still maintained by artificial means. Brain death is said to be when all the functions of the brain have permanently and irreversibly ceased. We are however extremely hesitant about embodying in a statute (which is not always susceptible of speedy amendment) an expression of present medical opinion and knowledge derived from a field of science which is continually progressing and inevitably altering its opinions in the light of new information. If a statutory definition of death were to be enacted there would, in our opinion, be a risk that further knowledge would cause it to lose the assent of the majority of the medical profession. In that event, far from assisting the medical profession, for example in cases of organ transplants, the definition might be a hindrance to them. Moreover, while there might be agreement that the statutory definition was defective, there might be differences of view about the proper content of any new definition. An additional reason for not recommending a definition of death is that such definition would have wide repercussions outside offences against the person and the criminal law. A legal definition of death would also have to be applicable in the civil law. It would be undesirable to have a statutory definition confined only to offences against the person, which is the extent of our present remit. For these reasons therefore we are not recommending the enactment of a definition of death.

See also *Malcherek* [1981] 2 All ER 422, section 3.2.3.4, p 61.

■ *Question*

The Criminal Law Revision Committee (CLRC) was unwilling to recommend any definition because, to put the matter simply, medical advances cause the goalposts to be shifted. This is, perhaps, a convincing argument against a statutory definition of death. But who defines death in a case where it is relevant?

Airedale NHS Trust v Bland

[1992] UKHL 5, House of Lords, http://www.bailii.org/uk/cases/UKHL/1992/5.html

(Lords Keith of Kinkel, Goff of Chieveley, Lowry, Browne-Wilkinson and Mustill)

B was very seriously injured in the Hillsborough disaster. He suffered irreversible brain damage which left him in a persistent vegetative state. All medical opinion was that there was no hope of recovery or improvement. The Health Authority sought a declaration that it would be lawful to discontinue all life-sustaining treatment including all medical and nutritional support except so as to allow B to die peacefully with the least pain. The House of Lords held that it would be lawful to discontinue the treatment even though in this case there was no consent by B. As the time had come when B had no further interest in being kept alive, the necessity for the treatment had gone and it would not be unlawful to omit to perform what had previously been a duty.

[Lord Keith of Kinkel:]

Where one individual has assumed responsibility for the care of another who cannot look after himself or herself, whether as a medical practitioner or otherwise, that responsibility cannot lawfully be shed unless arrangements are made for the responsibility to be taken over by someone else.... [I]t is of course true that in general it would not be lawful for a medical practitioner who assumed responsibility for the care of the unconscious patient simply to give up treatment in circumstances where continuance of it would confer some benefit on the patient.

See section 4.3.1.1, p 76, for the discussion in relation to failures to keep alive and positive acts terminating life.

The Mental Capacity Act 2005, s 4, deals with the circumstances in which treatment or its withdrawal is in the best interests of the patient. It is stipulated in s 4(5) that where the determination of what is in the best interests of the person relates to life-sustaining treatment, the person making the decision 'must not in considering whether the treatment is in the best interests of the person concerned, be motivated by a desire to bring about his death'.

In its review of the homicide offences, the Law Commission declined to engage in reform of mercy killings and euthanasia, preferring to see that as part of a free-standing review: LC304, para 1.6.

The Court of Appeal reiterated in *Inglis* [2010] EWCA Crim 2637 that mercy killings constitute murder. This is not altered by the benevolent motives for the killing. V was involved in an accident and suffered catastrophic head injuries, which left him in a vegetative state. D, his mother, injected him with a fatal dose of heroin, as she believed she needed to relieve her son of his suffering. Her first attempt at doing this failed and D was charged with attempted murder, but she succeeded on her second attempt and was found guilty of murder. The Lord Chief Justice stated:

37. On any view this case is a tragedy, not only for the appellant, who has lost a precious and loved son, but for the father and brothers of the deceased and the extended family. There is a wider public interest in the case because the issues to which it gives rise are immensely sensitive and difficult, and they have attracted an increasing measure of public interest and concern. Therefore we must underline that the law of murder does not distinguish between murder committed for malevolent reasons and murder motivated by familial love. Subject to well established partial defences, like provocation or diminished responsibility, mercy killing is murder. The offences of which the appellant was convicted, and for which she fell to be sentenced, were attempted murder and murder. The sentence on conviction for murder is mandatory. The judge had no alternative but to order imprisonment for life. He then had to assess the length of the minimum period to be served before the possibility of release from prison on licence could arise for consideration. In making that assessment he was obliged to have regard to the statutory provisions in schedule 21 of the 2003 Act.

38. We must also emphasise that the law does not recognise the concept implicit in the defence statement that [V] was 'already dead in all but a small physical degree'. The fact is that he was alive, a person in being. However brief the time left for him, that life could not lawfully be extinguished. Similarly, however disabled [V] might have been, a disabled life, even a life lived at the extremes of disability, is not one jot less precious than the life of an able-bodied person. [V's] condition made him especially vulnerable, and for that among other reasons, whether or not he might have died within a few months anyway, his life was protected by the law, and no one, not even his mother, could lawfully step in and bring it to a premature conclusion. Until Parliament decides otherwise, the law recognises a distinction between the withdrawal of treatment supporting life, which, subject to stringent conditions, may be lawful, and the active termination of life, which is unlawful.

39. We cannot decide the case on the basis of whichever of the contradictory strands of public opinion in this extremely sensitive area happens to coincide with our own views, assuming that is, that if we had allowed our personal feelings to impinge on our discussions, that there would be any coincidence of views. How the problems of mercy killing, euthanasia, and assisting suicide should be addressed must be decided by Parliament, which, for this purpose at any rate, should be reflective of the conscience of the nation. In this appeal we are constrained to apply the law as we find it to be. We cannot amend it, or ignore it.

■ *Questions*

1. V has been in a serious road traffic accident and his heart has stopped beating. He is in the emergency room at the hospital and the surgeon is about to start working on him. The surgeon is very confident that V will be capable of being revived. A colleague goes outside to tell D, V's wife, the prognosis. D is very disappointed. She hates V. D dashes into the emergency room and stabs V with a scalpel before the surgeons can resuscitate V. Is D guilty of murder? If not, of what?

2. Should there be a partial defence of 'compassionate killing'? See H. Keating and J. Bridgeman, 'Compassionate Killings: The Case for a Partial Defence' (2012) 75 MLR 697.

15.2.4 The Queen's Peace

'Alien enemies' who are actually engaged in hostile operations against the Crown will not be within the Queen's Peace. Their killing will not, therefore, amount to murder: *Page* [1954] 1 QB 170. An argument that an Egyptian national who had been murdered in an Egyptian village by a British soldier serving there was not within the Queen's Peace, was rejected. Killings by armed forces personnel of enemy forces will be criminal if the enemy agents have already surrendered. Note that murder committed by a British citizen outside England can still be tried by English courts: OAPA, s 9. (See further P. Rowe, 'Murder and the Law of War' (1991) 42 NILQ 216.) Note that the civilian criminal law applies to police and armed forces using lethal force on citizens. (See cases discussed on self-defence, in particular see *Clegg* [1995] 1 AC 482.) M. Hirst, 'Murder Under the Queen's Peace' [2008] Crim LR 541, argues that 'The killing must be committed by a person to whom, and in circumstances to which, the English law of murder applies. One could perhaps say, instead, that it must be committed under (or against) the Queen's peace.'

15.3 Mens rea

The mens rea for murder is that D must have malice aforethought, that is, D must have intended to kill or cause grievous bodily harm.

15.3.1 Subjective nature of test

The prosecution have to satisfy the jury so as to make them sure that the accused had the requisite state of mind, whatever it is, when he did the fatal act. This was not always clear. In *DPP v Smith* [1960] 3 All ER 161, [1961] AC 290, D, fearing that V, a police officer, was about to discover stolen goods in his car, drove off at high speed with V clinging on to the bonnet. D drove at increasing speed for 130 yards, during which time his car struck three oncoming vehicles, until V was finally thrown off into the path of another vehicle and killed. Restoring D's conviction for murder, Viscount Kilmuir LC, with whom all their lordships concurred, said (at 167):

> The jury must, of course, in such a case as the present make up their minds on the evidence whether the accused was unlawfully and voluntarily doing something to someone. The unlawful and voluntary act must clearly be aimed at someone in order to eliminate cases of negligence or of careless or dangerous driving. Once, however, the jury are satisfied as to that, it matters not what the accused in fact contemplated as the probable result or whether he ever contemplated at all, provided he was in law responsible and accountable for his actions, that is, was a man capable of forming an intent, not insane within the M'Naghten Rules and not suffering from diminished responsibility. On the assumption that he is so accountable for his actions, the sole question is whether the unlawful and voluntary act was of such a kind that grievous bodily harm was the natural and probable result. The only test available for this is what the ordinary responsible man would, in all the circumstances of the case, have contemplated as the natural and probable result.

Few cases can have attracted such a barrage of hostile criticism from the commentators. It was considered in, though not formally overruled by, *Hyam*, *Moloney* and *Hancock*. Lord Diplock did say in *Hyam* [1974] UKHL 2 that it was wrongly decided, and Lord Bridge in *Moloney* [1984] UKHL 4 and Lord Scarman in *Hancock* [1985] UKHL 9 said that in so far as it laid down an objective test it did not represent the common law. Another view expressed (by Lord Hailsham in *Hyam* among others) was that there was no need to overrule it because its effect had been modified by the Criminal Justice Act 1967, s 8 (section 5.2, p 109). As we have seen, however, s 8, properly construed, does not affect the mens rea required for any crime.

The section is concerned with how intention or foresight must be proved, not when they must be proved.

The issue had to be met, as it were, head on, in *Frankland and Moore* [1987] UKPC 3. The appellants had been convicted on a *Smith* direction on the Isle of Man at a time when the Isle of Man had no provision equivalent to s 8. Since the common law is the same in this matter as the common law of England, it was necessary to decide whether *Smith* correctly stated the common law. It was forthrightly held by five Law Lords that it did not. While decisions of the Privy Council cannot overrule decisions of the House of Lords, it seems safe to assume that the decision in *Smith* is not, and never was, the law of England.

15.3.2 Definition of mens rea for murder

The current law is that the definition of malice aforethought is satisfied by proof of an intention (direct or oblique) to kill or do really serious harm.

The mental element required for the crime of murder, as for the crime of manslaughter, has varied over the centuries. Prior to the Homicide Act 1957, s 1, a person who killed in the course of committing a felony involving violence (eg robbery) was guilty of murder. The abolition of that doctrine of constructive malice must be the starting point of a discussion of the mental element in murder though it tells us more about what the mental element for murder is not than what it is. Section 1 provides:

1. Abolition of 'constructive malice'

(1) Where a person kills another in the course or furtherance of some other offence, the killing shall not amount to murder unless done with the same malice aforethought (express or implied) as is required for a killing to amount to murder when not done in the course or furtherance of another offence.

(2) For the purposes of the foregoing subsection, a killing done in the course or for the purpose of resisting an officer of justice, or of resisting or avoiding or preventing a lawful arrest, or of effecting or assisting an escape or rescue from legal custody, shall be treated as a killing in the course or furtherance of an offence.

The section uses the expression 'malice aforethought' to describe the mens rea of murder. Traditionally the mens rea of murder was always described as malice aforethought but the term is unhelpful: 'malice' does not mean ill will and 'aforethought' tells us no more than that the mens rea must not come as an afterthought. It is simply a label used to refer to those mental states (whatever they are) that suffice for murder.

15.3.3 Intention to kill

Section 1 refers to two kinds of malice aforethought: 'express' and 'implied'. 'Express' malice must be a reference to whatever was considered as express malice at common law. What that was has nowhere been judicially defined nor has there been any explanation of it in the case law since the Homicide Act. What did Parliament (or the draftsman) have in mind when it was enacted that express malice sufficed for murder? The term was used by the institutional writers to denote those whose conduct was intentional. The earlier writers (Hale, Hawkins) did not restrict the term to those who intentionally caused death, but it now appears that the term 'express malice' means 'with intent to kill', and 'implied malice' means 'with intent to do serious bodily harm'.

The leading cases on intention are now *Moloney*, *Hancock* and, particularly, *Woollin*, section 5.2.1 pp 103–113, but the earlier decision of the House of Lords in *Hyam* may still require consideration. D can be liable for murder if he holds an oblique intention to kill or cause serious harm.

Hyam v Director of Public Prosecutions

[1974] UKHL 2, House of Lords, http://www.bailii.org/uk/cases/UKHL/1974/2.html

(Lord Hailsham of St Marylebone LC, Viscount Dilhorne, Lords Diplock, Cross of Chelsea and Kilbrandon)

In the early hours of the morning H set fire to a house after deliberately pouring petrol through the letterbox. Mrs Booth, the householder, and her son escaped alive through a window; Mrs Booth's two daughters died. H's reason for the attack was her jealousy of Mrs Booth and Mrs Booth's relationship with Mr Jones. H claimed to have started the fire only with the intention of frightening Mrs Booth into leaving the neighbourhood, and that she did not intend to cause death or grievous bodily harm.

Lord Hailsham LC: ...

The judge directed the jury:

> 'The prosecution must prove, beyond all reasonable doubt, that the accused intended to (kill or) do serious bodily harm to Mrs Booth, the mother of the deceased girls. If you are satisfied that when the accused set fire to the house she knew that it was highly probable that this would cause (death or) serious bodily harm then the prosecution will have established . . . the necessary intent. It matters not if her motive was, as she says, to frighten Mrs Booth.'

The judge explained that he had put brackets round the words 'kill or' and 'death or' because he advised the jury to concentrate on the intent to do serious bodily harm rather than the intent to kill.

There were other passages in the summing-up to the same effect, but this was the vital passage, and the judge reduced it to writing and caused the jury to retire with it into the jury room. As the case proceeded, it is the only passage in the judge's summing-up to which I need draw attention, and gives rise to the only point which was argued before your Lordships' House. The Court of Appeal [[1973] 3 All ER 842, [1974] QB 99] dismissed the appeal 'not without some reluctance', and, in giving leave to appeal to the House of Lords, certified that it involved the following point of law of general public importance, namely, the question:

> 'Is malice aforethought in the crime of murder established by proof beyond reasonable doubt that when doing the act which led to the death of another the accused knew that it was highly probable that that act would result in death or serious bodily harm?'

[Having rejected the argument that a consequence foreseen as highly probable is intended, Lord Hailsham continued:]

But this, again, does not dispose of the matter. Another way of putting the case for the Crown was that, even if it be conceded that foresight of the probable consequences is not the same thing as intention, it can, nevertheless, be an alternative type of malice aforethought, equally effective as intention to convert an unlawful killing into murder. This view, which is inconsistent with the view that foresight of a high degree of probability is only another way of describing intention, derives some support from the way in which the proposition is put in Stephen's *Digest* where it is said that malice aforethought for the purpose of the law of murder includes a state of mind in which there is:

> 'knowledge that the act which causes death will probably cause the death of, or grievous bodily harm to, some person, whether such person is the person actually killed or not, although such knowledge is accompanied by indifference whether death or grievous bodily harm is caused or not, or by a wish that it may not be caused'.

If this is right, Ackner J's direction can be justified on the grounds that such knowledge is itself a separate species of malice aforethought, and not simply another way of describing intention. . . .

But what are we to say of the state of mind of a defendant who knows that a proposed course of conduct exposes a third party to a serious risk of death or grievous bodily harm, without actually intending those consequences, but nevertheless and without lawful excuse deliberately pursues that course of conduct regardless whether the consequences to his potential victim take place or not? In that case, if my analysis be correct, there is not merely actual foresight of the probable consequences, but actual intention to expose his victim to the risk of those consequences whether they in fact occur or not. Is that intention sufficient to reduce the crime to manslaughter notwithstanding a jury's finding that they are sure that it was the intention with which the act was done? In my opinion, it is not...It is the man's actual state of knowledge and intent which, as in all other cases, determines his criminal responsibility. Nor, for the like reason, does this set up an irrebuttable presumption. It simply proclaims the moral truth that if a man, in full knowledge of the danger involved, and without lawful excuse, deliberately does that which exposes a victim to the risk of the probable grievous bodily harm (in the sense explained) or death, and the victim dies, the perpetrator of the crime is guilty of murder and not manslaughter to the same extent as if he had actually intended the consequence to follow, and irrespective of whether he wishes it. That is because the two types of intention are morally indistinguishable, although factually and logically distinct, and because it is therefore just that they should bear the same consequences to the perpetrator as they have the same consequences for the victim if death ensues.... for the reasons I have given in my opinion the appeal fails and should be dismissed.

[Viscount Dilhorne said that whether or not knowledge that certain consequences are highly probable is to be treated as intent (he was inclined to think it was), it had been established for at least 100 years that such knowledge amounted to malice aforethought. The jury had not been misdirected. Lord Cross took a similar view but was not prepared to decide without further argument whether intention to cause, or foresight of the probability of, serious bodily harm was sufficient. On the footing that *Vickers*, section 15.3.4, was rightly decided, he would dismiss the appeal. Lord Diplock, with whom Lord Kilbrandon agreed, dissenting, held that an intention to do serious bodily harm was not enough. There must be an intention to do an act likely to endanger life (see section 15.3.4, p 538).]

Appeal dismissed

■ *Questions*

1. Is there any life left in *Hyam* if the law is as stated in *Woollin* and, indeed, in *Moloney*?

2. As discussed previously, the jury is left with a considerable degree of moral elbow room in determining whether D intended to kill or cause serious harm. Given the seriousness of the allegation and the consequences of conviction, is such flexibility more, or less, desirable than in other crimes?

A. Norrie, 'After *Woollin*'
[1999] Crim LR 532

There has always been a deep-seated problem in the murder cases because what they have given with one hand, a narrow foresight of virtual certainty test, they have taken back with the other, through a broader foresight of probability approach in the guidelines. The guidelines in *Moloney* proved a Trojan Horse by virtue of which *Hyam* recklessness remained a part of the mens rea of murder. While declaring an orthodox subjectivist principle to be at the core of the law, the appeal courts undercut it by what they said judges should tell juries. It is not surprising, given the passage quoted [in *Woollin*] from *Nedrick*, that the trial judge in *Woollin* instructed his jury according to foresight of virtual certainty one day and according to foresight of substantial risk the next, because *Hancock* and *Shankland* and *Nedrick* sanction both approaches....

In *Woollin*, Lord Steyn declares that the words 'entitled to infer' in the model *Nedrick* direction should be replaced with the clearer 'entitled to find'. Professor Smith applauds the move, but wonders if the change in wording will remove one problem with the original formulation. If indirect intention is a species of intention, then to identify foresight of a virtual certainty in the accused's mind is to identify that she intended the crime. The use of the word 'entitled' however suggests that the jury may so identify intention, but, alternatively may not do so. 'Entitled' is permissive rather than obligatory, so that the formulation 'involves some ambiguity with the hint of the existence of some ineffable, undefinable, notion of intent, locked in the breasts of the jurors' . . .

I have previously argued that the idea of a mysterious gap between the law of intention and a factual finding of foresight of a virtual certainty owed its initial existence to some loose talk in *Moloney* about the place of foresight in the law of indirect intention. Lord Bridge wanted to distinguish recklessness from indirect intention, but he did so by suggesting that 'intend' and 'foresee' 'connote two different states of mind'. What he should have said, to be consistent with his analysis of indirect intention, was that the relevant distinction was between the mental states of 'foresight of a moral certainty' and 'foresight of a consequence within the range of probability'. Having said what he said, however, he then had to deal with the question of how the accused's foresight could be relevant to the law of (indirect) intention. His answer was that it played an evidential role so that indirect intention could be inferred from it. How this was logically possible given Lord Bridge's initial premise was never made clear, but the result of his argument was the idea of a gap between evidence of foresight of moral certainty and the law of indirect intention such that the former may, but need not, lead to a finding (previously an inference) of intention. This idea has remained an idée fixe of the law ever since, despite Professor Smith's best efforts to disabuse the judges of it. . . .

A narrow account of th[e] law makes *Woollin* and *Moloney* manslaughterers, a broad account makes them murderers, but neither the broad nor the narrow account actually captures the moral essence of the judgment that lies behind, but is mediated through, the law. . . .

In *Hyam*, the judges opted for the broad approach, but while the test of foresight of probable or highly probable consequence covered Mrs Hyam, it did not catch the essence of her moral wrongdoing. While 'foresight of a probable consequence of death or serious injury' carries moral information, it is still a relatively neutral way of describing the reckless animus with which Mrs Hyam addressed her victims. Still, unlike 'foresight of moral certainty', the lesser degree of risk enables her conviction. Again the test reflects the desired moral conclusion, but does not embody it. . . .

[T]he broader spirit of *Hyam* has always lurked within the indirect intention cases even when they have denied it, and this is as true of *Woollin* as the others. The case law contains both foresight of virtual certainty and foresight of (high) probability elements precisely because neither approach adequately embodies the moral judgments required by the murder label. For the same reason *mutatis mutandis*, the cases also leave the door ajar to a narrower, direct intention only, interpretation of the law in the manner of *Steane*.

Foresight of virtual certainty, even if it is not 'intention', is a condition precedent to liability; and foreseeing that the result was highly probable is materially different from foreseeing that it was virtually certain. But Professor Norrie's article suggests that the present formula leaves open the possibility of the addition of a further ingredient in the mens rea.

■ *Question*

What is the judge to say if the jury tell him they are unanimous that D foresaw that the result was virtually certain, but are divided as to whether he intended it, and seek guidance as to how they should decide?

The best practical advice to the judge is probably to fudge the issue: 'Members of the jury, intention is an ordinary word of the English language. It is a matter for you, applying your common sense and knowledge of the world.' This tells the jury nothing but it may result in a verdict. Would a more honest instruction to the jury be: 'If, in the light of all the evidence you have heard, you are satisfied D deserves to be convicted of murder, call his state of mind intention and convict. Otherwise acquit him of murder and convict him of manslaughter.' It may be that is how the jury do it anyway. And Professor Norrie's article suggests—in effect—that this may be the right answer.

It is already the law (section 17.3, p 615) in gross negligence that the test is whether the negligence is 'bad enough' to be condemned as criminal. This direction makes sense if it is treated as bad enough to be manslaughter (section 17.3.3, p 628). That approach has long been heavily criticized on the ground that it leaves a question of law to be determined by the jury (cf *Misra* [2004] EWCA Crim 2375, section 17.3.3.1, p 629). But if we are to have a law of manslaughter by gross negligence—and we do—there is probably no other way. There is no logical compulsion for a similar principle in murder; but should it be adopted as a matter of policy where it is not alleged that it was D's purpose to cause death or GBH? Should the judge be required to tell the jury in all such cases—not waiting to be asked: 'If you are sure that D knew the result was virtually certain, then, and only then, are you entitled to convict him of [murder]. But you will do so only if you are sure that, in the light of all the evidence, his conduct in causing death was bad enough to deserve condemnation as murder'?

This would explain the judges' strange reluctance to treat foresight of virtual certainty as intention in murder cases and insist that it is only evidence; but would it be fair to allow this escape route for hard cases where it is not D's purpose to kill, while excluding any escape route for D where death or GBH is his purpose? The mercy killer acts with the purpose of causing death, and his is perhaps the hardest case of all. The surgeons in *Re A (children) (conjoined twins)* were not guilty of murder, not simply because of their impeccable motives, but because the killing of Mary was necessary to defend the life of Jodie or was justified by a more general defence of necessity.

15.3.4 Intention to cause grievous bodily harm

Section 1 of the Homicide Act 1957 tells us not only that express malice suffices for murder but also that implied malice suffices. As with express malice, the reference to implied malice is simply a reference, and an unhelpful one, to whatever was understood to be meant by 'implied malice'. The term was again one frequently used by the institutional writers—East, Coke, Hawkins, Hale, Foster, etc—who gave various interpretations of it.

It is quite clear that s 1(1) abolished the rule that death caused in the course or furtherance of committing a felony—typically, robbery, burglary or rape—was murder. The section also clearly abolished the rule that a killing was murder simply because the death was caused in the circumstances described in s 1(2). Beyond that, the section told us nothing about the meaning of 'malice aforethought'—it remained a question of common law.

R v Vickers
[1957] 2 All ER 741, Court of Criminal Appeal

(Lord Goddard CJ, Hilbery, Byrne, Slade and Devlin JJ)

The appellant broke into the cellar of a shop which was occupied by an old woman of 73, Miss Duckett, intending to steal money. At the shop Miss Duckett carried on a prosperous business of grocer and tobacconist, and she lived alone on the same premises in two rooms above the shop; she was a small woman and the appellant, who lived in lodgings a short distance away, knew that she was deaf. While the appellant was in the cellar, Miss Duckett came down the stairs leading to it and saw the appellant. She asked him what he was doing and came towards him, whereupon the appellant attacked her with his fists and struck her several blows; she fell down. The medical evidence was that Miss Duckett was struck by 10 to 15 blows and was kicked in the face by the appellant, and that death was caused by shock due to general injuries;

the medical evidence was also that the degree of force necessary to inflict the injuries sustained by Miss Duckett would be moderately severe to quite slight force.

The appellant appealed against his conviction for murder, *inter alia*, on the ground that the judge misdirected the jury when he told them that malice aforethought could be implied if the victim was killed by a voluntary act done with the intention of causing grievous bodily harm.

[Lord Goddard CJ delivering the judgment of the court:]

Murder is, of course, killing with malice aforethought and 'malice aforethought' is a term of art. Malice aforethought has always been defined in English law as either an express intention to kill such as could be inferred when a person, having uttered threats against another, produced a lethal weapon and used it on him, or an implied intention to kill, as where the prisoner inflicted grievous bodily harm, that is to say, harmed the victim by a voluntary act intended to harm him and the victim died as the result of that grievous bodily harm. If a person does an act on another which amounts to the infliction of grievous bodily harm he cannot say that he did not intend to go so far. It is put as *malum in se* in the old cases and he must take the consequences. If he intends to inflict grievous bodily harm and that person dies, that has always been held in English law, and was at the time when the Act of 1957 was passed, sufficient to imply the malice aforethought which is a necessary constituent of murder.

It will be observed that s 1 preserves the implied malice as well as express malice and the words 'where a person kills another in the course or furtherance of some other offence' cannot in our opinion refer to the infliction of the grievous bodily harm, if the case which is made against the prisoner is that he killed a person by having assaulted the person with intent to do grievous bodily harm and from the bodily harm which he inflicted that person dies. The furtherance of some other offence must refer to the offence that he was committing or endeavouring to commit other than the killing, otherwise there would be no sense in it. It was always the English law that if death were caused by a person in the course of committing a felony involving violence, that was murder. Therefore, in this particular case it is perfectly clear that the words 'where a person kills another in the course or furtherance of some other offence' must be attributed to the burglary which the appellant was committing. The killing was in the course or furtherance of that burglary. He killed that person in the course of the burglary because he realised that the victim recognised him and he therefore inflicted grievous bodily harm on her, perhaps only intending to render her unconscious, but he did intend to inflict grievous bodily harm by the blows he inflicted on her and by kicking her in the face, of which there was evidence.

Section 1(1) of the Act of 1957 then goes on:

'the killing shall not amount to murder unless done with the same malice aforethought (express or implied) as is required for a killing to amount to murder when not done in the course or furtherance of another offence.'

It would seem clear, therefore, that what the legislature is providing is that where there is a killing, though it may be done in the course or furtherance of another offence, that other offence must be ignored. The other offence is not taken into consideration. What has to be considered are the circumstances of the killing; and if the killing would amount to murder by reason of the express or implied malice then that person is guilty of capital murder. It is not enough that he killed in the course of the felony unless the killing is done in a manner which would amount to murder ignoring the felony which is committed. It seems to the court, therefore, that here you have a case of a burglar attacking a householder to prevent recognition. The householder died as the result of blows inflicted on her—blows or kicks or both—and if s 1 of the Act of 1957 had not been passed there could be no doubt that the man would have been guilty of murder. He is guilty of murder because he has killed a person with the necessary malice aforethought being implied from the fact that he intended to do grievous bodily harm.

I will now briefly refer to the summing-up of Hinchcliffe J, which the court thinks is quite impeccable . . .

The court desires to say quite firmly that in considering the construction of s 1(1), it is impossible to say that the doing of grievous bodily harm is the other offence which is referred to in the first line and a half of the sub-section. It must be shown that independently of the fact that the accused is committing another offence, that the act which caused the death was done with malice aforethought as implied by law. The existence of express or implied malice is expressly preserved by the Act of 1957 and, in our opinion, a perfectly proper direction was given by Hinchcliffe J, to the jury, and accordingly this appeal fails and is dismissed.

Appeal dismissed

There were those who took the view that the rule that intent to cause GBH was the mens rea of murder was a form of constructive malice and that it had been abolished. The argument to this effect was 'dismissed out of hand' in *Vickers*—per Lord Mustill in *A-G's Reference (No 3 of 1994)* [1997] UKHL 31, section 15.1, p 529. The reasoning in *Vickers* was promptly criticized by J. W. C. Turner who pointed out ([1958] Crim LR 15) that causing GBH with intent was a felony under the OAPA, s 18; so s 1(1) could, and he argued, should, be read to say that it is not murder merely because D caused death in the course of causing GBH with intent.

The correctness of *Vickers* was doubted by Lord Diplock, with whom Lord Kilbrandon agreed, in *Hyam*. In an elaborate argument Lord Diplock concluded that D could not be convicted of murder on proof that he had caused death with intent to cause GBH, and, of course, still less if D had merely foreseen GBH as probable or highly probable. He thought that the GBH doctrine in murder was subsumed within constructive malice which had been abolished by the Homicide Act, s 1. Lord Diplock was thus able to conclude that the mens rea of murder was either (i) an intention to kill; or (ii) an intention to cause bodily injury knowing that it is likely to cause death. Looked at as a matter of principle, the views expressed by Lord Diplock in *Hyam* have much to commend them but they do not represent the current law. Lord Hailsham LC and Viscount Dilhorne said that *Vickers* had been correctly decided. That left Lord Cross with a casting vote which he declined to cast, reaching his decision '*on the footing that R v Vickers was rightly decided*' (his lordship's emphasis).

The sufficiency of an intention to cause really serious harm as a mens rea for murder was considered directly by the House of Lords in 1981.

R v Cunningham
[1981] 2 All ER 863, House of Lords

(Lord Hailsham LC, Lords Wilberforce, Simon, Edmund-Davies and Bridge)

The appellant attacked the deceased in a pub and hit him repeatedly with a chair. The deceased died from his injuries. The judge directed the jury that the appellant was guilty of murder if he intended to cause really serious harm. The Court of Appeal dismissed his appeal and he appealed to the House of Lords, relying on the speeches of Lords Diplock and Kilbrandon in *Hyam*, section 15.3.3, p 535.

Lord Hailsham LC:

... The real nerve of Lord Diplock's argument, however, does, as it seems to me, depend on the importance to be attached to the passing in 1803 of Lord Ellenborough's Act (43 Geo 3 c 58) by which, for the first time, wounding with the intent to inflict grievous bodily harm became a felony. This, Lord Diplock believes, rendered it possible to apply the doctrine of 'felony murder' as defined in Stephen's category (c), abolished in 1957, to all cases of felonious wounding, where death actually ensued from the wound. The abolition of 'felony murder' in 1957 was thus seen to enable the judiciary to pursue the mental element in murder behind the curtain imposed on it by the combined effect of the statutory crime of felonious wounding and the doctrine of constructive malice, and so to arrive at a position in which the mental element could be redefined in terms either of an intention to kill, or an intention actually to endanger human life, to correspond with the recommendations of the Fourth Report of Her Majesty's Commissioners on Criminal Law (8th March 1839).

It seems to me, however, that this highly ingenious argument meets with two insuperable difficulties. I accept that it appears to be established that the actual phrase 'grievous bodily harm', if not an actual coinage by Lord Ellenborough's Act, can never be found to have appeared in print before it, though it has subsequently become current coin, and has passed into the general legal jargon of statute law, and the cases decided thereon. But counsel, having diligently carried us through the institutional writers on homicide, starting with Coke, and ending with East, with several citations from the meagre reports available, only succeeded in persuading me at least that, even prior to Lord Ellenborough's Act of 1803, and without the precise label 'grievous bodily harm', the authors and the courts had consistently treated as murder, and therefore unclergiable, any killing with intent to do serious harm, however described, to which the label 'grievous bodily harm', as defined by Viscount Kilmuir LC in *DPP v Smith* [1960] 3 All ER 161 at 171, [1961] AC 290 at 334, reversing the 'murder by pinprick' doctrine arising from *R v Ashman* (1858) 1 F & F 88, 175 ER 638, could properly have been applied. It would be tedious to pursue the citations all in detail. We were referred successively to 3 Co Inst 47–52, 1 Hale PC 424–477, 1 Hawk PC 85–88, 4Bl Com 191–201, Foster's *Discourse on Homicide (Crown Law)* 255–267 and 1 East PC 103, 214–233. But the further we went into these passages the more hopeless appeared to be the view that, irrespective of constructive malice, malice aforethought had ever been limited to the intention to kill or endanger life. On the contrary, these authorities reinforced the conclusion arrived at by Stephen's original Note XIV (in the Sturge edition Note VIII). This is the more striking in that the last few lines of the note demonstrate clearly that the possible combined effect of the felony-murder rule and the existence of a statutory crime of felonious wounding was consciously present to the author's mind.

There is a second difficulty in the way of treating Lord Ellenborough's Act as providing the kind of historical watershed demanded by Lord Diplock's speech and contended for in the instant appeal by the appellant's counsel. This consists in the fact that, though the nineteenth century judges might in theory have employed the felony-murder rule to apply to cases where death ensued in the course of a felonious wounding, they do not appear to have done so in fact. No case was cited where they did so. On the contrary, there appears to be no historical discontinuity between criminal jurisprudence before and after 1803. Stephen never so treated the matter (either in his text, or, except in the last few lines, in his Note XIV). It was not so treated in the Australian case of *La Fontaine v R* (1976) 136 CLR 62 (after *Hyam*, but in a jurisdiction in which the constructive malice rule still applied). It was pointed out by counsel for the Crown that the relevant felony created by Lord Ellenborough's Act was limited to cutting or stabbing and did not extend, for example, to beating, which would effectively have excluded the felony-murder doctrine from many cases where death ensued from an act intended to inflict grievous bodily harm. For myself, I think that there is a logical difficulty not based on this narrow point of construction, which prevented the judges from adopting the principle. Felonious wounding intrinsically involves proof by the prosecution of the requisite intention and therefore gives no added force to the earlier law, if I have correctly interpreted the learning before 1803. The way is thus clear on any view to accept as decisive what I myself had always understood to be the law prior to 1957. This is contained in the statement of Lord Goddard CJ representing the court of five judges in *Vickers* [1957] 2 QB 664 at 670; cf [1957] All ER 741 at 743 [in the previous extract, p 538].

Appeal dismissed

In *A-G's Reference (No 3 of 1994)* [1997] UKHL 31, [1997] Crim LR 829, in *Powell & Daniels and English* [1997] UKHL 57 and in *Woollin* [1998] UKHL 28, [1998] Crim LR 890, HL, Lords Mustill and Steyn criticized what Lord Mustill called the 'conspicuous anomaly', that an intention to cause GBH is the mens rea of murder, as an instance of 'constructive crime'—that is, where the mens rea of a lesser offence is sufficient to ground liability for a greater: 'The fault element does not correspond to the conduct leading to the charge, ie the causing of death. A person is liable to conviction for a more serious crime than he foresaw...' '...a defendant may be convicted of murder who is in no ordinary sense a murderer.'

'Anomaly' implies something irregular or exceptional. In the context of offences against the person, the murder rule is hardly an anomaly. The law of offences against the person abounds in constructive crime—it appears to be the general rule. Under the OAPA, s 20, unlawfully and maliciously inflicting GBH, it is enough that D foresaw some harm, not necessarily grievous harm: *DPP v Parmenter* [1992] UKHL 1. Under s 47, assault occasioning ABH, it is not necessary to prove that D foresaw any harm—the mens rea of common assault, a mere summary offence, is enough.

■ *Questions*

Is it correct to describe the murder rule, as Lord Mustill does, as 'a fiction'? Do we pretend that an intention to cause GBH is an intention to kill? Or is this, and the related rules, simply a matter of policy? But is the policy a sound one? Does it allow the conviction of murder of a person 'who is in no ordinary sense a murderer'?

The Select Committee of the House of Lords on Murder and Life Imprisonment (1989, HL Paper 78-1) stated:

52. Two main criticisms have been made of the present definition of murder. The first is that it is too broad in so far as it requires the conviction of murder of a person who kills, intending to cause serious bodily harm but not to kill and who may not even foresee the possibility of death occurring...

53. The second criticism is that the definition is too narrow in that it does not cover the killer who displays outrageous recklessness; for example the terrorist who kills by an act done with intent to cause fear of death or injury, but does not intend to cause death or serious, or indeed any, bodily harm.

The Committee recommended that the first criticism be met by implementing the definition of murder proposed by the Law Commission (following the CLRC) in the Draft Code. After considering much evidence, including the argument by Lord Goff of Chieveley in favour of the Scottish concept of 'wicked recklessness' ('The Mental Element in the Crime of Murder' (1988) 104 LQR 30, below and the reply by Glanville Williams, 'The Mens Rea for Murder: Leave it Alone' (1989) 105 LQR 387), the Committee concluded that the proper place for reckless killings in English law was in the law of manslaughter. The principle of the Code definition should not be distorted to deal with the reckless terrorist and other wickedly reckless killers, who will in any event be liable to imprisonment for life (para 76).

Robert Goff, 'The Mental Element in the Crime of Murder'
(1988) 104 LQR 30

...I turn from intention to kill to intention to cause grievous bodily harm. In *Hyam* Lord Diplock, in a dissenting speech, suggested that the historical basis for the existence of this alternative form of the mental element in murder was unsound; he considered that, if the defendant did not intend to kill, he 'must have intended or foreseen as a likely consequence of his act that human life would be endangered.' But Lord Diplock's historical interpretation was emphatically rejected by the House of Lords in the later case of *Cunningham*. It is now settled by that case, for the time being at least, that this alternative form of the mental element, i.e. intention to cause grievous bodily harm, does indeed exist in English law, and further that (following a statement to the like effect by Viscount Kilmuir in *Smith*) grievous bodily harm means, quite simply, really serious bodily harm.

But the most serious objections exist to this as a form of the mental element in the crime of murder. The most fundamental objection is that the crime of murder is concerned with unlawful killing of a particularly serious kind; and it seems very strange that a man should be called a murderer even though not only did he not intend to kill the victim, but he may even have intended that he should not die. There are cases known to occur where the defendant does indeed intend not to kill but only to cause serious injury—as, for example, in the case of terrorists who punish traitors from their ranks by 'knee-capping' them—shooting them in the knee with a gun. This they do with a positive intent not to kill but to leave the victim maimed, *pour encourager les autres*. If a man so injured were to die in consequence, perhaps because he contracted an infection from his wound, the man who 'kneecapped' him would, in English law, be held to have murdered him, even though he positively intended not to kill him.

In case the point may be thought to be fanciful, let me give an example from my own practical experience. In certain areas of England there is a horrible practice called 'glassing.' A man takes a pint-size beer glass, knocks the top off on the edge of a table leaving a jagged edge, and then rams the jagged edge into the face of his victim—obviously causing dreadful cuts and scarring to his face. I found myself trying a young man for murder at Nottingham. He had gone out to a local public house with his uncle. They both had too much to drink. Another young man was there, who was regarded as an enemy. 'Glass him!' said the uncle to his nephew, and the boy proceeded to do so. But for some reason—perhaps the victim moved slightly—he caught not his face but the side of his neck, and severed his jugular vein. The victim staggered outside, covered with blood, and died shortly afterwards. The assailant and his uncle were both charged with murder. The facts were beyond dispute. The two defendants were ready to plead guilty to manslaughter; but the prosecution was not prepared to accept the plea, and the trial proceeded on the charge of murder. I summed up to the jury, as was my duty, on the basis that, if the jury were sure that the assailant had intended to kill his victim, or to cause him really serious bodily harm, then they should convict him of murder. The jury acquitted the defendants of murder but convicted them of manslaughter, and I sentenced them accordingly. Now it was plain to me, and must have been plain to the jury, that the assailant did indeed intend to cause the victim really serious bodily harm; yet they could not bring themselves to call him a murderer. This was a feeling with which I entirely sympathised, for the simple reason that, not merely could it never have crossed the assailant's mind that there was any risk of causing death to his victim, but he was horrified when he died. It may interest you to know that a colleague of mine on the English Bench had exactly the same experience in another case involving glassing.

The truth is that, for the reasons I have given, an intent to cause really serious harm should not be of itself sufficient to constitute the mental element in the crime of murder. Considerations such as these have led some law reformers to propose that a gloss should be placed upon this form of mental element. Such was the recommendation of the Criminal Law Revision Committee in its 14th Report (1980), to which I have already referred. I think it right that I should at this stage set out their recommendation in full:

'We therefore conclude that it should be murder:

(a) if a person, with intent to kill, causes death and

(b) if a person causes death by an unlawful act intended to cause serious injury and known by him to involve a risk of causing death.'

In addition, the Committee proposed a third possible category (to meet fears expressed about terrorism) as follows:

'That it should be murder if a person causes death by an unlawful act intended to cause fear (of death or serious injury) and known to the defendant to involve a risk of causing death.'

It is of course with recommendation (b) that we are at present concerned. To me there are two serious objections to this formulation. The first is that it is restricted to cases where there is an intention to cause serious injury. But why is it so limited? If a defendant does an unlawful act known by him to involve the risk of causing death, it would appear that (on this formulation) it is the knowledge of that risk which renders him a murderer. So what of the case where he only intends to cause a slight injury, or indeed no injury at all, but knows that his action involves a risk of causing death? Why should that be any different? For example, a nick in the skin of a haemophiliac could be as dangerous to life as a more serious wound to a normal man. Again, a man may project some missile in the vicinity of another, not intending harm but realising that there is a risk that, if it strikes some vital part, the other man may die; on the Committee's approach, if the victim was so struck, and died, that could not be murder. The for-mulation reeks, therefore, of a gloss upon an old but objectionable formula, rather than being a refor-mulation of the requisite intent. But there is a second objection, that as well as being too narrow (in the sense I have indicated) it is also, in another sense, too wide. The criterion chosen is that the defendant's act is known by him to involve a risk of causing death. But is that enough? For one may recognise a risk, and discount it as unrealistic; one may recognise a risk, and hope to avoid it. If a man does so, should he be called a murderer? For myself, I doubt it. Something more is, I think, required.

The additional suggestion, chosen to meet fears about terrorism, appears to me to be subject to the same objections. Indeed, it leads to the startling consequence that if a terrorist, not intending to cause fear of death or serious injury, but realising that his action involves a risk of causing death, blows up a national monument in order to publicise his cause and thereby kills the night watchman, then that cannot be murder. But I feel that this proposed category should not in any event constitute a separate category; and I also feel that, if one could look deep under the skin of category (b), it might be possible to discern a reformulation which would, on a more satisfactory basis, embrace both category (b) and the additional category designed to deal with terrorist.

> [In Scots law] 'when death results from the perpetration of any serious or dangerous crime, murder may have been committed, although the specific intent to kill be absent. This is so where the crime perpetrated involves either wilful intent to do grave personal injury, or the wilful use of dangerous means implying wicked disregard of consequences to life.'

If this approach is right, then both English and Scots law should abandon intention to cause grievous bodily harm or grave personal injury as constituting of itself a sufficient mental element for the crime of murder, if indeed this be Scots law.

■ *Questions*

Can the GBH rule be defended as (i) reflecting a general principle that the law imposes an obligation on an attacker to take the unforeseen consequences of his actions (J. Horder, 'Two Histories and Four Hidden Principles of Mens Rea' (1997) 113 LQR 9)?

Or (ii) as an appropriate response in cases of death caused by an 'attack' (W. Wilson, 'Murder and the Structure of Homicide' in A. Ashworth and B. Mitchell (eds), *Rethinking English Homicide Law* (2000), pp 44–46)?

15.4 Reform

■ *Question*

Given the difficulty in defining the core elements, should murder and manslaughter be abol-ished and replaced with a crime of unlawful killing?

The Law Commission, in its Report No 290, *Partial Defences to Murder* (2004) urged the Government to permit a review of the law of murder. Part 2 of that Report provided a useful

summary of the defects in the present law: http://lawcommission.justice.gov.uk/docs/lc290_
Partial_Defences_to_Murder.pdf.

The Commission concluded that:

2.74 The present law of murder in England and Wales is a mess. There is both a great need to review the law of murder and every reason to believe that a comprehensive consideration of the offence and the sentencing regime could yield rational and sensible conclusions about a number of issues. These could include the elements which should comprise the substantive offence; what elements, if any, should elevate or reduce the level of culpability; and what should be the appropriate sentencing regime. We recommend that the Law Commission be asked to conduct a review of the law of murder with a view to:

(1) considering the definition of the offence, together with any specific complete or partial defences which may seem appropriate.

(2) considering whether the offence of murder should be further categorised on grounds of aggravation and/or mitigation and if so what those categories should comprise.

(3) in the light of (1) and (2), considering the application of a mandatory life sentence to the offence of murder or to any specific categories of murder.

(4) Examining how each of (1), (2) and (3) may differently be addressed where the offender is a child.

15.4.1 Consultation Paper No 177, A New Homicide Act for England and Wales

The Law Commission published Consultation Paper No 177, which recommended a radical restructuring of the offences.

'First degree murder' (mandatory life penalty):

(1) intentional killing.

'Second degree murder' (discretionary life maximum penalty):

(1) killing where the offender did not intend to kill but did intend to do serious harm.

(2) recklessly indifferent killing, where the offender realised that his or her conduct involved an unjustified risk of killing, but pressed on with that conduct without caring whether or not death would result.

(3) cases in which there is a partial defence to what would otherwise be 'first degree murder'.

'Manslaughter' (fixed term of years maximum penalty):

(1) killing through gross negligence;

(2) killing through an intentional act intended to cause injury or involving recklessness as to causing injury.

'Other offences':

(1) infanticide; complicity in suicide.

Defences reducing 'first degree murder' to 'second degree murder'

(1) provocation (gross provocation or fear of serious violence).

(2) diminished responsibility.

(3) duress (threat of death or of life-threatening injury).

On the Commission's proposals, see: W. Wilson, 'The Structure of Criminal Homicide' [2006] Crim LR 471; A. Norrie, 'Between Orthodox Subjectivism and Moral Contextualism: Intention and the Consultation Paper' [2006] Crim LR 486; G. R. Sullivan, 'Complicity for First Degree Murder and Complicity in an Unlawful Killing' [2006] Crim LR 502; C. Wells and O. Quick, 'Getting Tough with Defences' [2006] Crim LR 514; V. Tadros, 'The Homicide Ladder' (2006) 69 MLR 601; J. Rogers, 'The Law Commission's Proposed Restructuring of Homicide' (2006) 70 J Crim L 223.

15.4.2 Law Commission Report No 304

In its final recommendations in Report No 304, the Law Commission made some significant changes to the provisional proposals. Most significantly, the Law Commission extended the proposed offences:

(1) First degree murder (mandatory life penalty)

    (a) Killing intentionally.

    (b) Killing where there was an intention to do serious injury, coupled with an awareness of a serious risk of causing death.

(2) Second degree murder (discretionary life maximum penalty)

    (a) Killing where the offender intended to do serious injury.

    (b) Killing where the offender intended to cause some injury or a fear or risk of injury, and was aware of a serious risk of causing death.

    (c) Killing in which there is a partial defence to what would otherwise be first degree murder.

(3) Manslaughter (discretionary life maximum penalty)

    (a) Killing through gross negligence as to a risk of causing death.

    (b) Killing through a criminal act:

        (i)   intended to cause injury; or

        (ii) where there was an awareness that the act involved a serious risk of causing injury.

    (c) Participating in a joint criminal venture in the course of which another participant commits first or second degree murder, in circumstances where it should have been obvious that first or second degree murder might be committed by another participant.

J. Horder, 'The Changing Face of the Law of Homicide'
in J. Horder (ed), *Homicide Law in Comparative Perspective* (2008)

2. The Fault Element for First Degree Murder

Under the Commission's proposals, first degree murder will be committed when someone kills intentionally, or kills with an intention to do serious injury, in the awareness that there is a serious risk of causing death. This involves a change from the provisional proposals in the Consultation Paper, where the proposal was that first degree murder should be confined to intentional killing. There was considerable support amongst the Commission's consultees for confining first degree murder (and, hence, the mandatory life sentence) to intentional killing. That said, the Commission decided that to confine it so closely would have meant that some killings morally just as heinous as intentional killings would have escaped categorisation as first degree murder. An example might be the person who tortures his victim in hideous ways over a prolonged period, but the victim dies of a resulting heart attack before the torturer has forced the information from him. In such a case, the desire to continue the application of the torture is inconsistent with an intention to kill through the act of torture, as such, but there are compelling grounds for regarding the torturer as guilty of murder. The torturer has intentionally inflicted serious injury. Further, in cases of prolonged and severe torture he or she is bound to be aware of a serious risk that the victim will die in the course of the torture whether or not the information demanded has yet been revealed. Under the expanded definition of first degree murder the Law Commission is now recommending, the torturer in such cases will therefore be guilty of first degree murder. In more commonplace cases the expanded definition also gives greater reassurance that a charge of first degree murder is appropriate. If, say, D shoots or stabs V in the head or heart, then, in the absence of any special explanation about his intentions, D can readily be found to have had the fault element for first degree murder.

The recommended definition of first degree murder does little more than update the proposal made for reform of the law of murder in England and Wales in the Draft Criminal Code of 1989. What are different are the recommendations for the new middle-tier offence of second degree murder. Second degree murder is made to do a great deal of work under the Commission's recommendations. It functions both as a free-standing offence in two different situations and as the crime to which first degree murder is reduced when a plea of provocation, diminished responsibility or half-completed suicide pact is successful on a first degree murder charge. I shall be concerned here with its function as a free-standing offence.

3. Second Degree Murder: Cases of Intending Serious Injury

The first situation in which second degree murder is committed, as a freestanding offence, is when someone kills having intended to do serious injury, even if they were *un*aware of a serious risk of causing death (compare first degree murder, above). Under the current law, killing in these circumstances is murder. Broadly speaking, that reflects the position in jurisdictions in, or influenced by, the English-speaking world, although in mainland European jurisdictions killing in such circumstances would commonly be a lesser offence. The current position in English law can lead to injustice, because it means that the mandatory sentence of life imprisonment must be passed on someone who may have had no idea that his or her actions might cause death. Such a person should not fall within the highest category of homicide, as is recognised by those jurisdictions that treat it as second degree murder or as some other offence. Under the draft code of 1989, someone who killed having intended to do injury regarded as serious by the jury would have been guilty of manslaughter. The Commission does not now regard this as a satisfactory solution. Manslaughter is widely considered to be an over-broad crime even at it stands. It would have become still wider with the inclusion of killing where there was an intention to do serious injury. This would have been a serious matter, because it is likely that a large proportion of killings currently categorised as murder take place when there is an intention to do serious injury but no intention to kill. Moreover, there are sound moral reasons for thinking that killing with intent to do serious injury should be treated as a crime of murder, even if not as first degree murder. The nature of the harm intentionally done will in many cases mean that the defendant has made death a foreseeable consequence of his or her action. To launch an attack of that severity against another person demonstrates a disregard for the vital interests of others deserving of the label 'murderous', even if it would not be right to regard the crime as one of first degree murder. Liability for second degree murder is justified by the fact that when death occurs, albeit unforeseen, D is not being held responsible for harm done out of all proportion to the harm intended. Consequently, there is no need to add, as the 1878–9 Bill does, the further restriction that the intentional infliction of serious injury must have been for the purpose facilitating the commission of a range of specified offences. The history of such 'felony murder' provisions has not been a happy one although, as indicated above, many jurisdictions have retained them and they have a small band of spirited and ingenious contemporary defenders. Such provisions lead to the drawing of arbitrary distinctions between offenders. They entail secondary litigation, often leading to further complexity and arbitrariness, over the meaning of terms such as 'for the purpose of facilitating'. We are better off without them.

4. Second Degree Murder: Tackling Reckless Killing

Under the Commission's recommendations, the second situation in which second degree murder is committed as a substantive offence will be when D intends to cause some injury, or a fear or risk of injury, in the awareness that he or she is posing a serious risk of causing death. [T]he Commission's recommendation now eschews use of the term 'recklessness'. . . . The first kind of reckless killer meant to fall within second degree murder is (in general terms) the kind regarded under the old law as acting out of malice aforethought, and hence guilty of murder, but currently falling outside the scope of murder because there is no actual intent to kill or to inflict serious injury:

> **Recklessness Case 1**: D injects V with an illegal drug, realising that the drug may amount to an overdose or contain potentially lethal impurities. The drug is an overdose or does contain such impurities, and V dies in consequence.

> **Recklessness Case 2**: D sets fire to V's house where V is asleep, intending to cause V to run in terror from the house, but knowing that V may be killed if he or she does not escape. V fails to escape and is killed.

In both cases, D's potentially harmful act is aimed at V in the knowledge that the act poses a risk of death. Under the Commission's provisional proposals, in both cases D could be regarded as acting with 'reckless indifference'. The question was to be whether D's attitude towards injecting V was 'if this causes V's death, so be it', or 'so what?'.

The second kind of killer meant to be caught by the provisional proposal was one who, without aiming any potentially harmful act at V, none the less acted with such a high degree of recklessness that his or her attitude could be regarded as one of indifference:

> **Recklessness Case 3**: D overloads a lorry with people hoping to obtain entry to Britain illegally. Although (as D knows) there is no way of ensuring that fresh air enters the locked compartments where the people are hidden, D completes a long journey into Britain without stopping to check on the people's condition, in order more quickly to obtain his payment. A number of people in the compartments are suffocated to death.

In this example, likewise, it seems plausible to suppose that D's attitude is 'if death is caused, so be it'. That would make him recklessly indifferent, and hence guilty of second degree murder even though no act of his was aimed at causing injury or the fear or risk of injury. The insistence that a lethal act manifest reckless *indifference*, if it is to amount to second degree murder, was meant to ensure that not all killing by advertent risk-taking became second degree murder:

> **Recklessness Case 4**: D is an electrician. D has installed wiring that he or she knows does not meet official safety standards, because he or she is highly sceptical about the value of the 'officious meddling' involved in setting standards. The poor quality of the wiring leads to V being electrocuted and killed.

In this case, it seems unlikely that D could fairly be said to be manifesting a callous attitude towards potential victims, although his or her conduct is reprehensible and in a basic sense 'reckless'. D's misplaced distrust in officialdom explains his or her actions better than a disregard for the safety of electricity users. D could be found guilty of manslaughter by gross negligence, but should not (at least on these facts) be guilty of second degree murder. Commentators on the Commission's provisional proposals were sharply critical of 'reckless indifference' as a test of liability, principally on the grounds that it was too vague or left too much unstructured discretion to the jury. There would certainly be no improvement on the present law if a whole series of cases had to be taken to the appeal courts to determine meaning of 'reckless indifference'. Consequently, in its final recommendations, the Commission has the reckless indifference term and substituted a test with clearer language, the test of whether D 'intended to cause injury, or a fear or a risk of injury, and was aware of a serious risk of causing death'. The question is whether that test fulfils the same function as the test of reckless indifference. How does it apply to the recklessness cases 1–4 above? In case 1, D can be found guilty of second degree murder under the Law Commission's recommendations because D intended to cause injury (in the shape of the injection) and was aware of a serious risk of causing death.... [T]he Law Commission's recommendations for second degree murder extend to cases in which D intends to cause a *fear or risk* of injury, in the awareness that a serious risk of death is being posed. There is good reason for extending the mental element in this way, and it is illustrated by case 2.... D intended that V should fear injury, and hence D falls within the scope of second degree murder because D was also aware of a serious risk that V might be killed. The Commission further extends the scope of second degree murder... to cover cases where D intends to create a risk of injury, aware that there is a serious risk of causing death. What kinds of cases does this extension cover?

Recklessness Case 5: D intends to play 'Russian roulette' with V. D puts a single bullet into a revolver, spins the barrel and points the gun at V's head while V is not looking. Without checking to see whether the gun will actually fire, D pulls the trigger. The gun goes off, killing V.

Here, D intends to subject V to a risk of injury and is aware that in so doing there is a serious risk of causing V's death. If the Commission's recommendations had stopped short at intending to cause a *fear* of injury, then whether D was guilty of second degree murder in this kind of example would have turned on whether or not V was sufficiently aware of what D was about to do to fear injury. The boundary between homicide offences ought not to turn on such an issue.

The Law Commission's Report on Homicide is also considered in A. Ashworth, 'Principles, Pragmatism and the Law Commission's Recommendations on Homicide Law Reform' [2007] Crim LR 333.

The Law Commission proposals on the redefinition of murder were not all incorporated in the Coroners and Justice Bill 2009 which became the Coroners and Justice Act 2009. The Government decided only to implement the Law Commission's proposed reforms to provocation and diminished responsibility. The other reforms to homicide remain unimplemented. The reformed partial defences to murder are considered in full in Chapter 16.

More recently, in *Homicide and the Politics of Law Reform* (2012) Professor Horder has questioned the aspiration for enacting a fully codified law of homicide in a single statute, preferring more piecemeal reform. He also argues that the citizenry has become dispossessed in debates over reforms of the law of homicide, as the public's opinion has become largely irrelevant in the law reform process. He states that this is especially pernicious in the context of murder and manslaughter as they are forms of 'violative' offence, meaning that they violate the victim him or herself, rather than merely that person's rights. Without consulting the public on the law of homicide, it will lack the necessary moral authority. To combat this, Horder states that any proposals for reform must contain a mechanism whereby the views of the citizenry can be ascertained on a periodic basis. He recommends that the merits of morally controversial legal reforms ought to be automatically subjected to periodic review every 15 to 20 years. Do you think this is a good idea?

FURTHER READING

H. Briggs, *Euthanasia, Death with Dignity and the Law* (2002)

A. du Bois-Pedain, 'The Duty to Preserve Life and its Limits in English Criminal Law' in

J. Horder and D. Baker (eds), *The Sanctity of Life and the Criminal Law* (2013)

B. Mitchell, 'Culpably Indifferent Murder' (1996) 25 Anglo Am LR 64

B. Mitchell, 'Public Perceptions of Homicide and Criminal Justice' (1998) 38 British J Criminology 453

B. Mitchell, 'Further Evidence of the Relationship Between Legal and Public Opinion on the Homicide Law' [2000] Crim LR 814

J. Munby, 'Medicine and the Law of Homicide: A Case for Reform?' (2012) 23 KCLJ 207.

J. Temkin, 'Pre-natal Injury, Homicide and the Draft Criminal Code' (1986) 45 CLJ 414

W. Wilson, 'Murder and the Structure of Homicide' in A. Ashworth and B. Mitchell (eds), *Rethinking English Homicide Law* (2000)

16

Voluntary manslaughter

16.1 Introduction

Manslaughter is a complex crime. Three types traditionally called voluntary manslaughter deal with the situations where the defendant kills with the fault required for murder but, because of the presence of a particular extenuating circumstance recognized by law, the offence is reduced to manslaughter. Three other types—'involuntary manslaughter'—consist of killings committed with a fault element less than that required for murder but recognized by the common law as sufficient to found liability for manslaughter. These are dealt with in the next chapter. The statutory offence of corporate manslaughter was dealt with in Chapter 9.

It should be emphasized that regardless of the categories there is only one offence. Whether the defendant is guilty of the voluntary or the involuntary variety, the verdict is simply manslaughter. The only qualification to this is that, where diminished responsibility has been left to the jury, it is the practice for some judges to invite the jury to inform him when giving their verdict of guilty of manslaughter whether it is on that ground.

A life sentence is mandatory for murder but for manslaughter the maximum is life and there is no minimum. It is an offence which may be committed with a wide variety of culpability and sometimes may be properly dealt with by a fine or a conditional or absolute discharge.

The law in relation to voluntary manslaughter was altered significantly as a result of reforms introduced by the Coroners and Justice Act 2009. The new law has been in force since October 2010. Although this chapter will focus on the new law, at times it will also be necessary to examine what it replaced. This is helpful not only to assist in elucidating the proper interpretation of the new provisions but also to evaluate whether they have achieved the aims intended of them. Three partial defences to murder exist:

(i) where D kills with the mens rea for murder but he has lost his self-control and one of the qualifying triggers is satisfied (governed by ss 54 to 56 of the Coroners and Justice Act 2009)—see section 16.2;

(ii) where D kills with the mens rea for murder but qualifies for the defence of diminished responsibility (under s 52 of the 2009 Act)—see section 16.3, p 577;

(iii) where D kills in pursuance of a suicide pact—see section 16.4, p 588.

16.2 Loss of control

The common law recognized a defence of provocation for centuries. The most authoritative statement of the common law defence was found in *Duffy* [1949] 1 All ER 932 in which Devlin J stated that murder was reduced to manslaughter where D killed with the mens rea for murder provided that at the time of the killing he had been subjected to:

some act, or series of acts, done by the dead man to the accused, which would cause in any reasonable man, and actually causes in the accused, a sudden and temporary loss of self-control, rendering the accused so subject to passion as to make him or her for the moment not master of his mind.

The common law defence was modified by s 3 of the Homicide Act 1957. The three elements of provocation as stipulated in the Act were that if D, when he killed, had the mens rea for murder, he would be guilty of manslaughter if:

(i)   things said or done provoked him;

(ii)   he suffered a sudden and temporary loss of self-control; and

(iii) the provocation was enough to make a reasonable man do as D did (with the reasonable man sharing those of D's characteristics that would affect the gravity of the provocation but not those which affected his ability to exercise self-control).

The defence was extremely controversial. One of the most powerful criticisms made of the defence was that it operated in a discriminatory fashion. Individuals who killed their abusive partners had to adduce evidence that they suffered from a 'sudden and temporary loss of control'. This was often difficult for women to demonstrate. Owing to a relative lack of physical strength, it is uncommon for women to lash out in this way. For example, in *Ahluwalia* [1992] 4 All ER 889 D suffered years of physical and psychological abuse at the hands of V, her husband. After he threatened to beat her again, D waited until V had gone to bed before pouring petrol on him and setting him alight. V died from his injuries six days later. There was evidence that the killing was premeditated. D was convicted of murder. The Court of Appeal mitigated the harshness of the 'sudden and temporary loss of control' requirement by stating that the partial defence could arise as a result of a 'slow burn' reaction rather than an immediate loss of control. Nevertheless, female victims of domestic abuse who killed their abusers were often forced to rely on diminished responsibility to avoid conviction for murder, which many thought unfairly stigmatized them.

The serious problems with the provocation defence prompted calls for reform. Law Commission papers examined numerous options for reform, including abolition of the partial defence altogether. The Law Commission summarized the problems with the defence in Report 290.

Law Commission Report No 290

3.20 There was widespread dissatisfaction among consultees both with the theoretical underpinning of the defence of provocation and with its various component parts. It is not underpinned by any clear rationale. There is widespread agreement that the concept of provocation has become far too loose, so that a judge may be obliged to leave the issue to the jury when the conduct and/or the words in question are trivial. The concept of loss of self-control has proved to be very troublesome. The supposed requirement of a sudden and temporary loss of self-control has given rise to serious problems, especially in the 'slow burn' type of case. There is much controversy about the supposed objective test (that the provocation was enough to make a reasonable person do as the defendant did), which has been interpreted by the majority of the House of Lords in *Smith (Morgan)* in a way that may enable a defendant to rely on personal idiosyncrasies which make him or her more short tempered than other people. . .

3.36 Powerful arguments can be advanced for and against the abolition of provocation as a defence. Abolitionists argue that a person who is sane and who kills another person unlawfully, with the intent required for murder, ought to be guilty of murder however great the provocation may have been. Provocation may be a mitigating circumstance which should be taken into account in passing sentence, but not in defining the offence. Assessing sentence requires a balanced appraisal of all the circumstances of the case (aggravating as well as mitigating), and this is a judicial rather than a jury function.

Not only is it inappropriate that provocation should be singled out among other possible mitigating circumstances as providing a special partial defence, but there are great difficulties in trying to define what may amount to provocation and how serious it has to be in order to amount to a partial defence.

3.37 Those who argue for the retention of some form of provocation defence, whether or not the mandatory sentence is retained, say that there are moral and practical reasons for doing so. Where the defendant's conduct was precipitated by really serious provocation, it is morally right that this should be reflected in the way that society labels and sentences the defendant; and it is desirable that the factual and evaluative question whether the defendant was provoked in that sense should be taken by the jury. A short sentence (or even in some circumstances a non-custodial sentence) for a provoked killing will be more understandable by, and acceptable to, the public if it results from a conviction by a jury of an offence not carrying the title of murder, than a decision by a judge after a conviction for murder. The existence of such a partial defence is justifiable in the law of murder, although there is no similar partial defence to non-fatal offences of violence, not only because the sentence for murder is fixed by law but also because of the unique gravity and stigma attached to murder. The real problem with provocation is not the underlying concept, but the way it has developed. It needs to be reshaped.

For criticism, see R. D. Mackay and B. Mitchell, 'But is this Provocation? Some Thoughts on Law Commission Report No 290' [2005] Crim LR 44.

The final provisions as enacted derive from Law Commission Report No 304, *Murder, Manslaughter and Infanticide* (2006). However, there are significant differences between the Law Commission's recommendations and what was finally enacted in ss 54 to 56 of the Coroners and Justice Act 2009, which states as follows.

Coroners and Justice Act 2009

54. Partial defence to murder: loss of control

(1) Where a person ('D') kills or is a party to the killing of another ('V'), D is not to be convicted of murder if—

   (a) D's acts and omissions in doing or being a party to the killing resulted from D's loss of self-control,

   (b) the loss of self-control had a qualifying trigger, and

   (c) a person of D's sex and age, with a normal degree of tolerance and self restraint and in the circumstances of D, might have reacted in the same or in a similar way to D.

(2) For the purposes of subsection (1)(a), it does not matter whether or not the loss of control was sudden.

(3) In subsection (1)(c) the reference to 'the circumstances of D' is a reference to all of D's circumstances other than those whose only relevance to D's conduct is that they bear on D's general capacity for tolerance or self-restraint.

(4) Subsection (1) does not apply if, in doing or being a party to the killing, D acted in a considered desire for revenge.

(5) On a charge of murder, if sufficient evidence is adduced to raise an issue with respect to the defence under subsection (1), the jury must assume that the defence is satisfied unless the prosecution proves beyond reasonable doubt that it is not.

(6) For the purposes of subsection (5), sufficient evidence is adduced to raise an issue with respect to the defence if evidence is adduced on which, in the opinion of the trial judge, a jury, properly directed, could reasonably conclude that the defence might apply.

(7) A person who, but for this section, would be liable to be convicted of murder is liable instead to be convicted of manslaughter.

55. Meaning of 'qualifying trigger'

(1) This section applies for the purposes of section 54.

(2) A loss of self-control had a qualifying trigger if subsection (3), (4) or (5) applies.

(3) This subsection applies if D's loss of self-control was attributable to D's fear of serious violence from V against D or another identified person.

(4) This subsection applies if D's loss of self-control was attributable to a thing or things done or said (or both) which—

   (a) constituted circumstances of an extremely grave character, and

   (b) caused D to have a justifiable sense of being seriously wronged.

(5) This subsection applies if D's loss of self-control was attributable to a combination of the matters mentioned in subsections (3) and (4).

(6) In determining whether a loss of self-control had a qualifying trigger—

   (a) D's fear of serious violence is to be disregarded to the extent that it was caused by a thing which D incited to be done or said for the purpose of providing an excuse to use violence;

   (b) a sense of being seriously wronged by a thing done or said is not justifiable if D incited the thing to be done or said for the purpose of providing an excuse to use violence;

   (c) the fact that a thing done or said constituted sexual infidelity is to be disregarded.

(7) In this section references to 'D' and 'V' are to be construed in accordance with section 54.

(8) The fact that one party to a killing is by virtue of this section not liable to be convicted of murder does not affect the question whether the killing amounted to murder in the case of any other party to it.

Provocation has thus now been abolished and replaced with loss of control. The partial defence comprises three main elements. There must be:

(1) A loss of self-control (not necessarily sudden).

(2) D's loss of control must have been attributable to one or both of two specified 'qualifying triggers':

   (a) D's fear of serious violence from V against D or another identified person; and/or

   (b) things done or said (or both) which:

   (i)   constitute circumstances of an extremely grave character, and
   (ii) cause D to have a justifiable sense of being seriously wronged.

(3) A person of D's sex and age, with a normal degree of tolerance and self-restraint and in the circumstances of D, might have reacted in the same or a similar way to D.

Each of these elements will be examined in turn, in addition to some other features of the defence.

16.2.1 No considered desire for revenge

The best place to start when considering loss of control is s 54(4) which states:

(4) Subsection (1) does not apply if, in doing or being a party to the killing, D acted in a considered desire for revenge.

Even if all the other elements of the defence are otherwise present, the defence cannot apply if D acted in a considered desire to revenge. In *Clinton* [2012] EWCA Crim 2 (discussed more fully in section 16.2.6.2), Lord Judge CJ observed that the greater the level of deliberation, the less likely it will be that the killing followed a true loss of self-control. The Lord Chief Justice explained:

> 10. In the broad context of the legislative structure, there does not appear to be very much room for any 'considered' deliberation. In reality, the greater the level of deliberation, the less likely it will be that the killing followed a true loss of self control.

However, there is no guidance in the statute as to what is meant by 'considered'. To illustrate the difficulty in identifying whether there is a considered desire for revenge when D has lost control, it is useful to consider examples from the old law. There was held to be sufficient evidence of provocation to go to the jury in *Thornton* [1992] 1 All ER 306 where a wife had previously declared an intention to kill her brutally abusive husband, and after a fresh provocation she went to the kitchen, took and sharpened a carving knife and returned to another room where she fatally stabbed him. Is that a considered desire for revenge? Similarly, under the old law, in *Pearson* [1992] Crim LR 193, although DD had armed themselves in advance with the fatal weapon and the killing was a joint enterprise, provocation was left. Is arming oneself evidence of a considered desire for revenge? In *Baillie* [1995] Crim LR 739, where D, being greatly enraged, fetched a gun from an attic and drove his car to V's house (stopping for petrol on the way) before shooting him, provocation was also left to the jury. Would this be regarded as a considered desire for revenge? Although there is no guidance in the Act as to what is meant by 'considered desire for revenge', the minister did state the following:

> the expression 'considered desire for revenge' achieves the right balance in ensuring that thought-out revenge killings are excluded without automatically barring every case where revenge may be part of a complex range of motivations.

■ *Question*

Does the inclusion of this restriction have the potential to undermine one of the aims in replacing provocation with loss of control, namely to ensure that women who are the victims of domestic abuse can plead loss of control if they kill their abusers. Would the defendant in *Ahluwalia* have been able to plead loss of control?

16.2.2 A loss of control

This element of the defence marks a significant departure from the Law Commission's proposals. The Law Commission had proposed abandoning the requirement that there be a loss of control. This was ultimately rejected by the Government. It was feared that omitting the requirement that D killed as a result of a loss of control would result in those who committed so-called 'honour' and gang-related killings would be able to avoid liability for murder by successfully pleading loss of control. As will be seen, there are those who argue that the reintroduction of this requirement has undermined the aims of the defence and rendered it conceptually incoherent. Although this element of loss of control is similar to provocation, it differs in that s 54(2) explicitly states that:

> (2) For the purposes of subsection (1)(a), it does not matter whether or not the loss of control was sudden.

However, it might be wondered how the jury will be able to determine whether D in fact lost her self-control if her reaction was not sudden. Indeed, Edwards argues that habituated gender thinking will continue to impress on the construction of this, as well as other, elements of the defence. Given that anger is typically regarded as signifying that someone has lost his or her self-control, the jury might be inclined to believe that D was acting out of a considered desire for revenge if her reaction does not conform to this societal stereotype. It is argued that this has the potential to undermine one of the central aims of the new defence. See S. Edwards, 'Loss of Self-Control: Why His Anger is Worth More Than Her Fear' in A. Reed and M. Bohlander (eds), *Loss of Control and Diminished Responsibility: Domestic, Comparative and International Perspectives* (2011).

In *Dawes* [2013] EWCA Crim 322 in a series of three conjoined appeals, the Court of Appeal sought to clarify a number of points in relation to the loss of control defence. Two of the appeals concerned the refusal to leave loss of control to the jury. In the third case the appellant argued that the judge had failed adequately to direct the jury fully as to loss of control and that his summing-up failed to deal with both sides fairly. Dawes was alleged to have stabbed a man in the neck having found him with D's wife on their sofa in the early hours (D claimed to be acting in self-defence). The second appellant, Hatter, stabbed his partner in the neck and claimed to have done so in a bizarre accident—the evidence was he had taken the knife to the scene and was angry as she was about to leave him. The third appellant, Bowyer, burgled a house and tortured and killed the occupant (a man he was competing with for the affections of a local prostitute).

The Lord Chief Justice stated that whether there was a loss of control is a question of the subjective state of mind of D. His lordship went on to observe that:

> Provided there was a loss of control, it does not matter whether the loss was sudden or not. A reaction to circumstances of extreme gravity may be delayed. Different individuals in different situations do not react identically, nor respond immediately. Thus for the purposes of the new defence, the loss of control may follow from the cumulative impact of earlier events. For the purposes of this first ingredient, the response to what used to be described as 'cumulative provocation' requires consideration in the same way as it does in relation to cases in which the loss of control is said to have arisen suddenly. Given the changed description of this defence, perhaps 'cumulative impact' is the better phrase to describe this particular feature of the first requirement.

Dawes was relied upon recently in *Jewell* [2014] EWCA Crim 414.

■ *Questions*

1. Does this explanation help? If the members of the jury assume they know what a loss of control looks like, and this assumption is based upon the male stereotype, might they be inclined to find that D's act was one of premeditated murder if her reaction does not conform to this stereotype?

2. Carol Withey suggests that if a loss of control is deemed to be central to the defence, then it would have been better to formulate a separate defence for domestic abuse cases where there would be no loss of control requirement. Do you agree? See C. Withey, 'Loss of Control, Loss of Opportunity?' [2011] Crim LR 263.

It has also been argued that the requirement that there be a loss of control has rendered the defence conceptually incoherent. Remember that the Government decided to retain the Law Commission's proposals in relation to the qualifying triggers but then also added the loss of control element. The following extract explains how this came about and also what the implications might be from a philosophical perspective.

A. Norrie, 'The Coroners and Justice Act 2009—Partial Defences to Murder (1) Loss of Control'
[2010] Crim LR 275

Loss of Control

The story of the law's reform away from and then back to loss of control is slightly complex. It begins with a concern of the Law Commission to exclude unmeritorious cases while admitting others. The problem was to permit the inclusion of, say, the abused woman who kills, but who acts with some apparent degree of premeditation, and to exclude other cases such as those of 'honour killing' or a case like *Baillie*, in both of which there is a strong motive of revenge. In light of this worry about the unworthy case of revenge creeping in under cover of the moral approach, the Law Commission proposed what became s.54(4) on 'considered desire for revenge', but also considered alternatives to strengthen the position, including that the defendant should have acted out of 'extreme emotional disturbance' or 'immediately' following the provocation.

The problem was that a person should be able to claim the defence who has acted out of a justifiable sense of being seriously wronged, in response to a grave provocation, but not in a situation where they have converted their justifiable anger into a cold calculation for revenge. What is required is that the person act out of anger 'in the moment'. The example of honour killing is slightly beside the point here, because it would be excluded on the basis that there was no justifiable sense of being seriously wronged. *Baillie* is perhaps nearer the mark, where the defendant drove to a drug dealer's house and killed him, acting as 'self-appointed judge, jury and executioner'. The Law Commission accordingly, in addition to the no 'considered desire for revenge' requirement, sought a marker for the 'in the moment' nature of the anger. This could be indicated either by a defendant's 'extreme emotional disturbance', or by immediacy in point of time between the provocation and response. The former would, however, add a different, jarring, element to the new moral basis for the defence. As well as acting out of justified anger, one would need to be emotionally disturbed. This involved bringing loss of self-control back into the picture, and was therefore inconsistent with the new rationale of the defence as stated by the Commission. The latter was perhaps more promising, since it linked the reaction to the time when 'the blood was up'. However, the problem with this approach was that it was thought that it could not apply equally to the fear trigger—why is not stated, but it may be that there was a worry that in the case of the abused woman, bringing in an immediacy requirement would undermine the core idea that the partial defence could be used in cases of non-imminence or improper pre-emption. Still, one might have thought that the clear stipulation that the person not have acted out of considered revenge would have been enough to indicate the moral scope of the new law in relation to either the anger or fear triggers, and this was in fact where the Law Commission left the matter.

Not so with the Government. When we come to the new law, we find that it is concerned that there is a risk of the partial defence being used inappropriately, in honour killing and also gang-related cases, and even in appropriate cases such as those of the abused woman who kills. Even there, there,

> 'is still a fundamental problem . . . where a defendant has killed while basically in full possession of his or her senses, even if he or she is frightened . . .'.

At this point, the Government jumps tracks on the Law Commission's approach, for under it, the angry or fearful defendant *is* in control of their senses, albeit acting out of anger or fear. The Law Commission relied on judges and juries (in terms of ss.54(4) and (6)) to distinguish acting out of justified anger or serious fear from killing in cold-blooded revenge, but it opened the door to this departure from its proposals by acknowledging that the stipulation against revenge might be insufficient. If it is right that the immediacy requirement was rejected because it would counteract the fear trigger in cases of pre-emptive violence, that only left 'extreme emotional disturbance' as a means of checking revengeful violence. That however, as I have said, is only a hop and a skip away from loss of self-control. Hence, the Government, picking up the Law Commission's hesitancy, reintroduced loss of self-control into the defence, and, indeed, even called it that.

What will be the practical effect of this change? We need to consider its impact on the two modes of provocation under the new and old law. The first is imperfect justification. Here, the defendant acts out of fear of serious violence or where something that has been said or done is extremely grave and causes a justifiable sense of being seriously wronged. These are the qualifying triggers which permit, under the new law, a loss of self-control. That loss, however, must not be in conditions where the defendant acted from a considered desire for revenge. In addition, that person must have lost their self-control, though this need not be 'sudden'. What does this add to the law? On the one hand, it may make no substantial difference to an actual case, since it might be thought that any person who kills out of anger *must*, at some level, have lost their self-control— why else would they have killed? That the killing could not take place out of revenge already means that that problem is covered. A loss of self-control may just become another way for the jury to test that the person did not act in revenge. On the other hand, however, the idea of loss of self-control must have some substance, and though the removal of the 'sudden' requirement may help where the defendant's provoked reaction is delayed or gradual, there can now still be an argument as to whether there was a loss of self-control. In the case of the abused woman who acts after a time delay, will this not take the law back into disputes about whether there was a loss of self-control, and from there, into questions of suddenness, for, it might be thought, a test for and constitutive feature of any loss of self control in anger is that it have an element of suddenness? How else does one identify a loss of control, except as a moment of departure from being in control? The concern may be that, with both the anger and the fear triggers, the reintroduced requirement for loss of control will work against the new understanding that killing out of anger or fear represents a form of imperfectly justified action. Now, as well as a legitimately grounded sense of anger or fear, the defendant must also show a loss of self-control. Will that not work against the core logic of the new defence? Will it return defendants to the difficulty in pleading both reasonable self defence and a mitigatory defence based on loss of control?

■ *Questions*

Was it a mistake for the Government to include the requirement that D must have lost self-control? What might this element have been replaced with? Consider the following extract and evaluate whether 'provoked extreme emotional disturbance' would be preferable to loss of self-control.

B. Mitchell, 'Years of Provocation, Followed by a Loss of Control'
in L. Zedner and J. Roberts (eds), *Principles and Values in Criminal Law and Criminal Justice: Essays in Honour of Andrew Ashworth* (2012)

The loss of self-control requirement

At the heart of the new law there remains the need for a loss of self-control, and it is difficult to avoid the conclusion that this will necessarily prevent much of the reform and improvement in the law which had been sought. The Law Commission was worried that a loss of self-control requirement would inevitably favour men over women and thought that there was no overriding need to replace it with some other form of subjective requirement; rather, it would be sufficient to stipulate that the provocation had not been triggered by a considered desire for revenge, that the defendant should not have 'engineered' or incited it, and that either judges could exclude undeserving cases or that juries could be trusted to do so. Ashworth though criticized that Commission's approach [see A. Ashworth, *Principles of Criminal Law* (2009)] on theoretical rather than practical grounds—it 'seeks to detach the provocation defence from one of its true rationales, which is that a good reason for partially excusing such defendants is that they acted during a distinct emotional disturbance resulting from what was done to them'. Ashworth's concern is not with the proposal to abolish the loss of self-control requirement but with the suggestion that there should be nothing put in its place. Interestingly, Horder had earlier floated the idea [see J. Horder, 'Reshaping the Subjective Element in the Provocation Defence' (2005) 25 OJLS 123] of what he called 'provoked extreme emotional disturbance' as a substitute for the subjective requirement. Indeed various alternatives to the loss of self-control element have been offered, some of which also seek to put emotional disturbance at the core of the subjective test. Such suggestions have been criticized for their uncertainty. Regrettably, though, the government's preferred condition, that there must be a loss of self-control, remains undefined and vague and there is no apparent reason to assume that the case law on it will be any more consistent that it was under the old common law.

...

The paradigmatic provocation case under the old common law was based on the idea that the defendant 'exploded' with anger (and lashed out with fatal violence), and the anger then subsided. But whether the new law will be noticeably different in this respect from the common law is open to doubt. It has already been suggested that this distinction between the old and the new law ought not in fact to make much difference. A loss of self-control can only occur 'as a moment of departure from being in control'. Moreover, the decision to admit evidence of cumulative provocation over a lengthy period, so as to provide the context in which the final incident (which may have been relatively trivial) occurred, effectively undermined the element of suddenness. Conversely, as has already been indicated, the new plea will automatically fail if the defendant acted in a considered desire for revenge, and the longer the time gap between the trigger and the fatal assault, the greater is the risk that the court will infer that the killing was vengeful.

Thus it has elsewhere been suggested that rather than focus on the physical nature of the defendant's reaction, the law should concentrate on the impact of the trigger (provocation) on his mind—after all, the defendant receives and processes the trigger in his mind; the physical response flows from that and is merely (ambiguous) evidence of the impact of the trigger. Arguably, therefore, the law should instead put some form of mental or emotional disturbance at the heart of the plea. One consequence of this would be the avoidance of the problem in both the old and the new law satisfactorily reconciling the loss of self-control requirement with acceptance of a time lapse before the fatal assault.

As has already been pointed out, whether there was a loss of control is a subjective question. However, in *Dawes* the Lord Chief Justice made the following observation which could be interpreted as injecting an element of objectivity into the first stage of the defence. Might this have the potential to make it more difficult for women who are the victims of domestic abuse to plead the defence?

For the individual with normal capacity of self-restraint and tolerance, unless the circumstances are extremely grave, normal irritation, and even serious anger do not often cross the threshold into loss of control.

16.2.3 The qualifying triggers

There are two potential qualifying triggers and the statute makes clear that D can rely on them individually or in combination.

(i) D's *fear of serious violence* from V against D or another identified person and/or

(ii) *things done or said* (or both) which:

(a) constitute circumstances of an *extremely grave character*, and

(b) cause D to have a justifiable sense of being seriously wronged.

The words 'attributable to' connote a causal requirement, however the statute does not provide any further clarification on this issue. As a preliminary matter of interpretation, it is important to bear in mind that Lord Judge CJ in *Dawes* [2013] EWCA Crim 322 stated that the circumstances in which the qualifying triggers will apply is much narrower than under the equivalent provisions in the former defence of provocation. Also, in *Clinton* [2012] EWCA Crim 2, it was held that each of the elements in the respective qualifying triggers requires objective evaluation.

16.2.4 Qualifying trigger 1: D's fear of serious violence

The inclusion of this qualifying trigger was one of the Law Commission's proposals and marks a significant departure from the old law. The purpose of including this element of the defence was for the benefit of women who suffer domestic abuse and kill their abuser. Section 55(3) provides:

> This subsection applies if D's loss of self-control was attributable to D's fear of serious violence from V against D or another identified person.

It is important to appreciate at the outset the constraints placed upon this qualifying trigger. D must fear *serious violence* from the individual he then goes on to kill. It will not suffice if she fears anything less than this. The fear of serious violence must be against D himself or an *identified* third party. Thus D will not be able to establish the existence of this trigger if he fears serious violence from V against an amorphous class of people. Finally, the fear must emanate from V, no one else.

This first limb may be one relied on well beyond the domestic violence setting, including in cases of householders who kill using excessive force and those who kill using excessive force in bar brawls. There is scope for the defence to be used in a very broad range of killings that are currently classed as murder and which previously attracted no defence. For example, D who stabs V in a fight in the pub might claim that he stabbed V having feared that V was going to stab him first. Even if D has used excessive force given the threat he thought he faced, and even if D has made an unreasonable mistake about the need for any force at all, he will, if the jury believe his story may be true and that he lost control, be convicted only of manslaughter. This is a significant change in the law.

It is also necessary to appreciate that this element of the defence encroaches upon the territory normally occupied by self-defence. See Chapter 11. There are, however, important distinction between loss of control and self-defence.

- loss of control is only available on a charge of murder, whether as a principal or secondary participant. Self-defence is available as a defence to any charge;

- if D successfully pleads self-defence it leads to a full acquittal, whereas if D successfully pleads loss of control his liability is merely reduced from murder to manslaughter;

- self-defence is available if D believes in a threat to him or others of *any* violence. Loss of control is only available if D believes himself or an identified other to be at risk of *serious* violence;

- if the degree of force used by D is, viewed objectively, excessive, that will deprive D of a defence of self-defence, but will not automatically deprive D of this defence. This is because it suffices if a person with a normal degree of tolerance and self-restraint *might* have acted in the same or a similar way as D did;

- if D seeks to plead self-defence, he must be reacting to an imminent attack. Imminence is not necessary with loss of control, provided that there is a fear of serious violence.

In *Dawes* [2013] EWCA Crim 322, the Lord Chief Justice observed that:

59. The loss of control defence is not self-defence, but there will often be a factual overlap between them. It will be argued on the defendant's behalf that the violence which resulted in the death of the deceased was, on grounds of self-defence, not unlawful. This defence is now governed by s.76 of the Criminal Justice and Immigration Act 2008. In the context of violence used by the defendant there are obvious differences between the two defences and they should not be elided. These are summarised in *Smith and Hogan, 13th Edition*, at p 135. The circumstances in which the defendant, who has lost control of himself, will nevertheless be able to argue that he used reasonable force in response to the violence he feared, or to which he was subjected, are likely to be limited. But even if the defendant may have lost his self-control, provided his violent response in self-defence was not unreasonable in the circumstances, he would be entitled to rely on self defence as a complete defence. S.55(3) is focussed on the defendant's fear of *serious* violence. We underline the distinction between the terms of the qualifying trigger in the context of loss of control with self-defence, which is concerned with the threat of violence in any form. Obviously, if the defendant genuinely fears serious violence then, in the context of self-defence, his own response may legitimately be more extreme. Weighing these considerations, it is likely that in the forensic process those acting for the defendant will advance self-defence as a complete answer to the murder charge, and on occasions, make little or nothing of the defendant's response in the context of the loss of control defence. As we have already indicated, the decision taken on forensic grounds (whether the judge believes it to be wise or not) is not binding on the judge and, provided the statutory conditions obtain, loss of control should be left to the jury. Almost always, we suggest, the practical course, if the defence is to be left, is to leave it for the consideration of the jury after it has rejected self-defence.

In addition to the potential confusion between this qualifying trigger and self-defence, there are a significant number of ambiguities in the legislation itself. For example, what constitutes 'serious violence'? Does psychological abuse fall within this category? Further, must the fear be a reasonable one, or does it suffice that it is genuinely held? For example, what of D who hears her husband coming home from work and putting his key in the front door, signalling to D that further physical abuse is potentially imminent? To anyone not in D's situation, it would be perceived as an overreaction if she then goes on to lose her self-control and kill V. However, it could be argued that D has a heightened perception of her future safety that is incomprehensible to someone who has not been the victim of domestic abuse. See S. Edwards, 'Loss of Self-Control: Why His Anger is Worth More Than Her Fear' in A. Reed and M. Bohlander (eds), *Loss of Control and Diminished Responsibility: Domestic, Comparative and International Perspectives* (2011).

When considering the relationship between this qualifying trigger and s 55(6)(a), it should be borne in mind what Lord Judge CJ stated in *Dawes*, namely that an individual who is out to incite violence would be unlikely to 'fear' serious violence and if this is the case the trigger will not be present. This restriction is considered in section 16.2.6.

16.2.5 Qualifying trigger 2: things said or done...

This qualifying trigger bears the closest resemblance to the old law of provocation, however there are a number of differences. Section 55(4) provides:

(4) This subsection applies if D's loss of self-control was attributable to a thing or things done or said (or both) which—

(a) constituted circumstances of an extremely grave character, and

(b) caused D to have a justifiable sense of being seriously wronged.

D must raise evidence both that the thing done or said constituted circumstances of an extremely grave character *and* that they caused D to have a justifiable sense of being seriously wronged. Although it was intended that victims of domestic abuse would primarily rely on the fear of serious violence qualifying trigger, it has been suggested that they ought to rely on this trigger. If domestic abuse is understood as a form of coercive control and a breach of trust, then why should victims not rely on this qualifying trigger? See J. Herring, 'The Serious Wrong of Domestic Abuse and the Loss of Control Defence' in A. Reed and M. Bohlander (eds), *Loss of Control and Diminished Responsibility: Domestic, Comparative and International Perspectives* (2011).

At the outset it is important to point out that there must be a thing said or done by someone; mere circumstances, such as a traffic jam, will not suffice. In this respect the new defence mirrors the old. Under the 1957 Act the source of the provocation was limited to acts of human agency. This limitation is open to criticism. For example, Mitchell cogently argues that the insistence that the loss of control stems from human conduct makes the resultant killing resemble a form of revenge and so undermines the justificatory aspect of it. See B. Mitchell, 'Loss of Self Control Under the Coroners and Justice Act 2009: Oh No!' in A. Reed and M. Bohlander (eds), *Loss of Control and Diminished Responsibility: Domestic, Comparative and International Perspectives* (2011).

16.2.5.1 'circumstances of an extremely grave character'

For the purposes of this second qualifying trigger, the threshold is that that things said and/or done must constitute circumstances of an 'extremely grave character.' The intention is to restrict the scope of the defence. This element renders the defence much narrower than the previous law. It is intended to be an objective test but in assessing the gravity of the situation some subjective assessment of D's circumstances may be relevant. As Lord Judge commented in *Clinton* [2012] EWCA Crim 2:

> the question whether the circumstances were extremely grave and whether the defendants sense of grievance was justifiable require objective evaluation.

This was reiterated in *Dawes* [2013] EWCA Crim 322, in which the Lord Chief Justice stated that whether a circumstance is of an *extremely* grave character and that it leads to a *justifiable* sense of being seriously wronged requires objective assessment by the judge at the end of the evidence. The existence of a qualifying trigger is *not* defined solely on the defendant's say so.

16.2.5.2 'justifiable sense of being seriously wronged'

The defendant must have been caused by the things done or said to have a 'justifiable sense of being seriously wronged'. This obviously imports an objective evaluation of the thing said or done and is intended significantly to limit the scope of the defence. As an example of how this aspect of the defence might work, consider some scenarios from the old law. In *Doughty* (1986) 83 Cr App R 319 it was assumed that the crying of a newborn baby could constitute a provocative act. D was thus able to escape liability for murder when he suffocated the baby to get it to stop crying. Under the new law, even if it was accepted that the baby's incessant crying constituted circumstances of an extremely grave character, the jury would not find that it caused D to have a justifiable sense of being seriously wronged. In *Mohammed* [2005] EWCA Crim 1880, D sought unsuccessfully to plead provocation when he killed his unmarried daughter after finding her having sex, which was against his religious beliefs. This would clearly not fall within this limb of the defence as it could not cause D to have a justifiable sense of being seriously wronged. Although D may argue that he felt seriously wronged, such is not sufficient to establish that this is justified.

Once again, this aspect of the defence contains a number of ambiguities. For example, must the things said or done be directed at D or does it suffice that they are directed at a third party and cause D to have a justifiable sense of being seriously wronged?

16.2.6 Other limitations on the defences

16.2.6.1 No defence if either trigger is self-induced

Section 55(6) places constraints on what can constitute a qualifying trigger. The first constraint is contained in s 55(6)(a) and (b), which states:

> (6) In determining whether a loss of self-control had a qualifying trigger—
>
> (a) D's fear of serious violence is to be disregarded to the extent that it was caused by a thing which D incited to be done or said for the purpose of providing an excuse to use violence;
>
> (b) a sense of being seriously wronged by a thing done or said is not justifiable if D incited the thing to be done or said for the purpose of providing an excuse to use violence;

It is unclear whether this alters the law or is a codification of the common law. The ambiguity is caused by the requirement that it must have been D's *purpose* to provide an excuse to use violence. Need it be his sole purpose? Compare the position in self-defence in section 6.6, p 176 and the case of *Hatton*.

The leading case under the old law of provocation was *Johnson* (1989) 89 Cr App R 148. In *Johnson* J and R had been drinking at a nightclub. J made threats of violence to R's female friend and to R himself. A struggle developed between J and R. J was carrying a flick knife. He stabbed R and killed him. He was convicted of murder and appealed on the ground that the judge ought to have, but did not, direct the jury on provocation.

Watkins LJ:

There was undoubtedly evidence to suggest that, if the appellant had lost his self-control, it was his own behaviour which caused others to react towards him in the way we have described.

We were referred to the decision of the Privy Council in *Edwards v R* [1973] AC 648. In that case the trial Judge had directed the jury thus:

> 'In my view the defence of provocation cannot be of any avail to the accused in this case . . . it ill befits the accused, having gone there with the deliberate purpose of blackmailing this man—you may well think it ill befits him to say out of his own mouth that he was provoked by any attack. In my view the defence of provocation is not one which you need consider in this case.'

The full Court in Hong Kong held that this direction was erroneous. The Privy Council agreed with the full Court. On the particular facts of the case Lord Pearson, giving the judgment of the Board, said (page 658): 'On principle it seems reasonable to say that (1) a blackmailer cannot rely on the predictable results of his own blackmailing conduct as constituting provocation . . . and the predictable results may include a considerable degree of hostile reaction by the person sought to be blackmailed; (2) but if the hostile reaction by the person sought to be blackmailed goes to extreme lengths it might constitute sufficient provocation even for the blackmailer; (3) there would in many cases be a question of degree to be decided by the jury.' Those words cannot, we think, be understood to mean, as was suggested to us, that provocation which is 'self-induced' ceases to be provocation for the purposes of section 3.

The relevant statutory provision being considered by the Privy Council was in similar terms to section 3. In view of the express wording of section 3, as interpreted in *Camplin*, which was decided after *Edwards*, we find it impossible to accept that the mere fact that a defendant caused a reaction in others, which in turn led him to lose his self-control, should result in the issue of provocation being kept outside a jury's consideration. Section 3 clearly provides that the question is whether things done or said or both provoked the defendant to lose his self-control. If there is any evidence that it may have done, the issue must be left to the jury. The jury would then have to consider all the circumstances of the incident, including all the relevant behaviour of the defendant, in deciding (a) whether he was in fact provoked and (b) whether the provocation was enough to make a reasonable man do what the defendant did.

Accordingly, whether or not there were elements in the appellant's conduct which justified the conclusion that he had started the trouble and induced others, including the deceased, to react in the way they did, we are firmly of the view that the defence of provocation should have been left to the jury.

Conviction for murder quashed. Conviction for manslaughter substituted

The Court of Appeal in *Dawes* [2013] EWCA Crim 322 offered guidance on the continuing validity of *Johnson*. Lord Judge CJ held that, for the purposes of loss of control, the impact of *Johnson* has been diminished, but not wholly extinguished by the legislative provisions in ss 54 to 56 of the Criminal Justice Act 2009. His lordship stated that:

One may wonder (and the judge would have to consider) how often a defendant who is out to incite violence could be said to 'fear' serious violence; often he may be welcoming it. Similarly, one may wonder how such a defendant may have a justifiable sense of being seriously wronged if he successfully incites someone else to use violence towards him. Those are legitimate issues for consideration, but as a matter of statutory construction, the mere fact that in some general way the defendant was behaving badly and looking for and provoking trouble does not of itself lead to the disapplication of the qualifying triggers based on s.55(3)(4) and (5) unless his actions were intended to provide him with the excuse or opportunity to use violence.

■ **Questions**

1. Would it have been preferable for the Court of Appeal simply to have held that the legislation in effect overturned *Johnson*? Does its retention add unnecessary complication?

2. Is the recognition of the continued validity of *Johnson* inconsistent with Lord Judge's earlier statement in *Clinton* [2012] EWCA Crim 2 that, 'The full ambit of the defence is encompassed within these statutory provisions'?

16.2.6.2 Sexual infidelity

In a case involving the second qualifying trigger, s 55(6)(c) provides that:

the fact that a thing done or said constituted sexual infidelity is to be disregarded.

This provision was not contained within the Law Commission's proposals, but was added by the Government. The following reason for its addition was given by the minister.

The history of the partial defence of provocation has led to a commonly held belief that that defence can be abused by men who kill their wives out of sexual jealousy and revenge over infidelity. That erodes the confidence of the public in the fairness of the criminal justice system . . . we want to make it clear that it is unacceptable for a defendant who has killed an unfaithful partner to seek to blame the victim for what occurred. (Hansard HC, Public Bill Committee, 3 March 2009, col 439 (Maria Eagle))

The provision was designed to demonstrate a clear shift in policy. The Ministry of Justice in its summary of proposals stated that:

It is quite unacceptable for a defendant who has killed an unfaithful partner to seek to blame the victim for what occurred. We want to make it absolutely clear that sexual infidelity on the part of the victim can never justify reducing a murder charge to manslaughter.

The inclusion of this provision proved to be extremely controversial and in fact was defeated in the House of Lords but was then reinstated in the Commons.

The provision gives rise to a number of issues.

- What constitutes sexual infidelity, in particular what types of relationship are encompassed by that term?
- Can words constitute sexual infidelity? For example, what if D is told by X that his wife, V, is having an affair.
- Can sexual infidelity be considered by the jury as part of the context in which D killed V?

The Court of Appeal gave guidance on a number of issues in the following case.

R v Clinton

[2012] EWCA Crim 2, Court of Appeal, Criminal Division, http://www.bailii.org/ew/cases/EWCA/Crim/2012/2.html

(Lord Judge CJ, Henriques and Gloster JJ)

There were three conjoined appeals against convictions for murder, but it was only the facts of *Clinton*'s case that raised the issue of the proper interpretation of the sexual infidelity clause. D and V had been married for a number of years. D and V were in financial difficulties. In addition, V had developed a relationship with another man she had met on a social networking site. V left the family home for a trial separation two weeks before being murdered. D showed signs of a suicidal ideation. V visited the family home and it was D's evidence that she told him in graphic detail about the affairs that she had been having with various men. In addition, D stated that V had taunted him about his intention to commit suicide, saying that he did not have the courage to go through with it. Finally, D stated that V had threatened to leave him to care for their children alone. D stated that he then lost his control and strangled V to death. It was the Crown's case that the murder of V was an act of revenge, evinced by the fact that D had previously set fire to V's car and had written what appeared to be a murder/suicide note prior to the fatal attack. D sought to plead loss of control but the judge refused to leave the defence to the jury on the basis that there was no evidence that there was a loss of control attributable to one of the qualifying triggers. This ruling was based on the fact that the judge disregarded what V had told D about the extent of her infidelity. It was this ruling that D appealed.

[In ruling that the defence ought to have been left to the jury and ordering a retrial, Lord Judge CJ stated:]

16. We immediately acknowledge that the exclusion of sexual infidelity as a potential qualifying trigger is consistent with the concept of the autonomy of each individual. Of course, whatever the position may have been in times past, it is now clearly understood, and in the present context the law underlines, that no one (male or female) owns or possesses his or her spouse or partner. Nevertheless daily experience in both criminal and family courts demonstrates that the breakdown of relationships, whenever they occur, and for whatever reason, is always fraught with tension and difficulty, with the possibility of misunderstanding and the potential for apparently irrational fury. Meanwhile experience over many generations has shown that, however it may become apparent, when it does, sexual infidelity has the potential to create a highly emotional situation or to exacerbate a fraught situation, and to produce a completely unpredictable, and sometimes violent response. This may have nothing to do with any notional 'rights' that the one may believe that he or she has over the other, and often stems from a sense of betrayal and heartbreak, and crushed dreams.

17. [Counsel for D] drew attention to and adopted much of the illuminating and critical commentary by Professor Ormerod at pp.520–522 in Smith and Hogan's *Criminal Law*. To begin with, there is no definition of 'sexual infidelity'. Who and what is embraced in this concept? Is sexual infidelity to

be construed narrowly so as to refer only to conduct which is related directly and exclusively to sexual activity? Only the words and acts constituting sexual activity are to be disregarded: on one construction, therefore, the effects are not. What acts relating to infidelity, but distinguishable from it on the basis that they are not 'sexual', may be taken into account? Is the provision directly concerned with sexual infidelity, or with envy and jealousy and possessiveness, the sort of obsession that leads to violence against the victim on the basis expressed in the sadly familiar language, 'if I cannot have him/her, then no one else will/can'? The notion of infidelity appears to involve a relationship between the two people to which one party may be unfaithful. Is a one-night-stand sufficient for this purpose?

18. Take a case like *R v Stingel* [1990] 171 CLR 312, an Australian case where a jealous stalker, who stabbed his quarry when he found her, on his account, having sexual intercourse. He does not face any difficulty with this element of the offence, just because, so far as the stalker was concerned, there was no sexual infidelity by his victim at all. Is the jealous spouse to be excluded when the stalker is not? In *R v Tabeel Lewis* . . . an 18 year old Jehovah's Witness killed his lover, a 63 year old co-religionist, because on one view, he was ashamed of the consequences, if she carried out her threat to reveal their affair to the community. She was not sexually unfaithful to him, but he killed her because he feared that she would betray him, not sexually, but by revealing their secret. [Counsel for D] asked rhetorically, why should the law exclude one kind of betrayal by a lover but not another?

19. [Counsel for the Crown] agreed that 'sexual infidelity' is not defined. He suggested that its ambit is not confined to 'adultery' and that no marriage or civil partnership ceremony or any formal arrangement is required to render the violent reaction of the defendant to the sexual infidelity of the deceased impermissible for the purposes of a qualifying trigger. He suggested however that the concept of 'infidelity' involves a breach of mutual understanding which is to be inferred within the relationship, as well as any of the more obvious expressions of fidelity, such as those to be found in the marriage vows. Notwithstanding their force, these considerations do not quite address the specific requirement that the infidelity to be disregarded must be 'sexual' infidelity. The problem was illustrated when [counsel for the Crown] postulated the example of a female victim who decided to end a relationship and made clear to her former partner that it was at an end, and whether expressly or by implication, that she regarded herself as free to have sexual intercourse with whomsoever she wanted. After the end of the relationship, any such sexual activity could not sensibly be called 'infidelity'. If so, for the purposes of any qualifying trigger, it would not be caught by the prohibition in section 55(6)(c). In such a case the exercise of what [counsel for the Crown] described as her sexual freedom might possibly be taken into account in support of the defence, if she was killed by her former partner, whereas, if notwithstanding her disillusionment with it, she had attempted to keep the relationship going, while from time to time having intercourse with others, it could not.

20. [Counsel for D] and [counsel for the Crown] could readily have identified a large number of situations arising in the real world which, as a result of the statutory provision, would be productive of surprising anomalies. We cannot resolve them in advance. Whatever the anomalies to which it may give rise, the statutory provision is unequivocal: loss of control triggered by sexual infidelity cannot, on its own, qualify as a trigger for the purposes of the second component of this defence. This is the clear effect of the legislation.

21. The question however is whether it is a consequence of the legislation that sexual infidelity is similarly excluded when it may arise for consideration in the context of another or a number of other features of the case which are said to constitute an appropriate permissible qualifying trigger. The issue is complex.

22. To assist in its resolution, [counsel for the Crown] drew attention to the formal guidance issued by the Crown Prosecution Service on this issue. This provides that 'it is the issue of sexual infidelity that falls to be disregarded under sub-section (6)(c). However certain parts of the case may still amount to a defence under section 55(4)'. The example is given of the defendant who kills her husband because he has raped her sister (an act of sexual infidelity). In such a case the act of sexual infidelity may be disregarded and her actions may constitute a qualifying trigger under section 55(4).

23. This example is interesting as far as it goes, and we understand it to mean that the context in which sexual infidelity may arise may be relevant to the existence of a qualifying trigger, but in truth it is too easy. Any individual who witnesses a rape may well suffer temporary loss of control in circumstances in which a qualifying trigger might well be deemed to be present, although in the case of a rape of a stranger, insufficient to cause the defendant to have a sense of being seriously wronged personally. A much more formidable and difficult example would be the defendant who kills her husband when she suddenly finds him having enthusiastic, consensual sexual intercourse with her sister. Taken on its own, the effect of the legislation is that any loss of control consequent on such a gross betrayal would be totally excluded from consideration as a qualifying trigger. Let us for the purposes of argument take the same example a little further. The defendant returns home unexpectedly and finds her spouse or partner having consensual sexual intercourse with her sister (or indeed with anyone else), and entirely reasonably, but vehemently, complains about what has suddenly confronted her. The response by the unfaithful spouse or partner, and/or his or her new sexual companion, is to justify what he had been doing, by shouting and screaming, mercilessly taunting and deliberately using hurtful language which implies that she, not he, is responsible for his infidelity. The taunts and distressing words, which do not themselves constitute sexual infidelity, would fall to be considered as a possible qualifying trigger. The idea that, in the search for a qualifying trigger, the context in which such words are used should be ignored represents an artificiality which the administration of criminal justice should do without. And if the taunts by the unfaithful partner suggested that the sexual activity which had just been taking place was infinitely more gratifying than any earlier sexual relationship with the defendant, are those insults—in effect using sexual infidelity to cause deliberate distress—to be ignored? On the view of the legislation advanced for our consideration by [counsel for the Crown], they must be. Yet, in most criminal cases, as our recent judgment in the context of the riots and public order demonstrates, context is critical.

24. We considered the example of the wife who has been physically abused over a long period, and whose loss of self control was attributable to yet another beating by her husband, but also, for the first time, during the final beating, taunts of his sexual activities with another woman or other women. And so, after putting up with years of violent ill-treatment, what in reality finally caused the defendant's loss of control was hurtful language boasting of his sexual infidelity. Those words were the final straw. [Counsel for the Crown] invited us to consider (he did not support the contention) whether, on a narrow interpretation of the statutory structure, if evidence to that effect were elicited (as it might, in cross-examination), there would then be no sufficient qualifying trigger at all. Although the persistent beating might in a different case fall within the provisions for qualifying triggers in section 55(4)(a) and (b), in the case we are considering, the wife had endured the violence and would have continued to endure it but for the sudden discovery of her husband's infidelity. On this basis the earlier history of violence, as well as the violence on the instant occasion, would not, without reference to the claims of sexual infidelity, carry sufficient weight to constitute a qualifying trigger. Yet in the real world the husband's conduct over the years, and the impact of what he said on the particular occasion when he was killed, should surely be considered as a whole.

25. We addressed the same issue in discussion about the impact of the words 'things said' within subsection 55(6)(c). Everyone can understand how a thing done may constitute sexual infidelity, but this argument revolved around finding something 'said' which 'constituted' sexual infidelity. [Counsel for the Crown] accepted that no utterance, as such, could constitute sexual infidelity, at any rate as narrowly construed. Professor Ormerod suggests the example of a defendant hearing a wife say to her lover, 'I love you'. On close examination, this may or may not provide evidence of *sexual* infidelity. However it does not necessarily 'constitute' it, and whether it does or not depends on the relationship between the parties, and the person by whom and to whom and the circumstances in which the endearment is spoken. It may constitute a betrayal without any sexual contact or intention. [Counsel for D] raised another question. He pointed out that in the case of *Clinton*, Mrs Clinton

confessed to having had an affair on the day before she was killed, but earlier she boasted that she had had sex with five men. If the boast, intended to hurt, was simply untrue, how could those words 'constitute' infidelity?

26. We are required to make sense of this provision. It would be illogical for a defendant to be able to rely on an untrue statement about the victim's sexual infidelity as a qualifying trigger in support of the defence, but not on a truthful one. Equally, it would be quite unrealistic to limit its ambit to words spoken to his or her lover by the unfaithful spouse or partner during sexual activity. In our judgment things 'said' includes admissions of sexual infidelity (even if untrue) as well as reports (by others) of sexual infidelity. Such admissions or reports will rarely if ever be uttered without a context, and almost certainly a painful one. In short, the words will almost invariably be spoken as part of a highly charged discussion in which many disturbing comments will be uttered, often on both sides.

27. We must briefly return to the second example suggested by Professor Ormerod, that is the defendant telling his spouse or partner that he or she loves someone else. As we have said, this may or may not provide evidence of *sexual* infidelity. But it is entirely reasonable to assume that, faced with such an assertion, the defendant will ask who it is, and is likely to go on to ask whether they have already had an affair. If the answer is 'no' there would not appear to be any sexual infidelity. If the answer is 'yes', then obviously there has been. If the answer is 'no', but it is perfectly obvious that the departing spouse intends to begin a full relationship with the new partner, would that constitute sexual infidelity? And is there a relevant distinction between the defendant who believes that a sexual relationship has already developed, and one who believes that it has not, but that in due course it will. Situations arising from overhearing the other party to a relationship saying 'I love you', or saying to the defendant, 'I love someone else', simple enough words, will give rise to manifold difficulties in the context of the prohibition on sexual infidelity as a qualifying trigger.

28. This discussion of the impact of the statutory prohibition in section 55(6)(c) arises, we emphasise, in the context, not of an academic symposium, but a trial process in which the defendant will be entitled to give evidence. There is no prohibition on the defendant telling the whole story about the relevant events, including the fact and impact of sexual infidelity. To the contrary: this evidence will have to be considered and evaluated by the jury. That is because notwithstanding that sexual infidelity must be disregarded for the purposes of the second component if it stands alone as a qualifying trigger, for the reasons which follow it is plainly relevant to any questions which arise in the context of the third component, and indeed to one of the alternative defences to murder, as amended in the 2009 Act, diminished responsibility.

29. We shall return to the question whether, notwithstanding that it must be disregarded if it is the only qualifying trigger, a thing done or said which constitutes sexual infidelity is properly available for consideration in the course of evaluating any qualifying trigger which is not otherwise prohibited by the legislation.

. . .

Sexual infidelity—conclusion

34. We must now address the full extent of the prohibition against 'sexual infidelity' as a qualifying trigger for the purposes of the loss of control defence. The question is whether or not sexual infidelity is wholly excluded from consideration in the context of features of the individual case which constitute a permissible qualifying trigger or triggers within section 55(3) and (4).

35. We have examined the legislative structure as a whole. The legislation was designed to prohibit the misuse of sexual infidelity as a potential trigger for loss of control in circumstances in which it was thought to have been misused in the former defence of provocation. Where there is no other potential trigger, the prohibition must, notwithstanding the difficulties identified earlier in the judgment, be applied.

36. The starting point is that it has been recognised for centuries that sexual infidelity may produce a loss of control in men, and, more recently in women as well as men who are confronted with sexual infidelity. The exclusion created by section 55(6) cannot and does not eradicate the fact that on occasions sexual infidelity and loss of control are linked, often with the one followed immediately by the other. Indeed on one view if it did not recognise the existence of this link, the policy decision expressly to exclude sexual infidelity as a qualifying trigger would be unnecessary.

37. In section 54(1)(c) and (3) the legislation further acknowledges the impact of sexual infidelity as a potential ingredient of the third component of the defence, when all the defendant's circumstances fall for consideration, and when, although express provision is made for the exclusion of some features of the defendant's situation, the fact that he/she has been sexually betrayed is not. In short, sexual infidelity is not subject to a blanket exclusion when the loss of control defence is under consideration. Evidence of these matters may be deployed by the defendant and therefore the legislation proceeds on the basis that sexual infidelity is a permissible feature of the loss of control defence.

38. The ambit of section 55(3) and (4)—the second component, the qualifying triggers—is clearly defined. Any qualifying trigger is subject to clear statutory criteria. Dealing with it broadly, to qualify as a trigger for the defendant's loss of control, the circumstances must be extremely grave and the defendant must be subject to a justifiable sense of having been seriously wronged. These are fact specific questions requiring careful assessment, not least to ensure that the loss of control defence does not have the effect of minimising the seriousness of the infliction of fatal injury. Objective evaluation is required and a judgment must be made about the gravity of the circumstances and the extent to which the defendant was seriously wronged, and whether he had a justifiable sense that he had been seriously wronged.

39. Our approach has, as the judgment shows, been influenced by the simple reality that in relation to the day to day working of the criminal justice system events cannot be isolated from their context. We have provided a number of examples in the judgment. Perhaps expressed most simply, the man who admits, 'I killed him accidentally', is never to be treated as if he had said 'I killed him'. That would be absurd. It may not be unduly burdensome to compartmentalise sexual infidelity where it is the only element relied on in support of a qualifying trigger, and, having compartmentalised it in this way, to disregard it. Whether this is so or not, the legislation imposes that exclusionary obligation on the court. However, to seek to compartmentalise sexual infidelity and exclude it when it is integral to the facts as a whole is not only much more difficult, but is unrealistic and carries with it the potential for injustice. In the examples we have given earlier in this judgment, we do not see how any sensible evaluation of the gravity of the circumstances or their impact on the defendant could be made if the jury, having, in accordance with the legislation, heard the evidence, were then to be directed to excise from their evaluation of the qualifying trigger the matters said to constitute sexual infidelity, and to put them into distinct compartments to be disregarded. In our judgment, where sexual infidelity is integral to and forms an essential part of the context in which to make a just evaluation whether a qualifying trigger properly falls within the ambit of subsections 55(3) and (4), the prohibition in section 55(6)(c) does not operate to exclude it.

40. We have proceeded on the assumption that legislation is not enacted with the intent or purpose that the criminal justice system should operate so as to create injustice. We are fortified in this view by the fact that, although the material did not assist in the construction of section 55(6)(c), our conclusion is consistent not only with the views expressed in Parliament by those who were opposed in principle to the enactment of section 55(6)(c) but also with the observations of ministers who supported this limb of the legislation.

[Lord Judge found support for this approach in the statements made by ministers as the Bill was proceeding through Parliament]

44. Our approach to the legislative structure is entirely consistent with these responses.

■ *Questions*

1. As a result of *Clinton*, is it now clear what is excluded by the terms of the Act?

2. Does this provision have the potential to operate to the disadvantage of female defendants, the very constituency that it was designed to protect?

3. Does permitting sexual infidelity to be considered as part of the context undermine the policy rationale for the prohibition or does it mitigate an otherwise unfair aspect of the legislation?

4. Should each qualifying trigger be compartmentalized, so that it has to stand or fall on its own merit? For this argument, see D. Baker and L. Zhao, 'Contributory Qualifying and Non-Qualifying Triggers in the Loss of Control Defence: A Wrong Turn on Sexual Infidelity' (2012) 76 J Crim L 254.

16.2.7 Mistakes in relation to either trigger

What if D honestly, but mistakenly, believes that V is going to inflict serious violence on him? Similarly, what if D mistakenly believes things were said or done, but in fact they were not? This might arise, for example, if D mistakenly thinks that V has directed a racial slur at him. The question is whether D can still plead loss of control despite his mistaken belief? The legislation is silent on this particular issue. In relation to the first qualifying trigger, self-defence is available if D holds a genuine though mistaken (even if unreasonable) belief of the threat to him of *any* violence. Arguably therefore, the new defence should be available if D genuinely believes himself to be at risk of *serious* violence. In relation to the second qualifying trigger, if D honestly believes that things were said or done which, when *viewed objectively* (see *Dawes*, section 16.2.2, p 556) constituted circumstances of an extremely grave character and caused him to have a justifiable sense of being seriously wronged, he ought to be able to plead the defence. This was the position the Law Commission adopted. Of course, it might be difficult for the jury to believe that D had a *justifiable* sense of being seriously wronged if he was unreasonably mistaken about the thing being said or done.

16.2.8 Combined triggers

The legislation explicitly states that D can rely on one or both of the qualifying triggers—that he killed having lost control because he was in fear of serious violence and had a justifiable sense of being seriously wronged. The two limbs might be relied on by the woman who kills her abusive partner after years of torment when she lost control fearing another violent attack by him. In *Dawes* [2013] EWCA Crim 322, the Lord Chief Justice alluded to the possibility that the defendant will often seek to rely on the existence of more than one qualifying trigger, so that this scenario will become the norm rather than the exception. His lordship went on to make the point that, as the legislation recognizes in s 55(5), there are unlikely to be many cases where the only feature of the evidence relating to the qualifying trigger that deals with fear of serious violence will be something completely isolated from things done or said within s 55(4). Therefore, in most cases, the qualifying trigger based on a fear of violence will almost inevitably include consideration of things said and done: a combination of the features identified in s 55(3) and (4).

■ *Questions*

What if D seeks to rely on both qualifying triggers and there is insufficient evidence of each limb in isolation but a combination would satisfy s 54(5)? Should the judge leave the defence to the jury?

16.2.9 Degree of tolerance and self-restraint

In addition to the loss of control and the existence of a qualifying trigger, the final limb of the defence imports a requirement of an additional objective requirement. Section 54(1)(c) provides:

> (c) a person of D's sex and age, with a normal degree of tolerance and self restraint and in the circumstances of D, might have reacted in the same or in a similar way to D.

Further clarification is offered in s 54(3):

> (3) In subsection (1)(c) the reference to 'the circumstances of D' is a reference to all of D's circumstances other than those whose only relevance to D's conduct is that they bear on D's general capacity for tolerance or self-restraint.

In order to understand this element of the defence, it is necessary to have some knowledge of what it replaced. Under the 1957 Act, the courts struggled to reach a clear position on the extent to which it was necessary or desirable to take into account the characteristics of the particular defendant when assessing the likely response of the reasonable person to the provocation. There were numerous visits to the House of Lords on this issue with a worrying lack of consistency in the answers provided. In deciding that D's age and gender was relevant, the House of Lords in *Camplin* [1978] 2 All ER 168 stated that:

> Although it is now for the jury to apply the 'reasonable man' test, it still remains for the judge to direct them what, in the new context of the section, is the meaning of this apparently inapt expression, since powers of ratiocination bear no obvious relationship to powers of self-control. Apart from this the judge is entitled, if he thinks it helpful, to suggest considerations which may influence the jury in forming their own opinions as to whether the test is satisfied; but he should make it clear that these are not instructions which they are required to follow: it is for them and no one else to decide what weight, if any, ought to be given to them.
>
> As I have already pointed out, for the purposes of the law of provocation the 'reasonable man' has never been confined to the adult male. It means an ordinary person of either sex, not exceptionally excitable or pugnacious, but possessed of such powers of self-control as everyone is entitled to expect that his fellow citizens will exercise in society as it is today. A crucial factor in the defence of provocation from earliest times has been the relationship between the gravity of provocation and the way in which the accused retaliated, both being judged by the social standards of the day.

The House of Lords in *Smith* [1998] 4 All ER 387 went on to expand the type of characteristics that could be included for consideration to encompass those that impacted upon D's capacity to exercise self-control irrespective of whether they were also relevant to the gravity of the provocation. This left the jury with no benchmark against which to assess D's conduct in killing when out of control. In *A-G for Jersey v Holley* [2005] UKPC 23, a specially convened nine-member Board of the Privy Council concluded by a majority that *Smith* was wrongly decided. The majority held that within the objective limb of provocation a distinction should be drawn between characteristics of D that were to be taken into account because they affected the gravity of the provocation he faced and those relating to the ability to exercise self-control. The latter were not to be taken into account in assessing the defence.

On one interpretation, the provisions in the Coroners and Justice Act 2009 might be seen as simply codifying the decisions in *Camplin* and *Holley*. However, there are a number of features of the third limb of loss of control that are important and which make it quite different from the law it replaced.

- Unlike the former law, reference is made to 'tolerance' in addition to self-restraint. Tolerance and self-restraint are two distinct qualities. This element was included in the Law Commission's drafts to reflect the idea that in addition to a comparison with a person of normal self-control, the defendant's conduct should be compared to that of a person who is not 'a bigot'. It excludes the person with unacceptable attitudes as well as those with an unacceptable temper. See R. Taylor, 'The Model of Tolerance and Self-Restraint' in A. Reed and M. Bohlander (eds), *Loss of Control and Diminished Responsibility: Domestic, Comparative and International Perspectives* (2011).

- The words that a person '*might* have reacted in the same or similar way to D' is more generous to D than the requirement in s 3 of the 1957 Act which was that 'the provocation is enough *to make* reasonable man do as he did'. In this respect, loss of control is arguably more generous than provocation. The word 'reacted' is not defined.

- The words 'in the circumstances of D' may enable a jury to adopt a more generous approach when judging D's response than might have been possible under s 3 as interpreted in *Holley*. It is important to note that s 54(3) clarifies s 54(1)(c) so that the reference to 'the circumstances of D' includes '*all* of D's circumstances' except those which bear on D's 'general capacity for tolerance and self-restraint' (eg a propensity to violent outbursts). This opens up a broader range of subjective considerations than under the *Holley* test. However, Mitchell argues that this reproduces the law after the decision in *Holley* so that the individual characteristics of D will only be attributable to the 'person with normal tolerance and self-restraint' if they are relevant to the triggering event. See B. Mitchell, 'Years of Provocation, Followed by a Loss of Control' in L. Zedner and J. Roberts, *Principles and Values in Criminal Law and Criminal Justice* (2012).

- Section 54(3) excludes circumstances 'whose only relevance to D's conduct is that they bear on D's general capacity for tolerance or self restraint.' That restriction is similar to the old law in *excluding* certain features. However, there is now no positive requirement that D's individual circumstances have to affect the gravity of the triggering conduct in order for them to be *included* in the jury's assessment of what the person of D's age and sex might have done. This represents a reversal of the *Camplin* test, which focused expressly on whether D's characteristics affected the gravity. *Any* circumstances are now relevant unless their only relevance bears on the general capacity for tolerance and self restraint.

■ *Questions*

1. Why were age and sex singled out as opposed to other attributes, such as race? Is this not superfluous since these attributes would fall to be considered as a 'circumstance'?

2. Does the inclusion of sex perpetuate the misperception that a sexed capacity for self-control exists and ultimately have the potential for dubious claims to be made about the ability of abused women who kill to control their behaviour? See N. Cobb and A. Gausden, 'Feminism, "Typical" Women and Losing Control' in A. Reed and M. Bohlander (eds), *Loss of Control and Diminished Responsibility: Domestic, Comparative and International Perspectives* (2011).

16.2.9.1 Can voluntary intoxication constitute a relevant 'circumstance'?

R v Asmelash
[2013] EWCA Crim 157, Court of Appeal, Criminal Division, http://www.bailii.org/ew/cases/EWCA/Crim/2013/157.html

(Lord Judge CJ, Rafferty LJ and Simon J)

D and V had spent the day together drinking alcohol. D claimed that V had been verbally abusive towards him and had tried to sexually assault him when they returned to the hostel in which they both resided. D took a knife, intending to scare V, but swung the knife at V when he began to advance towards him. The knife entered V's back, killing him. D pleaded loss of control. In directing the jury as to the elements of the defence, the judge stated:

Are you sure that a person of [D's] sex and age with a normal degree of tolerance and self restraint and in the same circumstances, but unaffected by alcohol, would not have reacted in the same or similar way?

D appealed on the basis that the judge was wrong to direct the jury that they were to ignore the fact that he was voluntarily intoxicated.

[In agreeing with the judge's direction, **Lord Judge CJ** stated:]

16. This unequivocal direction is criticised in a careful submission by [counsel for D]. The argument involves an analysis of s.54(1)(c) and s.55 of the Coroners and Justice Act 2009 (the 2009 Act). S.54 provides:

[His lordship set out the provisions of the Act.]

17. Focussing on the circumstances of D, [counsel for D] suggested that, assuming the provisions of s.54(1)(a) and (b) were engaged (and for present purposes we assume that they were) the fact that the appellant was drunk at the material time was one of his 'circumstances' to be considered in accordance with s.54(1)(c). The appellant should not be precluded from advancing the partial defence simply because, entirely coincidentally, he happened to be intoxicated. It would be otherwise if he had been drinking to give himself Dutch courage for some violent action, but the partial defence should be available so as to ensure that D would not be in any worse position than a sober person who might have acted as he did in similar circumstances. [Council for D] was not contending that the defendant should be entitled to take advantage of his self-induced intoxication, but that the fact of such intoxication should not of itself preclude him from advancing the partial defence. He drew attention to the first supplement to the Current Crown Court Bench Book where, in the context of s.54(3) of the 2009 Act, it is stated that 'D's circumstances would include the consumption of alcohol. The jury will no longer be directed that a reasonable man is a sober man. The jury will need to decide whether a man in these circumstances (including the consumption of drink) but nevertheless possessing a normal degree of tolerance and self-restraint might act as D did. It is suggested that the jury may still be directed that D's conduct is to be judged by the standard of the person who retained a normal degree of tolerance and self-restraint even if that person had consumed alcohol as D did.'

18. [Counsel for D] also drew attention to a paper written by Professor Ormerod published in November 2010 where the then new 'loss of control' provisions were analysed. At paragraph 73 Professor Ormerod observes that 's.54(3) only appears to exclude a circumstance on which D seeks to rely if its *sole* relevance is to diminish D's self-restraint. This could open the opportunity for D to adduce all sorts of evidence. In particular, D might claim that his intake of alcohol or other intoxicants was a relevant circumstance and that the intoxication did not simply diminish his self-restraint, but also had some other relevance—e.g. that it caused a relevant mistake. This may amount to no more than a plea of lack of intent on grounds of intoxication, but it will make directing the jury more complex'. These observations are effectively repeated in Smith and Hogan's *Criminal Law, 13th edition*, at p.526. The current edition of *Blackstone* is to much the same effect. (B1.34–B1.37)

19. [Counsel for the Crown] submitted that the judge's direction to the jury was correct, entirely in accordance with well understood principle. Everyone agreed that the appellant was drunk as the result of self-induced intoxication. No one suggested that this caused him to be mistaken about anything that was going on at the relevant time, or about what he was doing. Accordingly the only relevance of the drunkenness was that it affected the appellant's self-restraint, and caused him to act in a way in which he would not have acted if sober. Such drunkenness was an irrelevant consideration. It may have had some relevance to his general capacity for tolerance or self-restraint: but no more.

20. [Counsel for the Crown] suggested that the relevant passage in the Crown Court Bench Book ignored the effect and the wording of s.54(3). He further pointed out that the views expressed by Professor Ormerod did not appear to support the proposition that self-induced intoxication was excluded as a circumstance for the purposes of s.54(3) in so far as it might reduce the defendant's capacity for self-restraint. Rather Professor Ormerod was suggesting that it was possible that self-induced drunkenness might be relevant if, for example, in drink the defendant acted on the basis of a mistaken belief. By contrast, [counsel for the Crown] drew attention to the *Law Commission Report.* (Law Commission No. 34) on Murder, Manslaughter and Infanticide (published in 2006). He reminded us that the 2009 Act had not fully or faithfully followed all the recommendations of the Law Commission, and that in some respects, it had ignored them. Nevertheless in the present context the statutory provisions had followed the Law Commission recommendations very closely. At 5.41, where the report is directing attention to temporary intoxication rather than chronic alcoholism, the Law Commission reported that 'abnormal states of mind, such as intoxication or irritability, should also be left out, as should other factors that affect a general capacity to exercise adequate self-control'. This approach is consistent with very well understood policy considerations, robustly summarised by the observations of the trial judge in his summing up. In the absence of any express provision to the effect contended for by [counsel for D] the court should proceed on the basis that the law was unchanged. What is more, the issue of self-induced intoxication has already been considered in this court in the context of newly enacted provisions related to diminished responsibility in *R v Dowds* [2012] 1 Cr App R 34, at para 35. In that context, the defence could not be founded on voluntary intoxication, even if acute.

21. The question for decision in this appeal is whether the voluntary consumption of alcohol falls within the ambit of s.54(1)(c), as amplified by s.54(3) of the 2009 Act, when consideration is being given to the question whether a person of the defendant's sex and age 'with a normal degree of tolerance and self-restraint and in all of D's circumstances other than those whose only relevance to D's conduct is that they bear on D's general capacity for tolerance or self-restraint might have reacted in the same or a similar way to D'.

22. It has of course been long understood that the consumption of alcohol, or indeed the taking of drugs, may diminish the ability of an individual to control or restrain himself, so that, in drink, or affected by drugs, he may behave in a way in which he would not have behaved when sober or drug free. Although it may sometimes impact on the question whether the constituent elements of a crime, in particular in relation to the required intent, have been proved, self-induced intoxication does not provide a defence to a criminal charge. This principle was applied to the defence of provocation in *McCarthy* [1954] 2 QB 105, and in the context of the law of Jersey which corresponded with s.3 of the Homicide Act 1957, underlined in *Attorney General for Jersey v Holley* [2005] [2 AC] 580. Indeed for several decades now, judicial directions to the jury considering the provocation defence in the context of the voluntary consumption of alcohol, referred to the reasonable sober person in the position of the defendant. If [counsel for D]'s submission is correct, a remarkably benign development to the issue of alcohol has been adopted as part of the statutory ingredients of the loss of control defence when, simultaneously, the defence itself is in many ways much more restrictive than the former provocation defence. In *Dowds*, after a valuable analysis of the policy reasons underlining the approach of the criminal law to the issue of self-induced intoxication, headed *Voluntary Drunkenness in English Criminal Law*, the court observed:

'The exception which prevents a defendant from relying on his voluntary intoxication, save upon the limited question of whether a "specific intent" has been formed, is well entrenched and formed the unspoken backdrop for the new statutory formula. There has been no hint of any dissatisfaction with that rule of law. If Parliament had meant to alter it, or depart from it, it would undoubtedly have made its intention explicit.'

23. As Hughes LJ explained in *Dowds*, on occasions when recasting a defence in statutory form, express provision is made about the approach to self-induced drunkenness (see s.75(5) of the Criminal

Justice and Immigration Act 2008 which put the law of self-defence into statutory form). On other occasions, however, a new statute simply proceeded on the basis of the well established principles of law, and specific legislative provision was unnecessary.

24. In essence, therefore, [counsel for D]'s submission proceeds on the basis that in the absence of any express statutory provision, in the context of 'loss of control', a new approach to the issue of voluntary drunkenness is required. We disagree. We can find nothing in the 'loss of control' defence to suggest that Parliament intended, somehow, that the normal rules which apply to voluntary intoxication should not apply. If that had been the intention of Parliament, it would have been spelled out in unequivocal language. Moreover, faced with the compelling reasoning of this court in *Dowds* in the context of diminished responsibility, it is inconceivable that different criteria should govern the approach to the issue of voluntary drunkenness, depending on whether the partial defence under consideration is diminished responsibility or loss of control. Indeed, given that in a fair proportion of cases, both defences are canvassed before the jury, the potential for uncertainty and confusion which would follow the necessarily very different directions on the issue of intoxication depending on which partial defence was under consideration, does not bear contemplation.

25. Our conclusion does not bear the dire consequences suggested by [counsel for D]. It does not mean that the defendant who has been drinking is deprived of any possible loss of control defence: it simply means, as the judge explained, that the loss of control defence must be approached without reference to the defendant's voluntary intoxication. If a sober individual in the defendant's circumstances, with normal levels of tolerance and self-restraint might have behaved in the same way as the defendant confronted by the relevant qualifying trigger, he would not be deprived of the loss of control defence just because he was not sober. And different considerations would arise if, a defendant with a severe problem with alcohol or drugs was mercilessly taunted about the condition, to the extent that it constituted a qualifying trigger, the alcohol or drug problem would then form part of the circumstances for consideration.

26. In our judgment the judge was right to direct the jury as he did. This ground of appeal fails.

■ *Questions*

1. If D had been able to raise evidence that his voluntary intoxication was relevant to something other than his general capacity for tolerance and self-restraint, such as that it induced him mistakenly to believe that V was attempting to sexually assault him, should it have been left to the jury as a 'circumstance'?

2. If V had taunted D about the fact of his voluntary intoxication, should this have been left to the jury as a 'circumstance'?

16.2.10 The underlying philosophy

As a concluding matter it is worth considering how the defence fits into the typical excuse/justification dichotomy. Norrie explains the new defence in the following terms:

A. Norrie, 'The Coroners and Justice Act 2009—Partial Defences to Murder (1) Loss of Control' [2010] Crim LR 275

In their first report, the Law Commission distinguished two approaches to provocation, one with a justificatory, the other with an excusatory basis. While acknowledging that this was problematic, the Commission felt it did produce helpful arguments, and the distinction between the two operates to identify two different philosophies of provocation. What are these? The first is that of what I shall call *imperfect justification*, and it is this which informs the Law Commission's own thinking. In this view, anger is not a morally impermissible emotion, for it reveals a normal and, at one level, appropriate, even perhaps virtuous, response to certain forms of words or action. How this insight fits with the law is complex and operates at two different levels. Some would argue that 'anger cannot ethically afford any ground for mitigating the gravity of deliberately violent action', but the counter-argument is that it 'can be an ethically appropriate emotion and that . . . it may be a sign of moral weakness or human coldness not to feel strong anger'. Even in this view, however, anger cannot justify outright a violent response, certainly not a killing. Nevertheless,

> 'a killing in anger produced by serious wrongdoing is ethically less wicked, and therefore deserving of a lesser punishment, than, say, killing out of greed, lust, jealousy or for political reasons'.

Where a 'belief that the provoked [person] has been wronged by the provoker . . . is justified, it does not justify the provoked person in giving vent to his or her emotions by resorting to unlawful violence, however great the provocation. Two wrongs do not make a right. However, . . . there is a distinction in moral blameworthiness between over reaction to grave provocation and unprovoked use of violence.'

This idea of responding by way of an action that requires a nuanced and complex judgment of *both* its particular rightfulness *and* its overall wrongness I seek to catch by the term 'imperfect justification'. Note that in this approach, no reference need be made to a loss of self-control, for on this account, it is the way that anger righteously informs action, albeit in a context of overall wrongness, that provides the element of justification to set against the overall sense of a wrongdoing. On this model, it would be inappropriate to require a loss of self-control as a part of the defence. The defendant need not be out of control, though he or she acted when the 'blood was up'. Indeed to be out of control might take the moral edge off what has been done in righteous, but sanctionable, anger. Note also that what is true of anger is also true of fear, for fear too may be an appropriate and justified, if overall wrongful, emotional response. With both anger and fear, 'there is a common element namely a response to unjust conduct'.

If this is the approach of the Law Commission, how does it compare with the previous law and its underlying theoretical approach? As the Law Commission point out, the approach informing the 1957 Act was not one of justification but one based on excuse. Though they do not elaborate it, I would call it one of *compassionate excuse*. This reflects the fact that the person is held to have lost self-control, so that their act is intrinsically marked from the first as wrong. It is (arguably) one thing to act out of morally appropriate anger, remaining in control of one's actions, the new approach. It can never be right at any level to lose one's control, for this entails a defect in one's rationality, the sine qua non of moral action. Loss of self-control, hijacking reason, is a problem from the start. At the same time, it can in appropriate circumstances be understood, sympathised with, and therefore be partially condoned or excused. The law condemns the act both for the wrong done *and* the loss of control, but still extends a compassionate hand to the actor. This is the basis for the idea that provocation is a concession to human frailty, for the loss of self-control and its consequence is condemned, but the weakness it represents is viewed with sympathy. Note in this, by the way, the crucial rider 'in appropriate circumstances', for it is not every loss of self-control that will produce sympathy. Much will depend on the moral quality of the provocation to which there was a reaction, as well as to the particular human circumstances of the defendant. What was it about both the provocation and the provoked defendant that caused her to lose self-control, and is the 'ordinary person' sympathetic to their plight? Is their weakness something that can be condoned on a 'there but for the grace of God go I' basis? In sum, if the moral mark of the new Law Commission approach is that conduct is imperfectly rightful, and therefore both condemned and partially vindicated, the mark of the old law was that conduct was partially excused, both wrongful and partially condoned on ground of compassion. This, as we shall see, marks out two different territories for the old law of provocation and the new law of loss of control. I now return to the core problems that led to change in the law.

16.3 Diminished responsibility

Section 2 of the Homicide Act 1957 introduced a new defence to murder: 'diminished responsibility'. The defence has been substituted with one of the same name contained in s 52 of the Coroners and Justice Act 2009. The new provisions have been in force since October 2010. Unlike provocation, the defence of diminished responsibility was a relatively recent import into English law and in fact originated in Scotland in the middle of the nineteenth century. As with loss of control, diminished responsibility is only a defence to a charge of murder and if successfully pleaded it reduces murder to manslaughter. By s 2(2) of the 1957 Act, the burden of proof is on D. This is in contrast to loss of control, where the burden of proof is on the Crown to disprove that D lost his control if he adduces sufficient evidence to raise it as an issue. In *Foye* [2013] EWCA Crim 475 this reverse burden was upheld as being compatible with Article 6 of the European Convention on Human Rights (ECHR). Lord Hughes rationalized the different approach of the two defences in the following terms:

> In particular, it is plain beyond a peradventure that the reverse onus is applied by Parliamentary statute to diminished responsibility and not to loss of control. That is deliberate and entirely comprehensible. Diminished responsibility depends on the internal mental condition of the defendant. Loss of control depends on an objective judgment of his actions as a reaction to external circumstances.

Before the changes introduced by the 2009 Act, diminished responsibility comprised the following four elements:

(i)   an abnormality of mind;

(ii) which arose from one of the specified conditions set out in the Act;

(iii) which substantially impaired;

(iv) D's mental responsibility

None of these elements was defined with any precision and it was often said that the courts colluded with psychiatrists to keep the elements of the defence as vague as possible so that the mandatory life sentence for murder could be avoided in deserving cases where it would otherwise apply. There were numerous calls for reform. In its Report No 290, *Partial Defences to Murder*, the Law Commission concluded that there was 'overwhelming support' for reform. The Law Commission recommended that reforms to the law of diminished responsibility be postponed until after the implementation of its proposed reforms to murder. The Government decided, however, to enact the reforms to diminished responsibility without making the recommended reforms to murder. See L. Kennefick, 'Introducing a New Diminished Responsibility Defence for England and Wales' (2011) 74 MLR 750.

The defence is now found in s 52 of the Coroners and Justice Act 2009 which provides:

> (1) In section 2 of the Homicide Act 1957 (c. 11) (persons suffering from diminished responsibility), for subsection (1) substitute—
>
> '(1) A person ("D") who kills or is a party to the killing of another is not to be convicted of murder if D was suffering from an abnormality of mental functioning which—
>
> (a) arose from a recognised medical condition,
>
> (b) substantially impaired D's ability to do one or more of the things mentioned in subsection (1A), and
>
> (c) provides an explanation for D's acts and omissions in doing or being a party to the killing.

(1A) Those things are—

    (a) to understand the nature of D's conduct;

    (b) to form a rational judgment;

    (c) to exercise self-control.

(1B) For the purposes of subsection (1)(c), an abnormality of mental functioning provides an explanation for D's conduct if it causes, or is a significant contributory factor in causing, D to carry out that conduct.'

(2) In section 6 of the Criminal Procedure (Insanity) Act 1964 (c. 84) (evidence by prosecution of insanity or diminished responsibility), in paragraph (b) for 'mind' substitute 'mental functioning'.

Section 2(2) to (4) of the Homicide Act 1957 remains unaffected by the 2009 Act:

(2) On a charge of murder, it shall be for the defence to prove that the person charged is by virtue of this section not liable to be convicted of murder.

(3) A person who but for this section would be liable, whether as principal or as accessory, to be convicted of murder shall be liable instead to be convicted of manslaughter.

(4) The fact that one party to a killing is by virtue of this section not liable to be convicted of murder shall not affect the question whether the killing amounted to murder in the case of any other party to it.

The four elements of the defence are now as follows:

  (i)   an 'abnormality of mental functioning';

  (ii)   the abnormality must arise from a 'recognised medical condition';

  (iii) D's 'mental responsibility' must be substantially impaired. This means that his ability to do one of more of the three things in s 2(1A) must be substantially impaired. The three things are:

    (a) to understand the nature of D's conduct;

    (b) to form a rational judgement;

    (c) to exercise self-control.

  (iv) the abnormality of mental functioning from a 'recognised medical condition' must be a cause or a contributory cause of D's conduct in killing.

What should immediately be clear is that although the defence retains the title 'diminished responsibility' it no longer requires an evaluation of D's responsibility for killing. Indeed, the term 'responsibility' is to be found nowhere in the new provisions. Might this be a problem when the principle of fair labelling is considered?

Each of the elements of the new defence will be examined in turn.

16.3.1 An 'abnormality of mental functioning'

Under the old s 2 test (of 'abnormality of mind') the determination of 'abnormality' could be left to the jury as was explained by Lord Parker CJ in *Byrne* [1960] 2 QB 396 in the following terms:

'Abnormality of mind,' which has to be contrasted with the time-honoured expression in the M'Naughten Rules 'defect of reason,' means a state of mind so different from that of ordinary human beings that the reasonable man would term it abnormal. It appears to us to be wide enough to cover the mind's activities in all its aspects, not only the perception of physical acts and matters, and the ability to form a rational judgment as to whether an act is right or wrong, but also the ability to exercise will power to control physical acts in accordance with that rational judgment. The expression 'mental responsibility for his acts' points to a consideration of the extent to which the accused's mind is answerable for his physical acts which must include a consideration of the extent of his ability to exercise will power to control his physical acts.

This formula was appropriate under the old law, when the jury had to consider a concept as loose and general as the 'mind' and were being asked to evaluate whether D's mind deviated from the norm. However, the new provision is much stricter and more reliance will be placed upon expert evidence. As such, it may be wondered whether there is much for the jury to do in this respect. In *Bunch* [2013] EWCA Crim 2498, the court held that the new defence did not diminish the authority of cases under the old defence which held that medical evidence, though not formally required by the Act was a 'practical necessity' if the defence was to succeed: *Dix* (1982) 74 Cr App R 306.

16.3.2 'recognised medical condition'

The abnormality of mental functioning must arise 'from a recognised medical condition.' This is designed to be wider than the familiar list of bracketed causes in the original definition in s 2 of the 1957 Act. It is intended to produce clearer expert evidence from psychiatrists and psychologists and to allow sufficient flexibility for the new defence to develop in line with medical understanding and practice. Two obvious questions arise when considering this element of the defence: what kind(s) of medical condition; recognized by whom?

16.3.2.1 'medical condition'

This new element of the definition was intended to provide a clearer foundation for the defence. As the Royal College of Psychiatrists explained, it will:

encourage reference within expert evidence to diagnosis in terms of one or two of the accepted internationally classificatory systems of mental conditions (i.e. the World Health Organisation: International Classification of Diseases (ICD-10); and the American Psychiatric Association: Diagnostic and Statistical Manual of Mental Disorders (DSM-IV); see CP 19/08 fn 13) without explicitly writing those systems into the legislation.

It should be noted that *any* medical condition will suffice. This will include physiological conditions in addition to those of a psychological and psychiatric nature.

16.3.2.2 'recognised'

It is important to note that whether the condition that D was suffering from at the time he committed the killing is a 'recognised medical condition' is a question of law. Just because a condition is recognized by the medical community does not mean it will fall within the terms of the Act. The Court of Appeal clarified this point in the following case.

R v Dowds

[2012] EWCA Crim 281, Court of Appeal, Criminal Division, http://www.bailii.org/ew/cases/EWCA/Crim/2012/281.html

(Hughes LJ, Simon and Lang JJ)

D was convicted of murdering his partner, V, by stabbing her 60 times. Their relationship had been a violent one. D and V engaged in binge drinking, and on the night of the killing they had consumed 2 litres of vodka. At trial, D claimed that he had no recollection of the attack and that he lacked mens rea and also relied on the partial defences of diminished responsibility and loss of self-control. D sought to rely on diminished responsibility by claiming to have an abnormality of mental functioning arising from his 'recognised medical condition', namely 'acute intoxication' (which is listed in ICD-10), and that substantially impaired his capacity as defined in the section.

The trial judge refused to accept that 'acute intoxication' was a 'recognised medical condition' for the purposes of the defence: (a) on the grounds of policy because the Law Commission and Parliament could not have intended with the new formulation of the defence to allow voluntary intoxication to qualify for the defence and (b) because the state of acute intoxication was temporary.

[Dismissing D's appeal and upholding his conviction, Hughes LJ stated:]

10. It was established in 1975 in *R v Fenton* (1975) 61 Cr App R 261 that the effect on the mind of voluntary intoxication could not give rise to diminished responsibility. The defendant, who had shot four people in two different locations, had a number of other conditions, including paranoid psychopathy, which did raise the possibility of diminished responsibility, although the jury had rejected that defence. The trial judge had directed the jury to consider those but to leave out of account the defendant's heavy intoxication. This court held that the judge had been correct. The reasoning of Lord Widgery CJ, at pp 263–264, was brief:

'We recognise that cases may arise hereafter where the accused proves such a craving for drink or drugs as to produce in itself an abnormality of mind; but that is not proved in this case. The defendant did not give evidence and we do not see how self-induced intoxication can of itself produce an abnormality of mind due to inherent causes.'

It is perhaps significant that counsel for the defendant had felt able to argue his case only on the basis that a craving for, or an inability to resist the temptations of, drink was a feature of psychopathy, and thus became relevant to diminished responsibility indirectly. No one suggested that simple drunkenness could found a defence of diminished responsibility, and on the facts of the case a craving for, or inability to resist the need of, drink was not shown.

11. The law as explained in *R v Fenton* was never significantly questioned. It was in due course endorsed by the House of Lords in *R v Dietschmann* [2003] 1 AC 1209. That case resolved an uncertainty about how to approach the case of a defendant who *both* suffered from a mental abnormality and was also intoxicated. The House of Lords held that the correct approach was for the jury to ignore the effects of intoxication and to ask whether, leaving out the drink, the defendant's other condition(s) of mental abnormality substantially impaired his responsibility for the killing. It was treated as axiomatic that simple voluntary drunkenness was incapable of founding a plea of diminished responsibility.

12. As foreshadowed in *R v Fenton* the courts also had to deal with cases where the defendants' condition went beyond simple drunkenness into physical or psychological addiction such as, arguably, to amount to a mental abnormality. In dealing with such cases it was once again treated as axiomatic that simple voluntary drunkenness without such additional condition was incapable of founding the plea of diminished responsibility. See, most recently, *R v Wood* [2009] 1 WLR 496, 507—in particular para 23—and *R v Stewart* [2009] 1 WLR 2507, in particular paras 26 and 29.

13. This court's judgment in *R v Wood* usefully explains what is very clearly the case. The axiomatic rule that simple voluntary drunkenness, without more, cannot found diminished responsibility, is not a rule special to the partial defence. It is but one example of the general approach of English criminal law to voluntary drunkenness. Sir Igor Judge P, as he then was, put it in this way in *R v Wood*, para 23:

'Dealing with the point very broadly, the consumption of alcohol before a defendant acts with murderous intent and kills cannot, without more, bring his actions within the concept of diminished responsibility. On its own, voluntary intoxication falls outside the ambit of the defence. This is consistent with the general approach of the law that, save in the context of offences of specific intent, and proof of that intent, criminal acts committed under the influence of self induced intoxication are not for that reason excused. Public policy proceeds on the basis that a defendant who voluntarily takes alcohol and behaves in a way which he might not have behaved when sober is not normally entitled to be excused from the consequences of his actions.'

14. It is true that in the particular case of diminished responsibility under the original form of section 2 of the 1957 Act, there was an additional reason why simple voluntary drunkenness could not found the defence. That was because it could not readily be brought within the expression 'inherent cause' and clearly had none of the other sources listed in the bracketed clause in the section. But there can be no doubt that independently of the particular statutory language, the general principle to which Sir Igor Judge P referred in *R v Wood* does indeed underlie English criminal law.

[His lordship then set out the general approach that English and Welsh criminal law adopts towards voluntary intoxication, namely that it is not a defence but merely one way of negating mens rea in the case of crimes of specific intent.]

Amending section 2 of the Homicide Act 1957

[His lordship then discussed the background to the Law Commission report leading to the 2009 Act.]

26. The report contains no further discussion at all of the law relating to voluntary intoxication. We infer that that was because nothing had changed since 2004 when the existing law had been so clearly commended [in *Dietschmann*]; there had so far as we are aware been no significant discussion about it in any public quarter. The Commission did slightly amend its formulation of diminished responsibility into what was substantially the form adopted by the Coroners and Justice Act 2009. (There was a suggested addition of developmental immaturity which was not adopted by Parliament but that is irrelevant to the present issue.) For present purposes the significant change in formulation was to move from 'an abnormality of mental functioning *arising from an underlying condition*' (2004) to 'an abnormality of mental functioning *arising from a recognised medical condition*' (2006) (our emphasis).

27. The Commission explained the reasons for this slightly altered formulation in paras 5.114–5.120. They were: (i) the law ought no longer to be constrained by a fixed set of causes of mental malfunction but should be responsive to developments in medicine and psychiatry; and (ii) the altered formulation would help to make clearer the relationship between the role of the medical expert and the role of the jury.

28. As to the first of those, the Commission quoted at length from, and endorsed, evidence given to it by the Royal College of Psychiatrists. The college was concerned to establish that the partial defence should be grounded in valid medical diagnosis, rather than in imaginative or idiosyncratic fringe opinion. In that context the college had said this, at para 5.114:

'It would also encourage reference within expert evidence to diagnosis in terms of one or two of the accepted internationally classificatory systems of mental conditions (WHO ICD 10 and AMA DSM) without explicitly writing those systems into the legislation . . . Such an approach would also avoid individual doctors offering idiosyncratic "diagnoses" . . .'

It is apparent from this, and from the total silence in the 2006 report on the subject of voluntary intoxication, that the altered formulation owed nothing whatever to any intention in any quarter to alter the law on that topic.

. . .

41. If we had concluded that the defence of diminished responsibility ought to have been left to the jury, we should have been unable to accept the Crown's invitation to hold that it could not have succeeded in any event because of what must have been the findings of the jury. We agree that the jury must have rejected the defendant's assertion that he had been so drunk as to be unable to form the

intention to kill or to do serious bodily harm. We agree that his use of the telephone in the immediate aftermath of the killing tends quite strongly to suggest that he was in much better control of himself than was suggested. We agree that there were good grounds on which it may well be that the jury rejected also his assertion that he had no recollection of events. We agree that the jury rejected the argument that he had lost self-control in circumstances in which a reasonable man might have done as he did. But if it had been the law that voluntary acute intoxication could found diminished responsibility, the level of drunkenness involved would not necessarily have to reach inability to form an intent, nor would the loss of self-control necessarily have to be such as might have led a reasonable man to do as the defendant did. On our very clear conclusions, however, these considerations do not arise. Voluntary acute intoxication, whether from alcohol or other substance, is not capable of founding diminished responsibility.

■ *Questions*

1. If not all the conditions 'recognised' by psychiatrists in DSM-V and ICD-10 are 'recognised' in law for the purposes of the new defence, which ones are? How is the judge to decide?

2. Hughes LJ stated: 'It is enough to say that it is quite clear that the re-formulation of the statutory conditions for diminished responsibility was not intended to reverse the well established rule that voluntary acute intoxication is not capable of being relied upon to found diminished responsibility. That remains the law. *The presence of a "recognised medical condition" is a necessary, but not always a sufficient, condition to raise the issue of diminished responsibility*' (emphasis added). So what is the missing element that makes a condition in DSM-V 'sufficient' to qualify?

The DSM and ICD manuals contain thousands of medical conditions. If it was sufficient that any one would suffice for this element of the new defence it would render it available to an enormous range of people. The manuals contain some striking examples of conditions such as 'unhappiness' (R45.2), 'irritability and anger' (R45.4), 'suspiciousness and marked evasiveness' (R46.5), 'pyromania' (F63.1), 'paedophilia' (F65.4), 'sado-masochism' (F65.5) and 'kleptomania' (F63.2). DSM-V includes similar conditions such as 'exhibitionism', 'sexual sadism' and 'intermittent explosive disorder'. The Government expressed the view that the legislation must be sufficiently flexible to cater for emerging medical conditions. However, there are those who argue that this element of the defence will deprive it of sufficient flexibility that was one of the benefits of the former law.

R. D. Mackay, 'The Coroners and Justice Act 2009—Partial Defences to Murder (2) The New Diminished Responsibility Plea'
[2010] Crim LR 290

Recognised medical condition

The concept of a recognised medical condition is of itself nothing new. For example, it has been the subject of judicial comment within the context of disability litigation. However, its introduction as a requirement for a diminished responsibility plea is novel—but viewed as necessary by the MOJ,

> 'to accommodate future developments in diagnostic practice and encourage defences to be grounded in a valid medical diagnosis linked to the accepted classificatory systems which together encompass the recognised physical, psychiatric and psychological conditions'.

The relevant classificatory systems referred to by the MOJ are the two cited above by Baroness Murphy. However, while the phrase 'recognised medical condition' will clearly encompass all relevant mental disorders which fall within ICD-10 and DSM-IV, it is not restricted to these, and, as the MOJ concedes, must cover both 'psychological' and 'physical' conditions. Clearly, therefore, it is not limited to recognised mental disorders and must include conditions like epilepsy, sleep disorders and diabetes. In short, this is a concept which is capable of covering any and all medical conditions and as such is wider than the bracketed causes in s.2(1) of the 1957 Act which it replaces. These bracketed causes were open to criticism in that they were not psychiatrically recognised and their meaning had taxed the courts. However, it was clear that to succeed in a plea under s.2(1) the abnormality of mind had to fall within one or more of these bracketed causes, thus restricting the plea's availability. There is no such restriction relating to the scope of 'recognised medical condition' in s.52 of the Coroners and Justice Act 2009, so it is to the new plea's other requirements which one must turn for this. Before doing so, however, three additional remarks may be made about 'recognised medical condition'.

First, although it has been suggested above that this concept is wider than its counterpart in the original s.2(1) of the 1957 Act, there is ironically a danger that—because it focuses exclusively on the need for a defined and demonstrable condition which is medically recognised—it may fail to include those 'mercy killing' cases which currently qualify for a diminished responsibility plea. The reason for this is that because the wording of the current plea is so obscure, the court and the experts are sometimes able to enter into a benevolent conspiracy, thus permitting the psychiatric evidence to be stretched so as 'to produce a greater range of exemption from liability for murder than its terms really justify'. In short, therefore—having regard to the difficulty which psychiatrists experienced in bringing such cases within 'abnormality of mind' under the original s.2 of the 1957 Act—the concept of 'recognised medical condition' may exacerbate this difficulty. Secondly, in his article on the new loss of control plea, Alan Norrie makes it clear that as this new plea is narrower than the provocation plea which it replaces, cases such as *Humphreys* (emotional immaturity) and *Acott* (low intelligence) are unlikely to fall within its scope. And the same is likely to be true in relation to s.52 of the Coroners and Justice Act 2009, as its requirements—including the need for a 'recognised medical condition'— lack the flexibility of the original s.2 of the 1957 Act, which it turn often permitted both pleas to be combined; a defence strategy which is now much less likely to succeed owing to the fact that both new pleas are drafted in a manner which militates against possible overlap. Finally, by whom does the condition need to be recognised? Most of us can 'recognise' certain conditions of a medical nature. Presumably, however, what is meant here is that in order to fall within s.52 of the Coroners and Justice Act 2009, it must be a professionally accepted medical condition; although such recognition it seems will no longer be restricted to those with psychiatric expertise but will include, where relevant, all other branches of the medical profession and psychologists.

16.3.3 A 'substantial impairment of mental ability'

Whereas under the old s 2 of the 1957 Act, the matter that had to be substantially impaired was D's *mental responsibility* for acting as he did, the matter that now has to be shown to be substantially impaired is D's *ability to do* any of the things mentioned in the new s 2(1A). Therefore, what was a test of moral responsibility for the jury's determination under the former regime has become a medical one which will require expert evidence to resolve.

In *Ramchurn* [2010] EWCA Crim 194, the Lord Chief Justice gave the following explanation of 'substantial', as it was understood under the old law.

'Substantially' is an ordinary English word which appears in the context of a statutory provision creating a special defence which, to reflect reduced mental responsibility for what otherwise would be murderous actions, reduces the crime from murder to manslaughter. Its presence in the statute is deliberate. It is designed to ensure that the murderous activity of a defendant should not result in a

conviction for manslaughter rather than murder on account of any impairment of mental responsibility, however trivial and insignificant; but equally that the defence should be available without the
defendant having to show that his mental responsibility for his actions was so grossly impaired as to
be extinguished. That is the purpose of this defence and this language. The Concise Oxford Dictionary
offers 'of real importance' and 'having substance' as suggested meanings for 'substantially'. But, in
reality, even the Concise Oxford Dictionary tells us very little more about the ordinary meaning and
understanding to be attached to the word 'substantially'.

Again, there will be significant reliance placed upon the evidence of the expert in determining
whether D's impaired ability to do one or more of the specified things deviates so far from the
norm that it could be considered 'substantial'. This was confirmed as being applicable under
the new law by the Court of Appeal in *Brown* [2011] EWCA Crim 2796.

16.3.3.1 'to understand the nature of D's conduct'

This is similar to the first limb of the insanity plea. An example provided by the Law
Commission of how this element might be satisfied was of a 10-year-old boy with a recognized medical condition (amended to reflect the provision as enacted):

who has been left to play very violent video games for hours on end for much of his life, loses his
temper and kills another child when the child attempts to take a game from him. When interviewed,
he shows no real understanding that, when a person is killed they cannot simply be later revived, as
happens in the games he has been continually playing.

It has been observed that defining the expression 'nature of D's conduct' could prove to be a
'judicial nightmare'. What aspects of D's conduct bear upon the 'nature' of it? See R. Fortson,
'The Modern Partial Defence of Diminished Responsibility' in A. Reed and M. Bohlander
(eds), *Loss of Control and Diminished Responsibility: Domestic, Comparative and International
Perspectives* (2011).

16.3.3.2 'to form a rational judgment'

Although the Act states that the thing that must be impaired is D's ability to form a rational
judgement, strictly speaking this is not the proper way to express this aspect of the defence.
It is more accurate to say that it is D's ability to rationally form a judgement which must be
impaired. What matters is the ability, not the outcome.

The Law Commission gave the following examples (some of which have been amended for
these purposes):

(i)   a woman who has been diagnosed as being in a state of learned helplessness, conse-
       quent upon violent abuse suffered at her husband's hands, comes to believe that only
       burning her husband to death will rid the world of his sins;

(ii)   a mentally subnormal boy believes that he must follow his older brother's instructions,
       even when they involve taking take part in a killing. He says, 'I wouldn't dream of diso-
       beying my brother and he would never tell me to do something if it was really wrong';

(iii) a depressed man who has been caring for many years for a terminally ill spouse, kills
       her, at her request. He says that he had found it progressively more difficult to stop her
       repeated requests dominating his thoughts to the exclusion of all else, so that 'I felt
       I would never think straight again until I had given her what she wanted.'

16.3.3.3 The 'ability to exercise control'

This is a significant change and if construed widely could render the defence available in a
broader range of circumstances than either (a) or (b).

16.3.4 An explanation (or cause) of the killing

The defence is narrowed further by the requirement that the abnormality of mental functioning, arising from a recognized medical condition substantially impairing the defendant's ability in a relevant manner, must also 'explain' his acts in killing. By s 2(1B) 'an explanation' for D's conduct is provided 'if it causes, or is a significant contributory factor in causing, D to carry out that conduct.' The issue that immediately arises is whether this provision imports a strict causal requirement. Section 2(1B) does not say that for the defence to succeed a sufficient explanation can only be provided if the abnormality of mental functioning is a cause. On this basis, a causal link is just one of the ways in which the killing might be 'explained'. There may be cases where the abnormality provides an explanation sufficient to mitigate the conduct to manslaughter even if there is no causal link. However, the language in debates was clearly envisaging a causal link. In debates, the minister stated that:

> We do not believe that the partial defence should succeed where random coincidence has brought together the activity of the person and the recognised medical condition . . . there must have been at least a significant contributory factor in causing the defendant to act as he did. We do not require the defence to prove that it was the only cause or the main cause or the most important factor, but there must be something that is more than a merely trivial factor. (Hansard, 4 March 2009, col 416)

The need for any causal requirement has been challenged by some.

R. D. Mackay, 'The Coroners and Justice Act 2009—Partial Defences to Murder (2) The New Diminished Responsibility Plea'
[2010] Crim LR 290

Provides an explanation for D's acts and omissions in doing or being a party to the killing

This provision follows the recommendation of the Law Commission. Initially the Commission recommended a stronger causal provision which was as follows,

> 'the abnormality was a significant cause of the defendant's conduct in carrying out or taking part in the killing'.

However, after consultation the Commission decided that such a requirement might be problematical and instead opted for the provision (which now appears in subs.(1)(c) of the 1957 Act as amended) stating,

> 'we have framed the issue in these terms: the abnormality of mind, or developmental immaturity, or both, must be shown to be 'an explanation' for D's conduct. This ensures that there is an appropriate connection (that is, one that grounds a case for mitigation of the offence) between the abnormality of mental functioning or developmental immaturity and the killing. It leaves open the possibility, however, that other causes or explanations (like provocation) may be admitted to have been at work, without prejudicing the case for mitigation.'

Both the MOJ and government ministers have repeatedly opined that a stronger causal requirement is necessary. As a result subs.(1B) of the 1957 Act as amended provides:

> 'For the purposes of subsection (1)(c), an abnormality of mental functioning provides an explanation for D's conduct if it causes, or is a significant contributory factor in causing, D to carry out that conduct.'

The MOJ has been adamant that, 'there must be some connection between the condition and the killing for the partial defence to be justified'. In its response to its consultation exercise the MOJ further opined:

'With regard to the link between the impairment and the defendant's conduct, we have carefully thought through the various comments made but have concluded that it is right to maintain the position set out in the consultation paper. We are satisfied that it is right that, while it need not be the sole cause of the defendant's behaviour, it should be a significant contributory factor in causing the conduct—that is, more than a merely trivial factor. The partial defence should certainly not succeed where the jury believes that the impairment made no difference to the defendant's behaviour—he would have killed anyway.'

The Attorney General explained this further during debate on the Bill in the House of Lords saying:

'The Government consider it is necessary to spell out what connection between the abnormality of mental functioning and the killing is required for the partial defence to succeed. Otherwise a random coincidence would suffice. It need not be the sole cause or even the most important factor in causing the behaviour but it must be more than merely a trivial factor. We believe this gets the balance about right.'

The reference to 'random coincidence' seems strange. How—it may be asked—can this be possible if the defendant is able to prove that his abnormality of mental functioning gave rise to a substantial impairment of one or more of the abilities specified in subs.(1A) of the 1957 Act as amended? Surely, if such is the case then the killing cannot have been a 'random coincidence'. In any event, why, if the defendant proves that this is so, is this not enough? On possible line of argument is that subs.(1B) of the 1957 Act as amended is merely making express provision for what is already impliedly provided for in the original s.2(1). Two sources might be used to support this approach. The first is the following remark made by Lord Hutton in *Dietchschmann*:

'I think that in referring to substantial impairment of mental responsibility the subsection does not require the abnormality of mind to be the *sole cause* of the defendant's acts in doing the killing. In my opinion, even if the defendant would not have killed if he had not taken drink, the *causative effect of the drink* does not necessarily prevent an abnormality of mind suffered by the defendant from substantially impairing his mental responsibility for his fatal acts.'

The second is the Judicial Studies Board Specimen Direction on diminished responsibility which states:

'Substantially impaired means just that. You must conclude that his abnormality of mind was *a real cause* of the defendant's conduct. The defendant need not prove that his condition was the sole cause of it, but he must show that it was more than merely a trivial one [which did not make any real/appreciable difference to his ability to control himself].'

The following points can be made about these sources. First, Lord Hutton's reference to 'sole cause' has to be read in the context of the facts of the case, namely the causative relationship between the effect of alcohol and abnormality of mind. There is no suggestion in *Dietchschmann* that his Lordship was seeking to express an opinion on the need for some more general causal requirement in s.2(1) of the 1957 Act. Secondly, the reference in the Specimen Direction to 'real cause' is nowhere to be found in Lord Hutton's judgment. Despite this the Specimen Direction was used by Maria Eagle MP, the Parliamentary Under-Secretary of State, to support her conclusion that:

'While there is no reference to causation in [the] statute, we believe that the existing requirement that the abnormality substantially impairs mental responsibility for the killing implies a causative connection and that in practice the law is applied in this way. We therefore do not consider that the approach we are taking here represents any real departure from current law and practice or indeed from the Law Commission proposal.'

However, such a conclusion seems highly contentious for, as is mentioned above, there is no real support for such a strict causal requirement within the original s.2(1) of the 1957 Act. Not only that, no other diminished responsibility plea contains any such express requirement. In particular, none is to be found in the New South Wales revised plea upon which s.52 of the 2009 Act is modelled. Finally, it seems worth in this connection turning to the insanity defence. The *M'Naghten Rules* do not contain any such similar causal requirement. All the Rules require is 'a defect of reason, from disease of the mind'. What is necessary is that a 'disease of the mind' cause 'a defect of reason'. There is no additional need to prove that the 'disease of the mind' *caused or was a significant contributory factor in causing, D to carry out his conduct.* As a result one is compelled to ask whether it will not now be easier for a defendant whose mental state at the time of the offence satisfies all the elements of both pleas (with the exception of this causal requirement) to prove insanity within the *M'Naghten Rules* rather than the new diminished responsibility plea.

There are those who argue that the problems arising from the causal requirement are more illusory than real. Rudi Fortson QC gives the following three reasons:

(i)   the abnormality need not be the sole cause of D's conduct;

(ii) the provision arguably just gives legislative effect to what was the existing law as expounded in *Dietschmann*; and

(iii) since *Walton v The Queen* [1978] AC 788 the jury must consider all the evidence that is relevant to the question of whether the partial defence is made out.

See R. Fortson, 'The Modern Partial Defence of Diminished Responsibility' in A. Reed and M. Bohlander (eds), *Loss of Control and Diminished Responsibility: Domestic, Comparative and International Perspectives* (2011).

16.3.5 Intoxicated defendants

Two situations need to be considered:

(i)   D who is acutely intoxicated, but not alcoholic (see section 16.3.2);

(ii) D who has a recognized medical condition (including alcoholic dependency syndrome) and is drunk.

(i) In *Dowds* (section 16.3.2), Hughes LJ stated that acute voluntary intoxication is not a 'recognised medical condition' for the purposes of the defence.

(ii) If D suffers from some 'recognised medical condition' and also happens to be intoxicated at the time he kills V? In *Dietschmann* [2003] UKHL 10 Lord Hutton held that:

even if the defendant would not have killed if he had not taken drink, the causative effect of the drink does not necessarily prevent an abnormality of mind suffered by the defendant from substantially impairing his mental responsibility for his fatal acts.

So in this situation, the question under the new law seems to be whether, *ignoring the intoxication*, there was an abnormality of mental functioning arising from a recognized medical condition. If so, whether that abnormality of mental functioning substantially impaired D's ability in a relevant way and, if so, whether that abnormality of mental functioning was a cause of the conduct by which D killed. D should be entitled to the defence even if D might not have killed had he not been drunk, provided the abnormality of mental functioning arising from the recognized medical condition nevertheless explains his conduct in killing. If D would have killed even if he had not been suffering from an abnormality of mental functioning, whether D can plead the partial defence depends on whether s 2(1A) is interpreted as importing a causal requirement. See further, M. Gibson, 'Intoxicants and Diminished Responsibility: The Impact of the Coroners and Justice Act 2009' [2011] Crim LR 909.

16.4 Suicide pacts and assisting suicide

A further partial defence to murder is provided by the Homicide Act 1957, s 4. The defence is only partial, as with diminished responsibility and loss of control, and the successful plea will result in a conviction for manslaughter.

Homicide Act 1957, s 4

(1) It shall be manslaughter, and shall not be murder, for a person acting in pursuance of a suicide pact between him and another to kill the other or be a party to the other . . . being killed by a third person.

(2) Where it is shown that a person charged with the murder of another killed the other or was a party to his . . . being killed, it shall be for the defence to prove that the person charged was acting in pursuance of a suicide pact between him and the other.

(3) For the purposes of this section 'suicide pact' means a common agreement between two or more persons having for its object the death of all of them, whether or not each is to take his own life, but nothing done by a person who enters into a suicide pact shall be treated as done by him in pursuance of the pact unless it is done while he has the settled intention of dying in pursuance of the pact.

The provision in s 4 must be read alongside the Suicide Act 1961, which deals with those cases in which D does not cause V's death but assists or tries to help V to commit suicide.

Suicide Act 1961, s 1

The rule of law whereby it is a crime for a person to commit suicide is hereby abrogated.

Coroners and Justice Act 2009, s 59, amending Suicide Act 1961, s 2

(2) In section 2 (criminal liability for complicity in another's suicide), for subsection (1) substitute—

'(1) A person ("D") commits an offence if—

(a) D does an act capable of encouraging or assisting the suicide or attempted suicide of another person, and

(b) D's act was intended to encourage or assist suicide or an attempt at suicide.

(1A) The person referred to in subsection (1)(a) need not be a specific person (or class of persons) known to, or identified by, D.

(1B) D may commit an offence under this section whether or not a suicide, or an attempt at suicide, occurs.

(1C) An offence under this section is triable on indictment and a person convicted of such an offence is liable to imprisonment for a term not exceeding 14 years.'

(3) In subsection (2) of that section, for 'it' to the end substitute 'of a person it is proved that the deceased person committed suicide, and the accused committed an offence under subsection (1) in relation to that suicide, the jury may find the accused guilty of the offence under subsection (1).'

(4) After that section insert—

'2A Acts capable of encouraging or assisting

(1) If D arranges for a person ("D2") to do an act that is capable of encouraging or assisting the suicide or attempted suicide of another person and D2 does that act, D is also to be treated for the purposes of this Act as having done it.

(2) Where the facts are such that an act is not capable of encouraging or assisting suicide or attempted suicide, for the purposes of this Act it is to be treated as so capable if the act would have been so capable had the facts been as D believed them to be at the time of the act or had subsequent events happened in the manner D believed they would happen (or both).

(3) A reference in this Act to a person ("P") doing an act that is capable of encouraging the suicide or attempted suicide of another person includes a reference to P doing so by threatening another person or otherwise putting pressure on another person to commit or attempt suicide.

2B Course of conduct

A reference in this Act to an act includes a reference to a course of conduct, and a reference to doing an act is to be read accordingly.'

■ *Questions*

1. Does the relationship between these suicide-related offences/defences present a coherent law?

2. D and V decide to kill themselves. They sit in V's car with a hose from the exhaust pipe. D turns the ignition on and V dies but D is saved by paramedics. What offence has D committed? What difference would it make, if any, if V had turned the ignition key?

3. Don decides to commit suicide. He closes his eyes and throws himself from a fifth-floor window into the street below. He lands on Paul. Paul's neck is broken and he dies. Don breaks both his legs but, after six months in hospital, is now fully recovered. Is Don guilty of any offence?

4. Dick and Dora agree that they will die together. They are found in a gas-filled room. Dora is dead, but Dick recovers. Dick cannot remember who turned on the gas-tap and there is no evidence on the point. Can Dick be convicted of an offence under the Suicide Act or under the Homicide Act, s 4? Might it be different if Dora had been shot and it was impossible to prove whether she shot herself or was shot by Dick?

5. Eric and Ernie, who belong to a strange religious sect, agree that they will inflict mutilations on each other, amounting to grievous bodily harm. They believe that this will put them in a state of grace. They carry out their agreement. Are they guilty of an offence? (See Chapter 18.) If Ernie dies of the injuries inflicted by Eric, is Eric guilty of homicide?

16.4.1 Substantive or inchoate liability

Is the offence an inchoate offence or a full offence in its own right which can be attempted? Even though it is drafted in terms of assisting, it is not a form of secondary liability but a principal offence.

R v S

[2005] EWCA Crim 819, Court of Appeal, Criminal Division

(Rix LJ, Holman J and Sir Michael Wright)

D was alleged to have aided and abetted his 15-year-old girlfriend to commit suicide by jumping from a stone jetty into the sea. He encouraged her to do so, plied her with alcohol and dictated a suicide note for her. She jumped from the jetty. He then left the scene and did not call the emergency services for an hour and a half. She was found alive at the bottom of the jetty.

D claimed he had neither done nor said anything to encourage or assist his girlfriend to commit suicide and that he had not seen her fall. The judge directed the jury that there were two separate ingredients: (i) D intended that she should kill herself (ignoring whether she wanted to commit suicide) and (ii) D did some act—whether it was a physical act or whether it consisted of words of encouragement—which constituted an attempt to aid, abet, counsel or procure her to do so.

[In dismissing the appeal Rix LJ observed that:]

... The fact that that intention to aid and abet the suicide or attempted suicide of another would be impossible in circumstances where that other had no intention herself to commit suicide or even attempt to commit suicide, merely means that on the facts of such a case the attempt would merely be the attempt of an impossibility. But it is clear from the House of Lords decision in *R v Shivpuri* [1987] AC 1 [section 14.5, p 513] that it is no impediment to the offence of an attempted crime that the actual crime would have been impossible on the facts of the case, such as attempting to pick an empty pocket or attempting to handle goods which have not been stolen, or attempting to murder not a person but a bolster in a bed....

... [Rix LJ went onto state that:] it may in many circumstances be implicit in an intention to aid and abet a suicide or suicide attempt, that the defendant has a belief in the other person's intention or willingness to attempt suicide or, at any rate, in that other person's contemplation of suicide. But in certain circumstances such a belief may fade into almost nothing, or into nothing itself, as where a defendant attempts to aid and abet a person to commit suicide merely on the whim that if he, the defendant, can provide enough assistance, then any person at all, even someone who would never have contemplated suicide could be brought to the point of taking the final step.

■ *Questions*

1. V is suicidal and stands on top of the local multi-storey car park threatening to jump. D is exasperated by the traffic congestion this causes which is making D late for an appointment. D shouts 'Jump, you loser' as he drives by. V jumps and dies. Has D committed an offence?

2. V is terminally ill. She would like to control the manner and time of her death. She persuades her husband, D, to travel with her to Switzerland to a clinic where D will be given a lethal cocktail of drugs to give to V to drink. D is given the drugs by Dr Death at the clinic and he assists V in taking them. V dies. Is D guilty of an offence?

16.4.2 Assisted suicide

There have been recent attempts to clarify when an individual who assists someone who would otherwise be unable to commit suicide will be prosecuted. In the landmark case of *R (Purdy) v DPP* [2009] UKHL 45, P challenged the lawfulness of the failure of the DPP to issue a crime-specific policy identifying the facts and circumstances that would be taken into account when deciding whether to prosecute an individual for assisting suicide. The House of Lords agreed that P's rights under Article 8(1) of the ECHR were engaged and that the failure to promulgate a crime-specific policy meant that the infringement was not justified under Article 8(2). As a result of the judgment, the DPP published the policy mandated by the House of Lords. More recently in *(R) Nicklinson v Ministry of Justice* [2013] EWCA Civ 961 the Court of Appeal held that the DPP's blanket prohibition on assisting suicide was not a disproportionate interference with Article 8. However, the court went on to find that the guidelines in relation to medical professionals who assist their patients to commit suicide were not sufficiently clear to satisfy the requirements of Article 8(2); some indication of the weight that the DPP accorded to the fact that the helper was acting in his capacity as a health-care professional and the victim was in his care was necessary. See further F. Stark, 'Necessity and *Nicklinson*' [2013] Crim LR 949.

16.4.3 Reform

In its Consultation Paper No 173, *Partial Defences to Murder*, the Law Commission recommended abolishing the partial defence of assisted suicide. In its Report No 304, Part 7, the Commission examined the defence in the context of mercy killing and reliance on the suicide defence by those caring for terminally ill individuals. It recommended retention of the defence.

Joint suicide and complicity in suicide

7.42 Section 4 of the Homicide Act 1957 enables D to be convicted of manslaughter rather than murder if D kills V pursuant to a suicide pact. Section 2(1) of the Suicide Act 1961 [as it then was] provides that a person who 'aids, abets, counsels or procures' V to commit suicide is guilty of an offence ('complicity in suicide') punishable with a term of imprisonment not exceeding 14 years. Section 2(2) provides that a person may be convicted of the section 2(1) offence on a charge of murder or manslaughter.

7.43 In some suicide pacts where the intention of D and V is that each should die together, D kills V by setting in train a series of events that results in V's death. In such cases a verdict of manslaughter under section 4 is available but a verdict of complicity in suicide under section 2(1) is not.

7.44 In the CP, we queried whether this was fair given that in 'die together' suicide pacts there may well have been mutual assistance and support in the acts leading up to the attempt to commit suicide together. The verdict of complicity in suicide is not available because, perhaps by chance, the survivor was the one who performed what is taken to be the key conduct which caused V's death.

7.45 We invited views on whether on an indictment for murder or manslaughter, it ought to be possible for D to be convicted of complicity in suicide if the conduct that killed V was meant by D and V to end both their lives. The views of consultees were fairly evenly divided. In the absence of strong support for such a change, we are not minded to recommend it.

Final thoughts and recommendations

7.46 Although we are not making any recommendations for an offence or partial defence of 'mercy' killing, we make the following observations.

7.47 First, Professor Mitchell's surveys suggest that public opinion is generally not unsympathetic to those who believe that they are killing as an act of mercy, particularly if V has expressed a wish to be killed. The surveys reveal very little support for the imposition of a mandatory sentence of life imprisonment in genuine cases of 'mercy' killing. In addition, there is no clear evidence of a majority favouring no kind of prosecution in such cases.

7.48 Secondly, Parliament has already afforded statutory recognition to killings committed as acts of mercy. It has identified killing out of mercy as a potentially mitigating factor in fixing the length of the minimum term following a conviction for murder. There are three reasons why it is arguable that it would be more satisfactory if, in cases of rational 'mercy' killing, Parliament were to make 'mercy' killing a partial defence rather than purely a matter going to mitigation of the minimum term. First, for a genuine 'mercy' killer, a life long licence seems neither necessary nor appropriate. Secondly, if there is a dispute of fact as to D's motive for killing V, it might be thought better that the jury, rather than the trial judge, should decide the issue. Thirdly, a partial defence would avoid the need for the practice, which concerns some of our consultees, of dressing up rational 'mercy' killing cases as ones of diminished responsibility by means of a sympathetic report from a pliant psychiatrist which the court and prosecution are content not to challenge.

7.49 We recommend that the Government should undertake a public consultation on whether and, if so, to what extent the law should recognise either an offence of 'mercy' killing or a partial defence of 'mercy' killing.

7.50 We recommend that, pending the outcome of any public consultation, section 4 of the Homicide Act 1957 should be retained.

FURTHER READING

Diminished responsibility

R. D. Mackay, 'Diminished Responsibility and Mentally Disordered Killers' in A. Ashworth and B. Mitchell (eds), *Rethinking English Homicide Law* (2000)

E. Tennant, *The Future of the Diminished Responsibility Defence to Murder* (2001)

Loss of control

A. Ashworth, 'The Doctrine of Provocation' (1976) 35 CLJ 292

J. Horder, *Provocation and Responsibility* (1992)

J. Horder, *Homicide and the Politics of Law Reform* (2012), Ch 8

A. Howe, '"Red Mist" Homicide: Sexual Infidelity and the English Law of Murder (Glossing Titus Andronicus)' (2013) 33 LS 407

B. J. Mitchell, R. D. Mackay and W. J. Brookbanks, 'Pleading for Provoked Killers: In Defence of *Morgan Smith*' (2008) 124 LQR 675

V. Norse, 'Passion's Progress: Modern Law Reform and the Provocation Defense' (1997) 106 Yale LJ 1331

Suicide

K. Wheat, 'The Law's Treatment of the Suicidal' [2000] Medical L Rev 182

17

Involuntary manslaughter

17.1 Introduction

The previous chapter examined those categories of manslaughter in which the defendant killed with the mens rea for murder, but qualified for one of the partial defences which reduced his crime to one of voluntary manslaughter. In this chapter we examine those types of manslaughter committed where the defendant lacks the mens rea for murder—called involuntary manslaughter. There are various forms of the offence and the culpability involved can range from just short of murder to just worse than accident—sometimes it may even be properly dealt with by a fine or a conditional or absolute discharge.

In recent years Parliament has also introduced a range of statutory crimes of homicide. These include many driving-related offences and the offence under the Domestic Violence, Crime and Victims Act 2004, s 5, relating to causing or allowing the death of a child or vulnerable adult in the household. On the merits of specific statutory offences as opposed to common law manslaughter offences, see A. Ashworth, 'Manslaughter Generic or Nominate Offences' in C. Clarkson and S. Cunningham (eds), *Criminal Liability for Non-Aggressive Death* (2008). The offence of corporate manslaughter is examined in Chapter 9. That offence cannot be committed by a human actor, either as a principal or as an accessory.

Leaving aside the statutory homicide offences, the law of involuntary manslaughter might be summarized as follows:

A person is guilty of involuntary manslaughter where:

(1) he is not guilty of murder by reason only of the fact that, because of voluntary intoxication, he lacked the fault required (Chapter 6); or

(2) he kills another:

(a) by an unlawful and dangerous act (section 17.2, p 594); or

(b) being grossly negligent as to death (section 17.3, p 615); or

(c) being reckless (in the *Cunningham* sense) as to death or serious bodily harm (section 17.4, p 637).

Throughout the chapter we will be considering whether the types of involuntary manslaughter, each of which results in a conviction bearing the same label, share a similar degree of blameworthiness. It should be noted from the outset that there are difficulties in definition. In part this stems from the offence's common law status, and in part because it must be a flexible offence capable of covering all unlawful killings (other than murder and cases caught by specific statutory provisions). The Law Commission concluded that the offence of manslaughter was at risk of being devalued by being left as a 'residual amorphous, catch all homicide offence' (Law Com Report No 304, *Murder, Manslaughter and Infanticide* (2006), para 2.19).

The difficulties of defining involuntary manslaughter were described by Lord Atkin in *Andrews v DPP* [1937] AC 576, [1937] 2 All ER 552, section 17.3, p 618:

My Lords, of all crimes manslaughter appears to afford most difficulties of definition, for it concerns homicide in so many and so varying conditions. From the early days, when any homicide involved penalty, the law has gradually evolved 'through successive differentiations and integrations' until it recognises murder on the one hand, based mainly, though not exclusively, on an intention to kill, and manslaughter on the other hand, based mainly, though not exclusively, on the absence of intention to kill, but the presence of an element of 'unlawfulness' which is the elusive factor.

Some of the controversies that will be examined in this chapter include the following:

(i) whether the unlawful act manslaughter offence is too wide because there is minimal subjective fault required;

(ii) whether the unlawful act manslaughter offence is too vague;

(iii) whether a supplier of drugs can be liable for manslaughter if V dies from having taken them;

(iv) whether gross negligence manslaughter infringes the European Convention on Human Rights (ECHR).

17.2 'Unlawful act' manslaughter

The doctrine of constructive murder, now abolished, was mentioned previously. That led to a murder conviction where D killed in the course of a felony (section 15.3.2, p 532). There existed a similar doctrine of constructive manslaughter where death was caused during the commission of an 'unlawful' act (short of a felony). The doctrine of constructive murder was narrowed down by the judges before being abolished by the Homicide Act 1957. Somewhat similarly, the doctrine of constructive manslaughter has been narrowed down but, despite recommendations of the Criminal Law Revision Committee and the Law Commission (section 17.5, p 639), has not been abolished.

The current law is that D is guilty of manslaughter if he causes V's death by an unlawful and dangerous act. The only mens rea required is an intention to do that act and any fault required to render it unlawful. Provided that a reasonable person would have been aware of the circumstances making the conduct dangerous, it is irrelevant that D is unaware that it is unlawful or that it is dangerous, or that he is unaware of the circumstances which make it dangerous, or whether D himself ought to have been aware of those circumstances.

The elements of the offence are:

• an unlawful act,

• which is performed intentionally,

• which is dangerous in the eyes of a reasonable person, and

• which causes death.

The crime of manslaughter is 'constructed' on the fact that D is committing an unlawful and dangerous act. This explains why the offence is sometimes known as 'constructive manslaughter'. Identifying that base crime on which manslaughter is constructed is essential. In all cases it is useful to ask: what would be charged against D if no one had died? By way of example, if D throws a brick at a greenhouse knowing that V is standing nearby, if V dies when a shard of glass enters his eye, D may be guilty of unlawful act manslaughter. The base offence would be criminal damage.

17.2.1 An 'unlawful' act

Simply stating that the law requires the Crown to prove that D performed an 'unlawful' act opens up a whole raft of questions: must the 'unlawful' act be more than a mere tort or breach of contract? Must it involve the commission of a crime? If so, must all elements of the crime be proved? Will any type of crime suffice or must it be an offence of violence against the person? Is it sufficient that the crime is one of strict liability? Can unlawful act manslaughter be committed by omission?

17.2.1.1 Requirement that D commits a crime

Historically, the offence of unlawful act manslaughter was committed where D killed someone in the course of committing a tort. For example, in *Fenton* (1830) 1 Lew CC 179, Tindal CJ directed the jury that throwing stones down a mine shaft was a trespass and therefore it followed that the defendant was guilty of manslaughter where, as a result of his throwing a stone down the shaft, some scaffolding broke, a corf overturned and miners were killed. However, in *Franklin* (1883) 15 Cox CC 163, Sussex Assizes, it was settled that the unlawful act must amount to a criminal offence committed by the defendant before there can be an unlawful act manslaughter conviction. In that case, Field J stated that 'the mere fact of a civil wrong committed by one person against another ought not to be used as an incident which is a necessary step in a criminal case. I have a great abhorrence of constructive crime'. This decision had the obvious effect of narrowing the scope of the offence somewhat. As will be seen, at various stages in history judges have sought to contract and expand the scope of unlawful act manslaughter, thereby demonstrating what an amorphous offence it is.

In the following case the Court of Appeal clarified certain aspects of the offence, in particular that the unlawful act amounts to a criminal offence.

R v Lamb
[1967] 2 All ER 1282, Court of Appeal, Criminal Division

(Sachs LJ, Lyell and Geoffrey Lane JJ)

As a joke, Lamb pointed at his best friend a revolver with five chambers. It had bullets in two of the chambers but neither of these was opposite the barrel. He therefore thought it was safe to pull the trigger. His friend was also treating the matter as a joke. Lamb pulled the trigger and shot his friend dead. The revolver functioned in such a way that, when the trigger was pulled, the chambers rotated, bringing the loaded chamber opposite the barrel, before the firing pin struck. Lamb was charged with manslaughter and set up the defence of accident. The judge directed that the pointing of the revolver and pulling of the trigger was an unlawful act even if there was no intent to injure or alarm and that the jury did not need to consider whether the pointing of the gun was an assault.

[Sachs LJ, reading the judgment of the court:]

Counsel for the Crown, however, had at all times put forward the correct view that for the act to be unlawful it must constitute at least what he then termed 'a technical assault'. In this court, moreover, he rightly conceded that there was no evidence to go to the jury of any assault of any kind. Nor did he feel able to submit that the acts of the appellant were on any other ground unlawful in the criminal sense of that word. Indeed no such submission could in law be made: if, for instance, the pulling of the trigger had had no effect because the striking mechanism or the ammunition had been defective no offence would have been committed by the appellant. Another way of putting it is that mens rea being now an essential ingredient in manslaughter (compare *Andrews v DPP* [[1937] AC 576 at 582,

[1937] 2 All ER 552 at 555, 556; section 17.3, p 618] and *Church* [[1965] 2 All ER 72 at 76, [1966] 1QB 59 at 70; section 17.2.3, p 599] this could not in the present case be established in relation to the first ground except by proving that element of intent without which there can be no assault. It is perhaps as well to mention that when using the phrase 'unlawful in the criminal sense of that word' the court has in mind that it is long settled that it is not in point to consider whether an act is unlawful merely from the angle of civil liabilities. That was first made clear in *Franklin* [(1883) 15 Cox CC 163]. The relevant extracts from this and from later judgments are collected in *Russell on Crime* (11th edn, 1958), pp 651–658. The whole of that part of the summing-up which concerned the first ground was thus vitiated by misdirections based on an erroneous concept of the law; and the strength with which that ground was put to the jury no doubt stemmed from the firm view of the trial judge, expressed more than once in the course of the discussion on law in relation to the undisputed facts: 'How can there be a defence to the charge of manslaughter? Manslaughter requires no intent.' . . . [His lordship discussed the judge's direction on criminal negligence.] The general effect of the summing-up was thus to withdraw from the jury the defence put forward on behalf of the appellant. When the gravamen of a charge is criminal negligence—often referred to as recklessness—of an accused, the jury have to consider amongst other matters the state of his mind, and that includes the question of whether or not he thought that that which he was doing was safe. In the present case it would, of course, have been fully open to a jury, if properly directed, to find the accused guilty because they considered his view as to there being no danger was formed in a criminally negligent way. But he was entitled to a direction that the jury should take into account the fact that he had indisputably formed this view and that there was expert evidence as to this being an understandable view. Strong though the evidence of criminal negligence was, the appellant was entitled as of right to have his defence considered but he was not accorded this right and the jury was left without a direction on an essential matter. Those defects of themselves are such that the verdict cannot stand . . .

Appeal allowed

■ *Questions*

1. Could Lamb, in the view of the court, be guilty though he believed his conduct was perfectly safe?
2. What would have been the position if:

(a) Lamb had intended to alarm his friend by pointing the gun but the friend was not alarmed?
(b) Lamb did not intend to alarm his friend, or foresee that he might be alarmed, but the friend was in fact alarmed?

In *Scarlett* [1993] 4 All ER 629, D, a licensee, killed a trespasser by using excessive force while lawfully expelling him from his pub. D's conviction for manslaughter was quashed because the judge had directed that D was guilty if he had used unnecessary and unreasonable force—which would have been the tort of battery. To be guilty of manslaughter it was necessary to prove that D committed the crime of battery, not just the tort. That meant proving that D's use of force was excessive in the circumstances *which D believed to exist—Gladstone Williams*, section 11.6.1.1, p 415.

In assessing whether a base crime has been committed on which the manslaughter charge might be constructed, it is important to have regard to whether all the elements of that offence can be proved and any defences disproved. In *Slingsby* [1995] Crim LR 570, D had vaginal and anal sex with V with her consent. Then, also with her consent, he penetrated her vagina and rectum with his hand. V suffered cuts caused by a signet ring on D's hand. She did not realize for some time that the injuries were potentially very serious. Eventually she was admitted to hospital but died from septicaemia. D was charged with manslaughter by an unlawful and dangerous act. Judge J, as he then was, ruled that, putting the Crown's case at its highest, there was no manslaughter. The injuries were suffered as a result of vigorous sexual activity with V's consent. In other words, V consented to the battery and the sexual acts. There was no base crime committed on which manslaughter could be constructed. It would, in Judge J's judgement, be contrary to principle to treat as criminal activity that which would not otherwise amount to an assault merely because in the course of that activity an injury occurred. The Crown offered no evidence and a verdict of not guilty was returned.

The acts done by D to V in *Slingsby* would plainly have been assaults or batteries if V had not consented to them. Since in law it is possible for V to consent to assault and in fact she did so, there was no crime. In *Meachen* [2006] EWCA Crim 2414, the level of injury caused by D inserting his fingers into V's anus was serious. The question for the court was whether D had a defence of consent to that injury (GBH under s 20 OAPA). D did have a defence provided (i) V consented to it in fact or D believed she did, and (ii) the law was prepared to recognize that that level of injury could be consented to in the performance of vigorous sex (see section 19.4.2, p 686). The Court of Appeal quashed D's conviction. He had a genuine belief in her consent. If V had done there would have been no base crime.

In *A* [2005] 69 J Crim L 394, D's post-exam celebrations included pushing V into a river where he drowned. D claimed that he was entitled to a defence of belief in consent, his actions being mere horseplay. The Court of Appeal confirmed that if D had caused V to fall in the river by a non-accidental act and D did not have a genuine belief in V's consent to the assault, D would be liable for manslaughter if all sober and reasonable people realized it was dangerous in the sense discussed below. It is vital to check that D has committed the base crime.

17.2.2 An intentional act

What mens rea must D have in the commission of the unlawful act or 'base crime'? Is it sufficient that he performs a voluntary act that is in fact unlawful? Is it necessary for the Crown to prove that D had the mens rea that is required by the terms of the base crime?

In the *A-G's Reference (No 3 of 1994)* [1997] UKHL 31, D had stabbed his pregnant girlfriend in the abdomen and the foetus was injured. The foetus was born alive but died from injuries sustained in the womb. The trial judge ruled that there was no offence of murder on such facts, and the Attorney General referred the case to the Court of Appeal and ultimately to the House of Lords. In the course of the discussion of murder and transferred intention, see section 15.2.3.2, p 528, the House of Lords also addressed the possible application of unlawful act manslaughter to such facts:

The first point to be made here is that to require the prosecutor to prove beyond reasonable doubt that it was reasonably foreseeable that an unlawful act such as that which was committed in this case would result in the risk of injury to the child some time after being born would make it very difficult in practice for him to obtain a conviction.

The intention which must be discovered is an intention to do an act which is unlawful and dangerous. In this case, the act which had to be shown to be an unlawful and dangerous act was the stabbing of the child's mother. There can be no doubt that all sober and reasonable people would regard that act, within the appropriate meaning of this term, as dangerous. It is plain that it was unlawful as it was done with the intention of causing her injury. As the defendant intended to commit that act, all the ingredients necessary for mens rea in regard to the crime of manslaughter were established, irrespective of who was the ultimate victim of it. The fact that the child whom the mother was carrying at the time was born alive and then died as a result of the stabbing is all that was needed for the offence of manslaughter when the actus reus for that crime was completed by the child's death. The question, once all the other elements are satisfied, is simply one of causation. The defendant must accept all the consequences of his act, so long as the jury are satisfied that he did what he did intentionally, that what he did was unlawful and that, applying the correct test, it was also dangerous. (per Lord Hope of Craighead at 958)

Must the defendant have any mens rea beyond that required for the base offence? Must he be reckless as to death or the risk of death or even the risk of injury?

Director of Public Prosecutions v Newbury and Jones

[1976] UKHL 3, House of Lords, http://www.bailii.org/uk/cases/UKHL/1976/3.html

(Lords Diplock, Simon of Glaisdale, Kilbrandon, Salmon and Edmund-Davies)

The defendants were two boys who pushed a part of a paving stone off a railway bridge into the path of an oncoming train. It went through the cab window on the train and killed the guard. They were convicted of his manslaughter.

Lord Salmon:

The point of law certified to be of general public importance is:

'Can a defendant be properly convicted of manslaughter, when his mind is not affected by drink or drugs, if he did not foresee that his act might cause harm to another?'

The learned trial judge did not direct the jury that they should acquit the appellants unless they were satisfied beyond a reasonable doubt that the appellants had foreseen that they might cause harm to someone by pushing the piece of paving stone off the parapet into the path of the approaching train. In my view the learned trial judge was quite right not to give such a direction to the jury. The direction which he gave is completely in accordance with established law, which, possibly with one exception to which I shall presently refer, has never been challenged. In *Larkin* [[1943] 1 All ER 217 at 219] Humphreys J said:

'Where the act which a person is engaged in performing is unlawful, then if at the same time it is a dangerous act, that is, an act which is likely to injure another person, and quite inadvertently he causes the death of that other person by that act, then he is guilty of manslaughter.'

I agree entirely with Lawton LJ that that is an admirably clear statement of the law which has been applied many times. It makes it plain (a) that an accused is guilty of manslaughter if it is proved that he intentionally did an act which was unlawful and dangerous and that that act inadvertently caused death and (b) that it is unnecessary to prove that the accused knew that the act was unlawful or dangerous. This is one of the reasons why cases of manslaughter vary so infinitely in their gravity. They may amount to little more than pure inadvertence and sometimes to little less than murder.

I am sure that in *Church* [section 17.2.3, p 599] Edmund Davies J, in giving the judgment of the court, did not intend to differ from or qualify anything which had been said in *Larkin*. Indeed he was restating the principle laid down in that case by illustrating the sense in which the word 'dangerous' should be understood. Edmund Davies J said [[1965] EWCA Crim 1, [1966] 1QB 59 at 70, [1965] 2 All ER 72 at 76]:

'For such a verdict [guilty of manslaughter] inexorably to follow, the unlawful act must be such as all sober and reasonable people would inevitably recognise must subject the other person to, at least, the risk of some harm resulting therefrom, albeit not serious harm.'

The test is still the objective test. In judging whether the act was dangerous, the test is not did the accused recognise that it was dangerous but would all sober and reasonable people recognise its danger . . .

Appeal dismissed

Since the judge did not direct the jury that it must be proved that the defendant foresaw harm to anyone, the question for the House was whether a person doing what the defendants did but not foreseeing harm to anyone could properly be convicted. *Newbury* is a difficult case to reconcile with *Lamb* since it is unclear what offence DD would have been charged with had no one died. Remember the first step when considering unlawful act manslaughter is to establish all the elements of the base offence. When DD threw the concrete slab over the parapet they were not guilty of assault or any of the usual offences against the person, since these require mens rea. The more recent case of *Kennedy (No 2)* [2007] UKHL 38 supports the view that a criminal act must be identified and proved for unlawful act manslaughter.

■ *Questions*

1. Why is foresight of injury to or alarm of V necessary if D points a revolver at V but not necessary if he throws a paving stone from a parapet?

2. Will D be liable for manslaughter if he commits a crime of strict liability? Suppose that in *Alphacell v Woodward*, section 7.3.2, p 197, a swimmer in the river had ingested some of the effluent and died as a result. Would this amount to manslaughter? Cf *Andrews* [2003] Crim LR 477 and commentary (strict liability medicines prescription offence).

Remember it is helpful to ask when considering this element of the offence what crime D would be convicted of had no one died. All elements of the so-called base crime must be proved in full. In addition to proving the mens rea and actus reus of the base offence, the prosecution must disprove any defences to the base offence raised by D.

17.2.3 Dangerousness

Consider when reading the following case whether it is necessary for D to appreciate that his act is dangerous. Is it sufficient that the reasonable person considers it dangerous? What amounts to danger? A risk of death? A risk of some lesser injury? What do you think the test ought to be?

R v Church

[1965] EWCA Crim 1, Court of Criminal Appeal, http://www.bailii.org/ew/cases/EWCA/Crim/1965/1.html

(Edmund Davies, Marshall and Widgery JJ)

The appellant, according to his account, took a woman, Mrs Nott, to his van for sex. He was unable to satisfy her. She reproached him and slapped his face. They had a fight and he knocked her unconscious. He tried unsuccessfully for about half an hour to wake her, panicked, dragged her out of the van and put her in the river. Mrs Nott drowned.

At the trial, the appellant said for the first time that he thought she was dead when he put her in the water. The judge directed the jury that if Mrs Nott in fact was alive when thrown into the river, whether the appellant knew it or not, that was manslaughter. The jury convicted him of manslaughter.

[Edmund Davies J having cited the judge's direction on this issue:]

Such a direction is not lacking in authority; see, for example, *Shoukatallie v R* [[1962] AC 81, [1961] 3 All ER 996], in Lord Denning's opinion [[1962] AC 81 at 86, 92, [1961] 3 All ER 996 at 998, 1001], and Dr Glanville Williams' *Criminal Law* (2nd edn) at p 173. Nevertheless, in the judgment of this court it was misdirection. It amounted to telling the jury that, whenever any unlawful act is committed in relation to a human being which resulted in death there must be, at least, a conviction for manslaughter. This might at one time have been regarded as good law: see, for example, *Fenton* [(1830) 1 Lew CC 179]. It appears to this court, however, that the passage of years has achieved a transformation in this branch of the law and, even in relation to manslaughter, a degree of mens rea has become recognised as essential. To define it is a difficult task, and in *Andrews v DPP* [[1937] AC 576 at 582, [1937] 2 All ER 552 at 555; section 17.3, p 618] Lord Atkin spoke of the element of ' "unlawfulness" which is the elusive factor'. Stressing that we are here leaving entirely out of account those ingredients of homicide which might justify a verdict of manslaughter on the grounds of (a) criminal negligence, or (b) provocation or (c) diminished responsibility, the conclusion of this court is that an unlawful act causing the death of another cannot, simply because it is an unlawful act, render a manslaughter verdict inevitable. For such a verdict inexorably to follow, the unlawful act must be such as all sober and reasonable people would inevitably recognise must subject the other person to, at least, the risk of some harm resulting therefrom, albeit not serious harm ...

If such be the test, as we adjudge it to be, then it follows that, in our view, it was a misdirection to tell the jury *simpliciter* that it mattered nothing for manslaughter whether or not the appellant believed Mrs Nott to be dead when he threw her in the river ...

[The court dismissed the appeal on the ground that judge's direction on criminal negligence was an adequate one and, quite apart from that, the principle of *Thabo Meli*, section 2.4.2, p 35, applied to manslaughter (following Glanville Williams, *Criminal Law* (2nd edn), p 174) and the jury were entitled to regard the appellant's conduct as a series of acts which culminated in her death.]

Appeal dismissed

■ *Questions*

1. What was the crime with which Church could have been charged had no one died?

2. What does 'at least, the risk of some harm resulting therefrom, albeit not serious harm ...' mean? What type of risk? What degree of harm?

3. D, aged 11, is throwing stones at a tin can he has perched on the edge of a bridge over a canal. One stone thrown misses the can and lands on a passing barge beneath, hitting V, aged 2, who is killed. Is D liable for manslaughter? What further information do you require to determine his liability?

4. Professor Horder argues that in most cases the additional requirement that the act be dangerous is superfluous as danger is inherent in the unlawful itself. Do you agree? See J. Horder, *Homicide and the Politics of Law Reform* (2012).

See further R. A. Duff, 'Whose Luck is it Anyway?' in C. Clarkson and S. Cunningham (eds), *Criminal Liability for Non Aggressive Death* (2008).

In *Arobieke* [1988] Crim LR 314, D who was 'looking for' V, pursued him on to railway lines. V was killed by a train. There was no evidence that D had actually threatened V, so no actus reus of assault could be established. The conviction for manslaughter was quashed.

In the *A-G's Reference* case (section 17.2.2, p 597) involving the stabbing of the pregnant woman, Lord Mustill stated (at 950):

All that is needed, once causation is established, is an act creating a risk to *anyone*; and such a risk is obviously established in the case of any violent assault by the risk to the person of the victim herself (or himself). In a case such as the present, therefore, responsibility for manslaughter would automatically be established, once causation has been shown simply by proving a violent attack even if (which cannot have been the case here) the attacker had no idea that the woman was pregnant. On a broader canvas, the proposition involves that manslaughter can be established against someone who does any wrongful act leading to death in circumstances where it was foreseeable that it might hurt anyone at all; and that this is so even if the victim does not fall into any category of persons whom a reasonable person in the position of the defendant might have envisaged as being within the area of potential risk.

Difficulty arises in cases where the victim has some characteristic that makes D's act dangerous in circumstances where it would not be so if V did not have the characteristic. The rule is that the characteristic is only relevant if it would have been known to the sober and reasonable observer of the event (ie the commission of the base crime), even if it was not known to D. For example, in *Watson* [1989] 2 All ER 865 D burgled V's house. V was a frail, 87-year-old man. It was held that the base crime of burglary became 'dangerous' as soon as V's frailty and age would have been obvious to the reasonable observer. The unlawful act continued through the 'whole of the burglarious intrusion' so that when V died of a heart attack that was caused by D's continuing in the burglary after it had become dangerous, he was guilty of manslaughter. This can be contrasted with *Dawson* (1985) 81 Cr App R 150 in which V had a weak heart and died during an attempted robbery. V was standing behind armour-plated glass and D was brandishing a replica firearm. It was held that D was not guilty of manslaughter because the reasonable observer would not, at any point in the continuance of the base crime—robbery—have known of V's peculiar susceptibility. Therefore the act of robbery was not 'dangerous' in the *Church* sense.

However, there remains uncertainty over the extent to which the reasonable bystander is endowed with the knowledge of the accused. For example, D intends to rob a bank but does not wish to harm anyone. For this reason he buys what he has been told is a replica shotgun. Unbeknownst to D, the shotgun is in fact real. When D points the gun at V and pulls the trigger the gun fires and kills him. Would the reasonable bystander have the same knowledge as D that the gun was a replica? In *Dawson* Watkins LJ stated:

this test [ie the dangerousness test] can only be undertaken upon the basis of the knowledge gained by a sober and reasonable man as though he were present at the scene of and watched the unlawful act being performed…he has the same knowledge as the man attempting to rob and no more.

This could indicate that the reasonable bystander would also think the gun a replica.

However, this was doubted in *Ball* [1989] Crim LR 730 in which it was observed that:

…*Dawson's* case goes no further than showing that the sober and reasonable man must look at the unlawful act to see if it is dangerous and not at the peculiarities of the victim.

Ball can, however, be distinguished from *Dawson* on its facts. In that case D took a shotgun and loaded it with cartridges from his pocket. The pocket contained both live and blank cartridges and D had no way of knowing what he had loaded his shotgun with. The reasonable bystander would surely have thought there was the risk of some harm, given that it was just as likely that D had loaded the shotgun with live cartridges as with blanks. In his comment on the case, Professor Smith stated:

The sober and reasonable man cannot be treated as having come on the scene at the moment of the fatal act with no knowledge of any earlier events. His knowledge must surely include awareness of the preparatory acts done by the defendant—in the present case his taking up a handful of cartridges from a pocket which he knew to contain both live ones and blanks. It was this act which made the subsequent pulling of the trigger dangerous and the sober and reasonable person would have recognised it as such.

17.2.3.1 Unlawful act manslaughter does not necessarily include gross negligence manslaughter

In *Watts* [1998] Crim LR 833, there was evidence that D, a nurse and devoted mother of a severely handicapped child, had removed a tracheotomy tube from the child's throat after an operation. She was charged with murder and convicted of manslaughter. The judge directed the jury as to the ingredients of unlawful and dangerous act manslaughter. Defence counsel had raised the issue of manslaughter by gross negligence in his speech to the jury and the judge referred to that point in his summing-up but did not direct as to the ingredients of that form of the offence. D appealed on the ground that the jury might have convicted of that offence without being aware of, or satisfied about, its constituents. The Crown argued unsuccessfully that the unlawful and dangerous act direction, as in *Church*, was a sufficient basis for the jury to convict of gross negligence manslaughter. D's appeal was allowed. *Church* does indeed require gross negligence. Since an element is that 'all sober and reasonable people would inevitably recognise the risk' it must surely be grossly negligent not to recognize it; but (i) in unlawful act manslaughter it need be a risk of only some slight harm, whereas grossly negligent manslaughter requires foreseeability of death and (ii)— the crucial point in *Watts*—the negligence must be considered bad enough by the jury to justify conviction of manslaughter. Such badness is not an ingredient of unlawful act manslaughter. A properly instructed jury which is sure that D is guilty of unlawful act manslaughter is not by any means necessarily sure that he is guilty of manslaughter by gross negligence. D's appeal had to be allowed because the judge did not direct the jury as to the requirements of the offence.

17.2.3.2 D's act directed at V?

Must D's act be a direct cause of death? In *Goodfellow* (1986) 83 Cr App R 23, [1986] Crim LR 468, G, wanting to move from his council house but having no chance of exchanging it, set fire to the house, attempting to make it appear that the fire was caused by a petrol bomb. His wife, another woman and his son died in the fire. He appealed from conviction of manslaughter on the ground that the jury had been misdirected as to '*Lawrence* recklessness' (section 5.3, p 122). The Court of Appeal, having held that there had been no such misdirection, said there was also a case for an 'unlawful and dangerous act' direction. The appellant argued that the acts were not 'directed at' the victim, but the court rejected the argument that 'there must be an intention on the part of the defendant to harm or frighten or a realisation that his acts were likely to harm or frighten'.

17.2.4 Can there be manslaughter by an unlawful and dangerous omission?

In *Khan and Khan* [1998] Crim LR 830, the court said that manslaughter by omission is no more than an example of manslaughter arising from a grossly negligent breach of duty. Certainly the fault alleged in omission cases will usually be gross negligence. But is gross negligence the only form of manslaughter available for omissions? There can be a murder conviction based on an omission in breach of a duty to act, with intent to cause grievous bodily harm: *Gibbins and Proctor* (1918) 13 Cr App R 134, section 4.4, p 94, and it seems logical that, if the intent was to cause some lesser degree of harm, the offence should be manslaughter. This falls into the 'constructive' category rather than that of gross negligence. However, there is authority saying that a criminal omission can never be an 'unlawful act' for the purposes of constructive manslaughter: *Lowe* [1973] 1 All ER 805, [1973] QB 702 (Glanville Williams, TBCL 276). However, that case was forcefully and cogently criticized by the editor (Ashworth) in [1976] Crim LR 529: 'In the absence of strong and clear arguments in favour of treating homicide by neglect as less serious than other forms of homicide, the distinction set out in *Lowe* can only be based on superstition.'

17.2.5 Causing death

The unlawful, intentional, dangerous act by D must cause V's death. The ordinary principles of causation discussed in Chapter 3 apply here. In some cases, the causal link between the unlawful act and the death can be very difficult to establish.

The next case illustrates how difficult the offence of unlawful act manslaughter can be, with issues as to the unlawfulness, dangerousness and causation all arising. The extract is a relatively long one to allow for examination of each of these problems in a complex case.

R v Carey
[2006] EWCA Crim 17, [2006] Crim LR 842, Court of Appeal, Criminal Division, http://www.bailii.org/ew/cases/EWCA/Crim/2006/17.html

(Dyson LJ, Tomlinson and Andrew-Smith JJ)

The victim, Aimee Wellock (aged 15), and three friends were walking in a park area. The three defendants had spent the afternoon there drinking alcohol. When Aimee and her group met Carey's group by chance, Carey and her group began to abuse Aimee's group verbally. Carey struck one of Aimee's group, James, from behind and he moved away from both groups. Carey then punched another of Aimee's group, Shelley, in the face three times, causing her to fall over. Carey carried on the assault by kicking her on the nose, mouth and top of the right arm while she was down. Carey finally attacked Aimee, who was about 10 metres away from where Shelley had been assaulted. The attack on Aimee and her friends lasted about one minute. Aimee ran off, covering a distance of 109 metres over rough grass and up a slight slope. Aimee felt faint, collapsed and died that same night. The post-mortem revealed that the immediate cause of death was ventricular fibrillation (dysrhythmia). Aimee suffered from a severely diseased heart. Even the doctors who had treated her for certain other medical conditions were unaware of it. Aimee appeared physically fit and participated in dancing and other physical activities. The experts found that Aimee might not have died if she had not run 109 metres. Both experts accepted that the event 'most proximate to the collapse and therefore most likely to have been the precipitating factor which led to Aimee's death was her running away from the incident'.

The unlawful act (base crime) alleged against Carey was an affray contrary to the Public Order Act 1986, s 3:

(1) A person is guilty of affray if he uses or threatens unlawful violence towards another and his conduct is such as would cause a person of reasonable firmness present at the scene to fear for his personal safety.

(2) Where 2 or more persons use or threaten the unlawful violence, it is the conduct of them taken together that must be considered for the purposes of sub-section (1).

(3) For the purposes of this section a threat cannot be made by the use of words alone.

Carey was convicted of unlawful act manslaughter and appealed.

Dyson LJ [dealt with the facts, and issues relating to the appeal against conviction for affray]:

26. This being a case of alleged unlawful act manslaughter, it is not in issue that the Crown had to prove three elements, namely (i) that there was an unlawful act, (ii) which was dangerous in the sense that the unlawful act subjected Aimee to the risk of physical harm, and (iii) that the unlawful act caused her death.

27. At the close of the Crown case, Mr Harrison submitted that count 1 should be withdrawn from the jury. He contended that causation was not made out because (i) there was no evidence that the affray caused Aimee to run away (and thereby suffer the ventricular fibrillation), and (ii) in any event, there was no evidence that anyone would have recognised that running as she did would subject Aimee to the risk of harm. The judge rejected both arguments. He held that causation was a question of fact for the jury. As regards the second argument, he said that 'the necessity of establishing at least a risk of physical harm is a self-contained requirement that has nothing to do with causation, but is concerned only with the dangerousness of the unlawful act. If the act was unlawful and dangerous in the *R v Church* sense and caused the deceased's death, unlawful act manslaughter will be made out.'

28. The unlawful act relied on in this case is affray. It is important to emphasise at the outset that the Crown chose not to rely on C's assault on Aimee as the unlawful act in question. They could have attempted to secure convictions for manslaughter against C on the basis that she was Aimee's direct assailant and against the other defendants on the basis of joint enterprise liability for that assault.

■ *Question*

Could a conviction be secured on the basis that Carey caused Aimee to apprehend unlawful violence (base crime of assault) and that in reasonable response Aimee fled and died as a result?

[His lordship continued:]

The second element of the offence of unlawful act manslaughter is that of dangerousness. The act must be recognisably dangerous. This is a relatively recent limitation on unlawful act manslaughter and was clearly articulated in those terms by the Court of Appeal in *Larkin* [1943] 1 All ER 217. [His lordship referred to *Larkin* and then to *Church*.]

31. The *Church* test was subsequently approved by Lord Salmon in *Newbury* [1977] AC 500, 507C–E [section 17.2.2, p 598], saying that he was sure that in *Church* the court did not intend to differ from or qualify anything that had been said in *Larkin*. We are inclined to agree with Mr Harrison that, *pace* Lord Salmon, there is a difference between the tests for dangerousness set out in these two cases. *Larkin* requires that the act is likely to injure another; *Church* only requires a risk of some harm resulting. As Mr Harrison points out, as a matter of ordinary language, there is a difference between foresight that an act is likely to injure another, and foresight that there is a risk of some harm resulting. But the difference is not material in the present case. We propose to adopt the *Church* formulation on the grounds that it is more recent, was expressly approved in *Newbury* and is more satisfactory . . .

34. In later cases, the Court of Appeal explained both the type of harm which should have been foreseen, and the knowledge and attributes which could be ascribed to the reasonable person by whose response it is determined whether the act was dangerous. Two cases are of particular relevance to the present appeal. [His lordship referred to *Dawson* and *Watson* [section 17.2.3, p 601] . . .

35. Thus, in considering whether the unlawful act is dangerous in the context of manslaughter, it may be relevant to have regard to the attributes of the victim. Of course, a punch which causes a person to fall will almost inevitably satisfy the test of dangerousness. That is why a defendant who punches a victim who falls and suffers a fatal head injury as a result is guilty of manslaughter. It is foreseeable that the victim is at risk of suffering some physical harm from such a punch (albeit not serious harm), and that is sufficient. Physical harm includes shock. The reason why the death resulting from the attempted robbery of the 60 year old petrol station attendant was not manslaughter was that the attempted robbery was not dangerous in the relevant sense. It was not foreseeable that an apparently

healthy 60 year old man would suffer shock and a heart attack as a result of such an attempted robbery. On the other hand, the jury properly found that it was foreseeable that an obviously frail and very old man was at risk of suffering shock leading to a heart attack as a result of a burglary committed at his home late at night.

36. . . . Mr Harrison rightly conceded that there may be circumstances in which a verdict of unlawful act manslaughter can properly be entered where the alleged unlawful act is affray. Suppose that a very old and obviously frail man is the victim of an affray in which a number of youths participate; and suppose further that he is not physically assaulted, but each of the youths uses and/or threatens violence (but not by words alone) such that a person of reasonable firmness present at the scene would fear for his personal safety; and finally suppose that, as a result of the incident, the man suffers a heart attack from which he dies. On such facts, the jury might well conclude that the affray would be dangerous in the sense of being an act which sober and reasonable people would recognise subjected the old man at least to the risk of some harm resulting from it (shock), and so could properly find the youths guilty of manslaughter. The case would be analogous to *Watson*.

37. But, in our view quite rightly, the judge declined to leave the manslaughter charge to the jury on the basis that the affray had caused Aimee to suffer shock leading to her heart attack. In his summing up, the judge explained to the jury that they should 'take shock out of this case' because the difference between emotional upset, which is not physical harm, and shock, which is, is a 'grey area'. We agree with this observation, but would go further. Even if the affray had caused Aimee to suffer shock as opposed to emotional upset, the affray lacked the quality of dangerousness in the relevant sense. This is because it would not have been recognised by a sober and reasonable bystander that an apparently healthy 15 year old (or indeed anyone else present) was at risk of suffering shock as a result of this affray. In our view, this affray was less dangerous in the relevant sense than the attempted robbery of the 60 year old petrol station attendant in *Dawson*. The risk of that victim suffering shock leading to a heart attack would have been recognised by a sober and reasonable person as more likely than the risk of Aimee suffering shock leading to a heart attack as a result of the affray.

38. But the judge did accept the submission of Mr Myerson [counsel for the Crown] that it was sufficient that, in determining whether the affray subjected Aimee to the risk of at least some physical harm, it was legitimate to aggregate the infliction of violence on her two friends to the violence on herself, and to decide that that aggregated violence satisfied the test of dangerousness. The only remaining question was whether that aggregated violence was a cause of death. That this was the judge's view appears more clearly in his summing up than in the judgment that he gave when he ruled on the submission at the close of the Crown case. . . [His lordship quoted from the judge's summing-up.]

41. Thus, in deciding whether any appellant had committed an unlawful act against Aimee which was dangerous in the relevant sense, the jury could take into account the violence inflicted on all three of the victims and not just that inflicted on Aimee. It followed that the jury did not have to be sure that the assault on her by C was a cause of Aimee's death; it was sufficient if the violence by all defendants on all three victims was causative of death.

[His lordship considered the offence of affray.] . . .

46. In the present case, the only dangerous act in the relevant sense was the assault by C on Aimee. A punch to the face is a dangerous unlawful act. If Aimee had fallen against a hard surface and suffered an injury from which she had died, C would have been guilty of manslaughter on a straightforward application of *Church* principles. But in the circumstances of this case, Aimee's death was not caused by injuries that were a foreseeable result of the assault in the sense that the risk of such injuries would have been recognised by a sober or reasonable person having the knowledge that the appellants had. As we understand it, Mr Myerson accepts this. The slight injuries caused by the assault cannot be said to have been a cause of her death. That is why the judge did not direct the jury that it

was necessary for them to be sure that the physical harm actually inflicted was a cause of her death before they could convict of manslaughter.

47. It follows from the fact that (a) the only dangerous act perpetrated on Aimee (C's punch) did not cause her death, and (b) the other acts and threats of violence used in the course of the affray were not dangerous in the relevant sense as against Aimee, that none of the appellants was guilty of manslaughter.

48. By way of postscript, we should say a word about 'escape'. There are circumstances where the *actus reus* of a crime is completed by the act of the victim rather than that of the offender. Thus, where the victim injures himself in a fall whilst attempting to escape from an attack by the offender, the latter may be regarded as having caused that injury. Or take the case of the defendant convicted of assault occasioning actual bodily harm to his victim who was injured jumping from his moving car after he had assaulted her in that car: *Roberts* (1971) 56 Cr App R 95.

49. In his summing up, the judge directed the jury: 'if, however, you conclude that Aimee was still reasonably in fear of being attacked and that running away was a reasonable thing to do, you may conclude that the affray was a significant cause of death.' Mr Harrison and Mr Watson both submit that there was no evidence that Aimee was running away in order to escape from the possibility of further attack, rather than because she wanted to get home as quickly as possible. They say that the judge should not have left that issue to the jury, since it was impossible for the jury to decide why she ran away. Indeed, they say that there was no evidence that she was running away from her assailants: they were heading in the opposite direction and there was no actual or threatened violence present at the time when Aimee ran.

50. Mr Myerson did not rely on the death caused by the running away as analogous to the injury caused during the attempted escape in *Roberts*. He did not advance the case as an 'escape' case in that sense. He does not submit that Aimee ran off in fear of being attacked or threatened with violence. Rather, he submits that the running away was part of 'one overall incident which comprises the necessary crime antecedent to the death. Escape was not relied on. It was simply part of the overall picture which the jury had to consider because the case involved the run uphill and that was the last thing Aimee did.' . . . Viewed in that light, it seems to us that the running away does not require any modification of what we have already said. We do not understand Mr Myerson to submit that, if we reject his other arguments, the manslaughter conviction should be upheld by reason of the running away point . . .

53. For the reasons that we have given, to hold these appellants liable for the death of Aimee in circumstances such as occurred in this case would involve an unwarranted extension of the law. In our view, such an extension would come close to saying that if X commits an unlawful act but for which Y would not have died, X is criminally liable for the death of Y. That is not our law. Our law requires that X commits an unlawful act which is dangerous in the sense that it is recognised by sober and reasonable persons as subjecting Y to the risk of some physical harm which in turn causes the death. The only act committed against Aimee which was dangerous in that sense was C's assault on her, but physical harm resulting from the assault itself did not cause Aimee's death. It must follow that none of the appellants was guilty of manslaughter.

Appeal against the conviction for manslaughter allowed

In relation to what the court has to say about those cases where V dies in the course of fleeing from D, the later case of *Lewis* [2010] EWCA Crim 151 is instructive. Here, the Court of Appeal upheld the judge's direction to the jury that they should consider whether V running away from D was one of the responses which might reasonably be expected from someone who found himself in V's situation. If it was, D would remain liable. In cases of death during flight from an unlawful act, it is necessary to show that but for the unlawful act, flight and therefore death would not have occurred. See section 3.2.3.5, p 64 for further discussion.

■ *Questions*

1. What was the unlawful act committed by Carey? Why did the Crown not rely on the assault on Aimee and the flight by her to avoid that assault? Cf *Roberts* (1971) Cr App R 95.

2. Was the act dangerous? Was it only dangerous when viewed in combination with the acts of others?

3. Is the court right in its analysis of aggregating the conduct of many? If D1 is waving a machete around and D2 is shaking his fist at V, their affray comprises their combined conduct. Likewise, the dangerousness of the acts is properly assessed by looking at the combination of their conduct. It is submitted that there is no problem in aggregating the conduct of D1, D2 and D3 towards V1 and V2. Take a case where in the course of a robbery D1 issues serious threats against V1 and D2 issues threats to V2, and the obviously frail V2 died from a heart attack induced by the shock. It is submitted that the actions of D1 and D2 could be aggregated in determining whether the conduct was sufficiently 'dangerous' in the sense required by *Church*.

4. Did the unlawful and dangerous act cause Aimee's death? If not, what did?

The Court of Appeal considered *Carey* in the following case and rejected an interpretation of the elements of unlawful act manslaughter that would have considerably narrowed its scope.

R v M (J) and another

[2012] EWCA Crim 2293, Court of Appeal, Criminal Division, http://www.bailii.org/ew/cases/EWCA/Crim/2012/2293.html

(Lord Judge CJ, Roderick Evans and Thirlwall JJ)

This case was a prosecution appeal against the trial judge's direction that there was no case to answer. The defendants, DD, had been drinking in a nightclub and were ejected by the club's bouncers after becoming troublesome. DD sought to gain re-entry to the club by kicking a door. V was one of the bouncers who attempted to stop DD from re-entering the nightclub. An affray ensued but it was accepted that there was no evidence that V had been subjected to direct physical violence. Unbeknownst to V or anyone else, V was suffering from a renal artery aneurysm. V died. DD were charged with unlawful act manslaughter, the base crime being the affray. The prosecution alleged that the rupture of the aneurysm was consequent on shock and a sudden surge in blood pressure due to the release of adrenalin into the circulation during the attack by DD on the group of doormen. The prosecution alleged further that the rupture occurred either while the affray was in progress or in its immediate aftermath. The trial judge directed that the question was whether D died 'as a result of the sort of physical harm that any reasonable and sober person would inevitably realise the unlawful act in question risked causing'. This requirement was said to have been derived from *Carey*.

[In allowing the appeal, **Lord Judge CJ** stated]:

18. Without contradiction from [counsel for D2], [counsel for D1] (who did not appear in the court below) accepted that the judge misdirected himself when he required the Crown to establish the fourth ingredient, that is, that the reasonable and sober person envisaged in *R v Church* must realise that that was a risk that the unlawful act would cause the sort of physical harm as a result of which the victim died. We agree that such a requirement provided a gloss on the ingredients of this offence which is not justified by the authorities and does not follow from the reasoning in *R v Dawson* 81 Cr App R 150 and *R v Carey*. Indeed, the observations at the end of the judgment appear to elevate the requisite risk from an appreciation that some harm will inevitably occur into foresight of the type of harm which actually ensued and indeed the mechanism by which death occurred. Of course, unless

the Crown can prove that death resulted from the defendant's unlawful and dangerous act, the case of manslaughter would fail on causation grounds. However a requirement that the bystander must appreciate the 'sort' of injury which might occur undermines the 'some' harm principle explained in *R v Church*, and on close analysis, is not supported or suggested by *R v Dawson* or *R v Carey*.

19. It is indeed striking that in *R v Carey* the court plainly accepted that if 'the facts had arguably supported' the case that the affray had caused the victim to suffer shock from which she died, the manslaughter issue should properly have been left to the jury. The heart of the judgment on this question is that the affray lacked the necessary quality of dangerousness. Although reference is made to the risk of 'suffering shock' as a result of the affray, that has to be seen in context as a reference to the fact that no one would have recognised any risk of this 15-year-old suffering any harm or injury as a result of the particular affray.

20. In our judgment, certainly since *R v Church* [1966] 1 QB 59 and *Director of Public Prosecutions v Newbury* [1977] AC 500, it has never been a requirement that the defendant personally should foresee any specific harm at all, or that the reasonable bystander should recognise the precise form or 'sort' of harm which did ensue. What matters is whether reasonable and sober people would recognise that the unlawful activities of the defendant inevitably subjected the deceased to the risk of some harm resulting from them.

21. As we emphasise, in the present case we are concerned with and confine our decision to the circumstances of an affray in which the deceased was personally involved in the fighting which constituted the affray, rather than an individual who happened to be walking down the street and came to the scene of the fight without getting involved in it. The question whether the reasonable sober person would inevitably recognise the risk of harm going beyond concern and fear and distress to physical harm in the form of shock would have to be resolved as a question of fact rather than law.

■ *Questions*

Can *M (J)* really be distinguished from *Carey*? Do such piecemeal attempts to define the scope of the offence indicate that unlawful act manslaughter needs to be placed on a clear statutory footing? See the case comment by Professor Ashworth at [2013] Crim LR 335.

17.2.5.1 Problem cases of causation in unlawful act manslaughter: (i) suicide

R v D

[2006] EWCA Crim 1139, Court of Appeal, Criminal Division, http://www.bailii.org/ew/cases/EWCA/Crim/2006/1139.html

(Sir Igor Judge P, Henriques and Fulford JJ)

D had struck his partner a minor blow on the forehead and she had then committed suicide. This was against a lengthy background of domestic abuse by D amounting to psychological but not psychiatric injury of V. D was charged with manslaughter. Issues arose as to whether his single act of striking her was a sufficient unlawful act. The problem was that the victim's suicide was a free, deliberate and informed act; it broke the chain of causation. The alternative of treating the whole of D's abusive course of conduct to V as the unlawful act was problematic because the acts did not amount to anything other than psychological harm falling short of a recognized psychiatric injury which would amount to actual or grievous bodily harm (see section 18.2.1.1, p 643). The trial judge held that the infliction of mere psychological harm would not suffice to construct a manslaughter charge. However, in an *obiter dictum*, the Court of Appeal left open the possibility that a manslaughter conviction might be available:

> where a decision to commit suicide has been triggered by a physical assault which represents the culmination of a course of abusive conduct, it would be possible ... to argue that the final assault played a significant part in causing the victim's death.

■ *Questions*

Can D ever be liable for manslaughter where V has committed suicide and D's act is not at that moment a continuing and operative cause of death? Is it sufficient that V fears D's immediate attack in physical terms? Is it sufficient that V fears D's continued psychological abuse? Can suicide ever be a reasonably foreseeable response to violence or further psychological harm? To what extent must D take his victim as found 'psychologically' as well as physically? In none of the reported 'flight' cases does it appear that the victims have chosen to commit suicide; rather, they have behaved in a dangerous fashion, being aware that their choice of escape may expose them to danger of injury or death. Is a charge of gross negligence manslaughter preferable in these cases?

J. Horder and L. McGowan, 'Manslaughter by Causing Another's Suicide'
[2006] Crim LR 1035

...A cause of death is still cause, in law, even if it is only one of a number of operating causes. So, the fact that the defendant's final assault could only be understood as playing a minor causal role in the victim's suicide, does not prevent that final assault being a cause of her suicide. That being so, what is then the legal significance of the preceding years of abuse causing the psychological trauma? It is that evidence of years of abuse bolsters the case for saying that the final assault was indeed, in law, a cause of the victim's suicide. In that regard, we need to distinguish two kinds of case. In the first kind of case ... there is an assault shortly before the suicide that triggers the suicide, whereas in the second kind of case ... there is no such assault.

[Direct assault cases]

...if, a blow causes someone to commit suicide, so long as the blow is still regarded as an operating and substantial cause of V's death (even if not the only or main cause) manslaughter is committed. Suppose that D assaults V on a single occasion, for the first time in the relationship. V, perhaps moved by mixed motives of shame and fear, commits suicide in consequence. Can D be straightforwardly regarded as the cause of V's death, in such a case?

There have been cases in which it is the victim's own reaction—typically, in seeking to escape an impending assault—that explains the harm the victim suffered. In such cases, there is authority for the view that if the defendant's conduct is to be regarded as one of the causes of the victim's reaction, that reaction must have been within a range of responses that might reasonably have been expected in the situation in question. According to the Court of Appeal in *Mackie* [(1973) 57 Cr App R 453 at p 460 (per Stephenson LJ)], if it is still to be regarded as caused by the defendant's conduct the victim's reaction must be: 'the natural consequence of the assault charged, not something which could not be expected, but something which any reasonable and responsible man in the assailant's shoes would have foreseen.'

...in a case where the victim's reaction is one of deliberate self-harm (something not at issue in *Mackie*) it might seem difficult to satisfy the *Mackie* test when it is a first-time assault by D that has led to V's suicide. In a case like *Dhaliwal*, however, it might seem easier to satisfy the test. The final assault is the latest episode in a history of abuse. So, the fact that the victim has been subject to such abuse makes it more likely that a jury will accept that her reaction in committing suicide was within the range of what might be considered 'natural'. To this must be added the fact that cultural and religious influences on the victim made self-harm a more likely (a more natural) response in the longer term to the defendant's ongoing abuse.

. . .

[Indirect cases]

In many cases, there will be no final assault of a 'back-breaking straw' kind, that leads the victim to commit suicide. Suppose that D, who has subjected V to years of abuse, has been away abroad for some weeks on business, but is due to return shortly. Unable to face the prospect of resuming their abusive relationship, V commits suicide before D's return. Has D caused V to commit suicide? In such a case, the prosecution's argument will be that the cumulative effect of abuse for, inter alia, of non-fatal offences committed over a period of time, readily explains the victim's decision to commit suicide. This brings her suicide within the range of natural (i.e. not wholly unnatural) reactions to the abuse. There can be no doubt that, in some circumstances, the law does permit the effect of blows, or other wrongs, to be aggregated or assessed cumulatively so that the whole is regarded as, in law, greater than the sum of the parts. Individual injuries forming a part of a single attack can, for example, be aggregated for the purpose of judging whether the bodily harm done was 'grievous'. Individual actions can also be assessed cumulatively in deciding whether they amount to a course of 'harass-ment'. By analogy, it may be argued that (at least in some cases) the persistence of abuse, if not any one violent incident, is what establishes a causal link between that abuse and a consequent suicide. As has already been pointed out, moreover, it ought to be all the easier to establish such a link when sui-cide is much more likely to have been perceived by a victim of abuse as 'the only way out' for reasons such as religious and cultural background.

. . . When a relationship is characterised by persistent domestic abuse (especially in the kind of cul-tural and religious context to be found in *Dhaliwal*), the experience of living with the abuse is liable to affect the victim's decision-making processes, and to influence the range and character of actions she regards as legitimate, inevitable or natural. Through the way in which it shapes her world and her self-perception, the abuse may establish a controlling influence over how the victim understands and responds to her situation. . . .

It might be that a decision on the part of a victim of abuse to commit suicide is best explained, in straightforward causal terms, by a depressive condition induced by the abuse. In that event, the de-fendant will be liable for manslaughter on the basis that his abuse triggered the operation of a spe-cial vulnerability of the victim. On our account, however, the causal link between the abuse and the suicide can be (lack of) freedom-based, and need not be based on a victim's special vulnerability. An abuse-based controlling influence can, in this context, make a decision to commit suicide something that the victim was not truly free to avoid, because other avoiding actions were in practical terms ruled out by the effect of that influence. In that regard, the nature and degree of abuse suffered before the decision to commit suicide was taken should be an influential but not a decisive factor in establish-ing a casual connection between the abuse and the suicide. The understandable development of a suicidal state of mind may be as much a product of the very fact that domineering control has been established and maintained over a long period, as by the direct effects of the abuse that underpins that control.

■ *Question*

Do you agree that someone like Dhaliwal has caused his wife's death?

17.2.5.2 Problem cases of causation in unlawful act manslaughter: (ii) drug misuse cases

In a series of cases since the 1990s, the Court of Appeal struggled with the situation where D supplies V with drugs, V self-injects what turns out to be a fatal overdose and D is prosecuted for manslaughter. On a charge of unlawful act manslaughter, requiring proof of an unlawful, intentional and dangerous act causing death, there is a requirement to prove that D committed an unlawful act (the base crime). The Crown repeatedly relied on two options: (i) that D administered a noxious substance contrary to the Offences Against the Person Act 1861, s 23, or (ii) that D was an accessory to V's injection. Both were fundamentally flawed. D was not guilty of administering since V himself administered the drugs. V's act, if it was free and informed, broke the chain of causation. Nor could D be liable as a secondary party—V committed no offence to which D could be an accessory. It is not an offence to inject drugs or to kill oneself.

The principal problem with the decisions was that they ran contrary to the orthodox principle of causation: V's free, voluntary, deliberate, informed act should, on well-established grounds, break the chain of causation. As Glanville Williams explained:

> The new intervening act (*novus actus interveniens*) of a responsible actor, who had full knowledge of what he is doing, and is not subject to mistake or pressure, will normally operate to relieve the defendant of liability for a further consequence, because it makes the consequence too remote... What a person does (if he has reached adult years, is of sound mind and is not acting under mistake, intimidation or other similar pressure) is his own responsibility, and is not regarded as having been caused by other people. (*Textbook of Criminal Law* (2nd edn, 1983), p 391)

Despite the very basic nature of these propositions, the Court of Appeal in a series of cases created enormous confusion. In *Kennedy (No 1)* [1999] Crim LR 65, it had been held that D was a party to V's self-injection and that V's free, informed, deliberate act did not break the chain of causation. This was plainly wrong. In *Dias* [2000] 2 Cr App R 96, it was recognized that D could not be a secondary party in these circumstances since V commits no crime in which D can assist. That was correct. In *Rogers* [2003] 2 Cr App R 160, [2003] Crim LR 555, *Dias* was distinguished where D held the tourniquet for V while he injected; in those circumstances it was held that D was playing a part in the mechanics of the injection as a principal. That has now been held to be wrong (see the House of Lords' decision in *Kennedy (No 2)* in the following extract). In *Finlay* [2003] EWCA Crim 3868, the Court of Appeal suggested that D could be liable provided he was a factual cause of V's death unless V's act of self-injection was extraordinary. That too was plainly wrong. See also *Richards* [2002] EWCA Crim 3175. Because of the decision in *Dias*, Kennedy brought a second appeal against his conviction, arguing that the decision in *Kennedy (No 1)* had subsequently been undermined by decisions such as *Dias*. In *Kennedy (No 2)* [2005] EWCA Crim 785, the court reviewed the many controversial and often inconsistent decisions on this issue but managed only to perpetuate the errors. The Court of Appeal in *Kennedy (No 2)* (at [42]) sought to create an exception to the general principle that V's free, informed, voluntary act breaks the chain of causation where D is acting in 'joint concert' with V:

> ...if a defendant is acting in concert with the deceased, what the deceased does in concert with the defendant will not break the chain of causation, even though the general principles as to causation have to be applied. This was recognised by Lord Steyn when he qualified the general position when saying in *R v Latif & Others* [1996] 2 Cr. App. R. 92 at p 104: 'The free, deliberate and informed intervention of a second person, who intends to exploit the situation created by the first, *but is not acting in concert with him* is held to relieve the first actor of criminal responsibility.' (emphasis added)

This reasoning was fundamentally flawed. See section 3.2.3.3, p 56. See D. Ormerod and R. Fortson, 'Drug Suppliers Manslaughter (Again)' [2005] Crim LR 819.

R v Kennedy (No 2)

[2007] UKHL 38, House of Lords, http://www.bailii.org/uk/cases/UKHL/2007/38.html

(Lords Bingham of Cornhill, Rodger of Earlsferry, Baroness Hale of Richmond, Lords Carswell and Mance)

Kennedy lived in a hostel with Marco Bosque and Andrew Cody, who shared a room. On 10 September 1996, Kennedy visited their room. Bosque was drinking with Cody. According to Cody, Bosque told the appellant that he wanted 'a bit to make him sleep' and Kennedy told Bosque to take care that he did not go to sleep permanently. Kennedy prepared a dose of heroin for Bosque and gave him a syringe ready for injection. Bosque then injected himself and returned the empty syringe to Kennedy who left the room. Bosque then appeared to stop breathing. An ambulance was called and he was taken to hospital, where he was pronounced dead. The cause of death was inhalation of gastric contents while acutely intoxicated by opiates and alcohol. Kennedy appealed against the decision of the Court of Appeal's decision in his second appeal to uphold his conviction. The question certified by the Court of Appeal Criminal Division for the opinion of the House of Lords was:

> When is it appropriate to find someone guilty of manslaughter where that person has been involved in the supply of a class A controlled drug, which is then freely and voluntarily self-administered by the person to whom it was supplied, and the administration of the drug then causes his death?

Lord Bingham [stated the facts and continued:]

Manslaughter

6. It is well-established and not in any way controversial that a charge of manslaughter may be founded either on the unlawful act of the defendant ('unlawful act manslaughter') or on the gross negligence of the defendant. This appeal is concerned only with unlawful act manslaughter and nothing in this opinion should be understood as applying to manslaughter caused by gross negligence.

7. To establish the crime of unlawful act manslaughter it must be shown, among other things not relevant to this appeal,

(1) That the defendant committed an unlawful act;

(2) That such unlawful act was a crime (*R v Franklin* (1883) 15 Cox CC 163; *R v Lamb* [1967] 2 QB 981, 988; *R v Dias* [2001] EWCA Crim 2986, [2002] 2 Cr App R 96, para 9); and

(3) That the defendant's unlawful act was a significant cause of the death of the deceased (*R v Cato* [1976] 1 WLR 110, 116–117).

There is now, as already noted, no doubt but that the appellant committed an unlawful (and criminal) act by supplying the heroin to the deceased. But the act of supplying, without more, could not harm the deceased in any physical way, let alone cause his death. As the Court of Appeal observed in *R v Dalby* [1982] 1 WLR 425, 429, 'the supply of drugs would itself have caused no harm unless the deceased had subsequently used the drugs in a form and quantity which was dangerous'. So, as the parties agree, the charge of unlawful act manslaughter cannot be founded on the act of supplying the heroin alone.

8. The parties are further agreed that an unlawful act of the appellant on the present facts must be found, if at all, in a breach of section 23 of the Offences against the Person Act 1861 ...

9. As it now effectively reads, section 23 of the 1861 Act provides:

'**Maliciously administering poison, etc, so as to endanger life or inflict grievous bodily harm**

Whosoever shall unlawfully and maliciously administer to or cause to be administered to or taken by any other person any poison or other destructive or noxious thing, so as thereby to endanger the life of such person, or so as thereby to inflict upon such person any grievous bodily harm, shall be guilty of [an offence] and being convicted thereof shall be liable ... to [imprisonment] for any term not exceeding ten years ...'

The opening and closing words of the section raise no question relevant to this appeal. The substance of the section creates three distinct offences: (1) administering a noxious thing to any other person; (2) causing a noxious thing to be administered to any other person; and (3) causing a noxious thing to be taken by any other person. It is not in doubt that heroin is a noxious thing, and the contrary was not contended.

10. The factual situations covered by (1), (2) and (3) are clear. Offence (1) is committed where D administers the noxious thing directly to V, as by injecting V with the noxious thing, holding a glass containing the noxious thing to V's lips, or (as in *R v Gillard* (1988) 87 Cr App R 189) spraying the noxious thing in V's face.

11. Offence (2) is typically committed where D does not directly administer the noxious thing to V but causes an innocent third party TP to administer it to V. If D, knowing a syringe to be filled with poison instructs TP to inject V, TP believing the syringe to contain a legitimate therapeutic substance, D would commit this offence.

12. Offence (3) covers the situation where the noxious thing is not administered to V but taken by him, provided D causes the noxious thing to be taken by V and V does not make a voluntary and informed decision to take it. If D puts a noxious thing in food which V is about to eat and V, ignorant of the presence of the noxious thing, eats it, D commits offence (3).

13. In the course of his accurate and well-judged submissions on behalf of the Crown, Mr David Perry QC accepted that if he could not show that the appellant had committed offence (1) as the unlawful act necessary to found the count of manslaughter he could not hope to show the commission of offences (2) or (3). This concession was rightly made, but the committee heard considerable argument addressed to the concept of causation, which has been misapplied in some of the authorities, and it is desirable that it should be clear why the concession is rightly made. . . .

18. The criminal law generally assumes the existence of free will. The law recognises certain exceptions, in the case of the young, those who for any reason are not fully responsible for their actions, and the vulnerable, and it acknowledges situations of duress and necessity, as also of deception and mistake. But, generally speaking, informed adults of sound mind are treated as autonomous beings able to make their own decisions how they will act, and none of the exceptions is relied on as possibly applicable in this case. Thus D is not to be treated as causing V to act in a certain way if V makes a voluntary and informed decision to act in that way rather than another. There are many classic statements to this effect.

[His lordship dismissed the argument based on causation, holding that the victim's free voluntary act broke the chain of causation between D's act of supply and the death of V. Nor was it possible to argue that D caused V to take or caused to be administered to V since V's act broke the chain of causation, see section 3.2.3.2, p 56.]

19. The sole argument open to the Crown was, therefore, that the appellant administered the injection to the deceased. It was argued that the term 'administer' should not be narrowly interpreted. Reliance was placed on the steps taken by the appellant to facilitate the injection and on the trial judge's direction to the jury that they had to be satisfied that the appellant handed the syringe to the deceased 'for immediate injection'. But section 23 draws a very clear contrast between a noxious thing administered to another person and a noxious thing taken by another person. It cannot ordinarily be both. In this case the heroin is described as 'freely and voluntarily self-administered' by the deceased. This, on the facts, is an inevitable finding. The appellant supplied the heroin and prepared the syringe. But the deceased had a choice whether to inject himself or not. He chose to do so, knowing what he was doing. It was his act.

20. In resisting this conclusion Mr Perry relied on *R v Rogers* [2003] 1 WLR 1374. In that case the defendant pleaded guilty, following a legal ruling, to a count of administering poison contrary to section 23 of the 1861 Act and a count of manslaughter. The relevant finding was that the defendant physically assisted the deceased by holding his belt round the deceased's arm as a tourniquet, so as to raise a vein in which the deceased could insert a syringe, while the deceased injected himself. It was argued

in support of his appeal to the Court of Appeal that the defendant had committed no unlawful act for purposes of either count. This contention was rejected. The court held (para 7) that it was unreal and artificial to separate the tourniquet from the injection. By applying and holding the tourniquet the defendant had played a part in the mechanics of the injection which had caused the death. There is, clearly, a difficult borderline between contributory acts which may properly be regarded as administering a noxious thing and acts which may not. But the crucial question is not whether the defendant facilitated or contributed to administration of the noxious thing but whether he went further and administered it. What matters, in a case such as *R v Rogers* and the present, is whether the injection itself was the result of a voluntary and informed decision by the person injecting himself. In *R v Rogers*, as in the present case, it was. That case was, therefore, wrongly decided.

21. It is unnecessary to review the case law on this subject in any detail. In *R v Cato* [1976] 1 WLR 110 the defendant had injected the deceased with heroin and the present problem did not arise. In *R v Dalby* [1982] 1 WLR 425 the deceased had died following the consumption of drugs which the defendant had supplied but the deceased had injected. There was apparently no discussion of section 23, but it was held that the supply could not support a conviction of manslaughter. At the trial of the present appellant there was no consideration of section 23 and the trial judge effectively stopped defence counsel submitting to the jury that the appellant had not caused the death of the deceased. In dismissing his first appeal the Court of Appeal said:

> 'We can see no reason why, on the facts alleged by the Crown, the appellant in the instant case might not have been guilty of an offence under section 23 of the Offences against the Person Act 1861. Perhaps more relevantly, the injection of the heroin into himself by Bosque was itself an unlawful act, and if the appellant assisted in and wilfully encouraged that unlawful conduct, he would himself be acting unlawfully.'

But the court gave no detailed consideration to the terms of section 23, and it is now accepted that the deceased's injection of himself was not an unlawful act.

22. In *R v Dias* [2002] 2 Cr App R 96 the defendant had been convicted of manslaughter. He had prepared a syringe charged with heroin which he had handed to the deceased, who had injected himself. The court recognised that the chain of causation had probably been broken by the free and informed decision of the deceased, and noted the error in the decision on the appellant's first appeal as to the unlawfulness of the deceased's injection of himself.

[His lordship referred to the Court of Appeal's suggestion that the liability might rest on a principle of joint administration.]

24. It is possible to imagine factual scenarios in which two people could properly be regarded as acting together to administer an injection. But nothing of the kind was the case here. As in *R v Dalby* and *R v Dias* the appellant supplied the drug to the deceased, who then had a choice, knowing the facts, whether to inject himself or not. The heroin was, as the certified question correctly recognises, self-administered, not jointly administered. The appellant did not administer the drug. Nor, for reasons already given, did the appellant cause the drug to be administered to or taken by the deceased.

25. The answer to the certified question is: 'In the case of a fully-informed and responsible adult, never'. The appeal must be allowed and the appellant's conviction for manslaughter quashed. The appellant must have his costs, here and below, out of central funds.

Much of the difficulty and doubt which have dogged the present question has flowed from a failure, at the outset, to identify the unlawful act on which the manslaughter count is founded. It matters little whether the act is identified by a separate count or counts under section 23, or by particularisation of the manslaughter count itself. But it would focus attention on the correct question, and promote accurate analysis of the real issues, if those who formulate, defend and rule on serious charges of this kind were obliged to consider how exactly, in law, the accusation is put.

Appeal allowed

> ■ *Questions*
>
> 1. Was V's act really a free act if he was a heroin addict and D had heroin to offer?
>
> 2. Lord Bingham stated that 'informed' adults are treated by the law as autonomous beings. Does this impose a threshold of knowledge that V must possess and if he does not the supplier could be guilty of manslaughter if V dies from taking the drug? For example, what if, unbeknownst to V, the heroin was of a higher purity than he was accustomed to and D did not inform him of this fact?
>
> 3. Should 'using' prohibited drugs be an offence? If so, V would have committed an offence and D would have aided and abetted that offence. There would be an unlawful act on which to base D's liability for manslaughter if V died.

In *Burgess* [2008] EWCA Crim 516, the Court of Appeal subsequently suggested that had the matter fallen for consideration (on the facts D had pleaded on a basis that could not stand in the light of the House of Lords' decision), D raising the vein for V would suffice as an act of administering. It was held that 'if a defendant may be convicted on the basis that the fatal dose was jointly administered then it follows that he is not automatically entitled to be acquitted if the deceased rather than the defendant physically operated the plunger'. There is obviously a difficult borderline between contributory acts which might properly be regarded as administering a noxious thing and acts which might not. The evidence is likely to be patchy: one participant is dead and the other, the defendant, likely to have been heavily intoxicated. *Burgess* might therefore serve as an example falling just the other side of the line from *Rogers*. Whether the necessary proximity existed between the actions of D and V is for the jury to determine. Liability for manslaughter will exist where D has provided the drugs to V whose act of self-administration was not free and voluntary.

See further W. Wilson, 'Dealing with Drug Induced Homicide' in C. Clarkson and S. Cunningham (eds), *Criminal Liability for Non-Aggressive Deaths* (2008). Cf the approach in the case of *HM Advocate v McAngus* (2009), High Court of Justiciary, which decided not to follow *Kennedy (No 2)*.

It is important to point out that while there cannot be liability for unlawful act manslaughter in the drug misuse cases (subject to the caveats mentioned earlier), that is not to say that D is therefore not guilty of any offence. D may be guilty of gross negligence manslaughter. This issue will be considered in the next section.

17.3 Manslaughter by gross negligence

The elements of the offence are now established to be:

- a duty of care owed by the defendant;
- a gross breach of that duty which created a risk of death;
- breach of which caused death.

Before turning to the leading decision of the House of Lords in *Adomako*, it is helpful to consider the decision of the Court of Appeal in *Prentice, Adomako, Holloway* [1993] 4 All ER 935, [1994] QB 302, and the cases leading up to it.

At the time of the decision there were two tests of 'recklessness' in the criminal law. There was the subjective (*Cunningham*) test which requires foresight of consequences and which applies now throughout the law, and there was the objective (*Caldwell/Lawrence*) test, section

5.3, p 117, which applied until 2003, at the least, to offences of criminal damage. Following *Caldwell* and *Lawrence* there was a move, spearheaded by the House of Lords (there was less enthusiasm for it in lower courts), to adopt the single *Caldwell/Lawrence* test for recklessness and, in particular, to replace gross negligence manslaughter by reckless (ie *Caldwell/ Lawrence* recklessness) manslaughter. This development came to a head in the House of Lords' decision in *Seymour* [1983] 2 All ER 1058, [1983] 2 AC 493, a case of so-called motor manslaughter (on which see the observations of Lord Mackay LC, in *Adomako*, later in the section) and in the Privy Council decision in *Kong Cheuk Kwan v R* (1985) 82 Cr App R 18, [1985] Crim LR 787. This development placed the Court of Appeal in a dilemma in considering the appeals in *Prentice, Adomako, Holloway*.

In *Adomako*, next considered, the trial judge had given a 'traditional' direction on gross negligence on which the defendant was convicted and his appeal was dismissed. In *Prentice* and in *Holloway*, however, the jury had convicted of manslaughter following a *Caldwell/ Lawrence/Seymour* direction.

In *Prentice*, D, a junior doctor, under the supervision of E, administered an injection to a patient. Owing to a series of errors and misunderstandings between D and E, D administered the wrong drug with fatal results. Quashing the convictions of D and E, the Court of Appeal said:

In effect, therefore, once the jury found 'that the defendant gave no thought to the possibility of there being any such risk', on the learned judge's directions they had no option but to convict. [Counsel's] point is that if the jury had been given gross negligence as the test, they could properly have taken into account 'excuses' or mitigating circumstances in deciding whether the necessary high degree of gross negligence had been established. The question for the jury should have been whether, in the case of each doctor, they were sure that the failure to ascertain the correct mode of administering the drug and to ensure that only that mode was adopted was grossly negligent to the point of criminality having regard to all the excuses and mitigating circumstances in the case.

In *Holloway*, D, an electrician, who had done the electrical work on a central heating system in a house, returned to check the system after complaints that contact with the radiators caused electric shocks. His checks failed to reveal, as they should have done, that there was a fault in the wiring. V was subsequently electrocuted and died. It was held by the Court of Appeal, quashing D's conviction, that the proper issue for the jury's consideration was not whether D had given no thought to the serious risk but whether he was grossly negligent in forming the view that the installation was safe.

The Court of Appeal appears to have taken the view in these cases that the *Caldwell/ Lawrence* test was too strict for manslaughter. But is this right? Given that there is a risk of death or serious harm (ie a risk to which any sensible person would have adverted), why should a failure to advert to such a risk not constitute gross negligence?

R v Adomako

[1995] AC 171, House of Lords, http://www.bailii.org/uk/cases/UKHL/1994/6.html

(Lord Mackay of Clashfern LC, Lords Keith of Kinkel, Goff of Chieveley, Browne-Wilkinson and Woolf)

During an operation at which the appellant was assisting as anaesthetist, the tube carrying oxygen from the ventilator to the patient became disconnected. The appellant failed to notice the disconnection and some six minutes later the patient suffered a cardiac arrest from which, despite efforts at resuscitation, he died. At no stage did the appellant check the integrity of the equipment. The case against the appellant was that he had been grossly negligent in failing to notice or respond appropriately to obvious signs that a disconnection had occurred and that the patient had ceased to breathe.

Lord Mackay of Clashfern, LC:

...On behalf of the appellant it was conceded at his trial that he had been negligent. The issue was therefore whether his conduct was criminal....

The jury convicted the appellant of manslaughter by a majority of 11 to 1. The Court of Appeal, Criminal Division dismissed the appellant's appeal against conviction but certified that a point of law of general public importance was involved in the decision to dismiss the appeal, namely:

'In cases of manslaughter by criminal negligence not involving driving but involving a breach of duty is it a sufficient direction to the jury to adopt the gross negligence test set out by the Court of Appeal in the present case following *R v Bateman* (1925) 19 Cr App Rep 8 and *Andrews v DPP* [1937] 2 All ER 552, [1937] AC 576 without reference to the test of recklessness as defined in *R v Lawrence* [1981] 1 All ER 974, [1982] AC 510 or as adapted to the circumstances of the case?'

The decision of the Court of Appeal is reported at [1993] 4 All ER 935, [1994] QB 302 along with a number of other cases involving similar questions of law. The Court of Appeal held that except in cases of motor manslaughter the ingredients which had to be proved to establish an offence of involuntary manslaughter by breach of duty were the existence of the duty, a breach of the duty which had caused death and gross negligence which the jury considered to justify a criminal conviction; the jury might properly find gross negligence on proof of indifference to an obvious risk of injury to health or of actual foresight of the risk coupled either with a determination nevertheless to run it or with an intention to avoid it but involving such a high degree of negligence in the attempted avoidance as the jury considered justified conviction or of inattention or failure to advert to a serious risk of going beyond mere inadvertence in respect of an obvious and important matter which the defendant's duty demanded he should address; and that, in the circumstances, the appeals of the two junior doctors and the electrician would be allowed and the appeal of the anaesthetist, namely Dr Adomako, would be dismissed. The reason that the Court of Appeal excepted the cases of motor manslaughter and their formulation of the law was the decision of this House in *R v Seymour* [1983] 2 All ER 1058, [1983] 2 AC 493 in which it was held that where manslaughter was charged and the circumstances were that the victim was killed as a result of the reckless driving of the defendant on a public highway, the trial judge should give the jury the direction which had been suggested in *R v Lawrence* [1981] 1 All ER 974, [1982] AC 510 but that it was appropriate also to point out that in order to constitute the offence of manslaughter the risk of death being caused by the manner of the defendant's driving must be very high.

In opening his very cogent argument for the appellant before your Lordships, counsel submitted that the law in this area should have the characteristics of clarity, certainty, intellectual coherence and general applicability and acceptability. For these reasons he said the law applying to involuntary manslaughter generally should involve a universal test and that test should be the test already applied in this House to motor manslaughter. He criticised the concept of gross negligence which was the basis of the judgment of the Court of Appeal submitting that its formulation involved circularity, the jury being told in effect to convict of a crime if they thought a crime had been committed and that accordingly using gross negligence as the conceptual basis for the crime of involuntary manslaughter was unsatisfactory and the court should apply the law laid down in *R v Seymour* [1983] 2 All ER 1058, [1983] 2 AC 493 generally to all cases of involuntary manslaughter or at least use this as the basis for providing general applicability and acceptability.

Like the Court of Appeal your Lordships were treated to a considerable review of authority. I begin with *R v Bateman* (1925) 19 Cr App Rep 8 and the opinion of Lord Hewart CJ, where he said (at 10–12):

[Lord Mackay quoted extensively from Lord Hewart's judgment, pp 10–13, concluding:]

'The foregoing observations deal with civil liability. To support an indictment for manslaughter the prosecution must prove the matters necessary to establish civil liability (except pecuniary loss), and, in addition, must satisfy the jury that the negligence or incompetence of the accused went beyond a mere matter of compensation and showed such disregard for the life and safety of others as to amount to a crime against the State and conduct deserving punishment.'

Next I turn to *Andrews v DPP*, which was a case of manslaughter through the dangerous driving of a motor car. In a speech with which all the other members of this House who sat agreed, Lord Atkin said at pp. 581–582:

'of all crimes manslaughter appears to afford most difficulties of definition, for it concerns homicide in so many and so varying conditions. From the early days when any homicide involved penalty the law has gradually evolved "through successive differentiations and integrations" until it recognises murder on the one hand, based mainly, though not exclusively, on an intention to kill, and manslaughter on the other hand, based mainly, though not exclusively, on the absence of intention to kill but with the presence of an element of "unlawfulness" which is the elusive factor. In the present case it is only necessary to consider manslaughter from the point of view of an unintentional killing caused by negligence, that is, the omission of a duty to take care. I do not propose to discuss the development of this branch of the subject as treated in the successive treatises of Coke, Hale, Foster and East and in the judgments of the courts to be found either in directions to juries by individual judges or in the more considered pronouncements of the body of judges which preceded the formal Court of Crown Cases Reserved. Expressions will be found which indicate that to cause death by any lack of due care will amount to manslaughter; but as manners softened and the law became more humane a narrower criterion appeared. After all, manslaughter is a felony, and was capital, and men shrank from attaching the serious consequences of a conviction for felony to results produced by mere inadvertence. The stricter view became apparent in prosecutions of medical men or men who professed medical or surgical skill for manslaughter by reason of negligence. As an instance I will cite *Rex v. Williamson* (1807) 3 C. & P. 635 where a man who practised as an accoucheur [a male midwife], owing to a mistake in his observation of the actual symptoms, inflicted on a patient terrible injuries from which she died. "To substantiate that charge"—namely, manslaughter—Lord Ellenborough said, "the prisoner must have been guilty of criminal misconduct, arising either from the grossest ignorance or the most criminal inattention." The word "criminal" in any attempt to define a crime is perhaps not the most helpful: but it is plain that the Lord Chief Justice meant to indicate to the jury a high degree of negligence. So at a much later date in *Rex v. Bateman*, 19 Cr.App.R. 8 a charge of manslaughter was made against a qualified medical practitioner in similar circumstances to those of *Williamson's* case.'

Lord Atkin then referred to the judgment of Lord Hewart C.J. from which I have already quoted and went on, at p. 583:

'Here again I think with respect that the expressions used are not, indeed they were probably not intended to be, a precise definition of the crime. I do not myself find the connotations of mens rea helpful in distinguishing between degrees of negligence, nor do the ideas of crime and punishment in themselves carry a jury much further in deciding whether in a particular case the degree of negligence shown is a crime and deserves punishment. But the substance of the judgment is most valuable, and in my opinion is correct. In practice it has generally been adopted by judges in charging juries in all cases of manslaughter by negligence, whether in driving vehicles or otherwise. The principle to be observed is that cases of manslaughter in driving motor cars are but instances of a general rule applicable to all charges of homicide by negligence. Simple lack of care such as will constitute civil liability is not enough: for purposes of the criminal law there are degrees of negligence: and a very high degree of negligence is required to be proved before the felony is established. Probably of all the epithets that can be applied "reckless" most nearly covers the case. It is difficult to visualise a case of death caused by reckless driving in the connotation of that term in ordinary speech which would not justify a conviction for manslaughter: but it is probably not all-embracing, for "reckless" suggests an indifference to risk whereas the accused may have appreciated the risk and intended to avoid it and yet shown such a high degree of negligence in the means adopted to avoid the risk as would justify a conviction. If the principle of *Bateman's* case, 19 Cr.App.R. 8 is observed it will appear that the law of manslaughter has not changed by the introduction of motor vehicles on the road. Death caused by their negligent driving, though unhappily much more frequent, is to be treated in law as death caused by any other form of negligence: and juries should be directed accordingly.'

In my opinion the law as stated in these two authorities is satisfactory as providing a proper basis for describing the crime of involuntary manslaughter. Since the decision in *Andrews v DPP* [1937] 2 All ER 552, [1937] AC 576 was a decision of your Lordships' House, it remains the most authoritative statement of the present law which I have been able to find and although its relationship to *R v Seymour* [1983] 2 All ER 1058, [1983] 2 AC 493 is a matter to which I shall have to return, it is a decision which has not been departed from. On this basis in my opinion the ordinary principles of the law of negligence apply to ascertain whether or not the defendant has been in breach of a duty of care towards the victim who has died. If such breach of duty is established the next question is whether that breach of duty caused the death of the victim. If so, the jury must go on to consider whether that breach of duty should be characterised as gross negligence and therefore as a crime. This will depend on the seriousness of the breach of duty committed by the defendant in all the circumstances in which the defendant was placed when it occurred. The jury will have to consider whether the extent to which the defendant's conduct departed from the proper standard of care incumbent upon him, involving as it must have done a risk of death to the patient, was such that it should be judged criminal.

It is true that to a certain extent this involves an element of circularity, but in this branch of the law I do not believe that is fatal to its being correct as a test of how far conduct must depart from accepted standards to be characterised as criminal. This is necessarily a question of degree and an attempt to specify that degree more closely is I think likely to achieve only a spurious precision. The essence of the matter, which is supremely a jury question, is whether, having regard to the risk of death involved, the conduct of the defendant was so bad in all the circumstances as to amount in their judgment to a criminal act or omission.

My Lords the view which I have stated of the correct basis in law for the crime of involuntary manslaughter accords I consider with the criteria stated by counsel although I have not reached the degree of precision in definition which he required, but in my opinion it has been reached so far as practicable and with a result which leaves the matter properly stated for a jury's determination.

My Lords in my view the law as stated in *R v Seymour* [1983] 2 All ER 1058, [1983] 2 AC 493 should no longer apply since the underlying statutory provisions on which it rested have now been repealed by the Road Traffic Act 1991. It may be that cases of involuntary motor manslaughter will as a result become rare but I consider it unsatisfactory that there should be any exception to the generality of the statement which I have made, since such exception, in my view, gives rise to unnecessary complexity. For example, in *Kong Cheuk Kwan v R* (1985) 82 Cr App Rep 18, it would give rise to unnecessary differences between the law applicable to those navigating vessels and the lookouts on the vessels.

I consider it perfectly appropriate that the word 'reckless' should be used in cases of involuntary manslaughter, but as Lord Atkin put it 'in the ordinary connotation of that word'. Examples in which this was done, to my mind, with complete accuracy are *R v Stone, R v Dobinson* [1977] 2 All ER 341, [1977] QB 354 and *R v West London Coroner, ex p Gray* [1987] 2 All ER 129, [1988] QB 467.

In my opinion it is quite unnecessary in the context of gross negligence to give the detailed directions with regard to the meaning of the word 'reckless' associated with *R v Lawrence* [1981] 1 All ER 974, [1982] AC 510. The decision of the Court of Appeal, Criminal Division in the other cases with which they were concerned at the same time as they heard the appeal in this case indicates that the circumstances in which involuntary manslaughter has to be considered may make the somewhat elaborate and rather rigid directions inappropriate. I entirely agree with the view that the circumstance to which a charge of involuntary manslaughter may apply are so various that it is unwise to attempt to categorise or detail specimen directions. For my part I would not wish to go beyond the description of the basis in law which I have already given.

In my view the summing up of the learned judge in the present case was a model of clarity in analysis of the facts and in setting out the law in a manner which was readily comprehensible by the jury. The summing up was criticised in respect of the inclusion of the following passage:

> 'Of course you will understand it is not for every humble man of the profession to have all that great skill of the great men in Harley Street but, on the other hand, they are not allowed to practise medicine in this country unless they have acquired a certain amount of skill. They are bound to show a reasonable amount of skill according to the circumstances of the case, and you have to judge them on the basis that they are skilled men, but not necessarily so skilled as more skilful men in the profession, and you can only convict them criminally if, in your judgment, they fall below the standard of skill which is the least qualification which any doctor should have. You should only convict a doctor of causing a death by negligence if you think he did something which no reasonably skilled doctor should have done.'

The criticism was particularly of the latter part of this quotation in that it was open to the meaning that if the defendant did what no reasonably skilled doctor should have done it was open to the jury to convict him of causing death by negligence. Strictly speaking this passage is concerned with the statement of a necessary condition for a conviction by preventing a conviction unless that condition is satisfied. It is incorrect to treat it as stating a sufficient condition for conviction. In any event I consider that this passage in the context was making the point forcefully that the defendant in this case was not to be judged by the standard of more skilled doctors but by the standard of a reasonably competent doctor. There were many other passages in the summing up which emphasised the need for a high degree of negligence if the jury were to convict and read in that context I consider that the summing up cannot be faulted.

For these reasons I am of the opinion that this appeal should be dismissed and that the certified question should be answered by saying:

> 'In cases of manslaughter by criminal negligence involving a breach of duty, it is a sufficient direction to the jury to adopt the gross negligence test set out by the Court of Appeal in the present case following *R v Bateman* (1925) 19 Cr App Rep 8 and *Andrews v DPP* [1937] 2 All ER 552, [1937] AC 576 and it is not necessary to refer to the definition of recklessness in *R v Lawrence* [1981] 1 All ER 974, [1982] AC 510, although it is perfectly open to the trial judge to use the word "reckless" in its ordinary meaning as part of his exposition of the law if he deems it appropriate in the circumstances of the particular case.'

We have been referred to the consultation paper by the Law Commission, *Criminal Law, Involuntary Manslaughter An Overview* (Law Com no 135), and we have also been referred to a number of standard textbooks. I have also had the opportunity of considering the note by Sir John Smith in [1994] Crim LR 292 since the hearing was completed. While I have not referred to these in detail I have derived considerable help in seeking to formulate my view as a result of studying them.

I have reached the same conclusion on the basic law to be applied in this case as did the Court of Appeal. Personally I would not wish to state the law more elaborately than I have done. In particular I think it is difficult to take expressions used in particular cases out of the context of the cases in which they were used and enunciate them as if applying generally. This can I think lead to ambiguity and perhaps unnecessary complexity. The task of trial judges in setting out for the jury the issues of fact and the relevant law in cases of this class is a difficult and demanding one. I believe that the supreme test that should be satisfied in such directions is that they are comprehensible to an ordinary member of the public who is called to sit on a jury and who has no particular prior acquaintance with the law. To make it obligatory on trial judges to give directions in law which are so elaborate that the ordinary member of the jury will have great difficulty in following them, and even greater difficulty in retaining them in his memory for the purpose of application in the jury room, is no service to the cause of justice. The experienced counsel who assisted your Lordships in this appeal indicated that as a practical matter there was a danger in over-elaboration of definition of the word 'reckless'. While therefore I have said in my view it is perfectly open to a trial judge to use the word 'reckless' if it appears appropriate in the circumstances of a particular case as indicating the extent to which a defendant's conduct must deviate from that of a proper standard of care, I do not think it right to require that this should be done and certainly not right that it should incorporate the full detail required in *R v Lawrence* [1981] 1 All ER 974, [1982] AC 510.

[Lords Keith of Kinkel, Goff of Chieveley, Browne-Wilkinson and Woolf agreed.]

Appeal dismissed

■ *Question*

Does the test operate unfairly against doctors given that they have little control over whether they deal with circumstances which pose a risk of death?

17.3.1 A duty of care: a civil standard of negligence?

R v Wacker
[2002] EWCA Crim 1944, [2003] 4 All ER 295, Court of Appeal, Criminal Division, http://www.bailii.org/ew/cases/EWCA/Crim/2002/1944.html

(Kay LJ, Colman and Ouseley JJ)

The defendant used his HGV to transport 60 illegal immigrants into the UK via Dover. The only ventilation to the container on the HGV was a small vent. The vent was shut and remained closed for over five hours. Fifty-eight of the people hidden in the container suffocated. The defendant was convicted of 58 offences of manslaughter. At his trial the Crown accepted the general proposition that the principle of *ex turpi causa non oritur actio* applied in determining whether there was a duty of care in considering a charge of manslaughter by gross negligence, just as it did in determining whether a civil claim for damages for negligence could succeed.

The judge held that a proper distinction could be drawn between those criminal activities for which the passengers were solely responsible, those for which there was a shared responsibility and those for which the defendant and others were solely responsible. He ruled that the defendant's failure to ensure that the concealed illegal immigrants had sufficient air was incidental to their role but critical to the defendant's own role so that, in establishing the necessary duty of care, since the immigrants would be 'relying' on a matter incidental to their criminality, they would not be 'relying' upon their own unlawful conduct. The defendant appealed against the manslaughter convictions contending that no duty of care could be said to have been owed by him to the illegal immigrants because they shared the same joint illegal purpose; and that the judge had been wrong in his directions to the jury as to the circumstances in which a duty of care would arise. He also appealed against sentence. The Attorney General referred to the court the sentences for manslaughter as being unduly lenient, although he did not contend that the total sentence should be increased but only to the way in which the total of 14 years had been made up.

Held: As a matter of public policy there was no justification for concluding that the criminal law should decline to hold a person as criminally responsible for the death of another simply because the two were engaged in some joint unlawful activity at the time or because there might have been an element of acceptance of a degree of risk by the victim in order to further the joint unlawful enterprise. Nor could the duty to take care be permitted to be affected by the countervailing demands of the criminal enterprise. It was not necessary to examine whether the distinction between matters for which the immigrants were responsible and those incidental to their illegality was a proper one; how matters might have been characterized in a civil claim had no relevance to the issue that the jury had to decide. Accordingly, the approach taken in the court below had been too favourable to the defendant. In every other respect the necessary ingredients of the offence of manslaughter had been properly left to the jury and there were no reasons to doubt the safety of those convictions.

Kay LJ: [his lordship stated the facts:]

11. At the conclusion of the prosecution case, Mr Michael Lawson QC on behalf of the defendant submitted to the trial judge that there was no case for the defendant to answer on each of the manslaughter charges. He took as the foundation for his submission, the observation of Lord Mackay of Clashfern LC in *R v Adomako* [1994] 3 All ER 79 at 86–87, [1995] 1 AC 171 at 187 [section 17.3, p 618]:

'...in my opinion the ordinary principles of the law of negligence apply to ascertain whether or not the defendant has been in breach of a duty of care towards the victim who has died. If such breach of duty is established the next question is whether that breach of duty caused the death of the victim. If so, the jury must go on to consider whether that breach of duty should be characterised as gross negligence and therefore as a crime.'

12. Mr Lawson therefore submitted that the first question to be decided was whether applying 'the ordinary principles of the law of negligence', the defendant owed to those in the container a duty of care. He submitted that one of the general principles of the law of negligence, known by the Latin maxim of *ex turpi causa non oritur actio*, was that the law of negligence did not recognise the relationship between those involved in a criminal enterprise as giving rise to a duty of care owed by one participant to another. In his ruling Moses J summarised Mr Lawson's submission on the facts of the case:

'Mr Lawson contends that a failure to produce sufficient air or ventilation stems directly from the criminal activity in which both driver and passengers were engaged. It was essential to the criminal activity of all that secrecy be maintained. The closure of the vent, and the failure to reopen it during the course of the journey on board the ferry, which caused the death by suffocation of the 58 occupants, arose directly, he contends, from an enterprise the very essence of which was that secrecy was maintained. Secrecy could only be maintained by keeping the vent closed, since if it was open voices might be heard and, as the evidence of at least one of the survivor's revealed, the occupants had been told only to speak when the vent was open. Moreover, it is not possible for the court to determine the appropriate standard of care to be exercised by the driver. What is the appropriate standard of care to be applied in the case of a driver seeking, as part of a joint criminal exercise, to conceal the presence of 60 occupants of his lorry? In other words, the criminal activity on which all were engaged does, so he submits, have a bearing upon the appropriate standard of care. That standard cannot be ascertained without regard to the clandestine nature of the joint criminal activity. It was the driver's job to increase the chance of entry without detection, the very object which the passengers themselves sought to achieve.'

...

35. [L]ooked at as a matter of pure public policy, we can see no justification for concluding that the criminal law should decline to hold a person as criminally responsible for the death of another simply because the two were engaged in some joint unlawful activity at the time or, indeed, because there may have been an element of acceptance of a degree of risk by the victim in order to further the joint unlawful enterprise. Public policy, in our judgment, manifestly points in totally the opposite direction.

36. The next question that we are bound to ask ourselves is whether in any way we are required by authority to take a different view. The foundation for the contention that *ex turpi causa* is as much a part of the law of manslaughter as it is a part of the law of negligence is the passage from the speech of Lord Mackay of Clashfern LC in *R v Adomako* [1994] 3 All ER 79, [1995] 1 AC 171 set out at [11], above. In particular it is Lord Mackay's reference to 'the ordinary principles of the law of negligence'.

37. *R v Adomako* was a case where an anaesthetist had negligently brought about the death of a patient. It, therefore, involved no element of unlawful activity on the part of either the anaesthetist or the victim. We have no doubt that issues raised in the case we are considering would never have crossed the minds of those deciding that case in the House of Lords. In so far as Lord Mackay referred to 'ordinary principles of the law of negligence' we do not accept for one moment that he was intending to decide that the rules relating to ex turpi causa were part of those ordinary principles. He was doing no more than holding that in an 'ordinary' case of negligence, the question whether there was a duty of care was to be judged by the same legal criteria as governed whether there was a duty of care in the law of negligence. That was the only issue relevant to that case and to give the passage the more extensive meaning accepted in the court below was in our judgment wrong.

Appeals dismissed

How is D to know what duties of civil law will be sufficient to trigger potential criminal liability? In *Yaqoob* [2005] EWCA Crim 1269, the defendant was a manager of a minicab firm and he had failed to inspect the tyres of a minibus involved in a fatal accident. It was held that it was open to the jury to find that there was a duty to inspect and maintain beyond that required for a MOT test, council inspections and other duties imposed by regulation. Moreover, the jury did not require expert evidence to assess that duty.

There are established categories where a duty of care has been recognized to exist in the context of gross negligence manslaughter, such as between husband and wife (*Meeking* [2012] EWCA Crim 641); parent and child (*Evans* [2009] EWCA Crim 650); when one stores materials of an extremely hazardous nature on one's premises (*Winter and Winter* [2010] EWCA Crim 1474); and when a duty is voluntarily assumed (*C* [2011] EWCA Crim 3272). However, as the next section shows, there are more difficult categories on the periphery.

17.3.1.1 Gross negligence manslaughter: drug misuse cases

In *Kennedy (No 2)* the House of Lords stated emphatically that a supplier of drugs cannot be guilty of unlawful act manslaughter if the person to whom he supplies the drugs dies from having taken them, as long as that person is a fully informed and responsible adult and chooses to take the drugs voluntarily. However, a different approach is taken in the context of gross negligence manslaughter. As the following case demonstrates, the supplier of drugs can be guilty of gross negligence manslaughter and the fact that V self-administered them does not break the chain of causation. By extending the doctrine that was first propounded in *Miller* [1982] UKHL 6 (section 4.3.3.4, p 86) a five-member Court of Appeal based D's liability for gross negligence manslaughter on her having created *or contributed to* a dangerous situation. The duty arose when D realized or ought to have realized that V was suffering from a life-threatening reaction to the heroin she had supplied.

R v Evans

[2009] EWCA Crim 650, Court of Appeal, Criminal Division, http://www.bailii.org/ew/cases/EWCA/Crim/2009/650.html

(Lord Judge CJ, Moore-Bick LJ, Calvert-Smith, Christopher Clark and Holroyde JJ)

D supplied V, her 16-year-old half-sister, with heroin. After V self-injected the heroin, she developed symptoms that D recognized as being consistent with an overdose. D and her mother, X, who was also in the house, believed that they were responsible for V but did not seek medical assistance as they feared getting into trouble. V was put to bed but was found dead the next morning. The cause of death was heroin poisoning. X was convicted of gross negligence manslaughter on the basis that she owed V a duty of care, as she was her mother. The Crown based D's duty of care towards V not on the fact of their familial relationship, but on the fact that D did not seek medical attention when it became apparent that V was having a life-threatening adverse reaction to the drug that D had supplied her. In essence, this was a case of liability arising from an omission. D appealed her conviction, arguing that the judge had been wrong to conclude that D owed V a duty of care.

Lord Judge CJ:

20. The question in this appeal is not whether the appellant may be guilty of manslaughter for having been concerned in the supply of the heroin which caused the deceased's death. It is whether, notwithstanding that their relationship lacked the features of familial duty or responsibility which marked her mother's relationship with the deceased, she was under a duty to take reasonable steps for the safety of the deceased once she appreciated that the heroin she procured for her was having a potentially fatal impact on her health.

21. When omission or failure to act are in issue two aspects of manslaughter are engaged. Both are governed by decisions of the House of Lords. The first is manslaughter arising from the defendant's gross negligence: *R v Adomako* [1995] 1 AC 171. The second arises when the defendant has created a dangerous situation and when, notwithstanding his appreciation of the consequent risks, he fails to take any reasonable preventative steps: *R v Miller* [1983] 2 AC 161. Gross negligence manslaughter and unlawful act manslaughter are not necessarily mutually exclusive: *R v Willoughby* [2005] 1 WLR 1880. The same applies to the aspects of manslaughter presently under consideration. Indeed care needs to be taken to avoid the risk of allowing the convenience of addressing the different circumstances in which manslaughter may arise to be converted into a compartmentalised, mutually isolated series of offences each inconveniently described by the same word, 'manslaughter'.

22. Miller's duty to act arose after he fell asleep in a squat while holding a lighted cigarette. He woke up and found that his mattress was smouldering. He left the room in which he had been asleep and went back to sleep in an adjoining room. He wholly ignored the smouldering mattress. The house caught fire. He was convicted of arson. In the House of Lords argument ranged over whether his omission to act engaged what was described as the 'duty theory' espoused by Professor J C Smith or whether his reckless omission to rectify the consequences of his earlier unintended act attracted the 'continuing act theory' supported by Professor Glanville Williams. It was submitted that there was no liability in criminal law for an omission unless there was a legal duty to act imposed by common law or by statute, and that no statutory provision imposed a duty neglect of which involved criminal liability, and no common law duty to extinguish an accidental fire or fire innocently started had previously been 'declared'.

23. The decision of the House of Lords was expressed in the single opinion of Lord Diplock. Both theories, he said, led to an identical result. The 'continuing act' basis for liability was not disavowed, but the duty theory was adopted only on the basis that it was easier to explain to a jury, provided the word 'responsibility' rather than 'duty' was used. In fact, the issue has continued to be addressed in the context of 'duty' rather than responsibility, and we shall continue to do so. More important, however, Lord Diplock observed, at p 176, that he could see

'no rational ground for excluding from conduct capable of giving rise to criminal liability, conduct which consists of failing to take measures that lie within one's power to counteract a danger that one has oneself created, if at the time of such conduct one's state of mind is such as constitutes a necessary ingredient of the offence . . . I cannot see any good reason why, so far as liability under criminal law is concerned, it should matter at what point of time before the resultant damage is complete a person becomes aware that he has done a physical act which, whether or not he appreciated that it would at the time when he did it, does in fact create a risk that property of another will be damaged; provided that, at the moment of awareness, it lies within his power to take steps, either himself or by calling for the assistance of the fire brigade if this be necessary, to prevent or minimise the damage to the property at risk.'

24. The mens rea necessary for arson was, and thereafter the analysis focussed on, recklessness. But the reasoning in the decision does not exclude liability where a different mens rea is required. And if, for example, the result of the fire in *R v Miller* had included the death of a fellow squatter, it appears to us that Miller would properly have been convicted of manslaughter by gross negligence as well as arson: *R v Willoughby* [2005] 1 WLR 1880.

25. Adomako was an anaesthetist and the deceased was his patient. He plainly owed him a duty of care. Lord Mackay of Clashfern LC in the only speech, expressed the opinion that [1995] 1 AC 171, 187: 'the ordinary principles of the law of negligence apply to ascertain whether or not the defendant has been in breach of a duty of care towards the victim who has died.' He answered the certified question, at p 188: 'In cases of manslaughter by criminal negligence involving a breach of duty, it is a sufficient direction to the jury to adopt the gross negligence test set out by the Court of Appeal in the present case...'

26. Our attention was drawn to a number of subsequent authorities. In *R v Khan (Rungzabe)* [1998] Crim LR 830 a young woman was supplied by the appellants with heroin. This was probably the first occasion on which she had used heroin. She took ten times the recommended therapeutic dosage and twice the amount likely to be taken even by an experienced user of heroin. She became 'obviously very ill'. She needed medical attention. The appellants, who were drug dealers, left her where she was and did nothing to assist. On the next day they returned and found that she was dead. If she had received medical attention she would probably have survived.

27. The jury was directed that they could consider a manslaughter verdict on the basis of omission. This could arise only if the appellants had set in train 'a chain of events' which gave rise to a risk of harm to the deceased. The relevant act was the supply of heroin to her. The second necessary ingredient was knowledge or awareness of the obvious risk that, having taken the heroin, the deceased would or might be harmed, and that they deliberately took no steps to rectify it. The effect of the direction was 'to extend the duty to summon medical assistance to a drug dealer who supplies heroin to a person who subsequently dies'. This court held that that might be correct (*sed quaere* today, in the light of *R v Kennedy (No 2)* [2008] AC 269), but the issue needed to be closely addressed with the jury. The summing up in relation to manslaughter by omission was flawed. The convictions were quashed. The issue which arises in the present appeal was not directly addressed, although impliedly at any rate it appears that the court would not have rejected criminal liability on this basis.

28. *R v Sinclair, Johnson and Smith* (1998) 148 NLJ 1353 raised similar issues. For these purposes the detailed facts need no narrative. Johnson's conviction for manslaughter was quashed on the basis that his conduct had not demonstrated a 'voluntary assumption of a legal duty of care'. What he had done was rather 'a desultory attempt to be of assistance'. The facts were not capable of giving rise to a legal duty of care in his case. Sinclair, however, was in a different position. He was a close friend of the deceased. They lived together, almost like brothers. Sinclair paid for and supplied the deceased with the first dose of methadone and helped him to obtain the second dose. He knew that the deceased was not an addict. He remained with the deceased throughout the period of his unconsciousness. For a long time he was the only person who was with him. On this basis there was material on which the jury, properly directed, could have found that Sinclair owed the deceased a legal duty of care. That accords with the present case.

29. In *R v Willoughby* [2005] 1 WLR 1880 the appellant was convicted of manslaughter on the basis of arson. He owned some premises which he decided to destroy by fire. He recruited a man called Drury to help him set fire to the premises. In an explosion the premises collapsed and Mr Drury died. The court accepted that a duty to look after the deceased did not arise merely because the appellant owned the premises which collapsed and in which he was killed. But that fact, taken together with the additional facts that the destruction of the premises was for his financial benefit, that he enlisted the deceased to take part, and that his role was to spread petrol inside the premises, were sufficient, 'in conjunction' to be capable of giving rise to a duty of care: para 20.

30. In *R v Wacker* [2003] QB 1207 the appellant's convictions for manslaughter arose from the horrific deaths of 58 illegal immigrants hiding in a container loaded on to a trailer. The appellant was the lorry driver. It was suggested that he owed no duty of care to any of the deceased because they were parties to the same illegal purpose. The court, at para 38, had 'no difficulty in concluding that . . . the [appellant] did voluntarily assume the duty of care [for those in the container]', and he was aware that 'no one's actions other than his own could realistically prevent [them] from suffocating to death'. The appeal was dismissed on the basis that, once the jury decided that the appellant knew about those travelling in the container, it was a very plain case of gross negligence manslaughter.

31. These authorities are consistent with our analysis. None involved what could sensibly be described as manslaughter by mere omission and in each it was an essential requirement of any potential basis for conviction that the defendant should have failed to act when he was under a duty to do so. The duty necessary to found gross negligence manslaughter is plainly not confined to cases of a familial or professional relationship between the defendant and the deceased. In our judgment, consistently with *R v Adomako* [1995] 1 AC 171 and the link between civil and criminal liability for negligence, for the purposes of gross negligence manslaughter, when a person has created or contributed to the creation of a state of affairs which he knows, or ought reasonably to know, has become life threatening, a consequent duty on him to act by taking reasonable steps to save the other's life will normally arise.

[The Court of Appeal also made clear that whether a duty of care exists between D and V is a question of law not fact and is for the judge to determine. The jury are to be directed on what the law is—ie whether a duty of care existed—if they find certain facts to be established.]

45. In some cases, such as those arising from a doctor/patient relationship where the existence of the duty is not in dispute, the judge may well direct the jury that a duty of care exists. Such a direction would be proper. But if, for example, the doctor were on holiday at the material time, and the deceased asked a casual question over a drink, it may very well be that the question whether a doctor/patient relationship existed, and accordingly whether a duty of care arose, would be in dispute. In any cases where the issue is in dispute, and therefore in more complex cases, and assuming that the judge has found that it would be open to the jury to find that there was a duty of care, or a duty to act, the jury should be directed that if facts a + b and/or c or d are established, then in law a duty will arise, but if facts x or y or z were present, the duty would be negatived. In this sense, of course, the jury is deciding whether the duty situation has been established. In our judgment this is the way in which *R v Willoughby* should be understood and, understood in this way, no potential problems arising from article 6 and article 7 of the Convention are engaged.

■ *Questions*

1. Why did V's self-injection not break the chain of causation? Is *Evans* inconsistent with *Kennedy (No 2)*? See D. Baker, 'Omissions Liability for Homicide Offences: Reconciling *R v Kennedy* with *R v Evans*' (2010) 74 J Crim L 310.

2. How much of a 'contribution' to a dangerous situation must D make before the duty of care crystallizes?

3. Could D have avoided liability by quickly leaving the scene after handing over the heroin so that she would have been unaware of whether V had had an adverse reaction or not? If so, does this possibility mean that prosecutions in cases such as *Evans* will be rare?

4. Would D have been liable if the circumstances were the same but it had been X who supplied the heroin? Consider *Phillips* [2013] EWCA Crim 358 where the allegations against D were as follows:

i) having supplied [V] with a quantity of diarmorphine (heroin), a controlled drug of Class A, [D] owed him a duty of care;

ii) in breach of that duty and knowing that the state of affairs had become life-threatening, [D] failed to take reasonable steps to ensure that [V] received appropriate medical treatment;

iii) that breach of duty amounted to gross negligence;

iv) that negligence was a substantial cause of the death of [V]

Is it the supply of drugs that gives rise to the duty of care? Is that what was decided in *Evans*? Does the supply of heroin (or any drug) necessarily create or contribute to a dangerous situation?

17.3.2 Risk of death

Though Lord Mackay refers to a risk of death, it was not completely clear whether if D created a risk of causing serious bodily harm to V that would be sufficient. But in *Gurphal Singh* [1999] Crim LR 582, the judge directed: 'The circumstances must be such that a reasonably prudent person would have foreseen a serious and obvious risk not merely of injury or even serious injury but of death.' The Court of Appeal has now confirmed in *Misra* that a risk of death is required.

R v Misra and Srivastava

[2004] EWCA Crim 2375, Court of Appeal, Criminal Division, http://www.bailii.org/ew/cases/EWCA/Crim/2004/2375.html

(Judge LJ, Deputy Chief Justice of England and Wales, Treacy and Bean JJ)

M and S were doctors who, on duty in a hospital, failed to recognize that a knee-surgery patient had developed toxic shock syndrome. The poison built up in his body and he died. The prosecution relied not on M and S's failure to diagnose the precise condition, since that was a rare one and failure to identify it may well not have amounted to negligence at all. The Crown relied on their failure to appreciate that the patient was seriously ill, despite his showing persistent signs of infection and notwithstanding suggestions by other members of the medical team. M and S did not obtain the blood results that someone had ordered nor did either make any inquiry about the results. They did not seek help from senior colleagues. An expert for the prosecution testified that if he were examining a third- or fourth-year medical student, and the student failed to diagnose infection in such circumstances, he would have thought of failing the student on that basis alone.

49. No issue arises whether both appellants owed a duty of care to the deceased, or were negligently in breach of it. There was however helpful argument about the nature of the relevant risk. Was it, as the judge directed the jury in the present case 'serious risk to life', or was it much broader, extending to serious risk to safety as well as life? In its original formulation in *Bateman*, Lord Hewitt CJ referred to 'disregard to the life and safety of others' in the sense of serious injury. In *Seymour*, the risk was confined to the risk of death. In *Stone* [1977] QB 554 and *West London Coroner, ex parte Grey* [1988] QB 467, [1987] 2 All ER 129 reference was made to risks in broader terms, extending to health and welfare. Although Lord Mackay spoke in approving terms of these decisions in a different context, it is clear that his approval was directed to the deployment of the word 'reckless'. He was not addressing, and it would have been inconsistent with his own analysis of the legal principles if he were approving, the wider basis for identifying risk described in *Stone* and *West London Coroner ex parte Grey*. It is also striking that Lord Mackay did not expressly adopt or approve the broader formulation of risk made by Lord Taylor CJ in *Prentice*. Since *Adomako*, this issue has been addressed in this court, in *R (on the*

application of Gurphal) v Singh [1999] CLR 582 and the Divisional Court in *Lewin v CPS*, unreported, 24 May 2002. In *Gurphal Singh*, this court strongly approved the trial judge's direction in a case of manslaughter by gross negligence that 'the circumstances must be such that a reasonably prudent person would have foreseen a serious and obvious risk not merely of injury, even serious injury, but of death'. In *Lewin*, the Divisional Court applied that direction.

50. Mr David Perry, on behalf of the Attorney General, informed us that, as a matter of policy, when making a decision whether to prosecute for this offence in cases like the present, the Director of Public Prosecutions looks for evidence of an obvious risk of death, and that, if the extent of the risk were limited to the obvious risk of serious injury, and no more, prosecution would not follow.

51. The editors of *Blackstone's Criminal Practice* suggest that the law needs clarification, and that, if it were clarified, some 'degree of symmetry' between murder and manslaughter would be achieved if, for the purposes of gross negligence manslaughter, the risk should extend to grievous bodily harm. Professor Smith took the contrary view, suggesting that 'if we are to have an offence of homicide by gross negligence at all, it seems right that it should be...limited. The circumstances must be such that a reasonably prudent person would have foreseen a serious risk, not merely of injury, even serious injury, but of death.'

52. There will, of course, be numerous occasions when these distinctions are entirely theoretical. From time to time, however, they will be of great significance, not only to the decision whether to prosecute, but also to the risk of conviction of manslaughter. In our judgment, where the issue of risk is engaged, *Adomako* demonstrates, and it is now clearly established, that it relates to the risk of death, and is not sufficiently satisfied by the risk of bodily injury or injury to health. In short, the offence requires gross negligence in circumstances where what is at risk is the life of an individual to whom the defendant owes a duty of care. As such it serves to protect his or her right to life.

■ *Question*

D performs an act which is lawful (therefore not unlawful act manslaughter) and which does not objectively pose a risk of death, but his action causes V's death. Can D be charged with manslaughter? See section 17.4, p 637.

17.3.3 Grossness of the breach

This aspect of the test has been very heavily criticized. The question is whether the negligence was bad enough to amount to a crime and conduct deserving of punishment. This is easy enough to state, but difficult to apply. Consider driving as an example; every instance of driving without due care and attention is a crime and it can scarcely be the law that every such case would be manslaughter if the driving happened to cause death. How bad does the negligence have to be to be gross? As *Andrews* decided, even causing death by *dangerous* driving is not *necessarily* manslaughter.

In *Litchfield* [1998] Crim LR 507, the master of a square-rigged schooner which foundered off the Cornish coast was convicted of manslaughter by gross negligence by steering an unsafe course, knowing that he might need to rely on the vessel's engines and that they might fail through contaminated fuel. The judge, in the time-honoured fashion, directed the jury that negligence must have been 'so bad that it could properly amount to a criminal act...' Sir John Smith commented on the decision ([1998] Crim LR 508) that:

Section 27(2) of the Merchant Shipping Act 1970 makes it an offence, punishable by two years' imprisonment, for a master of a ship to do or omit to do anything which causes or is likely to cause, *inter alia*, loss or destruction of or serious damage to his ship, or the death of or serious injury to any person, if the act or omission amounts to a breach or neglect of duty. Two counts under this section were included in the original indictment but the prosecution decided not to lay them before the jury.

In so deciding the prosecution were apparently making a judgement that the negligence alleged went beyond, not merely a matter of compensation between parties, but beyond anything which could be adequately dealt with by conviction and sentence under the 1970 Act. It was argued on appeal that—

'...if the facts proved do indeed amount to a statutory crime it is illogical and contrary to public policy to ask a jury to determine whether the conduct found is so bad that it *ought* to be judged a crime.'

So it was said that—

'there is no room (or virtually no room) in the law for a shipping manslaughter case'. The court dismissed this argument as 'impossible'.'For a start it makes nonsense of *Adomako*... Secondly, of course, it would quite inappropriately benefit those who are made subject to a statutory criminal liability. Why, one wonders, should mariners be advantaged over doctors'?

Everyone will agree that there is no reason why mariners (or dangerous drivers) should be immune from prosecution of manslaughter; but does not the argument suggest that it is absurd to ask a jury to decide whether the negligence goes beyond a mere matter of compensation between parties? The negligence may go well beyond that while falling well short of what is required for manslaughter. Is not the real question, not whether the negligence is bad enough to deserve punishment but *whether it is bad enough to be condemned as the very grave crime of manslaughter and punished accordingly*? (In *Litchfield* the judge did say 'way above' and 'so bad, so obviously wrong...that it can properly be condemned as criminal, not in some technical sense of the word, like somebody might be regarded as criminal if they did not have light on the back of their bicycle, but in the ordinary language of men and women of the world.') If the statutory offence and manslaughter were charged in the same indictment, how could the judge explain their task to the jury other than by telling them that the manslaughter charge required a higher degree of fault?

17.3.3.1 Is the gross negligence test too uncertain?

In *R v Misra*, section 17.3.2, p 627, the Court of Appeal addressed these concerns.

Judge LJ [reading the judgment of the court:]

28. Mr Michael Gledhill QC on behalf of Dr Misra submitted that manslaughter by gross negligence is an offence which lacks certainty. As presently understood, it requires the trial judge to direct the jury that the defendant should be convicted of manslaughter by gross negligence if they are satisfied that his conduct was 'criminal'. Indeed, the effect of his argument was that it is a separate additional ingredient of this offence that the jury has to decide whether the defendant's conduct amounted to a crime. Relying in particular on the Law Commission paper on Involuntary Manslaughter (Law Com. No. 237) as a convenient summary of a good deal of the debate by distinguished academic commentators, he suggested that the current test is 'circular'. It is this circularity which leads to uncertainty. Mr Gledhill drew attention to, and adopted for the purposes for his argument, the way in which the Law Commission identified the potential problems arising from linking the civil and the criminal law concepts of negligence where the allegation against the defendant arose from omission. This was such a case. 'It is by no means certain that the scope of liability for negligent omissions is the same in criminal law as it is in tort.' The principles were 'so unclear' that it is difficult to tell whether 'the law as currently understood represents a change, and if so, what the implications might be.' The relevant part of the Law Commission paper ends, 'It is possible that the law in this area fails to meet the standard of certainty required by the European Convention on Human Rights (ECHR).' In Mr Gledhill's submission this is an understatement: the standard of certainty is not met.

29. To develop his argument on uncertainty, Mr Gledhill focussed our attention on art 7 of the ECHR, entitled 'No punishment without law', which provides:

'7(1) No-one shall be held guilty of any criminal offence on account of any act or omission which did not constitute a criminal offence under national or international law at the time when it was committed nor shall a heavier penalty be imposed than the one that was applicable at the time the criminal offence was committed.'

In our view the essential thrust of this Article is to prohibit the creation of offences, whether by legislation or the incremental development of the common law, which have retrospective application. It reflects a well-understood principle of domestic law, that conduct which did not contravene the criminal law at the time when it took place should not retrospectively be stigmatised as criminal, or expose the perpetrator to punishment. As Lord Reid explained in *Waddington v Miah* [1974] 2 All ER 377, [1974] 59 Cr App R 149 at p. 150 and 151,

'There has for a very long time been a strong feeling against making legislation, and particularly criminal legislation, retrospective. . . . I use retrospective in the sense of authorising people being punished for what they did before the Act came into force.'

[His lordship reviewed English common law authorities for the principle of legality.]

34. . . . In summary, it is not to be supposed that prior to the implementation of the Human Rights Act 1998, either this Court, or the House of Lords, would have been indifferent to or unaware of the need for the criminal law in particular to be predictable and certain. Vague laws which purport to create criminal liability are undesirable, and in extreme cases, where it occurs, their very vagueness may make it impossible to identify the conduct which is prohibited by a criminal sanction. If the court is forced to guess at the ingredients of a purported crime any conviction for it would be unsafe. That said, however, the requirement is for sufficient rather than absolute certainty.

[His lordship referred to the ECHR case law on the requirement of certainty and continued:]

37. Since the implementation of the Human Rights Act, the issue of uncertainty has also been addressed on a number of occasions in this court. It has been decided that the offence of making indecent photographs of children was sufficiently certain to satisfy arts 8 and 10 of the Convention (*R v Smethurst* [2001] EWCA Crim 772, [2002] 1 Cr App Rep 50, 165 JP 377); that the offence of publishing an obscene article satisfies the requirements of art 7 of the Convention (*R v Perrin* [2002] EWCA Crim 747); and that the offence of causing a public nuisance, by sending an envelope through the post containing salt, which was suspected to be anthrax, contrary to common law, was also sufficiently certain to satisfy the requirements of art 7, 8 and 10 of the Convention (*R v Goldstein* [2003] EWCA Crim 3450, [2004] 1 Cr App R 388). In each case the uncertainty argument was rejected. In *Goldstein* itself, at p. 395, Latham LJ commented:

'The elements of the offence are sufficiently clear to enable a person, with appropriate legal advice if necessary, to regulate his behaviour. . . . A citizen, appropriately advised, could foresee that the conduct identified was capable of amounting to a public nuisance.'

In our judgment, the incorporation of the ECHR, while providing a salutary reminder, has not effected any significant extension of or change to the 'certainty' principle as long understood at common law.

[His lordship dealt with the issues of recklessness and gross negligence discussed later in the chapter.]

58. We can now return to the argument based on circularity and uncertainty, and the application of arts 6 and 7 of the ECHR. The most important passages in the speech of Lord Mackay on the issue of circularity read:

'. . . The jury must go on to consider whether that breach of duty should be characterised as gross negligence and therefore as a crime. This will depend on the seriousness of the breach of duty committed by the defendant in all the circumstances in which the defendant was placed when it occurred. The jury will have to consider whether the extent to which the defendant's conduct departed from the proper standard of care incumbent upon him, involving as it must have done a risk of death to the patient, was such that it should be judged criminal.

It is true that, to a certain extent, this involves an element of circularity, but in this branch of the law I do not believe that is fatal to its being correct as a test of how far conduct must depart from accepted standards to be characterised as criminal . . . The essence of the matter which is supremely a jury question is whether, having regard to the risk of death involved, the conduct of the defendant was so bad in all the circumstances as to amount in their judgment to a criminal act or omission.'

59. Mr Gledhill suggested that this passage demonstrated that an additional specific ingredient of this offence was that the jury had to decide whether the defendant's conduct amounted to a crime. If the jury could, or was required to, define the offence for itself, and accordingly might do so on some unaccountable or unprincipled or unexplained basis, to adopt Bacon, the sound given by the law would indeed be uncertain, and would then strike without warning. Mr Gledhill's argument then would be compelling.

60. Looking at the authorities since *Bateman*, the purpose of referring to the differences between civil and criminal liability, whether in the passage in Lord Mackay's speech to which we have just referred, or in directions to the jury, is to highlight that the burden on the prosecution goes beyond proof of negligence for which compensation would be payable. Negligence of that degree could not lead to a conviction for manslaughter. The negligence must be so bad, 'gross', that if all the other ingredients of the offence are proved, then it amounts to a crime and is punishable as such.

61. This point was addressed by Lord Atkin in *Andrews* at p. 582, when he referred to *Williamson* (1807) 3 C&P 635:

'. . . where a man who practiced as an accoucheur, owing to a mistake in his observation of the actual symptoms, inflicted on a patient terrible injuries from which she died.'

To substantiate that charge—namely, manslaughter—Lord Ellenborough said, 'The prisoner must have been guilty of criminal misconduct, arising either from the grossest ignorance or the most criminal inattention.' The word 'criminal' in any attempt to define a crime is perhaps not the most helpful: but it is plain that the Lord Chief Justice meant to indicate to the jury a high degree of negligence. So at a much later date in *Bateman* (1925) 18 Cr. App. R 8 a charge of manslaughter was made against a qualified medical practitioner in similar circumstances to those of *Williamson's* case . . . I think with respect that the expressions used are not, indeed they were probably not intended to be, a precise definition of the crime.

62. Accordingly, the value of references to the criminal law in this context is that they avoid the danger that the jury may equate what we may describe as 'simple' negligence, which in relation to manslaughter would not be a crime at all, with negligence which involves a criminal offence. In short, by bringing home to the jury the extent of the burden on the prosecution, they ensure that the defendant whose negligence does not fall within the ambit of the criminal law is not convicted of a crime. They do not alter the essential ingredients of this offence. A conviction cannot be returned if the negligent conduct is or may be less than gross. If however the defendant is found by the jury to have been grossly negligent, then, if the jury is to act in accordance with its duty, he must be convicted. This is precisely what Lord Mackay indicated when, in the passage already cited, he said, '. . . The jury must go on to consider whether that breach of duty should be characterised as gross negligence and therefore as a crime' (our emphasis). The decision whether the conduct was criminal is described not as 'the' test, but as 'a' test as to how far the conduct in question must depart from accepted standards to be 'characterised as criminal'. On proper analysis, therefore, the jury is not deciding whether the particular defendant ought to be convicted on some unprincipled basis. The question for the jury is not whether the defendant's negligence was gross, and whether, additionally, it was a crime, but whether his behaviour was grossly negligent and consequently criminal. This is not a question of law, but one of fact, for decision in the individual case.

63. On examination, this represents one example, among many, of problems which juries are expected to address on a daily basis. They include equally difficult questions, such as whether a defendant has acted dishonestly, by reference to contemporary standards, or whether he has acted in reasonable self-defence, or, when charged with causing death by dangerous driving, whether the standards of his driving fell far below what should be expected of a competent and careful driver. These examples represent the commonplace for juries. Each of these questions could be said to be vague and uncertain. If he made enquiries in advance, at most an individual would be told the principle of law which the jury would be directed to apply: he could not be advised what a jury would think of the individual case, and how it would be decided. That involves an element of uncertainty about the outcome of the decision-making process, but not unacceptable uncertainty about the offence itself.

64. In our judgment the law is clear. The ingredients of the offence have been clearly defined, and the principles decided in the House of Lords in *Adomako*. They involve no uncertainty. The hypothetical citizen, seeking to know his position, would be advised that, assuming he owed a duty of care to the deceased which he had negligently broken, and that death resulted, he would be liable to conviction for manslaughter if, on the available evidence, the jury was satisfied that his negligence was gross. A doctor would be told that grossly negligent treatment of a patient which exposed him or her to the risk of death, and caused it, would constitute manslaughter.

65. After Lord Williams' sustained criticism of the offence of manslaughter by gross negligence, the House of Lords in *Adomako* clarified the relevant principles and the ingredients of this offence. Although, to a limited extent, Lord Mackay accepted that there was an element of circularity in the process by which the jury would arrive at its verdict, the element of circularity which he identified did not then and does not now result in uncertainty which offends against Article 7, nor if we may say so, any principle of common law. Gross negligence manslaughter is not incompatible with the ECHR. Accordingly the appeal arising from the question certified by the trial judge must be dismissed.

[His lordship reviewed the facts.]

Appeals dismissed

■ *Questions*

1. How will a defendant know with certainty whether the conduct he is engaged in performing negligently will be regarded as being so grossly negligent as to constitute the offence of manslaughter?

2. The court explains that 'a doctor would be told that grossly negligent treatment of a patient which exposed him or her to the risk of death, and caused it, would constitute manslaughter' (at [64]). What should the response be when the doctor then asks how gross his negligent conduct has to be in order to be convicted? How can the relevant standard be described to the doctor otherwise than by reference to whether the jury thinks that it is criminal?

3. Should gross negligence manslaughter be abolished? See O. Quick, 'Medicine, Mistakes and Manslaughter: A Criminal Combination?' (2010) 69 CLJ 186.

For further criticisms of the test, see V. Tadros, 'The Limits of Manslaughter' in C. Clarkson and S. Cunningham (eds), *Criminal Liability for Non Aggressive Death* (2008).

17.3.4 Gross negligence and mens rea

In *Misra*, the appellants also argued that in the light of the decision of the House of Lords in *G* (section 5.3, p 117), the gross negligence manslaughter formulation should be abandoned in favour of a test of subjective reckless manslaughter. The Court of Appeal rejected this ground of appeal.

39. After he had fully considered the recent decision of the House of Lords in *R v G and Another* [2003] UKHL 50, [2004] 1 AC 1034, [section 5.3, p 117] Mr Gledhill deployed an additional argument which was not before Langley J. In essence, he submitted that with the exception of causing death by dangerous driving, no serious criminal offence could be committed without mens rea. He relied on what Lord Bingham, at para 32, described as a 'salutary principle that conviction of serious crime should depend on proof not simply that the defendant caused (by act or omission) an injurious result to another but that his state of mind when so acting was culpable'. Unless some element of mens rea, such, for example, as recklessness, was a necessary ingredient of manslaughter by gross negligence, this essential principle was contravened. . . .

55. It is convenient now to address the argument that the decision in *R v G and Another* should lead us to reassess whether gross negligence manslaughter should now be replaced by and confined to reckless manslaughter. As we have shown, precisely this argument by Lord Williams of Mostyn was rejected in *Adomako*. We also note, first, that Parliament has not given effect to possible reforms on this topic discussed by the Law Commission and, second, notwithstanding that *Adomako* was cited in argument in *R v G and Another*, it was not subjected to any reservations or criticisms. Indeed in his speech Lord Bingham of Cornhill emphasised that in *R v G* he was not addressing the meaning of 'reckless' in any other statutory or common law context than s 1(1) and (2) of the Criminal Damage Act 1971. In these circumstances, although we gave leave to Mr Gledhill to amend his grounds of appeal to enable him to deploy the argument, we reject it.

56. We can now reflect on Mr Gledhill's associated contention that if recklessness is not a necessary ingredient of this offence, the decision in *Attorney General's Reference (No. 2 of 1999)* [2000] QB 796, [2000] 3 All ER 182 led to the unacceptable conclusion that manslaughter by gross negligence did not require proof of any specific state of mind, and that the defendant's state of mind was irrelevant. In our judgment the submission is based on a narrow reading of the decision that a defendant may properly be convicted of gross negligence manslaughter in the absence of evidence as to his state of mind. However when it is available, such evidence is not irrelevant to the issue of gross negligence. It will often be a critical factor in the decision (see *R (on the application of Rowley) v DPP* [2003] EWHC 693). In *Adomako* itself, Lord Mackay directed attention to 'all' of the circumstances in which the defendant was placed: he did not adopt, or endorse, or attempt to redefine the list of states of mind to which Lord Taylor CJ referred in *Prentice*, which was not in any event 'exhaustive' of possible relevant states of mind. It is therefore clear that the defendant is not to be convicted without fair consideration of all the relevant circumstances in which his breach of duty occurred. In each case, of course, the circumstances are fact-specific.

57. Mr Gledhill nevertheless contended that even so, the problem of mens rea remains. This, he argued was a necessary, but absent ingredient of the offence. We have reflected, of course, that if the defendant intends death or really serious harm, and acts in such a way to cause either, and death results, he would be guilty of murder. If he intends limited injury, and causes death, he would be guilty of manslaughter in any event. We are here concerned with the defendant who does not intend injury, but who in all the contemporaneous circumstances is grossly negligent. As a matter of strict language, 'mens rea' is concerned with an individual defendant's state of mind. Speaking generally, negligence is concerned with his failure to behave in accordance with the standards required of the reasonable man. Looked at in this way, the two concepts are distinct. However the term 'mens rea' is also used to describe the ingredient of fault or culpability required before criminal liability for the defendant's actions may be established. In *Sweet v Parsley* [1970] AC 132, [1969] 1 All ER 347, Lord Reid explained that there were occasions when gross negligence provided the 'necessary mental element' for a serious crime. Manslaughter by gross negligence is not an absolute offence. The requirement for gross negligence provides the necessary element of culpability.

■ *Question*

Is the gross negligence formula more favourable to the defendant than the *Caldwell* recklessness form of mens rea?

A difference between recklessness and gross negligence is that the recklessness test did not
include the requirement that the jury must be satisfied that D's conduct was bad enough to be
a crime. A direction in *Caldwell* terms deprived D of the chance of acquittal on that ground.
In *Prentice*, for example, there were many strongly mitigating factors in the doctors' conduct,
which were irrelevant if the jury were concerned only with what was foreseeable, but highly
relevant to the question whether their behaviour was bad enough to deserve condemnation
as manslaughter.

Like Lord Atkin in *Andrews*, Lord Mackay in *Adomako* considers it 'perfectly appropriate'
that the word 'reckless' should be used in cases of manslaughter but, again agreeing with Lord
Atkin, 'in the ordinary connotation of that word'. But what is the 'ordinary connotation of
that word' which Lord Atkin and Lord Mackay had in mind?

Lord Mackay in *Adomako* gives as an example of where recklessness was used 'with complete accuracy' the case of *Stone and Dobinson* [1977] 2 All ER 341, [1977] QB 354, CA. There S
and D, S's mistress, allowed S's sister to lodge with them. The sister became infirm while lodging with them and died of toxaemia from infected bed sores and prolonged immobilization. S
and D had made only half-hearted and wholly ineffectual attempts to secure medical attention
for the sister. Upholding the convictions of S and D for manslaughter, the court said (at 347):

> The duty which a defendant has undertaken is a duty of caring for the health and welfare of the infirm
> person. What the Crown has to prove is a breach of that duty in such circumstances that the jury feel
> convinced that the defendant's conduct can properly be described as reckless. That is to say a reckless
> disregard of danger to the health and welfare of the infirm person. Mere inadvertence is not enough.
> The defendant must be proved to have been indifferent to an obvious risk of injury to health, or actu-
> ally to have foreseen the risk but to have determined nevertheless to run it.

■ *Questions*

1. Is this statement entirely clear? Does it suggest, with its contrasting tests of indifference *or*
foresight, that D may be accounted indifferent without actual foresight of the risk?

2. The risk as to which it is stated D must be reckless, is a risk not of death but merely of 'health
and welfare'. What does that mean? Is it now the law that if on a charge of manslaughter the
case against D proceeds on the basis of gross negligence, the prosecution must prove that the
reasonable man would have foreseen that the conduct in question involved a risk of death, but
if it proceeds on recklessness it is enough to prove that D was indifferent to or foresaw some
risk much less than death? If so, is this defensible?

17.3.4.1 Proof of D's subjective recklessness

In *DPP, ex p Jones* [2000] Crim LR 858, DC it was acknowledged that experience shows that
a jury is more likely to convict of manslaughter when there is evidence of subjective recklessness than when there is not. This seems to be common sense. Where the prosecution
case is expressly based on gross negligence, which does not require proof of any subjective
element, should such evidence be admissible or is it precluded by the principle of *Sandhu*
(section 7.2, p 181)?

R (on the application of Rowley) v Director of Public Prosecutions

[2003] EWHC 693 (Admin), Queen's Bench Division, Divisional Court, http://www.bailii.org/ew/cases/EWHC/Admin/2003/693.html

(Kennedy LJ and Hooper J)

R's profoundly disabled son died when in a care home run by a local authority. The carer responsible for bathing him left him unattended in the bath and he drowned. R sought a review of the decision not to prosecute. The DPP considered that a factor favouring prosecution was that a severely disabled person was left unsupervised in the bath posing an obvious risk of death, but the lack of awareness of risk on the part of the carer was treated as a factor weighing against that finding. The DPP maintained the decision not to prosecute, and R applied for judicial review. One issue for the court was whether the carer's state of mind was a factor that the jury might take into account in the carer's favour when considering whether her conduct was so bad as to amount to gross negligence.

[Kennedy LJ set out the facts:]

28. It is clear from what Lord Mackay said [in *Adomako*] that there is a fifth ingredient: 'criminality' (albeit defining the ingredient in this way 'involves an element of circularity') or 'badness'. Using the word 'badness', the jury must be sure that the defendant's conduct was so bad as in all the circumstances to amount 'to a criminal act or omission'. Lord Hewart C.J. in *Bateman* used the words: 'to amount to a crime against the state and conduct deserving punishment' that is, conduct which does not merely call for compensation but for criminal punishment.

29. It is clear that subjective recklessness (actual foresight of risk) is not a pre-requisite for a conviction for gross negligence manslaughter. The thrust of the case against Dr Adomako was that he had failed to notice or respond to the obvious signs. If he had noticed that a disconnection had occurred or that breathing had stopped he would have taken action- but he had not. It is also clear that the presence of subjective recklessness may be taken into account by the jury as a strong factor demonstrating that the defendant's negligence was criminal. This was confirmed in *Attorney-General's Reference (No 2 of 1999)* [2000] QB 796 and in *R v DPP ex parte Jones* [2000] IRLR 373, a decision on which Mr Hunt places considerable reliance.

30. In the first of those cases the Attorney-General asked the Court of Appeal Criminal Division to consider two questions arising out of the ruling of a trial judge in relation to the prosecution of a railway company for gross negligence manslaughter which was said to have been a cause of a train crash. The questions were—

'(1) Can a defendant be properly convicted of manslaughter by gross negligence in the absence of evidence as to that defendant's state of mind?

(2) Can a non-human defendant be convicted of the crime of manslaughter by gross negligence in the absence of evidence establishing the guilt of an identified human individual for the same crime?'

31. The court answered the first question in the affirmative, and the second question in the negative. At 809 Rose LJ said in relation to question 1—

'Although there may be cases where the defendant's state of mind is relevant to the jury's consideration when assessing the grossness and criminality of his conduct, evidence of his state of mind is not a prerequisite to a conviction for manslaughter by gross negligence. The *Adomako* test is objective but a defendant who is reckless as defined in *R v Stone* may be the more readily found to be grossly negligent to a criminal degree.'

In the case of *Stone* Geoffrey Lane LJ had said at 363 that where a defendant had undertaken a duty of care for the health and safety of an infirm person the prosecution had to prove—

'A reckless disregard of danger to the health and welfare of the infirm person. Mere inadvertence is not enough. The defendant must be proved to have been indifferent to an obvious risk of injury to health, or actually to have foreseen the risk but to have determined nevertheless to run it.'

32. In *R v DPP ex parte Jones* the facts were as follows. Mr Martell, the Managing Director of a company called Euromin, had arranged for a dockside crane to be adapted, so that with the jaws of the grab bucket open bags could be attached to hooks fitted within the bucket. Jones was in the hold of a ship loading bags onto the hooks when the jaws of the bucket closed and he was decapitated. In deciding not to prosecute the managing director and the company for gross negligence, the lack of subjective recklessness on the part of Mr Mantell was 'dispositive' (see paragraph 36 of the judgment of Buxton LJ). In paragraph 23 of his judgment Buxton LJ referred to *Adomako* and the passage at page 809 of the *Attorney-General's Reference* case which we have already set out, and at paragraph 24 he continued—

'The law is, therefore, quite clear. If the accused is subjectively reckless, then that may be taken into account by the jury as a strong factor demonstrating that his negligence was criminal, but negligence will still be criminal in the absence of any recklessness if on an objective basis the defendant demonstrated what, for instance, Lord Mackay quoted the Court of Appeal in *Adomako* as describing as:

"failure to advert to a serious risk going beyond mere inadvertence in respect of an obvious and important matter which the defendant's duty demanded that he should address."

That is a test in objective terms.'

33. The issue raised in the present case by Mr Hunt is whether the state of mind of the defendant is a factor which the jury may take into account in the defendant's favour when considering whether his conduct is so bad as to amount to a criminal offence. Mr Hunt submitted that subjective recklessness may help to establish a prosecution case, but that otherwise the state of mind of the proposed defendant is irrelevant.

34. That seems to us to be an unrealistic approach which the authorities do not require, which no judge would enforce, and which no jury would adopt. Once it can be shown that there was ordinary common law negligence causative of death and a serious risk of death, what remains to be established is criminality or badness. In considering whether there is criminality or badness, Lord Mackay makes it clear that all the circumstances are to be taken into account.

35. An examination of the Court of Appeal decision in *Prentice* also shows that Mr Hunt's submission is not supported by authority...

[His lordship referred to the decision in *Prentice* (section 17.3, p 616).]

38. The fact that Dr Prentice was 'inexperienced, reluctant to give the treatment and wholly unaware...of the likely fatal consequences' were all factors which the jury were entitled to take into account in the defendant's favour. Likewise in Dr Sullman's favour, his belief and his understanding could be taken into account.

39. There is further authority for the proposition that the state of mind of the defendant is a factor which the jury may take into account in the defendant's favour in the passage which we have cited from the *Attorney-General's Reference* case and which was cited by Buxton LJ in *Jones*. Rose LJ makes it clear that the defendant's state of mind is relevant to the jury's consideration when assessing the grossness and criminality of his conduct.

40. It follows that it is relevant to look at all of the circumstances, many of which may cast light upon the defendant's state of mind...

The application was dismissed

■ *Question*

Is the decision consistent with that in *DPP, ex p Jones*?

17.4 Reckless manslaughter

Manslaughter by advertent recklessness, that is, conscious risk-taking, still survives as a separate head of manslaughter.

It is necessary for this offence to exist in order to deal with cases where D kills, but has not performed an unlawful dangerous *act* (that form of manslaughter applies only to acts) and his conduct is such that it does not satisfy the test of gross negligence because, for example, it does not pose a risk of death. As we have seen, where D killed by an act (not unlawful apart from the fact that it is done recklessly) knowing that it was highly probable that he would cause serious bodily harm, before the decision in *Moloney* this would have been murder (*Hyam*). It must still be manslaughter. Where death is so caused, the jury do not have to decide whether it is 'bad enough' to amount to a crime. That question is appropriate only when we are concerned with degrees of negligence. The jury are not asked this question in non-fatal offences against the person which may be committed recklessly, so it would be quite inconsistent if it applied when death is caused. What is uncertain is whether there is a sufficient fault:

(i)   when D's awareness of an unreasonable risk is of less than high probability; or

(ii) where the risk he foresees is of bodily harm, less than serious bodily harm.

It is submitted that the better view is that reckless manslaughter includes (i) but not (ii). Arguably, it should include (i) because a distinction based solely on the degree of probability is unsatisfactory since that is only one of many factors which may determine whether conduct is properly characterized as reckless. It should not include (ii) because, by analogy with murder, manslaughter should be limited to cases where the known risk is of serious bodily harm.

R v Lidar (Narinder Singh)
(1999) Court of Appeal, Criminal Division (unreported)

(Evans LJ, Alliott and Jackson JJ)

The deceased, Kully, was killed when he was hanging on to a car, with half his body through the car window, fighting with the appellant who was driving. He was carried about 225 m when his feet caught in the nearside rear wheel and he fell to the ground and was run over, suffering fatal crush injuries.

Evans LJ [his lordship reviewed the facts and the evidence:]

The relevant direction of law as regards manslaughter was this:

> 'In order for manslaughter to be proved in this case, the Crown have to prove that the defendant acted recklessly. Recklessly in this context means that the defendant foresaw that some physical harm, however slight, might result to Kully from driving the car as he did and yet ignoring that risk he nevertheless went on to drive as he did. Mere inadvertence is not enough. The defendant must have been proved to have been indifferent to an obvious risk of injury to health or actually to have foreseen the risk but to have determined nevertheless to run it. If you are sure that the defendant acted recklessly you find him guilty of manslaughter. If you are not sure you fif him not guilty'.

[His lordship reviewed the grounds of appeal.]

Mr Beckman applied for leave to add a further ground, which is to the effect that the judge ought to have directed the jury that this was a case of 'gross negligence' manslaughter which they should approach in accordance with the House of Lords' judgment in *Adomako* [1995] 1 AC 171. Whether the submission was that the 'gross negligence' direction should be given in addition to or in substitution for the 'recklessness' direction in fact given was not made entirely clear, but there was no complaint about the terms in which the direction was given, if 'recklessness' was appropriate. The application to add this ground of appeal was not opposed by Mr Milmo QC for the prosecution, and we gave leave because of the connection which must exist between the proper definition of the offence of manslaughter and the relevance of the suggested defences of self-defence and necessity to it ...

[His lordship dealt with the issue of self-defence.] ...

In *Adomako* the House of Lords affirmed the characteristics of 'gross negligence' manslaughter and further held that there is no distinction in principle between motor manslaughter and other cases where gross negligence is the basis of criminal liability. The House of Lords also held that juries might properly be directed in terms of recklessness although the precise definition derived from *Seymour* [1983] 2 AC 493 should no longer be used (188A). Lord Mackay LC said this:

> 'I consider it perfectly appropriate that the word "reckless" be used in cases of involuntary manslaughter, but as Lord Atkin put it "in the ordinary connotation of that word." Examples in which this was done, in my mind with complete accuracy are *Reg v Stone* [1977] QB 354 and *Reg v West London Coroner ex parte Gray* [1988] QB 467... I entirely agree with the view that the circumstances to which a charge of involuntary manslaughter may apply are so various that it is unwise to attempt to categorise or detail specimen directions. For my part I would not wish to go beyond the description of the basis in law which I have already given' (187H–188B).

Nothing here suggests that for the future 'recklessness' could no longer be a basis for proving the offence of manslaughter: rather, the opposite. *Smith & Hogan* records that 'For many years the courts have used the terms "recklessness" and "gross negligence" to describe the fault required for involuntary manslaughter ... without any clear definition of either term. It was not clear whether these terms were merely two ways of describing the same thing, or whether they represented two distinct conditions of fault' (page 375). After referring to *Adomako*, the learned author continues

> '*Reckless manslaughter*. Gross negligence is a sufficient, but not necessarily the only fault for manslaughter. To some extent manslaughter by overt recklessness, conscious risk-taking still survives' (p.377).

He goes on to ask whether it is necessary for the offence of reckless manslaughter that the risk foreseen is of serious, rather than non-serious, bodily harm.

In our judgment, the judge was correct in his view that this was a case of 'reckless' manslaughter and to direct the jury accordingly. We reject the alternative submission that he was wrong not to direct the jury as to gross negligence manslaughter, whether in place of or in substitution for the direction as to recklessness. Indeed, in a case such as the present, we find it difficult to understand how the point of criminal liability can be reached, where gross negligence is alleged, without identifying the point by reference to the concept of recklessness as it is commonly understood: that is to say, whether the driver of the motor vehicle was aware of the necessary degree of risk of serious injury to the victim and nevertheless chose to disregard it, or was indifferent to it. If the gross negligence direction had been given, the recklessness direction would still have been necessary. The recklessness direction in fact given made the gross negligence direction superfluous and unnecessary.

. . .

Recklessness

The direction given by the judge might be said to be open to criticism for failing to specify, first, that there had to be a high probability of physical harm to Kully, and secondly, that the risk was of serious injury rather than, as the judge put it, 'injury to health' and 'some physical harm, however slight'. This criticism was not advanced as a ground of appeal, but we should nevertheless consider what force there might be in it. In our judgment, there is none, because in the circumstances of this case both requirements undoubtedly were satisfied. The risk of harm to Kully, of which the jury has found that the appellant was aware, was clearly and unarguably a high degree of risk of serious injury to him. In the circumstances, therefore, we are satisfied that the verdict could not be considered unsafe if there was a mis-direction in this respect.

Appeal dismissed

There is a great difference between subjective recklessness and a case of inadvertent negligence, like *Adomako*. Adomako was quite unaware of the risk his failure was causing to the life of the patient but the prosecution's case against Litchfield (section 17.3.3) was that 'With his vast experience of sailing, he must have appreciated the obvious and serious risk of death to his crew'; and 'he knew the risk he was running in using contaminated fuel…and chose to run the obvious and serious risk of death by doing so.' The fault involved—subjective recklessness—is different, not merely in degree, but in kind, from the neglect which satisfies the Merchant Shipping Act, so the question of reconciling the two does not, or should not, arise.

17.5 Reform

17.5.1 Law Com No 237

The Law Commission (Law Com Report No 237, *Involuntary Manslaughter* (1996)) proposed the abolition of the common law offence of involuntary manslaughter and its replacement by two offences as follows:

1.—(1) A person who by his conduct causes the death of another is guilty of reckless killing if—

    (a) he is aware of a risk that his conduct will cause death or serious injury; and

    (b) it is unreasonable for him to take that risk having regard to the circumstances as he knows or believes them to be.

  (2) A person guilty of reckless killing is liable on conviction on indictment to imprisonment for life.

2.—(1) A person who by his conduct causes the death of another is guilty of killing by gross carelessness if—

    (a) a risk that his conduct will cause death or serious injury would be obvious to a reasonable person in his position;

    (b) he is capable of appreciating that risk at the material time; and

    (c) either—

        (i) his conduct falls far below what can reasonably be expected of him in the circumstances; or

        (ii) he intends by his conduct to cause some injury or is aware of, and unreasonably takes, the risk that it may do so.

  (2) There shall be attributed to the person referred to in subsection (1)(a) above—

    (a) knowledge of any relevant facts which the accused is shown to have at the material time; and

    (b) any skill or experience professed by him.

  (3) In determining for the purposes of subsection (1)(c)(i) above what can reasonably be expected of the accused regard shall be had to the circumstances of which he can be expected to be aware, to any circumstances shown to be within his knowledge and to any other matter relevant for assessing his conduct at the material time.

(4) Subsection (1)(c)(ii) above applies only if the conduct causing, or intended to cause, the injury constitutes an offence.

(5) A person guilty of killing by gross carelessness is liable on conviction on indictment to imprisonment for a term not exceeding [ ] years.

17.5.2 Law Com No 304

In relation to unlawful act manslaughter, the Law Commission's latest proposal (in Law Com Report No 304, *Murder, Manslaughter and Infanticide* (2006)) is that the offence will be recast as killing another person:

(a) through the commission of a criminal act intended by the defendant to cause injury, or

(b) through the commission of a criminal act that the defendant was aware involved a serious risk of causing some injury ('criminal act manslaughter').

The Law Commission's latest proposals on gross negligence as part of the *Murder, Manslaughter and Infanticide* Report are that the offence be recast as follows:

A person is guilty of gross negligence manslaughter if:

(1) a person by his or her conduct causes the death of another;

(2) a risk that his or her conduct will cause death . . . would be obvious to a reasonable person in his or her position;

(3) he or she is capable of appreciating that risk at the material time; and

(4) . . . his or her conduct falls far below what can reasonably be expected of him or her in the circumstances.

The Law Commission recommends abolition of reckless manslaughter. The Commission suggests that all cases will now be adequately catered for in either (i) the new second degree murder offence where D realizes there is a serious risk of death from his conduct and intends to cause injury, or (ii) the new version of gross negligence proposed above. The Commission has overstated the case here. Consider D who engages in an activity which 'because of his specialist knowledge' he realizes carries a risk of injury. That risk is not of a type that a reasonable person would appreciate. D kills V in the course of his activity. D cannot be liable for gross negligence: even though D's mental state can be considered by the jury in evaluating whether his conduct is grossly negligent, there is no objective risk of death. Nor is D guilty of second degree murder unless he sees a risk of death.

FURTHER READING

Unlawful act manslaughter

C. Clarkson and S. Cunningham (eds), *Criminal Liability for Non-Aggressive Death* (2008)

B. Mitchell, 'Minding the Gap in Unlawful and Dangerous Act Manslaughter: A Moral Defence for One-Punch Killers' (2008) 72 J Crim L 537

B. Mitchell, 'More Thoughts About Unlawful and Dangerous Act Manslaughter and the One-Punch Killer' [2009] Crim LR 502

B. Mitchell and R. D. Mackay, 'Investigating Involuntary Manslaughter: An Empirical Study of 127 Cases' (2011) 31 OJLS 165

W. Wilson, 'Dealing with Drug Induced Homicide' in C. Clarkson and S. Cunningham (eds), *Criminal Liability for Non-Aggressive Deaths* (2008)

Gross negligence manslaughter

S. Gardner, 'Manslaughter by Gross Negligence' (1995) 111 LQR 22

Law Commission Report No 237, *Involuntary Manslaughter* (1996), Part III

J. Stannard, 'From Andrews to Seymour and Back Again' (1996) 47 NILQ 1

G. Williams, 'Gross Negligence Manslaughter and Duty of Care in "Drugs" Cases: *R v Evans*' [2009] Crim LR 631

Reform

J. Horder, *Homicide and the Politics of Law Reform* (2012)

H. Keating, 'The Restoration of a Serious Crime' [1996] Crim LR 535

M. Wasik, 'Form and Function in the Law of Involuntary Manslaughter' [1994] Crim LR 883

18

Non-fatal offences against the person

18.1 Introduction

The conduct examined in this chapter ranges from a trivial tap on the shoulder to levels of harm threatening life itself. The relevant offences are archaic in their definition and lacking in any coherent structure. They are, however, extremely important. Not only are they frequently prosecuted, but they also give rise to interesting questions on issues central to the criminal law, such as how the autonomy of the individual should be respected.

The controversies that will be examined in this chapter include the following:

(i) whether psychiatric illness can amount to an offence against the person;

(ii) what level of harm constitutes 'actual' bodily harm as opposed to 'grievous' bodily harm;

(iii) whether actual bodily harm must be 'inflicted' or merely caused.

Although there is no formal ladder or hierarchy of offences, it is traditional to begin with the two offences which involve the least harm.

18.2 Assault and battery

An assault is any act by which D, intentionally or recklessly, causes V to apprehend immediate unlawful personal violence. A battery is any act by which D, intentionally or recklessly, inflicts unlawful personal violence upon V. But 'violence' here includes any unlawful touching of another, however slight.

Assault and battery are two separate offences, and each is also a core element of more serious aggravated offences—for example, assaulting a police officer in the execution of his duty, assault occasioning actual bodily harm, etc. Understanding the offences of assault and battery is therefore extremely important. It is also important to appreciate that an allegation of battery does not also include an allegation of assault. The Court of Appeal made this clear in *Nelson* [2013] EWCA Crim 30. Keith J stated that:

> 7. As we have said, the offence of common assault is committed when the defendant does something of a physical kind which causes someone else to apprehend that they are about to be struck. It follows that an ingredient of the offence of common assault is that that has to have been apprehended by the person who is alleged to have been the victim of that assault. Such an apprehension, however, is not required for the offence of assault by beating. As *Smith & Hogan's Criminal Law* (2011), 13th ed, says at p 623:
>
> > 'It used to be said that every battery involves an assault; but that is plainly not so, for in battery there need be no apprehension of the impending violence. A blow from behind is not any less a battery because [the victim] was unaware that it was coming.'

It follows that because one of the ingredients of the offence of common assault is not among the ingredients of the offence of [battery] an allegation of [battery] does not amount to or include, whether expressly or by implication, an allegation of common assault.

Criminal Justice Act 1988, s 39

Common assault and battery shall be summary offences and a person guilty of either of them shall be liable to a fine not exceeding level 5 on the standard scale, to imprisonment for a term not exceeding six months, or to both.

The CPS charging standards advise that the appropriate charge is assault or battery (rather than aggravated assaults) where the injuries sustained amount to no more than: grazes, scratches, abrasions, minor bruising, swellings, reddening of the skin, superficial cuts or a 'black eye'.

18.2.1 The elements of assault and battery

18.2.1.1 Apprehending/suffering unlawful violence

In assault the victim must apprehend (ie anticipate rather than be in fear of) immediate unlawful violence; in battery he must suffer such violence. As the following case shows, not only might the level of violence may be very minor, but the question of its lawfulness may give rise to considerably greater complexity than would be expected in such a minor offence.

Collins v Wilcock
[1984] 3 All ER 374, Queen's Bench Division

(Robert Goff LJ and Mann J)

The respondent and another police officer saw the appellant and another woman apparently soliciting for the purposes of prostitution. The appellant was not a known prostitute and when asked to get into the police car for questioning, she refused and walked away. The respondent walked after the appellant with a view to ascertaining her identity and, if in fact she was suspected of being a prostitute, to cautioning her in accordance with police practice before charging her with being a prostitute. The appellant refused to speak to the respondent and again walked away. The respondent then took hold of her by the arm to restrain her whereupon the appellant became abusive and scratched the respondent's arm with her fingernails.

The appellant appealed against her conviction for assaulting a police officer acting in the execution of her duty. The judgment of the court was delivered by:

[Robert Goff LJ, having quoted from the case stated, continued:]

The magistrate then stated the following question for the opinion of the court:

'The question for the consideration of the High Court is whether a Police Constable is acting in the execution of her duty when detaining a woman against her will for the purpose of questioning her regarding her identity and her conduct which was such as to lead the Constable to believe she may have been soliciting men.'

...

[His lordship explained the need to consider whether the officer was in the execution of her duty and the distinction between assault and battery.]

We are here concerned primarily with battery. The fundamental principle, plain and incontestable, is that every person's body is inviolate. It has long been established that any touching of another person, however slight, may amount to a battery. So Holt CJ held in 1704 that 'the least touching of another in anger is a battery': see *Cole v Turner* (1704) 6 Mod Rep 149, 90 ER 958. The breadth of the principle reflects the fundamental nature of the interest so protected; as Blackstone wrote in his Commentaries, 'the law cannot draw the line between different degrees of violence, and therefore totally prohibits the first and lowest stage of it; every man's person being sacred, and no other having a right to meddle with it, in any the slightest manner' (see 3 Bl Com 120). The effect is that everybody is protected not only against physical injury but against any form of physical molestation.

But so widely drawn a principle must inevitably be subject to exceptions. For example, children may be subjected to reasonable punishment; people may be subjected to the lawful exercise of the power of arrest; and reasonable force may be used in self-defence or for the prevention of crime. But, apart from these special instances where the control or constraint is lawful, a broader exception has been created to allow for the exigencies of everyday life. Generally speaking, consent is a defence to battery; and most of the physical contacts of ordinary life are not actionable because they are impliedly consented to by all who move in society and so expose themselves to the risk of bodily contact. So nobody can complain of the jostling which is inevitable from his presence in, for example, a supermarket, an underground station or a busy street; nor can a person who attends a party complain if his hand is seized in friendship, or even if his back is (within reason) slapped (see *Tubervell v Savage* (1669) 1 Mod Rep 3, 86 ER 684). Although such cases are regarded as examples of implied consent, it is more common nowadays to treat them as falling within a general exception embracing all physical contact which is generally acceptable in the ordinary conduct of daily life. We observe that, although in the past it has sometimes been stated that a battery is only committed where the action is 'angry, or revengeful, or rude, or insolent' (see 1 Hawk PC c 62, s 2), we think that nowadays it is more realistic, and indeed more accurate, to state the broad underlying principle, subject to the broad exception.

Among such forms of conduct, long held to be acceptable, is touching a person for the purpose of engaging his attention, though of course using no greater degree of physical contact than is reasonably necessary in the circumstances for that purpose. So, for example, it was held by the Court of Common Pleas in 1807 that a touch by a constable's staff on the shoulder of a man who had climbed on a gentleman's railing to gain a better view of a mad ox, the touch being only to engage the man's attention, did not amount to a battery (see *Wiffin v Kincard* (1807) 2 Bos & PNR 471, 127 ER 713; for another example, see *Coward v Baddeley* (1859) 4 H & N 478, 157 ER 927). But a distinction is drawn between a touch to draw a man's attention, which is generally acceptable, and a physical restraint, which is not. So we find Parke B observing in *Rawlings v Till* (1837) 3 M & W 28 at 29, 150 ER 1042, with reference to *Wiffin v Kincard*, that 'There the touch was merely to engage a man's attention, not to put a restraint on his person.' Furthermore, persistent touching to gain attention in the face of obvious disregard may transcend the norms of acceptable behaviour, and so be outside the exception. We do not say that more than one touch is never permitted; for example, the lost or distressed may surely be permitted a second touch, or possibly even more, on a reluctant or impervious sleeve or shoulder, as may a person who is acting reasonably in the exercise of a duty. In each case, the test must be whether the physical contact so persisted in has in the circumstances gone beyond generally acceptable standards of conduct; and the answer to that question will depend on the facts of the particular case.

The distinction drawn by Parke B in *Rawlings v Till* is of importance in the case of police officers. Of course, a police officer may subject another to restraint when he lawfully exercises his power of arrest . . . But, putting such cases aside, police officers have for present purposes no greater rights than ordinary citizens. It follows that, subject to such cases, physical contact by a police officer with another person may be unlawful as a battery, just as it might be if he was an ordinary member of the public. But a police officer has his rights as a citizen, as well as his duties as a policeman. A police officer may wish to engage a man's attention, for example if he wishes to question him. If he lays his hand on the man's sleeve or taps his shoulder for that purpose, he commits no wrong. He may even do so more than once; for he is under a duty to prevent and investigate crime, and so his seeking further, in the exercise of that duty, to engage a man's attention in order to speak to him may in the circumstances be regarded as acceptable (see *Donnelly v Jackman* [1970] 1 All ER 987, [1970] 1 WLR 562). But if, taking into account the nature of his duty, his use of physical contact in the face of non-co-operation persists beyond generally acceptable standards of conduct, his action will become unlawful; and if a police officer restrains a man, for example by gripping his arm or his shoulder, then his action will also be unlawful, unless he is lawfully exercising his power of arrest. A police officer has no power to require a man to answer him, though he has the advantages of authority, enhanced as it is by the uniform which the state provides and requires him to wear, in seeking a response to his inquiry. What is not permitted, however, is the unlawful use of force or the unlawful threat (actual or implicit) to use force; and, excepting the lawful exercise of his power of arrest, the lawfulness of a police officer's conduct is judged by the same criteria as are applied to the conduct of any ordinary citizen of this country.

We turn finally to the question posed by the magistrate for our consideration. As we have already observed, this question is in wide general terms. Furthermore, the word 'detaining' can be used in more than one sense. For example, it is a commonplace of ordinary life that one person may request another to stop and speak to him; if the latter complies with the request, he may be said to do so willingly or unwillingly, and in either event the first person may be said to be 'stopping and detaining' the latter. There is nothing unlawful in such an act. If a police officer so 'stops and detains' another person, he in our opinion commits no unlawful act, despite the fact that his uniform may give his request a certain authority and so render it more likely to be complied with. But if a police officer, not exercising his power of arrest, nevertheless reinforces his request with the actual use of force, or with the threat (actual or implicit) to use force if the other person does not comply, then his act in thereby detaining the other person will be unlawful. In the former event, his action will constitute a battery; in the latter event, detention of the other person will amount to false imprisonment. Whether the action of a police officer in any particular case is to be regarded as lawful or unlawful must be a question to be decided on the facts of the case.

Having regard to the facts of the present case, we have no doubt that the magistrate framed his question having in mind the act of the respondent in taking hold of the appellant's arm to restrain her, which we have held to be a battery and so unlawful. But, having regard to the distinctions we have drawn, we consider the question itself to be so widely drafted as not to be susceptible of a simple answer. We therefore prefer not to answer it; and we shall exercise our power to amend the case by adding the following further question which arises on the facts of the case, viz whether, on the facts found by the magistrate, the respondent was acting in the course of her duty when she detained the appellant. That question we shall, for the reasons we have already given, answer in the negative.

Appeal allowed; conviction quashed

■ *Questions*
1. Was this a case of battery or assault?
2. D pats V, a complete stranger, on the back in an exuberant fashion at V's birthday party. Why is D not guilty of battery?

Robert Goff LJ said in delivering the judgment of the court (in the previous extract, p 543) that, 'The law draws a distinction, in terms more easily understood by philologists than by ordinary citizens, between assault and battery.' However difficult it may be for the ordinary citizen to understand the distinction, it is essential for lawyers to do so. Assault and battery are distinct crimes with distinctive features. The distinction between the two has become blurred partly because the word 'assault' is commonly used (the *Oxford English Dictionary* so uses it) to include a battery, and partly because one and the same act (a punch on the nose, a kick on the shin) commonly amounts to both an assault and a battery. But, as Robert Goff

LJ goes on to explain, a battery involves an unlawful and unwanted contact with the body of another while assault involves causing another to apprehend an unlawful unwanted contact.

Since assault and battery are separate offences (see Criminal Justice Act 1988, s 39, section 18.2, p 642) it was held in *DPP v Taylor; DPP v Little* [1992] 1 All ER 299, [1992] QB 645, DC, that an information (ie a charge before the magistrates' court) alleging that 'L ... did unlawfully assault and batter J' was bad for duplicity (ie for charging more than one offence in the same information). In *Lynsey* [1995] 3 All ER 654 at 656, CA, the court found it unnecessary to express any opinion on the criticisms that had been made of that decision (J. C. Smith [1991] Crim LR 900). Comparing s 39, above, with the next section, s 40 (where 'common assault' is used in a context where the only sensible meaning it can carry is that of both 'common assault or battery'), Henry LJ observed in *Lynsey*: 'At this point angels prepare to dance on needles and legal pedants sharpen their quill pens.'

■ *Questions*

What offences does D commit in the following circumstances:

(i)   he sneaks up on V and strikes V on the back of the head with a blunt instrument;

(ii) he sneaks up on V intending to strike V on the back of the head, swings his weapon but misses;

(iii) he aims a gun, which he knows to be unloaded, at V's face and threatens to shoot V and V believes the gun is loaded;

(iv) he aims a gun at V which he knows to be unloaded and threatens to shoot V and V also knows the gun is unloaded;

(v)   he aims a gun at V which he believes to be unloaded and threatens to shoot V and V also believes the gun to be unloaded but, unknown to both, the gun is in fact loaded and when D pulls the trigger V is shot and injured?

One very controversial question which had been debated for centuries was whether there could be an assault by words alone—can D cause V to apprehend immediate unlawful violence as much by shouting at V as by shaking his fist at V?

R v Ireland; R v Burstow

[1997] 4 All ER 225, House of Lords, http://www.bailii.org/uk/cases/UKHL/1997/34.html

(Lords Goff, Slynn, Steyn, Hope and Hutton)

Ireland made repeated silent telephone calls, mostly at night, to three women who consequently suffered psychiatric illness. His conviction on three counts of assault occasioning actual bodily harm (s 47) (section 18.4, p 652) was upheld by the Court of Appeal, holding that since repeated telephone calls could cause the victim to apprehend immediate and unlawful violence, his conduct was capable of amounting to assault and that psychiatric injury could amount to actual bodily harm.

Burstow had conducted an eight-month campaign of harassment against a woman, including both silent and abusive telephone calls. She was fearful of personal violence and a psychiatrist testified that she was suffering from a severe depressive illness. B's appeal against conviction on one count of unlawfully and maliciously inflicting grievous bodily harm contrary to s 20 of the 1861 Act (section 18.4, p 652) was dismissed by the Court of Appeal on the ground that psychiatric injury could amount to GBH under s 20. At the time the Protection from Harassment Act 1997 had not been enacted.

[Lord Goff and Lord Slynn said they agreed with the speech of Lord Steyn.]

Lord Steyn:

My Lords, it is easy to understand the terrifying effect of a campaign of telephone calls at night by a silent caller to a woman living on her own. It would be natural for the victim to regard the calls as menacing. What may heighten her fear is that she will not know what the caller may do next. The spectre of the caller arriving at her doorstep bent on inflicting personal violence on her may come to dominate her thinking. After all, as a matter of common sense, what else would she be terrified about? The victim may suffer psychiatric illness such as anxiety neurosis or acute depression. Harassment of women by repeated silent telephone calls, accompanied on occasions by heavy breathing, is apparently a significant social problem. That the criminal law should be able to deal with this problem, and so far as is practicable, afford effective protection to victims is self-evident.

From the point of view, however, of the general policy of our law towards the imposition of criminal responsibility, three specific features of the problem must be faced squarely. First, the medium used by the caller is the telephone: arguably it differs qualitatively from a face-to-face offer of violence to a sufficient extent to make a difference. Secondly, ex hypothesi the caller remains silent: arguably a caller may avoid the reach of the criminal law by remaining silent however menacing the context may be. Thirdly, it is arguable that the criminal law does not take into account 'mere' psychiatric illnesses.

[His lordship considered the use of offences under the Telecommunications Act (now the Communications Act 2003, s 127) and the offences under the Protection from Harassment Act 1997.]

It is now necessary to consider whether the making of silent telephone calls causing psychiatric injury is capable of constituting an assault under s 47. The Court of Appeal, as constituted in *R v Ireland*, answered that question in the affirmative. There has been substantial academic criticism of the conclusion and reasoning in *R v Ireland* (see *Archbold News*, Issue 6, 12 July 1996, *Archbold's Criminal Pleading, Evidence and Practice* (1995), Supplement No 4 (1996) pp 345–347, Smith and Hogan *Criminal Law* p 413, Jonathan Herring 'Assault by Telephone' [1997] CLJ 11, and 'Assault' [1997] Crim LR 434 at 435–436). Counsel's arguments, broadly speaking, challenged the [Court of Appeal] decision in *R v Ireland* on very similar lines. Having carefully considered the literature and counsel's arguments, I have come to the conclusion that the appeal ought to be dismissed.

The starting point must be that an assault is an ingredient of the offence under s 47. It is necessary to consider the two forms which an assault may take. The first is battery, which involves the unlawful application of force by the defendant upon the victim. Usually, s 47 is used to prosecute in cases of this kind. The second form of assault is an act causing the victim to apprehend an imminent application of force upon her (see *Fagan v Metropolitan Police Comr* [1968] 3 All ER 442 at 445, [1969] 1 QB 439 at 444).

One point can be disposed of, quite briefly. The Court of Appeal was not asked to consider whether silent telephone calls resulting in psychiatric injury is capable of constituting a battery. But encouraged by some academic comment it was raised before your Lordships' House. Counsel for Ireland was most economical in his argument on the point. I will try to match his economy of words. In my view it is not feasible to enlarge the generally accepted legal meaning of what is a battery to include the circumstances of a silent caller who causes psychiatric injury.

It is to assault in the form of an act causing the victim to fear an immediate application of force to her that I must turn. Counsel argued that as a matter of law an assault can never be committed by words alone and therefore it cannot be committed by silence. The premise depends on the slenderest authority, namely an observation by Holroyd J to a jury that 'no words or singing are equivalent to an assault' (see *Meade's and Belt's Case* (1823) 1 Lew CC 184 at 185, 168 ER 1006). The proposition that a gesture may amount to an assault, but that words can never suffice, is unrealistic and indefensible. A thing said is also a thing done. There is no reason why something said should be incapable of causing an apprehension of immediate personal violence, eg a man accosting a woman in a dark alley saying 'come with me or I will stab you'. I would, therefore, reject the proposition that an assault can never be committed by words.

That brings me to the critical question whether a silent caller may be guilty of an assault. The answer to this question seems to me to be 'Yes, depending on the facts'. It involves questions of fact within the province of the jury. After all, there is no reason why a telephone caller who says to a woman in a menacing way 'I will be at your door in a minute or two' may not be guilty of an assault if he causes his victim to apprehend immediate personal violence. Take now the case of the silent caller. He intends by his silence to cause fear and he is so understood. The victim is assailed by uncertainty about his intentions. Fear may dominate her emotions, and it may be the fear that the caller's arrival at her door may be imminent. She may fear the *possibility* of immediate personal violence. As a matter of law the caller may be guilty of an assault: whether he is or not will depend on the circumstance and in particular on the impact of the caller's potentially menacing call or calls on the victim. Such a prosecution case under s 47 may be fit to leave to the jury. And a trial judge may, depending on the circumstances, put a commonsense consideration before [the] jury, namely what, if not the possibility of imminent personal violence, was the victim terrified about?

I conclude that an assault may be committed in the particular factual circumstances which I have envisaged. For this reason I reject the submission that as a matter of law a silent telephone caller cannot ever be guilty of an offence under s 47. In these circumstances no useful purpose would be served by answering the vague certified question in *R v Ireland*.

Having concluded that the legal arguments advanced on behalf of Ireland on s 47 must fail, I nevertheless accept that the concept of an assault involving immediate personal violence as an ingredient of the s 47 offence is a considerable complicating factor in bringing prosecutions under it in respect of silent telephone callers and stalkers. That the least serious of the ladder of offences is difficult to apply in such cases is unfortunate. At the hearing of the appeal of *R v Ireland* attention was drawn to the Bill which is annexed to Law Commission report, *Legislating the Criminal Code: Offences Against the Person and General Principles* (Law Com Consultation Paper No 218) (1993). Clause 4 of that Bill is intended to replace s 47. Clause 4 provides: 'A person is guilty of an offence if he intentionally or recklessly causes injury to another.' This simple and readily comprehensible provision would eliminate the problems inherent in s 47. In expressing this view I do not, however, wish to comment on the appropriateness of the definition of 'injury' in cl 18 of the Bill, and in particular the provision that 'injury' means 'impairment of a person's mental health'.

18.2.1.2 Immediacy

Earlier cases showed a tendency to take a generous view of 'immediacy'. In *Lewis* [1970] Crim LR 647, D was uttering threats from another room. In *Logdon v DPP* [1976] Crim LR 121, it was held that D committed an assault by showing V a pistol in a drawer and declaring that he would hold her hostage. In *Smith v Chief Superintendent of Woking Police Station* (1983) 76 Cr App R 234, [1983] Crim LR 323 (assault by looking through the window of a bed-sitting room at V in her night clothes with intent to frighten her), Kerr LJ limited his decision to a case where D 'is immediately adjacent, albeit on the other side of a window' and distinguished, without dissenting from, the opinion in the fourth edition of *Smith and Hogan* that 'there can be no assault if it is obvious to V that D is unable to carry out his threat, as where D shakes his fist at V who is safely locked inside his car'. There may be an assault although D has no means of carrying out the threat. The question is whether he intends to cause V to believe that he can and will carry it out and whether V does so believe. This is consistent with offences against the person being result crimes rather than conduct crimes.

In *Ireland*, the House did no more than reject the submission that a silent telephone caller can *never* be guilty of assault. Lords Slynn and Hutton made it clear that the House was not deciding how the concept of immediacy should be applied or whether it was satisfied in *Ireland*. If the caller says, 'There's a bomb under your house which I am about to detonate' there would seem to be a clear case of assault. What about Lord Steyn's suggestion of the caller who says, 'I will be at your door in a minute or two'? Notice that it is not enough that the victim is immediately alarmed. He must anticipate that something is going to happen *immediately*. In *Constanza* [1997] 2 Cr App R 492, [1997] Crim LR 576, D made numerous silent telephone calls, sent over 800 letters to V, repeatedly drove past her home and on three occasions wrote offensive words on her front door. She received two letters on 4 and 12 June which she interpreted as clear threats. D's conviction of assault occasioning actual bodily harm was upheld. It is easy to accept that V was immediately put in fear but did she really apprehend *immediate* violence when she read letters at the breakfast table? See also *Cox* [1998] Crim LR 810 and commentary. Is the offence of assault fitted to deal with an ongoing campaign of this kind?

Lord Hope in *Ireland* says that, in the case of a telephone call, the silence conveys a message to V and that it is, perhaps, otherwise where the parties are in the same room. The caller does something more than remain silent; he rings up. What if he is present and merely gives a hard stare, or glowers? Is the question for the jury simply 'Are you sure that D's conduct caused V to apprehend immediate violence and that D intended that it should, or knew that it might?' Is there any difference in principle between a gesture (which can certainly be an assault) and a glare?

■ *Question*

D aims a blow at V who is asleep. V awakes and dodges the blow. Since battery is triable only summarily, there is no offence of attempted battery. Is D guilty of an assault?

18.2.1.3 Mens rea

For assault, the defendant must intend or be subjectively reckless as to whether the victim apprehends immediate unlawful violence. For battery, the defendant must intend or be reckless as to whether he causes unlawful personal violence to the victim.

R v Venna

[1975] 3 All ER 788, Court of Appeal, Criminal Division, http://www.bailii.org/ew/cases/EWCA/Crim/1975/4.html

(James and Ormrod LJJ and Cusack J)

The appellant and others were creating a disturbance in a public street. The police were sent for and during a scuffle which ensued as the police sought to arrest him, the appellant kicked out with his feet. In so doing he struck the hand of an officer and caused a fracture which resulted in his being convicted of an assault occasioning actual bodily harm.

[James LJ read the following judgment of the court:]

On the evidence of the appellant himself, one would have thought that the inescapable inference was that the appellant intended to make physical contact with whoever might try to restrain him. Be that as it may, in the light of the direction given, the verdict may have been arrived at on the basis of 'recklessness'. Counsel for the appellant cited *Ackroyd v Barett* [(1894) 11 TLR 115] in support of his argument that recklessness, which falls short of intention, is not enough to support a charge of battery, and argued that, there being no authority to the contrary, it is now too late to extend the law by a decision of the courts and that any extension must be by the decision of Parliament.

Counsel for the appellant sought support from the distinction between the offences which are assaults and offences which by statute include the element contained in the word 'maliciously', eg unlawful and malicious wounding contrary to s20 of the Offences against the Person Act 1861, in which recklessness will suffice to support the charge: see *Cunningham* [[1957] 2 QB 396, [1957] 2 All ER 412]. Insofar as the editors of textbooks commit themselves to an opinion on this branch of the law, they are favourable to the view that recklessness is or should logically be sufficient to support the charge of assault or battery: see Glanville Williams [*Criminal Law* (2nd edn, 1961), p 65, para 27]; Kenny [*Outlines of Criminal Law* (19th edn, 1966), p 218, para 164]; Russell [*Russell on Crime* (12th edn, 1964), vol 1, p 656] and Smith and Hogan [*Criminal Law* (3rd edn, 1973), pp 283, 286]. . . .

We see no reason in logic or in law why a person who recklessly applies physical force to the person of another should be outside the criminal law of assault. In many cases the dividing line between intention and recklessness is barely distinguishable. This is such a case. In our judgment the direction was right in law; this ground of appeal fails. . . .

For these reasons we dismiss the appeal.

Appeal dismissed

The reference to recklessness in *Venna* is clearly a reference to *Cunningham* recklessness, that is, requiring foresight by the defendant of the risk of the physical contact to another which occurs (battery) or the apprehension by another of physical contact (assault) and going on to take that risk. Post-*Caldwell*, *DPP v K (a minor)* [1990] 1 All ER 331, [1990] 1 WLR 1067, DC, applied *Caldwell* recklessness to assault. *DPP v K (a minor)* was thought by the Court of Appeal in *Spratt* [1991] 2 All ER 210, [1990] 1 WLR 1073 to have been wrongly decided. Although *Spratt* was overruled in *Savage, Parmenter* [1991] 4 All ER 698, this was in relation to the Court of Appeal's ruling as to the mens rea of an assault occasioning actual bodily harm. *Venna* and *Cunningham* were expressly approved by the House of Lords in *Savage, Parmenter*. Since *G* [2003] UKHL 50 (section 5.3, p 119) there can be no suggestion that *Caldwell*-type recklessness has any part to play in offences against the person.

Hostility

Robert Goff LJ addresses the issue of hostility in *Collins v Wilcock*, section 18.2.1.1, p 643, and appears to conclude that hostility is not an ingredient of assault and battery. His lordship says that nobody can complain of the jostling which is inevitable in a supermarket, underground station or a busy street. It is not unknown, for example, for numbers of football supporters returning from a game to dash through shopping precincts, shouting obscenities and rudely pushing shoppers aside. Do they commit a battery? If so, is this because their jostling is accompanied by rudeness or hostility or for some other reason?

In *Brown*, section 19.4.2, p 686, the case of sadomasochists injuring each other, Lord Jauncey appears to accept that hostility is an ingredient of assault but concludes, 'If the appellants' activities in relation to the receivers [of the painful injury] were unlawful they were also hostile and a necessary ingredient of assault was present.' But if the act is unlawful, as it must be to constitute an assault or battery, does it add anything to the ingredients of the crimes to say that it is therefore hostile? In *B* [2013] EWCA Crim 3 in which D was charged with common assault for force-feeding V, the Court of Appeal stated *obiter* that:

The element of assault frequently and usefully described as hostility is a means of conveying to the jury that some non-hostile contact is an ordinary incident of life to which we all impliedly consent.

■ *Questions*

D pats V, a complete stranger, on the back in an exuberant fashion at V's birthday party. Why is D not guilty of battery? Is it because there is no hostility? Is it because he has a genuine belief in the consent of V to that action?

18.2.1.4 Unlawfulness

■ *Question*

The physical contact which D must cause V to apprehend in assault and actually cause in a battery must be unlawful violence. Must D also be aware that the violence is unlawful?

Blackburn v Bowering

[1994] 3 All ER 380, Court of Appeal, Civil Division

(Sir Thomas Bingham MR, Leggatt and Roch LJJ)

D was convicted of assaulting V, an officer of the court, contrary to s 14(1)(b) of the County Courts Act 1984. His defence was that he did not believe V was a bailiff—he thought he was using reasonable force against a trespasser. The judge ruled that s 14, like s 51 of the Police Act 1964 (now replaced by s 89 of the Police Act 1996), creates an offence of strict liability, and that D's mistaken belief was no defence. He remarked on the extraordinary situation that if D had been charged with 'an ordinary' assault (ie not one of assaulting a police officer in the execution of his duty) he would have had a defence.

[Sir Thomas Bingham MR, referring to the cases up to the present day:]

... *R v Maxwell and Clanchy* (1909) 2 Cr App Rep 26 and *McBride v Turnock* [1964] Crim LR 456. It has sometimes led to surprising results (as in *McBride v Tunnock*), and has not been immune from academic criticism (see, for example, Smith and Hogan *Criminal Law* (7th edn, 1992) p 417) but a similar view (despite very powerful dissents) has prevailed in Australia (see *R v Reynhoudt* (1962) 107 CLR 381) and there is no directly contrary authority. It is therefore clear that in a prosecution under s 51 of the Police Act 1964 [see now the Police Act 1996, s 89] or a prosecution or complaint under s 14 of the County Courts Act 1984 it is not incumbent on the prosecutor or complainant to establish as part of his case that the defendant knew or believed that the victim of the alleged assault was (as the case may be) a police or court officer. This makes good sense, given the public policy of giving such officers special protection when carrying out their difficult and sometimes dangerous duties.

Counsel for the defendants did not make any frontal challenge to this line of authority. His argument was more indirect, and I think involved these steps.

(1) It is not every contact between one person and another which amounts to an assault or battery. To be criminal, the show or application of force must be unlawful. It is not tautologous to define assault as an unlawful offer or application of force.

(2) In deciding whether a defendant exerted reasonable force in defending himself, a court must judge him on the basis of what (reasonably or unreasonably) he believed to be the facts and not on the basis of what the facts actually were.

(3) If a defendant applies force to a police or court officer which would be reasonable if that person were not a police or court officer, and the defendant believes that he is not, then even if his belief is unreasonable he has a good plea of self-defence.

(4) Since the state of belief of these defendants was, accordingly, relevant to their liability, the judge was wrong to rule as he did.

The first of these steps is, in my judgment, established in *R v Kimber* [1983] 3 All ER 316, [1983] 1 WLR 1118 and *R v Williams* [1987] 3 All ER 411. The second and third steps are made good by *R v Williams and Beckford v R* [section 11.6.1.1, p 415]. It accordingly seems to me that the fourth step follows, subject to the important qualification that the mistake must be one of fact (particularly as to the victim's capacity) and not a mistake of law as to the authority of a person acting in that capacity (*R v Fennell* [1970] 3 All ER 215, [1971] 1 QB 428).

[Leggatt and Roch JJ delivered concurring judgments.]

Appeal allowed

The appeal came before the Civil Division of the court because the offence was in the nature of a contempt, but the case is an authority on the criminal law.

■ *Questions*

1. Is the offence one of strict liability? Or is it a 'constructive crime' (section 7.2, p 182)?

2. D throws a pebble at V, a tramp. The pebble misses V and, unforeseen by D, hits X, a constable on duty. Is D guilty of assaulting a constable in the execution of his duty? Should he be?

18.3 Consent and assault

The subject of consent to offences against the person is dealt with in detail in the next chapter. For present purposes it is sufficient to note that consent will only be valid if:

(i)   V has given true consent—not therefore where, for example, V has been deceived or acts under threats or duress; and

(ii) the level of harm consented to (or which D believes V has consented to) is assault or battery or a greater level of harm arising in an exceptional activity (surgery, sports, etc).

The courts have not resolved expressly whether consent is an element of actus reus or a defence? Does it matter?

18.4 Occasioning actual bodily harm, wounding, inflicting GBH and causing GBH

Three closely related offences under the Offences Against the Person Act 1861 (OAPA) require consideration. They are, in ascending order of gravity:

Section 47

Whoever shall be convicted upon an indictment of any assault occasioning actual bodily harm shall be liable [to imprisonment for five years] . . .

Section 20

Whoever shall unlawfully and maliciously wound or inflict any grievous bodily harm upon any other person either with or without any weapon or instrument, shall be guilty . . . [of an offence and liable to imprisonment for five years].

Section 18

> Whosoever shall unlawfully and maliciously by any means whatsoever wound or cause any grievous bodily harm to any person...with intent...to do some grievous bodily harm to any person, or with intent to resist or prevent the lawful apprehension of any person, shall be guilty...[of an offence and liable to imprisonment for life].

CPS charging standards recommend charging s 47 where there is a loss or breakage of teeth, loss of consciousness, extensive or multiple bruising, displaced broken nose, minor fractures, minor non-superficial cuts or psychiatric injury. By comparison, examples of what would usually amount to s 20 include: injury resulting in permanent disability or permanent loss of sensory function; injury which results in more than minor permanent, visible disfigurement; broken or displaced limbs or bones, including fractured skull; compound fractures, broken cheek bone, jaw, ribs, etc; injuries which cause substantial loss of blood, usually necessitating a transfusion; injuries resulting in lengthy treatment or incapacity; psychiatric injury (CPS Charging Standard http://www.cps.gov.uk/legal/l_to_o/offences_against_the_person/index.html#a15).

18.4.1 Section 47: occasioning actual bodily harm

The offence under s 47 can be committed by D assaulting V or battering V and causing V a level of injury amounting to actual bodily harm. D's mens rea need only be an intention or subjective recklessness as to the assault or battery (see *Venna*, section 18.2.1.3, p 649). It is not necessary to prove that D intended or was reckless as to causing any actual bodily harm.

In *DPP v Smith* [2006] EWHC 94 (Admin), D sat on top of V and cut off the pony tail at the back of her head, without her consent. The victim accepted that there were no cuts to her scalp or other breaks of the skin caused while her hair was being cut. D submitted that there was no actual bodily harm and the critical ingredient of the offence had not been established. The justices acceded to that submission. The prosecution appealed by way of case stated. The Divisional Court held, allowing the prosecutor's appeal, that having regard to the dictionary definitions, in ordinary language 'harm' was not limited to 'injury' and extended to 'hurt' or 'damage'. 'Bodily', whether used as an adjective or adverb, was 'concerned with the body'. It was settled law that evidence of external bodily injury, or a break in or bruise to the surface of the skin, was not required for there to be an assault occasioning actual bodily harm. It applied to all parts of the body including the victim's organs, his nervous system and his brain. Furthermore, an assault occasioning actual bodily harm might be committed by words or gestures alone, without the need for any physical contact between the assailant and the body of the victim. Therefore, physical pain consequent on an assault was not a necessary ingredient of the offence. It followed that the respondent's actions in cutting off a substantial part of the victim's hair in the course of an assault on her, was capable of amounting to an assault which occasioned actual bodily harm. Whether it was alive beneath the surface of the skin or dead tissue above the surface of the skin, the hair was an attribute and part of the human body. It was intrinsic to each individual and to the identity of each individual. Previous authority establishes that actual bodily harm comprises 'any hurt or injury calculated to interfere with the health or comfort of the victim': *Donovan* [1934] 2 KB 498.

Smith is authority *only* for the proposition that on these facts the magistrates would be entitled to find that cutting off a *substantial* amount of a person's hair without consent is *capable* of amounting to actual bodily harm.

It has been accepted by the House of Lords in *Ireland* that actual bodily harm can include either physical injury or psychiatric injury.

R v Ireland; R v Burstow

(section 18.2.1.1, p 646), http://www.bailii.org/uk/cases/UKHL/1997/34.html

Lord Steyn:

It will now be convenient to consider the question which is common to the two appeals, namely whether psychiatric illness is capable of amounting to bodily harm in terms of ss 18, 20 and 47 of the 1861 Act. The answer must be the same for the three sections...

Courts of law can only act on the best scientific understanding of the day. Some elementary distinctions can be made. The appeals under consideration do not involve structural injuries to the brain such as might require the intervention of a neurologist. One is also not considering either psychotic illness or personality disorders. The victims in the two appeals suffered from no such conditions. As a result of the behaviour of the appellants they did not develop psychotic or psychoneurotic conditions. The case was that they developed mental disturbances of a lesser order, namely neurotic disorders. For present purposes the relevant forms of neurosis are anxiety disorders and depressive disorders. Neuroses must be distinguished from simple states of fear, or problems in coping with everyday life. Where the line is to be drawn must be a matter of psychiatric judgment. But for present purposes it is important to note that modern psychiatry treats neuroses as recognisable psychiatric illnesses (see *Liability for Psychiatric Illness* (Law Com Consultation Paper No 137) (1995) Pt III (The Medical Background) and Mullany and Handford *Tort Liability for Psychiatric Damage* (1993), discussion on 'A medical perspective' pp 24–42, esp p 30, footnote 88). Moreover, it is essential to bear in mind that neurotic illnesses affect the central nervous system of the body, because emotions such as fear and anxiety are brain functions....

[His lordship referred to developments in the civil law.]

The criminal law has been slow to follow this path. But in *R v Chan-Fook* [1994] 2 All ER 552, [1994] 1 WLR 689 the Court of Appeal squarely addressed the question whether psychiatric injury may amount to bodily harm under s 47 of the 1861 Act. The issue arose in a case where the defendant had aggressively questioned and locked in a suspected thief. There was a dispute as to whether the defendant had physically assaulted the victim. But the prosecution also alleged that even if the victim had suffered no physical injury, he had been reduced to a mental state which amounted to actual bodily harm under s 47. No psychiatric evidence was given. The judge directed the jury that an assault which caused a hysterical and nervous condition was an assault occasioning actual bodily harm. The defendant was convicted. Upon appeal the conviction was quashed on the ground of misdirections in the summing up and the absence of psychiatric evidence to support the prosecution's alternative case. The interest of the decision lies in the reasoning on psychiatric injury in the context of s 47. In a detailed and careful judgment given on behalf of the court Hobhouse LJ said ([1994] 2 All ER 552 at 558–559, [1994] 1 WLR 689 at 695, 696):

'The first question on the present appeal is whether the inclusion of the word "bodily" in the phrase "actual bodily harm" limits harm to harm to the skin, flesh and bones of the victim...The body of the victim includes all parts of his body, including his organs, his nervous system and his brain. Bodily injury therefore may include injury to any of those parts of his body responsible for his mental and other faculties.'

In concluding that 'actual bodily harm' is capable of including psychiatric injury Hobhouse LJ emphasised that—

'it does not include mere emotions such as fear or distress or panic nor does it include, as such, states of mind that are not themselves evidence of some identifiable clinical condition.'

He observed that in the absence of psychiatric evidence a question whether or not an assault occasioned psychiatric injury should not be left to the jury....

The proposition that the Victorian legislator when enacting ss 18, 20 and 47 of the 1861 Act, would not have had in mind psychiatric illness is no doubt correct. Psychiatry was in its infancy in 1861. But the subjective intention of the draftsman is immaterial. The only relevant inquiry is as to the sense of the words in the context in which they are used. Moreover the 1861 Act is a statute of the 'always speaking' type: the statute must be interpreted in the light of the best current scientific appreciation of the link between the body and psychiatric injury.

For these reasons I would, therefore, reject the challenge to the correctness of *R v Chan-Fook* [1994] 2 All ER 552, [1994] 1 WLR 689. In my view the ruling in that case was based on principled and cogent reasoning and it marked a sound and essential clarification of the law. I would hold that 'bodily harm' in ss 18, 20 and 47 must be interpreted so as to include recognisable psychiatric illness . . .

Expert evidence is required to prove a 'recognizable psychiatric illness'. Even where V can give evidence of headaches and physical pain, capable of being abh and occurring after the assault (*stricto sensu*—not a battery), there must be expert evidence to prove that these were caused by psychiatric injury: *Morris* [1998] 1 Cr App R 386. Serious psychiatric injury is gbh.

■ *Questions*

Does the expert or the jury decide whether it is 'serious'? Is it really feasible to prove that the defendant foresaw that he would or might cause (i) a condition that the expert witness subsequently diagnoses as a recognizable psychiatric injury, (ii) a condition which a judge and jury is not competent to recognize?

In *D* [2006] EWCA Crim 1139, in the course of its discussion of manslaughter (section 17.2.5.1, p 608), the Court of Appeal held that psychological injury, not amounting to an identified or recognized psychological condition, could not amount to 'bodily harm'. *Chan-Fook* (1994) 99 Cr App R 147 drew a clear distinction between psychiatric illness on the one hand and other psychological harm or states of mind on the other. The distinction drawn in *Chan-Fook* (upheld in *Ireland; Burstow* [1998] AC 147) was consistent with authority in the civil law, where it had been applied in claims for personal injury. In *D*, the Crown argued that 'bodily harm' encompassed psychological harm other than a recognized psychiatric illness or condition. This amounted to an argument that the clear line in *Chan-Fook* should be blurred, or a degree of elasticity should be introduced to it. To do so, although easy in theory, would go beyond the well-understood principles by which the common law developed incrementally and logically. The extension sought by the Crown would introduce a significant element of uncertainty about the true ambit of the relevant legal principles to which the concept of 'bodily harm' in the 1861 Act applied, which would be compounded by the inevitable problems of conflicting medical opinion in what was a constantly developing area of practice. By adhering to the principle of recognizable psychiatric illness, although some medical experts might be concerned with the way in which the definitions were arrived at, the issue required to be addressed could be clearly understood and those responsible for advising the prosecution and defence could approach their cases with a degree of certainly.

In *Santana-Bermudez* [2003] EWHC 2908 (Admin), S-B, a drug user, had assured a police officer about to search him that he was carrying no 'sharps'. The officer stabbed her finger on a syringe needle in his pocket during the search. Applying *Miller*, section 4.3.3.4, p 86, Maurice Kay J said:

. . . where someone (by act or word or a combination of the two) creates a danger and thereby exposes another to a reasonably foreseeable risk of injury which materialises, there is an evidential basis for the actus reus of an assault occasioning actual bodily harm. It remains necessary for the prosecution to prove an intention to assault or appropriate recklessness.

18.4.2 Section 20

Section 20 creates two offences: malicious wounding and maliciously inflicting grievous bodily harm.

18.4.2.1 Malicious wounding

Malice is interpreted to mean subjective recklessness: see *Cunningham* (section 5.3, p 117). In *Brady* [2006] EWCA Crim 2413, the Court of Appeal held that *G* (section 5.3, p 119) on subjective recklessness does not require proof that D had foreseen 'an obvious and significant risk' in order to establish that he had acted recklessly. D was drunk when he climbed on railings at a nightclub and fell onto the dance floor below causing serious injuries to V. The court allowed the appeal, because the judge had failed to direct the jury as to recklessness in sufficiently clear and careful terms.

In order to constitute a wound, the continuity of the whole skin must be broken. Where a pellet fired by an air pistol hit V in the eye but caused only an internal rupturing of blood vessels and not a break in the skin, there was no wound: *C (a minor) v Eisenhower* [1984] QB 331. It is not enough that the cuticle or outer skin be broken if the inner skin remains intact. Where V was treated with such violence that his collarbone was broken, it was held that there was no wound if his skin was intact: *Wood* (1830) 1 Mood CC 278. It was held to be a wound, however, where the lining membrane of the urethra was ruptured and bled, evidence being given that the membrane is precisely the same in character as that which lines the cheek and the external skin of the lip.

> ■ *Question*
>
> Why should the criminal law provide a specific offence labelled as 'wounding' rather than treat such cases as grievous or actual bodily harm as necessary? See on the significance of appropriate labelling to reflect the moral differences in harms caused, J. Gardner, 'Rationality and the Rule of Law in Offences Against the Person' (1994) 53 CLJ 520.

18.4.2.2 Maliciously inflicting grievous bodily harm: s 20

'Grievous bodily harm' was formerly interpreted to include any harm which seriously interferes with health or comfort; but in *DPP v Smith*, section 5.2, p 100, the House of Lords said that there was no warrant for giving the words a meaning other than that which they convey in their ordinary and natural meaning. Grievous bodily harm may cover cases where there is no wounding as, for instance, the broken collarbone in *Wood*. Conversely, there might be a technical 'wounding' which could not be said to amount to grievous bodily harm (see previous section). Psychiatric injury is sufficient for an offence under s 20 (*Ireland* (section 18.2.1.1, p 646)).

Whereas s 18 uses the word 'cause', s 20 uses 'inflict'. In a series of cases from 1861 to 1983 it was held or assumed that the words 'inflict' and 'wound' both imply an 'assault'. The effect was that D could be convicted of an offence under s 20 only if it was proved that he wounded or caused grievous bodily harm by committing an assault. The House of Lords in *Wilson* [1984] AC 242 at 260, resolved the matter by deciding, following the Australian case of *Salisbury* [1976] VR 452 at 461, that 'inflict' does not, after all, imply an assault. Arguably, the case decided no more than that; but Lord Roskill cited the opinion of the Australian court that 'inflict' has a narrower meaning than 'cause' and requires 'force being violently applied to the body of the victim'. The leading case was *Clarence*, but the decision in that case has now been rejected as the following extracts confirm.

R v Ireland; R v Burstow

(section 18.2.1.1, p 646), http://www.bailii.org/uk/cases/UKHL/1997/34.html

[Lord Hope considered on the meaning of 'inflict' in s 20:]

The decision in *R v Chan-Fook* opened up the possibility of applying ss 18, 20 and 47 in new circumstances. The appeal of Burstow lies in respect of his conviction under s 20. It was conceded that in principle the wording of s 18, and in particular the words 'cause any grievous bodily harm to any person', do not preclude a prosecution in cases where the actus reus is the causing of psychiatric injury. But counsel laid stress on the difference in legislative intent: inflict is a narrower concept than cause. This argument loses sight of the genesis of ss 18 and 20. In his commentary on the 1861 Act Greaves, the draftsman, explained the position in *The Criminal Law Consolidation and Amendment Acts* (2nd edn, 1862) pp 3–4:

> 'If any question should arise in which any comparison may be instituted between different sections of any one or several of these Acts, it must be carefully borne in mind in what manner these Acts were framed. None of them was re-written; on the contrary, each contains enactments taken from different Acts passed at different times and with different views, and frequently varying from each other in phraseology, and . . . these enactments, for the most part, stand in these Acts with little or no variation in their phraseology, and, consequently, their differences in that respect will be found generally to remain in these Acts. It follows, therefore, from hence, that any argument as to a difference in the intention of the legislature, which may be drawn from a difference in the terms of one clause from those in another, will be entitled to no weight in the construction of such clauses; for that argument can only apply with force where an Act is framed from beginning to end with one and the same view, and with the intention of making it thoroughly consistent throughout.'

The difference in language is therefore not a significant factor.

Counsel for Burstow then advanced a sustained argument that an assault is an ingredient of an offence under s 20. He referred your Lordships to cases which in my judgment simply do not yield what he sought to extract from them. In any event, the tour of the cases revealed conflicting dicta, no authority binding on the House of Lords, and no settled practice holding expressly that assault was an ingredient of s 20. And, needless to say, none of the cases focused on the infliction of psychiatric injury. In these circumstances I do not propose to embark on a general review of the cases cited: compare the review in Smith and Hogan *Criminal Law* (8th edn, 1996) pp 440–441. Instead I turn to the words of the section. Counsel's argument can only prevail if one may supplement the section by reading it as providing 'inflict *by assault* any grievous bodily harm'. Such an implication is, however, not necessary. On the contrary, s 20, like s 18, works perfectly satisfactorily without such an implication. I would reject this part of counsel's argument.

But counsel had a stronger argument when he submitted that it is inherent in the word 'inflict' that there must be a direct or indirect application of force to the body. Counsel cited the speech of Lord Roskill in *R v Wilson (Clarence); R v Jenkins (Edward John)* [1983] 3 All ER 448 at 454–455m [1984] AC 242 at 259–260, in which Lord Roskill quoted with approval from the judgment of the full court of the Supreme Court of Victoria in *R v Salisbury* [1976] VR 452. There are passages that give assistance to counsel's argument. But Lord Roskill expressly stated that he was 'content to accept, as did the [court in *Salisbury*], that there can be an infliction of grievous bodily harm contrary to s 20 without an assault being committed' (see [1983] 3 All ER 448 at 455, [1984] AC 242 at 260). In the result the effect of the decisions in *R v Wilson* and *R v Salisbury* is neutral in respect of the issue as to the meaning of 'inflict'. Moreover, in *R v Burstow* [1997] 1 Cr App Rep 144 at 149 Lord Bingham of Cornhill CJ pointed out that in *R v Mandair* [1994] 2 All ER 715 at 719, [1995] 1 AC 208 at 215 Lord Mackay of Clashfern LC observed with the agreement of the majority of the House of Lords: 'In my opinion . . . the word "cause" is wider or at least not narrower than the word "inflict". Like Lord Bingham of Cornhill CJ

I regard this observation as making clear that in the context of the 1861 Act there is no radical divergence between the meaning of the two words'.

That leaves the troublesome authority of the decision of the Court for Crown Cases Reserved *in R v Clarence* (1888) 22 QBD 23, [1886–90] All ER Rep 133. At a time when the defendant knew that he was suffering from a venereal disease, and his wife was ignorant of his condition, he had sexual intercourse with her. He communicated the disease to her. The defendant was charged and convicted of inflicting grievous bodily harm under s 20. There was an appeal. By a majority of nine to four the court quashed the conviction. The case was complicated by an issue of consent. But it must be accepted that in a case where there was direct physical contact the majority ruled that the requirement of infliction was not satisfied. This decision has never been overruled. It assists counsel's argument. But it seems to me that what detracts from the weight to be given to the dicta in *R v Clarence* is that none of the judges in that case had before them the possibility of the inflicting, or causing, of psychiatric injury. The criminal law has moved on in the light of a developing understanding of the link between the body and psychiatric injury. In my judgment *R v Clarence* no longer assists.

■ *Question*

We are told that 'cause' and 'inflict' are not synonymous but there is no 'radical divergence' of meaning. Is there *any* difference of meaning?

Lord Hope suggests: 'the word "inflict" implies that the consequence of the act is something which the victim is likely to find unpleasant or harmful.' But what about *Brown* [1993] 2 All ER 75, [1994] 1 AC 212, HL, section 19.4.2, p 686? Everyone was having a jolly good time. If grievous bodily harm had been proved (it was not), would the House really have held that, though there was an unlawful wounding contrary to s 20, there was no unlawful 'inflicting' contrary to that section?

In *Dica* [2004] EWCA Crim 1103 (section 19.3.1, p 681), the Court of Appeal held:

29. In *R v Ireland: R v Burstow*, . . . Lord Steyn recognised that the two words, 'inflict' and 'cause', are not synonymous. In relation to '*Clarence*', he acknowledged that the possibility of inflicting or causing psychiatric injury would not then have been in contemplation, whereas nowadays it is. In his view the infliction of psychiatric injury without violence could fall within the ambit of s.20. Lord Steyn described *Clarence* as a 'troublesome authority', and in the specific context of the meaning of 'inflict' in s.20 said expressly that *Clarence* 'no longer assists'. Lord Hope similarly examined the consequences of the use of the word 'inflict' in s.20 and 'cause' in s 18. He concluded that for practical purposes, and in the context of a criminal act, the words might be regarded as interchangeable, provided it was understood that 'inflict' implies that the consequence to the victim involved something detrimental or adverse.

30. Such differences as may be discerned in the language used by Lord Steyn and Lord Hope respectively do not obscure the fact that this decision confirmed that even when no physical violence has been applied, directly or indirectly to the victim's body, an offence under s.20 may be committed. Putting it another way, if the remaining ingredients of s.20 are established, the charge is not answered simply because the grievous bodily harm suffered by the victim did not result from direct or indirect physical violence. Whether the consequences suffered by the victim are physical injuries or psychiatric injuries, or a combination of the two, the ingredients of the offence prescribed by s.20 are identical. If psychiatric injury can be inflicted without direct or indirect violence, or an assault, for the purposes of s.20 physical injury may be similarly inflicted. It is no longer possible to discern the critical difference identified by the majority in *Clarence*, and encapsulated by Stephen J in his judgment, between an 'immediate and necessary connection' between the relevant blow and the consequent injury, and

the 'uncertain and delayed' effect of the act which led to the eventual development of infection. The erosion process is now complete.

31. In our judgment, the reasoning which led the majority in *Clarence* to decide that the conviction under s.20 should be quashed has no continuing application. If that case were decided today, the conviction under s.20 would be upheld. Clarence knew, but his wife did not know, and he knew that she did not know that he was suffering from gonorrhoea. Nevertheless he had sexual intercourse with her, not intending deliberately to infect her, but reckless whether she might become infected, and thus suffer grievous bodily harm. Accordingly we agree with Judge Philpot's first ruling, that notwithstanding the decision in *Clarence*, it was open to the jury to convict the appellant of the offences alleged in the indictment.

18.4.3 Section 18: grievous bodily harm with intent

Each of the elements has been considered earlier in this chapter. Note that the offence carries a maximum of life imprisonment.

In every case the Crown must establish an ulterior intent which may be either intent to do grievous bodily harm or intent to resist or prevent the lawful apprehension or detainer of *any* person. Recklessness is not enough. Where the allegation is of intentionally causing GBH, it is sufficient that D intended to cause the harm he did, irrespective of whether he would regard that as really serious harm. Where, under s 18, the charge is of causing grievous bodily harm with intent to do grievous bodily harm, the word 'maliciously' obviously has no part to play. Any mens rea which it might import is comprehended within the ulterior intent. Even if 'wounding' is not foreseen, it is 'malicious'.

Where the charge is of malicious wounding or causing grievous bodily harm with intent to resist lawful apprehension, 'maliciously' is important and must be proved according to its usual definition: *Morrison* (1989) 89 Cr App R 17 (D seized by a Woman Police Constable (WPC) as she was arresting him. D dived through a window pane and the WPC was dragged with him suffering serious facial injury. D clearly *intended* to resist arrest. The Court of Appeal held he must also be subjectively (*Cunningham*) reckless as to the grievous bodily harm). A mere intent to resist lawful apprehension should not found liability for a charge of wounding or causing grievous bodily harm. It is submitted that the Court of Appeal went too far in *Mowatt* [1968] 1 QB 421 at 426–427, in saying that 'In section 18 the word maliciously adds nothing.' In cases such as *Morrison* it clearly does.

Research has suggested that the moral distinction between the s 18 and s 20 offences has been eroded by the availability of the alternative verdicts and the frequency with which they are returned. In one study only 23 per cent of those indicted for s 18 were convicted of that offence, whilst 53 per cent were convicted of s 20 and only one in ten of the contested s 18 trials led to an outright acquittal: E. Genders, 'Reform of the Law of the Offences Against the Person: Lessons from the Law in Action' [1999] Crim LR 689.

18.5 Racially aggravated assaults

The Crime and Disorder Act 1998 created a new category of racially aggravated crimes and in the wake of 9/11, the Anti-Terrorism, Crime and Security Act 2001 extended these to include religiously aggravated offences. (See E. Burney, 'Using the Law of Racially Aggravated Offences' [2003] Crim LR 28. See generally, M. Malik, 'Racist Crime: Racially Aggravated Offences in the Crime and Disorder Act 1998' (1999) 62 MLR 409; M. Idriss, 'Religion and the Anti-Terrorism, Crime and Security Act 2001' [2002] Crim LR 890.)

Crime and Disorder Act 1998, s 28

28. Meaning of 'racially or religiously aggravated'

(1) An offence is racially or religiously aggravated for the purposes of sections 29 to 32 below if—

    (a) at the time of committing the offence, or immediately before or after doing so, the offender demonstrates towards the victim of the offence hostility based on the victims membership (or presumed membership) of a racial or religious group; or

    (b) the offence is motivated (wholly or partly) by hostility towards members of a racial or religious group based on their membership of that group.

(2) In subsection (1)(a) above—'membership', in relation to a racial or religious group, includes association with members of that group;

    'presumed' means presumed by the offender.

(3) It is immaterial for the purposes of paragraph (a) or (b) of subsection (1) above whether or not the offenders hostility is also based, to any extent, on any other factor not mentioned in that paragraph.

(4) In this section 'racial group' means a group of persons defined by reference to race, colour, nationality (including citizenship) or ethnic or national origins.

(5) In this section 'religious group' means a group of persons defined by reference to religious belief or lack of religious belief.

A person commits an offence under s 29 of the 1998 Act if he commits an offence:

    (i)   under the OAPA, s 20 (malicious wounding or grievous bodily harm, section 18.4, p 652); or

    (ii)   s 47 of that Act (section 18.4, p 652); or

    (iii) a common assault (section 18.2, p 642)

which is 'racially or religiously aggravated' for the purposes of s 29.

Offences (i) and (ii) are punishable on indictment with seven years' imprisonment (compared with five years for the basic, non-aggravated offence) and offence (iii) with two years, the basic offence being triable only summarily. In cases where offence (i) or (ii) is charged, a jury could convict of the basic offence if they were satisfied that it had been committed, but were not satisfied that aggravation was proved. A jury could not, however, convict of a common assault because that is triable only summarily.

'Race' is widely defined to include colour, nationality (including citizenship) or ethnic or national origins. It has been held that 'African' does not denote an ethnic, but does denote a racial group (*White* [2001] Crim LR 576). The courts have taken an extremely wide view of what constitutes a race and racial group. It has been accepted that the terms are satisfied by non-inclusive expressions as where D demonstrates hostility to V by calling him 'non-white' or 'foreign'. It has been said, *obiter*, that a racially aggravated assault might be committed by one white person on another if the former were, for example, to call the latter 'nigger lover': *DPP v Pal* [2000] Crim LR 756.

'Religious group' means a group of persons defined by reference to religious belief or lack of religious belief. The Act gives no further guidance. Given the broad interpretation in Article 9 of the European Convention on Human Rights (ECHR), it would seem likely that the domestic courts will interpret the offence as affording protection to a religion as widely understood. By analogy with the interpretation of race, non-inclusive terms will suffice, for example 'gentile': *DPP v M* [2004] EWHC 1453 (Admin).

R v Rogers

[2007] UKHL 8, House of Lords, http://www.bailii.org/uk/cases/UKHL/2007/8.html

(Lords Mance, Hoffmann, Hope of Craighead, Walker of Gestingthorpe and Baroness Hale of Richmond)

The appellant was riding a mobility scooter along the pavement on his way home from a pub. He tried to pass three young Spanish women walking on the pavement. He then pursued them in an aggressive manner into a local kebab house where they had gone to avoid him. He called them 'bloody foreigners'. He was charged with an offence under s 4 of the Public Order Act 1986 of using threatening, abusive or insulting words or behaviour intending them to fear immediate unlawful violence or to provoke it. The question was whether his use of the term 'bloody foreigners' and telling them to 'go back to your own country' demonstrated hostility based on their membership of a racial group so as to render it an aggravated offence under the 1998 Act.

Baroness Hale delivered the unanimous opinion:

4. The issue in this appeal is whether using the words 'bloody foreigners' and 'get back to your own country' can transform the offence of using abusive words and behaviour with intent to cause fear or provoke violence, contrary to section 4 of the Public Order Act 1986, into the racially aggravated form of that offence, contrary to section 31(1)(a) of the Crime and Disorder Act 1998.

5. Sections 29 to 32 of the 1998 Act create racially or religiously aggravated versions of some frequently encountered offences which vary greatly in their intrinsic seriousness: assaults falling short of grievous bodily harm with intent (section 29), criminal damage (section 30), certain public order offences (section 31) and harassment (section 32). If racially or religiously aggravated, the maximum penalties are higher. The justification for treating such conduct more severely than the basic versions of these crimes is helpfully summarised by Ivan Hare ('Legislating Against Hate—The Legal Response to Bias Crimes' (1997) 17 OJLS 415, 416–7):

'The case of principle for an explicit response to the phenomenon rests fundamentally on the realization that crimes motivated by hatred for the group to which the victim belongs are in some sense of a qualitatively distinct order of gravity. This perception arises from intuitive feelings of retribution and from awareness of the impact such offences have on the immediate victims and on society as a whole. In addition to being the target of an act of violence the victim is likely to feel a sense of injustice at having been discriminated against on the basis of his membership of, or association with, a particular group. The more general strain of the argument is that hate crimes entail a threat to public welfare which makes it appropriate to punish them more severely.'

6. The court must first be satisfied that the basic offence has been committed and then that it is racially or religiously aggravated within the meaning of section 28 of the 1998 Act. Subsection (1) provides that the offence is racially or religiously aggravated if either of two different circumstances exists:

'(a) at the time of committing the offence, or immediately before or after doing so, the offender demonstrates towards the victim hostility based on the victim's membership (or presumed membership) of a racial or religious group; or

(b) the offence is motivated (wholly or partly) by hostility towards members of a racial or religious group based on their membership of that group.'

One limb is therefore concerned with the outward manifestation of racial or religious hostility, the other with the inner motivation of the offender. Here we are concerned with the former but the point at issue arises in relation to both. Hostility, demonstrated or meant, is required for both, but hostility to what?

7. The point at issue is the meaning of 'racial group'. This is defined in section 28(4):

'In this section, "racial group" means a group of persons defined by reference to race, colour, nationality (including citizenship), or ethnic or national origins.'

[Her ladyship recited the facts.]

8. It is accepted on his behalf that had he called them 'bloody Spaniards' or any other pejorative word associated with natives of the Iberian peninsular, he would have been guilty. But it is argued that the hostility must be shown towards a particular group, rather than to foreigners as a whole. Mere xenophobia, it is said, does not fall within the ordinary person's perception of hostility to a racial group.

9. This may be true, but the definition of a racial group clearly goes beyond groups defined by their colour, race or ethnic origin. It encompasses both nationality (including citizenship) and national origins. This was quite deliberate. In *Ealing London Borough Council v Race Relations Board* [1972] AC 342, a majority of this House declined to interpret 'national origins' in the list of prohibited grounds of discrimination under the Race Relations Act 1968 so as to include 'nationality': discriminating against the non-British was allowed. Following this decision, the list of prohibited grounds was deliberately expanded in the Race Relations Act 1976 so as to include nationality. The list of grounds contained in the 1976 Act was adopted for the purposes of defining racial groups in the 1998 Act. An obvious advantage is that it helps to reduce argument about whether particular terms of abuse which are generally considered racist are or are not covered: does 'Paki', for example, demonstrate hostility towards everyone who might hail from the Indian subcontinent or only towards citizens of Pakistan?

10. Nevertheless, it is argued for the appellant that the Act requires that the group be defined by what it is rather than by what it is not. Hence it is argued that Spaniards are covered but foreigners, that is the non-British, are not. The same argument would presumably be made about a person who showed hostility towards all non-whites, irrespective of the particular racial group to which they belonged. This cannot be right as a matter of language. Whether the group is defined exclusively by reference to what its members are not or inclusively by reference to what they are, the criterion by which the group is defined—nationality or colour—is the same.

11. There are, as Mr David Perry QC for the respondent has pointed out, other indications that the statute intended a broad non-technical approach, rather than a construction which invited nice distinctions. Hostility may be demonstrated at the time, or immediately before or after, the offence is committed (section 28(1)(a)). The victim may be presumed by the offender to be a member of the hated group even if she is not (section 28(1)(a)). Membership of a group includes association with members of that group (section 28(2)). And the fact that the offender's hostility is based on other factors as well racism or xenophobia is immaterial (section 28(3)).

12. This flexible, non-technical approach makes sense, not only as a matter of language, but also in policy terms. The mischiefs attacked by the aggravated versions of these offences are racism and xenophobia. Their essence is the denial of equal respect and dignity to people who are seen as 'other'. This is more deeply hurtful, damaging and disrespectful to the victims than the simple versions of these offences. It is also more damaging to the community as a whole, by denying acceptance to members of certain groups not for their own sake but for the sake of something they can do nothing about. This is just as true if the group is defined exclusively as it is if it is defined inclusively.

13. The offences do not require particular words to be used: the necessary hostility could be demonstrated in other ways, such as the wearing of swastikas or the singing of certain songs. But it will normally be proved by the use of some well known terms of abuse. Fine distinctions depending upon the particular words used would bring the law into disrepute. This case shows that only too well but it is easy to think of other examples. 'Wogs begin at Calais' demonstrates hostility to all foreigners, whereas 'bloody wogs' might well be thought to have specific racial connotations. 'Tinted persons' could in certain circumstances demonstrate hostility to all non-Caucasians, while 'blacks' might refer to a particular racial group. But 'black' might equally refer to several different racial groups whose members may have very black skin. All are defined by reference to their race, colour, nationality, or ethic or national origins, whether there are many, several, or only one such group encompassed by the words used.

14. It therefore comes as no surprise that the Divisional Court and Court of Appeal have generally taken the same view, as did the Court of Appeal in this case. In *Director of Public Prosecutions v M* [2004] EWCA 1453 (Admin), [2004] 1 WLR 2758 the Divisional Court held that 'bloody foreigners' could, depending on the context, demonstrate hostility to a racial group. In *Attorney General's Reference No 4 of 2004* [2005] EWCA Crim 889, [2005] 1 WLR 2810 the Court of Appeal held that 'someone who is an immigrant to this country and therefore non-British' could be a member of a racial group for this purpose. In *R v White (Anthony)* [2001] EWCA Crim 216; [2001] 1 WLR 1352, it was held that 'African' could demonstrate hostility to a racial group, because it would generally be taken to mean black African. However, it was doubted whether the same would apply to 'South American'. It is not easy to imagine a scene in which hostility to South Americans as such is demonstrated, but as with 'African', it is quite easy to imagine a scene in which hostility is demonstrated to racial, national or ethnic groups within that continent. The context will illuminate what the conduct shows.

15. A case which might be thought to go the other way is *Director of Public Prosecutions v Pal* [2000] Crim LR 756. There the Divisional Court dismissed the prosecution's appeal when magistrates acquitted the defendant, of Asian origin, who had assaulted the victim, also of Asian origin, and called him a 'white man's arse-licker' and a 'brown Englishman'. It was held that this did not demonstrate hostility towards Asians. But it is difficult to understand why it did not demonstrate hostility based on the victim's presumed association with whites (within the meaning of section 28(2)). That would undoubtedly cover, for example, a white woman who is targeted because she is married to a black man. It may well be that this way of looking at the matter did not feature in the case presented to the Divisional Court.

16. The late Sir John Smith, commenting on *Pal*, was critical of what he saw as a further complication of our already over-complex law of offences against the person in order to meet a problem which could equally well be met by sentencing guidelines. But as Mr Perry has pointed out, there is an advantage for the accused in differentiating between the basic and the aggravated offence. The fact finders, whether a jury or magistrates, have then to decide whether the offence was indeed racially or religiously aggravated. If they decide that it was not, then the offender should be sentenced on that basis. If the offence is not covered by these provisions, it is for the sentencer to decide whether it was racially aggravated and, if it was, to treat this as an aggravating factor in sentencing (Criminal Justice Act 2003, section 145).

17. The Court of Appeal in this case [2005] EWCA Crim 2863, [2006] 1 WLR 962, para 24, expressed some concern that

> '[t]he very width of the meaning of racial group for the purposes of section 28(4) gives rise to a danger that charges of aggravated offences may be brought where vulgar abuse has included racial epithets that did not, when all the relevant circumstances are considered, indicate hostility to the race in question.
>
> If that is what the evidence suggests, of course, the normal criteria for bringing proceedings would not be met. There is no reason for the Crown Prosecution Service to be any more hesitant about charging these offences, if they are properly supported by the available evidence, than about any other.

18. The question certified by the Court of Appeal was: 'Do those who are not of British origin constitute a racial group within section 28(4) of the Crime and Disorder Act 1998?' The answer is 'yes', as would it be to the question whether 'foreigners' constitute such a group. Whether the evidence in any particular case, taken as a whole, proves that the offender's conduct demonstrated hostility to such a group, or was motivated by such hostility, is a question of fact for the decision-makers in the case.

Appeal dismissed

■ *Questions*

1. Is there a danger of every trivial dispute with an assault or public order offence or criminal damage becoming a racially aggravated offence if D calls V some racial or religious name in the process? Should such prosecutions be used for the racially aggravated offences so as to deter the use of racist slurs?

2. Lord Monson in the debates on the Crime and Disorder Bill anticipated this problem and described the section as Orwellian in that it seeks to police people's emotions (Hansard HL, 12 February 1998, col 1266). Do you agree?

3. Why are these particular offences (only) capable of being aggravated? Why not theft or robbery or rape?

4. At present, only insults relating to religion and race are criminalized in this way. Should the law extend the aggravated offences to include hostility on the basis of disability, sexual orientation or transgender identity? See the Law Commission Consultation Paper No 213 (2013).

It is important to appreciate the difference between cases under s 28(1)(a) and those under s 28(1)(b).

18.5.1 Section 28(1)(a): demonstration of hostility

Cases under s 28(1)(a) involve proof that D demonstrated hostility (an objective test). It is irrelevant what his motivations were and whether he had multiple reasons for demonstrating the hostility. It is also sufficient that D has demonstrated hostility based on V's presumed membership of a racial or religious group. So, for example, D calling V a 'Paki' would be sufficient even if V was in fact from India not Pakistan. Under s 28(1)(a), a raft of cases makes it clear that the offence extends to cases which may have a racially neutral gravamen but in the course of which there is hostility demonstrated towards the victim based on his presumed race. (See Maurice Kay J in *Woods* [2002] EWHC 85 (Admin) at [11].) In *Johnson v DPP* [2008] EWHC 509 (Admin), J appealed by way of case stated against the trial judge's decision in the Crown Court to uphold his conviction for a racially aggravated public order offence. J, who was black, had been involved in an argument with two white parking attendants in the course of which J told them 'This is our patch not yours' and 'You don't belong here' and in particular J said 'Why don't you [go and deal with] your white uncles and aunties'. J was convicted of the racially aggravated form of s 5 of the Public Order Act 1986. J argued that the mere fact that reference was made to the colour of the parking attendants and to leaving the black community alone was not sufficient to constitute racial hostility. The Crown Court dismissed his appeal as did the Divisional Court, concluding that it was reasonably open to the court to conclude that the words used by J had demonstrated a racial hostility at least in part. It was clear from the language that J had been talking in racial terms.

In *Johnson* it did not matter whether the hostility displayed was partly racial and partly directed at a general class of individuals, namely parking attendants.

18.5.2 Section 28(1)(b): motivated by hostility

Under s 28(1)(b), the prosecution must prove that D was motivated by hostility on grounds of race or religion. That is a subjective test. In addition, it does not matter whether D presumed anything about V's race or religion.

In *DPP v Howard* [2008] EWHC 608 (Admin), H chanted 'I'd rather be a Paki than a cop' at his neighbours who were police officers. H was convicted of using threatening, abusive or insulting words or behaviour within the hearing or sight of a person likely to be caused harassment, alarm or distress contrary to the Public Order Act 1986, s 5, but the magistrates concluded that there was insufficient evidence on which they could be satisfied that the racially aggravated offence under the Crime and Disorder Act, s 28, had been made out. They found that the evidence showed that H's hostility was motivated *only* by his intense dislike of X and not even as a result of his intense dislike of the police. The prosecution appealed by way of case stated, arguing that no reasonable magistrate, properly directed, could conclude that this was not racially aggravated. The Divisional Court dismissed the appeal, concluding that the magistrates were entitled to come to the conclusion they did: there was an abundance of evidence that the *sole* motivation for H's chanting was his hostility toward X personally. Moses LJ suggested that at para 12:

prosecutors should be careful not to deploy [s 28(1)(b)] where offensive words have been used, but in themselves have not in any way been the motivation for the particular offence with which a defendant is charged. It diminishes the gravity of this offence to use it in circumstances where it is unnecessary to do so and where plainly it cannot be proved.

In terms of the broader social objective of the legislation, the section may well be regarded as a success if it deters individuals from using racist language in *any* context. Whether this will be the effect or whether those convicted will bear such resentment at the stigma as to become more racist is debatable. See generally E. Burney and G. Rose, 'Racially Aggravated Offences: How is the Law Working?' (2002) HORS 244, and E. Burney, 'Using the Law on Racially Aggravated Offences' [2003] Crim LR 28.

■ *Question*

V arrives late for his tennis match and can find no parking place. He parks his car in the car parking space at the local church next door to the tennis club. Damien, the church warden, comes out shouting at him and kicks V. As he does so, Damian shouts 'You unbeliever'. Is this a case of religiously aggravated battery?

18.6 Administering poison, etc

Offences Against the Person Act 1861, s 23

Whosoever shall unlawfully and maliciously administer to or cause to be administered to or taken by any other person any poison or other destructive or noxious thing, so as thereby to endanger the life of such person, or so as thereby to inflict upon such person any grievous bodily harm shall be guilty of [an offence], and being convicted thereof shall be liable . . . to [imprisonment] for any term not exceeding ten years . . .

Offences Against the Person Act 1861, s 24

Whosoever shall unlawfully and maliciously administer to or cause to be administered to or taken by any other person any poison or other destructive or noxious thing, with intent to injure, aggrieve, or annoy such person, shall be guilty of [an offence], and being . . . convicted thereof shall be liable to [imprisonment for a term not exceeding five years].

18.6.1 A poison or noxious thing

Sections 23 and 24 both speak of 'any poison or other destructive or noxious thing' which suggests a common definition. But the definition appears to have reference, under s 23, to the effect it is required to have and, under s 24, to the intentions of D. Thus if D, intending to kill, places a small amount of cyanide in his victim's glass of milk (cf *White*, section 14.1, p 497) he is guilty of attempted murder but not of the offence under s 23 if the amount was so small that the victim was in no danger of suffering death or grievous bodily harm. D would, however, commit the offence under s 24 because he has administered a noxious substance and his intent to kill is more than enough to satisfy an intent to injure, aggrieve or annoy. Cyanide remains a noxious thing though administered in an amount too small to cause harm. It was held in *Marcus* [1981] 2 All ER 833, [1981] 1 WLR 774, CA, that a thing which would not ordinarily be described as noxious (in that case it was a sedative but it would embrace many proprietary medicines) was noxious if administered in a sufficient amount to injure, aggrieve or annoy.

R v Cato

[1976] 1 All ER 260, 270n, Court of Appeal, Criminal Division, http://www.bailii.org/ew/cases/EWCA/Crim/1975/5.html

(Lord Widgery CJ, O'Connor and Jupp JJ)

The appellant, with V's consent, administered heroin to him with a syringe. This caused his death. He was convicted of manslaughter and of an offence under s 23.

Lord Widgery CJ [delivering the judgment of the court, dealt with the conviction for manslaughter, section 17.2.5.2, p 611, and continued:]

Thus, a number of things have to be proved in order to establish the offence [under s 23] and the two which are relevant to the argument of counsel for Cato are 'maliciously' and 'noxious'. The thing must be a 'noxious thing' and it must be administered 'maliciously'.

What is a noxious thing, and in particular is heroin a noxious thing? The authorities show that an article is not to be described as noxious for present purposes merely because it has a potentiality for harm if taken in an overdose. There are many articles of value in common use which may be harmful in overdose, and it is clear on the authorities when looking at them that one cannot describe an article as noxious merely because it has that aptitude. On the other hand, if an article is liable to injure in common use, not when an overdose in the sense of an accidental excess is used but is liable to cause injury in common use, should it then not be regarded as a noxious thing for present purposes?

When one has regard to the potentiality of heroin in the circumstances which we read about and hear about in our courts today we have no hesitation in saying that heroin is a noxious thing and we do not think that arguments are open to an accused person in a case such as the present, whereby he may say: 'Well the deceased was experienced in taking heroin: his tolerance was high', and generally to indicate that the heroin was unlikely to do any particular harm in a particular circumstance. We think there can be no doubt, and it should be said clearly, that heroin is a noxious thing for the purposes of s 23.

18.6.2 Administer, cause to be administered or cause to be taken

To complete the offence D must 'administer or cause to be administered to or taken by' the victim the poison or other destructive or noxious thing. In *Gillard* (1988) 87 Cr App R 189, [1988] Crim LR 531, CA, D was convicted of conspiring to commit an offence (the offence being that of administering a noxious thing contrary to s 24) contrary to s 1(1) of the Criminal Law Act 1977 in agreeing with others to spray CS gas (a potent eye, throat and skin irritant) into the faces of P and others. Delivering the judgment of the court, McNeill J said:

Where . . . the learned recorder was in error was in holding that 'administering' and 'taking' were to be treated effectively as synonymous or as conjunctive words in the section: on the contrary, the repeated use of the word 'or' makes it clear that they are disjunctive. The word 'takes' postulates some 'ingestion' by the victim: 'administer' must have some other meaning and there is no difficulty in including in that meaning such conduct as spraying the victim with noxious fluid or vapour, whether from a device such as a gas canister or, for example, hosing down with effluent. There is no necessity when the word 'administer' is used to postulate any form of entry into the victim's body, whether through any orifice or by absorption. [T]he proper construction of 'administer' in s24 includes conduct which not being the application of direct force to the victim nevertheless brings the noxious thing into contact with his body.

R v Kennedy (No 2)
[2007] UKHL 38, House of Lords, http://www.bailii.org/uk/cases/UKHL/2007/38.html

(Lords Bingham of Cornhill, Rodger of Earlsferry, Baroness Hale of Richmond, Lords Carswell and Mance)

The appeal arose from a manslaughter conviction where K prepared a syringe of heroin and handed it to V who self-injected and died from the effects. See section 3.2.3.3, p 57. The certified question for the House of Lords was:

When is it appropriate to find someone guilty of manslaughter where that person has been involved in the supply of a class A controlled drug, which is then freely and voluntarily self-administered by the person to whom it was supplied, and the administration of the drug then causes his death?

The Committee in a remarkably short unanimous judgment delivered by Lord Bingham, concluded that the Court of Appeal had been in error.

Lord Bingham [his lordship stated the facts and discussed the manslaughter offence—see section 17.2.5.2, p 611:]

8. The parties are further agreed that an unlawful act of the appellant on the present facts must be found, if at all, in a breach of section 23 of the Offences against the Person Act 1861. Although the death of the deceased was the tragic outcome of the injection on 10 September 1996 the death is legally irrelevant to the criminality of the appellant's conduct under the section: he either was or was not guilty of an offence under section 23 irrespective of the death.

[His lordship referred to s 23.]

9. The opening and closing words of the section raise no question relevant to this appeal. The substance of the section creates three distinct offences: (1) administering a noxious thing to any other person; (2) causing a noxious thing to be administered to any other person; and (3) causing a noxious thing to be taken by any other person. It is not in doubt that heroin is a noxious thing, and the contrary was not contended.

10. The factual situations covered by (1), (2) and (3) are clear. Offence (1) is committed where D administers the noxious thing directly to V, as by injecting V with the noxious thing, holding a glass containing the noxious thing to V's lips, or (as in *R v Gillard* (1988) 87 Cr App R 189) spraying the noxious thing in V's face.

11. Offence (2) is typically committed where D does not directly administer the noxious thing to V but causes an innocent third party TP to administer it to V. If D, knowing a syringe to be filled with poison instructs TP to inject V, TP believing the syringe to contain a legitimate therapeutic substance, D would commit this offence.

12. Offence (3) covers the situation where the noxious thing is not administered to V but taken by him, provided D causes the noxious thing to be taken by V and V does not make a voluntary and informed decision to take it. If D puts a noxious thing in food which V is about to eat and V, ignorant of the presence of the noxious thing, eats it, D commits offence (3).

13. In the course of his accurate and well-judged submissions on behalf of the Crown, Mr David Perry QC accepted that if he could not show that the appellant had committed offence (1) as the unlawful act necessary to found the count of manslaughter he could not hope to show the commission of offences (2) or (3). This concession was rightly made, but the committee heard considerable argument addressed to the concept of causation, which has been misapplied in some of the authorities, and it is desirable that it should be clear why the concession is rightly made.

. . .

19. The sole argument open to the Crown was, therefore, that the appellant administered the injection to the deceased. It was argued that the term 'administer' should not be narrowly interpreted. Reliance was placed on the steps taken by the appellant to facilitate the injection and on the trial judge's direction to the jury that they had to be satisfied that the appellant handed the syringe to the deceased 'for immediate injection'. But section 23 draws a very clear contrast between a noxious thing administered to another person and a noxious thing taken by another person. It cannot ordinarily be both. In this case the heroin is described as 'freely and voluntarily self-administered' by the deceased. This, on the facts, is an inevitable finding. The appellant supplied the heroin and prepared the syringe. But the deceased had a choice whether to inject himself or not. He chose to do so, knowing what he was doing. It was his act.

20. In resisting this conclusion Mr Perry relied on *R v Rogers* [2003] 1 WLR 1374. In that case the defendant pleaded guilty, following a legal ruling, to a count of administering poison contrary to section 23 of the 1861 Act and a count of manslaughter. The relevant finding was that the defendant physically assisted the deceased by holding his belt round the deceased's arm as a tourniquet, so as to raise a vein in which the deceased could insert a syringe, while the deceased injected himself. It was argued in support of his appeal to the Court of Appeal that the defendant had committed no unlawful act for purposes of either count. This contention was rejected. The court held (para 7) that it was unreal and artificial to separate the tourniquet from the injection. By applying and holding the tourniquet the defendant had played a part in the mechanics of the injection which had caused the death. There is, clearly, a difficult borderline between contributory acts which may properly be regarded as administering a noxious thing and acts which may not. But the crucial question is not whether the defendant facilitated or contributed to administration of the noxious thing but whether he went further and administered it. What matters, in a case such as *R v Rogers* and the present, is whether the injection itself was the result of a voluntary and informed decision by the person injecting himself. In *R v Rogers*, as in the present case, it was. That case was, therefore, wrongly decided.

21. It is unnecessary to review the case law on this subject in any detail. In *R v Cato* [1976] 1 WLR 110 the defendant had injected the deceased with heroin and the present problem did not arise. In *R v Dalby* [1982] 1 WLR 425 the deceased had died following the consumption of drugs which the defendant had supplied but the deceased had injected. There was apparently no discussion of section 23, but it was held that the supply could not support a conviction of manslaughter. At the trial of the present appellant there was no consideration of section 23 and the trial judge effectively stopped defence counsel submitting to the jury that the appellant had not caused the death of the deceased. In dismissing his first appeal the Court of Appeal said:

> 'We can see no reason why, on the facts alleged by the Crown, the appellant in the instant case might not have been guilty of an offence under section 23 of the Offences against the Person Act 1861. Perhaps more relevantly, the injection of the heroin into himself by Bosque was itself an unlawful act, and if the appellant assisted in and wilfully encouraged that unlawful conduct, he would himself be acting unlawfully.'

But the court gave no detailed consideration to the terms of section 23, and it is now accepted that the deceased's injection of himself was not an unlawful act.

22. In *R v Dias* [2002] 2 Cr App R 96 the defendant had been convicted of manslaughter. He had prepared a syringe charged with heroin which he had handed to the deceased, who had injected himself. The court recognised that the chain of causation had probably been broken by the free and informed

decision of the deceased, and noted the error in the decision on the appellant's first appeal as to the unlawfulness of the deceased's injection of himself.

...

24. It is possible to imagine factual scenarios in which two people could properly be regarded as acting together to administer an injection. But nothing of the kind was the case here. As in *R v Dalby* and *R v Dias* the appellant supplied the drug to the deceased, who then had a choice, knowing the facts, whether to inject himself or not. The heroin was, as the certified question correctly recognises, self-administered, not jointly administered. The appellant did not administer the drug. Nor, for reasons already given, did the appellant cause the drug to be administered to or taken by the deceased.

Appeal allowed

In *Burgess* [2008] EWCA Crim 516, the Court of Appeal subsequently suggested that had the matter fallen for consideration, D's act of raising V's vein would make him responsible for the administration. It was held that 'if a defendant may be convicted on the basis that the fatal dose was jointly administered then it follows that he is not automatically entitled to be acquitted if the deceased rather than the defendant physically operated the plunger'.

■ **Question**

Consider D's liability if:

(i)   he puts cyanide in V's tea and hands V the tea;

(ii) he puts cyanide in V's tea and leaves the cup by V's bedside;

(iii) he puts cyanide in V's tea and gets X, V's 9-year-old child, to take it to him.

What difference does it make in each of these examples if V knows that the tea contains cyanide?

18.6.3 Maliciously

R v Cunningham
[1957] 2 All ER 412, Court of Criminal Appeal
The case is set out in section 5.3, p 117.

R v Cato
(section 18.6.1, p 666), http://www.bailii.org/uk/cases/UKHL/2007/8.html

Lord Widgery [the court considered *Cunningham* [1957] 2 All ER 412 at 413 in a passage which is set out in section 5.3, p 117, and continued:]

No doubt if the injury to the victim is indirect, then the element of foresight arises and the element of foresight will be taken from the words of Byrne J in *Cunningham*. But these problems do not arise when the act complained of is done directly to the person of the victim, as it was in this case. We think in this case, where the act was entirely a direct one, that the requirement of malice is satisfied if the syringe was deliberately inserted into the body of Farmer, as it undoubtedly was, and if Cato at a time when he so inserted the syringe knew that the syringe contained a noxious substance. That is enough, we think, in this type of direct injury case to satisfy the requirement of maliciousness.

Appeal dismissed

■ *Questions*

Does it make sense for the purposes of s 23 to draw, as was done in *Cato*, a distinction between injuries directly and indirectly done? Where the injury is directly done, in what precise respect does Lord Widgery see the mens rea as differing from a case where the injury is caused indirectly?

In *Hill* (1985) 81 Cr App R 206, CA; revsd (1986) 83 Cr App R 386, HL, D, who admitted he was attracted to young boys, gave Tenuate Dospan tablets to boys of 11 and 13. He told them they were 'speed' tablets which would make them feel cheerful. These tablets were available only on prescription (D got them on the black market) as slimming tablets and a side effect of them, of which D was aware, was that if taken at the wrong time or in excess of the appropriate dose they could cause sleeplessness. The prosecution's case was that D's intention in giving the tablets was to disinhibit the boys so as to cause them to lose their natural reserve and be more inclined to do things that they would otherwise not do. One of the boys who stayed with D spent a sleepless night but D made no sexual advances. Both boys suffered from diarrhoea and vomiting. The Court of Appeal quashed D's convictions under s 24 on the ground that the trial judge's direction to the jury left it open to them to convict if D's intention had been only to keep the boys awake. The following question was then certified: 'whether the offence of administering a noxious thing contrary to s 24 ... is capable of being committed when a noxious thing is administered to a person without lawful excuse with the intention only of keeping that person awake.' The House, restoring D's convictions, held that the trial judge's direction did not leave it open to the jury to convict if they found that D's intention was only to keep the boys awake and accordingly found it unnecessary to answer the certified question. 'It is,' said Lord Griffiths (at 390), 'in any event, a question which it is not sensible to attempt to answer without knowing the factual background against which it is asked. If the noxious thing is administered for a purely benevolent purpose such as keeping a pilot of an aircraft awake the answer will almost certainly be no, but if administered for a malevolent purpose such as a prolonged interrogation the answer will almost certainly be yes.' This appears to have been the view of the Court of Appeal. In *Weatherall* [1968] Crim LR 115 (HHJ Brodrick), D administered a drug called Tuinal to his wife to make her sleep more soundly so that he could search her handbag for letters which he thought might prove her guilty of adultery. The judge ruled that there was no evidence of an intent to annoy or aggrieve. Do you agree?

■ *Question*

Suppose that when Cunningham (section 5.3) pulled the gas meter from the wall he had realized that the gas would escape into the adjoining house but had thought that the occupants would be no more than mildly discomfited. Could he be convicted of the offences under s 23 and s 24?

18.7 Slavery and torture

The Coroners and Justice Act 2009, s 71, created new offences of holding another in slavery, servitude or compulsory labour where D knew or ought to have known that the person is so held. The offences are based on Article 4 of the ECHR. The maximum penalty on indictment is 14 years' imprisonment.

71. Slavery, servitude and forced or compulsory labour

(1) A person (D) commits an offence if—

    (a) D holds another person in slavery or servitude and the circumstances are such that D knows or ought to know that the person is so held, or

    (b) D requires another person to perform forced or compulsory labour and the circumstances are such that D knows or ought to know that the person is being required to perform such labour.

(2) In subsection (1) the references to holding a person in slavery or servitude or requiring a person to perform forced or compulsory labour are to be construed in accordance with Article 4 of the Human Rights Convention (which prohibits a person from being held in slavery or servitude or being required to perform forced or compulsory labour).

In *A-G's Reference (Nos 2, 3, 4 and 5 of 2013)* [2013] EWCA Crim 324 Lord Judge CJ made the following observations on the new offences.

6. Section 71 of the Coroners and Justice Act 2009 . . . created an offence capable of being committed in three different ways. This new offence does not require that the victim should have been trafficked, and does not address or create a new offence relating to immigration crime. The first offence involves slavery, the second, servitude, and the third, forced or compulsory labour. In the order of seriousness, slavery is the most grave offence, followed by servitude, and then forced or compulsory labour. Although this is the least serious form of these offences, it remains a serious offence in its own right.

7. The distinction between these three forms of the same offence is illuminatingly described by this Court in *Moore* [2001] EWCA Crim. 1691 applying the jurisprudence of the European Court of Human Rights in *Saliadin v France* . . . and *Van Droogenbroeck v Belgium* . . .

'we have found assistance on what may be described as the hierarchy of the denial of personal autonomy to which Article 4 and thus s.4 of the 2004 Act relate in *Clayton's and Tomlinson's "The Law of Human Rights"*, 2nd Edition, volume 1, paragraphs 9.17 to 9.20 (on the concepts of "slavery" and "servitude") and paragraph 9.25 (on the concept of "forced or compulsory labour"), where the following commentary appears:

"9.17 . . . 'Slavery' involves being in the legal ownership of another—a concept which is sometimes referred to as 'chattel slavery'. It has been suggested that this concept has evolved to encompass various other forms of slavery which are also based on the 'exercise of any or all of the powers attaching to the right of ownership.' In practice, issues concerning slavery have not arisen under the Convention because legally sanctioned slavery does not exist in any of the states which are parties to it.

9.18. 'Servitude' also embraces the totality of the status or condition of a person. However, it is distinguishable from slavery in that servitude does not involve ownership, but concerns less extensive forms of restraint. For Convention purposes 'servitude' means an obligation to provide one's services that is imposed by the use of coercion.

9.19. Servitude can be differentiated from forced labour. In the *Van Droogenbroeck* case, the Commission stated that: In addition to the obligation to provide another with certain services the concept of servitude includes the obligation on the part of the 'serf' to live on another's property and the impossibility of changing his condition . . .

9.25 . . . Forced labour connotes direct compulsion whereas compulsory labour impliedly includes *indirect* forms of compulsion as well . . . In most cases the distinction between the two is unnecessary."

In descending order of gravity, therefore, "slavery" stands at the top of the hierarchy, "servitude" in the middle, and "forced or compulsory labour" at the bottom.'

Section 134 of the Criminal Justice Act 1988 introduced a new offence of torture into English law.

A public official or person acting in an official capacity, whatever his nationality, commits the offence of torture if in the United Kingdom or elsewhere he intentionally inflicts severe pain or suffering on another in the performance or purported performance of his official duties.

The offence carries a maximum sentence of life imprisonment.

18.8 Reform of the law of offences against the person

The Home Office Consultation Document, *Violence: Reforming the Offences Against the Person Act 1861* (February 1998) acknowledged that, 'That Act was itself not a coherent statement of the law but a consolidation of much older law. It is therefore not surprising that the law has been widely criticised as archaic and unclear and that it is now in urgent need of reform.' Lord Ackner has agreed with the blunter criticism that the Act is a ragbag of offences brought together from a wide variety of sources with no attempt, as the draftsman frankly acknowledged, to introduce consistency as to substance or as to form: *Savage* [1991] 4 All ER 698 at 721. But, notwithstanding the admitted urgency, nothing more has been heard (as at February 2014) from the Home Office since February 1998, so lawyers and students must continue to grapple with the archaic and unclear law.

The Home Office Consultation Document included a draft Bill. The Bill is based on the recommendations first made by the Criminal Law Revision Committee, Fourteenth Report, *Offences Against the Person* (1980), Cmnd 7844, adopted in the Law Commission Draft Code and then, in a modified form, in Law Commission Report No 218 (1993).

The law in this area is far from satisfactory, for a variety of reasons. The Law Commission commented that it 'was defective on grounds both of effectiveness and of justice' (Consultation Paper No 122, *Legislating the Criminal Code: Offences Against the Person and General Principles* (1992)). It is an area of law which is very clearly in need of reform. The Law Commission Report No 218 contained recommendations, but these have been superseded by those in the Home Office, *Consultation Paper on Violence* (1998), on which see J. C. Smith, 'Offences Against The Person: The Home Office Consultation Paper' [1998] Crim LR 317. Relevant clauses provide as follows:

1. Intentional serious injury

(1) A person is guilty of an offence if he intentionally causes serious injury to another.

(2) A person is guilty of an offence if he omits to do an act which he has a duty to do at common law, the omission results in serious injury to another, and he intends the omission to have that result.

(3) An offence under this section is committed notwithstanding that the injury occurs outside England and Wales if the act causing injury is done in England and Wales or the omission resulting in injury is made there.

(4) A person guilty of an offence under this section is liable on conviction on indictment to imprisonment for life.

2. Reckless serious injury

(1) A person is guilty of an offence if he recklessly causes serious injury to another.

(2) An offence under this section is committed notwithstanding that the injury occurs outside England and Wales if the act causing injury is done in England and Wales.

(3) A person guilty of an offence under this section is liable—

(a) on conviction on indictment, to imprisonment for a term not exceeding 7 years;

(b) on summary conviction, to imprisonment for a term not exceeding 6 months or a fine not exceeding the statutory maximum or both.

3. Intentional or reckless injury

(1) A person is guilty of an offence if he intentionally or recklessly causes injury to another.

(2) An offence under this section is committed notwithstanding that the injury occurs outside England and Wales if the act causing injury is done in England and Wales.

(3) A person guilty of an offence under this section is liable—

(a) on conviction on indictment, to imprisonment for a term not exceeding 5 years;

(b) on summary conviction, to imprisonment for a term not exceeding 6 months or a fine not exceeding the statutory maximum or both.

4. Assault

(1) A person is guilty of an offence if—

(a) he intentionally or recklessly applies force to or causes an impact on the body of another, or

(b) he intentionally or recklessly causes the other to believe that any such force or impact is imminent.

(2) No such offence is committed if the force or impact, not being intended or likely to cause injury, is in the circumstances such as is generally acceptable in the ordinary conduct of daily life and the defendant does not know or believe that it is in fact unacceptable to the other person.

(3) A person guilty of an offence under this section is liable on summary conviction to imprisonment for a term not exceeding 6 months or a fine not exceeding level 5 on the standard scale or both.

5. Assault on a constable

(1) A person is guilty of an offence if he assaults—

(a) a constable acting in the execution of his duty, or

(b) a person assisting a constable acting in the execution of his duty.

(2) For the purposes of this section a person assaults if he commits the offence under section 4.

(3) A reference in this section to a constable acting in the execution of his duty includes a reference to a constable who is a member of a police force maintained in Scotland or Northern Ireland when he is executing a warrant, or otherwise acting in England or Wales, by virtue of an enactment conferring powers on him in England and Wales....

(5) A person guilty of an offence under this section is liable on summary conviction to imprisonment for a term not exceeding 6 months or a fine not exceeding level 5 on the standard scale or both.

6. Causing serious injury to resist arrest etc.

(1) A person is guilty of an offence if he causes serious injury to another intending to resist, prevent or terminate the lawful arrest or detention of himself or a third person.

(2) The question whether the defendant believes the arrest or detention is lawful must be determined according to the circumstances as he believes them to be.

(3) A person guilty of an offence under this section is liable on conviction on indictment to imprisonment for life.

7. Assault to resist arrest etc.

(1) A person is guilty of an offence if he assaults another intending to resist, prevent or terminate the lawful arrest or detention of himself or a third person.

(2) The question whether the defendant believes the arrest or detention is lawful must be determined according to the circumstances as he believes them to be.

(3) For the purposes of this section a person assaults if he commits the offence under section 4.

(4) A person guilty of an offence under this section is liable—

  (a) on conviction on indictment, to imprisonment for a term not exceeding 2 years;

  (b) on summary conviction, to imprisonment for a term not exceeding 6 months or a fine not exceeding the statutory maximum or both.

FURTHER READING

On assault and battery

M. Hirst, 'Assault, Battery and Indirect Violence' [1999] Crim LR 557

J. Horder, 'Reconsidering Psychic Assault' [1998] Crim LR 392

J. E. Stannard, 'Sticks, Stones and Words: Emotional Harm and the English Criminal Law' (2010) 74 J Crim L 533

On HIV transmission

S. H. Bronitt, 'Spreading Disease and the Criminal Law' [1994] Crim LR 21

D. Ormerod and M. J. Gunn, 'Criminal Liability for the Transmission of HIV' [1996] 1 Web JCLI

J. Slater, 'HIV, Trust and the Criminal Law' (2011) 75 J Crim L 309

K. J. M. Smith, 'Sexual Etiquette, Public Interest and the Criminal Law' (1991) 42 NILQ 309

On racially and religiously aggravated assaults

M. A. Walters, 'Conceptualizing "Hostility" for Hate Crime Law: Minding "the Minutiae" when Interpreting Section 28(1)(a) of the Crime and Disorder Act 1998' (2014) 34 OJLS 47

19

Consent and offences against the person

19.1 Introduction

In the previous chapter we examined the range of offences against the person. In this chapter we examine the controversial question of whether and, if so, when a sane adult should be permitted to consent to harm to himself or to the risk of harm to himself.

The controversies that will be examined in this chapter include the following:

(i)   the threshold of harm—should V be permitted to consent to any level of harm or only to minor harms;

(ii) whether a person should be permitted to consent to different levels of harm in certain activities: surgery, boxing, horseplay, etc;

(iii) whether the transmission or risk of transmission of diseases or infections can be consented to;

(iv) what constitutes 'true' consent.

The law in this area is heavily influenced by policy considerations, as the following case demonstrates.

R v Barnes
[2004] EWCA Crim 3246, Court of Appeal, Criminal Division, http://www.bailii.org/ew/cases/EWCA/Crim/2004/3246.html

(Lord Woolf CJ, Cresswell and Simon JJ)

D caused V a serious leg injury during an amateur football match. D was prosecuted for an offence of unlawfully and maliciously inflicting grievous bodily harm on the basis that the tackle was late, unnecessary, reckless and high up the legs. D claimed that the tackle had been a fair, if hard, sliding challenge and that any injury had been accidental. The jury were directed that D could only be guilty if the prosecution had proved that what had occurred had not been by way of 'legitimate sport'. D was convicted and appealed.

Lord Woolf CJ:

6. When criminal proceedings are justified, then, depending upon their gravity, the prosecution can be for: assault; assault occasioning actual bodily harm contrary to Section 47 of the 1861 Act; unlawfully wounding or inflicting grievous bodily harm contrary to Section 20 of the 1861 Act; or wounding or causing grievous bodily harm with intent contrary to Section 18 of the 1861 Act. If, unfortunately, death results from the assault, the charge could be one of manslaughter or even murder depending upon the defendant's intent.

7. When no bodily harm is caused, the consent of the victim to what happened is always a defence to a charge. Where at least bodily harm is caused, consent is generally irrelevant because it has been

long established by our courts that, exceptional situations apart, as a matter of law a person cannot consent to having bodily harm inflicted upon him.

8. To this general rule, there are obvious exceptions. A patient can lawfully consent to having an operation performed upon him by a surgeon, even though he will inevitably suffer bodily harm while the operation is being performed. Another exception is physical injury in the course of contact sports such as football or boxing. Boxing is different from football in that it is inherent in boxing that the combatants intend to injure each other. This should not be the position in football, albeit that taking part in a football match does give rise to a risk of injury and even grievous injury.

9. There is authority to support what we have said so far. The relevant authorities were exhaustively considered by the House of Lords in the course of their speeches in *R v Brown* [1994] 1 A.C. 212. [discussed in section 19.4]... The speeches in that case make it clear that the rule and the exceptions to the rule that a person cannot consent to his being caused actual harm, are based on public policy. The position is dealt with, with particular clarity, by Lord Mustill in his speech in *Brown* at page 262 et seq. Lord Mustill deals first with prize-fighting and boxing and then contact sports such as the various codes of football. (While Lord Mustill dissented as to what the result should be of adopting a public policy test in that case, his analysis of the case law is still of the highest authority.)

10. The same public policy approach is adopted in the very recent decision of this Court in *R v Dica* [2004] Q.B. 1257 [discussed in section 19.3.1]. *Dica* considers the position where, as a result of having sexual intercourse with two women, a male defendant who is HIV positive infects them so that they both are subsequently diagnosed as being HIV positive. This Court held that the man would be guilty of an offence contrary to Section 20 of the 1861 Act if, being aware of his condition, he had sexual intercourse with them without disclosing his condition. On the other hand, this Court considered that he would have a defence if he had made the women aware of his condition, but with this knowledge because they were still prepared to accept the risks involved and consented to having sexual intercourse with him.

11. The advantage of identifying that the defence is based upon public policy is that it renders it unnecessary to find a separate jurisprudential basis for application of the defence in the various different factual contexts in which an offence could be committed. For example, it explains why boxing, despite the fact that participants intend to hurt each other, is ordinarily considered a lawful sport, whereas prize-fighting is not. It also means that changing public attitudes can affect the activities which are classified as unlawful, as the judgment in *Dica* demonstrates. However, so far as contact sports are concerned, the recognition that public policy is the foundation of the defence should not detract from the value of recognising that public policy limits the defence to situations where there has been implicit consent to what occurred.

19.2 How to approach the issue of consent

It is necessary to address two different problems:

(i) situations in which V cannot be said to have given true consent—where, for example, V has been deceived or acts under threats or duress; and

(ii) cases where V gives factual consent but this is treated as a matter of policy as being ineffective in the eyes of the law.

By way of introduction, it must be emphasized that the law is far from straightforward. The most logical approach is, it is suggested:

(1) Ascertain whether V has consented in fact:

   (a) V's apparent consent may have been vitiated by fraud or force;

   (b) if V has not consented consider whether D has a genuine belief in V's consent.

(2) Consider the level of harm inflicted:

(a) if the level of harm is:

(i) one to which V may in law consent (assault or battery) and either V may have consented ((1)(a) above), or

(ii) D may have a genuine belief in V's consent to that harm ((1)(b) above),

D is entitled to be acquitted;

(b) if the level of harm is such that V may not generally consent in law (ABH, wounding, GBH, etc) D will be guilty even if V consented in fact unless either:

(i) the conduct in question represents an exceptional category in which V's consent will be recognized (sports, surgery, boxing, etc) and D has V's consent or a genuine belief in it, or

(ii) D intended only to cause a level of harm to which V's factual consent would be legally recognized (assault or battery) and V had consented to that lower level of harm, or if V had not, D nevertheless genuinely believed that V had.

19.3 Factual consent

The Crown must establish that V was not consenting.

In *H v CPS* [2010] EWHC 1374 (Admin), the Divisional Court sought to emphasize that consent cannot be implied. V was a teacher at a school for children with emotional, behavioural and social needs. D committed battery on V and sought to argue that V, by accepting employment at a school specializing in the education of children with emotional and behavioural issues, had accepted that there would be incidents where relatively minor violence would be used against him by pupils, and that they would have to use physical force to restrain pupils. In rejecting this argument, Cranston J stated that implied consent was limited to cases in which the injury arose in sports and should not be extended to encompass such situations.

19.3.1 Apparent consent vitiated by force or fraud: (1)(a)

V's apparently factual consent may be vitiated by force, or fraud as to the nature of the act or the identity of the actor. Factual consent is used here in the sense that V agreed to the infliction of the force in question, be it a slight touching or force of a more grievous nature.

R v Diana Richardson
[1998] 2 Cr App R 200, Court of Appeal, Criminal Division

(Otton LJ, Turner and Dyson JJ)

R was a dentist. She was suspended from practice by the General Dental Council. She continued to practise as a dentist and treated patients including performing drilling of teeth and fixing of fillings, etc.

In the Crown Court at Nottingham, before HHJ Matthewman QC, following a ruling by the judge the appellant changed her pleas to guilty on six counts of assault occasioning actual bodily harm. She appealed her conviction.

Otton LJ:

The agreed basis upon which the plea of guilty was tendered was that the appellant had practised while suspended, that the treatment was of a reasonable standard and was carried out on willing patients who had presented themselves for such treatment, and that all of the complainants had been treated by her before her suspension, without complaint.

Miss Caroline Bradley on behalf of the appellant now concentrates her argument on the issue of consent. She acknowledges that without consent the surgical procedures carried out were capable of amounting to an assault in law.

The general proposition which underlies this area of the law is that the human body is inviolate but there are circumstances which the law recognises where consent may operate to prevent conduct which would otherwise be classified as an assault from being so treated. Reasonable surgical interference is clearly such an exception. Counsel relies upon the *dicta* of Lord Lane CJ in *A-G's Reference (No 6 of 1980)* (1981) 73 Cr App Rep 63, [1981] QB 715 where it was held that an assailant was not guilty of assault if the victim consented to it but that an exception to that principle existed where the public interest required. Lord Lane said at p 66 and p 719:

> 'Nothing which we have said is intended to cast doubt upon the accepted legality of . . . lawful chastisement . . . reasonable surgical interference . . . etc. The apparent exceptions can be justified as involving the exercise of a legal right, in the case, of chastisement . . . or as needed in the public interest, in other cases.'

Thus it can be accepted that a person may give lawful consent to the infliction of actual bodily harm upon himself and is justifiable as being in the public interest where reasonable surgical treatment is concerned. But the question then arises, what is the effect on the validity of consent, if any, if the complainant has had concealed from them the true nature of the status of the person who, in the guise of performing a reasonable surgical procedure, subsequently inflicts bodily harm.

Professor J C Smith QC, in Smith and Hogan *Criminal Law* (8th ed), at p 420 states:

> 'Fraud does not necessarily negative consent. It does so only if it deceives P as to the identity of the person or the nature of the act.'

This statement of principle is derived from *Clarence* (1888) 22 QBD 23 where the victim [D's wife] consented to sexual intercourse with the accused and although she would not have consented had she been aware of the disease from which D knew he was suffering, this was no assault. Wills J stated at p 7:

> 'That consent obtained by fraud is no consent at all is not true as a general proposition either in fact or in law.'

Stephen J stated at p 44:

> '. . . The only sorts of fraud that so far destroy the effect of a woman's consent as to convert a connection consented to in fact into a rape are frauds as to the nature of the act itself, or as to the identity of the person who does the act.'

There is a clear line of authority concerning fraud and the nature of the act. In *Williams* [1923] 1 KB 340 the appellant, a choir master, had sexual intercourse with a girl of sixteen years of age under the pretence that her breathing was not quite right and that he had to perform an operation to enable her to produce her voice properly. The girl submitted to what was done under the belief, wilfully and fraudulently induced by the appellant, that she was being medically and surgically treated by the appellant and not with any intention that she should have intercourse with him. The Court of Criminal Appeal held that the appellant was properly convicted of rape. Lord Hewart CJ referred to *Case* (1850) 4 Cox CC 220 where a medical practitioner had sexual connection with a girl of fourteen years of age upon the pretence that he was treating her medically and the girl made no resistance owing to a bona fide belief that she was being medically treated. It was held that he was properly convicted of an assault and might have been convicted of rape. The Lord Chief Justice also referred with approval to the *dicta* of Branson J in *Dicken* (1877) 14 Cox CC 8:

> 'The law has laid it down that where a girl's consent is procured by the means which the girl says this prisoner adopted, that is to say, where she is persuaded that what is being done to her is not the ordinary act of sexual intercourse but is some medical or surgical operation in order to give her relief from some disability from which she is suffering, then that is rape although the actual

thing that is done was done with her consent, because she never consented to the act of sexual intercourse. She was persuaded to consent to what he did because she thought it was not sexual intercourse and because she thought it was a surgical operation.'

In *Harms* (1944) 2 DLR 61 the Supreme Court of Canada considered s 298 of the Canadian Criminal Code which established that in order to vitiate consent the false or fraudulent misrepresentation had to be as to the nature and quality of the act. Harms had falsely represented himself to be a medical doctor. Although the complainant knew that he was proposing sexual intercourse she consented thereto because of his representations that the intercourse was in the nature of a medical treatment necessitated by a condition which he said he had diagnosed. Harms was not a medical man at all. The court held that a jury was entitled to conclude that the nature and quality of the act as far as the complainant was concerned was therapeutic and not carnal. In other words, the complainant had consented to a therapeutic act, which it was not, and had not consented to a carnal act which it was. The consent induced by the fraudulent representation was held to have been vitiated.

The later case of *Bolduc and Bird v R* (1967) 63 DLR (2d) 82 was held to be on the other side of the line. The Supreme Court of Canada considered the case of a doctor who falsely represented that his colleague was a medical student and obtained the complainant's consent to the colleague's presence at a vaginal examination. It was held that there was no indecent assault because the fraud was not as to the nature and quality of what was to be done. It was observed that the defendant's conduct was 'unethical and reprehensible', but did not have the effect of vitiating the consent.

In *Papadimitropoulos* (1957) 98 CLR 249 the High Court of Australia considered the case of a complainant who had sexual relations with a man whom she believed to be her husband. Unknown to her no valid marriage ceremony had ever taken place. The complainant had consented to sexual intercourse under the belief, fraudulently induced, that she had contracted a valid marriage to the man whom she believed to be her husband. It was held that in these circumstances this did not support a conviction for rape. [His lordship referred to the Australian Court's findings.]

This result is not altogether surprising, for otherwise every bigamist would be guilty of rape.

The Law Commission in their Consultation Paper No 139 'Consent in the Criminal Law', having considered fraud and consent generally proposed a lesser offence of obtaining consent by deception and stated (at para 6.27) that:

'consent should not in general be *nullified* by deception as to any circumstances other than the nature of the act and the identity of the person doing it, but that deception as to other circumstances should give rise to liability for a lesser offence than that of non-consensual conduct. Where the defendant is aware that the other person is or may be mistaken about the nature of the act or the defendant's identity, we think that the other person's consent should be nullified as if the mistake by fraud ... If a deception as to circumstances in question would give rise to liability *only* for our proposed offence of obtaining consent by deception, as distinct from the more serious offence of acting without any consent at all, liability for taking advantage of a self-induced mistake as to that circumstance could at *most* be for the lesser offence.'

It is, thus, unremarkable that neither counsel has been able to cite any authority in which the complainant in a sexual case has been deceived as to the identity of the assailant and her apparent consent has held to have been vitiated by fraud. It is to be noted that section 1(3) Sexual Offences Act 1956 provides that a man can be guilty of rape if he induces a married woman to have sexual intercourse with him by impersonating her husband. However this only covers the type of case where the woman is legally married and for some reason believes that the person with whom she is having sexual relations is her husband when in fact he is not. [This provision has now been repealed and replaced by the Sexual Offences Act 2003, s 76, on which see section 20.2.1.5, p 715.]

Miss Bradley who argued the case ably contends that the complainants were deceived neither as to the nature or quality of the act nor as to the identity of the person carrying out the act. The statutory offence was created to punish such conduct as took place here.

Both before the judge and before this Court the respondent expressly disavowed reliance upon the nature or quality of the act. Mr Peter Walmsley succinctly submitted that the patients were deceived into consenting to treatment by the representation that the defendant was a qualified and practising dentist and not one who had been disqualified. He further submitted that the evidence of the patients was unequivocal: had they known that the defendant had been suspended they would not have consented to any treatment. If the treatment had been given by a person impersonating a dentist it would have been an assault. There was no distinction to be drawn between the unqualified dentist and one who is suspended. On this basis there was a mistake as to the true identity of the defendant.

We are unable to accept that argument. There is no basis for the proposition that the rules which determine the circumstances in which consent is vitiated can be different according to whether the case is one of sexual assault or one where the assault is non-sexual. The common element in both these cases is that they involve an assault, and the question is whether consent has been negatived. It is nowhere suggested that the common law draws such a distinction. The common law is not concerned with the question whether the mistaken consent has been induced by fraud on the part of the accused or has been self induced. It is the nature of the mistake that is relevant, and not the reason why the mistake has been made. In summary, either there is consent to actions on the part of a person in the mistaken belief that he or they are other than they truly are, in which case it is assault or, short of this, there is no assault.

In essence the Crown contended that the concept of the 'identity of the person' should be extended to cover the qualifications or attributes of the dentist on the basis that the patients consented to treatment by a qualified dentist and not a suspended one. We must reject that submission. In all the charges brought against the appellant the complainants were fully aware of the identity of the appellant. To accede to the submission would be to strain or distort the every day meaning of the word identity, the dictionary definition of which is 'the condition of being the same'.

It was suggested in argument that we might be assisted by the civil law of consent, where such expressions as 'real' or 'informed' consent prevail. In this regard the criminal and the civil law do not run along the same track. The concept of informed consent has no place in the criminal law. It would also be a mistake, in our view, to introduce the concept of a duty to communicate information to a patient about the risk of an activity before consent to an act can be treated as valid. The gravamen of the appellant's conduct in the instant case was that the complainants consented to treatment from her although their consent had been procured by her failure to inform them that she was no longer qualified to practice. This was clearly reprehensible and may well found the basis of a civil claim for damages. But we are quite satisfied that it is not a basis for finding criminal liability in the field of offences against the person.

We have arrived at this conclusion without any real difficulty. It is our considered view that the common law has developed as far as it can without the intervention of the legislature. For the better part of a century, the common law concept of consent in the criminal law has been certain and clearly delineated. It is not for this Court to attempt to unwrite the law which has been settled for so long. This is an area in which it is to be hoped that the proposals of the Law Commission will be given an early opportunity for implementation.

Finally, we feel obliged to observe that we are left with a state of unease at the procedure which was adopted in this case. We are concerned about the wisdom of the Crown being prepared to accept 'reasonable surgical intervention' as the factual basis of the plea. If the allegations of assault occasioning actual bodily harm had been persisted in and proved in accordance with the committal statements there would have been little or no room for the defence of consent. The nature of the dental treatment (if proved) would have gone far beyond the treatment that was either contemplated or consented to by the patients or their parents.

Accordingly, we must allow the appeal and quash the convictions.

Appeal allowed. Convictions quashed

■ *Questions*

How could the prosecution both (i) agree that the treatment was of a reasonable standard and (ii) allege that it constituted actual bodily harm? Is a dentist properly drilling a diseased tooth (or a surgeon properly amputating a limb to save life) causing 'harm'? If consent had been vitiated—for example, there had been a misrepresentation of identity—there would have been an assault but, if the treatment was necessary and competently done, would it have been an assault occasioning actual bodily harm? In the circumstances of *Richardson*, would it have been an assault occasioning actual bodily harm if the treatment had been harmful? Does V's consent to proper treatment negative D's assault if the treatment by D is improper? What if the treatment amounts to *grievous* bodily harm?

The Sexual Offences Act 2003, s 76, provides that it shall be conclusively presumed that V was not consenting where D has deceived V as to the nature or purpose of his acts or as to his identity. In relation to non-sexual offences, the question remains whether a deception as to the quality or purpose of the act, as opposed to its nature, will vitiate consent. See section 20.2.1.5, p 715.

R v Dica

[2004] EWCA Crim 1103, Court of Appeal, Criminal Division, http://www.bailii.org/ew/cases/EWCA/Crim/2004/1103.html

(Lord Woolf CJ, Judge LJ and Forbes J)

D was charged with two offences under the Offences Against the Person Act 1861, s 20, where, knowing that he was HIV positive, he had unprotected intercourse with two sexual partners causing each to be infected with the virus. He did not disclose his HIV status to either partner. He was convicted and appealed on the basis that (i) the trial judge had, notwithstanding *Clarence* (1889) 22 QB 23, held that it was open to the jury to convict D, and (ii) the trial judge had ruled that whether or not the complainants knew of D's condition, their consent, if any, was irrelevant and provided no defence (this issue is dealt with in section 20.2.1.5., p 715).

Lord Justice Judge [his lordship stated the facts and continued]:

10. It is perhaps important to emphasise at the outset that the prosecution did not allege that the appellant had either raped or deliberately set out to infect the complainants with disease. Rather, it was alleged that when he had consensual sexual intercourse with them, knowing that he himself was suffering from HIV, he was reckless whether they might become infected. Thus, in the language of the counts in the indictment, he 'inflicted grievous bodily harm' on them both.

11. It was not in dispute that at least on the majority of occasions, and with both complainants, sexual intercourse was unprotected. Recklessness, as such, was not in issue. If protective measures had been taken by the appellant that would have provided material relevant to the jury's decision whether, in all the circumstances, recklessness was proved.

12. Although both women were willing to have sexual intercourse with the appellant, the prosecution's case was that their agreement would never have been given if they had known of the appellant's condition. The appellant would have contended that he told both women of his condition, and that they were nonetheless willing to have sexual intercourse with him, a case which in the light of the judge's ruling, he did not support in evidence. The suggestion would have been strongly disputed by them both.

. . .

(a) The Crown's case

Concealment of the truth by the appellant

33. The judgments of the majority in *Clarence* included considerable discussion about the issue of fraud (in the sense of concealment), and the consequences if consent were vitiated. Again, however, the observations have to be put into the context of the perceived requirement that in the absence of an assault Clarence could not be guilty of the s.20 offence, and the deemed consent of the wife to have sexual intercourse with her husband....

36. Clarence did not face a charge of rape or indecent assault, yet the concept of his wife's notional consent to the act of sexual intercourse was inextricably linked with the quashing of his convictions for offences of violence. He was not charged with an offence under s 3(2) of the Criminal Law Amendment Act 1885, until recently, s.3 of the Sexual Offences Act 1956, and now in slightly different terms, s.4 of the Sexual Offences Act 2003....

37. The present case is concerned with and confined to s.20 offences alone, without the burdensome fiction of deemed consent to sexual intercourse. The question for decision is whether the victims' consent to sexual intercourse, which as a result of his alleged concealment was given in ignorance of the facts of the appellant's condition, *necessarily amounted to consent to the risk of being infected by him* (emphasis added). If that question must be answered 'Yes', the concept of consent in relation to s.20 is devoid of real meaning.

38. The position here is analogous to that considered in *R v Tabassum* [2000] 2 CAR 328. The appellant was convicted of indecently assaulting women who allowed him to examine their breasts in the mistaken belief that he was medically qualified. Rose LJ considered *Clarence*, and pointed out that in relation to the infection suffered by the wife, this was an additional, unexpected, consequence of sexual intercourse, which was irrelevant to her consent to sexual intercourse with her husband. Rejecting the argument that an 'undoubted consent' could only be negatived if the victim had been deceived or mistaken about the nature and quality of the act, and that consent was not negatived 'merely because the victim would not have agreed to the act if he or she had known all the facts', Rose LJ observed, in forthright terms, 'there was no true consent'. Again, in *R v Cort* [2003] 3 WLR 1300, a case of kidnapping, the complainants had consented to taking a ride in a motor car, but not to being kidnapped. They wanted transport, not kidnapping. Kidnapping may be established by carrying away by fraud.

> 'It is difficult to see how one could ever consent to that once fraud was indeed established. The "nature" of the act here is therefore taking the complainant away by fraud. The complainant did not consent to that event. All that she consented to was a ride in the car, which in itself is irrelevant to the offence and a different thing from that with which Mr Cort is charged.'

39. In our view, on the assumed fact now being considered, the answer is entirely straightforward. These victims consented to sexual intercourse. Accordingly, the appellant was not guilty of rape. Given the long-term nature of the relationships, if the appellant concealed the truth about his condition from them, and therefore kept them in ignorance of it, there was no reason for them to think that they were running any risk of infection, and they were not consenting to it. On this basis, there would be no consent sufficient in law to provide the appellant with a defence to the charge under s.20.

...

In *Dica*, the victims had been defrauded as to the risk of infection (and hence had not consented to bodily harm), but had not been defrauded as to the nature of the act of sexual intercourse (and hence had not been raped).

The Court of Appeal finally lays to rest that aspect of *Clarence* relating to implied consent. Thus, where V is unaware of D's infected state, by consenting to the act of unprotected sexual intercourse she cannot be said to have impliedly consented to the risk of infection from that intercourse. In principle, this aspect of the decision is welcome. True consent is based on an informed choice being made only when V has *all* 'information' relevant to the decision. The decision respects the principle.

■ *Questions*

1. To what extent is D obliged to inform his sexual partners where D merely suspects that he is HIV positive?

2. Does D have a right not to know what his own HIV status is? Cf V. Tadros, *Criminal Responsibility* (2006), p 247.

John Spencer has written that:

To infect an unsuspecting person with a grave disease you know you have, *or may have*, by behaviour that you know involves a risk of transmission, and that you know you could easily modify to reduce or eliminate the risk, is to harm another in a way that is both needless and callous. For that reason, criminal liability is justified unless there are strong countervailing reasons. In my view there are not. (J. Spencer, 'Liability for Reckless Infection: Part 2' (2004) 154 NLJ 385, 448)

In contrast, M. Weait ('Criminal Law and the Sexual Transmission of HIV: *R v Dica*' (2005) 68 MLR 121) writes:

While it may be right and proper to affirm that consent to intercourse itself should not be taken to imply consent to the risk of resultant harm, it is arguable that *Dica* does not—at least so far as its interpretation of *Clarence* is concerned—mean that consent to intercourse will necessarily imply an absence of consent to harm where other conditions are met—i.e. where the defendant is ignorant of his HIV positive status or where he knows and his partner is aware of the fact. If it were otherwise, *Dica* would mean that a person who was ignorant of his HIV positive status could not lawfully have unprotected consensual intercourse with anyone, nor could a person who knew of a partner's HIV positive status give a legally recognised consent to intercourse with them. If such a couple were to have sexual intercourse it seems counter-intuitive to suggest that they are not having consensual intercourse, but are instead having non-consensual intercourse in respect of which there has been consent to the risk of HIV transmission. Such an interpretation would render the distinction between conduct of this kind and rape so fine as to be unsustainable—a conclusion which the Court of Appeal was keen to preclude.

See further M. Weait, *Intimacy and Responsibility: The Criminalisation of HIV Transmission* (2006); M. Weait, 'Knowledge, Autonomy, Consent: *R v Konzani*' [2005] Crim LR 763. On whether the mens rea for an offence of transmission following *Dica* and *Konzani* involves D's knowledge that he is infected, see S. Ryan, 'Reckless Transmission of HIV: Knowledge and Culpability' [2006] Crim LR 981.

Note that the CPS has a special policy on prosecuting sexually transmitted infection cases: http://www.cps.gov.uk/publications/prosecution/sti.html.

■ *Questions*

1. Is D taking a risk of transmission where he knows that he is HIV positive and uses a condom, being aware that even so there is 'a' risk of transmission and infection? Is this a *justified* risk for him to take? Is it a justified risk irrespective of disclosing his status to V?

2. To what extent is V's consent dependent on accurate information?

R v Konzani

[2005] EWCA Crim 706, Court of Appeal, Criminal Division, http://www.bailii.org/ew/cases/EWCA/Crim/2005/706.html

(Judge LJ, Grigson J and Radford HHJ)

K had been informed that he was HIV positive, and he subsequently had unprotected sexual intercourse with three complainants, having not revealed to any of them that he was HIV positive. Each of the three contracted HIV. K was charged with inflicting grievous bodily harm on each of them contrary to the Offences Against the Person Act 1861 (OAPA), s 20. K argued that by consenting to the intercourse, each consented to the risks associated with sexual intercourse. The judge directed the jury that the consent of the complainant might provide the defendant with a defence only if that consent was an informed and willing consent to the risk of contracting HIV. The jury convicted. The defendant appealed on the basis that (i) the judge had failed to leave to the jury the issue whether the defendant might honestly, even if unreasonably, have believed that the complainants had consented to the risk of contracting the HIV virus; and (ii) that the judge had misdirected the jury on the issue of consent.

Judge LJ:.

...5. Notwithstanding their evidence that he withheld vital information about his condition from them, and that each complainant expressly denied that she consented to the risk of catching the HIV virus from him, counsel on his behalf addressed the jury on the basis that by consenting to unprotected sexual intercourse with him, they were impliedly consenting to all the risks associated with sexual intercourse. He argued that as infection with the HIV virus may be one possible consequence of unprotected sexual intercourse, the complainants had consented to the risk of contracting the HIV virus from him. Accordingly he should be acquitted. By their verdicts, the jury found that none of the complainants consented to the risk of contracting the HIV virus.

...

Consent

34. Referring to HIV, the judge directed the jury that they had to be sure that the complainant in each individual case:

'...did not willingly consent to the risk of suffering that infection. Note that I use the phrase "to the risk of suffering that infection" and not merely just "to suffering it". That is an important point which Mr Roberts rightly drew to your attention in his speech to you this morning. He put it this way, it is whether she consented to that risk, not consented to being given the disease which is, as he put it graphically, a mile away from the former. That is right, but note that I use the word "willingly" in the phrase "willingly consent", and I did that to highlight that the sort of consent I am talking about means consciously.'

He returned to the clear and important distinction between 'running a risk on one hand and consenting to run that risk on the other', pointing out that the prosecution had to establish that the complainant 'did not willingly consent to the risk of suffering the infection in the sense of her having consciously thought about it at the time and decided to run it'. He added that the appellant should be acquitted, if, in relation to any complainant, she had thought of the risk of getting HIV, and nevertheless decided to take the risk. In answer to a question from the jury, he returned to emphasise that before the appellant could be convicted, the prosecution had to prove that she 'did not willingly consent to the risk of suffering that infection', and he repeated that for the purposes of his direction, 'willingly' meant 'consciously'. He again repeated the distinction between 'running a risk on the one hand and consenting to run that risk on the other', adding that the 'willing' consent involved knowing the implications of infection with the HIV virus.

35. In short, the judge explained that before the consent of the complainant could provide the appellant with a defence, it was required to be an informed and willing consent to the risk of contracting HIV...

42. The recognition in *R v Dica* of informed consent as a defence was based on 'but limited by' potentially conflicting public policy considerations. In the public interest, so far as possible, the spread of catastrophic illness must be avoided or prevented. On the other hand, the public interest also requires that the principle of personal autonomy in the context of adult non-violent sexual relationships should be maintained. If an individual who knows that he is suffering from the HIV virus conceals this stark fact from his sexual partner, the principle of her personal autonomy is not enhanced if he is exculpated when he recklessly transmits the HIV virus to her through consensual sexual intercourse. On any view, the concealment of this fact from her almost inevitably means that she is deceived. Her consent is not properly informed, and she cannot give an informed consent to something of which she is ignorant. Equally, her personal autonomy is not normally protected by allowing a defendant who knows that he is suffering from the HIV virus which he deliberately conceals, to assert an honest belief in his partner's informed consent to the risk of the transmission of the HIV virus. Silence in these circumstances is incongruous with honesty, or with a genuine belief that there is an informed consent. Accordingly, in such circumstances the issue either of informed consent, or honest belief in it will only rarely arise: in reality, in most cases, the contention would be wholly artificial.

43. This is not unduly burdensome. The defendant is not to be convicted of this offence unless it is proved that he was reckless. If so, the necessary *mens rea* will be established. Recklessness is a question of fact, to be proved by the prosecution. Equally the defendant is not to be convicted if there was, or may have been an informed consent by his sexual partner to the risk that he would transfer the HIV virus to her. In many cases, as in *Dica* itself, provided recklessness is established, the critical factual area of dispute will address what, if anything, was said between the two individuals involved, one of whom knows, and the other of whom does not know, that one of them is suffering the HIV virus. In the final analysis, the question of consent, like the issue of recklessness is fact-specific.

44. In deference to Mr Roberts' submission, we accept that there may be circumstances in which it would be open to the jury to infer that, notwithstanding that the defendant was reckless and concealed his condition from the complainant, she may nevertheless have given an informed consent to the risk of contracting the HIV virus. By way of example, an individual with HIV may develop a sexual relationship with someone who knew him while he was in hospital, receiving treatment for the condition. If so, her informed consent, if it were indeed informed, would remain a defence, to be disproved by the prosecution, even if the defendant had not personally informed her of his condition. Even if she did not in fact consent, this example would illustrate the basis for an argument that he honestly believed in her informed consent. Alternatively, he may honestly believe that his new sexual partner was told of his condition by someone known to them both. Cases like these, not too remote to be fanciful, may arise. If they do, no doubt they will be explored with the complainant in cross-examination. Her answers may demonstrate an informed consent. Nothing remotely like that was suggested here. In a different case, perhaps supported by the defendant's own evidence, material like this may provide a basis for suggesting that he honestly believed that she was giving an informed consent. He may provide an account of the incident, or the affair, which leads the jury to conclude that even if she did not give an informed consent, he may honestly have believed that she did. Acknowledging these possibilities in different cases does not, we believe, conflict with the public policy considerations identified in *R v Dica*. That said, they did not arise in the present case.

45. Why not? In essence because the jury found that the complainants did not give a willing or informed consent to the risks of contracting the HIV virus from the appellant. We recognise that where consent does provide a defence to an offence against the person, it is generally speaking correct that the defendant's honest belief in the alleged victim's consent would also provide a defence. However for this purpose, the defendant's honest belief must be concomitant with the consent which provides a defence. Unless the consent would provide a defence, an honest belief in it would not assist

the defendant. This follows logically from *R v Brown* [see section 19.4.2]. For it to do so here, what was required was some evidence of an honest belief that the complainants, or any one of them, were consenting to the risk that they might be infected with the HIV virus by him. There is not the slightest evidence, direct or indirect, from which a jury could begin to infer that the appellant honestly believed that any complainant consented to that specific risk. As there was no such evidence, the judge's ruling about 'honest belief' was correct. In fact, the honest truth was that the appellant deceived them.

46. In our judgment, the judge's directions to the jury sufficiently explained the proper implications to the case of the consensual participation by each of the complainants to sexual intercourse with the appellant. The jury concluded, in the case of each complainant, that she did not willingly or consciously consent to the risk of suffering the HIV virus.

Appeal against conviction dismissed

19.3.2 D genuinely but mistakenly believes V has consented to an assault or battery: (1)(b)

Consistent with the decisions in *Kimber* [1983] 3 All ER 316, and *Gladstone Williams* (1987) 78 Cr App R 276, section 11.6.1.1, p 415, it was held in *Jones* (1986) 83 Cr App R 375, [1987] Crim LR 123, CA, that there is no assault where D genuinely believes in the other's consent, and it is irrelevant whether that belief is reasonably held or not.

■ *Questions*

D has unprotected sex with V. What is D's liability for an offence against the person if:

(i)   D knows he is HIV positive and he believes that V knows this but he has not told her himself?

(ii) D suspects he may be HIV positive and he believes that V is aware that he, D, may be, but he has not discussed it with her?

19.4 Consent recognized in law

19.4.1 Level of harm capable of being consented to in law: (2)(a)

On the level of harm to which V may in law consent see *Brown* in the following extract.

19.4.2 V may give valid factual consent to assault or battery and higher levels of harm in exceptional categories of conduct: (2)(b)

Beyond assault and battery, the *general* rule is that V may not give valid consent. Only in exceptional cases (surgery, sport, etc) may V consent to the infliction or risk of infliction of more serious injury than assault and battery. This is a controversial approach.

R v Brown

[1992] UKHL 7, House of Lords, http www.bailii.org/uk/cases/UKHL/1992/7.html

(Lords Templeman, Jauncey of Tullichettle, Lowry, Mustill and Slynn of Hadley)

The appellants belonged to a group of sadomasochists who willingly cooperated in the commission of acts of violence against each other for sexual pleasure. Their activities included whipping and caning on the bare buttocks, branding, the application of stinging nettles to the genital area and inserting map pins or fish hooks into the penis. There was no permanent injury done, no infection of the wounds and no evidence that any of the men had sought medical treatment. Their actions were carried out in private and there was no complaint made to the police who found out about these activities by chance when they were investigating other matters. The appellants were convicted of assault occasioning actual bodily harm contrary to s 47, and, in three cases, of malicious wounding contrary to the OAPA, s 20.

These convictions were upheld by the Court of Appeal which certified the following point of law of general public importance:

Where A wounds or assaults B occasioning him actual bodily harm in the course of a sado-masochistic encounter, does the prosecution have to prove lack of consent on the part of B before they can establish A's guilt under section 20 and section 47 of the 1861, Offences Against the Person Act?

Lord Templeman:

Three of the appellants pleaded guilty to charges under section 20 when the trial judge ruled that the consent of the victim afforded no defence.

In the present case each of the appellants intentionally inflicted violence upon another (to whom I refer as 'the victim') with the consent of the victim and thereby occasioned actual bodily harm or in some cases wounding or grievous bodily harm. Each appellant was therefore guilty of an offence under section 47 or section 20 of the Act of 1861 unless the consent of the victim was effective to prevent the commission of the offence or effective to constitute a defence to the charge.

In some circumstances violence is not punishable under the criminal law. When no actual bodily harm is caused, the consent of the person affected precludes him from complaining. There can be no conviction for the summary offence of common assault if the victim has consented to the assault. Even when violence is intentionally inflicted and results in actual bodily harm, wounding or serious bodily harm the accused is entitled to be acquitted if the injury was a foreseeable incident of a lawful activity in which the person injured was participating. Surgery involves intentional violence resulting in actual or sometimes serious bodily harm but surgery is a lawful activity. Other activities carried on with consent by or on behalf of the injured person have been accepted as lawful notwithstanding that they involve actual bodily harm or may cause serious bodily harm. Ritual circumcision, tattooing, ear-piercing and violent sports including boxing are lawful activities.

In earlier days some other forms of violence were lawful and when they ceased to be lawful they were tolerated until well into the 19th century. Duelling and fighting were at first lawful and then tolerated provided the protagonists were voluntary participants. But where the results of these activities was the maiming of one of the participants, the defence of consent never availed the aggressor; see *Hawkins Pleas of the Crown* (1824), 8th edn, chapter 15. A maim was bodily harm whereby a man was deprived of the use of any member of his body which he needed to use in order to fight but a bodily injury was not a maim merely because it was a disfigurement. The act of maim was unlawful because the King was deprived of the services of an able-bodied citizen for the defence of the realm. Violence which maimed was unlawful despite consent to the activity which produced the maiming. In these days there is no difference between maiming on the one hand and wounding or causing grievous bodily harm on the other hand except with regard to sentence.

When duelling became unlawful, juries remained unwilling to convict but the judges insisted that persons guilty of causing death or bodily injury should be convicted despite the consent of the victim.

Similarly, in the old days, fighting was lawful provided the protagonists consented because it was thought that fighting inculcated bravery and skill and physical fitness. The brutality of knuckle fighting however caused the courts to declare that such fights were unlawful even if the protagonists consented. Rightly or wrongly the courts accepted that boxing is a lawful activity.

In *R v Coney* (1882) 8 QBD 534, the court held that a prize-fight in public was unlawful . . .

The conclusion is that a prize-fight being unlawful, actual bodily harm or serious bodily harm inflicted in the course of a prize-fight is unlawful notwithstanding the consent of the protagonists.

In *R v Donovan* [1934] 2 KB 498 the appellant in private beat a girl of seventeen for purposes of sexual gratification, it was said with her consent. Swift J said, at 507 that:

'It is an unlawful act to beat another person with such a degree of violence that the infliction of bodily harm is a probable consequence, and when such an act is proved, consent is immaterial.'

In *A-G's Reference (No 6 of 1980)* [1981] 2 All ER 1057, [1981] QB 715 where two men quarrelled and fought with bare fists Lord Lane CJ, delivering the judgment of the Court of Appeal, said at 719:

'...It is not in the public interest that people should try to cause, or should cause, each other bodily harm for no good reason. Minor struggles are another matter. So, in our judgment, it is immaterial whether the act occurs in private or in public; it is an assault if actual bodily harm is intended and/or caused. This means that most fights will be unlawful regardless of consent. Nothing which we have said is intended to cast doubt upon the accepted legality of properly conducted games and sports, lawful chastisement or correction, reasonable surgical interference, dangerous exhibitions, etc. These apparent exceptions can be justified as involving the exercise of a legal right, in the case of chastisement or correction, or as needed in the public interest, in the other cases.' [Cf *Slingsby*, section 17.2.1.1, p 596.]

Duelling and fighting are both unlawful and the consent of the protagonists affords no defence to charges of causing actual bodily harm, wounding or grievous bodily harm in the course of an unlawful activity.

The appellants and their victims in the present case were engaged in consensual homosexual activities. The attitude of the public towards homosexual practices changed in the second half of this century. Change in public attitudes led to a change in the law.... [Lord Templeman referred to the Wolfenden Report and subsequent legislation.]

My Lords, the authorities dealing with the intentional infliction of bodily harm do not establish that consent is a defence to a charge under the Act of 1861. They establish that the courts have accepted that consent is a defence to the infliction of bodily harm in the course of some lawful activities. The question is whether the defence should be extended to the infliction of bodily harm in the course of sado-masochistic encounters. The Wolfenden Committee did not make any recommendations about sado-masochism and Parliament did not deal with violence in 1967. The Act of 1967 is of no assistance for present purposes because the present problem was not under consideration.

The question whether the defence of consent should be extended to the consequences of sado-masochistic encounters can only be decided by consideration of policy and public interest. Parliament can call on the advice of doctors, psychiatrists, criminologists, sociologists and other experts and can also sound and take into account public opinion. But the question must at this stage be decided by this House in its judicial capacity in order to determine whether the convictions of the appellants should be upheld or quashed.

Counsel for some of the appellants argued that the defence of consent should be extended to the offence of occasioning actual bodily harm under section 47 of the Act of 1861 but should not be available to charges of serious wounding and the inflicting of serious bodily harm under section 20. I do not consider that this solution is practicable. Sado-masochistic participants have no way of foretelling the degree of bodily harm which will result from their encounters. The differences between actual bodily harm and serious bodily harm cannot be satisfactorily applied by a jury in order to determine acquittal or conviction.

Counsel for the appellants argued that consent should provide a defence to charges under both section 20 and section 47 because, it was said, every person has a right to deal with his body as he pleases. I do not consider that this slogan provides a sufficient guide to the policy decision which must now be made. It is an offence for a person to abuse his own body and mind by taking drugs. Although the law is often broken, the criminal law restrains a practice which is regarded as dangerous and injurious to individuals and which if allowed and extended is harmful to society generally. In any event the appellants in this case did not mutilate their own bodies. They inflicted bodily harm on willing victims. Suicide is no longer an offence but a person who assists another to commit suicide is guilty of murder or manslaughter. [NB: his lordship is wrong on this. See section 16.4, p 588.]

The assertion was made on behalf of the appellants that the sexual appetites of sadists and masochists can only be satisfied by the infliction of bodily harm and that the law should not punish the consensual achievement of sexual satisfaction. There was no evidence to support the assertion that sado-masochist activities are essential to the happiness of the appellants or any other participants but the argument would be acceptable if sado-masochism were only concerned with sex, as the appellants contend. In my opinion sado-masochism is not only concerned with sex. Sado-masochism is also concerned with violence. The evidence discloses that the practices of the appellants were unpredictably dangerous and degrading to body and mind and were developed with increasing barbarity and taught to persons whose consents were dubious or worthless.

A sadist draws pleasure from inflicting or watching cruelty. A masochist derives pleasure from his own pain or humiliation. The appellants are middle-aged men. The victims were youths some of whom were introduced to sado-masochism before they attained the age of 21 [then the age of consent for men to have sex with men]. In his judgment in the Court of Appeal, Lord Lane CJ said that two members of the group of which the appellants formed part, namely one Cadman and the appellant Laskey:

> '... were responsible in part for the corruption of a youth K ... It is some comfort at least to be told, as we were, that K has now it seems settled into a normal heterosexual relationship. Cadman had befriended K when the boy was 15 years old. He met him in a cafeteria and, so he says, found out that the boy was interested in homosexual activities. He introduced and encouraged K in "bondage affairs". He was interested in viewing and recording on videotape K and other teenage boys in homosexual scenes ... One cannot overlook the danger that the gravity of the assaults and injuries in this type of case may escalate to even more unacceptable heights.'

[His lordship referred to various of the sadomasochistic acts which had been performed, that while the appellants had not contracted AIDS, two members of the group had died from AIDS, that the assertion that the instruments were sterile could not remove the risk of infection, that cruelty to humans had been supplemented by cruelty to animals in the form of bestiality, and that, given the nature of the acts, it was not surprising there had been no complaint to the police.]

In principle there is a difference between violence which is incidental and violence which is inflicted for the indulgence of cruelty. The violence of sado-masochistic encounters involves the indulgence of cruelty by sadists and the degradation of victims. Such violence is injurious to the participants and unpredictably dangerous. I am not prepared to invent a defence of consent for sado-masochistic encounters which breed and glorify cruelty and result in offences under sections 47 and 20 of the Act of 1861 ...

■ *Questions*

1. Were the defendants engaged in violence or sexual activity?

2. Counsel for some of the appellants argued that consent should be a defence to a charge under s 47 but not to serious wounding or serious bodily harm under s 20. Lord Templeman rejected this because 'differences between actual bodily harm and serious bodily harm cannot be satisfactorily applied by a jury in order to determine acquittal or conviction'. But is this not a distinction which juries are regularly called upon to make?

Lord Jauncey of Tullichettle:.

... It was accepted by all the appellants that a line had to be drawn somewhere between those injuries to which a person could consent to infliction upon himself and those which were so serious that consent was immaterial. They all agreed that assaults occasioning actual bodily harm should be below the line but there was disagreement as to whether all offences against section 20 of the Act of 1861 should be above the line or only those resulting in grievous bodily harm. The four English cases to which I have referred were not concerned with the distinction between the various types of assault and did not therefore have to address the problem raised in these appeals. However it does appear that in *Donovan; A-G's Reference (No 6 of 1980)*, and *Boyea* (1992) 156 JP 505, [1992] Crim LR 574, the infliction of actual bodily harm was considered to be sufficient to negative any consent. Indeed in *Donovan* and *Boyea* such injuries as were sustained by the two women could not have been described as in any way serious. Cave J in *Coney* also appeared to take the same view. On the other hand, Stephen J in *Coney* appeared to consider that it required serious danger to life and limb to negative consent, a view which broadly accords with the passage in his digest to which I have already referred. A similar view was expressed by McInerney J in the Supreme Court of Victoria in *Pallante v Stadiums Property Ltd* [1976] VR 331.

I prefer the reasoning of Cave J in *Coney* and of the Court of Appeal in the later three English cases which I consider to have been correctly decided. In my view the line properly falls to be drawn between assault at common law and the offence of assault occasioning actual bodily harm created by section 47 of the Offences Against the Person Act 1861, with the result that consent of the victim is no answer to anyone charged with the latter offence or with a contravention of section 20 unless the circumstances fall within one of the well known exceptions such as organised sporting contests and games, parental chastisement or reasonable surgery. There is nothing in sections 20 and 47 of the Act of 1861 to suggest that consent is either an essential ingredient of the offences or a defence thereto . . .

[I]n considering the public interest it would be wrong to look only at the activities of the appellants alone, there being no suggestion that they and their associates are the only practitioners of homosexual sado-masochism in England and Wales. This House must therefore consider the possibility that these activities are practised by others and by others who are not so controlled or responsible as the appellants are claimed to be. Without going into details of all the rather curious activities in which the appellants engaged it would appear to be good luck rather than good judgment which has prevented serious injury from occurring. Wounds can easily become septic if not properly treated, the free flow of blood from a person who is HIV positive or who has AIDS can infect another and an inflicter who is carried away by sexual excitement or by drink or drugs could very easily inflict pain and injury beyond the level to which the receiver had consented. Your Lordships have no information as to whether such situations have occurred in relation to other sado-masochistic practitioners. It was no doubt these dangers which caused Lady Mallalieu to restrict her propositions in relation to the public interest to the actual rather than the potential result of the activity. In my view such a restriction is quite unjustified. When considering the public interest potential for harm is just as relevant as actual harm. As Mathew J said in *Coney* (1882) 8 QBD 534, 547:

'There is however abundant authority for saying that no consent can render that innocent which is in fact dangerous.'

Furthermore, the possibility of proselytisation and corruption of young men is a real danger even in the case of these appellants and the taking of video recordings of such activities suggest that secrecy may not be as strict as the appellants claimed to your Lordships. If the only purpose of the activity is the sexual gratification of one or both of the participants what then is the need of a video recording?

My Lords I have no doubt that it would not be in the public interest that deliberate infliction of actual bodily harm during the course of homosexual sado-masochistic activities should be held to be lawful. In reaching this conclusion I have regard to the information available in these appeals and of such inferences as may be drawn therefrom. I appreciate that there may be a great deal of information relevant to these activities which is not available to your Lordships. When Parliament passed the Sexual Offences Act 1967 which made buggery and acts of gross indecency between consenting males lawful it had available the Wolfenden Report (1957) (Cmnd 247) which was the product of an exhaustive research into the problem. If it is to be decided that such activities as the nailing by A of B's foreskin or scrotum to a board or the insertion of hot wax into C's urethra followed by the burning of his penis with a candle or the incising of D's scrotum with a scalpel to the effusion of blood are injurious neither to B, C and D nor to the public interest then it is for Parliament with its accumulated wisdom and sources of information to declare them to be lawful.

There was argument as to whether consent, where available, was a necessary ingredient of the offence of assault or merely a defence. There are conflicting data as to its effect. In Coney Stephen J referred to consent as 'being no defence', whereas in *A-G's Reference (No 6 of 1980)* [1981] 2 All ER 1057, [1981] QB 715 Lord Lane CJ referred to the onus being on the prosecution to negative consent. In *Collins v Wilcock* [1984] 1 WLR 1172, 1177F Goff LJ referred to consent being a defence to a battery. If it were necessary, which it is not, in this appeal to decide which argument was correct I would hold that consent was a defence to but not a necessary ingredient in assault. . . .

I would . . . dismiss the appeals.

[Lord Lowry made a speech dismissing the appeals.]

Lord Mustill:

. . . I ask myself not whether as a result of the decision in this appeal, activities such as those of the appellants should *cease* to be criminal, but rather whether the Act of 1861 (a statute which I venture to repeat once again was clearly intended to penalise conduct of a quite different nature) should in this new situation be interpreted so as to *make* it criminal. Why should this step be taken? Leaving aside repugnance and moral objection, both of which are entirely natural but neither of which are in my opinion grounds upon which the court could properly create a new crime, I can visualise only the following reasons:

1. Some of the practices obviously created a risk of genito-urinary infection, and others of septicaemia. These might indeed have been grave in former times, but the risk of serious harm must surely have been greatly reduced by modern medical science.

2. The possibility that matters might get out of hand, with grave results. . . . If this happened, those responsible would be punished according to the ordinary law, in the same way as those who kill or injure in the course of more ordinary sexual activities are regularly punished. But to penalise the appellants' conduct even if the extreme consequences do not ensue, just because they might have done so would require an assessment of the degree of risk, and the balance of this risk against the interests of individual freedom. Such a balancing is in my opinion for Parliament, not the courts. . . .

3. I would give the same answer to the suggestion that these activities involved a risk of accelerating the spread of auto-immune deficiency syndrome, and that they should be brought within the Act of 1861 in the interests of public health. The consequence would be strange, since what is currently the principal cause for the transmission of this scourge, namely consenting buggery between males, is now legal. Nevertheless, I would have been compelled to give this proposition the most anxious consideration if there had been any evidence to support it. But there is none, since the case for the respondent was advanced on an entirely different ground.

4. There remains an argument to which I have given much greater weight. As the evidence in the present case has shown, there is a risk that strangers (and especially young strangers) may be drawn into these activities at an early age and will then become established in them for life. This is indeed a disturbing prospect, but I have come to the conclusion that it is not a sufficient ground for declaring these activities to be criminal under the Act of 1861. The element of the corruption of youth is already catered for by the existing legislation; and if there is a gap in it which needs to be filled the remedy surely lies in the hands of Parliament, not in the application of a statute which is aimed at other forms of wrong-doing.

Leaving aside the logic of this answer, which seems to me impregnable, plain humanity demands that a court addressing the criminality of conduct such as that of the present should recognise and respond to the profound dismay which all members of the community share about the apparent increase of cruel and senseless crimes against the defenceless. Whilst doing so I must repeat for the last time that in the answer which I propose I do not advocate the decriminalisation of conduct which has hitherto been a crime: nor do I rebut a submission that a new crime should be created, penalising this conduct, for Mr Purnell has rightly not invited the House to take this course. The only question is whether these consensual private acts are offences against the existing law of violence. To this question I return a negative response. I would allow these appeals.

[Lord Slynn made a speech and said that he would allow the appeals.]

Appeals dismissed

■ *Questions*

1. How should Parliament define the limits of consent to injury or physical harm (or the risk thereof) in criminal law?See P. Roberts, 'The Philosophical Foundations of Consent in the Criminal Law' (1997) 17 OJLS 389.

2. Is the level of harm to which one is permitted to consent clearly defined?

The judges in *Brown* seem to agree that consent is a complete defence to common assault and (except for persons under 16 and those with mental illness) that it would have been a defence to the charge of indecent assault (now repealed, see Sexual Offences Act 2003); yet in *Donovan*, where V consented to being caned, it was held that, but for misdirection, D's convictions for common and indecent assault would have been upheld; and that view seems to have been generally accepted. Lord Lowry, however, [1993] 2 All ER at 97, finds this aspect of *Donovan* hard to follow: 'If the jury, properly directed, had found that consent was not disproved, they must have acquitted the appellant of the only charges brought against him. How, then, could they have convicted the appellant of either of those charges or of the offence of assault, occasioning actual bodily harm, with which he was *not* charged?'

19.4.3 Is D's conduct in causing the impermissible level of harm within an 'exceptional' category? (2)(b)

D will not be liable if the conduct in question represents an exceptional category in which V's consent will be recognized (sports, surgery, boxing, etc) and D has V's consent or a genuine belief in it.

What are the exceptional categories listed in *Brown*?

■ *Questions*

1. What do the following activities have in common: surgery, sports, boxing, horseplay, tattooing, ritual male circumcision? Are they all likely to result in the same level of harm? Do they all necessarily involve the infliction of harm, or merely the risk of the infliction of harm? Are they all accepted by society generally to be beneficial to the person on whom the resulting injury is inflicted?

2. Does this list of exceptions based on policy grounds reflect a coherent and desirable approach to the limits of consent? See Law Commission Consultation Paper No 139, *Consent in the Criminal Law* (1995).

In *Wilson* [1996] 2 Cr App R 241, [1996] Crim LR 573, D branded his initials with a hot knife on his wife's buttocks. She had wanted his initials to be tattooed thereon, but, as he did not know how to do that, she had agreed to the branding instead. D was charged with assault occasioning actual bodily harm, contrary to s 47. The judge held that he was bound by *Brown* to direct the jury to convict. The Court of Appeal quashed D's conviction, saying that they shared the trial judge's disquiet that the proceedings should have been brought. *Brown* was not authority for the proposition that consent was no defence to a charge under s 47 in all circumstances. *Brown* concerned sadomasochism involving torture, danger of serious physical injury and blood infection. The act in *Donovan* was done for the purposes of sexual gratification and had an aggressive element. There was no aggressive element on D's part. D was assisting W to acquire a physical adornment, not logically different from a tattoo. The court asked itself, did public policy and the public interest demand that D's activity should be visited by the sanctions of the criminal law—that is, should the *offence* be extended, and answered, no. In *Brown*, Lord Templeman thought that the question was whether the *defence* of consent should be extended to the consequences of sadomasochistic activity; and answered, no. Compare the approach of Lord Mustill in *Brown*. May the result then depend on how the court poses the question?

■ *Questions*

Is the effect of *Wilson* that bottom-branding is to be added to a list of exceptions—manly sports, male circumcision, ear-piercing, tattooing, etc—where consent is a defence to a charge under s 47 or s 20? Or does it mean that consent is, after all, a defence to those charges—*except* where public policy demands it should not be? Would the result have been different if Wilson had admitted that he derived sexual gratification from the performance of the operation? Should it be different?

In *Emmett* (1999) The Times, 15 October, E participated in sadomasochistic practices with his partner, which included igniting lighter fuel poured over her breasts and applying ligatures to her neck. E was convicted under the OAPA, s 47. The Court of Appeal upheld the conviction, distinguishing *Wilson* on the basis that a s 47 offence had not been committed, there was no evidence of significant harm in that case and the parties had been married (in the present case the parties had only married since the incident). Is this a convincing basis for distinction? Is it a distinction that would withstand challenge under Article 8 and Article 14 of the European Convention on Human Rights (ECHR)? See section 19.5, p 697.

R v Dica

(section 19.3.1, p 681), http://www.bailii.org/ew/cases/EWCA/Crim/2004/1103.html

[The court referred to the cases of *Brown*, *Boyea*, *Donovan*, etc.]

46. These authorities demonstrate that violent conduct involving the deliberate and intentional infliction of bodily harm is and remains unlawful notwithstanding that its purpose is the sexual gratification of one or both participants. Notwithstanding their sexual overtones, these cases were concerned with violent crime, and the sexual overtones did not alter the fact that both parties were consenting to the deliberate infliction of serious harm or bodily injury on one participant by the other. To date, as a matter of public policy, it has not been thought appropriate for such violent conduct to be excused merely because there is a private consensual sexual element to it. The same public policy reason would prohibit the deliberate spreading of disease, including sexual disease.

47. In our judgement the impact of the authorities dealing with sexual gratification can too readily be misunderstood. It does not follow from them, and they do not suggest, that consensual acts of sexual intercourse are unlawful merely because there may be a known risk to the health of one or other participant. These participants are not intent on spreading or becoming infected with disease through sexual intercourse. They are not indulging in serious violence for the purposes of sexual gratification. They are simply prepared, knowingly, to run the risk—not the certainty—of infection, as well as all the other risks inherent in and possible consequences of sexual intercourse, such as, and despite the most careful precautions, an unintended pregnancy. At one extreme there is casual sex between complete strangers, sometimes protected, sometimes not, when the attendant risks are known to be higher, and at the other, there is sexual intercourse between couples in a long-term and loving, and trusting relationship, which may from time to time also carry risks.

48. The first of these categories is self-explanatory and needs no amplification. By way of illustration we shall provide two examples of cases which would fall within the second.

49. In the first, one of a couple suffers from HIV. It may be the man: it may be the woman. The circumstances in which HIV was contracted are irrelevant. They could result from a contaminated blood transfusion, or an earlier relationship with a previous sexual partner, who unknown to the sufferer with whom we are concerned, was himself or herself infected with HIV. The parties are Roman Catholics. They are conscientiously unable to use artificial contraception. They both know of the risk that the healthy partner may become infected with HIV. Our second example is that of a young couple, desperate for a family, who are advised that if the wife were to become pregnant and give birth, her long-term health, indeed her life itself, would be at risk. Together the couple decide to run that risk, and she becomes pregnant. She may be advised that the foetus should be aborted, on the grounds of her health, yet, nevertheless, decide to bring her baby to term. If she does, and suffers ill health, is the male partner to be criminally liable for having sexual intercourse with her, notwithstanding that he knew of the risk to her health? If he is liable to be prosecuted, was she not a party to whatever crime was committed? And should the law interfere with the Roman Catholic couple, and require them, at the peril of criminal sanctions, to choose between bringing their sexual relationship to an end or violating their consciences by using contraception?

50. These, and similar risks, have always been taken by adults consenting to sexual intercourse. Different situations, no less potentially fraught, have to be addressed by them. Modern society has not thought to criminalise those who have willingly accepted the risks, and we know of no cases where one or other of the consenting adults has been prosecuted, let alone convicted, for the consequences of doing so.

51. The problems of criminalising the consensual taking of risks like these include the sheer impracticability of enforcement and the haphazard nature of its impact. The process would undermine the general understanding of the community that sexual relationships are pre-eminently private and essentially personal to the individuals involved in them. And if adults were to be liable to prosecution for the consequences of taking known risks with their health, it would seem odd that this should be confined to risks taken in the context of sexual intercourse, while they are nevertheless permitted to take the risks inherent in so many other aspects of everyday life, including, again for example, the mother or father of a child suffering a serious contagious illness, who holds the child's hand, and comforts or kisses him or her goodnight.

52. In our judgement, interference of this kind with personal autonomy, and its level and extent, may only be made by Parliament....

60. In view of our conclusion that the trial judge should not have withdrawn the issue of consent from the jury, the appeal is allowed....

R v Konzani

(section 19.3.1, p 684), http://www.bailii.org/ew/cases/EWCA/Crim/2005/706.html

Judge LJ:

...35. In short, the judge explained that before the consent of the complainant could provide the appellant with a defence, it was required to be an informed and willing consent to the risk of contracting HIV. ...

40. *R v Dica* represented what Lord Mustill in *R v Brown* described as a 'new challenge', and confirmed that in specific circumstances the ambit of the criminal law extended to consensual sexual intercourse between adults which involved a risk of the most extreme kind to the physical health of one participant. In the context of direct physical injury, he pointed out that cases involving the '... consensual infliction of violence are special. They have been in the past, and will continue to be in the future, the subject of special treatment by the law'. In his subsequent detailed examination of the 'situations in which the recipient consents or is deemed to consent to the infliction of violence upon him', activity of the kind currently under consideration did not remotely fall within any of the ten categories which he was able to identify. *Brown* itself emphatically established the clear principle that the consent of the injured person does not form a kind of all purpose species of defence to an offence of violence contrary to s 20 of the 1861 Act.

41. We are concerned with the risk of and the actual transmission of a potentially fatal disease through or in the course of consensual sexual relations which did not in themselves involve unlawful violence of the kind prohibited in *R v Brown*. The prosecution did not seek to prove that the disease was deliberately transmitted, with the intention required by s 18 of the 1861 Act. The allegation was that the appellant behaved recklessly on the basis that knowing that he was suffering from the HIV virus, and its consequences, and knowing the risks of its transmission to a sexual partner, he concealed his condition from the complainants, leaving them ignorant of it. When sexual intercourse occurred these complainants were ignorant of his condition. So although they consented to sexual intercourse, they did not consent to the transmission of the HIV virus.

■ *Questions*

1. Why should V be permitted to consent to the *risk* of a potentially fatal infection of HIV by sex, but not to the *risk* of infection from the use of implements in genital torture?

2. Are the categories of exceptional conduct clearly defined?

In relation to injury or the risk of injury in sport, a number of categories need to be separated.

First, if the rules of the sport permit an unacceptably dangerous act, the law need not recognize the validity of V's factual consent. That is a matter of public policy. Boxing continues to be lawful despite the potentially life-threatening injury and participants' intention to cause grievous bodily harm. See J. Anderson, *The Legality of Boxing: A Punch Drunk Love?* (2007). Should cage fighting be treated as a lawful sport alongside boxing?

Secondly, where unlike boxing and martial arts, playing within the rules of the particular sport does not *necessarily* involve D causing actual bodily harm, but D intentionally inflicts actual bodily harm or worse, V's consent is irrelevant and D commits the offence: *Bradshaw* (1878) Cox CC 83.

Thirdly, and most difficult in practical terms to apply, if in playing such a sport D was reckless only as to the causing of the injury the question will be whether V impliedly consented to the risk of that level of injury in the context in which it was inflicted. The question of whether the conduct was within the rules of the game is not the sole determinant of liability. It would be too simplistic to suggest that V's consent is only valid within the rules of the game. V may well, as a matter of fact, impliedly consent to the *risk* of injury occurring in conduct outside the rules as in a late tackle in football, or an illegitimate bouncer in cricket: *Moore* (1898) 14 TLR 229. It is therefore necessary to look to a broader range of factors. In *Barnes* [2005] EWCA Crim 3246, the Court of Appeal preferred to adopt an objective evaluation of these circumstances as in Canada (see *Cicarelli* (1989) 54 CCC (3d) 121) and advocated by Law Commission Consultation Paper No 134, *Consent and Offences Against the Person* (1994). That approach was criticized by S. Gardner, 'The Law and the Sportsfield' [1994] Crim LR 513, but received generally favourable responses: LCCP 139, paras 12.6–12.23. Although one important factor will be whether the injury was inflicted when D was acting outside the rules of the game, it is submitted that this may require qualification so as to emphasize that only rules designed to protect against injury are considered: it should not, for example, be relevant that the impugned tackle occurred when D was breaking the off-side rule.

For an analysis questioning the objective approach to consent in sports, but denying the need for a uniform approach throughout the criminal law, see B. Livings, 'A Different Ball Game' (2007) 71 J Crim L 534, cf C. Elliott and C. de Than, 'The Case for a Rational Reconstruction of Consent in Criminal Law' (2007) 70 MLR 225.

19.4.4 The level of harm caused is impermissible, but D intended only to cause consensual permissible harm or harm within an exceptional category with consent (2)(b)

D is not guilty if he intended only to cause a level of harm/harm in a context in which V's factual consent would be legally recognized and V had consented to that type of harm, or if V had not, D nevertheless genuinely believed that V had.

In *Meachen* [2006] EWCA Crim 2414, D administered a date rape drug to V. There was a dispute between the Crown and defence whether V consented to taking the drugs. D's case was that he penetrated her anus with several fingers while she was straddled on top of him bouncing up and down, as a result of which she suffered permanent and very serious injuries to her anus. D claimed that V had consented to anal penetration by his fingers and that he had not intended or foreseen injury to her. The Court of Appeal held that liability under s 20 requires proof that D intended to cause injury or was subjectively reckless as to whether he might cause injury. In this case, although the level of injury was GBH and therefore V could not in law consent to it, D was entitled to be acquitted if he intended only to inflict a battery on V by penetrating her anus (or was reckless about doing so) and he had her consent to that activity or he genuinely believed he had her consent to that activity. The decision clarifies the law substantially over the previous explanations offered by the Court of Appeal.

The problems had derived from an overbroad statement in the *A-G's Reference (No 6 of 1980)* [1981] QB 715, where two youths aged 18 and 17 settled an argument by a fist fight and one sustained a bleeding nose and bruises to his face, it was held that the other was guilty of assault occasioning actual bodily harm. 'It is not in the public interest that people should try to cause or should cause each other actual bodily harm for no good reason. Minor struggles are another matter. So, in our judgment, it is immaterial whether the act occurs in private or in public; it is an assault if actual bodily harm is *intended and/or caused*. This means that most fights will be unlawful regardless of consent.' This should now be read subject to *Meachen*.

■ *Questions*

D (an adult) spanks V (an adult) with her consent. Is D guilty of an offence if:

(i) he intended to inflict bodily harm, as V desired, but was too timid in his delivery and inflicted only a battery;

(ii) he intended to cause only a minor battery (as V desired), but he misjudged his strength and inflicted actual bodily harm?

19.5 Consent and the ECHR

In *Laskey v UK* (1997) 24 EHRR 39, the European Court heard an application made by the defendants in *Brown* alleging breaches of Article 8—the right to respect for private life. The European Court held unanimously there was no violation:

36. The Court observes that not every sexual activity carried out behind closed doors necessarily falls within the scope of Article 8. In the present case, the applicants were involved in consensual sado-masochistic activities for purposes of sexual gratification. There can be no doubt that sexual orientation and activity concern an intimate aspect of private life (see, *mutatis mutandis*, the *Dudgeon v the United Kingdom* judgment of 22 October 1981, Series A no. 45, p. 21, § 52). However, a considerable number of people were involved in the activities in question which included, *inter alia*, the recruitment of new 'members', the provision of several specially-equipped 'chambers', and the shooting of many video-tapes which were distributed among the 'members' . . . It may thus be open to question whether the sexual activities of the applicants fell entirely within the notion of 'private life' in the particular circumstances of the case.

However, since this point has not been disputed by those appearing before it, the Court sees no reason to examine it of its own motion in the present case. Assuming, therefore, that the prosecution and conviction of the applicants amounted to an interference with their private life, the question arises whether such an interference was 'necessary in a democratic society' within the meaning of the second paragraph of Article 8. . . .

38. In support of their submission, the applicants alleged that all those involved in the sado-masochistic encounters were willing adult participants; that participation in the acts complained of was carefully restricted and controlled and was limited to persons with like-minded sado-masochistic proclivities; that the acts were not witnessed by the public at large and that there was no danger or likelihood that they would ever be so witnessed; that no serious or permanent injury had been sustained, no infection had been caused to the wounds, and that no medical treatment had been required. Furthermore, no complaint was ever made to the police—who learnt about the applicants' activities by chance. . . .

39. The applicants submitted that their case should be viewed as one involving matters of sexual expression, rather than violence. With due regard to this consideration, the line beyond which consent is no defence to physical injury should only be drawn at the level of intentional or reckless causing of serious disabling injury.

40. For the Government, the State was entitled to punish acts of violence, such as those for which the applicants were convicted, that could not be considered of a trifling or transient nature, irrespective of the consent of the victim. In fact, in the present case, some of these acts could well be compared to 'genital torture' and a Contracting State could not be said to have an obligation to tolerate acts of torture because they are committed in the context of a consenting sexual relationship. The State was moreover entitled to prohibit activities because of their potential danger.

The Government further contended that the criminal law should seek to deter certain forms of be-haviour on public health grounds but also for broader moral reasons. In this respect, acts of torture—such as those at issue in the present case—may be banned also on the ground that they undermine the respect which human beings should confer upon each other. In any event, the whole issue of the role of consent in the criminal law is of great complexity and the Contracting States should enjoy a wide margin of appreciation to consider all the public policy options. . . .

43. The Court considers that one of the roles which the State is unquestionably entitled to under-take is to seek to regulate, through the operation of the criminal law, activities which involve the infliction of physical harm. This is so whether the activities in question occur in the course of sexual conduct or otherwise.

44. The determination of the level of harm that should be tolerated by the law in situations where the victim consents is in the first instance a matter for the State concerned since what is at stake is related, on the one hand, to public health considerations and to the general deterrent effect of the criminal law, and, on the other, to the personal autonomy of the individual.

45. The applicants have contended that, in the circumstances of the case, the behaviour in question formed part of private morality which is not the State's business to regulate. In their sub-mission the matters for which they were prosecuted and convicted concerned only private sexual behaviour.

The Court is not persuaded by this submission. It is evident from the facts established by the na-tional courts that the applicants, 'sado-masochistic activities involved a significant degree of injury or wounding which could not be characterised as trifling or transient. This, in itself, suffices to distin-guish the present case from those applications which have previously been examined by the Court concerning consensual homosexual behaviour in private between adults where no such feature was present (see the *Dudgeon v the United Kingdom* judgment cited above, the *Norris v Ireland* judg-ment of 26 October 1988, Series A no. 142, and the *Modinos v Cyprus* judgment of 22 April 1993, Series A no. 259).

46. Nor does the Court accept the applicants 'submission that no prosecution should have been brought against them since their injuries were not severe and since no medical treatment had been required.

In deciding whether or not to prosecute, the State authorities were entitled to have regard not only to the actual seriousness of the harm caused—which as noted above was considered to be signifi-cant—but also, as stated by Lord Jauncey of Tullichettle . . . , to the potential for harm inherent in the acts in question. In this respect it is recalled that the activities were considered by Lord Templeman to be 'unpredictably dangerous' . . .

■ *Questions*

Do you agree that the English law is sufficiently certain? Do you agree that criminalization is necessary and proportionate so as to fall within Article 8(2)?

FURTHER READING

M. Allen, 'Consent and Assault' (1994) 58 J Crim Law 183

N. Bamforth, 'Sadomasochism and Consent' [1994] Crim LR 661

M. Giles, 'Consensual Harm and the Public Interest' (1994) 57 MLR 101

D. Kell, 'Social Disutility and Consent' (1994) 14 OJLS 121

Law Commission, Consultation Paper No 134, *Consent and Offences against the Person* (1994)

Law Commission, Consultation Paper No 139, *Consent in Criminal Law* (1995)

D. Ormerod, 'Consent and Offences Against the Person: Law Commission Consultation Paper No 134' (1994) 57 MLR 928

D. Ormerod and M. J. Gunn, 'Consent—A Second Bash' [1996] Crim LR 694

P. Roberts, 'The Philosophical Foundations of Consent in the Criminal Law' (1997) 17 OJLS 389

S. Shute, 'Something Old, Something New, Something Borrowed—Three Aspects of the Consent Project' [1996] Crim LR 684

J. Tolmie, 'Consent to Harmful Assaults: The Case for Moving Away from Category Based Decision Making' [2012] Crim LR 656

20
Sexual offences

20.1 The background to the Sexual Offences Act 2003

The law governing sexual offences is now found in the Sexual Offences Act 2003. The 2003 Act provisions are based on research from the Home Office consultation paper, *Setting the Boundaries, Reforming the Law on Sexual Offences* (see N. Lacey, 'Beset by Boundaries' [2001] Crim LR 3). See also, for an interesting comparison, Scottish Law Commission Discussion Paper No 131, *Rape and Other Offences* (2006).

The Act was prompted by calls for urgent reform due to concern over attrition rates (ie the proportion of those cases reported as sexual assaults which did not lead to a successful conviction) rising dramatically in the 1980s and 1990s. See the *Report of the Joint Investigation into the Investigation and Prosecution of Cases Involving Allegations of Rape* (2002) HMCPSI. See further J. Temkin and B. Krahe, *The Justice Gap* (2008).

For detailed criticism of the old law, see J. Temkin, *Rape and the Legal Process* (2nd edn, 2002). Most of the relevant law was contained in the Sexual Offences Act 1956, but that was itself merely a consolidation of various statutes dating back to the late nineteenth century. The law was widely regarded as: incoherent; discriminatory; failing to reflect the morality, prevalent sexual attitudes and practices of the twenty-first century; and providing inadequate protection for the vulnerable, while also failing to respect the sexual autonomy of those capable of making informed choices about their sexual behaviour. Many aspects of the old law were so discriminatory as to be incompatible with European Convention on Human Rights (ECHR) obligations: for example, offences such as gross indecency between males breached Article 8: *ADT v UK* (2000) 31 EHRR 803. The Government review in *Setting the Boundaries* set out to produce coherent and clear offences which protect individuals, especially children and the more vulnerable, from abuse and exploitation. It also aimed to enable more appropriate punishment of abusers, and to create a statutory framework which would be fair and non-discriminatory in accordance with the ECHR and the Human Rights Act 1998.

The 2003 Act redefines many of the offences found in the old legislation, but introduces a great number of new offences. It has been subjected to stringent and cogent criticism: see especially J. Temkin and A. Ashworth, 'Rape, Sexual Assaults and the Problems of Consent' [2004] Crim LR 328. It is impossible to deal with all of the offences in this chapter. The focus is on the non-consensual offences.

Some of the controversies that will be examined in this chapter include the following:

(i) Parliament's failure to define core elements of the offences, such as 'consent' and 'sexual' and the attempts by the courts to fill these lacunae;

(ii) whether a deception perpetrated by the defendant necessarily vitiates the complainant's consent;

(iii) the overly wide breadth of some of the offences;

(iv) the effect of voluntary alcohol consumption on the complainant's ability to consent to intercourse;

(v) the normative underpinning of the offences, that is, whether the rationale for their enactment is the protection of autonomy or some other value;

(vi) the excessive use of strict liability.

20.2 Non-consensual offences

20.2.1 Rape

Sexual Offences Act 2003, s 1

(1) A person (A) commits an offence if—

(a) he intentionally penetrates the vagina, anus or mouth of another person (B) with his penis,

(b) B does not consent to the penetration, and

(c) A does not reasonably believe that B consents.

(2) Whether a belief is reasonable is to be determined having regard to all the circumstances, including any steps A has taken to ascertain whether B consents.

Note that the Act adopts an odd style, with the offender always referred to as 'A' and the complainant or victim as 'B'. We follow that approach in this chapter.

20.2.1.1 The actus reus

For the first time in England and Wales, the 2003 Act extended rape to include non-consensual oral sex. It was argued by some that this inclusion devalues 'real' rape. The Court of Appeal has emphasized that in sentencing terms there is no distinction based on which orifice is penetrated: *Ismail* [2005] EWCA Crim 397. Prosecutors should specify which orifice is alleged to have been penetrated, but there is only one offence: *K* [2009] 1 Cr App R 131. The offence can be committed as a principal offender only by a man. Note that s 2 (section 20.2.2) provides a new offence of sexual penetration by objects other than the penis. Section 79(3) makes clear that surgically reconstructed body parts are included as parts of the 'body'. A, with his surgically reconstructed penis, can rape B with her surgically reconstructed vagina. This closes a loophole under the old law: see M. Hicks and G. Branston, 'Transsexual Rape—A Loophole Closed?' [1997] Crim LR 565.

Under the 1956 Act, it was held that sexual intercourse was a continuing act, and if B withdrew consent at any time during the act, A would commit the actus reus of rape: *Kaitamaki v R* [1985] AC 147, PC. Rape is now defined in terms of 'penetration' rather than 'sexual intercourse', and s 79(2) provides that penetration is a continuing act. Section 44 of the 1956 Sexual Offences Act (now repealed) provided that it was not necessary to prove the completion of intercourse by the 'emission of seed'. There is no such provision in the 2003 Act.

■ **Question**

Should all acts of sexual penetration by whatever object be classified as rape?

20.2.1.2 Consent

The crucial element of rape remains the absence of consent. Without that, penile penetration is not merely not criminal, it is an explicit expression of intimacy. Sections 74 to 76 of the 2003 Act seek to provide a clear definition of consent that can be applied consistently. These sections create three separate routes by which the prosecution may seek to establish absence of consent:

- s 74: general definition of consent;
- s 75: rebuttable presumptions; and
- s 76: conclusive (irrebuttable) presumptions.

Despite this purported clarification, defining consent remains problematic.

■ Questions

1. Is it possible to define 'consent' in statutory language in a way that can be applied in practice?

2. Why is the absence of consent an element of the actus reus? Could it be a defence? Cf the argument by M. Madden Dempsey and J. Herring, 'Why Sexual Penetration Requires Justification' (2007) 27 OJLS 467.

3. Is the act of sexual intercourse prima facie 'wrong'? Should the penetrator need to justify his action of penetration in every case?

20.2.1.3 Section 74

Section 74 provides that:

a person consents if he agrees by choice, and has the freedom and capacity to make that choice.

This definition, based on 'free agreement', is intended to emphasize that the absence of B's protest, resistance or injury does not necessarily signify B's consent. Although the Act is silent as to the precise moment at which B's consent or agreement must be present, it is clear that the relevant time is that of the alleged sexual wrongdoing.

J. Temkin and A. Ashworth (section 20.1, p 700 [2004] Crim LR 328) point out that freedom is only used to rule out the suggestion of some or all of its antitheses, (see at 336, citing J. Austin, 'A Plea for Excuses' in H. Morris (ed), *Freedom and Responsibility* (1961), p 8).

The interpretation of s 74 has been considered in a number of instances and it is clear that the question of whether or not B consented to sexual activity is highly context-dependent. The difficulty lies in deciding whether conduct by A can be sufficient in law and fact to vitiate B's freedom to choose whether to engage in sexual activity. A related problem lies in deciding whether only those deceptions by A listed in s 76 (as to identity, nature and purpose) can ever negate B's consent or whether a deception that does not fall within s 76 can nevertheless vitiate consent if the jury finds that it denies B freedom to choose within s 74. The courts seem to accept that there are forms of deception that will negate consent because they fall within s 74 even though they are not listed within s 76. A literal textual analysis of the Act might conclude that once it has been held that the deception perpetrated on B falls outside the limited scope of s 76, it is no longer relevant. One way of explaining the courts' approach is to say that deception may negate B's agreement, capacity or freedom and this explains why deception might fall to be considered in s 74 even though it is not listed as a factor in that section. As the following cases demonstrate, difficulties arise in delineating what types of deception by A ought to fall within s 74.

R (F) v Director of Public Prosecutions
[2013] EWHC 945 (Admin), Divisional Court, http://www.bailii.org/ew/cases/EWHC/Admin/2013/945.html

(Lord Judge CJ, Fulford and Sweeney JJ)

This case was an application for judicial review of a decision not to initiate a prosecution for rape. A and B were a married couple. A (referred to as the 'intervener' in the extract below as this is a judicial review case) displayed a domineering attitude towards B and was physically and verbally aggressive when they had sex. In addition, A would often demand sex from B. B was adamant that she did not want to have any more children, but was unable to use the contraceptive pill for medical reasons. Although they sometimes used a condom, A did not like doing so, and therefore their preferred method of contraception was withdrawal. B did not object to having intercourse in this manner, provided that A withdrew before he ejaculated. One afternoon, B agreed to have intercourse with A, but he failed to withdraw before he ejaculated. The issue was whether ejaculation without consent could transform consensual intercourse into rape. The CPS decided not to prosecute A for rape. The DPP's senior legal adviser conducted a review of this decision and agreed with it.

[In directing the CPS to reconsider whether to prosecute, **Lord Judge CJ** stated:]

22. At the time when the review was written [counsel for the CPS] did not have the advantage of the judgment of the Divisional Court in *Assange v Swedish Prosecution Authority* [2011] EWHC 2849 (Admin). It was submitted to the Divisional Court that as the complainant had consented to sexual intercourse only on the basis that Assange would use a condom, even if he did not, that fact was or would be irrelevant. She had consented to intercourse. Sir John Thomas, President of the Queen's Bench Division, explained, at para 86:

> 'The question of consent in the present case is to be determined by reference to s.74. The allegation is clear and covers the alternative; it is not an allegation that the condom came off accidentally or was damaged accidentally. It would plainly be open to a jury to hold that, if (the complainant) had made clear that she would only consent to sexual intercourse if Mr Assange used a condom, then there would be no consent if, without her consent, he did not use a condom, or removed or tore the condom without her consent. His conduct in having sexual intercourse without a condom in circumstances where she had made clear she would only have sexual intercourse if he used a condom would therefore amount to an offence under the Sexual Offences Act 2003, whatever the position may have been prior to that Act.'

23. Having reached that conclusion, the Divisional Court addressed the question whether Mr Assange's conduct in having sexual intercourse without a condom, or in continuing with it after removing, damaging or tearing the condom was 'deceptive'. The point did not require a firm conclusion, but it was accepted that 'it could be argued that sexual intercourse without a condom was different to sexual intercourse with a condom, given the presence of a physical barrier, a perceived difference in the threat in the degree of intimacy, the risks of disease and the prevention of a pregnancy; moreover the editors of *Smith and Hogan* (12th Edition at p.866) commented that it had been argued that unprotected sexual intercourse should be treated as being different in nature to protected sexual intercourse'. However, the court was not inclined to accept this approach, noting that the editors of *Smith and Hogan* approached the possible deception in relation to the use of a condom as 'likely to be held to remove any purported free agreement by the complainant under s.74'. The court further noted a view to similar effect expressed in the well known text book *Rook and Ward on Sexual Offences* (4th edition at paragraph 1.216.)

24. We must emphasise that we are not addressing the situation in which sexual intercourse occurs consensually when the man, intending to withdraw in accordance with his partner's wishes, or their understanding, nevertheless ejaculates prematurely, or accidentally, within rather than outside his partner's vagina. These things happen. They always have and they always will, and no offence is committed when they do. They underline why withdrawal is not a safe method of contraception. Equally we are not addressing the many fluctuating ways in which sexual relationships may develop, as couples discover and renew their own levels of understanding and tolerance, their codes of communication, express or understood, and mutual give and take, experimentation and excitement. These are intensely private matters, personal to the couple in question.

25. The facts suggested by the evidence in this case are quite different. It is inappropriate to examine the incident of sexual intercourse in February 2010 in isolation from the well evidenced history (including his own admissions) of the intervener's sexual dominance of the claimant and her unenthusiastic acquiescence to his demands. Given that essential background, the evidence about the incident in February 2010 is reasonably open to this analysis. Consensual penetration occurred. The claimant consented on the clear understanding that the intervener would not ejaculate within her vagina. She believed that he intended and agreed to withdraw before ejaculation. The intervener knew and understood that this was the only basis on which she was prepared to have sexual intercourse with him. There is evidence from the history of the relationship, as well as what he said when sexual intercourse was taking place, and his observations to the claimant afterwards, that although he never disclosed his intention to her (because if she had known he knew that she would have never have consented), either from the outset of penetration, or after penetration had begun, he intended that this occasion of sexual intercourse would culminate in ejaculation within her vagina, whatever her wishes and their understanding. In short, there is evidence that he deliberately ignored the basis of her consent to penetration as a manifestation of his control over her.

26. In law, the question which arises is whether this factual structure can give rise to a conviction for rape. Did the claimant consent to this penetration? She did so, provided, in the language of s.74 of the 2003 Act, she agreed by choice, when she had the freedom and capacity to make the choice. What Assange underlines is that 'choice' is crucial to the issue of 'consent', and indeed we underline that the statutory definition of consent provided in s.74 applies equally to s.1(1)(c) as it does to s.1(1)(b). The evidence relating to 'choice' and the 'freedom' to make any particular choice must be approached in a broad commonsense way. If before penetration began the intervener had made up his mind that he would penetrate and ejaculate within the claimant's vagina, or even, because 'penetration is a continuing act from entry to withdrawal' (see s.79(2) of the 2003 Act) he decided that he would not withdraw at all, just because he deemed the claimant subservient to his control, she was deprived of choice relating to the crucial feature on which her original consent to sexual intercourse was based. Accordingly her consent was negated. Contrary to her wishes, and knowing that she would not have consented, and did not consent to penetration or the continuation of penetration if she had any inkling of his intention, he deliberately ejaculated within her vagina. In law, this combination of circumstances falls within the statutory definition of rape.

■ *Question*

Dr Rogers states that in a case such as this one there should be no liability for a non-consensual sexual offence as the offences in the 2003 Act are designed to protect a person's sexual autonomy, not their sexual health or their desire not to have a baby. Do you agree? See J. Rogers, 'The Effect of "Deception" in the Sexual Offences Act 2003' (2013) 4 Arch Rev 7.

In *R v EB* [2006] EWCA Crim 2495, the defendant had had unprotected sexual intercourse with the complainant without disclosing that he was HIV positive. The question arose whether evidence of his HIV status was admissible. The Court of Appeal held that:

17. Where one party to sexual activity has a sexually transmissible disease which is not disclosed to the other party any consent that may have been given to that activity by the other party is not thereby vitiated. The act remains a consensual act. However, the party suffering from the sexual transmissible disease will not have any defence to any charge which may result from harm created by that sexual activity, merely by virtue of that consent, because such consent did not include consent to infection by the disease.

. . . as a matter of law, the fact that the appellant may not have disclosed his HIV status is not a matter which could in any way be relevant to the issue of consent under section 74 in relation to the sexual activity in this case.

> ■ *Question*
>
> In *Assange* it was argued that the reason why the defendant in *EB* was not liable was because he had not lied to the complainant about his being HIV positive; she had just never asked. Should a failure to reveal any sexually transmissible disease vitiate B's consent?

The issue of whether B's consent has been vitiated due to her having been deprived of 'choice' has been considered in a number of rather unusual circumstances, as the following case illustrates.

R v McNally

[2013] EWCA Crim 1051, Court of Appeal, Criminal Division, http://www.bailii.org/ew/cases/EWCA/Crim/2013/1051.html

(Leveson LJ and Kenneth Parker and Stewart JJ)

A, aged 17, was a transgender man, having been born female. When aged 13, A started an online relationship with B who was a similar age. A did not tell B that he had been born female and B claimed that she remained ignorant of that fact. After a number of years A and B met in person, on four occasions. On each occasion A penetrated B's vagina, both orally and digitally. B purchased condoms so that they could have full intercourse, but A declined. A was eventually confronted by B's mother and confirmed that he had been born a female. A complaint was made to the police and A subsequently pleaded guilty to committing assault by penetration, contrary to s 2 of the Sexual Offences Act 2003.

[In upholding A's conviction, **Leveson LJ** made the following comments in relation to s 74:]

23. The case for the Crown was that [B]'s consent was obtained by fraudulent deception that the appellant was a male and that had she known the truth, she would not have consented to acts of vaginal penetration. [Counsel for A] argues that deception as to gender cannot vitiate consent; in the same way deception as to age, marital status, wealth or, following *EB*, HIV status being deceptions as to qualities or attributes cannot vitiate consent. Thus, he submits that *Assange* and *R(F)* can be distinguished as the deceptions in those cases were not deceptions as to qualities or attributes but as to the features of the act itself.

24. We reject this analysis. First and foremost, *EB* was not saying that HIV status could not vitiate consent if, for example, the complainant had been positively assured that the defendant was not HIV positive: it left the issue open. As [counsel for the Crown contends], the argument that in *Assange* and *R(F)* the deceptions were as to the features of the act is not sustainable: the wearing of a condom and ejaculation are irrelevant to the definition of rape and are not 'features' of the offence and no such rationale is suggested. In the last two cases, it was alleged that the victim had consented on the basis of a premise that, at the time of the consent, was false (namely, in one case, that her partner would wear a condom and, in the second, that he would ejaculate outside her body).

25. In reality, some deceptions (such as, for example, in relation to wealth) will obviously not be sufficient to vitiate consent. In our judgment, Lord Judge's observation that 'the evidence relating to "choice" and the "freedom" to make any particular choice must be approached in a broad common-sense way' identifies the route through the dilemma.

26. Thus while, in a physical sense, the acts of assault by penetration of the vagina are the same whether perpetrated by a male or a female, the sexual nature of the acts is, on any common sense view, different where the complainant is deliberately deceived by a defendant into believing that the latter is a male. Assuming the facts to be proved as alleged, [B] chose to have sexual encounters with a boy and her preference (her freedom to choose whether or not to have a sexual encounter with a girl) was removed by the appellant's deception.

27. It follows from the foregoing analysis that we conclude that, depending on the circumstances, deception as to gender can vitiate consent...

■ *Questions*

1. If A tells B that he is very wealthy and knows that this is the only reason B will ever have sex with him, why (per Leveson LJ) does this deception not nullify B's freedom to only have sexual intercourse with wealthy men, thus making A guilty of rape?

2. Why does deception as to some attributes negate consent, while for others it does not? Applying a 'broad commonsense' approach, how are we to decide?

3. B is vehemently anti-Semitic and tells A that she will not have sex with anyone of Jewish descent. A is in fact Jewish, but does not disclose this to B and he proceeds to have sexual intercourse with her anyway. Should the law protect B's freedom to practise her anti-Semitism, thus making A guilty of rape? See A. Sharpe, 'Criminalising Sexual Intimacy: Transgender Defendants and the Legal Construction of Non-Consent' [2014] Crim LR 207.

4. Is *McNally* distinguishable from *EB* (earlier in this section)? What is the difference between A actively deceiving B and A not disabusing B of a false assumption he knows that B has made?

One of the elements central to s 74 is that of the victim's 'capacity'. That term is not further defined. Is what matters whether B has the *mental* capacity to choose to perform the specified act with A on the occasion in question? It is unclear to what extent B must have the capacity to understand the consequences of the action as well as its nature. For example, must B understand the risks of disease and pregnancy from unprotected intercourse in cases of penile penetration? No further clarification, indeed only obfuscation, is generated by cross-referring to the offences protecting those with a mental disorder in s 30(2) whereby:

(a) he lacks the capacity to choose whether to agree to the touching (whether because he lacks sufficient understanding of the nature or reasonably foreseeable consequences of what is being done, or for any other reason), or

(b) he is unable to communicate such a choice to A.

In *C* [2009] UKHL 42, B was a 28-year-old woman with a history of serious mental disorders. Her mental disorders could manifest themselves in episodes of impulsive and aggressive behaviour, delusions, hallucinations, depression or manic episodes. At the time of the offences she was living in supervised accommodation. She developed irrational concerns for her safety if she remained in the area, and so she left her accommodation. She met A who had offered to help her. A gave her crack cocaine and made her perform oral sex on him and a co-defendant. In interview B said that she had performed the acts out of fear of violence. A was convicted of an offence of sexual activity with a person with a mental disorder impeding choice contrary to the Sexual Offences Act 2003, s 30(1). The Court of Appeal allowed A's appeal against conviction and certified the following question of general public importance:

Whether the decision of the Court of Appeal...has unduly limited the scope of section 30(1) of the Sexual Offences Act beyond that which Parliament intended. Specifically (a) in holding that a lack of capacity to choose cannot be person or situation specific; (b) in holding that an irrational fear that prevents the exercise of choice cannot be equated with a lack of capacity to choose; (c) in holding that to fall within section 30(2)(b) a complainant must be physically unable to communicate by reason of his mental disorder.

The House of Lords allowed the appeal, reinstated A's conviction and in doing so answered the three certified question in the affirmative. Baroness Hale, speaking for a unanimous House, clarified a number of points in relation to the section. First, whether an individual has the capacity to consent is both person- and circumstance-specific. Secondly, the section is interpreted as being able to encompass a wide range of circumstances, including an irrational fear, as was the case here. It is sufficient if B has an irrational fear and it is this irrational fear that leads her to acquiesce to the sexual contact. Finally, an inability to communicate is not limited to those cases where B is physically unable to communicate. Rather, section 30 is wide enough to encompass cases where B's inability is attributable to a mental disorder.

■ *Questions*

1. Does the 2003 Act provide a clear workable set of definitions of consent and capacity that can be applied?

2. B has a mental disorder and an irrational fear of men with Welsh accents. A, from Wales, is unaware of that. He makes sexual advances to B and she is too afraid to resist. Is A guilty of rape? Or an offence under s 30?

3. C. Elliott and C. De Than, 'The Case for a Rational Reconstruction of Consent in Criminal Law' (2007) 70 MLR 225 argue that the test of capacity under s 74 should be based on whether B was capable of understanding at the material time the nature and reasonably foreseeable consequences of the act and able to communicate her consent effectively (at 242). Is this preferable to the court's approach?

4. Given that the definition of rape now encompasses oral penetration, in *C* above why was A not charged with the rape of B? Baroness Hale gave two reasons why a charge under s 30 might be preferable. First, because 'the prosecution has only to prove the inability to refuse rather than that the complainant actually did not consent.' Secondly, because the mens rea under s 30 is easier to prove than that required for rape. The reason for this is that all that needs to be shown to make D guilty under s 30 is that the defendant knew the complainant had a mental disorder and therefore is likely to be unable to refuse. Do you find either of these explanations convincing?

Intoxicated consent

A very practical problem is at what point self-induced intoxication vitiates consent. Under the 1956 Act, if a complainant, through alcohol or drugs, was not capable of exercising a judgement on consent, she was not consenting—that was a matter of law. The Government rejected a suggestion for a provision in the 2003 Act that 'someone who is inebriated could claim they were unable to give consent—as opposed to someone who was unconscious for whatever reason, including because of alcohol' on the ground that it would give rise to 'mischievous accusations'.

In *Dougal* (2005) Swansea Crown Court (discussed in *Bree* below), the trial judge directed the jury to enter a 'not guilty' verdict when the prosecutor informed the judge that he did not propose to proceed further because the prosecution were unable to prove that the complainant had not given consent because of her level of intoxication. The decision was controversial since all that B had said was that she 'could not remember'. Following the furore over that case, the Government raised the issue in a Consultation Paper, *Convicting Rapists and Protecting Victims* (2006) asking 'Does the law on capacity need to be changed. Should there be a statutory definition of capacity?' Subsequently, the Court of Appeal has sought to pre-empt the need for legislative intervention by encouraging trial judges to leave the issue to the common sense of the jury where there is evidence that B might not have been consenting owing to intoxication. On jury attitudes to intoxicated rape complainants, see also E. Finch and V. Munro, 'Breaking Boundaries; Sexual Consent in the Jury Room' (2006) 26 LS 303.

R v Bree

[2007] EWCA Crim 256, Court of Appeal, Criminal Division, http://www.bailii.org/ew/cases/EWCA/Crim/2007/804.html

(Sir Igor Judge P, Hallett LJ and Gloster J)

D, aged 25, and M, aged 19, had been drinking together. Both had voluntarily consumed large amounts of alcohol. M and D returned to M's student flat. M accepted her account of events was 'very patchy'. She agreed that she did not say 'no' to sexual intercourse, although she did remember saying 'no' when asked if she had a condom. D testified that he was 'absolutely positive' that she was awake and conscious throughout. She had removed her own pyjamas and responded to his touching positively by moaning quietly, and rolling on to her back and opening her legs. It was agreed that they had 'brief sex'. D was convicted of rape.

[Sir Igor Judge P delivered the judgment of the court. His lordship set out the facts and s 74.]

One of the objectives of the Sexual Offences Act 2003, which came into force on 1 May 2004, was to bring coherence and clarity to the meaning of consent. The provisions relating to consent represented the result of substantial discussion and Parliamentary debate about the principles which should apply to the acutely sensitive and intensely personal area of sexual relationships, whether they arise in the context of a long established marriage, or partnership, or a casual sexual encounter between total strangers. Arguments about consent abound just because consent to sexual intercourse extends from passionate enthusiasm to reluctant or bored acquiescence, and its absence includes quiet submission or surrender as well as determined physical resistance against an attacker which might expose the victim to injury, and sometimes death. The declared objective of the White Paper, *Protecting the Public* (Cm. 5668, 2002) was to produce statutory provisions relating to consent which would be 'clear and unambiguous'. As enacted, the legislation on this topic has not commanded totally uncritical enthusiasm. For some it goes too far, and for others not far enough. The law in the area, and our decision, must be governed by the definition of consent in section 74.

Neither 'freedom', nor 'capacity', are further defined or explained within section 74 itself, nor indeed in sections 75 and 76, which create evidential presumptions relating to consent. We note the analysis in the illuminating article, *The Sexual Offences Act 2003, Rape, Sexual Assault and the Problems of Consent*, (2004) CLR 328 by Professor Temkin and Professor Ashworth, that 'it might be thought that "freedom" and "choice" are ideas which raise philosophical issues of such complexity as to be ill-suited to the needs of criminal justice—clearly those words do not refer to total freedom or choice, so all the questions about how much liberty of action satisfies the "definition" remains at large'. Notwithstanding these philosophical difficulties, it is clear that for the purposes of the 2003 Act 'capacity' is integral to the concept of 'choice', and therefore to 'consent'.

Section 75 and section 76 of the 2003 Act [see sections 20.2.1.4 and 20.2.1.5] address the issue of consent in practical situations which arise from time to time in cases of alleged sexual offences including rape. They are not, however, exhaustive. The presumptions in section 75 are evidential and rebuttable, whereas those in section 76 are irrebuttable and conclusive. In this appeal we are not concerned with either of the conclusive presumptions relating to consent specified in section 76. The common characteristic of the particular situations covered by the evidential presumptions in section 75 is that they are concerned with situations in which the complainant is involuntarily at a disadvantage. Section 75(2)(f) is plainly adequate to deal with the situation when a drink is 'spiked', but unless productive of a state of near unconsciousness, or incapacity, this paragraph does not address seductive blandishments to have 'just one more' drink. Section 75(2)(d) repeats well established common law principles, and acknowledges plain good sense, that, if the complainant is unconscious as a result of her voluntary consumption of alcohol, the starting point is to presume that she is not consenting to intercourse. Beyond that, the Act is silent about the impact of excessive but voluntary alcohol consumption on the ability to give consent to intercourse, or indeed to consent generally.

It is perhaps helpful to identify a number of features of the law relating to consent which although obvious are sometimes overlooked. On any view, both parties to the act of sexual intercourse with which this case is concerned were the worse for drink. Both were adults. Neither acted unlawfully in drinking to excess. They were both free to choose how much to drink, and with whom. Both were free, if they wished, to have intercourse with each other. There is nothing abnormal, surprising, or even unusual about men and women having consensual intercourse when one, or other, or both have voluntarily consumed a great deal of alcohol. Provided intercourse is indeed consensual, it is not rape.

In cases which are said to arise after voluntary consumption of alcohol the question is not whether the alcohol made either or both less inhibited than they would have been if sober, nor whether either or both might afterwards have regretted what had happened, and indeed wished that it had not. If the complainant consents, her consent cannot be revoked. Moreover it is not a question whether either or both may have had very poor recollection of precisely what had happened. That may be relevant to the reliability of their evidence. Finally, and certainly, it is not a question whether either or both was behaving irresponsibly. As they were both autonomous adults, the essential question for decision is, as it always is, whether the evidence proved that the appellant had sexual intercourse with the complainant without her consent.

Before the 2003 Act, it was not difficult to identify the relevant legal principles, and for a judge to explain the law relating to the voluntary consumption of alcohol (or drugs) by a complainant. Thus, for example, in *R v Malone* [1998] 2 CAR 447 the Court of Appeal upheld the direction:

'She does not claim to have physically resisted nor to have verbally protested. She says the drink has disabled her from doing either . . . she has told you she did not consent . . . you must be sure that the act of sexual intercourse occurred without (her) consent. Submitting to an act of sexual intercourse, because through drink she was unable physically to resist though she wished to, is not consent. If she submits to intercourse because of the drink she cannot physically resist, that, of course, is not consent. No right thinking person would say that in those circumstances she was genuinely consenting to what occurred. What occurred . . . not wishing to have intercourse but being physically unable to do anything about it . . . would plainly, as a matter of common sense be against her will. It would be without her consent'.

We record this direction as illustrative of what was regarded as an appropriate direction in the circumstances of an individual case to a particular jury, rather than a learned disquisition of the law of consent as applied to rape. We should however highlight *R v Lang* [1976] 62 CAR 50 which summarised the relevant principle. The jury sought guidance from the judge on the question of whether the complainant's alcohol consumption may have vitiated her consent to sexual intercourse. The court observed

'. . . there is no special rule applicable to drink and rape. If the issue be, as here, did the woman consent? The critical question is not how she came to take the drink, but whether she understood her situation and was capable of making up her mind. In *Howard* [1965] 50 CAR 56 the Court of Criminal Appeal had to consider the case of a girl under 16. Lord Parker CJ . . . said: . . . "in the case of a girl under 16 the prosecution . . . must prove either that she physically resisted, or, if she did not, that her understanding and knowledge was such that she was not in a position to decide whether to consent or resist". In our view these words are of general application whenever there is present some factor, be it permanent or transient, suggesting the absence of such understanding or knowledge . . . None of this was explained to the jury. Their attention was focussed by the judge upon how she came to take drink, not upon the state of her understanding and her capacity to exercise judgment in the circumstances.'

In the context of the statutory provision in section 74, it is noteworthy that *Lang* decided thirty years or so ago, directly focussed on the 'capacity' of the complainant to decide whether to consent to intercourse or not. These are the concepts with which the 2003 Act itself is concerned.

We are not aware of any reported decisions which deal with this aspect of the new legislation. We should however refer to the much publicised case of *R v Dougal*, heard in Swansea Crown Court, in November 2005. Having heard the evidence of the complainant, the Crown decided to offer no further evidence. Before the jury counsel for the Crown explained:

> 'the prosecution are conscious of the fact that a drunken consent is still a consent and that in the answer, in cross examination, she said, in terms, that she could not remember giving her consent and that is fatal to the prosecution's case. In those circumstances the prosecution will have no further evidence on the issue of consent. This is a case of the word of the defendant against that of the complainant on that feature It is fatal to the prosecution's case . . .'

The judge (Roderick Evans J) directed the jury that as the prosecution was no longer seeking a guilty verdict, there was only one verdict which could be returned, and that was an acquittal. He added that he agreed with the course the prosecution had taken.

Without knowing all the details of the case, and focusing exclusively on the observations of counsel for the Crown in *Dougal*, it would be open to question whether the inability of the complainant to remember whether she gave her consent or not might on further reflection be approached rather differently. Prosecuting counsel may wish he had expressed himself more felicitously. That said, one of the most familiar directions of law provided to juries who are being asked to conclude that the voluntary consumption of alcohol by a defendant should lead to the conclusion that he was too drunk to form the intention required for proof of the crime alleged against him, is that a drunken intent is still an intent. (*R v Sheehan and Moore* [1975] 60 CAR 308 at 312). So it is, and that we suspect is the source of the phrase that a 'drunken consent is still consent'. In the context of consent to intercourse, the phrase lacks delicacy, but, properly understood, it provides a useful shorthand accurately encapsulating the legal position. We note in passing that it also acts as a reminder that a drunken man who intends to commit rape, and does so, is not excused by the fact that his intention is a drunken intention.

Some of the hugely critical discussion arising after *Dougal* missed the essential point. Neither counsel for the Crown, nor for that matter the judge, was saying or coming anywhere near saying, either that a complainant who through drink is incapable of consenting to intercourse must nevertheless be deemed to have consented to it, or that a man is at liberty to have sexual intercourse with a woman who happens to be drunk, on the basis that her drunkenness deprives her of her right to choose whether to have intercourse or not. Such ideas are wrong in law, and indeed, offensive. All that was being said in *Dougal* was that when someone who has had a lot to drink is in fact consenting to intercourse, then that is what she is doing, consenting: equally, if after taking drink, she is not consenting, then by definition intercourse is taking place without her consent. This is unexceptionable.

In our judgment, the proper construction of section 74 of the 2003 Act, as applied to the problem now under discussion, leads to clear conclusions. If, through drink (or for any other reason) the complainant has temporarily lost her capacity to choose whether to have intercourse on the relevant occasion, she is not consenting, and subject to questions about the defendant's state of mind, if intercourse takes place, this would be rape. However, where the complainant has voluntarily consumed even substantial quantities of alcohol, but nevertheless remains capable of choosing whether or not to have intercourse, and in drink agrees to do so, this would not be rape. We should perhaps underline that, as a matter of practical reality, capacity to consent may evaporate well before a complainant becomes unconscious. Whether this is so or not, however, is fact specific, or more accurately, depends on the actual state of mind of the individuals involved on the particular occasion.

Considerations like these underline the fact that it would be unrealistic to endeavour to create some kind of grid system which would enable the answer to these questions to be related to some prescribed level of alcohol consumption. Experience shows that different individuals have a greater or lesser capacity to cope with alcohol than others, and indeed the ability of a single individual to do so may vary from day to day. The practical reality is that there are some areas of human behaviour which are inapt for detailed legislative structures. In this context, provisions intended to protect women from sexual assaults might very well be conflated into a system which would provide patronising interference with the right of autonomous adults to make personal decisions for themselves.

For these reasons, notwithstanding criticisms of the statutory provisions, in our view the 2003 Act provides a clear definition of 'consent' for the purposes of the law of rape, and by defining it with reference to 'capacity to make that choice', sufficiently addresses the issue of consent in the context of voluntary consumption of alcohol by the complainant. The problems do not arise from the legal principles. They lie with infinite circumstances of human behaviour, usually taking place in private without independent evidence, and the consequent difficulties of proving this very serious offence. The jury were rightly directed that an essential requirement before the appellant could be convicted was that M did not consent to intercourse. They were told that 'a person consents if he agrees by choice and has the freedom and capacity to make that choice'. The statutory definition having been read, no further elucidation was given. Our attention was drawn to *R v Olugboga* [1981] 73 CAR 344, decided after the enactment of the Sexual Offences (Amendment) Act 1976. As Professor Temkin and Professor Ashworth explain, the report *Setting the Boundaries: Reforming the Law on Sexual Offences* (2000) which echoed a much earlier report by an advisory group chaired by Heilbron J in November 1975, suggested that the broad approach to consent and submission adopted in *Olugboga* should be abandoned. In our view, even if these criticisms are justified, the judgment contains passages of continuing value. The court rejected the submission on behalf of the Crown that a trial judge was required 'merely to leave the issue of consent to a jury in a similar way to that in which the issue of dishonesty is left in trials for offences under the Theft Act'. Because of the myriad circumstances in which the issue of consent may arise, the judgment continued, 'We do not think that the issue of consent should be left to a jury without some further direction. What this should be will depend on the circumstances of each case.'

In this case the jury should have been given some assistance with the meaning of 'capacity' in circumstances where the complainant was affected by her own voluntarily induced intoxication, and also whether, and to what extent they could take that into account in deciding whether she had consented. Moreover, the judge did not address the changed way in which the prosecution put its case against the appellant. There is a significant difference between an allegation that the complainant was unconscious and for that reason not consenting to intercourse, and an allegation that, although she was capable of giving consent, despite her state, she was not in fact consenting to intercourse and was giving clear indications that she was rejecting the appellant. The potential for confusion was compounded by the fact that the complainant herself asserted, more than once, that she was unconscious at different stages of the encounter. At the same time the Crown conceded that what she believed to be and said were periods of unconsciousness should for the purposes of the trial be treated as moments of memory deficit caused by drink. Of course if the Crown was not contending that she was unconscious, that at least was consistent with the appellant's case that she was indeed conscious throughout. . . .

Appeal allowed

■ *Questions*

1. Do you agree with the court that the definition of consent is clear?
2. Should the Court of Appeal have focused more on B's lack of capacity to consent, rather than whether or not she 'actually' consented? See G. Firth, 'Not an Invitation to Rape: The Sexual Offences Act 2003, Consent and the Case of the "Drunken" Victim' (2011) 62 NILQ 99.

In *Hysa* [2007] EWCA Crim 2056, a 16-year-old girl on a New Year's Eve celebration in London became separated from her friends and after drinking half a bottle of vodka, and taking cannabis, ended up in a car with three strangers. One allegedly raped her and fingered her vagina. She confirmed in her evidence that she did not want to have sex with the man, that she did not think that she did so willingly and she did not think that she would have consented. She said she could not remember what she had said to the man because she was drunk. When pressed in cross-examination, she said she could not recall what she was thinking or saying. Counsel for the Crown argued that it was clear that the complainant meant she could not say whether she had actually said 'yes' or 'no'. The Court of Appeal concluded that the judge erred in withdrawing the case:

> It was for the jury, not the judge, to decide, on the basis of the evidence called, whether, on these facts, in this case, the complainant had the capacity to consent and/or in fact consented to intercourse or not. . . . Issues of consent and capacity to consent to intercourse in cases of alleged rape should normally be left to the jury to determine. It would be a rare case indeed where it would be appropriate for a judge to stop a case in which, on one view, a 16 year old girl, alone at night and vulnerable through drink, is picked up by a stranger who has sex with her within minutes of meeting her and she says repeatedly she would not have consented to sex in these circumstances.

■ *Questions*

1. B is drunk. A knows that B has been drinking but is unsure how much. A penetrates B with his penis. B does not resist or give positive encouragement. What must the prosecution show in order to secure a conviction for rape?

2. What should the jury be told in such a case?

20.2.1.4 Section 75: evidential presumptions

If A is proved to have performed the relevant act to which s 75 applies (in the case of rape that is penile penetration), and it is proved that any of the circumstances listed in s 75(2) exists and A knows it exists, the complainant is taken not to have consented and A not to have a reasonable belief in her consent unless sufficient evidence is adduced to raise the issue.

The circumstances in s 75(2) and (3) are:

(2) ...

    (a) any person was, at the time of the relevant act or immediately before it began, using violence against the complainant or causing the complainant to fear that immediate violence would be used against him;

    (b) any person was, at the time of the relevant act or immediately before it began, causing the complainant to fear that violence was being used, or that immediate violence would be used, against another person;

    (c) the complainant was, and the defendant was not, unlawfully detained at the time of the relevant act;

    (d) the complainant was asleep or otherwise unconscious at the time of the relevant act;

    (e) because of the complainant's physical disability, the complainant would not have been able at the time of the relevant act to communicate to the defendant whether the complainant consented;

    (f) any person had administered to or caused to be taken by the complainant, without the complainant's consent, a substance which, having regard to when it was administered or

> taken, was capable of causing or enabling the complainant to be stupefied or overpowered at the time of the relevant act.
>
> (3) In subsection (2)(a) and (b), the reference to the time immediately before the relevant act began is, in the case of an act which is one of a continuous series of sexual activities, a reference to the time immediately before the first sexual activity began.

In Parliament, Baroness Scotland of Asthal explained:

> In order for these presumptions not to apply, the defendant will need to satisfy the judge from the evidence that there is a real issue about consent that is worth putting to the jury. The evidence relied on may be, for example, evidence that the defendant himself gives in the witness box, or evidence given on his behalf by a defence witness, or evidence given by the complainant during cross-examination. If the judge is satisfied that there is sufficient evidence to justify putting the issue of consent to the jury, then the issues will have to be proved by the prosecution in the normal way. If the judge does not think the evidence relied on by the defendant meets the threshold, he will direct the jury to find the defendant guilty. (Hansard HL, 17 June 2003, col 670)

Any one of the circumstances must be 'proved' before the presumption bites. A has to *know* that 'those circumstances existed' (s 75(1)(c)). But the requirement is only that any *one* circumstance is proved (s 75(1)(b)). The presumption only applies in the first place if three issues are proved by the prosecution—the sexual act (in rape that is penile penetration), the specified circumstance and A's awareness of it.

■ *Questions*

Why do these presumptions apply to the issue of consent rather than merely to A's belief? There is no requirement that the existence of the circumstances listed in (a)–(f) *caused* B's lack of consent. Should there be?

A problem stems from the fact that there is no direct match between the issues proved by the prosecution in s 75(1) and the issues about which A is obliged to raise evidence. The prosecution are establishing the act, the circumstance and the awareness of the circumstance. A is not required to rebut those directly. He has to rebut the presumed legal consequences of the elements that have been proved by the prosecution—A rebuts consent/reasonable belief in consent. For example, the prosecution prove that A had sex and that the circumstance existed—B was unconscious and produced some evidence that A was aware of that circumstance. A then raises an issue that although he was aware of the unconsciousness, he reasonably believed in B's consent but does not challenge that sex occurred nor that she was unconscious. It seems that the presumption still applies in relation to the absence of consent. The prosecution might prove absence of consent merely by proving the three initial elements of the presumption in s 75(1). Is it for the judge to decide whether or not A's evidential burden is discharged.

If the trial judge decides that there is sufficient evidence to raise an issue as to whether the complainant consented and/or the accused reasonably believed the complainant was consenting, then the judge will put the issues to the jury and s 75 has no part to play. In the relatively rare cases where the judge decides that there is not sufficient evidence on one or both of the issues, a s 75 direction must be given on that issue. See *White* [2010] EWCA Crim 1929 at [10].

As to what is necessary before A discharges the evidential burden, Lord Judge CJ in *Ciccarelli* [2011] EWCA Crim 2665 stated that there must be some evidence that A's belief was reasonable. In that case, the reasonableness of A's belief was based on a single flirtatious advance that B denied had occurred. The Court of Appeal held that the trial judge was correct to hold that this was insufficient to raise any issue for the consideration of the jury. In *Mba* [2012] EWCA Crim 2773 the Court of Appeal held that because the jury had found A guilty of committing grievous bodily harm with intent on B, this negated any question as to consent on the part of B or reasonable belief in her consent and so therefore A's conviction was safe despite the deficiencies in the judge's summing-up.

Threats of violence

The threat of/actual violence in (a) and (b) need not emanate from A. The 2003 Act has no section to replace the Sexual Offences Act 1956, s 2 (procuring sexual intercourse by threats).

■ *Questions*

1. Why is the element in s 75(2)(a) one of immediate violence? What if A threatens B that he will get her 'one day' unless she has sex with him now? Will the court interpret this as flexibly as in the case of offences against the person? What of threats less than those of force/violence?

2. A threatens to shoot B unless she has sex with him. She acquiesces. Rape?

3. A threatens to expose B's adultery unless she has sex with him. She acquiesces. Rape?

4. Has the new law dealt adequately with the need to criminalize sexual conduct where B claims that she was not consenting although she offered no physical resistance and was not threatened with violence by A? Is English law compatible with the obligation to protect complainants from sexual attack (amounting to inhuman and degrading treatment contrary to Article 3 of the ECHR)? Cf *MC v Bulgaria* (2005) 40 EHRR 20.

Unconscious victims

It seems uncontroversial that when B is unconscious she cannot consent to sexual acts.

■ *Questions*

1. A and B agree that they will have sex later that evening when they return from the party they are both attending. By the time they leave the party B is so heavily intoxicated that she cannot walk and A carries her home. He has sex with her while she is unconscious. Rape?

2. A touches B sexually (note that the presumption applies to offences of touching and not just penetrative acts) as she sleeps. This is a gesture of intimacy to wake her. Is A presumed to have acted without her consent? What would A have to show to rebut the presumption?

See also *Bree*, section 20.2.1.3, p 708, on intoxication and unconsciousness.

Stupefying complainants

This provision was introduced late in the Bill's progress as a response to the growing concern over 'drug-assisted rape'. See E. Finch and V. Munro, 'Intoxicated Consent and the Boundaries of Drug Assisted Rape' [2003] Crim LR 773; 'The Sexual Offences Act 2003: Intoxicated Consent and Drug Assisted Rape Revisited' [2004] Crim LR 789. Under the old law there was a much narrower offence under s 4(1) of the 1956 Act applicable to administering drugs to women with intent to stupefy or overpower in order only to facilitate intercourse. The new presumption of non-consent applies to complainants of both sexes and to sexual acts other than vaginal intercourse.

Although targeted at drugs which induce states of incapacity such as Rohypnol and GHB, (gamma hydroxyl butyrate acid), there is no statutory limitation on the type of substance which will trigger the presumption. Alcohol is certainly capable of satisfying the definition, so A who surreptitiously laces B's soft drink with spirits will be caught. If B's consumption is purely voluntary and fully informed, the presumption does not apply. The section does not apply to the 'seductive blandishments to have "just one more drink"' per Igor Judge P in *Bree*, at [24] (section 20.2.1.3, p 709).

■ *Question*

B indicates at the beginning of the date that she would not have sex with A. A surreptitiously laces B's drink with potent alcohol and B later willingly engages in sexual activity with A (not being unconscious or stupefied), her inhibitions having been lowered. Is A nevertheless presumed to be acting without consent?

20.2.1.5 Section 76: conclusive presumptions

If A performed the relevant act (in the case of rape that is penetration—it will differ as between the other non-consensual offences) and any one of the circumstances specified in s 76(2) existed, it is to be *conclusively presumed* that the complainant did not consent to the relevant act, and that A did not believe that the complainant consented. The circumstances in s 76(2) are:

(a) the defendant intentionally deceived the complainant as to the nature or purpose of the relevant act;

(b) the defendant intentionally induced the complainant to consent to the relevant act by impersonating a person known personally to the complainant.

■ *Questions*

1. A impersonates B's husband and has sex with B. B knows that A is not her husband but wants to have sex with A anyway. She does not tell A that she knows he is not her husband. Is A guilty of an offence? Is B?

2. Why are these frauds under s 76(2) conclusive of anything beyond A's absence of a belief in consent?

Section 76(2)(a): nature or purpose

The 2003 Act changes the law quite significantly in respect of frauds vitiating consent. It is important to distinguish between frauds as to the nature of the act, frauds as to the purpose of the act and frauds as to peripheral issues.

Under the 1956 Act, frauds by A as to the nature of the act would vitiate B's consent. In *Flattery* (1877) 2 QBD 410 (approved in *Williams* [1923] 1 KB 340), A told B, aged 19, that he could cure her of her fits by performing a surgical operation upon her. She allowed him to have intercourse with her, believing that the act was a surgical one.

■ *Questions*

If in this case B did not understand what sexual intercourse was (ie she had no sexual education at all), would this be an offence under s 76(a)? What if B knew what sexual intercourse involved (ie the mechanics of the act), but not the social implications of having sex?

It has been held that a defendant's failure to disclose his HIV status did not affect the issue of consent in rape where there were no allegations that A had deceived B, rather that he had forcibly attacked B. The evidence of his HIV status should have been excluded: *EB* [2006] EWCA Crim 2945 (section 20.2.1.3). There was an argument that although under the old law a deception as to HIV-infected status was only a deception as to an attribute, and not the nature of the act, there could be no rape, the new law might prompt the courts to take a different view. In *EB*, the Court of Appeal rejected this idea. If A has not disclosed his HIV positive status to B, he will be at risk of conviction under the Offences Against the Person Act 1861, s 20 (section 18.4, p 652). The courts' view is thta he has defrauded B as to the risk of infection, but he has not defrauded B as to the nature of the act of sexual intercourse. Do you agree?

Frauds as to the purpose of the Act are much more difficult to deal with under the old law. In *Linekar* [1994] EWCA Crim 2, [1995] Crim LR 321, A was charged with raping a prostitute, B. A approached B and she agreed to have intercourse with him for £25. Having had intercourse D left without paying. Was that a fraud as to the purpose? Is it the purpose of the act or the actor that matters?

R v Jheeta

[2007] EWCA Crim 1699, Court of Appeal, Criminal Division, http://www.bailii.org/ew/cases/EWCA/Crim/2007/1699.html

(Sir Igor Judge P, Simon J and HHJ Goldsack QC)

The victim, B, was a student who had had a sexual relationship with A. She started receiving text messages and telephone calls of a threatening nature, for example, 'We are going to kidnap you'; 'We are going to convert you'; 'We are going to kill you'. She told A. He was responsible for all the messages, but hid this fact from her and offered to arrange protection for her. He claimed to have alerted the police on her behalf and sent her text messages purporting to be from a police officer: PC Ken. Regular text messages were sent to B asking her for details of the phone calls and messages she had received, and requiring her to submit statements by text. 'PC Ken' told B that A would be able to watch her house and arrange for security including undercover protection at a cost of £1,000 annually. She paid. PC Bob took over from PC Ken—he too was a fiction created by A. PC Thomas was created and he sent more messages. Whenever she sought to break off with A, she would receive text messages from the different police officers, telling her that A had tried to kill himself and that she should do her duty and take care of him. She was told that she should sleep with A, and that she would be liable to a fine if she did not. She received something like 50 such demands over a four-year period. On each occasion B had intercourse with A in a hotel room. But for the messages from the fictitious police officers, she would not have done so. Eventually A's subterfuge was uncovered.

[Sir Igor Judge P reviewed the facts and A's response in police interview.]

In answer to the direct question, 'when you had sex with [B] on those occasions, did you have true consent?', he responded 'No'. He admitted that she had intercourse with him because of the texts. She would have been content with intercourse from time to time, but he wanted greater frequency. These admissions assume considerable significance when the basis of plea is examined. . . .

[His lordship referred to the indictment and the possible pleas that had been considered and then to ss 74 to 76 of the Act.]

Our particular concern is with section 76(2)(a), the 'nature and purpose' of the 'relevant act'. For the purposes of sections 75 and 76, relevant act is defined by section 77. In the context of rape the relevant act is 'the defendant intentionally penetrating, with his penis, . . . another person ("the complainant")'. The provisions relating to consent are not confined to rape, but do not at present require further examination. Perhaps more important, the offence of procuring a woman to have sexual intercourse by false pretences ceased to exist when the 2003 Act came into force....

This consideration provided part of the foundation for the submission by [counsel for the Crown] that a statute which brought together all the offences of a sexual nature cannot have been intended to decriminalise deliberate conduct designed to deceive a woman into having sexual intercourse. Here, the appellant's purpose was to deceive the complainant into having sexual intercourse with him in order to alleviate or remove the problems which she, having been deceived by him, believed she faced. The result was that she submitted to intercourse because of those extraneous pressures. These submissions broadened from the narrow consideration of section 76(2)(a) of the Act into the wider question of consent as defined in section 74. The appellant's actions deprived the complainant of her freedom to choose whether or not to have intercourse with him. He pleaded guilty on the basis that at least on some occasions her freedom to choose was constrained by his actions. For the moment we shall confine our attention to the irrebuttable presumption in section 76(2)(a).

[Counsel for the appellant] submitted that the Act incorporated the common law on these issues into statute, and created the irrebuttable evidential presumptions. The fact that the presumptions in section 76 are conclusive reinforced the need for circumspection about an extended interpretation of the 'nature or purpose' of the relevant act. The deception, within the limits described in the basis of plea, is conceded, but it was not a deception about the nature or purpose of the relevant act. The complainant was sexually experienced. She was aware of the nature and purpose of intercourse, and the identity of the applicant. The advice given to the appellant was incorrect in law. There was no deception operating on the mind of the complainant about the nature or purpose of the Act. The conclusive presumptions could not be established. The plea was tendered after legal advice which did not accurately reflect the statutory provisions. Therefore the convictions are unsafe.

Our approach is to address the ambit of section 76 in the context of the creation of an irrebuttable evidential presumption, with wide application to effectively every incident of sexual touching. Professor Temkin and Professor Ashworth explained one possible consequences of a wide interpretation of 76 in their valuable article, *The Sexual Offences Act 2003 (1) Rape Sexual Assault and the Problems of Consent* (2004) CLR 328 at 338.

> 'Those who are uncomfortable with the full implications of sexual autonomy may not share the view that a conclusive presumption of absence of consent should apply where D has sex with C who is asleep at the time. The provisions of the Act on consent apply not only to rape and assault by penetration but also to touching which falls within sexual assault or causing sexual activity. A conclusive presumption of absence of consent and absence of reasonable belief in consent, if applied to all situations where C was asleep at the time, would render D liable for sexual assault if he sexually touched his partner C while C was asleep even though D was in the habit of doing so and C had not objected to this in the past'.

The writers point out that a complaint, and subsequent prosecution, would be unlikely. However it would seem pretty surprising to couples sharing a bed to be told that the law prohibited either of them from intimately touching the other while asleep, and that they would be potentially liable to prosecution and punishment, for a sexual touch of the sleeping partner as a preliminary to possible sexual activity which the sleeping partner, on awakening, might welcome. The article also addresses 'the problem' of the repeal of the offence of procuring sexual intercourse by false representations. It explains that convictions for this offence were rare, adding that 'in the unusual case where this issue occurs, the vague terms of section 74 now assume a heightened importance'.

The starting point in our analysis is to acknowledge that in most cases, the absence of consent, and the appropriate state of the defendant's mind, will be proved without reference to evidential or conclusive presumptions. When they do apply, section 75 and section 76 are directed to the process of proving the absence of consent to whichever sexual act is alleged. They are concerned with presumptions about rather than the definition of consent. The evidential presumptions in section 75 continue to require the prosecution to disprove consent if, in the circumstances defined in the section, there is sufficient evidence to raise the issue. These presumptions are not conclusive, merely evidential. However section 76 raises presumptions conclusive of the issue of consent, and thus where intercourse is proved, conclusive of guilt. They therefore require the most stringent scrutiny.

In our judgment the ambit of section 76 is limited to the 'act' to which it is said to apply. In rape cases the 'act' is vaginal, anal or oral intercourse. Provided this consideration is constantly borne in mind, it will be seen that section 76(2)(a) is relevant only to the comparatively rare cases where the defendant deliberately deceives the complainant about the *nature or purpose* of one or other form of intercourse. No conclusive presumptions arise merely because the complainant was deceived in some way or other by disingenuous blandishments of or common or garden lies by the defendant. These may well be deceptive and persuasive, but they will rarely go to the nature or purpose of intercourse. Beyond this limited type of case, and assuming that, as here, section 75 has no application, the issue of consent must be addressed in the context of section 74.

It may be helpful to reinforce these observations by reference to a number of cases at common law which provide examples of deceptions as to the nature or purpose of the act of intercourse.

[His lordship referred to *Flattery* and *Williams*, section 20.2.1.5, p 715.]

Deception as to purpose is sometimes said to be exemplified in *R v Tabassum* [2000] 2 CAR 328, a decision described by the late Professor Sir John Smith as a 'doubtful case'. A number of women agreed to participate in a breast cancer research programme at the behest of the appellant when, as a result of what he said or did, or both, they wrongly believed that he was medically qualified or trained. They consented to a medical examination, not to sexual touching by a stranger. 'There was consent to the nature of the act, but not to its quality'. However section 76 (2)(a) does not address the 'quality' of the act, but confines itself to its 'purpose'. In the latest edition of *Smith and Hogan Criminal Law*, (11th edition) Professor David Ormerod identifies a better example, *R v Green* [2002] EWCA Crim 1501. Bogus medical examinations of young men were carried out by a qualified doctor, in the course of which they were wired up to monitors while they masturbated. The purported object was to assess their potential for impotence. Although the experiment did not involve any form of intercourse, it illustrates the practice of a deception as to the 'purpose' of the physical act.

These examples demonstrate the likely rarity of occasions when the conclusive presumption in section 76 (2)(a) will apply. For example, *R v Linekar* [[1994] EWCA Crim 2]] would not fall within its ambit. The appellant promised to pay a prostitute £25 if she had intercourse with him. It was a promise he never intended to keep. On this aspect of the case, that is, that the defendant tricked the prostitute into having intercourse with him, the judge left it to the jury to consider whether his fraud vitiated her consent which was given on the basis that he would pay. The conviction was quashed. The consent given by the complainant was a real consent, which was not destroyed by the appellant's false pretence. If anything, he was guilty of an offence under section 3 of the 1956 Act, that is an offence identical to the offence alleged in counts one and two of the present indictment. Linekar deceived the prostitute about his intentions. He undoubtedly lied to her. However she was undeceived about either the nature or the purpose of the act, that is intercourse. Accordingly the conclusive presumptions in section 76 would have no application.

With these considerations in mind, we must return to the present case. On the written basis of plea the appellant undoubtedly deceived the complainant. He created a bizarre and fictitious fantasy which, because it was real enough to her, pressurised her to have intercourse with him more frequently than she otherwise would have done. She was not deceived as to the nature or purpose of intercourse, but deceived as to the situation in which she found herself. In our judgment the conclusive presumption in section 76 (2)(a) had no application, and counsel for the appellant below were wrong to advise on the basis that it did. . . .

Appeal against conviction dismissed

■ Questions

1. About what, if anything, had B been deceived in this case? Did she understand the physical nature of the acts? Was she deceived about with whom she was doing them?

2. How would *Tabassum* be decided under the 2003 Act?

3. What of A, a doctor, who tells B, accurately, that an intimate medical examination is necessary. She allows this to happen. X, A's friend, derives sexual gratification from watching covertly (cf *Bolduc & Bird* (1967) 63 DLR (2d) 82). Is there a deception as to 'the purpose' of the acts?

In *Piper* [2007] EWCA Crim 2151, A invited young women who were 'willing to flaunt it' to attend interviews for 'modelling work'. They had to strip to their underwear and A secretly video-recorded them. A measured them for bikinis and 'was more careless with his hands than one might have expected him to be if he were doing it with any sense of appropriateness'. He pleaded guilty to sexual assault and 'acknowledged that the women would not have consented to allow themselves to be measured or take their clothes off if they had appreciated that it was a charade'.

■ Question

What were the 'wannabe' models deceived about?

A more bizarre twist on this problem arose in *Devonald* [2008] EWCA Crim 527. The complainant, was a 16-year-old boy who had been in a relationship with A's daughter. The relationship had broken down and, believing B to have treated his daughter badly, A sought to teach him a lesson by deliberately embarrassing him. A set up a fake email account pretending to be a young woman. A then corresponded with B over the internet and persuaded B to masturbate in front of a webcam. A was convicted of an offence of causing a person to engage in sexual activity without consent, having changed his plea to guilty following a ruling by the judge. The trial judge ruled that the Sexual Offences Act 2003, s 76(2)(a), would apply. The Court of Appeal dismissed an application for leave to appeal. It was open to the jury to conclude that B had been deceived as to the purpose of the masturbation.

■ Questions

1. Has B been deceived as to the nature of the act of masturbation? Was B deceived as to A's purpose in getting him to masturbate? Under s 4 it is arguable that it is this latter act which is the one about which B must be deceived—see s 77 of the Act which defines the 'relevant act' about which B must be deceived as being 'the defendant intentionally causing another person to engage in the activity where the activity is sexual'.

2. A tells B that his sexual technique is guaranteed to give her an orgasm. Because of this B has sex with him. A's performance is totally disappointing and B fails to have an orgasm. Has A raped B?

On one interpretation, it could be said that the decisions in *Jheeta* and *Devonald* conflict. The Court of Appeal resolved this conflict in *B* [2013] EWCA Crim 832 and held that, to the extent that there is any inconsistency between the two cases, *Jheeta* ought to be followed. In doing so, Hallett LJ stated that because s 76 contains a conclusive presumption, it ought to be narrowly interpreted and will only apply in rare cases.

R v B

[2013] EWCA Crim 832, Court of Appeal, Criminal Division

(Hallett LJ, Bean J and HHJ Pert QC)

B had been in a sexual relationship with A for five years. A contacted B on Facebook using the false name 'Grant'. B developed an online relationship with Grant, to the extent that she sent him pictures of herself posing topless. Grant then threatened B that if she did not engage in various sexual acts over the internet, he would send the compromising pictures to her employer and post them on the internet. B obeyed. B eventually confided to A about what Grant was making her do. A told B that she should lure Grant to a secluded place so that he could put the blackmail to and end. A subsequently told B that he had killed Grant and showed her a picture of a man with a gun to his head. A few weeks later, B was contacted on Facebook by A, who was now posing as 'Chad'. Chad told B that he was a friend of Grant's and knew what he had done. Chad claimed to be in possession of the topless photographs and told B he would send them to her employer if she did not do as he demanded. As a result of this, B carried out further acts involving penetration of her vagina and anus with objects. Eventually B contacted the police who discovered that it was A who had been posing as Grant and Chad. A denied that he believed that B was not consenting. A was found guilty of causing a person to engage in sexual activity without consent, contrary to s 4 of the Sexual Offences Act 2003.

Hallett LJ [gave the following guidance on the interpretation of s 76]:

9. Miss Kidd for the prosecution relied heavily upon a decision of this court in *R v Devonald* [2008] EWCA Crim 527. Devonald was a renewed application for leave to appeal against conviction on the basis the judge wrongly allowed reliance upon section 76.

[Her Ladyship set out the facts of *Devonald* and continued:]

10. Here, Miss Kidd observed, the complainant was led to believe that she was performing sexual acts for one or two complete strangers, under threat that if she failed to comply her place of work would be informed and the intimate pictures distributed. Thus, the deceit was threefold: as to the identity of the recipients of the web feed, the motivation of the recipients and the consequences of the failure to submit to the demands. Miss Kidd argued it would be artificial to divorce one of those facts from another. They should be looked at in the round and if so together they amounted to a clear case of deceit as to *purpose* of the relevant act.

11. Mr Bindloss for the defence submitted that section 76 did not apply. He preferred to rely upon the decision in *R v Jheeta* [2007] 2 Cr App R 34 in which the Court considered a full appeal against conviction as opposed to an application for leave.

[Her Ladyship then set out the facts of *Jheeta*, quoting the extract earlier in this section, and also of *Assange* before continuing:]

15. Nevertheless the judge chose to follow *Devonald*. He noted that the conclusive presumptions under section 76 should only apply in a very limited number of cases but was persuaded by Miss Kidd's arguments that the facts of the present case were very similar to those of *Devonald*. If, therefore, section 76 was applicable in *Devonald*, it was applicable in this case. He rejected Mr Bindloss' argument that the cases of *Jheeta* and *Devonald* conflicted and that *Jheeta* ought to be followed. He decided he would leave the issue of whether the complainant had been deceived as to purpose of the acts to the jury, but direct them that if they found deceit proved, the conclusive presumptions applied. He directed the jury in these terms (page 4G):

'The remaining issues in the case are to do with consent or reasonable belief in consent. Before I deal with consent and reasonable belief in consent in more detail, let me refer you to a question that Miss Kidd asked you Mr Bindloss took a different view about it. Miss Kidd said, "Did the defendant deceive Miss X?" Mr Bindloss said rightly, "That is not the right question." The question is not, "Did the defendant deceive Miss X?" It is accepted that he did deceive her as to who was sending messages. The question you have to ask yourselves in fact is did the defendant deceive Miss X as to the purpose of the acts? What the prosecution say is that she was deceived by the defendant by him pretending that he was one of two complete strangers whom she had never met, by threatening to tell her work what she had been doing on the internet or to publish pictures or footage of her on websites if she did not do as he told her, whereas in fact the reality was that he wasn't one of two complete strangers. He was her boyfriend. He was doing it for his own gratification or perhaps to get back at her for using Facebook, or to test loyalty, or to teach her to say no. This were various things that were raised by him during the course of his interviews. He said that since he was her boyfriend, he would never have published anything which harmed her.

So the question, members of the jury, is: has the prosecution made you sure that he deceived her as to the purpose of the acts? By deceiving her as to who it was and making all the threats, was he deceiving her to the purpose of the acts? If you are sure that he did deceive her as to the purpose of the various acts then, members of the jury, as a matter of law you must find that she did not consent to those acts and that the defendant did not believe that she consented to those acts. So if you are sure that he deceived her as to the purposes of the acts, you do not need to go on in detail the question of whether the prosecution has proved she was not consenting or whether they had proved that the defendant did not reasonably believe she was consenting.

It is only if the prosecution has not proved that she was deceived as to the purpose of the acts, only then would you have to go on to consider consent or reasonable belief in consent.'

Throughout the remainder of the summing-up the judge repeatedly referred to whether or not there had been 'deceit as to purpose' with no further explanation of what that meant. In his explanation of the route to verdict, he confirmed that if the jury was satisfied that the complainant had been 'deceived as to the purpose of the act', that was the end of the matter; their verdicts must be guilty.

16. There is but one ground of appeal and that was that the judge was wrong in law so to rule and so to direct. Mr Bindloss maintained his argument before us that there was here no 'deceit as to *purpose*'. He provided a dictionary definition of the word '*purpose*' namely: 'the reason for doing something' or the 'objective in doing something'. Taking those as the definitions of *purpose* he was prepared to accept that the decision in *Devonald* was correct because the applicant Devonald plainly misled the complainant as to his purpose for the sexual act. His true purpose was the complainant's humiliation not, as the complainant thought, sexual gratification.

17. Here, Mr Bindloss argued that the motive was clearly sexual gratification. That was the Crown's own case. The complainant was never asked as to what she understood the purpose or the motive of the person at the end of the webcam to be. One presumes she would have assumed the motive was sexual gratification; if so she was not misled as to the purpose.

18. In any event, Mr Bindloss argued the judge failed to give the jury an adequate direction on the application of section 76. It was incumbent upon him to give the jury clear directions as to the limited extent of the meaning of the word *purpose* and to identify the relevant evidence going to that issue. In reality, he simply adopted the prosecution approach of a global summary of the evidence coupled with the question: 'was the complainant thereby deceived as to purpose?'. He rolled up the various deceitful elements of the appellant's conduct. At no time did he direct the jury that deceit as to identity or deceit as to consequences would not be enough standing alone (see *Jheeta*).

19. There is no definition of the word *purpose* in the Act. It is a perfectly ordinary English word and one might have hoped it would not be necessary to provide a definition. It has been left to the courts and academics to struggle with its meaning in the context of a sexual act. We say 'struggle' advisedly because it may not be straightforward to ascertain the *purpose* of a sexual act. Those engaging in a sexual act may have a number of reasons or objectives and each party may have a different objective or reason. The Act does not specify whose *purpose* is under consideration. There is, therefore, a great danger in attempting any definition of the word *purpose* and in defining it too widely. A wide definition could bring within the remit of section 76 situations never contemplated by Parliament.

20. We shall, therefore, simply apply the normal rules of statutory construction and echo what was said in *Jheeta*. Where, as here, a statutory provision effectively removes from an accused his only line of defence to a serious criminal charge it must be strictly construed. We respectfully adopt the approach of the court in *Jheeta*. If there is any conflict between the decisions in *Jheeta* and *Devonald*, we would unhesitatingly follow *Jheeta*. Thus, it will be a rare case in which section 76 should be applied.

21. Is this one of those rare cases? Miss Kidd reminded the court of the extent of the deception and the affect upon the complainant. It was not unlike the extent and effect of the deception in *Jheeta*. Just as in *Jheeta*, this appellant undoubtedly deceived his girlfriend in a cruel and despicable way. However, the fact that there was a catalogue of deception of an unpleasant kind begs the question as to whether it was deception as to *purpose* so as to trigger the operation of section 76. We have our doubts.

22. The complainant was never asked what her purpose or understanding of the purpose of the act was and the appellant's purpose seems far from clear. His accounts varied but the most likely explanation, as the prosecution argued, was some kind of perverted sexual gratification. The complainant knew full well what she was being asked to do and what she did in fact do, namely perform a sexual act for the benefit of the camera. She could have been in no doubt that the motive was at least in part sexual gratification. If so, on one view, even if one were to extend the definition of *purpose* to include the appellant's intention, as has been suggested, there is here no evidence going to the issue of deceit as to his purpose.

23. Further, we see force in Mr Bindloss's submission that if reliance was to be placed on section 76, which effectively withdrew the accused's only line of defence, it was incumbent upon the judge to identify the evidence which went to the issue of 'deceit as to purpose'. Here there was no such analysis, and the jury were never directed that the word had a restricted meaning—see *Jheeta*. They were not informed that deceit as to what some commentators have called 'peripheral matters' was not enough.

24. For those reasons we are troubled by the way in which the prosecution put their case and by the way in which it was left to the jury. We understand how prosecuting counsel and the judge may have thought that the decision in *Devonald* applied and appeared to support reliance on section 76. However, as we have indicated, reliance upon section 76 in this case, on these facts and this evidence, was misplaced. The prosecution needed to look no further than the provisions of Section 74. It provides that 'a person consents if he agrees by choice and has the freedom and capacity to make that choice'. If the complainant only complied because she was being blackmailed, the prosecution might argue forcefully she did not agree by choice.

25. We turn to the question of safety. Miss Kidd argued there was ample evidence here to establish guilt. The complainant was a compelling witness and her distress obvious to all concerned. Miss Kidd submitted there cannot in truth have been any defence on actual consent or even reasonable belief in consent. Had the jury been directed solely by reference to section 74 she submitted the verdict would have been the same.

26. We see considerable force in the submission that the complainant was a compelling witness and was dreadfully distressed by the appellant's behaviour. However, whatever one thinks of him, he was entitled to a fair trial. He had only one avenue of defence, and given the admitted level of his deceit, that defence was effectively taken from him. Reluctantly, therefore, we feel we have no option but to declare the conviction unsafe.

■ *Questions*

1. Has s 76 now been rendered obsolete? In what circumstances might it apply?

2. Section 76 deals with cases in which there is a deception as to identity only where A was impersonating someone known to B. Was Grant 'known' to B?

J. Herring, 'Mistaken Sex'
[2005] Crim LR 511

Throughout history people have used all manner of deceptions to persuade others to have sex with them. And some things never change. ... Yet the law has traditionally been reluctant to criminalise the use of deception in sexual relationships. Consider this: Ted tells Mary he loves her and would like to marry her. As a result she buys him presents and lends him money. They also engage in sexual relationships. In fact Ted is a rogue. He has no feelings towards Mary and is known to have behaved in this way towards many women. If the facts could be proved there would be little difficulty in obtaining a conviction for obtaining property by deception. But it is generally thought that there would be no sexual offence; nor should there be. But why not? Is the law willing to protect property to a greater extent than sexual autonomy? ...

The traditional approach asks whether the victim's mistake is sufficient to negate her consent. The proper question should be: is the defendant's act that to which the victim has consented? ...

We could formulate a legal rule that would look something like this:

If at the time of the sexual activity a person:

(i) is mistaken as to a fact; and

(ii) had s/he known the truth about that fact would not have consented to it

then s/he did not consent to the sexual activity. If the defendant knows (or ought to know) that s/he did not consent (in the sense just described) then s/he is guilty of an offence.

Included within the word 'fact', in this test, would be the state of mind of the defendant. The mistake need not be to an issue which would be regarded as material to the reasonable person, if it was a pre-requisite to consent for the particular victim. Nor is there a need for the defendant to have caused the victim's mistake by a deception. So if A does not disclose his criminal past to his sexual partner, B, where B would not have consented to the activity had she known of it, B should be taken to have not consented. For A to engage in sexual activities with B knowing that B would not be consenting if A revealed facts about himself amounts to a fundamental lack of respect for B's sexual autonomy. Of course many people will be uninterested in their partner's past and that will not be relevant to a decision as to whether or not to consent to sexual relations. Further the mens rea requirement ensure that defendants will not be prosecuted when they did not (or should not have) realised that their partners would regard a particular fact as fundamental to their consent.

... The proposal is straightforward and explicable to juries. The Sexual Offences Act 2003 provides the courts with an opportunity to consider again the meaning of consent and to develop it along the lines proposed in this article. ...

■ *Questions*

Do you agree? Is there a difference between A deceiving B and B making a mistake? For a critique of the proposition that the purpose of sexual offences is to vindicate sexual autonomy, see J. Rubenfeld, 'The Riddle of Rape-by-Deception and the Myth of Sexual Autonomy' (2013) 122 Yale LJ 1372.

Hyman Gross, 'Rape, Moralism and Human Rights'
[2007] Crim LR 220

Jonathan Herring has proposed that the law of rape be extended to cover cases in which a man has deceived a woman about his feelings for her and about his intention to marry her in order to get her to have sex with him. If the man is right about the importance to her of love and marriage and is successful in seducing her through his deception he can be charged with rape. Herring's proposal rests on certain innovative ideas about consent. He suggests more generally that a woman is entitled to be informed about any facts that would make a difference to her decision to have sex. Any deception regarding such a fact would nullify her consent. His proposal does not stop there. If the man knew, or ought to have known, that the woman was mistaken about something that would make a difference to her decision, he is criminally liable since there was not valid consent to having sex.

This is an ambitious proposal. The law places strict limits on the kinds of deception that nullify consent. If the woman is deceived about what is going on, or about who she is doing it with, any consent she may have given is a nullity. If she is duped into thinking it is a medical procedure rather than intercourse, or deceived into thinking that the man in the darkened room is her boyfriend rather than someone else at the party, the man has had sex without valid consent. The law does not require the man to tell the woman the truth about whatever might be of concern to her in deciding whether to have sex.

Herring, however, is encouraged by s.76 of the Sexual Offences Act 2003 which provides that intentional deception as to the purpose of the act creates a conclusive presumption both that the woman did not consent to the act and that the man did not reasonably believe she did. In the Sexual Offences Act 2003 deception as to the purpose of the act is presumably meant to cover with greater precision of language than the common law provided the sort of case where a singing teacher told his student he needed to make an air passage to assist her in her singing and proceeded to have intercourse with her. Herring, however, argues that the purpose of the act should be extended to include what the parties understood the act of sexual intercourse to be about. If the man deceives the woman about his feelings and his intentions, under this enlarged conception of purpose he would be deceiving her about the purpose of the act. He is falsely representing the act as a way of expressing his feelings and expectations for the future. Having deceived her about the purpose of the act, he has vitiated any consent she may have given.

. . .

The first thing to be said is that s.76 is not on the books to punish men's deception, but to provide women with the protection they need when sex for a purpose is proposed. Consent to sex, like consent to other activities, may be strictly qualified, and the interests of the woman which the law protects by requiring consent remain protected against violation outside the bounds of the consent that is given. When a woman consents to engaging in intercourse for a particular purpose her consent is limited to sexual activity for that purpose. The purpose of an activity is determined by what the person engaging in it intends to accomplish by it. If it is a joint activity, as sex is, the two people engaging in it must both intend to accomplish the same thing for the activity to have that thing as its purpose. If it is not the man's intention to accomplish through intercourse what the woman intends to accomplish, their intercourse is not for the purpose that the woman supposes and so she has not consented to the intercourse they have. The singing teacher did not in fact intend to improve the singing ability of his gullible student by having sex with her, as he said, and so there was not consent to the sex they had. Had he truly believed the sex would open her air passages and help her singing their sex would be for the purpose he said and so her consent would be effective. Cases such as this are cases of sex for an ulterior purpose, an instrumental activity prompted by something to be achieved that marks its success. Such sex stands in stark contrast to the commonplace recreational activity that sex usually is. Sex simply for the pleasures of sex is not consented to conditionally, and though in deciding to have such sex a woman may well have made certain assumptions and may entertain certain expectations her willingness will not be conditional upon those expectations being pursued through the sex.

Herring's proposal for extending rape liability amounts to giving certain moral strictures legal effect. The proposed obligation not to deceive in obtaining consent comes down simply to making the telling of lies to get sex a punishable offence, at least when what is lied about is important to the woman. Placing the sex act on an elevated moral plane is an essential part of the argument. For

Herring, prevailing social attitudes are a disappointment, and public education to change them would be needed once the law of rape is extended as he suggests. What now are regarded as gambits in a game of seduction would be seen as fraudulent misrepresentations that corrupt a high-minded activity in which the participants are entitled to rely on mutual respect and honesty. On this view, in deciding to engage in sexual intercourse the woman is putting at risk her sexual autonomy and the preservation inviolate of the most intimate part of her person. Surely she is entitled to be protected by the law against the ignoble designs of some trickster.

■ *Question*

Do you agree?
See also J. Herring's spirited response, 'Human Rights and Rape: A Reply to Hyman Gross' [2007] Crim LR 228.

Section 76(2)(b)

By virtue of the Criminal Justice and Public Order Act 1994, s 142(3), it was rape for a man to induce a woman to have intercourse with him by impersonating her husband. At common law, this was extended to include impersonation of long-term (heterosexual) partnerships: *Elbekkay* [1994] EWCA Crim 1. Section 76(2)(b) extends the law beyond any particular category or duration of relationship, it also extends beyond the offence of rape to other acts of penetration and sexual activity. See also R. Williams, 'Deception Mistake and the Vitiation of the Victim's Consent' (2008) 124 LQR 132.

■ *Questions*

1. In s 76(2)(b) are all people B has ever met 'known personally to' B? Is it only those with whom B has had some greater degree of intimacy? Can B be known personally to a person by email correspondence? Consider the couple who arrange to meet after internet dating. A gets cold feet and decides he cannot face meeting B. X, his friend, steps in and assumes A's name. Is there a conclusive presumption that B was not consenting to any subsequent sexual activity?

2. If B visits a doctor's surgery and is told that the doctor on duty is Dr A, and B allows A to perform an intimate examination, which frauds by Dr A should negative B's apparent consent? That 'A' is really called 'X'? That A is not medically qualified? Which frauds are caught by s 76? See *Richardson* [1998] 2 Cr App R 200, [1999] Crim LR 62, section 19.3.1, p 677. Does it matter whether the examination is necessary?

3. Should rape be subdivided into offences of sex by force, sex by fraud, sex while B is intoxicated, etc? See V. Tadros, 'Rape Without Consent' (2006) 26 OJLS 515.

20.2.1.6 The mens rea of rape

The current test of mens rea as set out in s 1 of the 2003 Act (section 20.2.1, p 701) is markedly different from that proposed by the House of Lords in one of the most controversial decisions in the last few decades: *DPP v Morgan* [1975] 2 All ER 347, HL. There must be mens rea as to the penetration and also as to whether B is consenting. Despite the use of the word 'intention', in *Grewal* [2010] EWCA Crim 2448, relying upon *Heard* [2007] EWCA Crim 125, the Court of Appeal confirmed that rape is a crime of basic intent.

After *Morgan* and following the Heilbron Report (Cmnd 6352, 1975), rape was redefined in the Sexual Offences (Amendment) Act 1976, s 1(1), to include the case where the defendant was reckless as to whether the victim consents. The courts defined the mens rea as a state where A was reckless in the sense that he 'couldn't care less' whether B consented. The test was subjective. Someone cannot be said not to care less about something unless he has realized that there is a risk of it, and carried on. It might be that he has not in fact thought about it and if he had he would not have cared less, but that was not the test. It remained the case that A's unreasonable beliefs that B was consenting, if believed by the jury, would lead to an acquittal. There was little categorical evidence that *Morgan* defences were successfully run, so jurors were presumably not readily believing defendants' spurious claims. Nevertheless, the plea was easy to run and difficult to disprove, and sent an undesirable message—that it is acceptable to take unreasonable risks as to someone's consent to sexual conduct. See J. Horder, 'Cognition, Emotion and Criminal Culpability' (1990) 106 LQR 469 at 477; T. Pickard, 'Culpable Mistakes' (1980) 30 U Toronto LJ 75; C. Wells, 'Swatting the Subjectivist Bug' [1982] Crim LR 209.

One of the most significant effects of the 2003 Act is to reverse *Morgan*: a genuine but unreasonable belief in consent will be a sufficient mens rea for the offences in ss 1 to 4.

The mens rea in rape and the other non-consensual offences (ss 1 to 4) is that A does not reasonably believe B consents. Assessing whether a belief is reasonable is to be determined having regard to all the circumstances, including any steps A has taken to ascertain whether B consents.

Several issues remain controversial.

- Complexity—there are in effect two reasonableness elements. D's belief must be reasonable and, in assessing that, the process by which he came to that belief must be reasonable.

- Lack of a purely objective test—the question is whether A has a reasonable belief in consent. This must relate to A's personal capacity to evaluate whether B is consenting. A who does not think about B's consent is guilty, as is A who considers and wrongly concludes that B is consenting—unless that mistake is reasonable. The possibility of a purely objective test—whether the reasonable person would have believed B was consenting—was considered, but rejected in favour of this test which pays some heed to A's physical and mental capabilities. See for discussion of alternatives, H. Power, 'Towards a Redefinition of the *Mens Rea* of Rape' (2003) 23 OJLS 379.

- Ambiguity over how s 1(2) applies—is the correct question as to (i) A's purely subjective belief about consent measured against a standard of reasonableness applied by the jury or magistrate, or (ii) A's assessment that his own belief as to consent was reasonable?

- Is *Morgan* successfully abolished? Can A who is of limited mental capacity, who genuinely but unreasonably holds the belief that B is consenting, still run the defence that *he* made such efforts as *he* considered reasonable?

- Uncertainty over which of A's characteristics are to be considered when assessing whether it was reasonable for him to hold that belief in B's consent. The Government's view was that 'it is for the jury to decide whether any of the attributes of the defendant are relevant to their deliberations, subject to directions from the judge where necessary'. 'All the circumstances' would appear to include all circumstances that might be relevant to whether a belief is reasonable. Ministerial statements in Parliament have made it clear that 'circumstances' are not limited to surrounding facts: Lord Falconer of Thoroton, Hansard HL, 2 June 2003, vol 648, col 1076. Furthermore, in response to concerns expressed in Parliament that the New Zealand approach (where the reasonableness of

D's belief is assessed wholly objectively, without any heed to his capacity or state of mind) might be adopted, Baroness Scotland of Asthal provided reassurance, ibid, 17 June 2003, vol 649, col 678:

> We fully expect that characteristics such as mental incapacity and extreme youth will be taken into account in line with existing case law in such issues. We would not expect our courts to follow the New Zealand approach. We believe we can rely principally on case law as regards reasonableness.

The Court of Appeal in *Braham* [2013] EWCA Crim 3 considered the issue of whether a belief that B was consenting that was based upon A's delusional state of mind brought about by metal disorder was reasonable. Hughes LJ stated that:

> Unless the state of mind amounted to insanity in law, beliefs in consent arising from conditions such as delusional psychotic illness or personality disorders had to be judged by objective standards of reasonableness and not by taking into account a mental disorder that induced a belief which could not reasonably arise without it.

Therefore the trial judge was correct to direct the jury that they should leave A's mental illness out of the equation when asking whether any belief that he may have had in consent was reasonable, but that if there might, independently of the illness, have been a reasonable belief, that would result in a verdict of not guilty. The court did recognize, however, that there may be cases in which A's personality or abilities might be relevant to whether his positive belief in consent was reasonable, but that was an issue for determination on specific facts. So, for example, a defendant with Asperger's might not understand subtle and non-verbal cues to desist. Such beliefs would not be so irrational as to be ignored under the Act. This obviously leaves scope for some fine distinctions to be drawn in future cases.

■ *Questions*

1. Will A's lack of sexual experience be relevant? His learning disability? His extreme youth and lack of understanding of sexual mores? Surely not his voluntarily intoxication through alcohol or drugs? What of A's knowledge of B's previous sexual history?

2. Is a reasonable but wholly irrational belief in consent a contradiction in terms?

Mistakes and consent

What of D who claims that he thought on reasonable grounds X would be consenting to the sexual penetration which he then mistakenly performed on Y? Can D claim he has a reasonable belief in consent? In *Whitta* [2006] EWCA Crim 2626, A had agreed with X that they would have sex later after the party they were both attending. Both A and X were adults but drunk. A, having removed his glasses, later entered a bedroom and digitally penetrated B, the sleeping 51-year-old mother of the party host. B was also very drunk. A desisted as soon as he realized his mistake. The trial judge ruled that mistake as to the identity in this context was irrelevant—liability was strict.

■ *Questions*

A had penetrated the vagina of another, B? Is that enough? Does the express statutory reference to a specific person '(B)' rather than use of the words 'of another' itself alter things? Is the question then whether A has reasonable grounds for believing the person that he did penetrate would be consenting or whether he can rely on the reasonable belief in the consent of the person he thought he was penetrating?

The trial judge ruled that:

> Are the jury entitled to consider mistaken identity as a relevant circumstance in assessing reasonable belief or is the phrase 'having regard to all the circumstances' limited to whatever took place between the defendant and the complainant named in the indictment?
>
> In my view, it is the narrow view which must be adopted in that the wording of the section and of the indictment clearly relate to a named complainant in section 1(1) and the requirement in subsection (2) cannot widen the scope of such consideration so as to allow for the defendant's state of mind in relation to any third party.
>
> It is therefore not the jury in this case to be allowed to consider the circumstances which may have prevailed had the person whose vagina he penetrate been some person other than the complainant.

The Court of Appeal, in a sentencing appeal referred by the Attorney General, noted that:

> We disagree with this analysis of the ruling. The effect of the judge's ruling is that it is not a defence to a charge under sections 1 or 2 of the SOA if the defendant has made a mistake, however reasonable, as to the identity of the person to whom the sexual activity is directed. In his ruling the judge did not decide that the offender's belief was not reasonable or that he had omitted to take the necessary care. He decided that the offender's belief was irrelevant because he did not believe that C consented.
>
> If the ruling is right, then the three offences are offences of strict responsibility *as far as and only as far as* the identity of the complainant is concerned. This being so, the judge must determine the level of the defendant's culpability, if any, in order to determine the appropriate sentence.
>
> We note in passing that a possible alternative way of dealing with this very rare set of circumstances would be to hold that the offence is committed if a reasonable (and therefore sober) person would have realised that the person being penetrated or sexually touched was not the person whom the defendant thought he was consensually penetrating or touching.

■ Question

A is on holiday with his partner, X. He falls asleep on the sunbed with X snoozing in the sunbed next to his. He half awakes, reaches out his hand and pats the bottom of the person lying on the next sunbed assuming it is X. It is not X, but B a 12-year-old girl who has occupied the sunbed when X went for a swim. What offences has A committed? See section 20.3.1.

20.2.2 Assault by penetration

Sexual Offences Act 2003, s 2

> (1) A person (A) commits an offence if—
>
>   (a) he intentionally penetrates the vagina or anus of another person (B) with a part of his body or anything else,
>
>   (b) the penetration is sexual,
>
>   (c) B does not consent to the penetration, and
>
>   (d) A does not reasonably believe that B consents.
>
> (2) Whether a belief is reasonable is to be determined having regard to all the circumstances, including any steps A has taken to ascertain whether B consents.

Penetration with fingers and inanimate objects such as knives and bottles is caught by this section. The issues of consent and mens rea are as discussed previously in relation to rape. The act of penetration is regarded as continuing until withdrawal. Since the degree of penetration need only be slight, and 'vagina' includes 'vulva', oral sex performed on a woman is caught by s 2.

It seems doubtful that there is an element of mens rea as to the 'sexual' nature of the penetration. As a matter of principle, each element of the actus reus ought to have a corresponding element of mens rea. (Cf the view of Lord Hope in *G* [2008] UKHL 37, section 7.6.1, p 204.) Penetration must be 'sexual' as defined in the following section.

■ *Questions*

1. Is A who forcibly penetrates B with an object solely as an act of violence and humiliation guilty under s 2?

2. A penetrates B's anus with his fingers in the course of an intimate search of B who is under arrest for drugs offences. Does A commit an offence? What if A secretly derives sexual pleasure from doing so?

20.2.2.1 Sexual

'Sexual' is defined in section 78:

Penetration, touching or any other activity is sexual if a reasonable person would consider that—

    (a) whatever its circumstances or any person's purpose in relation to it, it is because of its nature sexual, or

    (b) because of its nature it may be sexual and because of its circumstances or the purpose of any person in relation to it (or both) it is sexual.

See *H* (section 20.2.3, p 730).

The penetration must be intentional; there is no crime of reckless sexual penetration. However, following *Heard* [2007] EWCA Crim 125 (section 6.3.2.2, p 157), the voluntarily intoxicated defendant cannot rely on his intoxicated state to support his claim that his penetration of B with an object/part of his body was not intentional.

20.2.3 Sexual assault

Sexual Offences Act 2003, s 3

(1) A person (A) commits an offence if—

    (a) he intentionally touches another person (B),

    (b) the touching is sexual,

    (c) B does not consent to the touching, and

    (d) A does not reasonably believe that B consents.

(2) Whether a belief is reasonable is to be determined having regard to all the circumstances, including any steps A has taken to ascertain whether B consents.

Sexual is defined as in section 20.2.2.1.

'Touching' is defined in s 79(8):

Touching includes touching—

    (a) with any part of the body,

    (b) with anything else,

    (c) through anything,

and in particular includes touching amounting to penetration.

The 2003 Act focuses not on 'assault' as under the old law but on 'touching'. This may be significant. No hostility is required. Sexual words do not constitute a touching (but might have been assaults). D, who walks towards someone with his penis exposed, commits no touching, but this would have been indecent assault—*Rolfe* (1952) 36 Cr App R 4.

R v H
[2005] EWCA Crim 732, Court of Appeal, Criminal Division

(Lord Woolf CJ, Davis and Field JJ)

A approached B, a stranger, at 10 pm as she walked across a field and said to her 'Do you fancy a shag?' B ignored him whereon A grabbed B's tracksuit bottoms by the fabric, attempted to pull her towards him and attempted unsuccessfully to put his hand over her mouth. B escaped. A was convicted of sexual assault, contrary to s 3 of the Sexual Offences Act 2003. Two issues had arisen at trial:

(1) whether the touching of B's tracksuit bottoms alone amounted to the 'touching' of another person within the meaning of s 79(8) of the 2003 Act; and

(2) whether anything which had occurred amounted to what a reasonable person might regard as being 'sexual' within the meaning of s 78 of the Act, which provides:

> . . . penetration, touching, or any other activity is sexual if a reasonable person would consider that:
>
> (a) whatever its circumstances or any person's purpose in relation to it, it is because of its nature sexual, or
>
> (b) because of its nature it may be sexual and because of its circumstances or the purpose of any person in relation to it (or both) it is sexual.

The Lord Chief Justice [his lordship referred to Temkin and Ashworth [2004] Crim LR 328 (section 20.1, p 700), and to the relevant statutory provisions:]

8. In this case we are concerned with section 78(b). Miss Egerton who appears on behalf of the Crown accepts that (a) has no application. The nature of the touching with which we are concerned was not inevitably sexual. It is important to note that there are two requirements in section 78(b). First, there is the requirement that the touching because of its nature may be sexual; and secondly, there is the requirement that the touching because of its circumstances or the purpose of any person in relation to it (or both) is sexual.

9. Miss Egerton agreed with the view of the court expressed in argument that if there were not two requirements in (b), the opening words 'because of its nature it may be sexual' would be surplus. If it was not intended by the legislature that effect should be given to those opening words, it would be sufficient to create an offence by looking at the touching and deciding whether because of its circumstances it was sexual. In other words, there is not one comprehensive test. It is necessary for both halves of section 78(b) to be complied with.

10. It is no doubt because of this aspect of section 78(b) and the article in the Criminal Law Review that Mr West who appears on behalf of the appellant referred to *R v Court*. That case dealt with an alleged indecent assault. An assistant in a shop struck a 12 year old girl visitor twelve times, for no apparent reason, outside her shorts on her buttocks. The assistant was convicted. Both this court and the House of Lords dismissed the assistant's appeal. At pages 42B–43E of his speech Lord Ackner set out his general approach. On reading that passage it is understandable why the article should have made the comment to which we referred. It is quite clear to the court that the staged approach which we have observed in section 78 is reflected in Lord Ackner's speech. The only difficulty that we have with applying Lord Ackner's approach is that he referred to *R v George* [1956] Crim LR 52. In that case

the prosecution relied on the fact that on a number of occasions the defendant had removed a shoe from a girl's foot. He had done so, as he admitted, because it gave him a perverted sexual gratification. Streatfeild J ruled that an assault became indecent only if it was accompanied by circumstances of indecency towards the person alleged to have been assaulted and that none of the assaults in that case (namely the removal or attempted removal of the shoes) could possibly amount to an indecent assault.

11. We would express reservations as to whether or not it would be possible for the removal of shoes in that way, because of the nature of the act that took place, to be sexual as sexual is defined now in section 78. That in our judgment may well be a question that it would be necessary for a jury to determine.

12. The fact that in section 78(b) there are two different questions which we have sought to identify complicates the task of the judge and that of the jury. If there is a submission of 'no case' the judge may have to ask himself whether there is a case to be left to the jury. He will answer that question by determining whether it would be appropriate for a reasonable person to consider that the touching because of its nature may be sexual. Equally, the judge will have to consider whether it would be possible for a reasonable person to conclude, because of the circumstances of the touching or the purpose of any person in relation to the touching (or both), that it is sexual. If he comes to the conclusion that a reasonable person could possibly answer those questions adversely to the defendant, then the matter would have to be left to the jury.

13. We would suggest that in that situation the judge would regard it as desirable to identify two distinct questions for the jury. First, would they, as twelve reasonable people (as the section requires), consider that because of its nature the touching that took place in the particular case before them could be sexual? If the answer to that question was 'No', the jury would find the defendant not guilty. If 'Yes', they would have to go on to ask themselves (again as twelve reasonable people) whether in view of the circumstances and/or the purpose of any person in relation to the touching (or both), the touching was in fact sexual. If they were satisfied that it was, then they would find the defendant guilty. If they were not satisfied, they would find the defendant not guilty.

14. In that suggested approach the reference to the nature of the touching in the first half refers to the actual touching that took place in that case. In answering the first question, the jury would not be concerned with the circumstances before or after the touching took place, or any evidence as to the purpose of any person in relation to the touching.

[His lordship referred to s 62, 'Committing an offence with intent to commit a sexual offence' and outlined the facts revealed by the evidence in the present case.]

24. . . . Where a person is wearing clothing we consider that touching of the clothing constitutes touching for the purpose of the section 3 offence.

25. As against that approach Mr West relied on section 79(8) (set out above). He submits that under section 79(8)(c) touching through anything (through clothing), if pressure in some form is not brought against the body of the person concerned, there cannot be touching; there has to be some form of touching of the body of the individual who is alleged to have been assaulted, even if it be through clothing. Mr West submits that, having regard to the complainant's evidence in this case, there was no such touching.

26. It is important to note that the opening words of section 79(8) are 'touching includes touching' and in particular 'through anything'. Subsection (8) is not a definition section. We have no doubt that it was not Parliament's intention by the use of that language to make it impossible to regard as a sexual assault touching which took place by touching what the victim was wearing at the time.

27. The second unsuccessful submission made by Mr West for the case to be withdrawn from the jury was as to whether anything occurred which a reasonable person could regard as sexual within the meaning of the Act. The judge's view was that there were here clearly circumstances in which the offence was alleged to have occurred, including the words alleged to have been spoken beforehand, which could make the actions which took place properly to be regarded as being sexual. In his

approach at that time, and indeed in his summing-up, the judge did not take a two stage approach to section 78(b). He looked at the matter as a whole. The problem about that approach is that in a borderline case a person's intention or other circumstances may appear to show that what happened was sexual, although their nature might not have been sexual. For the reasons we have already given that approach is not one which we regard as appropriate, although we recognise that in the great majority of cases the answer will be the same whether the two stage approach is adopted or the position is looked at as a whole.

[His lordship dealt with other grounds of appeal.]

Appeal dismissed

In *Court* [1989] AC 28, A, an assistant in a shop, pulled a girl aged 12, who was in the shop, across his knee and spanked her clothed bottom. When asked why he did it, he said 'Buttock fetish'. The House held (Lord Goff dissenting) that because it was ambiguous whether the act was indecent it was legitimate to refer to A's motive. In circumstances where the act was unambiguously indecent there was no need to refer to A's motive. In cases where the act was unambiguously not indecent, A's indecent motive could not make it such.

■ *Questions*

Would Court be convicted under s 3? What if Court had pulled the girl's shorts down and spanked her, and done so in the belief that this was an appropriate punishment because he believed her to be shoplifting? Would the jury even be entitled to consider his motive or would his act be caught by s 78(a)?

In *H*, Lord Woolf CJ referred to the Temkin and Ashworth article which states that:

...as under the *Court* test, conduct, which on the face of it is not sexual, cannot be brought within that description by pointing to its circumstances and/or purpose. The *Court* test and its application have been criticised as 'vague' and unclear, but a superior alternative remains to be found. In practice, in most cases, it will not be difficult to apply the test in section 78(a). It will be in unusual cases only that section 78(b) will be brought into play. Whilst section 78 might require some fine-tuning, it was wise to have included a provision of this kind. In Canada a decision to exclude any such provision from the legislation has led to a costly proliferation of cases in which courts have been called upon to rule in what circumstances a particular assault may be described as sexual.

His lordship stated that 'the expectation indicated in that part of the article that it will only be in unusual cases that section 78(b) will be brought into play is probably over-optimistic, as the facts of this case indicate'.

■ *Questions*

1. Fetishes include such conduct as stroking shoes, touching hair. Is there any conduct that a reasonable person would conclude may *not* be sexual?

2. In *H*, the defendant touched only B's clothes. How can that be a touching of the 'person' as s 3 requires? What if A touches only the hem of B's skirt? Is that distinguishable from touching B's bikini-clad buttock? Would soaking B's flimsy T-shirt be a sexual touching? Does A have to be holding the implement that touches B where it is alleged that he touched with something?

The touching must be intentional. What then of A, who is drunk at the office party, and who gropes B and claims that any contact was 'accidental'? In *Heard* [2007] EWCA Crim 125 (section 6.3.2.2, p 157), the Court of Appeal held that although it had a requirement for intentional touching, the offence should be treated as one of basic intent: it is no excuse for A to rely on his voluntary intoxication that he intended to touch the complainant in a sexual manner. On policy grounds the court was clearly entitled to assume that Parliament had not intended to change the law (although it should be noted that under the pre-2003 law, the offence of indecent assault was not always a basic intent crime).

Lord Justice Hughes states that:

> To flail about, stumble or barge around in an unco-ordinated manner which results in an unintended touching, objectively sexual, is not this offence. If to do so when sober is not this offence, then nor is it this offence to do so when intoxicated. It is also possible that such an action would not be judged by the jury to be objectively sexual, on the basis that it was clearly accidental, but whether that is so or not, we are satisfied that in such a case this offence is not committed. The intoxication, in such a situation, has not impacted on intention. Intention is simply not in question. What is in question is impairment of control of the limbs.... '[A] drunken intent is still an intent', the corollary [is] that 'a drunken accident is still an accident'.

■ *Questions*

1. A takes LSD. He thinks he is at the centre of the earth stroking a strange mammal. He is in fact stroking B's breast. Is he guilty under s 3?

2. A is out drinking with his mates. He is drunk and showing off. As B, the barmaid, bends over to collect glasses nearby, A pretends to grope her from behind. He intends to miss but get a laugh from his mates. He misjudges and makes contact with her bottom. Is he guilty of an offence under s 3? Is the touching accidental or reckless?

20.2.4 Intentionally causing someone to engage in sexual activity

Sexual Offences Act 2003, s 4

(1) A person (A) commits an offence if—

    (a) he intentionally causes another person (B) to engage in an activity,

    (b) the activity is sexual,

    (c) B does not consent to engaging in the activity, and

    (d) A does not reasonably believe that B consents.

(2) Whether a belief is reasonable is to be determined having regard to all the circumstances, including any steps A has taken to ascertain whether B consents.

This is potentially a very useful offence, which has as one of its purposes criminalizing the actions of women who force men to penetrate them. Other examples of the offence would include A requiring B to masturbate A, or to masturbate B, or A requiring B to masturbate C, etc. The offence can be committed by words alone. See *Devonald* [2008] EWCA Crim 527 (section 20.2.1.5, p 719). It is commonly prosecuted for indecent text messaging where A incites B to have sex with him: for example, *A* [2006] EWCA Crim 2103; *Hinton-Smith* [2005] EWCA Crim 2575.

Sexual is as defined in section 20.2.2.1, p 729; touching is as defined in section 20.2.3, p 729. Sections 74 to 76 (consent and presumptions discussed in section 20.2.1.3 to 20.2.1.6, pp 702–725) apply.

Section 4(4) elevates the crime to an indictable offence with a maximum sentence of life imprisonment if it involves: penetration of B's anus or vagina; penetration of B's mouth with a person's penis; penetration of a person's anus or vagina by B with his body or otherwise; penetration of a person's mouth with B's penis.

Since A must 'cause' the action, it can be assumed that it is sufficient for A to be *a* cause without being the sole cause (see section 3.2.1, p 44).

■ **Questions**

A, aged 18, texts B, aged 18, to whom he has taken a fancy. He asks her to come round to his flat for sex that night. B has never shown any interest in A in a sexual manner. Is A guilty of the offence under s 4? What if B decides to go round anyway because she really likes A?

20.3 Offences against children

The child sexual offences are some of the most heavily criticized offences in the Act, in particular for their over-criminalization and undue reliance on prosecutorial discretion. The legislation makes no attempt to distinguish between exploitative sexual activity against a child under 16 (whether by older individuals or not) and that of informed consensual sexual experimentation between children under that age.

J. Spencer, 'The Sexual Offences Act 2003 (2) Child and Family Offences'
[2004] Crim LR 347

The new child sex offences are open to two obvious criticisms: complexity and obscurity, and 'legislative overkill'. . . . There was no need for this, because behind the specific crimes of consensual sex with children the Act provides a range of crimes that punish every form of non-consensual sex. So it would be have been safe as well as simple to exclude from the offences of consensual sex with minors, any consensual act between persons of the same or similar age. . . .

The concern about the potential over-criminalization was countered with the responses that the CPS would exercise appropriate discretion. But, as the Joint Parliamentary Committee on Human Rights observed:

Creating catch all offences and then relying on the prosecutor's discretion to sort things out satisfactorily undermines [the rule of law]. It leaves prosecutors to do the job that Parliament should be doing, and gives them discretion to prosecute (or not to prosecute) people who ought never to have been within the scope of criminal liability in the first place. (12th Report 2002–3 *Scrutiny of Bills: Further Progress Report* 2003 (HL 119; HC 765))

20.3.1 Children under 13

Sections 5 to 8 create offences against children under 13.

- Section 5 makes it an offence carrying a maximum life imprisonment for A intentionally to penetrate the vagina, anus or mouth of a person under 13 with his penis. Liability as to age is strict (see *G* [2008] UKHL 37, section 7.6.1, p 203). Lord Hoffmann stated:

The mental element of the offence under section 5, as the language and structure of the section makes clear, is that penetration must be intentional but there is no requirement that the accused must have known that the other person was under 13. The policy of the legislation is to protect children. If you have sex with someone who is on any view a child or young person, you take your chance on exactly how old they are. To that extent the offence is one of strict liability and it is no defence that the accused believed the other person to be 13 or over.

Note that A is guilty of this offence even if B was consenting or indeed initiated the conduct. B, 12 years old, who willingly performs fellatio on A, her 12-year-old boyfriend, thereby renders him a rapist. Is X, A's friend, who tells A that he should ask B to perform oral sex guilty of assisting or encouraging rape?

Baroness Hale, in *G*, stated:

Every male has a choice about where he puts his penis. It may be difficult for him to restrain himself when aroused but he has a choice. There is nothing unjust or irrational about a law which says that if he chooses to put his penis inside a child who turns out to be under 13 he has committed an offence (although the state of his mind may again be relevant to sentence). He also commits an offence if he behaves in the same way towards a child of 13 but under 16, albeit only if he does not reasonably believe that the child is 16 or over. So in principle sex with a child under 16 is not allowed. When the child is under 13, three years younger than that, he takes the risk that she may be younger than he thinks she is. The object is to make him take responsibility for what he chooses to do with what is capable of being, not only an instrument of great pleasure, but also a weapon of great danger.

Do you agree that there is nothing unjust in this? Is prosecutorial discretion enough to prevent this offence being misused?

- Section 6 creates an offence of penetration of the anus or the vagina. Consent is irrelevant. Liability is strict as to the age of the victim. The maximum sentence is life imprisonment. The penetration must be sexual so, for example, a vaginal examination of a girl under 13 performed by a medical professional is not caught by the offence.

- Section 7 creates an offence of intentional sexual touching of a child under 13. 'Touching' and 'sexual' are defined at sections 20.2.2.1 and 20.2.3, both at 729. The maximum sentence is 14 years on indictment; six months summarily. Is liability as to the 'sexual' nature of the touching strict? Does the law's denial of the factual consent of the under 13-year-old to engage in sexual touching clash with the law's willingness to accept such a child's capacity to consent to, for example, invasive medical procedures? What proportion of the population do you think might have committed this offence?

- Section 8 creates an offence where A intentionally causes or incites another person (B) to engage in an activity and B is under 13. Liability as to age is strict. Consent is irrelevant. The maximum sentence is life imprisonment if the act involved penetration. How many offences are created? See *Grout* [2011] EWCA Crim 299. Andrew, aged 14, asks Britney, aged 12, to give him a 'shiner' (see *B v DPP* [2000] UKHL 13 (section 7.3.1, p 185)), meaning for her to perform oral sex on him. In her naivety Britney mistakenly believes that Andrew wants her to give him a black eye, so she hits Andrew and causes him severe facial bruising. Consider the criminal liability of Andrew and Britney.

Note that there is no liability for aiding and abetting or counselling rape of a child under 13 if the actor's purpose is to protect the child from STD/pregnancy or to protect his or her physical safety or promote his or her emotional well-being, unless the actor's purpose is to gain sexual gratification or to cause or encourage the relevant sexual act: s 73. The doctor who provides contraceptives to the 12-year-old girl to protect her in her consensual sexual acts with her partner will not be aiding and abetting her 'rape'. What of the parent who takes the view that he would rather his daughter had sex with her boyfriend in the safety of her bedroom than, say, the local bus shelter?

20.3.2 Children aged over 12 and under 16

Sections 9 to 13 deal with cases where B is aged over 12 and under 16. Each section creates offences for A aged over 18. All charges under ss 9 to 12 against under 18-year-olds are triable either way and carry a maximum sentence of five years on indictment/six months summarily. Section 13 also makes these offences available (with different sentences) where A is under 18, in which case the sentence is one of six months summarily, five years on indictment: s 13. Section 13 aged over 12 and under does not distinguish between cases where the offence involves penetration or not.

The group of offences dealing with conduct towards children aged over 12 and under 16 demonstrates the unnecessary complexity and overlapping nature of the provisions in the 2003 Act.

- Section 9 creates an offence for A intentionally to touch B sexually, where B is aged under 16. If B is aged over 12 and under 16, A is not guilty if he has a reasonable belief that B is 16. The offence is indictable only and carries a maximum sentence of 14 years' imprisonment if the activity involves penetration. Consent is irrelevant. A, 18, who kisses or touches his consenting 15-year-old girlfriend is guilty of the offence if that is a 'sexual touching'—of course that falls to be decided by the jury. A, 18, who kisses his 12-year-old consenting girlfriend is guilty, even if she said she was 16. There is no defence for couples under 16, lawfully married in another country and visiting England or Wales. Does the section reflect the reality of sexual conduct of under 16-year-olds in the twenty-first century? During the debates in Parliament the Home Secretary offered champagne to anyone who could provide a more suitable code of offences. How might a better form of offences have been drafted?

- Section 10 creates an offence where A intentionally causes or incites another person (B) to engage in a sexual activity. If B is aged over 12 and under 16, A is not guilty if he has a reasonable belief that B is 16. Note that the offence is indictable only and carries a maximum sentence of 14 years' imprisonment if the activity involves penetration. The offence can also be committed by a person under 18; if so, the maximum sentence is one of six months summarily, five years on indictment: s 13.

- Section 11 creates an offence for A intentionally to engage in a sexual activity and for the purpose of obtaining sexual gratification, where he engages in it when another person (B) is present or can observe it, and A knows or believes that B is aware, or intends that B should be aware, that he is engaging in it. If B is aged over 12 and under 16, A is not guilty if he has a reasonable belief that B is 16. The maximum sentence is ten years on indictment, six months summarily. The offence can also be committed by a person under 18; if so, the sentence is one of six months summarily, five years on indictment: s 13. This is designed to tackle the paedophile who performs sexual acts in a child's presence to gain sexual gratification. Note that there must be a person under 16 who is able to see the act. An undercover officer alone witnessing the event will not suffice.

- Section 12 creates an offence where A, for the purpose of obtaining sexual gratification, intentionally causes B, aged under 16, to watch a third person engaging in a sexual activity, or to look at an image of any person engaging in an activity. If B is aged over 12 and under 16, A is not guilty if he has a reasonable belief that B is 16. The maximum sentence is ten years on indictment, six months summarily. The offence can also be committed by a person under 18; if so, the sentence is one of six months summarily, five years on indictment: s 13. The offence was included to deal with paedophiles who use pornography as part of their grooming process. They show pornographic images to children in an attempt to break down the child's inhibitions about engaging in sexual conduct. In *Abdullahi* [2006] EWCA Crim 2060, the Court of Appeal held that it was sufficient that A showed the images for the purpose of obtaining sexual gratification, either by enjoying seeing the complainant looking at the images or with a view to putting the complainant in the mood to provide sexual gratification to A later.

- Section 14 creates an offence for A intentionally to arrange or facilitate something that he intends to do, intends another person to do or believes that another person will do, in any part of the world, where doing it will involve the commission of an offence under any of sections 9 to 13. The section is subject to defences for child protection (protecting the child from sexually transmitted infection; the physical safety of the child; preventing the child from becoming pregnant; or promoting the child's emotional well-being by the giving of advice). The maximum sentences are 14 years on indictment, six months summarily. In *R* [2008] EWCA Crim 619, the court gave a wide interpretation to s 14. It was acknowledged to be wider than attempt because it does not require proof of any act that is 'more than merely preparatory' to one of the relevant child sex offences. The court held that it does not require any 'agreement'. A asked the prostitute to arrange a child prostitute but she did not do so and therefore A could not be said to have done more than attempt to commit the s 14 offence.

- Section 15 creates an offence commonly known as 'grooming'. It is an offence if A has met or communicated with B, aged under 16, on at least two occasions and (i) subsequently A intentionally meets B, or A travels with the intention of meeting B in any part of the world or arranges to meet B in any part of the world, or B travels with the intention of meeting A in any part of the world, *and* (ii) A intends to do anything to or in respect of B, during or after the meeting which if done will involve the commission by A of a relevant offence. If B is aged over 12 and under 16, A is not guilty if he has a reasonable belief that B is 16. The maximum sentence is ten years on indictment, six months summarily. A, aged 18, writes two love letters to B, aged 15, arranging to meet at the local club. A hopes that the evening will end in sexual activity. Is A guilty of the offence? In *G* [2010] EWCA Crim 1693 the Court of Appeal held that A can be guilty of grooming even though there was no communication or contact of a sexual nature on the two occasions before he met B to engage in conduct which would amount to an offence.

■ *Question*

The Act is supposed to modernize the law and to reflect the sexual mores of the twenty-first century. Having regard to the offences involving children, does it?

20.4 Other sexual offences

20.4.1 Abuse of trust

The Sexual Offences (Amendment) Act 2000 created new offences of abuse of a position of trust. The 2003 Act replaces them with four offences where A (aged over 18) who is in a position of trust to B (under 18):

(i)   sexually touches B (s 16);

(ii) causes or incites B to engage in sexual activity (s 17);

    (iii) engages in sexual activity in B's presence for the purpose of sexual gratification (s 18);

    (iv) causes B to watch a sexual image or activity for the purpose of obtaining sexual gratification.

The most notable feature of the sections is that the offences criminalize consensual conduct with those under 18. Although 16- and 17-year-olds may consent to sexual activity in other circumstances, they cannot do so with those who 'look after' them (see ss 21 and 22). No offence is committed where A has a reasonable belief that B is aged over 18 (unless B is under 13). There is a defence for A to prove that he was lawfully married to B (aged 16) or that immediately before the position of trust arose there existed a lawful sexual relationship between them. This covers cases where, for example, A and B had a sexual relationship before A became a trainee teacher at B's school.

20.4.2 Family offences

The 2003 Act creates two sets of offences to deal with offences within the family. In relation to children, ss 25 and 26 criminalize the same forms of activity as ss 9 and 12 (above):

- sexual touching and
- causing a child to engage in sexual activity.

Sections 25 and 26 differ from ss 9 and 12 in two important respects: B must be under 18 and A must be a family member. Family membership is defined in very broad terms in the Act, extending well beyond blood relationships to reflect the diverse structures of modern life. Family members include:

- blood and adoptive relationships (parents, current or former foster parents, grandparents, brothers, sisters, half-brothers, half-sisters, aunts and uncles);
- wider family members who live, or have lived, in the same household as the child or who are, or have been, regularly involved in caring for, training or supervising or being in sole charge of the child (step-parents, cousins, step-siblings, current or former foster siblings);
- others who are living in the same household as the child and who hold a position of trust or authority in relation to the child at the time of the alleged offence. This offence will not be committed if A has a lawful sexual relationship with the child after the familial relationship has ceased, even where the child is under 18.

The breadth of the extended family caught by the Act reflects the shift in emphasis in the legislation from a blood relationship-based offence of heterosexual intercourse (incest based on eugenics arguments) to one based on gender-neutral exploitation of sexual vulnerability in the home environment. There are defences in s 28 where A is lawfully married to B at the time of engaging in the sexual activity, and under s 29 where A proves that a lawful sexual relationship existed between A and B immediately before the familial relationship arose.

20.4.3 Offences involving mental disorder

The Act provides three specific groups of offences to protect those with a mental disorder. In each category the types of behaviour criminalized are roughly the same as those in relation to children. In short, the activities prohibited are:

- sexual touching of B;
- causing or inciting sexual activity by B;
- engaging in sexual activity in B's presence;
- causing B to watch sexual activity.

When these activities arise in an exploitative context they are criminalized. The three contexts are:

- ss 30 to 33 where B is mentally disordered and 'unable to refuse';
- ss 34 to 37 where B is mentally disordered and the activity is caused by 'threats or deception or inducement' (which need not vitiate consent under s 74);
- ss 38 to 41 where B is mentally disordered and A is 'in a relationship as a carer'.

There are numerous general improvements in the new scheme. Creating specific offences produces much fairer labelling—defendants are convicted of offences that better describe their actions. The language has been modernized, and gender specificity has been removed. This is not mere window dressing: for example, one result is that mentally disordered men are protected against heterosexual abuse. The offensive terminology of the 1956 Act has been replaced by the appropriate (but technical) language of the Mental Health Acts. However, as with the Act in general, there is tremendous complexity.

See *C* [2009] UKHL 42 (section 20.2.1.3, p 706) on the meaning of 'capacity'.

20.4.4 Preliminary and other offences

The Act also introduces offences of:

- intentional administration of a substance/causing it to be taken by B without consent with intent to stupefy/overpower to enable any person to engage in sex with B: s 61;
- committing an offence with intent to commit a sexual offence: s 62;
- trespass with intent to commit a sexual offence: s 63;
- intentionally exposing one's genitals with the intention that another person will see them and be caused alarm or distress: s 66;
- for the purposes of sexual gratification, observing another person doing a 'private act' (or recording or installing equipment to record that) in the knowledge that the other person does not consent to being observed for that purpose: s 67. Section 68 defines 'private act' as 'an act done in a place and in circumstances where the person would reasonably expect privacy and either the person's genitals, buttocks or breasts are exposed or covered only by underwear, or the person is using a lavatory or the person is doing a sexual act that is not of a kind ordinarily done in public';
- bestiality: s 69;
- necrophilia: s 70;
- engaging in sexual activity in a public lavatory: s 71.

FURTHER READING

CPS guidance: http://www.cps.gov.uk/legal/p_to_r/rape_and_sexual_offences

E. B. Freedman, *Redefining Rape* (2013)

H. Reece, 'Rape Myths: Is Elite Opinion Right and Popular Opinion Wrong?' (2013) 33 OJLS 1

J. Stanton-Ife, 'Mental Disorder and Sexual Consent: *Williams* and After' in J. Horder and D. Baker (eds), *The Sanctity of Life and the Criminal Law* (2013)

S. Wallerstein, '"A Drunken Consent Is Still Consent"—Or Is It? A Critical Analysis of the Law on a Drunken Consent to Sex Following *Bree*' (2009) 73 J Crim L 582

21
Theft

21.1 Introduction

The law governing theft and related offences is to be found in the Theft Act 1968. That Act was supplemented by offences introduced in the Theft Act 1978 and the Theft (Amendment) Act 1996. Significant sections of these latter Acts were repealed and replaced by the Fraud Act 2006 (see Chapter 25).

The law of theft as defined in England and Wales may appear to be unduly technical. Since the offence is designed to protect rights in relation to property, ownership, possession, etc which are concepts defined in civil law, the offence must necessarily rely on the civil law definitions of these concepts, and these tend to be complex ones. There is a tension between a general moral understanding of stealing and the technical definition in the offence.

> To steal something is to violate in some fundamental way another's right of ownership. Note that this is different from saying that stealing is merely a violation of some particular set of laws concerning property. To be sure, in modern, liberal societies, we tend to think of rights of ownership in legalistic terms, and the law of property certainly plays a significant role in shaping and informing our understanding of what it means to own things and to have them stolen. But the concept of stealing itself seems to be in some fundamental way pre-legal. Small children and primitive man both have a sense of what it means to own things and they undoubtedly have a sense that having such things involuntarily taken from them in some way constitutes a 'wrong'. (S. P. Green, *Lying, Cheating and Stealing: A Moral Theory of White Collar Crime* (2005), pp 89–90)

Some of the controversies that will be examined in this chapter include the following:

(i)   the extent to which the criminal law of theft conflicts with civil law concepts of property;

(ii) whether it is possible to steal property that belongs to oneself;

(iii) the types of property that may be stolen;

(iv) the extent to which it is possible to provide a definition of 'dishonestly'.

21.1.1 Interpreting the 1968 Act

The 1968 Act constitutes the authoritative, comprehensive and exclusive source of the law of theft. But, of course, a law of theft assumes the existence of laws relating to property and ownership. As we will see, the Theft Act 1968, s 5, states when property is to be treated as belonging to another for the purposes of theft, and it is immediately apparent that in order fully to determine key terms under that section (such as whether there is another with a 'proprietary right or interest' or whether property is 'subject to a trust') reference must be made to civil cases, whether decided before or after the coming into force of the Theft Act. These provide authoritative explanations of these concepts. Hence, whether D is guilty of theft may involve a consideration of the law of contract, the Sale of Goods Acts or principles of equity.

Aside from necessary reference to definitions of general application and to civil law concepts, the Theft Act represents a clean break with the past. In their interpretation the courts have aimed to give words and expressions their ordinary meaning so as to avoid undue technicality and subtlety. There is nothing wrong with that, of course, as a general precept of statutory interpretation but it led to a practice, endorsed by the House of Lords in *Brutus v Cozens* [1972] 2 All ER 1297, [1973] AC 854, of leaving the interpretation, at least of 'ordinary' words and expressions to be determined by a jury or magistrates as a matter of fact. This can be problematic as it is sometimes difficult to discern precisely what the 'ordinary' meaning of certain words is.

Consider throughout the chapter:

- to what extent are the appellate courts content to uphold the conviction of those who have been found to have acted dishonestly, even if the conviction for the offence charged is technically flawed;
- to what extent is theft treated as a 'dishonesty' rather than a 'property' based offence?

The law is technical and complex. Some have questioned whether the time has come for a redefinition which would simplify the law of theft, as has now occurred with the deception offences being replaced by the broad and non-technical fraud offences in the Fraud Act 2006.

In examining the courts' interpretation of the theft offence which was designed as part of a new code, it is worth considering the extent to which a more radical approach would be desirable in any new codification of the law. The pressure for reform is increased by the fact that, in some instances, the Act has been overtaken by technological advances.

■ *Question*

Consider Robinson's proposal in his Draft Code: 'You may not damage, take, use, dispose of, or transfer another's property without the other's consent. Property is anything of value, including services offered for payment and access to recorded information.'
Would that offer a workable offence?

Note that the Code would have a qualification that no prosecution should take place in any case too trivial to warrant the condemnation of a criminal conviction. See P. H. Robinson, *Structure and Function in Criminal Law* (1997), pp 211–225.

21.2 Basic definition of theft

Theft Act 1968, s 1(1)

A person is guilty of theft if he dishonestly appropriates property belonging to another with the intention of permanently depriving the other of it; and 'thief' and 'steal' shall be construed accordingly.

Theft Act 1968, s 7

7. Theft

A person guilty of theft shall on conviction on indictment be liable to imprisonment for a term not exceeding seven years.

Theft therefore comprises five elements: (i) appropriating (ii) property (iii) belonging to another (iv) dishonestly (v) with an intention permanently to deprive the other of the property. Each requires detailed consideration.

21.3 Appropriation

Theft Act 1968, s 3

3. 'Appropriates'

(1) Any assumption by a person of the rights of an owner amounts to an appropriation, and this includes, where he has come by the property (innocently or not) without stealing it, any later assumption of a right to it by keeping or dealing with it as owner.

(2) Where property or a right or interest in property is or purports to be transferred for value to a person acting in good faith, no later assumption by him of rights which he believed himself to be acquiring shall, by reason of any defect in the transferor's title, amount to theft of the property.

The meaning of 'appropriation' is fundamental in the law of theft and has been the subject of extensive litigation.

Three issues created problems of interpretation:

(i)   whether s 3 requires that D appropriated *all* of the rights of the owner over the item of property;

(ii)   whether D acting with V's consent in relation to the property could be held to be appropriating it (eg where V consents to D taking the property because D has tricked V);

(iii) whether D could appropriate property in which he obtained the entire proprietary interest by the transfer from V (eg where V makes D a gift of the property so that D has 'indefeasible title').

As the law now stands, there is an appropriation if D has assumed a right of the owner. There is no need for the Crown to establish that he has assumed *all* the rights. In addition, D can be guilty of theft even when he has an indefeasible title to the property in question, such as by way of gift.

All three issues were resolved by the House of Lords' cases of *Morris* [1984] UKHL 1, *Gomez* [1992] UKHL 4 and *Hinks* [2000] UKHL 53. *Morris* and *Gomez* were examined by the House of Lords in the controversial case of *Hinks* which follows.

It is important to bear in mind that the question whether D has appropriated property belonging to another is not the same as whether he is guilty of theft. Only if he has the dishonest intent permanently to deprive will he be a thief. When reading the following extract, consider whether the House of Lords has interpreted the elements of theft in such a way as to render it a 'thought crime' too dependent on mens rea?

R v Hinks

[2000] UKHL 53, House of Lords, http://www.bailii.org/uk/cases/UKHL/2000/53.html

(Lords Slynn, Jauncey, Steyn, Hutton and Hobhouse)

Hinks (H), a 38-year-old woman, was friendly with John Dolphin (JD). She described herself as Dolphin's main carer. There was evidence that JD was extremely naive and gullible. It would be easy to take advantage of him. But he understood the concept of ownership and was quite capable of making a gift. In a period of a few months, he withdrew about £60,000 from his building society account. The money was deposited in H's account. JD also gave H a television set. H was convicted of theft of money and the television. The question left to the jury was 'Was [JD] so mentally incapable that the defendant herself realised that ordinary and decent people would regard it as dishonest to accept a gift from him?' On appeal it was argued that, if the gift from JD to H was valid, the acceptance of it could not be theft. Rose LJ, dismissing the appeal, ruled:

... in relation to theft, one of the ingredients for a jury to consider is not whether there has been a gift, valid or otherwise, but whether there has been an appropriation. A gift may be clear evidence of appropriation. But a jury should not, in our view, be asked to consider whether a gift has been validly made.

H appealed.

[Lord Jauncey said he would dismiss the appeal for the reasons given by Lord Steyn.]

Lord Steyn:

Since the enactment of the Theft Act 1968 the House of Lords has on three occasions considered the meaning of the word 'appropriates' in s 1(1) of the 1968 Act, namely in *Lawrence v Comr of Police for the Metropolis* [1971] 2 All ER 1253, [1972] AC 626; in *R v Morris; Anderton v Burnside* [1983] 3 All ER 288, [1984] AC 320; and in *R v Gomez* [1993] 1 All ER 1, [1993] AC 442. The law as explained in *Lawrence's* case and *R v Gomez*, and applied by the Court of Appeal in the present case ([2000] 1 Cr App Rep 1) has attracted strong criticism from distinguished academic lawyers: see for example, JC Smith [1993] Crim LR 304 and [1998] Crim LR 904; Edward Griew *The Theft Acts* (7th edn, 1995) pp 41–59; ATH Smith 'Gifts and the Law of Theft' [1999] CLJ 10. These views have however been challenged by equally distinguished academic writers: PR Glazebrook 'Revising the Theft Acts' [1993] CLJ 191–194 [Peter Glazebrook's article does not in fact 'challenge' these views and the reference to it is omitted in [2001] 2 AC 241 at 244]; Simon Gardner 'Property and Theft' [1998] Crim LR 35. The academic criticism of *R v Gomez* provided in substantial measure the springboard for the present appeal. The certified question before the House is as follows: 'Whether the acquisition of an indefeasible title to property is capable of amounting to an appropriation of property belonging to another for the purposes of s 1(1) of the Theft Act 1968'. In other words, the question is whether a person can 'appropriate' property belonging to another where the other person makes him an indefeasible gift of property, retaining no proprietary interest or any right to resume or recover any proprietary interest in the property.

Before the enactment of the 1968 Act English law required a taking and carrying away of the property as the actus reus of the offence. In 1968 Parliament chose to broaden the reach of the law of theft by requiring merely an appropriation. The relevant sections of the Act are as follows:

[Lord Steyn set out the relevant provisions of the Theft Act and the facts of the case, and quoted from the trial judge's summing up and the judgment of the Court of Appeal; and continued:]

My Lords, counsel for the appellant has not expressly asked the House to depart from the previous decisions of the House. He did, however, submit with the aid of the writings of Sir John Smith that the conviction of a donee for receiving a perfectly valid gift is a completely new departure. Relying on the academic criticism of the earlier decisions of the House counsel submitted that their reach should not be extended. ...

V

The starting point must be the words of the statute as interpreted by the House in its previous decisions. The first case in the trilogy is *R v Lawrence* [1971] 2 All ER 1253, [1972] AC 626. The defendant, a taxi driver, had without objection on the part of an Italian student asked for a fare of £6 for a journey for which the correct lawful fare was 10s 6d. The taxi driver was convicted of theft. On appeal the main contention was that the student had consented to pay the fare. But it was clear that the appellant had not told the student what the lawful fare was. With the agreement of all the Law Lords hearing the case Viscount Dilhorne observed:

> 'Prior to the passage of the Theft Act 1968, which made radical changes in and greatly simplified the law relating to theft and some other offences, it was necessary to prove that the property alleged to have been stolen was taken "without the consent of the owner" (Larceny Act 1916, s 1(1)). These words are not included in s 1(1) of the Theft Act 1968, but the appellant contended that the subsection should be construed as if they were, as if they appeared after the word "appropriates". Section 1(1) provides: "A person is guilty of theft if he dishonestly appropriates property belonging to another with the intention of permanently depriving the other of it; and 'thief' and 'steal' shall be construed accordingly." I see no ground for concluding that the omission of the words "without the consent of the owner" was inadvertent and not deliberate, and to read the subsection as if they were included is, in my opinion, wholly unwarranted. Parliament by the omission of these words has relieved the prosecution of the burden of establishing that the taking was without the owner's consent. That is no longer an ingredient of the offence. Megaw LJ, delivering the judgment of the Court of Appeal ([1970] 3 All ER at 935, [1971] 1 QB at 376), said that the offence created by s 1(1) involved four elements: "(i) a dishonest (ii) appropriation (iii) of property belonging to another (iv) with the intention of permanently depriving the owner of it." I agree. That there was appropriation in this case is clear. Section 3(1) states that any assumption by a person of the rights of an owner amounts to an appropriation. Here there was clearly such an assumption. That an appropriation was dishonest may be proved in a number of ways. In this case it was not contended that the appellant had not acted dishonestly.' (See [1971] 2 All ER 1253 at 1254–1255, [1972] AC 626 at 631–632.)

Viscount Dilhorne expressly added that belief that the passenger gave informed consent (ie knowing that he was paying in excess of the fare) 'is relevant to the issue of dishonesty, not to the question whether or not there has been an appropriation' (see [1971] 2 All ER 1253 at 1255, [1972] AC 626 at 632). The appeal was dismissed. The *ratio decidendi* of *Lawrence's* case, namely that in a prosecution for theft it is unnecessary to prove that the taking was without the owner's consent, goes to the heart of the certified question in the present case.

The second decision of the House was *R v Morris; Anderton v Burnside* [1983] 3 All ER 288, [1984] AC 320, in 1983, a consolidated appeal involving two cases in each of which the defendant attached a price label to goods in a supermarket which showed a price lower than that which was properly payable for the goods. The defendant intended to pay the lower price at the checkout. In the first case the defendant's deception was detected at the checkout point and in the second he paid the lower prices at the checkout. He was convicted of theft in both cases. The House concluded that the defendant had been rightly convicted of theft on both counts. In each case the certified question was the rolled-up one whether there had been a 'dishonest appropriation' of goods. These questions were answered in the affirmative. However, in the single substantive judgment Lord Roskill made an observation, which was in conflict with the ratio of *Lawrence's* case and had to be corrected in *R v Gomez*. Lord Roskill said:

> 'If one postulates an honest customer taking goods from a shelf to put in his or her trolley to take to the check-point there to pay the proper price, I am unable to see that any of these actions involves any assumption by the shopper of the rights of the supermarket. In the context of s 3(1), the concept of appropriation in my view involves not an act expressly or impliedly authorised by the owner but an act by way of adverse interference with or usurpation of those rights.' (See [1983] 3 All ER 288 at 293, [1984] AC 320 at 332.)

It will be observed that this observation was not necessary for the decision of the case: absent this observation the House would still have held that there had been an appropriation. Lord Roskill took the view that he was following the decision in *Lawrence's* case. It is clear, however, that his observation (as opposed to the decision in *R v Morris*) cannot stand with the ratio of *Lawrence's* case. And as his observation, cast in terms of 'the honest customer', shows Lord Roskill conflated the ingredients of appropriation and dishonesty contrary to the holding in *Lawrence's* case.

The third decision of the House was in *R v Gomez* [1993] 1 All ER 1, [1993] AC 442, in 1992. The defendant was employed as an assistant shop manager. He agreed with two accomplices that goods would be supplied by the shop in return for cheques which he knew to be stolen. He told the manager of the shop that the cheques were as good as cash. The Court of Appeal held that there was a voidable contract between the owner of the shop and the dishonest receivers of the goods; that the transfer was with the consent of the owner; and that accordingly there was no appropriation. The Court of Appeal quashed the conviction arising from a plea of guilty. The following question was certified:

> 'When theft is alleged and that which is alleged to be stolen passes to the defendant with the consent of the owner, but that consent has been obtained by a false representation, has, a) an appropriation within the meaning of s. 1(1) of the Theft Act 1968 taken place, or, b) must such a passing of property necessarily involve an element of adverse [interference] with or usurpation of some right of the owner?' (see [1993] 1 All ER 1 at 4, [1993] AC 442 at 444.)

By a majority (Lord Lowry dissenting) the House answered branch (a) of the certified question in the affirmative and branch (b) in the negative. In crystalline terms Lord Keith of Kinkel speaking for all the numbers of the majority ruled the following ([1993] 1 All ER 1 at 12, [1993] AC 442 at 464). (1) The meaning of the relevant provisions must be determined by construing the statutory language without reference to the report which preceded it, namely the eighth report of the Criminal Law Revision Committee on *Theft and Related Offences* (Cmnd 2977 (1966)). (2) The observations of Lord Roskill in *R v Morris* were unnecessary for the decision of that case; that they were in clear conflict with the ratio of *Lawrence's* case; and that they were wrong. (3) *Lawrence's* case must be accepted as authoritative and correct, and 'there is no question of it now being right to depart from it'. At the same time Lord Keith ([1993] 1 All ER 1 at 12, [1993] AC 442 at 463), endorsed the judgment of Parker LJ in the civil case of *Dobson v General Accident Fire and Life Assurance Corp plc* [1989] 3 All ER 927, [1990] 1 QB 274 where Parker LJ highlighted the conflict between *Lawrence's* case and *R v Morris* and chose to follow *Lawrence's* case. (4) Any act may be an appropriation notwithstanding that it was done with the consent or authorisation of the owner. In *R v Gomez* [1993] 1 All ER 1, [1993] AC 442 at 448 the House was expressly invited to hold that 'there is no appropriation where the entire proprietary interest passes'. That submission was rejected. The leading judgment in *R v Gomez* was therefore in terms which unambiguously rule out the submission that s 3(1) does not apply to a case of a gift duly carried out because in such a case the entire proprietary interest will have passed. In a separate judgment (with which Lord Jauncey of Tullichettle expressed agreement) Lord Browne-Wilkinson observed:

> 'I regard the word "appropriation" in isolation as being an objective description of the act done irrespective of the mental state of either the owner or the accused. It is impossible to reconcile the decision in *Lawrence* (that the question of consent is irrelevant in considering whether this has been an appropriation) with the views expressed in *Morris*, which latter views in my judgment were incorrect.' (See [1993] 1 All ER 1 at 39, [1993] AC 442 at 495–496.)

In other words it is immaterial whether the act was done with the owner's consent or authority. It is true of course that the certified question in *R v Gomez* referred to the situation where consent had been obtained by fraud. But the majority judgments do not differentiate between cases of consent induced by fraud and consent given in any other circumstances. The ratio involves a proposition of general application. *R v Gomez* therefore gives effect to s 3(1) of the 1968 Act by treating 'appropriation' as a neutral word comprehending 'any assumption by a person of the rights of an owner'. If the law is as held in *R v Gomez*, it destroys the argument advanced on the present appeal, namely that an indefeasible gift of property cannot amount to an appropriation.

VI

Counsel for the appellant submitted in the first place that the law as expounded in *R v Gomez* and *Lawrence's* case must be qualified to say that there can be no appropriation unless the other party (the owner) retains some proprietary interest, or the right to resume or recover some proprietary interest, in the property. Alternatively, counsel argued that 'appropriates' should be interpreted as if the word 'unlawfully' preceded it. Counsel said that the effect of the decisions in *Lawrence's* case and *R v Gomez* is to reduce the actus reus of theft to 'vanishing point' (see Smith and Hogan *Criminal Law* (9th edn, 1999) p 505). He argued that the result is to bring the criminal law 'into conflict' with the civil law. Moreover, he argued that the decisions in *Lawrence's* case and *R v Gomez* may produce absurd and grotesque results. He argued that the mental requirements of dishonesty and intention of permanently depriving the owner of property are insufficient to filter out some cases of conduct which should not sensibly be regarded as theft. He did not suggest that the appellant's dishonest and repellent conduct came within such a category. Instead he deployed four examples for this purpose, namely the following. (1) S makes a handsome gift to D because he believes that D has obtained a First. D has not and knows that S is acting under that misapprehension. He makes a gift. There is here a motivational mistake which, it is submitted, does not avoid the transaction. (Glanville Williams *Textbook of Criminal Law* (1978) p 788). (2) P sees D's painting and, thinking he is getting a bargain, offers D £100,000 for it. D realises that P thinks the painting is a Constable, but knows that it was painted by his sister and is worth no more than £100. He accepts P's offer. D has made an enforceable contract and is entitled to recover and retain the purchase price (*Smith and Hogan* pp 507–508). (3) A buys a roadside garage business from B, abutting on a public thoroughfare; unknown to A but known to B, it has already been decided to construct a bypass road which will divert substantially the whole of the traffic from passing A's garage. There is an enforceable contract and A is entitled to recover and retain the purchase price. The same would be true if B *knew* that A was unaware of the intended plan to construct a bypass road. (Compare Lord Atkin in *Bell v Lever Bros Ltd* [1932] AC 161 at 224, [1931] All ER Rep 1 at 30.) (4) An employee agrees to retire before the end of his contract of employment, receiving a sum of money by way of compensation from his employer. Unknown to the employer, the employee has committed serious breaches of contract which would have enabled the employer to dismiss him without compensation. Assuming that the employee's failure to reveal his defaults does not affect the validity of the contract, so that the employee is entitled to sue for the promised compensation, is the employee liable to be arrested for the theft the moment he receives the money? (Glanville Williams 'Theft and Voidable Title' [1981] Crim LR 666 at 672).

My Lords, at first glance these are rather telling examples. They may conceivably have justified a more restricted meaning of s 3(1) than prevailed in *Lawrence's* case and *R v Gomez*. The House ruled otherwise and I am quite unpersuaded that the House overlooked the consequences of its decision. On the facts set out in the examples a jury could possibly find that the acceptance of the transfer took place in the belief that the transferee had the right in law to deprive the other of it within the meaning of s 2(1)(a) of the 1968 Act. Moreover, in such cases a prosecution is hardly likely and, if mounted, is likely to founder on the basis that the jury will not be persuaded that there was dishonesty in the required sense. And one must retain a sense of perspective. At the extremity of the application of legal rules there are sometimes results which may seem strange. A matter of judgment is then involved. The rule may have to be recast. Sir John Smith has eloquently argued that the rule in question ought to be recast. I am unpersuaded. If the law is restated by adopting a narrower definition of appropriation, the outcome is likely to place beyond the reach of the criminal law dishonest persons who should be found guilty of theft. The suggested revisions would unwarrantably restrict the scope of the law of theft and complicate the fair and effective prosecution of theft. In my view the law as settled in *Lawrence's* case and *R v Gomez* does not demand the suggested revision. Those decisions can be applied by judges and juries in a way which, absent human error, does not result in injustice.

Counsel for the appellant further pointed out that the law as stated in *Lawrence's* case and *R v Gomez* creates a tension between the civil and the criminal law. In other words, conduct which is not wrongful in a civil law sense may constitute the crime of theft. Undoubtedly, this is so. The question whether the civil claim to title by a convicted thief, who committed no civil wrong, may be defeated by the principle that nobody may benefit from his own civil *or* criminal wrong does not arise for decision. Nevertheless there is a more general point, namely that the interaction between criminal law and civil law can cause problems: compare Beatson and Simester 'Stealing One's Own Property' (1999) 115 LQR 372. The purposes of the civil law and the criminal law are somewhat different. In theory the two systems *should* be in perfect harmony. In a practical world there will sometimes be some disharmony between the two systems. In any event, it would be wrong to assume on a priori grounds that the criminal law rather than the civil law is defective. Given the jury's conclusions, one is entitled to observe that the appellant's conduct should constitute theft, the only available charge. The tension between the civil and the criminal law is therefore not in my view a factor which justifies a departure from the law as stated in *Lawrence's* case and *R v Gomez*. Moreover, these decisions of the House have a marked beneficial consequence. While in some contexts of the law of theft a judge cannot avoid explaining civil law concepts to a jury (eg in respect of s 2(1)(a)), the decisions of the House of Lords eliminate the need for such explanations in respect of appropriation. That is a great advantage in an overly complex corner of the law.

VII

My Lords, if it had been demonstrated that in practice *Lawrence* and *Gomez* were calculated to produce injustice that would have been a compelling reason to revisit the merits of the holdings in those decisions. That is however, not the case. In practice the mental requirements of theft are an adequate protection against injustice. In these circumstances I would not be willing to depart from the clear decisions of the House in *Lawrence* and *Gomez*. This brings me back to counsels' principal submission, namely that a person does not appropriate property unless the other (the owner) retains, beyond the instant of the alleged theft, some proprietary interest or the right to resume or recover some proprietary interest. This submission is directly contrary to the holdings in *Lawrence's* case and *R v Gomez*. It must be rejected. The alternative submission is that the word 'appropriates' should be interpreted as if the word 'unlawfully' preceded it so that only an act which is unlawful under the general law can be an appropriation. This submission is an invitation to interpolate a word in the carefully crafted language of the 1968 Act. It runs counter to the decisions in *Lawrence's* case and *R v Gomez* and must also be rejected. It follows that the certified question must be answered in the affirmative . . .

[**Lord Hutton** made a speech giving reasons why he would allow the appeal and quash the convictions.]

■ *Questions*

1. Was it unjust to convict Hinks of theft? Was she better described as a thief or a deceiver? Does it really matter?

2. Lord Steyn states that: 'Given the jury's conclusions, one is entitled to observe that the appellant's conduct should constitute theft, the only available charge.' Does this put the cart before the horse? Just because D 'should' be guilty of theft does not necessarily mean all the elements of the offence are present.

Lord Hobhouse:

Rose LJ said ([2000] 1 Cr App Rep 1 at 9):

> 'In our judgment, in relation to theft, one of the ingredients for a jury to consider is not whether there has been a gift, valid or otherwise, but whether there has been appropriation. *A gift may be clear evidence of appropriation.* But a jury should not, in our view, be asked to consider whether a gift has been validly made . . .' (My emphasis.)

The dismissiveness of this reasoning is in itself remarkable but the proposition which needs particularly to be examined is that which I have emphasised bearing in mind that the Court of Appeal draws no distinction between a fully effective gift and one which is vitiated by incapacity, fraud or some other feature which would lead both the man in the street and the law to say that the transfer was not a true gift resulting from an actual intention of the donor to give. Another aspect of the Court of Appeal's reasoning which also has to be examined is the relationship of that proposition to the concept of dishonesty. It is explicit in the Court of Appeal judgment that the relevant definition of the crime of theft is to be found in the element of dishonesty and *R v Ghosh* [1982] 2 All ER 689, [1982] QB 1053 and that this is to receive no greater definition than consciously falling below the standards of an ordinary and decent person and may include anything which such a person would think was morally reprehensible. It may be no more than a moral judgment.

The reasoning of the Court of Appeal therefore depends upon the disturbing acceptance that a criminal conviction and the imposition of custodial sanctions may be based upon conduct which involves no inherent illegality and may only be capable of being criticised on grounds of lack of morality. This approach itself raises fundamental questions. An essential function of the criminal law is to define the boundary between what conduct is criminal and what merely immoral. Both are the subject of the disapprobation of ordinary right-thinking citizens and the distinction is liable to be arbitrary or at least strongly influenced by considerations subjective to the individual members of the tribunal. To treat otherwise lawful conduct as criminal merely because it is open to such disapprobation would be contrary to principle and open to the objection that it fails to achieve the objective and transparent certainty required of the criminal law by the principles basic to human rights.

I stress once more that it is not my view that the resort to such reasoning was necessary for the decision of the present case. I would be reluctant to think that those of your Lordships who favour dismissing this appeal have fallen into the trap of believing that, without adopting the reasoning of the Court of Appeal in this case, otherwise guilty defendants will escape justice. The facts of the present case do not justify such a conclusion nor do the facts of any other case which has been cited on this appeal.

[Lord Hobhouse examined the 1968 Act, ss 1 to 6, and continued:]

Section 5 and, particularly, s 5(4) demonstrate that the 1968 Act has been drafted so as to take account of and require reference to the civil law of property, contract and restitution. The same applies to many other sections of the 1968 Act. For example, s 6 is drafted by reference to the phrase 'regardless of the other's rights'—that is to say rights under the civil law. Section 28, dealing with the restoration of stolen goods, clearly can only work if the law of theft recognises and respects transfers of property valid under the civil law, otherwise it would be giving the criminal courts the power to deprive citizens of their property otherwise than in accordance with the law.

Section 5 shows that the state of mind of the transferor at the time of transfer may be relevant and critical. Similarly, the degree of the transferee's knowledge will be relevant to the s 5 question quite independently of any question under s 2. For instance, where there has been a mistake on the part of the transferor, the position under s 5(4) can be different depending on whether or not the transferee was aware of the mistake.

Further, it will be appreciated that the situations to which s 5 is relevant can embrace gifts as well as other transactions such as transfers for value. The prosecution must be able to prove that, at the time of the alleged appropriation, the relevant property belonged to another within the meaning given to that phrase by s 5. Where the defendant has been validly given the property he can no longer appropriate property belonging to another. The Court of Appeal does not seem to have had their attention directed to s 5. The question certified on the grant of leave to appeal is self-contradictory [see [1998] Crim LR at 906. The House of Lords amended the question; see earlier in this section, p 743]. The direction of the trial judge approved by the Court of Appeal is inadequate. There is no law against appropriating your own property as defined by s 5.

[Lord Hobhouse examined s 2(1) of the 1968 Act and continued:]

Although s 2 is headed 'Dishonestly', this quotation shows that it is as much involved with the application of the concepts 'appropriation' and 'property belonging to another'. Paragraph (a) contemplates that the defendant believes that he has the right to appropriate the property and (b) his belief that he would have the consent of the person to whom the property belongs to appropriate it. If belief in such a right or such consent can prevent the defendant's conduct from amounting to theft (whatever the jury may think of it), how can it be said that his knowledge that he has such a right or the actual consent of the person to whom the property belongs is irrelevant? How can it be said that the right of the defendant to accept a gift is irrelevant—or the fact that the transferor has actually and validly consented to the defendant having the relevant property? Yet it is precisely these things which the judgment of the Court of Appeal would wholly exclude.

Section 2(1) is cutting down the classes of conduct which the jury are at liberty to treat as dishonest. They qualify the *R v Ghosh* approach and show that in any given case the court must consider whether it is adequate to give an unqualified *R v Ghosh* direction as the Court of Appeal held to be sufficient in the present case.

Gifts

The discussion in the present case has been marked by a failure to consider the law of gift. Perhaps most remarkable is the statement of the Court of Appeal that 'a gift may be clear evidence of appropriation'. The making of a gift is the act of the donor. It involves the donor in forming the intention to give and then acting on that intention by doing whatever it is necessary for him to do to transfer the relevant property to the donee. Where the gift is the gift of a chattel, the act required to complete the gift will normally be either delivery to the donee or to a person who is to hold the chattel as the bailee of the donee; money can be transferred by having it credited to the donee's bank account—and so on. Unless the gift was conditional, in which case the condition must be satisfied before the gift can take effect, the making of the gift is complete once the donor has carried out this step. The gift has become the property of the donee. It is not necessary for the donee to know of the gift. The donee, on becoming aware of the gift, has the right to refuse (or reject) the gift in which case it revests in the donor with resolutive effect. (See 20 *Halsbury Laws* (4th edn. reissue) paras 48–49 and the cases cited.)

What consequences does this have for the law of theft? Once the donor has done his part in transferring the property to the defendant, the property, subject to the special situations identified in the subsections of s 5, ceases to be 'property belonging to another'. However wide a meaning one were to give to 'appropriates', there cannot be a theft. For it to be possible for there to be a theft there will have to be something more, like an absence of a capacity to give or a mistake satisfying s 5(4). Similarly, where the donee himself performs the act necessary to transfer the property to himself, as he would if he himself took the chattel out of the possession of the donor or, himself, gave the instructions to the donor's bank, s 5(1) would apply and mean that that constituent of the crime of theft would at that time have been satisfied.

If one treats the 'acceptance' of the gift as an appropriation, and this was the approach of the judge and is implicit in the judgment of the Court of Appeal (despite their choice of words), there are immediate difficulties with s 2(1)(a). The defendant did have the right to deprive the donor of the property. The donor did consent to the appropriation; indeed, he intended it. There are also difficulties with s 6 as she was not acting regardless of the donor's rights; the donor has already surrendered his rights.

The only way that these conclusions can be displaced is by showing that the gift was not valid. There are even difficulties with s 3 itself. The donee is not 'assuming the rights of an owner': she has them already.

My Lords, the relevant law is contained in ss 1 to 6 of the 1968 Act. They should be construed as a whole and applied in a manner which presents a consistent scheme both internally and with the remainder of the 1968 Act. The phrase 'dishonestly appropriates' should be construed as a composite phrase. It does not include acts done in relation to the relevant property which are done in accordance with the actual wishes or actual authority of the person to whom the property belongs. This is because such acts do not involve any assumption of the rights of that person within s 3(1) or because, by necessary implication from s 2(1), they are not to be regarded as dishonest appropriations of property belonging to another.

Actual authority, wishes, consent (or similar words) mean, both as a matter of language and on the authority of the three House of Lords cases, authorisation not obtained by fraud or misrepresentation. The definition of theft therefore embraces cases where the property has come to the defendant by the mistake of the person to whom it belongs and there would be an obligation to restore it—s5(4)—or property in which the other still has an equitable proprietary interest—s 5(1). This would also embrace property obtained by undue influence or other cases coming within the classes of invalid transfer recognised in *Re Beaney (decd)* [1978] 2 All ER 595, [1978] 1 WLR 770.

In cases of alleged gift, the criteria to be applied are the same. But additional care may need to be taken to see that the transaction is properly explained to the jury. It is unlikely that a charge of theft will be brought where there is not clear evidence of at least some conduct of the defendant which includes an element of fraud or overt dishonesty or some undue influence or knowledge of the deficient capacity of the alleged donor. This was the basis upon which the prosecution of the appellant was originally brought in the present case. On this basis there is no difficulty in explaining to the jury the relevant parts of s 5 and s 2(1) and the effect of the phrase 'assumption of the rights of an owner'....

I would answer the certified question in the negative. But, in any event, I would allow the appeal and quash the conviction because the summing-up failed to direct the jury adequately upon the other essential elements of theft, not just appropriation.

Appeal dismissed

■ *Questions*

Do you find Lord Hobhouse's reasoning more compelling than that of the majority? Is he right that there was there no inherent illegality in what D did and, if so, does this necessarily preclude criminalization?

21.3.1 All or any of the rights of an owner?

The owner of property has the right to do as he will with it in terms of using it, selling it, offering to sell it, hiring it, destroying it, doing nothing with it, etc. The owner has all of those rights over his property. In *Morris*, discussed in *Hinks*, section 21.3, p 744, Lord Roskill rejected an argument that in s 3, section 21.3, p 742, 'the rights of an owner' means *all* those rights, saying that the later words 'any assumption of a right' in s 3(1) and 'no later assumption by him of rights' in s 3(2) militated strongly against that view: it was sufficient that D assumed one such right, for example labelling goods. In *Gomez*, Lord Keith said that Lord Roskill was 'undoubtedly right'. See also E. Melissaris, 'The Concept of Appropriation and the Offence of Theft' (2007) 70 MLR 581, who also concludes that Lord Roskill is right in this interpretation.

Note that Morris would now be guilty of an offence under the Fraud Act (see section 25.2, p 825).

21.3.2 Gifts and theft

It was generally accepted prior to *Hinks* that Parliament had intended the 1968 Act to be construed in such a way that there could be no theft where the conduct alleged to be an appropriation was something D was within his civil law rights to do. Thus, if D was made a gift of some property by V, it was his to retain and the civil law would protect that right. It was thought impossible for there to be an appropriation and theft for D to retain the gift in accordance with that civil law right, but *Hinks* holds that it can be theft.

For further critical discussion of Hinks, see [2001] Crim LR 263; A. T. H. Smith, 'Theft or Sharp Practice: Who Cares Now?' (2001) 60 CLJ 21; and for a defence of the decision, S. Shute, 'Appropriation and the Law of Theft' [2002] Crim LR 445. Shute suggests that dishonest conduct such as that in *Hinks*, although it might not constitute a civil law wrong, 'may nonetheless have a tendency to undermine property rights either directly by attacking the interests that they protect, or indirectly by weakening an established system of property rights and so threatening the public good that the system represents'.

Not all commentators agree that the House of Lords has interpreted the law in an undesirable fashion. Consider the following extract.

S. P. Green, *13 Ways to Steal a Bicycle*
(2012), pp 105–107

Unfortunately, though lack of consent clearly plays a significant role in defining the moral structure of theft, there is a danger in putting too much weight solely on that concept. For a start, it is clear that lack of consent does not *sufficiently* describe the wrongfulness of stealing, since there are many cases in which property taken without the consent of the owner does not constitute stealing, such as where the taker acts under a claim of right or (if the taker is the government) pursuant to its power of eminent domain, forfeiture or taxation.

The more difficult question is whether lack of consent should be regarded as a *necessary* condition for stealing. A trio of post-Theft Act cases in England might be thought to raise doubt about this contention.

[Green then describes the facts and outcomes of *Lawrence*, *Gomez* and *Hinks* before continuing:]

Do these cases really establish the proposition that lack of consent should no longer be regarded as a necessary element of theft? To understand why they do not, it is necessary to look more clearly into what is meant by *consent*. The problem is that consent (or lack of it) means different things in different contexts. Thus, those cases that at first seem to have eliminated lack of one form of consent as an element of theft may in fact still require lack of consent in a different form.

A good place to begin this inquiry is with the work of Peter Westen, who, though focusing primarily on the offence of rape, has provided insight into how we conceive of consent more generally. Westen describes four basic senses in which to talk about the concept, but for present purposes the key distinction is between factual attitudinal consent, factual expressive consent, and prescriptive consent. *Factual attitudinal consent* reflects the consenter's state of mind at the time she consents; it occurs when the consenter's 'all things considered' desire is to acquiesce in the requested conduct. Thus, a person who agrees to have sex or surrender property to avoid threatened physical injury can be said to have consented in the factual attitudinal sense of the term because, all things considered, she prefers to submit rather than to suffer the threatened harm. With *factual expressive consent*, the consenter not only acquiesces mentally to the proposed action, but also makes her acquiescence known to others. Factual attitudinal or expressive consent is involuntary if it is made under the pressure of coercion; it is unknowing if it is obtained through deception; and it is incomplete if it is given by one who is incapable of understanding that to which she consents. Such forms of consent are to be contrasted with *prescriptive consent*, which to be recognized by law as consent must be made voluntarily, knowingly, and competently.

Westen's framework is helpful for understanding the role that lack of consent plays in defining the moral content of theft crimes. Consider again the three House of Lords decisions discussed above. In each case, an argument can be made that, though the defendant gave his factual expressive consent, he did not give his prescriptive consent: In *Lawrence*, the victim taxi passenger's English was poor, he apparently did not understand how much the taxi fare should have cost, and he was presumably nervous and intimidated; in *Gomez*, the victim employer was deceived by the defendant into believing that the checks were 'good as cash'; and then in *Hinks* the victim was of low intelligence and was essentially under the coercive influence of the defendant. Thus, when the Law Lords said in each case that lack of consent was no longer an element of the offense, what they really meant is that lack of *factual expressive* consent is no longer an element of the offense, not that lack of *prescriptive* consent is no longer an element. Had the victims of *Lawrence*, *Gomez*, and *Hinks* not been duped or coerced into giving up the money that they did, the outcome of the cases would surely have been different.

■ *Question*

If Green is correct about the proper interpretation of the cases, does this not suggest that the more appropriate offence to have charged D with was fraud rather than theft?

21.3.3 Appropriation by keeping

D borrows V's lawnmower for a week, and at the end of the week D resolves that he will keep it. At the end of the week D leaves the mower where it is in his garage hoping that V will forget about it and intending to keep it. Is this an appropriation? Is this theft?

21.3.4 Where does the appropriation occur?

Although the House of Lords' interpretation of s 3 has made the law easier for prosecutors by extending the scope of the meaning of appropriation, it still leaves problems, and arguably creates more problems, in identifying when the appropriation occurred. The appropriation and the mens rea must coincide in time for there to be a theft.

In *Atakpu* [1993] 4 All ER 215, [1994] QB 69, CA, the convictions of the defendants for conspiracy to steal were quashed where they hired cars in Germany and Belgium with the intention of shipping them to England, altering their identity and selling them to unsuspecting purchasers. On the *Gomez* (and now *Hinks*) view, the cars were stolen in Germany and Belgium and the defendants could not steal again in England property which they had already stolen abroad. Cf G. R. Sullivan and C. Warbrick [1994] Crim LR 650.

21.3.5 Continuing appropriation?

It is often important to know how long a particular theft continued. For example, D may be guilty of a theft by aiding and abetting it while it is being committed by P, but D cannot aid and abet once the theft by P is over. When it finished is crucial. Similarly, D may be guilty of robbery if he uses force while theft is being committed but not by using force when the theft is at an end. See G. Williams, 'Appropriation: A Single or Continuous Act' [1978] Crim LR 69.

21.3.6 Section 3(2)

Section 3(2) provides:

> Where property or a right or interest in property is or purports to be transferred for value to a person acting in good faith, no later assumption by him of rights which he believed himself to be acquiring shall, by reason of any defect in the transferor's title, amount to theft of the property.

The Criminal Law Revision Committee (CLRC), in its Eighth Report on which the Theft Act was based, observed (Eighth Report, para 37):

> A person may buy something in good faith, but may find out afterwards that the seller had no title to it. . . . If the buyer nevertheless keeps the thing or otherwise deals with it as owner, he could, on the principles stated above, be guilty of theft. It is arguable that this would be right; but on the whole it seems to us that, whatever view is taken on the buyer's moral duty, the law would be too strict if it made him guilty of theft.

In *Adams* (1993) 15 Cr App R (S) 466, [1993] Crim LR 72, CA, D, in good faith, purchased motorcycle parts but did not suspect they were stolen until two or three days later. D's conviction for stealing the parts was quashed. At the time of the acquisition of the parts—the relevant time under s 3(2)—he believed he had become their owner and by thereafter exercising an owner's rights he could not be guilty of theft even though he realized that he had no title to the parts.

■ *Question*

Suppose Adams, after discovering the parts are stolen, sells them to V, an innocent purchaser, for £100. May Adams be convicted of (i) stealing the parts; (ii) stealing the £100?

21.4 Property

Theft Act 1968, s 4

4. 'Property'

(1) 'Property' includes money and all other property, real or personal, including things in action and other intangible property.

(2) A person cannot steal land, or things forming part of land and severed from it by him or by his directions, except in the following cases, that is to say—

(a) when he is a trustee or personal representative, or is authorised by power of attorney, or as liquidator of a company, or otherwise, to sell or dispose of land belonging to another, and he appropriates the land or anything forming part of it by dealing with it in breach of the confidence reposed in him; or

(b) when he is not in possession of the land and appropriates anything forming part of the land by severing it or causing it to be severed, or after it has been severed; or

(c) when, being in possession of the land under a tenancy, he appropriates the whole or part of any fixture or structure let to be used with the land.

For purposes of this subsection 'land' does not include incorporeal hereditaments; 'tenancy' means a tenancy for years or less period and includes an agreement for such a tenancy, but a person who after the end of a tenancy remains in possession as statutory tenant or otherwise is to be treated as having possession under the tenancy, and 'let' shall be construed accordingly.

(3) A person who picks mushrooms growing wild on any land, or who picks flowers, fruit or foliage from a plant growing wild on any land, does not (although not in possession of the land) steal what he picks, unless he does it for reward or for sale or other commercial purpose.

For purposes of this subsection 'mushroom' includes any fungus, and 'plant' includes any shrub or tree.

(4) Wild creatures, tamed or untamed, shall be regarded as property; but a person cannot steal a wild creature not tamed nor ordinarily kept in captivity, or the carcase of any such creature, unless either it has been reduced into possession by or on behalf of another person and possession of it has not since been lost or abandoned, or another person is in course of reducing it into possession.

Almost anything may be 'property' and, if it is possessed or owned by someone, it 'belongs to' him. While s 4 identifies certain kinds of property which cannot be stolen, it does not otherwise provide a definition of property, whether tangible or intangible, which is capable of being stolen. To determine what is property for this purpose, recourse has to be made to the civil law. Merely because something has a value does not mean that it constitutes property. For example, does a wifi signal constitute property under this definition? Should it?

In summary, s 4(1) treats as property: money (ie coins and banknotes); all other property (ie DVD players, iPhones, handbags, etc); things in action (types of property which can only be enforced by bringing a legal action—not things which can be taken physically, eg bank credits) see, for example, *Kohn* (1979) 69 Cr App R 395, *Hilton* [1997] EWCA Crim 661, [1997] Crim LR 761; other intangible property (eg export quotas (*A-G of Hong Kong v Nai Keung* [1987] 1 WLR 1339), patents (Patents Act 1977, s 30), copyright (Copyright, Designs and Patents Act 1988, s 213)). In addition, it was held in *Smith* [2011] EWCA Crim 66 that the definition of property includes items that it is unlawful to possess, in this instance drugs. The Court of Appeal explained its reasoning as follows:

10. In Smith's *Law of Theft*, 9th edn (2007), p.80, it is suggested that 'public policy which prevents the wrongdoer from enforcing a property right should have no application to criminal proceedings brought in the name of the Crown. The criminal law is concerned with keeping the Queen's peace, not vindicating individual property rights.' That observation articulates the principle to be applied in the present appeal.

21.4.1 Intangible property

Intangible property includes such things as debts, copyright or shares in a company. The most common forms of intangible property that are stolen are 'things in action', that is, types of property that can only be enforced by bringing a legal action, for example a debt.

The main difficulties lie not in determining what constitutes intangible property but in determining how such property is appropriated and the owner permanently deprived of it. Suppose that D without permission publishes V's poems. This is a breach of copyright but is the copyright stolen? Since D does not intend to deprive V *of the copyright* the case would seem to be analogous to a dishonest use by D of V's car which is not theft in the absence of intention permanently to deprive. So how does D set about stealing V's copyright?

21.4.1.1 Bank accounts

One case where it is easy to see how a debt is appropriated is where D causes V's account to be debited and his own credited. See *Chan Man-sin v A-G of Hong Kong* [1988] 1 WLR 196, [1988] 1 All ER 1, PC. Where a bank account is in credit, the relationship between banker and customer is that of a debtor and creditor. In law, the customer, V, does not have 'money in the bank'; there is no specific pile of money that is designated as his. The property that he has is a 'thing in action', a right to payment by the bank of the sum of money it owes him. If D dishonestly causes a bank to debit V's account, D does not appropriate V's money, he appropriates a thing in action belonging to V (V's right to payment of that sum from the bank) and is guilty of theft of that property. If V has an authorized overdraft with the bank, V has a right to payment from the bank of the sum up to the limit of that agreed overdraft, and that is property—a thing in action—that D may steal by dishonestly causing the bank to debit V's account. For example, in *Kohn* (1979) 69 Cr App R 395, D, an accountant, drew cheques on the company's account for his own personal items. He was convicted of theft of the company's thing in action (ie the company's right to sue the bank for £x had now been diminished). See E. J. Griew, 'Stealing and Obtaining Bank Credits' [1986] Crim LR 356 and R. Heaton, 'Cheques and Balances' [2005] Crim LR 747 (both written before the deception offences in the Theft Act 1968 were replaced by the Fraud Act 2006).

21.4.2 Stealing cheques

Where V writes a cheque payable to D (or in more formal language 'draws a cheque in his favour') in what circumstances can D be guilty of theft, and of what? As a matter of banking law, a cheque is a piece of paper which, if given for consideration, creates a thing in action—a right for D to sue V for the amount stated. When V writes a cheque payable to D, D obtains two items of property:

(i) the piece of paper which previously belonged to V (or the bank). The Court of Appeal, in *Clark* [2001] Crim LR 572, [2001] EWCA Crim 884, held following *Preddy* [1996] UKHL 13 in the House of Lords that a cheque cannot be stolen. For criticism, see the commentary at [2001] Crim LR 572. In *Roach* [2011] EWCA Crim 918, Elias LJ considered *Preddy* and held that the decision did not preclude a conviction for the theft of the physical cheque in circumstances where D had no intention ever to cash it, for example when the cheque was signed by someone famous;

(ii) a thing in action—a right to sue V's bank for the sum specified on the cheque. This item of property—the thing in action—obtained by D is *not* an item of property that previously belonged to V; the thing in action D obtains is *his* right to sue V's bank. This is a new item of property, distinct from the item of property which V owned before he wrote the cheque to D; the previous item of property was *V*'s right to sue his bank. D cannot be guilty of stealing that. J. C. Smith, 'Obtaining Cheques by Deception or Theft' [1997] Crim LR 396.

Where D dishonestly induced V to write a cheque in D's favour, and D attempted to cash the cheque he would, under the 1968 Act (before the Fraud Act came into force in 2007), have been guilty of attempting to obtain by deception from the bank contrary to s 15 of the 1968 Act. D would now be committing an offence of fraud contrary to the Fraud Act 2006, s 1, see section 25.1, p 822. If D presents the cheque at a bank to be credited to his own account, at that point D becomes guilty of theft of a different thing in action which does belong to V, namely V's credit balance (or right to overdraw if such a facility exists) at his bank: *Williams (Roy)* [2001] 1 Cr App R 362, [2001] Crim LR 253. At the latest, on presenting the cheque, D has assumed V's right to destroy that part of V's property: *Ngan* [1998] 1 Cr App R 331.

21.4.3 What *cannot* be stolen?

Section 4 provides that some kinds of property cannot be stolen in certain circumstances.

- land;
- wild flora unless for commercial purposes; and
- wild animals—the key distinction is between wild animals and animals that, although typically wild, have been reduced into possession, for example by being in a zoo. The latter can be stolen, as can tamed animals.

In addition to those items listed in s 4, the following cannot be stolen.

- electricity—there is a separate offence in s 13 of dishonestly abstracting electricity without due authority. Gas can, however, be stolen;
- confidential information—confidential information is often of enormous value to the person who possesses it, especially in the context of trade secrets, but it is not treated as 'property'. The next case prevents the offence of theft straying into such areas.

Oxford v Moss
[1979] Crim LR 119, Queen's Bench Division

(Lord Widgery CJ, Wien and Smith JJ)

In 1976, M was an engineering student at Liverpool University. He acquired the proof of an examination paper for a civil engineering examination at the university. O alleged that M had stolen certain intangible property, that is, confidential information, being property of the Senate of the university. It was agreed that he never intended permanently to deprive the owner of the piece of paper on which the questions were printed.

Held: by the stipendiary [district judge] at Liverpool: on the facts of the case, confidential information is not a form of intangible property as opposed to property in the paper itself, and that confidence consisted in the right to control the publication of the proof paper and was a right over property other than a form of intangible property. The owner had not been permanently deprived of any intangible property. The charge was dismissed.

On appeal by the prosecutor, as to whether confidential information can amount to property within the meaning of section 4 of the Theft Act 1968.

Held: there was no property in the information capable of being the subject of a charge of theft, ie it was not intangible property within the meaning of section 4.

Appeal dismissed

The law here has been affected in many cases by the Computer Misuse Act 1990. The decision gives rise to considerable difficulties in relation to the misappropriation of trade secrets, and reform has been proposed: see Law Commission Consultation Paper No 150, *Legislating the Criminal Code: Misuse of Trade Secrets* (1997) and comment by J. Hull, 'Stealing Secrets: A Review of the Law Commission Consultation Paper' [1998] Crim LR 246. For a more recent review of the criminal law's general protection for intellectual property, see C. Davies, 'Protection of Intellectual Property—A Myth?' (2004) 68 J Crim L 398; A. L. Christie, 'Should the Law of Theft Extend to Information?' (2005) 69 J Crim L 349.

■ *Question*

Is the definition of property anachronistic in that it does not encompass things that are considered valuable in today's society?

21.4.3.1 Corpses

A rather bizarre anachronism is that there can be no theft of a corpse as the corpse does not, in general, 'belong' to anyone. In *Kelly* [1998] EWCA Crim 1578, Rose LJ held that parts of a corpse are capable of being property if they have acquired different attributes by virtue of the application of skill, such as preservation techniques. Relying upon this, in *Yearworth v North Bristol NHS Trust* [2009] EWCA Civ 37, the Court of Appeal held that sperm was the property of the claimants (ie the men who had deposited it) and so D was liable for failing to store it in the proper conditions. Could the sperm have been stolen?

For an excellent discussion of the more conceptual issues surrounding the controversy over what forms of property ought to be capable of being stolen, see S. P. Green, *13 Ways to Steal a Bicycle* (2012), Ch 4.

21.5 Belonging to another

Theft Act 1968, s 5

5. 'Belonging to another'

(1) Property shall be regarded as belonging to any person having possession or control of it, or having in it any proprietary right or interest (not being an equitable interest arising only from an agreement to transfer or grant an interest)....

(5) Property of a corporation sole shall be regarded as belonging to the corporation notwithstanding a vacancy in the corporation.

At first sight it is a perfectly obvious proposition that a person may steal only the property of another and, equally, that he cannot steal his own property. Usually the issue is clear cut. So D is guilty of theft if, with mens rea, he snatches V's handbag; the handbag being owned and possessed by V and D having no proprietary interest in it whatever. Conversely, if D arranges for the 'disappearance' of his own property in order to perpetrate a fraud on insurers it may be that D will commit other offences but it is plain that he cannot be convicted of theft.

But property may 'belong to' more than one person. V may have some interest in the property less than ownership. The handbag snatched from V might have been lent by O (the owner) to P (who thereby acquired possession) and P has in turn asked V to hold it while P unlocks her car door. Here V has mere custody of the handbag but this suffices under s 5(1) and the handbag is stolen from her by D who takes it. It is also stolen from O and P but it is equally stolen from V.

There is nothing odd in extending theft to an appropriation of property from someone who is not the exclusive owner of the property. Nor is there any oddity in holding that a person may be guilty of theft though he himself has a proprietary right or interest in the property. If, in the illustration concerning the handbag, P (the possessor) dishonestly intending to keep it for herself, tells O (the owner) that it was stolen from her by D, then both in law and good sense it can be said that P has stolen it from O.

Even a person who is the owner in the strict sense may steal the property if there is another 'owner'. So in *Bonner* [1970] 2 All ER 97n, [1970] 1 WLR 838, CA, it was held that where property is held by a partnership, one partner, even though he is a joint owner of all partnership property, may steal partnership property if he appropriates it to himself intending to defeat the interests of the other partners. The essential idea is that D may be guilty of theft where in respect of particular property he acts so as to usurp the interests that *any* others have in that property.

It should be noted that s 5 encompasses both legal and equitable interests. Where property is subject to a trust, it belongs to both the trustee (legal interest) and the beneficiary (equitable interest) and it may be stolen from either.

The following sections will examine some instances where it is difficult to discern whether the property in question 'belonged to another.'

21.5.1 What constitutes possession or control by V?

One difficulty arises when the defendant alleges that the property he has appropriated was abandoned or 'ownerless'.

R v Woodman
[1974] EWCA Crim 1, Court of Appeal, Criminal Division, http://www.bailii.org/ew/cases/EWCA/Crim/1974/1.html

(Lord Widgery CJ, Ashworth and Mocatta JJ)

W, his son and another man who was acquitted took a van to premises and loaded a significant quantity of scrap metal. The premises from which they took this scrap metal were a disused factory, secured with barbed wire, belonging to English China Clays. The defendants were charged with stealing the property of English China Clays. The prosecution claimed that the factory had ceased work in 1970 and miscellaneous scrap metal was left on the site. English China Clays had sold the scrap metal to another company, the Bird Group, which had removed what they could but left some scrap that was inaccessible. The scrap remained on site until 1972 when the defendants removed it. The site was still owned by English China Clays.

[Lord Widgery CJ delivered the judgment of the court:]

…English China Clays took further steps to protect their property because a number of notices giving such information as 'Private Property. Keep Out' and 'Trespassers will be prosecuted' were exhibited around the perimeter of the site. A Mr Brooksbank, who was an employee of English China Clays, gave evidence that he had visited the site about half a dozen times over a period of two or three years, and indeed he had visited it once as recently as between January and March 1973. He did not notice that any scrap metal had been left behind, and it is perfectly clear that there is no reason to suppose that English China Clays or their representatives appreciated that there was any scrap remaining on the site after the Bird Group had done their work.... [His lordship set out the provisions of the Act and the recorder's decisions at trial.]

The contention before us today is that the recorder was wrong in law in allowing this issue to go to the jury. Put another way, it is said that as a matter of law English China Clays could not on these facts have been said to be in control of the scrap.

We have formed the view without difficulty that the recorder was perfectly entitled to do what he did, that there was ample evidence that English China Clays were in control of the site and had taken considerable steps to exclude trespassers as demonstrating the fact that they were in control of the site, and we think that in ordinary and straightforward cases if it is once established that a particular person is in control of a site such as this, then prima facie he is in control of articles which are on the site.

The point was well put in an article written by no less a person than Oliver Wendell Holmes Jnr, in his book *The Common Law* [(1881) pp 222–224], dealing with possession. Considering the very point we have to consider here, he said:

> 'There can be no *animus domini* unless the thing is known of; but an intent to exclude others from it may be contained in the larger intent to exclude others from the place where it is, without any knowledge of the object's existence...In a criminal case [*Rowe* (1859) 8 Cox CC 139], the property in iron taken from the bottom of a canal by a stranger was held well laid in the canal company, although it does not appear that the company knew of it, or had any lien upon it. The only intent concerning the thing discoverable in such instances is the general intent which the occupant of land has to exclude the public from the land, and thus, as a consequence, to exclude them from what is upon it.'

So far as this case is concerned, arising as it does under the Theft Act 1968, we are content to say that there was evidence of English China Clays being in control of the site and prima facie in control of articles on the site as well. The fact that it could not be shown that they were conscious of the existence of this or any particular scrap iron does not destroy the general principle that control of a site by excluding others from it is prima facie control of articles on the site as well.

There has been some mention in argument of what would happen if, in a case like the present, a third party had come and placed some article within the barbed wire fence and thus on the site. The article might be an article of some serious criminal consequence such as explosives or drugs. It may well be that in that type of case the fact that the article has been introduced at a late stage in circumstances in which the occupier of the site had no means of knowledge would produce a different result from that which arises under the general presumption to which we have referred, but in the present case there was in our view ample evidence to go to the jury on the question of whether English China Clays were in control of the scrap at the relevant time. Accordingly the recorder's decision to allow the case to go to the jury cannot be faulted and the appeal is dismissed.

Appeal dismissed

■ *Questions*

1. In *Woodman*, the appellants were convicted of stealing the metal from English China Clays. The court appeared to lay stress on the facts that the company had erected a barbed wire fence and had erected notices against trespassing. Would it have made any difference if the company had taken neither of these steps?

2. All the scrap on the site had been sold to the Bird Group. What would the position have been if the appellants had been charged with stealing the scrap from the Bird Group?

3. A terrorist hides his stash of explosives in farmer Giles's field, unknown to G. Fred, a local metal detector enthusiast, finds them and takes them home thinking they are WWII relics. Has Fred committed theft?

4. D is caught retrieving golf balls from the bottom of the lake at his local golf club. Is he guilty of theft? From whom? See *Rostron* [2003] EWCA Crim 2206.

See also R. Hickey, 'Stealing Abandoned Goods: Possessory Title in Proceedings for Theft' (2006) 26 LS 584, considering whether it would matter if the balls were in the ground (in a water feature or embedded, etc) or on the ground, and suggesting that the criminal courts ought to follow the civil law where the property is found on the land—asking whether the landowner had evidenced an intention to control the land and anything on it. Where the item is found in the land, title should be with the landowner.

Generally, possession or control is shown by some measure of control in fact accompanied by an intention to exclude others. Obviously, a householder retains possession or control (indeed, he retains ownership) of 'unwanted' items which he consigns to his attic or cellar even though he cannot itemize them. Even household rubbish consigned to the dustbin remains in his disposition for he would certainly not want any Tom, Dick or Harry (or tabloid journalist) looking for items of value in his dustbin. In *R (Rickets) v Basildon Magistrates' Court* [2010] EWHC 2358 (Admin) D was observed taking bags of clothes that had been left outside the front of one charity shop (British Heart Foundation) and also those that had been left in bins behind another (Oxfam). He was charged with theft. In dismissing D's claim for judicial review of the decision to commit him to the Crown Court for trial, Wyn Williams J stated that it could not be inferred that the property had been abandoned:

10. I deal first with what I shall call the British Heart Foundation charge. In my judgment, the following inferences were open to the court. First, that persons unknown had deposited the items outside the shop with the intention of giving the items to the British Heart Foundation. Second, it was a permissible inference that the British Heart Foundation would have been willing either to keep the items with a view to resale in its shop or to dispose of them. In either event, of course, at some stage the items would have become within the possession or control of the British Heart Foundation and it would have had a proprietary right in the items.

11. It does not seem to me, however, that it was open to the court to infer that at the moment in time when the appropriation took place the British Heart Foundation had acquired a proprietary interest in, or had taken possession or control of, the items.

12. In my judgment it cannot be said that the British Heart Foundation acquired possession of the items or assumed control of them or even acquired a proprietary interest in them simply by virtue of the fact that they were left in close proximity to the shop.

13. However, it is clearly the case, in my judgment, that it was open to the court to infer that the items had not been abandoned. The obvious inference on the bare facts before the justices was that persons unknown had intended the goods to be a gift to the British Heart Foundation. Those persons had an intention to give; they had also attempted to effect delivery. Delivery would be complete, however, only when the British Heart Foundation took possession of the items. Until that time, although the unknown would-be donor had divested himself of possession of the items, he had not given up his ownership of the items. I accept that it would have been more appropriate to lay a charge of stealing property belonging to persons unknown, though as I have said it is not material to the resolution of this case that the claimant was charged with appropriating items belonging to the British Heart Foundation.

14. In my judgment the above analysis shows that it was open to the court to conclude that there was evidence from which a court could properly determine that the property belonged to another

at the time of appropriation by the claimant. That being the case, in my judgment, the claimant was properly committed on that charge for trial. It will obviously be a matter for the prosecution to consider how best to frame the indictment when the claimant is actually indicted in the Crown Court.

15. I turn to the charge alleging theft from Oxfam since it is somewhat different on the facts. The claimant admits that the items taken from Oxfam were items which had been placed in bins in close proximity to the rear of the shop. In my judgment, it would be open to a court to infer either that would-be donors had placed the items in the bins for receipt by Oxfam or that employees of Oxfam had placed the items in the bins for onward disposal by the local authority. This analysis assumes of course that the bins belonged to or were controlled by Oxfam, which is not presently disputed.

16. Upon that assumption it would be open to a court to infer that Oxfam had taken delivery of the items once placed within the bins. Alternatively, it could infer that Oxfam had taken possession of the items and had then placed them in the bins for disposal. Either way, Oxfam were in possession of the items at the time of the appropriation by the claimant.

17. I am also of the view that it would be open to the court to conclude that the bins were controlled by Oxfam even if this is disputed. The bins were in close proximity to the rear of the premises. That of itself, in my judgment, raises a permissible inference, in the absence of any other evidence, that the bins were under the control of Oxfam. In any event, if the prosecutor so chooses he or she can allege in the indictment in the Crown Court that the property belongs to a person unknown. That cannot be objectionable for the reasons I have given earlier in this judgment.

■ *Questions*

1. D and E are refuse operatives working for the local authority. They separate out anything they consider might be valuable from the 'rubbish' left by householders before placing the other material in their employer's vehicle. Would they be guilty of stealing from their employer or from the householder or both?

2. Do 'freegans' (those who take food from supermarket refuse areas when it has been discarded because it has passed its sell-by date) commit theft? See S. Thomas, 'Do Freegans Commit Theft?' (2010) 30 LS 98.

21.5.2 Property belonging to another and bank transfers

If D induces V to transfer money electronically from V's account to D's account, what item of property is D alleged to have obtained?

R v Preddy, Slade and Dhillon
[1996] UKHL 13, House of Lords, http://www.bailii.org/uk/cases/UKHL/1996/13.html

(Lord Mackay LC, Lords Goff, Jauncey, Slynn and Hoffmann)

The facts appear sufficiently in the speech of Lord Goff.

Lord Goff:

The first question

Against the above background, I now turn to the first question which your Lordships have to consider, which is whether the debiting of a bank account and the corresponding crediting of another's bank account brought about by dishonest misrepresentation, amount to the obtaining of property within s 15 of the 1968 Act. [This offence of obtaining by deception has been repealed.]

Under each count, one of the appellants was charged with dishonestly obtaining, or attempting to obtain, from the relevant lending institution an advance by way of mortgage in a certain sum. In point of fact it appears that, when the sum was paid, it was sometimes paid by cheque, sometimes by telegraphic transfer, and sometimes by the CHAPS (Clearing House Automatic Payment System) system. However, in the cases where the sum was paid by cheque the appellants were not charged with dishonestly obtaining the cheque. A useful description of the CHAPS system is to be found in the Law Commission's *Report Criminal Law: Conspiracy to Defraud* (Law Com No 228) (1994) p 39, n 83. It involves electronic transfer as between banks, and no distinction need be drawn for present purposes between the CHAPS system and telegraphic transfer, each involving a debit entry in the payer's bank account and a corresponding credit entry in the payee's bank account.

The Court of Appeal in the present case concentrated on payments by the CHAPS system. They considered that the prosecution had to prove that the relevant CHAPS electronic transfer was 'property' within s 15(1) of the 1968 Act. They then referred to the definition of property in s 4(1) of the Act as including 'money and all other property, real or personal, including things in action and other intangible property'; and they concluded, following the judgment of the Court of Appeal in *R v Crick* (1993) Times, 18 August, that such a transfer was 'intangible property' and therefore property for the purposes of s 15(1).

The opinion expressed by the Court of Appeal in *R v Williams* on this point was, in fact, *obiter*. The case related to a mortgage advance, the amount having been paid by electronic transfer. The court however concluded that a sum of money represented by a figure in an account fell within the expression 'other intangible property' in s 4(1), and that the reduction of the sum standing in the lending institution's account, and the corresponding increase in the sum standing to the credit of the mortgagor's solicitor's account, constituted the obtaining of intangible property within s 15(1).

. . . [T]he Court of Appeal were identifying the sums which were the subject of the relevant charges, as being sums standing to the credit of the lending institution in its bank account. Those credit entries would, in my opinion, represent debts owing by the bank to the lending institution which constituted choses in action belonging to the lending institution and as such fell within the definition of property in s 4(1) of the 1968 Act.

My own belief is, however, that identifying the sum in question as property does not advance the argument very far. The crucial question, as I see it, is whether the defendant obtained (or attempted to obtain) property *belonging to another*. Let it be assumed that the lending institution's bank account is in credit, and that there is therefore no difficulty in identifying a credit balance standing in the account as representing property, ie a chose in action, belonging to the lending institution. The question remains, however, whether the debiting of the lending institution's bank account, and the corresponding crediting of the bank account of the defendant or his solicitor, constitutes obtaining of that property. The difficulty in the way of that conclusion is simply that, when the bank account of the defendant (or his solicitor) is credited, he does not obtain the lending institution's chose in action. On the contrary, that chose in action is extinguished or reduced *pro tanto*, and a chose in action is brought into existence representing a debt in an equivalent sum owed by a different bank to the defendant or his solicitor. In these circumstances, it is difficult to see how the defendant thereby obtained *property belonging to another*, ie to the lending institution.

Professor Sir John Smith, in his commentary on the decision of the Court of Appeal in the present case, has suggested that:

> 'Effectively, the victim's property has been changed into another form and now belongs to the defendant. There is the gain and equivalent loss which is characteristic of, and perhaps the substance of, obtaining.' (See [1995] Crim LR 564 at 565–566.)

But even if this were right, I do not for myself see how this can properly be described as obtaining property belonging to another. In truth, the property which the defendant has obtained is the new chose in action constituted by the debt now owed to him by his bank, and represented by the credit entry in his own bank account. This did not come into existence until the debt so created was owed to him by his bank, and so never belonged to anyone else. True, it corresponded to the debit entered in the lending institution's bank account; but it does not follow that the property which the defendant acquired can be identified with the property which the lending institution lost when its account was debited. In truth, s 15(1) is here being invoked for a purpose for which it was never designed, and for which it does not legislate.

I should add that, throughout the above discussion, I have proceeded on the assumption that the bank accounts of the lending institution and the defendant (or his solicitor) are both sufficiently in credit to allow for choses in action of equivalent value to be extinguished in the one case, and created in the other. But this may well not be the case; and in that event further problems would be created, since it is difficult to see how an increase in borrowing can constitute an extinction of a chose in action owned by the lending institution, or a reduction in borrowing can constitute the creation of a chose in action owned by the defendant. It may be that it could be argued that in such circumstances it was the lending institution's bank whose property was 'obtained' by the defendant but, quite apart from other problems, that argument would in any event fail for the reasons which I have already given. For these reasons, I would answer the first question in the negative.

[His lordship dealt with the issue of cheque frauds more generally.]

[Lord Goff declined to answer the third question regarding the intention permanently to deprive as it did not arise for decision.]

[Lord Mackay LC and Lords Jauncey, Slynn and Hoffmann agreed with the speech of Lord Goff.]

The decision led to the hasty enactment of the Theft (Amendment) Act 1996. See now the Fraud Act, s 1, section 25.1.

21.5.3 In what circumstances can D steal property in which he himself has a proprietary interest?

We have seen that a number of people might simultaneously have an interest in property, but can D be guilty of stealing his own property?

R v Turner (No 2)
[1971] 2 All ER 441, Court of Appeal, Criminal Division

(Lord Parker CJ, Widgery LJ and Bridge J)

Turner took his car to Brown's garage for repairs. Mr Brown claims that he did those repairs and then parked the car around the corner 10 to 20 yards from the garage. Brown kept the ignition key which Turner gave him. Turner called at the garage and asked if the car was ready. On being told that it was ready subject to being tuned, Turner said that he would return on the next day to collect it and pay. A few hours later, however, Mr Brown found that the car had gone. Whoever had taken it had had a key, because the key that Mr Brown had was still on his garage keyboard. He reported the matter to the police. Brown went round the neighbouring streets to see if he could find the car, and eventually several days later he found it parked in a street near to Turner's flat. Brown took the car back to his garage, took out the engine and then towed it back less the engine to the place from which he had taken it.

[Lord Parker CJ continued recounting the facts:]

...Meanwhile, the police made enquiries of the appellant and there is no doubt in the light of what happened afterwards, that he, the appellant, told lie after lie to the police. He said that Mr Brown had

never had his Sceptre car at all, that the car had never been to the garage, and the only work that Mr
Brown had done was to a Zephyr car on an earlier occasion. However, a time came when he abandoned those denials and agreed that he had taken the car to the garage, and that he had taken it away
and had never paid for it. In saying that, he however emphasised that he had taken it away with the
consent of Mr Brown. It was on those short facts that the jury, as I have said by a majority, found the
appellant guilty of the theft of his own car.

The trial lasted, we are told, six days, in the course of which every conceivable point seems to have
been taken and argued. In the result, however, when it comes to this court two points, and two only
are taken. It is said in the first instance that while Mr Brown may have had possession or control in fact,
that is not enough, and that it must be shown before it can be said that the property 'belonged to'
Mr Brown, those being the words used in s 1(1) of the Theft Act 1968, that that possession is, as it is
said, a right superior to that in Mr Brown. It is argued from that, in default of proof of a lien—and the
judge in his summing-up directed the jury that they were not concerned with the question of whether
there was a lien—that Mr Brown was merely a bailee at will and accordingly that he had no sufficient
possession.

The words 'belonging to another' are specifically defined in s5 of the Act. Section 5(1) provides:

> 'Property shall be regarded as belonging to any person having possession or control of it, or having
> in it any proprietary right or interest . . .'

As I have said, the judge directed the jury that they were not concerned in any way with lien and the
sole question was whether Mr Brown had possession or control. This court is quite satisfied that there
is no ground whatever for qualifying the words 'possession or control' in any way. It is sufficient if it is
found that the person from whom the property is taken, or to use the words of the Act, appropriated,
was at the time in fact in possession or control. At the trial there was a long argument whether that
possession or control must be lawful, it being said that by reason of the fact that this car was subject
to a hire-purchase agreement, Mr Brown could never even as against the appellant obtain lawful possession or control. As I have said, this court is quite satisfied that the judge was quite correct in telling
the jury that they need not bother about lien, and that they need not bother about hire-purchase
agreements. The only question was: was Mr Brown in fact in possession or control?

The second point that is taken relates to the necessity for proving dishonesty. Section 2(1) provides:

> 'A person's appropriation of property belonging to another is not to be regarded as dishonest—
> (a) if he appropriates the property in the belief that he has in law the right to deprive the other of
> it, on behalf of himself or of a third person . . .'

The judge, in dealing with this matter, said, and I am only taking passages from his summing-up:

> 'Fourth and last, they must prove that [the appellant] did what he did dishonestly and this may be
> the issue which lies very close to the heart of this case.'

He then went on to give them a classic direction in regard to claim of right, emphasising that it is immaterial that there exists no basis in law for such belief. He reminded the jury that the appellant had
said categorically in evidence: 'I believe that I was entitled in law to do what I did.' At the same time he
directed the jury to look at the surrounding circumstances. He said this:

> 'The Prosecution say that the whole thing reeks of dishonesty, and if you believe Mr Brown that
> the [appellant] drove the car away from Carlyle Road, using a duplicate key, and having told
> Brown that he would come back tomorrow and pay, you may think the Prosecution are right.'

What counsel for the appellant says on this point is this. He says again that if in fact one disregards lien
entirely as the jury were told to do, then Mr Brown was a bailee at will, and the car could have been
taken back by the appellant perfectly lawfully at any time whether any money was due in regard to
repairs or whether it was not. He says, as the court understands it, first that if there was the right, then

there cannot be theft at all, and secondly, that if and insofar as the mental element is relevant, namely belief, the jury should have been told that he had this right and be left to judge, in the light of the existence of that right, whether they thought he may have believed, and he said, that he did have a right.

This court, however, is quite satisfied that there is nothing in this point whatever. The whole test of dishonesty is the mental element of belief. No doubt, although the appellant may for certain purposes be presumed to know the law, he would not at the time have the vaguest idea whether he did have in law a right to take the car back again, and accordingly when one looks at his mental state, one looks at it in the light of what he believed. The jury were properly told that if he believed that he had a right, albeit there was none, he would nevertheless fall to be acquitted. This court, having heard all that counsel for the appellant has said, is quite satisfied that there is no manner in which this summing-up can be criticised, and that accordingly the appeal against conviction should be dismissed.

Appeal and application dismissed

■ *Question*

In *Turner* the jury was told to disregard the possibility that the repairer had a lien on the appellant's car. If there had been a lien this would have meant that V had a proprietary right in the car, namely the right to retain possession of it until the debt for the service work was satisfied. If there was no lien, how could the car be regarded as 'belonging to another', namely the repairer?

Compare the decision in the following case decided at first instance.

R v Meredith
[1973] Crim LR 253, Manchester Crown Court

(Judge John Da Cunha)

M parked his car in the street. It was towed away to a police station yard under a relevant parking regulation. The defendant went to the police station adjacent to the yard; it was crowded and he went to the yard not having paid any sum to the police. He found his car and, without consent or authority from the police, he drove the car away. Two days later he was seen by the police, to whom he handed back the Krooklok which they had fitted to his car in the yard. He was charged with its theft contrary to the Theft Act 1968, s 1.

While he was at the police station an entry relating to his car in the found property book was signed by him and his having received his car, the column relating to a £4 charge [under reg 17(1)(a)(iii)] being marked 'not paid' by a police officer. Later he was charged also with theft of the car, the property of the police, contrary to ss 1 and 7 of the 1968 Act, and with taking the vehicle without consent of the owner or other lawful authority, contrary to s 12 of the 1968 Act, and he was committed for trial on the three charges. Subsequently he received a demand from the police for £4, the cost of impounding his car. At his trial no evidence was offered on the count under s 12. At the close of the prosecution's evidence he submitted that he had no case to answer.

Held: upholding the submission, that the reality of the situation was that the police were removing the car to another situation for the owner to collect it subsequently. An owner was liable to pay the statutory charge only if the car originally caused an obstruction, and he had three choices on going to the police station: to pay the £4, admitting that his car caused an obstruction; to refuse to pay, whereupon inevitably he would face a prosecution for having caused an obstruction; or to agree to pay, and then, no doubt, receive a bill. In all three eventualities he would be allowed to take the car away, for the police had no right, as against the owner, to retain it. Consequently, a charge of theft against the defendant was improper. As to the count of theft of the Krooklok, not merely was it a (comparatively) minor offence, but so short was the time elapsing between its being taken and the defendant's admission that he had it, that he should no longer be in jeopardy of conviction for dishonesty. Accordingly, the jury would be directed to find the defendant not guilty on all three counts.

■ *Questions*

1. Can the decision in *Meredith* be reconciled with the decision in *Turner*?

2. Suppose Don lends his copy of *Smith and Hogan* to Vinnie for a day. Several days later Vinnie has still not returned it and Don sees it on Vinnie's desk. Don surreptitiously retakes his book and says nothing to Vinnie. Is Don a thief? Would it make any difference to your answer if Don subsequently sued Vinnie for the loss of the book?

Property may belong to a corporation just as much as an individual and may be stolen from the corporation. Such property may be stolen whether the person appropriating it is a stranger to, an employee of, a shareholder in, or the managing director of, the corporation.

21.5.4 Equitable interests

Despite the breadth of s 5(1), it would not be sufficient to offer protection in all circumstances. Section 5 provides additional protection by deeming someone other than D to have a proprietary right or interest in specified circumstances.

Section 5(2) deals with cases where the alleged theft is of trust property by a trustee. If special provision were not made, the trustee thief might argue that he had exclusive legal right to the property. It provides:

Where property is subject to a trust, the persons to whom it belongs shall be regarded as including any person having a right to enforce the trust, and an intention to defeat the trust shall be regarded accordingly as an intention to deprive of the property any person having that right.

21.5.5 Property received by D to retain and deal with

A circumstance in which s 5(1) would not be sufficient to offer protection is the case where D obtains property from V and is under an obligation to deal with it in a particular way. For example, V gives D, her flatmate, money on the understanding that D will use it to pay the gas bill. V (probably) has no proprietary right or interest in the money once it has passed and if D spent the money on herself rather than the gas she would not commit theft. Section 5(3) provides a solution to such problems.

Section 5(3) provides:

Where a person receives property from or on account of another, and is under an obligation to the other to retain and deal with that property or its proceeds in a particular way, the property or proceeds shall be regarded (as against him) as belonging to the other.

21.5.5.1 An obligation to retain and deal

This crucial element of the section was examined in *Hall* [1972] 2 All ER 1009. H had been running a travel agency in the course of which he took deposits from customers for future travel. H was prosecuted for theft when, in several cases, no flights materialized, no refund was made and H accepted that he was unable to make any repayment. H claimed to have paid into the firm's general trading account all the sums received by him. He claimed there could be no theft because the money became his own property and had been applied by him in the conduct of the firm's business.

[Edmund Davies LJ read the judgment of the court:]

What cannot of itself be decisive of the matter is the fact that the appellant paid the money into the firm's general trading account. As Widgery J said in *Yule* [[1964] 1 QB 5 at 10, [1963] 2 All ER 780 at 784], decided under s20(1)(iv) of the Larceny Act 1916:

'The fact that a particular sum is paid into a particular banking account…does not affect the right of persons interested in that sum or any duty of the solicitor either towards his client or towards third parties with regard to disposal of that sum.'

Nevertheless, when a client goes to a firm carrying on the business of travel agents and pays them money, he expects that in return he will, in due course, receive the tickets and other documents necessary for him to accomplish the trip for which he is paying, and the firm are 'under an obligation' to perform their part to fulfil his expectation and are liable to pay him damages if they do not. But, in our judgment, what was not here established was that these clients expected them 'to retain and deal with that property or its proceeds in a particular way', and that an 'obligation' to do so was undertaken by the appellant. We must make clear, however, that each case turns on its own facts. Cases could, we suppose, conceivably arise where by some special arrangement (preferably evidenced by documents), the client could impose on the travel agent an 'obligation' falling within s5(3). But no such special arrangement was made in any of the seven cases here being considered. It is true that in some of them documents were signed by the parties; thus, in respect of counts 1 and 3 incidents there was a clause to the effect that the People to People organisation did not guarantee to refund deposits if withdrawals were made later than a certain date; and in respect of counts 6, 7 and 8 the appellant wrote promising 'a full refund' after the flights paid for failed to materialise. But neither in those nor in the remaining two cases (in relation to which there was no documentary evidence of any kind) was there, in our judgment, such a special arrangement as would give rise to an obligation within s5(3).

It follows from this that, despite what on any view must be condemned as scandalous conduct by the appellant, in our judgment on this ground alone this appeal must be allowed and the convictions quashed.

The Court went on to offer some guidance on the use of s 5(3). Noting (a) that it is important that reference is made to dishonesty in any case under s 5(3); (b)'where the case turns, wholly or in part, on s 5(3) a careful exposition of the subsection is called for.' (c) Whether in a particular case the Crown has succeeded in establishing an 'obligation' of the kind coming within s 5(3) of the new Act may be a difficult question.... [Mi]xed questions of law and fact may call for consideration.

Section 5(3) requires careful consideration to be given to the precise terms of the obligation it is alleged D is under. The next case demonstrates how complex an investigation into whether s 5(3) applies can be. This complexity is compounded when there is a large group of investors, not all of whom may share an expectation that the property is to be dealt with in a particular way. If only some investors hold such an expectation, but their property is amalgamated with that of those who do not and it is money from this 'mixed fund' that D is alleged to have used for his own purposes, D cannot be guilty. This is because it would be impossible to tell whether D has utilized property that constituted restricted funds or whether he used property that was not subject to the restriction.

In *Foster* [2011] EWCA Crim 1192, F ran a scheme whereby work colleagues invested sums with him expecting him to pool the sums and place large bets on football and other sports. The funds invested were used by F for his own purposes. The trial judge allowed the counts of theft to be left to the jury based on s 5(3). The defendant claimed that not all the property that he obtained from investors had been subject to an obligation to retain or deal in that particular way and that he had made clear to investors that funds could be used at his discretion. The Court of Appeal quashed the conviction for theft:

23. The key issue under section 5(3) is whether the property was given to the defendant in circumstances where he had an obligation to retain and deal with it or its proceeds in a particular way. If so, it is deemed to belong to the investor. By contrast if monies are received as consideration for a particular benefit, and the monies are dishonestly appropriated without the benefit being provided, section 5(3) will not be engaged unless there was some restriction in the way in which the monies could be used. So, for example, on the particular facts in the case of *Hall* [1973] QB 126 where a travel agent was sent money for an airline ticket and took the money without providing the ticket, section 5(3) was held to be inapplicable, because the only obligation on the facts was to honour the contract. There was no specific duty for the funds to be used in any particular way.

24. The Crown's case was that the property was received by the applicant for the purpose of gambling and/or network marketing. It was not given to be used in any way the applicant thought fit. Mr Glen QC, counsel for the appellant, submits that that is precisely how the money was given. The terms and conditions on which the money was given provided expressly that 'use of funds at the discretion of KF Concept'. This is wholly inconsistent with the notion that the funds were subject to a legal obligation as to how they should be used. The only obligation was for the applicant to honour the guarantee to return the funds. Furthermore, he submitted that the very notion of a collective investment scheme is that money should be pooled, and that also is inconsistent with any limitation on how the funds can be used.

25. The judge accepted the submission from the Crown that, notwithstanding the words in the documentation which apparently gave an unfettered discretion as to the use of the funds, nevertheless, those words had to be considered against the background of what the investors had been told by the applicant and by managers at roadshows and other events. He held that there was evidence on which the jury would be entitled to conclude that the money was given for the particular purpose or purposes of gambling and networking only, and that once the money was used for a different purpose section 5(3) was engaged. If the taking was dishonest, that constituted theft.

26. The evidence came from four witnesses we are told, who stated that they understood from the circumstances in which they transferred the funds that there was an obligation on the applicant to be to use the funds in the limited way relied on by the prosecution.

27. In our view, the judge was right to say that this was a matter which should go to the jury. It was in accordance with authority for him to do so. As the courts have emphasised on many occasions, whether or not there is an obligation to use the funds in a particular way is an issue of fact for the jury (See *Dunbar* [1995] 1 Crim App R 28). It must be a legal and not merely a moral obligation, as a number of authorities make clear. In this case the judge was right to find that it was for the jury to decide whether the only obligation was to honour the guarantee without any duty to use funds in any particular way, in which case section 5(3) would not have been engaged because the property would not be deemed to be that of the investors or alternatively whether there was a duty to use it in a particular way.

28. Mr Glen, in his submissions today, made an additional submission why section 5(3) could not apply as a matter of law. He focussed on the word 'retained' in section 5(3) and suggested that it was fanciful to think that the funds could be retained. That is so, but they do not have to be. The funds may be spent or invested—as the reference in the section to 'proceeds' indicates—providing they are being dealt with in the permitted manner, although the duty to use the funds in a particular way then attaches to any proceeds. It is not necessary for section 5(3) to operate either that the property is kept or that each investor's funds should be kept in separate compartments.

. . .

Was all the property subject to a section 5(3) limitation?

34. But there is a final point, which was raised—I hope I do not say to disrespectfully—almost in passing by Mr Glen, which has caused us concern in this case. As we have said, there was certainly evidence from some persons that they understood that there was a duty on the appellant to use the funds in a particular way and why they did so. That evidence was necessary because of the wording in the document to the contrary. The judge properly directed the jury that they could look at those words in the context of what individuals were told at various meetings up and down the country. Mr Donne submits that there was really no conflict about this evidence. There were four witnesses to say unambiguously what their understanding was and how they anticipated the money would be spent. There was no cross-examination on their account and, therefore, there was no basis for assuming that these were not representative of the whole group of investors.

35. Mr Glen submits that there was in fact a dispute on this point and that there were certain witnesses who gave evidence to the effect that investments were made trusting in the ability of the appellant to maximize returns. There was perhaps an expectation that the money would be used on gambling and networking, but no such obligation. So, for example, if some very valuable investment opportunity came up, that would be something which the applicant could take advantage of without being in breach of any obligations to the investor.

36. We are not in a position to resolve whether there was that potential conflict of evidence or not. In any event, it can be said by Mr Donne that even if there was, the jury have, by their verdicts dealt with that conflict in the prosecution's favour. We did consider whether we should adjourn this matter for further evidence to be given and transcripts obtained to see exactly what was said in evidence to the jury, but we think in fact that the problem is more fundamental than that. It seems to us that in circumstances where there is such a large group of investors—as we have said somewhere in the region of 8,500—that it is simply not possible to say that four investors can be taken as a representative sample representing each and every one of those investors. There is no doubt, as the jury by their verdicts must have found, that the funds provided by some investors could only be used for limited purposes. But equally, it is hardly fanciful to think that there would be others whose circumstances were different and the same inference would not necessarily be appropriate. We do not think, in other words, that it is possible, absent some consent from the defence which would in practice never be forthcoming, to assume that what was said to some investors which led them reasonably to understand that their funds would be used for limited purposes would have been said to them all. This is particularly so where the documentation pointed against any obligation to use the funds in a limited way.

37. The problem thereafter is this: the funds which come from the investors will be mixed. If some of those funds are, if we can put it in this way, restricted funds, not to be used for other purposes than gambling and networking, but some of those funds can be used more generally, but the two funds are mixed and are not divided in some way—and in practice they will not be—then it is not possible to say whether the funds which were drawn upon to pay for the personal benefits was derived from the tainted section of the funds or the untainted section. If the situation is that some of those funds were given without restriction and they are used for personal benefits, that of course is dishonest but it is not an appropriation of another's property within the meaning of the Theft Act, because in those circumstances the property does not belong to the investors. Nor is it deemed to belong to them where it is not be caught by section 5(3). It will have been transferred, effectively to the appellant, and he could not then steal his own money.

38. It is for that reason that we have concluded that, whatever further material were to come from the transcripts of evidence before the jury, it would not resolve what we think is the fundamental difficulty in this case. Where each individual investor may have invested in different circumstances and with a different understanding of how the funds could be used, it is illegitimate to take a representative sample and treat it as binding across the piece for all those who invested in the operation. It cannot therefore be assumed that the whole of the funds are subject to the limited use so as to engage

section 5(3). Some of the funds may therefore have transferred to the appellant in circumstances where section 5(3) in not engaged. They are then his funds and he cannot steal from himself. We appreciate that this means that it will be virtually impossible to rely on section 5(3) in cases such as this where there are many investors, but no doubt other charges could be pursued.

39. For those reasons we quash the theft counts.

The obligation under s 5(3) must be a legal obligation. Whether, on given facts, a legal obligation arises is a question of law for the judge, but it is for the jury to determine the facts.

Without the existence of a legal obligation, it is not enough that D has acted dishonestly, even gravely so. In *Cullen* (1974) unreported, No 968/c/74, D, V's mistress, obviously acted dishonestly where she made off with money given to her by V to pay domestic bills. Roskill LJ said that 'one could hardly imagine a plainer case of theft'. It was, of course, a plain case of *dishonesty* but was it, bearing in mind *Balfour v Balfour* [1919] 2 KB 571, CA (and the intent to create legal relations for contract), a plain case of theft? Would there be an offence of fraud?

Section 5(3) applies only where property is 'received'. Normally this presents no problems, but problems may arise if the transfer is of intangible property by electronic means: see *Preddy*, section 21.1.2, p 761.

It is plain from the terms of s 5(3) that the obligation must be owed by D to the alleged victim of the theft, V. It is not enough to sustain a charge of stealing from V that D was under an obligation to a third party, X, to deal with the property for the benefit of V.

In *Lewis v Lethbridge* [1987] Crim LR 59, DC, it was held where D, following a charity event, received money from people who had sponsored him, that he was not under an obligation to account to the charity for the *money* or its *proceeds*; he was merely a debtor to the charity for the *amount* received. *Lewis v Lethbridge* was, however, disapproved in *Wain* [1995] 2 Cr App R 660, CA. D was unable to account for some £2,800 which he had received from various contributors during a charity fundraising and which he had initially paid into a separate account before transferring it to his own. Affirming D's conviction for theft, the court said that D was plainly under an obligation to retain for the benefit of another (the Trust), if not the actual notes and coins received, at least their proceeds. Putting the matter colloquially, it may be helpful to consider whether the property received by D is earmarked for onward transmission to another.

In *A-G's Reference (No 1 of 1985)* [1986] 2 All ER 219, [1986] QB 491, D, the salaried manager of a pub, who was contractually bound to sell only goods supplied by his employer, was found bringing in his own beer, intending to sell it and secretly retain the profit. It was decided that the judge had rightly held that there was no case to answer on a charge of going equipped to steal the profit he would have made. If an employee or agent, D, receives a bribe in contravention of his duty to his employer or principal, P, P may recover the amount of the bribe in a civil action; but whether D can be guilty of stealing the amount of the bribe depends on whether he is a mere debtor or holds the bribe on trust for V. This is a question of civil law. According to the Court of Appeal in *Lister & Co v Stubbs* (1890) 45 Ch D 1, D is a mere debtor; but the Privy Council in *A-G for Hong Kong v Reid* [1994] 1 All ER 1, [1994] 1 AC 324 has held that he is a trustee. See J. C. Smith (1994) 110 LQR 180. If the Hong Kong case is followed by English courts, the scope of the law of theft has been extended by this change in the civil law. However, recently in *Sinclair Investments (UK) Ltd v Versailles Trade Finance Ltd* [2011] EWCA Civ 347, the Court of Appeal declined to follow *Reid*. Lord Neuberger MR held that decisions of the Privy Council were not binding on the Court of Appeal and rejected the contention that it was axiomatic the Supreme Court, should the issue come before it, would decide to follow *Reid* rather than *Lister*.

The same issues arise where D makes an improper profit through the use of P's property, or his position as P's employee or agent, as in the case of the publican or *Cooke* [1986] 2 All

ER 985, [1986] AC 909. In all these cases, a prosecution under the Fraud Act 2006, s 4, may be more straightforward (section 25.4, p 845).

21.5.6 Property got by another's mistake

Like s 5(2) and (3), s 5(4) provides a deeming provision (ie a provision inserted into the legislation to clarify how something is to be treated or regarded) where as against D, property will be treated as belonging to another provided certain criteria are satisfied. In s 5(4), in addition to the property having been got by mistake, there must be a legal obligation to make restoration of the property or its value.

Section 5(4) provides:

> Where a person gets property by another's mistake, and is under an obligation to make restoration (in whole or in part) of the property or its proceeds or of the value thereof, then to the extent of that obligation the property or proceeds shall be regarded (as against him) as belonging to the person entitled to restoration, and an intention not to make restoration shall be regarded accordingly as an intention to deprive that person of the property or proceeds.

Of all the provisions in s 5, s 5(4) certainly appears to be the most complicated. As a simple example of the way in which s 5(4) was designed to operate, consider *A-G's Reference (No 1 of 1983)* [1984] 3 All ER 369, [1985] QB 182. D, a police officer, received her pay from her employer by way of direct debit. On one occasion she was overpaid by £74.74 but when she became aware of this she decided to take no action though she did not subsequently withdraw any of this money. At her trial for theft, the trial judge directed an acquittal. Lord Lane CJ, on behalf of the court, held that he was wrong to do so. Referring to s 5(4), Lord Lane said that D was under no obligation to restore the money or its proceeds (why?) but was under an obligation to restore the value thereof. But there is another point of interest in this case. D had not spent the overpayment; it remained in her bank account.

■ *Question*

Lord Lane assumed that D had appropriated the money and pointed out that by virtue of s 5(4) an intention not to make restoration 'shall be regarded accordingly as an intention to deprive that person of the property or proceeds'. But had D appropriated the money? Cf *Stalham* [1993] Crim LR 310, CA.

In *Chase Manhattan Bank NA v Israel-British Bank (London) Ltd* [1979] 3 All ER 1025, [1981] Ch 105, the X bank by mistake paid $2 million to the Y bank for the account of the Z bank. The Z bank subsequently went into liquidation. The X bank was entitled to a dividend in the liquidation but it sought to recover the whole of its loss. It was held by Goulding J that a person who pays money (or, presumably, delivers any property) to another under a mistake of fact retains an equitable interest in the money and the conscience of the recipient is subject to a fiduciary duty to respect his proprietary right. Accordingly, the X bank was entitled to the restoration of its money and was not restricted to a creditor's rights in the winding up. If this decision is correct, s 5(4) is unnecessary. In *Shadrokh-Cigari* [1988] Crim LR 465, CA, a bank in the United States in error credited the account of a child at an English bank with £286,000 instead of £286. D, the child's guardian, got the child to sign banker's drafts and when D was arrested only £21,000 remained in the account. Upholding D's conviction for theft from the English bank, the court said that the drafts belonged to the bank and although legal ownership passed to D by delivery, the bank retained an equitable interest by virtue of the principle in *Chase Manhattan*. It was accordingly not necessary to rely on s 5(4) though the subsection provided an alternative route to conviction.

21.6 Dishonesty

The mens rea of the offence comprises two elements: dishonesty and an intention permanently to deprive the other of the property.

Dishonesty is the element of mens rea in offences under the Theft Act 1968, the Fraud Act 2006 and at common law (eg conspiracy to defraud). It is surprising that it remains undefined by Parliament.

In theft, the principal element of mens rea in the offence of theft is that D was acting dishonestly in appropriating the property. Section 2 of the Act provides:

Theft Act 1968, s 2

2. 'Dishonestly'

(1) A person's appropriation of property belonging to another is not to be regarded as dishonest—

   (a) if he appropriates the property in the belief that he has in law the right to deprive the other of it, on behalf of himself or of a third person; or

   (b) if he appropriates the property in the belief that he would have the other's consent if the other knew of the appropriation and the circumstances of it; or

   (c) (except where the property came to him as trustee or personal representative) if he appropriates the property in the belief that the person to whom the property belongs cannot be discovered by taking reasonable steps.

(2) A person's appropriation of property belonging to another may be dishonest notwithstanding that he is willing to pay for the property.

Section 2 does not define dishonesty. It merely tells us that three specified beliefs negative dishonesty and that the intention specified in s 2(2) does not necessarily do so. But s 2 makes it clear that where it applies D's *belief* is of paramount importance. If D believes he has a legal right to property he should not be convicted of theft, however unreasonable his belief may be. If he believes that V would have consented to the appropriation he cannot be accounted dishonest, though only a fool (which D is) could have believed that V would give consent. If D finds and appropriates property in circumstances in which any man who gave thought to it would realize the owner could be traced by taking reasonable steps, D is not dishonest if this thought does not occur to him. But the definition in s 2 is only partial.

■ *Question*

Note that s 2 applies only in relation to theft and not to all offences in which dishonesty is an element. Should it be so limited? As to belief in legal right, note that s 2(1)(a) does not create an exception to the general principle that ignorance of the criminal law is no excuse. Suppose that T, the tenant of furnished premises leased by L, has read s 4 but has misunderstood it. T concludes from his reading that while it is theft for a tenant to appropriate fixtures, it is not theft to appropriate the furniture. If T appropriates a bookcase belonging to L he cannot rely on s 2(1)(a) to negative dishonesty. T has made a mistake of law but his mistake relates to what constitutes the actus reus of theft; it is a mistake as to the *criminal law* and, as such, affords no defence. But if in a different case T believes that he has a right in civil law having read some out-of-date textbook on tenants' rights, the relevant law here being the civil law, then T does not act dishonestly even though the law recognizes no such right. This is not to say that T has necessarily acted dishonestly, only that he cannot rely on s 2(1)(a) to show categorically that he has not. Whether T is dishonest may be considered in the light of the next case.

R v Ghosh

[1982] EWCA Crim 2, Court of Appeal, Criminal Division, http://www.bailii.org/ew/cases/EWCA/Crim/1982/2.html

(Lord Lane CJ, Lloyd and Eastham JJ)

The defendant was a doctor who, it was alleged, had treated private patients using NHS facilities and claimed money for doing so.

[**Lord Lane CJ** read the following judgment of the court:]

The grounds of appeal are simply that the judge misdirected the jury as to the meaning of dishonesty.
...The law on this branch of the Theft Act 1968 is in a complicated state and we embark on an examination of the authorities with great diffidence.

When *R v McIvor* [1982] 1 All ER 491, [1982] 1 WLR 409 came before the Court of Appeal, there were two conflicting lines of authority. On the one hand there were cases which decided that the test of dishonesty for the purposes of the Theft Act 1968 is, what we venture to call, subjective, that is to say, the jury should be directed to look into the mind of the defendant and determine whether he knew he was acting dishonestly: see *R v Landy* [1981] 1 All ER 1172 at 1181, [1981] 1 WLR 355 at 365 where Lawton LJ, giving the reserved judgment of the Court of Appeal said:

'An assertion by a defendant that throughout a transaction he acted honestly does not have to be accepted but has to be weighed like any other piece of evidence. If that was the defendant's state of mind, or may have been, he is entitled to be acquitted. But if the jury, applying their own notions of what is honest and what is not, conclude that he could not have believed he was acting honestly, then the element of dishonesty will have been established. What a jury must not do is to say to themselves: "If we had been in his place we would have known we were acting dishonestly, so he must have known he was." '

On the other hand there were cases which decided that the test of dishonesty is objective. Thus in *R v Greenstein; R v Green* [1976] 1 All ER 1 at 6, [1975] 1 WLR 1353 at 1359 the judge in the court below had directed the jury:

'...The question you have to decide and what this case is all about is whether these defendants, or either of them, carried out their stagging operations [a share-purchasing scheme] in a dishonest way. To that question you apply your own standards of dishonesty. It is no good, you see, applying the standards of anyone accused of dishonesty otherwise everybody accused of dishonesty, if he were to be tested by his own standards, would be acquitted automatically, you may think. The question is essentially one for a jury to decide and it is essentially one which the jury must decide by applying its own standards.'

The Court of Appeal, in a reserved judgment, approved that direction.

In *R v McIvor* [1982] 1 All ER 491 at 497, [1982] 1 WLR 409 at 417 the Court of Appeal sought to reconcile these conflicting lines of authority. They did so on the basis that the subjective test is appropriate where the charge is conspiracy to defraud, but in the case of theft the test should be objective. [His lordship referred to that passage and other judgments on conspiracy to defraud referred to therein.] In *Scott v Comr of Police for the Metropolis* [1974] 3 All ER 1032, [1975] AC 819 Viscount Dilhorne stated as follows ([1974] 3 All ER 1032 at 1036, [1975] AC 819 at 836–837):

'The Criminal Law Revision Committee in their eighth report on "Theft and Related Offences" (Cmnd 2977 (1966)) in para 33 expressed the view that the important element of larceny, embezzlement and fraudulent conversion was "undoubtedly the dishonest appropriation of another person's property"; in para 35 that the words "dishonestly appropriates" meant the same as "fraudulently converts to his own use or benefit, or the use or benefit of any other person", and in para 39 that "dishonestly" seemed to them a better word than "fraudulently". Parliament endorsed these views in the Theft Act 1968, which by s 1(1) defined theft as the dishonest appropriation of property belonging to another with the intention of permanently depriving the other of it. Section 17 of that Act replaces ss82 and 83 of the Larceny Act 1861 and the Falsification of Accounts Act 1875. The offences created by those sections and by that Act made it necessary to prove that there had been an "intent to defraud". Section 17 of the Theft Act 1968 substitutes the words "dishonestly with a view to gain for himself or another or with intent to cause loss to another" for the words "intent to defraud". If "fraudulently" in relation to larceny meant "dishonestly" and "intent to defraud" in relation to falsification of accounts is equivalent to the words now contained in s 17 of the Theft Act 1968 which I have quoted, it would indeed be odd if "defraud" in the phrase "conspiracy to defraud" has a different meaning and means only a conspiracy which is to be carried out by deceit.'

Later on in the same speech Viscount Dilhorne continued as follows ([1974] 3 All ER 1032 at 1038, [1975] AC 819 at 839):

'As I have said, words take colour from the context in which they are used, but the words "fraudulently" and "defraud" must ordinarily have a very similar meaning. If, as I think, and as the Criminal Law Revision Committee appears to have thought, "fraudulently" means "dishonestly", then "to defraud" ordinarily means, in my opinion, to deprive a person dishonestly of something which is his or of something to which he is or would or might but for the perpetration of the fraud be entitled.'

In *Scott* the House of Lords were only concerned with the question whether deceit is an essential ingredient in cases of conspiracy to defraud; and they held not. As Lord Diplock said ([1974] 3 All ER 1032 at 1040, [1975] AC 819 at 841), 'dishonesty of any kind is enough'. But there is nothing in *Scott* which supports the view that, so far as the element of dishonesty is concerned, 'theft is in a different category from conspiracy to defraud'. On the contrary the analogy drawn by Viscount Dilhorne between the two offences, and indeed the whole tenor of his speech, suggests the precise opposite.

Nor is there anything in *R v Landy* itself which justifies putting theft and conspiracy to defraud into different categories. Indeed the court went out of its way to stress that the test for dishonesty, whatever it might be, should be the same whether the offence charged be theft or conspiracy to defraud. This is clear from the reference to *R v Feely* [1973] 1 All ER 341, [1973] QB 530, which was a case under s 1 of the Theft Act 1968. Having set out what we have for convenience called the subjective test, the court in *R v Landy* [1981] 1 All ER 1172 to 1181, [1981] 1 WLR 355 at 365 continued:

'In our judgment this is the way *R v Feely* should be applied in cases where the issue of dishonesty arises. It is also the way in which the jury should have been directed in this case.

In support of the distinction it is said that in conspiracy to defraud the question arises in relation to an agreement. But we cannot see that this makes any difference. If A and B agree to deprive a person dishonestly of his goods, they are guilty of conspiracy to defraud: see *Scott*'s case. If they dishonestly and with the necessary intent deprive him of his goods, they are presumably guilty of theft. Why, one asks respectfully, should the test be objective in the case of simple theft, but subjective where they have agreed to commit a theft?

[The court considered the implications of the dishonesty test in the offences of deception.]

We feel, with the greatest respect, that in seeking to reconcile the two lines of authority in the way we have mentioned, the Court of Appeal in *McIvor* was seeking to reconcile the irreconcilable. It therefore falls to us now either to choose between the two lines of authority or to propose some other solution.

In the current supplement to *Archbold's, Pleading, Evidence and Practice in Criminal Cases* (40th edn, 1979) para 1460, the editors suggest that the observations on dishonesty by the Court of Appeal in *R v Landy* can be disregarded 'in view of the wealth of authority to the contrary'. The matter, we feel, is not as simple as that.

In *R v Waterfall* [1969] 3 All ER 1048, [1970] 1 QB 148 the defendant was charged under s 16 of the 1968 Act with dishonestly obtaining a pecuniary advantage from a taxi driver. Lord Parker CJ, giving the judgment of the Court of Appeal, said ([1969] 3 All ER 1048 at 1049–1050, [1970] 1 QB 148 at 150–151):

'The sole question as it seems to me in this case revolves round the third ingredient, namely, whether that what was done was done dishonestly. In regard to that the deputy recorder directed the jury in this way: "...if on reflection and deliberation you came to the conclusion that [the appellant] never did have any genuine belief that [the appellant's accountant] would pay the taxi fare, then you would be entitled to convict him..." In other words, in that passage the deputy recorder is telling the jury they had to consider what was in this particular appellant's mind; had he a genuine belief that the accountant would provide the money? That, as it seems to this court, is a perfectly proper direction subject to this, that it would be right to tell the jury that they can use as a test, although not a conclusive test, whether there were any reasonable grounds for that belief. Unfortunately, however, just before the jury retired, in two passages of the transcript the deputy recorder, as it seems to this court, was saying that one cannot hold that the appellant had a genuine belief unless he had reasonable grounds for that belief.'

Lord Parker CJ then sets out the passages in question and continues:

'...the court is quite satisfied that those directions cannot be justified. The test here is a subjective test, whether the appellant had an honest belief, and of course whereas the absence of reasonable ground may point strongly to the fact that that belief is not genuine, it is at the end of the day for the jury to say whether or not in the case of this particular man he did have that genuine belief.'

That decision was criticised by academic writers. But it was followed shortly afterwards in *R v Royle* [1971] 3 All ER 1359, [1971] 1 WLR 1764, another case under s 16 of the 1968 Act. Edmund Davies LJ, giving the judgment of the court, said ([1971] 3 All ER 1359 at 1365, [1971] 1 WLR 1764 at 1769–1770):

'The charges being that debts had been dishonestly "evaded" by deception, contrary to s 16(2)(a), it was incumbent on the commissioner to direct the jury on the fundamental ingredient of dishonesty. In accordance with *R v Waterfall* they should have been told that the test is whether the accused had an honest belief and that, whereas the absence of reasonable ground might point strongly to the conclusion that he entertained no genuine belief in the truth of his representation, it was for them to say whether or not it had been established that the appellant had no such genuine belief.'

It is to be noted that the court in that case treated the 'fundamental ingredient of dishonesty' as being the same as whether the defendant had a genuine belief in the truth of the representation.

In *R v Gilks* [1972] 3 All ER 280, [1972] 1 WLR 1341, which was decided by the Court of Appeal the following year, the appellant had been convicted of theft contrary to s 1 of the 1968 Act. The facts were that he had been overpaid by a bookmaker. He knew that the bookmaker had made a mistake, and that he was not entitled to the money. But he kept it. The case for the defence was that 'bookmakers are a race apart'. It would be dishonest if your grocer gave you too much change and you kept it, knowing that he had made a mistake. But it was not dishonest in the case of a bookmaker.

The deputy chairman of the court below directed the jury as follows:

'Well, it is a matter for you to consider, members of the jury, but try and place yourselves in [the appellant's] position at that time and answer the question whether in your view he thought he was acting honestly or dishonestly.'

(See [1972] 3 All ER 280 at 283, [1972] 1 WLR 1341 at 1345.)

Cairns LJ, giving the judgment of the Court of Appeal held that that was, in the circumstances of the case, a proper and sufficient direction on the matter of dishonesty. He continued ([1972] 3 All ER 280 at 283, [1972] 1 WLR 1341 at 1345):

'On the face of it the appellant's conduct was dishonest; the only possible basis on which the jury could find that the prosecution had not established dishonesty would be if they thought it possible that the appellant did have the belief which he claimed to have.'

A little later *R v Feely* came before a court of five judges. The case is often treated as having laid down an objective test of dishonesty for the purpose of s 1 of the 1968 Act. But what it actually decided was (i) that it is for the jury to determine whether the defendant acted dishonestly and not for the judge, (ii) that the word 'dishonestly' can only relate to the defendant's own state of mind, and (iii) that it is unnecessary and undesirable for judges to define what is meant by 'dishonestly'.

It is true that the court said ([1973] 1 All ER 341 at 345, [1973] QB 530 at 537–538):

'Jurors when deciding whether an appropriation was dishonest can be reasonably expected to, and should, apply the current standards of ordinary decent people.'

It is that sentence which is usually taken as laying down the objective test. But the passage goes on:

'In their own lives they have to decide what is and what is not dishonest. We can see no reason why, when in a jury box, they should require the help of a judge to tell them what amounts to dishonesty.'

The sentence requiring the jury to apply current standards leads up to the prohibition of judges from applying *their* standards. That is the context in which the sentence appears. It seems to be reading too much into that sentence to treat it as authority for the view that 'dishonesty can be established independently of the knowledge or belief of the defendant'. If it could, then any reference to the state of mind of the defendant would be beside the point.

This brings us to the heart of the problem. Is 'dishonestly' in s 1 of the 1968 Act intended to characterise a course of conduct? Or is it intended to describe a state of mind? If the former, then we can well understand that it could be established independently of the knowledge or belief of the accused. But if, as we think, it is the latter, then the knowledge and belief of the accused are at the root of the problem.

Take for example a man who comes from a country where public transport is free. On his first day here he travels on a bus. He gets off without paying. He never had any intention of paying. His mind is clearly honest; but his conduct, judged objectively by what he had done, is dishonest. It seems to us that, in using the word 'dishonestly' in the 1968 Act, Parliament cannot have intended to catch dishonest conduct in that sense, that is to say conduct to which no moral obloquy could possibly attach.

This is sufficiently established by the partial definition in s 2 of the Theft Act 1968 itself. All the matters covered by s2(1) relate to the belief of the accused. Section 2(2) relates to his willingness to pay. A man's belief and his willingness to pay are things which can only be established subjectively. It is difficult to see how a partially subjective definition can be made to work in harness with the test which in all other respects is wholly objective.

If we are right that dishonesty is something in the mind of the accused (what Professor Glanville Williams calls 'a special mental state'), then if the mind of the accused is honest, it cannot be deemed dishonest merely because members of the jury would have regarded it as dishonest to embark on that course of conduct.

So we would reject the simple uncomplicated approach that the test is purely objective, however attractive from the practical point of view that solution may be.

There remains the objection that to adopt a subjective test is to abandon all standards but that of the accused himself, and to bring about a state of affairs in which 'Robin Hood would be no robber' (see *R v Greenstein*). This objection misunderstands the nature of the subjective test. It is no defence for a man to say, 'I knew that what I was doing is generally regarded as dishonest; but I do not regard it as dishonest myself. Therefore I am not guilty.' What he is, however, entitled to say is, 'I did not know that anybody would regard what I was doing as dishonest.' He may not be believed; just as he may not be believed if he sets up 'a claim of right' under s2(1) of the 1968 Act, or asserts that he believed in the truth of a misrepresentation under s 15 of the 1968 Act. But if he is believed, or raises a real doubt about the matter, the jury cannot be sure that he was dishonest.

In determining whether the prosecution has proved that the defendant was acting dishonestly, a jury must first of all decide whether according to the ordinary standards of reasonable and honest people what was done was dishonest. If it was not dishonest by those standards, that is the end of the matter and the prosecution fails. If it was dishonest by those standards, then the jury must consider whether the defendant himself must have realised that what he was doing was by those standards dishonest. In most cases, where the actions are obviously dishonest by ordinary standards, there will be no doubt about it. It will be obvious that the defendant himself knew that he was acting dishonestly. It is dishonest for a defendant to act in a way which he knows ordinary people consider to be dishonest, even if he asserts or genuinely believes that he is morally justified in acting as he did.

For example, Robin Hood or those ardent anti-vivisectionists who remove animals from vivisection laboratories are acting dishonestly, even though they may consider themselves to be morally justified in doing what they do, because they know that ordinary people would consider these actions to be dishonest.

Cases which might be described as borderline, such as *Boggeln v Williams* [1978] 2 All ER 1061, [1978] 1 WLR 873, will depend on the view taken by the jury whether the defendant may have believed what he was doing was in accordance with the ordinary man's idea of honesty. A jury might have come to the conclusion that the defendant in that case was disobedient or impudent, but not dishonest in what he did.

So far as the present case is concerned, it seems to us that once the jury had rejected the defendant's account in respect of each count in the indictment (as they plainly did), the finding of dishonesty was inevitable, whichever of the tests of dishonesty was applied. If the judge had asked the jury to determine whether the defendant might have believed that what he did was in accordance with the ordinary man's idea of honesty, there could have only been one answer, and that is No, once the jury had rejected the defendant's explanation of what happened.

In so far as there was a misdirection on the meaning of dishonesty, it is plainly a case for the application of the proviso to s2(1) of the Criminal Appeal Act 1968.

This appeal is accordingly dismissed.

Appeal dismissed

Ghosh clarifies the earlier law in some respects—it confirms that the test is subjective—it still leaves the jury to determine as a matter of fact (i) whether D's conduct would be regarded as dishonest by the ordinary standards of reasonable and honest people; and (ii) whether D was aware that it would be regarded as dishonest by those standards (not by his own standards).

K. Campbell, 'The Test of Dishonesty in *Ghosh*' (1994) 43 CLJ 349, cogently argues that the second limb of the *Ghosh* test is superfluous if under the first limb the jury is properly directed to take account of all the circumstances. Taking the oft-quoted example of D who fails to pay a travel fare because he is new to the country and is accustomed to free public transport, it should not be necessary to rely on the second limb to conclude that D is not dishonest. A properly directed jury would so conclude under the first limb. Campbell suggests that if the aim is to provide this hybrid test it should be: whether a reasonable jury, applying ordinary standards of honesty, is prepared to excuse D's failure to recognize that his own behaviour would be regarded as dishonest by the standards of ordinary people.

■ *Question*

Would campbell's suggestion be an improvement on *Ghosh*?

In *Peters v R* [1998] HCA 7, D was convicted of conspiracy to defraud and the High Court of Australia, the highest court in Australia, had to decide whether the trial judge was correct to direct the jury in accordance with the *Ghosh* test. The *Ghosh* test had earlier been rejected by the Supreme Court of Victoria in the case of *Salvo* [1980] VR 401. In that case, the court held that dishonesty meant that D had obtained the property 'without any belief that he has in law the right to deprive the other of it'. D's contention was that the jury ought to have been directed in accordance with that subjective test. In rejecting the *Ghosh* test, Toohey and Gaudron JJ stated:

Dishonesty

15. There is a degree of incongruity in the notion that dishonesty is to be determined by reference to the current standards of ordinary, honest persons and the requirement that it be determined by asking whether the act in question was dishonest by those standards and, if so, whether the accused must have known that that was so. That incongruity comes about because ordinary, honest person determine whether a person's act is dishonest by reference to that person's knowledge or belief as to some fact relevant to the act in question or the intention with which the act was done. They do not ask whether he or she must be taken to have realised that the act was dishonest by the standards of ordinary, honest persons. Thus, for example, the ordinary person considers it dishonest to assert as true something that is known to be false. And the ordinary person does so simply because the person making the statement knows it to be false, not because he or she must be taken to have realised that it was dishonest by the current standards or ordinary, honest persons.

16. There are also practical difficulties involved in the *Ghosh* test. Those difficulties arise because, in most cases where honesty is in issue, the real question is whether an act was done with knowledge or belief of some specific thing or with some specific intent, not whether it is properly characterised as dishonest. To take a simple example: there is ordinarily no question whether the making of a false statement with intent to deprive another of his property is dishonest. Rather, the question is usually whether the statement was made with knowledge of its falsity and with intent to deprive. Of course, there may be unusual cases in which there is a question whether an act done with knowledge of some matter or with some particular intention is dishonest. Thus, for example, there may be a real question whether it is dishonest, in the ordinary sense, for a person to make a false statement with intent to obtain stolen property from a thief and return it to its true owner.

17. The practical difficulties with the *Ghosh* test arise both in the ordinary case where the question is whether an act was done with knowledge or belief of some specific matter or with some specific intent and in the unusual case where the question is whether an act done with some particular knowledge, belief or intent is to be characterised as dishonest. In the ordinary case, the *Ghosh* test distracts from the true factual issue to be determined; in the unusual case, it conflates what really are two separate questions, namely, whether they are satisfied beyond reasonable doubt that the accused had the knowledge, belief or intention which the prosecution alleges and, if so, whether, on that account, the act is to be characterised as dishonest. In either case, the test is likely to confuse rather than assist in deciding whether an act was or was not done dishonestly.

A *Ghosh* direction on dishonesty is not necessary in every case. If D claims that his appropriation of property was not dishonest because he believed that he had in law the right to deprive the other of it, or because he believed the owner would consent, or he believed the owner could not be traced by taking reasonable steps (these are all cases falling within the partial definition in s 2), then the only issue for the jury or magistrates is whether he did so genuinely believe. Or D may claim that he took the goods (a book from a bookshop, say) absent-mindedly and had no intention to steal. In such cases a *Ghosh* direction would be inapt and, indeed, misleading.

The CLRC said that dishonesty is 'something which laymen can easily recognize when they see it'.

■ **Questions**

1. Can you easily recognize dishonesty when you see it? Do you think that you would always agree with your friends on what is and what is not dishonest? If not, is it satisfactory to settle the matter by vote after discussion which is presumably what a jury would do where opinions differ?

2. Is dishonesty really an element of mens rea or a defence?

The Law Commission in Consultation Paper No 155, *Legislating the Criminal Code: Fraud and Deception* (1999) provisionally took the view that a Home Secretary could not safely be advised to make a statement of compatibility in relation to a Bill creating a general dishonesty offence. The Commission resiled from that view in its Report No 276, *Fraud*.

The present law under *Ghosh* has its critics (see eg E. J. Griew, *Dishonesty and the Jury* (1974) and 'Dishonesty, the Objections to *Feely* and *Ghosh*' [1985] Crim LR 341; and D. W. Elliott, 'Dishonesty in Theft: A Dispensable Concept' [1982] Crim LR 395); but it also has its defenders (see A. Samuels's book review of *Dishonesty and the Jury* [1974] Crim LR 493; R. Tur, 'Dishonesty and the Jury Question' in A. Phillips Griffiths (ed), *Philosophy and Practice* (1985).

E. J. Griew, 'Dishonesty, the Objections to *Feely* and *Ghosh*'
[1985] Crim LR 341

A1. More, longer and more difficult trials

If the law is right in principle, so be it; the fact that it tends to multiply and prolong trials cannot be a decisive objection. But as an addition to other objections it is of such practical importance that it should have pride of place. There are several distinct points.

(a) The question tends to increase the number of trials. Whereas a different approach to the dishonesty issue might make clear that given conduct was dishonest as a matter of law and therefore constituted an offence, the *Feely* question leaves the issue open. It may be worth a defendant's while to take his chance with the jury. . . . Defences such as these provide ground for a contest where, before *Feely*, the defendants might have felt constrained to plead guilty.

(b) The question tends to complicate and lengthen contested cases. For it is difficult to say of any evidence relating to the defendant's state of mind or to the special circumstances in which he acted that it is irrelevant to the *Feely* issue. Moreover, it must be in the interests of some defendants to extend and complicate trials in order to obfuscate the issue. This point is shortly stated but is surely of considerable importance.

(c) At the end of a trial the jury may have to be asked not simply whether the defendant acted with the state of mind he claims to have had, or in other circumstances that, as he suggests, may have rendered his act not dishonest, but also (if he may have done so) whether his act with that state of mind, or in those circumstances, was dishonest according to ordinary standards. If these matters are not kept separate the jury may be seriously misled. But their careful separation shows the complexity of the direction that the *Feely* question will dictate in some cases. Nor can that question be avoided even if a conclusion on it adverse to the defendant is the only one that a jury acting reasonably can reach. The matter must be left to the jury to determine. . . .

(d) The separate matters just referred to, that may need to figure in the judge's direction, must then be handled by the jury in their deliberations. They may find them hard to keep separate. The issues we present to juries should be as simple as possible; jury service, after all, imposes tasks on ordinary people that they are not accustomed to discharge. The *Feely* question involves complications that we are not justified in supposing that all jurors are competent to handle.

A2. Inconsistent decisions

The *Feely* question carries an unacceptable risk of inconsistency of decision. This objection has been voiced by many critics. The problem of inconsistency is likely, of course, to affect only a small proportion of cases. In most cases the issue is one as to the facts: what did D do? what was his state of mind? Once the facts are found there will usually be only one plausible answer to the *Feely* question. It is only in a minority of cases that the matter will truly admit of argument. But within this crucial marginal group different juries, as the presumptive embodiment of ordinary decent standards, may take different views of essentially indistinguishable cases. The law of the relevant offence will then vary as between different defendants. This must be unacceptable.

A3. Fiction of community norms

The *Feely* question implies the existence of a relevant community norm. In doing so it glosses over differences of age, class and cultural background which combine to give the character of fiction to the idea of a generally shared sense of the boundary between honesty and dishonesty. This is the more obvious in a society with the range of cultural groups that ours now has; and it is the more relevant since jury service was extended to the generality of electors between 18 and 65. [Note this has since been extended further.] It is simply naive to suppose—surely no one does suppose—that there is, in respect of the dishonesty question, any such single thing as 'the standards of ordinary decent people.' Although most people will unite in condemning, or in tolerating, some forms of behaviour, there are others as to which considerable divergence of view will exist. How juries cope with this obvious difficulty we do not know. Presumably some acquittals derive from the triumph of the most relaxed standard represented on the jury. The present objection is not to outcomes, however, but to the illegitimacy of the stated test as resting disreputably on a reference to a fictitious category.

A4. 'Dishonestly' as an 'ordinary word'

The foregoing objection to the *Feely* question is closely related to another. The jury are to consult their sense of ordinary standards because the word 'dishonestly' is 'in common use.' Jurors in their own lives 'have to decide what is and what is not dishonest'; they do not 'require the help of a judge to tell them what amounts to dishonesty.' For 'the meaning of an ordinary word of the English language is not a question of law.' This is the heart of the reasoning in *Feely*. The premise is that the issue is a semantic one; whether the defendant acted 'dishonestly' depends upon what 'dishonestly' means.

The conclusion is that the issue requires the application of ordinary 'standards.' Between the premise and the conclusion lies the proposition that the meaning of the word 'dishonestly' will be found by a reference to standards. This silent step in the argument is itself interesting but is not of present concern. What must be expressed here is a doubt about the 'ordinary word.' It simply does not follow from the truth that a word such as 'dishonestly' is an ordinary word that all speakers of the language share the same sense of its application or non-application in particular contexts. Once again, it is to the marginal case, where the issue is live and crucial, that this common sense objection particularly applies. Even judges, a relatively homogeneous group of uniformly high linguistic competence, have been known to differ on the application of the epithet 'dishonest' in a marginal case. It is not acceptable that the meaning of 'dishonestly' should be 'whatever in a particular case it conveys to the mind or minds of the tribunal of fact without any instruction as to the meaning . . .'

A5. Specialised cases

The *Feely* question is in any case unsuitable where the context of the case is a specialised one, involving intricate financial activities or dealings in a specialised market. It is neither reasonable nor rational to expect ordinary people to judge as 'dishonest' or 'not dishonest' conduct of which, for want of relevant experience, they cannot appreciate the contextual flavour. Their answer to the *Feely* question ought sometimes to be that ordinary people have no standards in relation to the conduct in question. Juries do not reply in this rebellious way. Again, we do not know how they cope. Perhaps in some cases they take their cue from the fact of prosecution ('the prosecution are sure it was dishonest; of course the defendant says it was not!') or from the evidence of witnesses who do understand the context; but then they are not applying the *Feely* test. Perhaps in others they acquit because, perforce, they are not satisfied that the arcane activities of which they have heard offend against 'ordinary' standards; and then the test may produce a pernicious result.

A6. Ordinary dishonest jurors

The general understanding is that the jury may be taken to represent the 'ordinary decent people' to whom the *Feely* question refers. That is why, without incurring the disapproval of the Court of Appeal either in his own case or in *Ghosh*, the trial judge in *Greenstein* spoke to the jury of their 'applying [their] own standards.' Yet a vast number of what must surely be theft, handling and minor fraud offences are committed by 'ordinary,' even 'ordinary decent,' people such as serve upon juries: theft at work ('perks'), handling stolen goods being offered in the neighbourhood ('from off the back of a lorry'), inflation of expenses claims, inaccuracy or concealment in the income tax return. These ordinary people, as jurors, will either apply their own standards, as being the prevalent standards of which they know; or they will demand of their defendants higher standards than they themselves attain. To the extent (if at all) that the former occurs, the Court of Appeal in *Feely* and *Ghosh* will have achieved a reduction in the scope of dishonesty offences which it certainly did not intend. We ought not, on the other hand, to view the latter, presumably more common, occurrence with complacency. It is perfectly acceptable for the law to require a jury to apply a standard higher than its own; it is not acceptable that the law should invite a jury to impose such a standard by an act of creative hypocrisy. The law in effect expects many jurors, in relation to very common kinds of offences, to have one conception of ordinary standards outside court and another conception inside. This is disreputable.

A7. 'Anarchic' verdicts

The *Feely* question, offered without qualification to the jury, is 'a question of moral estimation without guidelines' and permits ' "anarchic" verdicts which are not technically perverse'. A jury without stars or compass cannot be accused of bad navigation. The direction it takes may be deplorable but cannot be wrong. A consequence of this, it has been pointed out, is that members of unpopular groups may receive inadequate protection from the law. Nothing, in any case, can prevent a jury from refusing to convict where the victim of the theft or obtaining alleged is someone whom they regard as 'fair game.' Such a disregard of property rights is easier to achieve, however, if it does not involve rebellion against a judicial direction but can pass as the performance of the jury's own evaluative function.

A8. What is 'dishonest' should be a matter of law

Whether an individual defendant was dishonest is, of course, a question for the jury. But it should be so only in the sense that the jury will find the facts upon the strength of which, applying legal principles, they will be able to say whether the defendant acted dishonestly. Whether the facts that they find constitute a case of 'dishonesty' within the meaning of that word in the particular legal context is a matter of legal principle upon which they should be able to turn to the law for clear guidance.

. . .

A9. Dishonesty and defences

Leaving the dishonesty issue to the untutored application of community standards allows the issue a potentially unlimited function. The jury may be unwilling to condemn a defendant's conduct as 'dishonest' because they sympathise with his motive or are inclined to excuse what he did in the difficult circumstances in which he found himself; they may be still less willing if they are prepared to say that his conduct was justified in the circumstances. Thus the jury may create for their defendant a defence of necessity greater than any known to the law or a defence of pressure of circumstances where the law knows only a plea in mitigation. But the law of defences should develop in a disciplined way under judicial control, save indeed to the extent that it is statutorily defined.

The preceding paragraph assumes that a jury response such as sympathy with the defendant's motive or with his dilemma in an emergency is capable of affecting their judgment of his conduct as 'honest' or 'dishonest.' Similarly, a familiar objection to the *Ghosh* question (B5 below) assumes that it allows a defendant to claim that he did not know that his conduct would be regarded as 'dishonest' because he thought that right-thinking people would approve of it on moral grounds. These assumptions can be challenged. It may be said that sympathy with a motive, or an inclination to condone what is done in an emergency, has nothing to do with a judgment about honesty; that the question 'was it honest according to ordinary standards?' is a narrower question than 'was it justifiable or praiseworthy by ordinary standards?' That would, indeed, be a way of slightly limiting the mischief of *Feely* and *Ghosh*. The difficulty with it is that it would require an explanation to the jury of what is meant by 'dishonest' in the *Feely* question itself. But the jury do not need such an explanation; they know what the word means!

. . .

B. Objections to the *Ghosh* question

The second question is: Must the defendant have known that what he was doing was dishonest according to the standards of ordinary decent people?

B1. More, longer and more difficult trials

Compare objection A1. The *Ghosh* question (a) creates an additional ground for contested trials; (b) justifies the introduction of additional evidence; (c) further complicates the judge's direction; and (d) adds further to the complexity of the jury's task. There is no need to labour these points.

. . .

B3. Inept correction of error

Two cases after *Feely* had introduced reference to the question whether the defendant knew or believed that he was acting dishonestly (*Boggeln v Williams* [1978] 2 All ER 1061; *Landy* [1981] 1 All ER 1172). . . . *Ghosh* was an attempt to reintroduce order into a subject that had become inconsistent and confused. But the job was ineptly performed.

All that needed to be done was to point out that reference to the defendant's belief in the honesty of his own conduct was an inappropriate way of taking into account his 'state of mind.' It is true that, as the Court of Appeal has repeatedly asserted, proof of dishonesty requires reference to the defendant's state of mind. But it does so only in the sense that there must first be a finding as to whether he acted (or may have acted) with a belief (e.g. a claim of right), an intention (e.g. to take the valuable goods he has found to the police station) or an expectation (e.g. of an immediate power to repay) that is relevant under section 2(1) of the Theft Act 1968 or may be regarded by the jury as relevant to the *Feely* question. Once a relevant state of mind has been found, the only question remaining to be answered is whether section 2(1) or the jury's sense of ordinary decent standards makes the defendant's conduct with that state of mind dishonest. This is a question, not as to what state of mind the defendant had, but as to how that state of mind is to be characterised.

The confusion on this point in the *Ghosh* judgment is clear to see in the treatment of the hypothetical of a visitor from a foreign country where public transport is free. He travels on a bus without paying. Does he do so dishonestly? The court says that 'his conduct, judged objectively by what he has done, is dishonest.' The error enters the argument at this point. It cannot be right, as the structure of the court's argument plainly implies, that the visitor's conduct would be regarded as dishonest by ordinary decent standards. If the jury knew that he believed public transport to be free, they would say that, according to ordinary standards, he had not behaved dishonestly. There is no need to go further; his 'state of mind' has already been taken into account. But the court, having declared him dishonest when 'judged objectively,' has to introduce a further 'subjective' element to rescue him. That leads to the question: 'Did he know it was dishonest?'—an entirely unnecessary question.

B4. Mistake of law

The *Ghosh* question 'allows something like a mistake of law to be a defence.' The question is a mere addendum to the *Feely* question; it is the answer to the latter that determines the view to be taken of the defendant's conduct as in principle criminal. The jury's apprehension of current standards makes law for the case; the defendant's misapprehension of those standards is indeed 'something like a mistake of law.' It is not strictly one, of course; his failure to realise that ordinary people would call his conduct dishonest means (taking *Ghosh* literally) that it is not dishonest.

B5. The 'Robin Hood defence'

A person may defend his attack on another's property by reference to a moral or political conviction so passionately held that he believed (so he claims) that 'ordinary decent' members of society would regard his conduct as proper, even laudable. If the asserted belief is treated as a claim to have been ignorant that the conduct was 'dishonest' by ordinary standards (and it has been assumed that it might be so treated, and if the jury think (as exceptionally they might) that the belief may have been held, *Ghosh* produces an acquittal. The result is remarkable. Robin Hood must be a thief even if he thinks the whole of the right-thinking world is on his side.

B6. A further threat to standards

A person reared or moving in an environment in which it is generally regarded as legitimate to take advantage of certain classes of people—perhaps bookmakers or employers—may plausibly claim that he did not realise that his conduct, of which a member of such a class was a victim, was generally regarded as dishonest. It is not acceptable that a claim of that sort should be capable even of being advanced. It has been said that 'the [*Ghosh*] question presents an even greater threat to the standard of honesty than the [*Feely* question].'

■ *Questions*

Do you find these criticisms convincing? Are there reported instances of juries struggling with the concept? If not, why not?

21.6.1 Reform of dishonesty

Would it be possible and desirable to enact an exhaustive definition of dishonesty? Suppose the partial definition in the 1968 Act had been made an exhaustive definition; would this adequately meet the case? Alternatively, consider a provision that a person appropriating property belonging to another *is* to be regarded as dishonest unless one of the three present exceptions applies—

> or, (d) he intends to replace the property with an equivalent, having no doubt that no detriment whatever will be caused to the owner by the appropriation.

This would exempt the person who takes money from his employer's till, knowing that he is forbidden to do so, but intending, and having no doubt that he will be able, to replace it before it is missed. *Should* he be exempted from liability for theft?

   A. Halpin, 'The Test for Dishonesty' [1996] Crim LR 283 at 294 suggests the following redefinition:

> 1. The treatment by a person of the property of another is to be regarded as dishonest where it is done without a belief that the other would consent to that treatment if he knew of all the circumstances, unless the person believes that the law permits that treatment of the property. 2. The treatment by a person of the property of another is not to be regarded as dishonest if done (otherwise than by a trustee or personal representative) in the belief that the person to whom the property belongs is unlikely to be discovered by taking reasonable steps.

> ■ *Question*
>
> Is this any better than the present law?

More radically, D. W. Elliott ('Dishonesty in Theft: A Dispensable Concept' [1982] Crim LR 395 at 398) proposes dispensing with the word 'dishonestly' altogether and adding a new s 2(3): 'No appropriation of property belonging to another which is not detrimental to the interests of the other in a significant practical way shall amount to theft of the property.'

> ■ *Questions*
>
> Is this any improvement? D takes £20 from David Beckham's wallet. Theft? Would it matter if it was the only £20 in the wallet and Beckham could not get to an ATM?

Ghosh is not followed in most other common law jurisdictions. For example, when the Irish Law Reform Commission examined options for reforming the law it recommended defining dishonestly as, 'without a claim of right made in good faith'. The rationale for defining dishonestly was as follows: 'To by-pass the judge and leave the definition of fundamental legal concepts to the jury would be an unwarranted exercise in misguided populism'. Do you agree?

   Despite the cogent criticisms levelled at the test propounded in *Ghosh*, a five-member Court of Appeal was convened in *Cornelius* [2012] EWCA Crim 500 to put beyond any doubt its continued validity.

21.6.2 No requirement of intention to gain

Section 1(2) of the 1968 Act provides:

> It is immaterial whether the appropriation is made with a view to gain, or is made for the thief's own benefit.

This section is designed to deal with cases such as:

(i) D who takes V's original art work, leaving V the catalogue valuation price in cash. The fact that D paid is not determinative of his dishonesty;

(ii) D the shop worker who charges his friend, E, for only some of the goods in E's trolley. The fact that the gain was for E does not prevent D being a thief; and

(iii) D who throws V's iPod off a cliff. D is guilty of theft notwithstanding the fact that he intends only to cause loss to V and not gain for himself or anyone else.

In *Wheatley and Penn v Commissioner of Police of the British Virgin Islands* [2006] UKPC 24, Lord Bingham observed that:

It is certainly true that in most cases of theft there will be an original owner of money or goods who will be poorer because of the defendant's conduct. But in one of the two cases in *R v Morris* the defendant was arrested before paying the reduced price for the goods, so that the supermarket suffered no loss [section 21.3, p 742], and in *R (on the application of A) v Snaresbrook Crown Court* [2001] All ER (D) 123, para 25, it was accepted that the alleged theft was carried out for a purpose which could financially benefit the company. In providing that an appropriation may be dishonest even where there is a willingness to pay, [the section] shows that the prospect of loss is not determinative of dishonesty.

21.7 Intention permanently to deprive

The offence of theft can be committed irrespective of whether V is permanently deprived of his property. What matters is not that there is a permanent deprivation, but that D *intends* that V will be permanently deprived of the property.

In the ordinary run of cases the issue presents no problems. If D takes V's book he is a thief if he intends to keep it but guilty of no offence if he intends to restore it to V.

But some cases are not quite so ordinary. Several problematical situations had arisen under the old law and the 1968 Act sought to provide for them:

(i) cases where D borrowed V's property in such circumstances as to amount to a permanent deprivation;

(ii) cases in which D took V's property and offered to sell it back to V;

(iii) cases in which D took V's property and provided him with a means of recovering it (eg sending him the pawn ticket); and

(iv) cases where D returned the property to V with all its goodness gone (eg returning V's batteries once flat).

The CLRC was firm in its view that, special instances apart, dishonest borrowing should not in general be an offence and accordingly retained in the definition of theft the requirement for an intention permanently to deprive as had always been the case with larceny. The CLRC, however, proposed no elaboration of the words 'with the intention of permanently depriving the other of it' and seems to have assumed that the expression would be interpreted as it had been under the earlier law. But someone always knows, or claims to know, better and s 6 was added to the CLRC's Bill.

Theft Act 1968, s 6

> **6. 'With the intention of permanently depriving the other of it'**
>
> (1) A person appropriating property belonging to another without meaning the other perman-
>   ently to lose the thing itself is nevertheless to be regarded as having the intention of per-
>   manently depriving the other of it if his intention is to treat the thing as his own to dispose of
>   regardless of the other's rights; and a borrowing or lending of it may amount to so treating it if,
>   but only if, the borrowing or lending is for a period and in circumstances making it equivalent to
>   an outright taking or disposal.
>
> (2) Without prejudice to the generality of subsection (1) above, where a person, having possession
>   or control (lawfully or not) of property belonging to another, parts with the property under a
>   condition as to its return which he may not be able to perform, this (if done for purposes of his
>   own and without the other's authority) amounts to treating the property as his own to dispose
>   of regardless of the other's rights.

See on s 6 generally, J. R. Spencer, 'The Metamorphosis of Section 6 of the Theft Act' [1977]
Crim LR 653.

21.7.1 Interpreting s 6

Academic analysis of the section was highly critical, regarding it as confusing and obscure.
The courts soon came to agree.

R v Lloyd
[1985] 2 All ER 661, Court of Appeal, Criminal Division

(Lord Lane CJ, Farquharson and Tudor Price JJ)

The appellant, a projectionist at a cinema, removed films which were to be shown at the cinema
and took them to his accomplices who made a master videotape from which they were able to
reproduce large numbers of copies. The films were out of the possession of the owners for only
a few hours. The copies would be sold to the great advantage of the accomplices and financial
detriment of the owners. The appellant was convicted of conspiracy to steal.

> **Lord Lane CJ:**
>
> The trial judge issued his certificate by posing the following question:
>
> > 'Whether the offence of conspiracy to steal is committed when persons dishonestly agree to take
> > a film from a cinema without authority intending it should be returned within a few hours but
> > knowing that many hundreds of copies will be subsequently made and that the value of the film
> > so returned will thereby be substantially reduced?'
>
> The complaint by the appellants is this, that the judge misdirected the jury first of all in leaving the
> question for them to decide whether the removal of a film in these circumstances could amount to
> theft, and secondly, in allowing them to consider s6(1) of the Theft Act 1968 as being relevant at all in
> the circumstances of this case.
>
>   The point is a short one. It is not a simple one. It is not without wider importance, because if the
> judge was wrong in leaving the matter in the way in which he did for the jury to consider, it might
> mean, as we understand it, that the only offence of which a person in these circumstances could be
> convicted would be a conspiracy to commit a breach of the Copyright Act 1956. At the time when this
> particular case was being tried, the maximum penalties available for the substantive offence under
> the Copyright Act were minimal. Those penalties have now been increased by the provisions of the

Copyright (Amendment) Act 1983, and in the light of that Act it can be said that, although Parliament perhaps has not entirely caught up with this type of prevalent pirating offence, it is at least gaining on it. [NB: the Copyright offences have since been substituted in more recent legislation.]

We turn now to the provisions of the Theft Act 1968, the conspiracy alleged being a breach of that particular Act. Section 1(1) of the 1968 Act provides:

[His lordship read s 1(1). See section 21.2, p 741.]

On that wording alone these appellants were not guilty of theft or of conspiracy to steal. The success of their scheme and their ability to act with impunity in a similar fashion in the future, depended, as we have already said, on their ability to return the film to its rightful place in the hands of the Odeon cinema at Barking as rapidly as possible, so that its absence should not be noticed. Therefore the intention of the appellants could more accurately be described as an intention temporarily to deprive the owner of the film and was indeed the opposite of an intention permanently to deprive.

What then was the basis of the prosecution case and the basis of the judge's direction to the jury? It is said that s 6(1) of the Theft Act 1968 brings such actions as the appellants performed here within the provisions of s 1. The judge left the matter to the jury on the basis that they had to decide whether the words of s6(1) were satisfied by the prosecution or not. Section 6(1) reads as follows:

> 'A person appropriating property belonging to another without meaning the other permanently to lose the thing itself is nevertheless to be regarded as having the intention of permanently depriving the other of it if his intention is to treat the thing as his own to dispose of regardless of the other's rights; and a borrowing or lending of it may amount to so treating it if, but only if, the borrowing or lending is for a period.'

That section has been described by J. R. Spencer in 'The Metamorphosis of Section 6 of the Theft Act' [1977] Crim LR 653 as a section which 'sprouts obscurities at every phrase', and we are inclined to agree with him. It is abstruse. But it must mean, if nothing else, that there are circumstances in which a defendant may be deemed to have the intention permanently to deprive, even though he may intend the owner eventually to get back the object which has been taken…

[Counsel for D referred to a number of past authorities.]

In general we take the same view as Professor Griew in his book *The Theft Acts 1968 and 1978* (4th edn, 1982) para 2-73, namely that s 6 should be referred to in exceptional cases only. In the vast majority of cases it need not be referred to or considered at all.

Deriving assistance from another distinguished academic writer, namely Professor Glanville Williams, we would like to cite with approval the following passage from his *Textbook of Criminal Law* (2nd edn, 1983) p 719:

> 'In view of the grave difficulties of interpretation presented by section 6, a trial judge would be well advised not to introduce it to the jury unless he reaches the conclusion that it will assist them, and even then (it may be suggested) the question he leaves to the jury should not be worded in terms of the generalities of the subsection but should reflect those generalities as applied to the alleged facts. For example, the question might be: "Did the defendant take the article, intending that the owner should have it back only on making a payment? If so, you would be justified as a matter of law in finding that he intended to deprive the owner permanently of his article, because the taking of the article with that intention is equivalent to an outright taking." '

Bearing in mind the observations of Edmund Davies LJ in *R v Warner* (1970) 55 Cr App R 93, [1971] Crim LR 114, we would try to interpret s 6 in such a way as to ensure that nothing is construed as an intention permanently to deprive which would not prior to the 1968 Act have been so construed. Thus the first part of s 6(1) seems to us to be aimed at the sort of case where a defendant takes things and then offers them back to the owner for the owner to buy if he wishes. If the taker intends to return them to the owner only on such payment, then, on the wording of s 6(1), that is deemed to amount to the necessary intention permanently to deprive: see for instance *R v Hall* (1849) 1 Den 381, 169 ER 291, where the defendant took fat from a candlemaker and then offered it for sale to the owner. His conviction for larceny was affirmed. There are other cases of similar intent. For instance. I have taken your valuable painting. You can have it back on payment to me of £X,000. If you are not prepared to make that payment, then you are not going to get your painting back.

It seems to us that in this case we are concerned with the second part of s 6(1), namely the words after the semi-colon: 'and a borrowing or lending of it may amount to so treating it if, but only if, the borrowing or lending is for a period and in circumstances making it equivalent to an outright taking or disposal.'

These films, it could be said, were borrowed by Lloyd from his employers in order to enable him and the others to carry out their 'piracy' exercise.

Borrowing is ex hypothesi not something which is done with an intention permanently to deprive. This half of the subsection, we believe, is intended to make it clear that a mere borrowing is never enough to constitute the necessary guilty mind unless the intention is to return the 'thing' in such a changed state that it can truly be said that all its goodness or virtue has gone. For example *R v Beecham* (1851) 5 Cox CC 181, where the defendant stole railway tickets intending that they should be returned to the railway company in the usual way only after the journeys had been completed. He was convicted of larceny. The judge in the present case gave another example, namely the taking of a torch battery with intention of returning it only when its power is exhausted.

That being the case, we turn to inquire whether the feature films in this case can fall within this category. Our view is that they cannot. The goodness, the virtue, the practical value of the films to the owners has not gone out of the article. The film could still be projected to paying audiences, and, had everything gone according to the conspirators' plans, would have been projected in the ordinary way to audiences at the Odeon cinema, Barking, who would have paid for their seats. Our view is that those particular films which were the subject of this alleged conspiracy had not themselves diminished in value at all. What had happened was that the borrowed film had been used or was going to be used to perpetrate a copyright swindle on the owners whereby their commercial interests were grossly and adversely affected in the way that we have endeavoured to describe at the outset of this judgment. The borrowing, it seems to us, was not for a period, or in such circumstances, as made it equivalent to an outright taking or disposal. There was still virtue in the film.

For those reasons we think that the submissions of counsel for the appellants on this aspect of the case are well founded. Accordingly, the way in which the trial judge directed the jury was mistaken, and accordingly this conviction of conspiracy to steal must be quashed...

Appeals allowed. Convictions quashed

In *Warner* (referred to in *Lloyd*), D removed a toolbox from V's workshop next door and when questioned by the police denied that he had taken it. There had been some ill-feeling between D and V concerning the parking of cars and D later said that it was his intention to return the toolbox and that he told lies to the police because he had panicked. It was held that the trial judge had misdirected the jury in saying that D could be convicted of theft if his intention was that V should lose the use of his tools indefinitely.

■ *Question*

Consider *Oxford v Moss*, section 21.4.3, p 756. Was not the borrowing of the paper equivalent to an outright taking in that the examination paper, once its contents were disclosed, was valueless to the university?

In *Bagshaw* [1988] Crim LR 321, CA, D was charged with the theft of gas cylinders and claimed that he had borrowed them. His conviction for stealing the cylinders was quashed because the trial judge had not properly explained to the jury that D could be convicted only if he intended to retain the cylinders until all their 'goodness' had gone. But was all their goodness gone by the use of the gas they contained? D was not charged with the theft of the gas (and to such a charge he would appear to have had no defence) but with stealing the cylinders. If the cylinders could be refilled with gas, was all—or any—of their goodness gone?

■ *Questions*

The court in *Lloyd* said that the trial judge had given, as an example of permanent deprivation, the case where D takes a torch battery intending to return it only when the charge was exhausted. Do you agree? Would it be different if the battery was rechargeable?

A person borrows property when he intends to return that property. This is not the same thing as restoring its equivalent. D, short of money to buy his lunch, 'borrows' money from the petty cash float in his employer's office which he intends to repay with an equivalent amount at a later stage. D may have a defence to a charge of theft in that he is not acting dishonestly but he cannot claim that he has not deprived his employer permanently of the money (ie those pound coins) which he has taken: *Velumyl* [1989] Crim LR 299, CA.

When introducing s 6 to an expectant and hushed House of Commons, the Under Secretary of State for the Home Department said:

> The case which comes most readily to mind in this connection is that of a person borrowing, say, a season ticket. If he borrows it merely to keep it for any reason whatever as a piece of cardboard having an intrinsic value of a fraction of a penny, no offence can be committed under the [section]. But let us assume that he uses the ticket to gain admittance to a certain performance or series of performances—let us say he uses it for 19 or 20 performances. He has, by that act, used the season ticket in a situation which shows that he is not any longer acting as borrower but as . . . owner of the ticket.

■ *Questions*

1. Do you agree that the taker of the season ticket is (i) not guilty of theft on the first hypothesis—suppose he keeps it in his pocket until the season is over, but (ii) guilty of theft on the second?

2. Suppose that D offers to sell to V, an unusually gullible tourist, the Crown jewels for £500. Realizing that this is something of a bargain, V accepts and pays £500. Obviously a case of fraud but has D stolen the Crown jewels? Assuming that in such circumstances D has appropriated the property (as to which see *Pitham and Hehl* (1976) 65 Cr App R 45, [1977] Crim LR 285, CA), has D, by virtue of s 6, an intention permanently to deprive the owner? How do you think Lord Lane would have answered this question?

In *Chan Man Sin v AG of Hong Kong* [1988] 1 All ER 1, PC, an accountant forged cheques from his employer's cheque book and paid them to himself. He was charged with theft of the debts his employer's bank owed to his employer. He appealed to the Privy Council, contending that since the bank had no authority to honour a forged cheque and the employer was entitled to have the debit reversed if the bank did honour a forged cheque, there could be no debt owed by the bank to the employer and therefore no chose in action which D could steal. The Privy Council upheld his conviction for theft. By drawing, presenting and negotiating forged cheques on the companies' accounts at their bank the appellant was assuming the companies' rights as owners of the credit in the account. What had D stolen? Did anyone lose anything? Who? Did he intend anyone to lose?

In *Marshall* [2000] EWCA Crim 3530, [1999] Crim LR 317, the defendants were observed obtaining underground tickets or travel cards from members of the public passing through the barriers, and reselling them to other potential customers. Mantell LJ said at 287:

It is submitted [s 6(1)] . . . is to be construed narrowly and confined to the sort of case of which Lord Lane gave an example and of which the present is not one. However, this Court had to consider a similar situation in the case of *Fernandes* [1996] 1 Cr App Rep 175 where at p 188 Auld LJ giving the judgment of the Court said this:

'In our view section 6(1), which is expressed in general terms, is not limited in its application to the illustrations given by Lord Lane CJ in *Lloyd*. Nor in saying that in most cases it would be unnecessary to refer to the provision, did Lord Lane suggest it should be so limited. The critical notion, stated expressly in the first limb and incorporated by reference in the second is, whether a defendant intended to "treat the thing as his own to dispose of regardless of the other's rights." The second limb of subsection (1) and also subsection (2) are merely specific illustrations of the application of that notion. We consider that section 6 may apply to a person in possession or control of another's property who, dishonestly and for his own purpose, deals with that property in such a manner that he knows he is risking its loss.'

In our judgment and following *Fernandes* the subsection is not to be given the restricted interpretation for which the appellants contend.

The principal submission put forward on behalf of the appellants is that the issuing of the ticket is analogous to the drawing of a cheque in that in each instance a *chose in action* is created which in the first case belongs to the customer and in the second to the payee. So by parity of reasoning with that advanced by Lord Goff in *R v Preddy* [section 21.5.2, p 761], the property acquired belonged to the customer and not London Underground Limited and there can have been no intention on the part of the appellant to deprive London Underground Limited of the ticket which would in due course be returned to the possession of London Underground Limited. Attractive though the submission appears at first blush we do not think that it can possibly be correct.

'A "*chose in action*" is a known legal expression used to describe all personal rights of property which can only be claimed or enforced by action, and not by taking physical possession.' (See *Torkington v Magee* [1902] 2 KB 427, per Channell J at p 430.) On the issuing of an underground ticket a contract is created between London Underground Limited and the purchaser. Under that contract each party has rights and obligations. Theoretically those rights are enforceable by action. Therefore, it is arguable, we suppose, that by the transaction each party has acquired a *chose in action*. On the side of the purchaser it is represented by a right to use the ticket to the extent which it allows travel on the underground system. On the side of London Underground Limited it encompasses the right to insist that the ticket is used by no one other than the purchaser. It is that right which is disregarded when the ticket is acquired by the appellant and sold on. But here the charges were in relation to the tickets and travel cards themselves and a ticket form or travel card and, dare we say, a cheque form is not a *chose in action*. The fact that the ticket form or travel card may find its way back into the possession of London Underground Limited, albeit with its usefulness or 'virtue' exhausted, is nothing to the point. Section 6(1) prevails for the reasons we have given.

Preddy decided that, because the thing in action represented by the cheque never belonged to anyone but the defendant, *the cheque* could not be stolen or obtained by him. Was the court right to reject the argument that the same principle must apply to the tickets? The cheque and the ticket are both pieces of paper which, when given for consideration, create and represent a thing in action: the right to receive the amount of money for which the cheque is drawn and the right to travel to the named destination, or to enjoy some other service. In both cases, the thing in action belongs not to the drawer or supplier, V, but to the recipient, D. In neither case can D be guilty of the offence of obtaining *the thing in action* from V, or stealing it from him for that thing never is, nor could be, property belonging to V. The court did not explain what is the difference between the two pieces of paper. One possible difference is that the ticket continues (because an operative condition on it so provides) to belong to the company, V, throughout, whereas the cheque form belongs to the payee, D, when it is delivered to him. D can lawfully burn it or tear it up if he wants to. But is that a material difference? In the cheque case envisaged in *Preddy*, the cheque form belonged to V at the critical moment—the instant before it was delivered to D. The instant of delivery is the time when theft is committed. The paper on which both the cheque and the ticket is printed is considered to be the property of V at the moment of the alleged theft.

■ *Questions*

What then is the material difference, if any, between the cheque and the ticket? If the cheque is not stolen, as *Preddy* decides, is the ticket?

21.7.2 Intention

D must *intend* permanent deprivation. Suppose D takes V's car in London which he later abandons in Leeds. D realizes that the car may be restored to V but it is a matter of indifference to him whether it is or not. Does D *intend* permanently to deprive V? (Might he be said to be reckless?) Can it be said that he has treated the car as his own 'to dispose of regardless of the other's rights' and this is 'in circumstances making it equivalent to an outright taking or disposal'?

R v Mitchell
[2008] EWCA Crim 850, Court of Appeal, Criminal Division, http://www.bailii.org/ew/cases/EWCA/Crim/2008/850.html

(Rix LJ, David Clarke J and HHJ Stewart QC)

Mrs Davis, who was sitting in her husband's BMW late at night in a country lane in Essex, was physically attacked and thrown out of the car by a group of men who were in a car being pursued by the police. Mr Davis's BMW was driven off and was subsequently found an hour-and-three-quarters later, a few miles away with its hazard lights flashing. The men then took a Vauxhall Cavalier which they later left abandoned and burnt out. M, one of the four men involved, was convicted of robbery. He appealed against conviction.

[Rix LJ stated the facts and continued:]

11. . . . The question in this case was whether the facts laid by the prosecution established a case to go before the jury of violence in the pursuit of theft. Had there been an intention permanently to deprive Mr or Mrs Davis of ownership of the BMW?

[His lordship recited s 6 and continued:]

13. There has been some discussion in cases, as will be seen, as to whether s 6 waters down or extends or only exemplifies the underlying requirement for theft of an intention permanently to deprive. Taking the wording of s 6(1) by itself without regard to authority it would seem that there is the possibility of a s 6 intention, that is to say an intention to treat the thing as his own to dispose of regardless of the other's rights, as somewhat extending the intention permanently to deprive, because the section begins with the hypothesis that property belonging to another has been taken 'without meaning the other permanently to lose the thing itself'. Although those words carefully avoid the

word 'intention', since the word 'meaning' is used instead, or the word 'deprived' since the word 'lose' is used instead, nevertheless it would appear that the purpose of the section is to render a Defendant to be regarded or deemed as having the necessary s 1 intention of permanently depriving the owner of his property if the s 6(1) intention is established. Having said that, we observe that the jurisprudence discusses the extent to which s 6 goes beyond the essential underlying intention of permanently depriving the owner of his property.

[His lordship referred to *R v Warner* (1970) 135 JP 199, 55 Cr App Rep 93, [1971] Crim LR 114 (section 21.7.1, p 787); *R v Lloyd and others* [1985] QB 829, [1985] 2 All ER 661, 149 JP 634 (section 21.7.1, p 786) and continued:]

21. The next case is *R v Coffey* [1987] Crim LR 498. That concerned the obtaining of machinery by a worthless cheque. The Defendant had obtained the machinery in order to put pressure upon someone with whom he had a dispute. The appeal was again allowed because the summing-up was defective but in the course of this court's judgment it was observed that this was one of those rare cases where s 6(1) could usefully be deployed before the jury, but the jury should have been invited to consider whether the taking of the machinery in the circumstances obtaining in that case was equivalent to an outright taking or disposal.

22. In *R v Cahill* [1993] Crim LR 141 a package of newspapers had been taken by the Defendant and, he said, put outside the front door of a friend of his as a joke. Section 6(1) had been brought into play at the trial but in summing up the matter to the jury the recorder in that case had dropped from his directions the statutory words in their place 'to dispose of'. That was held to be a misdirection because this court approved what Professor Smith had said of those words in his book on *The Law of Theft* as follows:

> 'The attribution of an ordinary meaning to the language of section 6 presents some difficulties. It is submitted, however, that an intention merely to use the thing as one's own is not enough and that 'dispose of' is not used in the sense in which a general might 'dispose of' his forces but rather in the meaning given by the Shorter Oxford dictionary: To deal with definitely; to get rid of; to get done with, finish. To make over by way of sale or bargain, sell.'

So that appeal was allowed as well. A note by Professor Smith followed the extract of that report by way of commentary. Professor Smith pointed out that that case could have been dealt with without mentioning s 6 at all since the question was 'Did the Defendant intend the package of newspapers to be lost to the newsagent forever?'— as might well have been the case where that package had disappeared to some strange doorstep. If, however, s 6 was to be invoked at all, the question would be whether the virtue had gone out of the thing, even if the Defendant had believed that the newsagent would get his papers back the following day, but at a time when they would be quite useless to him. So upon that basis s 6 might have been correctly deployed.

23. Finally, in *R v Fernandes* [1996] 1 Cr App Rep 175 this jurisprudence was revisited in the context of a case where a solicitor had invested client's money at his disposal in his colleague's back street money-lending business where it was lost. It was argued that s 6 should not have been deployed in that case. But in his judgment Auld LJ accepted that this was a case of proper use of it, saying at 188E:

> 'We consider that section 6 may apply to a person in possession or control of another's property who, dishonestly and for his own purpose, deals with that property in such a manner that he knows he is risking its loss.
>
> In the circumstances alleged here, an alleged dishonest disposal of someone else's money on an obviously insecure investment, we consider that the judge was justified in referring to section 6. His direction, looked at as a whole, did not water down the requirement that the jury should be sure of an intention permanently to deprive as illustrated by that provision.'

24. It is in the light of that jurisprudence that we have to consider the ruling of the judge on the application of no case to answer. What was said to the judge was that in the circumstances of this case

there was no intention permanently to deprive Mr or Mrs Davis of their BMW, nor was there an intention within s 6, which the prosecution also relied upon, to treat the thing as the Defendant's own to
dispose of regardless of the owner's rights. The car had only been driven for a few miles before being
abandoned. The fact of abandonment showed that there was no intention permanently to deprive
the owners of it or to dispose of it irrespective of the owner's rights. The judge, however, considered
that there was either in the taking or in the use or in the abandonment of the vehicle evidence capable
of amounting to a disposal under s 6(1). Of those three matters—the taking, the use and the abandonment—the judge in particular had emphasised the abandonment where he said 'It appears to me
that abandonment in those circumstances might amount to a disposal. That is a matter which in my
judgment should be decided by a jury.'

25. In our judgment the judge erred in these considerations. So far as the abandonment itself of
the car was concerned, a matter which on this appeal Mr Jackson on behalf of the Crown has not
relied upon, that of course operated as a factor in favour of the defence. Moreover, the fact that its
hazard lights were left on emphasized that there was no intention to avoid drawing attention to the
car. So far as the use of the vehicle is concerned, again a matter not relied upon on this appeal by Mr
Jackson, its use amounted to being driven just a few miles before its abandonment. So far as the taking is concerned, that was the one matter which Mr Jackson stressed in his submissions to the court.
Those submissions proceeded in this way. When he was asked whether the red Fiesta, which was the
car into which Mrs Davis' assailants had decamped from the BMW later that night, had been stolen Mr
Jackson answered that question with the answer 'No'. He was then asked to state what the difference
was between the taking of the Fiesta and the taking of the BMW. His first response was to say that the
difference was the removal of Mrs Davis by force from the BMW and also the breaking of its windows.
Subsequently in his submissions he abandoned the breaking of the windows as being a critical difference. Ultimately he took his stand upon the removal of Mrs Davis by force. This for him was the critical
and distinguishing feature. This was the feature which showed that her assailants intended to treat
the car as their own to dispose of regardless of the other's rights.

26. At some point during his submissions Mr Jackson, before being reminded of the words 'to dispose of', which Professor Smith had emphasised in his *Law of Theft* (see above) and which this court
similarly picked up in *Cahill*, omitted those words and emphasised, as we can well understand him
saying, that the treatment of Mrs Davis showed an intention to treat the BMW as the Defendant's own
regardless of the other's rights (but omitting the words 'to dispose of'). Of course, everything about
the taking and use of the BMW, like any car taken away without the owner's authority, indicates an intention to treat such a car regardless of the owner's rights. That is the test of conversion in the civil law.
But not every conversion is a theft. Theft requires the additional intention of permanently depriving
the owner or the substituted intention under s 6(1). The fact that the taking becomes more violent,
thereby setting up a case of robbery, if there is an underlying case of theft, does not in itself turn what
would be a robbery, if there was a theft, into a case of robbery without theft. The theft has to be there
without the violence which would turn the theft into robbery.

27. Turning to the Vauxhall Cavalier which was destroyed at the end of the day because it was set
on fire, Mr Jackson accepted that even there was nothing about the circumstances of that case which
would entitle the case of theft of the Cavalier to be left to a jury. We are not so sure of that. If it were
the case that a car was taken for the purposes of destroying it, that would be a case of theft, and
where another's car has been set on fire that may be some evidence on which an intention permanently to deprive or a s 6(1) intention may be inferred. It seems to us, however, that in considering that
the cases of both the Fiesta and the Cavalier could not support, and indeed, as he told us, would not
be prosecuted, as a case of theft, Mr Jackson was going far to demonstrate that the case of the taking of the BMW cannot be regarded as a case of theft (or therefore robbery) either. In effect, subject
to Mr Jackson's necessary concession regarding the Fiesta, Mr Jackson's submissions would run the
danger of turning every case of taking and driving away without authority under s 12 of the Theft Act
[section 24.3, p 815] into a case of theft, whereas of course the whole point of s 12 is to get round the

problem that a car which is taken and driven away for a ride, only to be abandoned, is not easily found to be a case of theft.

28. In our judgment the facts of this case simply do not support a case to go before a jury of theft and therefore robbery of the BMW. The BMW was plainly taken for the purposes of a getaway. There was nothing about its use or subsequent abandonment to suggest otherwise. Indeed, its brief use and subsequent abandonment show very clearly what was the obvious *prima facie* inference to be drawn from its taking which was that the occupants of the Subaru needed another conveyance that evening. We therefore consider that the judge erred in being beguiled by s 6 into leaving this count of robbery to the jury.

29. . . . We think that the factors for the jury to consider were put before the jury but of course the recorder never directed them, for the purposes of s 6(1) and the jurisprudence which we have considered, to ask themselves whether those factors amounted to such an outright taking or disposal or an intention within the words of s 6(1) as to amount to the equivalence of an intention permanently to deprive. We consider that the authorities which we have reviewed in this judgment show that the purpose of s 6 is not greatly to widen the requirement of s 1's intention permanently to deprive. A slightly broader definition of that intention is there provided in order to deal with a small number of difficult cases which had either arisen in the past under the common law or might arise in the future where, although it might be hard to put the matter strictly in terms of an intention permanently to deprive, in the sense of meaning the owner permanently to lose the thing itself, nevertheless something equivalent to that could be obtained through the intention to treat the thing as his own to dispose of, regardless of the other's rights, remembering Professor Smith's Oxford English dictionary use of the words 'to dispose of'. Thus, the newspaper taken but only returned on the next day when it is out of date, or a ticket which has been used, or a cheque which is paid, or something which has been substantially used up or destroyed, or something which would only be returned to its owner subject to a condition, all these are the sorts of examples to be found in the jurisprudence which discusses s 6. All of these cases are of ready equivalence to an intention permanently to deprive. None of them go any way towards extending the scope of s 6 to a case, however violent, of the taking of a car for the purposes of its brief use before being abandoned with its lights on. It must be remembered of course that a car with its licence plates on, left on the road, is utterly unlike a bundle of newspapers which have disappeared from a newsagents shop to a place where they would not be found. . . .

Appeal allowed

■ *Question*

Could Mitchell have been charged with robbery of the petrol in the BMW?

Cf *Raphael* [2008] EWCA Crim 1014, where R had been convicted of conspiracy to rob V by forcibly taking his car and then inviting him to pay for its safe return. The court held that such conduct could indeed amount to robbery. Sir Igor Judge P said:

47. The express language of section 6 specifies that the subjective element necessary to establish the mens rea for theft includes an intention on the part of the taker 'to treat the thing as his own to dispose of regardless of the other's rights'. In our judgment it is hard to find a better example of such an intention than an offer, not to return [V's] car to him in exactly the same condition it was when it was removed from his possession and control, but to sell his own property back to him, and to make its return subject to a condition or conditions inconsistent with his right to possession of his own property.

48. This is not a case in which the vehicle was taken for what is sometimes inaccurately described as a 'joy ride'. Section 12 of the Theft Act has no application to it. It was only 'abandoned' after the purpose

of the robbery had been frustrated and its possible usefulness to the robbers dissipated. Equally the appropriation of the car was not conditional in the sense described in *Easom* (1971) 55 Cr App R 410, where it was held that theft was not established if the intention of the appropriator of the property was 'merely to deprive the owner of such of his property as, on examination, proves worth taking and then, on finding that the booty is to him valueless, leaves it ready at hand to be re-possessed by the owner'.

These authorities were analysed by the Court of Appeal in *Vinall* [2011] EWCA Crim 2652, [2012] Crim LR 386. Pitchford LJ stated that:

If the prosecution is unable to establish an intent permanently to deprive at the moment of taking it may nevertheless establish that the defendant exercised such a dominion over the property that it can be inferred that at the time of the taking he intended to treat the property as his own to dispose of regardless of the owner's rights (c.f. *Easom* in which the handbag was replaced approximately in the position from which it had been removed). Subsequent 'disposal' of the property may be evidence either of an intention at the time of the taking or evidence of an intention at the time of the disposal. When the allegation is theft a later appropriation will suffice; when the allegation is robbery it almost certainly will not. In *Smith* the manner in which the property was disposed of was evidence supporting the inference of the s.6(1) intention; in *Mitchell* the manner in which the car was abandoned, and in *Easom* the replacement of the handbag, could not support the inference.

■ *Question*
What is the difference beyond theft and a 'joy ride'?

21.7.3 Intention permanently to deprive by swapping V's property?

In *DPP v Lavender* [1994] Crim LR 297, DC, D had taken two sound doors from council property which was undergoing repair and used them to replace two damaged doors at another council property of which his girlfriend was the tenant. Remitting the case to the justices with a direction to convict of theft, the court said that the issue was whether D had treated the doors as his own to dispose of and took the view that he had. D had dealt with the doors regardless of the owner's rights not to have them removed and in so doing had manifested an intention to treat them as his own. Clearly, D had relocated the council's property but had he disposed of it?

■ *Question*
It does not appear what he did with the two damaged doors which he replaced. What if he had thrown them in a skip for removal to the council's tip; would that be theft?

21.7.4 Conditional intention

A problem which has much exercised the courts is whether D may be convicted of theft where his intention permanently to deprive is conditional, as where D has no specific property in mind but has resolved to steal if there is anything worth his while to take. Commonly, for example, criminals enter cars on the lookout for anything that may be of value to them while realizing that there may be nothing in the car that interests them. Obviously, the criminal cannot be convicted of theft if in fact he appropriates nothing, but may he be convicted of attempted theft and, if so, of attempting to steal what? D cannot be convicted of attempting to steal that which he does not intend to steal. If the car contains only articles (tissues, road maps) of no interest to D, D cannot be convicted of attempting to steal these. But if it is D's intention to steal the car radio then he may be convicted of attempting to steal the radio though the car has no radio. And if D is on a fishing expedition having no specific property in mind, it appears that he may be convicted of attempting to steal property of V from the car.

FURTHER READING

Appropriation

J. Beatson and A. Simester, 'Stealing One's Own Property' (1999) 115 LQR 372

A. L. Bogg and J. Stanton-Ife, 'Protecting the Vulnerable: Legality, Harm and Theft' (2003) 23 LS 402

S. Gardner, 'Property and Theft' [1998] Crim LR 35

P. R. Glazebrook, 'Revising the Theft Acts' (1993) 52 CLJ 191

S. Green, 'Theft and Conversion—Tangibly Different?' (2012) 128 LQR 564

S. Shute, 'Appropriation and the Law of Theft' [2002] Crim LR 445

J. C. Smith, 'The Sad Fate of the Theft Act 1968' in W. Swadling and G. Jones (eds), *The Search for Principle: Essays in Honour of Lord Goff of Chieveley* (1999), p 97

Property

R. Cross, 'Protecting Confidential Information under the Criminal Law of Theft and Fraud' (1991) 11 OJLS 264

R. Hammond, 'Theft of Information' (1984) 100 LQR 252

J. Hull, 'Stealing Secrets: A Review of the Law Commission Consultation Paper' [1998] Crim LR 246

J. C. Smith, 'Obtaining Cheques by Deception or Theft' [1997] Crim LR 396

J. C. Smith, 'Stealing Tickets' [1998] Crim LR 723

Belonging to another

D. W. Elliott, 'Directors' Thefts and Dishonesty' [1991] Crim LR 732

Dishonesty

K. Campbell, 'The Test of Dishonesty in *Ghosh*' (1994) 43 CLJ 349

D. W. Elliott, 'Dishonesty in Theft: A Dispensable Concept' [1982] Crim LR 395

E. J. Griew, 'Dishonesty, the Objections to *Feely* and *Ghosh*' [1985] Crim LR 341

A. Halpin, 'The Test for Dishonesty' [1996] Crim LR 283

A. Samuels, 'Dishonesty and the Jury' [1974] Crim LR 493

A. Steele, 'The Meanings of Dishonesty in Theft' (2009) 38 Common Law World Rev 103

R. Tur, 'Dishonesty and the Jury Question' in A. Phillips Griffiths (ed), *Philosophy and Practice* (1985)

Intention permanently to deprive

J. R. Spencer, 'The Metamorphosis of Section 6 of the Theft Act' [1977] Crim LR 653

G. Williams, 'Temporary Appropriation Should be Theft' [1981] Crim LR 129

22
Robbery

22.1 Introduction

Robbery is one of the most serious offences in English law and certainly one of the most serious in the Theft Act 1968. It carries a maximum sentence of life imprisonment, and can only be tried in the Crown Court. The reason it is regarded so seriously is clear once the basic ingredients of the offence are considered: stealing with the use or threat of force. This is a hybrid offence with elements of offences against the person and dishonesty.

Some of the controversies that will be explored in this chapter include the following:

(i) the level of contact that is necessary before it can be said that 'force' was applied to V;

(ii) the fact that it is not sufficient that the use of force was gratuitous. D must use force *in order to* commit theft.

22.2 Elements of the offence

Theft Act 1968, s 8

(1) A person is guilty of robbery if he steals, and immediately before or at the time of doing so, and in order to do so, he uses force on any person or puts or seeks to put any person in fear of being then and there subjected to force.

(2) A person guilty of robbery, or of an assault with intent to rob, shall on conviction on indictment be liable to imprisonment for life.

22.2.1 Theft

Robbery is essentially a form of aggravated stealing (synonymous with theft) so proof of theft is essential to a conviction. All of the elements of theft must be established.

22.2.1.1 Appropriation

The robbery is complete when the theft is complete, that is, when the appropriation takes place. So in *Corcoran v Anderton* (1980) 71 Cr App R 104, [1980] Crim LR 385, DC, where D and E sought to take V's handbag by force, it was held the theft was complete when D snatched the handbag from V's grasp though it then fell from D's hands and the defendants made off without it. Their argument that this was only an attempt was rejected since the snatching of the handbag from V constituted an appropriation.

In *Hale* (1978) 68 Cr App R 415, [1979] Crim LR 596, CA, D and E entered V's house and while D was upstairs stealing a jewellery box, E was downstairs tying up V. The Court of Appeal declined to quash their convictions for robbery even though D might have appropriated the jewellery box before the force was used. The court said (at 418):

the act of appropriation does not suddenly cease. It is a continuous act and it is a matter for the jury to decide whether or not the act of appropriation has finished. Moreover, it is quite clear that the intention to deprive the owner permanently, which accompanied the assumption of the owner's rights was a continuing one at all material times. This Court therefore rejects the contention that the theft had ceased by the time [V] was tied up. As a matter of common sense [E] was in the course of committing theft; he was stealing.

■ *Questions*

What impact has the decision in *Gomez* [1993] AC 442 (section 21.3, p 744) had on this aspect of the offence? How much earlier in time might a theft be complete?

22.2.1.2 Property belonging to another

The requirement that the property belongs to another is unlikely to present difficulties in a robbery case. There will be few cases in which D uses force to obtain an item of intangible property from V, or in which some other problematical form of property is appropriated. However, there might be an issue in circumstances where D believes that he is retrieving property that belongs to himself, even though it is currently in V's possession.

■ *Questions*

1. D in London telephones V in his office in the bank HQ in Halifax and threatens to detonate a bomb under V's desk unless V makes an electronic transfer of funds into D's account. Is this robbery?

2. D is infertile. He has begged his brother V to provide a sperm sample with which D's wife can be impregnated. V refuses. D threatens him with violence unless he complies. Is this robbery? Which offences under the Sexual Offences Act 2003 might be committed?

22.2.1.3 Dishonesty

The *Ghosh* test applies, see section 21.6, p 772. In *Robinson* [1977] Crim LR 173, CA, D ran a saving club to which V's wife owed £7. Meeting V, D and others threatened him and in the fight which followed £5 fell from V's pocket which D took, claiming he was still owed £2. Quashing D's conviction for robbery, it was held that all D had to raise was an honest belief in entitlement to the money and not that he honestly believed that he was entitled to take it in the way he did.

■ *Question*

Should a belief in a right to the property also entitle D to use force to obtain it?

22.2.1.4 Intention permanently to deprive

In *Raphael* [2008] EWCA Crim 1014, R had been convicted of conspiracy to rob V by forcibly taking his car and then offering V the opportunity to buy it back. The Court of Appeal referred to the Theft Act 1968, s 6 (section 21.7, p 785), and concluded that this was clearly capable of amounting to robbery. See section 21.7, p 785.

Difficulties can arise in distinguishing between the requirement that there be both an appropriation and also an intention permanently to deprive. Remember that each must be established; it is imperative not to conflate the two. As the following case demonstrates, this distinction can be particularly troublesome in relation to robbery. The case is also important for the observations made on how s 6 ought to be approached in the context of robbery.

R v Vinall

[2011] EWCA Crim 2652, Court of Appeal, Criminal Division, http://www.bailii.org/ew/cases/EWCA/Crim/2011/6252.html

(Pichford LJ and Andrew Smith and Popplewell JJ)

Two young men were cycling along a cycle path when they came across a group of three young men. The allegation was that one of the young men was punched from his bicycle and was chased away. The group of three then walked away with the bicycle. The bicycle was subsequently found abandoned 50 yards away from where it had been taken from its owner. The defendants were found guilty of robbery. In quashing the defendants' convictions, Pitchford LJ addressed the two issues of whether the defendants were appropriating and whether they had an intention permanently to deprive and, if so, at what point in time.

10. It is clear that the starting point for the offence of theft in the circumstances of the present case must be the taking, that is, the moments leading up to and including the removal of the bicycle from the place where [V2] left it. The appropriation could have occurred when [V2] was chased away or when the bicycle was wheeled away. It is noticeable that in his directions the judge did not expressly invite the jury to consider whether the appellants intended at the moment of the taking to deprive the owner of the bicycle permanently. He did, however, refer to the fact that the bicycle was *'taken'* before being abandoned ('not all that far from where it was taken'). That is hardly surprising because it was common ground that the bicycle was taken from the cycle path and left at the bus shelter. The jury could, the judge directed them, treat the act of taking and abandonment of the bicycle as an assumption of the rights of an owner and, therefore, an act of appropriation. In our view, this was a perfectly proper direction as to the first ingredient of the offence of theft based upon the opening words of s.3(1) ('Any assumption by a person of the rights of an owner amounts to an appropriation'). The judge then directed the jury that they could conclude that when leaving the bicycle at the bus stop, showing no regard to the rights of the owner, the appellants should 'be taken as intending permanently to deprive the owner' of it. At this point in the summing up, as it seems to us, with respect to the judge, the separate concepts of appropriation and intention permanently to deprive became fatally confused. Appropriation by the appellants, their dishonesty and their intention permanently to deprive must coincide. If the intent required for theft was not present until minutes after [V2] was chased away the requirements of s.8 could not be proved.

11. The first question for the jury, applying ss.1, 3 and 6, was: *Did the defendants: (1) appropriate the bicycle dishonestly by taking it; (2) intending permanently to deprive the owner of it or intending to treat the bicycle as their own to dispose of regardless of the other's rights?* The taking of the bicycle was itself a sufficient assumption of the rights of the owner to amount to an appropriation. The abandonment was capable of being additional *evidence* that by taking the bicycle the appellants were, when they took it, assuming the rights of the owner (s.3). The jury could not be sure of theft, however, unless they were also sure that at the time of taking the bicycle either the appellants had an intention permanently to deprive (s.1) or they intended to treat the bicycle as their own to dispose of regardless of the other's rights (s.6). The jury did not receive these directions.

12. If the charge had been theft only, and the jury was not sure that at the moment of taking the appellants dishonestly appropriated the bicycle with intent (actual or deemed) permanently to deprive, they could next consider whether there was a later appropriation at the time of the abandonment. In that event the question for the jury would be: *Did the appellants, when they abandoned the bicycle; (1) assume the rights of an owner; (2) intending permanently to deprive the owner of it or intending to treat the bicycle as their own to dispose of regardless of the other's rights?* If so, the offence of theft

was committed at the time of the abandonment. This, however, was a charge of robbery. The judge left to the jury the option of concluding that the act of theft was completed not at the time of taking but at the time of abandonment. If the theft was committed only at the moment of abandonment the prosecution case of robbery was fatally undermined. In those circumstances the prosecution could not prove that force or the threat of force was used before or at the time of and *in order to* steal.

13. The judge's direction to the jury leaves open the real possibility that the jury thought that they could convict of robbery if the requisite intention for theft was formed only when the appellants decided to abandon the bicycle. . . .

14. For these reasons, it is our view that the convictions are unsafe, the appeals must be allowed and the convictions quashed.

Robbery and section 6(1) of the Theft Act 1968

15. As will be apparent from our analysis, in reaching our conclusions we have assumed in the Crown's favour that the act of abandonment was capable of being evidence from which the jury could infer the appellants' intent *at the time of the taking* to treat the bicycle as their own to dispose of regardless of the owner's rights. There has, we are conscious, been much academic and judicial debate as to the scope of the first and generally expressed part of s.6(1).

[The court examined earlier case law and made reference to academic comment on s 6 and concluded:]

16. . . . What s.6(1) requires is a state of mind in the defendant which Parliament regards as the equivalent of an intention permanently to deprive, namely 'his intention to treat the thing as his own to dispose of regardless of the other's rights'. The subsection does not require that the thing has been disposed of, nor does it require that the defendant intends to dispose of the thing in any particular way. No doubt evidence of a particular disposal or a particular intention to dispose of the thing will constitute evidence of the defendant's state of mind but it is, in our view, for the jury to decide upon the circumstances proved whether the defendant harboured the statutory intention.

17. Nevertheless, the court made clear in *R. v Mitchell* [2008] EWCA Crim 850 that the taking of a vehicle for 'joyriding' and its theft are quite different offences and the distinction must not be blurred. The defendant had by force or the threat of force taken the loser's vehicle as a getaway car and abandoned it a few miles away with the engine running, lights flashing and the doors open, in order to change to another vehicle. He was charged with robbery. The court held that the evidence was not capable of supporting a charge of theft. At [26] Rix L.J. said:

'. . . Of course, everything about the taking and use of the BMW, like any car taken away without the owner's authority, indicates an intention to treat such a car regardless of the owner's rights. That is the test of conversion in the civil law. But not every conversion is a theft. Theft requires the additional intention of permanently depriving the owner or the substituted intention under s 6(1). The fact that the taking becomes more violent, thereby setting up a case of robbery, if there is an underlying case of theft, does not in itself turn what would be a robbery, if there was a theft, into a case of robbery without theft. The theft has to be there without the violence which would turn the theft into robbery.'

At [28] he concluded:

'In our judgment the facts of this case simply do not support a case to go before a jury of theft and therefore robbery of the BMW. The BMW was plainly taken for the purposes of a getaway. There was nothing about its use or subsequent abandonment to suggest otherwise. Indeed, its brief use and subsequent abandonment show very clearly what was the obvious *prima facie* inference to be drawn from its taking which was that the [defendants] needed another conveyance that evening. We therefore consider that the judge erred in being beguiled by s.6 into leaving this count of robbery to the jury.'

[His lordship referred to the case of *Raphael* earlier in this section.]

Conclusion

20. In the present case, we conclude that it was open to the judge to invite the jury to consider whether the later abandonment of [V2's] bicycle was evidence from which they could infer that the appellants intended *at the time of the taking* to treat the bicycle as their own to dispose of regardless of his rights. If that was the way the judge had chosen to leave the issue of intent to the jury, an explicit direction would have been required explaining that an intention formed only upon abandonment of the bicycle at the bus shelter was inconsistent with and fatal to the allegation of robbery. In the absence of such an explanation, it seems to this court that the verdicts were unsafe and must be quashed. This is not a case in which the court should substitute a conviction for theft or taking a pedal cycle. These alternatives were not left to the jury.

■ *Questions*

1. Do you think the jury would have been sure that the later abandonment of the bicycle was evidence that D intended at the time of the taking to treat the bicycle as his own to dispose of regardless of V2's rights?

2. When should the judge refer to s 6 when directing the jury as to the elements of robbery?

3. Is it always possible to substitute a conviction of theft for one of robbery?

A similar issue arose in *Zerei* [2012] EWCA Crim 1114. D and another man approached V in a car park. D told V that he was going to take his car. When V refused, a struggle broke out during which D punched V and took out a knife. V's car keys were taken from him and D drove off with his car. The car was found abandoned a while later. D was convicted of robbery and argued that the judge had given the jury the impression that the forcible taking of the car itself might amount to proof of an intention permanently to deprive. He argued that the judge in his summing-up had not made it clear that taking a car by violence, irrespective of the rights of the owner, was completely different to an intention permanently to deprive. In quashing the conviction, the Court of Appeal found three issues with the judge's directions to the jury. First, the judge did indeed give the jury the false impression that the forcible taking of the car was sufficient to constitute an intention permanently to deprive. The court made clear that it is not. Secondly, the distinction between an intention permanently to deprive and taking of possession which merely defeated the rights of the owner for a short period of time was not made sufficiently clear. Finally, the judge should have pointed out to the jury that the abandonment of the car a short period of time after it was appropriated was relevant to the issue of whether there was an intention permanently to deprive.

22.2.2 Force

A person is guilty of robbery contrary to the Theft Act 1968, s 8, if he steals, and immediately before or at the time of doing so, and in order to do so, *he [a] uses force on any person or [b] puts or [c] seeks to put any person in fear of being then and there subjected to force.*

Few difficulties arise in cases where it is alleged that D uses force. This could be a push, a punch, etc. However, there are marginal cases which are much more difficult. The High Court considered what constitutes force in the following case.

Director of Public Prosecutions v RP

[2012] EWHC 1657 (Admin), Divisional Court , http://www.bailii.org/ew/cases/EWHC/Admin/2012/1657.html

(Mitting J)

DD walked past V and asked her for a cigarette. V replied that she did not have a spare one. In response to this, D1 snatched the cigarette that V had in her hand. At no point did D1's hand ever make contact with V's. Although V was pushed after the incident, the prosecution did not put the case as a continuing act. DD were found guilty of robbery and appealed.

4. ...The case raised, therefore, a single and very narrow issue: does the snatching of a cigarette from between the fingers of a person smoking it, without physical contact between the snatcher and the person smoking it, amount to robbery, provided, of course, that the elements of theft are present? ...

5. Under the law as it existed before the enactment of the Theft Act 1968, the answer would unquestionably have been no. What the old law required was that greater force than was merely required to take an object was required to be applied before the offence became an offence of robbery. Section 8 of the Theft Act 1968 provides:

[His lordship recited s 8 of the Theft Act 1968.]

. . .

6. As a matter of language, it is important to note that the statute requires the use of 'force on any person' or putting 'any person in fear of being then and there subjected to force'. Although the old distinctions under the Larceny Act 1916 have gone, there remains a basic requirement for the commission of the offence that force is used on a person.

7. Ms Zentler-Munro, for the appellants, accepts that the snatching of a handbag from a woman holding it on her shoulder or in her hand will ordinarily amount to robbery because by the very act of pulling on the handbag force will inevitably be applied to the person of the woman from whom the handbag is snatched. Her concession is a proper and inevitable one in the light of the case law as it has developed since the enactment of the Theft Act 1968.

8. The starting point is *R. v Dawson and James* (1977) 64 Cr. App. R. 170. The facts were that at Liverpool Pier Head a sailor on shore leave waiting for the ferry was surrounded by two men, one standing on either side of him, who nudged him on the shoulder, causing him to lose his balance. While trying to keep his balance, a third man got his hand into the sailor's pocket and took his wallet. It was contended before the trial court that that did not amount to the offence of robbery. The judge left the offence to the jury, who convicted him. In giving the judgment of the court, Lawson L.J. said the following at 172:

> 'The choice of the word "force" is not without interest because under the Larceny Act 1916 the word "violence" had been used, but Parliament deliberately on the advice of the Criminal Law Revision Committee changed that word to "force". Whether there is any difference between "violence" or "force" is not relevant for the purposes of this case; but the word is "force". It is a word in ordinary use. It is a word which juries understand. The learned judge left it to the jury to say whether jostling a man in the way which the victim described to such an extent that he had difficulty in keeping his balance could be said to be the use of force. The learned judge, because of the argument put forward by [counsel for the appellant], went out of his way to explain to the jury that force in these sort of circumstances must be substantial to justify a verdict.
>
> Whether it was right for him to put that adjective before the word "force" when Parliament had not done so we will not discuss for the purposes of this case. It was a matter for the jury. They were there to use their common sense and knowledge of the world. We cannot say that their decision as to whether force was used was wrong. They were entitled to the view that force was used.'

The force there used, although not substantial on one view, was nonetheless direct force applied to the person of the sailor.

9. The next case in point is *R. v Clouden*, only reported, as far as I know, in the *Criminal Law Review* for 1987, p.56. The appellant approached a woman who was carrying a shopping basket in her left hand from behind and wrenched it down and out of her grasp with both hands and ran off with it.

He was convicted of robbery. In dismissing his appeal, the court observed (see holding at [1987] Crim. L.R. 56) that:

'The old cases distinguished between force on the actual person and force on the property which in fact causes force on the person but, following *Dawson* and *James*..., the court should direct attention to the words of the statute without referring to the old authorities. The old distinctions have gone. Whether the defendant used force on any person in order to steal is an issue that should be left to the jury. The judge's direction to the jury was adequate. He told the jury quite clearly at the outset what the statutory definition was, though thereafter he merely used the word 'force' and did not use the expression "on the person".'

10. It seems to me from that brief report of the decision that the court in *Clouden* had in mind the need for the prosecution to prove the use of 'force on any person' and not merely 'force', but concluded that despite the lack of repeated reference to 'force on any person' in the summing-up, it was nonetheless adequate because the judge had drawn attention to the statutory definition at some part of his summing-up. That decision attracted an interesting commentary from Professor Smith (the author of *The Law of Theft*) [1987] Crim. L.R. 56:

'Robbery at common law and under the Larceny Acts was governed by the principle stated by Garrow B in *Gnosil* (1824) 1 Car. & P. 304: "The mere act of taking being forcible will not make this offence highway robbery; to constitute the crime of highway robbery the force used must be either before or at the time of taking and must be of such a nature to show it was intended to overpower the party robbed and prevent his resisting, and not merely to get possession of the property stolen..." According to this statement, it would appear there was no evidence in the present case of robbery as it was before the Theft Act 1968 came into effect.

As the present court was aware, the Criminal Law Revision Committee did not intend that the draft bill which became the Theft Act 1968 should affect this rule. In their *Eighth Report* (Cmnd. 2997) para.65, the Committee stated: "We should not regard mere snatching of property such as a handbag, from an unresisting owner as using force for the purpose of the definition, though it might be so if the owner resisted." The present decision and Dawson and James, which foreshadowed it, show that the Committee would have been wise to state the principle in *Gnosil* in order to preserve it because the wording of the section left open the construction now put upon it. It is a warning to the codifier that, if he intends the refinements of the law he is codifying to be observed, he should state them. Opinions will of course differ on where lines should be drawn; but it may well be thought that conduct such as that in the present case is more akin to that of the pickpocket than the bank robber and is quite adequately dealt with by the offence of theft which is, after all, punishable with a maximum of ten years' imprisonment.'

The force of those comments is not reduced by the fact that the maximum sentence has now been reduced to seven years.

11. Other more recent authorities have been cited to me but they do no more than make passing observations and do not contain statements forming part of the decision of the court which bind me.

12. I refer finally to an extract from a work bearing Professor Smith's name but in fact now written by Professor Ormerod. If it is not Professor Ormerod's words that I am quoting, it shows that Professor Smith must have changed his mind. In para.7.08 of *Smith's Law of Theft*, 9th edn, the author observes:

'Force

The term "force" was preferred by the CLRC to "violence", which was used in the Larceny Act 1916 to designate an aggravated form of robbery. Though the difference, if any, between the words is an elusive one, it is probable that "force" is a slightly wider term. Thus it might be argued that simply to hold a person down is not violence but it certainly involves the use of force against the person. Force denotes any exercise of physical strength against another whereas violence seems to signify a dynamic exercise of strength as by striking a blow. In *Dawson*, it was held that, where D nudges V so as to cause him to lose his balance and enable D to steal, it is a question of fact for the jury whether the nudge amounts to "force". It is submitted that it would be better if the law gave an answer to the question—preferably in the affirmative. It is submitted that no jury could reasonably find that the slight physical contact that might be involved where D picks V's pocket would amount to a use of force.'

13. I agree with those observations. This case sits neatly in between the two paradigm examples given by the author. There was, on the facts found by the court, no physical contact between the hand of RP and the hand of [V]. The court was invited to consider the case on the basis that the mere snatching of a cigarette from between the fingers of [V] was sufficient to amount to the use of force on her person. I remind myself that borderline questions, such as a question of what amounts to the use of force on a person when the force used is minimal, are questions for the court at first instance and that it is not for an appellate court to put a gloss on the words in s.8 of the Theft Act 1968.

14. However, in the stated case, the court did not find as a fact that RP used force on [V]. What the court found clearly was that a cigarette was snatched, on the prosecution case, without there being contact with [V], that that amounted to the use of force by RP and that the force was used in order to steal the cigarette. Those findings were clearly all open to the court but they do not amount to a finding that force was used on the person of [V], unless the mere removal of a cigarette from between her fingers itself is capable of amounting to the use of force upon her person.

15. In my judgment, it is not. This case falls squarely on the side of pickpocketing and such like, in which there is no direct physical contact between thief and victim. It cannot be said that the minimal use of force required to remove a cigarette from between the fingers of a person suffices to amount to the use of force on that person. It cannot cause any pain unless, perhaps, the person resists strongly, in which case one would expect inevitably that there would be direct physical contact between the thief and victim as well. The unexpected removal of a cigarette from between the fingers of a person is no more the use of force on that person than would be the removal of an item from her pocket. This offence is properly categorised as simple theft.

16. I therefore allow the appeal of the three appellants against their conviction for robbery, substitute convictions for theft and leave the sentence undisturbed.

■ *Questions*

1. D pumps a noxious gas into a bank causing the occupants to be overcome by the fumes and D then steals from them while they are incapacitated. Has he robbed them?

2. Altering the facts of *DPP v RP*, what if the cigarette had been lit and when RP tried to snatch it from V it made contact with her hand? Would this suffice to constitute force?

3. Does the decision in *DPP v RP* have the potential to place the law on the path that it was on prior to 1968, in requiring there to be violence before D can be guilty of robbery?

In cases where D puts or seeks to put V in fear of force, rather than actually using force, the position is slightly more complicated, but the courts have glossed over the potential problems. The Divisional Court confirmed in *DPP v R* [2007] EWHC 739 (Admin), that robbery does not require proof that V was actually put in fear. It is submitted that this must be correct, otherwise the commission of the offence would turn on the courage of the victim. That case does not, however, answer the question whether it is necessary for the victim to *apprehend* that force will be used. Where the allegation is that D *put any person in fear of being then and there subjected to force*, in that form of the offence, it would seem to be a necessary element. Support for that proposition is derived from *Grant v CPS* (10 March 2000, unreported), QBD, although the court in *DPP v R* cast doubt on that case. Where D *seeks to put* V in fear of force there is no need for V to be in fear in fact, nor it seems for V to apprehend force; the offence turns solely on D's intention. It is important to emphasize that it is sufficient that D's intent is to produce a state of mind where V apprehends force; it is enough that D intends to put V in fear. *Tennant* [1976] Crim LR 133, Nottingham Crown Court, makes clear that D may threaten to use force and satisfy the requirement of the offence of robbery although V is not made to apprehend the immediate infliction of force on him which is necessary to constitute an assault.

22.2.2.1 In order to steal

Force must be used 'in order to' steal. If D knocks V senseless in a fight and then decides to make off with V's watch which has fallen from his pocket, it would not be robbery; it would be assault and theft. Conversely, if D steals property without using force but subsequently uses or threatens force to retain it or in effecting an escape, it would not be robbery.

Under the pre-1968 law it was not sufficient that force was used in the taking of the property: the force had to be used to overpower the person or prevent resistance from him. This was examined in *RP* in section 22.2.2.

■ *Question*

D is about to go out one day to steal a new suit from a shop. He tells his wife of his plan and she threatens to telephone the police. D pushes her into the bathroom and locks the door and does not free her until he returns later wearing his new suit. Is this robbery?

22.2.2.2 Force on any person

The force may be on *any* person. In *Smith v Desmond* [1965] AC 960, [1965] 1 All ER 976, HL, D and E were held to have robbed V and X, night watchman and maintenance engineer respectively, in a bakery, where force was used on them in order to steal from an office some distance away on the premises. V and X's employer's property was in their immediate care and protection. The case is obviously within the terms of s 8 which extends to any case in which force is used on any person in order to steal. The threat of force may similarly be made to any person; but the offence is committed only if D seeks to put that person in fear of being subjected to force. It is not sufficient that he seeks to cause that person to fear that someone else will be subjected to force: *Taylor (Richard)* [1996] CLY 1518 (D handing to V, bank cashier, a note saying that D had a gun pointed at a customer).

22.2.3 Reform

Ashworth ('Robbery Reassessed' [2002] Crim LR 851) questions whether the offence is necessary:

Robbery is an amalgamated offence. Like burglary, it combines two separate wrongs. Unlike burglary, the two wrongs in robbery are both crimes. The offence combines theft of property with the use or threat of force. It is not specified which wrong should be regarded as more important, but surely the amount of violence should be given the greater significance, on the ground that violence is generally a much greater attack on an individual's well-being. It is possible to conceive of a case where an enormous sum of money is taken by using a small amount of (threatened) force, but even then we should bear in mind that the maximum sentence for theft is seven years. In most cases of street robberies and robberies at building society branches, off-licences and so forth, the robber only sets out to obtain a modest sum and does so, and therefore the theft component of the sentence should be small and well below the maximum for that crime. More significant, surely, is the amount of force. . . . The law of offences against the person reflects the relative seriousness of violence and threats in a rather unsatisfactory way. If we had a reformed law on violence, it would distinguish the various offences according to the degree of harm and the degree of culpability, and would assign graduated penalties from the least serious up to the most serious. Robbery should mirror this, or have at least two degrees of seriousness.

A more radical proposal would be to abolish the offence of robbery. It would then be left to prosecutors to charge the components of theft and violence separately, which would focus the court's attention on those two elements, separately and then (for sentencing purposes) in combination. The principal difficulty with this is the absence from English law of an offence of threatening injury: between the summary offence of assault by posing a threat of force, and the serious offence of making a threat to kill, there is no intermediate crime. This gap ought to be closed; and, if it were, there would be a strong argument that the crime of robbery would be unnecessary.

■ *Question*

Do you agree that a crime of robbery ought to be unnecessary or is there something distinctive about force or the threat of force being used to commit theft? Consider this question in the light of the following extract.

S. P. Green, *13 Ways To Steal A Bicycle*
(2012)

Robbery was probably the first form of theft to be criminalized. It has a strong claim to being the most morally wrongful and socially harmful form of theft and, indeed, the empirical study described in Chapter 1 indicated that it occupied a class by itself in terms of blameworthiness. Little elaboration is presumably needed to explain why it is morally wrong to inflict unjustified pain or fear on others. Any theory of morality, whether consequentialist or non-consequentialist, will regard such acts as among the most wrongful. The seriousness with which robbery was viewed by the criminal law—Coke called it 'amongst the most heinous [of] felonies'—is evidenced by the fact that the penalties for robbery are invariably higher than for other forms of theft. In this, the law of robbery parallels the law of sexual assault, which normally treats forcible rape as a more serious crime than rape by deception or coercion. At the same time, it is worth nothing that despite the fear and loathing with which robbery is normally viewed, there are nevertheless cases in which robbing bandits are celebrated as heroes who (whether they intend to or not) serve an important societal function.

The secondary wrong in robbery is so significant that it tends to overshadow the primary wrong of misappropriation. As the [Model Penal Code] commentary puts it:

> The violent petty thief operating in the streets and alleys of big cities—the 'mugger'—is one of the main sources of insecurity and concern in the population at large. There is a special element of terror on this kind of depredation. The ordinary citizen does not feel particularly threatened by surreptitious larceny, embezzlement, or fraud. But there is understandable abhorrence of the robber who accosts on the streets and who menaces his victims with actual or threatened violence against which there is a general sense of helplessness.

At the same time, it is important not to underestimate the way in which the wrongfulness of robbery is colored by the element of property misappropriation. Consider the most recent legal debacle involving O.J. Simpson. In September 2007, Simpson and several associates burst into a room at a Las Vegas hotel, several of them brandishing guns, and seized various mementos, including many items previously autographed by Simpson. In his subsequent trial, Simpson maintained that he had been conducting a 'sting operation' to recover property that, he claimed, had been stolen from him years earlier by a former agent. Assuming for the moment that his factual contention was true, could the fact that Simpson owned the property legitimately serve as a defense to robbery? Interestingly the law varies. A handful or courts—such as the Nevada court in which Simpson was ultimately convicted—have said that the proper charge was robbery regardless of who owned the property. However, I believe that the better view is that the proper charge was not robbery, but rather assault, since, assuming Simpson actually did have a right to recover the goods, he would not have been attempting to violate anyone's rights to property.

It is also worth considering how robbery should be distinguished from mere larceny [ie theft] particularly in cases of pick pocketing. Jewish law takes a subjective approach: if the victim is aware of the physical taking from his person, the act is robbery, if not, the act is considered larceny. Anglo-American law takes a contrasting, objective approach. Simply having physical contact with the victim is not enough to merit charges of robbery, even if the victim is aware of the contact. For there to be robbery, there must be some objective violence or intimidation.

Unfortunately, the line between robbery and larceny is not always clear. Even relatively light force, such as barging into someone or tugging at a handbag in such a way that the owner's hand is pulled downwards, has been held to constitute force sufficient to constitute robbery. Yet, as Andrew Ashworth has suggested [in the article previously extracted], such cases are troubling. 'It is difficult', he says, 'to draw the line between sufficient and insufficient force, but if robbery is to continue to be regarded as a serious offence, triable only on indictment and punishable with life imprisonment, surely something more than a bump, a push, or a pull, should be required.' Indeed, as Ashworth points out, the law surrounding robbery, at least in England, is much less finely graded than that surrounding assault. Because of this, he argues that robbery, in its current form, plainly breaches the principle of fair labeling. He therefore recommends a statutory scheme that would reflect the moral distinctions between theft by means of a 'mere push' and theft by means of 'serious violence'.

I assume that Ashworth would prefer something like the approach to robbery taken in the United States. Under the [Model Penal Code], only those thefts involving the infliction or threat of immediate 'serious bodily injury' are treated as robbery and subject to heightened punishment. If the theft involves only minimal force, the [Model Penal Code] treats it as 'ordinary theft'. Many states have an even more finely graded robbery offence scheme, which distinguishes among offences such as simple robbery, armed robbery, first degree robbery, second degree robbery, purse snatching and car jacking. In general, the more aggravated forms of robbery tend to be those in which the offender uses a weapon or inflicts or threatens serious physical injury.

■ *Questions*

1. If O. J. Simpson had burst into a hotel room in England, would he have committed robbery?

2. Does English law's approach to robbery contravene the principle of fair labelling?

3. Is the approach taken in the United States to robbery more satisfactory than English law? What might be the downside of the scheme Green sets out?

4. Does the decision in *DPP v RP* begin to ameliorate some of the issues identified by Ashworth?

FURTHER READING

D. Ormerod, *Smith and Hogan's Criminal Law* (13th edn, 2011), Ch 20 and references therein.

D. Ormerod and D. H. Williams, *Smith's Law of Theft* (9th ed, 2007), Ch 7

23

Making off without payment

23.1 Introduction

The offences in the Theft Act 1968 proved ineffective in dealing with a range of circumstances. Examples included defendants who ate in restaurants and ran off without paying the bill or defendants who filled their cars with petrol at self-service garages before driving off without paying. It was difficult to prosecute for theft if D claimed that he only formed the dishonest intent after the proprietary interest in the property had passed to him (eg when the petrol was in the tank). If his claim as to the timing of dishonest intent was true, he did not dishonestly appropriate property belonging to another; by the time of his dishonest intent forming, it was already his property. Charges of obtaining by deception were sometimes possible, but this required a strained reading of deception to include continuing representations.

In this chapter we examine why it was necessary in the Theft Act 1978, s 3, to provide, exceptionally, for the non-payment of a debt to become criminal. (The other offences in the 1978 Act have been repealed and replaced by the Fraud Act 2006.)

23.2 Definition

Theft Act 1978, s 3

(1) Subject to sub-section (3) below, a person who, knowing that payment on the spot for any goods supplied or service done is required or expected from him, dishonestly makes off without having paid as required or expected and with intent to avoid payment of the amount due shall be guilty of an offence.

(2) For purposes of this section 'payment on the spot' includes payment at the time of collecting goods on which work has been done or in respect of which service has been provided.

(3) Sub-section (1) above shall not apply where the supply of the goods or the doing of the service is contrary to law, or where the service done is such that payment is not legally enforceable.

There are five elements of the offence:

   (i)   D makes off;

  (ii)   without payment;

 (iii)   for goods supplied or a service done;

 (iv)   knowing that payment on the spot is expected;

  (v)   intending to make permanent default.

On conviction on indictment the offence is punishable with two years' imprisonment.

23.3 Elements

23.3.1 Makes off

According to the *Oxford English Dictionary* 'makes off' means to depart suddenly 'often with a disparaging implication'. But while making off is usually thought of as carrying the disparaging implication of cowardice, secrecy or stealth, it is not confined to such cases. It simply means to decamp and in *Brooks and Brooks* (1982) 76 Cr App R 66 at 69, CA, the court, with a biblical flourish, said that it 'may be an exercise accompanied by the sound of trumpets or a silent stealing away after a folding of tents'.

The precise legal meaning of the term, however, remains unclear. One interpretation is that D cannot be said to make off when he leaves proof of identity by which V can enforce the debt. J. R. Spencer writes ([1983] Crim LR 573):

> Obviously, s 3 is partly concerned to prevent the legitimate expectations of restaurateurs, hoteliers, etc being disappointed by people failing to pay their bills. But equally obviously, the section is aimed at some specific mischief narrower than this. If non-payment had been all that Parliament was concerned with, presumably it would have phrased the offence as 'dishonestly failing to pay'. If mere failure to pay was the true mischief of the offence, there was no need for 'making off' as an ingredient in it at all, whether it means 'leaves' as Professor Smith and others say, or whether it means 'leaves with guilty haste' as Francis Bennion suggests. So we must assume, surely, that 'makes off' points to some additional element of mischief which renders the case significantly worse than simply failing to pay, and to see what 'making off' really is, we ought to consider what conduct is, in practical terms, significantly worse than merely failing to pay. It can hardly be *leaving* without paying, because this, as such, does not worsen the creditor's position. It must surely be *disappearing: leaving in a way that makes it difficult for the debtor to be traced*.
>
> On this view, 'making off' would cover, obviously, the man who runs away. It would also cover the man who tells a lie to get outside, and then runs away. It would also cover a man who leaves a cheque signed in a false name. But it would not cover the person who leaves his correct name and an address at which he may readily be found. Nor would it usually cover the person who leaves behind him a cheque, drawn on his own account, in circumstances where it is likely to be dishonoured. In this case, although D has left, he has not as a rule made it difficult for P to trace him.

Spencer also relied on the fact that s 3(4) created a specific arrest power. That power has now become unnecessary given the general availability of arrest following the reform in the Serious Organised Crime and Police Act 2005; s 3(4) was repealed. Spencer argued:

> Years ago the common law set its face against giving hoteliers, restaurateurs and suchlike the power to arrest those who merely fail to pay their bills. Yet if we interpret 'makes off' as synonymous with 'leaves' we give them precisely this. On this view, any customer who sought to leave having failed to pay his bill would—subject to what the jury make of 'dishonestly'—commit the offence of making off without payment, and the hotelier or restaurateur would be able lawfully to detain him. To me, at least, it seems highly undesirable that hoteliers, etc should be given this power, at any rate when they know who the non-paying customer is and where he may later be found. On the other hand, if 'makes off' is limited as I suggest, there is no question of the hotelier having the power to arrest a customer who leaves his name backed with some plausible identification.

■ *Questions*

1. D, being well known to V, a restaurateur, decides not to pay his bill and departs via the cloakroom window. Would he be guilty according to Spencer? Is there anything in the section to justify acquittal? (See also Bennion [1980] Crim LR 670.)

2. Should there be a crime of 'dishonestly failing to pay' available in all circumstances?

3. Is the effect of the offence to criminalize those who fail to pay a debt? Should the taxi driver or restaurateur not avail themselves of the civil law in order to recover the money owed to them? Why might the offence represent an awkward compromise?

23.3.2 Payment on the spot

In *Vincent* [2001] EWCA Crim 295, [2001] 2 Cr App R 150, [2001] Crim LR 488, D stayed at two hotels in Windsor and left without paying his bills. His defence was that he had arranged with the proprietors of the hotels to pay when he could, and payment was not expected on the spot when he left; that he had not acted dishonestly and that he had no intention of avoiding payment. The judge directed that a dishonestly obtained agreement to postpone payment could not be relied on to negate the expectation of payment on the spot and D was convicted. His conviction was quashed: the section did not permit or require an analysis whether the agreement was obtained by deception. The fact that the agreement was dishonestly obtained did not reinstate the expectation of payment on the spot.

■ *Questions*

1. Would this decision apply to all cases where consent is obtained by fraud?

2. If D 'pays' with counterfeit money or a forged cheque, including a handsome tip, and departs with the warm good wishes of the hotelier, has he paid 'as required or expected'? Has he 'made off'?

3. Does it make any difference that D has left his true name and address in the hotel register?

4. The court in *Vincent* said that the remedy for fraudulently obtaining agreement to postpone payment must be sought elsewhere in the Theft Acts. Where? Is it fraud?

Difficulties can arise in identifying the 'spot' at which payment is expected or required. The Court of Appeal considered this issue in *Morris* [2013] EWCA Crim 436. D was a taxi driver who collected four men from a casino. The men had been drinking and were behaving in a rowdy fashion. They told D that there would be two stops. At the first stop, three of the young men got out of the taxi and started walking away at fast speed without paying the fare. D, forgetting that the fourth passenger was still in the back of the taxi and would pay the fare, thought that the men were making without payment. In order to prevent the passengers from evading the fare, D drove his taxi onto the pavement and in doing so broke V's ankle. D was charged with dangerous (or alternatively careless) driving. D claimed he had a defence under s 3 of the Criminal Law Act 1967 (see Chapter 11), in that he was using force in the prevention of crime. The judge ruled that the offence would have been completed as soon as the men walked away from the taxi. On appeal, one of the issues for the court was whether the offence had already been committed by the time D drove his taxi onto the pavement. After considering the earlier case of *Aziz* (1993) Crim LR 708, Leveson LJ stated:

17. . . . if a passenger were to explain (honestly) to the taxi driver that he had to enter his house in order to obtain the fare, the moment for payment would be deferred for him to do so. A decision not to return to the taxi would mean that, from that moment, the passenger is making off without payment. The taxi driver would never be in a position to know precisely when the passenger decided not to pay and, in our judgment, must be able to follow the passenger to challenge him in an attempt to prevent the commission of the offence.

18. The same principle can be applied in relation to a restaurant bill. If a diner approached the reception, credit card in hand, was distracted and then walked away, the owner of the restaurant would not know whether (or, if so, when) a decision had been made dishonestly to make off without payment. It would be reasonable for him to follow the diner and stop him on the basis that he was seeking to prevent the commission of the offence of making off or (alternatively) reminding the diner that he had forgotten to pay. He should not thereby risk a complaint of assault. The fact is that a restaurant owner (or a taxi driver) should not be required to make an accurate assumption of the intention of the person who has not, in fact, paid the bill or fare: he needs to be able to find out all the while as the person involved is 'making off'.

■ *Questions*

Are there any principles governing how the spot at which payment is expected or required is to be determined? Can there be?

23.3.3 Goods supplied or service done

Goods may be supplied, or services done, even though many or all of the physical acts to bring about the transfer are done by D and not the provider. All commentators are agreed that fuel is supplied by V at self-service filling stations even though the customer serves himself. Similarly, a service is done by V at a self-service car wash despite the fact that V is not on the premises and the machinery is operated by D.

A more difficult case is the self-service store. Suppose that D takes goods from the shelves which he places in his pocket and leaves the store with them. Obviously this is theft but does he also commit the offence under s 3? A. T. H. Smith ([1981] Crim LR 590) thinks that this case is to be distinguished from the self-service petrol station because in the latter case 'the customer does not just take possession of the petrol, but makes himself owner of it by pouring it into his tank'.

■ *Question*

D and E visit a 'club' in a disreputable part of town. D uses the services of a prostitute on the premises, and E orders and eats a meal. Subsequently, D and E leave refusing to pay, both claiming that they found the services substandard. Are they liable under s 3?

23.3.4 Without having paid

The issue of whether payment is made ordinarily presents no problems. One problem concerns payment by cheque (although in the era of chip and pin instances of payment by cheque are much less common and may eventually die out). If the cheque is supported by a cheque card which the bank must then honour, it would seem clear that V has been paid even though

D has exceeded his authority as between himself and the bank. The same would follow where a credit card is used. But what if V accepts a cheque from D which D knows will not be honoured? There is a suggestion in *Hammond* [1982] Crim LR 611 that V has been paid because a cheque taken without a banker's card is always taken at risk by the recipient. The judge in *Hammond* added that he did not see how in such a case it could be said that D made off.

23.3.5 Intention to make permanent default

It was settled by *Allen* [1985] 2 All ER 641, [1985] AC 1029, HL, that s 3 requires an intention to make permanent default. Lord Hailsham said, at 643:

> The judgment of the Court of Appeal, with which I agree, was delivered by Boreham J. He said ([1985] 1 All ER 148 at 154, [1985] 1 WLR 50 at 57):
>
> > 'To secure a conviction under s 3 of the 1978 Act the following must be proved: (1) that the defendant in fact made off without making payment on the spot: (2) the following mental elements: (a) knowledge that payment on the spot was required or expected of him: and (b) dishonesty: and (c) intent to avoid payment [sc, 'of the amount due']'.
>
> I agree with this analysis. To this the judge adds the following comment:
>
> > 'If (c) means, or is taken to include, no more than an intention to delay or defer payment of the amount due, it is difficult to see what it adds to the other elements. Anyone who knows that payment on the spot is expected or required of him and who then dishonestly makes off without paying as required or expected must have at least the intention to delay or defer payment. It follows, therefore, that the conjoined phrase "and with intent to avoid payment of the amount due" adds a further ingredient: an intention to do more than delay or defer, an intention to evade payment altogether'.
>
> My own view, for what it is worth, is that the section thus analysed is capable only of this meaning. But counsel for the Crown very properly conceded that, even if it were equivocal and capable of either meaning, in a penal section of this kind any ambiguity must be resolved in favour of the subject and against the Crown. Accordingly, the appeal falls to be dismissed either if on its true construction it means unambiguously that the intention must be permanently to avoid payment, or if the clause is ambiguous and capable of either meaning. Even on the assumption that, in the context, the word 'avoid' without the addition of the word 'permanently' is capable of either meaning, which Boreham J was inclined to concede, I find myself convinced by his final paragraph, which reads:
>
> > 'Finally, we can see no reason why, if the intention of Parliament was to provide, in effect, that an intention to delay or defer payment might suffice, Parliament should not have said so in explicit terms. This *might* have been achieved by the insertion of the word "such" before payment in the phrase in question. It *would* have been achieved by a grammatical reconstruction of the material part of s 3(1) thus, "dishonestly makes off without having paid and with intent to avoid payment of the amount due as required or expected". To accede to the Crown's submission would be to read the section as if it were constructed in that way. That we cannot do. Had it been intended to relate the intention to avoid "payment" to "payment as required or expected" it would have been easy to say so. The section does not say so. At the very least it contains an equivocation which should be resolved in favour of [the respondent]'.
>
> There is really no escape from this argument. . . .

■ *Questions*

Do you agree? Should an intention to delay payment suffice?

FURTHER READING

F. Bennion, Letter, 'The Drafting of Section 3 of the Theft Act 1978' [1980] Crim LR 670

P. Rowlands, 'Minors: Can They Make Off without Payment' (1981) 145 JP 410

A. T. H. Smith, 'Shoplifting and the Theft Acts' [1981] Crim LR 586

J. R. Spencer, 'The Theft Act 1978' [1979] Crim LR 24

J. R. Spencer, Letter, 'Making Off without Payment' [1983] Crim LR 573

G. Syrota, 'Statutes: Theft Act 1978' (1979) 42 MLR 301

G. Syrota, 'Are Cheque Frauds Covered by Section 3 of the Theft Act 1978?' [1980] Crim LR 413

24

Miscellaneous offences contained in the Theft Act 1968

24.1 Introduction

The Theft Act 1968 contains numerous offences and constraint of space precludes discussion of them all in the current work. This chapter will deal with the following miscellaneous offences:

(i)   removing articles from places open to the public—s 11;

(ii)   taking conveyances—s 12;

(iii) blackmail—s 21.

Some of the controversies that will be explored in this chapter include the following:

(i)   the extent to which it is necessary to have very specific offences based on particular types of property to supplement the general theft offence;

(ii)   the arguments for offences based on temporary deprivation of a person's property;

(iii) in what circumstances demands with threats ought to be criminalized as blackmail.

24.2 Removal of articles from places open to the public

Theft Act 1968, s 11

(1) Subject to sub-sections (2) and (3) below, where the public have access to a building in order to view the building or part of it, or a collection or part of a collection housed in it, any person who without lawful authority removes from the building or its grounds the whole or part of any article displayed or kept for display to the public in the building or that part of it or in its grounds shall be guilty of an offence.For this purpose 'collection' includes a collection got together for a temporary purpose, but references in this section to a collection do not apply to a collection made or exhibited for the purpose of effecting sales or other commercial dealings.

(2) It is immaterial for purposes of sub-section (1) above, that the public's access to a building is limited to a particular period or particular occasion; but where anything removed from a building or its grounds is there otherwise than as forming part of, or being on loan for exhibition with, a collection intended for permanent exhibition to the public, the person removing it does not thereby commit an offence under this section unless he removes it on a day when the public have access to the building as mentioned in sub-section (1) above.

(3) A person does not commit an offence under this section if he believes that he has lawful authority for the removal of the thing in question or that he would have it if the person entitled to give it knew of the removal and the circumstances of it.

(4) A person guilty of an offence under this section shall, on conviction on indictment, be liable to imprisonment for a term not exceeding five years.

The creation of the offence was inspired by a number (there seems to have been barely a handful of them) of 'removals', such as the removal of Goya's portrait of the Duke of Wellington from the National Portrait Gallery and the removal of the Coronation Stone from Westminster Abbey. The thinking behind the creation of the offence appears to be that articles displayed to the public are often irreplaceable and are not as easily protected as articles on private premises. But are they any more vulnerable than books kept on the shelves of a university library, many of which are equally irreplaceable?

■ *Questions*

The section provides an excellent opportunity to test your statutory interpretation skills. Consider the following: D enters the grounds of a stately home that is open to the public (on payment of a fee) and, as a prank, he removes a statue from the garden and hides it in a groundsman's shed. Has he committed an offence under s 11? Does it matter whether the stately home is open for business?

24.3 Taking conveyances

Theft Act 1968, s 12

12. Taking motor vehicle or other conveyance without authority

(1) Subject to sub-sections (5) and (6) below, a person shall be guilty of an offence if, without having the consent of the owner or other lawful authority, he takes any conveyance for his own or another's use or, knowing that any conveyance has been taken without such authority, drives it or allows himself to be carried in or on it.

(2) A person guilty of an offence under sub-section (1) above shall be liable on summary conviction to a fine not exceeding level 5 on the standard scale, to imprisonment for a term not exceeding six months, or to both.

(3) [Repealed.]

(4) If on the trial of an indictment for theft the jury are not satisfied that the accused committed theft, but it is proved that the accused committed an offence under sub-section (1) above, the jury may find him guilty of the offence under sub-section (1) and if he is found guilty of it, he shall be liable as he would have been liable under sub-section (2) above on summary conviction. . . .

(5) Sub-section (1) above shall not apply in relation to pedal cycles; but, subject to sub-section (6) below, a person who, without having the consent of the owner or other lawful authority, takes a pedal cycle for his own or another's use, or rides a pedal cycle knowing it to have been taken without such authority, shall on summary conviction be liable to a fine not exceeding level 3 on the standard scale.

(6) A person does not commit an offence under this section by anything done in the belief that he has lawful authority to do it or that he would have the owner's consent if the owner knew of his doing it and the circumstances of it.

For s 12A, 'Aggravated vehicle-taking', see section 24.4, p 817.

In short, the elements of the offence are (i) the taking for one's own or another's use; (ii) of a conveyance; (iii) without consent.

24.3.1 Taking for one's own or another's use

Although this element of the offence seems straightforward, there are a number of issues that need to be considered. In *Bow* (1977) 64 Cr App R 54 the Court of Appeal held that 'use' means, and only means, use *as a conveyance*. So although in that case, where D released the handbrake on V's car causing it to roll some 200 yards down a narrow road in order to enable him to remove his own car, the conveyance had been moved, it would not have been *used as a conveyance*. One question that proved problematic was whether D could be guilty of the offence in circumstances where he was already in possession or control of the conveyance, but uses it in an unauthorized way. In *McGill* [1970] RTR 209, D was given permission to use V's car to drive E to the station on condition that he returned it immediately. He subsequently drove it elsewhere and did not return it for some days. D was convicted. In *McKnight v Davies* [1974] RTR 4 the conviction of a lorry driver was upheld when, instead of returning the lorry to the depot at the end of the working day, he used it for his own purposes and did not return it until the early hours of the next morning.

■ *Question*

Why should a taking of a vehicle not just be treated as theft?

24.3.2 A conveyance

Section 12(7) provides:

> For the purposes of this section—
>
> (a) 'conveyance' means any conveyance constructed or adapted for the carriage of a person or persons whether by land, water or air, except that it does not include a conveyance constructed or adapted for use only under the control of a person not carried in or on it, and 'drive' shall be construed accordingly; and
>
> (b) 'owner', in relation to a conveyance which is the subject of a hiring agreement or hire-purchase agreement, means the person in possession of the conveyance under that agreement.

'Conveyance' has been interpreted to mean a mechanical contrivance of some kind. While it obviously includes conveyances such as cars and motorcycles, it does not include horses.

24.3.3 Without the owner's consent or lawful authority

In the vast majority of cases, this will not prove to be an issue. However, what if the owner's consent has been procured by fraud? In *Whitaker v Campbell* [1984] QB 318 it was held that when the owner is induced to part with the conveyance through fraud, it could not be said 'in commonsense terms' that he had not consented to the taking. The position would be different, the court held, if the consent had been procured through force.

24.3.4 Mens rea

The taking must be intentional; it is not enough that the vehicle accidentally moves with D in it. Section 12(6) provides that a person does not commit an offence by anything done in the belief that he has lawful authority to do it or that the owner would have consented. It appears to be the case that the test is a subjective one.

24.3.5 Driving or being carried

An offence under s 12 may be committed not merely by one who takes the conveyance, but also by one who, knowing the conveyance has been taken without authority, drives it or allows himself to be carried in or on it.

24.4 Aggravated vehicle-taking

The taking of motor vehicles (sometimes called 'joyriding' or 'twocking') increased dramatically in the 1990s to an extent where it was described as 'epidemic'. There are significant risks when takers demonstrate their driving 'skills' and high-speed chases ensue in which takers are pursued by police. The Government felt it had to respond to the growing mischief. The Aggravated Vehicle-Taking Act 1992 adds a further section, s 12A, to the Theft Act 1968, creating the offence of aggravated vehicle-taking (the offence is confined to the taking of mechanically propelled vehicles). This requires proof:

(1) that D has committed the offence under s 12(1) of the 1968 Act (the 'basic offence'); and

(2) that after the vehicle was taken and before it was recovered, the vehicle was driven or injury or damage was caused in one or more of the aggravating circumstances:

   (a) that the vehicle was driven dangerously;

   (b) that, owing to the driving of a vehicle, an accident occurred by which injury was caused to any person. (In *Marsh* [1997] 1 Cr App R 67, the court held that the words 'owing to the driving of the vehicle' were plain and simple and no gloss ought to be provided by referring the jury to the manner of the driving. See [1997] Crim LR 205 and comment. If D has used the car as a weapon, he will still be caught by the section: 'accident' includes deliberate causing of injury: *B* [2005] Crim LR 388.) If injury is caused it matters not if it was caused deliberately or without fault;

   (c) that, owing to the driving of the vehicle, an accident occurred by which damage was caused to any property, other than the vehicle;

   (d) that damage was caused to the vehicle.

There are two offences (one punishable on indictment by imprisonment for two years, and one by imprisonment for 14 years where death is caused). Both offences are draconian. While aggravating circumstance (a) requires a degree of fault, liability is totally strict in relation to the others and the offence is committed though the vehicle taken was driven with due care.

■ *Questions*
Is an offence of this breadth fair? Is it necessary?

Moreover, liability for the offence extends not only to the driver but to all of the participants in the basic offence. It seems that if D slashes the seats of the taken vehicle, E, who is in the vehicle, is guilty of the offence though he seeks to dissuade D from damaging the seats or even if he seeks to prevent him. See *Dawes v DPP* [1995] 1 Cr App R 65 at 72.

24.5 Blackmail

Blackmail is a crime which conjures up images of secret deals and liaison shrouded in glamour and intrigue; hence, its popularity with dramatists and authors. Prosecutions for blackmail tend to involve nasty rather than exotic conduct, with individuals preying on the vulnerable. This is one of the reasons that blackmail is treated so seriously by the courts in sentencing.

Blackmail is also a rather more technical offence than is commonly understood. It raises several interesting issues including some of the more theoretical issues as to the wrongs and harms which the offence of blackmail might be said to involve. There seems to be little consensus about the precise harm the offence of blackmail seeks to guard against.

In summary, blackmail is an offence involving a threat by D, backed by an unwarranted demand by which D intends to gain or cause loss in terms of property.

24.5.1 Definition

Theft Act 1968, s 21

(1) A person is guilty of blackmail if, with a view to gain for himself or another or with intent to cause loss to another, he makes any unwarranted demand with menaces; and for this purpose a demand with menaces is unwarranted unless the person making it does so in the belief:

  (a) that he has reasonable grounds for making the demand; and

  (b) that the use of the menaces is a proper means of reinforcing the demand.

(2) The nature of the act or omission demanded is immaterial, and it is also immaterial whether the menaces relate to action to be taken by the person making the demand.

(3) A person guilty of blackmail shall on conviction on indictment be liable to imprisonment for a term not exceeding fourteen years.

The elements of blackmail are: (i) a demand; (ii) with menaces; (iii) the demand must be unwarranted; and (iv) a view to gain or intent to cause loss.

24.5.1.1 The demand

A demand may take any form and may be implicit as well as explicit. However, whether it is express or implied, there must actually be a demand. Although it will typically be the case that D will demand money or other property, s 21(2) of the Theft Act 1968 provides that 'the nature of the act or omission demanded is immaterial'. Despite this, the offence can only be committed if D has a view to gain or an intention to cause loss in money or other *property*.

24.5.1.2 Menaces

The word 'menace' is an ordinary English word and as such should not require further elaboration in the majority of cases. The Court of Appeal in *Lawrence and Pomroy* (1973)

57 Cr App R 64 suggested that a jury could easily understand this word and that the judge should not define it for them. In *Clear* [1968] 1 All ER 74, Sellers LJ held that, to constitute menaces, the threats must be 'of such a nature and extent that the mind of an ordinary person of normal stability and courage might be influenced or made apprehensive so as to accede unwillingly to the demand.' The more recent case of *Lambert* [2009] EWCA Crim 2860 emphasized that it is still blackmail if D threatened to do something to V that could not there and then be carried out. See also *Garwood* [1987] Crim LR 476.

24.5.1.3 Unwarranted demand

The demand must be unwarranted or there is no offence. The Theft Act specifies that a demand will be unwarranted unless made in the belief (i) that there are reasonable grounds for making it, *and* (ii) that the use of the menaces is a proper means of enforcing the demand. The test is a subjective one: did D believe in the reasonableness of the grounds for making the demand and the propriety of using a menace to enforce the demand? For example, D's belief in the reasonableness might derive from the fact that V owes him money.

Criminal Law Revision Committee, Eighth Report
(1966), paras 121–122

...

    At first we proposed to include a requirement that a person's belief that he has reasonable grounds for making the demand or that the use of the menaces is proper should be a reasonable belief. There would be a case for this in policy; for it may be thought that a person who puts pressure on another by menaces of a kind which any reasonable person would think ought to be blackmail should not escape liability merely because his moral standard is too low, or his intelligence too limited, to enable him to appreciate the wrongness of his conduct. The requirement might also make the decision easier for a jury; for if they found that the demand was unwarranted or that the menaces were improper, they would not have to consider whether the accused believed otherwise. But we decided finally not to include the requirement. To require that an honest belief, in order to be a defence, should be reasonable would have the result that the offence of blackmail could be committed by mere negligence (for example, in not consulting a lawyer ...). The requirement would also be out of keeping with the rest of the Bill, because all the major offences under it depend expressly or by implication on dishonesty. In particular, the provision in clause 2(1) making it a defence to a charge of theft that the defendant believed that he had the right to deprive the owner does not require that the belief should be reasonable.

    ...

24.5.1.4 View to gain or intent to cause loss

With 'a view to'

The Court of Appeal, in *Dooley* [2005] EWCA Crim 3093, approved the approach to this expression in *Smith and Hogan* (11th edn, 2005) when considering that expression in the context of possession of indecent images 'with a view to' distribution.

D. Ormerod, Case commentary on *Dooley*
[2006] Crim LR 544

The phrase 'with a view to' appears, as the court observes, in many hundreds of statutes and it is surprising that it has not attracted much previous judicial or academic comment. Where it has been discussed, e.g. in the context of false accounting under s.17 of the Theft Act 1968, the focus has tended to be on the consequence D acts towards achieving (in that instance whether he acts with a view to 'gain'): see *Smith and Hogan Criminal Law* (11th edn, 2005), pp.789–790. The courts have acknowledged that the expression does not connote motive: per Chitty L.J. in *J. Lyons and Sons v Wilkins* [1899] 1 Ch. 255 at 269–270, considering the offence under s.7 of the Conspiracy and Protection of Property Act 1875. See also *Bevans* (1988) 87 Cr.App.R. 64: D's unwarranted demand with menaces for pain killer was sufficient for blackmail as he did so with a view to gain even though his motive was to alleviate pain. The academic view of the expression where it appears in offences such as blackmail has been to treat it as simply a form of intention, see, e.g. G. Williams, *Textbook of Criminal Law* (2nd edn, 1983), p.830.

The trial judge [in *Dooley*] regarded it as sufficient for the prosecution to prove that D acted 'with a view to' if D saw it as likely that others might access the files. The Court of Appeal is, with respect, right to reject that as a sufficient form of mens rea. Foresight or awareness of a likelihood of the files being exposed to acquisition by others is not equivalent to an intention that they should be. Nor is proof of foresight of that likelihood sufficient proof that D acted 'with a view to'. The court's conclusion is that it is sufficient that 'one of' D's reasons for possessing the images in that form is so that the files will be accessible to others, drawing on the discussion in *Smith and Hogan*, p.807 in the context of blackmail.

... The trial judge sought to distinguish the expression from intention, as did the Court of Appeal. How do the two relate? As far as direct or purposive intent is concerned, it seems obvious that proof of purposive intent satisfies the requirement of acting 'with a view to'. The Court of Appeal also concludes that D acts 'with a view to' a proscribed consequence even if that is not his sole or primary purpose for acting provided it is one of his reasons. How much further does the definition of 'with a view to' extend? The court's discussion implies that 'oblique' intent will not suffice in this context. On an oblique intent approach, D would be liable if in achieving his purpose of downloading images for personal use, he realised that his conduct involved temporary storage of the images in a shared folder, and that it is virtually certain that the files will therefore be available to others. The court considers it unnecessary to engage in the debate on oblique intention, might D be said to have foreseen as virtually certain that the files would be accessible to others without that being 'one of his reasons' for acting in downloading and retaining them in the shared folder?

Gain or loss

Theft Act 1968, s 34(2)

For purposes of this Act—

   (a) 'gain' and 'loss' are to be construed as extending only to gain or loss in money or other property but as extending to any such gain or loss whether temporary or permanent; and—

      (i) 'gain' includes a gain by keeping what one has, as well as a gain by getting what one has not: and

      (ii) 'loss' includes a loss by not getting what one might get as well as a loss by parting with what one has...

Normally the blackmailer intends a gain to himself and a loss to the victim but either will suffice. D may commit blackmail where he secures paid employment by V (view to gain) through menaces even though his intention is to restore the failing fortunes of V's firm (not to cause loss to V). Conversely, D might by menaces cause V to do something—revoke a will, for example—which confers no benefit on D but causes loss to others (or might cause them not to get something which they might have been given).

In *Bevans* (1987) 87 Cr App R 64, [1988] Crim LR 236, CA, D, crippled by osteoarthritis, called a doctor, V, and at gunpoint demanded a painkilling injection which V administered.

D was convicted of blackmail and his appeal was dismissed. The drug was property which D had demanded with a view to gain for himself; it was irrelevant that D's ulterior motive was the relief of pain rather than economic gain.

FURTHER READING

P. Alldridge, 'Attempted Murder of the Soul: Blackmail, Privacy and Secrets' (1993) 13 OJLS 368

R. Epstein, 'Blackmail, Inc' (1983) 50 U Chicago LR 553

L. Katz, *Ill-Gotten Gains: Evasion, Blackmail, Fraud and Kindred Puzzles of the Law* (1996)

D. Ormerod and D. H. Williams, *Smith's Law of Theft* (9th edn, 2007), Ch 10

J. N. Spencer, 'The Aggravated Vehicle Taking Act 1992' [1992] Crim LR 69

S. White, 'Taking the Joy out of Joy-Riding' [1980] Crim LR 60

25

Fraud

25.1 Introduction

This chapter is concerned with the offence of fraud. It is a statutory offence that can be committed in one of three ways: by making a false representation, by failing to disclose information and by abuse of position. Each has a different actus reus and mens rea, but for the most part liability turns on whether D was dishonest. In addition, this chapter examines the related offences of obtaining services dishonestly, possession of articles for fraud and making or supplying articles for use in frauds.

Some of the controversies that will be explored in this chapter include the following:

(i) whether the general fraud offence extends the scope of liability too far;

(ii) the extent to which an individual can commit a criminal offence in circumstances where his conduct would not give rise to civil liability;

(iii) whether a representation can be committed by omission;

(iv) the fact that, unlike the Theft Act 1968, under the Fraud Act 2006 there is no guarantee of an acquittal where D thinks he has a right in law to act as he did;

(v) given the width of the actus reus of the general fraud offence, whether the effect of the Fraud Act 2006 is to criminalize lying;

(vi) whether the Fraud Act 2006 is compliant with Article 7 of the European Convention on Human Rights (ECHR).

25.1.1 The general fraud offence under the 2006 Act

The principal offence is the general fraud offence created by s 1 in the following terms:

(1) A person is guilty of fraud if he is in breach of any of the sections listed in subsection (2) (which provide for different ways of committing the offence).

(2) The sections are—

    (a) section 2 (fraud by false representation),

    (b) section 3 (fraud by failing to disclose information), and

    (c) section 4 (fraud by abuse of position).

Each form of the offence is based on dishonest conduct against property interests, and carries a maximum ten-year sentence on indictment. Fraud is an are incredibly wide offence, deliberately drafted to avoid technicality.

25.1.2 Background

The Fraud Act 2006 came into force on 15 January 2007. The immediate history of the Fraud Act 2006 can be traced to the Law Commission Consultation Paper No 155, *Legislating the Criminal Code: Fraud and Deception* (1999), the subsequent Law Commission Report No 276, *Fraud* (2002) and the Home Office Consultation Paper, *Fraud Law Reform* (2004) which developed the Law Commission's proposals. However, calls for reform of the dishonesty offences, and in particular those based on deception, have been circulating for many years.

The Fraud Act 2006 abolished all the deception offences in the Theft Acts 1968 and 1978 (including that inserted by the Theft (Amendment) Act 1996). It replaced the deception offences with a basic fraud offence with emphasis on the defendant's conduct rather than the actions or beliefs of the victim. It introduced very wide-reaching preliminary offences of possessing/making equipment to commit frauds. The offence of obtaining services by deception was replaced by obtaining services dishonestly. Controversially, conspiracy to defraud remains, but whether it can be safely abolished without leaving serious gaps in the law will be kept under review. Guidance has been issued by the Attorney General on when it is appropriate for prosecutors to rely on that charge.

25.1.2.1 The merits of a general fraud offence

The Fraud Act 2006 was enacted to remedy the defects in the various deception offences that it replaced. Some academic commentators argued that the only way of meeting the difficulties created by these offences was to reject them in favour of a general fraud offence. The merits of general fraud offences have been debated for decades. The core advantage offered is by shifting the focus of the offence from whether D made false representations that were believed by V and caused a specific result, to whether D's dishonest conduct was sufficiently fraudulent to give rise to criminal liability. See further G. R. Sullivan, 'Framing an Acceptable General Offence of Fraud' (1989) 53 J Crim L 92.

Over the years, proponents of a general fraud offence argued for a model requiring not only that the prosecution prove that the defendant behaved dishonestly and with intent to gain/cause loss but also that there were economic interests actually imperilled by the conduct. This would certainly pose fewer problems than the model on which the Fraud Act is based, where there is no requirement of proof of the conduct having the potential to imperil economic interests or of D having caused the victim to believe any representation.

When considering the matter, most commentators doubted, however, whether a general fraud offence could ever be drafted which does not extend potential criminal liability too far (see J. C. Smith, 'Fraud and The Criminal Law' in P. Birks (ed), *Criminal Justice and Human Rights—Pressing Problems in the Law* (1995), Vol 1, p 49). By the end of the chapter you will be able to assess for yourself how accurate their belief was.

The Fraud Act is based on recommendations of the Law Commission set out in its Report No 276, *Fraud* (2002):

1.6 In asking us to consider the law of fraud, the former Home Secretary was particularly interested in whether the introduction of a general fraud offence would improve the criminal law. We have now come to the conclusion that it would. We consider that it would improve the law in each of the respects raised by the former Home Secretary:

(1) It should make the law more comprehensible to juries, especially in serious fraud trials. The charges which are currently employed in such trials are numerous, and none of them adequately describe or encapsulate the meaning of 'fraud'. The statutory offences are too specific to offer a general description of fraud; while the common law offence of conspiracy to defraud is so wide that it offers little guidance on the difference between fraudulent and lawful conduct. Thus, at present, juries are not given a straightforward definition of fraud. If they were, and if that were the key to the indictment, it should enable them to focus more closely on whether the facts of the case fit the crimes as charged.

(2) A general offence of fraud would be a useful tool in effective prosecutions. Specific offences are sometimes wrongly charged, in circumstances when another offence would have been more suitable. This can result in unjustified acquittals and costly appeals. Furthermore, it is possible that excessively broad crimes, such as conspiracy to defraud, may result in prosecutors wasting resources on those who should never have been charged at all. A generalised crime which nonetheless provides a clear definition of fraudulent behaviour may assist prosecutors to weigh up whether they have a realistic chance of securing a conviction.

(3) Introducing a single crime of fraud would dramatically simplify the law of fraud. Clear, simple law is fairer than complicated, inaccessible law. If a citizen is contemplating activities which could amount to a crime, a clear, simple law gives better guidance on whether the conduct is criminal, and fairer warning of what could happen if it is. Furthermore, when a defendant is charged with a clear, simple law, they will be better able to understand their options when pleading to the charge; and, if pleading not guilty, they will be better able to conduct their defence.

(4) A general offence of fraud would be aimed at encompassing fraud in all its forms. It would not focus on particular ways or means of committing frauds. Thus it should be better able to keep pace with developing technology.

1.7 In line with these conclusions, we recommend that the eight offences of deception created by the Theft Acts 1968–96 should be repealed, and that the common law crime of conspiracy to defraud should be abolished. In their place we recommend the creation of two new statutory offences—one of fraud, and one of obtaining services dishonestly.

■ *Question*

Consider at the end of this chapter whether the Fraud Act 2006 does in fact improve the law in the ways the Law Commission envisaged.

Although the Fraud Act 2006 does make it easier to prosecute instances of fraud, the pitfalls of a general fraud offence are not to be underestimated. Consider the following passage.

D. Ormerod, 'Criminalising Lying' [2007] Crim LR 193, concludes at 218:

General fraud offences offer many practical advantages including the clearer expression of large scale criminality in one charge; the ability to render complex schemes more readily understood by jurors; the avoidance of fragmenting factual chronologies to meet technical requirements of spe- cific counts on the indictment; the removal of the risk of duplicity or of overloading the indictment; and the ease of cross-admissibility of evidence. These practical advantages must not, however, be allowed to produce a general offence that is overbroad, based too heavily on the ill-defined concept of dishonesty, too vague to meet the obligation under Art.7 of the ECHR, and other- wise deficient in principle. It is certainly questionable whether the Act has secured these practical advantages at the cost of undermining important principles. The offences are so wide that they provoke the kind of astonishment that Professor Green expresses when considering the lowest common denominator of the moral content of fraud: 'if fraud really were to encompass not just stealing by deceit, but also deceptive and non-deceptive breaches of trust, conflicts of interest, nondisclosure of material facts, exploitation, taking unfair advantage, non-performance of contractual obligations, and misuse of corporate assets, it would be virtually impossible to distinguish between different offenses in terms of their nature and seriousness, and even to know whether and when one had committed a crime.'

(See further S. P. Green, *Lying, Cheating and Stealing: A Moral Theory of White Collar Crime* (2005), p 151 and Ch 14 generally.)

What is important to appreciate about the Fraud Act 2006 before proceeding any further is that it is an offence drafted in the inchoate mode; D can be guilty of fraud without ever having caused any loss or having gained anything. In this respect, it is similar to other inchoate offences, such as attempts and conspiracy. Andrew Ashworth explains the new approach in the following way, with reference to the offence of fraud by making a false representation.

A. Ashworth, 'The Criminal Law's Ambivalence About Outcomes'
in R. Cruft, M. H. Kramer and M. R. Reiff (eds), *Crime, Punishment, and Responsibility: The Jurisprudence of Antony Duff* (2011)

It seems that what happened in 2006 was that the law relating to fraud moved from an objectivist model, in which the causing of a particular outcome by particular means was prohibited, to a broadly subjectivist model, focused on the defendant's culpability and on what the defendant intended to achieve...What is interesting about the impact of the 2006 Act is that the new, broader, subjectivist definition of fraud includes 'those that fail as well as those that succeed' in the substantive offence. Indeed, by dint of the new definition, they have not failed, because all that needs to be proved is that they tried—that they made the false representation. In effect, the new offence of fraud has moved into the space that was previously occupied by attempt to defraud...

25.2 Section 2: fraud by false representation

The offence created by s 1(2)(a) of the Act is incredibly broad. The offence is described in s 2, which provides:

(1) A person is in breach of this section if he—

    (a) dishonestly makes a false representation, and

    (b) intends, by making the representation—

        (i) to make a gain for himself or another, or

        (ii) to cause loss to another or to expose another to a risk of loss.

(2) A representation is false if—

    (a) it is untrue or misleading, and

    (b) the person making it knows that it is, or might be, untrue or misleading.

(3) 'Representation' means any representation as to fact or law, including a representation as to the state of mind of—

    (a) the person making the representation, or

    (b) any other person.

(4) A representation may be express or implied.

(5) For the purposes of this section a representation may be regarded as made if it (or anything implying it) is submitted in any form to any system or device designed to receive, convey or respond to communications (with or without human intervention).

Section 1 provides that the maximum sentence on indictment is ten years.

The actus reus requires proof that D made a false representation; and the mens rea requires proof that D knew the representation was or knew that it might be false, and acted dishonestly, and with intent to gain, or cause loss. Contrast the offence with those of deception under the old law: it had to be proved that D's conduct actually deceived V and caused him to do whatever act was appropriate to the offence charged—transferring property, executing a valuable security, etc. Under s 2, there is no need to prove: a result of any kind; that the alleged victim or indeed any person believed any representation; that any person acted on it; or that the accused succeeded in making a gain or causing a loss by the representation.

■ *Question*

Under the s 2 offence can D be liable in the following cases? D:

(i)   tells V that the T-shirt he is selling was worn by David Beckham. V knows that the statement is untrue, but likes the T-shirt so buys it anyway;

(ii)   tells V that he is authorized to use the credit card (with D's father's name on it). V does not care whether that is true or not and takes payment from the card;

(iii)   sends an email to V (and 10,000 others) offering to sell them a guaranteed way to make money on the stock market which would never fail and net them 100 per cent returns in a week. V does not read or even see the false statement as his email provider deletes it as spam;

(iv)   sends the email as in (iii), but his ISP automatically deletes it as spam before it is sent to anyone;

(v)   visits a self-service fuel station and, having filled his car, tells the cashier that he has an arrangement with the manager so that he does not need to pay;

(vi)   decides to fake his own death and claim the insurance money. He sets out in his canoe intending to fake an accident at sea. He paddles out and then abandons the canoe, swimming safely to shore. He then hides away with the help of his accomplice wife who makes the demand to the insurance company. After six months the company pay out to the wife; and

(vii) in order to ensure that his son is offered a place at the best local school, D provides his sister's address on the application form instead of his own, as it is within the school's catchment area.

In each case, consider also at what point in time D would have completed the offence under s 2.

25.2.1 Making a false representation

25.2.1.1 Making

A false representation can be 'made' by speech, writing or conduct. D satisfies this element of the offence as much by saying to a customer: 'this is a genuine Renoir I have for sale' as by describing the painting in those terms in his sale catalogue. Forms of physical conduct other than speech or writing will suffice, as where D nods assent in response to the question 'Is this a genuine Renoir?' Classic examples will be false representations on mortgage application forms or loan application forms. The s 2 form of the offence is also specifically designed to criminalize 'phishing' on the internet. D who posts on the internet a website purporting to be that of a bank or financial institution, encouraging account holders to reveal their passwords and confidential information, will commit the offence. It does not matter that the website is ignored by everyone; the making of the false representation suffices.

It is arguable that the representation is made either (i) as soon as D articulates it, (ii) only if it is also addressed to something, (iii) only when it is actually perceived as such by a person, that is, when it is communicated. It is submitted that under the Fraud Act 2006, s 2, there need not be a completed communication in the sense that a person must read or hear or see D's statement in order for it to constitute a representation. A representation would seem to be 'made' as soon as articulated, but in accordance with the ordinary use of the word, a representation must be made 'to' someone or something. Cf C. Withey, 'The Fraud Act 2006' (2007) 71 J Crim L 220, suggesting that the offence is not committed unless a communication is completed. This is difficult to square with the statutory wording and Parliament's intent.

■ *Question*

Dodgy, a final year student, wants to sell his old criminal law textbook. It is woefully out of date and worth practically nothing. Dodgy goes to the new Law School building before the start of term and persuades the security staff to let him pin a notice on the freshers' notice board advertising the book as 'the latest edition, an essential textbook to pass the course'. The new building will not be open to students for another week. On the first day of term, Mabel the cleaner removes the notice from the board and puts it in the bin before any student has entered the building. What crime, if any, has Dodgy committed?

The false representation element of the offence is so ill-defined that it is unclear whether D can be liable for the s 2 offence when he omits to rectify a belief V has formed. Section 3 of the Act expressly provides for an offence of fraud by failing to disclose (section 25.3, p 842). A broad reading of s 2 would overlap significantly with that section. However, s 3 is limited to cases in which the defendant is under *a legal duty* to disclose information. The position seems to be:

- if D makes a false representation he can be liable under s 2;
- if D makes a false representation, but at the time he makes it, he believes it to be true—it is submitted that if D discovers that the statement is false and thereafter does not seek to rectify any misunderstanding, he should be liable under s 2;
- if D makes a statement which is true, but which V misunderstands and on V's misunderstanding would render the statement false, D is not liable at the time he makes the statement. If D realizes that V has misunderstood him:
  - D is liable under s 3 if D is under a legal duty to inform V; but
  - if D is not under a legal duty to inform V, D's only liability may be under s 2; and
- if D makes a true statement, but circumstances change so that the statement becomes inaccurate and D realizes this, D may be liable under s 2. D will be liable under s 3 if he is under a legal duty to correct his statement. As the *Allen* case, later in this section, p 828, demonstrates, liability will turn on the facts.

In *DPP v Ray* [1974] AC 370 Lord Pearson referred to there being a 'continuing representation' in the 1968 Act deception offences: 'By continuing representation I mean in this case not a continuing effect of an initial representation, but a representation which is being made by conduct at every moment throughout that course of conduct…' Lord Hodson held that under the deception offences, while a party may be under a duty to communicate a relevant change of circumstances before the contract is made, he does not deceive the seller by failing to communicate such a change after the contract has been entered into.

In *Rai* [2000] 1 Cr App R 242, [2000] Crim LR 192, D obtained a grant from the city council to provide a bathroom for his disabled mother. Before it was installed, she died. D did not inform the council and allowed the work to proceed. He was convicted of obtaining services by deception. Rai argued that he had no legal or contractual duty to inform the council of his mother's death. The Court of Appeal rejected this argument and held that positive acquiescence could amount to deception.

This issue was considered more recently and with explicit reference to the Fraud Act 2006 in *Government of UAE v Allen* [2012] EWHC 1712 (Admin). A was a British national who obtained a mortgage from a bank in the United Arab Emirates. The mortgage was to be paid over a period of 20 years and the funds were to come from A's credit card account, which was held with the bank. A supplied the bank with an undated cheque made out for the amount of the loan as security in case she defaulted on the payments. Some 20 months later, A defaulted on her mortgage payments and the bank sought to cash the cheque, but it was dishonoured as A did not have sufficient funds in her account to cover the amount. A returned to the UK and was convicted in her absence in the UAE of an offence of issuing an uncovered cheque and was sentenced to three years' imprisonment. The UAE sought A's extradition and the issue for the Divisional Court to consider was whether the requirement of dual criminality was made out, that is, whether A would on those facts have committed an offence in the UK.

Toulson LJ referred to the cases mentioned previously and found that D would not have committed an offence in the UK.

> There are some circumstances recognised in the case law in which a person who has made a true representation will be under a duty to inform the representee if there is a significant change in the circumstances, as previously represented, before the representation has been acted upon. In particular, where a representation is made in the course of negotiations, it will be readily understood as intended to subsist up to the conclusion of the negotiations, so that if it becomes incorrect before it has been acted upon by the representee the representor will be guilty of misrepresentation by remaining silent.

On the facts of the case it was held that A gave her bank no undertaking that she would provide it with information about any later change in her circumstances. Further, Toulson LJ concluded that there was no principled basis for construing an implied continuing representation into the loan agreement. The court observed that implied representations are legal constructs intended to give effect to what honest parties involved in a transaction would reasonably read into each others' conduct.

It is said by commentators that the overriding principle should be that the criminal law ought to take its lead from the civil law; the maxim *caveat emptor* ought to operate to restrict the scope of liability. The issue was debated in the early parliamentary stages of the Bill and the Attorney General accepted that there are occasions when:

> something that most of us naturally might think of as a non-disclosure is transformed by a fiction of the law into an implicit misrepresentation. But it is a fiction; it is not how people think about it. People will frequently say, 'I was not misled because I understand that he was implicitly making this representation to me. He just did not disclose something; he was dishonest in not disclosing it; and the purpose of that was to make a gain or to do something else'. One can think of many other examples where that would be the true basis on which a charge would be laid. (Hansard HL, 19 July 2005, cols 1411–1412)

However, remember that in *Hinks* [2000] UKHL 53, [2001] Crim LR 162 (see section 21.3, p 742) the House of Lords was willing to find criminal liability in circumstances were there was no civil liability.

■ *Questions*

1. When would a court find that D was under an obligation to inform the other party of a change of circumstances, making a failure to do so an offence under s 2? Is it as soon as D becomes aware that the circumstances have changed, or must D have made an undertaking to inform the other party if the circumstances change in order to be criminally liable for failing to do so?

2. Do you agree with Toulson LJ's example that failure to bring to the other side's attention a change of circumstances when conducting a negotiation warrants criminalization? If there is to be any liability at all, should it not be for a contractual misrepresentation or the tort of deceit?

3. D establishes a website asking people to sponsor him to do the London Marathon in a year's time. D's training does not go so well and six months before the marathon he decides not to run it, but still intends to collect money for charity. Fraud? What if D had never intended to run the marathon?

25.2.1.2 'Attempted' false representation

Since the s 2 offence can be committed as soon as D has made a false representation, there is only limited scope for a charge of attempt. Possible examples include where D, having pre-pared documents containing false statements, is apprehended en route to post those to V or where D unwittingly tells the truth. In *Deller* (1952) 36 Cr App R 184, D induced V to purchase his car by representing, *inter alia*, that it was free from encumbrances, that is, that D had own-ership and was free to sell it. In fact, D had previously executed a document that purported to mortgage the car to a finance company and, no doubt, he thought he was telling a lie. He was charged with a deception-based offence. However, the document by which the transaction had been effected was probably void in law for the technical reason that it was as an unregis-tered bill of sale. If the document was void the car *was* free from encumbrances—'... quite accidentally and, strange as it may sound, dishonestly, the appellant had told the truth'. D's conviction was therefore quashed by the Court of Criminal Appeal, for, though he had mens rea, no actus reus had been established. The Court of Appeal considered *Deller* in *Cornelius* [2012] EWCA Crim 500. D made a number of representations on various mortgage appli-cation forms that turned out to be true. D's convictions were therefore quashed, as he had made no false representations. The Court of Appeal declined to substitute a conviction for attempted fraud as, contrary to the defendant in *Deller*, the court could not conclude that the jury were sure that Cornelius had intended to be dishonest in respect of these very technical representations. There was no evidence that he had turned his mind to the veracity or other-wise of the statements on the mortgage application forms.

■ *Questions*

1. Given how widely the offence is drafted, is what would typically be considered an 'attempt' to commit fraud contrary to s 2 in fact an instance of the full offence? Consider D, who goes to an elderly person's home and tells her that her roof needs extensive repairs that will cost £5,000. D begins to 'repair' the roof but runs away when the victim's son is called. Although D never received a deposit for the 'repairs', is he not guilty of the full offence as soon as he made the false representation with the requisite mens rea? For the contrary position, see *Ward* [2011] EWCA Crim 212. Think back to Ashworth, section 25.1.1, p 825.

2. Does the idea of attempted fraud extend the scope of criminal liability too wide or is it ne-cessary to catch the putative fraudster who inadvertently makes a true representation?

25.2.1.3 Express or implied representations

By s 2(4), a representation may be express or implied. Subsection 4 is included for the avoidance of doubt. The inclusion of the word 'implied' might prove problematic as it adds to the ambiguity of the scope of the offence. One of the acknowledged difficulties with the old law was that it presented problems for the courts in relation to implied representations: see *DPP v Ray* (section 25.2.1.1, p 827).

■ *Questions*

Consider what representations are made by:

(i) Darren and Delia who register as a married couple in a hotel when they are not married; and

(ii) Den, a motor trader, who states that the mileage shown on the odometer of a second-hand car 'may not be correct'.

25.2.1.4 Representations and cheques

In *Hazelton* (1874) LR 2 CCR 134, it was thought to be settled law that a person tendering a cheque impliedly makes three representations: (i) that he had an account at the bank on which the cheque is drawn; (ii) that he has had authority to draw on the bank for the amount specified; and (iii) that the cheque as drawn is a valid order for that amount. However, in *Metropolitan Police Comr v Charles* [1976] 3 All ER 112, [1977] AC 177, HL, it was held that in substance there is only one representation, namely that 'the existing state of facts is such that in the ordinary course the cheque will be met'—per Lord Edmund-Davies quoting with approval the words of Pollock B in *Hazelton*. The 'existing facts' may thus include D's present intention to pay money into the account, or his belief that someone else will do so. It makes no difference that the cheque is post-dated: *Gilmartin* [1983] 1 All ER 829, [1983] QB 953, CA. The position under the 2006 Act was considered in *Government of UAE v Allen* [2012] EWHC 1712 (Admin).

The facts are set out in section 25.2.1.1, p 828.

Toulson LJ referred to the facts of *Gilmartin* and stated as follows:

34. When one considers the commercial circumstances in which the defendant gave an undated cheque to the bank in the present case, and what a reasonable person would have understood from her conduct in doing so, there are a number of striking features.

35. The amount of the cheque was practically equal to the amount of the loan, but it was not the intended method of repayment. Repayment was to be by monthly instalments through the defendant's credit card account. The cheque was to be completed and presented upon a certain contingency, ie in the event of a default. It was required by the bank in order to provide a form of security in that event, which might occur at any time within a period of 20 years. Any banker would know that over 20 years there might be any number of reasons why a borrower might default, other than a deliberate intention to do so. Accident, illness, unemployment and economic downturn are all part of the hazards of human life. A commercial lender takes account of them when deciding the terms on which it will lend, including the rate of interest.

36. The provision of the loan was for the purpose of buying a property. No banker could have supposed the defendant to be suggesting that her financial circumstances at the time of taking out the loan were such that in the ordinary way she would be able to keep the amount of the loan in her bank account. If that had been her position, it is unlikely that she would have needed to take out the loan to buy the property, which was the purpose of the loan. The bank knew her financial circumstances, because she was required to disclose them as part of her application. There is no evidence that she did not make a full and frank disclosure of her financial circumstances.

37. The bank was entitled to insist as a term of the loan on her providing it with security in the form of an undated cheque for the amount of the loan, but it would have known that the value of that security was bound to depend on her circumstances at such future time as a default might occur, which might arise for any number of reasons. No reasonable banker could have inferred that she was thereby making a statement that her current economic circumstances were such that the cheque would be met 'in the ordinary course' if presented at any time during the term of the loan on the contingency of a default. Indeed, the expression 'in the ordinary course' does not lend itself to ready understanding in the present context. As I have said, illness, accident and unemployment are not outside the ordinary course of human events over a 20-year period. Was the defendant to be taken as saying that in such an event, resulting in a default, her circumstances at the time of the loan were nevertheless such that the cheque would be met, albeit that she was unable to fulfil her primary repayment obligations? It makes no sense.

38. . . .

39. To summarize, it is easy to see that a person who obtains goods or services by giving a cheque in payment which he knows that he is not going to be in a position to meet, but who does not disclose that fact to the supplier, carries out a form of deception. This was the point made by Robert Goff LJ in *R v Gilmartin* [1983] QB 953. However, I do not accept that a reasonable bank would have understood the defendant, by agreeing to its requirement that she provide an undated cheque as security against the contingency of a default, thereby to be representing impliedly that her current financial circumstances were such as to be able to say with confidence that in the event of that contingency occurring, at any time during the term of the loan, the cheque would 'in the ordinary course' be met.

25.2.1.5 Credit cards and debit cards

When a person presents his credit or debit card he makes a representation (i) that he has the authority to use that card, and (ii) that payment will be made. Under the old law this caused problems. That difficulty is now removed because under the 2006 Act the only requirements are that the representation made is false and that D intends to gain/cause loss by that false representation. However, the difficulty might be said not to be eliminated altogether, but to have shifted from an element of causation in the actus reus to one of mens rea. Under the old law it had to be shown to be by the false representation that D obtained. Under the new law it has to be shown that D intends that by his false representation he will gain.

Consider D who proffers a card which he has no authority to use. The fact that payment will be made by the card-issuing company means that D's representation as to payment will in most cases *not* be false. The debit card contains an undertaking by the bank that, if the conditions on the card are satisfied, the payment will be honoured. The position with credit cards is similar. The bank issuing the card enters into contracts with the trader, agreeing to pay the trader the sum shown on a voucher signed by the customer/confirmed by chip and pin when making a purchase, provided that the conditions are satisfied. In the case of credit cards, the contract between the bank and the trader precedes the purchase by the customer, whereas in the case of the debit card the contract is made when the trader accepts the customer's cheque/debit card, relying on the card which is produced. The trader accepting either type of card will usually do so simply because the conditions on the card are satisfied. He will not know whether the customer is exceeding his authority and using the card in breach of contract with the bank. He will get his money in any event.

Is D making a separate false representation that he is authorized to use the card? Some commentators argue that there is not even a false representation in such circumstances: 'there is no rule of law that the user of a cheque card or credit card is deemed to represent that he has authority to use it' (J. Parry et al, *Arlidge and Parry on Fraud* (3rd edn, 2007), para 4.068). The argument is that there can only be a representation as to authority by D if he thinks that it will matter to V, and since the trader, V, will not care whether D is authorized, there is no false representation. It is submitted this interpretation places too much emphasis on the likely significance to V. That issue is no longer of relevance under the 2006 Act because the question is not whether V might be deceived or believe a matter, but rather whether it is a representation to the trader that D has authority to use the card. If he did not, the trader would not accept it because otherwise the trader would be an accomplice to D's fraud on the bank.

The Law Commission in its Report No 276 stated, at para 7.16:

One of the defects of the present law identified in Part III above, however, is that the concept of deception arguably implies a *belief*, on the part of the victim, in the truth of the proposition falsely represented by the defendant. In general such a requirement would present no more difficulty than the requirement in the pre-1968 law that the property be obtained *by* the false pretence, because if the victim handed over the property despite *not* believing the pretence to be true then the required causal link would not be present. Even where the representation is successful in achieving the desired objective, however, in certain circumstances it is arguably unrealistic to speak of the representee *believing* it. The chief example is the misuse of credit cards and other payment instruments. We now believe that such conduct would be covered in a more convincing and less artificial way if the concept of deception were replaced by that of misrepresentation. Since the merchant who accepts the card in payment does not care whether the defendant has authority to use it, it is debatable whether the merchant can be said to be *deceived*. It is clear from *Charles* and *Lambie*, however, that by tendering the card the defendant is impliedly and falsely *representing* that he or she has authority to use it for the transaction in question. In our view that should suffice, even if the defendant knows that the representee is indifferent whether the representation is true. We have therefore concluded that this form of the new offence should be defined in terms of misrepresentation rather than deception. For most practical purposes, however, the distinction is immaterial.

Is it *by the* false representation as to the authority to use the card that D intends to gain/cause loss/expose to a risk of loss? See *Gilbert* [2012] discussed at section 25.2.5.3, p 839.

■ *Question*

Consider the liability of:

(i) Dim who is unaware of the banking practice whereby the trader is guaranteed to receive payment. What representations has he made?

(ii) Dastardly who is aware of the banking practice and knows that although he is not an authorized user of the card the trader will get his money.

Does it make any difference if the trader does not care whether D has authority?

25.2.1.6 Representations as to 'fact' or 'law' or opinion

Representations as to present facts will create little difficulty for the courts. If D asserts that he is selling a genuine Rolex watch and it is to his knowledge a fake, he commits the offence. Section 2(3) also expressly provides that 'any representation' as to law will suffice. Representations of law ought to be equally simple: for example, D and V are reading a will and D, V's solicitor, deliberately misrepresents its legal effect.

Section 2(3) also provides that a representation as to a state of mind of any person will suffice. A representation as to a present intention of either the accused or some other person will therefore be sufficient. Representations as to present intentions may be express or implied. In *Allen* (section 25.2.1.1, p 828) the Divisional Court held that a statement that amounts only to a promise of future action may have effect as a contractual promise, but will not come within the legal classification of a representation.

■ *Questions*

1. In response to V's demand for payment of his invoice, D sends an email saying he will pay V tomorrow. What is D's liability if:

(a) D had no intention of paying tomorrow and was just fobbing V off?

(b) D genuinely believed that he would be able to pay tomorrow provided D himself was paid today?

2. D advertises his beer as 'probably the best in the world'. Fraud?

3. D embellishes the qualifications on his CV in order to gain a succession of higher paying jobs. Fraud? See *AW* [2010] EWCA Crim 3123.

Problems arise in relation to quotations as to price. Under the old law it was held that it is a misrepresentation of fact for the accused to state 'that they [had] effected necessary repairs to a roof [which repairs were specified], that they had done the work in a proper and work-manlike manner and that [a specified sum] was a fair and reasonable sum to charge for the work involved': *Jeff and Bassett* (1966) 51 Cr App R 28, CA. The evidence showed that nothing needed to be done to the roof, what had been done served no useful purpose, and it could have been done for £5, whereas £35 was charged.

Under the old law, in *Silverman* (1987) 86 Cr App R 213, [1987] Crim LR 574, CA, D charged two elderly sisters grossly excessive prices for work done on their flat. The sisters trusted D and assumed that the price was a fair one. D's conviction for deception was quashed for other reasons but the court said, 'In such circumstances of mutual trust, one party depending on the other for fair and reasonable conduct, the criminal law may apply if one party takes dishonest advantage of the other by representing as a fair charge that which he, but not the other, knows is dishonestly excessive.'

Under the new legislation there are numerous cases in which individuals have been found guilty of fraud in circumstances where they have told the victim, only sometimes incorrectly, that remedial work was required on their property and have then gone on to charge excessive prices for it. For example, in *Wenman* [2013] EWCA Crim 340, D was found guilty of fraud for charging an elderly person £25,600 for work to his house that was actually valued at £800. In *Greig* [2010] EWCA Crim 1183, D was paid £6,850 for work that was unnecessary and in any event should only have cost £300. In this case the jury were invited to infer that D must have dishonestly misrepresented the value of the job given the discrepancy between its true value and what D was paid.

■ *Questions*

1. Suppose a car dealer, aware that the buyer does not know the first thing about cars, sells the buyer a car for £10,000 which he knows to be worth not more than £2,500. Fraud? To what extent does the fraud offence conflict with capitalist ideals of sharp business practice?

2. At V's request D provides a quotation for repair work to V's house. He inflates the actual cost by 20 per cent. Is D guilty of fraud? Does it matter that the reason for his inflating the cost is that D does not really want the job, but does not want to get a reputation for turning down work? Does it matter whether D has worked for V before? Why?

3. In the circumstances of question 2, would it make a difference if the buyer were elderly or otherwise vulnerable? Should it? Consider the previous cases. Could what would otherwise be considered sharp business practice if perpetrated against one 'type' of person constitute fraud if committed against another?

25.2.2 False representations and machines

The prevailing opinion under the old law was that it was not possible in law to deceive a machine. The problem of how to criminalize the 'deception' of a machine has become an acute one in recent years, as businesses become increasingly automated with, for example, facilities to pay by credit card via an automated telephone system or via the internet. The offence under s 2 is capable of meeting some of these difficulties and, coupled with the offence in s 11 of the 2006 Act (section 25.5, p 848), should offer adequate protection against electronic frauds across a wide range of circumstances. See also I. Walden, *Computer Crimes and Digital Investigations* (2007), paras 3.50–3.53.

According to the Explanatory Notes, s 2(5) is designed to put beyond doubt that:

fraud can be committed where a person makes a representation to a machine and a response can be produced without any need for human involvement. (An example is where a person enters a number into a 'CHIP and PIN' machine.) The Law Commission had concluded that, although it was not clear whether a representation could be made to a machine, such a provision was unnecessary [see para 8.4 of their report]. But subsection (5) is expressed in fairly general terms because it would be artificial to distinguish situations involving modern technology, where it is doubtful whether there has been a 'representation', because the only recipient of the false statement is a machine or a piece of software, from other situations not involving modern technology where a false statement is submitted to a system for dealing with communications but is not in fact communicated to a human being (e.g., postal or messenger systems).

Under s 2(5) it is sufficient if 'anything implying' a representation is made in any form to any device.

■ *Questions*

1. Is a document 'submitted' when the defendant saves the typing to his hard drive on his internet-ready computer, or is it only 'submitted' when he sends it via email?

2. Suppose D1 intends to circulate his sales brochure with false statements in it by email at 8 am the following day, and he puts this false prospectus in his 'mail waiting to be sent' box addressed to V. Has he committed the offence?

3. D2, an old-fashioned fraudster, types his sales brochure with false statements on an old typewriter. He puts the typed pages in the out tray waiting for his secretary to put them in an envelope and post them to V. Has he committed an offence?

4. Dodgy, a final year student, wants to sell his old criminal law textbook. It is woefully out of date and worth practically nothing. Dodgy persuades the IT staff to let him have the email addresses of the freshers. He sends an email advertising the book as 'the latest edition, an essential textbook to pass the course'. The IT adviser has unwittingly given D the wrong email prefix. The emails go off into the ether unread. What crime, if any, has Dodgy committed?

25.2.3 'False' representation

The representation must be false. This requires not only that it is untrue or misleading, but that D is aware that it is or might be untrue or misleading. The definition has an element of mens rea. It is necessary for the Crown to establish as a matter of actus reus that the representation is false or misleading aside from any issue about D's knowledge as to its truth or otherwise. However, the states of mind of the parties are likely to be important. Whether a representation is false usually depends on the meaning intended or understood by the parties. That will usually be a question for the jury, even where the statement is made in a document. There may, however, be exceptional cases where the issue is about the legal effect of a document. In those circumstances it is for the judge to decide.

What do the words 'untrue' or 'misleading' mean? The Home Office in its *Response to Consultees* (2004, para 19) accepted that misleading meant 'less than wholly true and capable of an interpretation to the detriment of the victim'.

If the representation is untrue or misleading, there is no explicit defence that the representation was made for good reason or with lawful excuse, as where D said he made the false representation in order to recover property which he believed belonged to him. In such a case the defendant must rely on the claim of a lack of dishonesty.

In *Augunas* [2013] EWCA Crim 2046, the Court of Appeal confirmed that the Crown must prove that D knew the representation was false; it is not sufficient that the reasonable person would have known it to be false. The test is subjective, not objective. McCombe LJ stated:

> A representation is 'false' if it is 'untrue or misleading' and 'the person making it knows that it is, or might be, untrue or misleading'. What is required is that the accused person knows that the representation is, or might be, misleading. It is not enough that a reasonable person might have known this; what matters is the accused person's actual knowledge. In our judgment, it not good enough for the prosecutor to satisfy the jury that the accused ought to have appreciated that the representation made by him was or might be untrue or misleading, nor is it enough that the circumstances must have given rise to a reasonable suspicion that the representation was, or might be, untrue or misleading. Of course, if an accused person wilfully shuts his eyes to the obvious doubts as to the genuineness of the misrepresentation that he is making, then he knows that it might be untrue or misleading and he would be guilty of the offence.

25.2.3.1 Untrue

The word is an ordinary English word and no doubt the courts will suggest that juries should be directed to approach it as such. The only potential difficulties in application relate to those representations made by the accused which are not *wholly* untrue. It should be noted that there is no requirement that the falsity relates to a material particular. The fact that D's representation relates to a peripheral matter will not *entitle* him to an acquittal.

■ *Questions*

1. Don advertises for sale a car: 'Genuine VW, 25,000 miles, one careful owner'. The first two statements are true. The third is not. Is Don guilty of fraud? What if Don claims that it is not *by that falsity* that he intended to gain or cause loss.

2. Delboy, a market trader selling football shirts, shouts that this is 'The one worn by Beckham in person'. All those assembled laugh at the banter. Victor buys the shirt not believing for one minute that it was worn by Beckham. Is Delboy guilty of fraud?

3. Don and Delia book into Victor's hotel as Mr and Mrs Smith. They are not married. At the end of their stay they pay the bill in full. Subsequently, Victor, a devoutly religious man, discovers the lie. He wants to bring a private prosecution against Don and Delia for fraud. Would you advise him that he is likely to succeed?

Problems may arise if the proving that D's statement was untrue requires the prosecution to prove a negative. What of D who advertises his goods for sale adding 'You cannot buy this cheaper anywhere'?

25.2.3.2 Misleading

Being 'untrue' and being 'misleading' are distinct. An untrue statement is one which is literally false—'this is a Renoir painting' when it is not a painting by Renoir. A statement can be
misleading even though it is literally true. Common examples are where D fails to provide a
comprehensive answer to a question.

■ *Question*

V, a potential purchaser, asks D, a car salesman, 'Have you had many faults reported with this
model' and D replies, 'Only one this year'. That is a true statement. D fails to reveal that there
were 200 faults reported the previous year. V does not buy the car in any event as he does not
like the colour. Has D committed a fraud offence?

25.2.4 Dishonesty

The principal element of mens rea for the offence is that of dishonesty. The Law Commission
and the Home Office intended that the *Ghosh* definition should apply, and this is confirmed in
the parliamentary debates (Hansard, HL Debs, 19 July 2005, col 1424 (Attorney General)). If
D is claiming a lack of dishonesty, the *Ghosh* test (taken from *Feely* [1973] QB 530 and *Ghosh*
[1982] QB 1053 (section 21.6, p 772)) provides a two-part mixed subjective and objective test.

(i)   Was what was done dishonest by the ordinary standards of reasonable and honest
      people? If no, not guilty; if yes, consider (ii).

(ii) Must D have realized that what he was doing was dishonest according to these stand-
      ards? If yes, guilty.

The test of dishonesty is based solely on *Ghosh*; there is no equivalent to the Theft Act 1968,
s 2, and therefore D's claims to be acting under a claim of right are no guarantee of acquittal.
If D has a claim of right to the property he should not ordinarily be at risk of criminal liability.
What of D who lies in order to recover property that is his and to which he is legally entitled
but cannot afford the lawyers' bills to recover in a civil action?

The Law Commission in Report No 276 stated:

7.66 We do not therefore recommend that a 'claim of right' should be a complete defence to the
offence of fraud, nor do we recommend that 'belief in a claim of right' should be a complete defence.
However, we believe that in the vast majority of such cases the requirements of *Ghosh* dishonesty will
suffice to ensure that justice is done, and that the civil and criminal law are kept closely in line with
each other.

7.67 The first limb of the *Ghosh* test requires the jury to consider, on an objective basis, whether the
defendant's actions were dishonest. If the defendant may have believed that she had a legal right to
act as she did, it will usually follow that the jury will be unable to conclude that they are sure that she
was dishonest, on an objective basis. In appropriate cases we believe it would be proper for a judge to
direct the jury to the effect that if that is the case then an acquittal should follow, without their having
to consider the second limb of the *Ghosh* test.

7.68 In some exceptional cases it may be important for the judge in summing up to emphasise to
the jury that the 'belief in a claim of right' should be considered in the context of the first limb of the
Ghosh test, rather than the second limb. Such cases may arise where a defendant recognises that
'reasonable and honest' people might consider his actions dishonest, despite also believing that he
had a legal right to act as he did. For example, D works for V plc as a shop manager, and has accrued
many hours of overtime. V plc has failed to pay him for his overtime, despite D's repeated requests

and complaints. D feels that he cannot sue the company for the money, because he would risk being sacked, but on the other hand he cannot afford to let the matter drop. Eventually D uses his position as a manager to take cash from V plc's account. Knowing that he is not authorised to take money from the account to pay himself, he falsifies the documentation. D states in evidence that he genuinely believed that he had a legal right to the money, that he was only taking that which he believed was already his by the only means available to him, but he concedes that he also believed that most reasonable, honest people would consider his actions dishonest. Although he would, on his own admission, have fallen foul of the second limb of the *Ghosh* test, if the jury were not satisfied that his actions were *in fact* dishonest, on the ordinary standards of reasonable and honest people, it would be wrong for them to convict D merely on the basis that he *erroneously* believed that reasonable, honest people would find his actions dishonest.

■ *Questions*
Should D in this example be prosecuted for fraud? Is he dishonest?

As noted in section 21.6, p 772, because *Ghosh* leaves a question of law to the jury to define, the *Ghosh* approach to dishonesty may also fall foul of the ECHR, Article 7, which proscribes retrospective criminalization. The Law Commission initially doubted the potential compliance with the ECHR, Article 7, of a general fraud offence based wholly on dishonesty (LC155, paras 5.33–5.53) and repeated that view in its final Report No 276, *Fraud*. The Fraud Act has been confirmed by the Home Secretary and the Attorney General as being ECHR compatible—as is required by the Human Rights Act 1998, s 19. The Joint Parliamentary Committee on Human Rights, in its Fourteenth Report (2005–6) (at para 2.14) concluded that the new offences were compatible with the ECHR, Article 7 and common law requirements of certainty:

the new general offence of fraud *is not* a general dishonesty offence. Rather, it embeds as an element in the definition of the offence some identifiable morally dubious conduct to which the test of dishonesty may be applied, as the Law Commission correctly observed is required by the principle of legal certainty. We are therefore satisfied that, as defined in the Bill, the new general offence of fraud satisfies the common law and ECHR requirement that criminal offences be defined with sufficient clarity and precision to enable the public to predict with sufficient certainty whether or not they will be liable.

The Committee did, however, confirm that:

a general dishonesty offence would be incompatible with the common law principle of legality. In our view it would also be in breach of the requirement of legal certainty in Articles 5 and 7 ECHR for the same reasons.

Despite the criticism levelled at the test, a five-member Court of Appeal stated emphatically in *Cornelius* [2012] EWCA Crim 500 that the decision in *Ghosh* remains good law.

■ *Question*
What 'morally dubious' element over and above dishonesty renders the conduct criminal?

25.2.5 With intent to gain or cause loss or to expose to a risk of loss

Section 5 defines the meaning of 'gain' and 'loss' for the purposes of ss 2 to 4.

(1) The references to gain and loss in sections 2 to 4 are to be read in accordance with this section.

(2) 'Gain' and 'loss'—

    (a) extend only to gain or loss in money or other property;

    (b) include any such gain or loss whether temporary or permanent;

    and 'property' means any property whether real or personal (including things in action and other intangible property).

(3) 'Gain' includes a gain by keeping what one has, as well as a gain by getting what one does not have.

(4) 'Loss' includes a loss by not getting what one might get, as well as a loss by parting with what one has.

The definitions are essentially the same as those in the Theft Act 1968, s 34(2)(a). Under these definitions, 'gain' and 'loss' are limited to gain and loss in money or other property. 'Property' in this context is defined as in the Theft Act 1968, s 4(1), section 21.4, p 754. The definition of 'property' covers all forms of property; the Act is coherent with the Theft Act. None of the special exceptions in s 4 of the 1968 Act apply: there can be fraud with intent to gain/cause loss of land, wild animals and flora, but they cannot be stolen. In *Idrees v DPP* [2011] EWHC 624 (Admin), D paid someone to impersonate him in order to ensure that he passed his driving test. The Divisional Court upheld D's conviction, demonstrating that 'gain' is not confined to financial gain, presumably the licence was the property.

■ *Question*

There is a separate offence in s 174 of the Road Traffic Act 1988 of knowingly making a false statement for the purpose of obtaining a driving licence. Should D have been charged with that offence rather than fraud?

In addition, there is no requirement that actual loss is caused, nor even that V's economic interests are imperilled. In its Report No 276, the Law Commission stated:

Arguably the full offence should not be committed unless the defendant has succeeded in *actually* causing a loss or making a gain: where the defendant has acted with *intent* to cause loss or make a gain, but that intent has been frustrated, a conviction of attempt would adequately reflect the criminality of the defendant's conduct. It may sometimes be debatable, however, whether a loss has actually been caused or a gain made, whilst it is clear beyond doubt that the defendant *intended* to bring about one or both of those outcomes. We think it would be unfortunate if, in such a case, it had to be determined whether there had in fact been gain or loss within the meaning of the Act, when that question had little bearing on the gravity of the defendant's conduct or the appropriate sentence. We think that, as in the case of those offences under the Theft Act 1968 whose definitions employ the concepts of gain and loss, it should be sufficient if the defendant acts *with intent* to make a gain or to cause a loss.

25.2.5.1 Loss or gain

In most cases 'an intention to gain' and an 'intention to cause loss' will go hand in hand; V's loss will be D's gain. The phrase 'intent to cause loss' is not, however, superfluous. There may be circumstances in which D intends to cause a loss to V without any corresponding gain to D, for example where D lies to V to pay X. Problems arose in some cases under the old law because the deception might cause a gain which did not correspond to a loss.

■ *Questions*

1. D works for Alpha Co. He starts a false rumour that a competitor Beta is going out of business. Fraud?

2. What if D intends to gain the formula to a drug that another pharmaceutical company, his arch rival, makes a lot of money from producing? Can such information constitute 'property' for the purposes of fraud? Think back to *Oxford v Moss* (1979) 68 Cr App R 183 (section 21.4.3 p 756).

25.2.5.2 Intention

Intention should bear its ordinary meaning, and should extend as elsewhere in the criminal law to include the foresight of a virtually certain consequence (see section 5.2.2, p 109). This may be significant in extending the scope of the offences. For example, it is sufficient that D makes a false representation foreseeing that it is virtually certain to cause loss to V although that is not his purpose, and although he hopes that V will not lose.

25.2.5.3 Remoteness

As noted, the causal issue of whether V was deceived to transfer property, etc, was an element of actus reus in the old deception offences. It has become an issue of mens rea in the Fraud Act offences. The question is whether it is '*by the*' false representation that D *intended* to make the gain or cause the loss. This is an important feature of the offence that must be proven in every case and was considered in *Gilbert* [2012] EWCA Crim 2392.

G, S and H were charged with various offences including a count of fraud contrary to s 2 of the Fraud Act 2006. The particulars were that between 1 December 2008 and 30 January 2009 they had dishonestly and with the intent made false representations to Lloyds Bank in that they had supplied false details in support of an application to open a bank account. When applying to open the bank account for a building company, a meeting with a bank official had taken place and a checklist form had been completed. During the meeting, H dishonestly informed the bank that savings and assets were available to fund property development. G then signed a form confirming the truth of the information they had provided. After the account was opened, the company acquired computers and office equipment by issuing post-dated cheques to the supplier. The company subsequently stopped the cheques, causing a loss to the supplier of approximately £130,000. G was convicted of fraud in relation to the dishonest representations made to the bank. However, it was not suggested that she was party to the fraudulent scheme to acquire the computer equipment. There was disputed evidence about who had written on the form that G had 'savings' that would be available.

The defence argued that without proof the word 'savings' had been written by G, there was no 'misrepresentation' under s 2 and further that the prosecution had never identified any particular loss or gain. The recorder allowed the case to go to the jury on the basis that G might gain from future legitimate property development, rather than a gain arising directly from any representation made at the meeting at the bank or directly from the opening of the bank account. The recorder also directed the jury that it was open to them to find that a gain could be inferred if they concluded that the opening of the bank account was simply to enable development or the sale of the company.

The Court of Appeal quashed the conviction.

> An intention to make a gain (or to cause loss to another or expose another to risk of loss) is not of itself enough to meet the requirements of the section. In order to commit fraud by representation, a defendant must (a) make a false representation as defined in s.2(2)–(5) of the Act, (b) do so dishonestly and (c) intend, *by making the representation*, to make a gain (or to cause loss to another or expose another to a risk of loss). The jury must, therefore, be sure that the defendant intended to make a gain or cause loss or exposure to loss by making the false representation and it is a matter for the jury on the facts of each case whether the causative link between the intention and the making of the false representation, required by the section, is established. (per Roderick Evans J at [29])

In this case, although the word 'savings' might have amounted to a false representation, it was not proved that it was *by that falsity* that the defendant intended to cause loss to the bank or make a gain.

■ *Questions*

1. How remote can D's intentions be? Suppose that D makes false representations to induce V, a wealthy lawyer, to marry him. Is he guilty of the s 2 offence if one intention is to enrich himself?

2. D, a journalist working for a tabloid newspaper, dresses up as an Arab sheikh and ingratiates himself with celebrities. He makes false statements to them about who he is and about his wealth. His aim is to get them to provide him with gossip which he can use in his column in the newspaper. Fraud?

25.2.5.4 Claims of entitlement to the gain

It is not necessarily a good defence that D believes he has a right to the gain or loss he seeks. If he has such a belief, then he might not be dishonest under *Ghosh*, but he still has the intention to gain (and/or to cause loss). D lies to V to get back the money V owes him. What is the 'gain' to D? In the false accounting case of *A-G's Reference (No 1 of 2001)* [2002] Crim LR 844, the Court of Appeal held that the element of intent to gain is satisfied by proof of an intention to 'acquire' property even if it is that property to which D is entitled.

■ *Questions*

1. D is sick and tired of V who has not returned the lawnmower that D lent him months ago. D tells V falsely that D's mother-in-law is coming and it is crucial that he mows the lawn. Fraud?

2. D is a generous character and usually lends V money when he asks. On this occasion V asks D for a loan and D denies it to him by saying falsely that he has no money to spare. Is D guilty of fraud?

25.2.5.5 Exposure to temporary loss

Unlike theft, there is no requirement that D acts with intent to deprive V permanently of any property. It would seem to be sufficient under s 2, for example, that D makes a false representation to V with intent to cause V to lend D property which D intends to return in an unaltered form. The offence comes close to criminalizing dishonest deprivation of the value of an item's usefulness. This strains the property-based foundation of the offence. It supports the argument that the offence is one centred on lying. See further, D. Ormerod, 'Criminalising Lying' [2007] Crim LR 193.

25.2.5.6 Intention to expose another to a risk of loss

It is sufficient that D intends that V will be exposed to the risk of loss; there is no need for the Crown to prove that D had a more specific intention that V will lose. D, who makes a false representation on his health insurance form, will be liable (under s 2). He intends the insurance company to be exposed to a risk of loss, even though he desperately hopes that he will remain healthy and they will not incur actual loss. How much of a risk must there be though? Should there be a defence of *de minimis* or would this be relevant to the issue of whether D was dishonest?

25.2.6 Knowing that the representation is or might be false

The third element of the mens rea in the s 2 offence is that D must know that the representation he makes is or might be false. The varieties of criminal knowledge that will satisfy this element are: knowledge that it *is untrue*; knowledge that it *might be untrue*; knowledge that it *is misleading*; knowledge that it *might be misleading*.

25.2.6.1 Knowledge

Knowledge is a strict form of mens rea. It is much stricter than 'belief', 'suspicion', 'having reasonable grounds to suspect' and even 'recklessness'. See section 5.5, p 138.

Definitions of knowledge in criminal cases in England were rare until relatively recently. In *Montila* [2004] 1 WLR 3141, the House accepted (at [27]) that:

A person cannot know that something is A when in fact it is B. The proposition that a person knows that something is A is based on the premise that it is true that it is A.

Subsequently, in *Saik* [2006] UKHL 18 the House of Lords concluded:

the word 'know' should be interpreted strictly and not watered down...knowledge means true belief.

In the present context, proof of knowledge will often be by inference—D must have known the statement was untrue having regard to the surrounding circumstances—rather than by express admission by D.

■ *Question*

In response to V's demand for payment of his invoice, D sends an email saying he will pay V tomorrow. What is D's liability if D genuinely believed that he would be able to pay tomorrow because he hoped he would receive payment from his debtors today?

It is sufficient that D is shown to have known that his representation *might* be false. Is the offence rendered too wide by this alternative mens rea?

■ *Questions*

D who sells works of art tells a customer that he has a Renoir for sale.

(i)   D knows that there is a risk, as with all art, that the painting might be a fake. D knows that the statement *might be* misleading. Fraud?

(ii)   What if D admits that he thought of the possibility of such a risk and dismissed it from his mind? Is that knowledge that the statement might be false?

(iii)   What of D who simply failed to check the provenance of the painting properly because he was in such a rush to open the gallery?

The Attorney General addressed this example:

> If an art dealer said, 'This is a painting by Renoir', knowing that that statement can have a huge impact on the value of the painting—but not knowing whether it is true and thinking that it might be untrue—it would be for a jury to decide whether he was dishonest. If he was dishonest, I see no difficulty in saying that he is guilty of fraud in those circumstances. (Hansard HL 19 July 2005, col 1417)

■ *Question*

Do you think it is right that the dealer is exposed to a prosecution for fraud in these circumstances?

25.3 Section 3: fraud by failing to disclose information

Section 3 provides the second form of the general fraud offence introduced by section 1.

A person is in breach of this section if he—

(a) dishonestly fails to disclose information to another person, which he is under a legal duty to disclose, and

(b) intends, by failing to disclose the information—

    (i) to make a gain for himself or another, or

    (ii) to cause loss to another or to expose another to a risk of loss.

The elements of the offence: failing to disclose information to a person; being under a legal duty to disclose; dishonestly, with an intention to make a gain/cause loss.

R v Razoq
[2012] EWCA Crim 674, Court of Appeal, Criminal Division

(Hallett LJ, Griffith Williams and Singh JJ)

D was a Syrian national who had fled Syria and sought asylum in the UK. D was a doctor and wished to practise in the UK. In addition to his working for an NHS hospital, D also began to work for a number of locum agencies. A few months into practising, D was subject to disciplinary proceedings and suspended from his work at the hospital. The letter notifying D of his suspension warned him not to undertake work for any locum agency during the period of his suspension. This was in addition to the guidelines sent to all doctors by the General Medical Council (GMC) stipulating the same thing. D said that he had not read these documents, as they seemed like common sense. The locum agencies that D had signed up to work for all stated in their terms of employment that they must be notified if D became subject to disciplinary proceedings; D failed to notify them that he had been suspended from work, as he claimed he had never seen these documents. The prosecution alleged that D was under a legal duty within the meaning of the Fraud Act to disclose any exclusion, either as an express term in the contract, as an implied term in the contract or because it was a contract of utmost good faith and it was a material matter to be disclosed. D's case was that he did not believe he was under a legal duty to disclose his exclusion or that it was material to the work from the locum service, because his GMC registration was unaffected. He did not intend to gain as a result and he was not acting dishonestly. He genuinely believed that he could do the work involved properly, he intended to do the work and he did the work. D stated that the failure to disclose had no effect on his qualifications or his capacity and intention to do the work. The judge directed the jury that they could either find that the duty was implied within the terms of the contract or that it existed because the contract was one of utmost good faith.

Hallett LJ:

...[Counsel] helpfully summarised the various elements of the offences. The actus reus of an offence contrary to section 2 is making a false, i.e an untrue, or misleading representation.

The mens rea, however, is three-fold. First, it is making a representation that the accused knows is or might be untrue or misleading. The second is the accused intends to make a gain by the representation. The third is the question of dishonesty.

Similarly the actus reus of an offence contrary to section 3 is making a misleading, i.e incomplete, representation when under a legal duty to disclose. The mens rea is the same, save for the fact that a further issue might arise as to whether an accused knows of the existence of a legal duty to disclose.

[Counsel] did not argue that it was necessary to prove that an accused knew of the existence of a legal duty, but he reminded the court properly that lack of knowledge of such legal duty would be relevant to dishonesty. The section 3 offence is, in effect, he submitted a narrower form of the section 2 offence.

As far as the legal duty was concerned, the judge, perhaps influenced by a number of commentaries in the textbooks about the effect of the Fraud Act, took a cautious approach. Having found as a matter of law on a submission of no case that a legal duty to disclose did exist via two routes, (1) as an implied term of the contract and the conditions under which the doctor was registered with the GMC and (2) because the contracts into which he entered were contracts of utmost good faith, having come to those conclusions as a matter of law, however he left the jury three possible routes as to how a legal duty might arise. He did not withdraw the issues of an implied term and contract of utmost good faith from them. He directed them that a legal duty might only be imputed by an express term if the express term had been brought to the doctor's attention. He therefore left to them the question of whether or not the contracts had been received by the doctor and he had been made aware of the express terms to disclose.

As we have indicated, he also left to them the question of whether or not there was an implied term, or whether or not the contracts were of utmost good faith.

The Court of Appeal stated that the question of what constitutes a legal duty is one of law for the judge, who should direct the jury that if they find certain facts proved they could conclude that a duty to disclose existed in all the circumstances. The court accepted that the evidence was overwhelming that D was legally bound to inform the various agencies of his exclusion. Further, the court observed that D must have received the vast majority of all the documents, if not all of them. For this reason, it was held that it was plainly open to the jury to conclude that the express terms were brought to his attention and he was contractually and legally bound to disclose his suspension.

■ *Questions*

Consider the relationship with s 2 (section 25.2, p 825). Are all cases under s 3 capable of being prosecuted under s 2? Does it matter? Note that neither s 2 nor s 3 creates an offence: both are forms of the s 1 offence. Is it fair to charge D with an offence under s 1 without specifying which form of the offence is being alleged?

25.3.1 Legal duty to disclose

The concept of 'legal duty' is explained in the Law Commission's Report, *Fraud*, which stated:

7.28 Such a duty may derive from statute (such as the provisions governing company prospectuses), from the fact that the transaction in question is one of the utmost good faith (such as a contract of insurance), from the express or implied terms of a contract, from the custom of a particular trade or market, or from the existence of a fiduciary relationship between the parties (such as that of agent and principal).

7.29 For this purpose there is a legal duty to disclose information not only if the defendant's failure to disclose it gives the victim a cause of action for damages, but also if the law gives the victim a right to set aside any change in his or her legal position to which he or she may consent as a result of the non-disclosure. For example, a person in a fiduciary position has a duty to disclose material information when entering into a contract with his or her beneficiary, in the sense that a failure to make such disclosure will entitle the beneficiary to rescind the contract and to reclaim any property transferred under it. For example where a person in a fiduciary position has a duty to disclose material information when contracting with a beneficiary, a failure to make such disclosure will entitle the beneficiary to rescind the contract and to reclaim any property transferred under it.

The statute is much narrower than original proposals which included breaches of moral duties or duties arising from an expectation in the mind of the person with whom D is dealing. Nevertheless, it opens an extremely broad vista of criminal liability. One limitation seems to be implicit: that there is to be no conflict with the civil law. The Attorney General confirmed that:

the Government believe that it would be undesirable to create this disparity between the criminal and the civil law; it should not be criminal to withhold information which you are entitled to withhold under civil law. (Hansard HL, 19 July 2005, col 1426)

A straightforward example of the operation of s 3 will arise where D fails to reveal relevant information on an application form for a loan, a mortgage, life insurance, etc.

■ *Questions*

1. Consider the facts of *Rai* in section 25.2.1.1, p 828. Would Rai be guilty under s 2 or s 3? Does it matter?

2. Do you think it appropriate that the defendant in *Razoq* was prosecuted for fraud or should this case have been dealt with by the GMC by way of disciplinary proceedings?

3. Given that there exists uncertainty in civil law about when an implied term will be read into a contract, is this really a suitable basis for criminal liability?

25.3.2 Failing to disclose information

The duty must be one which is to disclose 'information'. That concept is not defined.

Liability appears to be strict as to the existence of a duty. If D claims that he lacked the knowledge or awareness of the duty to disclose that will be subsumed within his plea that he was not dishonest. What of the person who claims that he disclosed the level of information he thought was necessary?

25.3.3 Dishonesty

The *Ghosh* test will apply, as discussed in section 21.6, p 772. The element of dishonesty will be especially important in cases where D claims that he was not aware of his duty and/or that he believed that he had satisfied that duty. This much is borne out by *Razoq*, section 25.3, p 842. Remember that D claimed he had been unaware of the existence of a legal duty to disclose his exclusion from the hospital, having regarded the decision whether to tell the locum agencies as one entirely for himself. The judge directed the jury that D's knowledge as to the existence of a legal duty, or lack of knowledge, went directly to the issue whether he had acted dishonestly.

25.3.4 Intent to gain or cause loss/expose to a risk of loss

This element of the mens rea is discussed at section 25.2.5. There is no requirement that the intention is to cause a loss by which D gains. Nor need there be any intention for the loss to be caused to the person to whom the duty is owed.

■ *Question*

D completes his private health insurance form and fails to mention that he is a heavy smoker. When challenged about this, he claims that he never intended that the health insurance company would be caused a loss as he never intended to become ill. Is he guilty of the offence under s 3?

25.4 Section 4: fraud by abuse of position

(1) A person is in breach of this section if he—

   (a) occupies a position in which he is expected to safeguard, or not to act against, the financial interests of another person,

   (b) dishonestly abuses that position, and

   (c) intends, by means of the abuse of that position—

      (i) to make a gain for himself or another, or

      (ii) to cause loss to another or to expose another to a risk of loss.

(2) A person may be regarded as having abused his position even though his conduct consisted of an omission rather than an act.

As with ss 2 and 3, the terms of the offence are easy to describe. The actus reus comprises abusing a position in which D is expected to safeguard the interests of another and the mens rea comprises acting dishonestly, an intention by the abuse to make a gain/cause loss. None of the essential terms—'position', 'expected', 'abuse', 'dishonesty'—are defined. Professors Ashworth and Horder state that this is the most controversial of the sections because, 'its key terms crumble into vagueness when scrutinized' (A. Ashworth and J. Horder, *Principles of Criminal Law* (2013), p 408).

The section is designed to catch the secret profiteers such as the wine waiter who sells his own bottles, passing them off as belonging to the restaurant and pocketing the proceeds of sale: *Doukas* [1978] 1 All ER 1071. It extends much wider than that narrow category of case. The CPS has listed examples of circumstances in which s 4 should be charged to guide prosecutors—see http://www.cps.gov.uk/legal/d_to_g/fraud_act/. These include: an employee of a software company who uses his position to clone software products with the intention of selling the products on his own behalf; a person employed to care for an elderly or disabled person with access to that person's bank account who abuses that position by removing funds for his own personal use; an employee who abuses his position in order to grant contracts or discounts to friends, relatives and associates; a trader who helps an elderly person with odd jobs, gains influence over that person and removes money from their account; the person entrusted to purchase lottery tickets on behalf of others. These demonstrate the reach of the offence.

25.4.1 A 'position'

The Law Commission explained the meaning of 'position':

> 7.38 The necessary relationship will be present between trustee and beneficiary, director and company, professional person and client, agent and principal, employee and employer, or between partners. It may arise otherwise, for example within a family, or in the context of voluntary work, or in any context where the parties are not at arm's length. In nearly all cases where it arises, it will be recognised by the civil law as importing fiduciary duties, and any relationship that is so recognised will suffice. We see no reason, however, why the existence of such duties should be essential. This does not of course mean that it would be entirely a matter for the fact-finders whether the necessary relationship exists. The question whether the particular facts alleged can properly be described as giving rise to that relationship will be an issue capable of being ruled upon by the judge and, if the case goes to the jury, of being the subject of directions.

Despite the Law Commission's explanation, Ashworth and Horder deride this element of the offence as having, 'the rigidity of a marshmallow' (A. Ashworth and J. Horder, *Principles of Criminal Law* (2013), p 409).

■ *Questions*

1. Mrs Hinks looks after a vulnerable old man, Mr Dolphin. She ingratiates herself with him. He makes gifts of £60,000 and a plasma TV to Hinks. What would the prosecution need to prove to succeed in a prosecution under s 4? Compare *Hinks* [2000] UKHL 53, section 21.3, p 742.

2. Dastardly is short of cash to pay the window cleaner who calls to collect his money. Dastardly raids his daughter's piggy back, taking the £20 she has saved over months. Fraud?

3. Devious, aged 42, is concerned that his elderly parents are spending too much of their savings in their retirement years. They keep taking expensive holidays and luxury cruises. He persuades them to let him have control over their finances and moves a large sum into his own personal account. He claims that he was only preventing them squandering the money and was protecting their long-term interests. Is he guilty under s 4?

4. V lends his neighbour, D, a door key to V's house to allow D access to the garden where D is repairing the fence between their properties. Whilst in the property, D answers a phone call on V's phone informing 'the householder' that he has won £25,000 in a prize draw. D accepts the money without telling V. Is D guilty of the offence under s 4?

25.4.2 'Occupies a position'

The section applies only in relation to the positions D 'occupies'. It is clear that the 'abuse' with intent to gain or cause loss must arise while D is in occupation of that position in order for s 4 to apply. According to the Solicitor General in the course of debates in the Standing Committee:

> A person can occupy a position where they owe a duty that goes beyond the performance of a job. A contract that is entered into that obliges a person to have duties of confidentiality, perhaps, can go well beyond the time when that employment ceases. The duty may, however, still arise. The person entered into the duty at the beginning of the employment and it exists indefinitely. Therefore a person may still occupy a position in which there is a legitimate expectation. That may well, by virtue of a contract and the agreement that the employee entered into voluntarily, go beyond redundancy or the point when he leaves the post. (Standing Committee B, 20 June 2006, col 23)

■ *Questions*

D is employed by Blue Co. He realizes that one of the deals they are negotiating might involve corrupt payments. He makes secret copies of the negotiation memos, against company policy, and retains them in case it becomes necessary to show that he was not involved in the corruption. Twelve months later D is made redundant for unrelated reasons. He offers to sell the negotiation memos to a tabloid newspaper. Does he commit the s 4 offence? When? Consider also liability under s 6, section 25.6, p 851.

25.4.3 'Expected' to safeguard

The scope of the 'position' is to some extent dependent on the definition of the term 'position in which he is expected to safeguard'. Whose expectation counts? If it is the victim's, this could be a very wide scope of liability subject to the defendant denying liability by way of a lack of dishonesty. If it is a test based on what D thinks his financial duties are, it might be very limited and difficult to prove.

The Government's decision not to limit the offence to cases in which the law imposes a duty of financial responsibility—trustee and beneficiary, employer and employee, etc—was controversial. That limit, if it had been adopted, would have provided a clear boundary to the scope of the offence.

Section 4(2) makes clear that the offence can be committed by omission as well as by positive action.

■ *Questions*

1. Doss, an employee of Arsenal Football Club, is given responsibility for securing a star player, Rolando, to play for them next season. Doss fails to do so. Consider his liability under s 4 if:

(a) Doss discovered that his friend Eddy who worked for Chelsea was interested in Rolando so did not bother bidding. Doss knew that Eddy needed to secure the deal to keep his job; or

(b) Doss simply forgot to make contact with Rolando's agent.

2. Dodgy, a final year student, wants to sell his old criminal law textbook. It is woefully out of date and worth practically nothing. Dodgy offers to pay Keith, a member of the IT staff, if he will let Dodgy have the email addresses of the incoming freshers. Dodgy intends to email them to offer the book for sale. What offences, if any, have been committed?

25.4.4 Dishonesty

The definition is as in *Ghosh* (section 21.6, p 772). In cases in which there is no legal or fiduciary duty on the accused, it is difficult to see what additional element of conduct which is morally dubious prevents the offence being one based solely on dishonesty. As the Joint Parliamentary Committee on Human Rights recognized, such an offence would be likely to infringe Article 7 (section 25.2.4, p 837).

It would appear that liability is strict as to whether D occupies a position in which he is expected to safeguard the financial interests of another. D's lack of awareness that he is in such a position must be subsumed in a plea of lack of dishonesty. There is no explicit mens rea requirement that the defendant must be aware of the existence of any expectation that he must safeguard the financial interests of another.

Like the other forms of the offence, the one in s 4 turns on dishonesty. In *Woods* [2011] EWCA Crim 1305, D appealed her conviction of fraud by abuse of position. D was the deputy manager of a betting shop. D was working alone in the shop when she was approached by a punter wishing to place a £1 bet at 9 to 1 on a horse running in a race in South Africa. Having received the betting slip and money, D altered the stake to £100 and returned the bottom copy to the customer. The appellant rang up the bet on the till as a £100 bet. The horse won. The customer returned to the counter, not realizing that his bet of £1 had been altered to £100; he was happy to receive his original stake of £1 and his £9 winnings. D handed him a £10 note. However, D then went to the safe, counted out £990, placed the money in envelopes and put the envelopes in her bag. When D completed her shift she left with the money in her bag. D knew that such conduct was against her employer's policy, but she contended that she was not guilty of fraud because she was not intending to cause loss or to make dishonest gain because had the horse lost she would have put £90 in the till to cover her personal bet. D's alleged abuse of position was in altering the stake from £1 to £100. D was found guilty and the Court of Appeal upheld her conviction.

■ *Questions*

Why was Woods not charged with theft of the money? Was it because when she appropriated the money from the safe, it in fact belonged to her as it constituted the proceeds of her winning bet? Does the decision in *Hinks* [2000] UKHL 53, section 21.5, p 757 mean that she could still be charged with theft even if the money were lawfully hers, provided that she was dishonest? Does this demonstrate that there is a significant overlap between fraud and theft? Why might a prosecutor decide to charge one rather than the other in a case such as this?

25.4.5 Intent to gain/cause loss

See section 25.2.5, p 837.

25.5 Section 11: obtaining services dishonestly

As the Law Commission explained in Report No 276:

8.1 Because it requires proof of deception, the offence under section 1 of the 1978 Act fails to catch a person who succeeds in obtaining a service dishonestly but without deceiving anyone. This may happen in various ways.

(1) The service may be obtained by the defendant's failure to disclose a material fact, rather than by a positive deception.

(2) The service may not be provided for the defendant *personally*, but for anyone who is there to receive it. For example, the defendant climbs over the fence of a football ground and watches the match without paying the admission charge.

(3) The service may not be provided directly by *people* at all, but through a machine. For example, the defendant downloads, via the internet, software or data for which a charge is made, or which is available only to those within a certain category of person who have paid to be included within that category, by giving false credit card or identification details; or receives satellite television transmissions by using an unauthorised validation card in a decoder.

(4) Some cases are a hybrid of types (2) and (3). For example, the defendant gives false credit card details to an automated booking system, or tenders a forged or stolen credit card to an electronic vending machine, and thus obtains a ticket for a journey or entertainment. There is no deception of the booking system (because it is not a person), nor of the staff who check the tickets of the passengers or audience (because the staff are only interested in whether each person has a ticket, not how they got it).

The Law Commission's proposal as endorsed by the Home Office was to remove the troublesome element of deception from the offence and to place the emphasis on dishonesty.

Section 11 now provides:

(1) A person is guilty of an offence under this section if he obtains services for himself or another—

(a) by a dishonest act, and

(b) in breach of subsection (2).

(2) A person obtains services in breach of this subsection if—

(a) they are made available on the basis that payment has been, is being or will be made for or in respect of them,

(b) he obtains them without any payment having been made for or in respect of them or without payment having been made in full, and

(c) when he obtains them, he knows—

(i) that they are being made available on the basis described in paragraph (a), or

(ii) that they might be, but intends that payment will not be made, or will not be made in full.

(3) A person guilty of an offence under this section is liable—

(a) on summary conviction, to imprisonment for a term not exceeding 12 months or to a fine not exceeding the statutory maximum (or to both);

(b) on conviction on indictment, to imprisonment for a term not exceeding 5 years or to a fine (or to both).

According to the Law Commission: 'This offence would be more analogous to theft than to deception, because it could be committed by "helping oneself" to the service rather than dishonestly inducing another person to provide it' (LC276, para 8.8).

The actus reus comprises (i) an act resulting in the obtaining; (ii) of services; (iii) for which payment is or will become due; and (iv) a failure to pay in whole or in part. The mens rea comprises (i) dishonesty; (ii) knowing that the services are to be paid for or knowing that they might have to be paid for; (iii) with intent to avoid payment in whole or in part.

25.5.1 An act

It is not possible to commit the offence by omission alone.

■ *Question*

D goes to watch his favourite film at the local cinema. At the end of the presentation he remains in his seat and ducks down so that no usher sees him. Twenty minutes later the film is shown again and D sits up and enjoys watching for the second time that evening. Has he committed an offence under the Fraud Act?

25.5.2 Obtaining

Unlike ss 2 to 4, this offence is not inchoate; it requires the actual obtaining of the service. The offence is drafted in similar terms in some respects to the offence under s 1 of the 1978 Act. The troublesome issue of whether a 'benefit has been conferred' is not replicated. There is still a causal element in this offence. D's dishonest act must be the cause of the service being obtained. The obtaining may be for D or another.

25.5.3 A service

'Service' is not further defined.

■ *Questions*

1. Suppose that H hires V to kill H's wife, W, and V does so. H gives in payment a cheque that H knows will not be honoured. Is H guilty of a s 11 offence?

2. By way of an elaborate scheme, D tops up his mobile telephone by charging the cost to unwitting victims, thereby accruing huge costs on their bills. Does D commit an offence under s 11? In *Mariusz Mikolajczak v District Court in Kalisz, Poland* [2013] EWHC 432 (Admin), Keith J held that this would not be an offence under s 11 as D was not obtaining a service, but rather was obtaining credit. Do you agree?

25.5.4 For which payment has been, is being or will be made

The offence is restricted in that it only applies to services for which payment is required. This follows the old s 1 offence under the 1978 Act. Some of the situations in which D obtains a service for free by making a false representation will be caught by s 2 (section 25.2). As under the old law, an application for a bank account or credit card will only be caught by this offence if the service is to be paid for.

In *Sofroniou* [2004] Crim LR 381, [2003] EWCA Crim 3681, the Court of Appeal dismissed S's appeal against conviction for obtaining a service by deception under the old s 1 offence when he used a false identity to deceive or attempt to deceive banks into providing him with banking services and credit cards. There was no charge for opening the bank accounts or issuing the cards. S overdrew on one account and exceeded the limit on one credit card. He was convicted under s 1 of the 1978 Act, and appealed on the basis that there was no evidence that the 'benefit' would be paid for. The court stated that 'there should no longer be any doubt but that dishonestly inducing a bank or building society to provide banking or credit card services is also within the section, provided the requirement as to payment is also satisfied'.

Section 11 catches D who climbs over the wall at his local cricket club and watches the game without paying the entrance fee. It also catches D who uses false network cards to enable his television to receive cable/satellite television channels for which he has no intention of paying. It was suggested that it would also catch D illegally downloading music.

25.5.4.1 Without payment

One problem which the s 11 offence was designed to tackle was where D obtains the relevant service by unauthorized use of a credit card or debit card. But does the offence work bearing in mind that even though the use of the card is unauthorized, the payment will be made by the bank/issuing company provided that the PIN is correct and the security number accurate, etc?

■ *Questions*

1. D makes a false representation to a machine by using the card when he is not authorized to do so. He obtains a service—say, a theatre ticket. Has he committed the s 11 offence?

2. Is D liable under s 2? What has he obtained?

25.5.5 Dishonesty

The *Ghosh* test applies (section 21.6, p 772).

25.5.6 Knowing that the services are to be paid for/might have to be paid for

The additional requirement that D knows that the services are to be paid for or knows that they might have to be paid for is a relatively strict test.

25.5.7 Intention that payment be avoided

The additional requirement that D acts with intent to avoid payment in whole or in part marks a departure from the old s 1 offence and narrows the offence. In many cases where D has made a false representation to obtain services, he will commit the s 2 offence and his claim that he was intending to pay may well be irrelevant unless it is sufficiently plausible to negative his intent to cause loss or dishonesty. The Law Commission were keen to emphasize the limits so that it will not apply, for example, where DD, parents of D, lie about their religion in order to get D into a private school where they will be charged and pay the full fees. The intention to pay precludes liability. This is narrower than the 1978 Act offence.

25.6 Section 6: possession of articles for use in fraud

Section 6 provides a wholly new offence. The Law Commission had proposed simply to replace the form of the s 25 Theft Act offence (see *Smith and Hogan* (13th edn), p 970) which covered 'going equipped' with implements for 'deception', with one covering going equipped for 'fraud'. The Home Office in its consultation exercise in 2004 (para 41) proposed much wider reform. The Home Office wanted an offence of mere possession of, for example, computer software for use in 'the course of or in connection with' a fraud. One particular concern of the Home Office was clearly the widespread use of software to read credit cards. Is s 2, section 25.2 (and inchoate versions of it) wide enough to meet these concerns?

Section 6 of the Fraud Act 2006 provides:

(1) A person is guilty of an offence if he has in his possession or under his control any article for use in the course of or in connection with any fraud.

(2) A person guilty of an offence under this section is liable—

    (a) on summary conviction, to imprisonment for a term not exceeding 12 months or to a fine not exceeding the statutory maximum (or to both);

    (b) on conviction on indictment, to imprisonment for a term not exceeding 5 years or to a fine (or to both).

25.6.1 'Article'

The 2006 Act provides a broad definition of the term in s 8:

> (1) For the purposes of—
>
>   (a) sections 6 and 7, and
>
>   (b) the provisions listed in subsection (2), so far as they relate to articles for use in the course of or in connection with fraud,
>
> 'article' *includes* any program or data held in electronic form.

The Home Office Explanatory Notes on the Act, para 26, state that:

> Examples of cases where electronic programs or data could be used in fraud are: a computer program can generate credit card numbers; computer templates can be used for producing blank utility bills; computer files can contain lists of other peoples' credit card details or draft letters in connection with 'advance fee' frauds.

There is no requirement that the program or data is designed exclusively for fraud. Any word processing or spreadsheet program is capable of being used to produce false invoices or false utility bills. It is difficult to see any restriction on the concept of an 'article' which might limit the offence. A printer and computer, or even a humble pen and paper, are articles and capable of being used in the course of or in connection with fraud and are capable of being possessed.

■ *Questions*

Is there anything that would not constitute an 'article' for the purposes of the Act? What about the bank account into which D intends to direct the proceeds of his various frauds?

25.6.2 Has in his possession

There is no requirement that the articles are held in possession in any particular venue. Any article in the possession of the person, whether at home, in public or at work, is capable of satisfying this element of the offence. The term applies to the possession of tangible items such as a deck of marked cards or false die and clearly extends to possessing data on a computer such as software to create false utility bills or for skimming credit cards.

■ *Questions*

1. D's son, E, has downloaded onto his laptop software to pirate DVDs. D is unaware of that fact. Does D commit the offence if (i) the computer remains in E's bedroom? (ii) D borrows E's laptop to take to a work conference? What must the prosecution establish that D knew? (iii) D sees the software on the laptop but does not know what its function is. Can he be liable under s 6?

2. D discovers the software on E's computer and realizes what it is, and then deletes it by moving it to the recycle bin on the computer. Does D remain liable under s 6? Cf *Porter* [2006] EWCA Crim 560, [2006] Crim LR 748.

25.6.2.1 Control

Use of the words 'possession' or 'control' must suggest that Parliament intended them to be capable of applying differently. The offence requires possession or control of the *article* that is used in the illicit manner or in connection with the fraud, not control of the illicit use per se. The Court of Appeal has considered this aspect of the s 6 offence in two cases.

In *Tarley* [2012] EWCA Crim 464, D and his co-accused were convicted of being jointly in possession of articles for use in fraud. D's case was that he had no proprietorial right to the property, nor did he exercise or could have exercised control over it. The judge stated that there was little in the Act to assist him in interpreting what was meant by 'possession' or 'control'. Any guidance derived from offences of being in possession of a firearm or drugs would be imperfect. The judge found that on a true construction of the statute D, if he shared a common purpose that the articles be used in the fraud and knew this was why they were carried, and thus exactly the 'scam' intended, was jointly responsible and consequently jointly in possession and had joint control. In upholding D's conviction, Rafferty LJ stated that, 'this is a classic joint enterprise case. We do not accept that an individual cannot be in joint possession and control of items in an application of the doctrine to facts such as these.'

In *Rasoul* [2012] EWCA Crim 3080, one of D's associates was arrested and four envelopes were seized from him. One of the envelopes was addressed to D and contained a National Insurance number, an immigration status document and a residence permit indicating a grant of indefinite leave to remain. The immigration document and residence permit were found to be wholly counterfeit, while the National Insurance number was a valid number issued to a British male last known to be living in Essex. It was never issued to D. D was arrested and pleaded guilty to being in possession of an article for use in fraud. On appeal, D claimed that the National Insurance card was never in his possession. It was in the possession of his associate, who was about to post it to him. The prosecution's contention was that D had control of it. D denied this also and cited the case of *Peaston* (1979) 69 Cr App R 203, [1979] Crim LR 183 in support of his argument:

18. Mr Whelan, counsel for the appellant, in an attractive argument, submitted that as a matter of law he did not even have control. He relied principally on the case of *Peaston* (1979) 69 Cr.App.R 203 which involved a charge under section 5 of the Misuse of Drugs Act 1971. In that case the question was whether the defendant had drugs in his possession. He had ordered the supplier to send drugs to his address and the envelope had arrived and been put through the letter box in the premises where he lived. In those circumstances the court held that he was properly to be regarded as in possession. The goods had been delivered at his invitation. Counsel relies upon the fact that the possession here resulted from the drugs actually having been received by him at his address. Section 37(3) of the Misuse of Drugs Act provides that a person shall be taken to be in possession of anything which is subject to his control, even if it is in the hands of a third party. The submission is that that would have been an easy route to finding possession in this case if the fact that he had ordered these drugs was sufficient, without actual delivery, to constitute possession. So counsel submits that on the authority of that case a mere direction to somebody to send the illicit goods cannot of itself constitute control.

19. We do not accept that submission. We think there are a number of difficulties with it. First, the issue of control and indeed section 37(3) itself was never referred to by the court in *Peaston*. The Court did not need to consider whether there was control, and therefore possession, even without delivery of the goods because that did not arise on the facts. Second, and in any event, as Mr Smith QC (counsel for the prosecution) submits, there may be a different principle in relation to the definition of control under the Fraud Act than there is in the Misuse of Drugs Act The two statutes have different objectives. Third, in this case we do not know precisely what the facts were concerning the relationship between the appellant and his co-accused who were involved in the drugs activity. There never was a trial and so the precise nature of the relationship between them was never explored.

20. We accept that there is a nice question whether or not it could be said that there is control in these circumstances, but we are far from satisfied that such a defence would probably have succeeded so that we can say that there is a clear injustice. In the circumstances, therefore, we reject the appeal against conviction. (per Elias LJ)

1. D, in England, subscribes to a service offered by a company in Russia which allows him online access to software which can pirate DVDs. Does he commit the s 6 offence?

2. Does the Court of Appeal, in the cases analysed previously, expand the scope of the s 6 offence too far by permitting guilt where there is arguably only constructive possession of the article in question? How should 'control' be interpreted?

25.6.2.2 For use in the course of or in connection with

The form of words used is extremely wide. The offences of fraud are so wide that the items which might be used in connection with such activities are endless. D possesses an article which he intends to use if only in the course of covering his tracks after the commission of an offence; would this be enough to found liability under s 6?

25.6.2.3 Any fraud

There is no guidance on the scope of this concept. Is this limited to frauds under the Act? Is conspiracy to defraud caught as well? Is it restricted to the commission of the offence as principal offender or as an accessory or conspirator? Logically, the use must relate to future use. Past illicit use can be evidence of a current intention as to future use.

■ *Questions*

1. D enters a cinema with a camcorder intent on recording the film. Does he commit the s 6 offence? What would the prosecution have to establish?

2. D, a journalist working for a tabloid newspaper, buys a new outfit to enable him to dress up as an Arab sheikh and ingratiate himself with celebrities. He plans to make false statements to them about who he is and about his wealth. His aim is to get them to provide him with gossip which he can use in his column in the newspaper. Is he guilty of the s 6 offence when he buys the outfit?

25.6.2.4 Mens rea

As the Home Office Explanatory Notes, para 25, make clear, a general intention to commit fraud will suffice. The Home Office response to consultation was that the prosecution 'should have to prove a general intention that the article be used by the possessor (or someone else) for a fraudulent purpose, though they should not have to prove intended use in a particular fraud.' Parliament confirmed that the offence was not one of strict liability. The intention is clearly for this offence to follow the mens rea of the s 25 offence. In interpreting that offence in *Ellames* [1974] 3 All ER 130, the court said that:

In our view, to establish an offence under s 25(1) the prosecution must prove that the defendant was in possession of the article, and intended the article to be used in the course of or in connection with some future burglary, theft or cheat. But it is not necessary to prove that he intended it to be used in the course of or in connection with any specific burglary, theft or cheat; it is enough to prove a general intention to use it for some burglary, theft or cheat; we think that this view is supported by the use of the word 'any' in s 25(1). Nor, in our view, is it necessary to prove that the defendant intended to use it himself; it will be enough to prove that he had it with him with the intention that it should be used by someone else.

In *Sakalouskas* [2013] EWCA Crim 2278, the Court of Appeal confirmed that the interpretation given to s 25 of the Theft Act 1968 in *Ellames* applied in relation to s 6. Mitting J stated:

7. In our judgment, the observations of the court in *Ellames* in relation to [section] 25 apply with equal force to an offence charged under section 6. If it were not so, then it is easy to see how an innocent person who knew that an article used by somebody else for the purpose of fraud would commit an offence under section 6 if he knowingly had it in his possession. That cannot have been the intention of Parliament. The intention of Parliament as in the case of section 25 was to prevent the possession of articles that were intended for use then or in the future, not those which had been used in the past.

■ *Questions*

1. D opens a drawer in his new office and is horrified to find a machine with the exclusive function of credit card cloning. It is for use in fraud only and has no legitimate function. Is he liable under s 6?

2. D opens the drawer in his new office and finds what he thinks is a credit card cloning machine. He is delighted at the prospect of using it. In fact, the machine is a useless piece of machinery which would never produce a plausible copy. Is he liable for any offence?

25.7 Section 7: making, adapting, etc articles for fraud

Section 7 provides for a further broad offence:

(1) A person is guilty of an offence if he makes, adapts, supplies, or offers to supply any article—

    (a) knowing that it is designed or adapted for use in the course of or in connection with fraud, or

    (b) intending it to be used to commit, or assist in the commission of, fraud.

(2) A person guilty of an offence under this section is liable—

    (a) on summary conviction, to imprisonment for a term not exceeding 12 months or to a fine not exceeding the statutory maximum (or to both);

    (b) on conviction on indictment, to imprisonment for a term not exceeding 10 years or to a fine (or to both).

There are in fact several distinct versions of the offence contained in s 7. There are obviously differences between making, adapting, supplying and offering to supply. Section 7(1)(a) is narrower in requiring that the article *is* for use in connection with fraud (otherwise there could be no knowledge that it is for such use: *Montilla* [2004] UKHL 50 and *Saik* [2006] UKHL 18). Under s 7(1)(b) there is no requirement that the article is so designed, etc provided D intends it to be used. Section 7(1)(b) is narrower in a different respect, being restricted to articles for use in the commission of fraud, whereas s 7(1)(a) is wider—encompassing use in connection with fraud.

The only example of its operation provided in the Explanatory Notes to the Act is that where:

a person makes devices which when attached to electricity meters cause the meter to malfunction. The actual amount of electricity used is concealed from the provider, who thus makes a loss.

25.7.1 Makes or adapts

These narrow forms of the offence seem to be uncontroversial. Interpretation of these terms will rely on similar expressions used, for example, in relation to weapons and elsewhere in the criminal law.

25.7.1.1 Supplies or offers to supply

Given that we are dealing with the supply of articles for illegal purposes, it is unlikely that the courts will take a restrictive or unduly technical approach to the term. The term 'offer to supply' should at least be restricted so as not to extend to cases of mere invitation to treat. A supply clearly does not have to be a commercial supply.

25.7.1.2 Knowing that it is designed or adapted for such use

The requirement is of knowledge. Unlike the offence of handling stolen goods, there is no alternative that D can be convicted on proof of belief alone. This is a relatively strict mens rea requirement. Knowledge involves a state of mind of true belief. Note that the requirement is that D makes, etc any article knowing that it *is* designed for use in the course of or in connection with fraud. The knowledge must exist at the time of the making, adapting, supply or offer to supply. Subsequent knowledge is insufficient.

25.7.2 Intending it to be used to commit or assist in committing

This is an alternative form of mens rea to knowledge. Intention here will presumably include not only direct intention in the sense of purpose, but also an oblique intention (section 5.2, p 98) where the defendant sees the use of the article for fraud as virtually certain. The section does not require an intention that the person who is the maker, adapter or supplier use the item for a fraudulent purpose himself: what is required is that the article will be so used. Who will so use it is immaterial. That intention will therefore embrace the supplier of an item which he knows will be used for, or to assist in, fraud undertaken by the recipient or another person.

As an example of the offence in operation, in *Kirtland* [2012] EWCA Crim 2127, D supplied forged first-class travel passes. A railway company operated a system whereby its contracted staff could travel first class whilst they were on duty. Staff were issued with an annual pass to enable them to do this. These were the passes that D forged and sold to his unwitting customers. D was convicted of an offence under s 7. What frauds were the passes designed or adapted to be of use in?

FURTHER READING

S. P. Green, *Lying Cheating and Stealing: A Moral Theory of White Collar Crime* (2005)

L. Katz, *Ill-Gotten Gains: Evasion, Blackmail, Fraud and Other Kindred Puzzles of the Law* (1996)

D. Ormerod, 'A Bit of A Con: The Law Commission's Proposals on Fraud' [1999] Crim LR 789

D. Ormerod, 'Criminalising Lying' [2007] Crim LR 193

D. Ormerod and D. H. Williams, *Smith's Law of Theft* (9th edn, 2007), Ch 3

26

Burglary and related offences

26.1 Burglary

Burglary involves D either (i) entering a building as a trespasser with intent to commit certain specified offences or (ii) having entered a building as a trespasser committing one of a list of specified offences.

26.1.1 Introduction

Some of the controversies that will be explored in this chapter include the following:

(i) there is disagreement as to the rationale for the existence of burglary as an offence separate from theft, etc. Some argue that burglary is an anachronism that has been made redundant because it is always possible to charge an attempt to commit the specified offences. Others argue that burglary embodies a distinct type of wrongdoing;

(ii) burglary has become an increasingly technical offence and the cases substantiating the requirements of certain elements of it conflict.

(iii) the offence relies on the notion of 'trespass', which is a civil law concept. D must have intention or be reckless to the facts which make him a trespasser. However, problems can arise when D has been invited to enter for a particular purpose or by a person in the household who is not the owner. In addition, the time at which D must be aware that he is a trespasser depends upon which form of burglary is charged;

(iv) burglary of a dwelling is a distinct offence from that of a non-dwelling. However, dwelling is not defined in the 1968 Act and there is no definitive case law either;

(v) aggravated burglary is a serious offence, with a statutory maximum sentence of life imprisonment. Within the offence are a number of important distinctions, depending on which form of the offence D would have committed.

Burglary is an offence that has existed for centuries, but was only codified in statute relatively recently. Although the non-legal understanding is that burglary consists of 'breaking and entering', the offence is no longer defined in that manner.

Under the Theft Act 1968 burglary can now be committed in one of four ways and it is important to appreciate the distinctions between each variation, given how technical they have become. The elements of the various forms of the offence are:

(1) D enters (a) a building or part of a building (b) as a trespasser (c) with intent (d) to commit an offence of theft, criminal damage or GBH; or

(2) D enters (a) a building or part of a building (b) as a trespasser (c) once in the building D steals or inflicts GBH on a person therein or attempts either of those things; or

(3) D enters (a) a dwelling or part of a dwelling (b) as a trespasser (c) with intent (d) to commit an offence of theft, criminal damage or grievous bodily harm; or

(4) D enters (a) a dwelling or part of a dwelling (b) as a trespasser (c) once in the building D steals or inflicts GBH on a person therein or attempts either of those things.

Burglary is one of the most serious offences contained in the 1968 Act, as reflected by the statutory maximum sentence of ten years' imprisonment upon conviction, or 14 years if the building is a dwelling. In addition, it is also one of the most prevalent offences that is committed in England and Wales each year. Given its seriousness and the frequency with which it is committed, it is surprising that it remains unclear precisely what harm the offence of burglary is designed to protect against. Is it: the invasion of private space and the associated sense of violation; the risk of violent confrontation; or aggravated forms of theft or violence? (See G. R. Sullivan and A. P. Simester, 'On the Nature and Rationale of Property Offences' in R. A. Duff and S. P. Green (eds), *Defining Crimes* (2005), pp 168, 192.) Perhaps it would be better to abandon the search for a single, overarching justification for the offence? For example, Stuart Green argues that the offence involves the primary wrong of theft, GBH, etc in addition to a secondary wrong, consisting of the violation of the victim's sense of security. (See S. P. Green, *13 Way To Steal A Bicycle* (2012), pp 122–123.)

26.1.2 The external elements

Theft Act 1968, s 9

(1) A person is guilty of burglary if—

(a) he enters any building or part of a building as a trespasser and with intent to commit any such offence as is mentioned in subsection (2) below; or

(b) having entered any building or part of a building as a trespasser he steals or attempts to steal anything in the building or that part of it or inflicts or attempts to inflict on any person therein any grievous bodily harm.

(2) The offences referred to in subsection (1)(a) above are offences of stealing anything in the building or part of a building in question, of inflicting on any person therein any grievous bodily harm . . . , and of doing unlawful damage to the building or anything therein.

(3) A person guilty of burglary shall on conviction on indictment be liable to imprisonment for a term not exceeding—

(a) where the offence was committed in respect of a building or part of a building which is a dwelling, fourteen years;

(b) in any other case, ten years.

> (4) References in subsections (1) and (2) above to a building, and the reference in subsection (3) above to a building which is a dwelling, shall apply also to an inhabited vehicle or vessel, and shall apply to any such vehicle or vessel at times when the person having a habitation in it is not there as well as at times when he is.

Note that burglary included entering a building as a trespasser with intent to rape a person therein, until this element of the offence was replaced by the Sexual Offences Act 2003, s 63—trespassing with intent to commit a sexual offence (see section 26.5, p ***).

■ *Questions*

1. Would it make sense to have different offences: trespass with intent to steal, trespass with intent to injure, etc? Would this ensure better conformity with the principle of fair labelling or would such distinctions make the law overly complex?

2. Is burglary an inchoate offence? Apart from the trespass, is it all a matter of mens rea?

3. Is Robinson correct in his assertion that burglary is a 'special form of codified attempt'? Why might it be accurate to conceptualize the offence in this way? (See P.H. Robinson, *Criminal Law* (1997), p 776.)

4. Might burglary's continued existence be justified by arguing that the offence compensates for the under inclusiveness of the actus reus of attempts? If D inserts a bamboo pole with a magnet attached through a letterbox with the aim of snatching car keys but is interrupted before he can do so, would he be guilty of attempted theft? Attempted burglary? Burglary? Which offence is the most appropriate one to charge D with? See the facts of *Mahoney* [2009] EWCA Crim 1234.

26.1.2.1 Entry

At common law the insertion of any part of D's body, however small—a finger through an opening—was a sufficient entry. It seems that Parliament assumed when passing the Theft Act 1968 that the common law would continue to apply (see Hansard, HL Debs, vol 290, cols 85 and 86). The courts have not done what was expected. In *Collins* [1972] 2 All ER 1105 (in the next extract), Edmund Davies LJ appears to suggest that the law has changed so that it now requires a 'substantial and effective' entry. In *Brown* [1985] Crim LR 212, however, it was held there was a sufficient entry where D's feet were on the ground outside a shop and the top half of his body was inside the broken shop window, as if he was rummaging for goods displayed there. The court said that the word 'substantial' did not materially assist but the entry must be 'effective' and in that case it was. Perhaps D was already in a position to steal? Similarly, in *Ryan* [1996] Crim LR 320, D became trapped by the neck with only his head and right arm inside the window. His argument that his act was not capable of constituting an entry because he could not have stolen anything was rejected. These latter cases seem to undermine the assertion of Edmund Davies LJ in *Collins* that entry must be 'substantial and effective'.

■ *Questions*

1. In what sense could Ryan's entry be said to be 'effective'?

2. Could Ryan have been guilty of attempted theft? Does the fact that he was charged with burglary tell us something about the purpose of the offence?

3. Why was Ryan not charged with attempted burglary instead?

Parliament cannot have intended that D must have got so far into the building as to be able to accomplish his unlawful purpose, as this would arguably undermine the rationale for the offence. D who enters intending to cause GBH to V is surely guilty of burglary when he enters through the ground-floor window though V is on the fourth floor. Thus it is hard to see that there is any requirement that the act be either an 'effective' or a 'substantial' entry. *Ryan* decided only that there was evidence on which a jury could find that D had entered. This suggests that it is open to a jury to find D had not. It is unsatisfactory in principle that it should be open to a jury to find that there is no entry when such facts are established. Is the best course to accept the continued existence of the common law rule? It at least has the benefit of being a relatively certain test and one that is easy to apply.

■ *Questions*

Has D 'entered' when he: (i) uses his 9-year-old child to climb through the window to steal; (ii) uses a trained animal to do so; (iii) pokes a telescopic grab handle through the letterbox to seize property inside the building; (iv) sends a letter bomb to V's house through the post?

26.1.2.2 As a trespasser

R v Collins

[1972] 2 All ER 1105, Court of Appeal, Criminal Division, http://www.bailii.org/ew/cases/EWCA/Crim/1972/1.html

(Edmund Davies and Stephenson LJJ, Boreham J)

The facts of this case are memorable given how extraordinary they are. The appellant, Stephen Collins, was convicted of burglary with intent to commit rape. (At that time the burglary offence included entering as a trespasser with intent to rape. That offence has been replaced with one discussed at section 26.3, p 871. For the purposes of the discussion of trespass, the case remains good law.) The complainant went to bed one evening with her bedroom window open; the bed being located somewhere near the open window. In the early hours of the morning, the complainant awoke to find the appellant standing naked (except for his socks) in her window with an erect penis. Importantly, the complainant was unable to remember whether the appellant was standing on the outside of the windowsill, or on that part of the sill which was inside the room. Thinking that the figure in the window was her boyfriend, the complainant sat up in bed. The appellant then descended from the window and the pair had sex. When the complainant realized that the man with whom she had had sex was not her boyfriend, she slapped him and he promptly left. The appellant told the police that he had been drinking at the time and that he had climbed the ladder to the complainant's bedroom with the intention of trying to have sex with her.

[Edmund Davies LJ delivered the judgment of the court:]

Now, one feature of the case which remained at the conclusion of the evidence in great obscurity is where exactly the appellant was at the moment when, according to him, the girl manifested that she was welcoming him. Was he kneeling on the sill outside the window or the inner sill? It was a crucial matter, for there were certainly three ingredients that it was incumbent on the Crown to establish. Under s 9 of the Theft Act 1968, which renders a person guilty of burglary if he enters any building or part of a building as a trespasser and with the intention of committing rape [note that this version of the offence has been repealed by the Sexual Offences Act 2003], the entry of the appellant into the building must first be proved. Well, there is no doubt about that, for it is common ground that he did enter this girl's bedroom. Secondly, it must be proved that he entered as a trespasser. We will develop that point a little later. Thirdly it must be proved that he entered as a trespasser with intent at the time of entry to commit rape therein.

The second ingredient of the offence—the entry must be as a trespasser—is one which has not, to the best of our knowledge, been previously canvassed in the courts. Views as to its ambit have naturally been canvassed by the textbook writers, and it is perhaps not wholly irrelevant to recall that those who were advising the Home Secretary before the Theft Bill was presented to Parliament had it in mind to get rid of some of the frequently absurd technical rules which had been built up in relation to the old requirement in burglary of a 'breaking and entering'. The cases are legion as to what this did or did not amount to, and happily it is not now necessary for us to consider them. But it was in order to get rid of those technical rules that a new test was introduced, namely that the entry must be 'as a trespasser'.

What does that involve? According to the learned editors of Archbold [*Criminal Pleading, Evidence and Practice* (37th edn, 1969), p 572, para 1505]:

'Any intentional, reckless or negligent entry into a building will, it would appear, constitute a trespass if the building is in the possession of another person who does not consent to the entry. Nor will it make any difference that the entry was the result of a reasonable mistake on the part of the defendant, so far as trespass is concerned.'

If that be right, then it would be no defence for this man to say (and even were he believed in saying), 'Well, I honestly thought that this girl was welcoming me into the room and I therefore entered, fully believing that I had her consent to go in'. If Archbold is right, he would nevertheless be a trespasser, since the apparent consent of the girl was unreal, she being mistaken as to who was at her window. We disagree. We hold that, for the purpose s 9 of the Theft Act 1968, a person entering a building is not guilty of trespass if he enters without knowledge that he is trespassing or at least without acting recklessly as to whether or not he is unlawfully entering.

A view contrary to that of the learned editors of Archbold was expressed in Professor J C Smith's book on *The Law of Theft* [then in its first edition (1968), pp 123, 124, para 462], where, having given an illustration of an entry into premises, the learned author comments:

'It is submitted that . . . D should be acquitted on the ground of lack of mens rea. Though, under the civil law, he entered as a trespasser, it is submitted that he cannot be convicted of the criminal offence unless he knew of the facts which caused him to be a trespasser or, at least, was reckless.'

The matter has also been dealt with by Professor Griew [then in its first edition *The Theft Act 1968*, pp 52, 53, para 4-05] who in his work on the Theft Act 1968 had this passage:

'What if D wrongly believes that he is not trespassing? His belief may rest on facts which, if true, would mean that he was not trespassing: for instance, he may enter a building by mistake, thinking that it is the one he has been invited to enter. Or his belief may be based on a false view of the legal effect of the known facts: for instance, he may misunderstand the effect of a contract granting him a right of passage through a building. Neither kind of mistake will protect him from tort liability for trespass. In either case, then, D satisfies the literal terms of section 9(1): he "enters . . . as a trespasser". But for the purposes of criminal liability a man should be judged on the basis of the facts as he believed them to be, and this should include making allowances for a mistake as to rights under the civil law. This is another way of saying that a serious offence like burglary should be held to require mens rea in the fullest sense of the phrase: D should be liable for burglary only if he knowingly trespasses or is reckless as to whether he trespasses or not. Unhappily it is common for Parliament to omit to make clear whether mens rea is intended to be an element in a statutory offence. It is also, though not equally, common for the courts to supply the mental element by construction of the statute.'

We prefer the view expressed by Professor Smith and Professor Griew to that of the learned editors of Archbold. In the judgment of this court, there cannot be a conviction for entering premises 'as a trespasser' within the meaning of s 9 of the Theft Act 1968 unless the person entering does so know-ing that he is a trespasser and nevertheless deliberately enters, or, at the very least, is reckless whether or not he is entering the premises of another without the other party's consent.

Having so held, the pivotal point of this appeal is whether the Crown established that the appellant at the moment that he entered the bedroom knew perfectly well that he was not welcome there or, being reckless whether he was welcome or not, was nevertheless determined to enter. That in turn involves consideration as to where he was at the time that the complainant indicated that she was welcoming him into her bedroom. If, to take an example that was put in the course of argument, her bed had not been near the window but was on the other side of the bedroom, and he (being determined to have her sexually even against her will) climbed through the window and crossed the bedroom to reach her bed, then the offence charged would have been established. But in this case, as we have related, the layout of the room was different, and it became a point of nicety which had to be conclusively established by the Crown as to where he was when the girl made welcoming signs, as she unquestionably at some stage did.

How did the learned judge deal with this matter? We have to say regretfully that there was a flaw in his treatment of it. Referring to s 9, he said:

> '. . . there are three ingredients. First is the question of entry. Did he enter into that house? Did he enter as a trespasser? That is to say, did he—was the entry, if you are satisfied there was an entry, intentional or reckless? And, finally, and you may think this is the crux of the case as opened to you by [counsel for the Crown], if you are satisfied that he entered as a trespasser, did he have the intention to rape this girl?'

The judge then went on to deal in turn with each of these three ingredients. He first explained what was involved in 'entry' into a building. He then dealt with the second ingredient. But he here unfor-tunately repeated his earlier observation that the question of entry as a trespasser depended on 'was the entry intentional or reckless?' We have to say that this was putting the matter inaccurately. This mistake may have been derived from a passage in the speech of counsel for the Crown when replying to the submission of 'No case'. Counsel for the Crown at one stage said:

> 'Therefore, the first thing that the Crown have got to prove, my Lord, is that there has been a tres-pass which may be an intentional trespass, or it may be a reckless trespass.'

Unfortunately the trial judge regarded the matter as though the second ingredient in the burglary charged was whether there had been an intentional or reckless entry, and when he came to develop this topic in his summing-up that error was unfortunately perpetuated. The trial judge told the jury:

> 'He had no right to be in that house, as you know, certainly from the point of view of [the girl's mother], but if you are satisfied about entry, did he enter intentionally or recklessly? What the Prosecution say about this is, you do not really have to consider recklessness because when you consider his own evidence he intended to enter that house, and if you accept the evidence I have just pointed out to you, he, in fact, did so. So, at least, you may think, it was intentional. At the least, you may think it was reckless because as he told you he did not know whether the girl would accept him.'

We are compelled to say that we do not think the trial judge by these observations made it sufficiently clear to the jury the nature of the second test about which they had to be satisfied before the appel-lant could be convicted of the offence charged. There was no doubt that his entry into the bedroom was 'intentional'. But what the appellant had said was, 'She knelt on the bed, she put her arms around me and then I went in'. If the jury thought he might be truthful in that assertion, they would need to consider whether or not, although entirely surprised by such a reception being accorded to him, this young man might not have been entitled reasonably to regard her action as amounting to an invita-tion to him to enter. If she in fact appeared to be welcoming him, the Crown do not suggest that he should have realised or even suspected that she was so behaving because, despite the moonlight, she thought he was someone else. Unless the jury were entirely satisfied that the appellant made an effective and substantial entry into the bedroom without the complainant doing or saying anything to cause him to believe that she was consenting to his entering it, he ought not to be convicted of the offence charged. The point is a narrow one, as narrow maybe as the window sill which is crucial to this case. But this is a criminal charge of gravity and, even though one may suspect that his intention was to commit the offence charged, unless the facts show with clarity that he in fact committed it he ought not to remain convicted.

Some question arose whether or not the appellant can be regarded as a trespasser ab initio. But we are entirely in agreement with the view expressed in Archbold [*Criminal Pleading, Evidence and Practice* (37th edn, 1969) p 572, para 1505] that the common law doctrine of trespass ab initio has no application to burglary under the Theft Act 1968. One further matter that was canvassed ought perhaps to be mentioned. The point was raised that, the complainant not being the tenant or occupier of the dwelling-house and her mother being apparently in occupation, this girl herself could not in any event have extended an effective invitation to enter, so that even if she had expressly and with full knowledge of all material facts invited the appellant in, he would nevertheless be a trespasser. Whatever be the position in the law of tort, to regard such a proposition as acceptable in the criminal law would be unthinkable.

We have to say that this appeal must be allowed on the basis that the jury were never invited to consider the vital question whether this young man did enter the premises as a trespasser, that is to say knowing perfectly well that he had no invitation to enter or reckless of whether or not his entry was with permission. The certificate of the trial judge, as we have already said, demonstrated that he felt there were points involved calling for further consideration. That consideration we have given to the best of our ability. For the reasons we have stated, the outcome of the appeal is that this young man must be acquitted of the charge preferred against him. The appeal is accordingly allowed and his conviction quashed.

Appeal allowed. Conviction quashed

■ *Questions*

1. When did Collins enter the building? At that time what intention did he have?

2. When did Collins make a 'substantial' entry into the building? For what purpose was that entry also 'effective'?

3. Was the daughter's permission to enter the building enough to prevent Collins being a trespasser?

R v Jones; R v Smith

[1976] 3 All ER 54, Court of Appeal, Criminal Division

(James, Geoffrey Lane LJJ and Cobb J)

Jones and Smith were convicted of burglary. Two television sets were removed in the early hours of the morning from the home of Smith's father (Alfred) without his knowledge or consent. The sets were subsequently found in the possession of the son Christopher Smith and his friend John Jones. At their trial for burglary, Alfred Smith said that Christopher would not be a trespasser in his house at any time. The Court of Appeal dismissed their appeal against conviction, holding that:

a person is a trespasser for the purpose of s 9(1)(b) of the Theft Act 1968 if he enters premises of another knowing that he is entering in excess of the permission that has been given to him, or being reckless whether he is entering in excess of the permission that has been given to him to enter, providing the facts are known to the accused which enable him to realise that he is acting in excess of the permission given or that he is acting recklessly as to whether he exceeds that permission, then that is sufficient for the jury to decide that he is in fact a trespasser. (per James LJ)

James LJ [having read s 9(1) stated that]:

The important words from the point of view of the argument in this appeal are 'having entered any building . . . as a trespasser'.

It is a section of an Act of Parliament which introduces a novel concept. Entry as a trespasser was new in 1968 in relation to criminal offences of burglary. It was introduced in substitution for, as an improvement on, the old law, which required considerations of breaking and entering and involved distinctions of nicety which had bedevilled the law for some time.

Counsel for the appellants argues that a person who had a general permission to enter premises of another person cannot be a trespasser. His submission is as short and as simple as that. Related to this case he says that a son to whom a father has given permission generally to enter the father's house cannot be a trespasser if he enters it even though he had decided in his mind before making the entry to commit a criminal offence of theft against the father once he had got into the house and had entered that house solely for the purpose of committing that theft. It is a bold submission. Counsel frankly accepts that there has been no decision of the court since this Act was passed which governs particularly this point. [His lordship referred to *Collins*, earlier in this section, p 860, where the court approved the interpretation suggested by J. C. Smith.]

Appeals dismissed

■ *Questions*

1. D must have mens rea as to his status as a trespasser. Would Jones have thought he was a trespasser? Would Collins have thought he was a trespasser when the complainant invited him in to have sex?

2. Suppose that in *Jones and Smith*, Smith had lived at the house with his parents. Would he have been guilty of burglary? Would Jones?

3. Dan, who is going out with Stella, knows that Peter, Stella's father, has formed a strong dislike of him and has forbidden him ever to enter Peter's house. But, at Stella's invitation, he enters Peter's house one evening without Peter's knowledge. Just before he leaves, Dan steals Peter's riding boots. Is Dan a burglar? Would it make any difference to your answer if Dan had accepted Stella's invitation only because he wished to steal Peter's riding boots?

4. Would it ever be possible for D to be a trespasser for the purposes of the criminal law, but not the law of tort? Should it be possible? Think back to what Lord Steyn said in *Gomez* [2001] 2 AC 241 in relation to the interpretation of 'appropriation' see section 21.3, p 742.

5. Glanville Williams thinks that the decision in *Jones and Smith* contradicts that in *Collins*, since in that case 'it must have been held . . . that the defendant was not a trespasser although, since he intended to commit rape if necessary, he knew that his intention was "in excess of the permission" (TBCL 849). The court in *Jones and Smith* evidently did not consider this aspect of it. If *Jones and Smith* is right, *Collins* should have been convicted of burglary'. Do you agree?

In *Barker* (1983) 47 ALR 1, High Court of Australia, D, asked to look after V's house during V's absence, entered and stole certain goods. His conviction for burglary was upheld. Murphy J, dissenting, said that to regard such a case as one of burglary would depart very far from the traditional concept of burglary; it would mean that one who accepted an invitation to dinner would be guilty of burglary if he intended to steal a teaspoon. See further P. J. Pace, 'Burglarious Trespass' [1985] Crim LR 716.

■ *Questions*

1. What must D do to render him a trespasser for the purpose of burglary?

2. For the purposes of staging a sit-in, students enter the main administrative offices of the university. They believe (wrongly) that, as students of the university, they are entitled to go anywhere on university premises. One of them steals a file from the registry office. Is he a burglar?

3. Why does burglary include the requirement that D enters the building as a trespasser? Should it not suffice that D enters the building with the requisite ulterior intent? Is Fletcher correct to state that this requirement ensures that the offence retains an element of 'manifest criminality' or is it simply redundant? (See G. P. Fletcher, *Rethinking Criminal Law* (2000), p 125.)

Where it is open to the prosecution to do so the prosecution will normally rely on s 9(1)(b) rather than s 9(1)(a) (eg where the burglar steals or attempts to steal in the building). The reason for that is that under s 9(1)(b) it is not necessary to prove that D entered with the relevant intent. But, whichever limb is relied on, the prosecution must prove that D entered as a trespasser. It is not enough that D becomes a trespasser, for example by hiding in a store until after closing time: *Laing* [1995] Crim LR 395, CA. D who does so may, of course, thereafter commit burglary by entering another 'part' of the store as a trespasser.

■ *Question*

In its Model Criminal Code, the Australian Institute of Criminology included the offence of 'break out', committed when D obtains entry to premises with consent, but remains on the premises after the initial consent has been revoked. Would the creation of such an offence in England and Wales be desirable or is the current law satisfactory?

26.1.2.3 Building or part of a building

In *Stevens v Gourley* (1859) 7 CBNS 99, a question arose whether a wooden structure measuring 16 by 13 feet and intended to be used as a shop was a building for the purposes of the Metropolitan Building Act 1855, though it was without foundations and merely rested on timbers laid on the surface. Byles J observed that a building must be 'intended to be permanent, or at least to endure for a considerable time'. So what of the portable cabins placed at building sites to provide eating and toilet facilities for those working on the site? Would it make any difference that the works are planned to take months or only a matter of days? In *B and S v Leathley* [1979] Crim LR 314, Carlisle Crown Court, a freezer container had been placed in a farmyard for goods storage. For some two or three years it had been resting on sleepers, was connected to the mains electricity and the doors were equipped with locks. It was held to be a building. Cf *Norfolk Constabulary v Seekings and Gould* [1986] Crim LR 167, Norwich Crown Court. Needing extra storage space, a supermarket had two lorry trailers towed to the site. There they were unhitched, left standing on their wheeled chassis and connected to the mains electricity. Steps were provided for access and entry was made by unlocking the trailer shutters. They had been in use for a year when D and E tried to effect an entry. It was held that the trailers remained vehicles and had not become buildings. What if their tyres had been removed to prevent anyone taking them from the site?

In considering the appropriate interpretation of 'building' in s 2 of the Cremation Act 1902, Lord Neuberger MR in *R (Ghai) v Newcastle City Council* [2010] EWCA Civ 59, stated that if one approaches the issue of what 'building' means by making a preliminary assumption, it would be incorrect to take a somewhat artificially narrow meaning of the word and then see whether the context justifies a more expansive meaning. It is more appropriate to take the word's more natural, wider, meaning and then consider whether, and if so to what extent, that meaning is cut down by the statutory context in which the word is used.

It is important to remember that s 9(4) of the Theft Act 1968 confirms that 'building' encompasses inhabited vehicles and vessels, including when they are unoccupied.

■ *Questions*

1. Would a wedding marquee set up on the lawn of the house of the bride's parents be capable of being burgled?

2. Why should it matter that the trespass is to a building? Does the inclusion of this element provide an indication as to what harm the offence is intended to protect against?

3. Should there be an offence of trespassing on property with intent to commit specified offences thereon?

The issue of a part of a building was addressed in *Walkington* [1979] 2 All ER 716, [1979] 1 WLR 1169, CA. D entered the 'counter area' (a rectangle made up from movable counters which housed a till and which was reserved to staff) of a department store and was seen to open and shut the till drawer. It was held, upholding D's conviction for burglary, that whether the counter area was sufficient to amount to an area from which the public were excluded was a matter for the jury; there was ample evidence from which the jury could conclude that it was such an area and that D knew it.

■ *Questions*

Does Dan, a law student, commit burglary in any of the following cases?

(i)   He enters a telephone kiosk with intent to break open the coin box and steal its contents.

(ii) He enters the law library and, seeing that no one is around, he goes behind the library counter and steals a bottle of juice that the library assistant had brought for her lunch.

(iii) He enters the departmental secretary's room intending to pass through into the office of the head of department in order to steal an examination paper, but is stopped by the secretary before he reaches the office.

(iv) He enters a hall of residence, intending to enter any room that might have been left unlocked, in order to steal therein.

(v)   He falls asleep in a cinema and wakes to find the building closed. On his way out through the foyer he helps himself to some sweets from the kiosk which stands near the entrance.

(vi) He enters the Law Department's computing facility intending to use a computer to order goods over the internet using an unauthorized credit card as payment for them.

26.1.3 Mens rea

The mens rea involves two elements: (i) as to the trespassory entry and (ii) as to the ulterior offence.

26.1.3.1 Mens rea as to trespassory status

Collins (section 26.1.2, p 860) shows that D must be proved to know (or be subjectively reckless as to) the facts which make him a trespasser.

26.1.3.2 Mens rea as to the ulterior offence

It must be shown that D either:

- in respect of s 9(1)(a), entered with intent to steal, or to inflict GBH, or to do unlawful damage to the building or anything therein; or

- in respect of s 9(1)(b), entered and committed, or attempted to commit, the offence of stealing or of inflicting GBH.

It is not immediately apparent why D, if he enters a building as a trespasser without intent to commit any offence, is not a burglar if he thereafter decides to set it alight but is a burglar if he steals some trinket.

26.1.4 The ulterior offences

26.1.4.1 Theft

Stealing clearly means theft contrary to s 1 of the 1968 Act.

■ *Questions*

1. In *Morris* (section 21.3, p 742), was the defendant a burglar? Are all shoplifters?

2. Was D in *Gomez*, section 21.3, p 742, a burglar?

3. What of D, a plumber, who on arriving at V's house in response to a call-out realizes she is vulnerable and confused. He decides to lie to her as to the extent of the repair necessary. When, if at all, does he become a burglar?

In *Downer* [2009] EWCA Crim 1361, D was convicted of aggravated burglary against V. D claimed that V was a drug dealer who had taken his money but failed to supply the drugs, and that D had gone to V's house to get either the drugs or his money back.

■ *Questions*

Can D be guilty of burglary if he enters a building as a trespasser with the genuinely held belief that he is retrieving property that belongs to him? Would such an argument constitute a true defence or does it negate an element of the offence? Note that in *Lopatta* (1983) 35 SASR 101, it was held that D's belief as to the law or facts does not have to be soundly based, provided it is genuinely held.

26.1.4.2 Grievous bodily harm

Grievous bodily harm must extend to those offences where the infliction of GBH is an offence (viz the Offences Against the Person Act 1861, ss 20 and 23). Following the decision in *Mandair* [1995] 1 AC 208 (removing the distinction between causes and inflicts), it surely extends to the s 18 offence which uses 'causes' rather than 'inflicts'. Whether it extends to murder is undecided but it would certainly be surprising if it did not do so: the greater may be taken to include the less. It is important to note that there are differences depending on whether reliance is placed on s 9(1)(a) or s 9(1)(b):

- in respect of s 9(1)(a) intent must be proved, and thus the offence must be that under s 18 (GBH with intent to do GBH);

- in respect of s 9(1)(b) offences of s 18, 20 or 23 of the Offences Against the Person Act 1861 would suffice.

Under s 9(1)(b), another distinction seems to be suggested by *Jenkins* [1983] 1 All ER 1000, CA. It will be noticed that while s 9(1)(a) refers to 'offences of…inflicting on any person therein any grievous bodily harm', s 9(1)(b) merely refers to the infliction (or attempt to inflict) any grievous bodily harm without specifying that it must be an offence. This led the Court of Appeal in *Jenkins* to give the following example (at 1004):

> An intruder gains access to the house without breaking in (where there is an open window for instance). He is on the premises as a trespasser and his intrusion is observed by someone in the house of whom he may not even be aware, and as a result that person suffers a severe shock with a resulting stroke…

The House of Lords allowed the appeal in *Jenkins* [1984] AC 242, [1983] 3 All ER 448, without expressing any opinion on this matter. Clause 147 of the Draft Criminal Code would make it clear that the causing of the harm must amount to an offence.

■ *Questions*

1. If D enters a building as a trespasser through an open window with an intention to rough V up a little, but leaves without actually doing so, is he guilty of an offence under s 9(1)(a)? Has he committed any offence? Suppose D takes advantage of his being in V's house and steals his most prized possession, what offence is D guilty of then?

2. Must there be some nexus between the invasion of the building and the commission of the ulterior crime? If D and E, two tramps, squat for the night in V's empty building, does D become a burglar because he attacks E and inflicts on him grievous bodily harm? Should he be?

3. In the example given by the Court of Appeal in *Jenkins*, would D commit burglary if V died from the stroke caused by severe shock?

26.1.5 Burglary in respect of a dwelling

Since the Criminal Justice Act 1991, burglary of a dwelling is a separate offence carrying a maximum sentence of 14 years' imprisonment. In addition, s 111 of the Powers of Criminal Courts (Sentencing) Act 2000 requires a judge to impose a minimum three-year custodial sentence upon conviction of a third 'domestic' burglary. Neither 'dwelling' nor 'domestic' is defined; however, s 9(4) of the Theft Act 1968 does state that references to dwelling encompasses inhabited vehicles and vessels, including when they are unoccupied. In *Flack* [2013] EWCA Crim 115, [2103] Crim LR 521, the Court of Appeal declined to give guidance as to how dwelling ought to be interpreted, instead holding that it is a question of fact to be decided by the jury in each case. However, when considering whether an empty house undergoing renovations was a dwelling, Macduff J in *Sticklen* [2013] EWCA Crim 615 stated that, 'the justification for treating a dwelling as being different from other properties (and the judge mentioned a shed or a factory) is the very fact that it is someone's home, occupied, with personal and sentimental property within it.... Those factors do not apply here: there were no occupants, there were no personal objects, this was not someone's home with personal space being violated—indeed, no new tenant or purchaser had yet been identified. The premises were not only unoccupied, they had been empty for many months and were bare and unfurnished.' (See K. Laird, 'Conceptualising the Interpretation of "Dwelling" in s 9 of the Theft Act 1968' [2013] Crim LR 656.)

■ *Questions*

1. Is D guilty of dwelling burglary by entering as a trespasser with the necessary ulterior intent in the following circumstances: the foyer of a block of flats; a hotel room; a prison cell?

2. What are the advantages of singling out the offence of domestic burglary? Does this re-categorization provide any insight into the principal harm against which burglary is designed to protect? Pay particular attention to what was said in *Sticklen*.

As 'dwelling' is an aggravating element in the offence warranting a higher maximum sentence of imprisonment, it should, in principle, import a requirement of mens rea.

26.2 Aggravated burglary

Theft Act 1968, s 10

(1) A person is guilty of aggravated burglary if he commits any burglary and at the time has with him any firearm or imitation firearm, any weapon of offence, or any explosive; and for this purpose—

    (a) 'firearm' includes an airgun or air pistol, and 'imitation firearm' means anything which has the appearance of being a firearm, whether capable of being discharged or not; and

    (b) 'weapon of offence' means any article made or adapted for use for causing injury to or incapacitating a person, or intended by the person having it with him for such use; and

    (c) 'explosive' means any article manufactured for the purpose of producing a practical effect by explosion, or intended by the person having it with him for that purpose.

(2) A person guilty of aggravated burglary shall on conviction on indictment be liable to imprisonment for life.

26.2.1 Articles of aggravation

These include (i) articles made for causing injury to a person; (ii) articles adapted for causing injury to a person; (iii) articles which D has with him for that purpose; (iv) any article made for incapacitating a person; (v) any article adapted for incapacitating a person; and (vi) any article which D has with him for that purpose.

26.2.2 At the time of the burglary

It must be proved that D had the article of aggravation with him at the time of the commission of the burglary. Where the charge is one of entry with intent (s 9(1)(a)) this is the time of the entry; where it is one of committing a specified offence, having entered, etc (s 9(1)(b)), it is the time of commission of the specified offence. In *Francis* [1982] Crim LR 363, CA, the Ds who were armed with sticks were allowed by V to enter after they noisily demanded entry. They then discarded their sticks and subsequently stole articles in the house. Their convictions for aggravated burglary were quashed; they may have entered with weapons of offence but there was no evidence that at the point of entry they intended to steal. But in *O'Leary* (1986) 82 Cr App R 341, CA, D's conviction for aggravated burglary was upheld where, having entered as a trespasser, he took a knife from the kitchen, went upstairs and forced the occupants to part with property at knifepoint. At the time of committing the offence under s 9(1)(b) he had with him the weapon of offence.

Importantly, in *Wiggins* [2012] EWCA Crim 885, Pitchford LJ confirmed that where the principal in an offence of burglary does not have with him at the time of the commission of the offence an article of aggravation, but a secondary party does, neither party can be guilty of aggravated burglary.

26.2.2.1 Has with him

'Has with him' has been interpreted to require knowledge by D that he has the article with him since what aggravates the burglary, and attracts the higher penalty, must be D's decision to have the article of aggravation with him: *Stones* (1989) 89 Cr App R 26, CA.

Under s 10, what appears to aggravate the burglary is not the use of the firearm, weapon of offence or explosive, but the *possession* of any of these articles at the time of the commission of the burglary. If at the time of commission D 'has with him' a firearm or a kilo of explosive it can be no defence that D did not use them in the course of the burglary and never intended to do so: *Klass* [1998] 1 Cr App R 453.

With 'weapon of offence' the position is slightly more complicated. Two categories must be distinguished:

(i) if the article is one made or adapted for use for causing injury or for incapacitating, D may be convicted of aggravated burglary though he neither uses nor intends to use the weapon in the course of the burglary;

(ii) if the article is intended by D for use for causing injury or for incapacitating, D may be convicted of aggravated burglary only if he had it with him for such use. But if D does have the article with him for such use, he may be convicted of aggravated burglary though he does not intend to use the article for such use during the course of the burglary. So D's conviction for aggravated burglary was upheld in *Stones* even though, as he claimed, he carried a knife in case he was attacked by a rival gang and had no intention of using it during the burglary. The mischief aimed at by s 10, the court said, included the case where the weapon was carried to injure a person unconnected with the burglary because D, if challenged, might use it during the burglary.

But the section requires that D 'has with him' the firearm etc at the time of the commission of the offence. In *O'Leary*, D, it may fairly be said, 'has with him' a weapon, the kitchen knife, at the time he threatened the householders since he had possession of it for some moments.

■ *Question*

Suppose D is in the kitchen in the course of stealing the food processor when he is surprised by the householder. D seizes a rolling pin and threatens the householder with this. Is this aggravated burglary? Cf *Kelly* (1992) 97 Cr App R 295, [1993] Crim LR 763, CA, and commentary.

26.3 Trespass with intent to commit a sexual offence

Sexual Offences Act 2003, s 63

63. Trespass with intent to commit a sexual offence

(1) A person commits an offence if—

    (a) he is a trespasser on any premises,

    (b) he intends to commit a relevant sexual offence on the premises, and

    (c) he knows that, or is reckless as to whether, he is a trespasser.

(2) In this section—

    'premises' includes a structure or part of a structure;

    'relevant sexual offence' [is all those in that Part of the Act];

    'structure' includes a tent, vehicle or vessel or other temporary or movable structure.

Note the significant differences from burglary: (i) the offence is wider, since any trespass is sufficient and there is no need to prove a trespassory entry; (ii) the trespass relates to 'premises', which is wider than the concept of a building or part of a building; (iii) the concept of 'structure' is widely defined; (iv) as with s 9(1)(a) there is no need for the ulterior offence to occur; (v) the ulterior offences are all those in Part 1 of the Sexual offences Act 2003.

■ *Questions*

1. Was the creation of this offence necessary? Consider this question in the light of *Heeney* [2009] EWCA Crim 1393. In that case D entered a woman's flat at 2 am and made his way to her bedroom where he pounced on her, pushed her onto the bed and then began to touch her sexually. The court observed that those facts arguably gave rise to a charge under s 63 or s 3 of the 2003 Act, D having originally been charged with attempted rape.

2. Would Collins have committed this offence?

26.4 Going equipped with housebreaking implements

The Theft Act 1968, s 25 makes it an offence for a person to have in his possession when not in his abode any article for use in the course of or in connection with any burglary or theft. The offence is described as 'going equipped'. Cf s 6 of the Fraud Act 2006, section 25.6, p 851.

FURTHER READING

K. Laird, 'Conceptualising the Interpretation of "Dwelling" in s 9 of the Theft Act 1968' [2013] Crim LR 656

P. J. Pace, 'Burglarious Trespass' [1985] Crim LR 716

27

Handling stolen goods and related offences

27.1 Introduction

Thieves and fraudsters, especially professional ones, need to dispose of their goods. The person who assists them in doing so by handling the stolen goods plays an important role, and arguably without the handler there would be less theft and fraud. Handling is treated very seriously. Because of the many ways in which property can be acquired dishonestly (theft, fraud, etc), and the many ways in which someone can assist in the disposal of the property, the offence is a complex one, extending more widely than might at first seem necessary.

Some of the issues that will be explored in this chapter include the following:

(i)   the significance of the circumstance element of a crime: the conduct of D in handling is only criminal if the goods remain stolen or are the product of stolen goods;

(ii)   the complexity of the statute in providing so many different forms that handling can take;

(iii) the relationship between theft and handling—can a thief be guilty of handling the goods he has stolen?;

(iv)   the relationship between handling and the money laundering offences in the Proceeds of Crime Act 2002.

27.2 Definitions

There must be stolen goods. Goods are 'stolen' for the purposes of the Act if they:

(1)   have been stolen contrary to the Theft Act 1968, s 1;

(2)   have been obtained by blackmail contrary to the Theft Act 1968, s 21;

(3)   have been obtained by fraud contrary to the Fraud Act 2006, s 1;

(4)   consist of money dishonestly withdrawn from a wrongful credit; or

(5)   have been the subject of an act done in a foreign country which was:

(a)   a crime by the law of that country and which

(b)   had it been done in England, would have been theft, blackmail or fraud contrary to the Theft Act 1968, s 1 or s 21, or the Fraud Act 2006, s 1.

The handler must act in relation to the goods in one of the following ways:

(1)   by *receiving* the goods;

(2)   by *undertaking* the retention, removal, disposal or realization of the goods for the benefit of another person;

(3) by *assisting* in the retention, removal, disposal or realization of the goods by another person; or

(4) by *arranging* to do (1), (2) or (3).

The handler must act dishonestly, knowing or believing the goods to be stolen.

Theft Act 1968

22. Handling stolen goods

(1) A person handles stolen goods if (otherwise than in the course of the stealing) knowing or believing them to be stolen goods he dishonestly receives the goods, or dishonestly undertakes or assists in their retention, removal, disposal or realisation by or for the benefit of another person, or if he arranges to do so.

(2) A person guilty of handling stolen goods shall on conviction on indictment be liable to imprisonment for a term not exceeding fourteen years.

24. Scope of offences relating to stolen goods

(1) The provisions of this Act relating to goods which have been stolen shall apply whether the stealing occurred in England or Wales or elsewhere, and whether it occurred before or after the commencement of this Act, provided that the stealing (if not an offence under this Act) amounted to an offence where and at the time when the goods were stolen; and references to stolen goods shall be construed accordingly.

(2) For purposes of those provisions references to stolen goods shall include, in addition to the goods originally stolen and parts of them (whether in their original state or not),—

(a) any other goods which directly or indirectly represent or have at any time represented the stolen goods in the hands of the thief as being the proceeds of any disposal or realisation of the whole or part of the goods stolen or of goods so representing the stolen goods; and

(b) any other goods which directly or indirectly represent or have at any time represented the stolen goods in the hands of a handler of the stolen goods or any part of them as being the proceeds of any disposal or realisation of the whole or part of the stolen goods handled by him or of goods so representing them.

(3) But no goods shall be regarded as having continued to be stolen goods after they have been restored to the person from whom they were stolen or to other lawful possession or custody, or after that person and any other person claiming through him have otherwise ceased as regards those goods to have any right to restitution in respect of the theft.

(4) For purposes of the provisions of this Act relating to goods which have been stolen (including sub-sections (1) to (3) above) goods obtained in England or Wales or elsewhere either by blackmail or [fraud within the Fraud Act 2006] as stolen; and 'steal', 'theft' and 'thief' shall be construed accordingly.

27.3 Stolen goods

27.3.1 What constitutes 'stolen goods'?

'Goods' are defined in s 34(2)(b) of the 1968 Act to include 'money and every other description of property except land, and includes things severed from the land by stealing'. The effect seems to be that, with minor exceptions, any property that can be the subject of theft can be the subject of handling. While things in action (as defined in section 21.4.1, p 755) are not expressly mentioned in s 34(2), they must be included in the words 'every other description of property except land'. They can be handled.

Perhaps a thing in action cannot be 'received' (a word more apt to describe taking control of tangible property) but there would seem to be no reason why a thing in action cannot be 'realized' or 'disposed of'. In *A-G's Reference (No 4 of 1979)* [1981] 1 All ER 1193 at 1198, CA, the court said:

> it is clear that a balance in a bank account, being a debt, is itself a thing in action which falls within the definition of goods and may therefore be goods which directly or indirectly represent stolen goods for the purposes of s 24(2)(a).

If D steals £500 and gives £250 in cash to E while opening a bank account in F's favour for the remainder, it would be absurd that E might be a handler while F could not. Cf *Forsyth* in section 27.3.1.1.

27.3.1.1 Proceeds of transfers of stolen goods: what becomes and remains stolen

A stolen article—for example, an Audi car—may pass through many hands by way of sale or exchange but it continues to be stolen goods until it is restored to its owner or other lawful custody or until the owner ceases to have a right to restitution in respect of it: s 24(3). Any person acquiring the stolen car may be convicted of handling it if he acquires it knowing or believing it to be stolen. But the law goes further. See s 24(2) in section 27.2. If D exchanges the Audi with E for a BMW, the BMW is now notionally stolen because it directly represents the proceeds of the stolen Audi *in the hands of the thief*, D. If E is aware that the Audi was stolen and he exchanges it with F for a Citroën, the Citroën is now also notionally stolen because it represents the proceeds of the stolen Audi *in the hands of the handler*, E.

To change the example, if D has a voidable title to the BMW (because he obtained it by fraud from E) and he sells it to H who buys it in good faith for £5,000, the BMW now ceases to be stolen goods; and, once stolen goods cease to be stolen goods, they cannot revert to being stolen because they are subsequently acquired by someone aware of their provenance. The £5,000 in D's hands, however, is 'stolen' because it indirectly represents the stolen goods in the hands of the 'thief', provided that the true owner has a right to restitution of the money which now represents his car. If so, anyone to whom he gave it would, if aware of its provenance, be guilty of handling. The position is more complex where D banks the £5,000. If the £5,000 represents all that D has in the account, money which D draws from the account is stolen goods and a person receiving it from D, having the requisite knowledge, would be guilty of handling. Where, however, D has other innocently acquired money in his account, say a further £5,000, it may be difficult to prove that a cheque drawn for £2,000 represented proceeds of the stolen £5,000—that it represented his share of the ill-gotten £5,000. A charge of attempted handling may be possible. It may be that the full offence as opposed to a mere attempt is established if it can be proved that D intended the £2,000 to represent the proceeds of the stolen money: *A-G's Reference (No 4 of 1979)* [1981] 1 All ER 1193 at 1199.

The problems which can arise when a stolen thing in action is assigned or converted into cash and vice versa are well illustrated by the next case.

R v Forsyth
[1997] 2 Cr App R 299, Court of Appeal, Criminal Division

(Beldam LJ, Bracewell and Mance JJ)

Because of the complexity of the facts, the following note is provided in place of the judgment of the court.

Forsyth (F) was convicted of handling stolen goods. The 'goods' alleged to be stolen were a thing in action, £400,000 of a balance in Polly Peck International (PPI)'s account at the M bank in London. It was alleged that Asil Nadir (N), chairman and chief executive of PPI, stole it on 17/10/89 by ordering the transfer of that sum, via other banks, to the X bank in Geneva. F in Geneva collected that sum, less commission, in cash from the X bank and deposited it with the Y bank, also in Geneva. On her instructions, the Y bank transferred £307,000 to a bank in England and F brought back the balance (after commission) of £88,050 in cash to England. It was alleged she dishonestly handled the proceeds of the theft by N, comprising (i) the thing in action of £307,000 and (ii) £88,050 in cash, by undertaking or assisting in the retention, removal, etc of this property. F's handling of the thing in action was taken to continue until credit was made to the Bank in England, so the offence was committed within the jurisdiction.

When the M bank opened for business on 17/10/89, PPI's account was in debit to the extent of £7m. There was no thing in action to steal. But the M bank was aware that very large sums of overnight interest were regularly credited to PPI's account and, indeed, some £11m was credited that day. If, when the M bank transferred the £400,000, PPI's account was overdrawn, the overdraft was increased (apparently without prior authority), there was no theft and no stolen goods to handle. The evidence as to whether the account was in debit or in credit at the time of the transfer was, in the court's word, 'inconclusive'. Nevertheless, the court held that there was evidence on which the jury could be sure that the account was in credit at that time. There was another problem of timing. It was argued that F may have been allowed to withdraw the cash before the electronic transfer of that sum to the X bank was complete so the cash could not be the proceeds of any disposal or realization of the stolen thing in action. Again, it appears that the judge ruled that there was evidence on which the jury could find that the transfer was completed before the withdrawal and the Court of Appeal agreed; but they thought it was at least arguable that, where a sum is 'credited out of order in well-founded anticipation of an imminent receipt which then follows', the credit directly or indirectly represents the thing in action.

Between the trial and the appeal came the decision of the House of Lords in *Preddy* (section 21.5.2, p 761), which was invoked by the appellant. When funds are transferred from A to B online or by telegraphic transfer, etc, *Preddy* [1996] AC 815 establishes that B does not obtain property 'belonging to' A. B has acquired a new thing in action which never belonged to anyone but him. The property in B's bank account cannot, as Lord Goff said ([1996] 3 All ER 481 at 490), be 'identified' with that which was in A's account; but it does not necessarily follow that it does not 'represent' it. The difficulty for the prosecution in *Forsyth* was that the bank (or succession of banks) to which the £400,000 was transferred was not dishonest—it was neither thief nor handler. That difficulty was overcome by the court's decision that the words of s 24(2), 'in the hands of', mean 'in the possession or under the control of' and that the new credit balance, including that in the X bank, remained under the control of the thief, N. Although it was a new, different property, it indirectly represented the stolen goods in the hands of N and was 'stolen'.

But F was not charged with handling the stolen thing in action consisting in the credit in the X bank. That *credit* may have been under the control of N and so 'stolen'; but the X bank's banknotes certainly were not. When they were set aside for the purpose, they perhaps represented the stolen thing in action but they were quite separate property, not in the hands or under the control of any thief or handler. When the bank's cashier counted out £400,000 in notes to pay to F, he was counting money which was the property of, and under the exclusive control of, the bank, which was certainly neither a handler nor a thief. The £400,000 which was passed across the counter to F represented the stolen thing in action but it was not stolen goods while in the hands of the bank clerk. F, however, was acting as N's agent in cashing the cheque. If N, the thief, had done it himself, the cash he received would have represented the stolen goods in the hands of the thief—himself—and so it would have been stolen goods. As F was N's agent, it was the same as if N had done it himself. F was not a receiver of stolen goods; the cash was not stolen before she received it. She was in possession of stolen goods but that is not an offence. F was, however, guilty of handling if, knowing or believing it to be stolen, she assisted in the retention, removal, etc of the stolen cash for the benefit of another person, N. F's conviction was, however, quashed because of an inadequate direction on the meaning of the word 'belief' (section 27.7.2, p 887).

Note the significance of the fact that F was cashing the cheque as agent for the alleged thief. If A steals money, pays it into a new bank account and, in payment of a debt, gives B a cheque, B, if he cashes the cheque, does not receive *or have* stolen money in his hands. The cash in the hands of the bank is not stolen and it is not possible to argue that B is a handler and therefore the goods are stolen because they are in his hands. That would be a circular argument. If B believes the money to be stolen, it is arguable that he is guilty of an attempt to handle but it may be that this is not so because his 'mens rea' arises from a mistake of criminal law, not merely one of fact or civil law. Charges of money laundering may be possible. See section 27.11, p 892.

27.3.2 When goods cease to be stolen

Attorney-General's Reference (No 1 of 1974)
[1974] 2 All ER 899, Court of Appeal, Criminal Division

(Lord Widgery CJ, Ashworth and Mocatta JJ)

A policeman found an unlocked car containing packages of new clothing. He suspected they were stolen. The officer disabled the car by removing the rotor arm in the engine. D appeared, got in and tried to drive off. On arrest, the goods proved to be stolen. A charge of theft of the goods was rejected because there was no evidence to support it. The charge of receiving the goods knowing them to be stolen was left to the jury. D submitted that there was no case to answer, relying on the Theft Act 1968, s 24(3).

Lord Widgery CJ: . . .

After hearing argument, the judge accepted the submission of the respondent and directed the jury that they should acquit on the receiving count. That has resulted in the Attorney-General referring the following point of law to us for an opinion under s 36 of the 1977 Act. He expresses the point in this way:

'Whether stolen goods are restored to lawful custody within the meaning of s 24(3) of the Theft Act 1968 when a Police Officer, suspecting them to be stolen, examines and keeps observation on them with a view to tracing the thief or a handler.'

One could put the question perhaps in a somewhat different way by asking whether on the facts set out in the reference the conclusion as a matter of law was clear to the effect that the goods had ceased to be stolen goods. In other words, the question which is really in issue in this reference is whether the trial judge acted correctly in law in saying that those facts disclosed a defence within s 24(3) of the 1968 Act.

Section 24(3) is not perhaps entirely happily worded. It has been pointed out in the course of argument that in the sentence which I have read there is only one relevant verb, and that is 'restore'. The section contemplates that the stolen goods should be restored to the person from whom they were stolen or to other lawful possession or custody. It is pointed out that the word 'restore', although it is entirely appropriate when applied to restoration of the goods to the true owner, is not really an appropriate verb to employ if one is talking about a police officer stumbling on stolen goods and taking them into his own lawful custody or possession.

We are satisfied that despite the absence of another and perhaps more appropriate verb, the effect of s 24(3) is to enable a defendant to plead that the goods had ceased to be stolen goods if the facts are that they were taken by a police officer in the course of his duty and reduced into possession by him.

Whether or not s 24(3) is intended to be a codification of the common law or not, it certainly deals with a topic on which the common law provides a large number of authorities. I shall refer to some of them in a moment, although perhaps not all, and it will be observed that from the earliest times it has been recognised that if the owner of stolen goods resumed possession of them, reduced them into his possession again, that they thereupon ceased to be stolen goods for present purposes and could certainly not be the subject of a later charge of receiving based on events after they had been reduced into possession. It is to be observed that in common law nothing short of a reduction into possession, either by the true owner or by a police officer acting in the execution of his duty, was regarded as sufficient to change the character of the goods from stolen goods into goods which were no longer to be so regarded. . . .

[Lord Widgery discussed *Dolan* (1855) 6 Cox CC 449 and *Schmidt* [1866] LR 1 CCR 15.]

Then there is a helpful case, *Villensky* [[1892] 2 QB 597]. Again it is a case of a parcel in the hands of carriers. This parcel was handed to the carriers in question for conveyance to the consignees, and whilst in the carriers' depot it was stolen by a servant of the carriers who removed the parcel to a different part of the premises and placed on it a label addressed to the prisoners by a name by which they were known and at a house where they resided. The superintendent of the carriers, on receipt of information as to this and after inspection of the parcel, directed it to be replaced in the place from which the thief had removed it and to be sent with a special delivery receipt in a van accompanied by two detectives to the address shown on the label. At that address it was received by the prisoners under circumstances which clearly showed knowledge on their part that it had been stolen. The property in the parcel was laid in the indictment in the carriers and an offer to amend the indictment by substituting the names of the consignees was declined. The carriers' servant pleaded guilty to a count for larceny in the same indictment. It was there held by the Court of Crown Cases Reserved:

> 'that as the person in which the property was laid [ie the carriers] had resumed possession of the stolen property before its receipt by the prisoners, it had then ceased to be stolen property, and the prisoners could not be convicted of receiving it knowing it to have been stolen.'

In the same report there is a brief and valuable judgment by Pollock B, in these terms [[1892] 2 QB 597 at 599]:

> 'The decisions in *Dolan* and *Schmidt* are, in my judgment, founded on law and on solid good sense, and they should not be frittered away. It is, of course, frequently the case that when it is found that a person has stolen property he is watched; but the owner of the property, if he wishes to catch the receiver, does not resume possession of the stolen goods; here the owners have done so, and the result is that the conviction must be quashed.'

We refer to that brief judgment because it illustrates in a few clear words what is really the issue in the present case. When the police officer discovered these goods and acted as he did, was the situation that he had taken possession of the goods, in which event, of course, they ceased to be stolen goods, or was it merely that he was watching the goods with a view to the possibility of catching the receiver at a later stage? I will turn later to a consideration of those two alternatives.

Two other cases should, I think, be mentioned at this stage. The next one is *King* [[1938] 2 All ER 662]. We are now getting to far more recent times because the report is published in 1938. The appellant here was convicted with another man of receiving stolen goods knowing them to have been stolen. A fur coat had been stolen and shortly afterwards the police went to a flat where they found the man Burns and told him they were enquiring about some stolen property. He at first denied that there was anything there, but finally admitted the theft and produced a parcel from a wardrobe. While the policeman was in the act of examining the contents of the parcel, the telephone bell rang. Burns answered it and the police heard him say: 'Come along as arranged'. The police then suspended operations and about 20 minutes later the appellant arrived and being admitted by Burns, said: 'I have come for the coat. Harry sent me.' This was heard by the police, who were in hiding at the time. The coat was handed to the appellant by Burns, so that he was actually in possession of it. It was contended that the possession by the police amounted to possession by the owner of the coat, and that, therefore, the coat was not stolen property at the time the appellant received it. It was held by the Court of Criminal Appeal that 'the coat had not been in the possession of the police, and it was therefore still stolen property when the appellant received it.'

Counsel for the Attorney-General, appearing in support of this reference, showed some hesitation in relying on this case, because he clearly took the view that it was perhaps a rather unlikely decision, the policemen having started to examine the coat and then stopped for 20 minutes until the prisoner arrived and then claiming that the coat was not in their possession. It might be thought to be a rather bold decision to say that the police action in that case had not reduced the coat into their possession. But nevertheless that was the view of this court in the judgment of Humphreys J. All the authorities, as I say, point in the same direction.

The most recent case on the present topic, but of little value in the present problems is *Haughton v Smith* [[1975] AC 476, [1973] 3 All ER 1109]. The case being of little value to us in our present problems, I will deal with it quite briefly. It is a case where a lorry-load of stolen meat was intercepted by police, somewhere in the north of England, who discovered that the lorry was in fact full of stolen goods. After a brief conference they decided to take the lorry on to its destination with a view to catching the receivers at the London end of the affair. So the lorry set off for London with detectives both in the passenger seat and in the back of the vehicle, and in due course was met by the defendant at its destination in London. In that case before this court it was conceded, as it had been conceded below, that the goods had been reduced into the possession of the police when they took possession of the lorry in the north of England, so no dispute in this court or later in the House of Lords was raised on that issue. It is, however, to be noted that three of their Lordships, when the matter got to the House of Lords, expressed some hesitation as to the propriety of the prosecution conceding in that case that the goods had been reduced to the possession of the police when the lorry was first intercepted. Since we cannot discover on what ground those doubts were expressed either from the report of the speeches or from the report of the argument, we cannot take advantage of that case in the present problem.

Now to return to the present problem again with those authorities in the background did the conduct of the police officer, as already briefly recounted, amount to a taking of possession of the woollen goods in the back seat of the motor car? What he did, to repeat the essential facts, was: seeing these goods in the car and being suspicious of them because they were brand new goods and in an unlikely position, he removed the rotor arm and stood by in cover to interrogate any driver of the car who might subsequently appear. Did that amount to a taking possession of the goods in the back of the car? In our judgment it depended primarily on the intentions of the police officer. If the police officer seeing these goods in the back of the car had made up his mind that he would take them into custody, that he would reduce them into his possession or control, take charge of them so that they could not be removed and so that he would have the disposal of them, then it would be a perfectly proper conclusion to say that he had taken possession of the goods. On the other hand, if the truth of the matter is that he was of an entirely open mind at that stage as to whether the goods were to be seized or not and was of an entirely open mind as to whether he should take possession of them or not, but merely stood by so that when the driver of the car appeared he could ask certain questions of that driver as to the nature of the goods and why they were there, then there is no reason whatever to suggest that he had taken the goods into his possession or control. It may be, of course, that he had both objects in mind. It is possible in a case like this that the police officer may have intended by removing the rotor arm both to prevent the car from being driven away and to enable him to assert control over the woollen goods as such. But if the jury came to the conclusion that the proper explanation of what had happened was that the police officer had not intended at that stage to reduce the goods into his possession or to assume the control of them, and at that stage was merely concerned to ensure that the driver, if he appeared, could not get away without answering questions, then in that case the proper conclusion of the jury would have been to the effect that the goods had not been reduced into the possession of the police and therefore a defence under s 24(3) of the 1968 Act would not be of use to this particular defendant.

In the light of those considerations it has become quite obvious that the trial judge was wrong in withdrawing the issue from the jury. As a matter of law he was not entitled to conclude from the facts which I have set out more than once that these goods were reduced into the possession of the police officer. What he should have done in our opinion would have been to have left that issue to the jury for decision, directing the jury that they should find that the prosecution case was without substance if they thought that the police officer had assumed control of the goods as such and reduced them into his possession. Whereas, on the other hand, they should have found the case proved, assuming that they were satisfied about its other elements, if they were of the opinion that the police officer in removing the rotor arm and standing by and watching was doing no more than ensure that the driver should not get away without interrogation and was not at that stage seeking to assume possession of the goods as such at all. That is our opinion.

Determination accordingly

■ *Questions*

1. In determining whether goods have ceased to be stolen, which issues are for the judge and which for the jury?

2. Considering *Haughton v Smith* [1975] AC 476, do you think that, had the prosecution not conceded the point, it would have been successfully argued that the goods on the lorry remained stolen goods, that is, they had not been restored to the possession or control of the police?

3. In *A-G's Reference (No 1 of 1974)*, was not the only possible interpretation of the police officer's conduct, and especially his immobilization of the car, that he had taken 'custody' of the car and its contents? If so, was not the trial judge right to withdraw the case from the jury? The police officer's intention may have been conditional (I will let D drive away with the goods in the back of the car only if he satisfies me that they are not stolen) but even if it was so conditioned, should this make any difference?

27.4 Forms of handling

The offence may be committed in the following ways: (i) by *receiving* the goods; (ii) by *undertaking* the retention, removal, disposal or realization of the goods for the benefit of another person; (iii) by *assisting* in the retention, removal, disposal or realization of the goods by another person; or (iv) by *arranging* to do (i), (ii) or (iii).

Before the Theft Act 1968, it was an offence to 'receive' stolen property. This was interpreted as requiring that D should have exclusive control over the property or should be acting in a joint venture with the thief so as to have joint control of the property. This meant that if, say, D helped E to load stolen goods onto a lorry, or allowed E to leave them in D's garage overnight, or put E into contact with a prospective buyer, D did not thereby become guilty of receiving.

The Criminal Law Revision Committee (CLRC) was in favour of enlarging the offence and s 22 extends not only to receiving but to what the CLRC referred to (Eighth Report (1966, Cmnd 2977), para 127) as 'other kinds of meddling with stolen property'. For this reason the current offence under s 22 can be committed in all of the ways listed above. The words of the section, it was said in *Deakin* [1972] 3 All ER 803 at 808, 'are obviously intended to throw the net very wide'.

The breadth of the offence is illustrated by the following case.

R v Kanwar

[1982] 2 All ER 528, Court of Appeal, Criminal Division

(Dunn LJ, Cantley and Sheldon JJ)

D was charged with dishonestly assisting in the retention of stolen goods for the benefit of her husband. Her husband had brought the stolen goods to their house where the goods were used in the home. D was not present when the goods were brought to the house. She was in hospital at the time. During a police search of the house, D arrived and was told of the object of the search. She replied: 'There's no stolen property here.' She was subsequently asked a number of questions with regard to specific articles which were in the house and in reply to those questions, she gave answers which were lies. Although the officer had had no intention of arresting her when he came to the house, he did arrest her and she was subsequently charged. D did not give evidence and the evidence of her lies to the police officer stood uncontradicted.

[Cantley J read the following judgment of the court:]

In *R v Thornhill*, decided in this court on 15 May 1981, and in *R v Sanders*, decided in this court on 25 February 1982, both unreported, it was held that merely using stolen goods in the possession of another does not constitute the offence of assisting in their retention. To constitute the offence, something must be done by the offender, and done intentionally and dishonestly, for the purpose of enabling the goods to be retained. Examples of such conduct are concealing or helping to conceal the goods, or doing something to make them more difficult to find or to identify. Such conduct must be done knowing or believing the goods to be stolen and done dishonestly and for the benefit of another.

We see no reason why the requisite assistance should be restricted to physical acts. Verbal representations, whether oral or in writing, for the purpose of concealing the identity of stolen goods may, if made dishonestly and for the benefit of another, amount to handling stolen goods by assisting in their retention within the meaning of s 22 of the Theft Act 1968.

The requisite assistance need not be successful in its object. It would be absurd if a person dishonestly concealing stolen goods for the benefit of a receiver could establish a defence by showing that he was caught in the act. In the present case, if, while the police were in one part of the house, the appellant, in order to conceal the painting had put it under a mattress in the bedroom, it would not alter the nature of her conduct that the police subsequently looked under the mattress and found the picture because they expected to find it there or that they caught her in the act of putting it there.

The appellant told these lies to the police to persuade them that the picture and the mirror were not the stolen property which they had come to take away but were her lawful property which she had bought. If that was true, the articles should be left in the house. She was, of course, telling these lies to protect her husband, who had dishonestly brought the articles there but, in our view, she was nonetheless, at the time, dishonestly assisting in the retention of the stolen articles.

In his summing up, the judge directed the jury as follows:

'It would be quite wrong for you to convict this lady if all she did was to watch her husband bring goods into the house, even if she knew or believed that they were stolen goods because, no doubt, you would say to yourselves, "What would she be expected to do about it?" Well, what the Crown say is that she knew or believed them to be stolen and that she was a knowing and willing party to their being kept in that house in those circumstances. The reason the Crown say that, and we shall be coming to the evidence, is that when questioned about a certain number of items, [the appellant] gave answers which the Crown say were not true and that she could not possibly have believed to be true and that she knew perfectly well were untruthful. So, say the prosecution, she was not just an acquiescent wife who could not do much about it, she was, by her conduct in trying to put the police officers as best she could off the scent, demonstrating that she was a willing and knowing part of those things being there and that she was trying to account for them. Well, it will be for you to say, but you must be satisfied before you can convict her on either of these counts, not only that she knew or believed the goods to be stolen, but that she actively assisted her husband in keeping them there; not by just passive acquiescence in the sense of saying, "What can I do about it?" but in the sense of saying, "How nice to have these things in our home, although they are stolen goods".'

In so far as this direction suggests that the appellant would be guilty of the offence if she was merely willing for the goods to be kept and used in the house and was thinking that it was nice to have them there, although they were stolen goods, it is a misdirection. We have considered whether on that account the conviction ought to be quashed. However, the offence was established by the uncontradicted evidence of the police officer which, looked at in full, clearly shows that in order to mislead the officer who had come to take away stolen goods, she misrepresented the identity of the goods which she knew or believed to be stolen. We are satisfied that no miscarriage of justice has occurred and the appeal is accordingly dismissed.

Appeal dismissed

R v Pitchley

(1972) 57 Cr App R 30, Court of Appeal, Criminal Division

(Cairns LJ, Nield and Croom-Johnson JJ)

On 5 November, D was handed £150 by his son, Brian, and was asked to look after it. On 6 November D paid the money into his Post Office savings account. The money was in fact stolen but D claimed that his son told him that he had won the money on the horses and, while he thought this explanation strange, he did not become aware that it was stolen until 7 November. Having become aware of this, he had no wish to take his son to the police so he allowed the money to remain in his account and it was still there when he was seen by the police on 11 November. D was convicted of handling the money.

Cairns LJ:

...The main point that has been taken by Mr Kalisher, who is appearing for the appellant in this Court, is that, assuming that the jury were not satisfied that the appellant received the money knowing it to have been stolen, and that is an assumption which clearly it is right to make, then there was no evidence after that, that from the time when the money was put into the savings bank, that the appellant had done any act in relation to it. His evidence was, and there is no reason to suppose that the jury did not believe it, that at the time when he put the money into the savings bank he still did not know or believe that the money had been stolen—it was only at a later stage that he did. That was on the Saturday according to his evidence, and the position was that the money had simply remained in the savings bank from the Saturday, to the Wednesday when the police approached the appellant. It is fair to say that from the moment when he was approached he displayed the utmost frankness to the extent of correcting them when they said it was £100 to £150 and telling them where the post office savings book was so that the money could be got out again and restored to its rightful owner.

But the question is: Did the conduct of the appellant between the Saturday and the Wednesday amount to an assisting in the retention of this money for the benefit of his son Brian? The Court has been referred to the case of *Brown* (1969) 53 Cr App Rep 527 which was a case where stolen property had been put into a wardrobe at the appellant's house and when police came to inquire about it the appellant said to them: 'Get lost'. The direction to the jury had been on the basis that it was for them to consider whether in saying: 'Get lost', instead of helping the police constable, he was dishonestly assisting in the retention of stolen goods. This Court held that that was a misdirection but there are passages in the judgment in the case of *Brown* (supra) which, in the view of this Court, are of great assistance in determining what is meant by 'retention' in this section. I read first of all from p 528 setting out the main facts a little more fully: 'A witness named Holden was called by the prosecution. He gave evidence that he and others had broken into the cafe and had stolen the goods, and that he had brought them to the appellant's flat, where, incidentally, other people were sleeping, and had hidden them there; and he described how he had taken the cigarettes out of the packets, put them in the plastic bag and hidden them in the wardrobe. Holden went on to say that later and before the police arrived he told the appellant where the cigarettes were; in other words, he said that the appellant well knew that the cigarettes were there and that they had been stolen.' There was no evidence that the appellant had done anything active in relation to the cigarettes up to the time when the police arrived. The Lord Chief Justice, Lord Parker, in the course of his judgment at p 530 said this: 'It is urged here that the mere failure to reveal the presence of the cigarettes, with or without the addition of the spoken words "Get lost", was incapable itself of amounting to an assisting in the retention of the goods within the meaning of the sub-section. The Court has come to the conclusion that that is right. It does not seem to this Court that the mere failure to tell the police, coupled if you like with the words: "Get lost", amounts in itself to an assisting in their retention. On the other hand, those matters did afford strong evidence of what was the real basis of the charge here, namely, that knowing that they have been stolen, he permitted them to remain there or, as it has been put, provided accommodation for these stolen goods in order to assist Holden to retain them.' Having said that the direction was incomplete, the Lord Chief Justice went on to say: 'The Chairman should have gone on to say: "But the fact that he did not tell the constable that they were there and said 'Get lost' is evidence from which you can infer, if you think right, that this man was permitting the goods to remain in his flat, and to that extent assisting in their retention by Holden."'

In this present case there was no question on the evidence of the appellant himself, that he was permitting the money to remain under his control in his savings bank book, and it is clear that this Court in the case of *Brown* (supra) regarded such permitting as sufficient to constitute retention within the meaning of retention. That is clear from the passage I have already read, emphasised in the next paragraph, the final paragraph of the judgment, where the Lord Chief Justice said (at p 531): 'It is a plain case in which the proviso [ie the power the Court of Appeal had at that time to uphold a conviction despite the error] should be applied. It seems to this Court that the only possible inference in these circumstances, once Holden was believed is that this man was assisting in their retention by housing the goods and providing accommodation for them, by permitting them to remain there.' It is important to realise that that language was in relation to a situation where there was no evidence that anything active had been done by the appellant in relation to the goods.

In the course of the argument, Nield J cited the dictionary meaning of the word 'retain'—keep possession of, not lose, continue to have. In the view of this Court, that is the meaning of the word 'retain' in this section. It was submitted by Mr Kalisher that, at any rate, it was ultimately for the jury to decide whether there was retention or not and that even assuming that what the appellant did was of such a character that it could constitute retention, the jury ought to have been directed that it was for them to determine as a matter of fact, whether that was so or not. The Court cannot agree with that submission. The meaning of the word 'retention' in the section is a matter of law in so far as the construction of the word is necessary. It is hardly a difficult question of construction because it is an ordinary English word and in the view of this Court, it was no more necessary for the Deputy Chairman to leave to the jury the question of whether or not what was done amounted to retention, than it would be necessary for a judge in a case where goods had been handed to a person who knew that they had been stolen for him to direct the jury it was for them to decide whether or not that constituted receiving...

Appeal dismissed

■ *Questions*

1. Are *Pitchley* and *Brown* authority for the proposition that handling may be constituted by omission?

2. Dan's wife, Ena, makes her living by stealing fur coats which she keeps in the garage at Dan's house. Dan is well aware of this but considers it no business of his to interfere as long as he can get his car in and out of the garage. Is Dan a handler?

In *Coleman* [1986] Crim LR 56, CA, it was proved that D's wife was stealing from her employers and was using the money as part of the living expenses of herself and D. D was convicted of handling on a count which alleged that his wife had paid £650 in solicitors' fees in relation to the purchase of a flat in their joint names. D admitted that he knew the £650 was stolen. Quashing D's conviction, the court said that the actus reus of the offence lay in *assisting* in the disposal of the money. This meant helping or arranging. It was not enough that D derived a benefit from what his wife did unless he had told his wife to use the money or agreed that she should do so.

■ *Question*

Suppose that D's wife had asked him what she should do with the money and he told her to invest it in shares. Would D be guilty of assisting in its disposal? See also the offences in section 27.10.1, p 889

27.5 'Otherwise than in the course of the stealing': the relationship between handling and theft

'It should be noted,' said the CLRC (Eighth Report, para 132) 'that a person guilty of handling stolen goods will often be guilty of stealing them at the same time. This is because what he does in relation to them will be likely to amount to an appropriation within the meaning of [section] 3 as it would if they had not been stolen'.

So why have an offence of handling if the handler is ordinarily guilty of theft? The CLRC gave two reasons. One was that the penalty is higher for handling than for theft (14 years as against then ten, now seven).

■ *Question*

Why should the penalty be higher for handling than for theft?

The second reason given was that certain evidence (relating to other stolen goods found in his possession and to previous convictions for handling or theft) was admissible evidence under s 27 on a charge of handling but was inadmissible on a charge of theft.

Since the introduction of the bad character provisions in the Criminal Justice Act 2003, it is more likely that previous convictions will be admissible on any charges without special provision such as those applying to handling.

27.5.1 Distinguishing handling and theft

Given the decision in the Theft Act 1968 to retain handling as a specific offence, it became necessary to find a formula to set apart handling from theft. Suppose, for example, that D and E enter an unlocked car; D removes the radio and hands this to E. D and E are clearly guilty of theft but unless some special provision is made both would become handlers: E by receiving goods which he knows to be stolen and D by assisting in the disposal of the stolen goods. The special provision is to be found in the words 'otherwise than in the course of the stealing'. Since D and E in this illustration are both clearly in the course of the stealing, they cannot be convicted of handling though they may of course be convicted of theft.

In *Pitham and Hehl* (1976) 65 Cr App R 45, [1977] Crim LR 285, CA, a man called Millman, knowing that his friend McGregor was in prison and in no position to interfere, planned to steal the furniture from McGregor's house. He told the appellants that he had some furniture to sell, took them with him to McGregor's house and there sold them such furniture as they wished to buy at a considerable undervalue. Millman was convicted of stealing the furniture and the appellants of handling it. They argued that as their handling was 'in the course of the stealing' they could not be convicted of handling. Affirming the conviction, the court said, at 48:

Section 22(1) of the Theft Act provides: 'A person handles stolen goods if (otherwise than in the course of the stealing)'—I emphasise the words 'otherwise than in the course of the stealing'—'knowing or believing them to be stolen goods he dishonestly receives the goods, or dishonestly undertakes or assists in their retention, removal, disposal or realisation by or for the benefit of another person, or if he arranges to do so.' Now, the two conflicting academic views can be summarised in this way. Professor Smith's view in his book [*The Law of Theft* (3rd edn, 1977)], para 400, seems to be that 'in the course of the stealing' can be a very short time or it can be a very long period of time. Professor Griew in his book [*The Theft Act* 1968 (2nd edn, 1974)] paras 8-18, 8-19, seems to be of the opinion that, 'in the course of the stealing', embraces not only the act of stealing as defined by section 1 of the Theft Act 1968, but in addition making away with the goods. In the course of expounding their differing views in their books on the Theft Act the two professors have both referred to ancient authorities. Both are of the opinion that the object of the words, 'otherwise than in the course of the stealing' was to deal with the situation where two men are engaged in different capacities in a joint enterprise. In those circumstances, unless some such limiting words as those to which I have referred were included in the definition of handling, a thief could be guilty of both stealing and receiving. An illustration of the sort of problem which arises is provided by Professor Smith's reference to the old case of *Coggins* (1873) 12 Cox CC 517. In his book on the Theft Act at paragraph 400, he summarises the facts of *Coggins* (supra) in these terms: 'If a servant stole money from his master's till and handed it to an accomplice in his master's shop, the accomplice was guilty of larceny and not guilty of receiving.' He added another example. It was the case of *Perkins* (1852) 5 Cox CC 554. He summarises that case as follows: 'Similarly, if a man committed larceny in the room in which he lodged and threw a bundle of stolen goods to an accomplice in the street, the accomplice was guilty of larceny and not guilty of receiving.'

In our judgment the words to which I have referred in section 22(1), were designed to make it clear that in those sorts of situations a man could not be guilty under the Theft Act of both theft and handling. As was pointed out to Mr Murray by my brother, Bristow J, in the course of argument, the Theft Act in section 1 defines theft. It has been said in this Court more than once that the object of that definition was to make a fresh start so as to get rid of all the subtle distinctions which had arisen in the past under the old law of larceny. Sub-section (1) of section 1 has a side heading, 'Basic definition of theft'. That definition is in these terms: 'A person is guilty of theft if he dishonestly appropriates property belonging to another with the intention of permanently depriving the other of it; and "thief" and "steal" shall be construed accordingly.' What Parliament meant by 'appropriate' was defined in section 3(1): 'Any assumption by a person of the rights of an owner amounts to an appropriation, and this includes, where he has come by the property (innocently or not) without stealing it, any later assumption of a right to it by keeping or dealing with it as owner.'

Mr Murray's submission—a very bold one—was that the general words with which section 3(1) opens, namely, 'Any assumption by a person of the rights of an owner amounts to an appropriation,' are limited by the words beginning 'and this includes'. He submitted that those additional words bring back into the law of theft something akin to the concept of appropriation, which was one of the aspects of the law of larceny which the Theft Act 1968 was intended to get rid of. According to Mr Murray, unless there is something which amounts to 'coming by' the property there cannot be an appropriation. We disagree. The final words of section 3(1) are words of inclusion. The general words at the beginning of section 3(1) are wide enough to cover any assumption by a person of the right of an owner.

What was the appropriation in this case? The jury found that the two appellants had handled the property *after* Millman had stolen it. That is clear from their acquittal of these two appellants on count 3 of the indictment which had charged them jointly with Millman. What had Millman done? He had assumed the right of the owner. He had done that when he took the two appellants to 20 Parry Road, showed them the property and invited them to buy what they wanted. He was then acting as the owner. He was then, in the words of the statute, 'assuming the rights of the owner'. The moment he did that he appropriated McGregor's goods to himself. The appropriation was complete. After this appropriation had been completed there was no question of these two appellants taking part, in the words of section 22, in dealing with the goods 'in the course of the stealing'.

It follows that no problem arises in this case. It may well be that some of the situations which the two learned professors envisage and discuss in their books may have to be dealt with at some future date, but not in this case. The facts are too clear.

Mr Murray suggested the learned judge should have directed the jury in some detail about the possibility that the appropriation had not been an instantaneous appropriation, but had been one which had gone on for some time. He submitted that it might have gone on until such time as the furniture was loaded into the appellant's van. For reasons we have already given that was not a real possibility in this case. It is no part of a judge's duty to give the jury the kind of lecture on the law which may be appropriate for a professor to give to a class of undergraduates. We commend the judge for not having involved himself in a detailed academic analysis of the law relating to this case when on the facts it was as clear as anything could be that either these appellants had helped Millman to steal the goods, or Millman had stolen them and got rid of them by sale to these two appellants. We can see nothing wrong in the learned judge's approach to this case and on that particular ground we affirm what he did and said.

■ *Questions*

1. In light of *Pitham and Hehl*, do you think the accomplices in *Coggins* (1873) 38 JP 38 and *Perkins* (1852) 16 JP 406 could be convicted of handling?

2. D and E, employed by V, agree to steal goods belonging to V. D is to steal the goods and place them in E's locker for removal by E. D steals the goods in the morning and places them in E's locker. E removes them just before leaving at 5 pm. Is E a handler? Cf *Atakpu* [1994] QB 69, section 21.3.4, p 753.

27.6 By or for the benefit of another

A thief steals property most often to dispose of it for his own benefit by selling it to another. The CLRC was concerned that the thief should not become a handler by disposing, etc for his own benefit the goods he had stolen and sought to do this by introducing the requirement that the disposal, etc be 'by or for the benefit of another'.

In *Bloxham* [1983] 1 AC 109, [1982] 1 All ER 582, HL, D, having purchased a car which he subsequently discovered had been stolen, sold it at an undervalue to E. The trial judge rejected a submission that he had no case to answer on a charge of handling and he pleaded guilty. His conviction was upheld by the Court of Appeal on the ground that another person, the buyer E, had benefited by D's disposal of the car at an undervalue. The House of Lords quashed D's conviction, holding that the sale of the car by D was not 'for the benefit of another' and thus gave the section its intended effect. Cf J. R. Spencer [1981] Crim LR 682, 684, '[Bloxham] did not "undertake...for the benefit of another" in that he did not act on another's behalf. And although he assisted another in the *acquisition* of the stolen goods that is not the same thing as assisting in their removal, retention, disposal or realisation by another.'

The drafting of s 22 (section 27.2, p 872) is clumsy in some respects and in the Draft Criminal Code handling is, by cl 172, defined as follows:

A person is guilty of handling stolen goods if (otherwise than in the course of the stealing) knowing or believing them to be stolen goods, he dishonestly:

(a) receives or arranges to receive the goods; or

(b) undertakes or arranges to undertake their retention, removal, disposal or realisation for the benefit of another; or

(c) assists or arranges to assist in their retention, removal, disposal or realisation by another.

27.7 Mens rea

The mens rea contains two elements: (i) dishonesty; and (ii) knowledge or belief that the goods are stolen.

27.7.1 Dishonesty

Dishonesty bears the same meaning as it does for other offences under the Act, see section 21.6, p 772 (but note that s 2 of the Act does not apply). If D intends to restore the goods to the owner he is obviously not acting dishonestly.

In *Roberts* (1986) 84 Cr App R 117, [1986] Crim LR 122, CA, insurers advertised a reward for the return of stolen paintings. D contacted them offering to return the paintings provided no attempt was made to arrest him. He was arrested as he collected the £10,000 reward and subsequently convicted of handling, the prosecution's case being that he was involved with the thieves. D appealed, *inter alia*, on the ground that dishonesty in s 22 must involve dishonesty vis-à-vis the owner of the property and not dishonesty in a more general sense. Dismissing D's appeal, the court said that whether D acted dishonestly in relation to the owner would in some circumstances be important, the question whether D was dishonest was a subjective one and it was not necessary that the jury must consider whether D was dishonest vis-à-vis the owner. But in the context of s 22, other than the owner, in respect of whom can the act be said to be dishonest? The go-between presents problems. The owner is often anxious to recover his property and is willing to pay for it. Suppose he employs D to contact the thieves to arrange for restoration of the property and D does so (see [1972] Crim LR 213). Literally, D assists in its disposal for the benefit of the thieves but his conduct cannot be accounted as dishonest at least if he gets no more from the owner than fair remuneration for his services.

■ *Questions*

Is D, a go-between, dishonest if, knowing of the great sentimental value of the property to the owner, he makes an extravagant charge for his services? What if in *Roberts* the thieves had approached D saying that the paintings would be delivered to him for restoration to the insurers, and that D could pay the thieves £9,000 and keep £1,000 for himself?

27.7.2 Knowing or believing

The interpretation of 'knowing or believing' has caused a lot of problems. It has been held a misdirection to tell the jury that it suffices that D suspected the goods were stolen, or that he believed it more likely than not that the goods were stolen, or that he closed his eyes to the obvious. In *Harris* (1986) 84 Cr App R 75 at 78, CA, it was said, 'In our judgment the words "knowledge or belief" are words of ordinary usage in English. In most cases, but not all, all that need be said to a jury is to ask them whether that which is alleged by the prosecution, namely receipt, knowing or believing that the goods were stolen, has been established.' In *Hall* (1985) 81 Cr App R 260 at 264, CA, the court had this to say:

We think that a jury should be directed along these lines. A man may be said to know that goods are stolen when he is told by someone with first hand knowledge (someone such as the thief or the burglar) that such is the case. Belief, of course, is something short of knowledge. It may be said to be the state of mind of a person who says to himself: 'I cannot say I know for certain that these goods are stolen, but there can be no other reasonable conclusion in the light of all the circumstances, in the light of all that I have heard and seen.' Either of those two states of mind is enough to satisfy the words of the statute. The second is enough (that is, belief) even if the defendant says to himself: 'Despite all that I have seen and all that I have heard, I refuse to believe what my brain tells me is obvious.' What is not enough, of course, is mere suspicion. 'I suspect that these goods may be stolen, but it may be on the other hand that they are not.' That state of mind, of course, does not fall within the words 'knowing or believing'.

In *Forsyth* (section 27.3.1.1, p 874) the judge based his direction on *Hall* and the conviction was quashed because it was potentially confusing. Judges have to be careful not to tell juries that 'mere suspicion is not enough' because that might lead them to think that 'great' suspicion is enough. The very greatest suspicion is, apparently, not enough, even when coupled with the fact that D deliberately shut his eyes to the circumstances. In fact, this seems to be exactly the situation which the CLRC thought would be covered by 'believing'—their example is of a person who buys goods at a ridiculously low price from an unknown seller whom he meets in a pub: Eighth Report, para 64. Is the best practical advice to the judge now that he should avoid any explanation of what 'believing', as distinct from 'knowing', means? Any explanation he gives is almost bound to be wrong. The Court of Appeal constantly tells us what 'believing' is not, but never tells us (except unsuccessfully, as in *Hall*) what it is. Professor Shute has suggested that knowledge constitutes a true belief, and belief includes acceptance of the proposition in question whereas knowledge does not (S. Shute, 'Knowledge and Belief in the Criminal Law' in S. Shute and A. Simester (eds), *Criminal Law Theory: Doctrines of the General Part* (2002), p 194). In *Montila* [2004] 1 WLR 3141, the House accepted (at [27]) that: 'A person cannot know that something is A when in fact it is B. The proposition that a person knows that something is A is based on the premise that it is true that it is A. The fact that the property is A provides the starting point. Then there is the question whether the person knows that the property is A.' Subsequently in *Saik* [2006] UKHL 18, the House of Lords concluded (at [26]): 'the word know should be interpreted strictly and not watered down. In this context knowledge means true belief.' See also Hooper LJ in *Liaquat Ali and others* [2005] EWCA Crim 87 (at [98]), [2005] 2 Cr App R 864.

Hall suggests that if D had direct evidence, he knows; if he has mere circumstantial evidence, he believes. But, it would surely be more accurate to describe knowledge in terms of the accuracy of the belief, not the directness of the evidence leading to the belief.

What the judge may do is to tell the jury that turning a blind eye to the obvious inference that the goods were stolen is *evidence* that he *believed* they were stolen; but then he would be advised to stress that they must be sure that he really did believe that. If the jury ask him what *is* this state of mind of which they must be sure, probably all he can properly do is to tell them that 'believing' is an ordinary word of the English language and that, provided they remember it is not suspicion, however great, its meaning is a matter for them, not him.

■ *Questions*

1. What is the best solution? Should the law require nothing less than that D knows that the goods are stolen? Or should it be sufficient that D has deliberately turned a blind eye to the possibility; or merely that he is aware that it is (i) highly probable, (ii) probable or (iii) possible that they are stolen?

2. Would there be a stronger argument for criminalizing reckless handling if the offence was specifically subdivided into offences treating separately professional handling and single incidents of low-value 'dodgy trading'?

27.8 Dishonestly retaining a wrongful credit

The increased credit balance procured by *Preddy*, section 21.5.2, p 761, would, before the decision of the House, have been 'stolen goods', and could be the subject of an offence of handling, contrary to s 22 of the 1968 Act. That is no longer so. The Theft (Amendment) Act 1996 filled this lacuna by a new s 24A of the 1968 Act, creating an offence of 'Dishonestly retaining a wrongful credit'.

27.9 Rewards for return of stolen goods

By s 23 of the Theft Act 1968 it is an offence publicly to advertise for the return of stolen goods indicating that no questions will be asked about how the person returning the goods came by them.

■ *Questions*

Should it be? Who does this offence seek to punish and why?

27.10 The Proceeds of Crime Act 2002

In addition to the offence of handling stolen goods, there are numerous other offences for which a person may be criminally liable for possessing, acquiring, transferring, concealing, etc property that derives from criminal conduct or property that represents the proceeds of criminal conduct. Part 7 of the Proceeds of Crime Act 2002 introduced three 'money laundering' offences: ss 327, 328 and 329. These are exceedingly technical and controversial offences. We offer only a brief introduction to them here.

27.10.1 Criminal property

Sections 327 to 329 of the Proceeds of Crime Act 2002 criminalize D's dealings (concealing, disguising, converting, transferring, acquiring, using, possessing, etc) with 'criminal property'. Section 340 defines what constitutes criminal property and is therefore central to their operation. It is a complex provision defining criminal conduct and criminal property:

> (3) Property is criminal property if—
>
>   (a) it constitutes a person's benefit from criminal conduct or it represents such a benefit (in whole or part and whether directly or indirectly), and
>
>   (b) the alleged offender knows or suspects that it constitutes or represents such a benefit.

It is immaterial who committed the offence which generated the criminal property.

> (5) A person benefits from conduct if he obtains property as a result of or in connection with the conduct.

The 'predicate offence' (as it is known) could be any crime.

> (9) Property is all property wherever situated and includes—
>
>   (a) money;
>
>   (b) all forms of property, real or personal, heritable or moveable;
>
>   (c) things in action and other intangible or incorporeal property.

Notice that the property only becomes criminal property if D knows or suspects it to be criminally tainted. It is not enough to show merely that the property constitutes someone's benefit from crime; there is an element of *mens rea* to be proved.

There must be criminal property in fact and D must know or suspect it to be such. In *Shah v HSBC* [2009] EWHC 79 (QB) at [39] per Hamblen J:

> If the property in question is not in fact 'criminal property' then no offence is committed.

The criminal property must be identified, but the predicate offence that it is alleged generated the property need not be specified with precision. There is no need to prove that someone was convicted of the predicate offence and the courts have held that there is no obligation to prove the precise form of the predicate offence: for example, *Anwoir* [2008] EWCA Crim 1354 at [21]:

> ...there are two ways in which the Crown can prove the property derives from crime, a) by showing that it derives from conduct of a specific kind or kinds and that conduct of that kind or those kinds is unlawful, or b) by evidence of the circumstances in which the property is handled which are such as to give rise to the irresistible inference that it can only be derived from crime.

For a review of the case law see *DPP v Bolah* [2011] UKPC 44.

27.10.2 The s 327 offence

Section 327 creates an offence where in relation to criminal property D: conceals; disguises; converts; transfers; or removes it from the UK. Section 327(3) defines concealing or disguising criminal property as including 'concealing or disguising its nature, source, location, disposition, movement or ownership or any rights with respect to it'. The offence is broadly drawn, and has the scope to apply in cases that would usually be thought of as classic instances of handling stolen goods. In *Thompson*, [2010] EWCA Crim 1216, for example, D was convicted under s 327 when he sold a train set to a specialist shop for £180 when its true value was £3,500. The train set had been stolen five days earlier. D claimed to have bought it at a car boot sale. The jury found that the property was criminal property because it was the proceeds of crime (theft) and D suspected as much.

There is no requirement to prove dishonesty. Nor is there any requirement that D is aware of the precise criminality which created the property. It is sufficient that he does one of the acts—concealing, disguising, etc—and knows or suspects the property is the proceeds of criminal conduct.

The mens rea requirement is very wide. Suspicion is an ordinary English word. In *Da Silva* [2006] EWCA Crim 1654 the judge directed the jury that:

> to suspect something, you have a state of mind that is well short of knowing that the matter that you suspect is true. It is an ordinary English word. . . . The dictionary definition of 'suspicion' [is] 'an act of suspecting, the imagining of something without evidence or on slender evidence, inkling, mistrust'. Therefore, any inkling or fleeting thought that the money being paid into her account . . . might be the proceeds of criminal conduct will suffice for the offence against her to be proved.

The Court of Appeal held that the meaning of the word 'suspect' and its affiliates was that the defendant had to think that there was a possibility, which was more than fanciful, that the relevant facts existed. A vague feeling of unease would not suffice; however, the statute did not require that the suspicion had to be 'clear' or 'firmly grounded and targeted on specific facts', or based upon 'reasonable grounds'.

27.10.3 The s 328 offence

Section 328 creates only one offence of entering into or becoming concerned in an arrangement which, D 'knows or suspects facilitates (by whatever means) the acquisition, retention, use or control of criminal property by or on behalf of another person'. In *Geary* [2010] EWCA Crim 1925, Moore-Bick LJ said:

> In our view the natural and ordinary meaning of section 328(1) is that the arrangement to which it refers must be one which relates to property which is criminal property at the time when the arrangement begins to operate on it. To say that it extends to property which was originally legitimate but became criminal only as a result of carrying out the arrangement is to stretch the language of the section beyond its proper limits. An arrangement relating to property which has an independent criminal object may, when carried out, render the subject matter criminal property, but it cannot properly be said that the arrangement applied to property that was already criminal property at the time it began to operate on it.

On this construction, there is no need for the criminal property to exist prior to the time the arrangement will take effect. D agrees that E (a drug dealer) can bring cash to D's bureau de change in a week's time. At the time D and E make that agreement, the criminal property does not exist as E has not yet sold his drug supply for the week. When the arrangement takes effect—when E delivers the money to the bureau—the criminal property will exist.

There is no requirement of dishonesty, etc. D must know or suspect that the property is criminal property. The concept of 'suspicion' was considered previously.

In *Dare v CPS* [2012] EWHC 2074 (Admin), the Divisional Court examined the potential overlap between handling and the offence in s 328. D was convicted of an offence under s 328 of the Proceeds of Crime Act 2002 of entering or becoming concerned in an arrangement which he knows or suspects facilitates (by whatever means) the acquisition, retention, use or control of criminal property by or on behalf of another person. D had been approached by someone he knew to be a car trader but who, as D knew, had been involved with stolen cars. D had been offered a car and arranged to meet the trader to negotiate. The sale to D never took place. The magistrates found that D had agreed to meet the trader for a second time in order to buy the car, albeit at a reduced price, and in doing so had entered into an arrangement within the meaning of s 328(1). The Divisional Court quashed the conviction. Under s 328, the 'arrangement' had to be one that 'facilitates', not one that 'will facilitate'. In this case the agreement was to meet with a view to arranging a price; it was not even a contract of sale. If the price had been negotiated and the car was handed over, that would have facilitated the future acquisition of the car by another. The court suggested that s 328(1) applies if in the precise moment of the arrangement one could say it 'facilitates' the acquisition of criminal property by or on behalf of another person, and therefore that other person had to be identified or identifiable. The court was clearly concerned that on the Crown's construction every case of handling stolen goods with a view to resale would constitute an offence under s 328(1), but would be criminal at a much earlier point in time. The court gave the example of a man who bought a stolen watch with a view to selling it on at a profit: such a person was undoubtedly guilty of handling stolen goods if he knew or suspected that the watch was stolen and, if the watch was stolen, on those facts the purchaser had entered into an arrangement which he knew or suspected would facilitate, in the future, the acquisition of criminal property by or on behalf of another. On the Crown's submission, both individuals would have committed a s 328 offence at the moment that those individuals arranged to meet with a view to the watch being sold.

27.10.4 The s 329 offence

Section 329 creates three offences of acquisition, use and possession of criminal property. Subsection 3 provides that for the purposes of this section:

> (a) a person acquires property for inadequate consideration if the value of the consideration is significantly less than the value of the property;
>
> (b) a person uses or has possession of property for inadequate consideration if the value of the consideration is significantly less than the value of the use or possession;
>
> (c) the provision by a person of goods or services which he knows or suspects may help another to carry out criminal conduct is not consideration.

The offence has a wide reach. The thief who retains possession of property that he has stolen commits an offence under s 329(1)(b) or (c). In this respect it is easier to prove than handling since there is no issue as to whether the money laundering occurred otherwise than in the course of theft. It has, however, been argued that the thief never obtains an interest (in the sense of a legal interest) in the stolen goods and that there is no criminal property to be laundered under s 329. The counter and, it is submitted, stronger argument is that the thief would acquire possession of the property, and that is treated, in the law of theft at least, as a proprietary interest. The ease with which these offences can be proved by comparison with the offences under the Theft Act 1968 has led to some controversial convictions, for example *Hogan v DPP* [2007] 1 WLR 2944.

Dishonesty is not required under s 329. D must know or suspect that the property in question is criminal property. Suspicion is considered in section 27.10.2, p 890.

Section 329 provides a defence if D has acquired the property for adequate consideration.

27.10.5 Defences to ss 327 to 329 offences

There are two defences common to ss 327 to 329. First, where a person makes an authorized disclosure to the authorities under s 338 or was intending to do so and had a reasonable excuse for failing to do. Secondly, D will have a defence if he knows, or believes on reasonable grounds, that the relevant 'criminal' conduct occurred (or is occurring) in a country outside the UK, and is not (or was not at that time) criminal in that country.

27.11 Charging money laundering or handling?

The overlap between the offences in the Proceeds of Crime Act 2002 and the offence of handling seems obvious. There are certainly advantages for the prosecutor in charging money laundering. There is no need to prove that D was dishonest, or that he 'knew or believed' that the property in question was stolen goods. Mere suspicion is sufficient mens rea for money laundering. Money laundering also has the advantage of capturing the conduct of the thief himself, who under s 22 and following *Bloxham*, cannot be convicted of handling unless he does so 'for the benefit of another'. Moreover, there are no difficulties in money laundering charges if the goods were allegedly stolen abroad.

FURTHER READING

Handling

L. Blake, 'The Innocent Purchaser and Section 22 of the Theft Act' [1972] Crim LR 494

D. W. Elliott, 'Theft and Related Problems— England, Australia and the USA Compared' (1977) 26 ICLQ 110, 135–144

S. P. Green, *13 Ways to Steal a Bicycle* (2012), pp 182–192

E. Griew, 'Consistency, Communication and Codification—Reflections on Two Mens Rea Words' in P. R. Glazebrook (ed), *Reshaping the Criminal Law* (1978)

A. T. H. Smith, 'Theft and/or Handling' [1977] Crim LR 517

J. R. Spencer, 'The Mishandling of Handling' [1981] Crim LR 682

J. R. Spencer, 'Handling, Theft and the Mala Fide Purchaser' [1985] Crim LR 92

Money laundering

V. Walters, 'Prosecuting Money Launderers: Does the Prosecution Have to Prove the Predicate Offence?' [2009] Crim LR 571

28
Offences of damage to property

28.1 Introduction

The offences of damage to property are heavily used, with most prosecutions occurring in the magistrates' court. Most of the cases involve relatively minor acts of damage, but the offences also encompass much more serious cases including arson and damaging property intending or being reckless as to whether life is endangered. Some prosecutions for criminal damage also take on an enhanced gravity in constitutional terms because, although the value of the property damaged might be small, the act of damage has been done by way of protest and free expression. All in all, criminal damage offences can involve points of greater legal difficulty than would at first appear.

The principal offences of damage to property are governed by the Criminal Damage Act 1971. This legislation followed from the work of the Law Commission: see the Law Commission Report No 29, *Criminal Law: Report on Offences of Damage to Property* (1970).

Some of the controversies that will be explored in this chapter include the following:

(i)   the ability to define damage;

(ii) the relationship between the elements of the offence, particularly D's mens rea as to circumstance elements;

(iii) the arguments for endangerment offences.

28.2 Destroying or damaging property of another

Criminal Damage Act 1971, s 1(1)

A person who without lawful excuse destroys or damages any property belonging to another intending to destroy or damage any such property or being reckless as to whether any such property would be destroyed or damaged shall be guilty of an offence.

Where the damage is caused other than by fire (see section 28.4, p 923) the offence is punishable by imprisonment for up to ten years.

28.2.1 Destroy or damage

The Act does not define 'destroy or damage'. The *Oxford English Dictionary* defines 'damage' as 'injury, harm, *esp* physical injury to a thing such as impairs its value or usefulness'.

28.2.1.1 Impairment of usefulness as damage?

The tenor of the cases under the Act indicates that, as under the former law, 'damage' embraces not only physical damage to the property but also any impairment, temporary or permanent, to the value of usefulness of the property: *Morphitis v Salmon* [1990] Crim LR 48, DC.

In *Samuels v Stubbs* [1972] 4 SASR 200 at 203, Walters J said:

> It seems to me that it is difficult to lay down any very general and, at the same time, precise and absolute rule as to what constitutes 'damage'. One must be guided in a great degree by the circumstances of each case, the nature of the article and the mode in which it is affected or treated. . . . It is my view, however, that the word . . . is sufficiently wide in its meaning to embrace injury, mischief or harm done to property, and that in order to constitute 'damage' it is unnecessary to establish such definite or actual damage as renders the property useless, or prevents it from serving its normal function . . .

And the judge then held that a 'temporary functional derangement' of a policeman's cap resulting from it being trampled upon constituted damage, even though there was no evidence that the cap might not have been restored to its original shape at no cost and without any real trouble to the owner.

■ *Questions*

1. Is the definition of damage dependent on whether the owner has to spend time and/or money on repair? Should it be?

2. Can it sensibly be said that the cap in *Samuels v Stubbs* was damaged if it could be pressed back into shape in a matter of moments?

In *Hardman v Chief Constable of Avon and Somerset Constabulary* [1986] Crim LR 330 (Judge Llewellyn Jones and justices), it was held that pavement drawings in water-soluble paint constituted damage when the local authority incurred expense in removing them with high-pressure water jets; and in *Roe v Kingerlee* [1986] Crim LR 735, DC, it was held that where D had smeared mud and graffiti on the wall of a police cell the justices were wrong to conclude that this was incapable of amounting to damage.

■ *Question*

In *Hardman*, the council clearly incurred expense in washing down the pavement. Would the pavement have been damaged had the council left it to the next downpour to wash away the paint?

In *A (a juvenile) v R* [1978] Crim LR 689, D's conviction for damaging a police officer's raincoat by spitting on it was quashed. 'Spitting at a garment,' Judge Streeter said:

> could be an act capable of causing damage. However, one must consider the specific garment which has been allegedly damaged. If someone spat upon a satin wedding dress, for example, any attempt to remove the spittle might in itself leave a mark or stain. The court would find no difficulty in saying that an article had been rendered 'imperfect' if, after a reasonable attempt at cleaning it, a stain remained. An article might also have been rendered 'inoperative' if, as a result of what happened, it had been taken to dry cleaners. However, in the present case, no attempt had been made, even with soap and water, to clean the raincoat, which was a service raincoat designed to resist the elements. Consequently, there was no likelihood that if wiped with a damp cloth, the first obvious remedy, there would be any trace or mark remaining on the raincoat requiring further cleaning.

> ■ **Questions**
>
> 1. Was Judge Streeter right to rule that the raincoat was not damaged because it could be wiped clean with a damp cloth? What if the police officer had insisted (perhaps not unreasonably) that the coat be dry-cleaned before he wore it again?
>
> 2. Is there (should there be) a principle of *de minimis* in relation to criminal damage?

In *Faik* [2005] EWCA Crim 2381, F, in detention in a police cell, placed his blanket down the lavatory and then flushed it repeatedly, causing his cell, and two adjoining cells, to become flooded. Obviously the blanket was wet as a result, although not visibly soiled. The water which caused flooding was clear water from the lavatory falling onto a waterproof cell floor. The blanket was unusable until it was cleaned and dry. The cells themselves had had to be cleaned by a contract cleaner before they were usable. F's conviction for criminal damage was upheld.

28.2.1.2 Damaging by dismantling

Under the former law, it was held that a machine may be damaged by removing an integral part (*Tacey* (1821) Russ & Ry 452); or by tampering with it so that it will not work (*Fisher* (1865) LR 1 CCR 7, DC); or by running it in a manner so as to cause impairment (*Norris* (1840) 9 C & P 241); or by dismantling it (*Getty v Antrim County Council* [1950] NI 114). As for damage to computers, see section 28.2.1.4, p 896 and see section 28.7, p 923.

To remove the rotor arm or electronic ignition component from a car constitutes damage to the car (though not to the rotor arm or component if this is removed without damaging it) since without the component the car will not go. But a mere denial of use of property does not constitute damage. If a landowner finding a car parked in his courtyard chooses to lock up his premises for the night, there is no damage to the car though its owner will have to wait until the following morning before he can drive it away.

> ■ **Questions**
>
> What if D, as a practical joke, hides the ignition key to V's car and the key to V's house? Is the car damaged because V cannot drive it away? Is V's house damaged because V cannot gain access? Is the door to the house damaged because V cannot open it?

A series of cases has considered whether wheel clamping a car might constitute damage. In *Lloyd v DPP* [1992] 1 All ER 982, DC, the court rejected a submission that, in the absence of any evidence that the clamping caused damage to the car, this constituted criminal damage. *Lloyd* was followed in *Drake v DPP* [1994] RTR 411, [1994] Crim LR 855 and commentary, the court holding that clamping involved no intrusion into the physical integrity of the car. There is now a specific offence contained in s 54 of the Protection of Freedoms Act 2012 of immobilizing a vehicle without lawful authority.

> ■ **Questions**
>
> 1. Deflating the tyres of a car would presumably amount to damage since the car, albeit temporarily, is deprived of its usefulness. So why not clamping? Additionally, in *Lloyd* D's car had 'a large yellow sticker affixed to its windscreen' alerting D to the clamping. Might this have constituted damage to the car?
>
> 2. Is a car damaged by (i) disconnecting the battery terminals; (ii) removing the ignition key; (iii) removing a wheel; (iv) clamping a wheel?

28.2.1.3 Damage undefined?

In *Henderson and Battley* (unreported but noted in *Cox v Riley* (1986) 83 Cr App R 54, [1986] Crim LR 460), the Court of Appeal said that ultimately whether damage was done was a question of fact for the jury; and in *Roe v Kingerlee*, the Divisional Court said that what constitutes damage is 'a matter of fact and degree and it is for the justices to decide whether what occurred was damage or not'. In *Samuels v Stubbs*, counsel for D submitted that the finding 'of fact' by the trial court that the hat had not been damaged ought not to be disturbed. Walters J said that not only was it the practice of Australian courts to distinguish between the determination of the evidence (a matter of fact) and the determination of the inferences to be drawn from those facts (a matter of law) but that this view was based on respected English authorities.

■ *Question*

Which view is to be preferred: is it fact or law?

It seems clear that damage can be held to be caused despite the property being enhanced in the view of the defendant or even some other people. For example, if someone were to paint a graffiti mural on a wall that would constitute damage to the wall even if D saw it as a vast improvement. What if the artist was Bansky? What if the owner of the wall hated Bansky's work? See also M. Watson, 'Graffiti—Popular Art, Anti Social Behaviour or Criminal Damage' (2004) 168 JP 668.

■ *Question*

Does D damage property by improving it (i) in his eyes, (ii) in the reasonable person's eyes (eg by painting over offensive slogans: *Fancy* [1980] Crim LR 171)?

28.2.1.4 Computers

The modification of the contents of a computer shall not be regarded as damaging any computer or computer storage for the purposes of the Criminal Damage Act unless its effect on that computer or computer storage medium impairs its physical condition. See the Police and Justice Act 2006, Sch 14, para 2.

28.2.2 **Property**

Criminal Damage Act 1971, s 10(1)

In this Act 'property' means property of a tangible nature, whether real or personal, including money and:

(a) including wild creatures which have been tamed or are ordinarily kept in captivity, and any other wild creatures or their carcasses if, but only if, they have been reduced into possession which has not been lost or abandoned or are in the course of being reduced into possession; but

(b) not including mushrooms growing wild on any land or flowers, fruit or foliage of a plant growing wild on any land.

For the purposes of this sub-section 'mushroom' includes any fungus and 'plant' includes any shrub or tree.

Law Com No 29, *Criminal Law: Report on Offences of Damage to Property* (1970), paras 34 and 35

Offences of criminal damage to property in the context of the present law connote physical damage in their commission, and for that reason we have not included intangible things in the class of property, damage to which should constitute an offence. On the other hand, in the context of damage to property there is no reason to distinguish, as does the Theft Act between land and other property . . . We recommend, therefore, that the property which can be the subject of an offence of criminal damage should be all property of a tangible nature, whether real or personal.

■ *Question*

Why should D be liable for digging up his neighbour's lawn, but not for stealing it?

28.2.2.1 Animals

In *Cresswell v DPP* [2006] EWHC 3379 (Admin), the Divisional Court considered whether badgers which had been enticed into traps set by officials from DEFRA had become 'property' for the purposes of the Criminal Damage Act 1971. The defendants sought to argue that the badgers were property and that they therefore had a defence to destroying the traps because by destroying the traps they were protecting property—the badgers. Keene LJ, rejecting the argument, stated (at [11]) that:

merely to entice a wild animal, whether it be a badger or a game bird or a deer, to a particular spot from time to time by providing food there, even with the objective ultimately of killing it in due course, does not form part of the a course normally of reducing it into possession. If the creature were thereby to become the property, say, of the landowner providing the food, it would mean that it could not then be lawfully shot by the adjoining landowner on or over whose land it passed.

Walker J was more hesitant, declining to express a concluded view on what constitutes property. His lordship did express some more general views on the concept of wild animals (at [38]):

In broad terms, (a) it is a question of law whether an animal is wild or domestic. . . . (b) Once a wild animal is killed or dies, absolute property in the dead animal vests in the owner of the land or, in a case where relevant shooting or sporting rights have been granted, in the owner of those rights. (c) While a wild animal is alive there is no absolute property in that animal. There may, however, be what is known as a qualified property in them in three circumstances. The first is described as a qualified property *per industriam*. Wild animals become the property of a person who takes or tames or reclaims them until they regain their natural liberty and have not the intention to return. Examples of that kind of property include animals such as deer, swans and doves. A second qualified property is described as *ratione impotentiae et loci*. The owner of land has a qualified property in the young of animals born on the land until they can fly or run away. A third type of qualified property is described as *ratione soli* and *ratione privilegii*. An owner of land who has retained the exclusive right to hunt, take and kill wild animals on his land has a qualified property in them for the time being while they are there but if he grants to another the right to hunt, take or kill them then the grantee has a qualified property.

28.2.3 Belonging to another

Criminal Damage Act 1971, s 10

(2) Property shall be treated for the purposes of this Act as belonging to any person:

(a) having the custody or control of it;

(b) having in it any proprietary right or interest (not being an equitable interest arising only from an agreement to transfer or grant an interest); or

(c) having a charge on it.

(3) Where property is subject to a trust, the persons to whom it belongs shall be so treated as including any person having a right to enforce the trust.

(4) Property of a corporation sole shall be so treated as belonging to the corporation notwithstanding a vacancy in the corporation.

The offence under s 1(1) may be committed only where D destroys or damages property 'belonging to another'. Since there are similar policy considerations, the Criminal Damage Act, s 10(2), is similar to, though not identical with, the Theft Act 1968, s 5 (section 21.5, p 757). It is accordingly enough that V has some proprietary interest in the property which D damages and it does not have to be shown that V is the owner of the property; D may, for example, own a book which he has loaned to V and which V has left in the custody of V2 while he goes for lunch. D may commit an offence against V1 and V2 if they have a proprietary interest in the property and D acts with mens rea. See *Seray-Wurie v DPP* [2012] EWHC 208 (Admin).

But if no party other than D has any interest in the property, D cannot by destroying that property, nor by authorizing its destruction, commit an offence under s 1(1), even if this is done in order to perpetrate a fraud by making a claim against insurers.

> ■ *Questions*
>
> D falls out with his wife and, out of spite, defaces the original Picasso which she bought him as a present. Is D liable for criminal damage? Should he be?

28.2.4 Mens rea: intention or recklessness

It is not enough to prove that D intentionally did the act (threw the stone, fired the gun) which caused damage, nor that D intended to cause damage to the property; it must also be proved that D intended to damage property of *another*.

R v Smith (David Raymond)
[1974] 1 All ER 632, Court of Appeal, Criminal Division

(Roskill and James LJJ, Talbot J)

The defendant rented a flat. He installed wiring for his music equipment. He also installed new panels and floorboards. As a matter of law, the boards became part of the property and belonged to the landlord. When D came to leave the property he damaged the panels to gain access to the wiring which D sought to remove. The damage caused was in the sum of £130. When interviewed by the police, the appellant said, 'Look, how can I be done for smashing my own property. I put the flooring and that in, so if I want to pull it down, it's a matter for me.'

[James LJ read the following judgment of the court:]

The offence for which he was indicted is in these terms:

'Damaging property contrary to section 1(1) of the Criminal Damage Act 1971. *Particulars of Offence:* [The appellant] and Steven John Smith on the 19th day of September 1972 in Greater London, without lawful excuse, damaged a conservatory at 209, Freemasons Road, E16, the property of Peter Frank Frand, intending to damage such property or being reckless as to whether such property would be damaged.'

... The appellant's defence was that he honestly believed that the damage he did was to his own property, that he believed that he was entitled to damage his own property, and therefore he had a lawful excuse for his action causing the damage [His lordship referred to the summing up.]

...

The offence created [by the Criminal Damage Act, s 1(1)] includes the elements of intention or recklessness and the absence of lawful excuse. There is in s5 of the Act a partial 'definition' of lawful excuse.... [His lordship referred to s 5(2), s 5(3) and s 5(5).]

It is argued for the appellant that an honest, albeit erroneous, belief that the act causing damage or destruction was done to his own property provides a defence to a charge brought under s 1(1). The argument is put in three ways. First, that the offence charged includes the act causing the damage or destruction and the element of mens rea. The element of mens rea relates to all the circumstances of the criminal act. The criminal act in the offence is causing damage to or destruction of 'property belonging to another' and the element of mens rea, therefore, must relate to 'property belonging to another'. Honest belief, whether justifiable or not, that the property is the defendant's own negatives the element of mens rea....

It is conceded by counsel for the Crown that there is force in the argument that the element of mens rea extends to 'property belonging to another'. But, it is argued, the section creates a new statutory offence and that it is open to the construction that the mental element in the offence relates only to causing damage to or destroying property. That if in fact the property damaged or destroyed is shown to be another's property the offence is committed although the defendant did not intend or foresee damage to, another person's property.

We are informed that so far as research has revealed this is the first occasion on which this court has had to consider the question which arises in this appeal.

It is not without interest to observe that under the law in force before the passing of the Criminal Damage Act 1971, it was clear that no offence was committed by a person who destroyed or damaged property belonging to another in the honest but mistaken belief that the property was his own or that he had a legal right to do the damage. In *Twose* [(1879) 14 Cox CC 327] the prisoner was indicted for setting fire to furze [a type of bush] on a common. Persons living near the common had occasionally burned the furze in order to improve the growth of grass but without the right to do so. The prisoner denied setting fire to the furze and it was submitted that even if it were proved that she did she could not be found guilty if she bona fide believed she had a right to do so whether the right were a good one or not. Lopes J ruled that if she set fire to the furze thinking she had a right to do so that would not be a criminal offence.

On the facts of the present appeal the charge, if brought before the 1971 Act came into force, would have been laid under s 13 of the Malicious Damage Act 1861, alleging damage by a tenant to a building. It was a defence to a charge under that section that the tenant acted under a claim of right to do the damage.

If the direction given by the deputy judge in the present case is correct, then the offence created by s 1(1) of the 1971 Act involves a considerable extension of the law in a surprising direction. Whether or not this is so depends on the construction of the section. Construing the language of s 1(1) we have no doubt that the actus reus is 'destroying or damaging any property belonging to another'. It is not possible to exclude the words 'belonging to another' which describe the 'property'. Applying the ordinary principles of mens rea, the intention and recklessness and the absence of lawful excuse required to constitute the offence have reference to property belonging to another. It follows that in our judgment no offence is committed under this section if a person destroys or causes damage to property belonging to another if he does so in the honest though mistaken belief that the property is his own, and provided that the belief is honestly held it is irrelevant to consider whether or not it is a justifiable belief.

In our judgment, the direction given to the jury was a fundamental misdirection in law. The consequence was that the jury were precluded from considering facts capable of being a defence to the charge and were directed to convict . . .

Appeal allowed. Conviction quashed

Smith made an error in thinking that the wiring he had installed belonged to him and not to the landlord but as long as he did believe this he could not be convicted of damaging property 'belonging to another'. Compare that with the following case.

R v Appleyard

(1985) 81 Cr App R 319, Court of Appeal, Criminal Division

(Lord Lane CJ, Skinner and Macpherson JJ)

The defendant and a man called Lawford were charged with arson. It was alleged that they had set fire to premises belonging to Pontefract Tape Ltd. The defendant was the manager of the company and the owner of the premises.

The Lord Chief Justice . . . [His lordship set out the detail of the allegation and defence counsel's argument.]

It was argued by him that since the appellant was in effect the owner of the premises, he must be entitled to set fire to them if he wanted to. It could not therefore be said that he was acting without lawful excuse as the statute requires. After a very lengthy submission indeed, the learned Judge rejected that submission, the trial continued and, as already indicated, the jury convicted.

The first and main issue at the trial was the question whether it was proved to the satisfaction of the jury so that they felt sure that this man had started the fire. The jury came to the conclusion, not surprisingly, that they were so satisfied.

The next problem was that raised by the words of the statute itself. [His lordship read s 1 . . .:]

The only point of this appeal is whether the judge was right in rejecting that submission or not. Mr Steer confines his argument today to section 1 and does not rely on the provisions of section 5(2), to which it is, therefore, not necessary for us to refer.

The basis of Mr Steer's submission, as he was eventually driven to concede, was a statement by this Court in *Denton* (1981) 74 Cr App Rep 81. Let me just read the headnote relating the facts of that case in order to show the way it is distinguished from the present circumstances. It reads as follows: 'The appellant, who was employed by one T, set fire to T's business premises and was charged with arson contrary to section 1(1) and (3) of the Criminal Damage Act 1971. At his trial he gave evidence that T had asked him to start the fire because T's company was in difficulties and a fire might improve the financial circumstances of the company. The appellant relied on section 5(2) of the Act of 1971 [section 28.2.5, p ***] providing him with a defence to the charge in that T had consented to the damage caused by the fire and intended to make a fraudulent insurance claim in respect of it. The trial judge ruled that 'entitled' in section 5(2)(a) carried a connotation of general lawfulness and that T could not be said to have been entitled to consent to damage for a fraudulent purpose, so that the defence under section 5(2) was not open to the appellant, whereupon the latter changed his plea to one of guilty. On appeal against the judge's ruling,

'*Held*, that no offence was committed under section 1(1) and (3) of the Criminal Damage Act 1971 by a person who burnt down his own premises; nor could that act become unlawful because of an inchoate intent to defraud the insurers; accordingly, the judge's ruling was wrong; and as the appellant's plea of guilty had been based upon that ruling, the appeal would be allowed and the conviction quashed.'

It will therefore be seen that the point at issue in that case was nothing to do with the point in issue in the present case. Moreover in that case it was the servant of the company who had set light to the machinery and not T. In the present case it is the managing director or, as Mr Steer chooses inaccurately to call him, the proprietor of the business who had, according to the jury's finding, set fire to the property.

Therefore in order to support his argument and, as he concedes, as the basis of his argument, Mr Steer relies upon a passage in the judgment of *Denton* (1981) 74 Cr App Rep 81, 84, which runs as follows: 'It was agreed on all hands for the purpose of this case that T was the person who, any evil motives apart, was entitled to consent to the damage. It was likewise conceded that the appellant Denton honestly believed that T occupied that position and was entitled to consent.'

Basing himself upon that and basing himself upon the similarity of the position of T to the position of the appellant in the present case, Mr Steer argues that therefore this appellant must be taken to have been entitled to consent to the damage.

The fundamental fallacy of that argument scarcely needs pointing out. It was a concession in *Denton* (supra) that was assumed for the purposes of argument, for the simple reason that it was the servant and not the so called proprietor who was being charged. To seek to base a proposition of law upon a concession which was made simply for the purpose of argument in another case, is a fruitless exercise.

There is nothing in this appeal and it is dismissed.

Appeal dismissed

■ **Questions**

1. How does *Appleyard*'s case differ from *Smith*'s? If he believed that he was 'in effect' the owner of the company and its premises, and however unreasonable his belief was, was he not entitled to an acquittal since he did not intend to destroy property belonging to another?

2. How is *Denton* different from *Appleyard*? What is being pleaded: (i) the property is mine; (ii) I believed the property was mine; (iii) I believed I had a right to damage the property belonging to another; (iv) I believed I had the permission of the other to damage the property?

R v G and another

[2003] UKHL 50, [2004] AC 1034, House of Lords, http://www.bailii.org/uk/cases/UKHL/2003/50.html

(The case is set out at and discussed in full at section 5.3, p 117)

The two defendants, aged 11 and 12, when on a camping expedition without their parents' consent, entered the yard of a shop, set fire to bundles of newspapers, leaving some lit newspaper under a large plastic wheelie bin. The newspapers set fire to the wheelie bin and the fire spread causing £1m worth of damage. The boys had expected the fires to extinguish themselves on the concrete floor; neither had appreciated that there was any risk of the fire spreading in the way that it did. They were convicted applying the *Caldwell* formula of recklessness (section 5.3, p 117), although the jury acknowledged some difficulty in applying fairly an objective standard to children whose capacity to see risk was limited by their immaturity.

The House of Lords quashed their convictions, overruling *Caldwell* [1982] AC 341.

Lord Bingham:

...Section 1 as enacted followed, subject to an immaterial addition, the draft proposed by the Law Commission. It cannot be supposed that by 'reckless' Parliament meant anything different from the Law Commission. The Law Commission's meaning was made plain both in its Report (Law Com No 29) and in Working Paper No 23 which preceded it. These materials (not, it would seem, placed before the House in *R v Caldwell*) reveal a very plain intention to replace the old-fashioned and misleading expression 'maliciously' by the more familiar expression 'reckless' but to give the latter expression the meaning which *R v Cunningham* ... and Professor Kenny had given to the former. In treating this authority as irrelevant to the construction of 'reckless' the majority fell into understandable but clearly demonstrable error. No relevant change in the mens rea necessary for proof of the offence was intended, and in holding otherwise the majority misconstrued section 1 of the Act.

[Lord Bingham confirmed that the definition of recklessness to be applied in criminal damage is now that found in cl 18(c) of the Draft Criminal Code:

A person acts recklessly within the meaning of section 1 of the Criminal Damage Act 1971 with respect to—

(i) a circumstance when he is aware of a risk that it exists or will exist;

(ii) a result when he is aware of a risk that it will occur;

and it is, in the circumstances known to him, unreasonable to take the risk.]

■ *Questions*

In considering *Smith* (earlier in this section), which elements of the crime are circumstances and which results? On an allegation of reckless criminal damage what must be proved in relation to each element of actus reus?

The courts have applied the new test from *G* unhesitatingly. For example, in *Booth v CPS* (2006) 170 JP 305, the Divisional Court upheld a conviction for criminal damage against D, a pedestrian who had stepped out into the path of a car, causing £517 worth of damage. D was drunk but aware of the risk of a collision and implicitly aware of the risk of damaging the car.

Obviously, mens rea cannot be supplied by an afterthought. If D inadvertently breaks V's window he cannot be liable when, having learned that V is a tax inspector, he rejoices in the harm caused. On the other hand, as *Miller* [1983] 2 AC 161, [1983] 1 All ER 978, HL (section 4.3.3.4, p 86), shows, if D inadvertently sets fire to V's property and subsequently becomes aware that he has done so, he may be criminally liable if, intending or being reckless that *further* damage may ensue to V's property, he lets the fire take its course when it lies within his power to prevent or minimize that further damage.

28.2.4.1 Transferred fault

The common law doctrine of 'transferred malice' or, to use a more modern term, 'transferred fault', is considered at section 2.4.1.1, p 24, with particular reference to the law of murder and other offences against the person. The Law Commission assumed that the doctrine would apply to their proposed Criminal Damage Act:

For the simple offence we think that the necessary mental element should be expressed as an intention to destroy or damage the property of another or as recklessness in that regard. The intention or the recklessness need not be related to the particular property damaged, provided that it is related to another's property. If, for example, a person throws a stone at a passing motor car intending to damage it, but misses and breaks a shop window, he will have the necessary intention in respect of the damage to the window as he intended to damage the property of another. But if in a fit of anger he throws a stone at his own car and breaks a shop window behind the car he will not have the requisite intention. In the latter case the question of whether he has committed an offence will depend upon whether he was reckless as to whether any property belonging to another would be destroyed or damaged. (LC29)

Glanville Williams agrees that the doctrine 'almost certainly' applies to the Act: TBCL (2nd edn) 907. But, while accepting that it may be right for offences against the person, he has argued that, in principle, it should not apply to criminal damage: (1983) 42 CLJ 85.

He argued that it results in 'unfair labelling' where the property damaged is more valuable than that which D intended to damage or foresaw that he might damage; whereas injury to one person—for example, a broken leg—is presumably as bad as the same injury to any other person. (Cf A. Ashworth, 'Transferred Malice and Punishment for Unforeseen Consequences' in P. Glazebrook (ed), *Reshaping the Criminal Law*, p 92.)

■ *Questions*

1. D throws a stone intending to smash V's cheap vase. Unforeseeably, the stone bounces off that cheap, but very solid, vase which is undamaged, and smashes V's priceless Ming vase. *Should* D be guilty of criminally destroying the Ming vase? Is the case materially different from that where D smashes the vase he aims at, believing it to have been bought by V at Poundland, when in fact it is priceless Ming? Assuming D is convicted, should the sentence, in either case, be related to the value of the Ming vase, or the cheap vase—or something in between?

2. A further interesting question arises as to whether arson is a different offence from criminal damage for the purposes of transferring malice. Though fire is only another means of causing criminal damage, Glanville Williams thinks not ((1983) 42 CLJ 85 at 86) because arson carries a higher maximum punishment. 'The reasonable view,' he says, 'is that arson is a separate offence, so that the intention cannot be transferred.' (Cf *Courtie* [1984] AC 463 which provides that as a general rule if one form of an offence carries a higher penalty than another form of that offence it is to be treated as a separate offence and charged as such. But what if the gas leak caused an explosion, without any attendant fire, which destroyed the premises? Jeremy Horder ('A Critique of the Correspondence Principle in Criminal Law' [1995] Crim LR 759 at 769–770) argues that what really matters is 'the representative label: is it right to label D as an arsonist if he did not intend to start a fire...?' Do you agree? Is this a sufficiently precise concept for the law to operate effectively?

3. Suppose that D, bent on stealing from a gas meter, knowingly fractures the gas pipe and this leads to a fire in which the premises are destroyed. D is clearly guilty of criminal damage to the pipe but is he guilty of arson? See section 28.4, p 923.

28.2.5 Lawful excuse

Criminal Damage Act 1971, s 5

(1) This section applies to any offence under section 1(1) above and any offence under section 2 or 3 above other than one involving a threat by the person charged to destroy or damage property in a way which he knows is likely to endanger the life of another or involving an intent by the person charged to use or cause or permit the use of something in his custody or under his control so to destroy or damage property.

(2) A person charged with an offence to which this section applies shall, whether or not he would be treated for the purposes of this Act as having a lawful excuse apart from this sub-section, be treated for those purposes as having a lawful excuse—

   (a) if at the time of the act or acts alleged to constitute the offence he believed that the person or persons whom he believed to be entitled to consent to the destruction of or damage to the property in question had so consented, or would have so consented to it if he or they had known of the destruction or damage and its circumstances; or

   (b) if he destroyed or damaged or threatened to destroy or damage the property in question or, in the case of a charge of an offence under section 3 above, intended to use or cause or permit the use of something to destroy or damage it, in order to protect property belonging to himself or another or a right or interest in property which was or which he believed to be vested in himself or another, and at the time of the act or acts alleged to constitute the offence he believed—

      (i) that the property, right or interest was in immediate need of protection; and

      (ii) that the means of protection adopted or proposed to be adopted were or would be reasonable having regard to all the circumstances.

(3) For the purposes of this section it is immaterial whether a belief is justified or not if it is honestly held.

(4) For the purposes of sub-section (2) above a right or interest in property includes any right or privilege in or over land, whether created by grant, licence or otherwise.

(5) This section shall not be construed as casting doubt on any defence recognised by law as a defence to criminal charges.

■ *Questions*

How many defences does s 5 provide? How many types of mistake is D entitled to make within this section?

Law Com No 29, para 49

In most cases there is a clear distinction between the mental element and the element of unlawfulness, and in the absence of one or the other element no offence will be committed, notwithstanding that damage may have been done to another's property. For example, a police officer who, in order to execute a warrant of arrest, has to force open the door of a house is acting with a lawful excuse although he intends to damage the door or the lock. On the other hand a person playing tennis on a properly fenced court who inadvertently hits a ball on to a greenhouse roof, breaking a pane of glass, acts without lawful excuse, but will escape liability because he has not the requisite intention.

The Law Commission says that in most cases there is a clear distinction between 'the mental element' and 'the element of unlawfulness' and the Act deals separately with these elements. It is not obvious that any such clear distinction can be drawn.

■ *Questions*

Was the conviction in *Smith (DR)* quashed because D lacked the mental element or because he had a lawful excuse? Does it matter to determine which? Cf *Jaggard v Dickinson* [1981] QB 527, section 6.6, p 177.

28.2.5.1 Belief in consent

In *Denton* [1982] 1 All ER 65, [1981] 1 WLR 1446, CA, section 28.2.4, p 900, D obviously contemplated a fraudulent claim against insurers and the trial judge ruled that he could not rely on s 5(2) because the section carried a general connotation of lawfulness and it could not be said that the owner was 'entitled' to consent to damage for a fraudulent purpose. Quashing D's conviction, the Court of Appeal pointed out that had T (the owner) been charged he would (on the admission made in that case) have to be acquitted since it is no crime for a man to set fire to his own property. But if the Crown's contention was right, someone whom the owner directed to set fire to the property could be convicted. The court concluded (at 68):

> Quite apart from any other consideration, that is such an anomalous result that it cannot possibly be right. The answer is this: that one has to decide whether or not an offence is committed at the moment that the acts are alleged to be committed. The fact that somebody may have had a dishonest intent which in the end he was going to carry out, namely to claim from the insurance company, cannot turn what was not originally a crime into a crime. There is no unlawfulness under the 1971 Act in burning a house. It does not become unlawful because there may be an inchoate attempt to commit fraud contained in it; that is to say it does not become a crime under the 1971 Act, whatever may be the situation outside of the Act.
>
> Consequently it is apparent to us that the judge, in his ruling in this respect, was wrong. Indeed it seems to us, if it is necessary to go as far as this, that it was probably unnecessary for the defendant to invoke s 5 of the 1971 Act at all, because he probably had a lawful excuse without it, in that T was lawfully entitled to burn the premises down. The defendant believed it. He believed that he was acting under the directions of T and that on its own, it seems to us, may well have provided him with a lawful excuse without having resort to s 5.

■ *Question*

On the face of it, the conduct of Denton falls four-square within s 5(2)(a) but the court thought he probably had a lawful excuse without it. Is s 5(2)(a) therefore superfluous?

Smith (DR) is overtly based on the premise (and *Denton* implicitly so) that the mens rea of criminal damage lies not merely in intentionally or recklessly damaging property but in intentionally or recklessly damaging property of *another*. 'It is not possible,' the court said in *Smith (DR)*, 'to exclude the words "belonging to another" which describe the "property". Applying the ordinary principles of *mens rea*, the intention and recklessness and the absence of lawful excuse required to constitute the offence have reference to property belonging to another.'

In other words, there must be mens rea as to the conduct, the circumstances (property belonging to another) and the consequences (damage or destruction).

No doubt D would commit an offence where, not sure whether property which was really V's belonged to himself or V, he nevertheless went ahead and destroyed the property.

Clearly, a belief that the owner has consented to the destruction or damage constitutes a lawful excuse within s 5(2)(a). In *Blake v DPP* [1993] Crim LR 586, DC, D, a vicar, protesting against allied action against Iraq in the Gulf War, wrote a biblical quotation on a concrete pillar at the perimeter of the Houses of Parliament. Charged with criminal damage, D claimed that he was carrying out the instructions of God and that he had a lawful excuse because he believed God was 'the person . . . whom he believed to be entitled to consent to the . . . damage to the property in question . . .' Perhaps not surprisingly the court held that a belief, however genuinely held, that D had God's consent was not a defence under 'the domestic law of

England'. Rumpole would commit no offence if he sets fire to the Old Bailey on the instructions of his wife—'she who must be obeyed'—if he believes, however unreasonably, that his wife is the owner or has been authorized by the owner.

■ **Question**

Suppose Rumpole gets what he believes is a message from God to set fire to the Old Bailey. Rumpole, being Rumpole, is hesitant but God assures him that He has consulted with the Lord Chancellor and the Lord Chief Justice and both have agreed. Rumpole sets fire to the Old Bailey. Advise Rumpole.

28.2.5.2 Protecting property: s 5(2)(b)

R v Hunt
(1977) 66 Cr App R 105, Court of Appeal, Criminal Division

(Roskill LJ, Wein and Slynn JJ)

D's wife took up a job as a deputy warden in a block of old people's flats. D helped his wife and his wife's employers by doing jobs at the flats. He discovered that the fire alarm and the emergency alarm did not work. D set fire to a bed in the guest room in a comparatively isolated part of the block of flats. He told his wife he could smell smoke: he then led her past the guest room in their search for the fire so that they 'discovered' the fire and broke the fire alarm in order to show that it was not working.

Roskill LJ:

...The appellant was convicted...of arson contrary to section 1(1) and (3) of the Criminal Damage Act 1971....

[His lordship read ss 1(1) and 1(3) of the Act (section 28.2, p 893 and section 28.4, p 923).]

Now, two defences were raised: the first was that he had a lawful excuse for what he did; secondly it was said that he was not reckless whether any such property would be destroyed. The learned judge withdrew the first defence from the jury after hearing an interesting argument, as we have heard, from Mr Marshall-Andrews, by whom this man was represented at the trial as in this Court. He left the issue of recklessness to the jury, and the jury, by a majority verdict, convicted him. Obviously, on the judge's direction, there was no lawful excuse.

Lawson J gave leave to appeal, in order that this Court might consider whether the judge was right in withdrawing the defence of lawful excuse from the jury.

That defence arises under section 5 of the same Act and it is necessary, in order to make the point plain, to read the whole section.

[His lordship read s 5 of the Act, section 28.2.5, p 903.]

...

Let it be assumed in the appellant's favour that he honestly believed that the council were failing in their duty in not having repaired the fire alarm. The question is whether, on those bare facts which I have related and assuming an honest belief in this case, he is entitled to say that he had a lawful excuse for that which he did? I should add that he originally denied having set fire to anything.

This must depend upon the true construction of section 5(2)(b). As I said earlier, there was an interesting argument before the learned judge and the learned judge said that those facts were incapable, as a matter of law, of entitling this man to the benefit of that defence. Therefore, he withdrew that defence from the jury. Mr Marshall-Andrews has strenuously argued in this Court that the learned judge was wrong and that the appellant was entitled to the benefit of the statutory defence.

It is known that some of the sections in the Criminal Damage Act 1971 can give rise to difficulties. Some of the problems are helpfully discussed at pp 532 to 536 of Smith and Hogan's *Criminal Law* (3rd edn, 1973).

Mr Marshall-Andrews' submission can be put thus: If this man honestly believed that that which he did was necessary in order to protect this property from the risk of fire and damage to the old people's home by reason of the absence of a working fire alarm, he was entitled to set fire to that bed and so to claim the statutory defence accorded by section 5(2).

I have said we will assume in his favour that he possessed the requisite honest belief. But in our view the question whether he was entitled to the benefit of the defence turns upon the meaning of the words 'in order to protect property belonging to another.' It was argued that those words were subjective in concept, just like the words in the latter part of section 5(2)(b) which are subjective.

We do not think that is right. The question whether or not a particular act of destruction or damage or threat of destruction or damage was done or made in order to protect property belonging to another must be, on the true construction of the statute, an objective test. Therefore we have to ask ourselves whether, whatever the state of this man's mind and assuming an honest belief, that which he admittedly did was done in order to protect this particular property, namely the old people's home in Hertfordshire?

If one formulates the question in that way, in the view of each member of this Court, for the reason Slynn J gave during the argument, it admits of only one answer: this was not done in order to protect property; it was done in order to draw attention to the defective state of the fire alarm. It was not an act which in itself did protect or was capable of protecting property. The learned trial judge, during the argument, mentioned quite correctly, that one, though not necessarily the only, purpose of this sub-section was to make provision whereby a person, in order to protect his own property, might destroy or damage the property of another without being guilty of criminal damage. There are cases of which it is easy to think of examples, in which a person, in order to protect his property in actual or imminent danger of damage, will take steps, maybe drastic steps, legitimately protecting either his property or the property of another. It is that kind of protective action to which this particular sub-section is directed though we do not suggest that that is exhaustive. But the sub-section, on its proper construction, cannot possibly extend to the situation which arose in this present case.

During the argument after the adjournment Slynn J gave an example of the position which might arise were the argument for the appellant to succeed. Let it be supposed that the roof of some famous cathedral or building, like Westminster Abbey, was in danger due to a defective beam suffering from dry rot; let it be supposed that the authorities are doing nothing to repair it; let it be supposed that some person, acting in good faith, is horrified at this lack of attention. In order to draw attention to what he regards as a dangerous position, he goes and sets fire to a hassock [a type of cushion]. Is that seriously to be said not to be an offence of criminal damage because it is done to draw attention to the defective beam on the roof of the Abbey? Mr Marshall-Andrews says that the section would, on those facts, provide a defence. We think that the question has only to be asked to be answered in the negative.

In those circumstances the learned judge was absolutely right in his decision and for the reasons which he gave. As Slynn J pointed out, even if, contrary to our view, the test were subjective, the appellant did not set fire to the bed in order to protect property: he merely did that act in order to draw attention to what was in his view an immediate need for protection by repairing the alarm.

I would only add that we had some discussion about the scope of the words 'in immediate need of protection' in paragraph (b)(i) of sub-section (2). That question is touched upon on p 534 of Smith and Hogan, *Criminal Law* (3rd edn, 1973). No question arises for decision under that part of section 5(2)(b) and we express no view about it.

In those circumstances the appeal against conviction is dismissed.

Appeal dismissed

■ *Question*

Consider the example given by Roskill LJ of the hassock burner. Roskill LJ said, 'Mr Marshall-Andrews says that the section would, on those facts, provide a defence. We think the question has only to be asked to be answered in the negative.' Do you agree with Roskill LJ that the answer is so plainly 'no'?

In *Ashford and Smith* [1988] Crim LR 682, CA, D and E were convicted under s 3 of the Act of possessing articles with intent to damage property. They were found in possession of equipment with which as part of a demonstration against nuclear weapons they had tried to cut a wire fence surrounding an RAF base. They claimed they had done this to protect the property of persons abroad and in this country by reducing the risk of nuclear war. The Court of Appeal held the trial judge was right to rule that their conduct did not fall within the definition of lawful excuse since whether an act was done to protect property was to be objectively determined and there was no evidence that any property was in immediate need of protection.

Hill and Hall (1988) 89 Cr App R 74, [1989] Crim LR 136, CA, were factually similar cases. D and E, also convicted under s 3, were carrying equipment to cut the fence surrounding a US Air Force base. At her trial, D claimed that the base was used to monitor the movements of Soviet submarines and thus was a prime target for a retaliatory or even pre-emptive Soviet nuclear strike which would devastate the property of herself and her neighbours. By cutting the wire the security of the base might be compromised and force its removal. The trial judge directed the jury that what D had done was really part of a political campaign and, objectively, could not be said to be done to protect property. Moreover, on D's own testimony, there was no evidence that she believed the property to be in *immediate* need of protection. Upholding the convictions, the Court of Appeal reaffirmed the correctness of *Hunt*:

> The trial judge, [said the court] had to decide (i) what was in [D's] mind (subjective test); (ii) whether it could be said, as a matter of law that, on the facts as believed by her, cutting the strand of wire could amount to something done to protect her own home or the homes of adjacent friends (objective test). The judge had rightly concluded that the proposed act was too remote from the eventual aim at which she had targeted her actions to satisfy the test. He had also to determine whether on the facts, as stated by [D], there was any evidence on which it could be said that there was a need of protection from immediate danger.

Similarly, in *Blake*, section 28.2.5.1, p 905, the defence was rejected because, said the court, adopting 'an objective view', the action taken by D was not capable of protecting property in the Gulf States.

■ *Questions*

The conduct of Hunt, Ashford, Smith, Hill and Hall, and Blake might be thought to be ineffective and misguided. However, if asked 'what was your object in doing what you did?' each could have honestly answered: to protect property belonging to myself or another. Does not this meet the requirements in the first part of s 5(2)(b)? What warrant is there for saying that the action taken by them must be in some way causally effective in protecting the property?

In *Kelleher* [2003] EWCA Crim 2486, D decapitated a statue of Baroness Thatcher, and explained his motive as being that he held her responsible for developments in world politics with which he disagreed and that he genuinely feared for the future of his son being brought up in such a world.

■ *Questions*

1. Should the defence under s 5(2)(b) be available to him? What property is he protecting?

2. Would D have a lawful excuse for burning down a local factory as long as D believed this to be reasonable because he believed that effluent from the factory was ruining his tomatoes? The courts have struggled with how far the subjectivity in s 5 is to be taken.

Unsworth v Director of Public Prosecutions
[2010] EWHC 3037 (Admin), Divisional Court

(Munby LJ and Lagstaff J)

D was engaged in a dispute with her neighbour over trees which D claimed blocked the light into her property. D wrote a number of letters asking that the trees be reduced in size, but to no avail. Eventually D decided that self-help was her only option and took a saw to the trees, causing substantial damage to them. D was charged with criminal damage and convicted. D sought to plead the defence in s 5(2)(b) of the Act, but this was rejected. D was convicted in the magistrates' court and her appeal against conviction was dismissed by the Crown Court. D appealed to the Divisional Court by way of a case stated.

[Munby LJ, in allowing D's appeal against conviction, stated:]

5. The lawful excuse which can be relied upon by way of defence may of course be a lawful excuse conferred upon the defendant by the civil law, for example if the defendant can demonstrate that in doing what she did she was lawfully exercising a right of abatement conferred upon her by the civil law. Section 5(2), however, provides an extended ambit to the defence of lawful excuse, providing so far as is material for present purposes as follows:

[His lordship set out the relevant provisions of the Act.]

6. It can be seen from an analysis of the language in subsection (2)(b) that there are two elements to the defence. The first element, which for ease of exposition I will refer to as limb (A), is that introduced by the words 'in order to protect property' and so on. The other element, which for ease of exposition I will refer to as limb (B), is the latter part of the subsection beginning with the words 'at the time of the act or acts alleged'. As will be appreciated limb (B) itself has two sub-limbs, those set out in subsection (2)(b) paragraphs (i) and (ii).

7. On a plain reading of the statute the test in relation to limb (B) is and is exclusively a test of the defendant's belief. What on the other hand is the nature of the test in relation to limb (A)? The answer to that question is in my judgment answered definitively by the decisions of the Court of Appeal, Criminal Division, in *R v Hunt* (1977) 66 Crim App Rep 105, followed by and elaborated upon in *R v Hill, R v Hall* (1988) 89 Crim App Rep 74.

8. In *Hunt* the judgment was given by Roskill LJ, who said this at page 108:

'But in our view the question whether he was entitled to the benefit of the defence turns upon the meaning of the words "in order to protect property belonging to another." It was argued that those words were subjective in concept, just like the words in the latter part of section 5(2)(b) which are subjective.

We do not think that is right. The question whether or not a particular act of destruction or damage or threat of destruction or damage was done or made in order to protect property belonging to another must be, on the true construction of the statute, an objective test.'

As I read that, Roskill LJ is clearly distinguishing between what I have referred to as limb (A) and limb (B), is clearly stating that limb (B) is 'subjective' but is accepting that in part at least limb (A) imports 'an objective test'.

9. That reasoning was accepted by Lord Lane LCJ, giving judgment in *Hill and Hall*, as being binding upon the court. However, at page 79 he added these important observations:

'But we add that we think that Hunt was correctly decided, for this reason. There are two aspects to this type of question. The first aspect is to decide what it was that the applicant, in this case Valerie Hill, in her own mind thought. The learned judge assumed, and so do we, for the purposes of this decision, that everything she said about her reasoning was true. I have already perhaps given a sufficient outline of what it was she believed to demonstrate what is meant by that. Up to that point the test was subjective. In other words one is examining what is going on in the applicant's mind.

Having done that, the judges in the present cases—and the judge particularly in the case of Valerie Hill—turned to the second aspect of the case, and that is this. He had to decide as a matter of law, which means objectively, whether it could be said that on those facts as believed by the applicant, snipping the strand of the wire, which she intended to do, could amount to something done to protect either the applicant's own home or the homes of her adjacent friends in Pembrokeshire.

He decided, again quite rightly in our view, that that proposed act on her part was far too remote from the eventual aim at which she was targeting her actions to satisfy the test.'

10. Reading that, not merely on its own but in conjunction with the earlier judgment of Roskill LJ, it is clear in my judgment that the discussion by the Lord Chief Justice there was exclusively by reference to limb (A) and not by reference to limb (B). The significance of the principle as there expounded is that limb (A) has, for the reasons explained by the Lord Chief Justice, two aspects: the one subjective, the other objective.

11. From those two judgments, as indeed from the structure and wording of section 5(2)(b) I conclude therefore that limb (A) has both a subjective and an objective aspect, whereas limb (B) has an exclusively subjective aspect. It is also important to bear in mind, not least in the light of certain submissions helpfully put before us by Ms Thomson on behalf of the respondent, the Crown Prosecution Service, that the focus in limb (A) is upon the single question of whether what was done was done 'in order to protect property', whether the property of the defendant or someone else or to protect some interest in property which the defendant believed was vested in himself or somebody else. The matters referred to in paragraphs (i) and (ii) at the end of subsection (2)(b), that is, whether the property was in 'immediate need of protection' and whether the means of protection were or would be 'reasonable having regard to all the circumstances', are to be found within limb (B) and are therefore, for the reasons I have given, subject to an exclusively subjective test.

12. The other authority to which we were referred was the decision of the Divisional Court in *Chamberlain v Lindon* [1998] EWHC Admin 329, [1998] 1 WLR 1252 . . . [His lordship referred to the facts and various parts of the judgment.] Sullivan J said this at paragraph 50 (page 1262C):

'In the criminal context the question is not whether the means of protection adopted by the defendant were objectively reasonable, having regard to all the circumstances, but whether the defendant believed them to be so. By virtue of section 5(3) it is immaterial whether his belief was justified, provided it was honestly held.'

18. That in my judgment is an entirely accurate if succinct summary of the statutory provisions set out in limb (B). Limb (B), to repeat, is on the authorities, as in my judgment on the plain reading of statute, entirely subjective. The question and the only question is honest belief. Whether that belief was reasonable or unreasonable is not of itself determinative of the presence or absence of honest belief. It is, as Sullivan J correctly observed, immaterial whether the belief was justified, a reading of the statute which is not merely as it seems to me implicit in the words of section 5(2)(b) but which is made explicit in section 5(3).

19. The final observation to be made on the statute is that although reasonableness as a concept does appear in section 5(2)(b)(ii), what is relevant under the statute is not whether in fact the means of protection adopted or proposed to be adopted by the defendant were or would be reasonable but whether the defendant believed that those means were or would be reasonable. In other words the honest belief which provides the defence includes an honest belief that what is being done is reasonable. If there is honest belief that what is being done is reasonable the fact that, assessed objectively, it is not reasonable is neither here nor there.

[His lordship set out some of the extracts from the Crown Court rulings in the present case and the difficulties posed by the language of the case stated.]

32. Bearing in mind the immediate causal link between the act of lopping off the trees which would *eo instanti* ameliorate the obstruction to Ms Unsworth's light, the present case, as in *Chamberlain*, is as far removed as can be imagined from the tenuous causal chain between action and consequence characterised by *Hill and Hall* and similar such cases. In just the same way as in *Chamberlain*, where the objective element in limb (A) caused no difficulties to the success of the defence, the objective element in limb (A) could not in this case, as it seems to me, be any difficulty in the way of Ms Unsworth establishing the defence.

33. Mr Myers appropriately focussed upon Sullivan J's reference (see paragraph 30) to the question of whether on the facts the steps taken 'could' ameliorate the damage to the property in that case and, in this case, the obstruction to the easement. Manifestly in the present case as in that case not merely were the steps which Ms Unsworth believed it proper to take steps which *could* ameliorate the problem; they were steps which of their very nature *would* ameliorate the problem and moreover do so immediately

34. Of course it is not for us to find the facts, and we are confined by the facts as set out in the Case, but there is not from beginning to end anything that I can detect in the Case which would indicate that the Crown Court took the view that the objective element in limb (A) was not in fact established, nor indeed anything in the Case which would have entitled the Crown Court to come to that conclusion. In the way in which it formulated the questions which, albeit erroneously, it sought to answer in paragraph 15, the Case demonstrates that the focus of the Crown Court's analysis appears to have been, as inevitably it seems to me it had to be on its approach, not upon the objective element in limb (A), which was taken as satisfied, but impermissibly upon the legally irrelevant question of whether, in the context of limb (B), what Ms Unsworth chose to do was objectively justifiable as being objectively reasonable. In my judgment, with great respect to the judge and his colleagues in the Crown Court, the analysis in paragraph 15 of the Case, which in truth lies at the heart of the decision to dismiss Ms Unsworth's appeal, is both confused and confusing and in any event unsound in law.

. . .

40. There is one final aspect which I should perhaps refer to. As will be apparent, the Crown Court was perturbed as to the possible implications in cases of this kind, if the statutory defence was available in circumstances such as arose in the present case. And, as we have seen, it was concerned about the implications of what Sullivan J had said in particular in paragraph 50 of his judgment in *Chamberlain*. From one perspective, one can perhaps understand such concerns, but it is to be borne in mind, as I have already said, that all that Sullivan J was doing, as all that we are doing, is loyally applying the law as laid down by Parliament.

41. The statutory defence in this particular case is perhaps unusual. The point is well made in Smith and Hogan, *Criminal Law*, ed 12, para 29.1.5.2:

> 'This provision [that is, I interpolate, section 5(2)(b)] is in line with general principles of defences in so far as it relates to beliefs in facts or circumstances; however, it goes well beyond that in so far as it provides D's *belief* that the means employed *were reasonable* will excuse. This must be contrasted with the position in self-defence and the prevention of crime where D may use such force as *is found by a jury to be reasonable* in the circumstances which D believed to exist. Under the common law defence, the defendant's belief in the trigger for the defence is assessed on a subjective basis but the response to it is assessed objectively.'

In other words, whereas many such defences have a double requirement, a requirement of honest belief coupled with the requirement that that belief be reasonable, this defence is founded exclusively, so far as concerns limb (B) on the honesty of the belief. And although, as we have seen, reasonableness comes into limb (B), it comes in not as an additional criterion to be met but as one of the ingredients of the defendant's honest belief.

42. *Smith and Hogan* goes on to observe that in theory the defence might be relied upon as justification for a defendant 'laying waste an oil refinery because he believes its effluent is damaging his geraniums'. The protection, the safeguard, against such extravagant attempts to rely upon the defence is of course, as the authors point out, that a jury is unlikely in the circumstances postulated to believe that the defendant did think or could possibly have thought that what he was doing was reasonable. In other words the safeguard here is not to be found, as in many such defences, with the super-riding requirement to demonstrate that the belief was reasonable; it is to be found in the pragmatic reality that the fact-finding tribunal, whether in the present case the Magistrates' Court or, in trials on indictment, a jury, is the more unlikely to accept that the defendant's belief was honest the longer the difficulty has been in existence and the more extreme the measures the defendant takes to remove it. A defendant who has tolerated some obstruction, whether it be an obstruction to a right of way such as in *Chamberlain* or an obstruction to a right of light as in this case, may find it the more difficult to establish the honest belief in the need to take 'immediate steps' the longer that state of affairs has gone on. After all, if you have tolerated something for a very long time how can it be said that you honestly believe that you have to take immediate steps? In just the same way the more extreme the steps taken to ameliorate the perceived damage the more difficult it will be to persuade the fact-finding tribunal that you honestly believed that what you were doing was reasonable.

43. It seems to me that the spectre conjured up and which troubled the mind of the Crown Court is not perhaps as great as it may have feared. The answer in all such cases lies in the good sense and common sense of the fact-finding tribunal in taking a realistic view as to whether the defendant can really honestly have believed that which he or she asserts, in particular if the steps taken are extravagant. It does not take much imagination to imagine what the outcome would be if, in the example given by *Smith and Hogan*, the gentleman who blew up the oil refinery tried to persuade a jury that he honestly believed that was a reasonable step to take to prevent damage to his flowers. In just the same way, although, perhaps unsurprisingly, she was able to establish the defence in the present case, because all that she had done was to lop the upper parts of the trees, Ms Unsworth might have had more difficulty if she had cut the trees down altogether and would, I can confidently assert, have had no prospect whatever of establishing the defence if the remedy of which she availed herself had involved not merely the cutting down of the trees but the demolition of part of the defendant's structure.

44. Be that as it may, the fact is that the defence is perhaps unusual in its width. For the reasons I have given this appeal must in my judgment be allowed.

The Divisional Court in *Unsworth* confirms that for the purposes of the statutory defence in s 5(2) (b) it is sufficient that D honestly believes that he needs to take immediate action to protect his property. It is not necessary to consider whether the belief is objectively justified. The second limb of the defence is exclusively subjective, unlike the first limb which has both an objective and a subjective element.

Immediacy

D must also believe, however, that the property is in 'immediate' need of protection within s 5(2)(b)(i). This suggests that the property must be immediately and not remotely threatened. So in *Hill and Hall*, the trial judge ruled that there was no evidence that D believed that the former Soviet Union was about to declare war or launch a pre-emptive strike. Nor could Hunt believe that a fire would break out next day, next month or even that a fire would ever occur. What Hunt no doubt believed was that *if* a fire ever did occur it might bring with it, in view of the fact that the alarms were not working, disastrous consequences. He had done, in writing to the warden and the council, all that he could do but this had been to no avail. Why could he not claim, within the section, that he believed the property was in *immediate* need of protection albeit the risk was a future one? Had the relevant fire authority been consulted they would surely have insisted on the alarms being repaired immediately and not at any remoter time. So was not the property in immediate need of protection?

In *Johnson v DPP* [1994] Crim LR 673, DC, D, a squatter, chiselled off the lock of the door of the house he was occupying and replaced it with his own lock. Charged with criminal damage, D claimed that the action he had taken was done to protect his property, viz the furniture he had moved into the squat. Upholding his conviction, the court said that D's property was not in 'immediate' need of protection as opposed to a 'speculative future need'. But the risk of theft, like the risk of fire, is always a future risk and neither may ever materialize. But does any reasonable person wait until the burglar calls before securing the door?

28.2.5.3 Relationship with other defences

Section 5(5) makes it clear that the definition of lawful excuse in the section is not exhaustive so that general defences such as self-defence, duress and necessity are available on a charge of criminal damage.

28.2.5.4 European Convention on Human Rights

In *Steele v UK* (1999) 28 EHRR 603, S, with 60 others, attempted to obstruct a grouse shoot. She was arrested for breach of the peace for impeding the progress of a member of the shoot by walking in front of him as he lifted his shotgun. At trial S was convicted of the Public Order Act 1986, s 5 offence and for breach of the peace. Other defendants were convicted for various other unrelated peaceful protest activities. S argued that this infringed her right to freedom of expression under Article 10.

Article 10 reads, so far as relevant, as follows:

1. Everyone has the right to freedom of expression. This right shall include freedom to hold opinions and to receive and impart information and ideas without interference by public authority and regardless of frontiers. . . .

2. The exercise of these freedoms, since it carries with it duties and responsibilities, may be subject to such formalities, conditions, restrictions or penalties as are prescribed by law and are necessary in a democratic society, . . . for the prevention of disorder or crime, . . . [or] for the protection of the reputation or rights of others. . . .

The European Court held:

90. The Government submitted that the protest activity . . . was not peaceful, and that Article 10 was not, therefore, applicable.

91. The Commission found that the measures taken against each of the . . . applicants amounted to interferences with their rights under Article 10.

92. The Court recalls that the applicants were arrested while protesting against a grouse shoot and the extension of a motorway respectively. It is true that these protests took the form of physically impeding the activities of which the applicants disapproved, but the Court considers nonetheless that they constituted expressions of opinion within the meaning of Article 10. The measures taken against the applicants were, therefore, interferences with their right to freedom of expression.

The Court found that in relation to S, the infringement of her freedom of expression was necessary and proportionate to a legitimate aim under Article 10(2). See [1998] Crim LR 893.

■ *Question*

Could a defendant who painted over racist slogans successfully claim that his conduct was an act of expression for the purposes of the European Convention on Human Rights, Article 10? Cf *Fancy* (section 28.2.1.3e, p 896).

Protestors charged with criminal damage have also sought to rely on a defence that they were acting to prevent illegality in international law. The House of Lords dealt with a number of conjoined appeals in which this plea was raised in the context of the Criminal Law Act 1967, s 3, but did not address the availability of defences under the Criminal Damage Act 1971. (See *Jones and others* [2006] UKHL 16, [2007] AC 136, section 11.3.2.9, p 376; the criminal damage defence was examined only in the Court of Appeal.

In *Pritchard and others* [2005] QB 259, [2004] 4 All ER 955, DD had been charged with conspiracy to cause criminal damage and with offences under s 3(b) of the Act. DD had been involved in causing and attempting to cause damage at the military base at RAF Fairford. The defence asserted that the UK's attack on Iraq was an unlawful act and that their acts at the Air Force base were to prevent that illegality. DD sought to rely on the defences of duress of circumstance, necessity, lawful excuse under s 5(2)(b) and the prevention of crime under s 3 of the 1967 Act. The court on a preliminary ruling held that the international crime of aggression could not constitute a crime for the purposes of s 3 of the 1967 Act (see section 11.3.2.9, p 376), and that under s 5(2)(b) the jury was only concerned with the question of DD's honestly held beliefs. Therefore, no issue could arise in relation to the defence under s 5(2)(b) of whether the war in Iraq was illegal. As noted in the commentary in the *Criminal Law Review* ([2005] Crim LR 122):

> ... the court's conclusion that the legality of the war is irrelevant to the *availability* of the section 5(2) defence seems correct. But, is the illegality relevant to its *application*? Surely the circumstances—the immediacy, potency, lawfulness etc—of the action will be important to the jury in its evaluation of D's belief that his conduct is 'reasonable' as the statute requires? The success of the defence on facts such as these nevertheless remains debatable. Is there sufficient immediacy of threat to property, particularly where the charges of conspiracy to damage? Which item of property (the defence does not apply to protect people: *Baker* [1997] Crim LR 497) is D seeking to protect?

In *Hutchinson v Newbury Magistrates' Court* [2000] EWHC 61 (QB), H appealed against her conviction for criminal damage after cutting a perimeter fence at an atomic weapons establishment. H contended that (i) the production of weapons at the establishment was unlawful in customary international law pursuant to an opinion of the International Court of Justice in 1996 on the legality of the threat of use of nuclear weapons; (ii) the establishment's activities were therefore also unlawful in English domestic law and, since H's actions had been intended to impede that unlawful activity, they were therefore not a criminal act; (iii) by English domestic law the forbidden conduct of the establishment was not only unlawful but also criminal. Buxton LJ observed that:

> It originally seemed to be contended, ... that the fact that Mrs Hutchinson was acting to impede, alternatively to protest about, activities that were unlawful under international law in itself provided her with a lawful excuse in English criminal law. No authority was cited for a claim as broad as that. That is because no authority supports it. It is clear that the claim, when scrutinised, is hopelessly wide. If D commits a crime only to stop X doing an unlawful but not criminal act, he cannot claim the latter unlawfulness alone as an excuse for his own criminal conduct. Quite apart from the lack of authority, the practical implications of such an argument, were it correct, are obvious. What D must do in such a situation is bring his conduct, if he can, under one of the recognised heads of public or private defence, such as the heads that were set out by the judge in the second of her two questions for the opinion of this Court.

28.2.5.5 Section 5(5)

In *Lloyd v DPP* [1992] 1 All ER 982, [1991] Crim LR 904, DC, D, a trespasser, had parked his car on private land aware of notices that said the cars of trespassers would be clamped and that a charge of £25 would be made for their removal. He returned that evening to find his car clamped but refused to pay the £25 for its removal. The following day D returned to remove the clamp using a disc-cutter. D was charged with criminal damage to the clamp. On D's behalf it was argued that he could rely on s 5(5) because at common law the clamping of his car constituted a trespass and he was accordingly entitled to take reasonable steps to recover his property. If this argument was correct, said Nolan LJ:

. . . the only remedy open to a landowner who finds a car parked without authority on his land is to remove the car using as little force as may be required and to place it either on the highway or, if he knows who the owner of the car is, back at the owner's property. The practical difficulties and dangers which that remedy would involve can readily be imagined: breaking into the car if locked in the first place; propelling it by some means onto the road with or without insurance cover; leaving it where it might cause obstruction at least, if not danger to other road users.

I mention that only to illustrate the problems inherent in this branch of the law and the need to my mind for them to be fully explored in civil proceedings. This court, exercising its criminal jurisdiction, is not concerned with the question whether Mr Lloyd could sue the landowners for trespass to his car and for the inconvenience caused to him or with the precise remedies open in civil law to the landowner. We are solely concerned with the question whether Mr Lloyd had a lawful excuse for damaging the property of South Coast Securities. We are concerned with the civil law only to the extent necessary for determining whether such an excuse existed for the purpose of the criminal law.

For that purpose it is sufficient to decide, as I do, that [the prosecutor's] alternative submission is well founded. It substantially reflects the conclusion of the justices in para 6(d) of the case [In para 6(d) the justices had said: 'The clamping of the appellant's motor vehicle, whether lawful or unlawful, and we considered it to be a trespass, was not such an act that the appellant could not in law consent to it. He consented to the risk of his vehicle being clamped. In this regard the signs erected around the car park were sufficiently clear and unambiguous.'] although that conclusion might more accurately have been expressed by saying that since the applicant had consented to the risk of his car being clamped the clamping was not a trespass. Mr Sharp submits that this conclusion cannot carry the day for the respondent because the appellant's consent to the clamping ceased on his return to the car park at 10.00 pm. Mr Sharp submits that the immobilisation of the car was plainly unlawful thereafter and the appellant was at liberty to exercise his right of recaption using such reasonable force as was necessary to do so.

To my mind, it would be a truly absurd state of affairs if the appellant, having consented to the risk of clamping, was at liberty to withdraw his consent with immediate effect once clamping had occurred and to proceed at once to recover his car by force. I am satisfied that this is not the law. Even assuming in the appellant's favour that the refusal of South Coast Securities to let him remove his car save on payment of £25 was an unlawful restraint, it would by no means follow that there was a lawful excuse for his subsequent action. He had a choice. He could have paid the £25 under protest, removed his car and taken action against South Coast Securities in the county court. Instead he chose to re-enter the car park, once again quite plainly as a trespasser, and to retrieve his car by causing some £50-worth of damage to the property of South Coast Securities.

In my judgment, the suggestion that there was a lawful excuse for his action is wholly untenable. At the worst what he had suffered was a civil wrong. The remedy for such wrongs is available in the civil courts. That is what they are there for. Self-help involving the use of force can only be contemplated where there is no reasonable alternative. . . .

Situations like those which have arisen in the present case are becoming increasingly common. They can cause intense irritation both to the motorist deprived of the use of his car, as he thinks, unreasonably, and to the landowner or other victim of the motorist's unauthorised parking. That makes it all the more necessary for it to be clearly stated that, at any rate as a general rule, if a motorist parks his car without permission on another person's property knowing that by doing so he runs the risk of it being clamped, he has no right to damage or destroy the clamp. If he does so he will be guilty of a criminal offence . . .

As has already been pointed out, there is now a separate offence in s 54 of the Protection of Freedoms Act 2012 of immobilizing a motor vehicle without consent. So although D may be guilty of an offence when he damages V's clamp, V may also be guilty of a separate offence for clamping D's vehicle in the first place.

> ■ *Question*
>
> Consent to being clamped negatives trespass; but does 'consenting' to the risk have the same effect?

28.3 Destroying, etc property with intent to endanger life

Criminal Damage Act 1971, s 1

> (2) A person who without lawful excuse destroys or damages any property, whether belonging to himself or another:
>
>   (a) intending to destroy or damage any property or being reckless as to whether any property would be destroyed or damaged; and
>
>   (b) intending by the destruction or damage to endanger the life of another or being reckless as to whether the life of another would be thereby endangered;
>
>   shall be guilty of an offence.

Law Com No 29, paras 21–27

> This proposed offence gives effect to our view that the policy of the criminal law is, and should continue to be, to select certain offences as attracting exceptionally high maximum penalties, because these offences are accompanied by aggravating factors. There are examples of this approach in ss 8–10 of the Theft Act 1968 dealing with robbery, burglary and aggravated burglary, which may be regarded as theft accompanied by aggravating circumstances . . . None of our commentators suggested that the test should be objective in the sense that one should look only to the consequences or potential consequences of the offender's conduct. All were agreed that the criterion for the aggravated offence was to be found in the offender's state of mind, namely, his intention to endanger the personal safety of another or his recklessness in that regard . . . [I]f no such offence is created, a considerable gap in the law is left, especially where the offender is reckless as to endangering personal safety and yet no injury is caused. In such a case the offender cannot be convicted of an attempt to commit an offence under the Offences against the Person Act 1861, in an attempt to commit an offence, intention and not merely recklessness is necessary . . . We think that the proper criterion should be related to the endangering of life, a concept which appears in s2 of the Explosive Substances Act 1883 and in s16 of the Firearms Act 1968. It is not, therefore, a novel one likely to give rise to difficulties of interpretation, and we think that it correctly expresses the necessary seriousness. It is true that in adopting the criterion of endangering life there may still be some overlapping with offences against the person . . .

■ *Questions*

Do you agree with the Law Commission that but for the creation of this offence 'a considerable gap is left in the law'? How does the offence differ from attempted murder? See further D. W. Elliott, 'Endangering Life by Destroying or Damaging Property' [1997] Crim LR 382.

The elements of the offence are:

- damage;
- to some property (whether D's or not);
- caused intentionally or recklessly;
- D must intend or be reckless that, *by the* damage that he intended or about which he was reckless, a life would be endangered;
- no life need be endangered in fact.

28.3.1 Damage

In *Meah v Roberts* [1978] 1 All ER 97, [1977] 1 WLR 1187, DC, D, after cleaning pipes in a bar, put some caustic soda 'stronger than that needed to remove paint from woodwork' in a lemonade bottle and left the bottle standing with other lemonade bottles. At this stage, and assuming that D does not intend to kill but is aware of the risk to life, it seems that D commits no offence if the bottle is empty, but commits the offence under s 1(2) if the bottle had contained some lemonade.

28.3.2 Property

The offence under s 1(2) may be committed though the property damaged is D's own property or is damaged with D's permission: *Merrick* [1996] 1 Cr App R 130, [1995] Crim LR 802, CA.

28.3.3 Intention or recklessness as to the damage

See the elements of mens rea in relation to the offence under s 1, section 28.2.4, p 898.

R v Martin Alan Cooper
[2004] EWCA Crim 1382, Court of Appeal, Criminal Division

(Rose LJ, Hughes and Gloster JJ)

D was a resident in a hostel which provides support for people with mental health problems. One evening, after warning the staff that there would be 'trouble later', badly burnt bedding was found outside D's room. There was smoke in D's room and a mattress was found to be scorched on the underside. D had used lighter fuel as an accelerant. When interviewed he was asked, 'Had it crossed your mind that you might have hurt anyone else while you were doing it?' He replied, 'I don't think so, it did cross my mind a bit but nobody would have got hurt anyway.' [The officer:] 'I know that no-one did get hurt, but obviously you could have been hurt.' The defendant replied: 'That is what my intention was.' The trial judge directed the jury in accordance with *Caldwell* and D was convicted. On appeal, the conviction was quashed.

[Rose LJ stated:]

In the light of the House of Lords speeches in *G*, the *Caldwell* direction was a misdirection. It is now, in the light of *G*, incumbent on a trial judge to direct a jury, in a case of this kind, that the risk of danger to life was obvious and significant to the defendant. In other words, a subjective element is essential before the jury can convict of this offence. Mr Tizzano [counsel for D] also put the matter in this way, in the light of those answers in interview to which we have rehearsed: 'If he realised there was a risk, but dismissed it as negligible, it cannot be said he realised he was taking an obvious and significant risk.' With that submission we agree.

28.3.4 Intending or being reckless as to life endangerment by the damage intended or about which D was reckless

R v Steer

[1987] 2 All ER 833, House of Lords, http://www.bailii.org/uk/cases/UKHL/1986/6.html

(Lords Bridge of Harwich, Griffiths, Ackner, Oliver of Aylmerton and Goff of Chieveley)

D went to the home of his former business partner against whom he bore some grudge and rang the bell waking the occupants who looked out of their bedroom window. D fired a shot aimed at the bedroom window and two further shots, one at another window and one at the front door. No one was hurt. It was never suggested that the first shot had been aimed at any person.

[All their lordships concurred in the speech delivered by Lord Bridge of Harwich:]

Arising from this incident the respondent was arraigned on an indictment containing three counts. He pleaded not guilty to possession of a firearm with intent to endanger life, contrary to s16 of the Firearms Act 1968 (count 1) and to an offence of damaging property with intent, contrary to s1(2) of the Criminal Damage Act 1971, which was alleged in the particulars as originally framed as having been committed 'intending by the said damage to endanger the lives of David Gregory and Tina Gregory or being reckless as to whether the lives of David Gregory and Tina Gregory would be thereby endangered' (count 2). He pleaded guilty to a separate offence of damaging property, contrary to s1(1) of the 1971 Act (count 3).

[His lordship read s 1 of the Act.]

It is to be observed that the offence created by sub-s(2), save that it may be committed by destroying or damaging one's own property, is simply an aggravated form of the offence created by sub-s(1), in which the prosecution must prove, in addition to the ingredients of the offence under sub-s(1), the further mental element specified by sub-s(2)(b). In this case presumably count 2 was intended to relate to the damage done by the shot fired at the bedroom window and count 3 to the damage done by one or other or both the other two shots. It is also significant to note the maximum penalties attaching to the three offences charged. For an offence under s16 of the 1968 Act it is 14 years' imprisonment, for an offence under s1(2) of the 1971 Act life imprisonment, and for an offence under s1(1) of the 1971 Act 10 years' imprisonment.

At some stage in the trial the particulars of count 2 were amended by deleting the words alleging an intent to endanger life and leaving only recklessness in that regard as the mental element relied on to establish the offence under s1(2). The prosecution, it appears, presented the case on the footing that counts 1 and 2 were alternatives and, if the case had been left to the jury, the judge would presumably have directed them that if they found that the respondent intended to endanger the lives of Mr and Mrs Gregory they should convict on count 1, but if they found that he was merely reckless with regard to such danger they should acquit on count 1 and convict on count 2.

At the conclusion of the case for the prosecution, however, counsel for the respondent submitted that there was no case to answer on count 2 on the ground that, in so far as the lives of Mr and Mrs Gregory had been endangered, the danger had not been caused by the damage done to the bungalow, but by the shot fired from the respondent's rifle. Of course, it is obvious that any danger to life in this case was caused by the shot from the rifle itself, not by any trifling damage done to the bedroom window or to any property in the bedroom. But the judge rejected counsel's submission and accepted the submission made for the Crown that the phrase in s 1(2)(b) of the 1971 Act 'by the destruction or damage' refers on its true construction not only to the destruction or damage to property as the cause of the danger to life on which the mental element in the aggravated offence under the sub-section depends, but also to the act of the defendant which causes that destruction or damage. On the basis of the judge's ruling the respondent changed his plea to guilty on count 2. He appealed against conviction on the ground that the judge's ruling was erroneous. The Court of Appeal, Criminal Division (Neill LJ, Peter Pain and Gatehouse JJ) ([1986] 3 All ER 611, [1986] 1 WLR 1286) allowed the appeal, but certified that the decision involved a question of law of general public importance in the following terms:

> 'Whether, upon a true construction of s1(2)(b) of the Criminal Damage Act 1971, the prosecution are required to prove that the danger to life resulted from the destruction of or damage to the property, or whether it is sufficient for the prosecution to prove that it resulted from the act of the defendant which caused the destruction or damage.'

The Crown now appeals by leave of your Lordships' House.

We must, of course, approach the matter on the footing, implicit in the outcome of the trial, that the respondent, in firing at the bedroom window, had no intent to endanger life, but accepts that he was reckless whether life would be endangered.

Under both limbs of s1 of the 1971 Act it is the essence of the offence which the section creates that the defendant has destroyed or damaged property. For the purpose of analysis it may be convenient to omit reference to destruction and to concentrate on the references to damage, which was all that was here involved. To be guilty under sub-s(1) the defendant must have intended or been reckless as to the damage to property which he caused. To be guilty under sub-s(2) he must additionally have intended to endanger life or been reckless whether life would be endangered 'by the damage' to property which he caused. This is the context in which the words must be construed and it seems to me impossible to read the words 'by the damage' as meaning 'by the damage or by the act which caused the damage'. Moreover, if the language of the statute has the meaning for which the Crown contends, the words 'by the destruction or damage' and 'thereby' in sub-s(2)(b) are mere surplusage. If the Crown's submission is right, the only additional element necessary to convert a sub-s(1) offence into a sub-s(2) offence is an intent to endanger life or recklessness whether life would be endangered simpliciter.

It would suffice as a ground for dismissing this appeal if the statute were ambiguous, since any such ambiguity in a criminal statute should be resolved in favour of the defence. But I can find no ambiguity. It seems to me that the meaning for which the respondent contends is the only meaning which the language can bear.

The contrary construction leads to anomalies which Parliament cannot have intended. If A and B both discharge firearms in a public place, being reckless whether life would be endangered, it would be absurd that A, who incidentally causes some trifling damage to property, should be guilty of an offence punishable with life imprisonment, but that B, who causes no damage, should be guilty of no offence. In the same circumstances, if A is merely reckless but B actually intends to endanger life, it is scarcely less absurd that A should be guilty of the graver offence under s1(2) of the 1971 Act, B of the lesser offence under s16 of the Firearms Act 1968.

Counsel for the Crown did not shrink from arguing that s1(2) of the 1971 Act had created, in effect, a general offence of endangering life with intent or recklessly, however the danger was caused, but had incidentally included as a necessary, albeit insignificant, ingredient of the offence that some damage to property should also be caused. In certain fields of legislation it is sometimes difficult to appreciate the rationale of particular provisions, but in a criminal statute it would need the clearest language to persuade me that the legislature had acted so irrationally, indeed perversely, as acceptance of this argument would imply.

It was further argued that to affirm the construction of s 1(2)(b) adopted by the Court of Appeal would give rise to problems in other cases in which it might be difficult or even impossible to distinguish between the act causing damage to property and the ensuing damage caused as the source of danger to life. In particular, it was suggested that in arson cases the jury would have to be directed that they could only convict if the danger to life arose from falling beams or similar damage caused by the fire, not if the danger arose from the heat, flames or smoke generated by the fire itself. Arson is, of course, the prime example of a form of criminal damage to property which, in the case of an occupied building, necessarily involves serious danger to life and where the gravity of the consequence which may result as well from recklessness as from a specific intent fully justifies the severity of the penalty which the 1971 Act provides for the offence. But the argument in this case is misconceived. It is not the match and the inflammable materials, the flaming firebrand or any other inflammatory agent which the arsonist uses to start the fire which causes danger to life, it is the ensuing conflagration which occurs as the property which has been set on fire is damaged or destroyed. When the victim in the bedroom is overcome by the smoke or incinerated by the flames as the building burns, it would be absurd to say that this does not result from the damage to the building.

Counsel for the Crown put forward other examples of cases which he suggested ought to be liable to prosecution under s 1(2) of the 1971 Act, including that of the angry mob of striking miners who throw a hail of bricks through the window of the cottage occupied by the working miner and that of people who drop missiles from motorway bridges on passing vehicles. I believe that the criminal law provides adequate sanctions for these cases without the need to resort to s 1(2) of the 1971 Act. But, if my belief is mistaken, this would still be no reason to distort the plain meaning of that sub-section.

Some reference was also made to damage caused by explosives. This is the subject of specific provision under the Explosive Substances Act 1883 as amended. The offence created by s 3(1)(a) of that Act, as substituted by s7(1) of the Criminal Jurisdiction Act 1975, of doing 'any act with intent to cause . . . by an explosive substance an explosion of a nature likely to endanger life, or cause serious injury to property . . .' obviates the need to resort to the 1971 Act when explosives are used. . . .

I can well understand that the prosecution in this case thought it necessary and appropriate that, even if they could not establish the intent to endanger life necessary to support a conviction under s16 of the 1968 Act, they should include a count in the indictment to mark in some way the additional gravity of an offence of criminal damage to property in which a firearm is used. But they had no need to resort to s1(2) of the 1971 Act. A person who, at the time of committing an offence under s1 of the 1971 Act, has in his possession a firearm commits a distinct offence under s17(2) of the 1968 Act: see Sch 1 to the 1968 Act, as amended by s11(7) of the 1971 Act. If the respondent had been charged with that offence in addition to the offence under s1(1) of the 1971 Act, he must have pleaded guilty to both and, if the prosecution were content to accept that there was no intent to endanger life, this would have been amply sufficient to mark the gravity of the respondent's criminal conduct in the incident at the Gregory's bungalow.

I would accordingly dismiss the appeal. The certified question should be answered as follows: on the true construction of s1(2)(b) of the Criminal Damage Act 1971 the prosecution are required to prove that the danger to life resulted from the destruction of or damage to property; it is not sufficient for the prosecution to prove that it resulted from the act of the defendant which caused the destruction or damage.

Appeal dismissed

Consider *Webster, Warwick* [1995] 2 All ER 168, CA. In the first case the defendants and others pushed a coping stone from the parapet of a bridge onto a passenger train passing beneath. The stone penetrated the roof but did not strike anyone; passengers were, however, showered with, though not physically injured by, debris dislodged from the roof by the falling stone. The court said the judge was wrong to direct the jury that the defendants could be convicted of the s 1(2) offence if they intended that life would be endangered *by the falling stone*. The conviction was upheld, however, on the ground that the jury's verdict implied that the defendants must have been reckless as to the lives of the passengers being endangered by falling debris. Would that still be the case now that G has overruled *Caldwell*?

In the second case D, in a stolen car, repeatedly rammed pursuing police vehicles while E, D's passenger, threw bricks at passing police cars, one of which shattered a windscreen and showered the officers therein with broken glass. It was held that D was properly convicted of the s 1(2) offence. D intended that property be damaged and was at least reckless as to the endangering of life since either action—the ramming of the police cars or the breaking of the window—caused damage which in turn might have put the lives of the police officers at risk.

Attorney-General's Reference (No 3 of 1992)
(1993) 98 Cr App R 383, Court of Appeal, Criminal Division

(Lord Taylor CJ, Schiemann and Wright JJ)

The complainants, V, maintained a night watch over their premises from a motor car. Early one morning the respondents arrived in a vehicle containing petrol bombs and threw towards V's car a lighted petrol bomb which passed over the car and smashed against a wall. They were charged with attempted aggravated arson, the particulars alleging recklessness whether life would be endangered. The trial judge ruled that, on a charge of attempt, intent to endanger life was required; recklessness was not sufficient. That was the point of law referred by the Attorney General. Before considering the attempts problem, however, the court considered what has to be proved for the completed offences of criminal damage and aggravated criminal damage.

Schiemann J:

So far as the completed simple offence is concerned, the prosecution needs to prove:

(1) Property belonging to another was damaged by the defendant.

(2) The state of mind of the defendant was one of the following:

(a) he intended to damage such property, or

(b) he was reckless as to whether any such property would be damaged.

In the case of the completed aggravated offence the prosecution needs to prove:

(1) the defendant in fact damaged property, whether belonging to himself or another;

(2) that the state of mind of the defendant was one of the following:

(a) he intended to damage property, and intended by the damage to endanger the life of another, or

(b) he intended to damage property and was reckless as to whether the life of another would be thereby endangered, or

(c) he was reckless as to whether any property would be damaged and was reckless as to whether the life of another would be thereby endangered.

It is to be noted that the property referred to under 1 (to which we shall hereafter refer as the first-named property) is not necessarily the same property as that referred to in 2 (to which we shall refer as the second-named property), although it normally will be. Thus a man who—

(1) owns a crane from which is suspended a heavy object and

(2) puts the rope (the first-named property) which holds the object with the result that

(3) the object falls and hits the roof of a passing car (the second-named property) which roof

(4) collapses killing the driver—

would be guilty if it could be shown that he damaged the rope, was reckless as to whether this would damage the car, and was reckless as to whether the life of the driver of the car would be endangered by the damage to the car.

All the foregoing is common ground. The problem which has given rise to this reference relates to an attempt to commit the aggravated offence in circumstances where the first-named property is the same as the second-named property—in the instant case a car. It amounts to this: whether, if the state of mind of the defendant was that postulated in 2(b) above, namely that he intended to damage property and was reckless as to whether the life of another would thereby be endangered, and whilst in that state of mind he did an act which was more than merely preparatory to the offence, he is guilty of attempting to commit that offence.

We turn to the law of attempt . . .

The difference between the full offence and the attempt seems to be minimal. If the attempt is committed at all, it is committed as soon as D does an act more than merely preparatory to damaging the crane by cutting the rope—for example, taking out his knife and moving to make the cut. If the full offence is committed, it is done as soon as he cuts the rope. The only remaining questions for both attempt and full offence concern D's state of mind.

The court seems to assume that D would be guilty of neither offence unless he was reckless (which applying *G* means that he foresaw that there was a risk and unjustifiably took it) that someone's life might be endangered by a crushed car roof or some other property damaged by the falling object, distinct from the danger from the falling object itself. The object is treated like the ricocheting bullet in *Steer* (earlier in this section, p 918). But is this right? The ricochet was not the product of any criminal damage. The object falls as the direct result of criminal damage to the crane. Would not the full offence have been committed if D foresaw that the object was likely to fall on a pedestrian? If D damages the braking system of a car, is it not sufficient to prove that he was reckless whether the damaged car might endanger the lives of pedestrians by running into them? Is it really necessary to prove that he foresaw that the car might damage some other property which would endanger life, as by knocking down a lamp post which might hit a pedestrian?

For recent examples of the application of this approach, see *Thakar* [2010] EWCA Crim 2136 and *Wenton* [2010] EWCA Crim 2361.

28.3.5 No life need be endangered

The offence under s 1(2) requires that some property be intentionally or recklessly damaged. However, it is not necessary to show that life was in fact endangered if D in fact intended, or was reckless as to, such endangerment. D may be accordingly convicted if he has the relevant mens rea, even though a house in which he starts a fire is unoccupied (*Sangha* [1988] 2 All ER 385, [1988] 1 WLR 519, CA) or the fire which he starts is doused before any endangerment in fact arises (*Dudley* [1989] Crim LR 57, CA). The brick thrown at the police car in *Warwick* might have missed the windscreen and caused only trivial damage to the police car. D would still be liable if it was thrown with the requisite mens rea; otherwise, said the court in *Warwick*, liability would depend on whether D was a good shot.

■ *Question*

Do we need an endangerment offence? On endangerment offences generally, see the discussion in K. J. M. Smith, 'Liability for Endangerment: English Ad Hoc Pragmatism and American Innovation' [1983] Crim LR 127; D. Lanham, 'Danger Down Under' [1999] Crim LR 960.

28.4 Arson

The Law Commission recommended that there should be no separate offence of damaging property by fire (see LC29, paras 28–33) but this recommendation proved unacceptable to Parliament and s 1(3) of the Act provides 'An offence committed under this section by destroying or damaging property by fire shall be charged as arson'. Since arson is punishable with life imprisonment, arson contrary to s 1(1) must be a separate offence under *Courtie* (which holds that if one form of an offence has a higher penalty it should be treated as separate from other forms of the offence).

A person may therefore be charged with an offence under s 1(1) and (3), to which the definition of lawful excuse in s 5 applies; or with an offence under s 1(2) and (3), to which the definition in s 5 does not apply. In order to constitute arson there must be some damage, however slight, done by fire.

In *Drayton* [2005] EWCA Crim 2013, D was charged under s 1(1) and s 1(3) of the 1971 Act, but the word 'arson' did not appear in the information. The Court of Appeal held that the charge was, in the context of the magistrates' court, a valid charge. The use of the word 'arson' was described as desirable, but the fact that the information alleged 'damage by fire' was sufficient. Since arson was specifically preserved because of the unique stigma attaching to that wrong, and the section is cast in mandatory terms ('shall be charged as arson'), the result is a surprising one.

28.5 Other offences

By s 2 of the Criminal Damage Act it is an offence to threaten to destroy, etc property, and by s 3 it is an offence to possess anything intending to destroy, etc property.

28.6 Racially or religiously aggravated criminal damage

The Crime and Disorder Act 1998 created a new category of racially aggravated crimes. A person commits an offence under s 28 of the 1998 Act if he commits an offence within the Criminal Damage Act, s 1(1), which is 'racially aggravated' for the purposes of s 29. The offence is punishable summarily by imprisonment for six months or a fine not exceeding the statutory maximum and, on indictment, by imprisonment for 14 years, or a fine, or both.

The Anti-terrorism, Crime and Security Act 2001, s 39, extended s 28 to 'religiously aggravated' offences. By s 39(5), 'religious group' means a group of persons defined by reference to religious belief or lack of religious belief. The Law Commission is currently consulting on whether or not these offences ought to be extended to include hostility based on gender identity, sexual orientation and disability. See Law Commission Consultation Paper No 213, *Hate Crime: The Case for Extending the Existing Offences* (2013).

28.7 A note on the Computer Misuse Act 1990

Computers, like any other machines, may be damaged as by taking a hammer to them and such damage falls within the Criminal Damage Act. But they are much more likely to be 'damaged' or interfered with by the alteration of programs or the deletion of data by electronic means which, unlike the use of a hammer, leave no visible signs of damage to the computer or its software.

In *Cox v Riley* (1986) 83 Cr App R 54, [1986] Crim LR 460, DC, D 'blanked' (ie erased by electronic means) the programs from a plastic circuit card which was used to operate a saw to cut wood to programmed designs. The card bore no visible signs of damage and could have been reprogrammed, after the expenditure of time and money, to perform its original function. D's counsel argued ('gallantly', it was said) that because the programs could not be seen or touched in the ordinary physical sense, they were not 'property of a tangible nature' within the Criminal Damage Act.

The court thought that this argument failed to take account of the fact that D was charged not with damaging the programs but with damaging the plastic circuit card. The value and usefulness of the card had been impaired because it would no longer perform the function for which it had been designed. In principle, the decision seems defensible. The card, like a key which has been physically deformed, would not perform its function and the card, like the key, is no less damaged because it can be re-formed, by whatever means, to perform its original function. *Cox v Riley* was followed by the Court of Appeal in *Whitely* (1991) 93 Cr App R 25, [1991] Crim LR 436.

The Law Commission (see Law Com Working Paper No 10, *Computer Misuse* and Law Com Report No 186, *Computer Misuse* (1989) took the view that the problem of computer misuse should be tackled directly and the outcome was the Computer Misuse Act 1990.

The Law Commission did not think that criminal damage should apply to a person who recklessly modified computer material. Section 3(6) dealt with this overlap. The section has been superseded by the Police and Justice Act 2006 which inserted a new s 10(5) into the Criminal Damage Act which provides that:

> for the purposes of the Criminal Damage Act 'a modification of the contents of a computer shall not be regarded as damaging any computer or computer storage medium unless its effect on that computer or computer storage medium impairs its physical condition.

The Law Commission was, with respect, entirely right to tackle the problem of computer misuse directly but the amendments to the Computer Misuse Act raise a number of questions, not least as to its breadth.

■ **Questions**

Olivia's husband David is a workaholic. Olivia goes into his study one evening and pulls the plug out of the socket on his computer, causing him to lose hours of valuable research. Is Olivia guilty of an offence? Should she be?

FURTHER READING

Criminal damage

D. W. Elliott, 'Criminal Damage' [1988] Crim LR 403

Law Commission Report No 29, *Criminal Law: Report on Offences of Damage to Property* (1970)

See also Law Commission Working Paper No 23, *Malicious Damage* (1969)

Index